Dolores : a novel of South America.

Harro Harring

DOLORES:

A

NOVEL OF SOUTH AMERICA:

BY

HARRO-HARRING.

AUTHOR OF "POLAND UNDER THE DOMINION OF RUSSIA" —"THE POLE" —"YOUNG
ALFRED — THE PRIVATE OF DENMARK" —"THE MONK"—"THE
BROKEN HEART"—"THE FUGITIVE"—ETC ETC ETC

No hammer forged the iron so fast
That it can last be broken at last,
[illegible] break [illegible] change
And [illegible] highest power is the mind of man

COMPLETE IN ONE VOLUME

NEW YORK.
PUBLISHED BY THE AUTHOR

MONTEVIDEO LIBRERIA HERNANDEZ

1846

The Duplicate Original of this work in German, will be published by CHARLES MULLER, 118 Nassau-street, N Y
A translation into Italian, will be prepared by F FORESTI,—into Swedish, by G C HEBBE.

INTRODUCTORY LETTER.

To Mrs M····ᴀ W·ᴅ

MADAM—Among the manifold perplexities into which an author may be betrayed, two are peculiarly disagreeable The one is, that in which he is placed by a publisher, who, instead of beginning, according to contract, the printing of a completed work, suddenly, under the pretence of "*Christian principles*" and "*biblical religious*" views, *breaks his word* The other is, that in which the author finds himself when he has written a most finished dedicatory epistle, to an interesting and amiable lady, and suddenly misses the manuscript, just as he is at length sending his work to press.

Both cases are here realized The public prints have already presented the first for your contemplation, and will, probably, occupy themselves still further with the affair, if the car of Themis shall produce the material.

The second case is of an entirely different sort, and is even less explicable to me than the fact of an *orthodox* and royalist *censure* in the United States, endeavoring to suppress the present work

After you, Madam, had given me the permission to dedicate to you my novel on South America, for whose title you, in quality of sponsor, chose the designation of "*Dolores*"—I wrote the dedicatory epistle In it, I pointed out my position as author, and the character of my work, as a manifest of the spirit of humanity, in its striving and struggle for the development of mankind—with a hint at the influence of "*Old Europe*" upon the judgement of a literary work in a republican spirit—in so far as the moral freedom of many "republicans" is fettered and contracted by regulations and prejudices which stand rigidly opposed to the progress of the age

You gave yourself the trouble, Madam, to read this epistle, and the first book of the manuscript of my work

The manuscript of the first part, (commenced at the beginning of August, 1844,) to which the dedicatory epistle was attached, was confided, on the 10th of November, 1845, to a publisher, with whom Mr W·····d, in December, 1844, had, according to his own friendly proposition, concluded the contract for the edition The succeeding parts of the work were likewise delivered for publication on the 13th of January, 1846, and the whole work was, in my presence, given by the publisher, Mr H····p··r,· to the director of his printing office, "to run it through the press immediately," in consideration of the increasing interest of such a work, with reference to the affairs of RIO DE LA PLATA ·

Instead of the expected proof sheets, I received, some days later, the manuscript of "Dolores," neatly parcelled, under the address of your house, accompanied by the anathema of a Censor, whose letter would be a remarkable document in the history of philosophy in the New World

The Censor, in his letter, addressed to Mr H····p··r, proscribes the spiritual fruits of study and thought, denies freedom of conscience, and insults the cultivated public of the United States, as being incapable of understanding "*a novel of sentiment and religious opinion, evincing decided ability, but of a peculiar kind,*" (as he expressed himself,) "*and by no means orthodox*"

This is true, Madam Dolores is a novel—a novel of sentiment and opinion—of noble and elevated sentiment, and of well founded religious, political, and social opinion, but by no means "British orthodox"

I never contracted with any publisher to write a British orthodox novel

The learned man seems not to be aware, that, even in the universities of monarchies, together with professors of *orthodox theology*, there are also professors of *philosophy*— (of whose systems he does not even know the *names*, and which he "casts away" as

INTRODUCTORY LETTER.

To Mrs. M· · a W· · d.

Madam—Among the manifold perplexities into which an author may be betrayed, two are peculiarly disagreeable. The one is, that in which he is placed by a publisher, who, instead of beginning, according to contract, the printing of a completed work, suddenly, under the pretence of " *Christian principles*" and " *biblical religious*" views, *breaks his word* The other is, that in which the author finds himself when he has written a most finished dedicatory epistle, to an interesting and amiable lady, and suddenly misses the manuscript, just as he is at length sending his work to press.

Both cases are here realized. The public prints have already presented the first for your contemplation, and will, probably, occupy themselves still further with the affair, if the car of Themis shall produce the material.

The second case is of an entirely different sort, and is even less explicable to me than the fact of an *orthodox* and royalist *censure* in the United States, endeavoring to suppress the present work

After you, Madam, had given me the permission to dedicate to you my novel on South America, for whose title you, in quality of sponsor, chose the designation of "*Dolores*"—I wrote the dedicatory epistle In it, I pointed out my position as author, and the character of my work, as a manifest of the spirit of humanity, in its striving and struggle for the development of mankind—with a hint at the influence of "*Old Europe*" upon the judgement of a literary work in a republican spirit—in so far as the moral freedom of many "republicans" is fettered and contracted by regulations and prejudices which stand rigidly opposed to the progress of the age.

You gave yourself the trouble, Madam, to read this epistle, and the first book of the manuscript of my work.

The manuscript of the first part, (commenced at the beginning of August, 1844,) to which the dedicatory epistle was attached, was confided, on the 10th of November, 1845, to a publisher, with whom Mr. W· · d, in December, 1844, had, according to his own friendly proposition, concluded the contract for the edition The succeeding parts of the work were likewise delivered for publication on the 13th of January, 1846, and the whole work was, in my presence, given by the publisher, Mr. H· · p· r, to the director of his printing office, " to run it through the press immediately," in consideration of the increasing interest of such a work, with reference to the affairs of Rio de La Plata.

Instead of the expected proof sheets, I received, some days later, the manuscript of " Dolores," neatly parcelled, under the address of your house, accompanied by the anathema of a Censor, whose letter would be a remarkable document in the history of philosophy in the New World.

The Censor, in his letter, addressed to Mr H· · p· r, proscribes the spiritual fruits of study and thought, denies freedom of conscience, and insults the cultivated public of the United States, as being incapable of understanding " *a novel of sentiment and religious opinion, evincing decided ability, but of a peculiar kind,*" (as he expressed himself,) " *and by no means orthodox.*"

This is true, Madam. Dolores is a novel—a novel of sentiment and opinion—of noble and elevated sentiment, and of well founded religious, political, and social opinion, but by no means " British orthodox."

I never contracted with any publisher to write a British orthodox novel.

The learned man seems not to be aware, that, even in the universities of monarchies, together with professors of *orthodox theology*, there are also professors of *philosophy*—(of whose systems he does not even know the *names*, and which he " casts away" as *transcendentalism*,) and that many philosophers have published instructive works that are " *of a peculiar kind, and by no means orthodox* " Even from the various translations of the *Koran*, and the works of *Swedenborg*, despotic censure has erased no precept, much less condemned them totally to death , and neither the Koran nor Swedenborg are British *orthodox*. From the *Bible*, however, several books have been erased, as is well known, by the censure of fanatical sects, as not " British orthodox."

The " hangman of thought" afterwards declared that he had only read two hundred pages of the manuscript, (about thirty printed pages like the present,) while the first part had lain in the desk of the publisher since the 10th of November.

The paper coffin of the methodistically executed " Dolores" reached, unopened, the hand of a friend, who carefully preserved the corpse Last evening, for the first time, I again saw the manuscript, when I despatched it to another press, under more favorable prospects for the fulfilment of a plighted word, and without risk of the " non-imprimatur" of a stupid censure, or the diplomatic intervention of an agent of the usurper of Rio de La Plata, *Don Juan*—Manuel de Rosas

The dedicatory epistle has vanished——— It would be impossible for me to write one of the same, or similar tenor Like almost every effusion of the sort, it owed its existence to a poetic inspiration, and the muse being of the female sex, I cannot command her, but must avail myself of the favorable moment when she approaches me My manly discretion prohibits me from seeking her, and the sought or solicited favors of the muse, as of every other female, are deficient, besides, (as is well known,) in the spiritual sympathy that is requisite to the true inward life in which the poet exists

In my lost epistle, I declared, among other things, that, as the author of full forty volumes, I had never written a work upon the order or commission of a bookseller or book manufacturer—that I had never done homage to the taste of a " literature à la mode," but, as author, and as man, represent a *principle*, the principle of *moral freedom*, in which the spirit moves that leads to the development of mankind I declared that, instead of serving the money speculations of a bookseller, I sought to form a public for *thought*, since I did not consider freedom (and likewise the freedom of the press) as the *goal* of a nation, but as a *means* to higher intellectual completeness I declared that I acknowledged only one power, the power of *mind*, and all material means as subordinate to its service.

Whether, and in how far, these sayings (corresponding with the spirit and contents of my work) bear reference to the mysterious disappearance of the dedicatory epistle, and to a publisher's breach of his word, must remain undecided I found myself, according to the above, in the singular embarrassment of replacing the lost epistle by these lines, since I must explain to you the circumstances under which the original had disappeared. I am placed, for the moment, as it were, in the position of a bridegroom, who, on his way to the altar, in the gloomy walls of an old monastery, suddenly finds that he has lost the wedding ring , or of a youth, who, at the entrance to a representation of " Love's Labor Lost," misses his ticket.

Thanking you once more for the interest you have manifested in me and my " Dolores," I remain, with sincere esteem,

Your friend,

PAUL HARRO-HARRING,

New York, March 5th, 1846 of Ibenshof, in Denmark.

DOLORES.

BOOK I.

CHAPTER I

THE MYSTERY

"Seven and twenty balls aimed at his breast, blindfolded, kneeling," said Padre Fernando, slowly, and with marked emphasis, addressing Señor Domingo, the keeper of the prison, who attended him to the gates.

"Seven and twenty balls aimed at his breast," repeated Señor Domingo, with equal deliberation, as he took a pinch of snuff from his silver box, and handing it to the reverend Padre, added, "can I serve you?"

The monk, by no means disdaining the nasal offering of his old acquaintance, drew up the left corner of his mouth towards his ear, while he insinuated the pinch of snuff into his right nostril, and then again addressed the officer of the Argentine Republic in a business manner, keeping back the most important matters until the last.

"You must send some one immediately to the Monastery of St Bento,* and summon Brother Celeste to the condemned. I have daily and nightly endeavored to bring him to confession, to give the name of the poet who wrote the infamous Unitarian† Elegies, but all in vain! He will confess nothing, denounce no one, he will of course be shot to-morrow morning at sunrise, here in the yard! You must send some one immediately to the Monastery of St Bento to summon Brother Celeste. Do you understand, Señor Domingo? Brother Celeste. Our office and profession oblige us to gratify and fulfil the last wish of a condemned person, who is allowed to choose his confessor by the rules of the only saving Church, which is protected and richly endowed by the grace and favor of our lord and master the Director.‡ May the Lord grant him a long life, and finally a happy end!"

"Padre Celeste, at the Monastery of St Bento," repeated Señor Domingo, and called to him Narcissus, a mulatto, who stood beside a sentry, before the gate of the edifice, on the threshold of which the conversation took place. He expressly ordered the mulatto to bring the confessor

* The names of many places, and of all the persons of this novel, have been changed, to veil the reality of its facts.
† A political designation, as will be seen by the following tale.
‡ Gubernador or President.

with the utmost speed, whereat the messenger departed, repeating over to himself all the while the names of the monk and the monastery—an hereditary custom of the African negroes, who rely very little on their memories.

Although political offenders were usually confined in the prison edifice which formed a part of the so called Palace of Justice, in the Plaza de Victoria, at Buenos Ayres, many of these prisoners were to be found in more remote and ancient prisons, for the same reasons that a hotel keeper hastily converts, for the occasion, a private house into "furnished lodgings," when an unusual number of guests requires such an arrangement.

"Is there then no pardon—no deliverance, Padre Fernando?" inquired the prison keeper, after a short pause, during which each took another pinch of snuff, "must the young Señor Alphonso be shot early to-morrow morning? Seven and twenty balls aimed at his breast, you say? seven and twenty! Then, probably at least half a dozen will hit his breast, and it is to be hoped that one at least will reach his heart."

"Seven and twenty," repeated the monk, significantly, "as many bullets as the hardened sinner counts years such is the will and command of our lord and governor, which is to be regarded as an especial favor, since we may anticipate, (as you very justly remark,) that at least one bullet will reach the guilt-laden heart."

"Guilt-laden! yes, indeed," interrupted old Domingo, "he certainly caused the publication of the infamous Unitarian poems in Monte Video; this is proved, as we knew long ago, by the report of our high police. It is certainly high treason against the most high person of our Director. Whether he is the author, whether he himself wrote them, is matter of little consequence; he caused them to be published, and privately circulated it is horrible! unparalleled!" affirmed the prison officer, "this all proceeds from the free press at Monte Video."

"It all comes from the spirit of rebellion in Europe," interrupted Padre Fernando," and from the culpable example of God-dishonoring freedom in North America, where the people even live without a king! without a king, Señor Domingo! what do you say to that? and where the Director or President has not absolute authority like our monarch Rosas, who, though to be sure he is as yet neither anointed nor crowned king, will be, before his death, as sure as I am Padre Fernando '

" Will be crowned king ?" repeated Señor Domingo slowly and thoughtfully " Do you think so, Padre Fernando ? do you really think that this will yet come to pass ?

" More is known among us than what goes on in the Sacristy, Señor Domingo,' whispered the venerable follower of the holy Franciscus, ' more is known among us ' Already it is all planned and supported by the legitimate powers of Europe —the legitimate Christian powers '—of whom, thank God, many still remain there He will be crowned king and sovereign of the La Platas and Patagonia, and three new bishopricks will be founded, and seven new monasteries built, and our order will be held in especial consideration I tell you, Señor Domingo, we shall yet live to see it ' But we must go to work earnestly against this spirit of riot and rebellion, which even here, in the unhappy days of the past, has once overturned the throne ' We must take hold, and assist in rearing the throne of legitimacy However, s to our prisoner, the infamous republican and enemy to religion, our Señor Alphonso, down there in the dungeon, you may give him whatever refreshments you may think best, if he wishes any , and brother Celeste may remain with him to-night, until early to-morrow morning, until his hour strikes "

The prison, at the gate of which this conversation took place, had been built for a monastery, in the good old days of the Jesuits, and now degraded to a barrack, while the solid inquisitorial subterranean dungeons were used for their original purpose

The conversation of the two public servants, was interrupted by the appearance of Señor Borrachezo, a commissary of police, attended by one of those officers who serve the police in secret, and openly endeavor to pass for something quite different

" Come with us," said Señor Borrachezo, to the two friends of snuff, " come in, I have something to say to you . let the office be opened, Señor Domingo," cried Señor Borrachezo, a square built figure, with a copper colored nose, and pendent nether lip , " walk in, reverend Padre Fernando "

The chief jailer selected the key of the " bureau of locked-up responsibilities," from a ring brought to him by the under-porter , he opened a double door, turned the blind, to throw in the feeble glimmer of departing twilight on the persons entering, and arranged some chairs All four took their places, and the deputy of police, having taken a pinch from Señor Domingo's box, began—

" Señor Alphonso will be executed early in the morning, as you know, it is to be hoped you have prepared him, Padre Fernando , have you drawn from him any thing in relation to the secret ?"

" Prepared, indeed !" replied the monk, " if a sinner can be prepared, who will neither acknowledge the authorities, nor receive the sacrament of the church from a follower of the holy St Franciscus "

" How so ! will not receive it ?" inquired the police officer, surprised " does he refuse the sacrament of the holy supper ?"

" Not that," interrupted the other, " but he refuses to receive it from me, and desires his special confessor, a Benedictine, Brother Celeste "

' We cannot deny him that," declared Señor Borrachezo " Have you not sent some one already to the monastery of St Bento, Señor Domingo ?"

" At your service," replied the latter, " I have sent my Narcissus, he must soon be back again Can I serve you ?" said he, in the most courteous manner to the police officer, again handing him his snuffbox

" Have you remarked nothing since, Señor Domingo ?" inquired the latter . ' no suspicious persons in the neighborhood of the building ? no visits without legal tickets of admission ? Has no one appeared who would excite the suspicion that he might be a confederate of the condemned ?"

" No one, Señor Consejero, (counsellor,) but the executioner, who came once to ask me if I could learn whether the next was to furnish any work for him, he inquired whether Señor Alphonso was, as usual, to be secretly beheaded, hanged, strangled, or, das' only shot, whereupon I could give him no information until now that Padre Fernando has made me aware of the execution to-morrow morning " Señor Domingo concluded this report with a stout pinch of snuff, and leaned back comfortably in the old arm chair, which he had especially reserved for himself

' Singular !' began the police officer, in an under tone, turning to Señor Falsodo, who had entered with him, " no one has been here, no one who can in the least serve us in finding a clue whereby to discover the author of those infamous Elegies It is true, he asserts that they are his , that he, and no one else is the author, but the literary college, which our most high director commissioned to investigate the matter, decided to the contrary Señor Alphonso is very generally known as a young man of talent and information, of profound study, and with the most brilliant prospects of a career in the service of the State , but talents go single, and those of a young diplomatist are of an entirely different nature from poetic genius and in opposition to it , and, most unfortunately, such is the opinion of the literary college, the infamous Elegies display a poetic genius which has hitherto never manifested itself on the Rio de la Plata A most surprising phenomenon that ! Unheard of ! magnificent ! poetical ! cannibalish ! is that production—it is a pity, a shame, that such a genius has debased itself to such purposes as rebellion, poetry, and the apostleship of an insane idea of the union of the States of South America, as a confederacy, with the imaginary government of a Central America, after the example of the United States of North America It is shockingly unprecedented that ! It would make a fatal alteration in the official department, many would lose their posts, and some perhaps even their heads, if this bloody poetry became reality It is an awful thought that !"

" We must make every endeavor to trace out the author," replied Señor Falsodo, a little lean mannikin, with a yellowish pock-marked visage, in worn-out black clothes, balancing on his knees a steeple-crowned straw hat with a broad brim ; " if we had only a single leaf of the manuscript, only a few lines of the handwriting, it would be something on which to institute inquiry! I have written to my correspondent at Monte Video to obtain information in the printing office, if possible to procure a leaf, but in vain! Instead of the writing which is so important to us, my correspondent unfortunately received—what do you suppose, Señor Consejero, that he received?'

The person entitled Counsellor allowed his hanging under lip to drop still lower, involuntarily opening his mouth wider, as if he would receive the news so much the sooner through the medium of his vice-hearing organs. "What happened to your correspondent, Señor Falsodo? what did he get in the printing office at Monte Video?"

"A beating! Señor Counsellor, a beating, and of the most disgraceful kind, because, probably, he conducted himself awkwardly, and very injudiciously gave cause for the supposition that he was in correspondence with me, or with some one of my occupation in Buenos Ayres!"

What! do you say that he got a beating?" exclaimed Señor Borrachezo.

'Yes, and was thrown down stairs in the most unfeeling manner, and was obliged to ship to Rio de Janeiro immediately, as his stay in Monte Video was prohibited in consequence."

'It is shocking!' sighed the police officer, 'tis shocking to receive a beating in any case, but above all when nothing comes of it—not the smallest sample to found our inquiries on in this case."

"Such beatings are to be sure compensated by the increase of wages, on the part of our liberal government,' remarked Señor Falsodo. "It is a very humane system, that of indemnification, but, for the moment, a beating is very severe, especially when it falls on a feeble body, as would be the case with me, Señor Consejero."

You must take care of yourself, Señor Falsodo, you must take warning by your correspondent at Monte Video! I will see that you receive an increase of salary without first being beaten, especially if you should succeed in finding out the author of the Elegies, and deliver him alive to us. A substantial price awaits the discovery," said Borrachezo, in a lower tone, "a very substantial price! and protection for family and connexions besides: think of that, Señor Falsodo, think well of it."

'The price is certainly conformable to the enterprise, answered the spy, while he took his straw hat between his knees, and wiped the perspiration from his brow. 'I know the price, it is certainly suitable, although not extraordinary, if you consider that one hazards his life in such cases. It cannot be unknown to you that the very uncomfortable use of all sorts of murderous weapons, and, above all, daggers, and sometimes poisoned daggers, is frequently practised against —against the truest servants, who are united to the government by such tender ties, that a single ray of the light or disclosure instantly severs them."

"No fear, Señor Falsodo," said the police officer, laughing, as he again had recourse to Señor Domingo's snuff box; "think rather of your future prospects, of the career which opens before you."

" It is a system worthy of the highest respect! that of rewarding the faithful servants of the state at the expense of rebels and other traitors," replied Señor Falsodo, "only the risk is too great, and there is no security against dagger strokes.'

"Cowardice" muttered the commissary of police, "want of talent for the office, faintheartedness without cause"—and turned to Padre Fernando to inquire concerning his last interview with the condemned. The result of all his questions, however, was wholly unsatisfactory. The monk declared that all his endeavors had been in vain to extort the least information from the hardened sinner. He described the condemned as being in a state of apathy, and remarked of him further, that he answered some of the questions put to him only in part, and others not at all, and that he at last begged to see the Benedictine, Brother Celeste, once more, and to pass the last hours of his life with him; first objecting, however, to the continuance of an examination which he thought was not authorized by any sacrament of the church. "He was condemned to death and desired the fulfilment—the execution of the sentence." "Those were his first and last words," sighed Padre Fernando, plunging still deeper into the snuff box of Señor Domingo, as if his nerves required an instant strengthening by means of some external excitement. A long pause ensued, during which the police officer looked straight before him. "A most unheard of event," said he at last, breaking silence, "one that has never happened before in my practice, a crime committed—high treason committed—evidence of the fact in existence, and the author not to be discovered, a volunteer places himself in the way of death, that he may carry with him to the grave the mystery that envelopes the act. Pardon has been offered him—the way has been opened for him to leave the prison perfectly free—to retain possession of his property, and live in all comfort, any where out of this country, if he will only inform against the author of these cursed Elegies, if he will only deliver the real criminal into the hands of justice—besides unconditional pardon for the high treason of which he has allowed himself to become guilty, as an accomplice, by circulating such punishable poetry. All this has been offered him, and he refuses to name the author."

"Or the authoress!" added Señor Falsodo, with emphasis.

"Hem! indeed—quite possible," rejoined Señor Borrachezo, slowly nodding his head; "indeed! it may be a lady! it is a possible case!"

'And becomes to me all the while more likely," insisted the spy, "especially as it is well known that the patriotism of the women of our country sometimes exceeds the zeal of the men! I engage we would more easily get rid of rebels if there were no women."

"It has become notorious, and is not the case in our country alone, the influence of women in church and state is undeniable,' said Señor Borrachezo, energetically; "the petticoat governs the monarchy, and the glance of beauty forms heroes for the battle, popes are elected—bishops created, by women. Yes! yes! gentlemen, woman rules the world, and when married, her husband besides. A married man has his reasons for not being dangerous to the state! If a woman has written the slanderous Elegies, we ought not to seek her in the married state, at least not in domestic happiness We must keep a register, Señor Falsodo," continued he, after a pause "a register of our young hero's female acquaintances and friends of all classes, there must be a private register made, with daily notes as to their familiar resorts and rendezvous, evening visits on balcony and terrace '

At this moment the mulatto, Narcissus, the factotum of all communication between the persons in the prison and the world outside, hastily entered the office, with the information that Brother Celeste was at his heels, which was verified by the personal appearance of the latter A young Benedictine monk, the habit of whose order was made of singularly fine stuff, greeted those present with the priestly salutation, and inquired for what purpose he had been summoned His form was noble, of the middle size, in air and manner bearing the stamp of a certain dignity, which seemed rather to have remained in him from his former connexion with the world, than what the severe monastic discipline could ever impress upon a youth, who, like so many cloister brothers, had entered into orders "from the dregs of the people"

The police officer informed him of the cause of his being summoned, which he apparently heard with the cold insensibility of a priest accustomed to view, in the condemned, the criminal rather than the man Church and state alike, usually concern themselves too late with the human heart When the sentence is about to be fulfilled, which tears a human being from life, when the ties have long been broken which bound him to mankind, the church first informs the sinner that, at least beyond the grave, love and justice are to be found

The rigid features of the monk's deathly pale countenance gave no sign even of sympathy, no look indicated the least personal interest in the fate of the unfortunate man, to prepare whom for his momentous and approaching departure he had been summoned to his presence Just as little did his features indicate either assent or willingness, when the police officer gave him to understand that the government expected important disclosures through the last confessional interview of the condemned with the servant of the church To avoid this degrading requirement, Brother Celeste inquired where the condemned was to be found, and desired to be conducted to him Señor Falsodo had rather obtrusively placed himself by the side of the monk, and seemed inclined to accompany him, when the Alcalde* called a turnkey and gave him the needful orders Brother Celeste declared, in few words, that his interview with the condemned must be without witnesses, according to the rules of the church in such cases The spy appeared greatly embarrassed at having his company thus declined, he cast a glance at the red nose of the police officer, who put a good face on a bad business, and with a shrug of the shoulder assented to the monk's decided demand, and then added, that he was well aware of his extreme desire to obtain the requisite information concerning the person who had been guilty of such high treason

"The criminal is condemned by the sentence of our Director," interrupted the monk ; "the

crime on his part was proved before sentence was pronounced. It must be fulfilled, and I know my office and my duty towards the criminal conduct me to his dungeon "

The police officer thought it would be better to conduct the prisoner to a room where he might pass the last hours of his life more comfortably. The monk opposed this apparently humane proposal, remarking, at the same time, that the privilege of choosing the place belonged of right to the criminal, according to the customary liberty of the so called "dungeon hours ' But previously he desired to speak with him alone in the dungeon, undisturbed, and with closed doors

The resolute and measured deportment of the young monk, the dignity which manifested itself in word and look, and in his whole person, involuntarily checked the opposition of those present, who yielded a silent assent to his wishes, and resumed their consultations, while the turnkey and the Benedictine disappeared behind doors and grates

CHAPTER II.

THE CONDEMNED

IF we examine the buildings of the Jesuits in all parts of the world, we find an analogy between their foundations, their very groundworks, and the basis of their world-embracing system, both manifest durability and firmness To the perseverance, allied with the depth of consolidation employed by the Jesuits to erect their politico-religious edifice, (as a system,) is alone to be ascribed the extension and effect of their soul-destroying efforts Unlimited command of the social and political, as well as of the religious forms of human society, is the true aim of their secret and open labors No order exercises such a decided authority over the human will, such a strenuous self-denial, (as the means of attaining a proposed aim,) as does the "Order of the Society of Jesus" These considerations embrace a truth which strikes us the more painfully, when it appears evident to us that the object of the society is to degrade mankind under the scourge of absolutism The power of the order attained such a height in past centuries that it even sought to set aside the absolutism of monarchy, to promote its particular aim to its own sole and exclusive rule, and, unhappily, it here and there succeeded. As the gigantic enterprises of the Jesuits, indicated by their colossal edifices, now among the multitude of other monuments of the past, disappeared in Europe, the world-embracing sovereignty of this order advanced with the more rapid strides in South America.

A tragic contrast is offered for our consideration; the thought suggests itself, what a society, on a similar basis of firmness and solidity , with the same energy and perseverance, might have undertaken and accomplished for the welfare of mankind, if their united efforts, after the example of the Jesuits, had acknowledged the principle of humanity, instead of the principle of self-

---

* Alcalde del carcel, Superintendent of the Prison.

aggrandizement, (of absolute egotism,) and had pursued (or rather would pursue) this object with the same unshakeable tenacity of purpose, as did the Jesuits then aim for universal spiritual dominion, for the paralyzing of mind

In building their monasteries, as in all the edifices of the Jesuits, particular regard was had to their vaulted foundations the under-ground apartments, torture chambers, dungeons, and cellars, were arranged on the most masterly plan *dungeons* to restrain the spirit of progress, *cellars* to preserve the spirit of the wine for the triumphal banquets of their confederates

In one of these dungeons, which might serve as a model for similar constructions of modern days in Russia and its dependencies, the other states of the European continent, Señor Alphonso, the condemned, was confined His form was thin and tall, on which an active nervous organization appeared to have overcome the material tendency to flesh and corpulency, his pale, sallow countenance evinced the proud dignity of the Spanish race, but he, in common with all the inhabitants of La Plata, regarded his Spanish descent with indifference, if not aversion, while they acknowledged their situation as South Americans In the progress of the age towards freedom and enlightenment, they seemed unwilling to remember their European extraction, inasmuch as it reached back to the blood-stained histories of former days, with whose horrors the annals of the new world were also filled

Alphonso's meagre countenance, surrounded by coal-black hair, which particularly adorns the Castilian, was animated by the glance of a deep-set dark eye, rich in that magnetic fluid which appertains to the human eye as the organ of the soul He was dressed in the costume of his social condition, enveloped in a soldier's frock, his hands and feet loaded with chains and fetters

The turnkey opened the double iron doors of the dungeon, whose subdued light hardly made visible the individuals whose entrance interrupted the loneliness of the prisoner The monk found himself inside of the narrow vault, the doors were carefully locked and bolted on the outside Uncertain whether the longed for friend of his heart approached, or whether another monk in a habit of the same order stepped over the threshold, the unhappy man awaited, speechless and motionless, the first greeting of him who entered

' Alphonso !'' cried a voice, whose sound awakened a thousand memories of childhood and youth in the breast of the South American "Alphonso ! Alphonso !'' exclaimed the monk again in the outburst of a soul rending sorrow

"Lorenzo, is it you ?" inquired the prisoner, in a low faltering voice, and a long silent embrace followed

There are moments in life when we find that human language is no fitting organ for the life of the soul, there is a glance of the eye which says more than words can compass, and which, even in night and darkness, reveals reciprocal emotion. And when words lose their might, the overpowering feelings of the deeply agitated human breast gush forth in tears The extreme emotion of these tender friends, united by the holiest ties, over whose destinies fate lowered so portentously, overflowed in those pearls of the speechless soul-life, which is born from suf-

fering, and whose value he only discovers down whose cheeks and on whose breast they fall

"Lorenzo !" sobbed Alphonso, at length returning with a strong effort to external life, "have you seen her ? spoken to her ? been with her ?"

"I have done all, without consulting you, that I should have expected from you, had you been in my place, I in yours," replied Lorenzo, as the monk called *Celeste* "Did you receive and destroy the billet of your nephew Horatio ?"

"The passage from Calderon," returned Alphonso "which any one could have read without understanding it, and of which I alone could comprehend the sense and meaning I received the leaf wrapped round some tobacco, as they have allowed me to receive anything from my friends '

"Good," continued Lorenzo, "but our moments are numbered, we must understand each other quickly Dolores is in safety, and we depart hence before day-break, if a single decisive event can be averted, if she can be dissuaded from the resolution to suffer death in your stead, to come here in disguise and remain behind, while you leave the dungeon in her garb, and in her stead go on board a vessel where Horatio already awaits her

' Dolores !'' sighed Alphonso, in a broken voice, "impossible ! no, never, never ! but a ray of light penetrates my soul ! Were it possible that she might appear here undetected as you would have arranged it—Lorenzo, you can conceive what prompts me—call it not selfishness, the wish that springs up within me, to take leave of Dolores—on condition, however, that the struggle may be over first, that she will approach in the last hours of my life, with that self-possession so peculiar to her character Tell me, how have you arranged the plan so as to overcome the impossibility of her appearance here in the dungeon ? I will then decide if I can allow of its fulfilment, or whether the preponderating risk makes it my duty to deny myself this gratification "

" Dolores,' replied Lorenzo, with forced composure " is here in the neighborhood, at the house of her friend, the English lady, furnished with the habit of our order, which I brought under my own, from my wardrobe, and delivered to her in person, consequently avoiding all privity of others Being the librarian of our monastery, I can visit the Englishman's house without ceremony, as he manages my correspondence with Ireland, and receives books and papers from thence, for us The passage from Calderon gave you the intimation that you might receive the Lord's supper at my hands, I require a brother of our order for the administration of the sacrament, Dolores is to appear as a Benedictine the time of night favors her entrance into the building, which no one will notice, as it is an ordinary everyday occurrence Although we can only remain here a moment, yet, you can—then—take leave of her—see her once more, but there must be here, (as you are sensible yourself,) no struggle, no conflict of the holiest feelings, which would betray you and—bring both of you to death "

"So be it, then," said Alphonso, in low decided tones, "so be it !—on condition that Dolores yields up her urgent wish to sacrifice herself for me, to the higher duty of devoting her talents and mental aspirations to the future. Let her remember that the idea of the confederacy of the United States of South America is illustrated and displayed in her exalted powers, in the might of her enthusiasm, in the majesty of her words. As the personified idea of the future, life on earth becomes to her a sacred duty. I was to pass away, and am the subordinate agent of that Providence which accomplishes my destiny—through Dolores. The tool which he formed for the service of that sacred object has become useless—it is broken by tyranny. The instrument vanishes from this earthly sphere, but as the genius of South America, she lives, and in her, the exalted, godlike idea of the future—of the foundation of the union of the South in the spirit of Humanity."

"I understand you," said Lorenzo, "and Dolores will as little mistake your resolve to reject her sacrifice of love."

"Once more, I beseech you," sighed Alphonso, convulsively seizing the hand of his friend, "once more I beseech you, hold fast to the condition. I know Dolores, I know her love to me, I feel that I require from her an unheard of, superhuman effort, yes, I require from her a resolution of which I myself should hardly be capable—to tear myself in such a moment from her arms—to resign her to death, as I now require of her in my own behalf."

Lorenzo seized the word as the prisoner concluded. "I hope to God that the sense of duty will vanquish in her the urgent desire of yielding herself a sacrifice, she should know that your very self-respect is a man would not permit such an offering of love on her part, and she should not deny you the last consolation of a farewell."

"The twilight has passed away into night since I came here," continued Lorenzo, after a pause. "thunder clouds increase the darkness—I will leave you now, and inform the door-keepers that I shall return about midnight, attended by my brother with the ciborium. I shall use a chalice belonging to myself, in order to avoid our sacristy. To evade all suspicion, I will institute the sacrament in the usual manner in the chapel in this edifice, but, on pretence of economy, no candles shall be lighted except the lamp of eternal light, which casts its mild rays upon the altar, but not sufficient to cause us to be observed. For a possible case, however, old Achilles, well disguised and strongly armed, shall attend us as a servant of the monastery, and afterwards conduct Dolores to the quinta of Mr. Walker, and then on board the vessel, he will never leave her—never lose sight of her, he will be her attendant on board, and wherever her fate may lead her."

Alphonso still pressed the hand of Lorenzo, trembling in all his limbs, less from personal fear, to which he was a stranger, than from apprehension and anxiety in behalf of the risk which Dolores incurred, so long as she remained in the territory of Buenos Ayres, or any where on this side of the mouth of the La Plata river.

At length compelled, through the urgency of the occasion, to deny himself the consolatory presence of Lorenzo, he dismissed his bosom friend to arrange a meeting, of which, an hour before, his boldest fancy would not have dreamed.

CHAPTER III.

THE NEGRO.

CELESTE gave a sign by violent knocking on the inner door, whereupon the outer door, and then the second, was opened, whose massive iron was so thick as to render it impossible for the most attentive listener to distinguish a syllable of the conversation which took place in the dungeon.

The Benedictine found old Domingo alone in his sitting room, near the principal entrance of the building opposite to the porter's cell, his guests, wearied with a fruitless consultation, had gone their way, and left him and his snuff box, each, in his own mode, resolving immediately to trace out the clue to the mysteriously concealed existence of the exalted poet.

Señor Domingo did not fail to offer to Brother Celeste a pinch of snuff, without which, as it appeared, he could think of no greeting or meeting, and politely invited him into the room, and requested him to be seated. Celeste, (Lorenzo,) who maintained the customary tone of high society in his worldly intercourse, would not damp the humbly subservient hospitality of the old officer by a repulsive priestly arrogance. He sought, on the contrary, by his evident condescension, to requite the pointed, and undoubtedly respectful attentions of the old man, with a deportment which was well calculated to heighten his confidence to a degree which he felt might be essentially requisite for the approaching eventful occasion.

He immediately took the offered seat, gave the necessary orders for the sacrament in the chapel, remarking at the same time, that he found the condemned in a most melancholy state, in which, instead of his mother tongue, he spoke in a confused mixture of French, Italian and Latin. Celeste availed himself of this list to prepare for an unrestrained interview in the French language, between Alphonso and Dolores, at which Señor Domingo might happen to be present. Señor Domingo informed him officially, that the officer of the guard had already appointed the seven and twenty men who were to execute the sentence.

As a singular mark of respect to the former social position of the condemned, the officer had sought for the most distinguished and certain shots in his company, and was to take command of them himself, which, in all other cases, was entrusted to an awkward corporal or sergeant.

Celeste commended himself to the kindness of Señor Domingo, bowed before the crucifix, which was suspended over a sort of house altar in the apartment, and withdrew slowly and with measured steps, in all the dignity of his office.

The daily bustle of a thickly peopled commercial town sank by degrees, like the waves of the swelling ocean, to the ebb of relaxation and quiet. Promenaders of various classes passed to and fro on the sidewalks of the principal streets, engaged in conversation on indifferent subjects, when not discussing the revolution in Rio Grande, and the ever-enduring daily article of war and peace between Buenos Ayres and Monte Video, which was discussed over the cradle of the present generation, and has, so to say, grown up with them, and according to appearances, will extend over the bier of the living, as a reiterated article for discussion at the cradle-side of a future generation

The pulperías* of the most frequented streets of the first and second classes were, like the French Cafés, filled with customers, who, taking their usual places, and sipping this or that drink, smoked cigarettes by the gross, and tried to build "castles in the air," when the subject of conversation had no foundation in reality.

Brother Celeste betook himself to his monastery by the most direct way, where Achilles awaited him near the garden wall

The family of Dolores was one of the most considerable in the country, whose wealthy possessions brought with them a crowd of domestic servants, of divers colors. The pedigree of old Achilles could be traced back a century, from the tribe of *Minas*, in Africa, without any intermixture of another race. One of his ancestors, brought from Africa as a slave, and purchased by the great-grandfather of Dolores as his lawful possession, had solemnly married a negress of the same race, and in such wise did his descendants in like manner continue in the Spanish family on the banks of the river La Plata—as a double household, whose children played and grew up together. The removal of bondage from the blacks, a consequence of the independence of the United Provinces of La Plata, had in nowise alienated the negro family from the relatives of Dolores. Humane treatment on the one side, gratitude and fidelity on the side of the inferiors, had wrought a bond of attachment, which in time became a habit, a relation thence proceeded, which reminds us of the patriarchal age of antiquity, and manifests itself at times in all countries where the feelings of humanity are not altogether oppressed by slavery.

The father of Achilles had served the family as coachman, and would not forego the honor of conveying the corpses of their beloved parents to the churchyard, in person, when the reconciling angel of death called them both, within a short interval, away from this earthly night of suffering and sorrow.

Dolores inhabited, with her uncle, (her mother's brother,) a quinta,† where Achilles, dressed according to the quasi station of major-domo, was, so to speak, considered in the family as a companion, and consulted in all the subordinate affairs of the house. His daughter, Corinna, grown up with Dolores from the cradle, held the post of her chambermaid and notwithstanding the ban of color, was treated by her lady with all confidence, which, interwoven, as it were, with the first sentiments of their childish hearts, effected the moral improvement of both. The race of *Minas* negroes in South America is universally preferred and protected, insomuch as prominent peculiarities distinguish their nationality, which last, nearly all the negroes endeavor to uphold. This is not the place to insert our views and observations on the morality and capacities of the negroes of South America. There are, to be sure, particular races, which, with relation to disposition and talents, seem to be endowed by Nature with a step-mother's portion, in return for which, however, other races not

only stand equal in moral respects with the whites in other countries, but excel the lower classes of many white populations. Under the last head, may be classed the Kabendas, Mandingos, Mozambiques, Minas, and many other races. The race of Minas, so called after their native province in Africa, (which is rich in metal,) are men of noble appearance—most of them tall, athletic figures—the form of their countenances bordering on the Caucasian. Their expression, like their character and whole deportment, is earnest, and combined with a certain thoughtful reserve, and natural dignity, which manifests itself even in their air and gestures, in this, and other respects, they bear a general resemblance to the Kabendas. Their chins are usually covered with a thick beard, which is deficient in many negro tribes. The fundamental peculiarities of the Minas race appear to be incorruptible honesty, diligence in every employment, technical talent for all sorts of business, unshakeable attachment to each other as friends, fondness for domestic life in the circle of their race, and unswerving submission, fidelity, and devotion, in their relations as slaves or servants to the whites, while they are regarded as men, and humanely treated. The negroes possess the remarkable peculiarity of distinguishing with surprising acuteness, the varieties of nationality in Europeans, as well as the prominent traits of human character. According to this so called instinctive knowledge of mankind, the negro directs his confidence or mistrust, his attachments or dislikes, probably without being conscious himself of the intuition which guides him.

Achilles was a perfect exemplar of a Minas negro, in all the distinctive marks of that race. His frame, in which there was more bone than muscle, authenticated his origin, by the proud bearing and innate perception noticed above. On account of the early development of the negro in tropical climates, he appeared old, and the hair of his head and his beard exhibited a slight sprinkling of grey, while his robust activity betokened manly strength, which defied the influence of the climate in which destiny had transplanted his fathers.

Achilles had sought a stone near the iron gate of the garden of the monastery, pointed out to him by the friend of his lady, when he left him, at which he should await him until his return to his cell. Seldom as the visit of a monk to any private house might appear strange, in this case, peculiar circumstances combined to render the direct interview of Celeste with a young lady in the hours of night, especially dangerous, as it tended to make a coincidence

The vigilance of the police greatly embarrassed the movements of the monk, and on the other hand, his relations with his order required the utmost caution, if he would not excite suspicions which might give occasion for an investigation on the part of the authorities.

Without any previous knowledge of what nature the interview with Alphonso might be, and to what decision it might lead, Celeste had taken measures to prepare, through the trustworthy Achilles, a medium of communication between Dolores and his unfortunate friend.

The quiet of night surrounded the monastery. An oppressive stillness, the precursor of a thunder storm, fettered the topmost boughs of the

---

* Pulperia, a shop—pulpero, shop-keeper.
† Country house.

high trees, which partly overhung the walls
The footsteps of single passers by, intercepted
from time to time the noiseless silence. But
they were not the tread of the Benedictine in his
light sandals, and Achilles listened intently, as
motionless as the broad leaf of the gigantic om-
bados,* whose night-like shadow enveloped that
portion of the garden where he waited with increasing impatience.

This old negro was a sort of sealed family
chronicle of the events of his house, transmitted
to him by tradition from his father and grandfather, and increased by his personal interest in
all which had befallen the family from his childhood to the present time, his heart was like the
covering of a paquet of important family papers,
preserved by a black Ethiopian seal of secrecy
The meditative silence, peculiar to his national
character, was much increased by the unlimited
confidence of his masters   The more deeply he
was received into the relations and affairs of the
family, the more was his pride aroused to enjoy
unlimited confidence, and the higher did his zeal
arise, to show himself worthy of his position

Besides himself and his daughter Corinna,
Alphonso was the only person who knew the
situation in which Dolores was placed   The intelligence that Alphonso would become at day-
break the victim of shameless tyranny, would
have been sufficient of itself to deprive him of all
resolution, but his pain was greatly enhanced by
the thought that the "wonderful spirit" of Dolores, as he called it, (without being able to
comprehend it,) had indirectly drawn destruction upon the head of her beloved   He especially admired and honored in this mysterious
being her "wonderful spirit," which he so designated, because he could find no more appropriate term   Sinking more and more deeply in
reflection, he involved himself still more in the
web of considerations, which made the thought
of the deliverance of both persons beyond the
limits of possibility   He had but a miserable life
to lose, and was resolved to sacrifice it joyfully,
if he could, by so doing, save the friend of his
mistress, and herself.   He felt himself the more
unhappy, the more he was penetrated by the
consciousness that his will was palsied by the
insurmountable force of circumstances. Sunk in
such sad musings, he had forgotten the world
without, when he felt himself suddenly aroused
from his revery by a hand on his shoulder, and a
manly voice sounding in his ear   "How goes
it, friend Achilles?" was the salutation, accompanied by a heavy blow on his right arm   Achilles, whom the appearance of any human being,
except the expected Celeste, would have terrified, felt all the more alarmed at the appearance
of a person who, even though in remote idea,
was connected with the former days and fate of
his lady Dolores   As if roused from real slumber, he rubbed his eyes, and looked anxiously
around him, while he dreaded the return of Celeste, to which, until now, he had looked forward
with increasing impatience.

"Good evening, Señor Perezoso—how do you
do?" he began, after a pause, which followed
the salutation, and rose up, and instinctively
prepared for all possible accidents which might

---

* A sort of elm.

occur from this unwelcome interruption to his
loneliness   The person who stood before him
was one of those consonants in the great book of
this bustling world, which, on this or that page
of a day's history, stand as consonants, without
any special meaning, and at most obtain a cha-
acter as letters, in connexion with some vowel,
or, like types in general, allow themselves to be
used in any composition, to-day serving in an
essay which sets forth the principles of freedom,
to-morrow appearing in the praise of some tyrant,
until they are thrown for re-casting into the
churchyard mass of corruption, by the hand of
death, which dissolves all human compositions

Perezoso was a little man, with a round face,
and a sharp, and, what people consider, *piercing*
eye   His dress differed as little from the daily
costume of an European of any nation, as one
form of printing type from all others in general,
in themselves an insignificant alphabet of a case
of letters   Should he, at any time, be placed in
any class which the collection of masses of men
create, Señor Perezoso would prefer to pass under the title of a "literary gentleman," while
he, like so many of his species, assumed the title
without being particularly acquainted with any
literature, although, on the other hand, he was
not deficient in many so called practical acquirements, and possessed a certain penetration   He
would also wish to be considered as a gentleman
among gentlemen

Perezoso lived in the above category, as
teacher of languages and translator, and as such
had an extensive acquaintance in the educated
circles of society, in whose outward forms he
was thoroughly versed, so that he might as
readily pass for a gentleman, as many other *gentlemen* without figure or appearance   He had
for years visited at the house of the family in
which the old Achilles figured as a member bestowing on the two young ladies, Theresa and
Dolores, instructions in French and Italian

"How is Señora Dolores?" he inquired of
poor Achilles, who was making every effort to
conceal his solicitude, which was excited by the
thought that Celeste might suddenly arrive, and
that his appearance might furnish occasion for
deep reflection to the teacher   Before he made
any reply, he bethought himself whether it
would not be better to lead off the unwelcome
old acquaintance from the gate of the monastery
—a measure which he instantly rejected, as this
was his appointed post, and as even the shortest
removal from it might prevent his meeting with
Celeste.

"Señora Dolores," he at length replied, mea-
suring the teacher from head to foot, "I thank
you, Señor Perezoso, is well, very well, so far as
I know   But I have not seen her this week,
however, she is not here, she is at our old
quinta, thirteen leagues from here, she will soon
be married, the good Señora Dolores."

"Married?" inquired Perezoso, with peculiar
curiosity—every piece of news being of the
highest importance to him, as material for conversation in the widely extended circle of his
acquaintance—"to whom is she to be married?"

"She marries a foreigner, an European, a
merchant, a young millionaire; his name is Señor Pepefy and company"

"What?" cried Perezoso, "is she going to

marry Señor Pepefy and company?' the young Señor Pepety ' with the long nose?'"

"So they say,' replied Achilles; "whether the young man's nose is any longer than yours I cannot tell, but he is going to-morrow to Valparaiso, and will marry the Señora when he returns"

"For Valparaiso, to-morrow! is that certain?" pursued Perezoso, with the most eager curiosity, for his thoughts reverted to a small sum of money which the said Señor Pepety owed him for instructions, and also for translations

Achilles had, according to the German proverb, "set a pan of blind hares running," in order to produce a train of thought in the mind of the unwelcome guest, that should remove him from the truth While he meditated springing a third hare, to produce an effect of all others the most desirable, namely, that of getting him away either spiritually or bodily, from the walls of the monastery, Señor Perezoso had already prepared to depart He laid for a minute the fore finger of his right hand on the right side of his nose, considering whether he should write Señor Pepety a billet, or rather, with all speed, present him a visiting card, thus reminding him in a delicate manner of the said debt He decided on the latter, and left the old negro without any particular ceremony of leave-taking Achilles drew a long breath, and followed the retreating figure of the literary gentleman with a look of unspeakable relief, which he enjoyed more and more, the greater the distance became between them The old man found his long waiting at the gate hazardous in the highest degree, since this visit had made the danger apparent to him, which a light suspicion of the true state of the circumstances that led him there might bring upon him

He feared to seat himself in his old place, and wandered slowly back and forth in the neighborhood of it, again so deeply absorbed that he hardly perceived a sound or an object of the world without, and at last remained standing near a pillar of the iron gate, against which he leaned himself Unconscious how long he had continued in this dream-like condition, he was again startled by the immediate neighborhood of a human figure, which stepped directly before him, and whispered his classical name in his ear

"Señor Lorenzo,' replied he, in a subdued voice, calling the monk by the name with which he had first greeted him when a boy.

"Are you asleep, Achilles? are you overcome after so many nights' watching?" said Celeste to him The old man sprang suddenly aside, and involuntarily felt in his girdle in search of his weapon, then wrapped himself more closely in the mantle which concealed it

"Señora Dolores will be allowed to see Alphonso to-night, if you can persuade her to relinquish the resolution which she has formed, to remain behind in the dungeon instead of him Alphonso's honor will not admit of it—his love still less, she must be convinced of its impossibility. In order to take leave of him, we must first arrange to bring her here to the monastery, the means are already at her disposal If she consents to Alphonso's request to see him, and to leave him without persisting in her design,

conduct her to this gate at eleven o'clock, dressed in the habit of the order, which I carried to her yesterday. I will meet you here, and you shall attend me to the prison'

"Señora Dolores take leave of Alphonso! Oh! oh! Señor Lorenzo! Señor Lorenzo! Señor Alphonso is to die! is to be shot early to-morrow!' Oh! oh! Señor Lorenzo!" cried the old negro, and a stream of scalding tears burst from his sparkling eyes, while the thought of the fulfilment of the sentence deprived him of speech

"Almighty God of whites and blacks!'" sobbed Achilles, after a short pause, while he tried to conceal his tears with his mantle "Almighty God! where are now the Unitarians, the brethren and colleagues of Alphonso? where are the republicans of La Plata, that they leave him in the dungeon, and do not storm the prison before he is shot?'

"Compose yourself, Achilles," interrupted Lorenzo, "compose yourself, our friends are paralyzed through the power of Rosas The most efficient languish in dungeons like Alphonso, or in banishment from the borders of the La Plata, hundreds stand aloof, and no one of them will approach the other, for fear of drawing upon himself a similar fate They reserve their strength for days to come, and what assistance would it be for the present to storm the dungeon, and increase the number of sacrifices by a bloody struggle, if they could not at the same time surprise the palace of Rosas, and strike the tree of curses at its root?

"Rosas has concealed himself," muttered the negro, "Rosas, the tiger, will not leave his den, and vultures watch for every lamb that approaches it, and every bird that flies over it Rosas lets his horse* be led before the people— he is represented in the person of his horse on his birthday Rosas allows his image† to be worshipped as God, and conceals himself, like God, invisible, and the people believe that he is almighty as God, while he makes money to pay executioners! And the people surrender the power into his hands! Stupid people, the whites and colored people on the Plata river!"

While he muttered these "black reflections," Celeste stood sunk in thought, to suggest a word of counsel for Dolores, in whose welfare he was deeply interested There remained to him no other means to influence the decision of Dolores, and bring the alternative home to her, than to lay before her, through Achilles, the question, "If she would see her betrothed under the above conditions, or would withhold from him this last consolation?"

After having again briefly impressed these conditions on the mediator, and particularly charged him to warn Dolores of every danger which a manifestation of her feelings in the prison might lead to, he committed the affair to the prudence and dexterity of the negro, and passed through the garden gate of the monastery.

---

*Instead of appearing personally before the people, Rosas at times, on particular feast days, caused his horse to be trotted out, led by officers of high rank
†The portrait of Rosas, surrounded with red ribbons and flowers, was at times lifted on high and carried in procession, attended by priests.

CHAPTER IV.

THE ENGLISHMAN

AMONG the numerous English families that seek their *comfort* in all parts of the world to which the waves of the ocean bear a keel, or where their *business* establishes a *home*, the Walker family lived, in Buenos Ayres, in all the splendor of an undisputed respectability. They inhabited one of the most eligible houses in the street Victoria, which name, it is true, was given before the Queen of Great Britain mounted the throne, and entered into intimate alliance with the Emperor of Russia, but now, as the address of the English house, it acquired peculiar value. It is the easiest thing possible to indicate the standing and style of living of this family, as we only need to mention that it was an *English family of respectability.* Their house was of course furnished in English style, and covered with English carpets. Iron chimneys lawfully cast in England, and shells from the British colonies on the mantelpieces, English blue and white china services, a supply of castor oil, a knocker on the house door, and a bull dog in the yard, were sufficient attributes of unimpeachable nationality.

Mr Walker stood high on the Exchange, and would long since have become British consul, had he not, in secret, sustained the much higher rank of quasi diplomat, which brought him into personal intercourse with the assembled ministers and private secretaries of the sole ruler of La Plata. He considered himself the actual British ambassador in Buenos Ayres, which dignity was known to himself alone. He maintained, in a measure, a standing similar to that of a cabinet maker in Berlin, whom Frederick the Great, in jest, named privy counsellor, on condition that, besides themselves, no soul must know of the title. As a Briton, through the liberty of the press in his fatherland, he had always been allowed political reading, and had selected politics as his darling pursuit. From a longing to display his abilities in parliament, for which he was qualified by his wealth, without possessing any prominent talent for rhetorical discussion, he had thrice sought to gratify his ambition to become a member of that honorable body. Thrice defeated, and at length discontented with his native land, he left England, and established himself in business on the banks of the La Plata, where he now by all methods endeavored to carry out his political *role*, without in the least degree taking any open share in political events.

One fixed idea of old Mr Walker was, the annexation of all the provinces of La Plata to the British Crown, with which he combined a yet more audacious project, which, in itself, was by no means to be despised. After long and profound study of the geography of South America, he made the discovery that a union of the rivers Amazon and La Plata by means of a canal was possible, and when that should be completed, a steam navigation might be established from the Equator through South America to the 36th or 37th degree of south latitude. This undertaking was, of course, only to be carried on under "*British protection*," although, perhaps, with foreign capital, on the supposition

that both shores of the united floods for several hundred miles east and west, would serve as British colonies, depots for British manufactures, and furnish offices for the portionless sons of the English aristocracy. In pursuance of this bold idea, he had opened a mediatorial correspondence in London, by means of which he might, at least, lay his project before the private secretary of some minister. While he sought to have it understood there, that he was the right hand man of Rosas in Buenos Ayres, and carried all the provinces of La Plata, so to say, in his pocket, he endeavored to make himself appear to the parvenues who composed the cabinet of Rosas, as a secret ambassador from Great Britain, who had in his vest pocket the gift of the crown to the Dictator, in case the latter would consent to conquer and reserve Monte Video for England, that is, to permit the British government to erect forts at the outlet of the La Plata and control the navigation, from Cape St Antonio, along that river, by way of the ideal canal, to the mouth of the river Amazon, where a British viceroyalty (Para) should be established—the government of which he reserved for himself, and afterwards for his son, Mr Robert William Walker.

With regard to the future political condition of South America, *under British protection* all was, of course, in the best order, in Mr John Walker's port folio, when he sought, in the meantime, to turn the present circumstances of the country to his more immediate advantage. He was interested in several mining companies which had been established by Englishmen in South America, and in such *business* stood with one foot in Brazil and with the other in Buenos Ayres. Stamped by nature as a diplomat, he was under the necessity of doing something *secret*, which should at the same time be directly profitable, and accordingly he indulged his ruling *passion for mystery* by the unlawful exportation of precious metals and diamonds. He was also secretly engaged, as the principal owner of some slave ships, in conveying fresh laborers to the mines in Brazil, in which he, of course, had a double interest. He was, as the English say, *fond of secrets*, and could not have slept quietly if he had not been excited by a secret some hours before he went to rest.

CHAPTER V

DOLORES

SENOR Rodeiigo B——, the uncle of Dolores, maintained the standing of a man of independent fortune, whose riches were rated very high. Induced by the well known *respectability* of this *foreigner*, Mr John Walker had sought his acquaintance as a neighbor on the banks of the La Plata, and had shown the peculiar condescension of introducing his daughter, Miss Fanny, as the playmate of Dolores and Theresa.

This condescension, on the part of a Briton, must have been most highly valued by a South American, of Spanish descent, and, of course, a foreigner. However well meant on the part of the Briton might have been the introduction of

Miss Fanny, as the future friend of the Señoras Dolores and Theresa, fate could hardly have brought together two beings more totally different than Miss Fanny and Señora Dolores

In Dolores, from her childhood, a mind was developed which seized upon all the appearances of nature as well as of life, with a glow of feeling that shone with crystal clearness in every thought of her active mind These images in effect caused, in her early childhood, volcanic eruptions of a powerful and inwardly pervading warmth of emotion, which took the form of poetry Unconsciously to herself her spirit was elevated to a height of intuition which made the earthly life, whose chaos swept around her, appear foreign and strange to her

Her mother had with maternal partiality comprehended the peculiarities of her beloved child, and without the least intention of forming a prodigy which might in time serve a museum as a happy acquisition for its public exhibitions, had conducted her education with peculiar care Providence had bestowed upon her another daughter, her first born whose mind with similar intensity, had developed a preference for religious meditation Her spirit, even when unrestrained, never elevated itself to that high sphere of inward life, by the light of which the caricatures of the social world of our century are exposed to view, while it too often loads the breast which nourishes this higher idea of existence, with pain, sorrow, and grief

Dolores was born and brought up at a quinta, whose gentle elevation imparted a romantic prospect to the west across the expansive stream from whence onward it became like a sea, or rather like the ocean, while to the east the boundless pampas, here and there interrupted by insignificant hills and woods, displayed themselves like portions of an endless world

The starry sky of the southern hemisphere, glittering in this climate with peculiar brilliancy, presented to the the child's contemplation an unfathomable wonder-world of various appearances The thunder, attended by those wild storms (pamperos) which chase over the unbroken plains, announcing, as it were, a breaking up of the forces of nature, and immediately succeeded by the returning stillness, united the heart of the child more closely to the charms of the surrounding scenery The sentiment of love, strengthened by her admiration of nature, was blended with holy reverence and adoration of an all-ruling Deity At the same time, with these impressions of nature, Dolores received the bloody image of the struggles and uprisings of a human sense of honor and right against oppression and tyranny, which filled the annals of that period Gifted with that unhappy depth of mind which received all external impressions with such vividness, that the joy or grief of others became ingrafted as a part of her very being, Dolores beheld the struggles of her nation for freedom and independence from the same elevated point of view from which her mind had imbibed its ideas of nature, creation, and God, and the principle of *love* as the first principle of all being. As it is a historical truth, that mental power elevates itself more boldly when despotism seeks to subdue it, and loses itself, now and then, amid the relaxation of material comfort, when the element of freedom opens the

way to progress so did the spirit of Dolores unfold itself to astonishing height and expansion, the more the scornful power of absolutism, represented through Rosas, sought to stifle the pure sentiments of patriotism in her country Her spirit felt itself all the more free as Rosas sought, by the cheap assistance of the priesthood, to re-establish darkness and moral slavery

After the foregoing remarks, it will appear to us the more natural, when we perceive in the countries of South America the undeniable strivings of mental power, seeking to release itself from the two-fold pressure of the Church and of political oppression, and availing itself of the national poetry as its organ

The people of those provinces, for the greater part of Spanish or Italian descent, possess in consequence a vivacity of mind which is diametrically opposite to the phlegm of the other European races Since the time of its discovery, South America, as a possession of the Spanish crown, has been fettered by the burning chains of the inquisition and sunk in the night of fanaticism; therefore the light of moral freedom must have penetrated the hearts of men more effectually, when a single decisive struggle released each province from the torture-block of an impertinent priestly tyranny The people found themselves in the way of progress and development guided by the patriotic sacrifices of distinguished men, whose names grace the annals of history, until the epoch in which a man, who undoubtedly might have been a very good soldier, rising from the dregs of the people, and vilifying the democratic principle from contemptible selfishness, threw himself as an usurper upon an extensive territory

It was *Rosas*, who, as an ignominious example of brutal power, gave the absolutism of monarchy the means to mock at the republican principle, and to proclaim the aim after which our century is striving, to be " impracticable and absurd, ridiculous and contemptible, to every reasonable man "

In harmony with the depth of her mind, a spiritual power developed itself in Dolores, in the form of poetry In accordance with the spirit of poetry, she followed the impulse of the inspiration, which produced its effusions as if involuntarily and irrepressibly

As all true talent more or less unconscious of its own strength and power, compares the spiritual fruit of its efforts and labors with the object that floats before the imagination, and is coupled with diffidence, and often sinks into despondency, so did Dolores appear not to be clearly aware of the worth and dignity of the gift imparted to her as a poetess She carefully concealed from every eye the product of her inspiration, the material of which was taken from religion, nature, and of the political development of her nation, which last she contemplated from the point of view of humanity, as a movement in the progress of all mankind

The confidential relations of several families with their parents, had tied the happy bond of childish attachment between Lorenzo and Alphonso, in intercourse with Dolores and her sister Theresa The two youths were as different in individuality, as were the two sisters, who were in a manner educated with them Lorenzo had embraced the Catholic religion as the element of faith, as the realm of unbounded imagination, in which it became the undeniable support of all the different arts, while it continued to uphold the *idea* of the unity of mankind in the principle of love, which, unhappily, through the blood-shedding absolutism of the church, (as a state form,) has now in reality become despised

Theresa appeared to him as faith personified, as the embodied principle of love, his love to her became religion, because it sprung from the depths of his religious heart She died in the early bloom of her development A crisis followed in the inward life of the youth, the result of which is easier to declare than approve He assumed the tonsure at the grave of his betrothed and had lived several years in the quiet retirement of the cloister, at the gate of which we lately left him

Alphonso, on the contrary, in direct opposition to his friend Lorenzo, considered religion as the basis of all development in mankind, so far as related to one *primitive religion*, which, revealing itself from age to age under different forms, as religion confirmed its influence from century to century, upon the development of the human race Churches and rituals appeared to him as forms and formulas, which sink and fall away, to give place to new uprisings of the spirit, which affirms its all controlling power as the *primitive spirit of humanity*

The principle of love in Alphonso, took the form of patriotism, insomuch as he felt himself united to mankind as a *man* through his nation, and looked upon unreserved sacrifices for the cause of the people as the most sacred condition of the love of mankind, of *humanity*

Penetrated by these sentiments, the mental phenomena which developed themselves in Dolores, must have wrought upon him with powerful attraction He loved in Dolores his country , the principle of freedom, which, so strong in himself, found utterance in her, and was likewise inwoven in the spirit of his beloved, who at the same point of elevation with himself, formed with him a harmony of being, that no power on earth might rend or loosen He was as unable to separate the sentiments of patriotism from his love to Dolores, as she would have been to cherish love for a heart to whom the *idea* was foreign which was illustrated in her

It being a well known psychological truth, that either love or grief, and often both, rock the cradle of poetic development, and that poetic talent pursues its career, attended either by the genius of love or the demons of sorrow and grief, it was perfectly natural that the poetic spirit of Dolores should suddenly unfold itself to a high degree, in the consciousness of Alphonso's love.

Dolores, deeply feeling her loneliness since the death of her sister, was little inclined to relinquish the acquaintance of Miss Fanny, as the latter had displayed from childhood a cordial womanly feeling. Miss Fanny was more easily able to appreciate the exalted mind of her young friend by means of *her feelings*, than with her *understanding* to comprehend her mysterious nature, which she revered in Dolores, as much as she had loved her as a playmate

She was descended on her mother's side from one of those numerous sects, which in England separate themselves from the established church ; and had grown up in that mental confusion, which, so often coupled with narrowness of conception, considers the unlimited observance of church forms as *religion*, and, based on fear rather than faith, acknowledges an *evil principle*, whose power on earth even the Deity was not able to overcome

Mr John Walker, as a man of the world, less anxious about church forms than his wife, under the mask of tolerance concealed that indifference to all religion which characterizes our times Without giving in his open life any offence to the general requirements of so called religion, he acknowledged the exchange as the temple of *business*, to which alone he looked for happiness—*mammon* as the God of our century, and he considered *credit* more important than faith He passed (in this respect) for an enlightened man, who had risen above many prejudices, and acknowledged the Christian religion only to take an oath in the way of his business, at the custom house, or as a witness before a court

Miss Fanny s religious bias showed itself principally in consequence of her mother s influence, in unlimited hatred and rigid aversion against the Catholic church, and all Catholics, of whatever nation they might be, while she pitied and looked down also upon all Protestant sects, with the same Christian compassion with which they despise the unfortunate infidels and gentiles, who incur eternal damnation by anticipation The only point of religious union between Miss Fanny and Señora Dolores, was found in the circumstance that the latter had long since released herself from the forms of the "only saving church," without having as yet, however, preferred any other church to the Romish, while she strictly separated the notions of *church* and *religion*, and regarded the ordinances of any established church as being in direct contradiction to the religion of Jesus

Through mental reflection, and the profound study of history, Dolores was brought to the conviction that the fundamental principles of love, equality, and righteousness, had been as little upheld or practised, on the part of the Romish, as of any other established church, since the foundation of the Christian church in the third century

As the principles of *humanity*, aroused in Dolores, by the condition and sufferings of her country, under the yoke of tyranny, proceeded from the depth of her religious convictions, so did religion appear in her whole being, as the ruling element of life, and of mental power. Her sympathy in the political events of the time, called out by the lawless outrages of a brutal tyrant, was not at all that petty "spirit of party" with which so many condemn the political movements around them, viewing every appearance as founded on the same personal interest which guides themselves She cherished from her heart the republican principle which she acknowledged as the basis of development in all nations, and which she saw most ignominiously despised and proscribed under the arbitrary power of an usurper

Dolores was penetrated by the principle of love, which especially reveals itself by *tolerance*, in opposition to the intolerance of all sects; in which, instead of love, the *fear of the devil* prevails, consequently she loved in Miss Fanny, the playmate of her childhood, without seeking in the smallest degree, to influence her religious views, any more than she would have suffered a proselyte maker to approach her, to win her to this or that religious sect

To conclude our statement of the relations in which Señora Dolores is to be considered almost as a member of the English family, we will only remark, that Mr Wilker was the only Briton in Buenos Ayres who knew of the young lady's distinguished poetic talent

CHAPTER VI

THE FAREWELL IN THE PRISON

It wanted a quarter to eleven—the silence of death reigned in the prison, interrupted only by the dull tread of soldiers without military bearing, who carried their muskets sometimes on the right, and sometimes on the left shoulder, yawning in the dusky night, one minute standing still, and the next walking back and forth

In the upper stories, appropriated as barracks, Morpheus seemed to have taken charge of the watch himself, having relieved the mercenaries from duty, producing a most inharmonious nasal concert, which would be insupportable to the hearers as long as they took no part in it themselves

From time to time the clanking of a chain was heard through the grating of a dungeon, caused by the noisy stirring of an unfortunate, who, perhaps turning himself sleeplessly on his hard bed, longed for a draught of Lethe in the arms of sleep but found not the solace Señor Domingo sat sunk in profound slumber in the wide arm-chair of his little room, with his snuff box in one hand, and an unused pinch of snuff between the fingers of the other, disturbed, from time to time, by the preponderance of his old gray head, which sank upon his breast, obeyed the laws of gravity, and every now and then nodded more profoundly

Narcissus, the restless factotum of all commissions, had taken his place opposite, and leaned his arm and head upon a table, while he slipped about upon a wooden bench, to which long usage had given a natural polish and lustre

The sentry before the door tediously counted the minutes of the last quarter of an hour of his nightly post, until at last it struck eleven A night watchman, with a lantern in his hand, appeared at a distance from the building, and cried, in a hoarse, twanging voice, "Viva la Confederacion! mueran los salvages Unitarios! viva la representacion! . . . las once! tiempo sereno! . . . el cielo lleno de estrellas!*

This announcement of fine weather, which at the moment by no means agreed with the truth, inasmuch as the sky was covered with thunder clouds, escaped involuntarily from this, as it did

from many other watchmen of Buenos Ayres, as if in honor of the name of the city, even when the sky was filled with clouds, and the rain was falling by buckets full

With the change of sentries, two monkish forms approached, attended by a negro in a wide cloak A loud challenge was succeeded by as loud a reply The corporal cast an official glance upon both monks, one of whom presented to him the crucifix with outstretched arm, crying, in a low voice, "Memento mori"

Surprised and almost terrified at the appearance of the personified Saviour, he stepped back, and pulled with one hand the bell handle of the gate, which operation set the perplexed porter in motion The gate opened, the monks stepped over the threshold, the soldiers bowed with bended knees, crossed foreheads and breasts, and then arose to discharge the watch for the night. The sentries of the former watch soon left their posts and entered the building, whose gate, creaking and rattling, closed behind them The porter, a secondary helper in the bloody tragedy, spurred to diligence by Señor Domingo's unwonted night watching, locked and bolted the entrance, hung a heavy double chain across the gate, bent reverently before the two monks, and threw himself on his knees, embracing the occasion to secure a holy benediction

"Let the cell of the condemned be opened for us at once," at length said Brother Celeste, breaking the death-like silence which was again prevailing, and addressing Señor Domingo, who met him, "and be pleased to await us in the chapel, while we prepare the condemned for the sacrament of the holy supper"

"It shall be done immediately, without fail," said the old officer, ordering the mulatto, Narcissus, to call the turnkey of the wing under which the dungeon vault lay, in whose gloomy obscurity Alphonso withered

Dolores was one of those charming forms of La Plata, whose fame, in respect to the symmetry of their persons, and their natural grace of carriage and movement, has been proclaimed by so many travellers from all parts of the world Enveloped in the black habit of the order, with white sleeves, she appeared like a young monk Her glossy black hair, besides being covered with the concealing white hood, was further disguised by a false tonsure An artificial beard, corresponding to the early age indicated by her grief-blanched countenance, covered her upper lip and chin With a trembling hand she bore the cup of the Lord She stood panting, and with a heaving breast, leaning against a pillar, near Celeste, who carried the crucifix, as if overpowered by the struggles of contending emotions, which raged more fiercely within her, the more she felt herself compelled to suppress their manifestation.

Narcissus appeared at last with the under turnkey, a robust mixture of the European and Patagonian; the latter omitted not to pay his reverence to the holy symbols, and awaited the orders of the two monks Celeste desired him to take the ciborium and crucifix to the chapel, and place them on the altar, there to remain until he was prepared for the sacred ceremony. He pointed out his attendant Achilles as a member of the watch of his monastery, and ordered him to remain near him.

---

* Long live the Confederation! death to the cursed Unitarians! long live the representation! Eleven o'clock! fine weather! the sky is full of stars!
2

The chapel, in the projection of a wing of the building, was opened The twilight glimmer of the " *holy lamp*,' the so called " eternal light," shone through the shadowy masses of the columns and narrow aisles, and the low tread of the monks, enveloped in their long garments, produced an echoing rustle in the death-like stillness. Both monks approached the altar, and ridding themselves of the consecrated objects, knelt down in fervent devotion, sending up an inward prayer to the Lord of all worlds, to the judge of all tyrants, who trieth the heart and searcheth it to its innermost depths

A stream of tears flowed from the beaming eyes of Dolores, convulsively clasping her hands, she besought of God shelter and defence, strength and firmness of soul, for the next hours of her troubled existence Sighing from an anguished breast, she prayed aloud ' We call upon thee, O Lord' Lord hear us' Easier is it, O Lord, to suffer death, than to tear ourselves from the arms of the friend, on the steps of the scaffold, to which he voluntarily offers himself for thy sake, while the night of slavery oppresses our people We cry to thee, O Lord, in this hour of despair Enlighten us with the light of thy truth, revive us by thy all-surrounding might, elevate us with the spirit of thy eternal love, strengthen our souls and bodies, that we may not shrink, nor tremble, nor faint, in the moment of parting from him—from him—whom thou knowest as he knoweth thee' Lead and guide us, that we sink not under the superhuman suffering which we endure for his sake, and thine, O God '"

Pervaded and sustained by supernatural strength, Dolores rose, and soon after Celeste Silent and speechless, each extended a hand to the other, while their tear-bedewed glances encountered each other

With hasty steps they left the altar, and passed the threshold of the chapel, accompanied by the turnkey, while Achilles, gazing earnestly on all sides, followed them

The fatal door was reached at length, lock and bolt creaked and rattled, the turnkey placed a dark lantern on the floor of the vault, released the condemned from his fetters, and then departed, intimating with a nod that all was now prepared for the entrance of the ghostly fathers

The two monks passed the threshold, Achilles followed, and the door was closed from the outside without being locked

There is a limit to mortal language, and a sway of feeling which no sound of the tongue serves to express—when even the tear of anguish is congealed There are moments in which the heart of man, rent by superhuman agony, appears to cease its pulsations for the maintenance of physical life, while the soul escapes from its mortal fetters, and raises itself to the bright regions of anticipation and of faith There are moments when this world, and all that encompasses it, become as foreign to men as if they no more belonged to it, in such moments they seem to abide as spiritual beings of a brighter world within the shell of earthly clay, which can have nothing in common with the spirit

Dolores and Alphonso struggled through such moments in speechless embraces, as if paralyzed to corpses by a nervous stroke, while their spirits, overstepping time and space on the wings of faith, floated in the element of divine love

The return to earth awakened that powerful organ of the souls' life—the *glance*, to glance directed, for whose expression no word is adequate They gazed on each other, as if reciprocally sending beam after beam, and receiving them within the depths of their congenial souls The story of all the sufferings of an agonizing separation lay in a single glance the softest emotions of the speechless breast were expressed by a single glance Faith resignation submission to the will of the Most High, anticipation of the future, and courage and spiritual strength for the present, were mutually proclaimed by a single glance

Each pressed the other's hand like two friends who unexpectedly meet again, and in the joy of re-union forget that they are about to be parted to meet no more forever At length an indescribable smile of sadness and grief flitted over the lips of both, as in transition to the flow of words which yet appeared not to be at their command

There is a union of two souls, a union in the element of love, by means of which the one anticipates, and feels, and experiences, all that which, however lightly, moves its kindred soul There is an understanding and being understood, a knowing and being known, without intercourse through words, and often even without the influence of the magnetic fluid of the eye-glance This perception, and comprehension of the most secret passions in the depth of congenial souls, is the effect and condition of the holiest sympathy

Love and friendship are different forms of one and the same attraction of soul in the element of sympathy The higher the soul in the scale of spiritual improvement and development, the purer and clearer are its depths, the more it approaches the same degree of elevation and purity, the more powerful the attraction, the closer the bond of sympathy, be it in the form of friendship or of love

Dolores and Alphonso, in the same scale of spiritual enlightenment, with equal clearness and depth of mind, reciprocally comprehended the slightest impulse of their worldless breasts strengthened by the mutual action of their exalted soul-sympathy, both (as if in magnetic *rapport*, soaring over the present) appeared to be in the appropriate sphere of their existence at last finding utterance, they speak and move like somnambulists, in an element of light, while their their mortal bodies remain prostrate and exhausted, unconscious of their physical sufferings

The earthly world, and its puppets of the so called " social world," with its shades of human errors and crimes, was far removed from them it was, as if feeble recollections slightly reminded them of past sufferings and afflictions, while they recognised themselves as souls in the spheres of light and love—in the consciousness of the unity of their existence, and the immortality of their being

"Farewell, Alphonso '" said Dolores, at length, and the sad smile which rested on her lip spread itself over her countenance like the reflection of the spiritual glory which streamed through her soul

"Farewell, Alphonso ' we shall meet again. What is a human life in the scale of sacrifice, when the human spirit knows the destiny which awaits it beyond the grave, to which on earth it never can attain. How joyfully do we embrace death, sustained by the thought that we shall soar above in the spheres of light—perhaps live anew in a nobler form upon another planet, this earthly covering being thrown aside, to endure some lesser struggle in the progress towards perfection—perhaps from planet to planet, ever wrestling and striving, a million times ennobled and enlightened, to approach the light of all being, the primitive source of all love—to become brighter and more refulgent, from *the vision of the Godhead*, until we, made after the image of God, borne upwards by faith, lighted by the glow of love, moving godlike from step to step, from star to star, at length *behold God*—the source of light, life and strength, perhaps, after millions of years of mortal reckoning, arriving for the first time at the *consciousness* of our immortal nature, as we here attain to the contemplation of our connexion with God, through *faith in God*, which here in the dust we may suspect, but which will be fast *known* beyond the grave.

' Farewell, Alphonso ' ' she exclaimed, with increasing emotion, " we part like two wanderers—two children of one faith, seeking herbs on separate desert plains, to prepare a drink that shall strengthen the human heart in the long hours of suffering, that shall purify the soul and lighten its struggle after virtue, that shall arouse the spirit, and raising it upwards into the element of freedom, shall cause it to glow with the self-consciousness of a mighty strength of will. Well for us if we find some flowers for such an exalted purpose, well for us, if we are permitted to demonstrate the existence of a healing power, as within the compass of possibility. Our Father now calls thee hence. It is his will, and his will be done. But he leaves me behind on earth, perhaps for years, perhaps for months, perhaps only for hours, at most but the momentary pulse-throb of time, is compared with charity ! The all-loving Father calls thee home. His will be done on earth as it is in heaven ! His kingdom come ! May the reign of that love be realized on earth which the Son of Man once proclaimed, who suffered for man's sake—endured the death of the cross, sealing his doctrine with his blood—the doctrine of equality, justice and the love of man. This doctrine we have maintained in the consciousness of our vocation, as members of the great confederacy of love. For the sake of this doctrine, thou, my Alphonso, goest to the death which awaits thee, as to martyrdom, and to which I shall perhaps also soon be summoned, when I shall have plucked another flower for the healing draught of mankind, in the name of God the Father, (the source of all things,) in the name of God the Son, (of man who proceeds from him,) in the name of the Holy Ghost, (who unites Father and Son,) in the name of the holy spirit of progress and improvement. Amen ! Amen !"

" Amen !" cried Lorenzo, while Dolores sank anew on the breast of Alphonso, elevated above the earth as before, and absorbed in the sense of her higher existence.

" I am ready for death—ready for the passage through darkness into light !" said Alphonso, after a long pause, during which Dolores had returned to the perception of outward life, and perhaps hardly knew what she had just spoken as in a dream—in the dream-like state similar to somnambulism, from which she had recovered. ' Partake with me the Lord's supper, the farewell supper of the Son of Man. Thou wilt present it to me, Dolores, I desire to receive it from thy hand, concluded Alphonso.

Dolores, joyfully surprised at this unexpected proposal, answered without words the soul-beaming glance which accompanied the request of Alphonso. Lorenzo gave a sign to the troubled and agitated negro, who now beheld in his mistress a seraph, whose presence filled him with awe.

Achilles, hardly able to contain himself, approached the closed door, to intimate to the guard that the condemned was to be conducted to the chapel. He found the turnkey fast asleep on the steps of a winding staircase near the door, and by his side a soldier, whose loud yawning indicated that he would gladly have followed the example of the wearied man, if his harder duty had not denied him the enjoyment of this comfort.

With a morose countenance, provoked by the tedious preparation of a criminal for approaching death, the turnkey seized the lamp whose glimmering light was hardly perceivable in the dungeon, and staggering like a horse left asleep, he ordered the soldier to close the procession and follow the monks.

———

CHAPTER VII.

THE CONSECRATION TO DEATH.

The crucifix and ciborium remained, in the silent gloom of night, as the monks had lately left them. Alphonso, with those accompanying him, silently crossed the threshold of the chapel, approached the steps of the altar with a firm and manly deportment, and knelt in prayer, his example was followed by the two monks, Achilles and the attendant guard.

At the conclusion of his prayer, Alphonso rose, and likewise Dolores and Lorenzo. Alphonso, strengthened in soul and nerves, by his spiritual intercourse with the beloved and ' wonderful being, now began to speak in the French language, which was not understood by the guard, who, besides, had already chosen their resting-places, and were gradually sinking to slumber. He said—

" In the name of the Father, who created the myriads of stars ! in the name of the Son, the carpenter's son ! who proclaimed the deliverance of mankind, in the name of the Holy Ghost, who united mankind with the Godhead, and is manifested as the spirit of progress and improvement from century to century. I take leave of you, and of this earthly world, and approach my death. Amen ! Amen !

" When the Son of Man was born in the Roman province of Galilee, his countrymen lived under the dominion of the Roman emperors. Mankind was sunk in unbelief, and selfishness, and idolatry, while, at the same time, no religion prevailed upon earth. Faith had expired, the glow of love was extinguished Mankind degraded by slavery, wallowed in sensuality at the footstools of pompous idols' Man worshipped forms instead of spirit' Man felt the need of love, and embraced a marble statue' He felt the promptings of faith, and believed in a Messiah And Jesus appeared—'a man who performed wonderful works,' and taught, in the spirit of truth, the principles of equality, justice, and love of man, in direct opposition to the slavery of loveless and right-despising despotism The Scribes and Pharisees beheld in him the effort to re-establish the primitive religion, to the subversion of their traditions and forms for the subjugation of the mind He was accused, and condemned as guilty, as having sought to elevate his countrymen as a people, on the basis of democracy, because he wished to free them from moral servitude, and he was betrayed and sold, and delivered to his enemies, and nailed to the cross as a rebel' Scoffed at as "Rex Judeorum" And as the hour of his death drew near, he proclaimed to his disciples the struggle of the human race, which has remained the same from century to century, until this day—saving *

"Think not that I am come to send peace on 'earth I come not to send peace, but a sword

"For I have come to set man at variance against his father, and the daughter against her mother And a man's foes shall be they of his own household

"But, beware of men, for they will deliver you to the councils, and they will scourge you in their synagogues

"And the brother shall deliver up the brother to death, and the father the child

"And ye shall be hated of all men for my name's sake, but he that endureth to the end shall be saved

"But when they persecute you in one city, flee ye into another

"And he that taketh not his cross, and followeth after me, is not worthy of me He that findeth his life shall lose it, and he that loseth his life for my sake, shall find it

"'And he, foreknowing the approach of his last hour, assembled his disciples on the eve of his martyrdom, to partake with him the farewell supper'"

At these words, Alphonso looked at the ciborium, and then gazed in the eyes of Dolores, which had hitherto been steadily fixed upon him, and whose beams apparently mingled with his own Slowly, and in tones full of expression, Dolores said—

"Spirit, strength, light, and love, are one, kindred rays emanating from one source, from God, the source of all, in whom we believe in the dust, whom we shall, hereafter, behold in light'

O, friend' What in the universe surrounds us
The Spirit 'tis, that keeps the stars in motion,
Th' eternal Spirit' call him God or Allah
From love he raised the hymn of all creation—
The exalted hymn of being. Bound to being
Are all created things, and love displaying
Its greatest power in life but through emotion
The universe were nought, without love's presence

Life would be no life, were there no disturbance,
For unexerted power no might displays

* Matthew, Chapter 10, verses 34, 35, 36—17, 21, 22, 23, 38, 39.

All forms of matter meet with sure destruction;
The spirit's working slumbereth not, nor rests,
From strife and death the ransomed spirit riseth
Which then, renewed and strengthened, takes new forms,
Disturbance, struggle, life, the form's destruction,
Are but the spirit in its upward strivings

Perplexed are human nature's gloomy thoughts
Of death—no death reigns in the universe,
Strife, motion, dissolution, is the warfare,
Where matter menaces itself and spirit
Our entrance on the morning dawn of death
Is only the perfection of our being.
Even the breath of worms dies not in vain,
As beauteous butterflies they live again

Perplex'd are man's ideas of annihilation—
Call it decay—there is no annihilation
Life's progress is the universal poem,
The spirit's soaring when the form is rent,
Still upward striving, to its source aspiring
The source's sanctuary is love and light,
The being God—his element is love,
Which neither darkness nor corruption prove.

Progress needs strife—development, rebellion;
Death elevates the spirit evermore
On its unbounded path Love is its strength,
The spirit wills that strength be exercised

Know then, my friend, thy being's high design?
What is thy life? this little space of time,
A span it is, the spirit's might increasing
A cypher in the realm of immortality
Despair will ever be love's sure attendant,
When to mankind thou giv'st thyself as man
The "Son of Man" died on the cross complaining,
While bitter pangs transpierced his bleeding heart

"Despair' no, not despair Did the 'Son of Man,' when upon the cross, for a moment feel himself 'forsaken of God?" It was thus that he made known to us his breaking human heart He despaired of the success of his doctrine of the deliverance of the human race at that period, but not of mankind His life, like his death, indicated human feelings, human sufferings—faith in humanity—faith in the elevation of mankind And mankind are advancing towards their destiny

"It is no dream," continued Dolores—

"It is no dream—it yet shall be fulfilled,
The nations yet shall rise in all their might,
And love on faith its heavenly throne shall build
And life progressive soar in morning light
At last man's suffering shall diminished be,
When to the world this truth is once made clear,
That all must live in love, who fain would see
The kingdom of the Lord established here

It is no dream, that in the human soul
Can raise forbodings of those better days,
When sacred charity shall each control
To bear the errors of a brother's ways,
When love shall steel the heart against the strife
With death—and faith shall bid the soul arise,
Above the shroud and grave, to endless life,
Loosened from earth, to flourish in the skies

It is no dream—the purer spirit-life,
The innate consciousness of inward strength,
Whose prescience in the human heart is rife,
And gives to weakness power to rise at length,
And struggle onwards towards its endless aim
E'en though the crowd to slavery will bend,
A man may, by his words and deeds, proclaim
Truth, by which nations may to life ascend

We hear a wond'rous music' from the heart
Of all the nations issues forth the sound,
The mighty symphony of souls its part
Of love assumes—and man to man is bound;
The kingdom of our God on earth shall bloom,
The nation's hatred, scorn, and doubt's deep gloom,
Be lost in love—love that survives the tomb.

All that is written, then shall be fulfilled,
 All that the Son of Man consoling spoke.
The Eastern Satan is already killed,
 Men shall as brethren love, nor fear his yoke,
And Mammon, pois'nous serpent, be expelled
 From Eden, which his trail has soiled full long,
And where, as sov reign, he the keys has held
 Of love's pure kingdom, which to man belong

Satan has vanished from the glorious East,
 We are no longer swayed by devilish fear,
The hours draw nigh, and in their speed increased,
 The Nazarene's pure doctrine all shall bear—
The damteon grace of mankind shall be void—
 Love's spirit, glittering in its own pure light,
Appear—and fraud and lies shall take to flight,
 And then shall God be known and served aright

Dolores breathed out the last words in the loftiest elevation of godlike inspiration, then, taking a consecrated wafer, she broke it, and sharing it with Alphonso and Lorenzo, she said in a gentler voice,—

"And he took the bread and gave thanks, and reached it to his friends and said, ' Take and eat and regard this bread as my body, which is broken for the healing of humanity, and as often as ye meet in spirit think of me,'" and taking the chalice she extended it to both friends, and conveyed it to their lips, saying " And he took the cup, and handed it to his disciples, and gave thanks, and said, Drink ye all of this, and think that it is my blood, the blood of the New Testament of my legacies to humanity, which is shed for many' I say unto you that I will drink no more of the growth of the vine' take ye and drink it, and think of me '"

A long pause followed this solemn act All three knelt down in silent prayer

Whoever is acquainted with the Catholic ritual, will have already perceived that this celebration of the Last Supper was by no means according to the prescribed ceremonials and regulations of that church This circumstance arose from the situation and relations of these Christians who, separated of necessity from the church as the state institution of tyrants, and with the comprehension of the divine idea of Christianity, availed themselves of such forms as most clearly indicated the primitive spirit of the Farewell Supper of Jesus

The constellation of the southern cross, invisible to the inhabitants of our northern hemisphere, suddenly shone through the rent masses of dark thunder clouds The light of these stars (all the more brilliant as the southern hemisphere is less distinguished by prominent constellations than the northern) cast its rays through a high bow window into the obscurity of the chapel Like the constellation of the great bear around the polar star of the north the cross revolving around the south pole of infinity (in which the human eye has discovered no polar star) had reached the altitude in which it became visible to the three mortals at the altar of the feast of death

"Dante!" suddenly cried Lorenzo, perceiving the light of the cross The friends raised their eyes and the aspirations of their spirits towards the symbol of martyrdom, which the most ancient, and perhaps the greatest poet of our Christian era, beheld centuries ago in wonderful vision, before any European, so far as we know,

had crossed the equator, and made known the constellations of the southern hemisphere *

" Dante " sighed Lorenzo, speaking after a short pause, during which his uplifted gaze remained as it were riveted to the constellation. " As Dante's spirit in holy contemplation beheld this constellation, centuries before it was known to any human eye north of the equator, so do our eyes behold the stars of the freedom of South America' as brilliant stars of the future—of *liberty, equality*, and *humanity*' As Galileo† was once condemned before a civil and ecclesiastical tribunal, for declaring that our earth revolved with other planets around the sun, in opposition to the letter of the Scriptures—as he asserted in his last words, " I believe *in the motion of the planets*'—so went thou also condemned for believing in motion of mankind, in the elevation of the human race in opposition to the despotic command of tyranny—"*Humanity, stand still!*"

Alphonso, who was suddenly brought back by the spirit of these words to his element, laid his right hand on his convulsed heart, and broke forth in the following declaration

" I believe in God and humanity, for this I have contended I see the stars of the future brighten—the brilliant stars of freedom—the stars of the unity of South America, and because I declared what I beheld, and acted according to my belief, I am compelled to die I die, but I have not lived in vain The spirit of the Lord appeared to me here as *love*, and I proclaimed the exalted tie of the love of mankind as the bond of the Lord upon earth, that shall bind and unite all nations' And my declaration was made in love I proclaimed that no people can satisfy the claims and conditions of the Deity, without the consciousness of nationality! Only as a *people* can they include themselves in the great bond of humanity, in like manner as each man on earth can only fully accomplish his high calling, and satisfy the demands of the Deity, as a *man*, acting as a man among his *people*, and as a *son of his fatherland* I studied the history of nations, and read the ' book of mankind,' in the reality of our present time And it appeared to me like a caricature a people without the consciousness of their nationality, and I saw it willless, wordless, and deedless—as an instrument in the hand of absolutism, ignorant of itself—sinking more deeply in slavery—nourishing hatred and enmity against kindred nations And I trembled at the reality of such a caricature I saw nation alter nation in such a condition of degradation ; and I sighed to God—' thy kingdom come'' the kingdom of love! for *love* is the essence of God,

---

* " Io mi volsi a man destra, e posi mente
 All' altro polo, e vidi quattro stelle
 Non viste mai fuor ch' alla prima gente,
 Goder pareva 'l ciel di fer fiammelle," etc etc.
Queste quattro stelle d' una bellezza superiore si presentarono allo guardo di Dante nella direzione del polo antartico, Amerigo Vespucci—compagno del gran Colombo nel secondo suo viaggio all' America—alla vista di quelle stelle—si ricordo della adotta quartina di Dante.   H

† Some royalist authors, of late, will insist that Galileo was not persecuted on account of his spiritual standing They appeal to documents in the archives of those dynasties in whose pay they write We shall soon look for a learned confutation of the poisoning of *Socrates*, or the burning of *John Huss*.   H

and *freedom* the element of humanity—the means of all development and improvement I saw nation after nation without nationality, incapable of fulfilling the duties of humanity towards other nations—every bond rent asunder by slavery I saw men without patriotism, renouncing their people and fatherland, disowning their duty to their country and I trembled at such depth of selfishness

"And I was penetrated with the light of an *idea*—as a ray from the source of love, the idea of the United States of South America on the basis of *humanity*, in the brilliancy of the star of the future' And I recognised the same idea in thee, Dolores, and like twin stars united on an endless path, our spirits struggled upwards to the *source* of *love*, imploring power to disseminate the idea, that its light might illuminate and warm, and rejoice the hearts of kindred people And thy *word* became *deed*, and the deed was looked upon as the crime of love, and the staff was broken over us

"I die' but the *idea* of the deliverance of South America, and the establishment of a *Union of States in the spirit of humanity*, dies not with me' The bullets of tyranny may, in a few hours, pierce my heart—may shatter my shell of clay' but they destroy not *the principle of love*, which was developed in me, and in whose glow, the idea of freedom becomes brighter and purer *God is love' the ELEMENT of humanity is freedom—freedom is the means to elevate and ennoble men in the spirit of humanity'* Make known these, my last words, to all conditions of our people—to all the nations of the earth, send my death-greeting to our confederates in Europe, persevere in the belief in God, and think of me in the hour of the uprising of the nations'"

Inspired by supernatural strength, the martyr, at these words, gazed once more upward towards the constellation of the cross and then in the eyes of Dolores—whose arm, fettered by the circumstance of her disguise, and the presence of the guard, might not press the beloved to her throbbing heart, as a last—last—farewell A glance and pressure of the mind remained alone to be indulged Alphonso seized her hand, and pressed it once to his quivering lips, suddenly he let it fall, kneeling down before her, and extending his right hand to heaven while he gave her a sign with the left to leave him to death, and repeated to himself, with inspiration, the following words

"Who for a nation's freedom dies, though by the hang man's hand,
Has won on earth the holiest prize from God—for fatherland'"

Dolores and Lorenzo stood motionless, in silent prayer Achilles, who all along had been, as it were, in a land of dreams, and had obscurely comprehended the signification of the farewell words in a strange language, more from the scene itself, than from the words, could no longer remain at a distance from the beloved of his mistress Impelled towards him by the powerful impulse of sacred veneration, he longed to bear away with him at least a look of the martyr's eye as a legacy

He glanced timidly around, to see if the half-sleeping guard might observe his movements—threw himself on his knees towards the altar,

and sought, by his supplicating air, to convey to the martyr a token of his pure, manly attachment and veneration

Alphonso, at parting, in looking around through the obscurity, appeared to appreciate the feelings of the worthy negro, and to understand him, he cast a glance upon him, while the faithful attendant of his beloved, entirely overcome, burst into tears His sobs awoke the attendant mercenaries of the tyrant who ascribed them to the condemned, without supposing that a feeling human heart could beat within the breast of a negro The eyes of Dolores rested upon Alphonso Lorenzo awoke out of profound reflection, raised his voice, and said,

"It is no dream—it yet shall be fulfilled,
The nations yet shall rise in all their might'"

then extending his hand over Alphonso, he continued "The Lord cause the stars of futurity to shine over our country, the Lord establish and elevate the United States of South America to the welfare of the nations who dwell therein, the Lord strengthen and sustain thee in the hour of thy death, as a martyr to this exalted idea, the Lord be with thee at the moment of passing from night to light' The Lord conduct thee from step to step of everlasting perfection, to the contemplation of his omnipotence and grandeur, the Lord unite us with thee in the splendor of his love in eternity Amen'" "Amen'" cried Alphonso and Dolores aloud, in joyful tones, which pervaded the deathlike silence, and awakened a light echo in the gloomy vaults of the chapel. The clock in the neighboring steeple, slowly, and with loud reverberating sound, struck midnight

Señor Domingo, aroused from his sleep, which had confined him during this time to his chair, mechanically felt for his snuff box, and sought to raise his spirits by a tremendous pinch, and counted aloud the strokes of the old clock bell, from one to twelve, as if to afford evidence to the monks that he, in conformity to his duty, had by no means slept

"Are you ready now, Brother Celeste" said he, rubbing his eyes, after a prolonged yawn, "it is midnight, and the sun rises very early at this time of the year, and before it has fairly risen the sentence'——

Lorenzo—Celeste, interrupted the old man, who regarded the execution of an unfortunate as business, with the same coolness as the merchant thinks of the expedition of a ship captain to another part of the world, with the difference, that he concerned himself less about the happy arrival of the doomed man at his destined port, than the merchant does himself in regard to the voyage of the captain, unless the ship and cargo should have been prudently insured

"I will myself announce to the condemned his hour," interrupted Lorenzo, "and will therefore remain here with him in his dungeon"

"Very well' very well'" answered Señor Domingo, "I would not cherish suspicion against your reverence, but the guard that remains here must be doubled, according to regulation You may remain here, but alone, your reverence, entirely alone, in obedience to the ordinance of our lord and ruler may God protect him, at least as long as I live——so that I may not lose my post"

He murmured the last words slowly to himself, yawned again took another pinch of snuff, offered the box to the monks, who were not inclined to make use of it, and ordered a long, lank fellow, dressed in a corporal's uniform, to conduct the condemned, together with one of the monks, to the dungeon

Alphonso, prostrate on his knees before the altar, felt the touch of Lorenzo's hand arousing him, who, at the same time, whispered in his ear that he would remain with him till the last moments of his mortal existence

Surprised by such a consolation, which he could hardly have expected under existing circumstances, he suddenly rose, and sank into the arms of his friend Dolores involuntarily approaching him once more seized the captive's right hand, imprinted a kiss on his forehead, and felt the imperative necessity of immediately quitting her beloved and the friend of her deceased sister, who had now become more than a friend to her

'Dolores,' whispered Celeste in the ear of the unhappy one, ' Dolores, we must separate, but not forever I shall see you again upon Earth—perhaps soon—God willing

Lorenzo!' exclaimed Dolores, trembling and joyfully agitated by this announcement of a purpose which at the instant remained obscure to her " Farewell, Lorenzo! Farewell, Alphonso—we shall meet again there—there—!" The beam of her expressive look lost itself in the down-streaming light of the southern cross

" Forward to the dungeon, if you please,' exclaimed the long, bony corporal, striding up to the condemned

' The Lord be with you !". said Dolores, in a tone corresponding with her disguise as priest he felt herself without strength to leave the altar and the friends, who, standing there in a silent embrace, had convulsively seized both her hands

' Separate yourselves—break loose! forward!" exclaimed the corporal, parting their hands with great difficulty and effort, while Dolores, supported by Achilles, suddenly gained the requisite presence of mind, collected herself, and with drooping head, slowly and with trembling steps left the chapel and the prison, by the side of Achilles, separated from Alphonso, who, in the arms of his friend, enlightened and strengthened by the love of the " wonderful being," regarded the moment of death as the passage from night into light

CHAPTER VIII

PUBLIC CONVERSATION

In the corner house of the " Calle de veinte y cinco de mayo,* and a street, the name of which, used as an address," would by no means serve as an attestation of *respectability*, was to be found a pulperia (shop) in which coffee and national tea and liquors of all sorts were sold, resembling the small estaminets or cafés of the European

continent, in which the peace-loving citizens of the middle classes chat away their evening hours

The pulperia of Señor Boto was notorious as the gathering place of the secret agents of the Rosas police, and was, on this account, in high repute with all the poor sinners of servility—creatures of meanness, and the like, who, in some way or other, sought to earn their daily bread in some office of the state, or had already gained the same in the Supreme Director's service, on the condition of never showing the diploma of their suspicious dignity

The spirit or character of the customary evening company in Boto's pulperia (if spirits could be found there, except among the contents of his bottles, and if a certain privileged want of character should pass for character) was conformable to the principles of despotic monarchy, which the government represented under the false flag of a republic To follow out the monarchical principle, is to license every vice that is founded on the egotism of man, to increase the instruments of blind despotism, while men yield themselves to all its purposes, to satisfy under the mask of civilization their animal desires, where they have no higher aim in life than the gratification of material wants of sensuality As the principle of despotism licenses each vice, in so far as it removes men from the higher aspirations of spiritual life, so does it despise and proscribe virtue (founded on moral self-consciousness) because it requires the fulfilment of the higher duties opposed to despotism

Moral slavery is the element of vice Moral freedom, in the consciousness of man's dignity, is the element of virtue The principle of despotism, proceeding from egotism, makes use of man as an *egotist*, while it permits him to make good his personal claims at the expense of others

The principle of *humanity* (as the basis of a republic) requires from men the sacrifice of their individuality, the sacrifice of all personal claims, for the welfare and best interests of their country—their *fatherland*

Monarchy desires *slaves*—slaves of sensuality and all the passions, because these degrade men into the will-less instruments of absolute despotism Republics require *men*—men in the consciousness of moral freedom and mental dignity, because without these no virtue, no sacrifice for people and fatherland is to be expected

If we consider the history of the revolutions of nations, of the struggles of the principles of freedom within the last half of the preceding century, despotism shows itself to us in its greatest nakedness, when it seeks the means of sustaining itself by degrading men to moral depravity—by the system of a *secret police*

As despotism, by means of a dishonoring censorship, disputes the right of men to avail themselves of the expression of their *words* for their thoughts and feelings,—so it heightens the crime of high treason in a nation, while, by means of its hireling creatures, it seeks to spy out the thoughts and emotions in the depths of the human breast, to hear the suppressed word, to catch up the sigh of despair, that it may fill its dungeons, and seal the diplomas of its disgrace with the blood of martyrs

The pulperia of Señor Boto was too notorious

---

* Street of the 25th May

as the gathering place of the before mentioned *creatures*, for any other person, however superficially acquainted with the localities of the city, to incur the risk of allowing himself to be listened to and spied upon there

Señor Boto was formerly, as a mechanic and citizen,-a zealous patriot, a rigid Unitarian, and was imprisoned as a member of a conspiracy against Rosas. The loneliness of the prison, combined with many sufferings from privation, (which a patriot can so seldom endure without becoming more or less shaken in his principles,) had in a short time turned Señor Boto At the first hearing, he already manifested himself apparently near to the "*state of grace*," and to the acknowledgement of "the only comfortable making" absolutism, and was subjected to still severer treatment. He received several dozen lashes upon his back, and at last confessed more than was asked of him, and especially besought, in penitent humility and misery, to be received into the secret service of the tyrant—who could make use of such creatures After several heads had fallen in consequence of his denunciation, and found their places of honor on the iron railing which surrounds the obelisk in the Plaza de la Victoria, Señor Boto was set at liberty, under secret and open police inspection He still endeavored to wear the mask of a patriot, behind which, however, the stamp of the knavery of his nature, was but too prominently legible Under the pretence that he had spent a great deal of money, and that his former business was ruined, he established a coffee house, while he held the post of a spy But it was with him, as with many of his kind in other despotic States, he was as stupid, as characterless, and soon involuntarily betrayed his position The party of the patriots lost nothing in him, and despotism did not gain much But he nevertheless drew a pension from the secret fund, which was at the same time the private purse of Rosas, and vegetated on, like a poisonous plant in a fruit garden

A group of fitting subjects for the future king of Rio de la Plata with red ribannds in their button holes, red handkerchiefs—some with red vests—others, besides these marks of the Rosas party, with red noses—were just discussing the day's topic, the execution of the infamous Alphonso, (as they, in their dutiful contempt, called him,) when Señor Falsodo entered, and ordered a glass of liquor

Attentively listening to the conversation, according to the custom of his secret profession, he held the glass to his lips, while he directed a searching glance upon those present, and last upon Señor Boto, silently inquiring of him whether he had learned any thing that would be of importance to him

What is the news, Señor Boto?" inquired he, in a low voice, apprehending that his look had not been sufficiently understood

"Nothing, but what you probably know already," replied the host, "what the gentlemen were just talking about—that his Excellency, the Supreme Director, has set a price on the discovery of the author of the Elegies, and will double the sum to the one who will take the author, living, into custody"

"Alas! I know that already," sighed Señor Falsodo

"Alas!" replied Señor Boto; "perhaps you are afraid that some one will gain the reward Do you fear that from interest for the unknown author?"

Several of the guests turned around with unrestrained astonishment towards the meagre person of Señor Falsodo, beholding in him a Unitarian, the arch enemy of confederative despotism "I! from interest in the author!" exclaimed he, evidently shocked at the slighest suspicion of such a monstrous supposition "I! I! from interest in the traitor? Señor Boto, what do you take me for? I said "alas," because, "alas," no man will gain the reward—at least there is yet small prospect of it, as far as I can understand from people who are in connexion with the officers of government, who ought to know something about it

"The '*Eleguas de la Plata*,' which set forth the idea of the union of South America as a republic—the Elegies of which we were just now speaking," interrupted one of the guests, with an unusually wide red riband in the button-hole of a fashionable dress coat, "are to be attributed to no one else but the condemned Señor Alphonso, himself!"

"People do not call a condemned traitor, *Señor*, rejoined a short, thick set fellow, with gray whiskers, taking him up at the word, and suddenly brought into such a state of confusion from loyal effervescence, that he put the wrong end of a newly lighted cigar in his mouth With the end of his tongue well burnt, and the ashes between his teeth, he made most singular grimaces, sputtering about, and cursing the entitling of a traitor

Involuntary laughter and merriment among the bystanders excited the wrath of the short man whose violent gestures were extremely comical

The man in the new dress coat, with the broad *dog's mark of Rosas' legitimacy* in his button-hole, was a so called handsome figure, such as the French would denominate "*bel homme*," with well cultivated, dark whiskers

As the Emperor of Russia, the King of Naples, and other legitimate potentates, have issued ordinances against the moustache and beard, so there was law in Buenos Ayres, making it the duty of every owner of a beard to shave his chin, in contradistinction to the European mode of a later period, which caused the beard to be shaved in a half circle, as a kind of border, or setting to the face Whether these modes originated from the so called *liberals*, or whether, on the contrary, they were fashioned after the "Royal military ordinance for the growth of the sappeurs' beards," we leave a matter for historic and scientific research upon the human beard, a study which already counts some literary works, among which is an octavo volume in the French language—"*Sur la barbe de l'homme*," —which appeared towards the close of the last century

In consequence of this singular fixed idea of despotism and its instruments that the opinions, views, and convictions of men depend on their beard, without reference to the rules of physiognomy, (which for good reasons do not enter into their considerations,) Rosas had, also, long since, manifested his decided antipathy to the full beard under the chin, by a special ordinance

Whether the Director or Gobernador of the

Argentine Republic, was as narrow minded as the European monarchs, who sought to extirpate convictions and emotions from men's minds, by means of shaving their beards (thus providing for the peace of the state, and the security of his throne) is a matter for controversy. We know that the Regent, Rosas, had a special dislike to the beard on the chin, because this, united with the whiskers, forms an U which, as the first letter of the words Unidad, Unitario, and Uruguay, was hated by him to extermination—at least to the extermination of the beard. This ordinance against beards was in full force in Buenos Ayres, and a special instruction expressly directed the observation of all the open and secret police officers to the *beard*. Each true subject of Rosas, and peace-loving citizen of the quasi republic, was constrained to manifest a humble submission to the all prevailing will of the despot, by a shorn chin, that it might be judged thereby what opinion he cherished, be it political, moral, or religious.

The short man, with the gray whiskers, appeared singularly overcome by the hearty laugh of the handsome man in the new coat, and involuntarily turned his close attention towards his person, for having entitled the infamous, condemned traitor, *Señor*.

"Sir, what do you mean by laughing at me? Who are you? You!—you are perhaps an Unitarian, and come here into the company of loyal confederados, to give the title of Señor to a traitor! It is true, upon my soul! you are a Unitarian, and wish to deceive and betray us with your new riband in your button-hole, which you evidently have just put there!" The short man becoming more and more violent, made a sort of upward spring at the suspected person, and passed his finger between his chin and cravat, in search of *a political conviction*. The handsome man, as has been observed before, wore his whiskers peculiarly long, in well tended curls. Notwithstanding his beard was legally shaven, according to statute and pattern, a part fell down of itself in front—whereby he became, in the eyes of the confederates, suspected of Unitarian sentiments, and of course "a refractory subject," and liable to punishment as a rebel.

The short man, who found no hair under the handsome man's chin, on which he and his conjectures might hold fast, shrank down before the suspected man, as suddenly as he had jumped up to him. The handsome man, now, in retaliation, (for the other's importunity,) yet with more coolness, seized on his cravat, and holding him before him with outstretched arms, inquired, in a calm voice, "Who, then, are you?" Most of the bystanders, already greatly amazed by the foregoing scene, could no longer restrain their laughter, while the short man, who was all the while in trouble with his singed tongue, entirely lost his presence of mind.

"I! I! who am I?" stammered he, now, with deep gaspings, in danger of being strangled, like a Unitarian under the hand of the executioner, "I! I am the barber, Antonio Pedrillo Gordo, living here in Buenos Ayres, over there, in the calle de veinte y cinco de mayo! Antonio Pedrillo Gordo, I am—barber—barber! Shaving is my business, and I am an unsuspected, practical, shaving confederado!"

"Oh!" cried the handsome man in the new dress coat, "you have then certainly an *interest*, if not a *right*, to seize a stranger by the chin and ascertain whether he is shaven or not; as to the rest, I would remark to you, that you must neither approach my chin nor my person, my name is known to the police, and if a police officer were here, I would claim his protection against such a grasp at my personal property. Waiter! give me another glass of punch," said he, in a lower tone, turning away from the barber, whom Señor Falsodo now courteously approached and offered a cigar in indemnification for his ruffled plumage.

"Recover yourself! compose yourself, Señor Pedrillo," whispered the spy—"compose yourself in your praiseworthy zeal, it is very praiseworthy indeed, very praiseworthy on your part, to be so observant in relation to the expressions and intentions of an unknown person, whose name I know, nevertheless," added he, in a low voice—"The stranger there, is a farmer, from the neighborhood of Rio Negro, from Patagonia—only a short time here, in Buenos Ayres, on business—he is an Italian by birth, his name is Guiuseppe Testa."

"Ah, indeed!" replied the barber coming to himself by degrees, while he pinched and squeezed the accepted cigar, and finally lighted it, "he seems to be well acquainted with the circumstances, as he expressed the opinion that the condemned might be the author of the elegies, and called him *Señor* into the bargain, an evident expression of respect, which casts the suspicion upon him of approving the ideas and principles of the author—of being on Unitarian."

"It suddenly appears very much so to me," said Falsodo, in a still lower tone, "it surprises me, I did not expect it from him, no one has had any suspicion of him until now. He came here in a Patagonian dress, with a drove from the Rio Negro—with horses and cattle, accompanied by the son of a famous native chief, he had modern clothing made for himself, as you see, and he wears the Rosas riband, and shaves himself under the chin."

"Shaves *himself*, do you say?" interrupted the barber, quickly and with a wild stare—"shaves himself, do you say?"

"Whether he, or an artist of your trade has fulfilled the regulation of the ordinance on his chin, I cannot certainly decide—enough, that he appeared in all form as a confederado, until the thoughtless and apparently very hasty expression"——

"Look after him closely, Señor Falsodo! look after him closely! do you not observe that"——

"That the suspicion may be confirmed of his being a *Unitarian*?"

"I hope not—I do not mean that."

"What then? what am I then to observe about him?"

"That the under part of his left whisker is cut crooked, a sign that he"——

"That he entertains crooked views as a confederado?" inquired Falsodo, examining the stranger, with blinking eyes.

"No! a sign that he *shaves himself*, and of course—and of course"—the barber 'Pedrillo pinched and squeezed his cigar anew, as if he would vent his rage upon it—"and of course—is—is—a man for whom I would not give six pence, with his knowledge of existing circumstances, and with his giving titles to traitors."

4

"Perhaps he did not shave at all on the Rio Negro, or he might have been obliged to shave himself," said Señor Falsodo, while he sharply considered the stranger, who had resumed the conversation about the condemned with the other guests

"Not shaved at all," grumbled Pedrillo to himself, "what barbarism! how I rejoice in the progress of civilization, which even directs legislation to the beard, and commands shaving, whether it be for the promotion of distinguished talent in art, or even, as in the present case, for the promotion of industry—of manufactures! for whoever shaves himself, or allows himself to be shaved, at least requires directly or indirectly one razor Russia and Naples are in advance of civilization by their wise legislation In England, as I hear, such legislation is not necessary, since the people, from patriotism, observe the universal law of *fashion* in encouraging the manufacture of the razor, and the industry of the barbers"

"In England the growth of the beard will not easily become the fashion—the Briton will not designedly ruin his own manufactures," observed Falsodo, and walked towards the group of guests, which had formed around the stranger, who appeared to know very well in what atmosphere he found himself, and had visited the pulperia either designedly or from curiosity

"I repeat," said the Italian, while he observed the approach of Señor Falsodo, "that the ground of my supposition, that the condemned is himself the author of these poems, lies in this that I cannot understand how a man, out of generosity and favor to another, could allow himself to be shot, particularly as I hear that he could have his freedom, and live heceforth in comfort any where else, if he would point out the author"—

"Or the authoress, you would say," suddenly interrupted a little fellow, who had entered the apartment not long before, and listened to the conversation, while he lighted his cigarette Many looks were directed towards the owner of this voice, and Señor Falsodo approached him quickly, with the words, "You are also of that opinion? How do you do, Señor Perezoso? I hope you find yourself well?"

It was, in fact, no other than the volunteer spy, whom we incidentally met at the gate of the monastery, near the negro Achilles—and who, without being yet in the service of Rosas, awaited some appointment from the favor and grace of the regent, and, in the meanwhile, diligently strove to show himself worthy of the same

Perezoso had received news of the betrothal of Señora Dolores to Señor Pepefy, with great interest, and left old Achilles in all haste, to take at least one step towards making good an inconsiderable claim on his former scholar, at the same time to gain what farther information he could respecting the projected marriage He betook himself straightway to the dwelling of Señor Pepefy—was very politely received by an old negro, who took his card with equal politeness The result of his inquiries as to Señor Pepefy's journey, was unsatisfactory He went from thence to a shoemaker, whom the uncle of Dolores from time to time visited with his custom, and hoped to discover from him where the young lady was at that time—whether in the country near the city, or at a distance from it,

as old Achilles had intimated In a long conversation with the artist in leather, on broken soles, upper leather, footings, and new boots, he arrived at more valuable objects—at broken hearts, the imprisonment of external relations, social footings and standings on a larger or smaller footing, from whence he quite accidentally mentioned Señora Theresa, as well as her sister Dolores, and then touched upon the rumor that Señor Pepefy was about to have his social relations new footed, or rather would stand on an entirely new footing

The shoemaker, quietly working on at his last, goodnaturedly heard and answered the announcements and inquiries of his old acquaintance, who had recommended many new customers to him Señor Perezoso quite accidentally learned, to his great surprise, that Señora Dolores was at that very time in the city, with her friend, Miss Walker, and apparently would remain there for some time—and, besides, that Mr Robert Walker was preparing for a journey, and, as he understood, was going by sea, in a Swedish ship, as far as Rio Janeiro

After having taken these steps, he returned to his headquarters, *Café Boto,* where we have just observed him "You are also of that opinion," interposed Señor Falsodo—"that the poem may belong to a lady?"

"A suspicion is always a certificate of uncertainty," replied the private teacher, with distinct pedantic accent "So far as I am acquainted with the literature, and a great portion of the writers of our country, I might doubt whether the poem was the production of a man who had ever published any thing before I think it is evidently the firstling of an unknown muse—not that it is by any means weak or insignificant—but (just the contrary) because it is so original, and, alas, fearfully magnificent and powerful—a style little known to us"—

"Therefore it is so strongly prohibited by law," remarked Señor Boto, "and therefore the sentence of death, pronounced against the person who disseminated it through the press, was one of the wisest and justest sentences which our Director has ever signed"

"I am entirely of your mind," averred Señor Falsodo turning again to Perezoso—"but now, if I may ask, Señor Perezoso, what further strengthens your suspicions with respect to the femuality of the person who wrote the 'Elegies?'"

"Hem! that I should certainly find it difficult to answer with precision Either, I opine—either a youth wrote the poems, as the firstling of his muse, or a woman, a maiden, a young lady, who has already written much, but from British fear of making herself ridiculous by her talents and acquirements, has, until now, kept her poetry entirely secret I say *British* fear, because in England it is'an especial disgrace for a woman to possess either talents or understanding, and the English, besides so many manufactures, Bibles, tracts, white and blue stockings, are likewise introducing among us fashion and prejudice"

"A very correct observation, Señor Perezoso," again interrupted Falsodo

"England and France are rivals in their influence over our State, as well as over all South America," continued the private teacher "England sends us fashion, France intellect—English mer-

cantile houses show us the pattern of civilization, for the members of their families seat themselves at table in yellow patent gloves, and
the French disseminate, here, literary works,
whose authors, even in France, are imprisoned in
consequence of their intellectual labors If the
author, or the presumed authoress, be a lady, and
somewhat in connexion with English families
here, it appears extremely natural that she
should always have kept her poetic talent a profound secret, that she might not appear ridiculous among the English women Had she, on
the contrary, lived in intercourse with French or
Italian families, it is evident that she would
have long since become known as a poetess, in
one way or another What among those might
make her ridiculous, among these would have
been accounted to her honor."

"How so?" suddenly exclaimed the barber,
Pedrillo, in conversation on the same subject with
Señor Boto, "the villain would not confess,
would not admit a confessor to see him?"

"You are mistaken, Señor Gordo" remarked
Señor Boto, "he by no means refused to admit a
confessor, only he desired his own, he wished
for some Benedictine instead of a Franciscan,
that is the mistake."

"A Benedictine?" inquired Señor Perezoso,
suddenly, stepping nearer to the bar while Falsodo would gladly have reserved to himself the
interesting discussion upon the standing of the
presumptive authoress, and have heard still
further

"A Benedictine—a Brother Celeste?" con-
tinued he "So I have just accidentally learned
Is it not so, Señor Boto? you certainly mean
Brother Celeste."

"The same—the same, as I was informed by
two guests, who were talking over the news of
the day, affirmed Boto

"Who is Brother Celeste?" inquired Perezoso
"What is his family name, is he a South American, or one of those Spanish priests—one of
the Jesuits of Don Carlos—who quarter themselves here?"

"It is the rich Señor Lorenzo de V——, who,
from love, (unfortunate love, as people call it,)
took up the idea of assuming the tonsure," asserted Señor Boto

"Lorenzo de V——?" exclaimed the private
teacher, with evident surprise "Ah! is it
possible! what do I hear? that might be," murmured he, half aside "Ah! the devil!—that
might be," and he sank into earnest and profound reflection, while Falsodo appeared disposed to seize him by the button and detain him,
not only until the former discussion was concluded, but until he had made a full confession of
what at that moment so fully occupied him
Perezoso, however, felt by no means disposed to
continue the discourse further, on the contrary,
he bitterly regretted that he had given hints
and intimations, the importance of which had
just now first become apparent to him, from the
connexion of ideas with the sister of the deceased, Señora Theresa, and her friendly relations with Alphonso P——, with which he now
combined the appearance of old Achilles by the
walls of the Monastery of St. Bento According
to the proverb, "to whom God gives an
office, he gives understanding," Falsodo, as a
spy of the police, might, without Perozoso's inti-

mations, perhaps, have hit upon the idea which
sudden as lightning, appeared to have been awakened in the mind of the latter, namely upon
the suspicion or probability, that a spiritual connexion existed between Alphonso and Dolores,
and that the former had not made choice of the
Monk Celeste for confessor without especial
reasons To bring the origin of the famous
poetry into connexion with the above events,
now busied the private teacher's thoughts the
more earnestly, from the circumstance that a
substantial reward was annexed to the discovery, which, in case he succeeded, would promote his establishment in office more than any
protection

Perezoso sought to lead the conversation to
other subjects, and gradually to break off the
discourse with the guest, he availed himself of
a moment while Falsodo was listening with particular attention to the proprietor from Rio Negro, and departed Hardly had the spy discovered that the well informed private teacher had
vanished, than he also hurried out of the door,
and looked to the right and left, like a hound
which suddenly loses the scent of another hound
that has carried away a piece of bread from under
his nose

CHAPTER IX

BUENOS AYRES AND JOHN BULL.

THERE is hardly a seaport town of the first
or second class, which is so inaccessible to ship
navigation as Buenos Ayres where there is no
harbor, in the proper sense of the word, but a
double road, extremely dangerous as an anchorage, which prevents the approach of large
ships

The gigantic stream, Rio de la Plata, increased
by the waters of the Parana and the Paraguay,
forms a basin which is about a hundred miles
wide at its mouth, on the northerly coast of
which Monte Video is situated, and at a distance
of one hundred and thirty miles up the stream,
on the opposite shore, lies Buenos Ayres, where
the stream, although but twenty-five or thirty
miles wide, hardly affords a view of the country to the north A sand bank, which extends
along the city of Buenos Ayres, divides the
road into two anchorages, the inner road, Balizas, where ships may enter which do not draw
above twelve feet water, and the outer road,
Amarradero, like the open sea, exposes them to
all the danger of the winds and waves, which
assert their peculiar power The scarcely there
perceptible movements of the tide, which in a
quiet atmosphere does not alter the height of the
water five feet at most, attains a power like the
flow of the ocean when attended by the *pamperos*, (southwest storms,) and operates with unexampled violence upon this anchorage. A current of the ocean presses round Cape St Antonio into the basin of the mouth, which creates a
circular motion, (similar to the *stream* in the
Gulf of Mexico,) whirls through this basin,
and finds its first outlet on the opposite coast
near Monte Video. Under such circumstances

the rapidity of the stream, as well upward as downward, instead of three miles an hour, is increased to six or seven, so that a ship, carried along by the stream, would easily sail that distance in an hour. Ships which anchor in the road, can enter into communication with the city by means of skiffs and lighters; boats which set passengers on shore, are stopped by the sand, and the passengers must mount a wagon, or a cart, to arrive at a firm footing. The lading and unlading of ships is only permitted by law at one single point of the city, that it may be watched the more easily, and contraband trading rendered more difficult, so that the cunning and hardihood of the smugglers are put in requisition, in the endeavor to elude the vigilance of the guard, by landing several miles above or below the required point.

The situation of the city, as the capital of an extensive country, has a decided influence upon the political circumstances and internal relations of the same, as an invasion or attack from the seaside would be rendered difficult in the neighborhood of the city, and by a march through the interior of the country, over the almost endless plains, sparsely cultivated and inhabited, would render the movements, or even the existence of an army, a problem of the lust of conquest.

It remains besides to be considered, that the original inhabitants (however small their number in proportion to the immense expanse of surface) are by no means insignificant in number, and consist of robust and warlike tribes, distinguished for physical activity and strength, a native cavalry, grown up in struggles with four legged bulls, and at all events able to defend themselves against a two legged bull—whether he present himself under this or another name.

As the landing of an enemy from the seaside, opposed to a defence by means of strong batteries and a good sized fleet, would be extremely hazardous, if not impossible, under the before mentioned circumstances, so it would be equally uncomfortable to maintain Buenos Ayres, as a conquest, as certain Britons (Sir Home Popham and Lord Beresford) relate at length, in their report of the fatal events which befel them there on the 12th of August, 1806.

The more the Argentine republic was protected from foreign invasion, by its situation and local advantages, the more injuriously and tragically did they operate at the period of our history, (whose epoch extends to the present time,[*]) during the supremacy of an individual raised up as an usurper out of anarchy, who knew how to avail himself of all these advantageous circumstances, to hold the people under the lash through his well known system of terror, and even to defy the reigning powers of Europe.

Considered from another side, the despots of Europe beheld in the Dictator of La Plata a colleague, who looked forward to the throne and crown, and having an understanding with them, sought indirectly to make the republican principle appear despicable and impracticable, as we have before mentioned.

Notwithstanding the prominent difficulties of the undertaking, that render the conquest of Buenos Ayres by force of arms, on the part of Great Britain or any other European power, extremely doubtful, that country, by dint of the perseverance which peculiarly characterizes it, by no means intermits its labors to cultivate, indirectly, in every way, its territory for the future, on the La Plata river, and to manure it with its egotism.

By a singular mistake, the British, since the middle of the last century, have been represented (especially in the popular novels and romances of the European continent) as a nation who personify, in a colossal body, the principle of freedom, and each Briton as a hero or demi-god by whose very contact an infection of liberalism is communicated, which, united with generosity appears as consolatory to each slave, as dangerous to every despot. The Briton appears in a nimbus of freedom and independence, which other nations denote by the expression, "British pride," and bow themselves the more profoundly before this splendor, the more they want the feeling of nationality from which this pride proceeds.

The more and nearer, however, the nations in their struggle for freedom and independence, come in contact with the British, so much the more does the result of experience tend to diminish the glory of Britannia, without, at the same time, refusing the acknowledgement of her national honor, or denying, or contesting, the more valuable points of national character in individuals.[*]

It requires but little sound common sense to perceive that the greatness and splendor of Great Britain is maintained at the expense of the liberties of other nations, that the Briton arrogates to himself the monopoly of freedom, and holds up to other nations the prospect of becoming British subjects, as a peculiar honor.

Perezoso, the so called private teacher, or modern philologist, acquainted with several living languages, had had occasion, as a teacher and interpreter, from his youth upward, to observe, in commercial and consular business, the peculiarities of various nations, and, as his conversation with Falsodo manifested, had, with tolerable correctness, seized upon and pointed out the influence of the British, upon the customs and fashions of the country. Although from manifold reasons it concerned him to pursue the inquiry after the author of the condemned Elegies, still, among the number of families and persons with whom he was casually brought in contact, he had almost forgotten the intelligent and intellectual Dolores, whose relation to Alphonso still remained a secret.

---❀---

CHAPTER X.

UNEXPECTED FATE.

Perezoso left the *Café Boto* in a state of confusion and bewilderment, so blinded by the light

---

* The author distinguishes *national character* and *national sentiments* from *cabinet intrigue* and *the principles of a government.* Some, and perhaps not the least interesting characters of this novel are *English*; they are not the worst, and we hope that they rather do honor to the nation than otherwise.   H.

of his suspicions, that he was neither able to distinguish the condition of the present, nor the concatenations of the past, much less was he able to determine upon even a single step which it behooved him to take under the circumstances Uncertain which way to turn himself at that moment, or whether to give to any member of the government a hint of which the consequences still remained so uncertain, he was apprehensive that, by a rash step, he might acquaint some person with his prospect of the gallows premium, who would know how to make use of his confidence to his disadvantage

More and more absorbed in such reflections he unconsciously approached the prison where Alphonso languished It was past eleven o'clock, and Celeste and Dolores, attended by Achilles, had just crossed the threshold, when Perezoso turned the corner of a street, whose perspective presented in the back ground the architectural monument of the Jesuits of former centuries He heard hasty steps behind him, and before he had reached the edifice, which he by no means designed to enter, he turned round, slowly, to retrace the path he had come, in the hope to discover, by the way, a means of accomplishing his design He was not a little astonished when he found himself suddenly encountered, nose to nose, by Señor Falsodo, who, after long spying about, had renounced all expectation of such a meeting

"Ah! a very good evening to you, Señor Perezoso' said the spy to him, "have you been at the barracks there?"

"Ah! a very good evening to you, Señor Falsodo,' replied the private teacher, in the same friendly manner, "have you any business at the barracks there?"

"I! Señor Perezoso—I? My way led me through this street I am taking a walk, and feel my head a little heavy after the two glasses of spirits which I drank at Boto's'

"Then I shall take the liberty to accompany you a little way, I can as well go home by an indirect route"

"I am much obliged to you, Señor Perezoso," returned Falsodo, who would gladly have learned whether the private teacher had paid any visits since he had been out of his sight Each had secretly formed a resolution to keep the other company for this evening, so long as to leave him no chance to give his testimony to an officer before the morning came

"That is a solid, massive architecture, the old monastery there, the barracks there," began Perezoso, in a tone of conversation, as they approached the fatal door at which the guard was discharged, whose office was at the same time that of a patrol The guard at the entrance was doubled, the corporal in command had received the strictest orders to take charge of every living being who should show himself in the neighbourhood of the building, and place him in security for the time being

Instead of joining in the admiration of the ancient building, Falsodo noticed that a patrol was approaching them, and before he could utter a word, a sharp "Who's there?" was directed to the two night wanderers "Friends' Friends!" answered both, nearly at the same time

"Very good! friends of the condemned, friends

of the traitor!" grumbled the corporal, who at last found an opportunity to show his official diligence by an arrest, and in such a manner hoped to commend himself to advancement as a sergeant

"Who are you? what do you want here?" demanded he now of both, while he suddenly surrounded them with soldiers

"We? we are peaceable citizens, on our way home," stammered both, nearly shivering with apprehension as it did not particularly suit either of them to pass a night under arrest, and neglect their important business

The corporal informed himself of their names and dwelling places, and found the latter in exactly an opposite direction to their promenade

"What business had you here at the door of the prison? I will give you time to answer this question to the commissary of police, to-morrow noon March! forward, march! to the guard house!"

Neither Falsodo nor Perezoso, found it to the purpose to protest long against the disagreeable command of the grumbling soldier, whose strict orders they were now too well acquainted with Both seemed of the opinion that a long debate with such a subordinate jurisdiction, would be utterly superfluous and useless, especially as the so named "police hours" were long passed, and, under existing circumstances, appearances were against them

The less the police spy had been able to discover of the plans of his companion, the more did he maliciously rejoice to see him, at least for a time, prevented from acting, while he relied upon secret protection, to get himself released from confinement

Perezoso, who had been long since aware of the position of his companion, no sooner perceived his present situation, than he already harboured the worst apprehensions at being exposed, by such a singular accident, to a false accusation, which he now might expect

Animated to an acceleration of their movements by several ungentle jogs from the muskets of the guard, the two poor sinners hurried on to the Plaza de la Victoria, and to their iron grated place of destination The officer of the guard received the corporal's report, and sent the two confederados to a cell, where they found a straw bed, and leisure to philosophize over the origin of the Elegies and their own bad luck

CHAPTER XI.

THE YOUNG SOUTH AMERICAN

A storm-threatening night, in the spring month of October, enveloped the banks of the river La Plata, over which the city of Buenos Ayres projected, like an indefinite shadow in the southwest, partly concealed by scattered groups of the masts of ships, from different ports of the world.

The Swedish brig "Nordstjernan,"* lay in the outer road, "Amarradero," prepared for sailing,

---

* North Star.

at a pretty good distance from shore A solemn stillness reigned on board and all around The two seamen of the watch walked to and fro upon the forward deck, directing a look from time to time, towards west southwest, whence they expected the captain's gig, which was to convey a young lady, with her servants, on board, whom, as the captain had intimated, he was to bring off that night

Two passengers were seen upon the quarter deck, apparently strangers to each other, the one, a youth, hardly past boyhood, who stood leaning on the bulwark, gazing earnestly in the direction where the boat should appear, his pale, delicate features, and dark brown eyebrows, surrounded by dark ringlets, betokened his Spanish descent, while the countenance in itself, as well as the bearing of the slender form, distinguished by a peculiarly small hand and handsome foot, indicated a certain natural nobility, which is to be found, here and there, in all nations He was dressed in dark, fashionable clothing, without the least appearance of dandyism On his white linen, partly concealed by the bow of a dark silk cravat, glittered a diamond of great value, a family heirloom for many generations, inherited by him from his father, a South American patriot, whose head had fallen under the axe of the executioner, at the command of the liberally-governing Rosas !

This was Horatio de P——, the nephew of the noble Alphonso, who was to have shortly followed that foregoing martyr to the freedom of South America , but by the special mercy of the tyrant, had been at last permitted to carry his head to the grave, unseparated from his body Long imprisonment in a dungeon, had reduced the yet undeveloped frame of the youth to a skeleton, for suspicion had fallen upon him, among others, as being the author of the Elegies, whose publication had cost his uncle his life Becoming less and less suspected, in consequence of strong justification, and through peculiar circumstances, he was saved by the urgent mediation of a powerful ecclesiastic, whose influence, as a " pillar of the church," was at least able to effect so much in the cabinet of the tyrant, that the youth, pronounced free from suspicion, was condemned to perpetual banishment from the province of La Plata , and after the confiscation of half his property, while the other half remained under administration, he had received permission to embark

The stamp of genius impressed on the inward being of this youth, was not to be mistaken As art in general is a unity, and the various branches of poetry, music, and the fine arts, flow from one source of intellectual life, the suspicion above referred to was, unhappily, by no means groundless The youth, who manifested a conspicuous talent for painting, might very naturally be accused of the crime of national poetry, the element of which mingles in this unity

Art, having been brought from higher spheres down to this gloomy world, as a ray of the pure life of the soul, exalting the spirit of man to the contemplation of the elevated and the beautiful, makes known its existence as " national poetry," in the struggles for freedom of all the nations of the earth The fine arts, on the contrary, can only exhibit themselves when a nation has passed through several stages of development, and reached a certain outward stage, which demands the employment of those forms in which painting and sculpture are exercised Most powerfully, however, does art reveal itself as poetry, in the struggle of a people for their sacred rights, and only in such struggles does each national poetry display itself, quite different from the elegant literature, (however rich,) of a people who have acquired neither union nor independence, neither a free country, nor the sense of nationality

In corroboration of this,' we behold, on the shores of the la Plata, a poetic constellation of manifold brilliancy, whose rays, like the aurora of a future freedom, break through the dungeon-night of slavery, and beam around the scaffolds of the martyrs, with whose blood the despairing muse writes those patriotic hymns and songs, the origin of which is watched by the executioner In like manner as moral freedom must precede as the condition of all intellectual development, of every improvement in the arts, so must a national poetry of freedom form the groundwork of all art, which, on the other hand, belies its worth, and falls short of its destiny as art, as soon as it degrades itself to the service of absolutism

The young Horatio, burning with enthusiasm for the elevated and the beautiful, and seeking, from internal impulse, after forms in which to clothe the spiritual poetry of his being, had already become a " thorn in the flesh" to the ruling gaucho, who, conformably with his absolutism, sought from a distance to throw the lazo over the neck of the Pegasus, and entrap him, like a wild colt of the pampas, that he might harness him before the triumphal car of his renown As intellectual life in itself, and every species of moral development, is an abomination to absolutism, so was the discovery of the spark of genius in this youth sufficient to direct upon him the scourge of the gaucho, to load him with execrations, and to deprive him of his fatherland, whose soil had drank the blood of his nearest relatives

Horatio lingered for hours, leaning upon the bulwark of the " Nordstjernan,' and gazing out into the night, which offered to his eye no consolatory object The rushing of the stream, which hastened to the ocean with remarkable rapidity and stormy violence, was the predominant melody—a symphony of nature in her magnificence, and in the immensity of her movement From time to time the creaking of a yard sounded above the monotonous rushing accompaniment of the night, until, at last, another hour had sunk into the sea of eternity The watch bells of all the ships, far and near, tolled in mystical, harmonious tones, in the various keys of the different metals which chance had brought together from distant parts of the world, to serve as a floating bell concert on the La Plata river

Incessantly, and with restless speed, did the waves of the Parana, increased and strengthened by the foaming mass of the Paraguay, and united to the gigantic grandeur of the La Plata, a waving sea, rush past the Nordstjernan, whose ponderous chain cables proved their iron solidity, as, from time to time, the ship was shaken by a heavy blow, in the dangerous raging of the element, against the keel of this fabric of human temerity. Many thunder clouds threatened each other by silent declarations of war, over the extensive dominion of the Gaucho, and in the direction of the Banda Orientale, but they delayed to send forth their destructive lightning, amidst the rattling thunder, ever changing the forms of their cloud bodies, whose colossal domes and summits were more gloomily prominent, the less the remaining starry sky was obscured by smaller clouds.

The mind of the youth, in whose agitated depths the grandeur of the universe was reflected only in broken images, seemed to present similar contrasts with the firmament partly enveloped in thunder clouds. The thought of the approaching death hour of the martyr of his people, whose fate he felt was so intimately connected with his own, by the ties of blood and affection, weighed down his spirit. In painful uncertainty, he awaited the deliverance of Dolores, whose destiny was no less painfully united to the life of the condemned, than to his own fate. Agitated and overpowered by a double affliction, he forgot his own lot, and his own sufferings.

There are moments in which the human heart, too deeply wounded through the fate of a beloved being, turns to the light of the future, forgetful of its own sorrow, and finds the burden of this earthly existence the heavier, from its inability to save that being by the sacrifice of its own life. These are the hours that try our confidence in divine Providence, the deciding hours of the elevation or fall of inward human dignity.

The spirit deeply depressed by anguish at the sufferings of others, either rises to the loftiest contemplation of this mortal life, through trust in God, manifesting its nobler human nature by submitting its fate to another's destiny, or it succumbs in the struggle of despair, breaks the band of love and confidence in God, looks upon life as a caricature without support, without a stay, without any connexion with a higher idea, seeks deliverance in egotism, and loses itself, and the consciousness of the exalted dignity of human nature, in the abyss of materialism.

In Horatio, the love of fatherland appeared to be religion, while the principle of universal philanthropy developed itself in him, as love of mankind, (humanity,) for which a man should sacrifice his individuality, all personal considerations towards himself, to the sufferings and the fate of his people, (as a part of mankind,) in the sense of nationality.

Horatio beheld, in the thrilling fate of his uncle, and in the impending danger of Dolores, the sufferings of beloved beings, and therefore more deeply did he feel the circumstances of the slavery, and the subjugation of his people, under the executioner's axe of a barbarian. Involuntarily, however, brought to higher views of things, through the influence of the principles and example of his relatives, he recognised in that period of terror in his country the struggle of life and death, through which alone the strength of the nation could be developed, or "*moral freedom*," as the basis of all *political freedom*, become established.

On the foundation of faith in the providence of God, there arose within him the belief in "*humanity*." This sunbeam of futurity, as the harbinger of a bright dawn, breaking through the night of suffering that surrounded him, lightened his heart.

Incapable, in his childlike purity, of comprehending the reality of absolute wickedness on earth, his unbounded abhorrence of oppression and tyranny, was more the result of the sufferings of his countrymen, than personal hatred against the enemies of truth and freedom, whom he considered as unfortunate, blinded creatures, who, from despicable egotism, and to their own degradation, scoffed at and trampled upon the rights of mankind.

Gazing to no purpose in the direction whence he expected the return of the captain's boat, he turned, from time to time, to look on that part of the city where the monastery was situated, which, used as a prison, confined the martyr whose last moments of life, like the sands in an hour glass, appeared to escape the faster, the nearer they approached the end of their allotted time. No human hand was able to seize the hour glass of this mortal's earthly existence, and quickly reverse it in the moment when the last grain of sand was running out.

Penetrated by corroding grief, a cold sweat overspread his forehead, his knees shook, and he sought a physical support by leaning more firmly against the bulwark, looking forward to the longed for coming of Dolores, as the last consolation which the present was able to afford him.

CHAPTER XII

INWARD LIFE

" THE boat is coming!" exclaimed a Swedish sailor, in his mother tongue, his seaman's eye, practised in seeing at a distance, having discerned the expected object, notwithstanding the darkness of the night, like a black speck, afar off. " There it comes!" he repeated in English, supposing that the young South American understood English, or, at least, knew as much of it as himself.

" Is the boat coming? Is the Señora coming? are there passengers in the boat?" hastily inquired Horatio, trembling with the eagerness of expectation, and following the sailor to a place where the best view could be obtained.

The sailor understood by the tone, and from the words " Señora and passengers," the sense of the question, and collected his stock of English in broken fragments to answer the youth, that he himself still wavered in uncertainty, that the boat was yet too distant, and that he could not distinguish the number of persons.

The other passenger, whose presence on deck has been before mentioned, had hitherto, with measured steps, and arms folded upon his breast, continued his promenade upon the quarter deck. He cast, from time to time, a sharp look, from his deep set blue eyes, upon the youth, whose mental agitation could not have escaped a less attentive observer. As a well bred man of the world, he had, since he came on board, observed that reserve towards his fellow passenger which discretion and delicacy required of him, although, without having in the least transgressed the rules of politeness in their accidental encounter, he had conducted himself towards Horatio with becoming civility. He was of slender form, of middling size, and apparently about thirty-five years old—his deportment was characterized by that youthful activity, which appears in a person whose education has been carefully directed towards bodily, as well as mental improvement, and who, in the pursuit of military or gymnastic exercises, has his body at his command. His countenance bore that uncertain national character, found as well in the natives of the Pyrennean peninsula as in the Scandinavian countries, distinguished by a regular profile, a high broad forehead, dark brown hair, black beard, and a lighter colored beard on his upper lip. Similar faces occur so frequently in those remote countries of Europe, that singular mistakes sometimes occur in confounding persons of both countries, far distant from each other. Such occurrences are interesting to the inquirer in the department of physiognomy, as they support the physiological and historical observation, that the primitive races of mankind continue to exist, unchanged and unchangeable, in spite of all intermixture. The unknown wore a garment between a monkey jacket and paletot, of dark grey cloth, a grey Pyrennean hat, with a wide brim, made of pliable goat's felt, which yielded to, and received external impressions, as easily as the susceptible mind of a suffering human being. By incidental inquiries respecting the number and relative positions of his fellow passengers, who were to share the cabin with him, he had before learned that the boat had gone ashore, to bring away the sister of the young Englishman, who was pointed out to him, as the son of one of the house by which the ship was freighted. The mental agitation of Horatio revealed itself so unmistakeably, as not a little to rouse the sympathy of the stranger, by means of which his attention was directed involuntarily towards him, without, however, showing it by a direct approach. Suddenly interrupted in his rapid promenade by the words of the sailor, but especially by their effect on his fellow passenger, he placed himself near the watchful group, peering into the distance, from time to time, to fix his own eyes upon the object of increasing attention.

The darkness of the night was gradually giving way to the dawn of approaching day. In the expression of his countenance, as in the whole behavior of the youth, an eagerness of expectation appeared, which, proceeding from the same source with his previous agitation, seemed to have grown to such violence from the same cause. The stranger in the paletot contented himself with silently observing the approaching boat, which, coming from the shore, above the city, was favored by the current, and soon approached so near that single persons could be distinguished in it.

"There are passengers in the boat," said the stranger, breaking silence, "at least two in the stern, if not three."

"Then it is she! then it is she!" exclaimed the youth involuntarily, drawing a long breath, as if his heaving breast was relieved from a part of the oppressive weight of anxiety and apprehension that burdened it.

Nature gives to men, as members of the great and sacred league of humanity, a letter of recommendation and legitimation, whose seal and signature, impressed upon the face, is never forged, and is more valid than all the diplomas of open or secret societies, a document that seldom lies, and cannot be purchased with gold, or under the guarantee of a third person. It is the intelligent and noble expression of the human features, the inward dignity, beaming forth in the open countenance, operating on congenial natures, through the chief organ of the soul, the magnetic fluid of the eye. In accordance with this, an attraction, and repulsion or indifference, in meeting or social intercourse, manifests itself, which as undeniably draws a man in confidence towards this or that person, as in the opposite case it would operate repulsively upon him. Both emotions, sympathy and antipathy, are founded in the sacred mystery of our divine nature.

This repulsion and attraction moves in an invisible element, (the magnetic fluid,) operating like electric contact. The soul perceives the beneficial influence of a congenial being, by means of this element, as clearly as it feels itself disagreeably excited and disturbed by the approach of another, directly opposite individuality, of a different sphere of life, without, at the moment, being able to give any account of either one or the other influence.

This attraction of sympathy, and repulsion of antipathy, displays itself in the intercourse of mankind with each other, in proportion to the development of the spirit and the sentiment. The higher the degree of development of the inward life, the more powerful is the sympathy of congenial or similar natures, and the greater is the antipathy of such persons against individuals, in whom this life is either not all unfolded, or exists in an inferior degree.

Men whose intellects are developed at the expense of their hearts, operate repulsively upon men of feeling, whose intellects have been cultivated in harmony with the purity and depth of their minds, of their souls. The more a man denies his spiritual life, and stretches his conscience by the calculations of the understanding, striving merely after material aims, the more directly is he opposed to the spiritual man in the higher stages of the soul's life, and consequently, the stronger also the repulsion. In one, materialism reveals itself, destroying the life of the soul, in the other, spiritualism, purifying and elevating the soul. The greater these extremes, the stronger the repulsion.

In accordance with these observations, we find, in heartless men, absolute indifference exhibited, since they are incapable of any sympathy for others, of any love, (in the purer sense of the word,) interested in nothing which does not concern *themselves*—their own personal existence.

It is not necessary to mention whether, and how far the youth, Horatio, was conscious of an attraction towards the unknown, it is certain that he had experienced as little repulsion, as had the stranger towards him, who felt himself drawn towards the suffering youth by a powerful attraction.

There are moments in which men, looking

forward to the fulfilment of their long wishes, are so severely tortured by uncertainty, and harrassed by doubt, that they hastily consider their approaching realization as an illusion

Horatio was in a similar state of agitation, on hearing the assurance that there were persons in the boat which was to bring Dolores

"No! No! it is not she!" cried he, suddenly seized with an inward convulsion, which seemed to impart itself to his frame—"it is not she!" repeated he, wringing his hands He sank, half unconscious, on the breast of the stranger, who hastily seized him under the arms, as his physical strength was prostrated by a fainting fit The stranger felt the throbbing heart of the unhappy youth on his warm, glowing, manly breast, unable to afford him the slightest relief, in his wild and bitter agony, which might be perceived from such a convulsion of his nature.

The sympathizing seamen of the watch, moved, after their manner, by the swoon of the youth, hurried to the water butt, to procure the medium of revival, which the unknown by no means disallowed, though it exercised, as he feared, but little influence

The boat, impelled by wind and stream, had gradually approached the ship A death-like silence prevailed, as before "Horatio! Horatio!" sounded from the boat, in a subdued tone of a female voice As if struck with lightning, or recalled from apparent death to life by galvanic power, the youth aroused, and started, with a strong gaze, speechless and motionless, towards the sky, but without seeing the stars

"It is your friend," said the stranger, in his ear, but the youth heard not The two sailors hurried to the ladder, to hold a lantern to those approaching, while Horatio, conducted by his unknown friend, reached the quarter deck with firm steps, without knowing that he had changed his place

With increasing expectation the man in the paletot gazed at the person who ascended from the boat, and now stood on the deck. It was Dolores, in male attire, with a Biscayan cap, and enveloped in the national mantle, attended by Achilles and Corinna

"Where is Horatio?" cried she, with a trembling voice, anxiously gazing around, whereupon, the stranger led the youth, still speechless, from emotion, to her arms

Roused by the pressure of her hand, he felt his cheek moistened by her tears. With a cry that resounded through the grave-like stillness of the night, the unhappy youth sighed from the depth of his wounded breast, and called, "Dolores!" and the two breasts beat against each other in a silent embrace, in the bliss of reunion, as it were at the foot of the martyr's scaffold, whose fate and whose death had confirmed in them that bond of sympathy which is a strange and rare phenomenon here on earth, and is only to be conceived and understood in the department of the higher spiritual life.

CHAPTER XIII

FREE LODGINGS

THE officer of the guard, in whose custody the two prisoners had been placed, desired to know no more than that they were "suspicious persons," who had been found in the neighborhood of the before mentioned edifice, in order to confine them with due rigor and contempt, to await their further fate He did not even consider it worth his while to acquaint himself of their names, but noted for his report, where, and how they had been seized, and in what number of the prison they were confined

The "hotel for public security," in the front hall of which, the military watchfulness of the capital had established its head quarters, was provided, for similar cases of noble minded hospitality, with many unfurnished cells Many of these uncomfortable retirements, not originally erected for numerous families, were, from the want of sufficient rooms for the tempory separation of the sexes, divided by a wall, whereby the number was increased These "unfurnished rooms for single gentleman," had about the compass of a roomy clothes press, whose walls, instead of oak, were made of solid freestone—an iron door, and a grated opening, through which daylight endeavored to intrude itself "around" the left corner," by all manner of windings and turnings, formed the only furniture There was not even a decent chain, nor a ring in the floor, still less a nail or hook in the wall, where one weary of life might arrange his neckcloth for the last time. The strong walled, solid "clothes press,' into which were now shoved the everyday wardrobe of two persons, stuffed with the owners thereof, was locked and bolted with due carefulness Silently, and without regarding each other, Falsodo and Perezoso had walked together until they came to the door If either of them had felt an emotion of sympathy prompting him to exchange a look with his companion, it would have been advisable, to do it before the squeaking iron door sprang to its lock behind them

The keys and bolts rattled, and without a special mandate from the "future sovereign of La Plata," the two prisoners were totally interdicted from looking at each other, by the pitchy darkness. They absolutely saw nothing at all Without a conception of the narrowness of the space in which they were placed, they tried to take a step on each side of the entrance, and to venture further into the interior of the apartment, to find a bench, or place of repose A knock, and a tingling and crackling in the brains of each head, which protruded from its well kept garments, was the shocking consequence of such unoffending, and by no means unlawful "progress" A long pause followed their duet cry, which was lost on the damp, mouldering walls.

"It appears to me that the prison is in reality no prison," sighed Perezoso, at last.

"So much the better," growled Falsodo, "if we are soon convinced of the truth of your conjecture, and—and"——

"I mean that it is a sort of stone chest, so contracted that we can hardly both sit down in it—not a real prison, I think."

"I wish that this infamous wall, against

which I just now knocked my head, were likewise no real wall, but a mattress, or any thing else, so it were less massive," grumbled Falsodo

Both now sought, with outstretched arms, to measure the cubic contents of the cell, which they could easily do without moving from their places, a proceeding which would have been attended with serious difficulties At last they contrived to find as much room as was necessary to seat themselves close to each other, in such a manner that the feet of one touched the hips of the other They both placed their backs and the soles of their feet against the opposite walls, a resting place, or position, which had to answer for the occasion, as little choice of any other remained open to them

They had hardly arranged themselves in their places, before they sought a vent for the ill humor and spite which had been gradually increasing within them

"What put it in your head, to take a walk so late at night?" grumbled Perezoso

"And what induced you to turn back with me, to accompany me? I was not going that way, I wanted to go on further with you," replied Falsodo, with the same moroseness

"Why did you not say so, then?" demanded Perezoso

"Because I did not think it worth while; and in fact, I had not remarked what street we were in"

"You know that to-night, or towards morning, the execution in the prison yard will take place, and that the building was, on that account, guarded with peculiar strictness?"

"That was in the highest degree indifferent to me," returned Falsodo, "I trouble myself, for the most part little, if at all, with politics and political crimes and punishments"

"It is, indeed, a most thankless occupation," muttered the private teacher, "I find, however, that a person may be involved in political affairs entirely against his will"

"I have thought so this long while, and unhappily feel it more severely in your valuable society. We both sit here, apparently as much against our will, as Señor Alphonso will be shot in the morning against his" The spy sought in this manner to lead the conversation, as if accidentally, to the circumstance which had been the original cause of their imprisonment But Perezoso saw through him, and forthwith sat or lay as if overtaken by sleep

Falsodo was trebly chagrined, as spy, as prisoner, and as poor devil, especially by the reserve of his companion, who appeared thoroughly disinclined to make confession to him It occurred to him that several governments made important discoveries by causing prisoners to be watched during their sleep, or even in fever, and overhearing their expressions ; a measure which the secret police of the Grand Duke Constantine knew how to make as useful in Poland, as the inquisition of Don Carlos in Spain

Señor Perezoso must certainly know something which had reference to the discovery of the author or authoress of the Elegies This idea had become a certainty to Falsodo That the poems were written by a lady, had already become not less probable to him. But what lady the private teacher had in his eye, was a question which sorely puzzled him.

In the hope that his companion might dream in his sleep, and might talk in his dreams, he resolved to make the official sacrifice of watching, throughout the whole night, in the aforesaid posture, that no confession of any sort might escape him

Perezoso's purpose of deceiving his dungeon companion by a feigned sleep, in order to break off the discourse with him, was fully attained, finding himself in a sort of moral and physical depression, he soon sank into a real sleep, instead, however, of talking in his dreams, he discovered a peculiar talent in snoring from a deep nasal bass The spy sought, by all manner of means, to ward off sleep, and soon became so absorbed, notwithstanding his chagrin, that at length he was extremely obliged to his companion for keeping him awake by means of his music, even though he did not give him the desired confession

Several hours passed by The private teacher snored on, and the police spy listened to the variations of the nasal bass with strict conscientiousness The stillness of death prevailed around their cell, which lay half under ground, in a corner of the court, separated from the corridor of the façade Neither the clang of weapons nor the order for dismissal, penetrated into this solitude Suddenly, however, footsteps were heard, not far from the iron door near which Falsodo watched, and the jingling sound of weapons approached A tremendous yawn from some sleepy head, who let a bunch of keys fall, and thus indirectly announced himself as the jailer, sounded through the midnight silence

"Here is number five," he growled—"you want the two in number five?"

"To be sure!" exclaimed a sergeant, whose color and *build* betrayed a mixture of African and Patagonian blood, "quick, now ! we are in a hurry ! we must be at the shore before the boat goes Come, out with them both !"

The jailer yawned again, set a dark lantern with a half extinguished light on the ground, opened the iron door which he had pointed out, and called out at the threshold "March ! out with you ! out with you both !"

"We ? both of us ? out ?" asked Falsodo, as much astonished as alarmed, "we ?"

"Yes ! who the devil besides ? there are only you two in this lodge That fellow there is asleep yet," said the lock-up man, in still surlier tones, uttering a tremendous oath

"Now, come ! how long must this last ?" grumbled the sergeant, "can't the sleepy blockhead there get on his legs ? must I help the fellow a little ?"

Falsodo, beside himself with alarm, strove to stammer out a question—why, and wherefore, and whither, they were taking them To all this the sergeant replied, with a contemptuous smile, that he himself knew as little about it as he was interested in it.

Perezoso had neither time for question nor alarm, for before he was fairly awake, the escort, in whose midst he found himself, was already in the street, and in rapid motion

Awaking thus, he considered the whole event as the continuation of a dream, and marched on, mechanically, until the escort reached the banks of the river, where they were thrust, with more prisoners, on board a boat, which, according to appearances, belonged to the navy of the sole ruler of the Argentine quasi republic

CHAPTER XIV

OFFICIAL DUTY

It was an hour before sunrise, when the sentries at the gate of the prison were doubled, and a subaltern officer passing through the middle of the street with about fifty men, defiled them in parallel columns, thus closing the approach to the principal entrance. The officer was a young man, whose countenance bore very little expression of either the jailer or the executioner; he dropped the point of his sword and walked slowly back and forth, with arms crossed upon his breast, and downcast looks, gazing vacantly before him.

The grates and blinds of the balconies, and windows of the nearer and more distant houses, remained fastened, notwithstanding the military tumult, which was not unusual in this neighborhood. Here and there, a human figure moved behind the laths of the aforesaid wooden gratings, which characterize the architecture of South American houses. Some of these were painted red, thus manifesting, by this favorite color of Rosas, the loyal confederado sentiments of their owner. No one dared to open a grated door, or a blind, for fear of betraying in his features an emotion of pain or compassion, which might compromise him to the Argus eyes of despotism, as sympathizing with the cause of the people. The silence of death prevailed around. The steps of the young man in uniform kept pace with those of the sentries, while their earnest gaze was averted from each other, and they dared not exchange a word by which to shorten the tedium of their mutual post.

The harbingers of dawn, the first beams of the expected sun, appeared to linger. Time itself seemed to pause, before admitting through its mighty floodgates, the passage of a moment which should add another blood spot to the soiled book of the people's history, to increase the debt of guilt of tyranny, the settlement of which will belong to the nations, when they shall awake to the consciousness of their dignity and their power.

The bells of the neighboring monasteries, sounded for early mass, and the dying reverberations of their tones, produced a plaintive melody, which lost itself in the returning death-like silence of the dawn. The young man in uniform suddenly stood still, putting his left hand into his breast pocket, to draw forth his watch, when a report of musketry, from the interior of the barrack yard, apparently caused him to quiver, and the color of his manly countenance changed to a deathlike paleness.

"It is fulfilled," said he, half aloud, and at the same instant he suddenly straightened himself into a military attitude, and thundered out a command, which had as much of curse as blessing in its sound. The two columns formed themselves into one opposite the gate, from which, after a few minutes, an ordinance officer came forth, and whispered an order in the ear of the young man in uniform, whereupon the latter, with his corps, re-entered the barrack. A Franciscan monk appeared at the gate before it was again closed. It was Padre Fernando, who, in the name of his saint, desired to speak to the superintendent, Señor Domingo, or to some other officer of the prison. The ordinance officer measured the figure of the monk with a searching look, from crown to sandal, as if examining into the identity of the monastic appearance, and then suffered him to pass, while at the same time he gave the mulatto, Narcissus, a command to conduct him to the apartment of the superintendent of the prison. The gate was then locked and bolted again, as hastily as it had been opened.

Old Domingo had been so sorely burdened by visits and disturbances of all sorts, in relation to the traitor Alphonso, that at last it seemed *enough*, and he desired rest, as a kind of right, even though his mind, hardened and blunted by similar occasions and long habit, required it less than his aged body.

Weary and dispirited with the fulfilment of his official duty, in which we have partly followed him, Señor Domingo sat on a bench, near the door of his private apartment, in a sort of front hall, which was bounded by a grating between the inner court and the principal entrance. His seat allowed him the prospect of both courts, which were separated from each other by rows of willows, forming a perspective, animated by a crowd of soldiers, officers, and functionaries of various ranks, among whom the grave-digger occupied, for the moment, the most conspicuous position; he had just dug a grave in a corner of the inner court, which was close by the chapel and a portion of the old prison, and in some respects, a kind of *consecrated ground*. Fernando approached his old acquaintance with the customary ecclesiastical greeting, and the formula of inquiry after his health, which the old man answered by a murmur of thanks, and the mechanical proffer of his snuff box. The monk had not come for the pinch of snuff, so much as for the most circumstantial information respecting the last moments of the so called traitor, whom he was known to have attended in his last days. He seemed to act upon the principle, that whoever seeks a favor from a parent must speak well of his child, or from a snuffler, must praise his snuff. In this case, it was desirable to put the old man in a talkative humor, and Padre Fernando hit upon the method, by finding the snuff exquisite, whereupon, each took an enormous pinch. The monk cast a searching look through the iron grating in the back ground, where a blood red pall (the color of Rosas, and of the throne mantles of all tyrants) covered an object that looked like a corpse.

"He is dead, then? executed! shot!"—inquired the Padre, with a movement of the head in that direction.

"Seven and twenty balls aimed at the breast," replied old Domingo, slowly, and with emphasis, "seven and twenty—but not blindfolded—that he would not consent to; he protested against it, and the officers granted him the favor and mercy of looking death boldly in the face—out of humanity, out of pure humanity."

"But kneeling?" interrogated the monk

"Kneeling! certainly," continued the other, "but only upon one knee, and he held his hands on his back"

"What do you say?—on one knee, and with his eyes open!" again interposed the monk, "met death face to face? but he confessed beforehand? and the Benedictine, Brother Celeste—or whatever he is called—who must step into my place—when did he go away? if I may inquire"

"Brother Celeste remained in the dungeon with the criminal until his last hour, at your service, Padre Fernando," replied the old man, "and when they had taken leave of each other"——

"Taken leave?" once more interrupted the monk, "taken leave? then they spoke to each other, even at the place of execution? Did you not hear what they said, Señor Domingo? May I ask you for another pinch? your snuff is alwaysso excellent—excellentissimo"

Señor Domingo yawned in the face of the inquisitive priest, while he mechanically placed the snuff box at his disposal, without replying to the question

"Then you did not hear what they said to each other? Pardon me the question, it proceeds from pure Christian interest in"——

"In the person executed, to whom neither your sympathy nor mine can now be of the least service," added the old man, unconsciously, laying his hands upon each other, as if he would fold them in prayer "You see, Padre Fernando," he continued, "when I have living criminals and condemned persons, in chains and bonds, in my custody, on my responsibility, then I am hard, firm, relentless, inexorable in every respect, because that concerns the fulfilment of my duty to my office, my bread, my existence, and besides, the security of the state depends upon it—that is plain enough But when the hour is over, when the head of my prisoner rolls from under the axe, in the sand—or when the shots rattle and the corpse lies there, then all my criminals appear to me in an entirely different light They are judged, and the thought very often occurs to me, that they go to appear as accusers, before a judge on high, as accusers! Padre Fernando! before a judge who will one day pass sentence upon the judges—upon the judges, I mean, who here sign sentences of death"

"Hem! to be sure!" replied the Franciscan, "but judgement must be exercised on earth, and government is God's handmaid" May I ask you, Señor Domingo, where the reverend Brother Celeste is to be found? I am under the necessity of speaking to him"

"So far as I know, he is still in our chapel"

"Ah! in the chapel, there, may I request you to open this grated door for me?"

"I regret extremely, Padre Fernando, that I cannot oblige you; it is not permitted," replied the superintendent, drily and readily, "as you know yourself, it is not permitted without a written order from the authorities Yesterday is not to-day; you appeared yesterday as the father confessor, who was to prepare the condemned for death—you found admittance, the criminal is no more, and that order is no more in force I regret it extremely, Padre Fernando Will you take another pinch?"

The snuff was, at this moment, far from being as excellent as before, the monk had hoped in all haste to encounter the colleague, who had taken his place, and perhaps to learn something more about the condemned, that might at least gratify his curiosity The firm precision of the superintendent had drawn a dash through his reckoning He propounded the question, however, whether a lay brother, or novice, had not accompanied Brother Celeste, the preceding night, as was customary The wearied old man nodded an affirmative, and added, that he was indeed accompanied by a brother of his own order, and a negro, one of those blacks in the service of the monastery"

"So! so!" cried the monk, "then a second brother of his order was with him! Did you not learn his name?"

"I cannot inform you, I do not know it," murmured old Domingo, a little gruffly, annoyed with so many questions, whose object did not appear to him particularly important, and too weary and sleepy, besides, to desire continuance of this useless interview Just then the porter opened the grated door, to allow a number of functionaries, who had been present as witnesses of the execution, to depart

Señor Domingo, cast a mute look upon his uninvited guest, in the uniform of the holy Francis, which sufficiently intimated that the latter had better take this remarkably good opportunity of passing over the threshold of the prison

"There were seven and twenty balls then?" inquired the monk, who understood the hint, and had approached the door—"and all pierced the breast?"

"Nine the breast, three the heart, four the right shoulder, and three the left—six entered the head, and two missed, making seven and twenty," grumbled the old man, very hastily "Your servant—farewell, Padre Fernando!"

The monk had scarcely time to send his cordial thanks for this *ball report* through the closing narrow door, which was opened in the middle of the great gate for similar *small visits*, before he could collect himself, it was locked behind him He remained a moment standing, in counsel with himself, and then hastened in the direction of the monastery of St Bento, either to await there the return of his colleague, Celeste, or, if possible, to meet with one of the attendants who had entered the prison the past night, and perhaps had learned something of importance

CHAPTER XV

THE MERCENARY AND THE REPUBLICAN.

OVER against the Mole, which is built out into the stream from about the centre of the city, the brig of war *La Caza** lay at anchor in the "*Amarradero*," the outer road, near the sand bank which divides it from the inner road, the *Balizas*. La Caza carried twelve guns, and was commanded by *Mr Tumble*, an Englishman in the service of Rosas, who found such a position lucrative, after having received an un-

---

* "The chase"—" pursuit "

sought for dismissal as midshipman under the British flag. He was one of those so called "able seamen," who understand how to command a crew and to empty a glass of grog, but from a defect in their mental education, do not know how to sustain a proper balance of character, nor even to live in harmony with their superiors. Such kind of "useful subjects" pass for "good captains," when a ship is accidentally entrusted to them, although the verdict of their subordinates does not harmonize with their reputation on shore.

"Five bells" of the morning watch had just sounded. Señor Enero, the second in command, a young man from the banks of the La Plata, walked to and fro upon the quarter deck, conversing with Señor Codo, another officer, an European Spaniard. From time to time Enero looked towards the city, whose white spires, domes, and cupolas, becoming gradually lighted by the rosy beams of dawn, stood forth, by degrees, on the back ground of a cloudy horizon, while the body of the city below them lay like a dark shadow.

"There will be another elegant crew," said Enero, after a pause in the desultory conversation, accompanying his words by an ironical smile, "we have but twenty men on board, at most, and require fifty, and among all we are able to procure, there are few experienced sailors to be expected."

"It is the same here, under our Rosas, as it is in Constantinople, where I have often superintended such a press gang," remarked Señor Codo. "When a Turkish ship is about to sail, a bridge is laid from the shore to the ship, then the drums and fifes play, and all the needy ragaruffins in the neighborhood, who are prompted by hunger and despair, run on board and become the crew. If a proportionate number of Greeks were not always unpressed, who command respect as sailors, it would have fared worse with the Turkish fleet than has been the case."

"I have heard of those Turkish press gangs," replied Señor Enero, "which are similarly managed in Brazil, and especially in Rio de Janeiro, as well for the marine as for the completion of the military battalions. Whoever goes out in the evening must be supplied with a ticket of residence. a document with which the police provides the stranger on his arrival, upon the delivery of his passport. If the patrol find any one whatever without such a document, they immediately seize him, carry him temporarily to the guard house, and then send him, without ceremony, to the militia, often directly against the rebels in the interior, or to Rio Grande, and then it will be very hard for the unlucky 'permanento'* to get out of his uniform jacket again."

"Perhaps the transport cutter may bring us, this morning, the same description of forced recruits for the crew of our Caza," remarked Señor Codo, "and many whom we shall now receive, dreamed not last night of their future fate before the mast, or behind the guns on board of a war brig."

"Rightly observed," rejoined the second in command, "this mode of making up the number of men, whether it be on land or water, does not particularly please me, and when we closely investigate the power of the Orientales,* displayed in their persevering obstinacy, in the contest against us, we are constrained to acknowledge a certain moral force, founded especially on the circumstance"—the young man hesitated to utter a truth redounding to the disgrace of his country—"on the circumstance," continued he, "that there a man fights for a principle, and here, with us, by command of our Dictator, for a few dollars."

"To be sure," murmured the other, "I know what you would say, the Orientals bear upon their banners, or at least, as the motto of their newspapers, words that point at a notion, which they may call a principle. They talk much about 'Igualdad, Liberdad, Humanidad,' (equality, freedom, and humanity)—words which, like so many other fashions, have come to our shores from Europe, but, according to my judgement, they are merely words—each word stands for nothing more than a word, with which no idea is connected."

"I know your principles," said Enero; "in Spain you were a Carlist, and fought after your manner, for Don Carlos and the Inquisition. Our commander, Señor Turnble—with all respect to his character as a marine officer—our commander is likewise a royalist, like all Britons, and we are here united under the Argentine flag—and the device of our government is also a word, and that word is 'Rosas'" and the idea that we should combine with it, is, the subjugation of the provinces of La Plata under the executioner, Rosas!"

'Executioner, Rosas?" cried Codo, suddenly standing still, and gazing on his comrade.

"Certainly," replied the other, "and I repeat the word, although so many a patriot is quietly shot, instead of being beheaded. Taken figuratively, the sceptre of Rosas is the axe, the executioner's axe."

"Do you not fear the axe, if it should become known that you uphold such sentiments," whispered the Spaniard, with a sinister smile.

"No one overhears us," answered the South American, briefly and earnestly—"I know to whom I am speaking—I know your royalist principles—I know you, also, as a seaman, and that is enough. I know that no man of war bears our flag, in which Rosas has not spies in pay, directly and indirectly, and, for the most part. foreigners. I know, also, that many of our comrades owe their advancement to denunciation—to espionage. But the element of the ocean endures no treachery! Wo to him who should be discovered as a spy on board the Caza. With regard to the Orientals," continued he, after a long pause, "we must respect them as enemies, the honor, which worthy opponents bring against us, reflects upon ourselves! The Orientals fight from conviction, and with enthusiasm, because they know wherefore they fight. Our people fight for their pay, at the command of Rosas. That is the difference. The Orientals combat for the principle of freedom, of a republic, against the principle of absolutism represented by Rosas. The Banda Oriental does not renounce the idea of the union of the pro-

---

* Regular soldier.

* Orientals—the people of the *Banda Oriental*—Monte Video

vinces of La Plata, but only the sovereignty of
Rosas, whose person stands in the way of their
union, while he either will not, or is unable to,
comprehend the idea which unfolds itself in
South America."

"It is very true that Rosas does not concern
himself much with ideas," replied Codo, "and
there he is in the right, but he remains, notwithstanding, one of the greatest men of our age
—ay, or any age, and yields not to Napoleon
in any respect"

"May historians, after the death of Rosas,
place him where he belongs," answered Enero
"His name belongs to history, the history of
South America, and he himself has written it,
with blood, upon the annals of the present, may
he answer for it. He may persecute the Unitarians—he will not eradicate the spirit of freedom,
nor extirpate the idea that lies at the bottom of
the struggle, the idea of the foundation of the
United States of South America"

"A fantastic idea," said Codo, smiling ironi-
cally, "which will hardly ever be realized!"

"Just so would a royalist thirty years ago
have said, in reference to the independence of
our provinces of the Spanish crown," rejoined
Enero, "and whoever had dreamed, eighty years
ago, of a collossal republic of the United States
of North America, which, before the end of the
first century, should compete with all the monarchies of the earth, in bloom and fruit, in
dignity and strength, would have been proclaimed a madman. No mortal—no Rosas, can
restrain the development and accomplishment
of an idea, when once its rays have entered
the hearts of the people Our Argentine republic exists as a republic; and as to myself,
I shall still fight for principle, because I
would rather see Monte Viedo united to us,
than that she should fall into the hands of the
British, who reckon upon it But the system of
our government, the system of terror, cannot
last Rosas is mortal Even the worst republic,
is better than the most tolerable monarchy, for
the fate of the people does not hang upon the
first born of a single family, the nation has its
sacred rights, and only as a republic can it assert
them Did we not break loose from the yoke of
the Spanish monarchy, in a struggle of life
and death! Is it not to be ascribed to the want
of enlightenment, to the influence of the priests,
and the speculations of usurers, that we are
once more ruled by despotism'"

"What you call despotism, appears to me absolutely necessary for the maintenance of public
order," said Señor Codo

"So the royalists justify every arbitrary act,
every execution of a patriot, who, from love of
fatherland, embraces the cause of the people
The population of Monte Video consists of no
other elements than ours, here, in Buenos
Ayres."

"The liberal ideas of Europe find more free
entrance there," returned Codo

"Good! you contradict yourself, Señor Codo
—can public order, and security of person and
property, exist in the Oriental republic by the
dissemination of the so called liberal ideas of
Europe? Why then does the axe of despotism
become an absolute necessity here, among us?
We know the customary phrase of the royalists,
that a nation is not ripe for freedom; but we find

no example in history, where despotism has
prepared a nation for freedom, while it robs people of their sacred rights, and, by gradually increasing oppression, drives them to despair,
until the chain is broken, and they seek deliverance"

"Your principles, Señor Enero, are entirely
those of a republican"

"Other principles would not be to my honor,
my country is a republic, and only as such has
it a future, as a free state of South America"

The first lieutenant turned away at these words,
looked at his watch, and ordered the officer to
call him, when the cutter, which he expected
from the city, approached

The Spanish royalist who, like so many
others, had entered the service of Rosas as an
adventurer, looked after the South American
with a thoughtful mien, and then, resuming his
measured step, walked to and fro upon the
planks of the quarter deck *La Caza* swayed
slowly with the movement of the stream, the
yards creaked in measured time, the morning
dawn brightened into daylight, over a sea-piece
with a city in the distance, whose moveable
figures balanced more and more in the foreground Beheld from another point of view,
the sea-piece appeared still more dreary and
uniform, while the opposite shore of the La
Plata, covered with clouds, was hardly visible.
In the centre of the picture, among the separate
groups of ships from various parts of the world,
appeared the Swedish brig "Nordstjernan," by
whose sails and rigging it was evident that she
was preparing to heave anchor

CHAPTER XVI

THE MONKS

THE early mass was over, the monks of the
Monastery of St Bento endeavored to pass the
interval until the general assembling to breakfast in the large refectory, each after his own
manner The father guardian walked up and
down in the shady paths of the spacious garden,
deeply engaged in conversation with father Ambrose, a monk of the same order, from Barcelona, who, a month before, had found an asylum
in Buenos Ayres Father Ambrose had touched
upon a bloody and eventful chapter in his life,
in seeking to answer the inquiries of the father
guardian, who had embraced this opportunity to
inform himself of the political relations of Spain,
which, as in so many other countries of our time,
manifestly stood in close connexion with the
church

"Believe me, father guardian," continued
Ambrose, in his communication, "believe me,
it goes ill with the church in Spain, especially
with our order, which is in a bad way as long as
Don Carlos is not victorious. A shudder seizes
me when I recur to that time—to those scenes
of blood, from which I escaped with difficulty"

"Will the Christinos, then—or however the
rebel party may choose to call themselves—will
they acknowledge no church, no religion?"

"Religion! church!" muttered father Ambrose, "there is only *one* church—our own, and I cannot conceive what the Christinos call church, when they demolish monasteries, dissolve our order, and compel us either to follow a trade, or to carry arms, or they make shorter work with us—they hang us up!"——

"Hang us up!" exclaimed the father guardian, while he involuntarily grasped his neck and felt the collar of his cowl, as if he would convince himself that no cord was yet attached to it

"Yes, I assure you, the rebels made short work, and there are yet particular parties of the insurgents—the republicans, for example, who, if not numerous, are still dangerous—who are as severely persecuted by the provisional government of Christina, as they both persecute us, the followers of Don Carlos This republican party first broke out in France, as you may have heard France, you know, is a country which is separated from Spain by the Pyrenees That is a rebellious nation, the French!—a bloodthirsty people, the French—a savage"——

"A savage?" interrupted the father guardian —"cannibals, like the *Botacudoes* in Brazil, or savages, like our Unitarians?"

"Not precisely cannibals, but savages, exactly like these Unitarians, only it makes very little difference whether men eat us or bury us when we are dead, we have no more feeling then, and it is loathsome enough, besides, to think that we shall be eaten by worms, that are not even men '

"Then the French are a wild, horrible people ' savages, like the Unitarians, and live in Europe?"

"In Europe," continued father Ambrose, "to the north and east of the Pyrenees, their capital is called Paris—as, perhaps, you have heard—the centre of all rebellion "

"Paris ' it seems to me that I have heard of it," returned the other, slowly and meditatively

"Among the French," continued father Ambrose, "there were philosophers in the last century, who misled the people to think, and to infidelity and heresy "

"Philosophers?" inquired the father guardian, "what sort of people are they?"

"Heretics," replied the enlightened Spanish monk, "heretics, who can read and write, and publish books against the Pope "

"Books against the Pope?" exclaimed the other, "and the government permits this? I cannot conceive that "

"Has not a rebel lately published here, poetry against Rosas, our lord and protector?" inquired Ambrose, smiling, coming to the assistance of his brother's contracted comprehension with an example

"I have heard of that," answered the guardian, hastily, "and the criminal has just been shot Brother Celeste has rendered him the last services I know it, but he had the poetry printed in Monte Video, not here, in Buenos Ayres "

"It may be," said Father Ambrose, with a smile ; "the first works of the French philosophers of the last century were, also, printed at Amsterdam, a city in the Netherlands, governed by heretics To be sure, as soon as these books were discovered in Paris, they were publicly burnt by the executioner "

"Bravo !" cried the guardian, "I approve of that ' and the heretics who wrote the books—were they also burnt?"

"Alas ' they were not, some were put in prison—others escaped, and were looked upon, in the neighboring countries, as great men—and from their philosophy, the idea of freedom was developed in the French people, and revolution broke out Paris lay as full of men's heads, as Buenos Ayres is of bullocks' heads

"Shocking! shocking!" exclaimed the horrified monk, "the French are real savages!"

"Yes ' but much remains to be told," continued father Ambrose "There was then a republic in France, and a little artillery lieutenant made a compact with the devil, and peformed miracles of bravery through witchcraft, and was advanced to be general, and took the Pope prisoner, and beat the armies of all the princes, who wished to restore the sovereignty of the Pope, and the kingdom in France, and became Emperor of the French, and married the daughter of an emperor—the Emperor of Austria, an empire without freedom, and composed of many nations—and named his son ' King of Rome,' and made his brother king of Spain And *los Salvages Franceses*, the French, came to us in Spain, and then our monasteries would have been abolished, if the British had not come to our assistance, and re-established the holy Inquisition among us "

"Oh the British ' *los Ingléses*," cried the father guardian, "I know them, they are the friends of our Rosas, they call themselves gentlemen, and wear patent gloves They are heretics, though, as I hear, who do not bow before our crucifix, nor take off their hats when they pass by a church "

"There are, it is true, Christians in England, Catholics," remarked father Ambrose, "one entire British race is Catholic, and lives on an island, and is used when England is at war, for they are brave soldiers, but in peace they are hated and persecuted, even to blood, and only exist through sufferance—and are merely permitted, as a favor, to pay taxes, and tithes, and be honored by the acceptance of their money "

"What then is properly the religion of the British, or English?" asked the guardian

"The religion of the British is Politics, and their church is the Exchange," replied the other, with peculiar earnestness, "and these same British, who once reinstated the Inquisition amongst us, now support our *Christinos*, our rebels, because their ' religion' makes it appear advantageous to them It is to be hoped, however, that Don Carlos will succeed, and restore our monasteries, and then the English will again stand up for the Inquisition "

"A very convenient religion, is the British, I must acknowledge," remarked the father guardian, after a pause, "but tell me now, honestly, father Ambrose, is that all true, which you have related to me concerning the little lieutenant? is that a true legend? Did the little lieutenant really live ' and did he take the Pope prisoner—our holy father?"

"All that I have related to you, is positively true," affirmed the Spaniard

"And what became of the imprisoned Pope ' how was he again set at liberty?"

"When the ' little corporal,' as his soldiers called him, wished to become emperor," continued the monk, he became reconciled with the church, and with the Pope, and with the nobility, and restored all that the republic had overthrown, and had himself crowned and anointed emperor by the Pope."

"How so ? the same little corporal, who once took the Pope prisoner, allowed himself to be crowned and anointed by the Pope ?"

"As I tell you "

"I cannot understand it "

"Nor I."

"And what became of the little corporal, who made himself emperor ?"

Ambrose delayed his answer, and at length said, "It is a long story, and there are books—profane books, to be sure—which treat at large of the history of the little corporal, I have not read any of them, but I have heard about them All the kings and princes of Europe combined together to destroy the little emperor, and they succeeded, after much slaughter and bloodshed, and when the little emperor found himself forsaken and disarmed, he fled on board an English man of war, as a passenger, and sought an asylum with his bitterest enemies, and the English betrayed him, and carried him prisoner to a lonely, rocky island, which bears the name of a female saint, between South America and Africa And he, who would once conquer the whole world, was, as a man, content with overcoming himself He who had once formed alliances with emperors and kings, was content with the alliance of a friend, who remained faithful to him in his misfortunes And so he died—without church penance—and lies buried in unconsecrated ground—upon that rock there, in the ocean, that bears the name of a female saint It is a pity that he did not become a monk in his youth; he would have been able to effect more for the church than the saint of all saints, our Ignatius Loyola, ever did "

A long pause ensued. The father guardian appeared absorbed in reflections, whose nature he indicated by the question, " Do you believe that our Rosas has ever heard of the history of the little corporal ?"

The Spanish monk could hardly restrain his laughter, and assented to the probability of this supposition.

"The little corporal was lieutenant, you say ?"

"And became emperor," said the other, in a very low and expressive tone

" Our Regent, Rosas, was a *Gaucho*,* and also became general, and is equal to an emperor at present Do you not believe that the Pope would acknowledge him as emperor, or as provisional king, our Rosas, and crown him ?"

"I do not know that he would crown him personally, since the distance is so great, but that he will acknowledge him as sovereign, will certainly come to pass, and the coronation can also take place, through our bishop It will only be necessary that Rosas should constantly follow the example of the little emperor, and cause every one to be shot who publishes a book against him, as the little emperor also did—at least he did so in Germany,† and people affirm

that this proceeding contributed greatly towards showing him worthy of the favor of the church "

The guardian sank into profound reflection, and then again took up the word " Do you think that our Rosas has heard of the treachery of the British to the emperor of the French ? He ought to be warned of it, for the British ambassador is so friendly with him If Rosas trusts himself to the British, it may happen to him as it did to the French emperor—what was his name ?"——

Ambrose was just about to answer, as a Franciscan monk approached, with tolerably hasty steps, and offered his ecclesiastical greeting from a distance It was Father Fernando The guardian looked at him inquiringly, informing himself in anticipation, at a glance, of what had brought the reverend pupil of the holy Francis there so early.

After some humble preliminary remarks, he brought forth his inquiries respecting brother Celeste

The father guardian deliberately declared that, so far as he knew, the reverend brother Celeste had passed the night in the prison, with the condemned " enemy of Rosas," but without either attendant or ciborium, since the criminal, in his sinful obduracy, had refused to receive the sacrament, and that he had not yet returned

The Franciscan gazed silently before him— doubts arose in his mind, as the receipt of the mass-money came in question, which had been outrageously diverted from his monastery by the stubbornness of the criminal, who had sent him away, and chosen a monk from another monastery. He was unable to suppress within himself the injured feeling for his order, which appeared more in his tone than in his words, while he stood in dutiful humility, as a subordinate brother, before the superior of a very rich monastery, whose rank and corpulence claimed all respect. He suddenly found himself in a most singular position If he acknowledged the probability that the condemned had received the sacrament, he thereby clearly recognised the right of the monastery to the collection of the mass-money If he yielded to the assertion of the father guardian, that no ciborium had been taken from the monastery, and that the sacrament had not been performed, then the right of collection remained a doubtful matter, as the church did not allow any one to read a death-mass for a sinner who had refused the sacrament He repeated the assertion that three persons from the monastery were seen in the prison at midnight

The father guardian considered this charge a renewed insult to his order, and declared it to be a fabrication which brought reproach upon his monastery, as if they would meanly enrich themselves by urging a sacrament, and by a collection, as its consequence

The three brethren of the cloister had strolled through one of the alleys of the garden, and through the cross-walk of the monastery, to the front building, where the father guardian caused the lay brother to be summoned who bore the office of porter, and asked him, in a loud voice, if brother Celeste had left the monastery on the preceding night, alone or in company, with or without ciborium ? The answer tended to the most profound humiliation of the Franciscan,

* *Gauchos*, the inhabitants of the pampas (plains) of South America, near the Plata River—descendants of Spanish emigrants.

† Palm, a publisher at Nuremberg.

as a contradiction of his assertion, and the father guardian measured him from his forehead to his sandals, with an expression almost of contempt

"Strange!" remarked brother Ambrose, the Catalonian monk, while a suspicious smile flitted over his thin lips "Strange! And so they asserted in the prison that three persons from our monastery were there last night?"

"Three persons," repeated the poor Franciscan, re-assured for the moment by this special inquiry of the foreign brother, which, at least, showed a certain faith in the validity of his assertion "Besides the reverend brother Celeste, there was a younger brother, in the habit of the order, and one of the watchmen of the monastery, a negro, or mulatto—I cannot be certain which Nevertheless, Señor Domingo, the warden of the prison, saw all three persons bodily I make no false assertion, and our monastery will willingly renounce the collection of the mass-money," added the wounded Franciscan

"That is incomprehensible," began the Catalonian, after a pause

"Incomprehensible, certainly, but not un-heard of in the chronicles of the cloister," affirmed the father guardian Are there not examples of wonderful apparitions in the history of the monastic world? and especially at midnight, and particularly in the case of persons condemned to death? examples of revenants, and of multipli-cation of individuals in chapels, or even in the open street? confirmed by the assertions of many witnesses, as our archives relate, which record wonderful facts and circumstances to the glory and sanctification of our order, to which has been given the power to work miracles, since the martyrdom of our sainted founder" He sud-denly made the sign of the cross, and the other monks and the lay brother devoutly did the same

"In what light stands brother Celeste in the Refectory?" inquired the Spanish monk, after a pause, who, as the guest of the monastery, did not seem as yet duly acquainted with the char-acters of the individual brethren

"In the odor of sanctity,' returned the father guardian, hastily and with pride, "he is libra-rian of our monastery, and aspirant to the priory, in spite of his youth, he takes upon himself, with Christian humility, the subordinate duties of the monastery—visits the sick in the meanest hovels, and is untiring in his zeal for the exten-sion of the only saving church, in his intercourse with heretics and infidels of all sorts and classes He increases the number of Christians, through proselytes from the upper ranks, and the reve-nues of the monastery, by his personal exertions"

Father Ambrose listened with marked atten-tion to this eulogium of the young monk, as he had done to all that preceeded it, while he seemed to pursue a train of ideas, whose contra-dictory effect expressed itself more and more in his countenance, notwithstanding his efforts to conceal his inward emotions. Father Fernando received, with no less indifference, the inspired words of the corpulent father guardian, in which he saw but little prospect of gaining the proposed object of his personal curiosity.

The Catalonian was just about to utter a query in relation to the young monk's reputation for sanctity, when there was a ring at the outer gate, and the brother porter, who had, until now,

listened with open mouth, hastened to fulfil the duty of his office. Celeste stepped over the threshold, greeted those present, and walked slowly past, apparently so deeply absorbed, that he did not recognise the individuals of the group, while each of them separately considered him from his own peculiar point of inward con-templation All eyes accompanied the grave steps of the learned librarian, until he disap-peared behind the distant pillars The three monks then silently looked at each other

"Will you accompany me to the prison, reve-rend brother?" said father Ambrose, at length, to the Franciscan, "I should like to speak to the overseer of the prison?"

"In the name of all the saints, whose exam-ple unites us in monastic harmony, I shall con-sider it a personal honor to conduct you wher-ever your duty calls you"

At these words, confirmed by humble obei-sance, father Fernando passed to the side of the Spanish monk, and both stepped over the threshold

CHAPTER XVII

MR JOHN WALKER AND CAPT FINNGREEN

Mr John Walker sat early in the morning in his private cabinet, near his office It was a small room, well furnished with maps and charts, books and statistical tables, whose veritable Eng-lish origin was recognised at the first glance He was a tall, well built man, with broad shoul-ders His head, from long habit, was a little in-clined to the right shoulder, from "long habit," likewise, he generally kept the right one of his clean gray eyes almost shut, when he conversed with any one, whom he always observed the more closely with the left, at the same time turn-ing with his right hand his watch key, which dangled from a gold chain His dark hair, from the effect of years, and of various climates, was here and there sprinkled with gray, while his whole appearance indicated vital force and ful-ness He appeared unusually busy, and his as-pect was peculiarly cheerful, for he had secrets upon secrets to keep, and to expedite, and the brilliant prospect of not being able, for months to come, to retire to rest before two or three o clock in the morning, from the unavoidable pressure of business, in regard to secrets

"Captain Finngreen!" called a clerk, through the half opened door

"Let him come in here," returned Mr Walker, continuing the writing with which he was so busily occupied. The clerk admitted the person announced, and went out, shutting the door

"Good morning, captain, how are you? Take a seat, captain," said Mr Walker, in a friendly manner, but without interrupting his employment

The captain was a well built, middle sized man, as elegantly dressed as the steam progress-ing civilization of England requires of men in all parts of the world, in order to appear as gentle-men

Even a layman in the province of physiognomy could not avoid remarking that he was a son of the ocean, a ship captain, while the acute observer, engaged in the study of the different races of men, would have recognised his Scandinavian origin in the peculiar traits of his regular features

Captain Finngreen delayed, for a moment, to take the seat pointed out to him, he walked up to a chart of the coast of Africa, and endeavoured to study it, while, in spirit, he was busied on board of his "Nordstjernan," and, in fact, gave little heed to the object which covered a portion of the wall

At length Mr Walker sealed the letter which had, until then, claimed his attention, wrote the address, laid the steel pen in its usual place, with the point towards him, turned the upper part of his office chair and himself round towards the captain, and pointed out to him the chair near himself, which waited to receive him

"All on board, captain?" inquired Mr John Walker, with a friendly countenance, after having again informed himself of the health of his visiter, "all the passengers on board?"

"When I left the brig, yesterday, there were only two passengers on board, besides your clerk," replied the captain, deliberately seating himself "The young Spaniard, or South American, arrived there the day before yesterday, and the foreigner, about whom I cannot make up my mind, came yesterday The young lady who has the honor to pass for your daughter, or, at least, for the sister of Mr Robert Walker, was to be taken on board this morning, in my own boat, I have given up my cabin to her, according to agreement, and will do my best to make the voyage as comfortable as possible to her I wish we could only once get safely out of the river again, without being visited"

"There is no danger of visits," said Mr Walker, smiling—"none at all, the officers visit no ship here when she is once cleared It is not here as in Rio de Janeiro To be sure, war often makes exceptions to the rule, sometimes a cutter comes up with an outward bound ship—officers go on board, examine the passports, and seek for some patriot who may have fled, nevertheless, if even that should take place, the secret on board the Nordstjernan would remain undiscovered"

"God grant it!" returned Captain Finngreen, with a deep sigh, drawing his stool nearer to Mr. Walker "Pardon me, Mr Walker, there are some things on board which are not stated in the manifest Perhaps these were forgotten."

"How so, captain? how so? forgotten? I do not know what they can be," replied the Briton

"You know, Mr Walker, there are two small boxes of minerals on the manifest," continued the captain, "the only ones that I have taken for any house here I protested against it a long time, and would not take the boxes on board There is war between Buenos Ayres and Monte Video, and I must be prepared for privateers and cruisers under all sorts of flags If a privateer, or man of war from Monte Video should board me, and examine my manifest, and find goods from Buenos Ayres, no matter what, they would think that the boxes contained gold or diamonds, or some such valuables, they will examine them, detain me, and confiscate my vessel in the bargain There was a Danish brig lately brought into Buenos Ayres as a prize, which had weapons and ammunition on board for Monte Video, it was English property under a false firm, but the bark was confiscated If I were to inform my owners that my Nordstjernan had been confiscated on account of two boxes of pebbles, or whatever else they may contain, they would hardly conceive how I would resolve to take them on board, nevertheless, I have discussed that matter long enough with your son, who insisted on taking the boxes with him I made the condition, that I should see the tenants, and assured myself that they were, in reality, worthless stones, minerals for a museum, of no especial value I am glad to do you a favor, and would not refuse your son's request, but now comes the point Instead of two boxes, there are, all at once, four boxes on board! God knows how the last two got there My two mates pretended not to know who brought them, and the matter is unexplainable, for the two extra boxes are marked just like the others The thing does not please me—I am captain of my brig, and am answerable for brig and cargo in danger by contraband goods The name of your house is too respectable for me to have apprehended it!" He spared the head of the respectable house an humiliation, and continued—"the thing does not suit me at all, Mr Walker, and I must insist that the two boxes be immediately removed from on board, or if not, then I will throw them overboard myself, so you may take your own course, and do as you like"

Mr Walker had listened to the Swedish captain of the Nordstjernan, with the same friendly smile, leaning his head on one side, as before, and turning and re-turning the watch key, according to his old custom, without in the least losing his selfpossession, or giving a sign of any other mental emotion, than approbation and delight

"All right! all right captain," he repeated with peculiar satisfaction, "all right captain, I perfectly understand you, I am entirely of your opinion! With regard to the two boxes, I must inform you that they are no concern of mine, this affair has nothing at all to do with the respectability of my house The two boxes of minerals are shipped by a house here—a house little known, it is true—an entirely unknown house, but my son, Mr Robert Walker, knows the circumstances, and is answerable for them I will speak to him about them He will soon be here, to take leave, before going on board I will mention the matter to him, you may rely upon it I agree with you entirely in respect to the danger of your being overhauled by a cruiser or privateer from Monte Video, on the lookout for goods from Buenos Ayres It is, in fact, an interesting risk! it is a secret of solid value! an interesting secret! You have one privateer to fear, the 'Mazzini,' she is a famous corsair!—commanded by a Genoese, Señor Barigaldi, under the Oriental flag, with the flag of 'Young Italy' on the foremast This is a famous craft ! a miserable little schooner ! I would not bid a thousand dollars for her, if she were put up at auction, she is such a walnut shell, with six cannons, and five and twenty men, all Italians, all Genoese He is a bold fellow, that Barigaldi ! Condemned to death in Italy as a patriot, he accompanied the famous expedition of Savoy in 1834, of which you may have heard ! He is an amazing fellow ! a dangerous fellow ! a furious corsair ! rash enough to attack an Argentine corvette, to say nothing of a Swedish brig ! He cruises there, between Cape St. Antonio and the Rio Grande, and watches the mouth of the La Plata, as a hawk does a dovecot You will be very likely to get a sight of the nutshell, with the Italian flag at the foremast "

Captain Finngreen appeared by no means edified by this imposing representation of the danger to which he exposed himself, by having the least portion of Argentine goods among his lading, not to mention the secret of a considerable amount of contraband on board his brig Obscure as the affair had been to him from the first, it became more incomprehensible from the singular composure and satisfaction with which Mr Walker described the danger It very naturally did not occur to him, that this very case resulted from a "passion for secrets ," which found in the subject of discussion an exhaustless source of disquiet and anxiety, and as it were, delighted itself with the anticipation of the sleepless nights which this shipment must inevitably cause

The captain, at last, interrupted the pause that followed, by saying, "Pardon me, Mr Walker , I desire that you will immediately give orders to have both the extra boxes sent on shore, since you so clearly perceive the danger to which I expose myself I cannot conceive why you did not before explain to me the difficulties which awaited me , for then I would not have received on board the first two boxes of paltry minerals—at least, not as Argentine property Mr Walker," added he, "I have no more time to lose, either you must send some one on board to receive the boxes, or—or I shall do as I have said—I shall relieve myself from all accountability, and make short work "

"I will speak to my son about it," replied the other, "you may rely upon it, you may entirely compose yourself with regard to the respectability of my house, it has never yet been compromised, and would not have been in this case I regret that the matter does not concern me at all , it is the affair of a young man, an acquaintance of my son, who has, as I suppose, begged this favor of him "

"I, as a ship captain, am also obliging," returned captain Finngreen, "and have made many sacrifices to oblige persons, which have been poorly requited, but every thing has its bounds, and if my brig should be confiscated in Brazil, or here in the road, then your son would refer me to the Spaniard, whose name, to be sure, is on the manifest, but will hardly be found in any baptismal certificate—at least, my acquaintances here know nothing of such a firm "

Mr Walker pulled the bell-rope, a negro entered, whom he ordered to bring a bottle of champagne and some glasses

"I hope that the young lady got safely on board," began Mr Walker, throwing his left leg over the right knee, and playing *con-amore* with his watch key

"My people waited until half-past one, at your country house, and I was very fearful that she would not come ; but then she came, thank God ! I say thank God, although I do not know her situation I know from you that it is very necessary she should go hence, and that she is a very honorable young lady, belonging to a family of high standing Whatever I may risk by having her on board, is of no import, it she is in danger, and perhaps in danger of her life, I am not the first ship captain that has saved a human life—a head on which a price was set, whether by the Emperor of Russia, the Pope, or Rosas, who, as it seems, is both Emperor and Pope here, but I will have nothing to do with smuggling, Mr Walker !"

The negro came with the wine and glasses, drew the cork, poured out the wine, and left the cabinet "Here's to the health of your passengers," said Mr Walker, handing a glass to the captain , "the interesting young lady, and her cousin, the young painter A lucky voyage to the Nordstjernan ! That Horatio is a charming young man, but very bashful and modest He might pass for a girl He had two uncles here, brothers of his father ; they were both staunch republicans, opponents of Rosas, one was beheaded two years ago, and the other——" He interrupted himself, and hastily replenished the glasses "It is a very odd thing, this suffering one's self to be beheaded or shot for patriotism, for freedom, and fatherland—it is a very ticklish thing, is it not, captain ? It is not every one who would have done it, or allowed it to be done, when the alternative was placed before him, of retaining his property, and living very comfortably at a distance, on condition that he would wear the red riband of Rosas before his departure from Buenos Ayres, and—and mention a name—and"——

"And let another be shot in his stead, you would say, Mr Walker , I understand it , I can imagine such things, and for the present, desire to know no more ! but I assure you, that if the young lady or her cousin were in danger of being beheaded or shot here, by order of Rosas, and it depended upon me to save them—I would risk my life to do it, although I have a wife and children at home—it is my natural feeling "

"Bravo ! excellent !" hastily replied Mr. Walker, "noble principles, captain ! it is a pity you are not an Englishman—those are real British sentiments ; you ought at least to sail under the British flag—to command an English ship."

"Thank you for your compliment, Mr. Walker," rejoined the Scandinavian ; thank you for your confidence. As regards the British flag, I should hardly have had the honor to be freighted by you, as the captain of an English ship."

"Certainly—certainly—that is quite another point," said Mr Walker, laughing, "it might have been the case, notwithstanding You Swedes, to be sure, sail for very reasonable freight, but ships of other nations are obliged to follow your example from time to time " Mr. Walker appeared to desire, as the freighter of a ship, to avoid the near contact with this particular point in the shipping trade It must very naturally have suited him, that Swedish vessels reduced the freight, from time to time, in all parts of the world, from the fact that they stood upon a proportionably cheaper footing than many others The excess of wood and iron in Sweden, the low wages for labor, the low price for living, the low monthly wages at sea, the excess of seamen from the position of the countries of the north, and the inclination of all coast dwellers, to a seafaring life—all these circumstances combined to effect the depreciation of freight, by the Swedish captains

"Besides," observed Captain Finngreen, "it is probably universally known that your English captains are not particularly careful with respect to their rigging An English captain keeps his deck in perfect order, but his care does not extend beyond the deck; he concerns himself little about the cargo, when he has once taken it in, and still less with what is above his head An English captain uses up and ruins more rigging and sails in one year, than one of us in five The owners must renew what is worn out, the sail makers in England must live, and the sovereigns must circulate; John Bull is fat, and must have exercise"

As much as an Englishman prefers his own country to all others, just as little does an English merchant hesitate to employ foreigners, in preference to his own countrymen and seaman, when it is his interest to do so, and agreeable to the dictates of his judgement Seldom as an Englishmen enters on board a foreign vessel as passenger, young Mr Walker had merely resolved, under the peculiar circumstances, to go as passenger to Rio de Janeiro, with Captain Finngreen

A young dandy, whose countenance resembled an unfilled bill of exchange, entered the cabinet of his principal, with the announcement that the captain's papers were in order, whereupon both left their seats, and emptied a farewell glass to a safe arrival at the destined port, "And to better freight," added the captain—the well known appendix of a ship captain to the Lord's prayer, of whatever nation he may be

"I shall not lose another word about the two boxes," said captain Finngreen, in a low voice, to Mr Walker, as they left the cabinet "I have told you my views and intentions about them, and release myself from all responsibility I shall know, at all events, how to maintain my position on board as captain"

"All right, all right," replied Mr Walker, smiling, and clasping the Swede on the shoulder, while he courteously allowed him to go before, and pushed him through the door of the cabinet into the office, where a half dozen young gentlemen were occupied in the consumption of English ink, and English paper, and English steel pens.

CHAPTER XVIII

SMUGGLER'S FANCIES

Captain Finngreen was by no means satisfied with the "all right" of Mr Walker He signed the last document, added to the last signature his usual flourishes and dots of embellishment, laid the pen deliberately aside, stuck the papers in a colossal pocketbook which could hardly find a place in the inside pocket of his visiting coat, and looked inquiringly at the old Englishman

"Now Mr Walker the shallop which I have bespoken lies there ready," said he, breaking silence, during which the latter regarded the seaman with his left eye, his head being inclined over his right shoulder "I shall expect my passenger, Mr Robert Walker, on the Mole in an hour, with bag and baggage, with all that is yet to go on board, and a man from your house who will take the two boxes in charge"

The old chief smuggler betrayed a little embarrassment at this announcement of the captain in the presence of the persons in the office The look and emphasis, however, with which it was made, convinced him at once that he had a man before him, who understood no jesting in serious matters He led the captain into his private room again, raised his head a little higher, into nearly a perpendicular position, left his watch key at rest for the moment, and began, in a low in voice—

"But, captain, how the devil do you expect me to get the boxes on shore again? Was not that a master stroke to bring the two boxes of Chili stones so far without duty? To bring them safely from Chili over the boundary without duty? And safely from here on board without duty? I will bet you captain, that the boxes shall reach St Petersburgh free of duty, be safely disembarked at St Petersburgh without duty!"

It is all one to me," grumbled captain Finngreen, "but not in my brig, from here to Rio"

"But just think, captain, it is not so much on account of the paltry duty, it is not to save a few hundred dollars at each frontier—who thinks of that? it is for the sake of the affair, for the sake of the secret! It is only on account of the anxiety and disquiet which await me until the boxes are safely in St Petersburgh, and calculate yourself how long it must be until I can receive the advices!"

The seaman appeared to wish to lose no time, by being drawn into the passion of the old monopolist of secrets

He took out his watch, cast a hasty glance at the hands, put it up as hastily, and made a movement for an immediate departure Mr Walker seized him by the arm, and repeated what he had before said, but the captain remained unshaken in his resolution, and declared once more—

"Well Mr Walker, I have not another minute to lose, I must yet go to the ship chandler's, if none of your people accompany me on board, who can take charge of the boxes, I shall throw them overboard, you can then complain of me to my consul, or wherever you will My name is Finngreen, my vessel is called "Nordstjernan"

"Now, then, captain, do you know what?" whispered Mr. Walker, in the greatest haste; "you can deliver the boxes to my clerk, Mr Daily"

"For my part, it is all the same to me, which of your people you send on board with me."

"He is now on board"

"How so? have you sent some one on board already?"

"Certainly—Mr Daily, who sails with you, he is the most adroit clerk I have ever known in my business

"He remains here, then? and you say that he sails with me! How am I to understand that?"

The old man drew near the captain, laid both hands on his shoulders, and whispered, "Captain, captain, only understand me rightly, you deliver the two boxes to my clerk, Mr Daily, who is on board, and imagine that Mr Daily has gone ashore in the shallop, with the boxes, and imagine that Mr Daily and the boxes are no longer on board when the shallop leaves you Call Mr Daily, Mr *Nightly,* if you choose, as long as he is on board, persuade yourself that he is not Mr Daily, that he is quite another clerk—and a prosperous voyage to you Rely upon Mr Daily—I can place full confidence in him, that is my man! he's a genius! I tell you, captain, he is able to make the two boxes vanish from on board, and neither you, nor I, nor any one else, shall know where they are "

"You are in good humor, Mr Walker, spare your jests for your dinner Farewell "

He pushed the old humorist's hands rather roughly from his shoulders, repeated his farewell with dignity and politeness, and departed, before Mr Walker could collect himself to lay hands on him again

CHAPTER XIX

PRIVATE INSTRUCTIONS

"OBSTINATE fellow!" grumbled old Mr Walker to himself, evidently not a little perplexed by the resolute demeanor of the seaman He reflected for a moment, and rang the bell

"Tell McGaul to come in here," said he, to the clerk who now entered

McGaul appeared, a systematic man of business, and besides, a so called "clever fellow," who knew how to take his way "round the corner" in order to attain an object under peculiar circumstances Mr Walker now whispered softly in his ear, what would here interest us less than it did him

"I understand, I understand," interrupted McGaul, from time to time, during the communication of his principal, "I will do my best—you may rely upon me," and at length left the cabinet as hastily as he had entered it Hardly had Mr Walker taken his place at the desk, when a young man, in a travelling dress, entered in "flying haste," stepped up to him with the announcement, "Now, father, I am ready," threw himself on a stool, and his legs one over the other

This was Mr Robert Walker, the hopeful son of the house, usually called by his father, when speaking to him, "*Bob, my boy* " Bob was one of those youthful figures which occasionally proceed from the great workshop of nature, to serve, as it were, for models of fine forms Bob was universally acknowledged a handsome youth, and through a certain natural unreserve of manner, was justly beloved in the circle of his acquaintance He was about twenty-three years old, and already a perfect man of business, as is general in England, or among Englishmen, where there are only boys and men Without the transition period of youth, (which, among other nations, is the most delightful in life,) the English boy suddenly enters upon the business path of his earthly calling, at least into a practical life, which he, for the time, considers his calling Mr Robert, when a boy, had come with his father from England, from the British atmosphere, in a British ship, with a transplantation of British comforts for South American ground He had, of course, never left his British element, while he grew up a real Briton

Mr Walker arranged a packet of letters and papers, which he had laid aside for the important expedition of his son, while the young man took up an English penknife, and corrected the rounding of the nail on the little finger of the left hand, in order to leave something on shore which would be superfluous on board

"In a moment, Bob, my boy," cried Mr. Walker, with a hasty nod of the head, and repeated, "in a moment" He then arranged some other packets, letters and papers, subscribed some more documents, laid them with the others, and at last turned around in his chair, towards the youth, who, with admirable coolness, in this important moment of departure from his father's house, was using his penknife, as if nothing required his attention so much as the trimming of his finger nails Mr Walker placed himself in position, threw the right leg over the left knee, dropped his head sideways, drew down his right eyelid, began his favourite amusement with his hand on his watch key, and spoke, saying—"Bob, my boy, you have just come in time to hear my instructions and admonitions, many of which, to be sure, I have written out systematically on some of these sheets, that you may read them on board Here Bob, my boy, ' Private Instructions' here is the document, the most important (excepting the general letter of credit in your name) which the packet contains I shall previously detail to you some points and rules by word and mouth, and what I say to you to-day, in taking leave, will serve you as an English appendix to the proverbs of Solomon, as a fragment of an English Jesus, the son of Sirach

"Mark my words, Bob, my boy, I have not lived in vain for fifty years, and gathered wisdom, that is to say, money Bob, my boy, mark this, first of all, wisdom is money, for without money, wisdom is nonsense You go out into the world, as the son of John Walker & Co, as the son son of Mr John Walker, I would say, and as the representative of our house, John Walker & Co, mark that, my boy! know your worth, inasmuch as you represent the name of our house, and the worth of your father is valued in you You know what I am worth, it is known on ' 'change,' all Buenos Ayres knows it, all England knows it, all the world knows it! I mean the business world, for there is no other world of any consequence

"' What is he worth?' men will ask, when they speak of you, and you may well feel your worth ' Feel' is a poor word, we do not require feelings You may reckon your worth, I will say, in short, you know your worth ' Faith works salvation, and credit brings business;' I hold on to the ' credit,' which I make over to you.

" Consider three things, Bob, my boy, and these three things are one, they are the British trinity Consider first, that you are an Englishman—secondly, that you are Bob Walker—and thirdly, that you are a gentleman, and each of these, singly, embraces the whole in itself Remember that all mankind are arranged in two classes, Englishmen and foreigners, the foreigners are, to be sure, separated into various classes, as, for instance, Dutchmen, Frenchmen, Indians, Irishmen, Gipsies, Scotchmen, Hottentots, Negroes, Americans, Cannibals, and so forth, but they are all foreigners Always consider that you are a Briton, and that Britain is where you are. As a Briton, you are the centre on which the world turns The destiny of man upon earth is ' to make money,' and the means to this end are business, business ' Bob, my boy, remember that

" There have been different periods in the history of the world, in which an idea prevailed. An idea ' what is an idea ' Just the reverse of reality Will a pawnbroker lend you sixpence upon an idea ' What is reality ' This—this is reality '" Mr John Walker drew a sovereign from his vest pocket, held it between the thumb and forefinger of his right hand, towards his hopeful son, and repeated, " this, here ' this is reality, Bob, my boy '

" There was an epoch, in which men suffered death for the sake of an idea—they called it ' faith,' ' religion ', the Catholics did so in their wars for the Holy Sepulchre, nonsense ' There was another epoch, when men attached value to art, and poetry, and philosophy, nonsense ' arrant nonsense ' There was also an epoch when men named this fixed idea, ' honor,' and even now there are foreigners who allow themselves to be killed for the idea honor What is honor without money ' nonsense, Bob, my boy ' nonsense ' Can you express honor in round numbers ' The world has grown older and wiser, mankind have descended from the ideal world to reality Men know the worth of money, and their own worth in money. That is the quintessence of all the practical philosophy of our century, mark that, Bob, my boy ' Maintain this position firmly, and never forget your worth; that is to say, your father's worth, which passes over to you, and which will be increased when the great cash book of my life shall be closed, when I shall make over my whole worth to you, and with my bills of exchange, drawn on eternity, shall be thrown upon the mercy of God " He sighed at these words, looked upwards, and continued, " In our times nothing is easier than to know the worth of a man, or to obtain an answer to the question in respect to a man, 'What is he worth '' Carry your worth, then, steadily before your eyes and in your head, and take care that you do not compromise yourself—that you do nothing inconsistent with your respectability Never forget that you are an Englishman, and manifest your nationality in opposition to all foreigners But keep at a distance from all Englishmen in foreign countries, so long as you do not know their worth ; you know what that means. Never compromise yourself by associating with any person whatever, whose worth is doubtful, or for whose respectability you have no references

" Love Britannia, our Old England, and all that it contains and produces ; but be indifferent to all Britons, when they do not enter into business with you Wear nothing which is not English, and of English fashion, go bareheaded rather than wear a hat which is not of English manufacture Wear no coat which is not made of English cloth, by an English tailor, or, at least, by a tailor in London Write not a line except with English steel pens, or with goosequills prepared in England, for all that you use of British manufacture promotes British industry Remember that, Bob, my boy ' Be a commercial man, not only because you are Robert Walker, but be a commercial man as a Briton Consider all commerce, from your position as a Briton, who has the whole world at command, as an article of commerce Hate foreigners, but love foreign countries, for they serve as a market for the exportation of our manufactures, and employ our custom houses in the transmission of them

" The basis of all speculation is Politics Politics are a fine business. By politics I do not understand the chase after a seat in parliament ; that belongs to ambition ' Ambition and business are of different natures, and one often ruins the other Politics, Bob, my boy, are the great world traffic, a sort of privileged slave trade, the traffic with men, with nations black or white, all the same ' This great world traffic is carried on with state papers, and embraces the money market Understand me right, Bob, my boy As all human worth is reduced to money, so, very naturally, the gold trade and the man trade are all one. Thus, if you are ruined in fortune, you are also ruined as a man, since you have lost your worth Games of hazard with cards are prohibited, but the great game of hazard with state papers is not only allowed, but promoted by all governments, and those who govern often play the highest This game of hazard, is the highest attainment of human effort in our times, it is played for the article man, as for sixpences and shillings, whole nations are pledged, as they pledge a watch at the pawnbroker's, but with the difference, that the nations must redeem themselves, and must pay the interest besides, while the great pawnbrokers' tickets (state papers, or stocks) pass from hand to hand, and many, alas ' become in reality worthless, like pawnbrokers' tickets after the expiration of the time, as, for instance, when the nation gets certain ideas in its head, and will not redeem them, will not pay the interest Such cases are critical events in trade they usually show themselves as revolution, rebellion, and the fatal, fixed idea, in the people, which brings on such a crisis, is most generally the idea of freedom Mark that, Bob, my boy, and maintain your conservative principles—I mean mine, which I have infused into you Conservative principles stand opposed to liberalism Both may be simply explained. Conserve what you possess, seek to increase your possessions, and avoid liberalism, that is to say, liberality, generosity, whether it be in sentiment or in material sacrifices ; both contradict the conservative principle, as well as the mercantile principle, and evidently lead to ruin. But if generosity must be practised, be rather generous in feeling than in expenses. In a political crisis there is always a wide field for speculation Rebellion and revolution, in themselves, likewise offer a good business—an excellent business, especially for us Britons, of whom alone we are speaking. Every rebellion requires weapons, and our Britannia requires consumption, exportation, for such articles. Have we not done a splendid business here in South America, a brilliant business! with both parties, as well with the Unitarios as with the Confederados? Have we not made a portion of our property by the delivery of weapons to both parties? and with the traffic in the papers of pledged nations, which we threw off at the right time, before this or that nation threw off the chains of this or that despotism. What protects the house of Walker & Co, from danger and from loss? thoroughgoing routine in business. Politics! politics! Bob, my boy, are an excellent business! but they must be studied! mark that, and follow the example of your father. Trade is calculation, politics, as business, are the higher mathematics of commerce—mark that, Bob, my boy! We English are a merchant people, a commercial nation, and as such, the first nation in the world. As a commercial nation, we must be conservative, a liberal trading people would be a contradiction in itself. We are free, and we are religious, very free and very religious, Bob, my boy. But we do not speak here of freedom and religion as principles, but as articles, as articles of traffic in circulation among us Britons, but only among Britons. Britannia's freedom is a gift of Providence to the chosen British nation, an inheritance that must remain in the family. It is an original painting which we must preserve, and of which we must only sell copies to other nations. Mark that, Bob, my boy! Britannia is the mistress of the world! 'Rule Britannia! Britannia for ever!' As the sovereign power of the world, we bestow the title of freedom upon other nations, black or white, whenever we find it our interest to do so. We give to foreign slaves the title of British subjects, without fundamentally altering their position. We help kings and princes to crowns and thrones, and stamp them as sovereigns, because we know the worth of a 'sovereign,' and foreign princes are British subjects, without even making a claim to the title. If we regard freedom as a principle, and not as an article, not as our family inheritance, we must grant it to all nations, and see a rival power to our rule over the world start up in every free nation. We would thereby sign our act of abdication of our sovereignty over the world. 'All Europe may be reduced to slavery, as long as Britannia's freedom only shines, and our world wide traffic extends itself,' said Mr Roebuck, one of our members of Parliament, a short time since, and he struck the nail on the head." We have lost many of our colonies in North America, and, at the present time,* they speak with evil forebodings of Canada. It is the fixed idea of freedom, which the people have taken into their heads, and thus despise all

---

the endeavors of our missionaries, who preach resignation and submission to the sceptre of Old England! Bob, my boy, beware of republican ideas, of democratic principles, for they stand in direct opposition to our position and our business as Britons. Britannia is only Britannia as a monarchy; and I repeat, that in the acknowledgement of the principle of national freedom lies her sentence of death." Mr Walker took hold of his watch chain, and then felt in his vest pocket and pulled out his gold watch, looked at the minute and second hands, and continued "Mark my words, Bob, my boy, be always, and everywhere, an Englishman, a merchant, and a gentleman, and hold fast to English fashions, as to English principles, and English articles. As to our fashions, I have nothing further to say to you, except this, remain as you are, and what you are. As you have learned to eat and to ride after the English fashion, observe English fashions, henceforth, forever and everywhere. Do not lose yourself in intercourse with foreigners, and do not allow yourself to be led to adopt foreign customs. Ride no foreign horse—never mount any other than an English race horse, and above all, do not allow yourself to be smitten with foreign beauty—the worst snare in which you could ever fall.

"Remember constantly, Bob, my boy, that an Englishman who marries a foreigner, or uses any other article of foreign industry, is outlawed, and rightly so, since he commits high treason against his nationality, and against his national industry. Let his wife be who she may, or what she may, she is, and ever remains, a foreigner, and that is enough, her offspring will be half-breed. Never leave a room without gloves, but wear no gloves that were not made in England. At table, especially, forget not to let people know that you are an Englishman before you have finished the first course. Never put the point of a spoon nor a knife to your mouth, never! never! Never take a fork in your right hand, except when you eat apple pie or plum pudding. Never be persuaded to wear a moustache, or to allow your beard to grow, 'à la jeune France!' never! it is shocking! shocking! Shave yourself, Bob, my boy—shave yourself twice a day, and never let your beard stand over, unless in one case, namely—if you should happen to lose your English shaving apparatus, and would be obliged to use a foreign razor, in that case only, let your beard grow for the time.

"And now, Bob, my boy, farewell, and write to me soon, on English paper, with English pens."

Mr John Walker rang, and a servant entered—while Mr Robert Walker rose, and stuck the papers into his pocket. Notwithstanding the apparent indifference with which he had at first listened to this lecture of private instructions, many words appeared to have made a deep impression upon him. Seriously and in silence he shook hands with his father, and hastily left the cabinet to make his final arrangements.

DOLORES.

BOOK II.

CHAPTER I.

THE DANGER

The Swedish brig, "Nordstjernan," displayed, on the morning of the opening day, her yellow and blue flag, as the signal of her approaching departure The crew was busied in that "regular confusion" which always characterizes the deck of a merchant ship, when about to sail Here and there sounded the "yo heave ho," of some of the sailors, who, with one accord, hung the whole weight of their bodies upon a rope, to bring the tackle into the right position and order, the deficiencies of which would only strike the practised eye of a seaman

Soren, the cook, a robust Jutlander, from the Cymbrian peninsula, was scolding in his syllable swallowing provincial Danish dialect, at Ottar, the cabin boy, a lank young Finn, from Abo, whose father wore Russian irons in Kamtschatka, because he, as ship captain, had once conveyed a Pole from Riga to England, who was destined for Siberia Soren insisted that the long Ottar had intentionally thrown a herring into the coffee, which he had carefully set aside for himself, from the mate's breakfast Ottar, to maintain his innocence, in his increasing animation, made use of so many Finnish words, with his broken Swedish, that Soren became more excited, because he could hardly understand him, and at last threw the subject of dispute at his head, but, missing his aim, the coffee soaked herring flew past Ottar, upon the quarter deck

"Halloo!" cried Lars, the sailmaker, at work near the mainmast, "there comes a flying fish— but it flies out of a pot instead of into one, as is the case sometimes"

"Ottar! Ottar! rejoice that Soren is not the Emperor of Russia, he would send you, on the spot, to your father in Kamtschatka" A command of the first mate sent the sailmaker out on the bowsprit.

Ottar's lean visage was almost brought to tears at the injustice of the cook, while Soren availed himself of the Swedish language, in order to curse right heartily, and sent a "hundred thousand barrels of devils," after the poor youth, as the latter hurried to his business in the cabin Swend Roluffs, a young sailor and a wag, by nature, who had played this trick on the cook, laughed aloud at the wry face with which he drank the salted coffee, "that it should not be wasted"

Corinna, one of those slender figures of Ethiopian beauty, whose narrow waist and swelling roundness many Europeans might envy, softly left the apartment of her mistress, and appeared in the cabin, busied in overhauling the baggage, assisted by Achilles, whose eyes red with weeping, could scarcely distinguish the objects before him She wore, over her light modern clothing, a piece of black shawl-cloth, about two yards wide and six long, which the negresses of South America know how to throw around them with peculiar taste, after the Ethiopian fashion, like the drapery on antique statues—in such a manner, that it covers the upper part of the body, with one end passing over the left shoulder, and hanging down the back in wide folds A cloth of dazzling whiteness covered her head, and was tightly drawn down to her eyebrows, forming a turban of cylindrical shape, intentionally contrasting with the dark brown color of her face, of which the serious expressive Minas features displayed pain, grief, and sympathy, for the afflictions of her mistress A string of pearls of some value, with a plain gold cross, adorned her neck and breast, as a memorial of the mother of Dolores—whose unhappy destiny now removed her from the paradise of her childhood, on the banks of the La Plata

Her father, Achilles, remained sunk upon his knees before an open trunk, unable to select the objects which Corinna was to take to their places in the inner apartment for the comfort of the voyage Without knowing what his hands took hold of, he stared at his daughter, while the big tears that rolled down his furrowed cheeks, gave a vent to his feelings.—"Father! father!" said Corinna, in her Ethiopian tongue, wiping away his tears, "compose yourself, father Father, do not weep, for the white slaves of Rosas may yet come on board, and see us, and if they observe that we are melancholy and disconsolate, they will suspect, and the Señora's life be in danger Father, think of Señora Dolores, and do not weep"

"O, Corinna!" sobbed the old man, "I do think of the Señora, and it is, therefore, I weep. O Dolores! Dolores!" he sobbed, and folded his hands, and stretched them out before him.

"Compose yourself, father!" cried Corinna, louder, with an almost threatening voice; "the

7

Señora is in danger through our tears." She dried the old man's tears with her shawl, and after a pause, said, with forced composure, "Give me the box with the little vials of medicine, father?" and both endeavored to assume the indifference of deportment which the occasion required, as much as then troubled state of mind opposed their efforts

Horatio, who, until then, had sat in a corner of the cabin, sunk in reflection, and appeared like one petrified, approached old Achilles, laid his hand on his shoulder, and whispered in his ear, "Compose yourself, Achilles we shall soon go to sea, and the murderers of my relatives will no more overtake us "

How far the youth believed in a happy and undisturbed departure, is uncertain, he sought, at least, to infuse that momentary confidence into his weaker minded companions, which the circumstances of the case required

"Be calm ! be calm !" sighed Achilles, softly, to himself, "yes, be cold and calm, yes, cold and calm as the grave of your uncle, and as the grave of Señor Sebastian, your father ! I will be quiet and dumb, for Rosas reigns ! Rosas, who, for his first murder, caused his teacher to be killed, when he entered upon his government the second time, caused him to be killed in his presence ! Rosas ! Rosas ! a million curses on his guilt-laden head !" said he, gnashing his teeth, and staring before him The intensity of these curses, as they flowed from his livid lips, formed a singular contrast with the benignant expression of the gentle youth, who, as Mr Walker had before observed, was like a woman, but who, notwithstanding, betrayed neither deficiency of character, nor irresolute weakness

In Horatio a childish, inoffensive disposition appeared, which sought, with conciliating love, to embrace life and the world, like the bud of a flower, bursting open before it was moistened by the poison dew of worldly corruption

As deeply wounded in his inmost soul, as a mortal can be, by the murder upon murder of his relatives, and broken hearted by their fate, which he regarded as a consequence of the subjugation of his people, he yet maintained his confidence in the human heart, his faith in mankind, and from these drew his hope for the future in relation to the freedom of his fatherland

Notwithstanding this gentleness, which probably descended to him as a costly inheritance on the part of his mother, his inward nature was by no means deficient in that moral strength, which is developed and sustained in the human breast by an early and severe conflict with misfortune and suffering, and which rises, proportionably, the more we are burdened with sorrows and grief

Achilles handed to his daughter the little box of medicine which she sought, whereupon she again returned to the apartment of her mistress, while the old man mechanically removed the different articles of baggage that were before him

Horatio added a few more words of encouragement, again clapped the old man cordially on the shoulder, and then betook himself to his former place, on a sofa, in a corner of the cabin

The stranger, about whom Captain Finngreen had not yet "made up his mind," (as he had declared to Mr. Walker,) was also busily occupied, during the passage of this scene in the cabin, in repacking some trunks, and in making himself as comfortable as possible Among his unpacked effects, were to be seen seamen's clothing for various climates, also a sextant, some charts, a marine sword, which was not too long to pass for a dagger, and lastly, a bundle of flags of a singular construction They were strips of the usual bunting, about a yard wide, and some two and a half yards long, of various colors, and some with particular marks These single strips were set lengthwise, with eyelet holes about two inches apart On the flagstaff side was a piece of sail yarn, somewhat longer than the stuff, with metal points, so that two or three of these strips could be fastened together in a few minutes, which then formed a convenient signal flag

If Horatio had been in a state of mind to direct his observations towards the stranger, it would not have escaped him, that he sought out the separate flag strips from different pockets of his garments, and from various bundles, and brought them into a certain systematic arrangement Why this system of concealment had been adopted, whether the voyager found these portions of an "airy symbolism" useful to ward off, or, at least, render difficult the visitation of watchful authorities, is undetermined

In contrast with such ocean gear, the voyager carried horse pistols, a bridle, spurs, horse trappings, a cavalry sabre, a Russian kantschu, and a blunderbuss, (musketoon,) which, according to the muzzle, might conveniently serve as a piece of artillery on board of a corsair No inference could be drawn with regard to the social position of the voyager from the titles of the books, in various languages, which lay round about him

Notwithstanding the intercourse which had casually taken place between Horatio and himself, on the previous night, the stranger continued to maintain the distance which tact made necessary, and which harmonized with his nature But this tact, which proceeds from internal development, and is distinct from stiff reserve, by no means interdicted him from a lively interest in the scene, of which he once more became a witness

Difficult as it had been for him on the last night to clothe his sympathy in expressions, it became harder still for him now to assume a tone of intercourse, for the purpose of entering into conversation. He was, for the present, to regard the events of the past night as a dream, since he must know nothing of the appearance of the young lady, whose incognita indicated the danger to which she was exposed

The stranger, who appeared on the captain's passenger list by the name of 'O O Hinango,' had, since that meeting scene, felt himself involuntarily drawn towards the youth, by the mysterious bond of the attraction of the soul, while his position required, for the present, apparent distance. He sank into reflections upon the situation of man towards man, in consequence of the civilization of our century, and while thus busied in thought, he arrived at the following conclusions

The more egotism and treachery become dangerous to the cause of the freedom of all nations, and but too frequently undermine it, the more personal and material interest guides the acts and endeavors of men, the more does the man who is penetrated by a higher idea and nobler sentiments, appear to the world, in our era, either suspicious or ridiculous, a designing rogue, or a visionary madman, an " enthusiast "

The more seldom true patriotism, enthusiasm for truth and freedom, self sacrifice from conviction, manifest themselves, the more frequently does the world consider the higher endeavors of men either as the absurd consequence of a so called " fixed idea," of a " boundless vanity," or as the thoroughgoing, sly calculation of a common speculator, who seeks to carry out, under such a mask, a concealed plan of selfishness at the expense of others

The rarer the appearance of a man of noble nature, capable, from conviction, of any sacrifice, the greater danger does he incur when he desires to act, of being misconceived in his higher endeavors of being considered and treated by egotists as one of themselves Instead of love to man, which, as a religious duty, should lie at the foundation of all the intercourse of man with his fellow men, mistrust has become the first condition of judgement in the so called daily intercourse of the world

The more faith in the human heart becomes endangered by treachery and deceit, the more does suspicion become the duty of the unfortunate, who is exposed to treachery The idea attached to the word " man," loses its value after the bond of humanity becomes decayed, after faith as a religious principle sinks into a low materialism, which even seeks to make a business of " religion '

The so called " reasonable man" of our time, does not even believe in the heart of man, when it bleeds in the struggle for the cause of humanity Egotism judges all the appearances around it, after itself, it mistakes and despises exalted ideas and noble sentiments, because it cannot comprehend the former, and is unable to entertain the latter Our age is the epoch of infidelity and indifference—and mankind would sink into materialism, if, from the seed-cup of the hearts of some individual men, there did not, as it were, pass over to a future generation the seed-pollen of the conception of a higher idea ——

Hinango continued to pack and arrange his effects, and uttered, from time to time, an indifferent remark about wind and weather, and cabin and ship, as if he had not even seen the youth the night before, and did not know who occupied the captain's state room, through the door of which the negress went in and out—The youth replied to these detached remarks in the same tone of conventional courtesy, without being drawn from the chaos of his reflections and feelings

" Probably you know this book?" inquired Hinango, after a long pause, handing him a duodecimo volume " De Lamenais—Paroles d'un Croyant," read Horatio, while he took the book with a friendly nod, " I have read it in Spanish, I hear it is translated into many European languages "

" No book of our time has reached the hearts of the nations of Europe with such a ray of electric light," replied Hinango, " but in England it found no public."

" Why not?" inquired the youth; " how do you explain that?"

" Because faith in mankind, in the resurrection and deliverance of the nations, upon the basis of nationality, and in the spirit of humanity, remains foreign to them

" The so called higher classes in England, would take the less interest in such a book, because it defends the cause of mankind—it treats of the sufferings and the misery of the people, to which the proud Briton is indifferent The Englishman is an egotist, he feels no interest in any thing that does not concern his own personal affairs and business, and therefore takes the less interest in the miseries of others England is divided into Sects, and every sect is a quarantine bar against humanity The more man surrounds himself with the forms of a particular sect the more his spirit becomes enchained—his heart shrinks within himself, repelling the feelings of humanity, which regards every people as a family of mankind, and each individual as a man In England, the man without money is a non-entity—the People, ' canaille,' and mankind, a phantom Even glorious philanthropy has become the Phariseeism of the privileged classes, ostentatiously distributing alms before the public, to keep the misery of the people at a distance from them

" England regards freedom as a monopoly, while the British nation itself lies yet more deeply sunk in misery, under the yoke of the aristocracy and of the manufacturers, than many others, and cannot even now comprehend the spirit of love which breathes through this little book "

" You are undoubtedly in the right," rejoined Horatio Even here, in South America, we have no great confidence in the freedom we should obtain through British protection For myself, I regard the book as the gospel of the future, as a prophetic appearance in the history of mankind "

" As such, it has also become known," interrupted Hinango, "in spite of all the materialism which despises this word of faith."

The youth took up the book, and read, partly aloud, the beginning of a chapter which accidentally came to his eye.

" When you see a man led to prison, or to the scaffold, be not in haste to say, ' That is a wicked man, who has committed a crime against mankind,' for perhaps he is a righteous man, who would have rendered a service to his fellow men, and who is therefore punished by their oppressors

" When you see a people lying in chains, and is given up to the executioner, be not in haste to say, ' That is a violent people, that would disturb the peace of the earth,' for perhaps it is a martyr people, that suffers for the welfare of mankind !

" It is now eighteen centuries since the high priests and kings of that time, in a city of the East, scourged with rods, and then nailed to the cross, a rebel, a blasphemer, as they called him "

Horatio, penetrated by the light of the godlike idea that lies at the foundation of humanity, gazed fixedly before him, then rousing himself from his revery, he turned over the leaves of the little book, and read silently to himself.

" And I saw the evils that have come upon the earth; I saw the weak oppressed, the righteous begging his bread, the wicked raised to honor and abounding in riches, the innocent condemned by unjust judges, and his children wandering about on the face of the earth And my soul was sad, and hope poured out of it on all sides, as from a broken vessel

"And God sent me a deep sleep. And I saw, in my sleep, a form of light, standing near me a spirit whose soft and piercing look penetrated into the depths of my most secret thoughts

"And I shuddered, not from fear, nor from joy, but from a sensation as of an indescribable mixture of both. And the spirit said to me, 'Wherefore art thou sad'

"And I answered, weeping, 'Alas! behold the sufferings that are upon the earth!'

"And the heavenly form began to smile with an ineffable smile, and the following words reached my ear 'Thy eye sees only through the delusive mirror that men call time. Time is only for thee, for God there is no time' And I held my peace, for I understood not Suddenly the spirit said, 'Behold!' and while there existed for me, from that time, neither 'Before' nor 'Afterwards,' I saw in the same moment, and at once, what men, in their feeble and imperfect language, call 'past, present, and future,' and all that was only one, but in order to tell what I saw, I must descend again into the lap of time, I must use the imperfect and feeble language of man

"And the whole human race appeared to me as a single man

"And this man had done much evil, little good, he had experienced many sorrows, and few joys. And there he lay, in his wretchedness, upon earth, now frozen with cold, now burning with heat, there he lay, pining, starving, suffering, oppressed with a faintness mingled with convulsions, bound down with chains that were forged in hell, his right hand burdened his left, and his left the right, and, tossed about by his evil dreams, he had so rolled himself up in his chains, that his whole body was covered with them, and locked together

"And that was man, I recognised him And behold, a ray of light went out from the east, a ray of love from the south, a ray of strength from the north, and these three rays united in the heart of this man

"And as the ray of light went forth, a voice said, 'Son of God, brother of Christ, know what thou should'st know!'

"And as the ray of love went forth, a voice said, 'Son of God, brother of Christ, love whom thou should'st love!'

"And as the ray of strength went forth, a voice said, 'Son of God, brother of Christ, do what should be done!'

"And when these three rays had united, the three voices united, also, and they formed one, which said, 'Son of God, brother of Christ, serve God, and serve him alone!'

"And what had seemed to me as one man, now appeared to me as a multitude of people and nations And my first look had not deceived me, and my second also deceived me not

"And these people and these nations, awaking upon their beds of anguish, began to say, among themselves, 'Whence come our sufferings and our feebleness, and the hunger and the thirst that torment us; and the chains that bend us down to the earth, and press into our flesh?'

"And their understandings were opened, and they comprehended that the sons of God, the brethren of Christ, had not been condemned to slavery by their father, and that slavery was the source of all their evils Each one of these sought to break his chains, but no one succeeded.

"And they considered each other with great sympathy, and love was manifest in them, and they said among themselves, 'We have all the same thoughts, why should we not have the same heart? Are we not all the sons of the same God, and the brothers of the same Christ? We will, then, be saved together, or die together'

"And as they said this, they felt in themselves a divine strength, and I heard the fetters break, and they fought——"

CHAPTER II

PASSENGERS

Horatio read the last words half aloud, more and more slowly, and with a subdued voice, he let his hand, which held the little book, fall upon his knee, as if wearied, and gazed upon the stranger with an expression of bitter grief, while a sad smile flitted over his lips

Himango returned the glance of the sufferer with the ray of sympathy, which shines forth from the most secret depths of the soul, and reveals, more eloquently than words, each emotion and ebullition of the feelings. He divined the youth's grief, who experienced the consolation of sympathy, for its own sake, while the position and relations of the stranger remained to him an impenetrable riddle, whose solution led him into a labyrinth of conjecture, which became more obscure, the more deeply he lost himself in it ·

The first mate opened the cabin door, conducting in a passenger who had just come on board, and was, in external appearance, "the most perfect gentleman" that ever trod a cabin floor as passenger He was a slender, youthful figure, with a strikingly regular face, whose peculiar form reminded one of antique beauty, while it wanted the intellectual expression which enobles many less handsome countenances

This was one of those stereotype figures of the civilization of our century, elegantly dressed from head to foot in the last fashion—a walking clothes stretcher, which might have found a situation before the shop of any merchant tailor, to exhibit the latest fashion to the passers by.

The young man looked round him with all the self consciousness of respectability, while the mate went on with the sentence which he had begun on entering the cabin, to point out to the passenger his berth

Two sailors followed with his baggage, which was, like his dress, of English manufacture throughout trunk, carpet bag, writing desk, dressing box, etc., of the well known "stereotype edition," as we find them on board of steam and packet ships, set in motion by means of British machines, which, under the British or any other flag, cruise the waters of all parts of the world —a reprinted edition, as it were, of the British fashions

Mr Wilhelm Rossbruck representative and son of the far famed house of H W C , and M R B Rossbruck and Co , of one of the former " Hanse Towns," would rather, in a case of decided necessity, have travelled without any baggage, than to have carried even one trunk, whose British origin was not to be known at the first glance

There was, as a matter of course, upon each trunk or box, a brass plate, with the name of ' William Rossbruck, Esq ," in real English round letters

The name of Rossbruck in itself, caused the young gentleman or " Esquire" continual uneasiness, real sorrow of soul

Mr Rossbruck had long desired nothing more earnestly than to get rid of this unfortunate German stamp, to translate it literally, as " Horsebridge, '—in order that he might proudly step forth, in English travelling costume, as William Horsebridge, Esquire

But, alas ! this just and reasonable desire of a young man, who acknowledged the imperative necessity of the " only respectable making ' English fashion, could not be so easily fulfilled, for manifold reasons By such a translation, for instance, he would lose his connexion with the firm, which was, in a degree, in the circle of his acquaintance, the basis of his personal respectability

Mr Rossbruck's features manifested, from time to time, an expression of melancholy and depression, which many ladies considered as symtoms of an " unfortunate love " This expression of melancholy, which soon disappeared when the locomotive of his business calculations was set in motion, proceeded from one single source ——his name

The fatal German name imposed a rigid bound to all the efforts and sacrifices of his Anglo-mania, which he, in his best will, could not once overstep

Mr Rossbruck cast a glance at the two passengers whom we have particularly described above, and said what he had occasion to say to the mate in English, to which the latter replied in German

The "would be English gentlemen" drew on his black patent gloves, from time to time pressed them down between the fingers—and inquired, among other things, after a box of wine, which had been sent on board the day before The second mate was called to give an account of it It appeared that the said box had been put temporarily in a cabin between decks Mr William Rossbruck wished to satisfy himself of the vicinity of his spiritual travelling companion, and was conducted to the indicated spot, in which were arranged some state rooms, for passengers of inferior rank

This visit to the between decks, disturbed a passenger in important business It was Mr Habakkuk Daily, the before mentioned clerk of the house of Walker & Co , who had taken up his quarters there, because, very naturally, it was not suitable that he should inhabit the same cabin with the son of the house.

Mr Hab' Daily (as he generally subscribed himself for shortness sake) was a square built, robust fellow, with a cheerful, round countenance, blinking gray eyes, coarse black hair, and whiskers to match, which reached from his temples to the corners of his mouth, in the refractory inflexibility of a hedgehog's bristles. He was just driving a nail in one of the four boxes, which had been given to his especial care, and stood near his luggage—among which appeared two large trunks, covered with ox hides, and made, according to South American fashion, high and narrow. This form appears suitable to the purpose, since the baggage, for the most part transported by mules, is fastened to their sides, and, calculated for being carried through narrow mountain passes, is made to occupy the least possible breadth Besides, the height or depth of the trunks would occasionally serve for a very good purpose to their owner, who had ordered them for a voyage, and had caused the interior to be carefully provided with a false bottom and concealed drawers

" What can I do for you, Mr Hem ?" said Mr Daily to the mate, Mr Storhjelm, whose name he would willingly have pronounced correctly, if its genuine foreign sounds had not, unfortunately, escaped him, notwithstanding he had spelled it over many times to himself He seated himself at these words, comfortably, upon one of the high trunks, and played with the hammer, as if he had not thought of any thing serious for a year and a day.

" Are you looking for something, Mr Hem ?" inquired he, hastily, without awaiting the answer to his first question

" Nothing but the box of wine there," returned Mr Storhjelm, pointing to the object of search, which Mr Rossbruck recognised, to his great content, and at the same time cast a contemptuous look upon the clerk and the articles surrounding him This look was intended to demonstrate the great indifference with which a real gentleman observes all appearances around him

" A pinch of snuff, Mr Hem ?" inquired Mr Daily, while he, in his peculiar hasty manner, drew a silver snuff box from his pocket, opened, and handed it to the mate The latter was too much occupied by the urgent business of the day to be able to bestow suitable attention and reply to his ceremonial offer He muttered some words of thanks, without interrupting the conversation with the young gentleman, buried the point of his forefinger in the sneezing powder, and carried it rather awkwardly to his nose, not being a proficient in this fine art

" Mr Storhjelm !" cried the loud voice of the long Ottar, down from the deck " Mr Storhjelm, there is a boat coming ! And there is another, that seems to be coming towards us !"

At this announcement, the mate and Mr Rossbruck hurried on deck. " That is the passenger, the German Doctor, or herb gatherer, or whatever he is !" grumbled Mr Storhjelm, to himself, while he directed his eye to the nearest boat, which the cabin boy pointed out

" Brig ahoy !" sounded from the boat, after some moments; " is this the Swedish brig for Rio de Janeiro ?"

" This is the Swedish brig Nordstjernan, for Rio de Janeiro," answered the mate, " whether there is another Swedish brig bound to Rio, I do not know "

The boatman declared, in the English language, with a Spanish accent, that the passenger he brought had not been able to tell whether the vessel which he sought was a brig, a bark, or a schooner

"Is not this the vessel that I was on board of?" inquired a little man, in the stern of the boat, who had, by this time, attracted the eyes of all those present on the deck of the brig The little man appeared like a colossal brown wood beetle, with a thick and almost square head, set upon a very small neck, and with proportionably small, thin legs. His very old hat was decorated, on the inside and out, with beetles, of all sorts and sizes, stuck upon pins, while his brown overcoat was covered, from top to bottom, like a travelling arbor, with branches of trees, leaves, creeping plants, and flowers of all sorts—part stuck in the buttonholes, and part carefully fastened to his arms and neck with packthread In his right hand our little man held an uprooted young tree, with a fresh top, some feet higher than himself, and which had, apparently, been taken from the earth but a short time, in his left hand was a large cigar box, perforated with holes The question of this wandering naturalist, whether he had already been on board of the brig, was followed by an involuntary chuckling laugh from most of the seamen, who were looking down into the boat, over the forward bulwark, accompanied by the reply of the mate, that such was probably the case, and that he had better come on board, and make himself comfortable

"It will be very difficult for me to get up there?" exclaimed the passenger, in the boat, "how I shall accomplish it I know not, especially and particularly, as I——" He interrupted himself, and inspected his coat, the side pockets of which, stuffed full, stood out from his body. "——especially and particularly, as I see that my eggs are in danger"

"Your eggs?" inquired the mate, laughing heartily, "how so?"

"Yes, indeed, my eggs! I have all my pockets filled with birds' eggs, and have been obliged, the whole long way from the city, to stand upright, as you see me here, and the deuced boat would hardly lie upon the water, but rocked and pitched hither and yon, and I had both hands full, as you see"

"But why then did you not pack up your eggs carefully, as we bring our eggs on board for stores?"

"You! your store eggs? how can you compare them to my eggs?" exclaimed the little man "What sort of eggs are your store eggs? ha! common hen's eggs, or duck eggs at the most! Eggs! truly—eggs which every miserable hen in Europe will lay for you, and you wish to compare them with my eggs! with my costly contributions for a royal museum! you would compare your insignificant, ordinary store eggs, to my eggs. What countryman are you? not a Swede? not the countryman of the great Linneus?"

"Will you please to step on board, and pay us our fare?" interrupted the boatman, in Spanish, while Mr Rossbruck could as little restrain his laughter, as the mate and crew.

"But why do you have the eggs so loose in your pockets, if they are of so much importance to you?" again inquired the mate, leaning comfortably against the bulwark, while the occurrence was taking up the time, and appeared to amuse him

"Why? because they are not yet classified—they have not yet been brought into system—and especially, because I only this morning discovered the 'Anser Merboldensis,' of which neither Humboldt, nor Blumenbach, nor Cuvier, made the least mention, and look here! look here! this is the egg, it is yet warm, the egg of the Anser Merboldensis! You know that I am Dr Merbold—the captain has my passport"

"Go to the devil with your eggs" exclaimed the boatman, suddenly, in English, "step up the ladder there, and let your baggage be taken on board," grumbled he in Spanish

"Now, how in the world am I to do that? you do not reason at all, I am more badly placed than you are! Here I stand with my eggs, and have both hands full," exclaimed Dr Merbold, in broken English, "and you sit there, with your club in your hand"—the learned man meant the tiller

While they were thus disputing, the mate ordered some sailors to jump into the shallop, and help the good doctor, and bring him and his effects on board as quickly as possible, but carefully and circumspectfully.

After a great deal of difficulty and exertion, Dr Merbold at length stood upon the quarter deck

"Mate," said he, looking around, inquiringly, "will you have some earth brought up to me, from your ballast, for a tree here? Perhaps you have a box, or an empty cask?"

"Earth? from our ballast?" repeated Mr Storhjelm, laughing aloud, "how? what do you mean by that, doctor?"

"Why, now! I meant some earth from your ballast! You generally carry some good, rich earth as ballast, and my 'simplex magnus Merboldensis' may grow in that, until we come to Rio de Janeiro?"

"Pardon me, my dear doctor," replied the Swede, a little at a loss, "we have nearly a full cargo, as you see, and if we had brought earth here as ballast, we must have thrown it overboard before we took in the cargo"

"So?" answered the learned man, in subdued tones, "I did not know that! I never thought of that, that is very probably the case So you have no earth on board? pity! if I had imagined that, I would have brought as much with me from shore, as I have need of—there is no scarcity of earth there Is there not a boat going to the shore again, that I may have the opportunity of bringing some earth on board?"

"None of our boats are going ashore again," replied the mate, "we are waiting for the captain, that we may go to sea."

"Hem," murmured Dr. Merbold, to himself, "then I shall hardly be able to send that 'simplex magnus Merboldensis' growing and green, to Berlin, and, unfortunately, I cannot draw a line, or else I should soon know how to help myself.

"Well, then," continued he, soliloquizing half aloud, "I will do as other renowned naturalists have done, who could draw as little as I, and have, nevertheless, published splendidly illustrated works about their travels. I will arrange it, thank you for your good will, Mr Mate," he exclaimed, aloud, and then sank into reflection on his newly discovered natural productions

———————✿———————

CHAPTER III

IMPORTANT ACQUAINTANCE

The arrival of the second sailboat, which the long Ottar had announced, interrupted the scene of the savant's debut on board the Nordstjernan Mr McGaul stepped on board, sought and found Mr Daily, and drew him immediately aside in conversation, concerning the taking of the two boxes of precious stones from on board, and landing them safely somewhere in the neighborhood of the country house which has been spoken of The attempt was in itself no trifle, the shore being rather strongly guarded, and no boat daring to approach any other than the appointed landing places in the city, without special permission from the custom house

Mr McGaul had received orders to take possession of the two boxes, to pass the day on the river, and then to endeavor to land them safely in the evening or night In the possible case of making an arrangement to have them shipped with another captain, he was to receive a second order in the neighborhood of the country house, in which case it would be easier to bring the contraband goods on board without touching the shore

Mr Daily put on a grave face, turned his head right and left, and moved it backwards and forwards, whenever his words required these accompanying gestures, and then sank again into reflection, in order to advise his colleague as to the best course to be pursued by him

The latter had been provided by Mr. Walker, with two water casks, which he brought with him in the boat, into which the two boxes were to be secreted and headed up. "Two water casks !" cried Mr Daily, half aloud, "excellent ! exquisite ! There we have our Mr Walker again ! he is indeed a capital smuggler ! he knows the ways and means so directly ! In water casks ! each box to be placed in a water cask— the head to be taken out first, and then put in again ! Excellent ! beautiful ! But what sort of people have you got with you ? can you rely upon them ."

"O ho ! as to that," whispered Mr McGaul, "they are trusty fellows, who have already done so much on their own account, that they must be silent, if they would not carry chains all their lives ! They cannot injure us, Mr. Walker has them in his hands, or rather in his pocket."

"All right" returned Mr Daily, in as low a voice, "then I will hand the two boxes over to you, in the presence of the mate, that he may be satisfied that they are the same which the captain will have sent from on board "

"Very well," answered the other, "do so'; call the mate aside, and have the boxes brought on deck "

It was done as they had agreed ; the mate examined the captain's seals, and found them unbroken on both boxes. These were put on board of the boat, which Mr McGaul soon after stepped into, and steered for the opposite shore When it had got off at some distance from the brig, he took out some fishing tackle, and prepared for fishing, as if he was on the stream simply for that purpose, and had never thought of precious stones (or smuggling) in all his life

Mr Rossbruck had observed the secret discourse of the two clerks, without taking any apparent notice of it The expedition of two boxes from on board just before the departure of the ship, appeared to him a little out of the ordinary course of business He threw a stolen glance, accompanied by a knowing smile, to the mate, who looked after the boat for a long time, and then, to amuse himself, went and sat down by Dr Meibold, who was still busied in freeing himself from his beetles and leafy covering, and in classifying and systematizing

"What have you there, in that box, doctor, if I may ask ?" said Mr Rossbrück, unintentionally exhibiting one of his German traits of character, in commencing a conversation, although it was entirely opposed to the manner and custom of a real gentleman

"The most interesting thing that a naturalist has ever brought from this country," answered the savant, and his broad, square face beamed with a radiant expression "Look, if you please, through one of the little holes, you will there see a newly discovered production of nature, in four specimens, two male and two female, the one pair is designed for Queen Victoria, and the other for the Emperor of Russia "

"They appear to be wood beetles , are they not, doctor ?" remarked the other, after a hasty look at the show box

"They certainly belong to the class of wood beetles, but this species has never yet been mentioned by naturalists I myself have discovered this beetle, and have given it my name, as I do with all my discoveries, to avoid misunderstanding, in regard to my right of property as a naturalist "

"The discovery may be very interesting and very important," remarked Mr Rossbruck , "it is a pity that I am no connoisseur, and understand so little about such things

"A pity, do you say ? it is, indeed, a pity," replied the little man, straightening himself up with arrogant importance , " it is, indeed, a pity that you are unacquainted with the science of entomology, for it is the first in the world It evidently penetrates into the most hidden depths of nature, for where no other creature can penetrate, a beetle will, and the study of beetles conducts us, also, where they penetrate Look here, sir ! a beetle will penetrate into a thick, hard piece of wood, and there cut and work out his way and his dwelling, you, with all your human intelligence, cannot do the like "

Mr Rossbruck was compelled to admit the justness of the above observation of the naturalist, who continued with vivacity his panegyric of beetles "Do you see this tree, which has cost me so much trouble to bring with me ? why does it interest me ? simply as a tree ? by no means; dendrology is not my province , it simply interests me because a beetle lives on it and in it, in the physiology, or rather psychology, of which I have spent some months Do you comprehend that, sir ? Do you see this egg here ? the egg of the *Anser Merboldensis?* Do you suppose that the goose interests me as a goose? Oh no! no goose has ever yet interested me But this, my goose, lives entirely on beetles, it eats nothing but beetles; the element of its life is beetles, and, therefore, it interests me, for I have devoted myself, my whole life, to the study of beetles—to beetles Do you understand that, Mr —— ? what is your name?'

"My name is Rossbrück," said the young man, a little embarrassed, and in a low voice, for he disliked to pronounce his fatal German name in the presence of Mr Daily, who had just approached him

"Then you are, also, a German? I am rejoiced, I am rejoiced to make your acquaintance," exclaimed the little man

"Fine weather to-day," began Mr Daily, while he held out his snuff box to the young gentleman; "a good wind, likewise, for going down the river?"

The young gentleman answered by a slight nod, stepped aside a few paces, and removed himself from the deck passenger.

Mr Daily was too much of an Englishman not to understand this negative reply, he by no means lost his self-possession, but repeated his observation about wind and weather, while he stepped close up to the little beetle man, and held out the box to him Dr Merbold replied with all kindness, agreed that it was very fine weather, —but as regarded the wind, which was required to go down the river, that was a matter with which the learned man was entirely unacquainted

Like so many others of his kind, Dr. Merbold lived in the narrow boarded up world of his particular study, in which he was sufficiently well versed But out of the domain of his study of beetles, he appeared as unconversant with the world, and as unacquainted with practical life, as many others of his kind

Entirely taken up with his beetles, he only bestowed a hasty look upon his travelling companion, whose advances were, however, not unwelcome to him He loved conversation and intercourse, without, however, interesting himself much in its subject, unless it was some kind of beetle

"How long have you been in this country?" inquired the clerk of him, after a pause in their discourse The learned man held a beetle before him on a needle, and said, "I caught this one the first week after my landing, it may be two months since Only see once! what a splendid specimen that is, they cost ten millreis a pair in Rio de Janeiro, and in Europe you would have to pay ten dollars for them"

"Is that true!" exclaimed Mr. Daily, "then you, who have embarked such a capital in the article, will make a good business and a great deal of money by it."

"As to money-making" rejoined the little man, there I am not so fortunate as other people, for I am not a merchant—not in the least; and besides, I am always too much absorbed in my occupation, in and for itself, to be able to concern myself with speculation and trade. I pursue this study simply as a study, and only from the love of knowledge."

Mr. Daily stared at the little man in astonishment, while he as little understood this unconscious confession of the naturalist, (so much to

his honor,) as he was able to conceive of the entire separation of science from the general knowledge of the world

"One can engage in business, and make money as a naturalist, as to that matter," continued Dr Merbold "When you go to Rio de Janeiro, you will find there naturalists, or at least those who call themselves so, who have acquired property by trading in miserable stones and pebbles—in minerals! I know a Mr Closting, there, who follows this business."

"So!" said Mr Daily, more attentive than before, "he deals in minerals! in stones did you say? probably in precious stones, brilliants—that is worth hearing"

"Precious stones! precious stones! brilliants!" grumbled the other to himself; "as if there was any thing precious in a stone! there is but one precious—one brilliant—the well known 'brilliant beetle!'"

"Do you know any European in Rio de Janeiro, who does a business in minerals and the like—I mean a naturalist, as you call him, who is not exactly a merchant?" inquired Mr Daily, after a pause

"Naturalist, or something of that sort, who does a good business? yes, I know one well, who understands how to make money out of stones If you require such a one, I will give you Mr. Closting's address, or go with you to him, when we come to Rio I, myself, will have nothing to do with him—may God keep me from it! but if I can do you a service as my travelling companion——"

Mr Daily became more and more attentive, for the few words respecting the unknown "brought water to his mill," and he inquired further—"I hope he does not stand in bad repute—the naturalist of whom you spoke?"

"In repute?" returned Dr Merbold, busily occupied in sticking down beetle after beetle "I have told you, already, he does a good business He has money, and whoever has money does not need reputation. As to 'how he has made' his money! that has nothing to do with his reputation I—I mean what people call reputation Only he who has no talent for business, and does not understand how to make money, stands in evil repute with all who have money, they endeavor to shun him, because they fear that he may occasionally expect certain favors of them They call him lazy and stupid, or, altogether too honorable, too honest"

Mr. Daily smiled with peculiar satisfaction at these remarks, in which more sound sense shone forth, although in broken rays, than could have been expected from the learned man, after what had taken place.

"Very true! excellent!" he exclaimed, while the other continued—"I know men in great commercial cities, of whom people say sometimes one thing and sometimes another: one has forged notes; another has made three fraudulent bankruptcies; a third has counterfeited the name of his king, and thus obtained money; and another has committed all of these crimes together so they say. And all of them, but especially the last, do a good business, and pass for clever fellows, and of course are in good repute as clever fellows. What more do you wish? Do you not think so too, Mr.——? what's your name?"

"Daily, Habakkuk Daily, is my name," answered the other, smiling as before, regarding the little man with individual interest, who, on his part, little suspected how important his information and remarks were to his travelling companion, if the latter should be permitted to apply them to the individual spoken of, whose acquaintance he hoped to make by means of this accidental introduction

" You must move all your things away from the deck, down below, between decks '" said the mate, interrupting the conversation, and approaching the naturalist, who had not troubled himself in the least about his berth and accommodations

" Down below, between decks ?" inquired the naturalist, without looking up from his beetles, " is there then such a hurry ' I love the fresh air, and am busy, as you see "

" So I see, indeed," replied the mate, " but we are going to be very busy here just now ourselves , the captain is coming with the last cabin passenger, and we must have the deck clear "

" Hem ' if it must be so, it must," grumbled Dr Merbold , but canrot you make yourself busy somewhere else besides here, where I and my things are ?"

The mate wavered for an instant between mirth and anger, but involuntarily broke into laughter, and called a sailor, to whom he gave the order to transport the little fellow, with all his trumpery, below, between decks, where his berth was prepared for him The naturalist put a good face on a bad business, while Mr. Daily lent a helping hand, and, with remarkable officiousness, assisted him in arranging his quarters In this manner they were brought into close personal contact, and had time and leisure, by degrees, to enter more and more into conversation with each other, although it would have been difficult for the naturalist to become, as the expression is, " better acquainted" with his travelling companion In fact, the learned man troubled his head very little about the clerk, as he was no beetle, and therefore did not particularly interest him

—────~~~~~✦~~~~~──

CHAPTER IV

THE UNITARIAN.

While these intermediate scenes of embarkation, were passing on board the Nordstjernan, it was not less lively on board the Argentine man of war, La Caza.

The second morning watch, including the time from four o'clock in the morning, until eight, had passed by before the expected cutter, or a snallop with the required crew, was any where to be seen

Mr. Tumble, the commander, appeared on the quarter deck, after having been waked to breakfast by the steward He was one of those broad shouldered figures, whose heads sit so close upon their bodies that the blood easily mounts into them, while the expression of his round face, " cut with a coarse chisel out of soft sandstone," presented a perpetual declaration of war.

Mr Tumble generally sailed on the waves of inflated self-conceit under a full wind of brutality, whereby men in similar posts impose upon their inferiors, and require, as a tribute of duty, the respect which would otherwise be denied to them The commander, Mr Tumble, belonged to the great class of men who offer little for their most intimate associates to love or respect , whose deeds of selfishness and meanness draw upon them universal contempt, while they themselves live under the mistake, that they command universal respect These imposing men are generally surrounded by creatures whose studied demeanor manifests this dutiful respect, without which they would evidently prejudice their own interests On the other hand, men of the world are often officially forced into contact with them, who possess sufficient tact to adapt their behavior to them, without disturbing the illusion of these " highly respected and universally prized" men , an attempt which would be in itself as impossible as thankless

The greater the obligation, in the social relations, which compels persons who are brought into contact with a man occupying a position like the above, to manifest a certain outward respect, the more difficult would it be, to infuse into his mind doubts, or even a suspicion that this respect does not proceed from " esteem," but is merely the maintenance of external forms Such an intimation would be as useless as fruitless, and would, besides, be lost upon the egotism of the " respected man " The natural consequence would be a heavy dose of official brutality against the friend who, from a noble motive, should dare to disturb such a happy illusion—to raise the veil from before the fatal reality—whereby he would only injure himself, and serve no other person

Two elements of the world's great theatre set aside this so called universal " public or personal respect" of a man, as unnecessary The two elements are · business and subordination, neither for the one nor the other of these purposes, does the man generally require this article, where these elements are replaced by others— for business by credit, and for subordination by rank

Respect, founded on moral worth, disappears by the tendency of the civilization of our century, in proportion as the " worth of man," in some countries, is estimated according to rank, title, and external dignity ; in others, according to the measure of money , and sometimes by both together Whoever possesses one or the other of these qualifications, will trouble himself very little about " personal esteem," the article in question, since he does not at all require it for the maintenance of his position At this point we encounter a universal evil of our time, an inevitable result of so called civilization, which excludes the idea of a sense of honor.——

Capt, Tumble drew his old ash-gray " southwester" (which, in consequence of long service, might have passed for the original hat of Jim Crow) farther over his right ear, cast a criticising glance at the rigging and deck, and then upon the midshipman of the watch. He gave a half-dozen orders in a thundering voice, and at a breath, which the midshipman would certainly have given had they been necessary, or if the time for them had arrived The young officer repeated each order separately, in the customary seaman's intonation, and with the rapidity which their execution allowed. The commander drew his telescope to a focus, with a dissatisfied air, and stepped to the bulwark to observe the cutter and a shallop, which showed themselves in the far distance, steering for the Caza At the end of half an hour, during which the officers had breakfasted, and the fragmentary crew had received their rations, both sails had come alongside of the Caza, and offered a singular spectacle in their cargo of living creatures, (food for the cannon of the Orientals) Besides the people who served to man the cutter and shallop, a variegated mixture was presented, of " forced passengers," of various ages, from the boy to the graybeard, and with as great variety of character and nationality

As great as was the contrast of individuality in this " muster-roll of neglected children," from the remotest corners of the earth, who were now treated by fate in such a stepmotherly manner, there was, nevertheless, a certain general expression predominating throughout the entire intricate picture, composed of every degree of wretchedness, want, grief, anxiety, discontent, and despair, whose colors were blended with each other, and presented a most tragical view to the feeling observer

More speedily than Dr. Merbold had left his shallop for the deck of the Nordstjernan, did the future defenders of the Argentine republic arrive on board the Caza, on the quarter deck of which, in the neighborhood of the mainmast, the ship's clerk had arranged his table, with paper and writing materials, in order to make out an inventory of the captured machines and blind tools, while the midshipman who commanded the cutter went up to the commander, and handed him several documents, which were, in a certain degree, to be considered as a " bill of lading" of the delivered articles

Señor Enero undertook the conduct of the inspection, and a scene took place similar to the recruiting muster of Falstaff, the details of which would overstep the prescribed limits of this novel. The officer caused the floating troop to be arranged into four divisions, in order more readily to assign to each individual the future employment for which his fate had destined him The divisions were as follows   Volunteers, who had announced themselves as willing to serve in the marine , and these, again, were divided into the two classes of sailors and marines   The last class embraced some who had already served as soldiers on shore, or had learned the use of arms   The volunteers were to be entitled to several dollars bounty money, from which a boatswain, who conducted a recruiting party in the city, had already made advances to release one and another out of some public house, where they had pledged themselves and their travelling bundles   Besides these, appeared the third, and certainly the most numerous class, of so called criminals, individuals who, under pretence that they were dangerous to society, were placed for the present in safe custody. This class embraced all the " disorderly fellows," taken up in their frolics out of the gutters and thrown into prison, with Unitarians—men who, from their feeling and enthusiasm for freedom and fatherland, had become suspicious and " dangerous to church and state."

The fourth class consisted of natives of the republic, subject to military duty, who were obliged to serve out their time, by land or by sea, as defenders of their country, or rather as servants of Rosas

Besides these divisions, the recruiting boatswain, who conducted the transport, thrust forward two individuals, who, strictly speaking, fell into neither of these categories, whom he had " picked up" quite accidentally, just before the embarkation

To avoid confusion afterwards, these two were first examined. The one was a tall, herculean fellow, with coarse hair, of a color between vermilion and chrome yellow, which sported in frizzled locks, and a weatherbeaten face A deep fold was formed on his singularly strong, muscular neck, whenever he held up his head, with a sort of independent carriage, which seemed peculiar to him   He wore a simple " sailor's negligée " wide sailcloth pantaloons, and a garment (which the overstrained morality of certain countries will not allow to be named) of unbleached calico, with a blue sailor's collar, and white trimmings   These two pieces of clothing formed his whole attire   At the small leather girdle above his hips, which protected his " inexpressibles from mischance or downfall, hung the" remnant, or rather back of a buckhorn handled knife, very nearly worn out by length of service To a piece of sailyarn, strung around his solid neck, dangled a small octave flute, the holes of which were so near to each other that it must require a twofold art to play upon the instrument with such clumsy fingers as those of its owner Hat, barret, cap, stockings, shoes, or boots, were out of the question

The neglected son of the muses sustained himself with his back against the mainmast, with an evident difficulty to conceal the exertion that it cost him to maintain a suitable posture before the officer without balancing.

To the question about his name and country, he replied with the utmost significance of expression

" My name is Patrick McCaffray, but the ladies call me Pat Gentleboy, your honor I am an Irishman by birth, a little drunk by accident, and an American by principle."

An involuntary shout of laughter from the officers near the clerk, called the commander from the hinder part of the ship, to the group, where he only saw, in the manly form of the newly arrived person, a " brilliant acquisition for his Caza "

Mr. Tumble now began, in good English, a private examination of Patrick, at whose answers he was as little able to restrain his laughter as before

It transpired, by degrees, that Pat Gentleboy was twenty-nine years old, and had been to sea twenty-one years, that he had served a long time in the British navy, and five years on board a United States corvette, which had discharged him in Monte Video according to documents in the best form, which he carried in a rusty round tin box near his flute.

" You are a fifer, as I see ? inquired the commander, in continuation of his examination.

" Yes, your honor, fifer by profession, and Catholic by religion Many an anchor has been raised by this fife, I assure your honor, and many capstans have been manned after it in dade ,"—and thereupon Patrick Gentleboy put his miniature instrument to his lips, and blew, in the clearest, shrillest notes that had ever sounded above the murmur of the waves, and with undeniable skill, the well known Irish melody, "My love is on the ocean," accompanying, as it were, the trills and runs with heart and soul, gazing fixedly in the air, and keeping the most exact time on the planks with his bare foot

A hearty applause on the part of the officers, followed the last, masterly executed passage, whereupon Señor Enero whispered in the clerk's ear

"Set him down in the list of voluntarios, with five pesos* bounty money "

Patrick, who understood the words " voluntarios" and " pesos," excused himself, and spoke with peculiar seriousness

"Cinco pesos? good! very good! I have nothing agin that, but not as Voluntario I beg your honor's pardon! I am not here as voluntario, but as a land traveller, as a passenger, your honor. It is my intention to travel to Rio Negro, where I have a brother, a carpenter, your honor He lives there in a little town or village on the coast My brother's name is Tom, your honor! Patrick is my name—Patrick Gentleboy—and by no manes a voluntario! But if your honor plazes to give me the cinco pesos, God bless your honor, and may the heavens be your bed!' I will accept thim for travelling expinces with plaisure And you may write all that in the book, Mr Officer! if you plase! Patrick Gentleboy—musicianer—Irishman by birth —and above all, if your honor would plase to put down the name of the place where my brother lives, for I'm afeared I've lost the bit of paper where I had it written down "

Captain Tumble laughed heartily, and endeavored, with great success, to translate this original request of the Irishman, verbatim, into good Spanish

"No mistakes, your honor," continued Patrick, in the matter of voluntarios, I am no voluntario at all, at all! I'm an American by principle, and this here, as far as I see, this here is a Rosas ship, an 'Ar-gentile' man of war, isn't it, your honor? and I'm by no manes willing to act agin my principles! by no manes at all, at all! note that in your book Patrick Gentleboy—passenger—American by principle Does your honor understand? No mistakes, for my brother is expectin' me on the coast of Patagonia No mistakes, your honor!"

The officers lingered as long by this volunteer against his will, as the urgency of the time permitted, and then handed him over for the present to the steward, for an extra breakfast, against which Patrick Gentleboy had " not the least objection in the world."

They waited now for the other individual, whom the boatswain brought forward with the following account.

"This man I found to-day, while I was waiting for the transport, he sat in a boat by the shore, and twanged on his guitar the cursed Spanish tune of freedom, by Rigas or Riego, however the song may be called, and muttered words to it

that induced me to arrest him and bring him on board "

All eyes were now directed to the prisoner He was a young man, apparently about thirty years old, of a middling size, and weak frame— whose features, furrowed by suffering and grief, were evidently stamped with the proud seriousness of Spanish nationality, which his whole person indicated

He wore black nether garments, a velvet spencer, with buttons which had once been gilt, a broad Pyrenean or Basque bonnet, with a long tassel fastened under the chin, an old threadbare cloak, or mantle, thrown over his shoulders, and in his right hand a Spanish mandoline

"Your name?" inquired Señor Enero, with a certain air of consideration, in consequence of the impression that his appearance made upon him

"Alvarez de la Barca," replied the prisoner, looking his interrogator boldly in the eye

"A Spaniard, then?" said the other

"A South American," replied Alvarez.

"Where were you born?"

"In Corrientes "

Enero continued, while the clerk wrote down the answers

"What is your standing, your profession?"

"Aristocrat among democrats, compositor by profession "

Singular as this answer might seem in itself, no one dared laugh at it, since the undeniable dignity of the prisoner suppressed the sense of the comic

"Were you ever in military life?" asked Enero

"A volunteer in the well known ' bataillon de la Blouse,' at Barcelona," replied Alvarez, without allowing an emotion of his mind to be visible

"What song were you singing this morning, when the boatmen met you?"

"A republican hymn, a South American song —fragment of the Elegias de la Plata "

The officers looked at one another with an expression of surprise

"Sing the song again," ordered the captain. "Sing it!" cried he, louder, while a scornful smile distorted his mouth, "I wish to hear it, as a sample of Unitarian poetry Sing on !"

"Do you then desire that I should sing the fragment?" asked the prisoner

The commander reiterated his order, and the South American, after preluding some passages upon his instrument, raised his powerful baritone voice in an air similar to that of the famous hymn of Riego, and sang the following strophe·

*"The waves of La Plata are beating
 On the shore—and with horrors they're gone,
Streams of blood there its waters were meeting,
 Through the crimes of the tyrant thereon !†"

"What !" cried Codo, whose royalist principles had sufficiently declared themselves during the quarterdeck promenade of the foregoing night "how do you dare to sing such a song here, on board the Caza?"

"I ordered it," interrupted the commander, in a harsh voice; "I wish to hear the song, do not disturb him "

The singer had continued his accompaniment,

---

* Dollars.

† Free imitation of the Spanish original.

without noticing the interruption, while Patrick Gentleboy had returned in all haste from the forward deck, and accompanied the air in a masterly manner, with his picolo flute

With increasing animation, during which a deathly paleness overspread his noble features, the South American sang the following stanzas, without being again interrupted:

"The flowing of time's ceaseless torrent,
　From the Pampas the tyrant would stem ,
With walls and with ramparts abhorrent,
　Its course he would willingly hem

His ramparts with corses are gory ;
　The dams are cemented with blood ,
And the hangman, so runs the sad story,
　Lacks stones to encumber the flood

From the high sunny hills in the distance,
　La Plata bears freedom's idea
To a people whose future existence,
　In the union of nations will be'

In the rush of her waves is her greeting,
　Their movement is harmony's might,
Although rulers the nation are cheating,
　Its sympathy goes with the right

The waves of La Plata shall nourish
　For Rosas contempt, while they run ,
Though hirelings the praises may flourish
　Of the Pampas' degenerate son

Let Rosas then be well attended,
　Grow rich at the cost of the state ,
Though by strangers and priests he's defended,
　Yet vengeance shall be his sure fate

The hero by flatt'rers surrounded,
　Ingulfed in time's current shall be ,
His name as a by-word be sounded,
　The scorn of the brave and the free

When nations are writing their story
　Of tyrants with blood-spotted fame,
Let each traitor who shines in such glory
　Be called ROSAS—a curse be his name "

The effect of the different verses upon the minds of the officers, and upon that portion of the crew who were more or less able to understand the signification of the words, rose above all expression, with the accompaniment which filled up the pauses of the song, while the singer, evidently carried away more and more by his enthusiasm, brought forth all the strength of his thrilling voice, in accordance with the depth of feeling, with which he pronounced the words

Patrick Gentleboy, although not particularly conversant with the Spanish language, had placed himself directly opposite the singer, and outdid himself in an able accompaniment to the refrain, the more the singer's expression of countenance, as it were, brought him out of his drunkenness and electrified his fingers

The effect, however, upon the various minds of the officers, reached its crisis with the last strophe, and it would be a fruitless attempt to describe it here

"Infamous Unitarian !" cried Señor Codo, as the last words had scarcely left the singer's trembling lips, "infamous ! and you dare here, on board—— ?" Throwing himself upon him with these words, he unsheathed his dirk, and would have seized the unfortunate man by the cravat, but Enero sprang between the two, and turned the blow aside, crying loudly, "Justice '—and no murder '—back ! back ' who gave you orders '

"Fair play ' fair play ' gentlemen ," cried Patrick who suddenly dropped his flute, and seizing the daring Unitarian, covered him with his colossal body, when the commander sprang forward, and, by his loud orders, assembled round him a dozen of his crew

"Seize that Irishman !" roared he, foaming with rage, and leave the Unitarian to me, I will despatch him myself !"

Hardly had he spoken these words, when Patrick Gentleboy was overpowered by several stronghanded sailors, and the unfortunate Alvarez stood exposed to the arbitrary powers of the British hireling of Rosas

"Miserable Unitarian !" growled he, with irrepressible rage, and seizing him with a nervous arm, he dragged him to the bulwark, and pitched him overboard with his mandoline

"Do not reach any thing to him, let him drown !" shouted he to the sailors in the shallop which had brought a part of the forced volunteers on board, "do not touch him ; let the hound drown ' the Unitarian dog !"

Out of breath, and still trembling with savage emotion, he went back to the quarterdeck, while a deathlike silence ensued, and no one dared to look overboard, for fear of manifesting a curiosity which might be ascribed to personal sympathy for the unfortunate man

— ⚜ —

CHAPTER V

THE ESCORT ON BOARD

Mr John Walker accompanied his son to the place of landing and departure, where a sailing shallop lay, ready to take the captain of the Nordstjernan on board his vessel, his own boat having taken the Señora Dolores, the night before, from the country house of the Briton to the brig

Captain Finngreen appeared under the friendly attendance of Mr Lund, a ship chandler's clerk, who gave him his company, for which his principal had already taken a per centage in his account Mr Lund, formerly a student in Upsala, had been, like so many Europeans, led to South America by the caprice of fortune, where he, for the time, laid by his jurisprudence, and had assumed the provisionary occupation in which we see him

"When I see the heads which are stuck on the grating of the Plaza del Victoria there," remarked the captain, as he encountered Mr Walker and his son, " my heart becomes heavy, and I feel inclined to have my own head insured before I cast anchor in the stream yonder The executioner appears here to be the prime minister of your Director or Dictator, as you call your Gobernador."

" That is, indeed," said Mr. Lund, smiling; " and red is not, without reason, the favorite color of Rosas."

" That color has made many a cloth dealer rich," interrupted Mr. Walker, while his son's effects, and the last articles sent from the ship chandler's, were arranged in the shallop, "and for all that," continued he, leaning his head on one side, and closing one eye, as usual, " for all that, this is a very liberal government, the most free in the world We can here do and follow what we will, pursue commerce as much as we choose, if we leave politics alone, shave the beards smooth under our chins, and wear a red vest, or even anything else that is red I desire no better government than that of Rosas If the Unitarians will strike their heads, I cannot help it, whoever wishes to get rid of his head, meets with prompt attention here. But merchants, like us, do not easily ' lose their heads' here. Do you understand me, gentlemen ?"

Mr Walker accompanied his wit with a hearty laugh, and handled his watch key

"Rosas was, also, a merchant himself, as I hear," added Captain Finngreen, " he must understand traffic well to buy men, as he is accustomed to do"

"Certainly,' replied Mr Lund, " he was clerk to a mercantile house in this city, and that is no disgrace to him That he understands how to do business, he shows plainly enough, he does it well, he keeps in with the merchants, because he knows that they are not easily excited to rebellion ; and he says to the lower classes, ' you are free,' and they are so stupid as to believe it He keeps in with the priests, who preach to the people, ' ye shall be in subjection to the magistrates,' and the priests here water the plant of stupidity diligently, with holy water Whoever is independent, and no merchant, is abhorred by him, for he fears the patriotism and disinterestedness of such men, he calls them Unitarios, causes them to be beheaded or shot, if they do not save themselves by flight, and confiscates their property, which he shares with his favorites, who know how to use money as well as he does himself"

"But he is, withal, a wisehead, a ' clever fellow,' who understands how to govern," asserted old Walker, " but he was never a 'merchant,' only a clerk, only a clerk !" At these words, he drew up his head for an instant, from his right shoulder to an upright position, and continued, " Rosas was born and brought up among his father's cattle in the pampas, and came to Buenos Ayres a calf, and became a clerk, and soon afterwards entered as a volunteer into the party war, and in the extermination of the aborigines, showed bravery, and became a chief And when he had a thousand men under his command, he became general, and as general, military chief of the republic, and then Supreme Director or Gobernado——"

"And was very liberal when he first came to the government," said the ship chandler's clerk. "He talked of enlightenment and the education of the people, and a free press and the like, until the priests took him to school, and the Jesuits from Spain taught him the secret of governing like a tyrant, and passing for liberal before the world That is the history of our Rosas, captain," added he, after a pause, " and so far as I know from Gazettes and books, the history of most rulers in Europe He follows the method of many discreet heads, who wear the crown, and relinquish the executive power to the executioner"

The unpretending clerk's sound common sense very justly indicated the position of Rosas in this explanation, and partly unravelled the singular riddle, how it had been possible for the despot of La Plata to assume such a position, and maintain it for so long a time

"But how the people here can allow themselves to be satisfied with such treatment, no one in Europe can easily understand," replied the captain

"And yet it is very easy to explain," returned Mr Lund, " when you think of the condition in which the people were, in all parts of South America, subject to the oppression of the priesthood, under Spanish or Portuguese sovereignty, under the influence of the priests, and especially of the Jesuits, who, as you see here, have built nearly all the colossal architecture of the country. The Spanish population of this ancient colony were, in a moral respect, entirely in the hands of the priests, and externally in slavery to the government—to absolute despotism The political developments of Europe, worked directly or indirectly to the progress of things here in South America, and many European seeds have here grown and thriven, with remarkable rapidity, to blossom and fruit Our country, however, is by no means the first and only one where the priests have known how to avail themselves of a certain ' republican freedom,' to effect their own purposes, to uphold the interest of the ruling powers, and unite them with their own, under the pretence of maintaining public order The priests of all orders, after they had once obtained a firm footing here, and had almost literally had possession of all the provinces, did not resign their position, even when the light of freedom, coming over from Europe, extended its rays here, and evidently (we cannot deny it) dazzled the people, like a blind man, who is pierced for the cataract, and seeing suddenly, is unable to distinguish between near and distant objects"

"What the devil !" suddenly exclaimed old Walker, " I thought you were a shipchandler's clerk, and you speak like a member of parliament—or a lord of the upper house ! you must have studied."

"A little, Mr. Walker," replied Mr Lund smiling, " but I see that our shallop is ready for sailing, and I will, in all haste, conclude my remarks The priests would not relinquish their position here, although a part of the population would no longer, as formerly, accept their papal letters of credit, but often sent back their ' bills of exchange on eternity' protested. They quietly sought to gain over Rosas, by making him understand that the despotism, by which alone he sustains himself, cannot subsist without the aid of the so called ' church.' Church and state here, also, formed an alliance, and Rosas became the instrument of the priests, while he retains the illusion that he uses the priests as instruments for the maintenance of ' public order,' a plant, as we see here, plentifully watered with blood, and for the growth of which corpses are used as manure. And now, captain, farewell, a happy voyage to you "

The former student from Upsala hastily gave his right hand to Captain Finngreen, while old Mr Walker as hastily seized his left, and overcome by a peculiar heartiness, exclaimed, " I will pay you a compliment, Mr. Lund. Is not your name Lund ? No, I will not pay you a compliment ; I am not fond of compliments, as you must know I—I have respect for you, all respect It is a pity you are not an Englishman Your qualifications would open a career before you, a brilliant career ! by my soul ! But how came you in a ship chandler's shop ! I should like to know.'

"The ways of fate are not always direct," returned Mr. Lund , " besides, I find my acquirements very convenient in my position as clerk in a ship chandler's store, since I can serve as interpreter in three or four languages, and become useful to many captains as well as to my principal, without, in my apprehension, degrading myself in the least, or having any thing with which to reproach my conscience "

Very honorable ! very honorable on your part," observed Mr Walker. " If you ever wish to better yourself, to increase your salary, come to me "

Mr Lund returned hearty thanks for this offer, while Captain Finngreen interposed the request that he would accompany him on board, adding, " You can and must give one more proof how useful you can become to a captain I have still to pass the man of war there, and if vessels are not generally hailed, it may yet be the case to-day that something of the kind may occur to me, and then, too, I am still uncertain whether the two boxes are sent from on board You know, Mr Walker, what I mean ? Come on board with me, Mr Lund In case the two boxes are still there, you shall at least witness that I throw them overboard "

"It's all right ! all right, captain," returned Mr Walker, smiling, " I have already sent out my McGaul, an hour ago, the boxes are disposed of, rely upon it But go on board with him, for all that," continued he, returning to the clerk ; " do the captain that favor, at my request I will call at your store, and inform your principal that I have made it

"No, indeed," returned Mr Lund , " why should I not go ? I accompany so many captains on board, that my principal finds it quite in order "

Mr. Walker now took leave of Captain Finngreen and his son, but he had no tears of emotion at his disposal, since he did not allow himself an overflow of feeling, which would disturb his business, and was not the fashion

"Now, Bob, my boy !" he at last exclaimed, " farewell ! take notice of my ' Private Instructions ;' read them over to-day, when you are comfortably on board , and read them often, very often ; act by them, live by them, as a gentleman, a Briton, and a Walker "

Bob Walker was just stepping into the cart which was to convey him on board the shallop, when some one tapped old Mr. Walker on the shoulder

"Good morning, Signor' Testa, come state, Signor' ?" he exclaimed, as loudly as before, to the gentleman who had saluted him It was Mr Joseph Testa, the Italian from Patagonia, whom we observed, the evening before, at the coffee house " I can give you the exchange on Genoa that you desired ; you can despatch it immediately It is all right. Come with me, if it suits you You came quite apropos, Signor' Testa, as if you had been sent for I have a secret for you You are my man. I

thought of you last night Come along " All these fragments flowed in such haste from Mr Walker's lips, that the Italian found no opportunity for reply

"All very well, Mr Walker," interrupted he, at length , " but I have first something here for Signor' Roberto Here, Signor' Bob," said he, turning to the young Mr Walker, while he hurried to the cart, and delivered him a letter, " here is a letter to one of your fellow passengers, Mr Hinango It contains a letter of introduction to our friend Horatio, and to yourself I desire that this traveller may be considered by you all as my friend and countryman He was not, to be sure, born in Italy, but my fatherland acknowledges him as a son Introduce him to our Horatio, and farewell "

The worthy Bob promised, with hearty good will, to take the best care of the letter, and thanked the Italian for thus procuring him an agreeable acquaintance , whereupon the other spoke to him for some time in a low voice, he then took leave of his papa, and hurried off

"Farewell, Bob, my boy ! God bless you ! Write to me soon from Rio Pleasant voyage !" cried Mr Walker, after him, while he seized Signor Testa under the arm, drew him along with him, and whispered in his ear—

"You are a good Catholic—are you not ? You can go into a monastery without difficulty, not as a monk—I do not desire that—I will not persuade you to celibacy—but with a secret to the monastery up there—that one there Come with me, first, into my cabinet "

Signore Testa followed the eccentric old man, without obtaining time to thank him for the arrangement of the exchange Mr Walker appeared happy to be once more in possession of a secret, and one, too, of so much importance that he dared not speak of it in the public streets, in the lightest whisper He forcibly drew along by the arm, the confidant who had appeared as if " sent for," as an English steamer tows an Italian bark up the Thames , and they soon disappeared amid the throng in the Calle del Victoria

CHAPTER VI

DELIVERANCE AND MEETING.

THE shallop steered for the brig Nordstjernan, which lay about a mile from the war brig, La Caza, in such a direction that her course would carry her past the latter.

The three men in the stern talked about wind, and weather, and war, and executions, while a favorable breeze hastened their voyage.

Mr Robert Walker furnished his two companions with cigars, and added the request that they should keep them lighted, that he might kindle another by them before they came on board, because the wind would render it difficult or impossible to light a match on the way. They were already past the Caza, the distance of two long rifle shots, when they descried an object on the waves, which suddenly fixed their attention. It was a person swimming, who, from time to time, held up something round above the water, (which a sailor pronounced to be a large shovel,) giving himself up at one time to be the sport of the waves, by allowing himself to be borne along by them, and then striking out and swimming again. The natural impulses of humanity were aroused in the most lively manner, in the breast of each man in the shallop, and, without a word of conceit, the boat was steered towards the singular appearance. It was no one else than the unfortunate Alvarez de la Barca, enfeebled by prolonged and powerful exertion, into a kind of apathy, a transition state to utter exhaustion—to death. To find a man in such a condition in the stream, and to consult whether they should save him by taking him into the shallop, never occurred to them. But the boatmen bestirred themselves the more to rescue the drowning man, when they came near to him, and Mr Lund recognsied in him an acquaintance, though not very intimate.

"My God!" exclaimed Mr Lund, "that is certainly the guitar teacher, who was lately at our store, seeking a passage for Bahia! I know him by his velvet spencer, with yellow buttons, and he has even yet his instrument in his hand!"

While Mr Lund was saying these words, the boatman threw a rope to the drowning man, and tried to bring the shallop near to him. He had hardly strength to hold the rope with both hands, until a sailor caught him by the collar of his spencer, and hastily drew him into the boat. Since he had entered the Caza, the band of the guitar had been slung round his neck, whereby the instrument, more accidentally than intentionally, had remained united to his fate, and had partly served him, as a kind of oar, until it became filled with water, when it had assumed the shovel movement, (which the sailor had noticed at a distance,) as he occasionally emptied it of its liquid contents. Young Mr Walker hurried to open his medicine chest, which stood near him, among his other baggage, and it required all the dilligence of his rescuers to bring the unfortunate man out of danger, and to the consciousness of his earthly existence.

"How in the world did you come to be in the water at this distance from the shore?" inquired Mr Lund. "Did you fall overboard from some vessel? I suppose you will hardly know me? I took you lately to a Danish captain, who was bound for Bahia."

Alvarez stared at the Swede a long while, and then at all the other persons in the shallop in turn, and finally appeared to become conscious of his situation, and to remember the clerk. He emptied a glass of Madeira wine, which Captain Finngreen held to his lips, and began his reply in a low, feeble voice.

"I remember you very well, sir, and I thank you again for your former kindness to me, by and by, perhaps, I shall find words to thank you all, gentlemen, for my rescue, though it is yet to be seen whether death or life be the greatest benefit to me. May I beg," said he, suddenly interrupting himself, and turning to one of the boatmen, "may I beg you to dry out my mandoline very carefully, if it is not already unglued, and then lay it in the shade."

The sailor to whom this request was addressed hastened to fulfil it, while the singer, with his feeble voice, continued to answer the above questions, and the shallop flew towards the Nordstjernan.

"Then you remember me, and perhaps as much of my circumstances, likewise, as I confided to the captain in your presence. I could find no employment as a printer here in Buenos Ayres, for I was proscribed as a Unitarian, and no one would compromise himself by employing me. As a teacher of the guitar, I required recommendations. My treasury stood at sixty-five pesos—so I sought a passage to Bahia, although that sum was hardly sufficient for it. In order to save my money for the voyage, I was obliged to lodge at a miserable public house, where the charges were low. Some rascals who stayed there, suspected or observed my intentions, and although I put my purse under the straw bed at night, it was stolen from me. I was now driven to despair, and was in constant danger of being apprehended as a Unitarian. I passed the last night under the open sky; and, sure enough, was arrested this morning by a press gang for Rosas' navy. Think what you will of me, when I assure you that I preferred death to such a service—to fight against my political friends. I found an opportunity, as I expected, to end my life—or, in the strange contradiction of my feelings, to save my life—to regain my freedom, and live hereafter as a Unitarian. I was taken on board the vessel, the man of war there. The commander ordered me to sing the song, of which the officer of the press gang had, this morning, heard a few passages, which I was repeating to myself, as a sort of morning prayer. I knew my situation and calculated on the consequences of such a song. They were verses from the 'Elegias de La Plata.' I selected those which were most bitter against the tyrant. I had scarcely ended, before a dirk was drawn upon me; it was held back, and in a second the commander, with his own hands, pitched me overboard with astonishing dexterity. Although at first I made no effort to save myself, the stream lifted me up on its waves. I was born on this river, and am a practised swimmer from childhood. Contradictory feelings arose within me. Providence does not yet seem to require my death. I find myself here, tolerably well—I still live—and there is a God—and his will be done!"

A long pause followed, during which the three men in the stern of the shallop looked thoughtfully at each other, and involuntarily considered about the immediate disposition of the rescued man. Captain Finngreen, who was sufficiently acquainted with Spanish to catch the sense of the relation, was the first to break silence, while he fixed his eyes earnestly upon Mr Walker and Mr Lund, saying in an under tone

"A singular situation, in which this unfortunate man has placed us, without intending it. We cannot throw him overboard again—he can as little go back to Buenos Ayres with you, Mr. Lund, he must go on board with me, and we may rest assured that the longboat of the cursed brig there, will be directly steered for the Nordstjernan, to reclaim him, and then they will be led to entertain other suspicions, and molest my cabin passengers, and I would gladly shield your sister from such visits, Mr. Walker."

A long silence again followed, during which Mr. Lund found himself in peculiar perplexity, from not knowing whether he ought to appear cognizant of a secret, about which the captain had confidentially consulted with him, before he had agreed to the request of Mr Walker to take the lady on board as passenger

"I take it for granted, captain, that you have made your countryman, Mr Lund, acquainted with the circumstances of my sister, so far as my father imparted them to you ?" at last began Mr Walker, who had read in the countenance of his third companion what was passing in his mind. He spoke these words in a very low voice, on account of the presence of the boatmen, upon whose discretion, very naturally, he could not count, in case they understood English

"Mr. Lund, my confidential friend," answered the captain, "knows as much as myself in relation to your sister, Mr Walker; but since we can only speak of the affair among ourselves, we must get on board , and this poor man must go with us—come what will. In no country of the world does there exist, according to my knowledge, a law which forbids taking a man out of the water when he is in danger of drowning Whether I may save a man's life by receiving him on board as a passenger, is another question, and we can only talk about it on board "

The captain now turned to Alvarez, as if he had not been speaking of any thing important to his friends , and asked him, with manifest sympathy, how he felt

The unhappy man, who appeared sunk in deep reflection upon his present situation, declared that he was quite well physically, and asked where the vessel was bound to which the shallop was making its way, and when it set sail

The captain named his place of destination, with the remark that he should weigh anchor, and go to sea immediately, in case the wind, which now appeared favorable, "held," and would carry him out of the mouth of the river A glance of the persecuted Unitarian said more than it would have been possible for his tongue to express

"I have a request to make to you captain," he began, after a fresh pause, while his lips moved as if the muscles of his organs of speech refused to obey the will "I have a request to make to you, captain, but I can only speak it when I am on board with you ' May I go on board with you ?"

In this last question lay evidently the withheld request, as little as it might have been his intention to utter it so plainly.

"We shall soon be on board," replied the captain, with a sailor's brevity "Come up with us, and at least take something warm, as soon as possible, if it is only a cup of tea or coffee It will do you good, and then we will talk of the rest. Here '" said he, to the crew of the shallop "here is a little drink money, for the lengthening of our passage while you were picking up this unfortunate man , for the deed itself, of saving his life, God will reward you, if I were rich, I would also offer you something "

With these words he handed the master of the shallop a gold piece, whereupon Mr Walker took out his purse, and gave them double the sum, for the moment already forgetting his father's admonition in relation to generosity. The design of securing the boatmen on their side, in case they fell in with the mercenaries of Rosas,

governed, undoubtedly, the conduct of both, especially as the situation of the young lady on board the Nordstjernan had become more dangerous, apart from the feelings of humanity which prompted them to the rescue of the unfortunate Alvarez

The shallop was now beside the Nordstjernan. The captain stepped on board, the others followed him, while he gave orders to remove the various goods and effects from the boat, and to hand the boatmen a couple of bottles of wine

"Make some good coffee for the cabin," cried he to the long Ottar, as he stepped upon the quarterdeck, "and now, gentlemen, come with me," added he, turning to his companions, while he took the enfeebled Alvarez under the arm, and led him to the cabin steps Hinango and Horatio stood among the passengers who were upon the quarterdeck, awaiting the captain's arrival Both had observed, through the telescope, the rescue of a man from the water, and had involuntarily taken a warm interest in the scene The nearer the shallop approached, the more lively did this feeling become in Hinango, who thought that he beheld, in the person rescued, a man whom he had seen elsewhere, either in reality or in a dream

Such cases of glimmering recollection, in which, as it were, we put in requisition all the powers of our memory, to follow out some clue of the past to the point of contact with the actual present, bring us into a state of reflection, as singular as painful Remembrance is a matter of sentiment, of the soul, memory is an affair of the understanding The clearness of our impressions often becomes conditional upon the greater or less excitement of feeling, through the susceptibility of the mind, at the moment when we receive them Impressions which we receive in the depths of our agitated souls, inweave themselves into our very existence— while others, which excited us more superficially, are more easily effaced, and lose themselves in the background of our perceptions, among the thousand-fold appearances of the external world

The richer the life of a man in events, the sooner do even the more lively impressions which he has received into the depths of his being become confused, and he must set aside a mass of "old and new images in the remembrance chamber of his mind," before he can find the impression of the appearance, whose search has involuntarily occupied him This displacing and search becomes often more difficult and painful when the mind, at the moment excited by important events, is receiving deep impressions, whose images glitter in all the liveliness of their colours on the foreground of the perception, and preferably occupy us

Hinango not only felt that he had actually met the stranger somewhere, whose life had just been saved, but there arose within him a faint remembrance that he had held intercourse with him at some eventful period, where and whenever it might have been. Musing more and more, without finding a clue which could lead him, through the labyrinth of his past life, to any spot, where the meeting had taken place, and at length despairing at the fruitless exertion of his powers of retrospection, he already experienced a sensation of physical suffering in the nerves of his brain, as Mr Rossbruck suddenly drew near him, and accidentally blew the smoke of a genuine Manilla cigar by his nose

Whether the olfactory organs of men are most closely connected with those fibres of the brain, through which the nerves extend whose spiritual fluid operates as memory, or whether some other impenetrable mystery of nature is the source of a train of thought which, at times, places us, with the speed of an electro-magnetic conductor, in one or another scene of the past, when an odour excites us which we there perceived with peculiar liveliness? Be that as it may, it belongs to the researches of physiology

Scarcely had Hinango felt the lightest breath of the Manilla smoke, when he found himself suddenly placed in a dilapidated monastery in Catalonia, in a spacious cell, severely wounded, and saw a physician near him, who blew the smoke of a Manilla cigar in his nose, thereby recalling him to life, while a comrade of his famed " Bataillon de la Blouse" had hold of his right hand, and cried out, in a joyful tone, " He lives !"

Just then Alvarez, with the captain, was approaching the entrance to the cabin, passing Hinango, when the latter, as if struck by lightning, still inhaling the Manilla perfume, as suddenly stepped up to the rescued Unitarian, gazed intently in his eyes, and under profound mental agitation, cried out to him, " He lives !"

The effect of this exclamation, accompanied by the appearance of a human form so suddenly stepping before him, as if out of the grave of the past, very naturally produced a shock in the nervous organization of the sufferer

As if dazzled, Alvarez gazed, with quivering eyebus, upon the countenance of the man from whom these words were directed to him, but quickly attained the consciousness of recollection, and involuntarily exclaimed, " Capitan ! Dios y Humanidad !" It was the watchword of that night, from before whose scenes the curtain was now rolled up to the unrestricted perception of memory

" Come quickly with us into the cabin !" whispered Captain Finngreen in the ear of Hinango, who thereupon followed the three men who had brought his comrade on board

--------··········--------

CHAPTER VII

THE TWO RIVALS

We return on board of the Argentine war brig La Caza   The death-like silence which followed the intended (and, to all appearance fulfilled) murder, was interrupted by the continuance of the inspection of the recruits, though the clerk addressed his questions in a somewhat subdued voice to the individuals who came in turn before him   The commander still puffed and fumed, in apparent transports of rage, walking up and down on the quarterdeck, and then, hastily drawing his telescope to a focus, he directed his attention to the shallop which was steering for the Swedish brig. The rapid movement of the stream had already carried

the victim of his savage fury to a considerable distance   At the same moment, when he had perceived the object of his scrutiny, it appeared to him, as if a human head raised itself out of the waves, and then suddenly disappeared behind the shallop whose sail partly concealed the movements of the people on board of it

" One of the recruits desires to have the honor of confiding to you something of importance, Captain Tumble," said Codo, who had quietly approached him

" What does the fellow want ?" grumbled he, without removing the glass from his eye, " probably some excuse to leave the ship, I know such important matters of old " —

" He intimates," returned Codo," that he is able to give information, concerning the author of the ' Elegias de La Plata,' for whose head it is known a reward is offered "

" Show him the yard there," replied the commander, sullily " and ask him if he wants his neck stretched ' if he wishes to have a rope around it, and swing there ?"

" He seems certain of being able to give up the author, or the authoress," returned Codo

" Could it be a woman ? Do you mean the authoress of the Elegies, of which the wretch there lately sung some verses !" inquired the commander, a little more attentive.

" So far as I have understood, he means the authoress of these Elegies," returned the other, " but he requires to return to the city, to a police officer, to register his deposition

" To return to the city ' there, you see ! 'tis all nonsense,' grumbled the commander, " the fellow is afraid of the sea air, and has the cannon fever, that is all "

" He speaks English, besides," continued Codo, " and desires nothing farther than to speak with you alone "

" Does he speak English ?" inquired Mr Tumble, taking his glass under his arm, and suddenly giving his entire attention to the officer's account

" He says he is a literary gentleman, from Buenos Ayres, in a condition to give the best references, upon influential English families there   He asserts that he was apprehended entirely by accident, without the least fault-on-his-part "

" Let the fellow come this way," said Mr. Tumble   Codo disappeared—and after some moments Perezoso stood on the quarterdeck, trembling like an aspen leaf, while the glance of the captain passed from his head to his feet.

" Who are you ? and what do you want ?" said Mr Tumble to him   " What have you to say to me ?"

The literary gentleman approached the commander as nearly as his extreme fear would permit, that he might speak to him in the lowest possible tones, from a needless precaution, lest his companion and rival, Señor Falsodo, who stood far from him, by the foremast, should overhear him

He answered the first questions concerning his person and position, with all brevity, in a faltering voice, for Señor Codo had not failed to whisper some words in his ear about the " yard " and " rope around his neck," and " dangling ;" and the fate of the guitar singer floated before his eyes.

The brutality of the commander diminished proportionably, the more fluently the prisoner continued to speak English, though with a Spanish accent

After he had heard the introduction to a disclosure, the object of which was in itself of so much importance, he beckoned the literary gentleman to follow him, and retired to his cabin.

Before he descended the stairs, he called to the first lieutenant, "Keep an eye on the shallop, yonder ! send an officer to her ! I wish to know whether they have drawn the Unitarian dog, dead or alive, out of the water ? If they have rescued him, and taken him on board the Swede, he must be brought from there, if not—if the dog is entirely dead, the shallop may pass "

"I will go myself, and meet the shallop," returned Señor Enero, and ordered the Spanish royalist to take his place in the inspection

The captain disappeared with Perezoso Codo placed himself near the clerk, and made a remark about the official diligence of the lieutenant, who very wisely made no reply

Enero stepped into a boat with twelve oars, and steered in the direction of the Nordstjernan, while the shallop, which had already discharged her passengers and their effects, now sailed towards him.

The mustering of the "instruments and tools" for the maintenance of despotism on the river La Plata went forward, under the guidance of Codo, who would certainly rather have commanded the boat, for various reasons The recruits passed in review, one after the other, and many who had no red riband, or did not wear some red thing or another, were sharply examined.

"What is your name ?" inquired the clerk, of a little fellow, dressed in black, with a broad brimmed straw hat, who came next in order

"Ignatius Loyola Falsodo," replied the prisoner.

"What are you ? what is your profession ?"

"I am an Agent of police, in the service of government, and have a special report to make to the Chief of the Police Department. I attend the Unitarian there, who has gone into the captain's cabin. I apprehended him last night in front of the prison in which the traitor Alphonso lay, who was shot this morning I had made the discovery that the plan was laid to free him. I maintained my incognito towards this Unitarian, because I was on special service You understand me, gentlemen ; the police must sometimes wear a mask, to go to work more surely. I know that this Unitarian, Perezoso by name, stands in intimate connexion with the friends of Alphonso, and has assisted in the dissemination of the damned ' Elegias de La Plata.' What step he is now taking to get on shore again, in what manner he is seeking to delude and outwit the commander, I can only suspect As concerns myself, I require to remain here on board as a prisoner, to write a report to Borrachezo, a commissary of police ; it will then be confirmed that I am in the service of government, and I shall be recalled to further duty in the city "

Codo heard this announcement with peculiar interest, and not without surprise. "Step aside," said he to the police spy ; he then beckoned to a midshipman to take his place at the inspection, and hurried down into the commander's cabin He found Mr Tumble in earnest conversation with Perezoso, which had lost the form of a hearing, and taken that of a secret conference, in which the subordinate situation of the literary gentleman was set aside by the importance of the disclosures

Codo asked pardon of the commander for disturbing him, and whispered some words in his ear ——

Thereupon Captain Tumble sprang up, in great agitation, from his seat, and with the violence peculiar to him, exclaimed, " It is, then, true, as I at first suspected, and the fellow was in the way to lead me thoroughly astray Wait now, you dog ! the rope is spun for you already !"

"Will you permit me to put some questions to the prisoner here, to arrive at the truth the sooner ?" said Codo, interrupting the pause, during which the commander had become lost in reflection

"Ask him !" he replied, as morose and brief as usual, and threw himself back upon the sofa, looking with a tiger's glare at the faithful partisan of Rosas, who was in danger of being despatched as a Unitarian.

"Do you know a man named Falsodo ?" inquired Codo of the prisoner, who, through this interruption, and the violent agitation of the captain, had nearly lost all selfpossession Less than ever did the muscles of his organs of speech comply with the urgency of the occasion With a quivering under lip, he replied, hesitatingly, " I only know him according to his position—no further. I stand in no further connexion with him "

"And what is the position in which you know him ?"

"He is known as a police spy—well known," stammered the poor devil, not thinking, in his deadly anxiety, that this title would here be the best recommendation he could give to his opponent.

"As a police agent, you would say," exclaimed Codo, now casting as triumphant a look at the commander, as if he had captured an enemy's corvette " Is any further confirmation required, sir ?" continued he, " does he not himself state in whose company he came on board ?"

"Unheard of! shameful !" exclaimed Mr Tumble ; " and to circumvent me with such cunning Me ! To endeavor to bring me upon his side ! Let the police officer come down here "

Codo flew up the cabin steps, and before Perezoso had time to wipe off, with his Rosas-red handkerchief, the sweat of anxiety which stood in great drops upon his forehead, Falsodo stood directly opposite to him.

The consciousness of displaying his official diligence under the protection of furious Confederados, seemed to have removed in the police spy all hesitation and fear, which often disturbed him when he found himself amidst opposing elements, as was too clearly manifest from his conversation with Borrachezo, the commissary of police, in the office of old Domingo.

"You are then in the service of government, as police agent ?" inquired the commander, looking him steadily in the eyes.

"For years, S'ñor Commander, as my chief,

S'ñor Borrachero will confirm, to whom I wish to send a report from here "

" And how came you in prison, then ?"

" As I had succeeded in disturbing this Unitarian in his plan, and having him arrested, I was forced to make up my mind to pass the night with him in the guard house, that I might not lose sight of him until I found an opportunity to commit to paper a report to my chief, which I have not been able to do until now

" It was past eleven, when we were arrested My position did not permit me to make a confident of the corporal or the lieutenant of the guard I knew sufficiently well the mode of proceeding in such cases Either I should remain until to-day in the guard house, and would then have summoned a servant of the police to inform my chief where I was, or that must happen which is now the case . I must find an opportunity to confide in some officer of a higher rank This I have quietly waited for here, while I gave my prisoner ample opportunity to unmask himself, inasmuch as I knew, beforehand, that he would make the attempt, under one pretence or another, to go from on board and regain his freedom "

" Miserable liar ! " exclaimed Perezoso between his teeth, while his knees shook, as if seized with an ague fit, and he tried to sit down in an arm chair, whose disjointed frame was almost broken, and cracked under him

" Stand up !" cried Codo to him , " prisoners do not sit here, in the cabin of the commander "

Mr Tumble had listened with great attention to the spy's communication, and recognised in it a certain appearance of probability, that seemed worthy of a closer examination

" You are then firmly convinced that this Unitarian stands in connexion with the friends of the traitor, who, as I hear, was shot this morning ?" he asked, looking steadily into the eyes of the " police officer "

" I am firmly convinced of it," answered Falsodo, more and more encouraged by the official protection of the marine officer. " I am firmly convinced that this Unitarian is not only engaged in a plot with the friends and coadjutors of the executed person, but that he knows the author or authoress of the infamous Elegies , and that he can at least be compelled to give the name "

A long silence again ensued, while all three sought to read the impression of this declaration on the countenance of the literary gentleman, which, like a book whose back is unglued, hardly held together, while his gaze wandered about unsteadily, and found no resting place

" I am no Unitarian !" he at length sighed, squeezing his red handkerchief together in a ball, " God knows, I am no Unitarian ! I am a Confederado, and a true follower of our Regent— our Director I will do all I am able to come upon the track of the author of the damned Elegies, when I am in the presence of a functionary with whom I can co-operate My life is in your hands, S'ñor Commander. If you choose to end it here, you make it impossible for me to operate for the interest of the government in this matter. Remember all the particulars which I gave you.—— Do with me what you will, only send me as prisoner on shore to trial, since what I have to depose falls within the province

of the police, of the judiciary, and not of the marine department Consider me Unitarian, until I can legally prove that I am a real Confederado, and the truest servant of our Rosas that ever wore his colors "

He drew a long breath, and involuntarily unfolded his red handkerchief like a flag, while the sweat of anxiety streamed out more and more, and required its constant use

This brief exculpation confused the commander, with respect to the position and prospects of the literary gentleman The blustering hurricane of his fury, which had threatened to overwhelm the lifeboat of the accused, became transformed into a " stiff breeze of official duty." The mysterious cargo of the literary gentleman appeared to be of some value, and might be of some use to himself From the late declaration made to him in private, it seemed evident to him that Perezoso was apparently sure, on his part, of arriving at the discovery of the author of the Elegies , so it very naturally remained, that he would reveal his secret to any one through whom he might be deprived of the reward that was affixed to the denunciation The accusation of Falsodo in regard to the literary gentleman's position as a Unitarian, might appear well founded in the eyes of the captain, as in the contests of the political parties of our day, it was by no means an impossible thing for a person to become, from self interest, a traitor to his own party, when a favorable opportunity should be offered In the accuser, Falsodo, he saw nothing but the " respectable police agent," who had maintained his incognito under the peculiar circumstances

Without the floating, " wooden world " of his vessel, our commander knew but little of the world and mankind His contracted world was the wooden district, with its cordage, copper, and iron, from the maintruck to keel, and from the flying jib-boom to poop-lanterns Officers and crew were subjected to his unrestrained command, by the fetters of subordination in the element of official duty He exercised only ship knowledge, not the knowledge of mankind. Nothing was so foreign to him as character and heart , the internal basis of the man, from whose rich or desolate soil his conduct proceeds He recognised neither noble nor base conduct, he knew only, ' Duty ' Man, as man, never came into his consideration, as humanity was a quality foreign to his nature , and he very naturally could not look for that in others, in which he himself failed, and of course he had not the least idea.

Without entering into Falsodo's notions, or perceiving his contemptible meanness, he saw in him only the " officer on service," and in the service too, of the same government from which he so regularly received his solid monthly, and which held out to him " brilliant prospects of advancement "

As an officer on duty, he saw himself placed accidentally beside the " clever and obedient police officer," Ignatius Loyola Falsodo, who had, in a manner, taken refuge on board of his Caza, in order, under his protection, and by his co-operation, to guard the Unitarian prisoner, Perezoso, and lead him to the confession of his secret. There immediately arose within him, a demand for official dilligence, to sustain, to the best of his power, the so called police officer. In the possible, though improbable case, that Falsodo was not in the service of government, (which might soon be ascertained,) he held himself, even on this supposition, secure of his person, and of course, no oversight of duty would occur on his part.

Some peculiar circumstances of his voyage required him to go on shore again, to an office of the admiralty After a brief consideration of the importance of the mystery which Falsodo so conscientiously escorted in the captured life-boat of the literary gentleman, he resolved to accompany his colleague in service to the office of the designated commissary of police, to convince himself, in person, of the reality of his relations

While these transactions took place in the commander's cabin, Señor Enero had approached the shallop in which Mr Lund was returning from the Nordstjernan After the preliminary inquiries upon which he had received orders, the lieutenant found it expedient to bring the shallop alongside of the Caza, that the commander might himself receive the information which he had obtained, and that he might be relieved of all further responsibility in this matter.

Mr Tumble had left the cabin with his two prisoners, and had gone to the quarterdeck, where he now waited for the long boat Enero stepped on board, and announced, in a serious official tone, that he had accomplished his errand.

" The master of the shallop, and the young man in the stern, there, a ship chandler's clerk from the city," continued he, " declare that they drew a man out of the water, and took him on board. He was, as they say, in such a state of phrensy, as led to the suspicion that he had intentionally thrown himself into the stream, which his further behaviour and his end confirmed He was hardly restored to consciousness, before he seized a fitting moment to thrust aside, with the strength of despair, those who had surrounded him, jumped overboard, and sank to rise no more From some words which he muttered in his delirium, it appeared evident that he took the Swedish brig for a man of war, and the fear of falling again into the hands of the *Confederados*, moved him to suicide "

Captain Tumble heard this report, like any other, without receiving any impression from it, which did not belong to the service, and muttered to himself—" The hardiness of his behavior here on board, as a first attempt to end his life upon a yard or in the stream, certainly agrees very well with his end. The fellow was crazy, like all Unitarians, and belonged to the madhouse, like them all 'Tis a pity that I did not first have him tied over a cannon He ought to have been soundly flogged, before I threw him overboard, it is vexatious to think that I neglected that. But I was heated, overcome by an impulse of generosity, of humanity, as the Unitarians call it It is a pity !''

" The barret and guitar of the madman lie there in the shallop," remarked Enero, with apparent indifference, while the commander cast a glance at Falsodo, whose presence warned him of the expedition to the police office.

" The guitar ? that appears worth more than the fellow himself," returned he, after a pause,

" let it be brought up here—I know a lady who can use it."

" And the barret, besides ?" inquired Enero, in the same tone as before, while the " confiscation of the effects " of the drowned man was taking place

" The barret ?" returned Mr Tumble, while he considered it anew ; " that has great similarity with a Scottish Highland bonnet, if it did not have that long tassel on it Let it be thrown into my cabin for the present "

" If you mean to keep it on board, Señor commander, do give it to the Irishman, the fifer, who has nothing upon his head but his fiery red hair," said Enero.

" The Irishman there," said the captain, " the fellow who sprang to the assistance of the damned Unitarian ? what ails you ? I would rather take off the tassel, and wear it myself " With these words, he snatched the barret from the hands of the boatman who had taken possession of the confiscated property, and threw it into his cabin, through the skylight.

" Is there nothing else left on board, that belongs to the Unitarian dog ?" he asked, while he leaned over the bulwark and looked down

" Nothing but the wet place here in the stern, where we laid him down," replied the boatman, with an ironical smile.

" What passengers did you take on board ?" inquired the commander, further

" Only one, S'ñor Capitan" replied he, " a young Englishman from the Calle del Victoria "

" Do you not know his name ?" The boatman looked at the ship chandler's clerk, as if to intimate that he could give the required information.

" It was Mr. Robert Walker, who went on board with the captain," answered Mr Lund

As Señor Perezoso heard this name, the muscles of his face were set in motion, and he was on the point of making a loud exclamation to the captain, but his rival, Falsodo, stood close to him, and, as it were, held the fibres of his countenance " under police control " The possibility that Señora Dolores might sail with young Mr. Walker was extremely probable to the literary gentleman, but, nevertheless, he dared not take any steps to direct the attention of others to the Swedish vessel, much less to point out the authoress of the Elegies, as long as he remained under a twofold arrest, and would thus, through the intrigues of Falsodo, lose all prospect of the expected reward

" What is the name of that Swedish brig there ?" inquired the captain, without any particular object

" Nordstjernan," replied Mr. Lund, with a movement in the stern of the shallop as if preparing himself to return to the city.

The commander appeared to recollect himself for a moment, and then exclaimed, " The shallop may pass off !" and turned to the lieutenant, saying, in a surly, official tone, " I am going ashore in the cutter, with these two here. A corporal and six men for the cutter !——choose trusty men of our old stock. Codo, with the long boat, to the brig there ! ——the passengers' passports must be strictly examined, the list of their names must be taken

" I see the brig is preparing to set sail," he added, hastily, looking at the Nordstjernan.

Lose no time, and besides, ' Pronto para hacerse á la vela !" (ready for sailing) before I return "

Codo received the order, as a starving man would the order to go to the baker for bread. He girded on his sword, stuck two pistols in his belt, and jumped into the longboat, at the same time that the commander, with his two prisoners, stepped into the cutter, and pushed off from the Caza.

CHAPTER VIII

OLD AND NEW ACQUAINTANCES

THE position of Alvarez, on board the Nordstjernan, had increased to the utmost the peril which hovered over Dolores But, nevertheless, the captain did not for an instant appear unresolved to keep the unfortunate man on board, if possible, and became the more confirmed in his highhearted purpose, as the meeting between him and Hinango gave a sort of moral guarantee in regard to the person of the persecuted man

"You know this man, then ?" inquired Captain Finngreen of Hinango, when they found themselves in the cabin, and he had thrown aside his hat, for his head was warm

"I know him as a man of honor, as a comrade in the Spanish war of the revolution," asserted Hinango, " and am, besides, under an obligation of gratitude to him, for the personal attachment and fidelity which he showed to me when my life was in danger "

"Well, then," said the noble seaman, " we must counsel together, how to get him away, how we can hide him, for we may be certain of a strict visit from the man of war, there "

"That will not long be delayed," observed Mr Walker, " for the commander of the Caza, is an Englishman, who understands his duty, and a diligent servant of our Don Juan Manuel de Rosas A good deal depends upon which of the officers he sends to us, I know nearly all of them, and have often breakfasted on board "

"So much the better," interrupted the captain, " but how shall we hide this friend here ? that is the question "

A long pause of silent consultation ensued, each seemed to meditate a plan, but to hesitate in producing it, in the hope of yet finding a better

"He must not go any more on deck; a glass from the man of war may be directed towards us, and then all would be lost," whispered the captain at last. The shallop will probably be hailed by the brig when it returns Our plan must be preconcerted " He directed the last words to Mr Lund, who replied with decision, " I will hurry on deck and speak to the boatmen, who have already received some gold pieces, that class of people may be relied upon, they are sailors, and will not bring an unfortunate man to the scaffold, who has committed no other crime than that of loving his country "—He disappeared at this remark, and Captain Finngreen continued. " This opening, here, leads into a narrow space, which is connected with the ship's hold by another. I will step down with our friend,

and let him slip in as far as possible, between barrels and boxes, and will then throw buffalo hides and sails, over the cargo, leaving as much air as is necessary for him to breathe Before the opening, down here, we will stow as many trunks and boxes as will go in the space, and on these we will stand a ship's chest The great hatch in the middle of the vessel is already covered Whoever wishes to examine into this space, must go down through the little forward hatch, and will have to creep a long while before he comes to the back part, where I will, with my own hands, take measures that they shall not easily discover him Explain this now as quickly as possible to the good man, in Spanish," continued he, turning to Mr. Walker, " and I will step down to work."

" You require a pair of hands to help," whispered Hinango in his ear " I will go down with you, captain, I am not entirely unaccustomed to such games of ' hide and seek ' "

Captain Finngreen thankfully accepted the passenger's offer, and both disappeared through the opening in the floor, while Mr. Walker disclosed to the unfortunate man the measures about to be taken for his deliverance, who, deeply moved, found few words to express his gratitude for so lively an interest in his fate

Mr Lund reappeared in the cabin, with the assurance that he had arranged every thing so as to gain over the boatman, and had no doubt that his plan would succeed, he required, however, for his purpose, the mandoline and cap of the rescued man, which had already been seen on board the Caza

" My mantle, besides, floats somewhere on the stream, or is hanging to the man of war," said Alvarez, entirely agreeing to the proposal of his friend

Mr Lund now took a hurried leave, since his longer continuance on board the Nordstjernan might excite suspicion; whereupon the shallop departed, and soon drew near to the longboat of the Caza, which, under Enero's command, glided over the waves towards them

While the packing of the living contraband article was taking place in the hold of the ship, Mr Robert Walker undertook the equally important measure of drawing his clerk, Mr. Daily, into his confidence, and then speaking to Mr Rossbruck, whose name he knew " on 'change," he requested him to be cautious not to say or do any thing to attract the attention of the German doctor

Horatio, who was hastily made acquainted with all the circumstances, was charged with the difficult task of tranquillizing the old negro and Corinna, from whose anxiety in relation to Dolores, the worst was to be feared. The youth explained the circumstances to them both, with the same firmness and selfpossession which we have before observed in him, and by his example, he unconsciously worked more effectually on the agitated minds of his auditors than by his words. He had just sent Corinna to Dolores, to prepare her for an investigation which might be carried even to the threshold of her apartment, when a sailor gave the announcement that the long boat of the Caza, was once more steering for the Nordstjernan

The refugee had just been carefully stowed away, in the hold of the vessel, and Captain

Finngreen and Hinango were already upon the quarter deck, where the other passengers assembled around them, all looking forward with earnest expectation to the arrival of the visiters, while the mate ordered the crew to keep on undisturbed in their preparations for sailing, without concerning themselves about the presence of the marines on board

The captain ordered one anchor to be raised, the more quickly to make sail if the impending danger should be happily passed through. The firm confidence of the seaman in the competency of his preparations for the approaching visit, unconsciously increased the courage of the anxious bystanders, and called out from many countenances an expression of tranquillity and carelessness which was more than necessary to meet the inquisitorial look of the officer.

"It is not the same officer who commanded the longboat when it hailed the shallop," remarked the captain, examining the fatal object with his telescope; "it is a smaller man, the other appeared to me tall and slender, and this time there are soldiers there, with bayonets"

"Bring a dozen glasses and some bottles of champagne up here!" cried he, to the cabin boy, after a pause.

"A dozen glasses and some bottles of champagne!" returned the long Ottar, as the mate and sailors repeat each order by itself, as soon as it sounds in their ears. "But the coffee for the cabin is ready, captain!" added he, and he was on the point of inquiring, whether he should take a cup to the newly arrived passenger, when he fortunately recollected himself, as the instruction suddenly occurred to him, that he must act as if he had not seen any wet passenger

"Then bring the coffee first!" cried the captain, after him! "Coffee first!" returned Ottar, as if it were "square the yards," and hurried to the cook in the caboose.

Mr. Robert Walker improved this moment of suspense, to hand the envelope of Mr Testa to his fellow voyager, Mr Hinango, who appeared to have expected such a parcel, and handed over the enclosed letter to Horatio with peculiar pleasure.

Joseph Testa, a jurist of Bologna, played a conspicuous part in the insurrection for the deliverance of Italy, in the years 1830–31, had been sentenced to death, like so many other patriots, and, having escaped as a refugee, was exiled. He succeeded in reaching Marseilles from Genoa, and from thence arrived at Buenos Ayres, where he lived for some years, until he purchased land in Patagonia. Originally addressed to the house of Walker and Co, as a travelling gentleman, he had entered into a business intercourse with old Mr Walker, and was intimately acquainted with many of the patriots of the country—among the rest, with Alphonso.

Horatio received the communication of his friends, and a gleam of joy and animation flitted over his countenance, which was lighted up still more as he read further into the letter that he held in his trembling hand

"Is it possible?" he exclaimed, in a smothered voice, stepping aside with Hinango, "is it possible! you are a confidential friend of

sake, to seek out our uncle, Alphonso, and Señora Dolores?"

"I came too late," said Hinango; "too late for Alphonso, and God grant that I may have come in the right time to save Dolores! I had already heard, in Monte Video, of your uncle's arrest. My errand referred especially to him, and to one of his most confidential friends, whose name you will easily guess. His fate was yet unknown in Monte Video. I did not find him, but I saw his head on the iron grating of the Plaza de la Victoria. The danger impending over Dolores was now all the greater, I, therefore, the more readily resolved upon the journey, sailed across the mouth of the river, and arrived, partly by land, at Buenos Ayres. Testa waited for me here. The strictest caution was necessary. To save Dolores, I must appear as if I did not even know her by name. All had to be managed through Testa. The fortunate concurrence of different circumstances, united in behalf of our taking ship, the freighting of the Nordstjernan, and the individuality of the captain, to whom, until to-day, I was, likewise, personally, a stranger. Send to your friend Dolores the consolatory information of my presence on board, for her succor. I perceive that, the young negress is initiated in all the secrets of our situation, let her take these lines, with the necessary explanations, to Dolores, but bring back the letter, for these leaves must be destroyed before the officer there steps upon the vessel."

Horatio hurried into the cabin to Corinna and Achilles, while Hinango handed a piece of paper out of the envelope to Mr Robert Walker, who read it over very hastily. "I am already advertised of this by word of mouth, through our friend Testa," returned the young Briton, with a good humored smile, as he glanced over the lines, "I am rejoiced to have a companion in the defender of my 'sister' We could now get clear, if that cursed longboat was only going from us, instead of coming to us You are heartily welcome, but I must confess that our friend Testa understands managing a secret better than my father, who never suspected your reasons for embarking"

"It is all right, if you know it now, Mr. Walker," said Hinango, smiling, "and if the captain learns it from you opportunely, when it shall be necessary, when circumstances shall require me to render him any assistance as a seaman."

"All right! all right!" exclaimed Mr. Robert Walker, "the whole management of the embarkation falls on me, and the captain," added he, very low, and half aside, "has acted like a fool, to send away the two boxes from on board"

Hinango did not understand the meaning of the last words, and felt no direct occasion to inform himself further in regard to them.

"Our secret requires the destruction of these letters," whispered he, in the ear of young Walker, as Horatio returned with his, and then said aloud, "Would you like a cigar, Mr. Walker? I am going to light mine presently."

"All right! all right!" cried Bob, helping himself to a "smoking stick," while the latter stepped to the caboose and burnt the papers.

CHAPTER IV

THE VISITATION.

HARDLY were these precautionary measures taken, before the Swedish brig was hailed from the longboat of the Caza, and Señor Codo, armed with sword and pistols, sprung upon the quarterdeck, and posted six so called marines (a woful looking set) with their guns as a guard

"Are you the captain of this vessel?" inquired Codo, as Captain Finngreen stepped up to him in the gangway

Captain Finngreen, at your service!" answered the latter

"What is the brig's name?"

"The Nordstjernan!"

"Call your passengers and crew on deck, and hand me your papers, passenger list, and muster roll, but first bring out the man that you have concealed here, that you brought on board in the shallop!"

"Passengers and crew, on deck!" cried the captain to the mate "Here are my papers, as to a man on board from the shallop, I know nothing about it, it must be a mistake!"

"Come, don't make a fuss about it, captain! produce him, or I shall have him searched for, and then you will fare hardly!"

"I am sorry that I cannot obey your commands in this respect If you will give yourself the trouble of searching my vessel, I cannot prevent you"

"Four men up here, to search the brig!" cried the officer, to the men in the longboat, and as the fourth man, appeared Patrick Gentleboy, who, notwithstanding, his position as land traveller and passenger on board the Caza, had been ordered into service in the longboat, as there was no superfluity of good rowers like him on board

"Stay in the boat!" roared Codo to him, "another man here! I cannot employ you here!"

"Beg pardon, your honor! and sure I've no nade of employment, intirely! for I am 'employed to rest,' an it's quite waried I am, wid the long pull you gev me," said the Irishman, falling back into the boat, to give place to another sailor

"Arrah! and if there isn't his cloak swimming, the poor crature!" exclaimed Patrick, as he seated himself, "and there it is, fast to an anchor buoy, and the tide is agin it, and it can't make sail wid this wind, sure"

All eyes were directed to the object thus pointed out, and the captain remarked

"That certainly seems like a cloak or mantle, and may have belonged to the unfortunate man, who threw himself overboard from the shallop, just after we had picked him up"

Señor Codo appeared to reflect for a moment, doubtful of the result of his proceedings, for he had until then suspected the assertion of the boatman, and sought to attain his end by his insolent demands

"Search the brig thoroughly, the fellow must be hidden somewhere!" he now repeated to the sailors, who stood there in a state of embarrassment, and appeared not to know where they should begin, while each of them would have been glad to creep into a hole, himself, and desert.

"Let the people search the vessel, lieuten-ant!" interposed Mr. Walker, "only accompany me first to the cabin door of my sister, who lies ill in her birth, overcome by sea sickness. I hope you will take this part of the search upon youself, and not disturb my sister"

"You are Mr ——?"

"Mr Walker! Mr Robert William Walker!"

"Oh, yes! we are already acquainted;" returned the officer, who held the list of passengers in his hand, and read the name there

"At your service! I am a friend of your commander, captain Tumble, as you know How is the commander? I hope he is very well?"

"Thank you, very well!" replied the other, in a dry tone. "You are then going to Rio Janeiro, and your sister is on board? Will you have the goodness to accompany me to her?"

"I believe she is asleep, just now. I will open the door for you I give you my word, that the man whom you are seeking, is not hidden with my sister, even if he were on board"

"I believe that readily, but I must, notwithstanding, be convinced of the presence of your sister on board"

At these words, Señor Codo followed the young Englishman, who softly opened the door of the private cabin, and the officer cast a sharp look into the interior

"Let me beg you not to wake her, ladies do not feel very comfortable on board at any time," whispered Mr. Walker, while Codo saw a female form in a berth, and a quantity of female travelling necessaries, behind which no Unitarian could find room to hide himself

"Pardon me that I was obliged to institute this search Your sister appears to have been born here, she has as fine, black, curling hair as a daughter of South America," added the officer.

"Our beauties of Albion not only vie with yours here on the La Plata in their curls, but also in all other endowments," returned the young Briton, with a proud smile

"And these persons are my attendants," he remarked in a calm serious tone "My old negro Achilles and his daughter Corinna, the waiting maid of my sister!"

"Why do they weep so? Their eyes are as red as the lees of Burgundy"

"They have never been away from the shore," replied the youth, "and are as afraid of the sea, as a hen of the pond"

The officer looked around in the great cabin, and then ascended to the quarterdeck.

"Do you believe that I, as a son of the house who have freighted this vessel," said young Mr. Walker to the officer, "do you really believe that I would have suffered a deserter or Unitarian to conceal himself on board, even if such a chance had occurred? It is to be hoped that you know my father's position—his confidential relations with the ministry. This vessel goes to sea under our name. The vagabond whom the people in the shallop drew out of the water, sprang overboard again before we could determine what was to be done with him. In any case we should have sent him back to the city, as a candidate for the madhouse or the house of correction—since the name of our house would have required it."

The officer heard the young Englishman's declaration with "half an ear," but appeared partly led astray by the unrestrained naiveté which accompanied it. He now proceeded to an examination of the passengers, compared the passports with the list of names, copied the last into his pocketbook, and examined each individual from head to foot, as if he hoped to discover the object of his search under one mask or another

"Mr Rossbrück appeared on deck, and was now examined, and gave his name

"Mr William Rossbruck," repeated Señor Codo to him, "what countryman ?"

"An Englishman !" answered he, not without some embarrassment, since Mr Walker stood near him.

"You an Englishman ?" inquired Mr Walker of him, with an ironical smile, but without any asperity in his tone, which might wound him—from consideration, which the secret on board, rendered necessary, in which the other was partly involved.

"Yes sir," returned the pseudo Briton, "my brother is established in London, and has married an English woman."

"Indeed !" said the other, smiling as innocently as possible, without asking whether he was the son of his brother, and the English woman

An involuntary redness had overspread the countenance of the young gentleman from the European continent, but his end was gained, he saw that the officer had added the word *Inglés* after his name

"Your standing and profession ?" further inquired the latter.

"Gentleman !" was the answer, for Mr Rossbrück had travelled in Germany and Switzerland, and had not only observed that every saddler, or shopkeeper from England, inscribed his name, with this title added to it, in the foreign registers, but also carved it with his own hand on the Rigi and the Weissenstein.

The naturalist came next in order, gave his name, and replied to the question about his nationality.

"I am an Anhalt-Bernburger, a subject of his Highness, the Duke of Anhalt-Bernburg "

"An-halt-Bern-bur-ger," repeated the Spaniard in the service of Rosas; "what nation is that ? I do not know the flag, the country must he somewhere in the interior of Europe

"It is one of the thirty-four small nations which supply princes and princesses for the European thrones, and emigrants for transatlantic and other colonies," returned Mr. Walker, very seriously

"Oh !" said the officer, and added the question, "what standing ? what profession ?"

"Entomologist; Doctor of Philosophy, Corresponding Member of the Royal, Imperial, and Grand Ducal Academies of Science, at Vienna, Berlin, Detmold and Kniephausen; Honorary Member of the Zoological Societies of St Petersburgh and Weimar; Member of the Basle Bible Society; and Honorary Member of the British Temperance Society "

"What is the man properly ?" inquired Señor Codo, quite confused by this string of titles, a yard long, of which he understood very little.

"Set him down as a literary gentleman," remarked Mr. Walker; "that will about express all the titles."

"What !" exclaimed the little man, evidently displeased; "literary gentleman ? Literary may

do, but gentleman—gentleman ! that I object to I am no gentleman—no Englishman, but an Anhalt-Bernburger, and will not dress myself in borrowed plumes I am neither a Prussian, nor a Saxon, nor a Wurtemberger. I know my home, and the name of my reigning prince, and when his birthday comes Spell it, now, correctly: An-halt-Bern-burger, not Anhalt-Dessauer—no sow "

The officer gave little heed to this exhortation, and went on with his inspection

"Your name ?" inquired he of the passenger in the monkey paletot

"Ormar Olafur Hinango," answered the latter, slowly and distinctly

Captain Finngreen, who stood near him, appeared suddenly so surprised by the sound of this name, that it evidently cost him great effort to conceal his inward emotion After a side glance at the mate, Mr. Storhjelm, he turned his eyes to the passenger, about whom, until now, he had not been able to make up his mind, and whose thoroughly northern name he now heard for the first time

"What nation ?" inquired the officer

"Scandinavian—born in Finland "

"Finland ! that belongs to the Swedish crown, if I am not mistaken ?"

"It belongs to Scandinavia, and was united to Sweden, but fell accidentally under Russian sovereignty."

"You are, then, a Russian subject ? What standing ?"

"Formerly Russian naval officer."

"What rank ?"

"Lieutenant commander of a brig "

"What was the name of your last brig in the imperial Russian navy ?"

"KamtschatRa "

The Spanish naval officer heard these replies with a certain nautical sympathy, which seldom is wanting in the heart of a seaman, as soon as he comes in contact with his equal, either from a strange race, or from one kindred to himself.

"Commander of a brig in the imperial Russian navy, at present out of service," he repeated, slowly, while he allowed his pencil to rest on his note book, and again observed his ocean comrade and his passport

"But you carry a French, not a Russian passport," remarked he, with peculiar intonation

"I find it more suitable to my situation to travel under French protection, especially as the French language is better understood in foreign countries than the Russian," replied Hinango, with indifference

"When did you leave your brig, and the naval service ?" inquired the other

"It is six years since I transferred from the navy into the marine department, at St Petersburgh."

"And you are travelling, now, for your pleasure ?"

"I sought a southern climate for the re-establishment of my health, and have now a notion of taking a merchant vessel—of purchasing one for myself. I came here on that account, having learned at Rio de Janeiro that a Danish brig, from St. Thomas, was offered for sale here, but I came too late. It is the little brig down there," continued he, pointing to a vessel in the distance; "she had already found one to fancy her "

"I know the brig," replied Señor Codo, "you have not lost much in her, she is a heavy old box—a wretched sailer. Would you not like to enter our service? Our government would gladly give you command of a corvette. Capable naval officers, who join us, find immediate advancement."

"I thank you for your confidence," replied the Russian naval officer, "I wish to see if I can procure a Baltimore schooner at Rio de Janeiro, which I have already inspected; if that is not the case, it is possible that I may arrange other plans for the future, and return hither again."

"In any case, you will find a welcome with us," Señor Codo remarked.

Captain Finngreen, who had perceived this amicable discourse of the two officers with great surprise, as well as to his inward relief, in respect to the immediate situation of the passengers, now stepped up to a bench on which bottles and glasses were set, and said, "Will you permit a seaman, who, indeed, wears no naval uniform, to empty a glass with you, to the welfare of the Argentine republic, and to the future destiny of our fatherland—Scandinavia?"

"Scandinavia! Scandinavia! star of the north, break brightly forth!" he whispered in the ear of the passenger in the monkey paletot, while their glances encountered each other.

Himango replied to the heart's greeting by an expressive glance.

"I have some passengers, and all the crew to examine," answered the officer, "but I will by no means decline your seaman's invitation, then Viva la Confederacion Argentina! mueran los salvages Unitarios! Viva Rosas! and the Emperor Nicholas!" he cried, while he raised his glass.

"Rosas and the Emperor Nicholas," repeated the two Northmen, without particular emphasis, although mentally added, "may they come to the gallows."

"And our Queen, Victoria!" exclaimed Mr. Walker.

"Her Majesty's, Queen Vic-tories' health!" cried Mr Rossbruck in his overflowing enthusiasm as an Englishman.

"And the illustrious dynasty of the house of Anhalt-Bernburg, his Highness! and all the Princes of the Germanic Confederation! If you are going to drink, I will drink with you," said the little beetleman, taking the glass which the captain handed to him.

"And the British Temperance Society, and all its travelling members!" said Mr Robert Walker, with a smile, and looking at the little man, who did not take it at all amiss.

"I hope there is no brandy in your champagne, captain!" he remarked, in reply to this look, "for I must not drink brandy; but a glass of wine; I will take a glass of wine, upon my conscience! now! gentlemen, altogether!" and the British temperance man drained his glass to the last drop, and then said, with a satisfied air, "Captain, that was right good—I have not drank such champagne for a long time."

"I am glad that you like it," replied Captain Finngreen, laughing, and replenishing the glasses.

"But you do not drink at all!" said he, perceiving a yet untasted glass, and near it Horatio, "Why do you not drink? the wine will not hurt you?" said he.

Horatio was just expressing his thanks and excuses, as Señor Codo suddenly directed his attention to him, and then hastily looked at the list of passengers.

"You are Horatio de P——?" he now asked the pale youth, with a look that expressed all the bitterness of a raging party spirit.

"My name is Horatio de P——!" replied the young man, looking the Dictator's mercenary boldly in the eye.

"Nephew of the traitor, Marco Alphonso, who was executed this morning?" added the officer, contemptuously, "only son of the rebel Hannibal Sebastian de P——?"

"I am the son of Hannibal Sebastian, and the nephew of Marco Alphonso," replied Horatio slowly, and with decision, while captain Finngreen was unable entirely to suppress his uneasiness, and cast an anxious glance at young Walker.

"My passport lies there, near the others," remarked the youth, with assumed indifference.

"You are banished then, and disinherited—at least disinherited in part."

"You seem to know my situation," replied the youth.

Señor Codo continued the examination of the passports, while Horatio placed himself in a solitary position, on the quarter-deck, and fixing his eyes upon the shore, repeated, mentally, the following verses:

"Farewell, my dear, my native land, farewell!
From which I am exiled by a despot's curse,
Farewell! but if forever—who can tell?
Beloved soil, which did my childhood nurse,
Farewell, my country—know thy destiny!
I could for whom my kindred blood was shed,
God lives! who shall from tyrants set us free?
Though still a youth, man's woes are on my head!"

A natural connexion of ideas, or relationship of feeling, suddenly called to his mind stanza from Walter Scott's "Lay of the Last Minstrel," which Dolores had translated into Spanish with many other gems of English poetry. Modern cosmopolitism, will most assuredly consider the mental malady of the enthusiastic youth, and the like poetical reminiscences quite superfluous, as it casts aside as useless baggage the terms "fatherland" and "patriotism," and makes of man a "respectable vagabond,"who with the freedom-papers of egotism, without duty towards his nation and humanity, wanders about the world, and places his marriage bed where he makes money to buy a mattress with. Notwithstanding this, Horatio repeated to himself, as he would a verse from a psalm, the following lines:

"Breathes there the man, with soul so dead,
Who never to himself hath said,
'This is my own, my native land?'
Whose heart hath ne'er within him burned,
As home his footsteps he hath turned,
From wandering on a foreign strand?
If such there breathe, go, mark him well;
For him no minstrel raptures swell,
High though his titles, proud his name,
Boundless his wealth as wish can claim,
Despite those titles, power, and pelf,
The wretch, concentered all in self,
Living, shall forfeit fair renown,
And, doubly dying, shall go down
To the vile dust, from whence he sprung,
Unwept, unhonored, and unsung."

10

He now turned to the captain, and his friends Olafur and Robert Walker, raised the glass, and, with tearful eyes, said, in a low voice, "Our farewell to the shores of the La Plata !"

"In the hope of a speedy return" replied Captain Prinzigren taking his glass If there is a city on earth upon whose road the seaman who has once been there joyfully casts his anchor again, it is Buenos Ayres, the city of hearty hospitality and true sociability Success to Buenos Ayres ! where a man meets with men ! Will you not empty your glass with us, lieutenant, to the happy voyage of this young friend ?" he now asked the officer of the Caza, who examined the passport of the banished youth with peculiar strictness, and did not condescend to reply

The little beetleman, who had understood the words of the officer in relation to Horatio and his uncle, appeared sunk in profound reflection, and held his fourth glass motionless in his hand

"Had your uncle, the traitor, amassed no collection of beetles ?" he at length inquired of the youth, in a peculiarly cordial manner

"I, myself, have on board a little box of beetles, and other natural productions, as a remembrance of my fatherland," sighed Horatio, answering, in all good humor, the naïve beetle in jury

"Have you, indeed ? you would eternally oblige me if you would do me the favor to show them to me, when it is convenient, perhaps there may be duplicates of a singular species, which might be in the highest degree interesting to me "

"As soon as I have time, I will open my little collection for you with great pleasure," replied Horatio

"You will eternally oblige me, Mr. ——, what's your name, sir ?"

The youth named his family name, and the little beetleman drew his eye brows up towards his forehead, and repeated the name several times so inconsiderately loud, that the officer, until then sunk in thought, suddenly became observant of him, and hastily stepped up to him, "Does that name so particularly interest you ?" he roared out, the little naturalist shrunk back, trembling and terrified, answering

"The name does indeed interest me; it does indeed, it is a famous name, from Peru, although no such name is known in the whole nomenclature of beetle science, either in Europe or elsewhere "

"What was your object in coming to Buenos Ayres ?" demanded the enraged officer, and began the strictest investigation which he had yet conducted to any of the passengers

Mr. Walker, stepping up to the side of the helpless voyager, as interpreter, endeavored to explain that the German savant concerned himself very little about the political relations of the country, but only with its plants and beetles, all which the latter loudly confirmed, and added—

"Politics ! politics ! what do I care about politics ? how in all the world do politics concern me ? What do you think of me, gentlemen ? what do you particularly take me for ? I consider this examination here on board very insulting ! I protest against all such accusations; as if I had ever troubled myself with the affairs of nations, whether in Europe or in South America I do not trouble myself with Germany, to say nothing of the Argentine republic What is all such stuff to me ? I have more important matters to attend to, than politics Do you consider me insane ? Do you take me for a conspirator, that is in connexion with revolutionists, rebels, and the like fanatics I protest against all such accusations, and refer you to the Prussian consul in Buenos Ayres, who knows me, and my position, as a member of the Royal Zoological Society in Berlin, if you wish to know it "

Bob Walker hastily rendered this exculpation as literally as possible into Spanish, whereupon, Señor Codo, himself, could not keep from laughing, and appeared quite convinced of the political innocence of the savant

One of his crew now appeared with the report, that the vessel had been searched in the strictest manner throughout, and no trace of a refugee found, whereupon, he passed in review Mr. Daily, and then the sailors of the Nordstjernan, and prepared to depart

"Klar til at segla !" (Prepare for sailing !) cried the captain, and then betook himself to his post upon the quarterdeck, from whence he issued his other commands, which soon brought all into order

Señor Codo, in the highest degree dissatisfied with the result of his expedition, suppressed his confederative rage in his farewell to the captain and Hinango, emptied several glasses more of champagne at parting, while Horatio, for manifest considerations, had withdrawn himself from his sight

"A prosperous voyage !" he said, at last, to the two men on the quarterdeck, and descended the ladder into the longboat, which immediately pushed off, and was set in motion by the oar strokes of the "forced volunteers "

"I might as well have the mantle of the poor drowned crature," whispered Patrick Gentleboy, to his next neighbor, while he struck out lustily with his oar It has got wound around a buoy, or a piece of wood, and the poor drowned crature doesn't nade it at all, at all "

"Loose the mantle there from the buoy, and throw it here in the stern," said Señor Codo to one of the men in the boat With these words, he steered in the direction indicated The man fulfilled the order, and as the relic of the "infamous Unitarian" was safely taken out of the water, the longboat was brought into a direct course for the Caza, while the sails of the Nordstjernan were unfurled in the most seamanlike order

CHAPTER X

DENUNCIATION AND DISCOVERY.

IN a spacious private audience chamber of the Palace of Justice, in the Plaza de la Victoria, sat Señor Petrozo, the Chief of the Police Department, dressed in black, with a Rosas-red vest, in a large easy chair, lined with Rosas-red velvet, before a table covered with red cloth. Around him, on smaller chairs, were seated Father Ambrose, the Catalonian monk, the corpulent father guardian of the Benedictine monastery, Father Fernando, the Franciscan; Señor Borrachezo, the Commissary of Police, and Señor Domingo, the superintendent of the prison"

Señor Petrozo, a lean, decrepid old man, with deep sunken, dead looking eyes, was chewing the end of a thick goosequill, he supported his wrinkled forehead upon his left hands, and looked down on a sheet of paper, which he was laboring, gradually, to fill From the precaution of not allowing even a secretary to be initiated in so important a secret as that which had occasioned the assemblage, he wrote the protocol with his own hand.

"Viva la Confederacion Argentina ! mueran los salvages Unitarios !"* murmurred Señor Petrozo to himself, as a priest would his litany, and inquired aloud, " You abide by your assertion, reverend father guardian, that Brother Celeste left the monastery towards midnight, last evening, without attendants, and that he took no ciborium from the sacristy ? Viva la Confederacion Argentina ! mueran los salvages Unitarios !" he repeated, in the same manner as before

" Viva !" responded the father guardian, "viva la Confederacion Argentina ! mueran los salvages Unitarios ! I repeat that I have questioned, in the name of our holy Saint Benedict, the porter of our monastery, the brother overseer of the garden, and Brother Urbano, who carries the keys of the sacristy, about this matter, and that the result of my inquiries is this—that the reverend Brother Celeste left the convent about half past ten o'clock last night, through the garden gate, alone and unattended, under the pretence of visiting the condemned sinner and arch enemy of our lord and ruler, in his prison Viva la Confederacion Argentina ! mueran los salvages Unitarios !"

Señor Petrozo wrote some lines on the margin of an already finished sentence, and turned around to Señor Domingo, saying, " Viva la Confederacion Argentina ! mueran los salvages Unitarios ! And so you repeat your assertion, Señor Domingo, that the aforesaid Brother Celeste crossed the threshold of your prison, last night, at eleven o'clock, in company with a young monk of the same Benedictine order, and a negro, or mulatto, as an ostensible watchman of the monastery ? Viva la confederacion Argentina ! mueran los salvages Unitarios !"

" I repeat my declaration—Viva la Confederacion Argentina ! mueran los salvages Unitarios !" returned old Señor Domingo, while he took a heavy pinch from his deep snuff box— " that the said Brother Celeste, dressed as a Benedictine monk, with a crucifix in his hand, appeared last evening, at the aforesaid hour, in the court of the prison, attended by a young monk of the same Benedictine order, who carried the ciborium, or, at least, a massive silver chalice, covered with black cloth; followed by a negro, or mulatto, whom Brother Celeste brought in as one of the watchmen of his monastery, and who, as such, departed with the young monk,

after they had administered the Lord's Supper to the condemned, in our chapel Viva la Confederacion Argentina ! mueran los salvages Unitarios !"

Señor Petrozo again wrote some lines, and then stuck his pen behind his ear, put a pair of spectacles on his nose, and turned to Father Ambrose " Viva la Confederacion Argentina ! mueran los salvages Unitarios ! And what inference do you, reverend Father Ambrose, draw from these thoroughly contradictory declarations, confirmed by the office and dignity of the deponents, and affirmed to by oaths administered beforehand ? Viva la Confederacion Argentina ! mueran los salvages Unitarios !"

" I maintain," said Father Ambrose, rising from his seat, and sticking his hands in the sleeves of his robe, " I maintain that there has been deception practised here, wilful deception, on the part of Brother Celeste, in favor of the condemned traitor "

" Viva la Confederacion Argentina ! mueran los salvages Unitarios ! How dare you presume—— !" exclaimed the father guardian, and would have continued, when Señor Petrozo, hastily, and loudly interrupted him.

" Viva la Confederacion Argentina ! mueran los salvages Unitarios ! Silence ! father guardian, no exceptions—no interruption of judicial proceedings You maintain," continued he, turning again to the Catalonian—" you maintain ?"

" Viva la Confederacion Argentina ! mueran los salvages Unitarios ! That a deception has been practised on the part of the librarian, Brother Celeste," answered the Spanish monk, briefly, and in a decided tone

Señor Petrozo diligently went to writing again, while Señor Domingo passed around his snuff box, and bowed to every one who " made an inroad upon his property "

" Señor Borrachezo," said Señor Petrozo, " send a police officer, immediately, to the Monastery of St Bento, to produce Brother Celeste here, without delay But understand, send him a polite invitation, be circumspect ! be circumspect ! and order them to lock the antechamber as soon as the said brother Celeste has entered this room Make haste, we shall proceed no farther until you return "

" Viva la Confederacion Argentina ! mueran los salvagos Unitarios !" Señor Borrachezo, after repeating this Rosas motto, bowed to his superior officer, and departed with hasty steps

A pause followed which the president of this council of the church and state, employed not only to look at, but sound his repeater, it struck two slow, and three rapid strokes ; of course it was a quarter before three, in the afternoon ; he counted the seconds and minutes of the absence of the police commissary, who did not make them wait long for him, but soon returned and resumed his seat

" Viva la Confederacion Argentina ! mueran los salvages Unitarios !" murmured the pater guardian, and asked, as Señor Petrozo brought his pen again to his paper, " May I put a question to the reverend Father Ambrose ?"

" Viva la Confederacion Argentina ! mueran los salvages Unitarios ! Speak—ask your question," answered Petrozo

" Pardon me, reverend Brother Ambrose," said the corpulent father guardian to the guest of

---

* " Long live the Argentine Confederation ! death to the cursed Unitarians." The well known motto of the Rosas government, which appeared as many as twenty-five or thirty times, and sometimes oftener, in every number of the official newspaper at Buenos Ayres, " La Gaceta Mercantil "

his monastery, " pardon me the question ! what, in the name of all the saints ! what induced you to make such an accusation against our universally honored librarian, Brother Celeste ? to accuse him of deception, after you had only this morning, when he was yet a stranger to you, received my testimony of his worth ? what grounds have you for such an accusation ?"

" Grounds that are sufficiently convincing," returned the monk from Barcelona, and threw himself back in his arm chair, playing with his rosary, and stretching out both his feet. " Grounds of conviction—after a long interview with this venerable functionary, Señor Domingo, confirmed by much experience in similar cases in our monasteries in Europe, where so many of the ' Lord's anointed,' like this Brother Celeste, walk before the world in the ' odor of sanctity,' who, nevertheless, infected by this cursed spirit of freedom, with the blasphemous aim of so called enlightenment, are long since alienated in heart from the only saving church, and nourish under the tonsure thoughts and ideas, the dissemination of which would undermine the foundations of the church, and lead to its entire overthrow, if we did not proceed with vigor— if we did not seek to eradicate the spirit wherever we behold the poisonous blossoms of such a shoot. In the present case, the poisonous blossoms have already matured into poisonous fruit.

" I am very certain in this affair,' continued he, after a pause, although at present I can neither see into the particular object of the deception, nor the well chosen means of its accomplishment. I assert, however, that a treasonable and sacrilegious connexion existed between the librarian and the condemned, and now executed rebel, and which further examination will manifest. I honor the faith and the personal confidence of the worthy father guardian, in relation to the suspected brother of our order, but I also know this spirit of freedom, this turbulent poison of thought, which in Europe not only endangers the church, but is even brewed by those who call themselves the " anointed of the Lord," and, as the true elixir of the devil, pervades and infects the veins of the churches. The holy Benedict forbid, that the name of one calling himself a priest, should pass my lips, who, seduced and blinded by Satan, has made such use of the abominable invention of printing as even to deceive the most tried adherents of the only saving church. The holy Benedict forbid, that I should, even in the most remote manner, designate a little book which a reprobate priest, who will be justly condemned to eternal punishment, has written in the language of the ' salvages Frauceses,'* which has been published by hundreds of thousands, in the languages of all the European nations, in which a priest receives the confession of a Christian ! Verily, verily, I say unto you !" he continued, in evident excitement, rising up and leaning forward, " verily I say unto you, those curse-laden and hell-concocted words—of a so called Believer,† have occasioned greater evil in the kingdom of Christianity, than the plague in the East, and the cholera morbus in Europe, and other parts of the world , and a follower of the holy Benedict, who, under the mask of

piety and sanctity, and under pretext of his office as librarian, not only tolerates such a book inside the walls of a monastery, but, under the seal of secrecy lends it to a younger brother to read, is capable of desecrating the habit of our order—of desecrating the sacrament of the supper—by conducting a friend or confederate of the rebel, disguised as a brother of our order, into the prison and prison chapel, and thus bringing upon himself the curses of all the saints, and the excommunication of the church !" He thundered out the last words in convulsive agitation, trembling in all his limbs, and sank, as if exhausted and unstrung, back into his arm chair.

" Viva la Confederacion Argentina ! mueran los salvages Unitarios ! Of what book do you speak, reverend Father Ambrose ?" said Señor Petrozo, interrupting the deathlike silence which followed the loud speech of the Spaniard, during which the assembled associates of the temporary inquisition stared at each other.

" I speak of this," said the monk, and drew from under the folds of his robe a duodecimo volume, bound exactly like a prayer book, which he threw upon the table of the president. " I speak of this book !"

Father Fernando's countenance turned pale, he made the sign of the cross, and was just on the point of leaving his seat to avoid the neighborhood of a book burdened with so heavy a curse of the church.

" Be composed—sit down ! reverend brother," cried Ambrose to him , " I take all the responsibility upon myself."

Señor Petrozo repeated his " Viva la Confederacion Argentina ! mueran los salvages Unitarios !" stretched his bony fingers slowly and hesitatingly out towards the infectious little book, ventured, at length, to take it up, and read the title half aloud to himself—" Palabras de un Creyente—por De La Menais." " Then a priest is the author, and is named De La Menais," he said " I have heard of this book , but our lord and ruler takes no notice of books, if they contain nothing against him. He does not read himself, and does not comprehend how other men can occupy themselves with books. But, nevertheless, the book may be dangerous, especially since the church so strictly forbids it. Where did you find it ?" he then asked of the Spanish monk.

" In the hand of a young brother of our order, the day before yesterday, early in the morning, in the garden of the monastery. The sinner tried to steal away and hide the book. I succeeded in bringing him to confession, and in getting possession of it. He confessed to me that the brother librarian, whose name I hardly knew, had entrusted him with such forbidden fruit, under the condition of the strictest secrecy."

" Viva la Confederacion Argentina ! mueran los salvages Unitarios ! But are you quite certain that the young brother of our order, in whose hands you found the book, can read ?" inquired the father guardian, still firmly believing in the integrity of Brother Celeste, who stood in high consideration with him, because he was able to read, not only Spanish, but even books in several other languages.

The monk from Barcelona replied to this question by a look expressive of deprecation, and

---

* French savages.   † Paroles d'un Croyant.

almost of contempt The question, however, could only appear singular to a monk from Europe, since the ignorance and stupidity of the South American " brethren of the cloister " is universally known, and has become a by-word there, and for which they will bear a comparison with their brethren in the monasteries of any other country

" Viva la Confederacion Argentina ' mueran los salvages Unitarios !'" now interposed Señor Petrozo " The crime of Brother Celeste, which can be proved by this book, belongs to the tribunal of your order, and can here only serve as presumptive evidence that the erring Brother Celeste, who, according to appearances, has been for a long time apostate from the church, has, also, committed a crime against the state, which we shall inquire into, and then hand him over to the inquisition of the church "

Father Ambrose, by a profound inclination of the head, gave his assent to this declaration, just as a light knock was heard at the door Señor Borrachezo hurried out, but instantly returned with the information, that one of his private agents, attended by a naval officer and a third person, desired to speak to him

" If it is about the affair of the condemned, or concerning the author of the Elegies," said the Chief of Police, " you may let the people come in here , if not, they must wait until the accused Brother Celeste is examined, because you, Mr Commissary, cannot leave here until then "

' My private agent, without there, informs me that the trace of the authoress of the ' Elegies ' has been discovered "

" The authoress !'" interrupted the Chief, " a lady, then ? I am very curious to hear about it Let the people come in here "

Borrachezo opened the door, and Captain Tumble, in uniform, and well armed, stepped over the threshold, accompanied by Señors Perezoso and Falsodo As a precaution, and for his own personal security, he commanded two of his marines to place themselves inside of the door, where he found himself in an unknown port, where various " strange flags " met his eye, which appeared connected with the Popedom, a naval power which he placed in the same scale with Tunis and Tripoli

" Are you Señor Borrach - ezo, the Commissary of Police ?" asked the commander of the Caza, of the officer who conducted him into the apartment, and as the latter assented, he continued, pointing to Falsodo, " And do you acknowledge this man as an agent in the service of government, in the Police Department ?"

The Commissary of Police hesitated with the answer, for it was a singular case to be called on to acknowledge, openly, the standing of a police spy, a case which had never occurred to him before in his practice , and the open acknowledgment of a secret agent would absolutely prevent his further operations, and, of course, must serve as a dismissal from secret service. Falsodo felt that his life hung upon the confirmation of the assertion, which he had made on board of the Caza, inasmuch as he might be assured that Captain Tumble would as certainly, and more punctually, keep his word in relation to rope and yard, as the Regent in respect to the reward for the discovery of the poet, and this feeling was any thing but comfortable A tiger

glance from the somewhat brandy-red eyes of the enraged commander, during the pause which followed this question, forced out the perspiration from the smooth forehead of the miserable sinner

After a long hesitation, Señor Borrachezo, at length, replied—" If this man, under peculiar circumstances in his service, has been induced and compelled to discover himself as commissioned on the part of the police, and the confirmation of such a position, on my part, can promote the affair, I shall, by no means, decline to interest myself in the matter "

Captain Tumble, as a seaman and captain accustomed to the extreme of brevity, had expected a decisive yes or no, the ifs and ands of the police diplomatist by no means suited him , he crossed his arms over his breast, took a firm position, and said, tolerably loud—

" I wish to know, sir, whether this man has heretofore been in your service or not ?"

" In my service ?" said Señor Borrachezo, smiling

" In the service of the police ," growled the commander, as loudly as before

" If he is really in the service of the police, it will be easy for him to prove his standing, by documents," answered the commissary, and Falsodo's confiscated visage again lost its color

" This man pretends to have orders to observe and apprehend the Unitarian there, as this Unitarian stands in connexion with the friends and confederates of an executed traitor "

" Very possible !'" replied Señor Borrachezo

" While the Unitarian, on the contrary, claims to be no Unitarian, but a zealous Confederado, and offers to name the authoress of the infamous Elegies of the Plata, and to deliver her person into the hands of justice "

" Indeed ' is it possible !'" interrupted the other, a little seriously , " that would certainly be interesting ," and turned to Perezoso with the question—

" Who are you ?'"

" I hope I have the honor of being long known to you, Mr Commissary ? My name is Perezoso, I am a philologist, as you must know "

In the tone of a man of business, who seeks to despatch one after the other Borrachezo now addressed Captain Tumble, while he pointed out an arm chair to him

" Take a seat, if you please, sir ' With whom have I the honor to speak ?"

" With a naval officer of the Argentine republic, as you see," returned Captain Tumble, with considerable brevity, and threw himself into the nearest armchair—" with the commander of the brig la Caza—with Captain Tumble "

" I am rejoiced to make your acquaintance," replied the commissioner, " you are a foreigner, as I hear ?"

" A foreigner ' I, a foreigner ? you are mistaken, sir ' I am an Englishman, and you are a foreigner ; I stand in the service of the republic, and desire that you would despatch my prisoners without circumlocation, without a long introduction I require your decided declaration, whether this man has heretofore stood in the service of the police or not ? If you confirm it, I will deliver him over to your responsibility ; if you deny it, I shall take him on board, and have him hung, for he has tried to circumvent me in service—in service ! on board of my brig ! As concerns the other, the Unitarian, I will leave it with you to obtain his confession in relation to the Elegies I require, however, pen, ink, and paper, to write down my report, in case the discovery and apprehension of the poetess, or of the poet takes place, since I have indirectly assisted in the discovery, and have my interest therein, do you understand ? my interest ?"

Captain Tumble seated himself, without ceremony, at the table, helped himself to the necessary writing materials, and began his report to the Minister of Justice

The decided language of the commander, confirmed by his domineering deportment, did not fail of its effect upon either Borrachezo or Falsodo, the former appeared inclined to take part with the spy, and the latter begged permission to throw himself into a chair, for his knees trembled, and his head swam in anticipation of the hanging

" Hasten your inquiries !" said Señor Petrozo, " there are cases in which the police must openly acknowledge their secret agents, and we are here, moreover, among ourselves, entirely among ourselves Lose no time, Mr Commissary—for it is to be hoped we shall soon begin an equally important examination He looked at his watch, and listened to a noise at the door, but it was not occasioned by the arrival of the Benedictine, Brother Celeste, but by the movements of the marines whom Captain Tumble had posted there

Borrachezo now beckoned to the spy, and went with him into the recess window, where they talked together for a long while

Falsodo disclosed the tragical events that had happened to him since their last interview in the office of the superintendent of the prison, and finally asserted that he had possessed himself, in the person of Perezoso, of the secret in relation to the Elegies

" Sit down," whispered Borrachezo to him, " compose yourself," and then beckoned to the private teacher, who took the vacant place left by the spy, and made his statement, and with peculiar confidence.

" I have ascertained," he asserted, after a brief introduction," who has written the infamous Elegies, and will engage to apprehend the author, if government will place the means at my disposal, of which I must avail myself, to attain my object "

" The author ? I thought it had been a lady !" interrupted the commissary

" Whether it be a man or a woman," replied the other, is my affair, since I only have as yet found the clue If I uttered, in the presence of Falsodo, the supposition that a lady wrote the Elegies, you will readily understand such a precaution, as I suspected Falsodo's position, and wished to reserve my secret for myself."

Borrachezo appeared to find this quite in order, and bestowed the more confidence on the clever fellow

" What means do you require at your disposal ?"

" Immediate appointment for life, as custom house officer, and unlimited power, as such, to search every house and every ship, without restriction, with armed attendance," replied the private teacher

" And if you do not deliver up the author ?"

" Then I will lay down my office again, and return to my private station; but I require an immediate private audience with the Minister of the Department of the Interior, and my appointment made out, that I may proceed to the arrest I have not a minute to lose "

Borrachezo hesitated, for the originality of these stipulations, surprised him He perceived the necessity of such a post, for unrestrained search under the pretext of the discovery of smuggled goods, but he equally acknowledged the " clever fellow's " presence of mind, in thus securing to himself a permanent situation

Without losing a word, he hurried to the chief, in the red armchair, and laid before him the requisitions of the zealous Confederado

" Here are my documents in our prosecuting partnership," exclaimed Captain Tumble, "write me a receipt, Mr Commissary, stating that I have delivered up to you the secret, for which a reward is offered, enveloped in the person of the literary gentleman "

" I will acknowledge the arrival of both persons here, in the Palace of Justice, in your company !"

" That is what I require "

Borrachezo took the pen which Captain Tumble handed to him, and had hardly written and subscribed an attestation, when there was another knock at the door.

" That must be the librarian, Brother Celeste," whispered he to the Chief of Police, " I will bring him in, and then accompany Señor Perezoso, in all haste, to the Minister of the Interior, that the search may proceed as speedily as possible "

" Do so, I will, for the moment, give the librarian a hearing "

Borrachezo left the room, but soon returned with a lengthened and colorless face

" The librarian of the Monastery of St Bento, Brother Celeste, has disappeared—there is no trace of him to be found ! The habit of the order, which he wore this morning, lay upon his bed A box, purporting to contain books for the library, stood open, and half empty, in his cell No one has seen him since eight o'clock, when he went into the church, and returned to his cell through the sacristy, he has not been seen since

" A miracle ! a miracle !" exclaimed the father guardian, addressing himself especially to the Franciscan. " Did I not say so ? did I not tell you so, this morning, Father Fernando ? that he is endowed with miraculous power ? that he can double his person ? as has been proved in the prison, where he appeared in a two-fold form, and as a negro or mulatto, besides ! did I not tell you so ? And now he has vanished bodily ! vanished like a bursted fire ball on the festival of the holy Benedict "

" A half emptied book chest stood in the cell, you say, Mr Commissary ?" inquired the Spanish monk, turning away, vexed, from the father guardian

" So says the police agent, without, there, who has been in the monastery "

" What is more probable than that a complete wardrobe was in the box, and the reprobate has taken himself off through the garden gate, in disguise !"

" Very probable," affirmed Señor Borrachezo.

" Highly probable," chimed in Señor Perezoso.

"Without doubt—unless a miracle has occurred!" added old Domingo

"Is it convenient for you to accompany me now to the Minister of the Interior?" whispered Perezoso, in the ear of the Commissary of Police, perhaps I may catch two heads with one lazo, but I repeat, I have no time to lose?

Señor Borrachezo now exchanged a few low words with the Chief, and took his hat

"Do not forget to give in my report," cried Captain Tumble after him

"It shall be punctually attended to," returned the other "I will add mine, verbally, in acknowledgement of your official diligence"

"Mr Commander, I thank you for your escort to this place," said Perezoso to the naval officer, "perhaps, and very probable, I shall yet have the honor to see you on board of your brig, or even in the stern of your cutter, if you remain on shore for an hour longer"

Captain Tumble pondered over these words, and endeavored to interpret their meaning, but did not seem to arrive at the connexion of ideas, and so let the matter rest, until some official order should bring him in contact with the vice agent and future custom house officer

'Come! come! I pray you, Mr Commissary, we must hurry," said Perezoso to his companion, who, at length, answered the last words of the Chief of Police with a "very natural!" and the two departed, leaving the college, which represented Church and State, to ponder over the twofold mystery of the authorship of the "Elegies," and the flight of the brother librarian from the Monastery of St Bento.

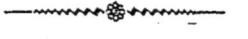

CHAPTER XI.

THE SONS OF THE OCEAN.

AFTER Captain Finngreen had given the order to prepare for sailing, and taken his place upon the quarterdeck, while the longboat of the Caza was on its way, he, in great haste, desired his passenger, Ormur Olafur, to have Alvarez come up into the cabin, and to take care to see him refreshed and strengthened, while he would bring the vessel in course

Ormur gave all the other passengers a hint to leave the deck, for he, as a seaman, knew the moment when nothing is so superfluous upon a vessel's deck as a passenger, and nothing so necessary as a captain who knows how to give his orders, and a crew that knows how to execute them

Captain Finngreen attended to the fulfilment of his duty as captain, with as much decision as if he had no passengers, much less refugees, on board, for whose heads a reward was offered According to the standing harbor laws, each captain, in Buenos Ayres, is bound to take a pilot to Point Indio, and only in case that no pilot is to be had, can he take his vessel out himself, and receive back his pilotage Captain Finngreen had asked for a pilot, but all were employed upon the river, and he would have to wait some hours, until one was placed at his disposal

From the apprehension that even a pilot might bely his loyalty as a seaman, and, observing something suspicious on board the Nordstjernan, might betray him, he the more readily resolved to go to sea without one, and, likewise, to renounce the pilotage, since he avoided appearing again in the pilot office at the moment of his departure His position was, consequently, one of great responsibility, and put in requisition the head of the seaman, as well as the heart of the man

We leave him to the performance of his duty, and betake ourselves to the cabin, whither Horatio, Ormur, Mr Walker, and Mr Rossbruck, had directed their steps, and were just then busied in bringing the refugee, Alvarez, out of his hiding place

The latter related that the sailors of the man-of-war had crept quite near to him, and nearly touched him, but from their low discourse, he had remarked that they would all have been glad to take his place, and fly from a service to which necessity compelled them "They were more afraid of finding me, than I was of being found,' said Alvarez, "for the poor creatures acknowledged their equal in me, and in misery a rough heart often feels noble sentiments"

Achilles took upon himself the office of the long Ottar, who was employed on deck, and performed the services of steward in the cabin, under Ormur's directions, to strengthen the physical force of the unfortunate Alvarez, by means of nourishment, while all, for particular reasons, avoided any reference to the circumstances of their present situation

Horatio desired his friend Ormur to lend him the "Paroles d'un Croyant" for the moment, for though he was not in a mood to occupy himself with reading, there was, on the other hand, no other book within reach, that was better adapted for his consolation The seaman hastily took out some books, to gratify the desire of the youth, whereby another little book accidentally fell to the floor, which Robert caught up Without looking at the title, he observed the heading of a chapter, "The sons of the Ocean," and excused himself to the owner for retaining it, he added, "If you will allow me, I will read it, since we must remain down here until our captain has the Nordstjernan on her course"

"Read it, if you like it," replied Hinango, and Robert threw himself into a corner of the sofa, and read attentively, to himself, the following pages·

"THE SONS OF THE OCEAN"

"As men in every station and condition of life, generally fall into particular divisions, a seafaring life admits of an arrangement of captains of vessels in three classes, distinct in their character from each other There are, among sea captains, as in all other kind of business, men who, from vocation and inclination, and others, who, by chance, or a whim of fate, follow the sea, and others, again, who enter this path, because no other remains open to them. For the designation of these three classes, particular generic names are necessary, which we shall here make use of for that purpose. There are, among ship captains, Seamen, Captains, and Skippers. The seaman feels himself born for the ocean, and however the circumstances of his childhood may shape themselves, he wears out his boy's shoes upon ship's deck, and already, while a boy, obtains, in a manner, an elevated view of life and of the world, from the main-mast top, where his commander sends him in storm and tempest. Accustomed to the adverse elements, deprived of tranquillity and comfort, his moral powers are developed by difficulties and dangers. Courage in him is moral self-reliance, and manifests itself as strength of mind, in perseverance and endurance, in self-denial and privation. This courage of the seaman has nothing in common with the so called 'courage' of the mercenary, which, for a few pence, he manifests, as the blind, willess instrument of absolute despotism. The seaman passes through all grades of service, from cabin boy to commander, and deports himself, in every station and situation, as a born seaman. The ocean is his element, the storm is his companion, the universe his world, and the central point of his life, his ship. The seaman, in his place as captain, regards the ocean as his home, his cabin as his dwelling, his quarterdeck as his promenade, his vessel as a part of his own being. The seaman on shore, longs to be on board again, as the youth longs for his beloved, all his thoughts and cares hover around his vessel. In conversation on different subjects, he is all the while thinking of his ship, and loves to talk of nothing so much as of the dangers he has gone through. He regards his vessel with pride, when he is leaving or returning to it, 'it is the joy of his stormy life.' The retired loneliness and the deep reflection which are at all times peculiar to his situation, develop in the seaman that depth of contemplation which regards life, from an elevated position, in accordance with the unconscious result of his nautical studies, which lead him into the boundless domain of astronomy. He considers our planet as an imperfect, insignificant thing, in mathematical relation, to other planets—the universe, as a region of eternal motion, where solar systems revolve around other solar systems. In such contemplations of creation, (forced upon him, so to speak, by his calling,) he feels the nothingness of earthly life, while he recognises the dignity of the human mind. As a spirit in a body of clay, he is able to fix the point of his momentary existence upon the ocean, with more or less precision. Conversant with the orbits of the stars, he arrives at the elevated degree of calculating by seconds the distances of the constellations, whose motions are as familiar to him as the course of his own ship. Through mathematical demonstration, faith becomes in him the conviction that a higher power exists, which directs the universe, and reveals itself upon our planet, through its works as nature, and governs the tides——the breathing of the ocean, under the influence of the moon, , the pulse-throb of a mysterious life. Opposed to the grandeur of the universe, worldly brilliancy appears to him in its insignificant nothingness, while his spirit feels itself allied with the all-governing primitive power, which reveals itself in the daring elevation of human intellect, calculating the rotation of the constellations. He is emboldened to follow the path of a comet—to enter the realms of infinitude , and shrinks back, with holy awe, before the impenetrable mystery of the magnet.

"The seaman treats his crew as men, and his officers as friends. Not forgetting that he has been a sailor himself, and borne the toils and hardships before the mast, he endeavors to lighten the lot of his crew. He observes a rigid fulfilment of his duties as captain, while he requires from each man equal exactitude in service, and equal respect as a man, on all occasions, and at all times. Beholding in his officers men who may become to-morrow what he is to-day, he treats them as he desired to be treated by his commander when in a similar position. More accustomed to thinking than to talking, the seaman is laconic in his discourse, and likes, least of all, the obtrusive speeches and far-fetched questions of tedious passengers, which are as strange to him as are life and the world to them.

"If accident brings him in contact with a man in whom he finds a harmony with his own feelings, whether it be with a passenger on board, or in social intercourse on shore, the polar crust of ice which encloses his heart easily melts, and his inward nature opens, under the reciprocal attraction, to unrestrained communion. Bountiful and generous, without extravagance, in his intercourse on shore, he displays his peculiar qualities in hospitality on board his ship. He relinquishes the details of providing for the crew to those whose office involves this duty, while he gives his particular attention to the supplying of pure water and sufficient stores. The instruments and charts required by his vocation, are especially dear to him, and his possessions of this sort approach to a luxury which he displays in nothing else.

"In his toilet he is neat and cleanly, as well as in his ship. He is less observant of the changes of fashion when on shore, than of the changes of the moon when on board, but takes care to have a wardrobe suitable to the variations of climate. He is fond of reading on board, and keeps on increasing a little cabinet library, though few authors serve him , he likes only those that ' sail deep,' and carry rich cargoes. At sea, he longs to see his voyage speedily ended , on shore, he wishes himself at sea again. His manly character is not only evinced in imminent danger, but more especially by his equanimity and patience in calms and other hindrances. Familiar with the dangers of the element from his youth up, he becomes equally familiar with the thoughts of death, with which he is threatened by every cloud that disturbs the horizon, and which may bring about his last hour. Although attached to life by the bonds of love and friendship, he does not fear death in the moment of danger. Feeling the responsibility which rests upon him, by having the lives of other men confided to his charge, who are placed under his unrestricted authority, and who, in a measure, are involved in his fate, within a limited space, are in dependance upon him, he maintains his firmness and presence of mind in decisive and critical moments. Without expecting miracles of a supernatural character, where human help fails, he sustains himself as man, upon the elevation of strength of mind, the greatest miracle on earth, since ' man, revealed in the seaman,' dares to brave and contend against the destructive power of the elements, 'a worm of the dust' floating upon the raging ocean, allied, as spirit, to the primitive power, whose breath pervades all nature, and roars in the storm and the hurricane

"In churchyards and burial places, we seldom see the memorial of a seaman. Born on the sea-shore—as a boy, growing up on board—as a youth, only on shore to go to sea again—the seaman, for the most part, ends his life in the waves—whereby the owners lose nothing, because ship and cargo are insured. The ocean on which his life was developed, most generally becomes his grave, and the storm which raged about his path, and proved his courage and hardihood, becomes the only witness of his death hour. But storm and tempest, raging above him in his last moments, offer no organ of renown. The murmur of the waves tells not to his people the last struggles of the seaman. No whispering of the billows in a calm, on the shore of his home, brings his last farewell to the objects of his affection, nor the last sigh, which, in the dismal distance of the raging elements, or within sight of the coast of his destination, is lost amid the howling of the storm, and the roaring of the breakers in whose companionship death embraces him. The fury of the tempest which caused his end, closing his bursting eyes in eternal night, and his heart in everlasting silence, is appeased, and has died away. The sunbeams which tanned the seaman's cheek, shines upon no flower, sparkles in no dew drop, upon the grassy sod of the seaman's grave. His fame disappears as tracklessly as the wake which he leaves behind him in circumnavigating the globe, while his name lives in the recollection of kindred hearts, which knew and acknowledged him in his worth, is a *man*. This is the 'seaman,' developed in struggles, braving every danger, in the conciousness of his mental power and manly dignity.

"Opposed to the Seaman, we see the 'Skipper.' The skipper has entered upon a seafaring life, because he was good for nothing on shore, he ran away from his apprenticeship to a tailor, and was not strong enough for a blacksmith or carpenter. He sails ten years before the mast, and at length becomes mate, because there is no one else who can write the account in a table of reckoning, and call 'stop!' when casting the log. He arrives, in twelve years, as second mate, so far that he can keep a 'log book,' and come tolerably near to the latitude by means of the sextant, when the horizon is not too uncertain, and the ship too 'crank.' At length he finds a captain who makes him first mate, and keeps him in his employ for years because he is as stupid as himself, and tolerates him because he, as mate, takes no notice of the captain's blunders. He becomes captain by his good name as a manager, by his marriage with a widow, by the caprice of an old woman, by the death of a captain, or by the influence of a sister or niece in the service of a merchant, and gets a ship, to repair the rigging, patch the sails, and take a crew over the sea on the 'starving system.' Having completely fulfilled the expectations of the stingiest of owners in this respect, a better vessel, with a more numerous crew, is confided to his 'hunger cure.' He is now captain, and remains so, and lays up money, that he may retire

as soon as possible. He traffics and cheats on board and on shore, and sells his own clothes to a sailor, in payment of his monthly wages. Instead of the 'Nautical Almanac,' he carries an old Low Dutch reckoning book. He knows nothing of the distances of the constellations, and has no acquaintance with any star in the heavens but the evening star, which once caught his attention, because it sparkled alone. He carries no chronometer, for he does not know how to use it. On a long course, he relies upon the accidental meeting of a ship which knows the longitude, and then boasts to his mate of his precision, if he has not made a mistake of more than 7°. He treats his crew like slaves, and his officers like servants; drinks a glass of wine or grog himself, but enjoins 'temperance' upon all besides, for he maintains that 'spirits and much meat are real poison at sea.' The provisions are given out to the crew in his presence, and he strictly controls the weight. If the ration is short by a half pound, he thinks it is 'very well' the next time more can be given.' His favorite seat is the water butt, upon the afterdeck, where he observes the clouds. The least unfavorable change in the wind sets his blood in a ferment, and in a contrary wind, or even in a calm, he loses his senses, he raves about like a madman, looks up the cabin boy, to find some fault with him, and seizes the nearest rope to cool his wrath upon him. If the wind becomes favorable, he chats with the man at the helm and with the cook, and promises the mate his influence to procure him a ship. In the neighborhood of the coast, he is thrown into a fever of anxiety, because he does not know where he is; he climbs the mast ten times a day, and insists that a sailor must see land where there is none. If he should, at length, find a pilot boat, he gets intoxicated for joy, gives over his ship to the pilot, and lays himself down in his berth.

On land he is a sea hero, and relates miracles of his ability as seaman. He is fond of associating with the captains with whom he once sailed before the mast, and allows himself to be treated by them at the ship chandler's and in hotels. As the time approaches for him to put to sea again, he becomes cross and discontented, for he fears the sea 'as a miserable sinner does the devil.' He keeps no mate with him for more than one voyage, and no sailor will hire with him who has ever met with any one who has sailed with him before. He cheats his owners, and knows how to save, in provisions and in the inventory, for them and for himself, and retains their good opinion of him as an 'able captain.' When he has raked money enough together, he retires to repose, and becomes a grocer or tavern keeper in the neighborhood of a harbor, frequented by sailors. He shudders at the thought of the sea, but allows himself, nevertheless, to be called 'captain,' and keeps a picture of the ship which he last had charge of, in a frame and glass. Such is the 'skipper,' as contrasted with the 'seaman.'

"The third, or, properly, the middle class, is represented by the 'Captain.' He is neither seaman nor skipper, and there is nothing further to be said of him, than that he is 'captain of this or that ship.'

"It is self-evident that the true seaman is to be found in all ranks; among the sailors of merchant vessels, as well as among the mid-shipmen of the navy, although many a skip-per and captain, favored by fortune, commands a frigate, which the seaman, who stands at the helm as a sailor, would be more capable of guiding In respect to the three above appella-tions, we remark, in conclusion, that the word ' seaman' is often used where a skipper or captain is meant, and in English may, perhaps, be re-placed by the word ' sailor ' But our notion of a good seamen is, evidently, something different from that of a good sailor, for every skipper and captain can be a good sailor—' if he has a good wind ' "

Bob Walker had finished reading, and still held the book in his hand, as if unwilling to part with it, when Captain Finngreen hastily entered the cabin, and unrolled a chart He marked his course, and called, through the open skylight, " Northeast by east ' "

" Northeast by east ' " repeated the man at the helm, and the captain left the cabin as hastily as he had entered it

CHAPTER XII

RETROSPECT AND REVELATION.

THE brig Nordstjernan had got under way about noon, and was favored by a moderate south breeze, for, like many other vessels, she sailed proportionably better before a half wind

Four and twenty hours had passed away, and as the seaman expresses it, ninety miles " had altered" in respect to the distance between her starting place, and the place where she now floated "

Many ships and fishing boats had sailed past her, in opposite direction, and this and that flag had, from far and near, saluted the Swedish colors Among the various sails, was likewise seen an Argentine man-of-war brig, easily to be distinguished as such, by the red stripe under the black bulwarks She passed up the stream, and seemed to take little notice of any merchant vessel, whatever flag it bore, while she sought to take advantage of the wind, and was probably under special instructions to reach the place of her destination as speedily as possible

The Nordstjernan had safely passed, in the above distance, by the " Bank of Ortiz" and " Point Espinilla," and was now distant from Monte Viedo some thirty miles, in the direction of " Memory Point," when the south breeze gra-dually became lighter, and at last almost died away. The weather was remarkable fine, and offered the passengers the most agreeable prome-nade, or at least a beneficial airing on deck, if their legs had not acquired the seaman's step for walking about

Excepting a cloudbank in the southwest, which appeared to contain the materials of a thunder storm, the heavens displayed the deep blue so peculiar to that zone, and through whose in-describable purity, the air itself becomes an ele-ment of invigoration, a balsam of life to the breast which inhales it.

Friendly " Cape pigeons," dazzling white

gigantic seagulls, and yet larger brownish grey fishhawks, circled around, and flew above the Swedish brig in all directions, from time to time dipping down into the " keel water," the exten-sion of which became constantly narrower in the decreasing breeze, and the foam of which constantly lessened

" We have now one thing, above all others, to fear," said Captain Finngreen, in a low tone, to Ormur, who walked at his side with hasty steps, up and down the quarterdeck, " I mean the chance that the secret police, notwithstanding all the precautions on the part of Mr Walker, may discover the trace of Señora Dolores, sus-pect her flight here on board, and that we shall yet have that cursed man-of-war after us "

" The chance is possible returned Ormur, " and not improbable, although that officer searched the ship thoroughly, and let the young lady in your cabin, pass for ' Miss Walker ' I can by no means deny my own anxiety in this res-pect, but we have at present a light wind, almost a calm, and must abide our fate "

" And the miserable brig-of-war, if she should really be sent after us, will probably have the current with her, and make her four or five miles an hour, with even as light a wind as we now have, while we lie here in a calm and contrary current, as if at anchor, that is the misfortune lieutenant "

" Lay aside that disagreeable Russian naval title," interrupted Ormur Call me Ormur, Ola-fur, or Hinango, whichever you prefer, but not by an imperial title, which was once forced upon me "

" It seems always like a dream to me, that you are here on board with me," said Captain Finngreen, who was acquainted with Ormur's position as a patriot, without having seen him personally " No one at home has heard a syl-lable about you in years We knew no more than that you were sent off to Kamtschatka, Siberia, or the Caucasus "

" And at present, hardly any one in my father-land knows where I am, except some officers of the Russian secret police, for a man in my cir-cumstances is deprived of even the last conso-lation of correspondence with friends and rela-tions I would as little write, and compromise my friends at home, by any communication with them, as a letter would be likely to reach them through the barriers of the secret police "

" You were, then, while ' Chef de Bureau' in the Marine Department, suddenly escorted to Circassia ?" asked the captain, after a pause

" I was stripped of my office and rank, de-graded to a common soldier, and placed for life in a cavalry regiment, which had taken the field against the Circassians "

" And the sole cause of this degradation, lay in your position as associate in a conspiracy ?"

" If you choose to call it so, captain, certainly, as far as an extensive, restless, and efficient con-spiracy excites the heart of nearly all the na-tions of Europe, against the present arrogance of despotism. Strictly speaking, however, the cause lay in myself, in my inward being, in my nature as a man. You know the predilection of my race, or our national talents as some call it, for poetry and music—the intellect of our people, which not even the knout of the Czar can suppress or eradicate. And Providence has also entrusted a pledge to me, of which I shall some time give an account—I mean the glowing, irrepressible impulse of the mind to express itself in the weight of word, in the great contest of our century. I was born with his impulse, it dwells within me as a part of my existence, and can as little be separated from me as I can think of being separated from myself.

It was sufficient to be known as a man, by the government, to draw upon me the closest observation of the secret police. I passed several years as an officer, in service, on board of a corvette in the Bosphorus, entered into connexion with some young Greeks in Constantinople, and indirectly into correspondence with patriots in Italy. By such means, some of my poetical manuscripts reached Paris. Promoted as lieutenant commanding of a small brig, the Kamchatka, of twelve guns, I found my station as a cruiser in the Grecian Archipelago. When the Kamschatka returned in the Neva, I was called from her, and placed in an office of the Marine Department, under the strictest supervision. The revolution broke out in Poland, and the sympathy of our Scandinavian race in this cause of humanity was closely watched in each individual man, for it was feared.

'I came under examination, respecting so called 'treasonable' correspondence with 'rebels' in Italy and France, and was then degraded. I served two years as a hussar in the war against the Circassians, and took an opportunity to go over to them, when I was wounded, and fell into their hands. I was cured, and treated by them as a man. They assisted me in my flight towards the Black Sea, and I escaped, by the way of Constantinople and Malta, incognito, to Marseilles. Italian refugees, young men of the first rank, in a social and intellectual respect, had found a temporary asylum there, and I discovered amongst them some of my early confidential correspondents.

"At the close of the year 1831, a political association, 'Young Italy,' was formed at Marseilles, whose committee, however, were expelled from France, and obliged to betake themselves to Geneva.

"The revolution in Italy was suppressed, as the Poles were disarmed, but, nevertheless, that spirit prevailed, and fermented throughout Europe, which neither chains nor dungeons were able to bind or eradicate.

"Oh! Captain Finngreen, it was an exalted epoch! It was a time, captain, in which a man might feel proud of his dignity as man—when the mind of the nations, the mind of all the nations of Europe, when all mankind, was aroused and in movement, in longing faith in a higher destiny, in faith in themselves, in faith in God!"

Ormur's eye sparkled with inspiration, he remained standing, and looking up into the azure of the heavens—pursuing a thought which, for the moment, led him away from earth! "It is a great period," continued he; "and whoever has lived through it, in open struggle against the 'confederates of tyranny, by the grace of God,' who have stained the thrones of Europe with the martyr blood of the noblest sons of all nations—whoever has lived through that time, as I have fought through it, will never more despair of the cause of humanity—never more despair of the uprising of the nations in the spirit of humanity!

"Once more, in regard to the peculiar appearances of that epoch,' he continued, as he again walked up and down with Captain Finngreen. ' I am telling you now of that spirit of truth and freedom, which we acknowledge in the history of the development of mankind, and which has revealed itself in the eternal struggle of the idea, so far as we can look back into the past. This spirit, which shone around me in its reality, and penetrated the hearts of all the nations of Europe, awaked simultaneously in Italy, in Poland, in Switzerland, in Spain, in Germany, and in France—after it had, for years before, manifested, in these nations, symptoms of its workings and strivings. It appeared in the barricades of July, in Paris, it extended from thence, arousing, as if by an electric shock, the strength of the people, through all those countries of Europe, contended, in all forms, in word and deed, with blood and life, through nearly four years, until treachery succeeded in disarming it, in Savoy, where it sought to concentrate its last forces, as the advanced guard of the future, Europe's sons, out of five nations——"

"Now, captain, about what time shall we be at Rio de Janeiro?" inquired the large beetle man, as he stepped in between Ormur and the captain, and stuck his hands into the wide pockets of his inexpressibles.

"When we shall have the 'Sugar Loaf' behind us, and pass the fortress of Santa Cruz," returned the captain, with a side glance at the seaman next him.

"I knew nearly as much as that myself," said the savant, who appeared a little embarrassed at having uttered the inquiry. "See there! there comes our young English woman, she has made her appearance at last!" he exclaimed, as Señora Dolores, in a black mantilla, led by Corinna, ascended the cabin steps, and took a seat in the shadow of a sail.

"She looks as if she was a little sea-sick. Advise her, captain, to take some gammon, with mustard, and then a little 'schnapps' after it. That is a good preventive of sea-sickness, I know that by experience."

Horatio and Robert Walker approached the ex-lieutenant of the Russian navy, to conduct him to Dolores at her request, in consequence of the written introduction of Señor Testa.

Dr. Meibold was curious to listen to the salutations of the voyagers, and was following at their heels, when Horatio's presence of mind, supplied him with a means of attraction to draw away the German savant for an instant.

"I will now show you my collection of beetles, doctor!" said he, "if you will accompany me to the cabin."

"With the greatest pleasure," replied the zealous entomologist, who almost leaped for joy, and hurried to the cabin steps, without casting a glance back at the "young English woman," and the two passengers.

Dolores gazed long, with a penetrating look, upon the "friend," who had been led to her, by so mysterious a union of events and of internal relationship, as the companion of her fateful voyage. Incapable, for the moment, of finding words by which to express her excited feelings, she held out her hand to the Scandina vian, and while she sought for utterance, she seemed to derive support and consolation in her grief, from the consciousness that a spiritual association existed in a distant part of the world, whose confederates, striving after the same goal of the future, in the spirit of love which animated her, also found the strength to act, to endure, and to suffer

"I hear, through Horatio, and indirectly through our friend Testa, on what mission you have come to us," she began, after this silence "I thank you for the sympathy and the sacrifices, which you offer to the cause of my fatherland, may your own consciousness say more to you, than these weak words are able to express

"Horatio has explained to me that you brought particular communications from our associates in Europe and in Monte Video, to two of our countrymen, both of whom—are no more !'" She ceased for a moment, pursuing the contemplations which this retrospect awakened in her, and then continued "The most confidential colleague of my friend, Alphonso, became a sacrifice before him, to the bloodthirsty tyranny which the foreign journalists (in the pay of Rosas) praise as a mild and liberal government Alphonso followed him——" She broke off again, evidently struggling with herself, and then cast a glance at Robert Walker, who had gone aside some paces, and leaned over the bulwark, from the discreet desire of not disturbing the interview

"Did you not learn yesterday morning, from our young friend, Mr Walker, the particulars of Alphonso's death—of his last moments ?'"

"I observed," returned Ormur, "that Señor Testa, spoke to Mr. Walker, in all haste, at the moment of embarkation, as he handed him the letter for me——" He hesitated to proceed further Dolores manifested, by the expression of her countenance, that she had attained sufficient firmness to receive the particulars of the execution, for which she had, in so elevated a spirit, sought to prepare her beloved

"Mr Walker will communicate to you, what Señor Testa whispered in his ear," said Ormur "Every inquiry on his part, after the condemned, would naturally be suspicious He appears, however, to have made out to learn that Alphonso——" He stopped again

"Proceed—you see I am composed"

"He appeared, however, to have learned that Alphonso left the earth with the strength of mind which was expected of him He had requested the 'favor' of meeting his death with unbandaged eyes The moment of his departure to another sphere did not, at least, aggravate his physical sufferings—many balls struck him, and one the heart"

"The heart !'" repeated Dolores, with an emphasis which no words can express, and although, she had thought herself sufficiently strong to receive this last account of the end of Alphonso without agitation, nevertheless, the bloody picture of the martyr's death appeared to have made a painful impression upon her soul Grief overpowered her Her countenance became deathly pale ; the convulsion which seized her heart, seemed to vibrate through her whole being, her lips quivered, but spoke not, and her tearless eyes were fixed on vacancy.

Ormur again found himself, as before with Horatio, in the most painful situation, agitated by compassion for suffering, for which he had, at his command, no expression of sympathy

After some moments, Dolores, by the exertion of all her moral force, succeeded in overcoming the anguish that pervaded her spirit, she looked calmly in the face of Ormur, and said "You are on a mission to my people, and were sent to Alphonso—it would be a consolation to me—a powerful consolation, if you would transfer to me the sacred trust with which our associates in Europe and in Monte Video honored Alphonso—I believe I have a right to make this request"

"As valid as is your right, so sacred is my duty to make the revelation to you" With these words, Ormur took his seat on the bench next to Dolores, that he might be able to speak lower, and said "I will, at another time, take the liberty of communicating to you a review of the internal movements of Europe, of latter years, in case many particulars should be still strange to you. I say internal movements, as the spirit of progress for the deliverance of the nations, as opposed to despotism, works, as it were, in subterranean intrenchments, and the faithful, who rely upon the uprising of mankind, must assemble in catacombs, as was done at the time of the dissemination of Christianity, to escape secret and open persecution After the people of Europe were roused anew to the consciousness of their sacred rights, by the overthrow of the legitimacy in France, in the year 1830, there succeeded, as you know, a *quasi* legitimacy, whose operations sought to suppress the cause of the people, by means of treachery, in France, as well as in the other countries of Europe

"The nations, however, were aroused, and fought, but the treachery of particular men, who formerly wore the mask of patriotism, and here and there usurped the rulership, sustained by the despicable venality of their fellows in all classes of the struggling nations, undermined the cause of freedom, and 'peace was re-established in Poland,' as in Italy and France, and only in Spain, until the present time, do the people contend against absolutism and the Inquisition—to find, nevertheless, under the control of the 'holy alliance' of legitimate and *quasi* legitimate powers, the much praised 'just medium,' which offers power to despotism, and liberty to the people, upon a piece of paper called a 'constitution'

"Men from five nations, for the most part condemned and banished on account of their patriotism, sought an asylum in France and Switzerland, drew together, led by the spirit which animated them, and united to make a decided armed insurrection, for the manifestation of the idea of the future, of the deliverance of Europe, of the establishment of an offensive and defensive union of the nations of Europe for mutual support, upon the basis of nationality, in the spirit of humanity.

"The association, 'La Giovine Italia,' has existed since the year 1831 The Italian refugees and exiles, particularly numerous, and more or less penetrated by the exalted spirit which strives to confirm words by deeds, lingered, for the most part, in Switzerland and in the south of France, and sought from thence to maintain their connexion with their country. The struggle in Italy was resolved upon and prepared Polish, French, and German refugees, more or less numerous, united with the Italians in Switzerland, and the Polish, German, and Spanish refugees, confederated in France

"Scandinavians, also, but few in number, and without claiming to represent our nationality, made themselves known to the exalted society which, at that time, had a spirit, but not a name

'The city of Chambery, in Savoy, was to have been our Jerusalem, from whence we hoped to send forth our gospel of freedom, written with the blood of martyrs, to all the nations of Europe The insurrection was fixed for the 12th of November, 1833, and we considered that we should be favored by the time of the year, as it would be difficult for the troops of legitimacy to pass the Alps and smaller mountains around us, whose valleys and gorges would make our defence more easy - at the same time, the Austrian troops stationed in Italy, would infallibly have put themselves in motion against us, vacating the garrisoned towns, and thereby giving the Italians an opportunity to rise

"The committee of 'La Giovine Italia,' under the presidency of Mazzini, (whose name and position are known to you,) was stationed at Geneva, in Switzerland

"Military prejudices, which prevail in the armies of all monarchies, had forced upon us, as General in Chief, a man who bore a great name in the gazettes, although in his office, as general in Poland, he had already conducted himself very ambiguously This was Ramorino, born in Savoy, and formerly a French cavalry officer He was then in Paris, and was to arrive in Geneva on an appointed day He came not! and sent a so called adjutant to us, with the excuse, that he hoped to gain a still great number of associates in France, and postponed the insurrection to an indefinite time There exists a work in the French language, which gives an explanation of the delay, as well as of the commencement and issue of the expedition * I will give it to you in Rio de Janeiro.

"We waited for Ramorino's determination with painful expectation. He had received from the treasury of our expedition an advance of 40,000 francs, and was amusing himself in Paris, sufficiently notorious as a bon vivant, and a passionate gambler

"You will find it conceivable that the committee of 'La Giovine Italia,' did not begin the insurrection without Ramorino There are relations and circumstances, however, in such associations, which cannot be investigated during the lifetimes of many individuals who were involved in them A strong protest against the nomination of the chief, was by no means wanting, but a great part of the considerable contributions to the expedition, which amounted, in all, to nearly two millions of francs, was sent from Italy, under the express stipulation that Ramorino, should take the command, since his newspaper reputation secured to him the necessary influence and consequence, especially amongst *the military."*

---

* Memoires sur La Jeune Italie, et sur les derniers evenemens en Savoye, Par Harro-Harring, 2 vol. Dijon et Paris, chez Derivaux, 1834.

Mr Robert Walker, who stood at a distance, and evidently was not intentionally listening, had accidentally caught the sound of the words, "two millions," without any connexion with the rest, and, from commercial instinct, could not help looking around, as the sound of such a sum had electrified him for the moment, it was the most interesting thing that he had ever heard from Ormur's mouth; he recovered himself, however, as suddenly, and again looked over at the waves

Ormur continued "After long delay, the day of insurrection was at length appointed, for the last of February, 1833 We endeavored to concentrate our associates in Switzerland on the Lake of Geneva, and to advance from Grenoble, in France, towards Pont d Echelles, in the mountains of Savoy Our number was nearly 800, mostly men and youths of the higher classes, well armed and equipped

"O, Señora!" he sighed, after a pause, "those days of insurrection were the most fatally eventful, but the most glorious days, of my desolate life The present moment, however, will not permit any lengthy account of them All the difficulties which treachery and intrigue could lay in the way of our enterprise were adapted, with the nicest calculation, to lame our strength, to nullify our plans, and to suppress a struggle, the consequences of which would, undoubtedly, have broken the neck of despotism in Europe, have dismembered Old Europe with its bloodstained throne, overthrown the prerogatives of tyranny, and called to life a Young Europe from the ruins of the sweat and blood drinking monarchies— a Young Europe that would have found its associates in the young unions of the United States of the transatlantic world

"The princes of Europe trembled, and their diplomatists hid themselves in secret conferences, they recognised the danger, and it was necessary to overthrow our work, but this overthrow could not be effected by an open contest, for in the armies of many monarchies lay the germs of revolution, as in the nation itself, and Old Europe trembled at the thought of our entrance into Savoy We could only be disarmed by treason "

"And you advanced to Chambery?" asked Dolores, hastily, with eager anticipation.

"Not without shame must I answer—No," returned Ormur, and he related further, with increasing animation. "I have seen nations at war, and survived the destruction of battles, but never did I witness such an appearance as that!

"The spirit, which, in spite of all the treachery, favored our insurrection, appeared like the uprising of the united strength of the European nations The banner of 'La Giovine Italia,' bore well known inscription, 'Libertà, Equaglianza, Umanità ' "

"The same device which Monte Video has adopted," interrupted Dolores

"The same," continued Ormur "One of the noblest ladies of Italy, one of whose sons ended his life in a dungeon, and whose two others marched in the advanced guard of our corps, had embroidered this banner with her own hands, the banner was unfurled in Savoy, and treachery—treachery undermined our enterprise

"I saw a phalanx with the flowers of the youth and manhood of five nations, in their glittering columns, and my heart was near to bursting, but the treachery was made more easy by the spirit of resignation, and sacrifice, and republican self-denial, which inspired each individual among us

"None of the spirited leaders of the cause of the people were willing to assume a rank, the noblest men of each nation entered the columns as simple volunteers Men who had singly sacrificed from thirty to forty thousand francs on equipments, marched with their muskets in the ranks of the advanced guard, and left their equipages to follow the rear guard, for the service of the wounded

"Mazzini himself. the founder and chief of the Association of 'La Giovine Italia,' entered the columns, and betook himself to an outpost of the advanced guard But this republican unpretendingness assisted treachery"

"The self-denial and absence of pretension was, undoubtedly, exalted in itself, a singular phenomenon of our time, in opposition to the spirit of many republics, in which self interest seeks after office, and *parvenues* press forward to the highest stations," observed Dolores

"Excuse me for to-day," continued Ormur, "from the details of that night at the foot of Mont Blanc, when the watchfires of the betrayed cause of the people blazed upon the hills—when our numbers were increased by men and youth from far and near—when women sent us weapons, and children brought us the munitions of their fathers

"The cunningly planned and well adapted treachery, which had been weaving for three months, rendered our enterprise impossible, the half of our columns were detained in Switzerland, so also in France. False orders of the infamous chief, even, divided our strength in Savoy. And he himself fled—fled like a coward, for he jumped out of a window at the moment when the bayonet of vengeance, which should have pierced him through, went into the wall near him He fled, and with him confidence from many hearts We returned back to Switzerland, And the same fate overtook the column near Pont d'Echelles Their chief, Volontiere, was wounded, taken prisoner, and soon afterwards shot at Chambery."

"Shot! like Alpnonso," sighed Dolores, and a long pause ensued

At length, Ormur continued "A new association has, however, grown out of this enterprise, the spirit of which has extended throughout Europe, and, flying across the Atlantic ocean, has shown itself on the Rio de La Plata. The founders of this expedition, betrayed and sold, wandered about in Switzerland, while hundreds of its numbers were apprehended, and exiled from the continent to England, the Botany Bay of the Holy Alliance

"And many of these men, of different nations, united themselves in an association for the future, at Bern, in Switzerland, founded upon the bloody ruins of the other destroyed edifice—the 'Association of Young Europe'

"For your perusal hereafter, and for communication to Horatio, I hand you, as a historical document in my relation, our 'Act of Fraternity,' and, at another time, will disclose to you upon what particular mission I have come to South America the second time" With these words, Ormur delivered to Dolores an envelope, just as Dr Merbold appeared on deck with Horatio

"Be sure you do not forget the name," said the entomologist *Simplex Merboldensis*—Simplex Mer-bol-den-sis' I have called it so, because it appears extremely simple, and because I discovered it, and my name is Dr Merbold, as you know I have already written down my report to the committee of the Society of Natural History, in Berlin, that I may send it from Rio, and you will know, by and by, from the newspapers, what a sensation my discovery makes it is one of the most important beetles, and the most interesting discovery in the entomology of our century, of that I am firmly convinced"

With these words, the savant followed Horatio, who had only, with the greatest effort, separated himself from Dolores and Ormur, whose discourse was equally interesting to him, as his new discovery was to the little beetleman

"Sit down by me, Horatio, and let us read together a document, the origin of which I will afterwards explain to you," whispered Dolores to the youth, and both now gave their undivided attention to the perusal of the "Act of Fraternity of Young Europe"

YOUNG EUROPE

LIBERTY—EQUALITY—HUMANITY.

Act of Brotherhood

We, undersigned, men of progress and liberty, believing in the

Equality and brotherhood of men, and the Equality and brotherhood of nations ·

Believing also ·

That the human race is destined to advance in a course of continual progress, and under the empire of the universal moral law, in the free and harmonious development of its powers, and the accomplishment of its mission in the universe.

That this can only be effected by the active concurrence of all its members in free associations

That free associations can only exist among Equals, since all inequality implies a violation of independence, and every violation of independence impairs the freedom of concert.

That Liberty, Equality, and Humanity, are equally sacred that they are the three necessary elements in every satisfactory solution of the problem of society and that, wherever any one of them is neglected from regard to the two others, the attempt to solve this problem must prove a failure

Being satisfied

That although the objects which the different branches of the human race aim at, are necessarily the same, and the general principles which direct their progress essentially similar—there are, nevertheless, a thousand different ways by which the common purpose may be effected

Being satisfied.

That each man and each nation has a peculiar mission, in which individuality consists, and through which it concurs in accomplishing the mission of the race in general :

Being satisfied. finally :

That associations of men and nations ought to combine security for the full accomplishment of the individual mission with certainty of concurring in that of the general mission of the race

Strong in our rights as men—strong in our consciences, and in the duty which God and Humanity impose upon every one, who is willing to devote his arm, his mind, his whole being, to the sacred cause of the progress of nations

We have formed ourselves into national associations, free and independent of each other, intended as the germs of

Young Poland, Young Italy, and Young Germany

Having met together in council to promote the general good, with our hands placed on our hearts, and in full confidence of a successful result, have agreed upon the following declaration

I

Young Germany, Young Poland, and *Young Italy*, republican associations, intended to effect the same general object, and having a common belief in Liberty, Equality, and Progress, hereby unite themselves into one brotherhood, now and forever, for all purposes belonging to the common object

II

A declaration of the principles that constitute the moral law, as applied to nations, shall be drawn in common, and signed by the three national committees It shall specify the belief, the object, and the general course of proceeding of the three associations, and no association can act otherwise than in conformity to this declaration, without a culpable violation of the Act of Brotherhood

III

In all matters not concerning the declaration of principles, and not of general interest, the three associations are severally free and independent of each other.

IV

An alliance, offensive and defensive, is hereby established among the three associations, as representatives of the nations to which they respectively belong , and each of them shall be authorized to claim the aid and cooperation of the others in every important enterprise for the promotion of the common object

V

The assembling of the three committees, or their delegates, shall constitute the Committee of *Young Europe*

VI

The members of the three associations shall regard each other as brothers, and discharge towards each other the duties belonging to that relation

VII

The Committee of *Young Europe* shall agree upon a badge to be worn by the members of the three associations, and a motto to be placed at the head of the proclamations.

VIII

Any other nation, which may desire to unite in this alliance, may do so by agreeing to and signing, through its representatives, the present Act

Done at Berne, (Switzerland,) April 15th, 1834
(Here follow the signatures)

CHAPTER XIII

THE PURSUIT.

Four and twenty hours more had passed over, and the fatal calm had only been occasionally interrupted by the variable caprices of the airy element, while the current in the distant mouth of the basin, round Point Piedras, was more like a whirlpool, which, delayed the voyage, rather than favored it

Under such circumstances, the Nordstjernan had altered her distance very little, and had only approached a few miles nearer, to the coast of Monte Video, whose mountain top had now become visible, and fixed the attention of the passengers, if only, as land, interrupting the uniformity of the voyage.

Dolores, however, as well as Ormur, Horatio, and Alvarez observed, with other sentiments than those of curiosity, a country whose history assumes so important a page in the annals of nations, in the sacred book of mankind

"Men have their sacred missions here on earth,
And nations have their mission—men there be,
Impressed with self consciousness of strength,
In freedom s path, who break the people s way.
And there are nations, by their station urged,
And through their sad and dreadful fate impelled,
To take the lead in mankind's bloody path
Of reformation—patterns to the world,
Loosing themselves from slavery and disgrace
Only by union and the consciousness,
Of nationality in freemen s hearts,
Can any nation raise itself in strength
Long as the world endures this truth shall stand.
Rob nations of their nationality,
The high consciousness of spiritual strength,
And down they sink to vilest slavery,
Without the power to act as freemen do,
in manhood's bonds, and in the fear of God."

We distinguish Monte Video by the above lines, the South Americans of la Banda Orientale, of Uruguay, their position and their struggle in our century , and even from the beginning of our century up to the present time

We admire, in reading the annals of antiquity, the strength and opposition, the courage and sacrifices of the Maccabees, and the Lacedemonians, in contending against an external foe. And many nations of the earth, who glory in their civilization and freedom, appear little inclined to acknowledge a nation which lies nearer to them in geographical position, than any other nation in historical, a people whose blood moistens the shores to which every day heavily freighted ships from different parts of the world. Are wafted, and for half a century have taken home with them superficial intelligence of the uninterrupted struggle of this people, " which disturbs commerce, and interferes with mercantile speculation "

As in Asia, the Circassians have contended for thirty years against the lust of conquest of a barbarian despotism, which, under the Jesuitical pretext of " civilizing the people," endeavors to introduce the knout there, in a savage war of extermination, and to subjugate the spirit , so have the people of the *Banda Oriental* struggled, for nearly half a century, against the asso-

---

* Moses zu Tanis, von Harro-Harring. Second volume of his works, New York edition.

ciated despotic power of two hemispheres, first freeing themselves from the Spanish yoke, then against the uninterrupted assaults of English lust of conquest, as against the monarchical pretensions of Brazil, and against a tyrannic power, for which the history of the nations has, as yet, no name, since, in itself, it stands without example—a people governed by a murderer, who, long ago, in the judgement of sound reason, deserved death by the hand of the executioner.

Much has been written and prated, by diplomatists and political tinkers, (with and without orders in their buttonholes,) upon the right and the system of the intervention and the non-intervention, of legitimate and *quasi* legitimate powers, in the contest of one or another nation, against outward enemies, and against the despotism of the Church and State within their boundaries, and nation upon nation contends for its most sacred rights, and sheds its noblest blood, and the question of intervention is decided by the " right of the strongest," through the brutal power of tyranny

If we consider the struggle for freedom of the South American people of the Banda Oriental, we do not see a petty strife, induced by boundary questions, as the archives of a decayed viceroyalty designate it, nor some shepherds' feud, about wells and pastures for their flocks The contest appears to us as a " hereditary war" on the part of a usurper, who first learned to read and write when the anarchy made use of his scourge and butcher knife in the war of extermination against the natives of the country, against the hardy tribes of the pampas of Patagonia, and against the " rebels" of the Banda Oriental, which proudly disregarded the documents of the archives of the Spanish viceroyalty.

We behold, in this exterminating war of the " usurper from the stable," the " principle of the antiquated letter," which was, perhaps, originally new to his ignorance, but which, in the history of national development, is sufficiently known, and repudiated with sufficient contempt

The usurper fights, with the scourge and axe, to sustain and reinstate a confederation of the Spanish hereditary provinces of La Plata, after the letter of the archives and the provisionary statutes, without regard to the mighty demands and progress of the spirit which tumbles into a heap crowns and thrones, together with their archives, and breaks its way to the goal of ennoblement, from century to century

Monte Viedo contends against the usurper, and contends at the sacrifice of life, for the principle of freedom as the basis of all political, moral, and religious development, for the idea of unity as an independent state in itself, and for the unity of all the South American States under the form of the United States of South America, in the spirit of humanity, as opposed to the letter of the archives of the United Provinces of La Plata, under the axe of the usurper

This is the position of the two foes This is the war of extermination and of conquest of the Gaucho, the war of despair of Monte Video, of the Unitarians of South America And this struggle of Monte Video against enemy upon enemy, now the Spaniard, now the Briton, now the Brazilian, now the mercenaries of Rosas—this struggle of a people, so small in numbers,

during half a century, for a principle, for an exalted idea, is unexampled in the history of nations, and of all times, from the graves of the last of the Maccabees, up to the present day *

" Monte Video !" exclaimed Dolores, in the circle of her-travelling companions and spiritual associates, and stretched her arms towards the blue promontory, which rested like a cloud upon the horizon. Soon, however, she pressed her right hand to her forehead, and depressed her head, while she supported herself by the bulwark, and sank into a revery, the feelings which gnawed at her heart were incapable of rhetorical effusion She sank into contemplations, similar to those which have just been presented to us, and then, looking into the future, at length sought words for the alleviation of her griefs, and said, in a low voice, turning to her surrounding friends, "How singularly that mountain projects, isolated, as if placed by nature, as a significant waymark of navigation, at the entrance to the river La Plata, and so does Monte Video stand forth, as a state, as an isolated, separated people, as if appointed by Providence, as a waymark of civilization—in the pure sense of the word, as a waymark to the nations of the earth, who contend for their sacred rights Monte Video rises above the blood polluted waves of the age, an eternal example of the power of the people, of steadfastness, and of resistance to conquest and subjugation"

" I hear you have been in Rio de Janeiro," said Mr William Rossbruck, interrupting the observation of the poetess of La Plata, as he approached the group with Mr Robert Walker, and addressed himself to Ormur Olafur, in his German dialect, " do you know, perhaps, one of your countrymen—I believe he is from a Russian province, like yourself—a certain Louis Closting? He is quite a celebrated man, and is shortly to become Brazilian *Charge d'Affaires* somewhere in Europe He is genealogist, or geologist, or mineralogist, or something of te sort"

" Louis Closting !" repeated Ormur, irritated by this interruption, " I have heard of the man, although he was not in Rio at the time of my arrival I have known one Louis Closting from my youth."

" Indeed ! I am very glad of tat," continued Mr Rossbruck, " ve are interested in great business negotiations vit him, respecting extensive colonization, in an undertaking vich

* The humane institutions of the Banda Oriental, in opposition to the self will of the despotic sovereign of Buenos Ayres, have been in existence since the year 1830, and are as follows
"An elective gobernador (president) and two chambers, the one nine senators, and the other twenty nine representatives
" Freedom of religion and the press Freedom of speech and of protest Education at the expense of the government Trial by jury. Public justice A citizen militia in all the nine departments of the republic No standing army. Only a garrison of five hundred men in the capital Code Napoleon as the law, with alterations in relation to local circumstances Each foreigner who settles in the country, has the privilege of citizenship Who ever is inclined to build there, receives sixty acres of land free from all taxes, for twenty years, and provisions, free of expense, until the next harvest After the expiration of twenty years, a yearly tax of ten dollars at the utmost, is imposed upon the sixty acres Abolishment of the slave trade and of slavery. Freeing of negro slaves, with indemnification on the part of the state to their former owners, etc., etc.

vill bring millions in circulation, a colony upon Santa Catharina '

Mr Bob Walker had followed the *pseudo* gentleman from curiosity, as he had hastily advanced to Ormur, and could not suppress a secret smile at such mistimed talkativeness, but he suddenly became extremely attentive

" Indeed!" replied Ormur, to this undesired communication ' Then I hope that we do not mean the same person, or that Mr Louis Closting his put on the new man' since his departure from the North "

' How so?" inquired the young merchant, apparently surprised at this remark

' The only question is, as to the identity of the person of whom we are both speaking About Louis Closting, whom I knew but too well in my youth, you can obtain sufficient information from a man whose address I will give you, in case you desire it "

" I thank you very kindly, beforeward, for your obligingness," interrupted Mr Rossbruck ' You can very well understand how important it must be to our house to obtain information respecting Mr Closting s former standing in Europe, especially ven te undertaking, of vich he has communicated to us te plan, vill bring some millions in circulation "

" I can, certainly, very well imagine such a circumstance,' rejoined Ormur, " but I still doubt the identity of the person of whom we speak "

" May I beg you to tell me, vitout circumstances, vat you have learned of te character and honesty of te Louis Closting, hom you mein Excuse te question, I have a peculiar interest in ts ting, especially as it ——"

" Concerns some millions," added Robert Walker, with a peculiar glance at Ormur

" I have no occasion to make any secret about facts in relation to a man who very little interests me, and whom I should not wish to consider among my acquaintance,' replied Ormur

" Did he play some tricks in his yout?" inquired Mr Rossbruck, evidently suffering from curiosity, until he received the expected information

' When I arrived in Rio de Janeiro, two years and a half since," related Ormur, " I found there an acquaintance of my youth, a certain Henry Fitz—an optician, and teacher of astronomy—whom I had been very fond of when a boy, he was brought up by a relation, in my native place In after years, I met him, here and there, in foreign countries The first word, so to speak, that I heard from him in Rio de Janeiro, was the name of Closting, since he probably thought it would be very interesting to me to hear something about him "

" And vat did he tell you about him, if I may inquire ?"

" That he lived in Brazil, and, to my question, who this Closting was, whom I had nearly forgotten, he reminded me of a certain prank, 'à la Cartouche,' as he called it, which Mr Closting had played in a Northern capital."

" I am verry curious "

" Mr Henry Fitz asserted that this was the same Mr. Closting who once disguised himself as adjutant of his king, and as such, presented a forged requisition for a certain sum in the war department, or upon some officer of the royal treasury, received the money, and took himself off with it "

" Vat do you say ? can tat be te same Mr Closting, he is negotiating vit our house, in respect to an undertaking tat vill bring some millions in circulation ?"

"On that point, you can receive ample information from the person I spoke of, in Rio de Janeiro, whose address I will give you If he should have changed his residence, it will be easy to inquire it out, for he is sufficiently well known "

" As an honorable man, I presume ?" interrupted Mr Rossbruck

" He is a man of great talent, but poor as a church mouse, and from thence it may easily be inferred that he makes no money at the expense of others So far as I know him, he is incapable of trickery, or deceit, but he is improvident in the highest degree, and does not know the worth of money, like a merchant He lived a long time in Paris, is more of a Frenchman, than a Scandinavian, and likes to pass for a Frenchman "

" I shall be exceedingly tankful to you, if you vill give me his address," said the young gentleman, taking out his letter case, ' tat it may not be forgotten, if I may ask it ' Ormur took a silver pencil, which was suspended from his neck, and asked permission to write the address of his countryman with his own hand, it was granted, and Mr Rossbruck then went into the cabin, to his writing desk, sunk in profound reflections upon the important discovery which he had just made

" That young man, may be the representative of a mercantile house," remarked Mr Walker, " but he is not a ' merchant ' If such a colonization project as he speaks of, is not yet decidedly concluded, this young man may be sorry that he has babbled here, what was by no means necessary Henry Fitz, optician, and astronomer,' said he to himself, in a low voice, with a stolen glance at Ormur, while he drew out a miniature memorandum book, and took into his hand a heavy gold pencil

" You desire to get to the windward of this gentleman's house, it seems," said Ormur, with a smile, in reply to the glance of the young Englishman

" I only wish to endeavor to give a sample of my abilities, as a man of business, to make my debut as a merchant

" I wish you good luck, Mr Walker," rejoined the Northern marine officer," if you know how to handle your instruments, and as I have little doubt, understand your trade a little better than our fellow voyager, you may easily cast anchor before the intended colony, some hours sooner than the other, and it requires no more time than that to get the start of any one, in order to plant your British flag any where "

" If this Mr Closting is really so thoroughgoing a fellow as his ' youthful pranks' would lead one to expect, remarked Mr Walker, " I do not doubt but that, after his long residence in the country, he may be very well able to give good counsel concerning colonization and the like, especially as I hear that he is a geologist. Perhaps he has even discovered mines, and for such a chance, I would infallibly seek to make his acquaintance, and——"

12

"Take care of yourself, Mr Walker," interrupted Ormur

"That he does not cheat me, do you mean? that he does not outwit me? Oh? there is no danger of that And besides, I do not trade alone, but have business friends in Rio—experienced people?"

"That he will not cheat you, that you will take care of, I have less anxiety about that than—than in an entirely different respect"

"How so, Mr Hinango? what do you mean by that?"

"You may have occasion to become acquainted with Madame Closting, his wife?"

"Is she, then, a dangerous person?"

"Dangerous! not at all! she is dazzlingly beautiful! and has a pair of Brazilian eyes—perhaps you have seen such eyes—their glances can kindle flames ——"

"You jest, Mr Hinango, but, jesting aside, does the lady stand a little in the shade? not particularly bright? you understand me?"

"Oh, no! by no means—so far as I know I have only casually met her a few times—a year and a half ago—and she struck me—not so much by the undeniable beauty of her face and her form, as by a certain expression of suffering—and that sort of suffering women—beautiful, besides, is dangerous, and often brought in danger, itself, by meeting with a youth like you, Mr Walker!"

"There is a brig in sight, behind us, Captain!" cried the man at the helm, through the open skylight

All eyes were now turned in the direction indicated, and Captain Finngreen appeared upon the deck with his telescope in his hand

"She has a better wind than we," said the mate, "but we shall soon obtain the same breeze"

Ormur, who had not observed the vessel at the horizon, owing to his conversation with Rossbrück and Mr Walker, threw a seaman's glance in the distance, and hurried to the cabin to get his own telescope In a second, he sprung upon deck again, and clambered to the mainmast top, without even looking at any one Deep silence reigned on deck, and the distant approaching rustle of an increasing westerly breeze made itself heard in the loud murmur of the waves

Dolores, standing beside Horatio, observed the point indicated with a fixed gaze, and unconsciously leaned upon the arm of the youth, as if in reality she required support, while her lips spoke nought of the fears which agitated her breast. Horatio dared as little express his anxieties and surmises, and both looked up to their friend in the mainmast top, as if they longed to receive the confirmation of their trembling surmises by a hint on his part, little expecting that their anxiety would prove to be unfounded

Capt Finngreen gave the telescope to Mr Storhjelm, the first mate, without uttering a word Mr Walker and Mr Rossbrück each used his own telescope, while Alvarez approached Dolores and Horatio, and said more with a look than both could have answered in words

Mr. Daily's attention, in his "between decks," was attracted by the sudden silence, and he had come upon deck, likewise, without disturbing his companion, Dr Merbold, who was so absorbed in the classification of his beetles, that he neither saw nor heard any thing in the outward world around him

Old Achilles and his daughter, busied with the preparations for dinner, remarked upon all countenances the peculiar expression of anxious expectation, but did not venture a syllable, and looked with mute inquiry at each other

After some ten minutes of portentous silence, Ormur again found himself upon the quarter-deck He answered the glance of Dolores, which had sought his, and she understood its expression, which was not in the least calculated to relieve her apprehensions She leaned more heavily upon Horatio's arm, and kept her eyes fixed upon Ormur, whom Capt Finngreen, just then, beckoned to follow him. The two seamen now stood opposite each other by the helm, and, as yet, had not spoken a word

"It is the man-of-war, friend Hinango!" at length said Capt Finngreen

"I am convinced of that," replied Ormur "She probably came out with the tide, yesterday, and has now a good breeze"

"And which will soon bring her up with us"

"But she does not sail as we do," remarked Hinango

"She did not appear as if she could, there in the road"

"And now we shall certainly have a breeze, also, but the brig has a cutter that sails faster than we, we cannot outsail it," remarked Capt Finngreen

"Impossible, captain, that is not to be thought of, and we shall soon see it" A long pause again ensued

"Captain Finngreen," at length continued Ormur, "I have something to propose to you"

"I am ready for it Speak, friend Hinango—speak as a seaman to a seaman There stands the South American lady, she is of more value than my ship and cargo Speak Hinango"

"I understand your meaning, captain, in relation to Señora Dolores, you meet me there half way But your ship and your cargo is lost, if once the cutter comes alongside, and an officer steps upon your deck"

"I feel that The brig would not chase us if she did not, certainly, know that we had eluded her visitation"

"Well then, captain, now for my question You know me as a naval officer, as a seaman who has trod the gangway for fourteen years, can and will you justify yourself to your owners, for relinquishing to me, for some hours, the command of your brig? and I will take it upon me to get rid of the cutter, and if the breeze does not leave us in the lurch, to bring her safely off"

"Friend Hinango," returned the captain, "you know my position as captain. Among a thousand cases, not one occurs in which a captain should relinquish the command in danger Never! never! But I confess to you, honestly and freely, I know no means of saving ourselves; none at all Do you know of any? I will take upon myself responsibility to my owners, for the half of the Nordstjernan belongs to me, and there's an end of that I accept your offer, I am your first mate from this moment; command the Nordstjernan. Mr Storhjelm!" cried he to the first mate, "this is Lieutenant

Hinango, a Russian naval officer Lieutenant Hinango commands the Nordstjernan from this moment, until we shall have lost sight of the brig there Inform the crew, and direct them to obey every order with thorough punctuality "

Hinango now hurried to Dolores and Horatio, who had from a distance observed each expression of the two seamen's faces, greatly strengthened by the inconceivable calmness and self-possession which they displayed

The sense of the Swedish words which the captain addressed to the mate, in a tolerably loud tone, was sufficiently clear to all the passengers, under the existing circumstances, although none of them understood Swedish

Ormur spoke a few tranquillizing words to Dolores and Horatio, hastily pressed a hand of each, as if to take a short farewell of them, since, for the present, as a seaman upon his post, he must be thoroughly apart by himself He now gave the orders necessary for profiting the most by the favorable breeze, which became stronger and stronger, although he would gladly 'have laid the brig by the wind,' to await the cutter's approach, if he could have been certain that the Caza, would not have gained upon him

Hardly, had he put the telescope again to his eye, when he called out to the captain, "The cutter is under sail "

"I see it, likewise," answered the vice captain of the Nordstjernan, "she comes after us as if she had steam aboard "

"The sooner here, the sooner decided," remarked Ormur

The Nordstjernan was what would be called "a heavy brig," of full three hundred and fifty tons burthen, she had been in use but a few years, and was built on the modern plan, sharp at the bow and keel, and widest at about three-fourths of her length, towards the bow, a construction which, with corresponding rigging, generally makes a good sailer Hinango observed, with a technical eye, the sailing of the brig on the preceding day, and had carefully marked her good properties He now observed, for a quarter of an hour, almost without turning away his eyes, the sailing of the brig and the cutter, which became the easier, as he could nearly calculate the relative difference in their sailing, in proportion as the latter left the former behind her

Besides a short interview between Captain Finngreen and Mr Walker, little was spoken

The unfortunate Alvarez, approached these two, and sought to express the disconsolateness, which burdened him, since he did not yet know but that the pursuit, on the part of the man-of-war, was occasioned entirely by his presence on board, and that he was the sole cause of bringing the brig into such danger The sincerity of his sorrow, and the grief which he manifested, moved the good Captain Finngreen to such a degree, that he proposed to Mr Walker, in English, to ask ' his sister' if she would consent to inform the Unitarian, for his consolation, who she was, as no treachery was to be feared from him

Mr Walker, having no objection, spoke to Dolores, led Alvarez to her, and whispered to him the name of the poetess from whose Elegies, he had sung those verses on board the Caza A scene followed, which it would be difficult to describe, since no language can express the emotions and sensations experienced by the ardent admirer of the South American poetess, which are as indescribable as a symphony and its effects

"The surprise which followed this announcement was so great, that Alvarez cast an indignant glance at Captain Finngreen, under the impression that he had given a hint to the young Englishman to indulge himself in a joke, and announce his sister as the authoress of the Elegies, whose name neither he knew, nor any one else out of the circle of her immediate friends It was only when Dolores, herself, assured him that all was true which had been revealed to him, that he believed it, and then he scarcely knew how to contain himself He thanked Providence, with tearful eyes, that it was permitted him to share the lot of the poetess He desired, as he expressed it, nothing more than to be a seagull, to hover around, and attend upon her from that time to her death, and then to die upon her grave Dolores acknowledged the sincerity of such profound veneration, but remarked that the gift of poetry, the power of words, was no merit of hers, which heightened her inward worth, but a spiritual gift, which Providence had intrusted to her, as the property of the nation. In the ensuing conversation, Alvarez related that he had been to Spain, to obtain all possible information concerning the fate of an uncle, (his mother's brother,) who had disappeared in a mysterious manner, in his youth

"What was the family name of your mother ?" inquired Dolores

"Garringos," returned the other

Dolores appeared suddenly agitated by the mention of this name, but exerted herself to conceal its effects upon her mind "Do you know," said she, at length, "at about what time your uncle disappeared in Spain ?"

"Precisely," was the reply, " on the 24th of May, 1512, at Madrid "

Dolores was shocked, and sought, by a glance at the approaching cutter, to conceal the working of her features, which the announcement of this date appeared to have produced

"The secret has gone to the grave with my mother !" whispered she, partly to herself, partly turning to Horatio, and was about to say a word to Alvarez, just as Ormur, approached the group, who, after continued consideration of the hostile sail, had spoken in a low tone to the captain and Mr Walker

The tranquillity which manifested itself in Ormur's countenance, was less remarkable than conceivable to all, since something of his stirring and eventful life, was known, which was certainly calculated to develop in him such firmness and moral strength in encountering danger On the other hand, the plan or means of defence which he intended to employ for their deliverance, were unknown, even to the captain The more each puzzled himself, and turned the question over in his mind, what he would do in a similar situation, the less able was he to answer it.

The brig carried four guns, which were nicely polished, and stood upon well painted carriages, intended more for ornament and for salutes, than for defence in cases similar to the present.

"I do not believe that I shall require the cannon," remarked Ormur, to Captain Finngreen, "but nevertheless, I wish them to be loaded, and our friend Alvarez, here, will be just the person to serve as gunner, and to load them." After some words in Spanish to his comrade of the Batallion de la Blouse, the men required, were placed in readiness to fulfil the gunner's directions.

"As concerning your Swedish flag," continued Ormur, "I will not compromise it, but will carry a flag which, to be sure, has never been displayed on any fleet, but whose associates we may very likely meet upon these waters." He gave orders to have his trunk brought on deck, and set himself to work, to lace together some flags, out of the before mentioned strips of bunting.

Dolores went up to him, and appeared to observe, with especial attention, this fastening together of the different strips, to which, after a while, she lent a helping hand.

"The flag will really be laced together, like a lady's corset," said Mr Rossbruck, "te method pleases me."

"And signals, without number, may be made after this manner, by altering the strips," remarked Mr Walker. "Probably you have, also, a flag dictionary?" said he to Ormur.

"One that is not yet published," he replied, and looking at his watch, he added to the captain.

"It is now one o'clock, captain, we can go to dinner in peace. It will be three or four hours before the cutter will overhaul us, perhaps even later, as we are getting more of this breeze every moment. We make five knots now, and I reckon that the cutter makes seven. It is nearly six miles from us, and, consequently, will require three or four hours to overhaul us, if we hold this breeze, which, it seems to me, is increasing. The man-of-war brig has a better

wind than we, and rather hangs back, she seems to sail six knots an hour at the most; with the same wind, that would carry us eight, and we shall, of course, gain two knots on her every hour. We have, then, only to deal with the cutter, and, God willing, I hope to be prepared for her."

"She appears strongly manned," remarked the captain, "and will carry a sufficiency of bayonets."

"Is that a schooner or a fishing sloop, there in the distance, lieutenant?" inquired the man at the helm.

Without replying, yet evidently not disagreeably surprised, Ormur left the composition of his flag, and hurried again to the mainmast top, while a conflict of contending emotions began in the minds of those on board the Nordstjernan, and none dared to inquire what this new appearance might be, or whether it drew near for their benefit, or to hasten their destruction.

"That seems to be a little devil!" said Capt Finngreen, partly to himself, with the telescope at his eye. "By her rig, she is a Baltimore schooner, but a little thing, and far, far distant, and the cutter will reach us first, at all events."

After some moments, Ormur descended to the quarterdeck, and, with his telescope under his arm, walked to and fro with hurried steps, wrapped in reflection, and without looking at any of those present.

He then again observed the new sail and the cutter once more directed his telescope towards the schooner, reflected again, and then stepped hastily to the open trunk, beside which lay the prepared flags.

"ORA E SEMPRE," said he, half aloud, and took up a green, red, and white flag, and handed it to the first mate, with the order, "To the foremast with this!"

"To the foremast!" repeated the other, sailorwise, and obeyed the command.

DOLORES.

BOOK III.

CHAPTER I

ENCOUNTER AND DEFENCE

SOME hours had again passed away, and the brig Nordstjernan, with her passengers, was like a floating deaf and dumb institute, except that it wanted the signs

The breeze had freshened more and more, and with the approach of the cutter, the eventful moment drew nigh that must deliver Dolores and Alvarez to the fury of ruthless party spirit, unless their good genius, in the person of the northern ex-naval officer, should carry out some master-stroke of presence of mind, the plan of which he, like a true seaman, still kept to himself

The air was clear and pure, and the grey-green waves spattered about the vessel, as if she floated there, only to interrupt the uniformity of their rustling motion and to serve them as a toy, that the eccentric dwellers of the earth had resigned to their consideration and discretion, notwithstanding they had already, in their ill humor, tossed about and destroyed a thousand similar brittle playthings

The same Cape pigeons which had, with devoted adherence, attended the vessel from Point Indio, circled and flew in all directions about the stern, and conspicuously dipped, from time to time, in the wake, the foam of which appeared to delight them, the longer the vessel by its rapid course preserved its fleeting existence

The man-of-war, "La Caza," had long since hoisted her lee-sails, in order to follow the cutter as speedily as possible, which, however, gained a considerable advance, and seemed to fly along more swiftly, the shorter the distance became between the three vessels, whose sailing propensities were gradually manifested, as the skilful seaman had calculated and pointed out

The lee-sails of the Nordstjernan lay, by Hinango's order, ready upon deck; but he deferred the order to hoist them He awaited, with a sort of painful impatience, the contact with the cutter, and allowed the Caza an approach, which could bring him into no particular danger, so soon as he should succeed in despatching the cutter

The Baltimore schooner, which had been observed in the far distance, had evidently got sight of the Nordstjernan, and seemed to hold a course which was calculated to contact with both, (the cutter and the Nordstjernan,) at a re-mote point, since she could take no other course if she did not wish to give up the Swedish brig

Hinango, with the glass at his eye, watched with increasing expectation, for the moment that would enable him to recognise the schooner's flag, which fluttered at the mainmast.

The minutes became hours to all on board the Nordstjernan, the hours appeared as if they would never terminate

Dolores, Horatio, and Alvarez, formed an inseparable group, as if the danger would become less, if they awaited it together, and this notion, in a moral point of view, might be very well founded Hinango stepped up to them, from time to time, to strengthen within them, by some words, the faith in a possible deliverance, which became fainter the nearer the cutter approached, and under surrounding circumstances and relations, might very well waver in hearts less penetrated by a confidence in Divine Providence, than were those of Dolores and her two companions

But the want of well founded sources of consolation, increased in Hinango the oppression and uneasiness with which these endless hours burdened him, since, after all his expressions of confidence, he saw himself flung back upon the deceitful element of "hope," upon which his designed plan of defence was built, and only too closely resembled the sea, since it, abstractly from his manly self-reliance, afforded no guarantee for the success of any enterprise, until the end itself was attained

Robert appeared to regard, with a certain stoical indifference, the approach of a crisis, which, at all events, might endanger his life, if an indiscreet bullet should be directed from the gun of a Confederado towards him, and pierce some vital part of his body Endeavoring to await the decision of the matter, as comfortably as possible, he had stretched himself out upon his cloak on the quarterdeck, smoking one cigar after another, and, from time to time, looking over the "Private Instructions" of his worldly wise father, many passages of which especially pleased him, at least he could not suppress his entire assent, at times, by a covert smile, and a half loud " Very good , very good, indeed ""

Mr William Rossbruck sat in the cabin, absorbed in his colonial speculation, "which was to put some millions in circulation," not a little provoked at being placed, by a fatal chance, with passengers who ought not to have shipped on board the same vessel with respectable people, since their suspicious position excluded them, as well from the society of business people, of any consideration, as from the higher circles of the social world, who did not trouble themselves with similar sacrifices for patriotism, and the like " unwarantable phantasies "

Dr Merbold, had at length remarked something wrong, and asked the captain what the singular silence of the passengers signified, and the thoughtful mien with which they had so long observed the " little fishing boat," and the vessel in the distance ' When he learned that this cutter would probably institute another visitation on board, and inquire after the refugee whose life they sought to save since they had drawn him out of the water, the savant lost his phlegmatic indifference.

" How could you have undertaken, captain, to keep a man on board who was reclaimed by the police, or even by the officers of justice ' You suspected, or knew, then, without doubt, that the man would be pursued ' you knew it before the shallop returned back to the city, and you kept him on board ' Hark you, captain ' this is not only unpardonable, but it is contrary to police regulations, and is treasonable, besides, and if I had suspected that you were capable of doing that, of taking demagogues, or patriots, or the like, on board, and keeping them on board, I certainly would not have gone to sea with you I will write a letter to the Prussian consul at Buenos Ayres, with my own hand, for having sent me in such a vessel, with such a captain And I will do it on the spot ' The boat that is coming there, will take away the fool, the demagogue—good ' I will then embrace the opportunity, and send back a letter to the Prussian consul in Buenos Ayres, and give him a piece of my mind It is enough to craze one," he muttered to himself, while he crept down to his berth " Has the captain gone crazy under the line ' that he undertakes in the face of day, to act so in opposition to the police ' to compromise all of us, as if we had even assisted in taking a suspicious fellow to sea, who has meddled with politics ?"

The two captains of the Nordstjernan observed the cutter and the schooner with equal attention The first had gradually approached so near, that the persons which she carried, were distinguishable

Two officers appeared in the stern, and near them a man in a civil dress, besides a crew of twelve men

The sending of the cutter, in itself, must, in any case, be regarded only as a provisory intimation that the Caza followed behind, and had a word to say to the Nordstjernan, since the cutter, unattended by the Caza, would hardly be in a condition to take the Swedish brig by force, as it, like many European vessels upon the Southern Atlantic Ocean, carried, besides several cannon, a well filled arm-chest, and an abundance of ammunition.

It would certainly have been possible to prevent the stepping of even a single man from the cutter upon the deck, considering the difficulty of climbing up from a small craft on board of a large vessel, well supplied with weapons of all sorts But such a method of escape did not enter into Hinango's plan, who would not put the peaceful crew of the Nordstjernan to such a test, which, if it failed, would bring the most fearful punishment upon them

Capt Finngreen had, long since, perceived that Hinango had not prepared for such a defence, without, on the other hand, having discovered what was his particular design—what means he intended to adopt for the deliverance of the Nordstjernan After all that he had learned, however, of the life and character of his countryman, (whose fate and misfortunes lived in the mouths and in the hearts of his people,) there arose within him an almost unbounded reliance upon him, as a man and as a seaman , and he looked forward with confidence, although not without painful expectation and disquiet, to the decisive moment

Hinango took the best axe from the carpenter's chest, examined the edge, and finding it in sufficiently good order, laid it upon the windward side of the quarterdeck, and again observed the schooner with his telescope Hardly had he caught sight of it, than he exclaimed, in joyful tones, " It is the Mazzini ' Look, captain ' the flag is green and yellow, without the Brazilian emblem of the solar system It is the revolutionary flag of Rio Grande, and on the foremast is the flag of ' La Giovine Italia '—green, red and white "

" The same which we carry—I recognised it immediately, when you unfolded it It is designated upon a flag chart as the Italian national flag, but, alas ' it is, as yet, borne by no fleet,' remarked Capt Finngreen

" Not at this time , but I assure you, captain, that there are many Italian naval officers who would gladly carry it, and maintain it with their lives "

" I have no doubt of it, and in the future they will verify its power "

Hinango now brought forward two flags, which he had previously arranged, and threw one to the mate, with the order, " Take down the flag from the foremast, and put this in its place , and this," throwing the other flag to him, " on the mainmast "

" The Mazzini has answered the Italian flag," and I know now where I am , perhaps he already suspects who we are," remarked Hinango " We will, however, make him understand it more plainly "

" Bravo '" cried Capt Finngreen, noticing the flag at the foremast " that is the flag of our Scandinavian Union—blue, white, and yellow—with the polar star in the blue field I know it from prohibited books; and if a spy were now to see my Nordstjernan, I should never dare to go back through the sound again."

" I believe you, indeed, captain , but you have relinquished to me, for the present, the command of the Nordstjernan, that it may not be taken back as a prize to Buenos Ayres, and as the proverb says, ' despair has no law ' If we succeed in despatching the cutter, it will not be easy to prove that you have carried the Scandinavian flag, here in the mouth of the river La Plata "

The mate, Storhjelm, delivered to Hinango the flag of " La Giovine Italia," cast a glance upon the Scandinavian flag, and observed, " The Danes and Norwegians would miss their red from the flag above there."

" They are the colors from the three crosses of

the ancient flags of our countries ," said Hinango; " the Swedish yellow, the Norwegian blue, and the Danish white, with the polar star, the symbol of the future unity of Scandinavia Blood red has, however, too often stained the history of our monarchies, and our race has been stirred up to fight against itself by the crimes of a tyrant, like Christian the Second May the remembrance thereof vanish from the hearts of the people, and the symbolic colors of the three crosses, likewise the colors of our Northern starry heavens, elevate our spirits to faith in the future destiny of nations "

Dolores, Horatio, Alvarez, and Robert Walker, had stepped up to the two captains, just as the name, Mazzini, was mentioned, and seemed now more than ever, solicitous about the issue of the eventful encounter

" It is a pity that the schooner was not a single mile nearer to us," said Robert Walker , " it will be impossible for her to reach us before the cutter "

" Certainly, she cannot," replied Hinango, " but she will be able to attack the cutter before she overhauls us "

" I see that well ! Her commander is said to be an Italian bandit," continued Robert Walker, with an ironical smile , " he must be a famous fellow "

' Certainly ! the Austrian gazettes call all the Italian patriots banditti, no matter how high their social position Barigaldi, who commands this schooner, is, to be sure, an Italian—condemned to death as a rebel—but he is a *gentleman*, who formerly moved in the great world as much as any courtier of Modena or Tuscany," replied Hinango

Dolores attentively considered the flag at the mainmast It consisted of three dark blue stripes, forming a surface—in the middle of which was a golden yellow star, surrounded by an oval light blue halo, which nearly filled the breadth of the central stripe *

Hinango now broke off from his conversation with Robert Walker, and looked with an undefinable expression of inward emotion upon Dolores, and then upward upon the flag

" May I ask, or guess," said Dolores, interrupting the deathlike silence of the moment— " may I guess what sort of flag this is—what this symbol signifies ?"

" You suspect, ' said Hinango, looking with sympathy in the eyes of Dolores, and seeing into her heart

" It is the flag of Humanity , the golden star is the dawning star of the religion of the future, which sends down its rays, through the misty circle of the materialism of our century, into the bleeding human heart," sighed she, again raising her tear-dimmed gaze to the significant symbol of a despised faith

" It *is* the flag of Humanity," said Hinango, " you are not mistaken , and I hope that all of us do not err, when we believe in a resurrection of the human race out of this night of infidelity, of indifference, of sectarian hatred, and of the fanaticism of forms without religion The star

of the future, whose rays illuminate our hearts with foreboding faith, will arise in the firmament of the path of the nations, and the religion of Jesus will shine forth as a higher *idea* than the *church* has heretofore recognised in it—a higher idea than the oriental dualism—the dispute between the evil and the good Mankind will be elevated by the knowledge of the *unity* of all strength, and *Satan* will no more give men free leave to *sin* on his account, and at his instigation The star of humanity will go before, to light the way of progress to mankind '

Dolores followed this inspired effusion with her whole soul, and reached her hand to her friend and champion, with a wordless glance

" The cutter comes near !" said Hinango, " we shall now see whether our flag of humanity floats here under God's protection Retire to your cabin, and do not tremble, and all of you, gentlemen, will leave the quarterdeck for a short time " With these words, he led Dolores to the cabin stairs, and all followed him, and went below

Hinango now ordered the first mate to summon " all hands on deck !" and immediately the whole crew stood, expectantly, by the mainmast

" Countrymen ! Scandinavians !" said he to them , " a short sea manoeuvre is about to take place, under the Scandinavian flag Upon the punctuality with which you execute my orders, depend our own lives, and the lives entrusted to the care of your brave captain Hear, then, and mark what I say The cutter will give a signal that we should ' lay by the wind ' I will give, through the trumpet, the necessary orders—you must fulfil them , but do not let go of the tacks and sheets Remain at your posts, and at the moment when I command, without the trumpet, ' brace full " bring the foremast yard in the direction in which it now stands, and fill the mainsail, likewise Have you understood me ?"

" We understand ! we understand !" cried all, with one voice

" Captain," said the seaman, now turning to Capt Finngreen, " cut off a rope there, and keep one end of it in your hand when you throw it to the cutter, at my command through the trumpet, and let the rope go entirely, when I give the order ' Let go for !' "

" I understand you, ' replied Capt Finngreen, and just then a round of musketry was fired from the cutter, for want of a cannon

The cutter was now near, and had lowered one sail, as she steered round the after part of the brig, to come under her lee Hinango hastily ordered the " boom over to the windward," which the commander of the cutter probably took as a civility, as if done to enable him to approach nearer, and to come alongside more conveniently, without endangering his masts

" Brace back the head yards ! throw out a rope !" cried Hinango, through the trumpet, then, throwing it aside, he seized the axe, and stationed himself on the windward of the boom-sheet, directing his eye towards the cutter's masts Availing himself, with calculation, of the moment when the masts of the cutter passed the bulwark, he now cut loose the sheet The colossal boom, loaded with sails, and driven by the wind, obeyed the laws of gravity, and slung over to the leeward, breaking both the cutter's masts like Cologne pipe stems, which, together with

---

* The above symbol, with the addition of others, was later—in 1841—engraved upon a seal ring, which the committee of "La Giovine Italia" in London, sent to their spiritual associate, De Lamenais, in his prison, in Paris.

their sails and rigging, plunged, with a crash, into the waves

"Let go for '" (let go ') he now cried to the captain who let go the rope which a sailor in the cutter had already served to fasten on to the brig

"Brace full '" thundered he to the sailors, who punctually carried out the required order

"Keep on your course '" he said, in a low voice, to the man at the helm, when all the orders were complied with He now looked, for the first time, upon the dismasted cutter, in which the confusion appeared so great that no one seemed to think of sending a bullet at the commander of the brig

The whole affair was the work of a moment, and the rapidity of its execution allowed no man to come to his recollection, or to reflect upon what was likely to happen, until the whole was executed, and the cutter dismasted Surprised to the utmost, officers and crew now gazed upon each other and then looked at Hinango, unable to find words to express their astonishment

CHAPTER II

COURSE AND DISTANCE

"We are saved '" Hinango exclaimed, and then hastened to convey to the South American lady the assurance of her safety, and returned to the deck with her, accompanied by all the cabin passengers

The expression of each countenance offered, for the moment, in indescribably rich field for observation, in case some psychologist on board, had found time and leisure to consider them

All could now be convinced of a deliverance, which, notwithstanding the confidence in Hinango, no one had, until now, thought probable, since the danger had become so imminent. All could now believe in their personal security, after their minds had been racked for nearly five hours, by a painful uncertainty, which must have paralyzed all their powers

This sudden transition, from fear and anxiety to tranquillity and joy, wrought in many minds a similar convulsion, as did the first moment of the man-of-war, like a speck in the horizon

"There is my letter, captain '" cried the German savant, from his hole, while he clambered up with effort, assisted by Mr Daily, and holding in his hand a sealed envelope "There is my letter, the shallop will now soon be here "

"I am very sorry," replied Captain Finngreen, that the opportunity has escaped you of sending your report to Buenos Ayres! There lies the cutter, and cannot, with the best intentions, take charge of your despatches "

"How so ' Not take charge of them ' Will she, then, not take charge of the fellow—the political fanatic—the fool there '

"Doctor '" interrupted Hinango, spare the titles with which your German royally privileged erudition insults the patriots of all nations, especially of your own You are here, on board of the Nordstjernan. Doctor, keep within the limits of your own narrow science, and remain within your beetle world Insult no one with your servility Consider that this vessel carries human beings, who are morally and mentally as far above the horizon of your learned perceptions, as men are above beetles Greet your Prussian consul in Buenos Ayres, and at Rio, and every servant of the king of Prussia, who, under the title of a savant, receives a report from you '

"Do not fly in a passion with a man who is, in the highest degree, deserving of our compassion, for his deadness and insensibility to the cause of the people," said Dolores, interrupting the vehement speech of Hinango, who, for the first time since he had been on board, allowed an ebullition of anger to appear

"Forgive me, Miss Walker '" he replied, while he left the insect man, and walked aside with Dolores," excuse this bitterness, towards a man who can as little insult either you or me, as he can understand us, in case he should ever learn our position My anger, however, does not extend to him alone, but to the whole class of servile literati, be they entomologists, or philologists, or theologists, who, for a breakfast from some creature of the court, not to mention a professorship, an order, or a pension, would betray and sell their own nation, and all the nations of the earth, if it were possible, and, in fact, be proud of such an action "

"I believe I know the man next to the officer in the stern of the cutter," said Horatio, who, using Hinango's telescope, had, until now, with the captain and Robert Walker, been viewing the cutter "I must be very much mistaken, or it is the private teacher of languages, Perezoso "

"That is very possible, and even probable," interrupted Robert Walker, "for the same person shewed himself very zealous in a little notorious coffee-house, on the evening before our departure, with respect to the discovery of the author of certain Elegies, as Señor Testa informed me, who observed him there "

Dolores and Hinango went up to their two companions, to give their attention likewise to the cutter, surprised by his last words, she inquired of young Walker '

"You appear to have known more respecting our danger than you have imparted to me "

"I learned from Señor Testa, that they were upon the point of discovering your incognito as a poetess, and that a certain Perezoso, whose name he learned in this famous coffee-house, was much to be feared "

"The wretch '" exclaimed Dolores; "here is another man who has the reputation of great learning, who understands a half dozen languages, and lowers himself to become a spy, that he may obtain some office under government "

"It's the old story," said Hinango, laughing, "but there he floats now, thank God ! and can do us no more harm for the present "

"Until his colleagues in Rio de Janeiro are informed," sighed Dolores again, "then, wherever I may hereafter find an asylum, the vengeance of despotism will follow me, though I went to the antipodes I am prepared for any future fate "

"Singular ! but perhaps easy to be explained,"

interrupted Hinango, "that, in this moment of deliverance, such gloomy despondency should come over you"

"How seldom are we able to account for even the lightest of our internal emotions," replied Dolores, "it is not fear that oppresses me, but rather a presentiment that I am only saved to encounter greater dangers"

"It is so with me, also," affirmed Hinango, "but with the consciousness of our calling, our mission, we are pervaded by a divine strength to brave danger, to bear our lot A life like ours is good, when it is *ended*"

Dolores replied with a glance at the flag of "Humanity," and remained silent

The Mazzini altered her course the moment when the masts of the cutter were shivered, and steered directly for the latter, while the Caza had nearly vanished behind the horizon, with all her canvass given to the wind, to support the cutter, and to take her, together with her crew, on board

For the understanding of the course and distance of the three sails, the following nautical explanation may be requisite

The Caza might have been about five miles from the object of pursuit, when she was perceived by Hinango, and sent out the cutter Although she had a better wind than the Nordstjernan, her average progress might be taken at about six miles an hour, while the latter sailed about seven, and the cutter eight The Nordstjernan had then made thirty-five miles in about five hours, the cutter forty, and reached the Swedish brig, with the addition of the five miles' variation in the distance, while the Caza had made thirty miles, and, of course, remained ten miles behind the cutter

All the endeavors of the Caza to save the cutter would, of course, be nautically impossible, as the Mazzini, at the time of this catastrophe, was at the utmost three miles from the place of encounter, where the cutter still lay, endeavoring to put up jury masts, in which, however, from want of sufficient materials, she was not likely to succeed

The Mazzini had constantly, in her diminished course, a half wind, and might reach the cutter in twenty minutes—a space of time which, with reference to the arrival of the Caza, was not to be taken into consideration

Hinango observed the movements of the Mazzini with redoubled interest, as an associate under the before mentioned flag, and, also, because he wished to enter into communication with the commander of the schooner, whom he had not met when he was at Monte Video

Although since the fortunate issue of the encounter with the cutter, he had ceased to consider himself in command of the Nordstjernan, he intimated to Capt. Finngreen that he should prefer "laying the brig under the wind," to await the result of the meeting between the two vessels, of which one only carried sails. Capt. Finngreen was entirely willing to comply with this request, and the Nordstjernan now lingered "under the wind," some two miles distant from the hull of the cutter, just as the Mazzini discharged a shot—expecting, as a reply, the signal of a "surrender at discretion."

Before, however, we consider more nearly the encounter of the cutter and the Mazzini, we must seek the requisite explanation of the despatch of the Caza from Buenos Ayres, and of the part occupied by the Mazzini in the history of our time.

CHAPTER III.

THE EXPEDITION

THE Police Commissary, Borrachezo, hurried from the Palace of Justice, to conduct Perezoso to the bureau of the statesman who was entrusted with the office of Minister of the Interior

The importance of the affair required a private audience, and Perezoso's offers and stipulations for the apprehension of the person to whose head the oft-mentioned price was affixed, were well received, and immediately accepted, without his having in the least allowed it to be perceived in what direction he would institute his investigations

His conditions and stipulations were confirmed in writing, and he, thereupon, required an authorization to have a man-of-war at his disposition, and, if possible, the brig La Caza, in case there should be any necessity for him to make an excursion upon the river La Plata The zealous spy, of course, desired to be sent as a personified despatch, whose contents the naval officer (as is often the case) should first learn when he was on board, and under sail—a wise precaution, for he still feared that he might be anticipated in this important and enticing affair

This expedition upon the river La Plata had, nevertheless, its difficulties, as it required a conference of the Minister of the Interior with the Minister of the Marine Department, which could not be so suddenly and hastily arranged, as the speculative office hunter desired, who was placed in a very critical position by the unavoidable delay of his voyage

Earnestly as he endeavored to induce his protector, Borrachezo, to use all possible haste, he felt himself exposed to the danger of directing his attention, by a single inconsiderate intimation, to the Swedish brig, and hazarding his secret. Perezoso now found himself in the critical position of every traitor and intriguer, who can only conduct his secret business with his equals, and know, beforehand, that the men with whom he operates are as cunning and unprincipled as himself, and would not hesitate, for a moment, to outwit him, and turn his secret to their own advantage

The high functionaries, who had to pass upon this matter, considered it, from their own particular point of view, as a business transaction of the government, and very naturally desired a moral (or, rather, an immoral) guarantee in regard to the person who so zealously offered "to serve the state"

Those of them who had acted the spy on former occasions, to arrive at their present posts, just as zealously as Perezoso now did, as office holders inwardly despised and detested the "traitor," while, at the same time, they were willing to make use of the "treachery" for the maintenance of the so called public order, for the security of the state, or for their own security and the security of Rosas.

Under such circumstances, four and twenty hours elapsed before Perezoso had obtained his full powers, and was handed over to the commander of the Caza, as Envoy Extraordinary for no Court, to be sure, but temporarily, upon the La Plata river, as *Chargé d'Affaires de poursuite et d'arrestation,* &c., &c.

Capt. Tumble received his guest and passenger on board with all respect, as he was in duty bound, by the high order of the Minister of the Marine Department, which obliged him to search strictly every vessel that the envoy should point out to him.

Perezoso did not disclose to him upon which vessel his attention was directed, until the Caza was under sail, to go down the river. And, even then, his prudence kept him silent as to what person he was in pursuit of, and what was the nation, sex, and standing of the individual.

Capt. Tumble was the more vexed at this mysterious reserve, as he had honored the Swedish brig with all the attention which the strictest official duty could require of him.

He ran over the passenger list with Señor Codo, which the latter had handed over to him, and after long consultation and fruitless examination, the suspicion of "revolutionary poetry," fell as well upon Robert Walker as upon his sister, upon William Rossbruck and Habakkuk Daily; and finally upon Dr. Merbold, who, as a "literary gentleman," had protested against that title, and was, therefore, the most suspicious person in the eyes of the commander of the Caza, so much so, that he resolved, beforehand, to bring him on board as a prisoner, on his own responsibility, let the *Envoy Extraordinary* apprehend whom he would.

The man-of-war, under the varying contrarieties of the wind, and favored by the current, went forward as fast as it well could, for the Caza had by no means thereputation of a "fast sailer," but rather served as a guardship to anchor at some appointed station. Many other vessels of the Rosas navy would have done better service in this case, but Perezoso had more "reference" to the character of the commander and officers, with whom he had already become acquainted, than to the deficiencies of the vessel, (unknown to him,) while from his past intercourse with Capt. Tumble and Señor Codo, he regarded them as furious Confederados.

As soon as the Caza had the Swedish brig in sight, which appeared as if fettered by flawing winds, the cutter was lowered and despatched, under Señor Codo's command. One midshipman and Señor Perezoso took their places likewise in her stern, and twelve of the strongest and most robust men of the crew, and among them *Pat Gentleboy,* all well armed, served at the same time as marines and as sailors.

CHAPTER IV.

HISTORICAL RETROSPECT

THE appearance of the Mazzini, which was now approaching the cutter, was no phantom of the imagination, brought down from the clouds and fixed on the La Plata river, still less was it a "flying Italian," (step-brother to the "Flying Dutchman,") but "a real, personal vessel," (as Pat Gentleboy appropriately expressed himself,) and as such it had, like other vessels, its origin and history, which, however, are so intimately connected with the historical events of South America, that we cannot recount the one without taking a retrospect of the other.

All the political movements of South America, as of the whole transatlantic "New World," are the fruits of the spirit which was developed in Europe. As yet, the New World has broached no *new idea*—no idea, the origin of which cannot be traced to the spiritual development of some one or other European nation. Many ideas of European intellect have, however, been realized (and either ennobled, or disfigured and degraded) in the New World, whose political soil, less encumbered by the unfruitful stoneheaps of ancient monarchy, offers a certain youthful vigor of nature, for the reception of spiritual seed, accelerating, as it were, with miraculous rapidity, the blossoming of a transplanted idea.

The foundation of the United States of North America (one of the most exalted phenomena in the history of mankind) is not the work of transatlantic originality, but the consequence and fruit of European intellect, which, as it were, in its strivings for development, flew across the ocean, to seek an asylum in the New World, and caused an explosion of strength there, which, in a measure, scattered in all the system of dominion "by the grace of God."

The awakened spirit of the age conquered the sooner in the New World, although, after a hard struggle, while the same spirit, at the same time, broke its fetters in Europe, contending for the cause of humanity, under less favorable circumstances, since it could hardly stir for the crowns and thrones which obstructed its progress.

The freedom of nations is never developed from external material conditions, it is no fruit of materialism, and where it proceeds entirely from material interests, it is not founded in spirit and in truth, but is a falsification of the idea, the coinage of a "constitutional convention," by the prevailing selfishness to promote its own speculations, while the principle of freedom is set aside.

Freedom, as the means of higher developments, is of a spiritual nature, and is only called forth by the spiritual life and moral strength of a nation. It is developed as an idea, and its vital energies are distributed equally through the several classes of the people, in like manner as nature's forces are distributed through the roots, trunk, and branches of a tree, to the outermost leaves.

But the distribution of the spiritual, vital energy of the idea of freedom, from the depths of inward life, (through which the spirit of God is manifested in the human mind,) is not the work of a few springs, like the branches of a tree, but of more or less extended periods of transition, of the long and desperate struggle of centuries, to overcome matter.

The history of South America shows us, as it were, the history of the European nations in a "mirage," a reflected image of the reality across the ocean horizon The Spanish and Portuguese provinces, (under which title they were inscribed as possessions in the archives of the kingdoms of the Old World,) first arose in the consciousness of their sacred rights, in consequence of the world-thrilling events of Europe, when the sacred inscription—*fraternity, equality*—was stamped with blood, in the French language, upon the banner of mankind. They then aroused, with that energy of self-consciousness which the awakened spirit brought with it, and which found, in the New World, the same elements to contend against, the same rubbish of decaying systems to remove out of the way, the same roots of antiquated prejudices to eradicate.

At the epoch of this relation, South America represented the three different conditions which are revealed in the history of mankind in all parts of the world "Absolute monarchy," the arbitrary rule of a single individual, under the hypocritical banner of a republic, in Buenos Ayres and Paraguay, a "constitutional monarchy" in Brazil, with all its contradictions of throne-sovereignty and the people's rights, which wants nothing but the sanction of sound reason, which will never justify the prerogative of birth before the laws of nature In the other states, the 'republic," organized, more or less, after the pattern of the United States of North America—not, however, regarding freedom as the end—but, (as for example, the republic of La Banda Oriental, and in Rio Grande,) striving, on the basis of freedom, to promote the dissemination and development of a higher idea, to further the progress of true civilization As the war of independence of the Spanish South American provinces, in the commencement of our century, was a consequence of events in Europe, which put in doubt the right to the throne "by the grace of God," we there behold, in the various states and provinces, up to the present time, the direct and indirect operations of European progress towards the deliverance of mankind.

The constitutional monarchy in Brazil was, for years, up to the period of our relation, undermined, as it were, by this spirit of progress.

The "political cholera" (as many diplomatists are wont to call this spirit of the age, whose nature, like that of the Asiatic cholera, still remains a riddle, concerning whose extension, whether contagious, or non-contagious, the learned are still engaged in discussion) had penetrated into Brazil This "poisonous disorder," which causes the strength of armies to waver, and plants "a moth in the ermine mantle of legitimacy," began to spread in Brazil, to the terror and dismay of the royalists, who, in all the revolutionary insurrections of Pernambuco, Rio Grande, Bahia, Para, and later in the Provinces of Minas Geraes, and St Paolo, saw nothing but the "political cholera," flown over from Europe, the dissemination of which, however, no quarantine was able to restrain.

The province of Rio Grande has stood out, for years in open resistance to the claims of the Brazilian monarchy The boundary connexion with the Banda Oriental, as well as the relationship of the population, through their Spanish, Italian, and Portuguese extraction ; a lively spiritual intercourse with those countries of Europe, which continually contend for the spirit of freedom, the moral influence of many families,

and isolated men, who, pursued by despotism, have sought an asylum in the New World all these circumstances promote in Rio Grande the spirit of progress, and develop the idea of freedom.

The members of the association of "La Giovine Italia," after the treachery in Savoy, were scattered throughout all parts of the world to become, more by chance than designedly, the apostles, as it were, of a new gospel of the future *

Individuals of this association had found an asylum in Monte Video and Rio Grande, where, as in Spain, they had immediate occasion to bear the sword for the common cause, inasmuch as the same principle was there contended for in the open field, on which their association was based Fragments from Mazzini's works, (of La Giovine Italia,) whose tendency agreed with the principles set forth in the "Fraternization Act" of Young Europe,† were printed in large editions in Rio de Janeiro, at the expense of a committee of Rio Grande, and distributed there with zeal.

On this historical basis, the schooner Mazzini was equipped by the provisionary government of Rio Grande, placed as a privateer under the command of Barigaldi one of the most distinguished Italian refugees, and mostly manned by Italians.

The Mazzini was what is called a "Baltimore schooner," of about seventy-five tons, built for "a fast sailer," and befitting her destination, with eight guns of various calibre and one peculiarly long cannon, which ranged in all winds, and could be used with good effect "on particular occasions." Her hull and yards were painted black, and the sails, bought like the whole vessel at second, or perhaps at "seventh hand," had already become rather grey with age, and were here and there spotted with a patch of new She bore the before mentioned revolutionary flag of Rio Grande, the Brazilian green and yellow, without the device of the solar system, which the flag of the empire displayed.

Four officers besides the commander, (two for navigation, and two for the armament,) twenty marines, and five sailors, formed the crew of this flying privateer, which especially served to prevent the debarcation of the enemies' hostile troops on the banks of the Rio Grande, from larger vessels of war, as she drew little water, and could slip in where her appearance was important, and not very agreeable to the enemy.

---

* The author touches in this relation, upon the secret associations of Europe and South America, inasmuch as many of their secrets have been discovered to the governments of various countries, through the diligence of their well paid private agents

Several documents which are inserted in, or appended to this work, have already, in the meritorious co operation, for the dissemination of the persecuted idea, been made public through the press, by different governments. The correspondence of Mazzini with the author, a course of philosophical letters, written in the years 1833–4, were stolen out of a trunk in London, in February, 1835, while he lingered in prison, in Ostend and Bruges, in Belgium

The author's correspondence with Mazzini, from Brazil, in the years 1840—1842—1843, was subjected to the well known opening of Mazzini's letters, by order of the British government, which led to the apprehension and execution of so many patriots in Italy and other countries The author makes known, in this work, what he considers essential for the defence of the sacred cause.

† See "Dolores," page 96

CHAPTER V.

THE SIGNAL OF DISTRESS

----VARIABLE winds, such as, for the last two days, had blown the pennant to all points of the compass, are considered as an ill-omen by the weatherwise in this zone, because they are the forerunners of a southwesterly storm, which, under the title of Pampero, asserts its sovereignty as "the might of the strongest," over the southern plains, and even over the river

Instead of a discharge of artillery, as the warlike answer from the cutter to the shot of the Mazzini, the significant thunder responded from a scarcely perceptible cloud on the horizon, and a pampero was now rather to be feared

After this hollow rumbling *entr'acte* of a mysterious orchestra, the second scene of the marine drama upon the river La Plata unfolded itself The schooner took in a sail, to approach the cutter more slowly, and to be able to hold discourse with her, but no sign followed that made known the design or intention of the commanding officer Barigaldi, the often mentioned commander of the Mazzini, stood upon his limited quarterdeck, observing his opponent with the telescope, who did not even put up a signal of distress, as an invitation to peaceable approach

"I will wager," said Barigaldi, to an officer near him, "the fellow has some designs upon us, he will let us come within musket shot, and then take aim at the 'Italian bandit,' as they call me "

"What good would that do him? our cannon would soon answer him," replied the other "You had better send him a dose from our four guns, and he will not hesitate much longer "

Barigaldi looked again through his telescope, and remarked "I believe I distinguish the commanding officer What do you think, Filippo?" said he to one of the crew, "can you blow away that officer out of the stern with our long tube?—that man who stands up there, with the naval hat, next to the man at the helm ?"

The man to whom this question was directed was an old artillerist by profession, grown gray on board a man-of-war, with a brownish red weatherbeaten countenance

"As you may command," replied he with the utmost sangfroid, walking up to the *long tube*, the moveable great gun of the Mazzini

"Await my order," said Barigaldi "I will ask a blind question, and if that is not answered, then, in God's name, self-defence is no murder "

A shot was now fired into the air, and the schooner laid "by the wind," but no signal yet appeared from the cutter

"Can he have resolved to be sunk ?" said the officer near Barigaldi, "as he lies there—dismasted—with scarcely any arms—threatened by a pampero, and, notwithstanding all, evidently having some design upon us ?"

"Every thing is to be expected from savage party spirit," replied Barigaldi. "He appears to honor us with a plan, and risks himself and his crew to remove from the river the famous Mazzini, or at least the Italian bandit who commands her "

"That appears to be his intention, indeed," affirmed the other.

"Make ready the long gun !" cried Barigaldi, again putting the glass to his eye, to contemplate the mark once more before the order to fire

"Halloa !" cried he, "there seems to be mutiny on board !" and just then a pistol shot was heard

"The officer in command, there, has shot a man, or at least, wounded one," continued he A musket shot followed—and Barigaldi appeared absorbed in contemplation of the scene, which, with the glass at his eye, he could observe tolerably well

Old Filippo stood motionless, with his hands on his knees, continually keeping his mark in view, and ten times already had the schooner's movement "warranted the shot," as he expressed it, and yet the unexpected order was not issued

"But now I do not see my man any more," said he, partly to himself, as the musket shot was heard

"The crew appear to have possessed themselves of the cutter," said Barigaldi, after a long pause, "the officer, there, was shot, and thrown overboard, the body of the sailor likewise—a man in citizen's dress is also despatched and thrown overboard—he may, perhaps, have been brought out as supercargo for the Swedish brig, yonder "

A pair of old breeches, fastened to a temporary mast of the cutter, confirmed the suspicion of the mutiny, this signal plainly indicating that foreign assistance was required

"Thanks, old Filippo, for your good will !" said the commander to the sharpshooter at the long gun

"It is a pity ! a great pity !" murmured the latter, "I should as surely have hit him as could be, for the Mazzini laid by the wind like a sleeping child in the cradle

The command to hoist sail and steer for the cutter was issued as soon as the signal was perceived, and in a few minutes they were so near that an interview could take place, by means of a speaking trumpet.

Without waiting for the schooner to hail, the question was asked, from the cutter, "if any one on board understood English ?"

A smothered roll of thunder, from the far distance, hindered the immediate reply to a question, that sounded comical enough to the officers of the schooner

Instead of replying with a simple " Yes," Barigaldi inquired, in tolerably good English ·

"What ship do you belong to ?"

"I do not belong to the damned man-of-war with the Rosas flag, nor to the cutter !" was the answer

Barigaldi looked at his officers with a smile, and then ordered the sail to be put up, that they might approach the cutter near enough to throw a rope on board of her, for this singular introduction promised an intercourse which would be difficult to carry on through the trumpet

The cutter was now fastened by the rope, and a midshipman was seen in the stern, with his hands tied behind his back, while a herculean figure, in a sort of temporary naval uniform with an officer's sword at his left side, and cocked hat upon his fiery red hair, still held the trumpet in his hand which he had used. It was our friend, Pat Gentlebo' vanced to the command of the cutter, and next to him stood a South American, with an officer's sword at his left side also He was boatswain of the Caza.

"Who are you?" said Barigaldi, now observing, attentively, the dismasted cutter, with the pantaloon flag, and the prisoner of war

"My name is Patrick McCaffray, your honor Very respectable young ladies call me, generally, Pat Gentleboy, as it is well known I am an Irishman be birth, and American be principle I was a passenger on board the man-of-war yonder, and they sent us out in the cutter to hail the Swedish brig there, and bother her, till the lazy ould thing could come up with us We had a spy on board—bad luck to him! He came out to arrest some of the passengers Does your honor understand? Very respectable people, so far as I know, and all for a little matther of poethry They were going to take them, and shoot them, or hang them, as they do there in Buenos Ayres And besides, your honor, I heard them say that a price was set upon somebody's head on board of the Swedish brig there, the raal living head, whether iv a gintleman or lady, the divil take me if I know: but the spy that we had on board, wanted to make me spy under him I was stupid, your honor understands—stupid as the ground I knew more than I choose to answer, but my friend, the guitar player, that was pressed as a passenger at the same time wid me, knows more than I.

"As to our cutter, I must take leave to tell your honor, that our officer did invent devilish means, to disable the Swedish brig, till the ould Cazey—split her timbers!—could come alongside He had a powder barrel and rockets on board, to shoot out of a musket, now, wasn't that the divil's invintion, your honor? If the brig hadn't consinted to take us on board, and to keep quiet, we must then fall astarn of her, where she couldn't hinder us, your honor, without lowering one of her boats, thin we were to drive this wooden wedge between her rudder and keel, so that she couldn't turn, and thin, your honor, heard you iver the like! we were to fix the powdther barrel, just under the starn, and fire six rockets into the powdther cask, and thin, your honor sees, the starn would be smashed, any way, and a part of the cabin blown up Well, your honor! we came up wid the brig, and it seemed as if she would take us on board without any fuss at all, at all, so all went on mighty well But see, your honor! whoiver the gintleman is that commands the Swedish brig, his head is in the right place, I can tell you, and his heart, too, and that I would testify to in writing, only I don't know how But I am tiring your honor's patience, and that I'd be loth to do, intirely So, to make a long story short, we lost our masts, and lay like an empty biscuit cask, with rats for passengers, until your honor was coming up with us, and thin our commanding officer wanted to try the powdther plan upon your honor, but he wanted a rope from you first, to come alongside Eight men were to return your fire, in case you fired on us first, and these four were to fasten the powdther cask to the starn, and thin the ould Cazey would have overhauled you; shocking enough 'to perish the Danes!'

"And so that's the whole, your honor, and the one that made the plan lies down below there,

and the spy, besides; and here is his pocket book, full of papers, that we took out of the rascal's pocket, before we gave him salt water to drink That one there, is a midshipman from the Rosas man-of-war, that we believe to be better than the others I tell your honor, plainly, none of my comrades here were willing to sarve the spy, to bring worthy people to the gallows; and here is a man that understands English as well as I do, his name is——what is your name, now?" he asked a Frenchman, from the Isle of Jersey, who had, likewise, been compelled, on some fine morning, to act the "volunteer against his will"

Barigaldi heard this long story with all the patience of a seaman in a calm, but not without interest, and now examined the Frenchman from Jersey, who spoke tolerably good Spanish, and, thereafter, became Patrick's interpreter

"The officer," answered Mr Toby, from Jersey, to a question of Barigaldi's—"the officer, whose name was Señor Cudo, ordered us to fasten the powder cask to your stern, and selected four people for that purpose, upon whom he especially relied When we knew all, we understood each other, without speaking a word, we only looked at each other, and the matter was settled. We loaded all our guns, six or eight, from which the rockets were to be fired The officer now ordered us to raise a signal of distress, to have you throw us a rope The man who was to put up the signal, refused, and the officer shot him, at the same moment, the Irishman levelled at the officer, and—there he lay The midshipman made no attempt to avenge him, and the spy had already received his sentence when we came on board, and we have conscientiously fulfilled it"

"Have you room for all of us on board, Mr Commander?" inquired Patrick McCaffray, alias Gentleboy, "we surrender ourselves to you at discretion or indiscretion, whichiver your honor plases"

"There is room enough for you all," replied Barigaldi "Fasten the cutter in tow, and come on board quickly For the present, we thank you for your noble refusal to deliver us over to the man-of-war, which would have been possible by such a method You have behaved like brave sailors, and as such you will be treated by us I pledge myself to send you free to Monte Video, but I am going first to Rio Grande"

"All right, captain, I thank you for us all," cried Patrick Did your honor say it was to Rio Grande, you was going? Och, then, it is a pity it is not to Rio Negro, for it is there I'd wish to go, my brother Tom is there, a carpenter by profession, your honor"

"You will easily find a passage out there from Monte Video," returned Barigaldi, who could hardly restrain from laughter, then casting a glance at the Nordstjernan, and at the distant thunder cloud, he stepped down into his confined cabin, to examine the pocket-book of Perezoso, which the honorable commander of the cutter, Pat Gentleboy, had handed to him

The disarmed midshipman of the Caza was obliged to have his hands untied, that he might use them in getting on board the schooner When he stepped on the deck he mentioned his name, and resigned himself to his fate as a prisoner of war The crew was now on board, and with them all their arms and ammunition   Barigaldi stepped hastily out of his cabin, and commanded the vessel's course to be directed to the Swedish brig.

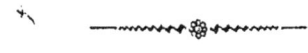

CHAPTER VI

THE TWO EUROPEANS.

THE distance of about two English miles, at which the Nordstjernan had awaited the surrender of the cutter, was soon passed over   The Mazzini was laid by the wind, and the cutter, in tow, was hastily used as a shallop, with which to come on board of the brig

The notorious "Italian bandit" was of the same age with Hinango, and resembled him in form and figure, while he also would have been readily recognised as belonging to the higher classes of the social world, let him appear in whatever dress he might

The lengthened form of his face, his pale complexion, sharply defined and somewhat curved nose, well formed lips, and deep set, dark eyes, with an expressive glance, black hair, and the peculiarly sonorous sound of a clear breast voice, all marked him as an Italian

He was dressed in a simple, dark blue uniform, armed with sword and pistols, and wearing on his head a marine hat, in the form of a shallop, (a wind splitter, as Patrick Gentleboy called it,) which displayed the same green, red, and white cockade that he had worn in Savoy

Hinango and Captain Finngreen awaited him at the gangway, for the usual welcome   He stepped upon deck, and the three seamen looked earnestly at each other, and pressed each others hands   Ormur presented his countryman, Capt Finngreen, to the commander of the Mazzini, as captain of the Nordstjernan

"Ormur !" said Barigaldi, and pressed him to his breast, while the eyes of both appeared to become moist, and their lips to quiver with the emotions that pervaded their manly hearts

The thunder, which was heard from time to time, between long intervals, gradually strengthened its voice, and again reminded them of an approaching southwest storm

"Welcome to me, old friend !" at length exclaimed Ormur. "we have much to say to each other "

"We must be brief," returned the other, "our minutes are numbered, a pampero is on its way, and we must go to sea with reefed topsails. I will keep you company to the latitude of Rio Grande What news do you bring from our friends in Europe ? But first, above all, what do you bring from Buenos Ayres ? What passengers—what fugitives or exiles have you on board ?"

Ormur hastily led his associate to the quarter-deck—to Dolores, Horatio, and Alvarez, and a scene of surprise, and a soul-felt greeting ensued, which shook the hearts of the bearded men, though long hardened in the storms of life and of the ocean

The universal interest which the songs of the poetess had excited, especially in Monte Video

and in Rio Grande, must naturally extend itself to her person, and increase with the danger to which they made her liable On the other hand, Barigaldi was an equally interesting personage to the associates on the southern banks of the La Plata, since he represented, as it were, the spirit of a European association, whose strength and resources, considered from so great a distance, appeared the greater, the more he proved their principles by his daring heroism

"The spy who was sent after you, to apprehend you," began Barigaldi, when the salutations were over, "is no longer able to molest you   The true sailor hearts of these people from the man-of-war were aroused against a treachery which would have destroyed us all   I will leave a man on board with you, who can relate to you, circumstantially, what danger we have escaped   So much for the moment, I have the pocket book of the spy in my possession, and perceive, by some of the papers, that the Benedictine monk, Celeste, is involved in your affairs, is exposed to the like danger, and has fled   They suspect him to be on board of this vessel   Is he here ?"

"Celeste !" exclaimed Dolores, involuntarily folding her hands, "then he has escaped ! Almighty God protect his flight ! be with him as thou art with us !"

"He is not on board, then ? that is well, for then, at least, they do not suspect where he has gone—they have no trace of him in and around Buenos Ayres   Fate, also, appears to favor him "

"May God grant it !" sighed Dolores again

"Has he any one of our friends as his confidant ?" inquired Barigaldi, hastily, as before

"Joseph Testa is in communication with him," replied Ormur

"Joseph Testa, from Rio Negro ?"

"The same, he was in Buenos Ayres, and assisted our embarcation," continued Ormur

"Well ! then, Brother Celeste is in good hands. with God's permission, we shall hear from him in good time   An Englishman, Mr Walker, is called to account for your flight, Señora, you have staid in his house," continued Barigaldi

"And what course did he take to clear himself ?" inquired Dolores, with anxiety

"So far as I learn by the spy's papers, he seems to be a clever old fellow   He affirmed that he knew nothing at all of your political position, and complained of his son for having probably carried you away, since the police, to his great terror, as he affirmed, had found his daughter remaining in Buenos Ayres, who was to have gone with his son to Rio de Janeiro, but instead of her, he supposed his son had probably taken you with him   He described the whole affair as a love adventure, and the police are not yet wholly satisfied as to the authorship   Only the spy, Perezoso, as he was called, appeared to know your true position, but as yet he had confided it to no one "

The ingenious turn given by old Mr Walker, to mask the sudden departure of Dolores, and to divert the suspicion from himself, of having favored her flight, was too comical not to excite a hearty laugh, in spite of the seriousness of the occasion

"That looks like old Mr. Walker," observed

Horatio "I can picture to myself exactly how he played his part before the police, and in fact there was no other way for him to extricate himself from this scrape into which his sympathy for us had led him"

"There was no other way," said Dolores, "but I am convinced that he is able to lead the police astray, and that many of them really believe him But what has become of Perezoso?"

"The people of the cutter, here, threw him overboard," answered the Italian

"My God!" cried Dolores, "drowned?"

"Drowned! like a cat," continued Barigaldi, "after having been shown to be the originator of this expedition for our overthrow He has found his reward as a police spy in the waves"

Dolores appeared absorbed in painful contemplations upon the death of the man, who, notwithstanding, had openly sold her life for gold

Barigaldi continued "Approve my counsel Señora remain quietly for the present in Rio de Janeiro, or the neighborhood Perhaps we may hereafter offer you a more secure asylum in Rio Grande, that is my desire In either case, you shall soon hear from me Ormur will, I hope, soon take a privateer, like mine, and come to us, but without protection on our part, you cannot remain in Brazil"

"These two friends," replied Dolores pointing to Horatio and Alvarez," will, I hope, remain in my neighborhood, and my old servant, the negro there, will not leave me, our enemies can only succeed by the most deeply planned and well executed measures, if at all, in isolating and capturing me"

"It is probable, notwithstanding the fate that has so speedily overtaken the betrayer, that your authorship and whereabouts may be discovered, and vengeance become more envenomed in proportion to its difficulty. Pardon me, if I repeat what you may consider a superfluous warning, "omit no precaution"

"My situation will be the more critical, because the customs and prejudices in regard to my sex oblige me to live with some family, who may be more or less indifferent to my fate"

"I feel that it is so," interrupted Hinango, "another case, that may well lead us to serious contemplation of the social position of the female sex, which we will discuss at some future time"

The thunder storm, whose lightnings were hardly visible in the far distant sky, reminded the commander of the Mazzini of the pressing need of haste, he handed some papers to Hinango, saying "We have mutual reports to make to each other upon the progress and present circumstances of our spiritual association, and upon South America, foreseeing the chance that we might speak to each other for a moment, I have arranged some extracts and several letters for you to deliver to our friends in Europe

I beg you, in case our voyage admits of it, to write down what you have to communicate to me from Europe, before we separate in the latitude of Rio Grande."

"I have already, like yourself, availed myself of some leisure hours here on board," replied Hinango, "to draw up my report for you, and I will hand it to you I would remark, however, that my statement of the circumstances of Europe, in respect to the extension of our association, can only serve as a hasty sketch, since the subject is too comprehensive, and I am not in the state of mind which is absolutely necessary for such a labor I will get the leaves for you"

He hurried down into the cabin—Dolores followed him with her eyes, and Barigaldi said, in a subdued voice

"A singular man, our friend Ormur, one of the most singular I have ever met with, the most reckless devotion to the cause of the people, with renunciation of all thought of acknowledgement, and even despairing of the result in our generation A man whose path from childhood has been in one direction, and whose spirit has taken a flight in which ordinary men cannot accompany him He is, with all his failings, defects, and weaknesses, one of the most disinterested men I know, but also one of the most unhappy Can you conceive of the greatest harmony and consistency in word and deed, a spiritual and moral unity, founded upon unshaken conviction, elevated by religious faith, united with the most deeply lacerated heart, with renunciation of all expectations in life, with hopelessness of a single hour of joy—a gloomy disconsolateness which endures life, and longs for the grave?"

Dolores heard this description of her protector, with profound emotion, and replied, in as low a tone

"Until now, I have neither sought, nor accidentally found the opportunity to touch the chords of his inward life, to awaken sounds which might indicate such a state of mind as you describe But I suspected, in a manner unaccountable to myself, a similar state of mind in our friend, and I can conceive it of him I can combine the unconditional consequence of individual suffering with renunciation and devotion to the cause of the people Only an egotist fastens himself on this earthly existence, because he believes in no higher"

"Figure to yourself," said the Italian, "a man who stands isolated in the midst of the social world, as far removed from them, as he is, here on board, remote from the firm land, a soul, with the deepest susceptibilities for love and friendship, whom, however, no woman did understand, not love, and who, proscribed by our political enemies, even often misapprehended by our associates, is frequently injured by our friends "—

"No woman, you say, did understand him, and has ever made him happy with her love? How is that possible, since he appears to possess many of the qualities with which a man should inspire affection?"

"Exalted mind, noble sentiment, and the firmness of a manly character, seem not to be always appreciated by woman, on the contrary, I suspect that the heart of our friend has been wounded and poisoned by a woman, in spite of his mind, sentiment, and character There is a secret in his soul, which, besides God, one being has ever known Whether this being yet lives, we, who know him as a friend, are ignorant You will know him better during your voyage, and before he leaves Rio de Janeiro; but the gloomy veil which envelopes his mind, will hardly be rent to your view Touch the veil, and you will behold in him a convulsive ebullition, the furies will be awakened in him He is an Orestes towards a Pylades, but an Orestes, also, pursued by Eumenides—only with the difference that he has found no 'sister,' whose deliverance from the bonds of tyranny may reconcile him with an offended God It seems as if his peace of mind were gone—as if the sanctuary of his inward life had been disturbed by some 'Vandalism'"

Hinango here returned on deck, and delivered the papers to his associate, saying, with a smile "We must, then, separate, to remain near each other, if you are willing to 'make little sail in a good wind,' that we may be able to follow you "

"I will endeavor to remain near you, that I may be at hand in case of need," replied the other "The man-of-war cannot overtake us, if the storm should even drive her after us We have passed the English Bank. Follow after me, I will be your pilot, even though you no longer require me Farewell ' It is to be hoped that we shall escape the Pampero as luckily as we have the sbirri of Rosas, and find a fine day, in the latitude of Rio Grande, to take leave, until we meet again in Rio Grande itself" After some heartfelt words from all, he was hurrying, with all speed, from the quarterdeck, as Capt Finngreen stepped up to him, and, after the sacred custom of Northern hospitality, refused to allow him to depart until he had emptied a glass of wine to "mutual prosperity and success, a good wind, and hopes of a better future to all the oppressed nations upon earth "

Barigaldi already stood with one foot upon the gangway steps, and then turned to the two captains of the Nordstjernan, with a look at the cutter, and exclaimed "Apropos ' what shall we do with the cutter ' She is a good prize, and I would take her after me, in tow, if some one else could not make better use of her "

He now turned to Patrick Gentleboy, who sat in the stern of the cutter, with a bottle from the stores of the Nordstjernan

"Son of the ever green Erin '" cried Barigaldi to him, "I give the cutter to you, for you honestly deserve it Come on board of the Nordstjernan, and go with it to the latitude of Rio Grande The cutter will find room here by the longboat, in case the Pampero becomes too strong, and threatens to break the tow line Shall it not be so, captain ' You will take them up—the man and the cutter ?"

"With pleasure," said Capt. Finngreen ; "I will send a couple of men down to bring the cutter to us again "

"Besides, I desire," said Barigaldi to Patrick, "that you should, circumstantially, relate to the captain, and some of the passengers, how you came to be with us You will find time enough for that at sea "

"All right, your honor !" cried Patrick, "and, faith ' I've enough to tell " Then putting the bottle to his lips, he exclaimed "Health, and long life, and good luck, to your honor ! and sure I'm much obliged to ye, and I'll take this hat, and sword, too, by your honor's lave, and thin I'll be a navy officer, with hat and sword, and a 'private privateer,' owner of my own vessel Glorious that ' is't not? If only the folks in ould Ireland could know of it !"

"We thank you, you have brought us all out of danger by your presence of mind ; perhaps a career, as a seaman, will soon be opened to you. If I equip a privateer, you shall be my first boatswain, if you desire it," said Hinango to him

"Thank your honor kindly, and heaven bless you all, gentlemen, but, for the present, I am captain of the cutter, and passenger on board the brig here, by your lave "

Some sailors of the Nordstjernan followed the commander of the Mazzini down into the cutter, which quickly passed to the schooner, and then returned. The cutter, and her lawful commander, Mr Patrick Gentlebov, soon found themselves on board of the Swedish brig, which hoisted sail and resumed her course

The waters at the mouth of the La Plata had assumed a loamy yellowish color, and here and there the foam curled over a tolerably high wave The cloud bank in the southwest had extended itself to a gray dusky veil, which nearly covered the entire horizon The seabirds soared in hurried flight around the sails and yards of both vessels, through whose rigging the outbreaking storm piped and howled, as through the sides of an Æolian harp

The Mazzini was under sail, and gave the farewell salute with a full round Capt Finngreen replied with his four cannon, which, loaded in such eventful hours, could scarcely have been fired under more fortunate circumstances.

The man-of-war, La Caza, appeared in the far distance, seeking her cutter and the Swedish brig, on whose mast commander Tumble expected to see the Rosas' flag, which Señor Codo had carried with him for this purpose What reflections occurred to him when he beheld the Nordstjernan under sail, and could see nothing of his cutter, and what curses he sent out into the roaring pampero, which, by degrees, carried away from him the object of his pursuit, we leave unmentioned

---

CHAPTER VII.

BRAZIL

THE Nordstjernan followed the Mazzini at a short distance, and carried as much sail as the constantly increasing storm would permit, to keep in sight of her leader, which, as Mr Walker had said, was tossed about like a "nutshell," indeed, from one foaming wave to another

Many of the passengers on board the Nordstjernan, did not feel very comfortable at being carried to sea in such weather, and Dr. Merbold asked the captain "why he did not cast anchor until the storm was over " The wind was in itself favorable, and a seaman would not have wished for a "better opportunity" to pass the sand banks at the mouth of the river

Dolores and her companions looked back upon the last few hours with excited feelings, their souls were like the ocean, which, after having been tossed about by the tempest, does not find rest when the storm ceases, but the sun breaks forth, but continues to raise on high its foam crested waves

The past danger lay behind her like a gloomy dream, in which were seen many figures of corpses, and which had threatened her with the grave The storm that now lay around her, gave her no alarm Persons who are penetrated by an exalted idea, who devote their lives to some inward conviction, know no fear of death, no anxiety from surrounding danger The consciousness of their free sacrifice is inwoven with a firm confidence in divine power, the source from which proceeds the light whose rays illuminate their souls—In such cases their faith urges upon fatalism, insomuch as they feel that the mission upon which they are sent, is not yet fulfilled on earth, and that the mysterious power which men call "providence," or "fate," conducts them, through storms and dangers, to their goal, to the completion of their mission

Hinango, whose mind was occupied with his next destination, his personal cooperation in the struggle of the Brazilians for the establishment of their freedom, sought a moment of leisure to look over the papers which Barigaldi had handed to him, and read hastily and cursorily the following—

FRAGMENT ON BRAZIL

Communication of a Brazilian, 1838

So far as I am acquainted with the representations of the political circumstances of Brazil in European pages, they give, for the most part, an obscure and confused view of the real state of affairs Nearly all the statements flow from foreign pens, and arise at the instance of some embassy or other, or at least proceed from persons who are dependant upon some European court, and most of whom travel at the expense of royalty, and, of course, endeavor to represent the monarchial principle, although, notwithstanding this, they do not deny the progress and development of the republican spirit in Brazil The conclusions of such articles in newspapers and reviews, are of a very peculiar character They deplore the disturbed state of our country, and prophesy the downfall of the state, by bankruptcy of the finances, or revolution, "if the European powers do not finally take the thing in hand, and restore peace and order amongst us"

The Brazilians may well smile, when they read, or hear such phrases, which have been 'worn threadbare for the last twenty years, while, since the first republican insurrection in Pernambuco in 1817, we have often given the European powers sufficient opportunity to gather the bloody experience, that, up to the present time, it has not been an easy matter to establish among us what they term "peace and order," by means of foreign bayonets This "most Christian," magnanimous, and diplomatically heroic co-operation of the European powers, for the maintenance of despotism in Brazil, has, unfortunately for them, thus far, failed in its object, since it has called forth the might of our people by an uninterrupted struggle, and strengthened them by means of internal excitement

In those "standing phrases" upon the future prospects of Brazil, through the influence and intervention of European powers, lies one of the diplomatic contradictions by which these people sometimes compromise themselves.

If Brazil as a monarchy approaches bank-

ruptcy, will the European powers generously pay our state debt? or will they, like England, (with equally magnanimous Great Britannical stipulations,) increase our public debt, by means of a loan, and thus still more derange our financial relations, thereby hastening the prophesied downfall of the state, and bringing about the fulfilment of the prophecy, instead of retarding it?

Will the European powers anticipate the downfall of the Brazilian monarchy, through revolution, by the intervention of their armed troops? Supposing that the revolutionary spirit in their own countries should permit them to despatch entire armies across the ocean, at whose cost is this to be accomplished? At Rothschild's?

Grant that such "disinterested intervention" should here and there introduce a republican insurrection, would these fantastic hosts then magnanimously withdraw, reship, and return home at Rothschild's expense? I have as yet as little conception of the generosity of the European diplomacy for the deliverance of the tropical monarchy, as they apppear to entertain of the position of our people I behold in their measures, instead of the deliverance and preservation of the monarchy, directly the reverse, the downfall of our state by dismemberment and division, after the European diplomatic method, and to avert this fate, is the first and most sacred duty of every Brazilian

I may be allowed to presuppose a superficial acquaintance with the history of Brazil, and point out, here, only the various epochs which have been inscribed with our blood upon the annals of the century

Brazil, under Portuguese sovereignty, presented the scandalous picture of an absolute monarchy, in which demoralization, proceeding from the court, went hand in hand with the stupifying system of the priesthood Portuguese aristocrats, for the most part adventurers, who, for various reasons, had removed from the mother country to seek their fortunes in the New World, formed here the basis of a social world, in which not even bigotry itself would thrive, which here, as everywhere else, should sustain the monarchy

The Europeans may, with justice, describe the former condition of Brazil as a sink of demoralization and barbarism What morality could flourish in a society whose founders left the Old World to despoil the gold mines of a country by means of negro slaves, and recognised sensual animal enjoyment as the aim of life, from the first Minister of the State, and the Prior of the monastery, down to the meanest lackey, who, like his lord, went to work, systematically, to increase the population by mulattoes Trades people, of different countries, who settled in the seaport towns, and whose number was as limited as trade itself, (then a monopoly of the Portuguese government,) cannot be considered as exercising any influence on manners and culture

The historical fact, however, that already, in the beginning of our century, a decided spirit of Brazilian nationality, founded upon morality, showed itself under this priestly government, which recognised the suspicious position of the European adventurers, and met with deserved contempt their plundering of the rich country, as well as their degrading treatment of the natives, the descendants of European ancestors all this appears to me more remarkable than the condition of licentious degradation, which must proceed, as a natural consequence, from the former element

If we consider the original white population of Brazil, descended from condemned criminals,[*] persecuted Jews, women thrust forth from society, aristocrats without nobility of soul, priests who evaded celibacy, soldiers who stood in the same class with galley slaves, (independently of the preponderating number of mulattoes,) it must certainly be an elevating phenomenon, that Brazil, notwithstanding all the systematic demoralization of Church and State, has become a nation, that, upon the slightest influence of historical events in Europe, has shown the spirit of progress, the desire for freedom, to be the condition of all civilization, and has often maintained it with her blood.

Indeed, this appearance of a nation, in the consciousness of its national dignity, in an uninterrupted, decided struggle for republican freedom, at the beginning of the third century[†] after its settlement, furnishes material for the most serious consideration upon the ennoblement of the human race, as a natural, self-consequent condition.

Different as may be the provincial character of the inhabitants, from Para to Rio Grande, all travellers, who have given the result of their observations to the world, unanimously acknowledge the Brazilians as an upright, hospitable people, susceptible of great cultivation, and striving after it, and endowed with high intellectual talents and capacities

None will deny that despotism, as well as priestcraft, made every exertion to retain the people under their yoke, and to undermine and choke down the spirit of enlightenment, the desire for freedom, in the heart of the nation Brazil was kept, as it were, in a perpetual quarantine, for the prevention of contagion from so called " liberal ideas " Europe sent over shiploads of priests, in monk's cowls and secular habits, and armies in the service of the crown, and yet, all these endeavors of absolute, as well as of constitutional monarchy, were in vain The country itself, which, up to the year 1810, had delivered to Portugal over 1,400,000 lbs of gold, and upwards of 20,000 lbs of diamonds, appeared to have relinquished into the hands of the monarchy all conceivable means of overwhelming the provinces with its power

And what has the Portuguese dynasty done for the welfare of mankind, with these millions ' What has Portugal accomplished, with such means, for the civilization of Brazil—for the civilization of Europe '

Portugal treated us as vassals of the crown, and, at the present time, every Portuguese *parvenue* considers our country as a Portuguese colony, detached by rebellion, but which will,

with the help of England, and other European powers, sooner or later, again become the property of the crown.

A second element of foreign disturbance was developed, when Portugal relinquished the monopoly system of export and trade, and, as it were, partly pledged, and partly sold, the whole monarchy to England   While England sought, in Brazil, a free market for her manufactures, she loaded the most important of our productions with an import duty of two hundred per cent , and received her handsome interest for the loan of three millions of pounds sterling, magnanimously offered under truly Britannic conditions

Moreover, England has possessed herself, by means of private enterprise, of nearly all the gold mines of the country, and supports the government, (which will transfer the country, with its land and naval forces, to the pawnbroker's shop—Britannia,) when the nation, wearied with such maltreatment, assert their rights, and contend for the " liberty" which the Briton has in his mouth while he helps to destroy it

Our constitutional government shows an annual deficit of almost a million of pounds sterling, (nearly one-third of the whole revenue,) and the European royalists appear to wonder, that hardly a year passes, in which a rebellion does not break out in one part of Brazil or another, the republican tendency of which they cannot themselves deny, and to suppress which, the state debt must be still more increased, by means of foreign bayonets, or, at least, by means of foreign money   The monarchical system is, more evidently, working its own downfall here, than in other countries, under similar circumstances, and whoever will still deny the hastening overthrow, must be as narrow-minded as the government which considers it possible to maintain itself by such a system.

The creatures at the head of the government, who also serve as its instruments, appear to perceive, very clearly, the approaching downfall of the last and only monarchy in South America, and even in this perception they seem to find an additional reason for the ruin of the finances   These high officers of Brazil steal with the same effrontery as the privileged and order-decorated crown thieves of Russia, or any other legitimate or quasi legitimate monarchy, while the heir to the crown (a tragical sacrifice to the principle he represents) is brought up under the influence of Austria, to become an emperor, whose person is intended to be every thing to the people, and a cypher to the ministers, which, in their political calculations, they place before numbers, where a cypher is of no value   Out of the above elements, three parties have been formed in Brazil · the *Caramuros*,[*] the Portuguese aristocratic party , the *Moderados*, the constitutional mercantile, (the *juste-milieu ;*) and the *Faroupilhas*, the republicans, with sword in hand

The preponderating number of the last was ascertained by the election of the regent, during the interregnum in the year 1835, which, by a great majority, gave the helm of state to the patriarch Feigo, formerly an ecclesiastic of the

---

[*] The above mentioned selection, for the later population of the country, offers brilliant facts in proof of the system of demoralization intended to uphold legitimacy there.

[†] During the first century after the discovery of Brazil, Portugal hardly took any notice of this New World—a neglect, the cause of which can only be traced to the narrow spirit of such a priest-ridden government.

[*] *Caramuros.*—An Indian word, signifying men with fire arms

Moderado.—Temperate, moderate

Faroupilhas.—Ragamuffins, sans culottes.

highest rank, and an abomination to the European powers, who, as the supporters of the Caramuros, used every means to bring about a state of anarchy, in order to disgust the venerable chief ruler of Brazil with the regency

Feigo[*] abdicated his office with resignation, since he probably perceived that the Brazilian monarchy was not to be saved by a single man, and his position was too elevated, that he, as a republican, should attach any value to being monarchical regent of his country.

We will now consider the position of the Portuguese and Britons

The Portuguese are attached to, and dependants of the Caramuros, and would as gladly reinstate the Portuguese absolute monarchy as the Britons, who would certainly patronise this "Christian work" as zealously as they once did the like in Spain—while in Brazil they endeavor to put down the people, by force of arms, wherever they stand up for their rights

The bitter hatred of the Brazilians, against the British and Portuguese, is, of course, a logical consequence, resulting from the nature of things

A nation cannot be more speedily led to the development of freedom, than when it is directly, or indirectly, under foreign dominion And who will deny that we are under foreign dominion? We are under British dominion, for we are pawned to England, and systematically drained of our wealth by England We are under the Portuguese yoke, for the majority of government officers are Portuguese parvenues, declared enemies to the Brazilian nation, under the influence of the European Great Moguls, who, through their ambassadors, directly rule the court, (their own workmanship,) and, in its dependance, their diplomatic plaything

Let no man wonder that the people, impoverished by direct and indirect extortions of foreign avarice and foreign usury, and despised by foreign selfishness, rise up in despair, and make "short work" with all the British and Portuguese, as they did in Para two years since, and as may well happen again in other places [†]

British travellers, who appear as authors, reproach us that we let the children of our negroes live in our families, and grow up with us and our own children, whereby they acquire a certain groundwork of moral culture, and these same Britons desire to be thought zealous "Abolitionists," and "Christian philanthropists"

I touch here upon this British inconsistency, because the matter is, in itself, more important than it appears

In no country is there so little prejudice against color and religion, and no where is tolerance towards black and white so prevalent as in Brazil The growing up together, and the relation to each other as playfellows, of black and white, has an important influence upon the moral condition of the people, which, undeniably, proceeds from it. In the great cities, as Rio de Janeiro, for example, the proportion of the white population to the black, is as one to three,[*] and the number of criminals, according to the official lists of the prisons, is an average of five whites, to one negro, or colored person, and, moreover, among these whites, the smallest number are native Brazilians, the majority are foreigners, who honor our country by coming to it as vagabonds, or chevaliers d'industrie. The fruit and vegetable trade, the fishery, the retail trade of subordinate necessaries, and the commonest handicrafts, are followed by free negroes, and colored people; and there is hardly a more honest and industrious class in any city of Europe, than our free colored people

While the slave trade is declared by our constitution to be abolished, the government, directly or indirectly, promotes and favors the introduction of negro slaves for the benefit of British mines and British plantations, and for the "fazendas[†]" of our aristocrats in the interior of the country

Proprietors of the middling class, (fazendeires,) in possession of a small number of negroes, cannot, very naturally, keep pace in the cultivation of the soil with British speculators and Portuguese aristocrats, who transport here, from Africa, whole cargoes of negro slaves for their plantations, and establish fazendas, and dig mines at pleasure The strict enforcement of the prohibition against the introduction of negro slaves, and the entire abolition of slavery, would be to the interest of the people, the inhabitants of the interior cultivating their lands as beneficially by the labor of free negroes, as under the above mentioned circumstances by slaves They have not the capital of the foreigners and aristocrats at their command, to keep some hundred negroes at work, and each negro is, to the less wealthy, a considerable property in himself, which cannot be insured against sickness or accident, while a richer person would suffer less from the loss of a single one

When our negroes in the insurrectionary provinces fought like lions by the side of their former owners, they did not fight with the savage thirst for blood, but with the "strength" of lions, and with manly consciousness The negro of Brazil is not so stupid as he sometimes appears, and the heart of a negro feels and suffers, at times, more deeply than the hardened hearts of white men.

This tolerance of the whites, and the setting aside of all prejudice against color, so that a mulatto can as well become minister of state as a Portuguese, is undeniably a cause and incitement to moral and physical ennoblement, while the negroes of other countries, who glory in their "freedom," despised and treated like brutes by the whites, become degraded below the brutes, to the disgrace of our century.

I close these fragmentary observations upon the political relations of Brazil, with the remark

---

[*] Diego Antonio Feigo, one of the most interesting and noble characters of our century, was apprehended in 1842, at the headquarters of the republicans in St Paulo, and carried prisoner to Rio de Janeiro, where the author became acquainted with him

[†] When the provinces of St Paulo and Minas Geraes had united with the republican revolution in Rio Grande, in 1842, and the rebels were only one day's march from Rio de Janeiro, the night was appointed in which all the British and Portuguese there should be put to the sword A defeat of the insurgents by a sudden attack of the government troops, in a narrow pass not far from Sabara, hindered, for the moment, the execution of this plan Among the numerous captures that were made on that occasion, the author saw the most respectable men of the higher classes, from the provinces as well as from the capital.

[*] Rio de Janeiro numbers 280,000 inhabitants, of whom 80,000 are white, the rest colored. (1838.)

[†] Farms.

that the constitutional monarchy, which at various times has driven deputies from the chamber with bayonets, and fired upon the representatives of the people, has already provisionally planned its own act of abdication, and has fired, in anticipation, a salute over its own open grave

The diplomatists of the European powers, and their mercenary writers, may describe the situation of affairs to their courts as their politics require, they will not alter with their pens the reality of facts, nor, at any future time, crush with troops, landed from their ships of war, the republic, which grows like a caterpillar in its chrysalis, and, like that symbol of life, awaits its hour to break forth.

A people, whose country is the richest and loveliest on earth—a people, whose patriotism embraces such a paradise—a people, who, for twenty years, have struggled for freedom, and deluged the soil with their blood, have a right to the blessings of liberty   And liberty is not the monopoly of certain races of men—not a blossom of certain zones   Brazil shall be free, and become a free state of South America !"

APPENDIX TO THE ABOVE FRAGMENT

——— THE republican insurrection of the province of Rio Grande, which the royalists ridicule, as an outbreak of " the infectious distemper" that has crept in there from the neighborhood of the Banda Oriental, was originally connected with the war of extermination against the Portuguese and Britons in *Para*, and with the proclamation of the republic in Bahia, in July, 1835.   The enemy must, at least, give to the negroes who fought at Bahia, in connexion with the whites, the glorious testimony, that it was with difficulty, and more by accident than by tactics, that they succeeded in burying the proclaimed republic alive for the present ———

——— Rio Grande, which is less mountainous than the provinces near the equator, and, lying outside of the torrid zone, is favored with a mild climate, offers to its population inexhaustible riches from agriculture and grazing, and presents, in common with the southern provinces of South America generally, a similarity to the patriarchal world of ancient days ———

From the early exchange of occupancy, the Spanish national character is there found mingled with the Portuguese, while a great number of Italians and Germans have likewise founded there a new fatherland for themselves

The recruiting for the Brazilian military service, which was carried on in the north of Germany, has, as is well known, since the year 1820, been the cause of the introduction of ship-loads of white slaves[*] to Rio de Janeiro—a traffic in men which is only distinguished from the African slave trade by the difference in the color of its subjects   The Brazilian government avails itself of an officer from the south of Germany as its principal agent, who even empties whole penitentiaries, and buys the prisoners of the governments, for body guards to the Brazilian court

These "jail birds," and similar vagabonds,

[*] *Escravos brancos.*—A nick-name which the negroes have given them.

were, however, dispersed amongst the great body of troops, which, commanded likewise by German officers, numbered among them many respectable men, who deserved a better fate than they found in Brazil, until they finally received their dismissal, and a part of them settled in Rio Grande

The disbanding of these German troops forms a tragical episode in the history of the monarchy of a country, one of the richest on earth in gold and silver, but which had not once punctually paid their wages, even in paper money. They shed their blood on credit, for the greater part of them were sent to fight against the republicans, in the southern and northern provinces, and there won the reputation of " brave soldiers," while the equally brave Brazilians, opposed to them, destroyed whole battalions, and sent the rest back as invalids to Rio de Janeiro

After a fruitless campaign against Monte Video, that ended with a chapter in which the Brazilian government did not assume the most brilliant position, a part of these troops returned to Rio de Janeiro, just as a revolution again broke out, in 1825—which was only suppressed, with difficulty, by troops landed from European vessels of war   These German regiments (all creditors of the monarchy so rich in gold) formed the centre of the insurgents, and even though the republican principle was not awakened in the hearts of many of them, the empty stomach, at least, demanded its natural right, and they fought with the courage of despair

Similar events, which we find inscribed in bloody paragraphs upon each leaf of the history of Brazil, indicate the nullity of a monarchy whose government, being a production of European power, becomes a gold mine to the intriguers who know how to advance themselves to its summit, and, with unexampled audacity, ruin the state finances, while, with like audacity, they increase their own

Under such circumstances, it remains, evidently, impossible for the most able and upright men in Brazil, when summoned by the voice of the people to a share in the government, to overcome difficulties which the diplomatists of European powers attribute, as a well known consequence, to the free press, and to the studies and travels of respectable Brazilians in France.

The influence of Austria and England upon Brazil is the more powerful, from their having two means at their command, the operation of which is more dangerous, as they know how to mask it·

Austria, which, in the year 1820, took under its protection the Jesuits driven out of Russia, not only seeks to extend the priestly government in Brazil, through the influence of the dynasty, but to hold the spirit of the people under bit and bridle, by the establishment of Italian monastic orders, under pretence of converting the savages, without considering the impossibility of causing the perpendicularity of the movement of the progress of the times to " stand still."

England pursues, in her own manner, but with more sagacity, the plan of a future sovereignty over Brazil, since she not only obtains a temporary right, by financial speculations, and gains a firm footing in Brazil by means of trade, but seeks to extend her influence in the interior of the country, by Missionaries of the English Church, though this particular object often remains unknown to many of the worthy missionaries themselves.

Britannia, with the trident of Neptune in one hand, and the bishop's pastoral staff in the other, evidently aims at the same spiritual sovereignty, or, rather, at the same spiritual oppression, as the Jesuits, whose intrigues she is in nowise behind

Upon these two elements is founded the rigid, and every day increasing, intolerance of English Protestantism against Catholicism, which last mentioned faith, under the guardianship of the Jesuits, has spread, in the transatlantic world, from Canada to Buenos Ayres, but is less dangerous to the principles of liberty in Brazil, since the Romish Church has here undermined its own credit, by the "scandalous chronicle" of the priesthood

In South America there are two extremes of Catholic clergy Men who have, long since, in their hearts, renounced the worm-eaten "sacred chair," and endeavor, on the contrary, to perfect themselves by philosophical reading, and, on the other hand, priests who are monuments of ignorance and sensuality

We find, in Brazil, numerous examples of monks, in their monastic garbs, becoming members of the so called "secret societies," in whose mysteries they, at least, "seek" the spirit of enlightenment and progress, as a thirsty man presses to the fountain—though it is doubtful whether the society to which they have recourse, is able to offer them a spiritually strengthening nectar

It is a fact of pyschological interest, that the Brazilian, undeniably endowed with comprehensive intellectual powers and natural strength of judgement, eagerly receives a new system or a new idea, and endeavors to examine it thoroughly, in proportion as he is removed from all bigotry and religious fanaticism The Brazilian is passionate, and for want of a careful education, is easily led astray by extravagance, but even his extravagances have in them a certain spiritual noble side, and seldom degenerates into meanness

European teachers, who have found opportunity to observe and examine the Brazilian youth thoroughly, give brilliant testimony in relation to their mental progress, with the remark, that a young Brazilian is able to learn more in a month, than some youth of another nation in a year—the ardour of their characters showing itself in a thirst for knowledge, but a certain levity, equally natural, often leaving them at a distance from their goal

Psychologists, who seek to trace the generations of men from their origin, attribute this intellectual geniality of the Brazilians to the unpassioned nature of their equally attractive and susceptible women, on the one hand, in happy marriages, and on the other, in the social aberrations of those females who find themselves deceived in their choice, and understand how to satisfy the claims of the heart, where there has been a marriage without love

The monastic seclusion of the female sex in family life, and their defective education in convents, only the more promotes the extravagance of adventurous episodes, which the moralist lays to the charge of the women, while they are founded for the most part upon the heartlessness and the character of the man himself, who degrades the sacrament of marriage to the license of his sensuality, who lies to a woman of love, and leads her to the altar to have a wife

The consequences of the irresponsible levity with which a union is concluded, that is not only to last for life, but affects the existence of a future generation, the most sacred condition of the human race, stand forth more boldly in the tropical flower-world of Brazil, than in many other countries ——

While Hinango read these fragments on Brazil, (which we should not have inserted here, but that each remark has a direct or indirect reference to the development and summing up of our narrative,) the pampero howled through the rigging of the Nordstjernan, as it followed the Mazzini, which now disappeared in a trough of the sea, and then, lifted on high by a foaming wave billow, seemed to float in the air until night came on, when Barigaldi sent up a rocket, from time to time, as a sign that he kept on his course in spite of the pampero

CHAPTER VIII.

SLAVERY AND LOVE

WE leave the two vessels on their course, being called, by the events of our history, to far distant places, on the western declivity of one of those colossal chains of mountains, from five to six thousand feet above the level of the sea, which pass through Brazil from the south to the north, in unbroken elevations, for many hundred miles in length.

These mountains form, in some places, sloping table lands, (campos,) and in others, valleys of proportionable extent, intersected by numerous rivers, and countless forest streams On the abovementioned declivity were situated many fazendas, upon natural terraces of miles in width, surrounded by the tropical luxuriance of a flourishing vegetation

The sun had almost ended his apparent daily course, from right to left, in the northern hemisphere, and cast his glowing rays upon the equally picturesque and gigantic chain of mountains Some of the naked rocky summits glittered in singular shapes, while others were gloomily separated from them, in broad shadowy masses. The light blue, transparent horizon, unknown in Europe, whose atmosphere shows plainly to the naked eye, objects at a distance of miles, and forms that airy perspective, the outlines of which we see so sharply defined in Chinese painting, and which, true to nature, embraces the characteristics of a tropical landscape

These naked masses of rocks were lost, some hundred feet further down, in the endlessly diversified extent of mountain summits, clothed with the primitive forest, down to a third gradation of the stupendous edifice of nature.

In these latter, lower, earth regions of the mountains of Brazil, the eternal creative sculptural power, appears to have chosen the cone as its favorite form, and has placed, as if for picturesque grouping, at various distances, isolated sugar-loaf shaped granite blocks, some thousand feet high, and likewise partly decorated with luxuriant foliage, which serve as mile stones for the traveller

These grand conical masses, of various sizes, singly form, as it were, the fore ground of a landscape, or the middle point of a panorama, whose description would overstep the limits of poetic narration

"We will then go into Madame Fesh's, at the next fazenda If you like, Senor Capitao, I will let my mules rest there for an hour, and then go on a couple of miles, to Villa Tasso, to our Signore Serafini's, where I hope to meet Mr Dujour You will remain to-night at Madame Fesh's, as if we had no understanding with each other, and then come early in the morning, and get possession of his person" These words were spoken by an European, in the ordinary dress of a Mineiro,* consisting of a velvet jacket, a broad brimmed straw hat, a light vest, and linen pantaloons, the lower part of which were covered with high buckskin boots, with heavy silver spurs, he was riding on a mule, near a man in uniform, whom he called captain, the latter was a Brazilian officer of the permanentos, which were distributed in small numbers in the different military stations, (Destacamentos) in the interior of the country, serving as gens d'armes, and occasionally for the apprehension of "suspected persons," or faroupilhas

Besides these main duties, the Permanentos gave protection and succour to every loyal subject of the government, especially when they helped to sustain public order by the espionage and denunciation of patriots

The officer, whose rank was that of lieutenant, was well pleased with the title of captain, as he was of Portuguese descent, and possessed the desire for titles, and the anxious servility that characterizes the "woodenshoed aristocracy" of that nation, which they imbibe with their mother's milk. He longed for nothing more earnestly, than to wear the red riband of the order of Santo Christ, in his buttonhole before he died, that the cross might be paraded on his coffin.

"I like your plan Senhor Luiz,"† he replied, "but it seems to me more suitable, not to go quite so early in the morning, at least not until the negroes are at work on the plantation I have, it is true, thirty men with me, but—Senhor Serafini is probably sufficiently supplied with arms—and there might be resistance—bloodshed—which I wish to avoid "

"I understand you Senhor Capitao—just as you please—come to-morrow about ten o'clock, and then they will not be so apt to suspect me of having met you, and travelled some days in your company."

A man on horseback trotted up behind the two travellers, and informed them that some of the negroes had got sore feet, and, therefore, could not follow so rapidly This was Mr Nols, the servant of the European, who, at the same time, performed the duties of any Arreiro de la tropa, (leader of the caravan,) and as Toccadero,* or driver "Lay on the chigote (whip) and cut them as much as is necessary to make them trot '" replied Mr Louis What possesses you, to come to me just now with such information, as if you were leading an expedition for the first time ·"

"But their feet bleed at every step, Mr. Closting Pardon my replying Some of these new ones from Africa can, in fact, hardly stand, much less walk "

"That may be—but they must—at least they must be at the fazenda yonder, at the Italian's, in an hour and a half from this time Use the chigote, and follow after us "

The officer looked back upon the caravan, at the head of which followed his soldiers, whose march was as painful as that of the slave merchant's negroes The most of these permanentos went barefoot, and carried their shoes hanging upon their bayonets The greater part of them were recruits, natives of the country, of all colors, from the blackest negro up to the tawny white Brazilian, intermixed with Mamelucos,† and some "civilized Botocudos " A spencer and pantaloons, with what is called a "bonnet de police," (uniform cap,) a sabre and cartridge box, and a rolled up "capote," which served them as a bed at night—was their whole equipment To the most of these poor devils of the armed force of the empire, who had gone barefoot through life from their childhood, the wearing of the heavy commissary shoes was a real misery, and plainly hindered their "progress" in military civilization

After the first vain attempts to march in shoes, had covered their feet with sores, and blisters, "they chose the least of two evils," and limped over sand, and gravel, and rough pieces of rock, like the negroes of the slave merchant in their company, marching barefooted, and marking many of their footsteps with their blood, but they knew the supple leathern instrument at the saddle of their officer, and dared not complain in the least, either to their arreiro on horseback, or to their corporal toccadero, like the new negroes from Africa, who were as yet but partially acquainted with the customs and whip usages of Brazil.

"In case we meet the grimpeiro,‡ Mr. Dujour, at Si Serafini's," continued Mr Closting, as they again rode forward alone, "I beg you will not speak to him of the affair, as if I had come to the knowledge of it through him. The suspicion of a communication with the authorities falls naturally upon him, and it is not impossible that the revenge of the faroupilhas, will be extended to him You see, captain, that I hazard my life, out of loyalty, from pure royalist sentiments "

"I acknowledge it," replied the other, "and shall know in what terms to speak of you in my report to Rio de Janeiro "

"But be, guarded in your expressions, captain '

---

* Inhabitant of the province of Minas Geraes.
† The Brazilians in their familiar intercourse, generally call each other by their Christain names

* A Brazilian caravan (tropa) generally consists of from twenty to twenty-five loaded mules, seven of which are driven by one toccadero

† A mixed race, derived from the Indians and whites.

‡ Grimpeiros.—People who search for gold mines, and wash gold dust without informing the government, as required by law.

be guarded," interrupted the informer, "letters do not go safely here, and if your report should fall into the wrong hands,"

"Do not concern yourself on that account, my report goes by the military escort, which will accompany the prisoner ——"

In thus conversing, the two riders approached the first fazenda which lay in their road, it was a good sized stone building, with an airy sort of front hall, generally used by the family as a sitting room. The terrific howl of a negro, under corporeal chastisement, resounded through the solemn stillness of the twilight, which threw, as it were, a purple veil over the romantic scenery around, before its hasty passage into night. The diversified chattering, the monkeys hopping about from twig to twig, sometimes screaming like the cries of a person in distress, sounded like a living echo to these fearful notes of despair, and awakened the discordant laughter of the parrots in the distant thickets of the gigantic forest.

Without taking the least notice of this daily occurring howl of chastisement, the two travellers fastened their mules to the stakes of an outbuilding of the fazenda, several of which were built in such a manner as to form a roomy courtyard between them, and were used as the dwellings of the negroes, and for household purposes.

A white man, in performing the duties of the principal overseer of the widow, received the two guests, and gave their mules in charge to some negroes.

"Our tropa will take up their lodgings here for the night," remarked the captain. "My people must give no one here any trouble; I have already given the necessary orders."

The tropa of the naturalist who traversed the country as both slave merchant, and pedler, consisted of ten mules, laden with various kinds of merchandise, and a horde of sixteen negroes and five negresses, likewise merchandise for sale.

Mr Nols, the arreiro, rode up to the building, and received his instructions for the approaching night, which he, like his negroes, in case they remained there, would have to pass under the open sky, unless, by the hospitality of the overseer, he should be allowed to sleep in some corner of an outhouse.

"Has not Banko come yet?" inquired Mr Closting of the arreiro.

"He is coming down this way, I heard him swearing just now, he is not far off," replied Mr Nols.

Banko was a German student, whom the celebrated naturalist had engaged as secretary, and brought out to Brazil, at his (Mr Banko's) expense, on his last voyage to Europe, as quasi envoy extraordinary, where he assumed all sorts of Brazilian titles.

"Have you collected your usual number of butterflies, to-day?" inquired Mr Closting, of the youth, who now approached in torn garments, and was almost burnt to a mulatto by the sun. "I shall examine them early in the morning—and if they are again worthless stuff, then I shall have something more to say to you," he added, without waiting for a reply.

"I neither in Dusseldorf nor Antwerp subscribed a contract to collect butterflies for you, not to mention a stipulated number," replied Mr Banko, whose countenance, embrowned as it was with the sun, showed an evident expression of European culture—and youthful unreserve.

"You at length undertake to reply to me, in an insolent manner?" said the naturalist, raising his gruff voice. "Do you not forget that you are in Brazil, and that we have here as good prisons for 'fantastical subjects' as in Europe?"

"If all the Europeans in Brazil should be imprisoned, who deserve it, without being 'fantastical' subjects, there would soon be no empty cells," replied the slave trader's secretary.

"Scoundrel! do you dare to say that to me in the presence of a Brazilian officer?"

"He hardly understands German," interrupted the other, "if you desire it, however, I can repeat it to him in Portuguese."

The answer to this remark, was a severe blow on the face, which the poor German student was compelled to take as the delayed postscript of the letters by which Mr Closting had engaged him in Europe "for scientific purposes."

"Captain, let this fellow be guarded to-night by your troop," said he, before the youth could come to his recollection, and who had just grasped his dagger, as some hobbling permanentos, at the order of the captain, pulled him backward before he had drawn his weapon from the sheath.

"Mr Closting!" he now exclaimed, suddenly recovering himself, and perceiving instantly the consequences which an immediate ebullition in defence of his injured honor would undoubtedly draw upon him. "Mr Closting, remember this I endure your ill usage, but I shall not forget it, I will take my opportunity to obtain personal satisfaction."

The prisoner disappeared behind the household buildings, and the two cavaliers now followed the howl of the person under chastisement, which had continued without intermission.

They entered the verandah of the dwelling house, and beheld Me Fesh upon a low chair, with a slate on her knees, near a wax light, protected from the wind by means of a glass shade. She was a robust, corpulent woman, about forty years old, with coarse features, and a still coarser expression. Her light hair hung in unconfined locks upon her yellowish brown neck. She counted and noted down, with a grim smile, the blows which a white man, her cousin, slowly laid on the unfortunate victim of her savage anger, while she held a watch, with second hands, in her left hand, and gave him a sign every time he was to strike *

The laws of esthetics will not permit us to take a look at the particulars of this bloody scene—but we must not leave, unobserved, three black corpses, which lay at a distance from the verandah, over the balustrade of which was extended the unfortunate slave, quivering with convulsive agony. One was the corpse of a young Mosambique female, of noble form, whose figure was like one of the antique group of Niobe, which is so frequently peculiar to the Ethiopian. Near her lay the corpse of a youth of the same race, as regularly formed, and not far from

---

* This, like so many other scenes of this novel, is entirely true, and is described as it actually occurred.

them, the body of a robust negro, from one of those tribes which dwell near the equator, in Africa, who, little favored by nature, possess countenances as " black as night," and whose bony frames cannot serve as models of manly beauty

" Is that you, Mr Closting " said the white widow, at length, after she had, without interrupting her tale, already cast several glances at the two guests, "I hardly knew you again—come nearer, I shall soon be through One hundred and forty-three," said she, in a low voice, to herself, and wrote some figures on the slate " I should wonder if he outlives the last seven Give it to him a little slower ' not before I tell you !" she called out to the white torturer, and then counted, with long pauses, after the minute hands of the watch The negro groaned, evidently in the last agony, while the heavy chigote (which bears a family resemblance to the Russian kantschu) wound itself, at each blow, round his body, and lacerated it in its tenderest parts

The hundred and fifty lashes, which his inhuman owner had appointed this evening for the slave's second dose, (after he had received the same number in the morning,) was counted A negro now brought, at her command, spirits of wine and pepper, to rub on the open and bleeding wounds, which nearly covered the whole body

The howl of the sufferer exceeded all human imagination, and whoever has not witnessed a similar scene, nor heard a sound of similar horror, to the disgrace of humanity, would scarcely be able to follow a description, which we avoid from consideration for the feelings of the reader

The fearful howl died away in hollow groans, and the rattling of the scarcely breathing chest, which gradually became fainter and weaker The rope, with which the half expiring body had been fastened, was loosed A young negress pushed the man with the pungent restoratives aside, as soon as the mistress went away She covered the dying man with a wet sheet, brought a garden watering pot, and sprinkled him, while another held vinegar and water to his lips, which did not move

" There lie, now, my two contos,* yes, if I say two contos and four hundred millreis,† at least," said Me Fesh to her guests, as she stepped into the room, of which the open door and window shutters, without glass windows, communicated with the verandah " May Satan take them all ' the damned black beasts ! Is it not enough to craze one, to live in this cursed country -" She then threw herself into an arm chair, gathered up her coarse hair, and endeavored to bind it with a handkerchief

" What has happened to you, Madame ?" inquired Mr Closting, who was seated by a table, set with wine and other refreshments, which the intendant, according to the custom of the country, had already provided.

" What has happened to me ?" screamed the lady of the house, gritting her teeth. " I will tell you It is infamous—unheard of ! Negroes are all the time becoming dearer, the importation of them is becoming more and more difficult, and I must take care that my growing children

inherit a sufficient number I have now four negresses who bring me, every year, a young one. Mulacks*, I tell you, black as ebony, and nearly all from one father—from Pluto, the robust fellow who lies there a corpse ! Nearly all from him ! And so, some months ago, I bought him another pretty black creature— Anastasia—a real model of beauty, smooth, I tell you, like black marble ! and I wished to give her to Pluto, and she refused ! Only think—she refused ! I observed, then, a young Mosambique, who had come from Africa with her, whom I had bought at the same time, I saw, in fine, that he liked her, and she him—also, that they were a love pair So I locked them in together, but nothing came of it, and then I agreed with Pluto that he should have Anastasia, in spite of her refusal, and gave Antinous, the lover of Anastasia, for a time, to the Frenchman, over there, who wanted to hire a negro, and agreed with him that he should lock up Antinous securely at night But what does Antinous do ? Neither lock nor key were of any avail, he ran away at night, and lay, as I was told, before the chamber below there, where I had locked in Anastasia with Pluto, and there he lay, and heard what was to be heard And what did he do ' He burst, like a madman, through the window, that Anastasia, perhaps intentionally, had not bolted on the inside, he sprang in upon them, I tell you And what did he do ? He stabbed his friend, his beloved, his wife, as he called her, Anastasia, and he stabbed Pluto, and then himself, last night Last night he stabbed them and himself, and there lie the corpses ! There lie my two contos—my two contos and a half? What do you say to that, Mr Closting ?"

" Nothing else, than that I could have told you beforehand how the song would end, my good Me Fesh, for I have had much experience in these matters The same case which has happened to you, occurred, with nearly the same symptoms throughout, and the same crisis, in Rio de Janeiro, sometime since, and in my neigborhood, in Maranham, where a white man played the part of Pluto, the black lover murdered him upon the bed of the one he called his beloved I know a third case of the sort, where a negress killed herself, when she was given to a ' Pluto,' instead of yielding to him, she stabbed herself Yes, yes, Me Fesh, these cattle are jealous, and feel love ! if one may use the word for cattle ! As the parental love of monkeys has become proverbial, we may far more justly make the love of the negro proverbial It they once feel love, it only expires with their lives "

" Stupid stuff !" replied Me Fesh, after a pause, " Stupid stuff ! love ! what is love ? Is it not all the same to such a creature, whether this or that one satisfies her—then one of those cattle is a woman for all, and can obtain what she desires—it is all the same from whom !" Me Fesh certainly did not reflect that she contradicted herself by acknowledging the womanly nature of the so called cattle, which she appeared to deny

" Do you suppose that I would have stabbed myself twenty years ago, when I was married," continued she " I was not asked whom I would marry, and it was all the same to me. My pa-

---

* A conto d'reis, is five hundred dollars.

† Four hundred millreis—two hundred dollars.

* A word used instead of negro.

rents gave me a husband, who possessed a handsome fortune, and when I first learnt to know any thing of matrimony, I found my lot very comfortable What you say about love, Mr Closting, is stupid nonsense How can such cattle feel it, when I have experienced no such sensation ?"

"You must consider " interrupted the naturalist, "that the negroes, of both sexes, are mere children of nature, and that love is a nervous disease, a matter of sentiment, which disappears among us whites, the more we advance in civilization Love is a disease madame ! a disease of the nerves, and in the female sex, it is subject to the influence of the moon I have made physiological observations, and have had sufficient proof on that subject Love is, however, a very dangerous nervous disease, if it is not overcome in time, and that is often difficult, especially with the negroes, who are very nervous Corpulent people are seldom attacked by this disease The more thickly the nerves are cushioned over, the more they are protected against external impressions and inward emotions, that is perfectly natural The only effectual remedy against love is civilization, which supersedes sentiment, and makes it ridiculous Among civilized people, this disease does not last long, and may be reckoned according to northern or southern climates The love of a civilized woman, under the influence of the moon, endures in the south only about two months—hardly two months, in the north, somewhat longer, but seldom three full moons ''

" Thank heaven !" said the lady, "that I have never been afflicted with this disease I had a husband—he is now in heaven—who suited me in every respect, and I lived very happy with him, night and day I have had eleven children, five of whom are living The world says, to be sure, that I used my husband ill, and worried him into his grave Let the world talk, it is nothing but envy, sheer envy, in other women who would be glad to have had as many children But I must take care, Mr Closting, to have young mulicks for my children, and there lie the corpses, and my Pluto is murdered May the devil take the cursed Apollino, who had his hand in the pie !"

" You mean the negro to whom you have just counted out his reckoning ?" inquired Mr Closting

" The same—Apollino, I mean Only imagine, he did not let loose my two great bloodhounds, ' Blackman ' and ' Nigger,' in the night, when all this happened, my two large chained bloodhounds, who would have torn Antinous as soon as he sprang over the garden wall And his consent, his black love service, shall cost him, also, his life Three and a half contos lie there in blood, and it is all the same to me if I lose six or seven hundred millreis more He shall die ! If he is alive, he shall receive his hundred and fifty early in the morning ! the infamous, miserable *kabendo !* that Apollino !"

" Then I have come as if sent for," began the slave trader, after a pause, " I have with me the most admirable samples of the male and female sexes; you can replace your loss immediately I will sell them at a moderate price, we will review them early in the morning Apropos !" said he, interrupting himself, while

- 15

he turned to the officer, who sat very quietly refreshing himself at the table, and consuming, with a good appetite, bread, and cheese, and bananas, and wine

" Apropos, captain, concerning our affair I will, then, immediately ride on to Villa Tasso, and leave my *tropa* here, and come back again, since I can make a trade here As to the fellow whom I placed in your charge as a prisoner, have the goodness to keep him safely to-night, and set him at liberty in the morning, when you break up Hand him over to my arreiro, Nols It is now nearly seven o'clock, I shall be at Villa Tasso by half-past eight, and that will be soon enough I hope Mr. Dujour will be there, waiting for me "

" Very well I give my full consent to the arrangement that we have spoken of," whispered the officer, " but will you ride alone ?'

" I shall take one of my negroes with me, and shall be here again in the morning My *tropa* can rest themselves Good night, then We shall meet in the morning, at ten o'clock, at Villa Tasso "

The officer accompanied the " confidant of the police to the verandah, where Mr Fesh had just received the intelligence that Apollino was no more

Curse after curse flowed from her angry lips; she did not seem so embittered by the loss, which she had evidently designed, as at the marred pleasure of taking her slate upon her knee, and the watch in her hand, and counting a hundred and fifty, the next morning Without returning Mr Closting's farewell, she went on, and at length burst into tears over the loss of the three contos, and some hundred millreis, and ordered the bodies of the four cattle to be buried in a filthy corner of the court

Isabenda, the young negress who had tried to soothe the wounds of the dying man by cooling applications, after a while, tremblingly approached her raging mistress, and, with downcast eyes, informed her that the corner of the court was rocky ground, and that it would be very difficult to bury the bodies there, since the rocks must first be blasted

" Then bury them, in the devil's name ! somewhere in the road, out there, where you will—so that I do not see the dead beasts in the morning "

Isabenda's deceit had gained her object, she dared to run the risk of her mistress discovering the incorrectness of her statement, for it certainly was not so difficult to dig a grave in that place, but her womanly heart, though in a dark colored body, risked ill treatment, and even death, which she might also, meet in a similar manner as it had snatched away her lover She acted according to her pure and deeply wounded feelings, for she lost a friend in Anastasia, and a lover in Apollino

The narrow mindedness, and insensibility of the mistress of the house, who considered nothing but her strong box, and saw nothing that could not be touched with the hand, did not permit her to look into the heart of a black, especially as she could with difficulty have suspected even an emotion of such sentiments in the heart of a white person, since she, like everybody else, judged others by herself, and was not able to think of any higher grade of feeling, or of mind, than the low one upon which she herself vegetated

Isabenda quickly departed, and hurried back to her friends, who, standing round the bodies in the unclean place, looked forward with anxious expectation to the result of the experiment planned by them Instead of giving the answer of the white fury in words, she sunk down, with tears and sobs, by Apollino's corpse The black bondsmen of the European lady stood around, in numerous groups, from the oldest greybeard to the youngest child Sympathy with the fearful fate of the victims, and suppressed feelings of vengeance against the Christian murderess, had assembled them to the burial, to the last service of love, from their human, feeling hearts They all gazed silently upon Isabenda, beholding in the outburst of her grief, a denial of her righteous wish, which none of them would have had the courage to express None dared to utter a question Isabenda suddenly rose, and gave them to understand, by a sign, that they were to take up the bodies and follow her She then hurried before them out of the court, across the road, to a hill, where a single palm tree reared its majestic head

"Here ! here !" she whispered in a trembling voice, anxiously looking back at the fazenda, as if she feared that the cursing voice of the white fury would yet reach her before the work should be fulfilled "Here ! but make haste," she repeated, and desired them to dig a large grave for three bodies, and a separate one for the corpse of Pluto

The burial was completed in deathlike silence The numerous hands, old and young, furnished with mattocks and spades from the fazenda, and urged on by sympathizing zeal, did not require much time, the graves were filled, and the piled up turf covered the place of rest All now knelt in a circle around the graves, as silently as they had accomplished their labor of love According to the various customs of the Ethiopian tribes, some crossed their arms over their heads towards the firmament The sentiment of their bleeding hearts was involuntary prayer, although, perhaps, not in the forms of a spiritless "wrapper to heaven," or even of another religious book of service, which Me Fesh bought of a peddling missionary, and gave to her amiable children, for the explanation of their Christian treatment towards the "negro cattle"

Fearing that if they remained long absent, some harm might be done to the fresh graves of the victims, all but Isabenda returned within the boundaries of the court Consoled in her anguish by the success of her bold resolution—consoled, if consolation for such grief is to be found on earth—she lingered alone by the grave of her beloved, who, although a despised negro slave, had sacrificed himself from brotherly love for a youth like himself, because he honored the power of that love in his friend, which he felt in the same degree in himself, and which he bore to his grave.

The moon rose above the distant chain of mountains in the east, and lighted the tear bedewed countenance of a woman, who, though despised by Christians, might, by her virtues and love, shame many Christians, since her heart was not yet laid waste by European "civilization."

CHAPTER IX

ARREST AND PLUNDER

VILLA TASSO was built upon one of the beforementioned terraces, which were formed by the collossal masses of granite composing the third gradation of the mountains, and whose varied valleys, partly covered with the richest layers of earth, produced the most flourishing vegetation

The main building was erected in the middle of the last century, by the ancestors of the present owner of the extensive plantation It was built in the Italian style, with high stories, and spacious saloons and chambers, with covered verandahs, on the balustrades of which was seen, here and there, the luxuriant foliage of an orange tree, while gigantic mangoes, Barbadoes cedars, jacarandas,* palm trees, and other ornaments of a tropical landscape, reached to the height of the roof, and rustled coolly, with their shady, fanlike branches, in the chambers of the upper stories. Many rooms of the first story afforded a beautiful prospect over a level space of many hundred square miles, whose hills and valleys offered an inexhaustible multiplicity and variety of the most idyllian and magnificent natural scenes, from the distant horizon to the surrounding foreground

In a room which fronted the east, simply furnished, after the European fashion, the verandah of which was peculiarly favored with similar prospects, sat Signore* Serafini, at breakfast, with his family, which was also partaken by some of the officers of his plantation, and by Mr Closting and Mr Dujour, who had agreed to meet each other at Villa Tasso

Although the family of Serafini had lived in Brazil for several generations, they still passed for Italian, since the language and customs were handed down from father to son, united with a love of art in all its branches

Several valuable oil paintings of the ancient Italian masters decorated the saloon, and various musical instruments pointed out the villa as the asylum of harmony, in this corner of the earth so remote from "civilization"

Carlo Serafini was a young man, not yet thirty years old, blessed in domestic happiness by the sacred bond of love, and considered the wealth inherited by him from his father, as a gift of Providence, by which he felt himself the more pledged to become useful to mankind, as far as lay in his power

Notwithstanding his predilection for the nation from which he originated, he passed among his country people, the Brazilians, for one of the most decided patriots, as had been the case with his ancestors

The susceptibility for the beautiful, the love of art that introduces the mind of man to an inner world, which, separated in a greater or less degree from outward life, gives the spirit a higher direction towards the perception of the great and the sublime, had been handed down in the family In accordance with this inheritance the element prevailed, in which alone this spirit is able to unfold itself, the element of moral free-

---

* Rosewood tree.

† Portuguese, Senhor ; Spanish, Senor ; Italian, Signore , the pronunciation is nearly the same.

dom With such endowments, the "man" was developed in Serafini, in the noblest sense of the word, in the consciousness of the duty of patriotism Sufficiently notorious as one of the most zealous Faroupilhas of Brazil, he took no less interest in the events of Europe, and especially in the struggles of the country of his fathers—in Italy's spirited and bloody struggles for nationality and freedom

'If you have letters to be despatched to Italy," said Mr Closting, in conversation at breakfast, " you ought only to confide them to me—I mean, especially, such letters as are of more importance than business correspondence You know who I am, you know my sentiments in relation to politics "

"I thank you, Senhor Luiz," replied the other, " I have, indeed, known you for years, as a naturalist, and negro trader, and tradesman I am much obliged to you, and will take the opportunity to avail myself of your passing through —— How does it happen," said he, turning to the other guest, evidently wishing to introduce another subject, " how does it happen, Mr Dujour, that your father calls himself *Daily*, and you bear a sort of translation of the name into French ? Pardon me this indiscretion, is it your stepfather who is called so ?"

" My father," said Dujour, (a man whose exterior indicated nothing peculiar.) " My father married when an emigrant in England, in the beginning of the year '90, and found it convenient, under peculiar family circumstances, to translate his name, Dujour, into English, though, perhaps, not very literally I returned this name during my first marriage, from which a son inherited it, who is now in a mercantile house in Buenos Ayres, and when I took my second wife, a very patriotic French woman, I looked up our old family papers, and made use of the French name, in judicial form, in Bahia, where I then lived "

"You are, then, married a second time ?" inquired Sra Serafini, who, with maternal tenderness, was endeavoring to feed, from a spoon, a beautiful boy, that she had lately weaned

" I *was* married a second time," replied Mr Dujour , " but, alas ! my second wife died in her first childbed, and I am a widower again An unlucky planet seems to hover over me and my family," sighed he, as he shelled a banana, and then, sunk in reflection, laid it out of his hand again " My father, you probably know, Senora —my father is—infirm in intellect , in a situation that I would rather not touch upon further Gold cannot bring happiness , on the contrary, I feel that the mines of Brazil have rather increased than lessened the miseries of mankind "

The lady of the house had too much delicacy of feeling to inquire further after the sufferings of old Dujour " Certainly," replied she, after a pause , " certainly the mania for seeking gold and making money, which comes upon so many men here like a disease of the climate, leads, in general, to no earthly happiness ; at least, we seldom see an example of a grimpeiro staying his thirst for gold-water, content himself with a modest income, and retiring to repose in some place where he may enjoy life, which here, in this paradise of the earth, presents so many charms, and offers a heaven upon earth, if our hearts would embrace an altar of love."

Serafini regarded Angelica, his wife, with a look expressive of his congenial perception of the truth which she had just uttered with such profound feeling, and in so gentle a manner Their glances met, Angelica's deep, dark eye sparkled, and her noble countenance beamed with that nimbus of love which, in the consciousness of the harmony of the soul, that feels itself transfigured in the soul of the beloved

"Yes ! life on earth is delightful—delightful and exalted, if we consider it as a spiritual existence, and all earthly goods only as means of more and more improving and perfecting our moral powers, and effecting the improvement of others, as far as we are able," said Serafini, in a serious tone

" Apropos !" interrupted Mr Closting, I hear that you have established a school for your negro children , is that true, or only a report ?'

" It is true," replied the planter, with a sharp glance at his interrogator , " I have erected schools for both sexes Why do you ask ?"

" Only because I found a connexion of ideas with the principles which you have just expressed That is very handsome of you , it does you honor "

" I considered it my duty, and my parents would have done it, long ago, if the priests here in our neighborhood had not endeavored to interrupt the measures for such an object by all sorts of intrigues Besides, you know I buy no more negroes since the slave trade is abolished by law , I am trying to carry out another system "

" I belong, it is true, at present, to the class of grimpeiros," said Mr Dujour, taking up the word, and addressing the lady , " you have also designated me with this class , but I am gradually in the way of turning my property into diamonds, into which I have partly converted the income that I have acquired by making gold into money, and I intend buying a fazenda I wish to follow the example of your husband, and perhaps become your neighbor "

The clerks left the table and the room, hastening to their employments, and the two guests remained alone with the family

" Our bargain is closed Mr Closting," he continued, in a lower tone , " you shall have the diamond for twenty contos, and take possession of it here, in the presence of my friend, Signore Carlo in payment, two-thirds in ready money, in gold and silver coin, a third part in exchange, upon houses of good standing, in Bahia and Rio de Janeiro "

" It is all in order," replied the naturalist , " three months from to-day we will meet here again, and I will deposite here the twenty contos "

" Very well, according to agreement," remarked Mr Dujour

" You have been prudent, Mr Dujour," whispered Sra. Serafini, " you have not allowed it to be suspected on the road that you carried the diamond with you ? Pardon me the question—you know that we, here, unfortunately, can confide in but few, even of our nearest acquaintance !"

" I thank you, Signora, for your sympathy," returned the grimpeiro " I have, alas ! long since, been compelled to exercise prudence from much bitter experience Mr Closting can never be displeased that I desired the rendezvous with him to take place here in your presence, since Sr Serafini has known him longer than I "

" Far from it," interrupted the negro trader, " how can I take ill of you, a prudential measure, which I should observe myself towards any business man in such a case especially here in Brazil ' You know, as well as I, that there are merchants in Rio de Janeiro, called ' respectable,' who, as is said, and can be proved, carry the brand of the galleys on their backs ' "

" I have heard of such individuals," replied Dujour, " and know many of them, personally, but would not appoint a rendezvous with one of that class, to sell him a diamond worth twenty or twenty-five contos '"

" I believe you, indeed ' I have no doubt of it," observed Mr Closting

" There come permanentos, mamma ' Mamma ' there come barefooted permanentos, and an officer on horseback '" cried a beautiful little boy, of some three years of age, who had left the breakfast table, and gone out on the verandah, where he was feeding his pet, an enormous cockatoo

" Permanentos '" exclaimed Angelica, slowly, with a look of amazement at her husband, who involuntarily sprang up, and hurried to the boy, while the mother, with the little one in her arms, followed him

" Permanentos '" cried Mr Closting, likewise, and gazed around him with an unsteady look

" They can, however, have nothing to do here '" said Dujour, partly aside, and both placed themselves near the family, on the verandah.

The prospect embraced a part of the extensive valley, intersected by a considerable stream, in which rivulet after rivulet emptied itself, led into every sort of curvature by the hills and masses of rocks, and here and there, under the strong light of the rising sun, presenting glittering, mirrorlike surfaces The lieutenant, whom we left in the fazenda of Mc Fesh, had just then ascended, with his troop, a hill not far from the villa, which had, until then, covered his march

" What can that signify '" inquired Angelica, on the arm of her husband, who, like herself, had until then, looked upon the unexpected visiters with an inquiring glance. Instead of answering, he pressed Angelica's hand, and said, softly. " Compose yourself, be prepared for all things , but prove that you are a South American, and ask yourself, at this moment, which lot you would prefer for your children—to leave them behind you as the slaves of a monarch, or as free citizens of a grand republic '"

He beckoned to a negress to take the youngest child away, and bade the elder boy go with her, and look at the permanentos down below The little fellow obeyed, and crying out again, " Barefooted permanentos '" went off in the nurse's hand

The officer encompassed the villa, as far as it was possible to 'do so with thirty men, whispered something in the ear of the two corporals and an ensign, and was lost to the gaze of the observing group, while he entered the villa, and, after some minutes, appeared in the room

Notwithstanding his military bearing, united to a certain degree of impudence, he seemed, for the moment, confused and embarrassed, when he espied his accomplice, Mr Closting, who did not dare to look him in the face.

" Sr Carlo Serafini '" inquired the officer, with a searching glance at the three men, and drew out a document that he unfolded with a trembling hand Perhaps Mc Fesh's coffee had been too strong, and affected his nerves a little

" I am he '" replied the planter, in a firm voice, stepping, with his wife on his arm, before the shirri, who now began .

" In the name of the commandant of the province, I have the honor——I am commissioned to secure your person, and conduct you to Porto Seguro, whence you will be shipped to Rio de Janeiro "

Angelica, overpowered by the sensation of the moment, and shocked by the lightning stroke which had suddenly descended upon the elysium of her domestic life, and injured the main pillar of the temple of her earthly happiness, tottered on the arm of her husband, who, encircling her with his right, reached out his left for the document that made him a prisoner

Hardly had Angelica's head rested so long on the breast of Carlo, as sufficed him to scan over the order for his apprehension, when, as if strengthened by a higher power, she suddenly resumed all her self-possession, and looked boldly around her

" Place a chair here for the officer, and hand him some wine," said she, in a decided tone of her melodious voice, to a negro, who quickly obeyed the order " Be seated, continued she, to the officer, who moistened an old faded handkerchief with the sweat of his brow, and then, surprised by the attention of the lady, sat down before her

" And on what account is my husband arrested '' she asked, with a glance, which, as it appeared, he was unable to bear, for he looked down before him on the floor

" Has my husband committed forgery ' has he wronged widows and orphans ' has he broken his plighted word ' If he has done any act which I must in like him, henceforward, unworthy of my respect, then let me know it, and take him with you, for the bond of the heart is loosened where respect ' has ceased , and no social duty can fasten the wife to a criminal who is unworthy of her love Answer me, if you are able What is the crime of my husband ' If he is dishonored, then take him , if not, then take us both ' I accompany my husband '"

Without awaiting the reply of the officer, who sat there, deadly pale, with a full glass in his hand, she turned towards Carlo, pressed his hand, kissed him on the forehead, and left the room

The moment permitted the husband no reply to the resolute actions of his wife

Absorbed in reading the order for his arrest, which at the same time contained some of the grounds of complaint, he had, nevertheless, heard Angelica's words, and found himself in a sort of absence of mind, from the twofold attention

Dujour, who had, until this time, lingered near the betrayer upon the verandah, now stepped up to his old acquaintance, the owner of Villa Tasso, and was hardly able to move his lips He placed himself near him, and took a look at the document

" On account of participation in secret associations, for the subversion of the Brazilian empire," he read, half aloud—"and to promote the founding of a republican confederation of the United States of South America

"On account of participation in an European republican association, called 'La Giovine Italia ' On account of active participation in the dissemination of rebellious writings—among others, Mazzini's epistle, 'To the Youth of Italy,' printed in Rio de Janeiro, at the instance of the said Carlo Serafini, and sent, by his procurement, to the headquarters of the rebels in Rio Grande"

Serafini looked from the document at Mr Dujour, as if he would ask, "What do you say to this?" cast a searching look upon the naturalist on the verandah, and then handed the paper to the officer, and asked him,

"When will you depart? When must I be ready to accompany you?"

"I have strict orders to depart without delay," replied the officer "I am sorry that I must trouble you to prepare yourself for the journey as soon as possible, as soon as my people have completed taking possession of your papers, and of all the weapons on your plantation "

"Possession of my papers," repeated Carlo, in an ironical tone, "by all means, but then your people will require my keys As concerns my weapons, I tell you plainly, beforehand, that I possess for my two hundred negroes, full two hundred guns with bayonets, and all necessary small arms besides, for the defence of my property, which is my right and my duty I think that a government which offers no personal security to its citizens, and gives them up as a prey to be plundered by every robber, ought not to prohibit its citizens from arming their people Your couple of hundred permanentos, as gens d'armes on service, will really not protect our province, and where am I to look for you, with your thirty men, if I should even be attacked by wild beasts?"

"As respects the protection of your property, a captain will be here to-day, or to-morrow, with a military division You may rest quite unconcerned on that score," said the officer

"I am acquainted with such administration, and thank the government for its care I know, a colonel in Rio de Janeiro, who commanded in Minas Geraes, under pretence of suppressing the rebellion, and returned, after four months, to Rio de Janeiro, with a property of fifty contos, with which he established himself in the rua do Ouvidor, as a livery stable keeper, but that does not interest you, and does not concern either of us "

It may appear strange to an English reader, that a colonel of cavalry should retire from service to establish a livery stable In respect to this, we may remark, that in Brazil the man makes the business honorable, and the business does not indicate the respectability of the man A washing establishment, for instance, is there a business, like that of a livery stable, which puts in circulation some hundred thousand dollars a year, and no family, of such fortune, would be ashamed to apply their capital in this manner. Manners and climate, in all countries, affect the estimation in which different occupations are held In Brazil, less hypocrisy and prejudice prevail than in many other lands, where a Chris-

tian capitalist speculates in building vessels for the slave trade, who would be ashamed to keep a livery stable ——

The ensign now entered the apartment, accompanied by two of the barefoot corps, with lowered bayonets and cocked muskets, they looked anxiously around, as if fearing that some one might shoot them down, without their having the courage to defend their sunburnt hides The subordinate spoke in a low voice, to his superior officer, who intimated to the prisoner that he might go about the house at his pleasure, under the escort of this guard, and prepare himself for his journey

Serafini was going out with the ensign, when the officer hastily called him back, and asked him—

"What is the family name of your wife?" and then opened his pocketbook, and held a pencil ready

"De la Barca!" was the answer, which the former noted

"Where was she born?"

"In Corrientes, on the Parana."

"Are her parents living?"

"No"

"What is her mother's family name?"

"Garringos"

"Has she sisters and brothers?"

"Only one brother "

"What is his name?"

"Alvarez de la Barca "

"Where is he now?"

"That is unknown to us," replied Serafini, and left the room, accompanied by his hobbling guard

Angelica had had the presence of mind to destroy all those papers of her husband which might have been used as evidence against him She met him in the corridor, and flew into his arms A long, speechless embrace followed, from which she then tore herself, to make further preparations for her journey

Carlo did not dare to oppose her, as he knew his companion, who now, in all haste, made the most important arrangements to leave her two children under the most secure protection possible The journey to Porto Seguro was long, and extremely difficult, as it could only be undertaken on horseback, and over many chains of mountains, full of hollows and precipices, and deserted inhospitable campas, and was attended with dangers and privations of all sorts

Mr Closting remained upon the verandah, as if he had been chained there, while an often despised, inward voice, which we call "conscience,' to his great astonishment, aroused itself within him, and, as it were, forbade him to look any one in the face, to say nothing of entering the apartment where the arrest had taken place

"Who are you?" now inquired the officer of the old acquaintance of the prisoner, since he, also, had, very naturally, become suspicious to the government, as the confidant of the faroupilhas

"Mr Dujour started, and mentioned his name, which the officer noted down, and demanded further "And you, there—you without' who are you?" cried he to the negro trader, as if he had never seen him before.

Encouraged by this firm demeanor, the informer then entered the room, and likewise passed a strict examination.

"You may depart, both of you," said the officer, after he had read over his *proces verbal.* "You had better make haste to go, the captain, who is coming here, is, perhaps, stricter than I "

Mr Dujour, although he had long resided in Brazil, felt his position very uncomfortable, under surrounding circumstances, and expressed a wish to travel in the company of the other guests

Without in the least suspecting how entirely he was coming into the finely spun plan of the betrayer, he was rejoiced by the consolatory assurance that Mr Closting could accompany him for some days, as far as the turning of the mountains, and would protect him with all his people, if he would first go with him a little out of his way, to Me Fesh's

Mr Dujour agreed to this proposal with cordial thanks, and gave a negro, who was arranging the room, the order to have their beasts saddled, whereupon Mr. Closting offered to attend to it himself, and hastily departed, that he might not again come under the observation of the laroupilha or his wife

A sumptuous breakfast was prepared for the officer and his ensign, after the patriarchal custom of Brazil, which offers refreshments even to an enemy, and shelter to a betrayer

Serafim appeared in an elegant national travelling costume, rich in gold buttons and precious stones, glittering on the vest and spencer, and upon the brilliantly white linen, the watchguard, the fingers, and on the spurs upon the buckskin boots A negro behind him carried the "poncho," the national mantle, of a peculiar cut, made of dark blue cloth, nearly five feet wide and eight feet long, with an opening for the neck in the middle, (and a gold or silver agrafe,) lined with red, and rounded at the corners

This form of the "poncho," originally borrowed from the Patagonians, is particularly suitable to its object, as it protects the arms of the equestrian traveller, and leaves his hands free, while it serves him for a covering to sleep under at night

"Pardon me, illustrissimo Senhor!" said the officer to his prisoner, in a tone of contemptuous politeness, "pardon me, that I am obliged to order your travelling toilet according to my instructions You must carry nothing of value about you—absolutely nothing, and instead of your spencer, you must wear a capote, which is somewhat warmer for the mountain heights You may take your "poncho" with you, I will answer for that, although I foresee it may bring a reprimand upon me Please to lay aside your clothes with gold and diamond buttons, and all that you carry about you. I will take them in charge to Porto Seguro, you need not be at all concerned about them "

Not in the least moved in his mind, but filled with contempt for such legalized plundering, which characterized the persecution of all rebels in Brazil, Carlo took off his jewellery, of the value of some five contos

Assured of such loss, he had, nevertheless, endeavored to save some of those valuables, the confiscation of which must be as indifferent to him, whether accomplished now, or afterwards, by the expected officer, who was to undertake the "administration of the plantation."

Angelica entered the apartment as her husband drew on the capote, which is recognised in Brazil as the dress of the meanest criminal, and, as such, indicates a sort of degradation

For a second she remained standing, as if petrified, and turned pale, while a large tear rolled down her cheek

Carlo, who was under the hands of some permanentos, who served as valets to the proscribed, observed the emotion of Angelica, and all that oppressed his heart, all that he felt of bitterness, contempt, love, and faith, was expressed in a single look, which, met the soulfelt glance of her eye

Angelica was attired in a European costume, with a long riding dress, and a broad brimmed beaver hat Her dress, like her husband's, was ornamented with jewels, after the custom of the country

At the first word of the sbirro's cringing servility, intimating that the lady must lighten herself of her ornaments, and confide them all to him, Carlo lost his self-command

"Lieutenant, or corporal, or whatever you may be," said he, to the driver of the barefooted troop, "leave my wife unmolested! If you dare to give an order to touch her—to plunder her as you have plundered me, I swear by the holy God you shall not pass alive over the Serra dos Esmeraldos, to Porto Seguro! Mark that well! I swear it yet again! Recollect that my wife is not your prisoner, but my wife, who accompanies me from her own choice, and is free in the eyes of the law! Mark that! and guide yourself accordingly! Disobey my command, and a hundred carabines of noble Brazilians shall blow you and your thirty men to atoms before we pass the next town "

During this objurgation, he had drawn on the frock of the "escravos brancos," and now reached his arm to his wife, to leave their home, perhaps forever

Angelica's resolution to depart without taking leave of her children, wavered like her steps, as she was entering the corridor—she left the arm of her husband, beckoned him to go before, down the broad granite stairs, and disappeared through a door which led into the apartment of the children

Carlo left the house To the father attached to his children with equal fondness, a farewell scene would have been impossible, for which the womanly spirit of the mother appeared armed with superior strength He would not have had the power to embrace them, perhaps for the last time, without, after leaving them, stabbing to the heart, with the nearest knife, the slave of tyranny who tore him from them—for he was a man

Angelica appeared in a short time, with teardimmed eyes, under the portal of the villa, and mounted her mule with the assistance of her husband She was followed by two women and two men, as servants, and to take charge of some animals laden with travelling necessaries The officer allowed the chain intended for the "rebel," to hang at his own saddle, that it might be at hand as quickly as possible, in case of need, and Mr. Dujour, and the lamenting house servants, took a hasty farewell of the prisoner and his noble wife.

CHAPTER X

THE SECRET PLAN

"THESE are troubled times!" said Mr Clost-ing, interrupting the long silence, as he rode along by Mr Dujour.

"Very troubled times, indeed!" replied the latter, and a long pause again ensued

Mr Dujour was one of those " peaceable citi-zens, who do not trouble themselves with poli-tics," when it might lead them into any danger to do so, but who are very zealous politicians, whenever their particular interest in connexion with this or that government requires it, when the prospect and hope of a situation or pension, the provision for a family, or the like, bring them in contact with the administration, or with any person who represents it

Mr Dujour was a grimpeiro, a gold specula-tor, and, as such, belonged to a class of men, who have thoughts for nothing but gold and gold's worth, and of course give themselves not the least trouble about their nation and country

This numerous and (through the tendency of our epoch) rapidly increasing class, find their peculiar element in countries where a false cul-tivation, or " civilization," makes a position for a man according to the value of his money Num-bers, of themselves, represent materialism, and words, spirituality Numbers are the means of material speculation, and the word, the com-munication of thought—the medium of spiritual elevation and of moral ennoblement

It is characteristic, that a man who occupies himself during his whole life with counting and with calculation, without, at the same time, " thinking" of something which lies without the circumference of his material gains, loses, by degrees, the particle of intellect which nature lent him, and becomes every day more one-sided, contracted, and stupid

In opposition to these remarks, we find that the higher intellectual men stand in their deve-lopment, the deeper they, led by the inspired word, penetrate into the realms of thought, the further, in the same proportion, are they re-moved from every calculation of material specu-lation, because every earthly good is only the means of pursuing their intellectual exertions

We touch here one of those fundamental points, from which the various tendencies of men universally proceed. In retrospect to for-mer intimations upon the inner life—attraction and repulsion, spirituality and materialism—we consider the life of the soul to be in spirituality, and materialism as the death of the soul—two poles, separated by the equator of indifference If we judge every man as the inner life is awakened within him, by the attraction towards the lofty pole of spirituality, and weigh, on the other hand, the humiliation of men who sink be-low the equator, to the earthly pole of material-ism, the endlessly varied degrees of inward life, and inward deadness, as it were, systematically present themselves

Nothing is more remarkable than the mutual attraction of those in whom the spiritual life pre-vails, and the business attraction to each other of those men who, more or less spiritually dead, vegetate as calculating machines, upon or under the equator of indifference.

As spiritual men, in whom the life of the soul unfolds itself, are drawn towards each other by means of a mysterious attraction, so do those who are inwardly dead, seem, as it were, to recognise each other by the mouldy smell proceeding from the rottenness of the heart, since they approxi-mate to each other with singular facility, where reciprocal speculation requires it

To get rich by calculation, at the expense of others, by overreaching and honest cheating, as elements of commerce, must become more diffi-cult every day—for men, warned by thousand-fold experience, will, also, relatively increase their prudential measures, if they do not be-come, at the same time, from day to day, more contracted in the above named slough of the spiritless world of calculation, and, notwith-standing all their business knowledge, become the prey of overreaching

In the same measure as mutual distrust in-creases, (since the man of business is prepared for deceit beforehand,) does strength of judgement appear to diminish The more a man gains in single-sided business routine, the less does he gather of knowledge of the world and mankind.

The deeper a man sinks into material specula-tion, the more he lives in figures, and thinks of nothing which he cannot reckon by a number, the less does he often observe the nearest objects around him.

It would, perhaps, have awakened a slight dis-trust in many men in Mr Dujour's situation, to have observed, with the smallest power of com-prehension, the deportment of his travelling com-panion, but the faculty of thought, of reflecting upon any subject whatever not connected with his gold speculations, was wanting in the grim-peiro, as in thousands of his kind

He looked upon his companion as a man of business, and the before intimated fellow feeling, caused by the perception of inward rottenness, had led to those relations of business traffic, in which the money bag alone has any weight, and the heart is held in the least possible considera-tion

" We shall be liable to meet the permanentos again," began Mr Closting, after one of the fre-quent pauses, " I mean the captain who is to take possession of Villa Tasso, and, perhaps, he may even take it in his head to search us, to see whether we carry secret papers about us, and he will find your diamond"

Mr Dujour, who was suddenly aroused from his speculations, and had scarcely heard what the other said, arrived, with difficulty, at a con-nexion of ideas, which made evident the danger that threatened him

" You are right," replied he, " an unlaid egg is not safe from such a band of robbers as our military here, or, at least, their officers, not to mention a diamond in the pocket of a traveller "

" Especially when the traveller is known as the intimate friend of a faroupilha "

" We are in danger of being seized and plun-dered as such "

" Indeed! the affair is serious—let us then ride a little faster!" With these words, the nat-uralist gave his mule the spur, and the grim-peiro followed him as fast as he could

S'nhor Luiz!" cried he, from a distance, and then said, in a lower tone, as he again overtook him, " may I beg a favor of you? Will you take the diamond in charge until we come to Mc Fesh's fazenda, or until we reach my dwelling You are more strongly armed than I, and besides, know better how to handle weapons Your looks would keep a man at a distance, and I—they would see my anxiety at the first glance—I am not the man for such cases "

" If you believe that the diamond will be any safer in my keeping than with you," replied Closting, " and I can do you a favor by carrying it, I will do so, willingly, with all my heart Before any one comes at my person, be it a captain, or a common permanento, I have at least four balls ready " He pointed to his pistols and his double barrelled gun

" I also carry a gun, to be sure, as it is a custom of the country, but I should hardly use it for my protection " He opened his spencer and his vest, and gave over to his companion a little box, which was suspended from his neck by a strip of leather, like an amulet

" There it is," he whispered softly, looking at his two negroes, who, with the naturalist's servant, followed them at a great distance, and of course could not see what went on

" If one only reflects upon it," remarked Mr Closting, as he hung the case about his own neck, in the same manner as it had been carried by its owner, " if one only reflects upon it, the value of such a stone is altogether imaginary, if I had not had an order to buy it for a German prince, I would not have offered twenty contos for it."

" And if I had not been certain that somebody or another, commissioned by a third person, would offer me such a sum for it, I would not have invested the money in it that I paid for it," replied Mr Dujour, smiling

" Then you did not wash* it yourself ?"

" Oh, no ! I bought it with gold dust A hundred years ago this stone would have been worth three times its present value. The price of diamonds diminishes, as the product of the washing diminishes "

" That is founded on political circumstances Crowns no longer sit as securely on the heads of princes, as formerly A king's crown, with all its diamonds, is no longer worth as much as it was a hundred years ago !"

" Very justly remarked ! very acute, Mr Closting ! One would soon perceive that you have studied "

" A man is better off with gold and silver : it is the measure of human worth, and will remain so, whilst British civilization advances

" Before England's influence extended itself over the world, a man had some value as a man, his character, his talent, his spirit, were worth something Now, however, it is entirely by his money that a man is valued , he may be a mean fellow, and the greatest blockhead in the world, and if he have only money, he is well received "

" Excellent ! and unhappily true—but too true."

" There is something very peculiar in the circumstance of the Britons' seeking to obtain a monopoly of all the gold on earth, and also seeking to usurp nearly all the mines here in Brazil ' Where the carcass is, there will the eagles be gathered together,' is Scripture—and where gold is, there do the Britons assemble ! If one even discover a mine, one must use the utmost circumspection, lest a Briton should come behind him, and get possession of it before he suspects it I know of a spot up there in your neighborhood," he continued, in a lower voice, and with a significant expression, "where a man could make himself rich !"

" How so ?" inquired Mr Dujour, hastily and inquisitively " Not a mine ? a fast mine ? Is it in strata, or flowing !"

The naturalist appeared unwilling to give a direct answer to these inquiries, but, on the contrary, heightened the curiosity of the grimpeiro by remarking

" If my business would permit me to stop with my negroes, which I have with me at present, for four months, in that corner of the mountains, I would buy ten dozen such diamonds as yours with ready money But I must first, formally settle myself there, and form a partnership with somebody, since I could not be always there myself "

At these words, the grimpeiro listened with heightened expectation, and would gladly have asked a direct question, if he had not feared that it might operate against his present desire

" Before we separate, and when we are up there in the neighborhood of the mine, just tell me one word about it, entirely as a matter of business ;" said he, slowly, and with emphasis " It is natural that in such a business some partner should be personally established there."

" I have no objection at all to meet you in this affair," replied Mr Closting, " but every thing must be done with the greatest prudence , and we will speak about it further, before we separate "

The two grimpeiros now reached the fazenda of Mc Fesh, and found her still cursing over the loss of her " contos in negro flesh," as she expressed herself

Placed under a necessity of purchasing a Pluto, and some other negroes and negresses, she had employed herself, during the absence of Mr Closting, in holding a review over his black merchandise She found herself in similar perplexity with many ministers of state, who have to select from genealogical lists some prince, for a princess or heiress to the throne, and must rely upon good luck in their choice, since the qualities for propagating a legitimate dynasty cannot, unfortunately, be ascertained and proved beforehand There existed only this difference, that as yet no Mahommedan prince has come upon such a list, to whom several princesses could be disposed of at once, if even, on the other hand, many Turkish customs are not entirely strange at European courts

After long hesitation, she chose a successor to Pluto, and a young negress to replace Anastasia, and deferred, to Mr Closting's dissatisfaction, the purchase of an Antinous and Apollino to better times, since ready money had, even for Mc. Fesh, a solid value, in comparison to which the life of some few black beasts was not to be considered—if it were not, that they, like other " stock cattle," cost ready money.

The negro trader hastened to proceed on his journey, for he had set his heart upon accompanying the grimpeiro into the mountains. He

---

* Technical expression for finding in the water.

called him aside, to return the diamond to him, in case he desired it, which the other confidingly refused, as he observed that the jewel would be better taken care of by his companion than by him—which might very well be the case

Mr Banko had debated with himself, and consulted with his fellow sufferer Mr Nols, whether he should immediately leave the negro trader, and wander alone to Rio de Janeiro, or Bahia, or endure his situation still longer Stripped of all means, without necessary clothing, a stranger in a country where even the government itself afforded no personal security, and where, apart from the countless perils and difficulties amongst Indian tribes and wild beasts, he was in danger of being thrust into a copote of the permanentos, and misused as a recruit, there remained in short, nothing for the poor youth, but for the present to abide by his fate, and run about for a time, through bushes and over rocks, to hunt butterflies, an employment which, in the tropical heat, by no means contributed to personal comfort

"Where are those that you took yesterday?" inquired the naturalist of him, when he had concluded his trade with Mr Fesh, and received his money

"Here!" grumbled the youth, and opened his box, in which appeared many particularly brilliant and uncommon specimens of beetles, as well as butterflies, the view of which softened the savage humor of the slave trader, which had been, besides, rendered less violent by the above sale of his ware.

"That will do very well," said he, I will not reckon so severely with you, for your impertinence of last evening"

"My demands on you for maltreatment I have noted down, along with other claims," interrupted Mr Banko," and your being satisfied with this capture will not ward it off I declare to you, that I shall only remain with you for a few days' journey, until we arrive in the neighborhood of a town, or meet a caravan to which I can join myself I consider myself released from our contract since last evening, as you have not fulfilled your part of it Here you are the stronger, and I defer my reckoning with you—until an opportunity presents itself " Mr Closting felt that the measures of the offended youth might bring under discussion certain former transactions, and he wished to give matters a favorable turn Mr Banko's clothing was entirely torn, as the natural consequence of his wandering about, through bushes and briars, wherever the harmless whims of a pair of butterflies led his steps after their fluttering flight He now desired some clothes and shoes, and necessary linen, and a straw hat, for the sun had burnt him apparently to a mulatto.

The naturalist granted his request, and had means enough at hand to comply with it immediately, as he carried with him ready made clothing for sale and exchange.

Banko equipped himself for his contemplated separation, as well as the apprehensions and the present good humor of his master permitted, of which he was obliged to make speedy use

Mr Closting appeared to agree the more readily to the demands of his penless and inkless secretary, as he evidently wished to set out immediately upon his journey, for the present, directed to an uninhabited grimpeiro village, near

exhausted gold mines, deep in the interior of a neighboring mountain, where Mr Dujour had his dwelling.

The tropa left, towards evening, the fazenda of the humane lady, and disappeared behind hills and rocks, as the expected military troop approached on its way to Villa Tasso, and did not, of course, trouble them, as their way led them from the so called highway into the mountains.

Mr Dujour felt particularly satisfied to escape the possible search, that might endanger his diamond, which he now felt to be the more secure, since he relied upon the weapons of his business friend, who had the jewel in safe keeping

---

CHAPTER XI.

THE MURDER AND ROBBERY.

The tropa of the naturalist proceed through vallevs and ravines, through brooks and swamps, over rocks and stones, and through " thick and thin." It had nearly completed the second day's journey, and was to pass the night at a Venda,* kept by a Brazilian family of Portuguese extraction

Mr Dujour, who had been travelling for some weeks, longed to see his old neighbors again, whose distance from his place of abode might, like so many other neighborhoods in these parts, be measured with " seven league boots," and a pretty long strip at that

"There is the fazenda of the ' pious English people,' as the family are called here," said the grimpeiro, riding up to his business friend, and pointing out a mountain summit at some miles distance, whose site formed a topographical angle with that of the old venda

"You may possibly have heard of them ·" he continued, " of the ' pious Englishmen,' there, who wish to prevent Sr Brega from furnishing travellers with drink on Sundays for their refreshments They are very God-fearing people, the gentlemen up there "

"It is a great while since I was in this mountain," replied Mr Closting " Is it really the case, that they would have the tavern keeper shut up on Sundays ? or are you joking ?"

"It is no joke at all—I am really in earnest. There has been a dispute for more than a year past, especially since a so called missionary has lived up there, formerly a brushmaker in London, who was sent here for the conversion of the Botacudos, and preaches English to the savages He is particularly indignant about the venda, because the negroes from the different fazendas sometimes meet there on Sundays, and entertain themselves, after their fashion, with music and singing, a harmless pleasure to the poor devils, who enjoy little relaxation through the week "

"I can now understand the matter easily enough," returned Mr. Closting, " such a Sunday festival may very well be an annoyance to the ' holy grimpeiros;' and yet I would wager that they would not refuse to examine a mine on the holy Sabbath, even though it were the one of which I have spoken to you, which lies here in

---

* *Venda.—Inn.*

the neighborhood, if they should happen to find it on a Sunday."

Mr Dujour again appeared as if suddenly electrified, he held in his mule, and stared around him, with an inquiring look.

"Here in the neighborhood?" whispered he, "not far from here? then it must be over there, somewhere?"

The lively curiosity of the grimpeiro, who would have deprived himself for days of nourishment and sleep, to satisfy himself of the existence of an untouched mine, if the prospect were opened to him of becoming a partner in it, did not escape his companion's observation

"I have now considered the affair," said Mr Closting, interrupting the long pause which followed this question ; "I will make you the offer to work the mine, with an equal number of negroes, and to bear half the expense, and have half the proceeds——"

"That is just the proposal I wished to make you," interrupted the other , "and, as concerns the management, in which you cannot take a part personally, you can send an attorney, who can take the control in your stead."

"That would be entirely superfluous, my worthy Mr Dujour," replied Mr Closting "I repose so much confidence in your integrity, and have already known you so long, through Senhor Serafini, that I would transfer to your charge, not only this mine, but my whole property, if peculiar circumstances should render it necessary for me to choose a credible man for such a purpose I would give you the preference in all Brazil '

"I am rejoiced at that," rejoined the other, with peculiar satisfaction "That delights me, especially since I have been recommended to you by Senhor Serafini The unbounded confidence of such an excellent man as Serafini, is worth more to me than the little property that I have acquired, without any detriment to others "

"I, also, agree with you in this testimony of a clear conscience A good name, and untarnished honor, are always the most valuable capital, which bears its own interest, notwithstanding the esteem of men for money, which belongs to our times We will, then, take a circuit through that valley there, towards the old venda It leads into a narrow dell, I have marked the passage."

He looked back upon the tropa, now approaching at a distance, and then both dismounted from their saddles. Mr. Closting beckoned to his arreiro, Mr Nols, who instantly galloped forward, and received the order to lead the tropa to the before mentioned venda, and bespeak quarters there for the night, while Mr Dujour would accompany him through the ravine, where they were to examine some veins of metal, and then follow after to supper. The trackless way, through this ravine, could only be undertaken on foot, wherefore Mr Nols was told to take both mules to the tropa, and lead them with him

Mr. Dujour was satisfied with every arrangement, and stood, as if on coals, to set out on a walk of several miles, which was to lead to such golden termination

"You can mount my mule," said Closting to his "secretary," who had come up with the negroes, and heard a part of the orders

"I thank you, Mr Closting," replied the youth, unfolding his long bamboo catcher "It is a remarkably fine afternoon, and the butterflies seem to enjoy it very much ; I hope still to take some splendid specimens on the way "

The naturalist was too deeply absorbed by his plan, to reflect much on the peculiar motives for this polite refusal, he praised the zeal of the young German, hung his double-barrelled gun and game-bag over his shoulder, gave some further directions to his arreiro, and departed with the expectant grimpeiro

The valley, which the tropa now traversed, was narrow, in comparison with the grand scale of Brazilian scenery, with a brook winding through it, that near its source, was reported to be possessed of golden sands, and, in bygone days, had afforded a rich supply of the so called "precious metal," which, up to this time, has contributed little towards improving the human heart.

A colossal, and nearly perpendicular wall of rock, several thousand feet high, towards the northwest, was here and there broken by rugged and fantastically formed masses of stone Gigantic blocks, apparently the overthrown portions of this exalted temple of nature, perhaps separated from it by a volcanic movement, and removed to the distance of miles from their former base, lay around in picturesque grouping, forming, with their vistas of expanded extent, and complicate forms, other valleys and ravines

A narrow passage of this description, only a few feet wide, led, on the other side of the brook, towards the south, to a marshy basin, shut in by similar gigantic rocks, which were no longer lighted by the rays of the evening sun, since one of the principal ridges, towards the northwest, had already darkened the whole landscape with the veil of its gloomy shadow

The two grimpeiro's went on, through the towering ravine, absorbed in discourse about their undertaking They were soon surrounded by a mysterious stillness, often broken in upon, nevertheless, by the screams of brilliant parti-colored birds, and by the disagreeable croaking of an enormous frog, of the size of a man's head flattened, which crept slowly through moss and mud, as it placed there for a bugbear, in contrast to the magnificence and splendor of nature Lizards, whose length approached a small crocodile's, ran about the overgrown path of the wanderers, and crawled, or glided with unexampled rapidity, up along the side walls of the rocks. The low ringing tones of fondling serpents resounded from the summits of the cliffs, which, warmed by the burning sun during the day, mysteriously concealed the nightly couch of fiery love

Brilliant butterflies, always in pairs, in obedience to the instinct of love, fluttered about the two grimpeiros, concluding their daily flight in the blissful dream of innocence, (unacquainted with the catcher of a naturalist, or his secretary,) and seeking a little place where to pass the night close to each other, and to await the re-awakening of the flowers, whose perfume forms their happy world

Faithful "inseparables," that little sympathetic race of bright green dumb parroquets, whose lives flow on, pair-wise, in one harmonious existence, and who build, in similar marshy places of Brazil, their asylum of love, on lonely, prominent trees, flew about anxiously, from limb to limb A loving little pair of these flying creatures of sympathy, seemed terrified by the presence of two living beings in this sanctuary of their solitude, although unacquainted with the death-dealing instrument of the Europeans

Both hovered about in tremulous flight, and lingered, as if fastened by magic, in the neighborhood of the naturalist, who dexterously brought down one of the delicate creatures on the wing It had hardly dropped, before its companion placed itself by the body of the slain one, and allowed itself to be captured ; and the hand that captured it, instantly wrung its head off

"The feathers are useful," said Mr Closting, and thrust the two birds into his game-bag

Mr Dujour, by no means known for his sensibility, experienced, at the moment, a cold, shuddering, creeping of the nerves—perhaps an attack of fever, in consequence of the altered temperature, and the evaporation from the confined marshy soil

An old, dead, dried up mango, (similar to the European oak,) which had been struck with lightning, stood at some distance, upon the height of a rock, and presented a singular and forbidding appearance The bare, leafless, variously distorted branches, resembled a numerous group of petrified serpents, twisted and twined together in every variety of convolution, distinguished as a dim shadowy outline from the western horizon, which now, in the tropical shortness of the twilight, suddenly lost its glow, and passed into a color that was almost a bright green

"Another pair of inseparables have lit there," whispered the naturalist, with a glance at the serpent tree, and hastily loaded his double barrelled gun He turned, however, as if accidentally, away from his companion, and slipped two bullets into the barrels, instead of bird shot

"Do not fire, Mr Closting," said his fellow-traveller," do not fire to-day at another living being You have shot enough ! You know that I am neither a sportsman nor naturalist—and it may be ridiculous, I admit—but it always gives me pain, when a pair of these little sympathetic creatures are killed What attachment does their instinct display ! The one always follows the other, and if you take one, you have them both "

"It is the stupidity of these narrow minded creatures—'tis all stupidity, Mr Dojour, nothing else. If these birds were a little more knowing, they would escape such a danger ; at least, the one would not allow itself to be seized when the other is killed, wounded, or caught."

"Permit me one question, Mr Closting," interrupted the other " do you take Sra Serafini for a stupid woman ?"

Closting started, and looked on the ground "Sra Serafini ? Why ? She is a woman, and does not want to pass her nights alone, for some months to come, but desires, if possible, to be in her husband's neighborhood, for the fulfilment of conjugal duties—which is very natural !"

Mr Dujour remained silent, and walked slowly by the side of his companion, whose company became more and more disagreeable to him, without his being able to account for an uneasiness which had evidently come over him

A half hour had passed by, and they were again among blocks of stone, the space between which hardly admitted the passage of a single person

"There ! there, at the end of that ravine—just there the vein lies—it is a gold vein, in regular strata !" whispered Mr Closting "The rock is granite, and contains some portions of hornblend and mica. The gold ore is mixed with ferruginous sandstone conglomerate, which is often the case, as you know You will find the earth there in cascalhao strata, intermixed with rock."

The grimpeiro's lust for gold hardly allowed him time to hear his companion to the end He stared at the entrance into the ravine, above described, and no power on earth could now have held him back, notwithstanding all his feverish symptoms, from examining the vein of ore, so technically described He swung his mineral hammer, as if he felt himself suddenly strengthened, in case of need, to devote three days to geological researches, without sleep or food, and hurried forward, at a quick pace The opposite ravine, which had been pointed out to him, was as narrow as that through which he had just passed His body soon stopped up the narrow passage, in which it would have been difficult for the grimpeiro to turn and look around him, if he had even, in his thirst for gold, thought of looking back at his companion The latter availed himself of this moment with great presence of mind, took aim as cooly as if he was going to shoot a monkey—and two bullets pierced the spine and breast of his companion, whose diamond hung in safe custody upon his own neck

The crashing echo of the double shot reverberated among the gigantic angular masses of rock, like rolling thunder For an instant the murderer stood there, like a statue, among the ruins of Gomorrah—observed by the young German, who had followed him at a distance, without being perceived

The murderer approached the victim of his frightful deed, with tottering steps ; he leaned upon his gun, and bent forward, as if to satisfy himself that the body was really a corpse He found no trace of life, and drew it aside a few steps, into the marsh from which the rocky masses arose He then felt an involuntary impulse to look towards the place where the youth's unaverted gaze rested upon him, but he saw nothing to discompose him, and hastily loading his gun, he sought his way through the swamp, feeling, from time to time, at the " amulet" enclosing the diamond worth twenty-five contos, which he had bought for twenty, and had just paid for.

CHAPTER XII.

MURDER FROM INTOLERANCE

NOTWITHSTANDING the different degrees of cultivation to which, (from the circumstances of their earlier lives,) Mr. Nols and Mr. Banko had attained, a certain intelligence existed between them, in relation to the character and dealings of their common master. Both had been brought into his service, by the caprices of chance, without their free choice, and they bore their lot with a degree of philosophy, inasmuch as it could not be altered, until they could find an opportunity to separate from him, without burdening their consciences by co-operation or participation in any wrongful act

Mr. Nols had perceived the design of the young man, and understood the reasons why he would not mount the mule

He went up to him as soon as the two grimpeiro's had disappeared behind the rocks and bushes, and gave him the saddled animal, ordering a negro, upon another mule, to wait near the place until Banko should mount it, and follow after the tropa with him This happened when the youth had been witness to a deed which filled him with horror, and remained indelibly impressed upon his mind

Decidedly as the repulsion of antipathy, founded in the nature of both, had hitherto separated him from his master, there now arose within him an equally bitter abhorrence of a man, who, infected with the contagious distemper of our times, "of making money at any rate," and, driven from crime to crime, had committed murder and robbery with the same coolness with which he had brought down a "sympathy bird"

Mr. Nols had reached the before mentioned venda, but instead of the expected accommodation, for him and his followers, he found wretchedness and despair

The waning moon already lighted the wild romantic landscape, in the foreground of which stood the venda, an old, massive stone building, surrounded by thickly leaved fruit trees, and numerous bananas, the gigantic leaves of which, (often twenty or more feet long, from the succulent handle to the point,) made a rustling, like sheets of paper blown against each other by the wind

On a granite block, before the door, sat Kilkenny, an old Irishman, who had honorably ended his military career, as a dragoon in the British service, and for many years had served the Brazilian family, as house steward and chief hostler.

He was one of those conscientiously exact people, who not only give a horse drink, and take care of him, because they have been hired to do such a service, but because the horse requires his food and drink regularly, and cannot procure it for himself.

He cast a distrustful glance at the approaching tropa and their white leader, who rode towards him on a short gallop, and bade him good evening

"Are you Protestant or Catholic?" inquired the old domestic of the venda, without returning his greeting, or rising up from his low seat

"Why do you ask that question?" inquired Mr. Nols, not a little astonished at being thus addressed, " I am the arreiro of this little tropa, and desire quarters for the night, my belief ought not to come in question here, if I carry the money with me for the reckoning."

"May the devil take me, if I ever harbor another Protestant here in the venda, till I turn my back upon it, which I hope will be soon," grumbled the old dragoon to himself.

"What is the matter with you? What has happened here? Are you alone in the venda? Is not the landlord here, or are you the landlord?"

"To be sure I am landlord, since Senhor Braga, with his son, and our four negroes, were murdered, last Sunday night, towards Monday, poisoned—the supper was poisoned the black beans and the *carne secco**, altogether, were poisoned , and, by good luck, the two Senhoras had ridden out on a visit I went with them, and we could not come home because of a thunder storm , and we came back about noon on Monday, and found the bodies—all the bodies ; and Senhor Braga lived some hours after, and declared, in his last moments, that no other had poisoned him and his but the people over there, the pious people, who, long ago, wanted to forbid us to receive people here on Sundays, and to let the negroes play the *marumba* and the *gourd fiddle*, and dance† here. All the bodies are buried down there—down below, by the cross there, and I was there to-day to set the other crosses—for each one must have his cross , and I will roll a stone there, and carve in inscription upon it—I, myself, with these hands And that is religion ! Bible religion ! Christian religion, that must be ! I rode into the town to the Juis de Foro and Capitam Mor, and informed them, and took my oath to the last words of the old Senhor. But what good did that do ? where was the proof ? And what a dying man says in a fever, said the justice, was not sufficient accusation, though everybody knows what has happened here during the last year—how the Bible pious people have cheated us, and tried to coax our negroes to become such saints as they are— the poor negroes, that neither know what is Protestant nor Catholic But the holy gentlemen up there use slaves as much for their gold washing, as we, Catholics, for our fazendas, and allow the negroes no recreation on Sundays, and call it 'Sabbath-breaking,' if the poor devils make merry in their way, among themselves—the poor negroes! with their miramba and their gourd fiddle !'"

Mr. Nols heard this effusion of old Kilkenny with increasing attention, and without interrupting him, as he could, by so doing, only arrive at the information which he required

"I took the two Senhoras into the town, to their aunt, and am only waiting here until the venda is sold," continued the Irishman, "for the Bragas cannot stay here any more No Catholic would dare to keep a venda here—that is natural To-day, or to-morrow, the same means would be taken to turn us out I hear an agent of the gentleman up there is already bargaining for the purchase of the venda Very naturally, the saints will now buy the venda, and when thirsty travellers come here on Sundays, they will put them off till Monday, and will establish a depot here for all sorts of merchandise That is very natural They are mad that I have escaped them, and I am not sure of my life here for an hour, for I am an Irishman, you must know—an Irishman, and a Catholic, and the brushmaker, who passes for a missionary, has often made proposals to me, to change my religion, and leave the Bragas

---

* Dried meat.

† The author vouches for the facts in these and similar episodes, which characterize the interior situation of South America, the description of which he has made his especial object.

"I have all respect for a missionary, whether Catholic or Protestant, if he is a man of education, and can instruct others; if he extends book knowledge, and teaches the people what is right and what is wrong, what is one's duty, and what is not, what should be done, and what should be left undone; but to set one's self up as the devil's outriding courier, to proclaim him, and that he follows after him, and will drive all Christendom to hell with his scourge! I can do that, too, myself, when I have no other way of earning my bread

"Here I have sat since Sunday, and waited until I could go away—afraid to eat or drink the least thing, for fear of being poisoned, and so I only eat bananas from the tree down there, and eggs as soon as the hen lays them, and if I am obliged to eat any thing else, I give it first to our makakas* to try—but I should be sorry, even to poison one of our makakas, for the old Senhor loved them, and gave them their breakfast, himself, the good old Senhor, he loved men and makakas, and would not have poisoned a makaka!"

The faithful servant of the Braga family continued, in this manner, to explain his present position, which by no means served to recommend the venda, for it was certainly critical to eat the least thing in it

In about half an hour, Mr Banko came galloping in, in company with the negro who had staid behind His countenance involuntarily betrayed that something shocking had occurred Hardly had Nols, however, with all brevity, called out to tell him what had happened to the family at the venda, than he had the presence of mind to attribute to this intelligence, the agitation which he evidently felt

Mr Nols made himself known to the old dragoon, as a comrade, as he also had been in the army for some years, and both assumed a cordial barrack style, in which the religious question came no more under consideration

We touch here upon a subject which may be misconceived by many of our English and American readers, and which, nevertheless, cannot be passed over: the operations of the missionaries of the English church, and of the Jesuits in South America, as the objects of both are political We consider the principles of the doctrine of Jesus, as the principles of equality, justice, and love to man, as the basis of all development of mankind, but we rigidly separate spiritless "forms" from the "spirit" of Christianity We honor and respect the missionary, of whatever sect, who, penetrated by the above mentioned convictions, endeavors to disseminate the principles of the religion of Jesus

The circulation of the Bible, as the word of God, and as a primitive historical record of the human race, can, however, only exercise a beneficial influence where a fundamental education has prepared the way for the spirit which lies at the foundation of the word

The Old Testament, written with the childlike unreserve of past ages, contains passages which openly violate the moral sentiments of the reader, awaken thoughts in the pure heart of youth, and burden the youthful imagination with images which can neither promote morality nor religion

If some of the Bible societies, would prepare

extracts from the Bible, with the omission of all dangerous, evidently immoral, passages about impurity, unchastity, incest, etc, retaining, instead, books full of truth and wisdom, and of historical importance, as, for example, the book of Jesus, the son of Sirach, and the books of Maccabees, which the English church has omitted in her edition of the Bible, if the Bible were diminished, by a third part, of its voluminous texts, the reading of it would be useful and wholesome, to a well instructed man, in whatever quarter of the world he might be, and could have no dangerous tendency for any boy or girl that is our view of the Bible

As regards temperance societies, the writer of this novel practices temperance, in consequence of a good education We doubt, however, whether any temperance society will ever attain its noble object of moral improvement, if the rational education of the so called lower classes, is not attended to, as zealously as the public abstinence from all spiritous liquors is inculcated The use of brandy has caused more moral and physical desolation than fire and sword can ever do

The passion for drink, is an abyss in which man is exposed to every other passion—for by degrading himself far below the brutes, he has ceased to be a man

Alcohol is a poison which takes hold of a man's whole being, palsies his physical and moral strength, and, by degrees so to say, "dissolves his spirit-by-combustion" To work against the desolation and destruction caused by such an evil, is the sacred duty of every man, but the renunciation of all spirituous drinks, in itself, does not, by any means, make a moral man, if passion and intemperance, in other respects, are not likewise uprooted at the same time, and the fulfilment of all the social duties is not recognised as an incumbent condition

According to Aristotle-Johnson, abstinence and temperance signify about the same thing, in the English language, but the etymology of these words leads to entirely different notions

Temperance is a requirement of nature and of reason, and should be recommended, especially to many people living "in the lusts of the flesh," in a twofold sense There are spices which operate as prejudically upon the blood and nerves, as alcohol, and which are used to excess in the English manner of living, as, for example, pepper, the direct effect of which, ought to be sufficiently well known Though married people may find the operation of pepper and similar spices convenient, they are always a destructive poison for growing children, who, according to the English custom, are, so to speak, fed with pepper Who knows the direct operation of mustard outwardly applied, acts just as unreasonably, when he lowers similar plasters into the stomachs of children We will not here comment upon the English custom, which poisons new born children, by the use of laudanum, or prepares them for national dulness. The dissemination of dietetic instructions, prepared by an experienced physician, would be, in our opinion, as useful and wholesome as the distribution of spiritless tracts, which show the "way to heaven," without pointing out the way to live rationally on earth But the English literature, up to the present

---

* Makaka.—Monkey

time, lies under a stronger censure than the German, Italian, Russian, etc; a censure which does not, as in those countries, keep down the human mind with bayonets, but which is sustained by the absolute paralysing of moral freedom by prejudice, and is kept up by hypocrisy

There prevails in England, and among English people, the absolute despotic law " not to touch upon certain subjects, because they ought to remain untouched " But this last reason is British absolute despotism, and is opposed to all enlightenment

No one ever contended more energetically against the sanctimoniousness of the rich, and the hypocrisy of external Sabbath keeping—against praying in the corner of the street, and the hypocritical Pharisees—than did Jesus

British censure* would forbid us to draw effective parallels between the church of our century and the Jewish priesthood, against whom Jesus contended, until the priests and Pharisees, at last, brought him to the cross The inspired sayings of Jesus would have received as heavy a censure from the Jewish priests and Pharisees, in Jerusalem, in case a press had existed there, as would a bookseller of the present day in London, who, against the censure of prejudice, should undertake the publication of the language of sound reason, in the exegesis of the admirable epistle of James,† which sets forth moral freedom, and places works above words and a blind faith

> " Sectarian methodists, and pietists !
> And what more we may ever call them , all
> But serve to show that each man feels desire
> To raise himself above this earthly clay,
> And stand erect in spirit—for the proof
> Of faith and of religion, the foundations
> Of inward life, which marks the difference
> Between the man and brute , for, even in brutes,
> We see instinct, which often puts to shame
> The dulness of mankind But the mind,
> In aspiration for a higher grade ,
> The soul's presentiment , the faith and thirst
> For spiritual life , the consciousness,
> Within himself, of spiritual nature,
> Belongs to " man alone Without it here,
> Man censes to be human—bears the form
> And figure of a man, and is a brute "‡

In our more elevated consciousness, lies the contemplation of this earthly life, from a higher point of view of moral freedom, without which there can be no virtue and no sin The notion of an earthly existence, " cursed by God" from its commencement, through the fall of man and original sin, contradicts, evidently, the notion of divine love and justice, which lie at the foundation of the religion of Jesus—for such an existence would burden, with the same " damning curse," all endeavors after moral improvement, every work and deed of love.

We return to our story The tropa was placed under shelter, in a building adjoining the venda, and as good a supper prepared, as was possible under surrounding circumstances, with security against poison

---

* When writing these lines, the author did not expect to meet the same censure of dulness in hypocrites in the United States, endeavoring to suppress the novel "Dolores."—[Note in correcting the proofs of "Dolores," April the 25th, 1846] HARRO.

† Which Luther wished to strike out, when he came to an understanding with the German princes.

‡ Fragment of a dramatic Poem. H.

Banko had little appetite, and often gazed thoughtfully before him, which did not particularly surprise his companion.

It was long before the naturalist appeared He came at last There was nothing in his manner that could have excited the least suspicion His countenance wore the same expression of cold insensibility which was always peculiar to him, and his eyes avoided, as they always did, meeting the eyes of any other man

" Is not Mr Dujour here yet ? How does that happen ?" he inquired, as he looked around him with adroit dissimulation. and received a negative answer to the first question " I left him down there in the ravine, using his mineral hammer, and I thought best not to disturb him A garimpeiro likes solitude in his researches. But he must be here soon "

" If he does not come within gunshot of one the saints, and his person is not mistaken for mine !" interrupted Kilkenny , and Mr Closting now learned in what manner the venda had been depopulated

" Dreadful !" exclaimed he, " unheard of ! murder upon murder ! And all this can happen here with impunity—without justice ! To what political party did this family belong " he further inquired " That is, unfortunately, the chief thing here Religion and politics are here one The English are no faroupilhas, but go with the Caramuros Probably your old master was an adherent of the faroupilhas "

" He was a Catholic, as I tell you," replied Kilkenny " As to politics, I only know so far as this, that we have sometimes hid faroupilhas here in their flight, and that the permanentos have, at times, held their inquisition here, or inspection, as they call it, and that the two young Senhors, who are betrothed to the two daughters, are both faroupilhas That is well known "

" Then, alas ! there is nothing to be done !" said the slave trader , "no accusation can be sustained, no process instituted. Every thing is against the two daughters , and who will testify against the Englishmen ?"

" That is just what the gentlemen in the town said !" replied Kilkenny , " they said the same thing, and the affair was suppressed ' Where there is no accuser, there is no judge ' And the venda will now be sold, and fall into the hands of the Englishmen—at least they will buy it, and have the control of it—that is very natural "

" Quite natural '' affirmed Mr Closting, and again expressed his surprise at the long stay of his companion

" I would not give two patacks for his life !" said Kilkenny , " for I know certainly that they waylay me, and it is only here at the venda that they will not shoot me They have some shame left—they dare not despatch me here at the door. If the fanatical brushmaker choses to offer a negro a couple of patacks, and at the same time holds up hell in flames before his eyes, and tells him that he can save himself from the devil, if he will shoot down or stab a Catholic, no traveller is safe here at twilight, whose skin is white, like mine, and who, like me, wears horseman's boots, a straw hat, and an old poncho, that Sr Braga presented to me—may God preserve it, for he gave it to me—he who lies below there He has his cross at his grave, and the others shall have theirs "

"The grimpeiro was dressed just as you have described," said Mr Banko, who was busied in emptying his master's game bags, which contained some birds, among which were the two "inseparables"

"It is not improbable," he continued, with a sharp look at Mr Nols, that he might have been shot or stabbed, through mistake

"The thing appears quite probable " interposed Mr Closting "I am only sorry that I did not stay near him. He seemed to think that he could discover another mine, and in such cases a grimpeiro likes to be left alone "

Nols had closely observed the countenance and the subsequent deportment of the youth, and had remarked more than enough to confirm his former suspicions The arrival of their master without attendance, removed all doubt respecting the fate of his travelling companion It appeared to Nols not only probable, but certain, that Mr Closting had made sure work with Mr Dujour, and put him quietly to rest, but he could not clearly understand the particular design, or the peculiar motive for the act, since, up to this time, neither he nor Banko knew any thing of the diamond He, nevertheless, followed the example of his confidant, and behaved as if he had not the least suspicion, as he hoped with time and with Banko's aid, to obtain some explanation of this mysterious affair

" Perhaps he went another way," observed he, taking a part in the conversation, " and has gone to a fazenda some distance from here We saw some houses up above there, as we passed the mountain "

" It is possible that he may have taken another way, and that we shall find him at home to-morrow evening, although he was on foot,' interrupted Mr Closting

" Sr Dujour Daily no go home a foot '" said Francisco, one of the two negroes in the service of the grimpeiro, who attended him on Minas horses as a sort of body guard

" Sr Dujour Daily come here to night, else he be dead, murdered ' No right for Sr Branco* leave he lone in hollow, in de mountains' dat no right I no had ride on wid Bastian if I tink dat Me ride now look what Sr Dujour Daily stay Come Bastian, we go look for S'nhor '"

The two negroes sprang upon their horses, and galloped off by the same way that they had come Banko expressed a desire to accompany them, which his master, however, found superfluous, remarking that he knew the grimpeiro to be a singular person, who often had strange fancies, and did not like to be observed and watched

" At any rate" continued he, " in the morning, we will set out on our journey to his dwelling, where it is to be hoped we shall find him If not, then I will take the needful steps—in reference to the suspicion that prevails here, in connexion with this dreadful murder of a whole family "

Banko had cleaned the two birds, and temporarily prepared them for preservation, designing them as memorials for himself, without allowing the murderer, in the least, to perceive that he had seen any thing, as he well knew that he would thereby endanger his own life Mr Closting had already lain down to rest, when Nols found a fit moment to speak to his confidant without being overheard

Banko related, with manifest embarrassment, and anxiety, what he had seen, and where the event took place, with all the attending circumstances, as well as he had been able to observe them at a distance, behind bushes and rocks

" I cannot tell what led me to suspect that something like this would happen," said Nols, ' but I had a singular presentiment, and you seem likewise to have experienced the same feeling, when you declined riding the mule We have yet to find out what was the object of this murder "

" Which we probably shall, when we go to the grimpeiro's dwelling Perhaps, Mr Dujour had given him his money, or something of great value, for safe keeping We can only learn that from his family His father, however, is deranged, as Sebastian has told us, and there will hardly be any thing reasonable got out of him, but he has some mulheres de cama,* up there, and probably one of them is acquainted with his circumstances "

The two negroes of the grimpeiro, who had followed upon his track, now returned. Sebastian sprang from his horse, and sought the two whites, to give them the information that they had actually found the corpse of their master

" S'nhor Branco shoot he !" cried they, with clenched fists, " and we make him pay for it ' S'nhor good branco, and no beat de nigger to death like S'nhora Branca,† down below dere she murder slave wid chigote You S'nhor have shoot our S'nhor Dujour !"

Nols hastily put his hand upon the negroes' thick lips, to indicate to him that he must be silent if he valued his life—since Mr Closting, in case the suspicion was well founded, would despatch him also, that he might tell no tales

The negro understood this, and thanked the white for the warning " But we must bury de body," continued Francisco, " him lie in marsh, and we no have spade "

" I must yet see the body myself,' whispered Nols, after a pause, " I will venture to go with these two, and help them "

" That will not answer now," said Banko, " we must arrange it differently Hark you, Sebastian !" said he to the negro " You two must not let it be known that you have found the body—do you understand ? Early in the morning, before we break up, you must ride back some distance, as if you were looking for your master, and then follow us slowly home, and there you must first tell that you have found the body, and where it lies Mr Dujour s mulheres will then desire to have it buried, and the affair will be more inquired into, at least, more known. If we inform our Senhor here, that you have found the body, he will order it to be buried, and the whole affair will remain a secret, for he can deny our testimony

The negro Sebastian had sufficient sound common sense to see into the propriety of this plan He burst into lamentations over the death of his good master, who had been very kind to his black people, and especially to the black women, and had given his slaves many free hours to work for

---

* White man

* Brazilian expression for concubine. † White lady.

themselves, and earn something, that they might, by degrees purchase their own freedom

Both negroes were again strictly enjoined to silence, especially towards the slaves of the tropa, with whose characters they were, for the most part, unacquainted They promised the necessary caution, and went to rest, that they might depart at an early hour in the morning

CHAPTER XIII

THE LUNATIC.

WHETHER the naturalist had pleasant dreams and a comfortable night's rest, as no one inquired the next morning, he did not think it worth his while to mention   Perhaps his sleep was not particularly refreshing, for he was stirring very early, urging his arreiro to break up, "and to quit this murderous place as soon as possible" The information that the two negroes of the grimpeiro had gone back to look for their master, did not appear to surprise him

"It is to be hoped that we shall find him at home, or that he will make his appearance there soon after us, and his two blacks, likewise," he observed, and mounted his mule

The venda of old Braga lay at the foot of a Serra,* up along the steep and broken sides of which the road now led, offering, at every step, to the traveller, who cherished a sense of the grandeur of nature, an extensive prospect over the romantic valley, and the various grouping of the rocks in the neighborhood, which assumed different forms at every turning of the badly constructed road.

The sun had already attained a considerable height, as Hanko, in his chase after butterflies, arrived upon a summit, which suddenly afforded a prospect into a second valley, if this word may be applied to a space bounded on the horizon, at a distance of full sixty miles, by an azure mountain chain, enclosing again, however, in an extended semicircle, mountain after mountain, campos after campos, valley after valley, in manifold variety, dotted over with farms and villages

Amid this scenery, upon a mountain ridge many hundred feet high, at some miles distance from the point where the youth was standing, there appeared, in an admirably picturesque situation, a tolerably large sized town, whose white spires and cupolas projected above the equally white walls of palace-like dwellings The town was encompassed by that variegated green, which there maintains the same freshness in one eternal summer, whose botanical nomenclature many assiduous naturalists, of worthier standing than Mr Closting, and less pedantic than Dr. Merbold, have set down in their reports, and preserved in their scientific works

The view of this town had something in it of magical surprise for the youth, from its being partly unexpected to him. Mr Closting seemed to have remained intentionally silent, as to what district they were in, and Mr. Nols's topographical knowledge did not suffice to give him the required information. His imagination was, at the time, occupied by the gloomiest images of scenes of murder ! The world, for him, had become a desert, peopled by bloodthirsty animals in human form

The whole scene bore the character of a majestic dignity, regulated by a cultivated taste and a sense of the beautiful, which was developed in this paradise, in the sublime grandeur of nature

The balm of a bracing atmosphere, aromatic with the various perfumes of spicy plants from the depths of the valleys, to the sparse vegetation waving over the gigantic heights, swelled the breast of the youth, and he remained standing, absorbed in reflections upon earthly life and sublunary happiness, upon life's sorrows and pleasures.

"Who can find fault with the Brazilians," thought he, "for being proud of their nationality, and loving their fatherland ? such a wonderfully charming fatherland ! and which, during so short a period of white population, has made such progress towards cultivation and improvement Who can blame them for hating the English, who turn up the earth here for gold—who carry away their gold and precious stones, and endeavor to plant British dulness in this highly favored soil   Not far from my home on the Rhine is a tavern, on which these words are displayed in large letters 'No ENGLISH ADMITTED HERE !' May this inscription also be placed over the gates of this Brazilian town, in order that the men who wish to enjoy themselves there in the lap of nature, may not be disgusted by British fashion and British arrogance "

Amongst the countless variegated butterflies, which fluttered around him, a peculiarly splendid pair rose up from the opposite valley

"And must I take you ?" thought he, following with his eyes, the sportive flight of the faithful pair, without moving his feet "Must I take you, and kill you ? You, at least, enjoy your short existence without stealing and robbing from your fellow creatures—inseparable in love—alone holier, perhaps, than the sensuality of many men who abuse the word   Shall I take you, that my master, as he calls himself, may make money out of you, and that a Briton, or Anglicised European, may judge you according to your beauty ? No ! but according to the money that they have paid for you   Fly away, and enjoy your lives I have committed too many murders upon your race   From this day, forward, I will violate no soul's life under a butterfly's covering "

The youth hurried after the limping negroes under similar, certainly very sentimental and unpractical reflections, and was forced to make up his mind to commit the appointed number of murders upon the symbols of the soul's life, until the evening approached, and the tropa reached the town of the grimpeiro

If money is the source of all evil, and all misery, it is not strange to meet with so much evil and human misery in full bloom, in the Eldorado of Brazil, as it now contains

In contrast with the charming variety of the environs, which had excited the youth's admiration on the summit of the rock, and here and there, almost daily until now, the prospect unfolded itself, by degrees, of an unfriendly, comfortless, depopulated desert   Dilapidated huts

---

* *Serra.*—A ridge of mountains.

and houses, part of them inhabited as ruins by poverty stricken human figures, villages without population, and, here and there, a little town that looked like a wretched village, a scanty vegetation in the gardens and plantations, from the neglect of human hands, were all united into a tragical whole. It was a region of gold mines, and diamond rivulets, stripped to the last little grain, and still dug through by the insatiable avarice of civilized men. Millions upon millions, had here been taken from the so called mother earth, and had been misapplied and abused by her degraded children

The ruins of Sodom and Gomorrah might convey an impression, similar to the one now created by these wrecks of a rich past—from which not a single pillar projects, that might serve, by its beauty and ornaments, as an evidence to future generations, that men here had a sense of noble forms, of the beautiful in art or nature. The fearful image of gain—which seeks to turn even the earth, with all its treasures, into money, with no higher aim, than to make money for money's sake, without any other object in life, without an intellectual enjoyment of life, became impressed more strongly upon the mind of the youth, the farther he advanced in the regions of Eldorado. Here were living skeletons, covered over with skins of every shade of light and dark complexion, that seemed as if only saved from starvation by the mild gifts of nature, which afforded them a scanty supply of Indian corn, bananas, and fresh water. Bound to their home by the habit of wretchedness, they crept around the huts of their black ancestors, who here had served the gold mania of licentious Europeans, while the later generations of mulattoes had become free by law, and impoverished, neglected, and breadless, by the exhaustion of the mines, and the heartlessness of their oppressors whom they had enriched

The wretchedness of similar places in the mountains of Brazil, which have enriched the world with millions in gold and diamonds, without alleviating the miseries of the people of Europe, in the countries to which all this wealth was transferred, is a subject for the most profound and serious contemplation, which we cannot here exhaust

The Europeans, by means of slaves, dig into the interior of the earth, without cultivating its surface, and affording the population the means of existence, from the resources of industry. They employed no mulatto or white person, on day wages, in their gold mines—because they either carried negro slaves with them, or could hire them there from speculators, who settled there, with their slaves, for this purpose alone, and in their *dolce fare niente*, pocketed the weekly or monthly hire, and in this manner enriched themselves likewise

As soon as such a mine became exhausted, the Europeans disappeared with their gold and their negroes, and the unfortunate inhabitants remained breadless. The wretchedness of such places, as, for example, the miserable village of Isambé, in Minas Geraes, has originated, it is true, the Portuguese proverb, " Das miserias de Isambé libera nos domine !" but they do not appear to have reflected, that it was the duty of men indirectly to relieve Isambé, and all other unprovisioned places, from their misery.

The tropa reached the mean dwelling of old Mr Daily, at the end of an equally mean village, through which flowed the brook that was the former source of this Eldorado. The old man was engaged in making gold. Regular ditches, cut crosswise, were dug on each bank of the brook, elevated on the edge with the sand that had been thrown out of them, and carefully dammed up at the ends. These served to intercept the gold enriched water, which was retained until it had deposited its sediment. The water was then slowly drawn off, and the sandy mud on the bottom of the artificial canal, contained gold dust, and, in other brooks, diamonds were obtained by a similar process

A gigantic negress, with a short Italian tobacco pipe in her wide mouth, did the honors to the guests. It was Sra Matura, one of the " mulheres de cama" of the lavendeiro, Mr Dujour

" Do not disturb him," whispered she to the naturalist, as he approached the old man, who, stretched upon the ground, groped about with both hands in the mud of a canal, and carefully took out the pebbles, putting them in a little box beside him. " Do not disturb him—he sometimes has convulsions when he is interrupted. He must first have his appointed quantity, there lie the scales, he weighs his gold and his diamonds, and packs them carefully away, and then he calls for his supper, and a negro brings him letters, as if the letter carrier had been here "

Mr Banko had placed himself near Closting, and looked upon the old man, whose countenance bore the distorted expression of quiet lunacy, amidst the traces of former noble features. Coarse white hair fell over his high, broad forehead, and his unsteady light brown eye stared into the mud, and saw nothing but gold and diamonds. Jacket and pantaloons, stiffened with the dirt of the ground in which he groped about, formed his attire. A tin star on his breast, many variegated ribands in his buttonholes, and a knit band under his knee, for the " order of the garter," were his ornaments

He ended his day's work, took up the scales, and appeared uncommonly satisfied with the result. He then placed himself in a commanding posture, while he addressed a troop of negroes whom nobody saw but himself. He praised one, and scolded another—complained of this one for having incurred the suspicion of swallowing a diamond, and ordered one of the others to shut him up, and give him a bur-glass full of castor oil, and not to let him out until it had operated. After these measures, he tottered to a bench near the door, slowly seated himself, all the while staring before him, without taking notice of any one, ordered his supper, and inquired if the letter carrier had come ' (who, by-the-bye, only made his appearance once a month at the utmost, unless a particular occasion required a letter bag to be forwarded into the mountains)

Nestor, an old servant of the house, came ' running out, and wiped the sweat from his brow with his bare hand, as if he had hurried there from a distance, and handed the newly arrived letters to the grimpeiro, which he had already unfolded a hundred times, they having been daily put into other envelopes

He prepared for reading with peculiar zeal, placed a pair of spectacles, without glasses, upon his meagre nose, and first contemplated the post mark and stamp of each cover, before he broke it open Without noticing whether he held the writing right or wrong side up, he read, after his manner, the important correspondence, extemporizing the contents of the letters with wonderful facility, and in an exhaustless variety enriched by his remarks, and manifested in his improvisations the fixed idea of his insanity

The unfortunate man had been in this situation, since he had sold, through an agent, a considerable supply of diamonds to an European court, and received the payment for them in government paper, which had, unfortunately, become worthless, and ruined him He considered himself now the minister of finance to the fallen dynasty, and wished to overturn the ancient dynasties in all parts of the world, and found new ones in their stead, that he might make a successful business, and marry his colored daughters to legitimate princes

" No letter to-day from my principal agent ? that is very singular!" he muttered to himself, contemplating the envelopes " O, yes ' here it is ' that is his handwriting and seal, and the Lisbon post mark ' Lisbon, the 1th of May' May ' this is the 15th of August—September, or January The date is correct, the letter has not been long coming ' May it please your Excellency—I have received your orders of the tenth of last month, and in a private audience with his majesty, I requested him to prolong your leave of absence six months, which he has been graciously pleased to grant '

" Excellent ' I can remain here six months longer, and direct the mines of Brazil in person , that is excellent '

" ' As concerning the marriage of your daughter, Senhora Amphitrite, with his royal highness the Grand Duke Alexander, his highness is approaching man's estate, and I have sent the Baron von Dachspot as envoy extraordinary in this matter, to St Petersburgh, who will return before the arrival of your excellency, and bring back the imperial consent with him.'

" Then that affair, is arranged ' excellent ' Senhora Amphitrite, will be Grand Duchess of Russia, and in time Empress

" ' I have learned that the great diamond of the Russian crown has been broken by a pistol shot, fired by the emperor at a rock in Poland , the ball bounded back in a most surprising manner, against the crown I have received the commission to replace it, with a new one of similar weight '

" Hem ' my son's diamond is not heavy enough, otherwise it would be an excellent opportunity , it has fire like a sun Well, I must see, and produce one for my Amphitrite's future father-in-law.

" ' It is a most remarkable fact in regard to the European crowns of modern days, that they will not sit steadily upon anointed heads, every now and then one falls down and breaks, and the boys in the streets, pelt each other with the diamonds.'

" The young dogs ' I will send over a dozen chicotes, that will soon subdue the ' rascals '

" ' Her royal highness, the Princess Victoria, begs your excellency to send her an Ethiopian prince, naturalized in Brazil, as chamberlain for herself, and as adjutant for her future husband

She sends you, herewith, the measure of the ' Apollo of Belvidere,' from the British museum, taken with her own hand, in height, hips, thighs, calves, etc , to be as far as possible identical It will be required, moreover, that the said mulatto prince should be legitimate on the mother's side, and musical , he must also possess dramatic talent, and be able to play Othello—from state economy, to save the enormous salaries of the singers in the Italian opera '

" Very well, I will take a note of that I know a legitimate Ethiopian princess , she belongs to our neighbor over the way, and is an exquisite laundress, she is old enough, and has grown up sons—mulattoes I will copy the measure , it is given here below, in the letter, in feet and inches, all correct It shall be seen too "

" ' There is good prospect of marrying all of your excellency's daughters to German princes, whose number is more than sufficient '

" Yes, I know that, but it does not suit me—such a duodecimo German prince, with two and a half soldiers for a garrison, and one and a half riding horses in the court stable No , my Senhoras aim a little higher ' nothing will come of that ' they never send over orders for crown diamonds Bohemian stones are even too high priced for them ' If it were a prince of Austria ' or Russia—or Bavaria—very well, that might answer , but Bavaria is constitutional, and I have nothing more to do with constitutions—I require legitimacy ' legitimacy, and a guarantee for my diamonds '

" ' There is quite a prospect for a couple of dozen dynasties in the United States of North America , they have no nobility, but there is a lively demand there for that article '

" Capital ' something may be made out of that ' I will reply by the next post , that must be attended to

" ' Valets of European princes are already sent to the United States, and received there with the greatest enthusiasm, as representatives of their monarchs and other sovereigns, furnished with secret dynastic commissions and powers ' Fifteen per cent increase in the price of cotton in fifteen years, guarantied to each dynasty—of course there is hardly a doubt but that the affair will succeed, especially in some particular States '

" That looks very reasonable I could not have heard any thing more desirable

" ' There is a great throng of future North American noblesse in the royal zoological gardens and menageries of European princes, as a debut and preparatory school for the necessary manners and etiquette '

" That is likewise quite in accordance with the spirit of the times, and can do no sort of harm

" ' Mrs Whiteskin a widow, who has become worth a million and a half, by the death of her husband, requires from you a garniture of diamonds, of about the value of half a million, that she may carry one third of her worth in plain sight She is going from here to Paris, for exhibition, to show herself in the Theatre Fran-çais, and in her box at the Italian opera '

" I will take note of that—of the order , the lady does quite right, but she is very modest Why does she not wear her whole worth in sight, like my Amarosa—who knows that her worth consists in her beauty, and goes almost entirely naked, not from vanity, but because she wishes to be married, and will not deceive any one   My future sons-in-law ' by the grace of God,' may know what they get   Many a man marries a woman, and when she is seen by the light, she is a skeleton, covered with untanned leather   ' All is not gold that glitters,' and cotton is just now a cheap article for the toilet.

" There is a letter from Buenos Ayres—from my chargé d'affaires there   I am very curious

' ' The monarchical principle makes the most brilliant progress here, where only the crown is yet wanting, for which you must furnish the diamonds, if possible, in exchange for buffalo hides, for Rosas has already sent the gold which is required for the crown, with all his other savings, to the bank of England, for safe keeping '

" In exchange for buffalo hides !   Is the future monarch of La Plata crazy, or is he a merchant ? What should I do with so many buffalo hides ? I should like to know !   There are oxen enough in Brazil, native and foreign, that carry their hides to market   I only use a few hides for my gold dust, and require no cargoes from Rozas ! That does not suit me at all !   No ! a dynasty that traffics with ox hides, cannot trade with me   I desire legitimacy and ready money—I will have nothing to do with legitimate oxen, I might, perhaps, barter diamonds against men—black or white, it makes no difference   The people must pay taxes for my diamonds, that is natural ' Tel est notre plaisir !' And so a quasi legitimate citizen, or oxen king, may sell his subjects, and his oxen, where he will, and to whom he will   Stupid stuff ! ox hides, for diamonds ! Who ever heard of such a thing before But what else can be expected from a Gaucho—an ox driver who wishes to be king, and will not spend much on his crown !   Let him marry a legitimate princess, and he will soon carry another ornament on his forehead, which has a great family likeness to the head ornaments of oxen "

After this monologue, the old man stared long before him, as if some image had attracted his fancy, and afterwards looked round on the bystanders, and at length upon Mr Closting

" Where have you left my son ? and where is his diamond ?" he inquired, rising from his seat, as if he would seize the stranger by the throat

The murderer turned pale, and stepped aside some paces, but by no means lost his self-possession, though he cast a glance sideways at his negroes, and beckoned to Matura to take hold of the old man   Matura, stepped between the guest and the lunatic, but appeared suddenly to have become observant of the protracted stay of her man, as she called Mr Dujour.

" Did not my man travel with your tropa ?" she asked the naturalist, " I thought he had only staid behind accidentally, and would be here directly ?"

" Who are you ? and where have you left my son ? and where is his diamond ?" repeated the lunatic, as Mr. Closting was about to begin his reply.

" Be quiet, father !" whispered Matura, in the old man's ear, at the same time taking his hand, " This gentleman is a friend of your son. Sr Xavier will soon be here   This gentleman knows nothing of the diamond !"

" Who are you !" said the lunatic to Closting, " an European ? Let us see you once ! What is written on your forehead ? I wish to read it !

Take off your hat ! take off your hat, I say, or I will call the life guard ! my grenadiers are down there, in front of the palace   Let me see you, I say ! I wish to read who you are ! the good God writes a legible hand, and men's countenances do not lie !   Show yourself, I tell you !"

" Let the old man be taken to bed," whispered Mr Closting in the ear of a young negress, who stood near him, with a mulatto child in her arms

" Now I see the writing through your straw hat—there it is ! but you, yourself, know best what you are worth, and the negroes here, have no occasion to know it, for they are negroes, and you are a branco   Ha, ha, ha !" he laughed, frightfully, " a branco ! a respectable branco !"

He observed him again, with a fixed gaze, and continued   " Of what nation are you ? What nation has the honor to call you son ? You must be a cosmopolite ! one of those who belong to any nation, where they can do a good business ! Quite right ! you are a cosmopolite, and wear the cloak of cosmopolitism, lined with philanthrophy ! That becomes you very well ! it's the fashion, now !"

Mr Closting heard this speech of the lunatic with the same apparent indifference which any one with a clear conscience would have maintained in his place, but he appeared to find such a string of titles superfluous, and was just about to withdraw, as Francisco, the negro of the murdered man, came galloping in, with his companion

" Where is my man ?" cried three black women ! " Where is my man ?" repeated Matura, letting go the hand of the old man, who continued to stare at the guest, with a piercing look

The danger of being seized, and perhaps strangled by the lunatic, threatened the murderer, who knew sufficiently the unbounded physical strength of a man under such circumstances, though the old man appeared to be so weak that a boy might hold him back

" He is murdered !" shrieked the lunatic, before the two negroes had uttered the same exclamation   " Do you see him there ? There lies the pretty Sevandija,* and his companion of the dirt, that rooted about with him, has murdered him ! There he lies ! And the other sevandija crawls about, unconcerned, but he has not stolen any thing from him—only the bright spark has gone from the breast of the murdered sevandija—it has gone, disappeared "

" Sr   Sevandija ! Sr   Branco Sevandija !" cried he to the slave trader, " come ! come ! sit down by me ! I have state affairs to discuss with you ! Do you wish to become chargé d'affaires ? I have a post for you !" He pursued this monologue, while the lamenting shrieks of the women broke forth, who had now received, from the negroes, the news of the murder   But he seemed not to hear it, and stared again at the spot in the sand, where he thought he saw the murdered muckworm

" He is murdered !" cried the negroes, without concerning themselves about the old man's soliloquy

" Murdered !" resounded from all mouths, and Mr Closting now stepped into the midst of the four concubines

* Muckworm

"How so? murdered?" he inquired of the negro, who leaped from the saddle and gave his horse to the charge of another.

"Tell what you know! where is Mr. Dujour?"

Francisco now reported, after his manner, in broken Portuguese, where he had found the corpse. He was interrupted by the weeping and lamentations of the four women, which knew no bounds, and permitted no one to pay the least attention to the circumstantial relation of the negro.

Mr. Closting now stepped up, as the friend of the murdered man, and endeavored to impose upon all present by his resolute behaviour. He informed himself, precisely, of all the circumstances, as far as the negroes were able to relate them, and gave the women the assurance that he would take upon himself the investigation for the discovery of the murderer, and would go back the next morning and bury the body.

But the women did not hear him, and went on lamenting, without cessation.

"Shut up the old man in his room!" he whispered in the ear of the negro, Francisco, continually apprehensive that he might spring upon him and strangle him. The lunatic, however, remained standing upon the spot where he had made the last outcry, and stared, as if petrified on the ground, at his murdered sevandija.

"Who disturbs me while I am reading my letters?" cried he, as Francisco approached him, with several negroes, to fulfil the order of the authoritative guest.

"We will attend you to your room, Senhor. You must read your letters there, Senhor!"

"First bury this sevandija for me, and erect him a monument, for he deserves as good a monument as any other 'homen sujo.'* Now I will read my letters, but do not let any one disturb me! Invite the guest to sup with me—the branco! He seems to me to be a gentleman! a perfect gentleman! The man pleases me! Take him into the 'rangers' room, and give him a jacket and fresh linen."†

The unfortunate Mr. Daily went into his room, and again opened some letters, while he laid himself down on an old cane bottomed sofa Francisco softly locked the door on the outside, and went back to Mr. Closting, who employed all his eloquence to console the survivors of the murdered man, and offered them his friendly services.

The women surrounded the Sr. Branco with the confidence of necessity, and were far from entertaining the least doubt and suspicion of him, since they had known him for years as the business friend of their fourfold man, and gradually dried their honest tears of grief, consoled by the circumstance that chance had brought a Sr. Branco to them, who, they hoped, would, in many respects, take the place of the murdered man.

Banko and Nols observed their employer, since the arrival of the two negroes, with the mute understanding that existed between them, and exchanged their thoughts by many stolen glances.

If Nols had not learned the fact of the murder, through the credible youth, and had not for a long time had many reasons for believing his

employer capable of such a deed, he would have doubled its reality.

If the deportment of the betrayer could work such an impression upon a man who had known him as such for years, it might very well strike the negroes dumb with amazement, who had entertained the strongest suspicions, and now saw them all weakened.

Francisco was unable to conceive of that degree of European civilization, by which a man is enabled to master every internal emotion before the world, and by means of a preparation for practical life, to maintain his self-possession in every situation, and, as was the case with the European in the present instance, to assume any mask that the occasion required.

The *stupid negro*, not possessing any knowledge of that sort, became more and more embarrassed, and could hardly understand how it was that he could have believed the Sr. Branco capable of the murder.

Mr. Closting saw very well that his assurance had produced its intended effect, whereby he gained a wider field in which to move without restraint.

Without having imagined that the wholesale murder in the venda of old Senhor Braga would serve him to lead the suspicion, in respect to the corpse of the grimpeiro, upon the "holy gentlemen," he had, in anticipation, (as the reader will recollect,) let fall some words, in conversation with the officer of the permanentos, signifying that he exposed himself to the vengeance of the faroupilhas, by promoting the apprehension of Serafini. Although the grimpeiro, Dujour, had not had the least to do with the affair, and Mr. Closting had never spoken to him about Serafini's political standing, he, nevertheless, represented him as the informer, that he might afterwards be able to make the intended murder, in case it were successfully accomplished, appear as a deed of vengeance on the part of the faroupilhas.

Accident had now doubly favored him, (as it has so many other rascals on earth, who are elevated by "success in business,") and he now availed himself, most judiciously, of these circumstances, in conversation with his two white attendants and the women of the murdered man, to divert suspicion from himself.

"If he be not murdered, through mistake, by the 'holy gentlemen,'" he remarked, among other things, "which will soon be ascertained, then the faroupilhas have had a hand in it, for suspicion rested upon him of having denounced Senhor Serafini It is not at all improbable," continued he, further, "that some negro, or white person with attendants, may have followed us from Villa Tasso, to revenge the treachery which Mr. Dujour, according to their view, had been guilty of towards Senhor Serafini We know, unhappily, by experience, the bloodthirsty vengeance of the faroupilhas, in such cases of treachery, as they call such a transaction, though a man, in committing it, may act in it—accordance to his convictions—for the public service In the other case, it is just as possible that one of the 'holy gentlemen's' negroes has mistaken him for the old dragoon There is as much to be said on the one side, as on the other."

All this was more than sufficient to screen the known business friend of the murdered man from

---

* A dirty, vulgar fellow—a muckworm

† A Brazilian custom on the arrival of any stranger.

all suspicion in the eyes of the guileless colored people, and even, if not to extinguish, at least to weaken, the suspicion of the faithful Francisco, so that he did not dare (as might have been expected before) to come forward against the "Senhor Bianco," with all the decision of a brave negro

The two white attendants of the latter had each their own thoughts, and often looked at each other significantly, with all respect for the practical dexterity of their employer

All measures for the discovery of the murderer, and the interring of the corpse, were settled in the best manner. Mr Closting decided upon making a circuit the next morning, to lodge an information of the affair in the above mentioned town, and, if possible, to conduct an examination from thence—at least, to give over the whole affair into the hands of the judge, where he knew, beforehand, that it would soon be forgotten

Banko had already learned the name of the town that he had seen, and, so far as concerned himself, had resolved to separate, the next day, from his employer. It happened that a young man of his acquaintance, from Europe, lived in this town, as a physician—at least, according to the information that he had obtained in Rio de Janeiro, he hoped to meet him there, and it was now more than ever evident to him that Mr Closting had concealed from him in what comarca they were

Mr Nols was obliged to remain some time longer in the service of the naturalist, for he had still a demand upon him for a considerable sum of arrears of salary, and Mr Closting had adopted the custom of the business men of our time, to put off the payment of money as long as possible. According to the above custom, he generally paid his subordinate creditors the interest of their claim with rudeness, for their urgency implied a doubt of his ability to pay, and, of course, was an insult to his respectability

The unfortunate widowed *mulheres de cama* wept through the comfortless night, each in the conviction that her man loved her in his heart above all others, and in case he, in the moment of his death, had found time to take leave, in spirit, of any one, he certainly had thought of her, and of her only

Mr Closting personally convinced himself, before he went to rest, that the door of the room in which old Mr Daily raved, was well fastened

He then betook himself to the before mentioned stranger's room, which was a very miserable one, to be sure but kept with Brazilian neatness. He carefully bolted his door and window shutters, examined the locks and loading of his pistols and his double-barrelled gun, and laid himself down to rest

Banko and Nols arranged their beds as comfortably as the circumstances permitted, in a corner of the hospitable house, where the negro Francisco had spread out some straw mats for them. The thought of the proverb, that "walls have ears," prevented them from speaking on the paramount subject which chased away their sleep. When all was quiet in the house, Francisco came again to the couch of the two whites to wish them good night, and whispered in their ears, "Your Senhor Bianco is innocent, or he is as great a Velhacaz* as there is in Brazil!"

"Pst! pst!" whispered Mr Banko to him; "if Francisco is prudent, he will not say any thing, or he runs the risk of being shot, like his master, by the Senhor Branco, who is, probably, a highly respectable velhacaz. Good night, Senhor Francisco!"

CHAPTER XIV

WOMAN

At the extreme boundary of the southern tropical zone, almost directly under the Tropic of Capricorn—where the sun is at its zenith when we, north of the equator, have the shortest days—nature has hollowed out a bay, nearly seventeen English miles in length, and varying from four to five in width, upon whose environs she seems to have expended all that she is able to effect upon our planet, in beauty and wealth, in grandeur and elevation, in variety and luxuriance, in idyllian charms and romantic wildness. It is the world-famed bay of Rio de Janeiro

Like the whole coast of Brazil, from Pernambuco to Rio Grande—bordered by a colossal chain of mountains, broken off at several places and retiring more or less into the interior, which penetrate the clouds in their sublime grandeur —the entrance into the "bay of tropical splendor and magnificence," is, also, surrounded by high mountains

Two conical masses of rock, hardly three quarters of an English mile apart, stand opposite to each other, and nearly perpendicular, appearing like the hewn pillars of a gate, and afford, even directly at their bases, safe navigation for the largest ships to enter the bay

As we enter from without, the so called "sugar loaf" rises, on the left hand a guide to the mariner, who does not see the entrance until he finds himself in a straight line before it, and who readily recognises the famous "sugar loaf," from the circumstance that it, unlike every other conical point along that coast, inclines to the southwest. At the foot of the opposite rocks of pure granite, and at an inconsiderable distance in front, extends the fortress of Santa Cruz. Inside of the "sugar loaf," upon a low rocky island, stands the bastion of St João, and between these two points, a view unfolds itself that fills with amazement the heart even of the traveller, who has admired the beauty and grandeur of nature in Europe, from the Archipelago to the North Cape

Towards the southwest, at the foot of a group of mountains, fully three thousand feet high, whose peculiar forms recall no landscape in Europe, lies the city of Rio de Janeiro, with the cultivated villages and suburbs of the bay, extending, in terrace-formed alternation, to a distance of some seven English miles

From the naked heights of the cloudcapt rocky summits, the ever fresh, green, and luxuriant vegetation descends in an endless variety of colors, down to the little hills, upon whose

---

* Scoundrel—pronounced veljacaz

misty back-ground stands the city, with its churches and unassuming palaces, with its monasteries and chapels, with its mass of dwellings, and its terraces, with its gigantic aqueduct and its fountains, overlooked by countless chacaras,* gent ally painted white, and kept neat and clean, and reflected in the dark bluish green of the sparkling waves, which play around the keels of vessels, arriving here from all parts of the world, decorated with the flags of every civilized nation upon earth -

Opposite to these rocky tops, on the other side of the bay, appeared the heaven-piercing pipes of the "Organ Mountains,' (Seria dos Orges,) which receives its name from its singular form It is about seven thousand feet high, and appears like a deep blue stone wall, sharp distinguished at almost all times of day, from the etherially clear horizon

The Organ Mountains descend, in the foreground, by various gradations in hills, valleys, and meadows, to the sandy shore of the bay, where the little towns of Praya Grande and St Domingo are seen, with their idyllian chacaras

Mountain upon mountain, near and remote, and countless islets rising above the ever murmuring waves, partly inhabited, and partly appearing as if placed there by nature, as altar steps in the mysterious temple of solitude, to remind the feeling human heart to bring its offering there in hours of devotion, in contemplation of the splendor and magnificence of divine ceation

The same moon which shone upon the hospitable dwelling of the murdered garimpeiro, in the interior of the country, cast its bright rays, through the clear tropical atmosphere, into the half open window of a chacara, which stood upon the ridge of a hill at the foot of the Corcovado †

The long leaves of the bananas rustled in the silence of the night above the fragrant tops of the blooming orange trees, and the waves of the bay beat against the beach, with a splashing noise, in the regular "pulse-throb of nature" Their advance and falling back were distinctly audible, far below, on the nearest shore, and far away from the granite foundations of the fortress of Santa Cruz, notwithstanding the distance of some miles

In strong contrast with the gloomy, almost black masses of mountains, above which the moon had just risen, and whose shadows still enveloped the walls of the fortress of Santa Cruz, glittered the mirrorlike surface of the bay, like an outspread silver veil, inwrought with myriads of sparkling diamonds, whose brilliancy was only exceeded by the inexpressible splendor of the cloudless firmament Although the southern hemisphere presents fewer constellations of prominent magnitude than the northern, it affords, in their place, by the indescribable ethereal clearness of its atmosphere, a view into the awe-inspiring regions of immensity, which agitates the soul, while, after long gazing, another universe of countless stars is revealed, to which there is no bound.

* Country houses.

† A rock of 3,000 feet high, at the foot of which, the church Nossa Senhora da Gloria, the monastery Santa Theresa, and a part of the city, are built

At the half open window sat a female form, with her unadorned head supported upon a hand of childlike delicacy, over which a luxuriant wealth of coal black hair rolled "in regular confusion" She appeared self-absorbed Her look was directed towards a bright sparkling star, without noticing it, for the long dark lashes were moist with tears, and the eye of the observer might penetrate into the inner world of a sorrow burdened soul

The gentle swelling form of a Venus de Medici was enveloped in a simple, dazzling white robe, fastened over the breast by an agrafe, the folds of which, like the artistically arranged drapery of an antique statue, revealed the form the more it veiled it

In natural harmony with such a noble figure, (which did not exceed the middling size of the antique models,) the expressive countenance bordered upon that admired Grecian form which the tropical nature of Brazil renders so glorious with luxuriant charms, while the hardly perceptibly projecting arch of the nose bordered on Roman beauty, and at the same time it often undeniably manifests a consciousness of womanly dignity, commanding reverence, and pride, which would repel, with contempt, every indiscreet approach

The charmingly formed lips had already assumed the impression so peculiar to the Brazilian women, which is manifested in the depressed corners of the mouth, and, in a greater or less degree, betrays inward contradiction, discontent with one's self and with the world, disregard of outward appearances, ill humor, and melancholy, which, however, according to the assertion of experienced psychologists, is founded on an early satiety of the pleasures of life, without love

Emulating the brilliancy of the star on which her gaze appeared to be fixed, the eye of the Brazilian lady was lighted by a peculiar expression

The dark ball of the cornea, appeared only one large, deeply black pupil, without even a shade of another color, surrounded by a bluish white, and rich, notwithstanding, in the magnetic fluid, which is often almost entirely wanting in dark eyes

The room, at the window of which this female sat, in an unpremeditated attitude, upon a divan, was simply furnished in the French style An open door near a forte piano, led into a sleeping apartment, in which reposed a little girl of some four years of age, that hardly any one would have taken for the daughter of the Brazilian lady, since she, herself, resembled a childish girl, and the child's features bore not the slightest resemblance to her own

Sunk in contemplations, which probably would have found no effusion, if her most confidential friend (in case she possessed one) had been present, she gazed upward at the starry night, unconscious of the lapse of time

A colossal bat, of the size of an owl, flitted about the window, and touched with its pronged wings the broad curtains, which lightly moved near her, under the breath of the wind Reminded of her earthly existence, she suddenly recollected herself, and awakened from her world of thought She hurried to the open door of the sleeping apartment, satisfied herself of the peaceful slumber of the little one, and pulled a bell rope An old negress appeared, who had once been her nurse, and now waited upon her as the attendant of her child •

"Where is the book that the doctor sent me, lately " she asked, with a feeble voice "Bring a light and look for it I cannot sleep, and must read something"

The old woman lit the wax candles, which stood ready upon a table, in silver candlesticks, under glass cylinders—sought for, and found the book, and would have left the room

"Are the pistols well loaded?" inquired the lady, "can I depend upon them?"

"Certainly, Senhora, certainly, I have loaded so many pistols in my life, and know how, as well as a man They lie there on the night table, by your bed"

"Then you may go to rest, but if you notice the least thing, if any one should be lurking about here, if you hear footsteps at the garden gate, come to me directly—without such disturbance, you may sleep on, but be at hand immediately, when I ring"

"Better, Senhora, to tie a string around my arm, and pass it through the key hole—if you want to wake me quickly, pull it, and I shall awake right away"

The lady agreed to this proposal, the old woman arranged the string as she had proposed, and left the room The title of the book, which the lady now took in her hand, was

"PSYCHOLOGY OF LOVE——1831 '

She seated herself in an armchair, threw her tamarcas* from her naked, childlike little feet, stretched them out upon a velvet footstool, stroked her locks, which rolled down to the floor, behind her ears, looked into the book, and read

WOMAN

A mighty, incalculable influence upon the education, and consequently, upon the condition of mankind, is effected by the female sex.

The female sex is able to decide the freedom or slavery, the deliverance or subjugation, of a rising generation The child receives the first impressions of life, the first foundation of education, from its mother, and grows up (as well the boy as the girl) under the mother's guidance Hardly ripened to youth, the man is placed anew under female influence, by the power of love

The character of a slavish mother will never develop freedom in the boy, and the power of the "love" of a slavish being, threatens danger and destruction to the moral freedom of the man, as well as of the youth

Woman is endowed, by nature, with the same capacities and abilities for moral independence, as man

Woman has the same right to social independence and moral freedom, as man

But woman has been degraded, by disgraceful prejudice, to slavery, to legal bondage, under man

Woman is degraded to a ware, which is bargained away by parents or relations, and if no one will take her "on commission," she sells herself for a personal existence—for a living

Marriage has become a contract by which for-

* Neat wooden slippers, with colored leather over the toes.

tunes are disposed of, and settlements, jointures, and life annuities, are created

Woman has become a secondary object in the sacrament of marriage, whereby two fortunes are united to each other

Woman is degraded to a propagating machine, to bear male and female slaves in lawful marriage, and sensuality has become the element of female existence

All social usuages indicate the moral condition of the nation in which they are current

The conditions of nature in woman, are as sacred and powerful as in man, but woman is deprived of the rights of nature, woman cannot seek a moral union with a man, under the yoke of senseless, unreasonable social laws

Falsification of the notions of virtue, innocence, and honor, indicate man to be a brutal, savage creature, whom no young woman can approach without the risk of losing "her virtue, her innocence, and her honor"

Where such social laws prevail, morality must have sunk low, indeed

Where confidence in virtue and honor is extinguished in the hearts of the people, there is full room made for the predominance of vice

A woman, driven to despair by circumstances, dares not seek refuge nor protection from a worthy man, but only from those who develop vice under the protection of the laws

Virtue finds no asylum in the breast of a man, unless he will hazard his "good name" and his honor, as a citizen, by innocent intercourse with the female sex

To destroy virtue, to subvert innocence, to lead women to suicide or wretchedness—all this in nowise injures a man's good name or honor, as a citizen, so long as he does not offend against "good manners" The woman, however, who has been seduced, has lost her honor, becomes despised or laughed at, and remains debarred from "respectable society!"

Education has, until now, instead of confirming morality and virtue, promoted vice and corruption of manners

Where virtue and morality have become chimeras, neither rules of deportment, nor governesses and teachers, will be able to awaken them.

If a young woman must be guarded like a wild turkey, to prevent her from coming into the society of a young man, miserable, indeed, must be the state of virtue in her heart

Where the innocence of a young woman is endangered, as soon as she goes alone into the garden or into the street with a young man, morality cannot be particularly flourishing in the hearts of youth

The education of the female sex has, until now, been directed to the training of an automaton, to dance, speak some phrases, sew, read and write, and fill the marriage bed

Where such an automaton possesses a considerable fortune, she is a pattern to the female sex, and becomes a wife and mother, to the joy of legitimacy

An excellent mother lays the foundation of her children's welfare by a careful training; she teaches them to pray before they can speak, keeps them from playing with other children who are in a lower station, and directs them to bow to a stranger, if he be well dressed

A good mother derives joy from the bringing

up of her children, when the daughters make good mothers, and the sons are doing a good business, or have obtained good situations under government, without being put in the pillory, or sent to the house of correction, when they are not slandered as being men of heads and hearts, who trouble themselves about the cause of humanity, and when they are not persecuted as "rebels"

It is only a wonder that the human race has not fallen lower, when we consider the morally wretched condition of woman, and weigh the influence of the female sex upon rising generations.

For the maintenance of public order and morality, a union of both sexes is necessary, which has, until now, been called "marriage"

The union of the two sexes should take place with harmony of character, under the guarantee of physical existence.

The alliance should be based on love

Where no sympathy of soul prevails, the union will become what, for the most part, marriage has been until now—a business alliance on speculation, or a legally sensual mode of living tediously together

The connubial relation exercises the most powerful influence upon the moral condition of future generations

So long as the female sex are not conscious of their dignity, mankind will remain fettered, as hitherto, in slavery

Luxury and fashion have become the world of women, and the dutiful mother, who may form an advantageous exception, gives to the state, at the utmost, creatures who are not "obnoxious to the police"

A woman who develops her moral powers, who manifests understanding and feeling, and is concerned for the lot of humanity, is considered an "enthusiast," who troubles herself about things which do not concern her

Youths and men, who have glowed in the cause of the people before they were enchained by slavish women, lose their honorable sentiments and their moral freedom in connubial union, and shake off their convictions, that they may propagate a race of slaves

The charms of sensuality, and the force of habit, lessen the power of resistance of oppressed humanity in the contest against every enemy, increasing the number of slaves, and the might of the oppressor.

Woman's duties are different from those of man, but the duties of reasonable beings upon earth, the duties of humanity, (of man towards mankind,) should be fulfilled, by woman, as well as by man

Notwithstanding the slavery in which woman is held, we recognise in her the most exalted being in creation, who not unfrequently surpasses man in power of mind and strength of soul, in fortitude under suffering, and courage and firmness in danger

The development of the human race will advance with giant strides, so soon as woman assumes the position in human society which is her due, according to the requirements of nature, and reason.——

The young lady had read to this place, with increasing attention—and now looked again at the title page of the book, as if seeking, by a view of the author's name, an intimate acquaintance with him, whose mind attracted her own towards it

"I should like to know if this man is, or has been married," said she, half aloud, to herself, "and I would like to know the woman who made him happy—and she, also, must have been happy in the love of a man who prizes our sex so highly" She read further "Marriage without Love"——and hesitated

"A fearful chapter! shall I read to night?" said she to herself "How came I to take it into my head to read this book to-night? Did the doctor give it to me intentionally? The doctor? Can he know my thoughts? my inner mind? but what has that to do with this chapter?"

She seemed again to sink into reflection, and then read

MARRIAGE WITHOUT LOVE

There is a crime, which is committed thousands of times under the sanction of the church and the state, and whose consequences are often brought before the tribunals of justice, without the legislation of any country being, as yet, able to remedy the evil, which is based upon the deficient organization of human society   It is the crime of marriage, without love

Love is the union of two beings in unity of soul, thought, attraction, upon a similar, or equal, grade of sentiment

Marriage, as an absolutely necessary social institution, should be founded upon love, upon relationship of the souls of two beings, brought together by spiritual sympathy   In any other case, (even if it be confirmed as a contract by church and state,) it becomes a crime against nature and humanity, and produces effects, which extend their destructive influence to the second generation, and even further

Woman serves as the ornament of creation—an ennobled being by reason of her delicate nervous organization, insomuch as we recognise the nervous system as the organ of spiritual life Woman has so much the more righteous claim to love, in proportion as she is susceptible of love, and is so much the more capable of returning love, in the higher sphere of sentiment ——

"Fearfully true!" sighed the lady, and read further."

—But if we consider the social position of woman, in all so called civil countries, we behold her a slave, deprived of her moral and personal freedom, subordinate to man, so soon as she forms a connexion against her convictions, and without love, upon which her future fate her whole earthly happiness depends ——

"Terrible!" sighed the lady, and read further ·

—As in the male sex, so do we observe in the female, various aims in the improvement of the heart and the understanding, various and endless gradations of the soul's life in spirituality, and of the soul's death in materialism.

But woman is the more capable of developing the life of the soul, the more sensitively and susceptibly the organ of the soul, the fluid of the nerves, is unfolded in her.

The heart (as the symbol of the soul) is the basis and the sanctuary of all ennoblement, and when, in woman, the so called understanding is developed at the expense of the heart, together with suppression of the feelings, she stands in contradiction with the nature of female existence, and its high destiny on earth.

Love is the element of the soul's life, and, as such, the absolute condition of spiritual existence Woman longs after love, so soon as she arrives at a consciousness of her dignity. In the reciprocation of this longing, or in its denial, (whenever she forms a connexion without love,) lies the difference between spiritual life and moral death ——

The book trembled in the lady's hand, she gazed before her, and then read further

—The more the men of our civilized century, sunk in materialism, choke the inward life within them, and recognise no higher aim than to satisfy the demands of a refined sensuality, by the most luxurious possible gratification of their physical wants, the more tragical becomes the lot of woman

She seeks, in man, a heart, a soul, and finds, at the utmost, the cold calculations of the understanding, material speculation, animal instinct, without spirit

Modesty, at the expense of the consciousness of inward worth, as well in woman as in man, is rather a weakness than a virtue A woman should feel whom she is capable of making happy She who does not value herself, renounces, also, the respect of others

A woman who renounces love, and, induced by so called reasonable motives, resolves upon an alliance in which the most sacred conditions of the race, the relation of man to mankind, comes into consideration, commits a crime against nature

A woman who, under pretence of a right to independence, endeavors to dispose of herself in exchange for the satisfaction of external wants, and proclaims the result of her "reasonable motives" as love, deceives, beforehand, the companion of her life, who, as a man, whoever he may be, has a right to require love, if he is able to return love

In thousands of cases, a woman believes that she loves, and, nevertheless, does not love, and her deceit is, of course, not intentional, but the man who, for material ends, feigns love to gain a woman, is guilty of the crime of soul murder

If woman enters upon the holiest connexion which human society has ever been able to institute, with a renunciation of love, that she may be outwardly provided for, if she expects no love from the man to whom she gives herself, in the most sacred and solemn sense of the word, she appears no longer like a woman, but an unnatural being, in contradiction with herself and with God She becomes dangerous to human society, and her whole life fashions itself into a succession of rugged contradictions She will, sooner or later, feel her self-deceit, and recognise the crime which she has committed against herself—against the divine nature in mankind ——

The lady shuddered, and was about to lay aside the book—then took another look at the name of the author, dried a tear from her long lashes and sighed · "No ! he cannot and will not injure a woman ! I forgive him these hard words Who knows what anguish has forced them from him ?" She read on :

—If we regard marriage as a holy institution of the Christian religion, (apart from the degradation of its sacredness by the church, which imparts its blessing, at a stipulated price, to every pair who announce themselves ready to pay,) the connexion appears to be a sacred symbol of the union of two souls in the element of love—insomuch as there is only one love existing upon earth, in whatever form it may be

A woman who resolves upon the holiest of all connexions, from "reasonable motives," and, with so called self-control, suppresses her feelings, calculating thus to secure her external subsistence, profanes and desecrates the sacrament of marriage, which should establish a union of souls on earth, that was "made in heaven," in the exalted region of spiritual life

Such a woman is only distinguished from so called *femmes entretenues* by her cunning and foresight, for with less faith in man's heart, she requires and abuses the formal bonds of the church, that she may attain a better guarantee for her future existence ——

"Who is the man that wrote this ?" the lady exclaimed, letting the book fall again , "I would choke him, strangle him, with my own hands, if he were here ! No !" continued she, after a pause , "no ! I would press his hand, and look him in the face ! Who will deny that he has told the truth ?" She read further

—The welfare of all mankind lies in marriage It is the spirit of love which breathes through the universe, and love is the mystery of all creation The man however, who, from sensuality, meddles with the Creator in his creation, wants the spirit of love and a second innocent generation suffers the penalty of his crime

A generation that owes its existence to the forced performance of so called "duty," stands on low scale in the fellowship of humanity, and bears the germ of slavery, the essence of selfishness, in itself ——

—Forced performance of so called duty ?" interrupted she "Forced · The good man who wrote that was never married A woman does not allow herself to be forced to any so called 'performance of duty,' or she must be a goose, and her husband a monster " She read on ·

—There is a sin against the Holy Ghost, it is the sin against the holy spirit of love, the contemning of moral freedom in the slavish service of legally privileged sensuality—opposed to the bugbear of the forced fulfilment of duty ——

"Why is he all the while prating about the forced fulfilment of duty ?" said she, again interrupting her reading "Where love is extinct, there is no longer any duty in this respect " She read further.

—on the other hand, stands the mourning genius of love, fettered and despised by the precepts of the Church and the State, which are based upon slavery, and mankind grope about, in chains and fetters, from generation to generation.

What, then, is love ? Th' attraction of the soul
To kindred soul—the striving after union,
Union of souls within the spirit's realm,
Fit consequence of light and purity
Love is the divine spirit 's spheral note,
In myst'ry sounding for the hastening on
Of the soul's elevation , source of light,
Piercing through matter's darkness clear and bright.
  The soul's attraction to its kindred soul,
Its longing its existence to extend,
As a part, still striving upward to th' unknown—

The source of life, whose tones encircle him –
Proud of the spirit's union to its like,
The nameless longing of th' excited soul,
To merge itself with others, and to soar
To being's heights upon the wings of thought,
That is true LOVE—the element of life,
Endless condition of the living soul,
From freedom's spirit indivisible
     Only through freedom can the soul prolong
Existence, and the more is granted her,
The more exalted the victorious strife
True love will, in its object, lose itself,
And sacrifice itself for whom it glows
     Love is so far estranged from selfishness,
It hopes, it suffers, and endureth all,
If matter rigidly opposes it
Its essence is allied to that of sound,
Or light, which know no circumscribed bound
It is the holy spirit of sacrifice
On the heart's altar, to God consecrated—
Its being, endlessness, eternity ——

" The man who wrote this, has felt what love is " sighed she, " whether he has ever found a being yet who understood him—that is another question." She read further

—If we recognise love as an unity, it follows that the sentiment which raises us in longing and faith to the idea of the Deity, (as religious love,) is one and the same with the consciousness of love which binds us on earth to one being, whose soul is united to ours on the same scale of sentiment

It is one and the same divine power, which, striving after ennoblement, seeks its point of spiritual support in higher spheres, and on earth The bond of souls, in love on earth, bears us upward to the idea of the Deity, and religious love (love of God) is again illustrated in us, in the union with a kindred soul. it is the divine blending of two being's natures in the idea, God !

It is the " point of Archimedes," without the corporeal world, upon which the two kindred natures are in a condition " to heave out of joint" the whole terrestrial universe, with its circumscribed relations

As every man is capable of religious love, (apart from all cultivation of the understanding,) so is every human heart susceptible of that love which is presupposed in the sacred institution of marriage, provided the spiritual life within it be not wasted and destroyed, and sunk into materialism In the latter case, a man is capable of neither the one love nor the other, and stands in the scale of brutes, that follow their instincts, and know no passion

The unity of the idea of love is proved in this, that men who substitute sensuality for love, and under the protection of the church and the state, lead a woman into a connexion which licenses sensuality are also incapable of religious love, and on the other hand, men, whose spiritual life has become extinct, and who are thus incapable of religious love, are also strangers to that love, which presupposes union of souls Where there is no spiritual life, no soul, there is also no religion, no love ——

The book dropped from her hand, while she tremblingly shrunk together, and with an expression of despair, sank upon her knees, and stretched her hands towards heaven Suddenly a bright ray of consolation appeared to pervade her soul. She gazed, with a smile of spiritual effulgence, upon a crucifix, that hung opposite to her, under a picture of Saint Theresa, and a gleam of spiritual peace overspread her counte-

nance What passed within her, who may know ? Who could know but the Allwise Being, who watched over, and looked into the soul of, this unhappy child of earth

A noise at the outside garden gate, as if some one were turning the lock, startled her She listened, and satisfied herself of the reality of the disturbance, then quickly pulled on the string before mentioned, hurried into the next room, seized a pistol, and awaited, trembling and shuddering, the entrance of the old attendant.

CHAPTER XV

SHORT WORK

THE old negress did not keep her mistress long waiting for her, ~~she found~~ her in the above mentioned situation, listening to the noise, which was repeated from time to time

" He seems to be trying a key," whispered the old woman, " but I have drawn both bolts carefully—he cannot get in—and the wall is too high "

" Take the other pistol, and follow me !" whispered the lady, " have it ready when I require it "

The old woman obeyed the command, while the young lady wrapped herself in a shawl, and stepped out on the verandah

The moon had risen considerably higher, and lighted the garden with almost the clearness of day The flowers had closed their chalices, and drooped their heads, diminutive lizards, of a beautiful species, scarcely an inch and a half long, glided around upon the white walls of the chacara and garden, caressing each other in the undisturbed happiness of their mysterious and useful lives, (for their glance arrests the mosquitoes, which they instantly swallow)

The lady stepped forward, silently and carefully, to avoid the least rustling, and approached the threatened gate, upon which fruitless efforts were still being made to open it

At the distance of about five paces, she aimed, with presence of mind, at a point above the usual height of a man, fired, and the bullet pierced through the gate

" The second bullet shall be aimed lower, if you do not take yourself off !" cried she, while she took the other pistol in her hand, and stepped up to the entrance " Mark that! you know what you have to expect "'

The departing steps of a man, evidently booted and spurred, at that instant clattered on the rocky ground, over which a footpath led to the chacara, and soon ceased to be heard The lady remained for a moment leaning, nearly exhausted, against the gate, then seizing the arm of the old negress, she tottered back to the room, and threw herself on the divan.

" Sit down, Anna," said she, after a long pause, during which, both listened attentively; " sit down; we are safe now, for to-night "

" It was certainly he, and no one else," said the old woman, while she set about reloading the pistols.

"'Tis very probable," replied the lady; "who else, would desire to intrude here? But how he has discovered our flight, and found us out, that is more inexplicable to me than his temerity, his insolence!'"

"Do you know how I can explain it, Senhora? how he discovered us?"

"How?"

"By your piano, by the tune you are so fond of playing—and music can be heard so far, far away!'"

"Indeed, Anna, you are right. I will play the melody no more! What you suspect, is very probable, but he did not inquire after me, when he was here yesterday?"

"When he knocked at the gate, I did not go to open it, but sent Maria, whom he would not so readily recognise, and Maria said it was he, she also described his figure and dress, and all agreed together. He asked her if there was not a room to let here, and when she told him no, he observed that the pavilion, over there, was uninhabited, he wished to hire it, so Maria said—"

"My God! why did you not tell me!'" interrupted the lady; "you only told me that he had made general inquiries after lodgings!'"

"I did not want to make you uneasy."

"But, Anna! if he should really hire the pavilion? what then? We must then move immediately!'"

"That is taken care of already," said the old attendant smiling, "When Maria went into the city to-day, I gave her an order to hurry to Senhor Moreto, and tell him to get possession of the pavilion next to us, and assume the right of letting it himself, that no one should come into it without your consent Senhora! and that I would speak to him about it myself, to-morrow, when Maria was here with you again. I told Maria that she must say to Senhor Moreto not, for any thing in the world, to tell any body who you were, or what your name was."

'I thank you my good Anna, for your forethought, that is like you. Indeed, if I could trust even one man on earth, I might desire that the pavilion were inhabited by some man on whom I could rely, who, however, must not know my situation. Perhaps some stranger may soon be casually informed of it, and I shall then make new enquiries——no one shall easily come to us, who is in the least suspicious."

"This pavilion will not stand empty long," remarked Anna, "the situation is too charming, and the prospect from here too well known, not to be inquired after, when a dwelling is to let here."

She had loaded the pistols again, and laid them both on the night table in the inner apartment.

"Go to bed now!" said the lady, "I feel myself strengthened—my mind is tranquil—tranquil as it can be—more tranquil than before I have prayed—and God has heard me!'"

"God indeed hears the prayers of the whites and the blacks," said Anna, "but he does not always grant them! So many thousands pray to him! how can he hear and attend to so many prayers at once? and then, in so many languages! Among us, here from Africa, we count forty different Ethiopian languages! forty, Senhora, and many tribes do not understand each other's language! and all pray to God! even if they have not been baptized! All pray to the Great Spirit, as we call him! and the Great Spirit must understand all these languages! I have thought, that, if he understood them, he would have freed us, long ago, from slavery to the white people!'"

"Every man has his invisible genius, Anna! we all have our gardian angels, who hover round us, and see into our hearts before the thoughts pass our lips in words! and God will deliver us—you blacks, and us whites—from all slavery, if we show ourselves worthy of freedom, and have God before our eyes and in our hearts, and take care that we consent to no sin."

"All the slaves in Brazil do not have such good times and feel so happy as we, with your parents and with you, if only your husband, our master, would not——"

"How? What?" cried the lady, who now contracted her strongly defined eyebrows, and suddenly burst into a passion.

"Do you presume to make remarks upon my husband? upon his treatment of negroes? Is there a white man in Brazil, who treats his negroes better? Is there any one who generally maintains a better character, a worthier man, in every respect, than my husband?"

Poor old Anna trembled, and seemed, with a low, hardly articulate voice, to repent having caused such a convulsive excitement in her mistress.

"Pardon me! pardon me! Senhora," said she, imploringly, and with repeated courtesies, "I will not say any thing more—I will never say any thing again about our master! never more! no, never!'"

"I don't thank you for that! Go now! get off with you! go to your room! march!'"

The old attendant gazed after her commandress, like a faithful dog at his mistress, who has given him a kick, because her husband's nightcap had fallen into the wash basin, which the poor animal had not touched.

Anna arranged the string, in case of the necessity of being again awakened, raised her right hand towards her mistress, according to Ethiopian custom, wished her good night in a mournful tone, and departed. Instead of replying, the lady tossed one of her tamancas from her with her foot, to vent her ill humor on some object.

"I wish the doctor had kept this miserable book to himself!'" grumbled she, throwing the book after the tamanca, and then disappeared behind the mosquito net in her sleeping apartment.

CHAPTER XVI.

HINANGO

"THERE is a light before us, captain!" cried Rolufls, the young sailor at the helm of the brig Nordstjernan, and pointed directly north.

Capt Fingreen was sitting with Hinango and Robert Walker, upon a bench on the quarterdeck, enjoying the fine breeze and mild atmosphere. They were engaged in conversation upon the movements among the Scandinavian races towards the foundation of a national unity

All three now sprang up, and Robert called down through the open skylight—"the light of the island of Raza, Señor Horatio! The light upon Raza!"

"True," said the captain, when he had observed it for some time, and counted the appearance of the revolving light by the second-hand of his watch. "We may be some twenty miles distant from it."

"Perhaps still further, captain," replied Hinango; "for nothing is more deceptive than the distance in a tropical atmosphere—though objects may appear near to us, through the purity of the air."

"At any rate, thank God! we have the light in view," remarked the other, and hurried to the cabin to his chart, to reckon the course of the vessel since he took the last latitude. Horatio and Alvarez did not long delay to take a view of the wished for light.

Dolores had heard the call of young Walther, and made her appearance in a wide mantilla, with a shawl wound round her head like a turban, for she was just on the point of retiring to rest. It was after midnight, and the moon, which lighted the walls of the chacara, at the gate of which the pistol shot had fallen, threw her dazzling light, from the same altitude, down upon the deck of the Nordstjernan.

"There, then, is land!" sighed Dolores, from an oppressed heart, "and to-morrow, perhaps, we shall step upon it, and it will unfold to us a 'new world' of personal relations."

"The coast, which we shall see early in the morning, forms a title-page vignette to a new division of our lives, which we shall begin there," remarked Hinango.

"And how rich in contents may many chapters be that our fate shall inscribe in the book of our lives. The so much talked of happiness, that man cannot see the distance of a span into the future, or, at least, cannot foresee, with certainty, the events which are likely to befall him," asserted Hinango, "is all that makes earthly life endurable, in the everyday routine of which existence would become wearisome to many intellectual men, if they might not hope for some alteration of things."

"I am of your opinion, and find, in the limitation of human knowledge in respect to the future, a sublime regulation of the Allwise God," said Dolores.

"As concerns our fate," said Hinango, "I maintain that every man is master of his own fate, every man spins the thread of his own fate, as far as his lot and his circumstances are developed from his actions. A youth, for instance, who goes to sea, ought not to complain of storm and shipwreck, and a maiden who, from her own free will, marries a man from so called 'reasonable motives,' ought not, as a wife, to wonder, if, instead of love, she finds heartlessness."

"Røet sa som hun går!" (steady as she is going!) cried Capt. Finngreen to the man at the helm, as he stepped upon deck again, and he added:

"Ottar! make a fire, and put on the teakettle. Heat some water for a bowl of punch—do you hear?"

"Put on the teakettle! water for a bowl of punch!" repeated the long Ottar, and hurried to the caboose.

"The levity with which people so often decide on the most important step of their lives," continued Dolores, "tends very little to the honor of their hearts, and what they call the result of their reason, often stands in contradiction to sound reason, and, for the most part, at least, to their feelings."

"Many men very soon extinguish their feelings, and, of course, generally act from cold calculation," replied Hinango "and those are the ones who are first wrecked upon the future, which cannot be calculated like the per centage of a business."

"The women of our day exceed the men in cold calculation,' remarked Dolores, "for they sell themselves, and often for a very small price, and the very suppression and extinction of feeling in female hearts, is a requisition of so called civilization, by which mankind are, at length, alienated from every exalted aim. The internal sentiments, in the depths of which lie the whole moral worth of mankind, especially in the female sex, are considered, according to the precepts of fashion, as in infamy, and everybody endeavors to make it ridiculous, whenever it shows itself. Civilization, as the term is usually understood, requires simply machines—not men."

"This truth would long since have driven me to despair,' rejoined Hinango, "if I did not regard men from a higher point of view, and consider our epoch as a transition period. Mankind press forward towards the design of their destiny, which will ever remain contracted, and eternally be confined within the bounds of their planetary mediocrity."

Dolores appeared to follow, with peculiar attention, the course of her friend's ideas, and now looked inquiringly at him, as if she desired an explanation of the last assertion. Instead of answering, the Scandinavian returned the look of the South American lady. He then cast his eyes upward, towards the stars, as if he would have said, "Accompany me!" and continued:

"Think of the universe, consisting of solar systems upon solar systems, as we express in mortal language the assemblage of a collection of worlds, think of the sun, as the material centre of motion of the planetary orbits, and myriads of suns, as similar centres of similar orbits, like planets with their satellites about a sun within suns, and again, myriads of these suns surrounding other suns, and all revolving about a spark of light—the idea of the Deity!

"Ask yourself where the space terminates, in which moves the most distant star that our eyes behold. Ask yourself when time began, upon whose wings our lives are borne, and when time will end? Think of an eternal continuation of spiritual development, from satellite to satellite, from planet to planet, from solar system to solar system, of which our system contains a greater number of larger planets than of smaller ones—and there are still smaller planets of our solar system than the human eye has hitherto discovered. Then think of our poor little earth, as a subordinate planet, in a solar system, which contains a greater number of planets, larger. Then measure, by this rule of the planetary proportions, man, as an inhabitant of the earth."

"You mount high, and fly swiftly!" said Dolores, after a pause, "but I follow you, from one elevation to another. I accompany you!"

"Accompany me then to a world of intuition, in which I have been at home from childhood, and whose spheres have drawn me upward, above this earthly world, by the mighty bond of attraction. Think of our spiritual life as a unity, this shell of clay only as the instrument, the organ of connexion with the corporeal world. Think of our spiritual existence as a reality, and this earthly life only as a dream, in whose fetters thousands live along without awakening to a consciousness of the spiritual reality—and accompany me now to my home."

"To your home?" inquired Dolores, with surprise! "How so? What do you mean by that?"

"Accompany me to Uranus."

"To Uranus!" she repeated, with an expression of amazement. "Oh, yes! I know—you are a poet, and your imagination may certainly have ventured on many an audacious flight!"

"Horatio, who was seated next to Hinango, held fast to his arm, and gazed upward, at him.

"Call it a flight of imagination—I have no name for the expansion of my spiritual life, which I seek to make evident to you. I lay at one time severely wounded—how I received the wound—whether I inflicted it upon myself—that must remain untold. I lay there, on the confines of this earthly existence, and hoped to die. It appeared to me as if I vanished from the earth, and suddenly awoke to a consciousness of spiritual reality. And my whole past existence was revealed to me in a single spiritual survey. And I knew that I was living here on earth for the second time."

"For the second time?" inquired Dolores, who listened to the revelation of her friend with increased attention.

"Behold the moon, there!" continued Hinango, turning to Horatio. "Did you ever long to return back to the moon?"

"Long to return back?" inquired both, as with one voice.

"Or, have you longed to be upon the moon? If I have too soon used the word back."

Both looked at each other, and remained silent.

"I have never found a man," continued the Scandinavian, "who would give me an affirmative reply to this question, while I have often found people who longed to reside upon this or that star."

"I must acknowledge," replied Horatio, "that the moon has for me something gloomy. I have, indeed, never experienced a wish to inhabit it."

"You explain sensations that I have often felt," began Dolores, looking earnestly at Hinango, "that have long darkly slumbered within me. I have indeed longed, a thousand times, to be upon some one of those sparkling stars, but never to live upon the moon—never!"

"In that state of spiritual intuition," continued Hinango, "it seemed to me, that we had all been upon the moon once, without being conscious of our existence there. Call my communication of to-night, madness, my madness has, at least, (like Hamlet's,) 'method' in it, and I ask of you to inform me of any contradiction in what I am going to state to you.

"The effect of the moon upon the physical nature of man, is incontestible, no observing physician, will deny it, let him be ever so much of a materialist. There exists an effectual telluric bond—a bond of existence, which is manifested in the nervous system, and especially in the female sex, whose nervous organization, is so much more delicate and sensitive than ours.

"In a state pronounced dead by my physicians and friends, my spirit flew through all my past existence, as thousandfold recollections occur to us in a single moment of joy, or of grief. I was upon the moon, the single satellite of a planet, which, forty-nine times greater than the moon, observed from thence, glittered in the zenith of the firmament, in wonderful majesty. And my existence was a longing after a brighter perfection, which this planet made perceptible to me, and my longing was borne upward towards the earth, in the full splendor of its rays, which there shone about me. And I was conceived and born, as a man on earth, by a loving being, to whom the operation of my longing, and the telluric influence of the moon, upon her inward life, remained a secret. I lived here a short dream-life, and died. And I rose from step to step of development, from planet to planet, from Jupiter to Saturn, from Saturn to Uranus. I stood then in the highest scale of being in our solar system, ready for the transition to one more perfect, for entrance into life upon the smallest planet of a brighter solar system, which is, nevertheless, larger and more perfect than Uranus.

"What I saw and felt in those spheres, was repeated within me like the recollection of a dream. There are dreams from which we awake, and they suddenly vanish, the last forms or appearances float around us, as if to take leave, the curtain falls, and we see them no more. The spheres of the dream-world form a separate spiritual region, into which no bridge leads that man can tread of his own will, and the arbitrary reminiscences of a dream are capable of exciting a nervous disturbance.

"The whole universe then lay before me, below me, like the garden of my home on earth, in which, I had played as a child and boy, a thousand remembrances awoke within me, and genii, who had been allied to me upon one and another planet, greeted me, and mourned over my fearful fate.

"Upon earth, words are the organ of the communication of thought, upon Ceres, perfume, like the aroma of the flowers, of which language we have an intimation, here on earth, in the strong perfume of flowers at the time of their fructification. Upon Jupiter, this organ is the array of colors, like the rainbow and the morning dawn, upon Saturn, tune—the sound of harmony, what we here call music, the acoustic ring of that planet, facilitating the circular movement of sound, stands in connexion with this expression. Upon Uranus however, where a higher degree of perfection exists, the ray serves as the medium of expression, similar to the spiritual fluid of the eye here on earth.

"What we are here unable to express in words, is there told by a ray, and the irradiating operation of magnetism here on earth, is an intimation of the interchange of thought and feeling by those who dwell upon Uranus In the same manner as a clairvoyant, or somnambulist, perceives and becomes sensible of the thoughts and slightest emotions in the soul of a distant person, is the spiritual intercourse of the beings upon Uranus carried on, when space divides them The invisible operation of magnetism in general, is only a feeble foreboding of the medium of communion, and connexion in the spiritual sphere of Uranus, the highest in our solar system, towards which our longings aspire on earth

"With the transition to the smallest planet of a brighter system, we first conceive the aspiration after the highest degree of the existence of the happy beings upon the largest planet of that solar system—and so onward, from step to step, from perfection to yet greater perfection The higher the planetary degree, the less is the soul fettered by matter, the more easy becomes the upward tendency towards the source of love, the more powerful the expression of the ray "

"The ray' similar to the spiritual fluid of the eye-glance'" interrupted Dolores "Your revelation penetrates me with a holy seriousness " She seemed to wish to say more, but interrupted herself, and said "Pardon me this interruption, I beg you will proceed "

The Scandinavian continued "As upon our planet, and upon all the others, progress through struggle, effort through motion, is the condition of all being, so it is, also, upon Uranus, and love is, also, there, the element of life

"Love and friendship, as one idea in various forms, here on earth, is only a foretaste of that which we shall feel in a higher degree of the soul's life, in the spheral world The less we are fettered by matter, the easier does the soul soar upward to the source of love, of light, and of strength, (if ever, a million times more capable of purity,) and so much more blissful is, also, the sentiment of love The nearer to the light, the more powerful is the spiritual ray that pervades and inflames us But there, also, is doubt, and there, also, is the foreboding of a higher existence And the consciousness of faith upon Uranus, bears the same relation, in clearness, to the dark forebodings of the inhabitants of earth, that the orbit of eighteen hundred millions of miles bears to an orbit of ninety-three millions But there, also, is a striving and struggling after the idea of freedom, as the condition of all spiritual development ——And the clearer the foreboding of a higher existence in a brighter solar system penetrated me, the more boldly I struggled upward, despising the ordinances of a corporeal world, which there, also, fetter the spirit, and bind it the more oppressively, the more it is already enfranchised by the consciousness of its dignity in the higher scale of being I contended for the idea of freedom as the means of ennoblement, and I loved, and I confounded the limits of love upon Uranus, with the limits of freedom beyond the sphere of Uranus, and I fell out with myself, and with the genius who loved me as I loved him I misunderstood his godlike love, because I suspected that he misunderstood me, and, in a moment of anguish and soul-rending emotion, at being misapprehended by the being whom I loved the most, I committed suicide.

"I was hurled back to Saturn, burdened by the curse of a horrible existence, which could only be delivered by love A nature allied to mine, with the same aspirations towards the divine source, with equal attraction towards the primitive idea, was to deliver me, by uniting our two beings in love, and reconcile me to the Deity through love, which, in my despair, I dared to despise I now sought the genius of deliverance, the atonement of love, but I found it not With the clear consciousness that a higher world existed, I was a stranger to the beings of Saturn for the most of them were embarrassed by doubt and unbelief, (like mortals here upon earth,) and when I taught them of the existence of a higher sphere of life, they ridiculed me, and called me an enthusiast, in the sharply significant expressions of their sound-language, and I was neither understood nor loved there In the glow of my longing after love, I drew near to a genius of Saturn, but the aspiration and faith were deficient in him, and he comprehended me not—he understood me not Powerfully agitated by the reality of the love in which mortals, there, strive upward towards God, borne along and floating upon the soarings of the melodiously harmonious world of sound, of harmony, I felt my unhappy fate, to live without love' and the convulsion of despair again pervaded me, and a step, similar to the one which had caused my departure from Uranus, threw me downward, back upon Jupiter Still less understood there than upon Saturn, I vainly sought after the atonement of love, the union of a kindred nature with my own, through spiritual attraction In vain' Mistaken and misunderstood, with hurt and wounded feelings, I again renounced the hope of love, bore my life without love, to the abyss of despair, and thus rushed, headlong, seeking love, and meeting injuries, from despair to despair, from planet to planet, downward and backward, until I came again upon earth, and I must still go backward to Venus, and then to Mercury,"——he rose, and continued, slowly "unless the Deity should strengthen me with supernatural power to bear such a loveless life to the grave, and to linger and to endure, until this earthly covering, that burdens my soul, falls away—until I am again called, by divine love, to the radiant region of my home upon Uranus "

A long silence ensued Dolores and Horatio looked, with unaverted gaze, at the friend who had honored them with a confidence that they knew how to appreciate Hinango stood there, deadly pale, with his eyes directed upward to the stars, and a bright tear glistened upon his eyelashes "Forgive me '" said he, at length, "forgive me, for having awakened your sympathy by my revelation, better, perhaps, that I had not done so "

"On the contrary," replied Dolores, "I thank you, with all the warmth of my heart, for the confidence you have bestowed upon us, but my sorrow is heightened by the thought, that our earthly language is too weak to afford you consolation "

"It is too late '" sighed Hinango "You are a woman, and are, therefore, the less able to heal wounds which——" He shuddered, and remained silent

Dolores observed that the unhappy man had touched that subject which Barigaldi had mentioned, and which she had, unwittingly, agitated

"I pray you, tell us something more about the world of spheres," entreated Horatio, to lead him away from his earthly griefs

Hinango seated himself by them again, and began

"Do you not find that there is, at times, something particularly significant in the names of men, as if they had been given them from prophetic inspiration, as, for example, Pitt, who, by his system, has dug a pit into which the whole empire of Great Britain may fall headlong

'Peel, Robert Peel, the 'peel' which covers the decaying trunk of British aristocracy, likewise, to 'peel,' to shell off to flay, insomuch as Peel's system 'pulls the wool over the eyes of the people,' &c

"Buonaparte, the family (of 'buonaparte,' of a good part, or good portion,) which portioned the whole of Europe among themselves

"Columbus, the dove, which, like the dove from Noah's ark, flew across the ocean, and confirmed the existence of the transatlantic world

"Lopez de Vega—vega, a broad, fruitful plain, a rich, blooming field, which agrees with the wide field of the rich dramatic productions of this poet

"Pfaff, a German polemic writer of the former century, who zealously endeavoured to maintain that Protestantism was more accordant with despotism than Catholicism   A true pfaff *

"Fourrier, the 'army commissary for the barrack system, by which he would supply all mankind with rations

"Cuvier, (from cuver, to hatch,) who hatched out a new system, and was capable of hatching out an entirely new set of animals from the bones of past ages

"Mirabeau, (mire, to aim,) who, as an orator, aimed beautifully, and often hit the centre

"Volontiere, who, as a volunteer, as the leader of a corps in Savoy, was the first prisoner taken and executed in 1834 †

"Washington, who was 'washing' the soil of the new world from the stain of British monarchy

"But enough ! it would be easy to sketch a numerous nomenclature in all languages

"As the names of so many men are strongly significant, and each often express what the men afterwards become, so, also, the planets, through a singular inspiration, have been named, throughout, with the same characteristic significance For example; Mercury, the god of merchants and thieves—Venus, the personification of sensuality Both planets stand far below our earth in respect to spiritual and moral development One of the lowest degree of the inhabitants of our solar system is that of Mercury, since the dirty, selfish interest of traffic, of gain, and of cheating, as the element of trade, prevails there The inhabitants of Mercury have no thoughts for anything but material gain, and the higher idea of love penetrates weakly and faintly through the mire of materialism in which they wallow They rob each other systematically, sell each

other, and sell themselves, and call it practical life'—while they despise the spiritual existence, and endeavor to dispose of every spiritual being among themselves, as a slave for their own service

'The despicable littleness of the selfish inhabitants of Mercury, is seventeen times meaner than that of the men of the earth, the dirty selfishness which prevails there, is seventeen times more contemptible than that of men

"The inhabitants of Venus, less thievish and usurious than those of Mercury, not in extravagant sensuality, and the ray of love but faintly penetrates the night of their existence, and often first affects a being, when it has already renounced love, and has become incapable of true love Many beings of Venus have already renounced, in the intoxication of sensuality, the love after which he longed, when penetrated by a ray of the spirit of love, which glimmers even there

"The beings of Venus consider sensual enjoyment as the destination of their existence, and brute propagation as a merit, on which they pride themselves

"Under the pretence of a fulfilment of the duty of propagation, they deaden themselves in sensuality, and hold themselves absolved from every other duty, whose fulfilment does not relate to them doubled and multiplied self

"They increase like rabbits, and, like them, willingly creep into the material of their planet, for the zealous performance of the so called duty of their existence

"Apart from the element of sensuality, the inhabitants of Venus resemble those of the earth, and approach, in their nature, so near to that of mankind, that there is no important difference.

"The transition of their entity into inhabitants of the earth often checks the progress of ennoblement, since their nature, here and there, shows forth, and binds the human being in moral slavery, through sensuality

'We are acquainted with the inhabitants of our earth The name earth in Greek (γαῖα, similar to gemo, to generate) is likewise suitable Man named his world according to his human, dark conceptions, while he regarded animal propagation as the principal object of life, and considered the earth as conceiving and propagating

"Less meanly material, and less dishonest than the inhabitants of Mercury, and less sensual than the hot-blooded beings of Venus, man, nevertheless, bears within himself a trace of both Our spiritual life contains a germ of the development which unfolds itself in higher regions, and the ray of the eye-glance here signifies an alliance with the mode of expression upon Uranus

"Man, in the bands of earthly imperfection, wallows in the dust of the ground, clogged by the matter in which his spiritual life is enclosed—while he receives, at the same time, the spiritual strength to subdue matter, by means of the freedom of his will

"Man was endowed with reason, as were also the inhabitants of Mercury and Venus, and it is easier for him than for them, to develope his spiritual life, if he will.

"But as the inhabitants of all planets and constellations carry with them the peculiarities of those stars which they have last left, so, also, do

---

* Priest.

† Some years later, Hinango might have, also, named Bandiera, the two immortal brothers, of "La Giovine Italia," who planted the banner (Bandiera) of their nationality, and moistened it with their blood They were executed at Cosenza, on the 25th of July, 1844

the peculiarities of Venus and Mercury characterize man Sordid material interest and low sensuality are the two elements in which the man moves upon earth, who denies in himself the presentiment of a higher degree of spiritual life These two elements sustain so-called 'human society'' And the more a man denies them, receiving within himself the ray of a higher existence, the more does he become a stranger to human society—a stranger upon the earth—and the more powerfully does the spiritual attraction draw him upward to the higher spheres

"The seed pollen of the spirit floats across from planet to planet, into the flower chalice of being, borne by the breath of love, for there are more perfect planets than ours, but as characteristically denoted by their names.

" The inhabitants of Mars are morally and spiritually stronger than we, and strive upwards with more manliness

"Believe me, the love of a being of Vesta, is a pure love, it imparts a felicity which I saw there, but did not enjoy Higher than the inhabitants of Juno, shine the beings of Pallas, exhalted in wisdom and divine knowledge

" Would that I could give you an idea of the brilliant, radiant world of Jupiter, as it once surrounded me, and as I now see it, at times, in the dreams of remembrance of my spheral life—in sleep—here, upon earth ' Even upon the transition stars, the four satellites of Jupiter, the operation of the ray is above all human conception As our earth appears to the inhabitants of the moon, forty-nine times larger than the moon to us—you may thereby imagine the aspect of Jupiter to those upon the first satellite, which is not farther from it than the earth from the moon, while Jupiter is sixty-eight thousand times larger than the moon The attraction of the ray is revealed in the whole universe, as the organ of spiritual life, as the organ of mysterious love The higher the degree of spheral life in our planetary system, so much the more powerfully, purely, and deeply, does the attraction of the ray penetrate the beings of the inhabitants of those higher and larger planets, and the more purely is the perception and intention of the Divinity developed in them , but they are, also, so much the more powerfully penetrated by the mysterious spheral light, in the anticipation of a higher state, and in the longing of love The spirit there, illuminated by such a radiant splendor, penetrated by such a powerful attraction, strives on, scarcely burdened by incorporation with clogging matter, upon the wings of its own developed strength, from satellite to planet, from planet to satellite and planet To find again kindred souls, as beings in a like degree recognise them again in the radiant brilliancy of such a firmament, embraces the bliss of such a spheral existence, increased by the extent of the means of expression of our sensations As, for instance, all proportions are a thousand times greater and grander upon Saturn than upon the earth, so, also, the communication of the soul, by the organ of the eye-glance, is a thousand times easier and more heartfelt, than by the language of the tongue upon earth

"As the inhabitants of Jupiter, at times, behold all four satellites at once, in their colossal grandeur, the radiant world of the seven satellites of Uranus, indescribably, different in size and ro-

tation, offers to the beings there a prospect which, in sublimity, approaches the effect which that radiant world exercises upon them spiritually As the eye-glance is the organ of the soul upon Uranus, upon Jupiter (as I have already told you) it is the colors caused by the refraction of rays The ray, in itself, can there express a thought by forms and images, as well as it is able to imbody the thought as an image *

"In accordance with the expression of the beings upon Saturn, as the sphere of sound, (of which we upon earth have obtained an idea by music,) the communication and fastening of thought takes place there (as by writing upon the earth) by means of those acoustic figures, in an easily moved bodily mass, which we can conceive of here on earth by the acoustic figures which may be made in sand, upon glass, by the sound of a musical string Such hieroglyphics are fastened in the moment of creation, and can serve for the future, like the written word upon earth As there the organ of expression is music of itself, the tone of the communication can, at the same time, produce and fasten a similar hieroglyphic writing in the element of sound

" As various is are the degrees of mental cultivation in the inhabitants of the stars, are the movements of their more or less material or ethereal bodies The subordinate, heavily material creatures of Mercury, creep about in the mire of their existence, in thieving and usury, and their 'progress' is seventeen times slower than the course of men upon earth. The sensual beings of Venus partly swim, and land in the moss-bedded caves of their luxurious 'social life'—in which, at times, they act without much restraint The ancients appear to have had an obscure recollection of the world of Venus, as their mythology makes Venus Aphrodite ascend out of the sea upon a mussel shell, as a symbol of sensual love Upon higher planets, movement is by soaring and flying, of which many a spiritual developed inhabitant of the earth may conceive an idea—in dreams—in the freed existence of the soul in the body—in which it moves in its sphere of presentiment "

"'Then you consider the state of dreams as the connecting medium with the spiritual world ?" interrupted Dolores

" Our dream-life, to be sure," replied Hinango , " but not all dreams, by any means " The realm of the dream-life is twofold There are animatic† and animal dreams The first compose the real dream-life, the latter are the effects of external or physical causes, as, for instance, digestion during sleep, the contact of any part of our body with another , as the weight of a hand that has fallen asleep, resting below the pit of the heart, (plexus cœliacus,) causes the nightmare The realm of the true dream-life is animatically free, foreign, and removed from all physical causes, as well as from the corporeal world. Only the dreams in this sphere are significant, as the continued spiritual life, during the rest of our body Every man dreams more or less livelily, in proportion to the development of his animatic, his spiritual life Animals and plants dream, also, in proportionate indistinctness The dreams of a Newfoundland dog can easily be observed, as he shows the motions of running and swimming in sleep, barks in a strange tone and whines, as if he were in suffering The uneasy neighing of a noble Arabian horse in his sleep, can also be considered as an evidence in this respect The dream-life of plants can only be supposed The *mimosa pudica* (sensitive plant) manifests susceptibility by movement, at outward touch, and experience in the department of magnetism shows us animatic life, as magnetic power, in many trees and shrubs Men in whom animatic life is oppressed by a predominance of the animal nature, likewise dream, without being conscious of their dreams when they awake—and they maintain that they seldom, or never dream The higher the degree of animatic life, so much the clearer is the perception of dreams, and so much the more extended is their province, which touches upon the boundaries of somnambulism, and, at times, affords a view, or a spiritual passage, into this mysterious realm of the soul-world '

' Men in whom the animatic power has been cultivated to a peculiarly high degree, often experience a continuation of their dreams after the interruption of waking, like the succeeding acts of a drama Such dreams are creations in the proper animatic sphere I, myself, for instance, frequently pass through the regions of my astral world, on such often interrupted visions "

" Permit me to ask one more question," again interrupted Dolores " If I have rightly understood you, there are sexes upon the higher planets, as upon earth '

" Certainly !" affirmed the ' spirit from Uranis ' " There are sexes wherever there are bodies, but there are higher planetary systems than ours, and with every degree of the endless progression towards perfection, the ethereal covering of beings is transfigured to a wonderful purity and beauty, in proportion to the purity of the soul and the degree of beatitude Love as the primitive principle of all being, is the spiritual element of the whole spheral world, and the attraction of everlasting love, received and returned by kindred souls, is the condition of all striving after eternal perfection, in the approach to the mysterious, primitive source of love But the higher the sphere, the less do the relations of sex come in consideration

" There are male, as well as female planets, as there are male and female plants—and the spiritual conception of the idea, of our planetary system, resembles the mysterious impregnation of plants upon the earth, by the wonderful, and to us inconceivable, transportation of the seed-pollen of a flower, in the unfolded susceptible cup of a kindred ' flower-soul '

" The awakened, susceptible mind of man, under the influence of the ray of the idea, (as a ray of light from the source of life, of love, and of strength,) resembles that state of susceptibility of a flower which is manifested by the fullness and increase of the aromatic fragrancy at the period of seed-conception, and affords us a presentiment of the spiritual life upon the planet Ceres

" I say there are male and female plants, in va-

rious senses of the word, as we upon earth connect ideas with it The same (to us) inexplicable presentiments, which I have before spoken of to you, (and by which ' Saint Just', for instance, was named when a child,) lead men upon earth to the suitable nomenclature of the planets Venus, Ge ja, Vesta, Juno, Pallas, Ceres, are female planets, the rest male But these terms do not relate as well to the bodily organization of the inhabitants, as to the system of spiritual conception, of the transportation of the divine idea, from a male planet to a female one Upon female planets, the female mind is predominant, as the conceiving and generating—(is man, without knowing why, called the earth ' Mother Earth', (the generating,) in its influence upon moral cultivation and ennoblement, as is the case upon our earth the woman governs

" The soul of itself, is of no sex, as little as God, himself (the primitive idea of being) neither of the male nor female sex Only the more or less material or ethereal covering of existence, of the soul, requires sex Therefore, our future existence, as a being of a higher spheral world, has not the least reference to sex, according to earthly ideas The meeting and recognition, hereafter, of spiritual kindred beings, whose attraction mutually bound them in holy sympathy upon this, or upon another subordinate star, is the everlasting, inexhaustible source of the blissful happiness of a higher existence, of eternal blessedness

" As Jesus has already intimated, (who, in divine clairvoyance, was acquainted with the highest spheres) there is, in the world to come, no earthly social bond, but love alone Beings of both sexes, who, from deception, mistake, or error, were bound to each other upon earth by social bonds, without sympathy, foreign to each other, and inwardly distant from each other as souls, do not hereafter find each other again Many an earthly being, which, in the abyss of materialism here upon earth, suppressed or choked in itself the spiritual life, at death awakes in the subordinate degree of Mercury or Venus, where the soul is allowed, as before, to receive in itself the light of divine love, clogged by heavier matter, to strive after a higher perfection, for another transition to a nobler degree, upon a higher star

' The being that perhaps upon earth was united with it by earthly bonds, knowing itself here below, and already strove upwards to a higher degree, is, also, separated from it there, in the consciousness of the divinity, which even upon earth elevates us from the dust, as love and as faith

" The struggle of the spirit with matter, which envelopes it as its instrument, is the everlasting condition of all effort—in every degree—upon every star The higher the sphere, the lighter and more ethereal is the body, the easier the victory of spirit, the higher and more exalted the happiness by the attraction of love, by a common striving onward after perfection, in the clearer and clearer contemplation and perception of the eternal, mysterious, primitive being—GOD "

" The captain begs to know if you will be so good as to take a glass of punch with him—all three of you—the lady, too " interrupted the long Ottar

19

This prosaic interruption broke up the communication of the Scandinavian

The captain approached them, likewise, with Robert Walker, and the "spiritual drink" was tried Dolores could not avoid touching a glass, when the captain cried out

"Good luck to the Mazzini !"

"Long life to our Mazzini !" cried Hinango, and the glasses clinked, after the Scandinavian custom.

"The Mazzini, it is to be hoped, is long since in Rio Grande !" remarked the captain

"Probably at Rio Negro, on the coast of Patagonia," replied Hinango "We are now sixteen days from the English bank, in the Plata river, and it is ten days since the Mazzini left us, in the latitude of Rio Grande Barigaldi intended to set his passengers from the cutter on shore there, and then to make a digression towards Rio Negro, where, perhaps, a land traveller might be greatly served, by finding a passage to Rio Grande "

"Do you really hope that Celeste may have escaped with Testa ?" inquired Dolores, in connexion with this intimation.

"I hope so, and it is probable No one would be likely to suspect that he has fled by land The flight on horseback, through the pampas, to Rio Negro, has few difficulties, so soon as the traveller is once out of Buenos Ayres, and that seems to have been the case, according to some papers in the portfolio of Perezoso

"God grant that we may soon receive intelligence and letters from Celeste and Barigaldi !" sighed Dolores

"God grant," exclaimed Hinango, "that St Paulo and Minas Gernes may soon unite with the insurrection of Rio Grande, and that the brave Mineiros may put aside the Brazilian emperor, and set up the cap of liberty upon the old Sugar Loaf there, behind Raza Island "

"And that Scandinavia may proclaim her unity—

'A free, united fatherland,
From North Cape to the Eider Strand '' '

cried Captain Finngreen

"A crisis will ensue in the history of all nations and all countries," remarked Hinango, "sooner or later ! Humanity strides onward Nothing, however, injures the cause of the nations so much as the spirit of littleness, the provincial meanness of the duodecimo rulers, who avail themselves of a corner of sovereignty to play their rôle as heroes of a day, and, instead of comprehending the idea of nationality, boast of provincial trash, preach provincial hatred, and despise the spirit of humanity And therein lies the evil which circumscribes the progress of all the nations The so-called 'liberals' are little-minded—miserably so. They steadfastly contemplate the provincial map of their birthplace, without surveying the general map of their fatherland. Their spirit moves in a cubic space of four feet, instead of soaring upwards to the contemplation of their epoch They imagine that they promote the cause of the people for the moment, and dismember their country. They cling to the letter of the past, without effort for the future They beg for the "favor of liberty, liberty of the press," like effeminate cowards, and forget that no people has ever yet become free without a bloody struggle For a long time the crowned heads of Europe have not been the bitterest enemies of the cause of the people , the bitterest enemies are the miserable Constitutional lick-spittles, whose hearts are as narrow as the bounds of the countries whose provincial sovereignty they maintain Pity that there is no devil, to carry away this inefficient rabble "

Dolores could not avoid laughing, and remarked, that it was already half-past one She stepped aside with Hinango, and thanked him, once more, in the most impressive manner, for the disclosure of his inward life, and added "You have bestowed your confidence upon me, and I know how to honor it You shrink from me, because I am a woman I feel that I am one, and I know my sex I know what a woman can be to a man, as his genius or his demon , as an angel or a fury , but do not, therefore, despair of the female sex '"

"Despair !" interrupted Ormur; "on the contrary, I build my faith in the deliverance of mankind wholly upon the influence of woman upon man, as boy, as youth, and as man

"The redemption of all mankind rests in the heart of woman, as maid, as wife, and as mother. May woman remember this, and feel her dignity and her destination, which is by no means attained when she approaches the altar

"As I sacrifice my individuality, my life, as an offering to the cause of mankind, I also separate my individual sufferings from the great sorrow which I sustain on account of the martyrdom of the nations For verily I say to you, that few men would have less cause to plead for the dignity of woman, to be the advocates of the female sex, than I "

The paleness of his countenance, and the quivering of his lips, evinced his violent agitation, which a retrospect of his past life appeared to awake once more within him

Dolores pressed the hand of her friend, and withdrew in silence She retired to her cabin, to rest for some hours, that she might be able to enjoy, with strengthened susceptibility, the entrance into the "bay of tropical splendor and magnificence."

DOLORES.

BOOK IV.

CHAPTER I

HABAKKUK DAILY.

HARDLY had Dolores left the deck, when a sailor of the watch brought the intelligence that he believed a little craft was "making for the brig," from the land

"That is a negro smuggler," remarked the captain, now likewise perceiving the object. "He takes us for a slave ship, and is willing to do us a service"

"And so he can!" interrupted Robert Walker, "he can smuggle our Mr Daily on shore, and then Sr Alvarez can take his passport, and land with us at Rio, unmolested"

Hinango seemed surprised at this forethought of their young friend, who, during the voyage, had taken every opportunity of being obliging to Alvarez

"Are you serious, Mr Walker?" inquired Ormur, "will you really do us this great service? I say us, because I take a great interest in the fugitive from the river La Plata"

"The captain knew my intention long ago," replied the youth, "and Mr Daily is already made acquainted with the affair It is, to be sure, forbidden, as you know, under a heavy penalty, to communicate with any of these vessels on the coast, but if we meet them, as appears likely to be the case at present, I will take upon myself the consequences" ·

"That is very noble of you! it does you honor!" rejoined Hinango

"I hope it is not the last thing that I shall do for the cause of the persecuted, I have not grown up with Sra Dolores in vain," said Robert

"It is a smack or 'sumacca,' as these vessels are called here," remarked the captain, who was observing the sail, "she bears directly for us, she wants to come up with us"

"At any rate, I will have Mr. Daily waked, that he may hold himself in readiness, if we can succeed in despatching him with this sloop," observed Mr. Walker, and gave orders to the long Ottar, to call his clerk in all haste

Ottar had a certain readiness at waking others, since (excepting at night) he found an opportunity to exercise himself every four hours, in "calling the watch" To awake himself, was somewhat more difficult for him. He went about his task of arousing the grandson of the

"European minister of finances" from his sleep, making use of the usual cry, with which he brought a deck watch upon their legs This instantly roused somebody between decks; but instead of the clerk, Dr Merbold stretched forth his nearly bald head, and cried, in a peevish tone, "Now! what's the matter?"

"Mr Daily! Mr Daily must come up here!" cried Ottar

"Am I asleep yet, and dreaming that I am Dr Merbold?" muttered the entomologist. "Am I Mr Daily? then wake me up properly, you stupid boy! that I may be brought out of my dream, for I dream as vividly, that I am Dr. Merbold, as if I were he in reality!"

Mr Daily had heard the disturbance, and at last his own name, and crept up, in all haste, in the moonshine, to the German savant

"Now?" the latter asked him, "are you Mr Daily, or am I? If you do not know it, upon my soul I don't, for I cannot get rid of my dream! the negligent boy, there, has only half waked me!"

"What's the matter? what's the matter?" inquired the other, rubbing his eyes, "what must I do?"

"Mr Walker wishes to speak to you, you must come on deck, I believe you are to go on shore!"

"Directly! directly!" replied he, and retired to put on, at least, a jacket

"On shore! on shore! but do you know, for certain, that you are Mr Daily and not Dr Merbold?" said the beetleman "I am not sure that there is not a misunderstanding, for I am still dreaming, vividly, that I am Dr Merbold, and if I wake up, by and by, and Dr Merbold has gone on shore, I do not, for my soul, know what will become of me!"

Habakkuk Daily scrambled hastily past the meditating savant, who did not, in fact, seem to be thoroughly awake, and who hurried quickly back to his mattress again, where he continued the dream that he was Dr Merbold, until he finally fell asleep again, and perhaps dreamed himself into the individuality of Habakkuk Daily

"Mr. Daily!" said Robert, meeting his clerk, "there is a sumacca, a sort of smuggling craft, and we will see if you can go on shore in her"

"All right, Mr Walker!" replied the other, "it will cost something, however!"

"That is my affair If you will only play

your part well, in case any officer should examine you "

" I ' play my part well ' As to that, you may rest entirely unconcerned ' I'll bet that I will play my part so well that you shall, yourself, take me for something else than I am."

" So much the better ' The sumacca will be here directly ' Get your baggage ready. Will you take all your things with you '"

" Certainly ' certainly ' I shall take my trunks with me ' for the sake of respectability A traveller with considerable baggage is always examined less than a fellow without any, or with two shirts in a bundle But I require something for my rôle—something seamanlike a sextant, a couple of old nautical almanacs, and such like."

" We will consult about that," replied Robert, " only make yourself ready, let your trunks be brought on deck "

" In a moment '" cried the other, and disappeared below. where he now kindled a light, and, as we say in English, " laughed in his sleeve "

Robert hurried back to the captain and Hinango, and informed them what Mr Daily required Both were ready to furnish the adroit actor with whatever he desired for the rôle he was to play as seaman, and Robert intimated that Mr Daily would punctually restore, at Rio, all that was confided to him.

" We do not doubt that, in the least," observed Captain Finngreen, and, at the same instant, the cry of " Brig ahoy '" was heard from the sumacca, followed by the question, in good English, " Where are you from ·"

" From Buenos Ayres '" returned the captain, through the speaking trumpet

" Have you not met a brig, bound for St Catharine's '"

" No '"

" Do you want some fresh fish ·"

" If you will not let the Guarda mor* know that we met you here "

" Nonsense ' we have as little desire to have any dealings with the Alfandega† as you "

" Throw them a rope '" ordered the captain, and it was not long before the spokesman of the sumacca, with two of his comrades, stood on the gangway, and a considerable quantity of very fine fish lay near them

" Arrah, now, and is that you, Dick '" cried Pat Gentleboy, who took his turn, as a sailor, in the watch, and was now looking attentively at the man who spoke as good English as himself.

" What, the devil ! Pat Gentleboy ' is it possible ' You don't say that's you ' All alive, and the same as ever '"

" But how did you come in this smack, honey ' Have you got to be a smuggler of slaves ' sorrow take you ' Didn't we two cruise together agin the slave ships, on the coast of Africa, long enough '"

" Hush ' Pat ' every one must make his trade with the article that is most wanted in the market You go as a sailor, I see, in this brig ; or are you working your passage ?"

" I go boatswain, here '" replied the other—clever enough not to let his old acquaintance know that he was ' commander of a cutter,' and had come into collision with " Ar-gentiles "

Mr Habakkuk Daily made his appearance, in a blue seaman's jacket, with yellow anchor buttons, a short sword at his side, and a pilot coat over it, an oilcloth cap on his head, and an extraordinary serious quarterdeck countenance, and stepped up to the people of the sumacca

" I want to be set on shore this side of the Sugar Loaf How much do you ask ?"

" There stands the captain," replied Dick—a former sailor in the British navy, and an old shipmate of Pat Gentleboy

" I am an English officer, said Mr Daily," in Spanish, to the captain of the sumacca " I wish to land this side the Sugar Loaf, as I am ordered to our ambassador at Bota Fogo Will you take me on board ' This brig is going to Bahia "

The Portuguese understood Spanish quite well, and particularly the words British officer, Bota Fogo, and ambassador He regarded the Englishman from head to foot, and replied, " That may be done."

To the question, how much he asked ' he replied, with seamanlike dryness, " A hundred millreis, if you wish to be landed immediately, and fifty, if you wait until I choose to go on shore "

" How long may that be ' When are you going to land ?"

" To-morrow, towards midnight, I shall go into a cove this side the Sugar Loaf "

" Well, I will give you thirty millreis, and wait until towards midnight to-morrow "

" You will give forty millreis, senhor—forty ? I cannot take you for less than that "

" Then I shall easily find another sumacca or felouque, before we reach the Sugar Loaf, I will give no more than the thirty millreis, except, perhaps, a half dozen bottles of Swedish brandy besides," added Mr Daily, and stepped on the quarterdeck, as if he commanded there

The negro smuggler reflected for a while, and seemed to perceive the possibility that the " English officer" might find a similar opportunity. Thirty millreis was, on the other hand, a very reasonable passage, which he could receive without going out of his course He resolved, then, to take the money, and drew near the quarterdeck to settle the affair

Mr Daily had stepped aside with Robert Walker, received the needful supply of money, and the address of the house in Rio where he might report himself, as soon as he had safely arrived

" The two boxes of minerals," remarked the clerk, " are in my berth It is a pity we had not kept the others on board, I could easily take them on shore with me now."

" This would certainly have been an excellent opportunity ' But—the captain would not risk it, and perhaps the boxes are already on board of another vessel "

" Let us hope that they have been taken good care of !" whispered Mr Daily, and stepped again, in his character of an English officer, to the smuggler, who imparted to him his decision. The captain bought the fish at a very reasonable price, and Mr. Daily's luggage, together with sufficient provisions for the twenty four hours, was lowered into the sumacca.

Mr. Daily desired the mate to present his compliments to the German doctor, who had, some time before, noted for him the address of the celebrated naturalist, and of a little tavern, where he might himselt be met with. After a hasty farewell to his "young master," and all those who stood near, he stepped down to his two trunks in the smuggling smack, which immediately pushed off, and pursued her course, to obtain intelligence of the slaver, expected at St Catharine's, from Angola

CHAPTER II.

THE OLD WIDOWER

THE immense French hotel, Faroux, situated close by a landing place of the bay, opposite to the station of the foreign vessels of war, in the neighborhood of the unpretending imperial palace, formed a sort of Palais Royal, as the gathering place of respectable and fashionable guests, in Rio de Janeiro, from all parts of the world

It was about five o'clock in the afternoon, the separate tables, designed for private dinners, of four to six persons, were, one after the other, nearly all occupied Men and youths, in the naval uniforms of legitimate, quasi legitimate, and republican powers, divided, for the most part, according to nationality and rank, were conspicuous amongst dandies and no dandies, in white linen spencers and considerably darker complexions

Men of different ages and stations, from the commodore of a ship of the line, and his excellency, a colored minister of state, down to the white partner of an inferior commercial house, were mingled together, according to the republican spirit of Brazilian customs, which is less clogged with narrow prejudices than those of many republics

"Respectable, and very respectable gentlemen," with yellow patent gloves, maintained their British fashions in spite of the climate, consuming, "in the sweat of their brows," their roast beef and beef steak, in thick cloth clothing of British manufacture, and, occasionally, (as an interesting topic of conversation) giving each other the assurance that it was "very warm—very warm indeed!

Gayer and more lively than at the British tables, were heard conversations in French Spanish, Italian, and Portuguese, and, here and there, in the German, Danish, and Swedish languages, while each group despatched its own dishes, and troubled itself but little about what the others ate or said

Entirely contrary to all British fashion or custom, a "degenerate gentleman," in a white linen hunting frock, sat among "foreigners" at a foreign table, spoke French, and drank claret instead of port and sherry. He was one of those stereotype British figures, whom we meet as cabin passengers, in every English steamer, on different courses, from Monte Video to Gottenburg.

Our gentleman was tall, robust, and broad shouldered, with a round, fresh colored visage and short neck His crown was nearly bald and adorned with weakly grown curling hair, somewhat gray, an inquiring and yet little observing look, a shade of red on the nose, a strong under jaw, (the muscles of which had acquired their strength by long service,) united with a careless expression, and an excellent appetite, formed a whole · This was Mr. George Thomson, brother-in-law and partner of Mr John Walker, and chief representative of the house of Walker and Company in Rio de Janeiro, a man about sixty years old, quick in his movements, lively in conversation, and gay and good humored, when he was not harassed by his sister.

Opposite to him sat Monsieur le Baron de Spandau, "chevalier of different orders, of various kinds of *industrie*," universally known as a very respectable gentleman, because he was a stated guest at the Hotel Faroux, often showed himself in a box at the Theatre de St Pedro de Alcantara, kept a couple of riding horses and a negro in livery, always wore clean gloves, and often waited for hours in the ante-chamber of this or that ambassador, till a valet informed him that his excellency was busy He was a lean little fellow, apparently forty years old, with blinking gray eyes, and sharply defined features, out of the centre of which arose a turn-up nose, the wings of which fell in, and peculiarly exposed the nostrils Small, hardly perceptible lips, closed a mouth which (except for operations similar to the present) was, for the most part, only opened in the endeavor to produce something piquant, in which he did not always succeed, and which he himself anticipated by a smile, in case no one else should laugh at his wit His narrow forehead was covered with dark hair, on which he appeared to bestow peculiar care, as it dripped with oil and pomatum, which the tropical heat dissolved into troublesome fluidity

Between the two, sat a tall, serious man, who might be rather above forty years of age, with regular features, and an expression of settled melancholy His whole aspect bore the stamp of inward cultivation, which is indicated by a certain something, which no barber can frizzle, and no tailor can fit, even according to all the rules of the fashioning art of our days, and after all the precepts of the last number of the "Journal des Modes"

"You have then been married four times, as your portraits at Bota Fogo, show?" inquired the little chevalier of the Briton, pursuing the conversation, while the third turned over the rich gastronomic bill of fare, and seemed to find little to tempt his appetiteless palate

"Strictly speaking, four times and a half!" replied Mr. Thomson, "for I was betrothed once, and, so to say, almost married, when my intended, whose presence made me happy at that time, died suddenly, of the yellow fever, in Havana"

"And your wives were all English women!"

"By no means—but they were stout and corpulent! they were all corpulent, for this quality was always my first requisite, when I made a choice, and where I found this, in connexion with other desirable qualities, I troubled myself little about the nationality, to the boundless vexation of my family, who fairly drove me from England on that account. My first wife weighed two hundred and three pounds! She was an Irish woman, of very respectable family, and beautiful! very beautiful, I tell you! that is, corpulent! stout as a man could desire a woman to be!".

"You appear to have Turkish notions of beauty," remarked the baron, "for stout, corpulent, and beautiful, are known to signify one and the same thing among the Turks"

"The Turks are perfectly right, as to that! perfectly right! entirely right! That shows that they are not so stupid, and I am quite of their opinion, for I love solidity! firmness! and if I were to find, to-night, or to-morrow, an object that particularly interests me—by a tendency to corpulency, well understood—I will not be positive that I would not once more pay my tax to the church, and marry for the fifth time!"

"You would do perfectly right!" replied the baron, "a man like you, with such a fortune!"

"I should not easily find again a lady like my last wife!" interrupted the old widower "She displayed a degree of corpulence, I assure you—a corpulence which exceeded all my former expectations, for it is a very singular thing, the corpulence of women! It has its crisis, after which the corpulence either increases or suddenly fails, and is entirely lost That was the case with my first wife, who brought it no farther than one hundred and eighty-two pounds, and then became suffering, hypochondriac, 'mysterical,' as the doctors call it, and grew as lean, I assure you, as a European horse, that will eat no grass here in Brazil, and so she died, the good woman!"

"As regards corpulence," remarked the baron, "you will hardly find a country, besides Turkey, where the women spread as they do here Many mothers of families, when they walk to church on Sunday, behind their generation, can evidently hardly move, from mere corpulence"

"Yes, so far as that goes," interrupted the widower, "it is not to be denied, that female corpulence increases here admirably! But the girls here marry at thirteen, and even younger! and the tendency to corpulence is then, for the most part, undecided! To be sure, most Brazilian ladies become corpulent in matrimony, but, Baron! the crisis, the crisis of which I have just spoken, that must be guarantied, and it often comes on very late, I mean, it may come on four, five, or even six years after marriage, and even later, when the house swarms with children, but, you see, that depends on circumstances, on relations A happy wife adds to her corpulence, and I maintain, from experience, that where a woman suddenly grows thin, and withers away, then it is not right with her heart, then there is mental disease. But still I will by no means assert that all women who do not feel happy in marriage grow thin, either suddenly, or by degrees, by no means! that depends on circumstances! I have experience in these matters, baron! and know what married life is! Indifference! indifference, baron! is a sure foundation for corpulence and domestic happiness! Sentiment, feeling, or the like qualities and endowments, are dangerous, and generally bring on the crisis of which I speak But there are, nevertheless, robust natures, who defy all attacks of sentiment, and do not grow thin, as, for example, my second wife, who was a Russian. She weighed a hundred and ninety-four pounds and three-quarters in her bloom, and only eight pounds less as a corpse She was a noble woman, I tell you! but often suffered from feeling, from sentiment! and up to this day, I cannot

conceive the cause, for she had all she required, she wanted for nothing! horses and carriage, and country house, and the like! and I gave her open credit with her milliner! and, notwithstanding all that, she had hardly reached the crisis, when she died—suddenly died! as I told you, in her bloom"

"Indeed!" said the third gentleman, who had listened, with particular attention, to the widower's experiences

"It happened nearly the same with my last wife," continued Mr Thomson, "who, it is true, only weighed a hundred and forty pounds when I married her, but she had a tendency to corpulency, a tendency of which I am a tolerable judge, and six months after her first confinement she weighed a hundred and ninety-three pounds, after the second, two hundred and thirty-six and three quarter pounds; but then came the crisis. She became melancholy, and learnt foreign languages She was an Italian by birth, and at last her mind became diseased, and she got certain notions that I did not love her, and the like stupid stuff, that women take into their heads And she wanted for nothing! she had all that she required, all that my other wives enjoyed, and with which the first and last were contented, until their happy end! A woman, let me tell you, is like a cylinder watch, like a repeater, which will often keep good time for years, if you wind it up regularly—but at length it stops, for the first time, and repeats incorrectly, it then requires a skilful watchmaker to set it a going again, without spoiling it, and the watchmakers and physicians of our time, generally handle their patients very superficially, and often do not know themselves what part of the works is out of order That was the reason my last wife died, for, I tell you, she was shrunk away to a skeleton, and her corpse only weighed eighty-three pounds! think of that! a hundred and fifty-three pounds difference, because the good woman was wanting in indifference! in indifference, I tell you!"

"You are yet in your best years, Mr Thomson," remarked the serious man next to him, who had laid aside the bill of fare, "you will marry again! I will make a bet with you, that you will at least be betrothed in a year and a day"

"I will rather bet the contrary with you, for I honestly admit that I cannot live without a wife; I am so accustomed to wedded life, from my youth upwards, and shall now look about me in earnest, once more, if I can find something according to my taste, with a tendency to corpulency and the other qualities But, alas! I shall never again meet with a wife like my last! It would, indeed, be a wonder if I should! She was from the Rio de la Plata, and, it is true, only weighed a hundred and forty pounds when I married her; but, she had a tendency to corpulence; a tendency, I tell you, which she developed to two hundred and thirty-six and three quarter pounds in four years, in four years, I tell you! and a better wife," he added, with a sigh, "a better wife I shall probably never meet with! such a comfortable wife as that! and if I marry again, which God grant may soon happen, I shall look for a lady from La Plata, and I have already written to my brother-in-law, in Buenos Ayres, about it. He knows my taste and the qualities I require I tell you what, gentlemen, you are fools, don't take it ill of me for saying so, you are fools in your bachelor's life, you will die in it, without having lived, I can tell you! There is nothing so pleasant as domestic happiness and married life, and whoever is not acquainted with them, does not know what day and night are, I tell you!"

"Marriage may have its charming side," replied the serious man "that I do not deny, but I, as a physician and unmarried man besides, know only the dark side of matrimony, and, above all, of marriage without love"

"Marriage without love!" cried Mr Thomson "the devil! what has love to do with marriage? A girl does not ask you, 'Do you love me?' but, 'Will you marry me?' Marrying is always the principal thing! and I know young ladies, of various ages, who would never ask a gentleman, 'Do you love me?' for fear he might honestly answer, 'No!' and draw back, it love is to be made a condition!"

"I am entirely of your opinion," affirmed the baron pouring a tremendous dose of vanilla over his ice "The fearful thought of remaining an old maid, has brought the gallopade into favor"

"You must marry, doctor," said Mr Thomson "You suffer with hypochondria and melancholy There is no such cure for them, as matrimony, I assure you! I know that, by experience Cream of tartar and castor oil will do no good Marriage is the only cure for melancholy!"

"Widowers, for the most part, soon marry again" remarked the doctor, "that is easily explained—it is the force of habit, and a widow, likewise, would not wait long and remain single, if she enjoyed the same freedom of choice as a man This freedom, I affirm, is founded in natural rights, and we should find less of nervous diseases and hysterical maladies, if women were differently situated, in many respects If they were allowed to choose freely, we should certainly witness less suffering and more happiness on earth"

"To be sure, many women remain single," observed Mr Thomson, "because they are deprived of the liberty of making a free choice, that is natural!"

"Pardon me, sir," said the baron, "I am by no means of your opinion, I doubt if the free choice of maids or widows would produce much benefit, for, as long as I have been in the world, I find always that a girl chooses rather from caprice than love, and, in hundreds of cases selects the most stupid and meanest of her admirers, who, however, may possess some exterior qualities A girl seldom, or never, chooses a man for his mental accomplishments"

"You have made a very just observation," asserted the doctor, "but, notwithstanding that, woman does not lose the right to a free choice—errors, and even crimes, do not destroy the principle of moral freedom"

"I agree with you entirely, doctor, as regards free choice," observed Mr Thomson "I assert that some nice woman would have chosen me, long ago—some nice woman, with a tendency! with a tendency!"

His two companions smiled.

"How many pounds of domestic happiness have you embraced, in all, Mr Thomson?" inquired the baron Have you ever summed up?"

"Eight hundred and forty-three and three quarter pounds!" quickly replied the old widower, "counted in the bloom, that is to say, counted in the very bloom! for I kept correct books, and weighed my wives every month, at the new moon!"

The baron laughed heartily, and nearly swallowed a fish bone

A poor, but cleanly dressed man, of a sickly aspect, slowly approached the table and handed the serious man a document, with an apology for troubling him The latter unfolded it, and cast a glance over it, then drew a millreis bill from his vest pocket, handed it to him, with the paper, and said, in a low voice, "there! but do not drink it up, give it to your wife, if this paper be not false!"

"False! false! Oh, God!" exclaimed the poor fellow, while he offered his heartfelt thanks "It is, alas! too true, I have been here eight years, as a sergeant of the German legion, and am now the father of a family, with six little children, and am sick, as you see!"

"That is all very well, my good man, but how can you have six children, when one, like yourself—according to your document, has only been married five years? Your wife, then, has twins?"

"No, my good sir, not twins, but—but, she is a French woman, from Provence, and——"

Mr Thomson burst into loud laughter, in which he was joined by his two companions.

"That is all very well, my good man," continued the physician, "but this privilege of parentage is contrary to reason I do not give you this alms, as the father of a family, for at the utmost I must consider your wife and children, for you, I have no consideration—none at all!"

"How so, sir?" inquired the invalid, a little embarrassed.

"Because it depended upon your free choice to marry, or not to marry, and because thousands of men must abstain from that which you sought in married life, thousands, who have the same claims to domestic happiness as yourself, but who make a conscience of connecting a being with their fate, who has likewise claims on life, and who then must share the sufferings of her husband If a person came to me, now, and said, 'Sir, I have had to struggle through my life in desolate loneliness, I have sacrificed myself, from conviction, for my nation and country, and have been obliged to deny myself all domestic happiness, I have enjoyed no love, and have even never become a 'husband,' which yet every dolt may be Sir! I know nothing of love and felicity—I stand alone on earth!' Whoever says this to me, for him I have consideration—him, I understand"

"According to your views, doctor," said the old widower, likewise bestowing a gift on the poor man, "according to your views, no one ought to marry"

"No one? Pardon me; you misunderstand me. Let him marry, who finds reciprocal affection, and feels himself in a condition to provide for his wife, and knows how to bring up his children, but let no one imagine that he possesses especial claims to the consideration of others, as the father of a family." The invalid offered his thanks again, and withdrew

"I consider family life as the most sacred

bond of human society," continued the doctor, "but not propagation, as the highest vocation or the first duty of man I consider education the most sacred requirement! The mass, or crowd of mankind, is not to be considered, but the cultivation There are shiftless creatures enough, who lie about the streets, and fill the prisons—led, by degrees, from wretchedness to crime, and the source of their crimes is the levity of their parents, in the 'gallopade to matrimony,' as our baron justly calls it "

"You attach my own words to very singular principles, doctor, which will hardly admit of defence," observed the baron

"I am, nevertheless, ready to maintain them The unanimous and universal complaint, in relation to the wretchedness of Europe, is sought to be explained by the over population, and the want of political and personal freedom I think it would be better if a man should first endeavor to establish a free fatherland for his family, before he increased the population in number, and, of course, only made the wretchedness greater "

"Those are evidently dangerous principles!" exclaimed the baron, " they would bring you to prison in Europe "

"I believe the European powers have spies enough to control the demagogue principles of an individual in Brazil, as well as on the La Plata, only, people do not always take much notice of their investigations "

"Do you really think that the European powers have spies here in Rio?" inquired the little man, with the turned-up nose

"I think that such scamps would be very indifferent to me, whenever and however they might seek a collision with me"

The Baron shelled a banana and filled his glass, while Mr Thomson again took up the word

"You are then opposed to all emigration from excess of population, doctor?"

"I would allow each one the personal liberty to travel and settle himself where he will, or as particular circumstances might lead him, but no nation on earth will ever become free through emigration As to the rest, I believe that excessive population is often an erroneous idea, and that only despotism and slavery make it difficult for men to live, while there would be room enough in the country for each nation to increase in numbers, if it were only politically free The wretchedness lies, for the most part, in the institutions of the country The government is certainly served by the great plurality of the population, which increases the income of the state by direct and indirect taxes Whoever feels no patriotism would be of no service to his country, and may therefore emigrate, in God's name "

"Certainly ; as to that, I cannot gainsay you," observed Mr Thomson

"Did you not tell me, lately," continued the physician, " of a young negro who would not marry his black sweetheart until he had purchased her freedom? he would not increase the number of his master's slaves?"

"Certainly ; the young woman belonged to me, and I gave her her marriage portion "

"Bravo! Mr Thomson, that looks like you; I must thank you for that, myself," returned the doctor. "I remember at least ten other cases of the sort here, which redound to the honor of our

mulacks But do you not find, in that, the direct reverse of what I affirm, in relation to the levity of the whites? It is a crime to bring slaves into the world, from convenience, without love, slaves of the circumstances under which they are born If not exactly bondmen, they often become criminals "

"Certainly! I understand you, now, and am entirely of your opinion," affirmed Mr Thomson, working away at his roast beef

"To leave an oppressed country," continued the doctor, "without assisting in the deliverance of one's fatherland, to wander away and help to increase the population of a free country, to enjoy the freedom for which a former generation shed their blood, any one can do, and I find nothing in this, either meritorious or honorable! Whoever thus leaves his nation and fatherland, from selfishness, to promote his personal happiness in some distant portion of the world, is, at least, evidently, an egotist, who only thinks of himself, and recognises no duty towards his nation That is my view Can you gainsay it?"

"No reasonable man could ever have an idea of contradicting you in that," observed Mr Thomson," for your principles are thoroughly patriotic, British principles, as we have manifested under Charles the First "

"To your happy betrothed, within a year and a day, Mr Thomson!" cried the baron, with his glass in his hand, and to the development of corpulence!"

"Thank you, baron!" returned the other, "I will avail myself of a good opportunity, if one offers itself "

An officer of the alfandega entered the apartment, and approached the Briton, on whom his look was directed, from the distance He addressed him very politely, and handed him a note "A Swedish brig, from Buenos Ayres, consigned to you, Senhor Thomson has just entered the Franquia * There are passengers of your family on board, a young Senhor Walker and his sister "

"Wh-a-t!" cried the old widower, with a glance at the note he had just received, "my nephew and niece on board? on board the Swedish brig! I thank you, Senhor Pedro ! thank you! Will you not take a glass of wine? I thank you for your attention!"

"I was on board, with the quarantine boat, and took charge of the letter bag, and the young Senhor desired me to hand you this note, as he was told that I was personally acquainted with you "

"Are there no other passengers on board?" inquired the doctor

"I can give you the names," replied the obliging custom house officer, and handed a card to the serious man

"Shall we go out Mr Thomson ?" whispered the latter, as soon as he had cast a glance at the list of names

The little baron burned with impatience to read the list likewise, and reached out his dry fingers towards the doctor.

"This instant I will go out! this instant!" answered Mr Thomson "I shall be very glad to have the honor of your company "

"I should like, besides, to take a pleasure ex-

---

* A part of the bay of Rio.

cursion on the bay, as I do frequently," continued the doctor "You came home very late, last evening," said he, to the baron, as they rose from the table "If I am not mistaken, you galloped past my chacara in great haste, after midnight, from the Gloria I recognised you by your spurs and your Chili hat It was a beautiful moonlight night"

The baron appeared for the moment, a little embarrassed, swallowed a slice of anana, coughed, and at length replied

"Very likely I just remember that I had been upon the Gloria, to enjoy the prospect by moonlight, and found it so lovely, that I was belate l

"Feared you had been attacked, for shortly before I saw you a shot was fired—a very heavy pistol shot, as it appeared, or a buck shot The weapon was heavily loaded"

"A shot? as I came down the hill? I did not hear a shot I was however, very much absorbed in meditation"

"So much the better that you know nothing of the shot, but the haste with which you passed my garden gave me a certain connexion of ideas, thank God, unfounded, for I did not hear the shot repeated"

"Are we ready, Dr Thorsin?" whispered the Englishman, who had poured out a couple of glasses of wine for the custom house officer

"I am at your service," replied the doctor Both took a courteous leave of the chevalier, who now scanned over the passenger list, which, however, the custom house officer demanded hastily, as he required it in his duties

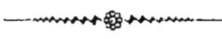

CHAPTER III

PECULIAR CIRCUMSTANCES.

The brig Nordstjernan had reached the Franquia, an inlet on the right shore between the fortresses of Santa Cruz and Da Vilhalcon, also called Do-Vilganhon, which latter is erected on a rocky islet in the middle of the bay

Dolores and her friends abandoned themselves, from the first ray of dawn, to astonishment and admiration of nature The gigantic rocky masses of the nearest coast presented the appearance of monuments of creation, formed from chaos, when the elements were separated for the formation of our planet. A constant succession of amazing natural scenes gradually unfolded themselves to their view, in the interior of the bay, like a panorama, whose several parts harmonized as well with the whole, as they produced a harmonious effect upon the minds of the voyagers

The Nordstjernan lay at anchor The shallops and boats of the authorities came out to her, according to the established regulations The quarantine boat had already returned to the city, as we have learned in the Hotel Faroux, and, with greater anxiety than perhaps the occasion required, Dolores and Alvarez awaited the visit of the guarda mor, who went in person on board of every newly arrived vessel, to take possession of the ship's papers and passports, and convince himself of their accordance with the passengers and cargo

"A long Felouque,* with an awning and a broad government flag, rowed by twelve negroes in light sailor's dress, with straw hats, on which fluttered broad black ribands, steered towards the brig It was the gondola of the guarda mor, who soon mounted the quarterdeck, attended by a subaltern officer He was a young man, of a highly respectable family, who spoke fluently five languages, and was not unknown as a satirical poet in the epigrammatic style

The appearance of this man, as the representative of a nation, on board of an arriving vessel, had in it something peculiarly imposing

A simple blue naval uniform, embroidered with gold, white pantaloons, a naval hat, and a valuable sword, adorned his slender figure, of a middling height His sallow countenance, with dark moustaches, was legibly stamped by God's hand with the impress of humanity

The whole appearance of this man was evidently calculated to give every new comer the most advantageous idea of his nation, and to infuse unbounded confidence in Brazilian national character †

He took possession of the ship's papers, and list of passengers in a serious, business-like manner, cast a penetrating glance upon the several persons, and, among the rest, upon Miss Fanny Walker and Mr Habakkuk Duly, and exchanged a friendly word with the captain, and this and that passenger He commanded the flag to be hoisted up the foremast, probably as a signal that his duty had been performed, and then declared that the passengers might land at their pleasure, and left the vessel The broad national flag waved over the awning of the long gondola—the twelve negroes dipped their oars in regular time in the mirrorlike wave, and the guarda mor,' with his subordinate, swung over to another vessel, which had likewise just cast anchor

With a less burdening heart Dolores now sat beside Horatio, and observed, with a wandering gaze, now one, and then the other, of the landscape groups of these wonderful environs, but the surrounding forms were too exuberantly rich and sublime for the eye to embrace a single scene, to say nothing of the entire panorama, in case the immediate situation of the homeless exiles had allowed them leisure to give themselves up to enjoyment

The sun gradually descended towards the western horizon The entire rocky mountains, the Devil's Flat, the Two Brothers, the Corcovado, the Gabia, the Tijuca, etc, at whose feet lay the city, with its countless forest of masts, glittered in the reddish purple atmosphere, which, notwithstanding the outlines of the forms and objects, could be seen through with Chinese distinctness Like the glance of a volcano, the sun darted upwards, behind the pointed forms of the rocky tops, while the white walls of all the

* Gondola
† He was incorruptibly strict against the illegal importation of negro slaves, and insisted upon the enforcement of the law His position but too frequently offered him opportunities of observing the system of the government, by which Brazil was evidently becoming diplomatically ruined, wherefore, his secession to the league of the Faroupilhas may more readily be explained. On a fine Sunday morning, in June, 1842, his house, in the Rua Direita, was entered by permanentos, but they did not find him—he had escaped. A noble Briton had offered him an asylum, and kept him concealed in his house for months, while they were looking for him at a distance.

buildings of the city and its environs, and the sails of the vessels, reflected a rosy hue, and were mirrored in the azure blue of the bay. Countless gondolas and barks, whose colored crews bore the appearance of neatness and cleanliness, in their light clothing, glided past in the foreground, and were lost behind the larger vessels, whose motion averted the thought that the whole was a wonderful picture and no reality, since the latter was hardly able to present such a panorama in any country in the world.

The passengers, by degrees, prepared themselves to make use of the permission of the guarda mor to leave the brig, in which they had encountered many dangers, and whiled away many an hour in cordial intercourse.

Di Merbold approached the Russian ex-naval officer, with German good humor, and endeavored, in the best way he could, to apologize for his peevish ebullition, in relation to the fugitive, Alvarez, on the La Plata river.

He explained that his ill humor, in that case, was to be attributed to an attack of seasickness, and, "like all other mental emotions," originated in reasons of the stomach. He gave the assurance that he was very liberal, and not at all behind the crown prince of Prussia, in that respect, with whose reign a new Aurora was to dawn upon the lauded land of the German Confederacy, and Prussia (if not all Germany) would become the most free country upon God's earth. "I assure you," added he, eloquently, "when the crown prince of Prussia assumes the government, we shall experience a new epoch in the history of the world, for his royal highness invented the powder with which his royal highness will blow all difficulties into the air, which have, until now, stood opposed to the union, in a legal manner, (of course,) of Germany, as required by the spirit of the times. I can assure you, he is the very genius of liberalism! The only thing that I fear, is that he may be too liberal for the German people, that would be bad, indeed! You will find this to be the case, and hereafter you will think of me! And if you should happen, in your travels, to discover a species of beetle which has, as yet, remained unknown, you would eternally oblige me, if you would send one or two well prepared specimens, addressed to me, Di. Merbold, and directed to some of the Prussian consuls. I would be, as I said, eternally obliged to you."

Hinango promised that he would think of him, and has probably kept his word, even if he could not succeed in discovering a new species of beetle, except the great crowd of tame "French haters," of various natures, who, on the accession of Frederick William the Third, crawled and buzzed about, in Prussia and the whole of Germany, and hummed the so called "Rhine song."

The captain had his shallop got ready to go on shore in the evening, to report himself at the bureau of the house to which he was consigned, but especially to place Señora Dolores and Mr Robert Walker on "terra firma," in case the officer of the alfandega had not met with the old uncle. He offered the same opportunity to the other passengers, and all set themselves in motion to pack their carpet bags, since the other baggage was to be left on board, to pass the inspection of the alfandega.

It was not long before the mate discovered a felouque making for the brig, and Mr Robert Walker recognised, by means of the telescope, his old uncle, whom he had seen in Buenos Ayres some years before.

"That is uncle George! and, as it seems, hale and hearty!" said he to his sister Fanny, who now felt, more than before, the oppressiveness of her situation, in being compelled to seek an asylum and receive hospitality in a strange family, of a strange nation, with foreign customs and foreign prejudices.

Notwithstanding the alleviation of her spirit, and all the decision of her intellectual character, she felt the painful restrictions which she, as a female, was subjected to by the regulations of the social world, which concede to a man the privilege of standing independently, while many men have less of moral independence than women. Dolores felt the contradiction, and even the ridiculousness, of the social idea of wishing to protect a female by contesting her right to protect herself, which many women are often better able to do than the men who deny all moral independence.*

The felouque approached, and Hinango discovered, with old Mr Thomson, one of his friends, whom we have previously noticed in the Hotel Laroux. Dr Thorun was, by birth, a Norwegian, who had practised as a physician in Odessa and Moscow, and was afterwards in the Russian navy, where he lived for some years, on board the same frigate with Hinango.

His ill health had served him as a pretext to his dismissal, in order to save himself from transportation to Siberia, as, on the other hand, it induced him to take up his residence in the beneficent and wholesome climate of Guenabara.† He lived quiet and retired, in the neighborhood of Rio, absorbed in the serious study of natural science, without exactly turning away the sick, who sometimes made demands on his experience, as a physician.

Robert Walker consulted with Dolores, if it would not be better for her to remain in her cabin, until he handed his father's letter to his uncle, and explained the existing circumstances. The unhappy one, who had taken leave of her beloved, at the foot of his scaffold, with so much strength of mind, now trembled before the entrance into relations, the elements of which were as distant to her as she was strange to the world which she was now approaching.

Sighing deeply, she gave her consent to all the measures which the confidant of her childhood thought proper to take for her, and withdrew from the quarterdeck.

"Halloo, Bob, my boy! halloo! How d'ye do? Welcome to Rio! Where's Miss Fanny? not seasick yet?" cried Mr Thomson, from the felouque.

"She is below, getting ready to go on shore," returned Bob.

"How you have grown Robert! you are fit for the London grenadier guard! you have become a fine young man, Bob! but you ought not to know that!"

Old Mr Thomson scrambled up the ladder,

* The situation and circumstances in which we here behold Dolores, are partly strange and unknown in North America, where women enjoy a greater degree of social independence than in any other country.

† The original name of the province of Rio de Janeiro.

and soon stood, with Dr Thorfin, on the gangway. A short, British, mutual introduction ensued. Hinango embraced his friend from the far north, and stepped aside with him, while Robert seized the arm of his uncle and led him to a bench on the quarterdeck.

"Here my dear uncle, in the first place, is a letter from my father, with a thousand verbal greetings. Read it, if you please. I will run down to Fanny, in the meanwhile, and tell her you are here."

"Thank you, but first get me a little fire for my cigar, which has gone out."

Robert gave the requisite order to the long Ottar, and hastily withdrew, that he might not be besieged with questions, before the old man had read the clear statement of circumstances in the letter. The latter was soon absorbed in reading, and his broad, good-humored, jovial countenance, offered a different expression at almost every line. First he drew his forehead into deep wrinkles, then he raised his eyebrows to the utmost height, and, at a particular place, cried out, "five thousand pesos upon her head, to whoever delivers her alive!" He then hurried on to the end of the third page, hastily sprang up, and exclaimed "Bob! Bob! its all right! you are welcome, with your sister! Ask Miss Fanny to come on deck, or perhaps I had better step down!"

Bob, who had waited with peculiar anxiety, at the door of Dolores' cabin, now beckoned her to follow him, and appeared with her, upon the quarterdeck, before his uncle.

"Heigho!" muttered the old widower to himself, as the majestic figure from La Plata came before him, "there is a tendency, there is a tendency to corpulence! that suits me right well! Thank you, brother John! you have executed my commission, well!"

With all the embarrassment of a female, in a strange country, exiled and condemned to a painful incognito, Dolores approached her future protector, whose exterior had in it nothing that was repulsive, if, on the other hand, it had no particular attraction for her.

Like a chamberlain in Buckingham Palace, at the appearance of Queen Victoria, only bowing less profoundly, Mr Thomson stepped up to the young lady, held out his hand to her, and said, in a carefully measured tone.

"Miss Fanny! as such, I have the honor to greet you. Receive the assurance, that Mr Walker has afforded me a high gratification, to receive you as my niece, and, as such, I shall be happy to receive you—that is, my sister, Miss Thomson, will, she is already informed of your arrival."

Dolores expressed her thanks for his sympathy, and assured him, in a voice full of emotion, that she should greatly regret, it her visit should be in the least troublesome to him or his sister. Whereupon the old widower interrupted her with protestations to the contrary, and, stepping backward a few paces, evidently contemplated his niece, from "top to toe," with increasing satisfaction.

"Do you think, then, my dear uncle," inquired Robert, "that Aunt Susan will keep the secret?"

"Aunt Susan? Miss Thomson keep the secret?" returned the old gentleman. "She must keep it! she shall be silent!—or—or I will show her that I am master of the house!'"

"I have no doubt of that, dear uncle. But if she should not be silent—if she should let out something, then it would be too late, even your anger—your just anger, my dear uncle, would do no good then!"

"I will rather make short work!" cried Mr Thomson. "Miss Susan is very anxious to be married—she is in love with a German baron, she may take him, or rather he may take her, and I will get a housekeeper, right away, and be alone—that will be best."

Without wishing to operate in the least against his aunt's desire for matrimony, Robert instantly made the very just remark, that her removal from his uncle's house would throw difficulties in the way of the young lady's reception.

"Difficulties! what difficulties!" inquired Mr Thomson. "I do not see any!"

"Excuse me, my dear uncle!" replied Robert, in very low tone, "if Señora Dolores might live alone with my housekeeper, it would be altogether more suitable that Aunt Susan should know nothing at all about her arrival, and she——"

"But she knows it already—she already knows, that Miss Fanny is here! I sent a negro, from the Hotel Faroux, to my house at Bota Fogo, to inform her, and to order my carriage to be sent to the hotel. Miss Susan knows it already."

"Very well, then, my dear uncle! Aunt Susan expects Miss Fanny, could we not tell her it was a misunderstanding? that you misunderstood the officer from the alfandega? that I only had come? We could then, of course, immediately engage a country house for Señora Dolores, and a trusty housekeeper?"

"That will not do! that will not do!!" Robert," cried Mr Thomson, like a pilot in a storm. "That is contrary to custom! that would never do!'"

"Excuse me, then, my dear uncle, but it would answer still worse for the Señora to live alone with you, with a housekeeper."

Mr. Thomson sighed, and bit off a piece of his cigar. "Hem! you are quite right, Robert! you are quite right! the stupid, miserable prejudices! I see it all, it will not do! and nothing remains for us, but to oblige Miss Susan to hold her tongue."

"Alas! there appears to be no alternative," observed Robert. "If she has still such a temper as at Buenos Ayres, where she would not once permit me to play the forte piano, for——"

"Yes, alas! alas!" sighed Mr Thomson, "that's it! there's the trouble! she becomes more insupportable every year. Nevertheless," said he, suddenly interrupting himself, for he felt that he had already said too much in the presence of the newly arrived stranger, "nevertheless, that is nothing to the purpose! I am master of my house, and——Miss Fanny, may I offer you my arm? Will you be so good as to hold yourself in-readiness?—We shall meet my carriage at the landing place."

Dolores withdrew, to give her attendants the necessary orders, and to complete her toilet for the voyage.

"Damn!" muttered the old widower to himself, as he looked after her with sparkling eyes,

' Damn ! there's a tendency ! there's a tendency ! my word for it "

"Oh, yes, my dear uncle! I assure you Señora Dolores possesses a poetical tendency, one of the most distinguished!——"

Mr Thomson found that he had muttered a little too loud, and immediately recollecting himself, he added

"More than a tendency, there appears already a blooming development! She must produce admirable works She must be a poetess of the first class, to have such a price set upon her head! Five thousand pesos make a thousand pounds sterling—the exchange is trifling, certainly the danger is great, because the temptation is great, and we must be prudent"

Hinango remained in the middle of the vessel, in earnest conversation with Dr Thorsen, while this introduction of the lady took place

"Your position is discovered,' continued the doctor, "and few of your former acquaintance will speak to you, if they meet you The fear of compromising themselves will naturally remove all those people from you, who formerly sought your society You were an object of curiosity to many, in consequence of your resignation in Russia and the fate that followed it Now you are an object of dread to your former friends, they will fly from you as from the cholera"

"That is all not new to me, my dear Thorsin rejoined Hinango, ' it is only a tragical re-edition of my situation and circumstances in Europe I know the world, and do not, therefore, hate or despise the men who comply with its regulations, and withdraw themselves from me, because the circumstances in which they are placed require it But nothing is more sacred to me, than the silent respect of noble men, who, even though controlled by the power of circumstances, acknowledge and honor the man in me '"

"There are letters for you from London, under cover to Falter and Vernon, but open—— they lie open in the envelope, and the documents in the letters also unsealed

"Why !" exclaimed Hinango, "the documents opened, too! You are joking!"

"Mr Vernon sent for me, and showed me the packet of letters and you may be satisfied that the letters to you were opened, where, and by whom, cannot be known No suspicion rests upon Falter and Vernon, for we know them sufficiently well. But the letters arrived by the English mail, and are dated at London Could they have been opened in England ?"

"Opened, and not sealed again, do you say ? Perhaps, this may have occurred through carelessness ?"

"You may soon convince yourself of the fact, mysterious as it is There is, besides, a fellow here who has got track of you, and, among others, has intruded himself upon Fitz—since he seems to know that you were friends in youth."

"A spy, then! probably a fellow who does a commission business for several princely houses, as we have already known such creatures "

"It appears so, I even suspect that he does business for Rosas, for he sneaks around here, amongst the Argentine fugitives, and probably this government also gives him commissions, for he has admittance to some ministers of the caramuro party "

"What is the fellow's name ?"

"He calls himself the Baron de Spandau. Where he came from, I do not know. According to his dialect, he is a Prussian."

"And the documents are probably lithographic circulars '" asked Hinango, interrupting himself

"Under the former title, certainly; but, very naturally, they can compromise no one besides you, you only are branded, because it is entirely impossible to discover any one of the names, for no one knows the book that serves you as a key "

"Very well! then through me no one will be easily compromised, and, as concerns myself, I have, long since, had no other object in life than to labor for the cause of the people, so far as I am able," replied Hinango

Mr George Thomson just then led his niece to the gangway, accompanied by Robert, who was followed by Achilles and Corinna

This was, of course, the moment in which Dolores must take leave of her travelling companions, Horatio, Hinango, and Alvarez A wide chasm of convenance and etiquette, whose steep sides, grown up with all the thorny bushes, thistle growth, and belladonna of social regulations and prejudices, must henceforth separate the young lady from social intercourse with the men to whose spirits hers was so nearly allied, and who had become so precious to her heart The perception of this reality appeared suddenly to awaken, in all its painfulness, her countenance lost the last trace of color, a tear dimmed her eye, and she seized the hand of Horatio, who waited by the steps with Alvarez and the two Scandinavians

"Señor Hinango," said she, and laid the hand of the youth in his, "if I have a right to your friendship, to your sympathy, and your remembrance, then take charge of our Horatio, or at least assist him to find a place of rest, somewhere here in Rio "

Hinango replied to this honoring request, with all the force of his peculiarly heartfelt language, while Mr Thomson threw a criticising glance upon the "foreigner," who, as it appeared, possessed, in such a high degree, the confidence of his niece

Robert informed himself of the hotel where Hinango would stop, and Dolores painfully felt the difficulties of her situation, which did not permit her to invite either Horatio or Hinango to visit her, since she, as a young unmarried lady, had no "Self "

She had, through the regulations of the social world, no independent existence, but was only a being, who must become by contract the lawful property of a man, before she could invite a man, as the "friend of her husband," to visit her, inasmuch as this "self" had then become "plural," in which the "singular" of female individuality was merged

Nothing can more strongly designate female nullity, in the social world, than the present situation of Dolores in contrast with her intellectual elevation. A being, whose inspired words were able to arouse the might of a whole people, and shake the throne, or divan, or chair of a tyrant, could not, without the guard of some governess or another, dictate a poem to a friend, read a literary work with him, or consult with him upon the most sacred concerns of humanity.

Why not? Because this being has the misfortune to be a woman

On the other hand, the pretensions of the most unintellectual man might require such a woman to give "herself to him," to enable her, thereby, to obtain the right to bear his name, or to purchase a new hat, or a new shawl, on his account, (which, however, must not be too dear,) and give the invitation to some acquaintance to "be so good as to come and see Us" If these and similar regulations are more or less strictly recognised by the whole civilized world, it would be well worthy of philosophical contemplation, to examine upon what basis such so called social laws are founded What was feared, when such laws were created? Immorality? In that case, such mistrust involves a coarse insult to the female sex, by a doubt of their dignity and honor Or was a forcible attack, an assault, upon honor, virtue and innocence apprehended? Then, indeed, were the insult not less against the male sex These laws would appear to indicate, by their necessity, the low degree of the morality of the so called educated classes, for whom they were especially created

In the very distrust, in the doubt of morality, lies an evidence of the prevailing immorality of those who maintain such regulations, since they judge others according to themselves, and deny all moral dignity, in even the noblest beings of both sexes Even the thought of abusing personal and moral freedom lies far remote from the moral dignity, which carries, within itself, the means and weapons to guard itself

Robert appeared involuntarily absorbed, in deep reflection, upon the situation of Dolores He was urged, by a silent congenial feeling, to beg his uncle to extend an invitation to the two friends of his playmate of La Plata—to open to them his hospitable house But the words died on his lips, and he deferred his intimation to the future, and took leave of both, with the remark, that he should soon take the liberty of calling on them He then stepped into the felouque, with Dolores and his uncle, while the captain, with his other passengers, took their places in the shallop, and both vessels steered towards the landing places of Rio de Janeiro

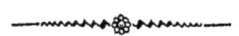

CHAPTER IV.

ROBERT

—There are hours, in the development of the inward life and character of a youth, in which he involuntarily, as it were, attains a consciousness of his powers, and becomes a man at once

The same youth who, seventeen days before, when just on the point of stepping over the threshold of his paternal home, to go into the world, sat trimming his finger nails in his father's cabinet at Buenos Ayres, now sat, with Dolores and his uncle, in the Brazilian shallop, and surveyed, with a single glance of the mind, the present and the future, of a being who required a protector from oppression and danger

Robert, who had grown up from boyhood with Dolores, had first recognised her mental worth when the consequences of her sublime poetic efforts had resulted in the necessity of her flight What long years of social intercourse had not revealed to him, had become suddenly evident since he saw her in such danger, and especially since he had become more and more acquainted with her inward nature, which had unfolded itself to Linango's kindred spirit in so many interviews and communications, to which he, as well as Horatio, had been a listener

The transparent purity of his youthful heart evinced itself, in the clear perception of his friend's situation He beheld now, in the playfellow of his sister, the persecuted poetess from La Plata, whose fate was to be placed at the mercy of a female, his aunt, who, "conceived and born in dullness," and brought up in prejudice and heartlessness, was a burthen to herself and others He suddenly recurred to what Brigaldi had revealed to them, in relation to the suspicions of the secret police and his father's presence of mind, which appeared to have succeeded in making the flight pass for an abduction, and in averting from Dolores the suspicion of being in reality the authoress of the Elegies

Pereroso, the only one who was convinced of this fact, had disappeared, and carried his secret with him into a watery grave

After sitting self-absorbed for some moments, unobservant of the strange and imposing appearances around him, he said, at length, to his uncle and Dolores

"Permit me to explain to you my views, and the ways and means which I find desirable for your safety My aunt ought, in no case, to know in what danger you are placed Far be it from me to doubt her character, or to expect that she may, in an ebullition of ill humor become intentionally prejudicial to you—far from it, I do not think of such a thing But, so far as I know my aunt, you are as remote and different from each other, as two women on earth can possibly be The very mental qualities in you, which should bespeak her protection, would call forth her decided antipathy"

"Bob, my boy!" said his uncle, "you speak like a man of experience and knowledge of mankind! say on"

"My father has declared to the authorities, in Buenos Ayres, that I have run away with you, and that you are any thing but a poetess"

"What? what?" cried Mr Thomson, "run away? run away?"

"Until now," continued Robert, "the authorities have in their hands no evidence of the contrary Aunt Susan is expecting my sister, and you appear As a fugitive, as a persecuted poetess, she would hardly receive you, and even were she to do so, it would soon become known here that you are the authoress of the Elegies. In short, Aunt Susan is Aunt Susan, and cannot hold her tongue! I therefore propose to conceal from her, altogether, the true cause of your departure, and follow exactly the path which my father has broken in Buenos Ayres, by telling her that I have carried you off—that you are my betrothed"

Mr Thomson suddenly made a grimace, like a pug dog to whom a piece of cake is held out and then quickly drawn away again

" As your betrothed !" cried he, and forget to close his lips again   Two cases presented themselves to him, like a landscape revealed by lightning in a dark night: the possibility that a secret understanding already existed between his nephew and his " niece;" or else that such a thing might come to pass, and, in the latter case, it appeared to him dangerous " to paint the devil on the wall," to proclaim a connexion which might make a bad stroke through his reckoning, especially as Señora Dolores had, in his eyes, an admirable tendency to corpulency, and in consequence of a former commission to his brother-in-law on the La Plata river, he had already laid out his plan

" But then you cannot live with us, Robert !" cried he, as quickly and loudly as before

" It is all the same," said Robert, " I will gladly renounce a daily intercourse with Señora Dolores, and will live wherever you think best, if I can only thereby avert from our friend the suspicion of her being the authoress of the Elegies, and promote her personal safety "

" Thank you, dear, noble Robert !" exclaimed Dolores, seizing his hand, which Mr Thomson found very confiding, and not exactly necessary , " I thank you for your sympathy and forethought, and recognise therein the brother of my friend Fanny "

" I think so too," interrupted the old widower, who had no objection whatever to Dolores' considering his nephew as the brother of his niece, though not as her betrothed, either in jest or earnest   " That is my opinion !   Robert and Fanny have one heart, one and the same heart exactly, and it is to be hoped that Robert will retain his !"

Without understanding the double meaning which the good uncle evidently, very slily, and really ingeniously attached to these words, Dolores assented to the congeniality and nobleness of heart of her two friends, and the old widower continued .

" I confess, Robert, that you see with a sharp glance into the position of things   I even doubt whether Señora Dolores would be safe in our house for one hour, if Miss Susan knew her to be a poetess   You know, Robert, she has her prejudices, and would go into convulsions, if she knew that Señora was an authoress, such as Lady Morgan, Lady Blessington, Madame de Stael, Madame Dudévant, or some such person, at whose names she loses her self-command, and wishes that the devil had all reading and writing in hell, except what relates to the literature of missions "

" I know all that," replied Robert, " and even admitting that her antipathy against intellectual effort in women were not so bitter, as is really the case, the way that my father has opened for us would still remain the only advisable one to deceive, yet further, the authorities of La Plata, who will not neglect to watch us here, through their agents."

" They will yield me no peaceable asylum here !" sighed Dolores, " there exists a secret association, extended to all parts of the world, the most efficient which has ever been organized, since the Jesuits gave them the example.   It is the association of espionage, the working in common of the secret agents of all the despotic powers on earth, for the persecution of the pa-

triots of all countries, for the extinction of the idea of the future, which, notwithstanding this, like the forebodings of the prophets before the birth of Christ, becomes extended and strengthened among all nations

Mr Thomson listened, with evident amazement, to these remarks of his niece, which evinced to him the clearness of his perceptions, and he exclaimed, when she had finished :

" Admirable ! admirably said ! showing, in so few words, the position of both the chief parties ! It corresponds with what I have read of you, Señora !   I have acknowledged and admired your penetration, after having read your Elegies."

" Thank you for the compliment Mr Thomson," replied the lady, with a slight blush. " Then you have read my Elegies, you say, dear uncle ? (for I must accustom myself to call you so)   Did Mr Walker send you a copy of the edition ?   It is to be hoped, however, that you learnt, for the first, from his letter to-day, that I am the authoress ?"

Robert awaited the answer with greater anxiety than herself, and looked, with a controlling glance, into the eyes of the old man, which evidently embarrassed him

" Certainly ! certainly !" he began, while he endeavored to compose himself, " Mr Walker sent me a copy of your Elegies, as a secret , you know he is very fond of secrets , he has a passion for mystery, and what he confides to me, that——"

" My God !" cried Robert, " he has not, surely, written to you, from Buenos Ayres, that Señora Dolores was the authoress, when he sent you the copy ?"

" To be sure !" replied Mr Thomson , " and if even—if he even did so, I know as well how to keep a secret as——"

Dolores looked at Robert with an expression that significantly said to his comprehension, " I am lost "

" Compose yourself, Dolores ! " said the youth, with inward excitement, " tranquillize yourself, my uncle has certainly given no one a hint which can——"

" Far from it !" cried the old widower, " what is the matter with you ? and, even if I had, you are now in Rio de Janeiro, and under my protection, and—and—as concerns myself, I shall, in time, find out ways and means for your personal safety, and to prepare you a comfort which no lady would lightly——"

Robert appeared so much shocked by the thought, that the two old men might, from want of judgement, have committed an indiscretion, that he found it advisable suddenly to break away from the subject, the explanation of which might awaken still more ground of discomposure

" We are then agreed among ourselves," said he, hastily, " that Miss Susan is not to know at all who you are   We will mention another family name, since we shall confide to her that I have carried you off, and before the world you will pass for my sister."

" So be it, then !" assented Mr Thomson, as if nothing had been said about the copy of Elegies ; " so be it, then , Robert's plan is indeed the best, and I will immediately look out for a pleasant country house for him.   Wait now ! I just happen to think of a pavilion—on da Gloria—a wonderful prospect   I occupied the pavilion myself, some years ago, when I came here alone, as a lonely widower We will make a circuit, and drive to Sr Moreto's in the Rua dos Ourives He will still be in his loja,* and, if possible, you can go there to-morrow You can stay to night at the Hotel Faroux, for we must be consistent ! You ought not to remain in the same house with your betrothed, not a single night !"

' To be sure not !" said Robert, laughing, "although Aunt Susan keeps the house, the world might be overthrown ! I mean the social world, with its anxiety, and its distrust, and its philanthropic care for the upholding of morals " The noble youth reddened as he was led to a topic which caused him to reflect upon the mean foundation of such measures

"The pavilion up there," interrupted his uncle, and pointed in the distance, "that's the one I mean I lived there once The hill there, with the white church, amongst the dark foliage—that is the church of Nossa Senhora da Gloria—and the whole surrounding parish is called so "

Dolores followed Robert's glance in that direction, and an idyllian landscape unfolded itself to their view, such as can nowhere be found, but in the bay of Rio A considerable hill, or mountain, which, being a peninsula, was nearly surrounded by the mirrorlike waters, and was built over with tasteful country houses in various styles, interspersed with lively green declivitous meadows and fields, with gigantic forests and low thickets projected from the misty back ground of the stupendous Corcovado, whose summit, already enveloped in darkness, as seen from this side, appeared like an obelisk on the apex of a pyramid

"Ah how lovely ! how charming !" sighed Dolores, how happy might men be in such a paradise !"

"Yes, indeed, Señora ! yes, indeed !" replied Mr Thomson, with a covetous glance at the "tendency" of the young lady of La Plata, "Yes, indeed, Señora ! man can be happy here—very comfortably happy, in the domestic relations—that is my opinion "

"Is that the mountain there, that we wish to purchase ?" asked Robert, contemplating another portion of the extensive and wonderful picture whose realities surrounded them

"We ! that is to say the English, have made proposals to purchase the Signal Mountain—that is it, there—with the old church of St Sebastian, but the present government has hitherto refused, and will not give it up "

"And the whole mountain is to be levelled ?"

"Yes, it is to be taken down and levelled, and the surface is to be built up as a city, as British property Do you understand that, Robert ? And then we shall have a firm footing here—and the rest will soon follow !"

"The hill appears about three hundred feet high——"

"And may be one and a half English miles in circumference, perhaps two, and lies, as you see, in the midst of the town, on the shores of the bay; it would be an admirable acquisition, an English city in the midst of the capital of Brazil ! We should then have the key to the wealth of all Brazil in our pocket, Robert ! What do you say of that ?'

---

* Shop.

"I think that the Brazilians will hardly sell us the mountain "

"Why ! because they suspect that there are gold mines in it ?"

"Even without gold mines in it They would not admit a British jurisdiction within their own "

"They must, Robert ! they will have to, at length ! We have already advanced them sufficient for such a purchase, and when it once comes to the crisis, and we require our millions back again, and when the empire becomes bankrupt, then—then, Robert, do you see our frigates and corvettes, and ships of the line ! They will lie there ! and we shall know, then, how far our cannon will reach, and the mountain there, the mountain is ours, with or without gold mines !"

The shallop glided past the station of the foreign fleet, which guards the Brazilian empire lest the Botocudos should steal it Again an imposing view was presented to the strangers, in the background of which was seen the pointed Organ Mountain, with its lofty pipes, like a misty dark blue shadow, contrasting with the transparent horizon

"Is not that the Danish flag ?" inquired Dolores, pointing to a small brig from St Thomas, which lay unpretendingly at anchor near a majestic United States corvette, as if it had been sent into the world out of irony, in testimony that Britain had forgotten at least one man-of-war, when she stole the Danish fleet, as a thief would a handkerchief out of a farmer's pocket

"The Danish flag, Señora ? yes, indeed, at your service ! It is the Danish flag, a small brig that has made an excursion on the Atlantic Ocean," replied Mr Thomson, involuntarily, a little embarrassed, as a very natural connexion of ideas, made him suspect that the political poetess from La Plata river had not mentioned the Danish flag without an allusion to the British speculation of the Signal Mountain

Like the unfortunate young Briton in the famous poem, "I Profughi di Parga," by the Italian Giovanni Berchet, Robert Walker stared straight before him, seized by a sentiment of shame—breathed upon by the curse of oppressed nations that howls around the British flag, which is gnawed through by the serpent of treachery.'

Shot after shot just then resounded from the neighboring fortress Do-Vilcalhon, and from the brazen mouths of the European and transatlantic fleet—for the sun, long since disappeared behind the mountain summits, had touched the nautical horizon of the longitude of Guenabara.

All around was again silent, and the oars of passing barks and gondolas dipped in the whispering waves Long boats of the navies of foreign nations, with stately officers in their sterns, floated by, returning from the landing-place at the Hotel Faroux, which the shallop now approached With a sorely oppressed heart, Dolores looked into the gloomy night of her cloud-covered future

"There is our carriage !" cried Mr Thomson, pointing out a stately vehicle, with negroes in livery, as coachman and footman. He offered his hand to the exile, who had already taken Robert's arm, to the smothered vexation of the old widower, who now ordered the coachman to drive through the Rua dos Ourives, and stop at Senhor Moreto's shop.

CHAPTER V.

ARRIVAL.

It was an hour after sundown when the five clerks and mercantile volunteers of the house of Rossbruck & Co., in the Rua da Alfandega sat at table, in the large dining room, on the first floor, and drank their tea socially together, according to the custom of European houses of business in Rio Janeiro. They were all amiable young men, from different counties in Europe, of unexceptionable families, and exemplary deportment. They were talking and joking in the best humor, and two negroes sprang round the long table, (which afforded room for thrice the number of guests,) and served the young senhors with Ethiopian attention and readiness. There was a knocking at the house door, as if a rhinoceros thumped against it.

"Who is making such a noise down there?" cried Mr Doubly, a young Swiss, who occupied the seat at the head of the table.

One of the negroes instantly ran down stairs, and, after some moments, a gentleman appeared in a travelling dress, attended by a negre de gagne,* who carried his carpet bag, with his umbrella and hat box.

The gentleman had, unfortunately, found no English knocker on the door, with which to cause, according to English custom, a dozen hasty taps of respectability to resound in quadruple time. He had, however, with surprising presence of mind, known how to help himself, by making, with the handle of his umbrella, the above "loud raps of respectability," in the fashionable quadruple time, as his respectability required.

"Is not Mr Francis Rossbruck at home?" inquired the gentleman, in broken English, stepping up to the table, with a disdainful glance at the youthful company.

"No!" answered Mr Doubly. "What do you wish?"

"Are none of te partners at home?" inquired the other, drawing on his patent gloves more tightly, and pressing them down between the fingers.

"No!" was again the reply, and all eyes rested upon the gentleman in a Mackintosh overcoat, which was, at that time, the height of fashion, but extremely warm for the gentleman, since he happened to be in Brazil.

"I am Mr William Rossbruck, and intent to stop here!" said the latter, observing from head to foot the young people, in their white jackets and coats, who must, of course, all be clerks, for no partner of the house made himself known among them.

"Abd el Kader!" cried Mr Doubly, "put the room up there in order for this senhor!" The negro, Marco, who bore this nickname in the house, hastened to fulfil the order, and carried the carpet bag of the Senhor Branco into the designated apartment.

"Take a seat, if you please," said Mr Doubly, now, in German, to the gentleman. "May I offer you a cup of tea, and what we have for supper?"

The gentleman partner of the house felt himself almost offended by such a solicitation, to seat himself at the same table with the clerks, and even to drink tea with them, an idea of the young man in the white spencer, which, according to the views of the gentleman, did not tend to the honor of his civilization.

"I tank you!" he muttered, turning his back on the company, and walked slowly and stiffly, into the room where the negro had carried his carpet bag.

The young people looked after him, and then at each other, but their lips to suppress a burst of laughter, and took up a thread of the interrupted conversation, as if no one had disturbed them.

The negre de gagne waited for his couple of vingtaines,* for porterage, and at length ventured to remind them of it.

"We will take it upon ourselves," whispered Mr Doubly to his companions, "and give the guest credit for a patack,"† and then paid the negro, who thanked him, and likewise departed.

The supper was ended, and each went into his cabinet, after having first agreed which of them should have the watch for the two following days—a holiday and a Sunday, as, according to old custom, one of them must take care of the house on such days. The watch for the next day was Mr Doubly's, who, besides, wished to stay at home, and occupy himself with music and reading.

"A young little goose flew over the Rhine
And came home a gander, fashionably fine!
Trala! trala! trala!"

sang a young man, with a clear toned voice, while he prepared, in his room, for a promenade in the cool of the evening.

"And how they hold a fork to eat,
And how they walk along the street,
Long since he learned to imitate!"

joined in Mr Doubly, just as loudly, and, seizing his guitar, he preluded, and sang, and accompanied, *con amore*, as if he had been alone in the house.

While this was going on in the Rua da Alfandega, the carriage of the real gentleman from Bota Fogo, had nearly made its half way home from the place from where it started, or at least had rolled through the Rua dos Ourives, where it stopped, in front of the loja before mentioned. A little, fat, pockmarked descendant of Vasco de Gamo ran out to the carriage door, and greeted his old acquaintance, Mr George Thomson.

The latter had, by this time, reflected, that it would be best for him, in pursuance of his particular plan, to quarter the young betrothed as far as it was any way possible from his country house in Bota Fogo, and he formed the determination to hire for him the villa, whose situation was as charming as respectable, which latter was naturally the first thing taken into consideration.

It turned out, that one of Sr. Moreto's two pavilions on "da Gloria" was to rent, and the very same one which Mr. Thomson had inhabited after the death of his third corpulency.

"And who lives in the other pavilion?" inquired Mr Thomson, in all haste.

"A young lady of my family, at your service, Sr. George, a widow, from St João del Rey, a very respectable person, whose neighborhood cannot be disagreeable to you, in any respect.

---

* *Negre de gagne.*—Slaves who serve as porters on their master's account.

* Copper coin, of 20 reis.　† About 20 cents.

She is here attending upon a lawsuit in Rio, and lives incognito—altogether incognito, and if it were not you, Mr George, I would not let the pavilion near her, but, upon my responsibility, the young lady will gladly admit the neighborhood of a gentleman of your house She is a very accomplished young lady, and I will answer for her respectability, you have long known me in that respect, Sr George, my assurance has its weight with you '"

"Certainly '" cried the old widower from the carriage, "certainly ' I would take your word for a hundred contos ' All in order ' Then tomorrow forenoon my nephew can go there '"

"As early as he pleases, nevertheless, it would be very well, if your nephew would take the trouble to call on my relation, since I have promised not to let the pavilion to any one, without her consent, and I like to keep my word, you know that, Sr George It is merely a formality, for I know, beforehand, that a connexion of your house, whom I recommend, will be welcome to my niece, it is merely a formality, and I will send some one to-night, to apprize her of the visit of your nephew"

"I will not fail to ride out there early to-morrow," replied Robert

Mr Thompson now inquired, in all haste, the month's rent, (with which he was already acquainted,) and Sr Moreto stepped back from the coach door, and the carriage rolled on, with flying Brazilian speed, through the Rua d'Ajuda, out to the Praya do Flamingo, and on to Bota Fogo

The shallop of Captain Finngreen had landed at the great stairs, which, farther up in the city, opposite the Ilhos das Cobras,* was surrounded, early and late, by captain's boats and negro canoes, and served as a connecting point between the city and the merchant vessels

Mr Rossbrück had stepped out, and, under the guidance of a cicerone, proceeded towards the neighboring Rua da Alfandega, without taking leave of the other passengers, as that was not written in his catechism of British fashion, in which (as we have already remarked) he had made great progress

Captain Finngreen hastened to report himself at the bureau of the house, with whose head he had already spoken, and was then, according to agreement, to meet his passengers, Hinango, Horatio, and Alvarez, in the Hotel du Nord, in the Rua Direita, whither the Scandinavian conducted the two latter

"I will see if Fitz is at home, and bring him here '" said Dr Thorfin to Hinango, as the three strangers were going up the steps, to take together a salon with adjoining chambers

"Well, do so, if you will take the trouble Then we will all take supper here," returned Hinango; "but come back soon, for we have much to talk about."

"I will go likewise to Vernon, and tell him that you are here," added the doctor, and hurried off, accompanied by the gratitude of the stranger for his kindness.

In a roomy atelier for astronomical and nautical instruments, sat a little man, with all sorts of expression on his weather browned face, unusually late at his work table, and filed, and polished, and sang, with a barbarous voice,

* Serpent Island.

21

"No general has such powerful might,
With all his hosts entire,
As a handsome woman, day or night,
In negligent attire '
In neg——li——gent—attire '"

It was Mr. Henry Fitz—"Chief Intendant of the Imperial Physical Cabinet at St Christova, and Unpatented Air Pump Controller to their Imperial Highnesses, the Princesses," as he called himself, without, however, receiving any stipulated salary from the court

Two haggard, meagre Mamaluco boys, whose bones were scantily cushioned over with dingy carne secco,* likewise pursued their labors, filing and turning on screws and rollers for an imperial Brazilian electrical machine, which stood there unfinished, on a broad pedestal, in the midst of the saloon

Some one approached the corridor on the outside, and Tycho Brahe (as Mr Fitz called one of the nearly transparent Mamalucoes) opened the door

Franco, a negro from the numerous colored attendants of the Hotel Faroux, entered and inquired for Sr Fitz, to whom he handed a card, and added, a Sr Inglés wished to know where Sr Closting lived, and, if possible, to see him, early in the morning

"Then the Sr Inglés will have far to ride this night, replied Mr Fitz, in his customary jesting mood "Sr. Closting lives, to be sure, somewhere in the city, when he is here, but, so far as I know, he is yet some hundred leagues off, in Mattogrosso, or Goyaz, or Minas Geraes, or somewhere else where there are mountains, and can hardly be seized early in the morning"

"If Sr Closting was not in town, then the Sr Inglés said, I should beg you to tell me who conducted his business here, and I was then to take the card there."

"Who has the difficult employment of conducting Mr Closting's business here, I can tell you Wait ' I will write down the address for you" He made the required note on the back of the card, and added "Ask for Sr Forro, No 164 Rua de Sabão, if he is not at home, he will certainly be somewhere else '"

The negro thanked him for the direction, and hurried down stairs

"No general has such powerful might——" recommenced Mr Fitz, when he was again disturbed by some one clapping his hands before the door, the customary Brazilian token of announcement, which takes the place of the European knocking on the door. Tycho Brahe hurried to open it again, and Dr Thorfin appeared on the threshold

"Make yourself ready, and come with me to the Hotel du Nord '" cried he, at the door, "an old friend has arrived"

"Not Hinango '" inquired the astronomer.

"How did you happen to think of him ?"

"I am sure I don't know myself, but I am sure it is he, and no one else"

"You have guessed rightly, now come with me"

"Step in, and sit down till I get ready. Where did the dev'lish fellow come from, that he is here again '"

"From the coast of Africa, by way of St. Helena and Monte Video."

* Dried meat.

" With his Iduua ?"

" Oh no! as a passenger, he has lost his Iduna."

" Lost ' I will not think it ' Where, and how ?"

" Come with me to the Hotel du Nord By and by he will tell you how he came here "

" From St Helena, as passenger, by the way of Monte Video ? and wants, perhaps, to purchase a ship here ?"

" And instruments of you," added Mr Thorfin

" I know of a schooner brig for him, she is called the Vesta, a lovely little thing ' a thing I tell you, that sails like vengeance, and is built and designed entirely for a privateer " He had partly put away his tools, and now took his hat, and left to his two Mamalucoes the atelier, and then carne secco for supper

Dr Thorfin and the astronomer took their way to the Hotel du Nord, and found Captain Finngreen with the new comers A mutual, hearty greeting ensued, as the latter also was acquainted with the " sextant mender," as he called him

CHAPTER VI

ABYSS, IN THE INTERIOR OF THE SOCIAL WORLD

THE conversation of the friends and acquaintances at supper, in the Hotel du Nord, touched upon many common reminiscences, and Hinango inquired after one and another with whom he had formerly held intercourse

" Dr. D—— and Signor F—— have lost their wives," said Mr Fitz to him

" Both ?" inquired Hinango " Was it with some infectious fever ?"

" I don't know whether it was infectious, but there seemed to have been a hot fever beforehand, at least in the mind Both have absconded—have abducted men——"

" What ? How ? You would say they have both been abducted "

" No, I will not say that, for I am free to doubt whether a woman ever yet was abducted I venture to affirm, that the woman carries off her lover—that no woman ever allows herself to be carried off—never ' No steam engine of sixty horse power can tear a woman away from her husband, unless she breaks loose herself "

" You always make original assertions, and I like you for it, when you are able to maintain them," remarked Hinango

" In the present case, we must both allow ourselves to be run away with, that I may support my assertion," replied Fitz ; " but I will add this much : you will never run away with any woman, if you remain true to your early principles, so far as I know them."

Hinango smiled, and assured him that the latter was the case.

" Still less will any woman run away with you," continued Fitz, " or she must have a very peculiar taste. You are far too sentimental, and too little agreeable to the female sex ; at least, to the married women "

" I thank you heartily for that. To be very

agreeable to married women is, in my opinion, the greatest misfortune that could befall a man."

" Certainly, according to your views, I know your ' platonic system,' and that is just what the women do not like "

" But to return to our two friends : is it jest or earnest ?"

" It is earnest," joined in Dr Thorfin ; " unhappily earnest ' Both have made the sorrowful discovery, that marriage without love was a very weak bond "

" Apropos ' Doctor !" cried the air pump controller, " a gentleman has just been making inquiries after Mr Closting I sent him to Senhor Forro—for it was a business affair, I suspect Have you heard, through his wife, when he returns ?"

" Madame Closting has gone away," replied the physician

" Gone away ?" interrupted the other, " what, for ever ? Gone away from Rio ? Perhaps to meet her husband ?"

" Where, I do not know ; and if for ever, that also I do not know It would, in many respects, be most advisable, if she would absent herself forever from her husband It is hard to be a physician for such evils, which have their seat in the heart, and are to be cured in the nerves "

" You are a pretty doctor '' said Fitz, " you use ' dissolving remedies' for conjugal relations Were you the physician of Senhora D——, and Senhora F—— ?"

" If I had been the physician of these two ladies, I should, at least, have known no means to restore or to establish sympathy of soul when there was none According to my view, the sacrament of marriage does not consist in the outward ceremony, (which any one can pass through for money,) but in love

" It is not the sacrament which binds, but love The profanation of every sacrament, is a prostitution of the Most Holy as he profanes the sacrament of the Lord's Supper who approaches the table of the Lord, without being penetrated by the spirit of the doctrine of Jesus

" The sacrament of marriage has grown old," observed Mr Fitz, " and when Brazil was Portuguese, one had first to write to Lisbon,* and it was often putrified and corrupt before it arrived here It is rotten, it is about fifteen hundred years old, if I am not mistaken, and dates from the Emperor Constantine. And what the church puts together, no longer holds so firmly ' The glue is good for nothing ' It is manufactured in great quantities for sale, of poor ingredients, and if it sticks until the first baptism is paid for, it is very well ! Let us rejoice that we have not Brazilians for our wives—who would turn their backs on us "

" As regards that," returned the doctor, " I am of another opinion I know Brazilian women who may be cited as patterns—both as wives and mothers—and am satisfied that the women of Brazil stand as high, as women, as those of any other nation, when they find a return of the love which they feel "

" But, on the other hand, we must willingly

* In those times, whoever wished to be married in Brazil, first had to obtain permission from the Archbishop of Lisbon.

admit that here, as everywhere else, there are women who cannot love," observed Hinango.

"How so? cannot love?" interrupted Mr. Fitz, "that would be curious, a woman who could not love?"

"It depends on what we call love," replied Hinango "Love presupposes heart, a development of soul, inward life, sentiment; and by many women the understanding is cultivated at the expense of the sentiment. The heart is lost The soul is oppressed by female pretensions Such women believe that they love, and do not, and no bond of church or state will bind them, for their hearts never have bound them ; they are the most dangerous beings in creation Such beings should never marry, for they abuse and desecrate the sacrament of marriage, which presumes love They would like to give away a heart, and have none. They do not look for a man of honor and character, but for a 'husband!' to satisfy their manifold wants Their element is sensuality, and their being changeableness, passion for diversion, with a constant desire to fill the inward void, without a heart Their whole life is a destructive caprice—with *variations en negligée* They are the women of *marriage à la mode*, and their number is legion They are the poisonous plants of humanity, whose effects destroy human life, and pass destructively over to the next generation. They represent the privilege of marriage—as the cluster of all demoralization"

"A terrible, but very, very true remark," said Captain Finngreen, "but there is also another class of women, capable of all love, who are circumvented by men who never loved them, and when the illusion vanishes, then such unfortunate women are to be pitied"

"Very true, captain," rejoined Dr Thorfin "Such women long all the more after love, from having been circumvented, when it becomes clear to them that they have never been blessed by reciprocated love The claims of the heart—the most sacred demands of nature—assert their rights, but then it is too late, and those nervous diseases come on, against which the physician only knows palliative remedies, and which are not to be cured so long as the cause cannot be removed which produces the disorder the unnatural connexion of marriage without love!"

"And this cause is generally not to be removed," added the captain

"And many women will not remove it," observed Hinango

"I assure you, gentlemen," said Dr. Thorfin, "whoever looks deeply, as a psychologist, into the cause from which such diseases proceed, may well shrink back from the basis on which the social world is founded I am entirely of our astronomer's opinion, and affirm that there are few, if any, wives who are abducted, but they run away with those whom they have captivated. And I go still further, and assert—maidens are seduced, married women seduce I offer, as a psychologist, to sustain this position, and to prove it by facts"

"I do not doubt it, but I trust you will not assert that these unfortunate women seduce intentionally?" said Hinango.

"Women of a noble character seduce certainly not intentionally," replied the doctor. "By no means; on the contrary, they are, for the most part, overcome by the unconquerable force of an inward motive, the longing after love It is the consciousness of an awakened inner life, whose organ is the nervous system, and this becomes so much the more susceptible, the more it is oppressed by disturbing influences"

"I understand you," remarked Hinango, "since I recognise the differences of individuality in spiritual life, and in materialism—the two poles of earthly existence Nothing operates more destructively upon the nerves than the forced suppression of repulsion—physical surrender with antipathy of soul"

"Very naturally," affirmed Thorfin, "and who can wonder, in the least, that these diseases are daily gaining ground, in an epoch in which marriage is made a 'business,' and in France is even arranged by specially established houses of business, by means of travelling clerks, and is considered, in the whole social world, as an object of speculation and convenience, or as a gratification of sensuality? Who can wonder at the deterioration of the human race, at the religious and moral indifference of our century, if we cast a glance at the desecrated and plundered sanctuary of generation? From a union formed with resignation of love, in levity and indifference, no generation can proceed such as God made man, 'in his own image' I do not wonder at the deterioration of the human race," continued the physician, "but rather that mankind has not sunk deeper under such desecration? There must be an indestructible divine strength in humanity, which will not suffer itself to be laid waste and destroyed, notwithstanding all the degradation of woman in the service of man without love!"

"I grant that married women seduce," said Hinango, "and are not seduced, but the foundation must be this inward disturbance, which manifests itself in the nervous system through repulsion The love of such a being is a destructive deity, which requires human sacrifices ; it destroys the inner life, and wo to the man, or the youth, who is selected as the victim in such a case!"

"He is lost, without redemption!" said Dr Thorfin ; "for even when he would play the part of Joseph, the embittered vengeance of injured womanhood would seek to destroy him! A rejected woman is capable of any murder."

"An English author says, in other words:

'Earth knows no curse like love to hatred turned, Hell has no fury like a woman scorned,'"

observed Mr Fitz, smiling

"Hell has no fury like a woman scorned?" repeated Hinango, with a deep sigh "The word 'scorned,' however, seems to me very badly chosen, for I can imagine to myself one case, in which a man would withdraw from a woman at such an eventful moment, and that, not by any means because he despised or 'scorned' her, but because he loved her, and out of love shrank back before her future—spared her weakness—Such a case may certainly belong to the rarities of our age; but I know that it may occur The consequences, however, remain ever the same, and the saying of the English poet remains in force."

"As concerns Joseph," said the air pump controller, "I do not rely much upon that affair.

I very much doubt whether the Egyptian chroniclers had hidden a stenographer in the apartment of Potiphar's wife! So far as I am acquainted with woman, in all zones, Joseph would hardly have become minister, if he had run away, like a young Scandinavian poet in Avignon, who left a Spanish lady, in the deepest negligée, in the lurch, as we have read of somewhere. As bitterly as this lady afterwards threatened him with a dagger, would Madame Potiphar have known how to revenge herself, also, in some way or another. There is no power so ragingly destructive as the bitter hatred of a woman in such unfortunate cases, for she is not mistress of herself."

"You seem to have had practical experience in these matters," remarked Hinango.

"My dear friend, I lived ten years in Paris, from my five and twentieth year until five and thirty, and as I had become acquainted with my ground by hearsay, I endeavored, at least, to come out of it with my life, and made all sorts of marginal notes upon the text of the suspicious history of Joseph."

The friends laughed, except Hinango, whose seriousness could not understand a joke where the most sacred concerns of humanity were treated of.

"And as regards my experience," resumed Dr Thorfin, "I obtained it during eight years of observation, as so called ladies' physician, in Odessa and Moscow. I sought, in the study of psychology, the basis of all healing knowledge, and arrived at the conviction, that in thousands of instances all medical treatment remains ineffectual, inasmuch as so many circumstances evidently contradict the unconditional requisites which the physician must prescribe. I saw my Hygeia in despair at the statutes of government. I stood by many biers, which held the victims of a powerfully suppressed repulsion, and lived to see suicide after suicide, of noble beings of both sexes, who were carried away by despair, when they learned, too late, that marriage without love is a crime that draws after it a hell, from which there is no redemption, but through the gate of death."

"Horrible!" sighed Hinango, "but in a thousand cases to one, the woman is innocent, or, at least, only guilty in having once given away, without love, what she can never get back again."

"I will give you a systematic survey of the loveless apathy of women," began Dr Thorfin, after a long pause, "and you may then the sooner arrive at clearness, in respect to many appearances of the reality about us here.

"We behold three other cases of marriage without love, (except the numerous class of women in marriage à la mode,) which are repeated a thousand times each.

"In the first case, we find the spiritual, noble woman the victim of circumstances, of self-deceit, or of treachery on the part of the man. She watches over-fulfilment of conjugal duties with lively diligence, labors on from one multiplication to another, and, from calls of business, has no time to reflect upon her lot nor to feel her animatic* life. She receives what is offered her of the pleasures of life, and often affords her hus-

---
* Animatic, from anima—soul.

band more than he requires, in the delusion that she is loving and beloved. In this manner, years pass away, and a single circumstance, a single movement, an accident, or destiny, suddenly rends the veil of illusion. The consciousness of the loveless reality crosses her mind, she becomes aware that the partner of her life has never loved her, that his heart has been no sanctuary of her love, that he neither understands her heart nor had been acquainted with her spirit, that he only loves himself in the possession of her charms, and, her heart is broken, her earthly happiness has fled! She awakes from a sensual illusion, and feels that she, also, does not love. Disturbance of the nervous system ensues, partly in consequence of physical causes, but mostly the effect of the repulsion, which this discovery brings with it. The luxuriant bloom of strength and beauty fades, like an aromatic flower in the poisonous night dews, and the suffering condition ensues for which the physician knows no other remedy than exactly that one, the want of which has brought on the disease—love—sympathy of soul. And granting that the woman has found love, their deliverance, through love, is forbidden by all the laws of church and state.

"In the second case, we behold the woman in a subordinate development of the spiritual life, with less depth of feeling, giving herself up to her vocation with the same passion, the fulfilment of which enervates her, and affords her the charm of life which satisfies her. Physical strength and abundance force the spiritual life more and more back upon itself, and by degrees it succumbs to the influence of material gratification. She wants no love, because the susceptibility for love is partly extinct in her, and because she considers that to be love which is no love. Whether she deceives herself, or is deceived, she lives on in illusion, and the material side of life affords 'her domestic happiness.' Her element is indifference. She is a so called exemplary wife, who knows no temptation, and whose virtue, of course, does not stand very high.

"In the third case, we see the woman as an intellectual being, of clear understanding and ennobled heart, a victim of circumstances, with a renunciation of love, sold like a slave to a man who is unworthy of her. Sophisms of the understanding led her to the resignation of love. She seeks to overcome her decided repulsion to her companion by the philosophy of life, and only lives for her 'duties.' She resigns herself to the guidance of Hymen, and through his instructions the fulfilment of her so called duties becomes gradually endurable, and at length an agreeable habit. But she lives in eternal contradiction with herself, and the inevitable disturbance of the nervous system soon ensues, that physical infirmity which is the reaction of the constraint upon her inner life, and her physical convulsions are the effects of her mental struggles. She feels herself fastened for ever to a man whom she can 'neither love nor respect,' while it becomes clear to her that he is universally despised for his selfish meanness; that he has never recognised in her either mind or heart, but only sought a woman for the satisfaction of his sensual desires.

"In respect to character, men do not judge each

other with such forbearance and consideration, as the wife her husband, for ' love makes one blind, and marriage deaf and dumb ;' and granting that the woman, in the above position, had not been blind, because she did not love, she would be deaf and dumb, as a wife, deaf, to all reports to the prejudice of her husband, and dumb, as to all that she feels against him   She believes it her duty to respect, in her companion, the husband whom she cannot love, she feigns towards him all reverence, in the presence of others, and seeks to make a virtue of the low hypocrisy through which the wife excuses, embellishes, and (in case of need) defends all the faults and meannesses of her husband, and, by degrees, even approves of them   Jean Paul calls marriage ' a double egotism,' but I maintain that marriage, without love, protects all crimes   No wife has ever yet given up her husband to justice   is a thief or counterfeiter   As no man is so vile that he does not possess some concealed so called ' good side,' the wife seeks to bring out this good side of her husband, judges him entirely according to it, and defends and smooths over his vices and crimes, compares him with others, and finds preference upon preference, and an unaccountable self-deceit makes the ' father of a family ' blameless, where the ' man ' would be condemned for his meanness   What was hypocrisy, 'then becomes demoralization of the heart'—the feeling is blunted which once rose against baseness   As the wife in her hypocrisy must despise herself for being a dissembler, so she renounces, by degrees, the judgement of public opinion, all that concerns the reputation of her husband, whose ' good qualities' satisfy her

"I can cite cases   one, in which the wife of a functionary of high rank, branded by public opinion as a rascal, a cheat, and a forger, even declared, to a confidential friend, every word to the prejudice of her husband, which had casually come to her ears, to be calumny and lies, while the same lady had long felt her love for him extinguished, and a strong repulsion had destroyed her nervous system   I attended this unhappy creature in hysterical convulsions, and recognised the impossibility of physical deliverance where moral rescue was impossible   So I at length renounced my brilliant practice as ladies' physician in Moscow, and went into the navy   I engaged in researches upon the nature of women and upon their social position, and asked myself. Can a lady who is really not wanting in understanding and sagacity, after many years of such intimate connexion, can she really not know the character of her husband? Can marriage without love blunt the feelings and the power of judgement? Can even conjugal familiarity weaken the intellectual capacities, as repulsion disturbs the nervous system ? I sought to explain, psychologically, how it was possible that a woman, in such a case, could steadily take up the defence of her husband in a confidential interview, and I beheld her sunk into the abyss of demoralization, which was effected by the union with a man of whose meanness and baseness she must partake   Why ? Because she is bound to him by the laws of church and state ? O no ! because he is her ' husband, the father of her children,' whom she possesses, or wished to possess, because she had given herself to him, whether

in the conceit of love, or from resignation of love   She is his wife, and his crimes are hers— his baseness is hers   The purchased negro slave can curse her owner, she can execrate him, in her prayers to God, for deliverance from degrading slavery, the wife, the lawful property of the man of our civilized world, must bless her owner, and intercede for him before the world, if she cannot intercede for him with God, she must feign for him so called fidelity and respect before the world, although he lies in prison, as a forger and cheat, or is taken to the scaffold, as a criminal and a murderer   She has, long ago, sacrificed herself to him, and from the moment when she denied him in her heart all respect, and feigned for him all respect before the world, she must also despise herself, in her demoralization and in her hypocrisy "

A long pause ensued, while all, even the ironical, light-hearted Henry Fitz, appeared shocked by the communication of the experienced physician

" Love ennobles, marriage without love destroys the heart '" at length remarked Hinango, " but I hope, to the honor of women, that many admit, to themselves, the baseness of their husbands "

" And, of course, the hypocrisy is so much greater," interrupted the astronomer, " for a so called cultivated woman will deny the baseness of her husband to her most intimate friend "

" And, for this trait in the character of woman, I seek for a word, in any language whatever, but I find none," interrupted Dr   Thorfin

" Frailty ! thy name is woman '" says Shakspeare, " there you have the word," added Mr   Fitz, laughing

" Who can find the way out of the labyrinth of contradictions, into which marriage without love leads a woman '" said Hinango, after a pause   " Marriage without love is a school of immorality and crime, and often is the remote cause of insanity   It is surprising that we so frequently find the most interesting, intelligent, and amiable women, married to men without character, and very frequently to men in the highest degree contracted and stupid "

" That will admit of explanation," joined in Mr Fitz   " A French woman once said to me, in confidence ' The most stupid men make the best husbands.' But it is the more inexplicable to me, that many sensible women think their stupid husbands intelligent "

" I every day less and less understand what is comprised under the notion of a husband," said Hinango   " The qualities of an admirable husband must apparently be common and easy to find, as every woman considers her husband perfect   At least, wo ! wo be to those who would express, in the presence of a wife, a doubt of the infallibility of her husband "

" The noblest woman acquires, by degrees, the base properties of her husband, while she thinks to ennoble him," observed Dr. Thorfin." She sinks down to him, while she believes that she has elevated him, and at length lies parallel with him, and then often feels very comfortable   She regards her companion as the most desirable one on earth ; at least, she would hardly exchange him for another. All this happens in marriage without love ; for where there is love, there is also ennoblement. A noble-minded woman elevates her husband to the most noble sentiment, when he loves her with the same sincerity as she loves him ?"

"I have known women that would suffer themselves to be beaten by their miserable husband," said Fitz, laughing; "beaten, I say, and yet they not only lived with them, but had the impudence to praise such unmanly canaille before the world, as a pattern of domestic virtue"

"Explain that to me psychologically," said Hinango to Thorfin.

"That I cannot, fills me with dread," replied the latter, "for I have known families, myself, in which the husband lived on the property of his wife, beat her, and she not only did not separate from him, but praised him to others, as the most excellent husband, and the finest gentleman, that was any where to be found !"

"A commercial house that I know here," remarked Mr Fitz, "was charged to send a young woman back to her friends in Europe, whose husband had sunk into debauchery, illtreated her, stole from her, and lived with other women. She refused to go away, and went back to her husband instead."

"May not physical causes lie at the bottom, in such a case ?" inquired the captain, "perhaps sensuality, and the force of habit ?"

"That would be bestiality, and then I would renounce my faith in humanity," cried Hinango

"Our two friends," began Mr. Fitz, after a pause, "D—— and F——, by no means illtreated their wives, and were certainly not bad fellows"

"And did Madame D—— leave her husband, and her property, and her two children ?" Hinango asked

"She felt that he did not love her," answered Thorfin, "and that she, also, had never loved him; they had 'merely married each other,' as takes place a thousand times When she awoke from the illusion, she became attached to another, of whose love she felt certain She must choose, and she chose him whom she loved

"The flight of this unhappy mother shows the consequences of marriage without sympathy, certainly, in a very striking light, and affords abundant material for observation upon such a disturbance of the female mind Even her children, as the fruits of her sensuality without love, appeared indifferent to her, if not abhorrent, when she became acquainted with the feeling of love, to which she had, until then been a stranger But wo to the unfortunate whom she found worthy of her love, when it was too late !

"Yet another !" said Mr. Fitz "Mr L——, whom you know, has become insane, has been taken back to Europe, and died."

"And was it through love ?" asked Hinango

"Alas !" replied Dr. Thorfin, "a 'mysterical' woman (as Mr Thomson expresses himself) had captivated him, and appeared to love him, and he loved her; and because he loved her, he wished to keep at a distance from her, but he could not—he fell a sacrifice ! The disturbed character of the lady showed itself, in all its caprices, in eternal contradiction with herself. She illtreated him like a negro, while she continued to live with her husband. He loved her, as a man's heart can love.

"The thought of the woman he loved, in the arms of another, whom she, as she declared, did

not love, made him deranged I was his physician He had lucid moments. His sufferings were unheard of, but his noble character showed itself, as well as his pure love; he forgave her all she had brought upon him by her ill usage A double image lay before him, and he could not banish it. Not far from the coast of England, he threw himself into the sea"

"I know the captain who had him on board as a passenger," said Captain Finngreen, after a pause "He must have been a noble man, but no one suspected the cause of his sufferings, as I learned from the captain"

"If he had always been able to confide in a friend, he might yet have been saved," continued Thorfin; "the necessity of silence brought on his illness, and his death"

"And the woman ' the unhappy woman ?' hastily inquired Hinango, "how did she bear the news of his death ?"

"Who can answer the question ?" replied Dr Thorfin "The very secrecy which he unconsciously respected, even in his derangement, naturally concealed her sufferings Her nervous disorder appears, besides, to have been subdued by time, and, with a certain 'philosophy of life,' she finds her comfort in her social relations."

All were silent, and the doctor continued

"Who can venture to decide upon what she felt, what she endured ? Willingly would I always, in every instance, intercede for the unfortunate woman, and proclaim her innocent—innocent before God Would you condemn a fever patient who, in a paroxysm, escapes from his watchers, and stabs a sleeping person ? or would you accuse a somnambulist of suicide, who should leave her bed, ascend to the roof of the house, and there, frightened from some accidental cause, fall and break her neck ? We must distinguish effect from cause The cause of this murder was marriage without love, the crime had its foundation in the past, in physical surrender without love, whose consequences disturb the nervous system, and all the other crimes proceed from such marriage"

A long pause again ensued, which was interrupted by Captain Finngreen.

"In Old England," he observed, "marriage without love appears to have been à la mode, at least, in 'good old times,' so far as we can infer from old songs, which, in general, aptly indicate the customs of a country. I once, quite accidentally, bought an old book of plays, in London, a volume of Dryden's words, for which I only gave sixpence, and it contains many verses that are worth six guineas Just at the beginning of 'Marriage à la mode,' we find an admirable song in the mouth of a lady I believe I can repeat it"

He recited, in a harmonious tone:

"Why should a foolish marriage vow,
Which long ago was made,
Oblige us to each other now,
When passion is decayed ?

We loved, and we loved, as long as we could,
'Till our love was loved out in us both,
But our marriage is dead, when the pleasure is fled.
'Twas pleasure first made it an oath.

If I have pleasures for a friend,
And further love in store,
What wrong has he whose joys did end,
And who could give no more ?
'Tis a madness that he
Should be jealous of me,

Or that I should bar him of another,
For all we can gain
Is to give ourselves pain,
When neither can hinder the other.”

“Excellent!” cried Hinango, while all laughed. “The demoralization of marriage à la mode, or a union without love, is displayed in this song, in all its revolting nakedness; for, surely, a woman who could cherish such sentiments could not easily captivate any man's heart. Such a woman was either incapable of love, or has destroyed her inward life by a marriage à la mode. She belongs to the numerous first classes of women, already indicated above.”

“Whoever should write such a song at the present day,” observed Dr. Thorfin, “would certainly encounter the reproach of immorality, as if he would make a jest of the sacrament of marriage.”

“That is sufficiently made a jest of by marriage à la mode, in all countries of Christendom,” interrupted Fitz.

“And an unfortunate husband,” continued Captain Finngreen, “expresses himself just as significantly in respect to his marriage de convenance. In another piece, ‘The Conquest of Grenada,’ this poor husband sighs thus:

‘Marriage! thou curse of love and snare of life,
That first debased a mistress to a wife!
Love, like a scene, at distance should appear
But marriage views the gross daubd landscape near
Love's nauseous cure thou cloy'st whom thou shouldst please,
And, when thou cur'st, then thou art the disease
When hearts are loose, thy chain our bodies ties
Love couples friends, but marriage, enemies
If love, like mine, continues after thee,
'Tis soon made sour, and turn'd by jealousy,
No sign of love in jealous men remains,
But that which sick men have of life—their pains.’ ”

“I know the ‘glorious John Dryden,’ as the tailor poet, Claud Halcro, in Walter Scott's ‘Pirate,’ calls him,” remarked Hinango, “and consider him classical in English literature. He appears, besides, to have known and deeply felt the sufferings of unhappy love. His Almanzor, in the ‘Conquest of Grenada,’ is a sort of Don Carlos, as represented by Schiller. How admirably tender are the dialogues between Almanzor and the queen!”

“The manners of Old England, in those days, may have been as licentious as they still are in many countries,” rejoined Dr. Thorfin, but Dryden proves, as the representative of his epoch, that pure true love, even then, found an altar in men's hearts.”

“And he subscribes his testimony to the acknowledgement of woman's worth,” concluded Captain Finngreen, “while he declares,

‘Your sex and beauty are your privilege.’ ”

“True enough,” affirmed the air pump controller, “only the fair but too frequently abuse their ‘privilege,’ at the expense of man's heart, and if we could examine the madhouses and graves, it would become ascertained that fewer females have become insane, or have ended by suicide, from unfortunate sympathy, than males. Women are generally more strongly constituted than men, and can bear a good deal, as well morally as physically.”

Another long serious pause followed.

“Do you believe that Madame Closting knows the character of her husband?” asked Hinango at length.

“They gave her a true picture of him before she married him,” replied Thorfin. “She declared it all to be lies and calumny, an outburst of envy against him and her.”

“She was of course blind,” observed Fitz, “and even before marriage deaf, lately she has also become dumb, and is now an exemplary wife, who called her negro to turn me out of doors when I once mentioned, incidentally, that I had known her husband in Europe!”

“Would it not be the duty of such a woman to part from her husband,” remarked Hinango, “before sympathy for another should overpower her, and she, perhaps, should captivate some noble youth, or man, and kindle a flame in him which might destroy him, and lead him to suicide, or burden him with an existence more terrible than death?”

“I have, as yet, known no case in which a woman has parted from her husband on account of his bad character, from moral conviction,” replied the physician. “Church and state promote demoralization. The moral baseness of a man, according to my knowledge, does not serve as valid grounds for divorce, if certain points be not proved.”

“The viler the fellow, so much the less will the woman separate from him,” observed Hinango, “for she is demoralized by him.”

“A dreadful truth, which the reality around us here confirms,” sighed the doctor. “A lady like Madame Closting may involuntarily commit a murder to-day, or to-morrow, if she should come in contact with some unfortunate for whom she feels a sympathy, and who, for the moment, forgets Seume's warning. You know what I mean.”

Mr. Fitz recited, with peculiar seriousness:

“Flee from the woman, friend! within whose snare
Is, first, intoxication, then despair—
And in the whole creation no where dwells
A being that with every angel gift
In which the blinded victim may delight,
Will pay thee more terribly with despite.”

“But Seume speaks entirely of wives, not of maidens,” added he, with his customary humor.

“Wo to those!” cried Hinango, “who attain such experience as we must pre-suppose in Seume, before he was able to utter such words of warning. I, as a man, would sooner send a bullet into my head than——”

He was interrupted by some one knocking at the door, and Robert entered the room, with a loud friendly greeting.

“I come in all haste to see my travelling companions in their comfort, and to wish them good night,” said he to the three newly arrived strangers. “I have taken my sister home, and am to stay at the Hotel Faroux to-night, to have a meeting with some one early in the morning on business. It is, to be sure, a holiday, but not an English one!”

His travelling companions returned the youth's pressure of the hand, he hastily drank a cup of tea, and inquired if he could be in any way useful to them, as he was ready to devote a part of the following day to them. The friends returned their thanks with the same heartiness with which the offer had been made. Robert then stepped aside with Hinango, and revealed to him under what mask Dolores had been presented to his aunt, and begged him, in case any thing was said of her, to guide himself in such a manner as to maintain her incognito Hinango seemed surprised at the cleverness and zeal with which he had conducted in this affair, and assured him of his sincere approbation The youth, thereupon, took leave as hastily as he had come, and departed

"Is he engaged to ——— ?" inquired Captain Finngreen, when Mr Walker left the room

"To the young lady you mean who accompanied his sister on board at Buenos Ayres ?" interrupted Hinango hastily, with a stolen wink, in reference to the presence of Mr Fitz, towards whom he entertained not the slightest distrust, but whose levity he knew "I believe not, captain," added he, "Robert's heart appears as yet untouched by the electric ray of love '

"He is an excellent young man !" observed the captain, "that he is, so far as I know him, and endowed by nature and by fate with all that might make a woman happy who is worthy of him He behaved nobly and resolutely in rescuing Alvarez. I should hardly have expected it of him."

"Nor I either, but the 'merchant' has not yet choked the 'man' in him," added Hinango "He has deep feelings, and his position is dangerous, he will often have to suppress them on the exchange "

"No one has any business there with mind and feelings," said Mr Fitz

Captain Finngreen looked at his watch, remarked that it was late, and rose to return to his vessel Horatio and Alvarez had taken little part in the conversation in the Norse language, and being, besides, wearied and exhausted, had withdrawn to their rooms

Mr Fitz attended the captain to his shallop, and Dr Thorfin remained alone with Hinango

CHAPTER VII.

PLANS OF MARRIAGE.

HINANGO had already, on board the Nordtsjernan, communicated, in all brevity, to his friend, Dr. Thorfin, the circumstances of the South American lady, whose personal security, before all things, lay near his heart

"You know old Mr Thomson, then, as it appears, very well ?" inquired he, now that they were alone, "do you believe that he is a man who would protect her, in case a cunning plan should be formed for carrying her off to Buenos Ayres

"I know the old man, and have great confidence in him. He is a genuine Briton, in the noblest sense of the word; who possesses many of the good qualities of his nation, but therewith, also, the individual originality which we generally find among Britons, and which exactly characterizes them.— So far as I know old Mr. George, it does not appear improbable to me, that he may come to the resolution to offer his hand to Dolores ' to marry her !"

Hinango, to whom laughter was not very familiar, suddenly underwent the involuntary violent shaking of the diaphragm, which, according to the assertion of physicians, is so conducive to health, and is not so easily smothered, he sank upon a sofa, and yielded himself to the influence of an intimation, which was certainly originally British, insomuch as two extremes were to meet

"No ! you joke !" cried he at length, drying the drops of Momus from his cheeks, "I hardly think that he can entertain such an idea "

"Why not ? he has had four wives, and is now looking out for a fifth, and, so far as I know his taste, such a majestic figure as your fellow-voyager, with a tendency to corpulency, as he calls it, and which he likes, is, for him, an alluring object "

"But, Mr George would be no alluring object for Dolores, so far as I know her," said Hinango, laughing

"Of that I am just as well satisfied "

"And the fellow, the spy, of whom you told me, visits at Thomson's ?"

"He has worked himself in there, as into many other families, less, however, as it appears, to spy there, than to make his court to Mr Thomson's sister She is an old maid, who possesses some property, and hopes, at length, through the baron, to wear the ring "

"You believe, then, that he designs to offer himself !"

"So it seems to me, a speculation on his part, to betake himself to repose, somehow, or to travel about more comfortably, to keep house here and there, to receive foreigners at home, and so act the spy more conveniently We see such perambulating social circles in many cities, where the elements of fermentation exist, which the European powers think it important to control "

"Yes, indeed, similar posts have been proposed to both of us, in our travels, and under very brilliant conditions, too "

"To you, as well as to me," assented Thorfin "Literati and physicians appear to be very useful subjects to the secret police The title of baron, whether true or false, always has its value with the English women, as a qualification of respectability, although a German baron certainly does not stand very high in England Whoever, as a foreigner, makes acquaintance in an English family, and wishes to marry, will do better to call himself count, and in three weeks he will make a good match "

"What sort of person is Miss Thomson ? how will she deport herself to a young lady, such as I have described Dolores to you ?"

"As lead to gold, and as pebbles to a diamond She is one of those females of English manufacture who proceed as marriageable from the always uniformly moving machine of English finishing She is a brilliant production of the British system of education, according to which children are forbidden to cry, or to laugh, and are rapped on the knuckles when they show a lively interest in any thing, as that, of course, manifests excitability of feeling She appears to be a masterpiece of such culture, since there is evidently no trace of feeling left in her. One would believe that such beings have no souls, and in consequence, do not operate with the attraction upon the manly heart, and so remain single, their characters becoming every year more soured and embittered, until, at length, a candidate for matrimony feels himself attracted towards them by their fortune, (in case they possess one,) and so ' the antiquity' is taken into the bargain

"This is the class to which Miss Thomson belongs."

"A bad governess for Dolores And you are Mr Thomson's family physician?"

"I am his physician, but not hers; she uses her English domestic quack-pharmacopæia, and, in special cases, very naturally, an English physician"

"Well! you visit at Mr Thomson's country house?"

"To be sure! I am very intimate with Mr Thomson"

"We shall by that means, on our part, then, be able to guard Dolores, and keep up a communication with her"

"So long as the country house at Bota Fogo is not, like Paris, surrounded by citadels, and declared in a state of siege, I hope to have admittance there"

"Whilst the old negro Achilles remains in her service, she has personal defence, besides her pistols, in case a formal attempt should be made to carry her off, which I do not expect I rather fear that they will endeavor to remove her, and get her in their possession by stratagem, especially if she, according to her intention, continues her literary efforts here, arranges her poems for an edition, and finally issues them"

"That would, perhaps, not be advisable"

"My dear Thorfin, is it altogether advisable on her part, or mine, to put our heads at hazard, and renounce all claims on life, from—how shall I call that which impels us? from a self-conviction of our vocation? from an irresistible inward impulse, which drives us to intellectual efforts? Is it not the requisition of the strength within her, as in me, to strive on in eternal movement, induced by the attraction of the idea whose rays penetrate us?"

"I understand you, Ormur! and in these words, you have defined your position and hers"

"My position is a peculiar one—I know myself, I stand low before God, for he knows that I bear this earthly life as a burden—that I long for death"

"Even this horrible longing for death!" interrupted Thorfin. "Poor Ormur! you are weak Can you then attain to no side of life which will give you a hold upon earthly existence?"

"None, but the duty yet to live for the cause of the nations I often feel myself bowed down, however, and from day to day become more desolate within. When I again saw, to-day, this paradise of Guenabara, I cannot tell you how entirely different it appeared to me from before It seemed to me as if a veil hung between me and nature, that separated me from her, that made me foreign to her, as if the whole panorama around me here were a pictured image, not through its originality, as at the first view, two years ago, but through a certain indescribable something in myself that isolated me—separated me from the world—the social world, to which I do not belong, which has thrust me forth because my mind recognises an aim, in advance of the age, that stands higher than our time, because

22

I have become a man, and the world only requires machines"

"God, who has assigned you the path, will arm you, also, with strength to tread it, to pursue your aim Continue in the consciousness of your strength, preserve your faith in humanity and in God And now, good night I have the chacara on St Theresa arranged for you to-morrow Horatio, and Alvarez can likewise come to me to-morrow, at my house on da Gloria I did not find Vernon at home, he will bring the letters to you himself early in the morning"

The friends separated, and Hiningo stepped out upon the balcony, gazed upward at the southern cross, and sank into meditations, to which we will leave him for the present

CHAPTER VIII

MISS SUSAN

MISS SUSAN Thomson sat in a shady arbor on the garden terrace of the country house at Bota Fogo, which she inhabited with her brother. She was a "young lady" on the wrong side of forty, slender, and without the slightest tendency to corpulency, in a pearl coloured satin dress, *à la Victoria*, with flounce trimmings, *à la Melbourne*. Her countenance, though tolerably regularly formed, was without expression, an empty leaf, that, as the title page of her heart, said nothing at all. A moderately large light gray eye contained so little "fluid ray," that it hardly entered the eyes of a person upon whom she looked, when in conversation, notwithstanding which, however, Miss Susan saw as keenly at a distance as a pilot on the coast of Old England. She was born in Berkeley street, near Berkeley square, London, of course, she was of substantial respectability. From the first little socks, that full forty years before she had worn on her little feet, to the certainly somewhat larger stockings whose silken fabric was suitable to the larger footing on which she lived in Rio, she had never worn a single thread that was not of British manufacture She was reading in Campbell's "Pleasures of Hope," in a book which had never seemed to her so interesting and attracting, as since she had become acquainted with the Baron de Spandau whose attentions had awakened thoughts in her, that almost bordered upon sentiment Hearing footsteps in a sidewalk of the park which led from the house to the terrace, she thrust the "Pleasures of Hope" into her reticule, and took out, instead, the Almanac of British Missions, in the reading of which she appeared absorbed, as a negro brought her a billet, in which Mr. Thomson informed her of the arrival of the relatives from Buenos Ayres, with the request that she would send the dark blue carriage to the landing place.

"Is it possible!" cried she; "Miss Fanny and Mr Robert Walker, from Buenos Ayres! is it possible?" and she hastened to give the requisite orders to the butler, who was, besides, chief intendant of the equipages.

When the negro had withdrawn, and Miss Susan found herself once more alone, at home, she ventured to pursue her worldly reading with the more security, since she was now sure that her brother would not come so soon Hardly, however, had she read some lines, when she was again disturbed, and again took in her hand the Almanac of Missions, being threatened by the danger of having her sinful propensity for worldly reading remarked

A negro in livery, on horseback, brought a flower pot, with a rare Chinese plant, and a written compliment, from Monsieur le Baron de Spandau, in which he commended this flower, from the Celestial empire of legitimacy, to her especial care, significantly adding "They call this flower (which will gradually unfold itself) l'Espérance de Chine, or "l'Amour de l'Empire Celeste?"

Miss Susan's pale countenance was suffused by a maiden blush, as she read the billet, which was directed to George Thomson, Esq, at Bota Fogo, and was unsealed

She considered, for a long time, whether she should give a millreis to the servant of the amiable baron, or whether such a gift would not compromise the baron's livery Not from economy, or avarice, but out of pure discretion in respect to the compensation of the negro, she at length decided to hand him a patack in copper, which the mulack on horseback received with thanks, and departed on a gallop

The suddenly ensuing twilight at length interrupted Miss Susan's reading, she walked through the tropical shrubberies of the "English park," into the apartment, furnished in English style, and placed the worldly book, among the less interesting books of her brother, which principally treated of the art of fishing, a favorite study of the old widower. In expectation of the relatives who were coming, she commanded the stranger's room to be put in order, and the tea table set for four persons, contemplating, from time to time, the plant de l'Amour de l'Empire Celeste, which only showed a very small, hardly perceptible bud, and at length the blue carriage rattled before the high gate of the English country house.

The strangers entered the garden, and Miss Susan walked slowly towards them, for a hurried step would have indicated a certain excitement of feeling, which was contrary to all fashion, and, besides, unknown in the ice cellar of her heart.

"Good evening Aunt Susan! how are you? always well and hearty?" cried Robert to her from a distance Aunt Susan made no reply, but directed her British critical glance towards that majestic form of the American lady, who appeared on the arm of the old widower, attended by Achilles and his daughter Corinna The rich, black, splendid hair, 'à l'enfant,' of the young lady, was evidently not the less dark hair of Miss Fanny Walker.

"What the devil is this?" she muttered to herself, "can I have lost my senses?"

"How are you, Miss Susan?" cried Mr. Thomson also. "Thank you for sending the carriage I have the honor to present to you the Señora Isabella Campana—the betrothed of our nephew Robert, who has run away with her from Buenos Ayres. Señora Isabella will pass for our niece

until we have obtained the consent of her parents Mark that! and keep a close mouth. Do you understand me, Miss Susan? And now be properly friendly, and give your hand to our future relative!"

Señora Dolores courtesied with the elegant dignity which was peculiar to her nature, but Miss Susan by no means held out her hand to her "So!" was all that, after a long pause, her thin violet blue lips uttered. She stood before the exile of La Plata, like a statue cast out of sulphur, *lunar caustic, and gall*

It was not merely a passing moment, it was 'an event' in her dry, lean life of forty years—an event that, agitated her hardly living nerves, in a degree to which no event upon this planet had ever yet affected and agitated Miss Susan Thomson Nothing—nothing in the world interested her beside the baron, since he had admired her really handsome, though rather large teeth Nothing could make any impression upon her but a visit of the baron, and the incidental intelligence that any young lady of her acquaintance (whether some weeks, months, or years younger than herself) was betrothed, was to be married, or even had already passed the line of female destiny With a contemptuous glance, the feeble ray of which did not, it is true, stream forth more than three inches from the point of her nose, she gazed upon the handsome, stately youth, and then again upon the embarrassed betrothed, who raised her hand to meet the expected pressure of Aunt Susan's The hardly grown "green youth" seized in her stead the hand of his "bride," and shook it right heartily, in good English style, and said.

"Come in, Señora Isabella! uncle George will show you your rooms, we will then drink tea, and I will hurry back to the city, to my hotel"

The words "to the city, to my hotel," fell upon Miss Susan's ear like a verse from a psalm, and at least intimated the speedy departure of her insufferable nephew from La Plata, who, "hardly out of school," had carried off a young lady, and, as it appeared, even had the fixed intention to marry her! an idea which certainly was enough to make a young lady like Aunt Susan crazy, as no youth on earth had ever sought to put in execution such an idea towards her, notwithstanding she was already some months older than this strange person

Mr Thomson led the young lady to the door of a room that stood ready for her, besought indulgence for the ill humor of his sister, and hurried back to her "to read her a text" upon such inhospitality towards a strange lady, whom their genial nephew had carried off from Buenos Ayres to Rio, as dexterously as so many old or young gentlemen in England have escorted a bride to Gretna Green

"George!" cried Miss Susan to her brother, anticipating his lecture, and pointing with the dry thumb of her right hand to a path surrounded by thick shrubbery, towards which she directed her steps; "George! I have something to say to you"

Mr. George followed the indication of the thumb, and entered the lonely corner, in which his sister came up to him, with both hands resting on her waist, and, staring at him from head to foot, asked him. "Have you dined at the Hotel Faroux?"

"To be sure, with the Baron de Spandau and Dr. Thorfin," replied the old widower.

"Then you are intoxicated?"

"I might ask you, in return, whether you are crazy, but it would be unkind, and, therefore, I shall only think as I please."

"Notwithstanding that, I repeat the question, what does this mean? What is it? what must I call it? You bring a foreigner into the house, and introduce her as Robert's betrothed, whom he has carried off from Buenos Ayres—"

"Carried off with the connivance of his father, Mr John Walker, although he could not own it in Buenos Ayres."

"With Mr John's consent? Have I heard rightly? And she is a Spanish woman! a South American, and, also, a Catholic?"

"Probably! and has brought with her a fortune of about a million two hundred thousand pesos in solid paper—for she is of age, and the consent of her parents, which she expects, is a secondary concern."

"Then she has property? and it is at her disposal? and she is of age? Of age? Then she is not so very young, and, indeed, that may easily be seen. She is no longer a child. But a Catholic! and I must live under one roof with her!"

"That is not necessary," said Mr. Thomson, laughing. "You can move into the pavilion, over there, that has a separate roof."

"Nonsense! You even permit yourself to jest with my religion, degenerate as you are, with all your Catholic wives! Four! four women has this man led to the altar, and a person like me has not even——" She suppressed her righteous lamentation, and burst into bitter tears. "And that simpleton, that booby, Robert, already thinks of matrimony, and is, at the utmost, two and twenty years old, and brings a Catholic into the house, who is, to be sure, not so very young. But what is the particular need of her being married just now? Are they in such a hurry?" She dried her righteous tears, and inquired further: "And the person is to pass for Miss Fanny?"

"Yes!" replied Mr George, briefly and positively. "No one must know but that she is Miss Fanny Walker, and if you undertake to betray, by a look, that she is not, I will forbid the baron the house, and he shall never cross my threshold again! Do you know what's trump? Hearts are played—take the trick, or follow suit".

"Shocking!" sighed Miss Susan, directing her feeble glance towards the summit of the Corcovado, into the cloudless ether. "And he talks in card-playing language to spite me, in the bargain, for he knows that I can as little endure card playing, as musical instruments and Catholics."

"Then the Baron de Spandau ought never to come to the house again," said Mr George, briefly and pointedly.

"How so? Good heavens! how so?" inquired she, hastily.

"Why, because he is a Catholic."

"A Catholic! The Baron de Spandau a Catholic?"

"To be sure, Miss Susan; a Catholic, from the land of Goshen, or Posen, in Prussia, or somewhere else. But he is a Catholic; that I know assuredly."

Miss Susan stood like a well spiced plum pudding overflowed with Jamaica rum, blazing up, and the blood mounted with such violence to her head, that the veins in her temples threatened to burst. She would gladly have made an exception to the rule, but she feared it might be too conspicuous, and found it expedient to bring into the world another long, long "So!" and at length inquired. "And Robert—he is not, then, to stay with her—with this person—this foreigner?"

"Robert will stay somewhere else until we receive the consent from Buenos Ayres, which is a mere form," returned Mr George, briefly, and more drily than before.

"And the Baron will come to dinner on Sunday?" inquired the *young lady*.

"He comes every Sunday, even if he is not invited, but I will tell him to come to-morrow, for I have to go to the Hotel Faroux. And now, Miss Susan, be properly friendly, and sit down to the tea table with us, and speak two or three words to Miss Fanny. Do not call her Señora Isabella. Do you hear? She speaks as good English as we—with a Spanish accent, it is true; but we must say here, what indeed is the truth, that our sister, Mrs Walker, died early, and that Miss Fanny was educated in the Spanish language. Do you understand? Take heed! and be properly friendly."

The million of the young lady's disposable property, her being at least arrived at majority, and the baron's Catholicism, had suddenly given another direction to the old English brig, Miss Susan, she now steered, under an augmenting breeze of tolerance around the reefs of her brother's obstinacy, which she had already run foul of so often, and laid her course for the Cap d'Espérance de Chine, or Cap d'Amour de l'Empire Céleste, without, however, allowing it to be perceived whither she was sailing.

"I will come to tea," said the slender young lady in a pearl colored dress, à la Reine Victoria, with a somewhat milder tone. "Robert, is going into town again, to the Hotel Faroux, I will come directly—perhaps, he may meet the baron. You can send him word, by Robert, that on Sunday he——"

"Give yourself no uneasiness, about that! he will be sure to come! I'll engage for that. But I'll write him a line, now, right away, Robert, can take it with him."

The gleamings of a 'better' humor suddenly flitted over Miss Susan's countenance, even if it were still far remote from 'good' humor. Her brother had now tried the bridle bit upon her, with which he hoped, with skill, to manage her, in case she should take it in her head to turn even one step aside from the prescribed path of silence. By these means, he saw the incognito of "the young lady," with an undeniable tendency to corpulency," assured for the present; and, what was most important to him, he had, quite incidentally, through Robert's own contrivance, obtained an admirable pretext to get his handsome young nephew out of the house. The intimacy with his betrothed, who was even to pass for his sister, appeared to the old widower, if not dangerous, at least superfluous.

Mr. Robert awaited the family, in the spacious garden saloon, the walls of which were decorated with four oil paintings, the portraits of Mr.

Thomson's four corpulent wives, painted during their lives, by various artists, in entirely different styles. One thing was, however, uniform on all four of the portraits, a precise threefold notice of weight: first, at the period of marriage; second, the highest matrimonial development; and third, the weight of the corpse, set down in the right hand corner of each picture, in gold letters and figures.

"Is that Robert's negro?" inquired Miss Susan, in a mild voice, when she espied old Achilles, whom she had not seen before, from pure gall, though he was all the while close to Dolores.

"It is Miss Fanny's coachman," replied Mr. Thomson, briefly and seriously, as before, "and the negress is his daughter, Miss Fanny's chambermaid. They are free, not slaves," added he. "Order our people to treat them as Miss Fanny's attendants."

"A coachman—corresponding with her property—certainly very respectable—'carriage people' then,' thought Miss Susan, and went into the salon with her brother, just as Miss Fanny was led in by an opposite door.

Mr. Robert, in accordance with his double station of brother and bridegroom, hastened to meet his bride, or his sister, (whichever we may entitle her,) offered her his hand, and led her to her place at the tea table, which Mr. Thomson thought very wellbred and civil, but, notwithstanding, superfluous.

"Were you long at sea, Miss Fanny?" inquired Miss Susan, in a peculiarly mild voice, and with the most humane glance possible.

"Sixteen days from the English Bank at the mouth of La Plata," replied the niece, and the conversation proceeded in a tolerable family tone, until Robert had drank his tea in haste, and received the billet from his uncle, which the latter had, in equal haste, written to Monsieur le Baron de Spandau.

Robert now lingered for a moment by Miss Fanny, and whispered in her ear some tranquillizing and consoling words, which the widower found not only superfluous, but in the highest degree indiscreet, as he did not understand them, and the entire relation of the young man to the imposing beauty from La Plata, appeared much too intimate for him to find Bob's daily presence, at breakfast, dinner, and tea, even endurable.

Silently rejoicing at the plan of his nephew, which made his living out of the house requisite, he enjoined it once more upon him to make his visit early on the morrow to Sr Moreto's relative on da Gloria, stuck the billet in his pocket, and availed himself of that opportunity literally to take the young man by the collar and put him out of the room, where his presence had become in the highest degree irksome to the old widower.

Mr Thomson now did the honors to the young lady, as the brother-in-law of Mr Walker, who had so urgently recommended her to him, while Mr Robert rode back to the city, where we have already seen him at the Hotel du Nord.

─⌁⌁⌁⌁❀⌁⌁⌁⌁─

CHAPTER IX

THE STRANGERS IN THEIR HOTELS

HARDLY had Robert seated himself on the following morning at breakfast in the Hotel Faroux, when the servant of the corridor on which his apartment opened, brought him a card, inscribed, "Forro & Co." The representative of this firm was conducted to the private parlor of the young Briton, who soon stood in his presence.

Sr Forro was a figure of the middle size, elegantly dressed in the Brazilian business costume, in white linen. His countenance bore a strikingly calculating expression, which undeniably intimated that he was a man of business, and would even make a profit on his physiognomy, if a Lavater were to make him an inviting offer to purchase it, for it was not very valuable to himself, giving him not much credit with others.

Robert spoke to the representative of the house of Forro & Co, in a brief, businesslike manner, and announced that he had casually heard that a geologist had projected various plans and proposals for the establishment of a mining colony on the coast of Brazil. He desired to enter into connexion with the geological gentleman, as he, or rather his house, were inclined to found a similar undertaking, in case no other mercantile house, of any nation whatever, had positively entered into the intended business; in such a case, he must apologize for having troubled him, as he should then withdraw his proposition, and consider it as if it had not been made.

The decided business tone of the young man, and especially the name of the firm of Walker & Co, appeared to please the agent of the geologist, and he replied, with brevity:

"The enterprise, of which you have accidentally heard, is, like every business of the kind, strictly a secret until the expiration of a certain time. As Mr Closting's agents, we are in negotiation with a certain house, and expect a partner of the house from Europe, via Buenos Ayres. According to our last agreement, the provisionary company is bound to sign the contract within four-and-twenty hours after the arrival of the partner in Rio, or, if not, it is at our option to proceed, or not, in the enterprise. According to the *Jornal do Commercio*, the expected partner arrived here last evening, and we require the decision to-day, before sundown. If no one applies, we are under no further obligation towards this house, and shall not be disinclined to open the whole project to you."

"In case no one should announce himself to you," replied Mr. Walker, "I shall expect you directly after sundown, this evening, at the bureau of our house, in Rua Direita."

"Very well!" assented Senhor Forro. "In that case, I will not keep you waiting, and, that you may not wait for me, I will send you word in case I shall not come, and it will remain as strictly a secret that I have had the honor to make you this visit, as the business has been until now."

"I am entirely agreed," replied the young merchant, and Mr Forro took a hasty leave, and left the parlor and the Hotel Faroux.

In the narrow billiard room of a German public house, in the Rua do Cano, (which certainly contained less stories, and corridors, and parlors, and chambers, than the Hotel Pharoux,) at this same time, sat a stranger, at a small, moderate, and neatly covered table.

It was his princely highness, Tobo Pontam, a Botocudo prince, without crown or sceptre, dressed in white linen. He bore a broad, triangular countenance, with long and thick raven hair, small Kalmuck eyes, a broad flat nose, yellowish brown complexion, thick lips, with a sort of bottle cork fastened in the under one, and similar ornaments displayed in his ears.

Tobo Pontam drank his national Brazilian drink of coffee, and opposite to him sat Dr Merbold, similarly employed, and near him a cigar box full of holes, containing the double specimen of the Simplex Merboldensis.

"You are, then, an Enger-eck-moung,"* said the savant, looking as intently upon his breakfast companion as he ever cared to look at any thing that was not a beetle, "an Engereckmoung! I am very happy to make your acquaintance, that is, here in the Rua do Cano—for at your home, there on the Rio Doce, your acquaintance might be somewhat unpleasant."

The honest Engereckmoung, who understood so much Portuguese as his education as a prince, in contact with half savage European princes, permitted, comprehended, at least, the words Rio Doce, and asked the 'Senhor Branco' if he had been there, among his tribe, on the Rio Doce.

"Have I been there?" said the little beetle-man, smiling, 'I should think so, Senhor Engereckmoung. I was a prisoner there, a prisoner, for two months, among your noble race. I lost myself there, one day, in the primeval forest, when I was hunting beetles upon the Rio Doce, and I could write a whole book upon the scientific aberration. Enough! I found, at length, amongst apes and parrots, a couple of human beings—perhaps a couple of the people of your tribe."

"Of your subjects, you should say, doctor," interrupted a waiter, in German, "that is a prince—he is here in Rio, in audience with the prince, and to acquire a notion of civilization."

"Hey! the devil! a prince! then a highness! a serene highness! I wonder whether he has as liberal views as our crown prince of Prussia? Do you know whether he is constitutional, or despotic? I assure you, that the prince by whom I was taken prisoner was very constitutional—not at all despotic. I have already told you, that my Botocudo prince kept me with him in the forest, as a prisoner of state—but he helped me to look for beetles, and laughed at me, for calling that my business! His naked bodyguard had taken away all that I carried about me, but all was carefully preserved—my whole baggage, and even my money. I had sixty-eight millreis with me, when they took me, every evening he took one millreis for board and lodging, as he gave me to understand. Well! the board was very simple, and the lodging was certainly the largest that a state prisoner ever inhabited—it was the wide primeval

forest! When I had dwelt sixty-three days with him, without a dwelling, and sat at his table, where there was no table at all, he at length gave me back my five millreis, for travelling expenses, and showed me the way out of the forest, to the banks of the river, and made me a present of a bow and arrows, as a keepsake, and of a handful of beetles, among which there was, unfortunately, no undiscovered species.'

His highness from Rio Doce had, during the relation, retired to his room. A negro announced the arrival of a traveller, who inquired for Dr Merbold.

"I know, already, who that may be! It is my travelling companion, the Englishman from Buenos Ayres, what was his name——?"

"He can have lodgings here!" cried the waiter, following on the lowest step of which, stood Mr Habakkuk Daily, who called himself Mr James John Stone. He had safely reached Brazilian ground, from the smuggling smack, on the shore of a bay outside the Sugar Loaf, and, with the sacrifice of a few sovereigns, (over the stipulated sum,) had been well served by his companions, in all that related to his incognito and his two heavy trunks, which were now borne near him, upon the woolly heads of two gigantic Loango negroes, who were just in the act of relieving themselves of the enormous burdens. By what means he had, since midnight, arrived in the city from the shore, the mules who had carried him and his trunks, and perhaps their drivers, knew better than he.

Enough, that Mr Stone had arrived at the German tavern, in the Rua do Cano, which Dr Merbold had serviceably informed him of, and now entered an unpretending department, where he safely bestowed his trunks for the present.

He learned, to his great dissatisfaction, that Mr Closting, the naturalist, was in the interior of the country, and was not expected back in some months, which certainly made a small "stroke through his reckoning," though it by no means annulled it.

Mr John James, or James John Stone, as he variously styled himself, (since the name was yet new to him,) made his toilet like a clerk who might pass for a "gentleman," took breakfast by himself, and then went to the neighboring Rua Direita, to announce his arrival at the bureau of his house, Walker & Co.

The three travelling companions from the river la Plata, who had gone to the Hotel du Nord, sat likewise at the aromatic coffee, which, drank at the "fountain head," in Brazil, appears like an entirely different beverage from what it is in Europe, since the beans partly lose their peculiar tropical flavor by the transportation across the ocean.

Gango, a negro, went out and in, and was particularly attentive to every call of Hinango, since he had already become acquainted with him two years before. The Scandinavian caused the two South Americans to observe the Ethiopian, by inquiring how he had been since he saw him last.

Gango thanked him, and replied that he had been very well.

* The proper name of the Botocudoes, the latter is a nickname which the Portuguese have bestowed upon them, in reference to the piece of wood on the under lip

"And do you still copy the Jornal do Commercio?" inquired Hinango, laughing, and related to his companions what he meant by the question:

"When I lived here two years ago, I came home very late one night, and found Gango busied in copying, as precisely as possible, with a pen and ink, the print of the Jornal do Commercio, to exercise himself in writing, as he did not appear to know that other letters existed for writing I assure you he had nearly attained to the perfection of caligraphy!"

The negro was embarrassed, and observed that he had practised long enough to be able to copy the letters properly.

"What do you say to this desire for cultivation, which you meet with here amongst the Brazilian negroes? I will take you to-day to a poor black tailor, who, without a teacher, has learned French by means of a grammar and dictionary, and now reads French authors in his leisure hours! Does not such a negro shame many of the whites of Europe, who can hardly read and write their mother tongue, and never take a book in their hands besides a cash book?"

"There goes an equipage with a white coachman and white footman," remarked Horatio, who had stepped out upon the balcony, "and a negro is sitting inside, elegantly dressed, with a young negress, like a dame à la mode!"

"That will not surprise you," replied Ormur, "when you become better acquainted with Rio, you will here find negresses and mulatto women at the balls of the elegant world The most celebrated minister of state under king John was a negro The capacity for cultivation, and the intellectual powers of the negro, never appeared strange to me; but one thing surprises me the intolerance and prejudice with which the whites of so called Christian nations treat the colored people; thrust them out as outlaws, while the Christian religion inculcates the principles of love and equality, and permits no distinction of person nor of color"

"The Protestants appear more intolerant in this respect than the Catholics,' observed Alvarez.

"The oppression of intolerance will corrupt and demoralize any people, as history shows," added Hinango "Tolerance and humanity will elevate any people, and any class. Brazil's better future is founded upon the tolerance which a man finds here, let him be of what religion or of what color he may!"

The negro Gango interrupted the conversation, with the announcement that Mr Vernon was there, and wished to speak to Mr. Hinango.

"I will come directly, show him to my room," replied Ormur, and then said hurriedly to his two companions

"Dr Thorfin has arranged an abode for you both in the house where he lives You, Sr. Alvarez, will for the present remain his guest, until you receive an answer from Bahia respecting the fate of your sister; you had better write to-day, at once, friend Robert will take care of your letter" He allowed the unhappy fugitive no time to express his grateful feelings, but left the room, and hurried to the apartment where Mr. Vernon was waiting for him.

CHAPTER X

HINANGO'S CONFESSION

MR VERNON, partner of a European house in Rio, greeted the ex-naval officer, Ormur Olafur Hinango, with measured civility, and handed him the open envelope which Dr Thorfin had already mentioned

"I thank you for your kindness," began Hinango "I know, already, the circumstances under which you have received this packet of letters for me, and regret that my friends in Europe have compromised me with you."

"And, also, me and our house," remarked Mr. Vernon

"Until now, the seal of a letter in England, and under British post regulations, has been an inviolable sanctuary—at least, it has passed for such, and if my friends, relying upon this institution, have availed themselves of the kind permission on your part, to send me letters under your address, I beg, in their name, for your indulgence, for forgiveness from yourself and partners, and take upon myself all the consequences of this affair No one can, or will, ever call you to account for an indiscretion, or whatever you may call it, committed by men in London, who are entire strangers to you"

"I by no means came, Mr Hinango, to reproach you with what has occurred I should not have said a word to you about it, if Dr Thorfin had not anticipated me I come to you as a friend, to a man who has been highly recommended and accredited to us by our business friends in Europe What a future you are rushing upon, Ormur! What a path you are pursuing! Where will your efforts lead you? To the fortress Do-Vilganhon, to the patriots of Rio Grande, and at length, to the wretchedness of a joyless existence"

"I understand you, friend Vernon," returned Hinango, slowly and seriously "I thank you for your warm interest As regards my path, it proceeds (like the aims and dealings of every man) from within, as the unconditional consequence of my convictions, of my perceptions, of my self-consciousness as a man You are now aware of my position, condemn me as a man of business, explain to me that I evidently act against my own interest, that I renounce my claims to earthly happiness and peace, to domestic life, and the enjoyment of terrestrial felicity, but do not break the staff over me as a man, for you can consider me from no other point of view Judge, with a clear perception, the 'man' in me"

"Whom I honor, even although I am not able to comprehend you," answered Vernon "I am aware of your former position in the Russian service, and know that you might now be commander of a frigate, if you had continued there. I know that you have sacrificed yourself for the cause of the Poles, and that you are sacrificing yourself now for the cause of Italy and South America, but what will be your fate? Do you really hope, or believe, that you will outlive the crisis of the political fermentation of our epoch? Do you expect to conquer before your death? to see the result of your efforts and endeavors realized?"

"No!" answered Ormur, in a decided tone.

"In the lonely nights, in the gloomy solitude of subterranean dungeons, I have surveyed the history of the nations, so far as it is known to us through their annals I, as a man, have ascertained my position towards mankind The development of the nations from slavery to the open struggle for freedom, to the confirmation of their nationality, was never the work of a short human life The idea, however, of freedom, of progress, of ennoblement, has been transmitted from one epoch to another, by individual men, who felt this vocation within them With their self-consciousness, the strength was, also, increased in them, to tread their path, to bear their lot, even to the grave at the foot of the scaffold Without a prospect of the realization of the idea, whose ray penetrated them, their death was a personal resignation, without claims to the acknowledgements of their contemporaries"

"I comprehend you, and your resignation shocks me Do you know that men, from the very countries for which you sacrifice yourself, despise you? So called liberals, even exiles, who have once been drawn, against their wills, into the whirlpool of the revolutionary excitement of their nation—exiles who do not know for what they contended, and now regret their 'youthful indiscretion'—despise you, and would laugh at you, if, in your banishment, you sunk into poverty and misery"

"I know that, I know that there are men who think that I am indebted to their nation, because I have written in their dead language, others, who boast that they have afforded me the opportunity to share the fame of having contended, according to their views of entering into a speculation, in furtherance of their cause, which, alas! like so many other enterprises, has miscarried" But, are such individual men, the 'nation,' for which I contended? How little does the scorn and contempt of individuals trouble me, if I, knowing myself, have a clear conscience? 'Each judges of another by himself'—this is an incontrovertible truth in the judgement of men Whoever, is incapable of making any sacrifice for the cause of mankind—whoever always acts with calculation to his own selfish interests, will not understand me, cannot judge me correctly—he only sees himself in me"

"And you cannot, and will not, turn aside from your path? betake yourself to repose somewhere? renounce all politics? seek for domestic happiness, and live in peace?"

"What do we understand by Politics, Mr Vernon? Is the cause of South America foreign to the cause of Europe? Is the principle of freedom, which is struggling in Monte Video and Rio Grande, different from the principle for which hundreds in Italy and Poland ended their lives in solitary dungeons? Can I, as a man, contemplate the cause of South America with indifference, without contradicting myself, when I look back upon Europe? You ask, it I will not seek-repose somewhere, and enjoy domestic happiness? Do you believe, that the intellectual force in me, as a force, will ever repose, which can only be 'force' in movement, and which impels me, because it is a part of my existence? Will you command this pulse to stop? Well, then death ensues! and the cessation of my spiritual motions would be, moral death! Do you understand me now?"

"Ever more and more; but I also pity you; you strive for a phantom!"

"Phantom!" exclaimed Hinango, suddenly turning pale, and staring at a point beside him, as if he beheld something He then recovered himself, just as quickly and proceeded, my heart could be broken, the peace of my soul could be destroyed. a "phantom" (in an entirely different sense from that in which you mean it, friend Vernon,) can hurl me into the grave, a convulsion can end my life, but not my faith in humanity,

"Humanity!" repeated Mr Vernon "You are in error, there is no humanity! What do you call humanity? the mass of the people, in which each individual takes care of his personal interest, and troubles himself but little about the fate of his neighbor? Observe the bustle here in the Rua Direita, the throng in and before the exchange, do you call that humanity? Seek me out, from among them, one who would not, this day, sell your whole so called humanity to the devil for a per centage, if he could make such a bargain?"

"What have a multitude of brokers and usurers to do with humanity? Does the exchange represent humanity? There are, to be sure, nations who have no thought for any thing but money, but I will not, on that account, give up all mankind," replied Hinango

"If you give a people their freedom," returned Vernon "they will only use it to make money"

"You would say, they would sink into materialism!" interrupted Hinango, "and make for themselves an idol, such as the Jewish nation set up, when Moses freed them from the yoke of Pharaoh They worshipped the golden calf!"

"Very true! and confirmed by examples in the present time"

"But Moses perceived this abyss of ruin, and gave laws to his people He established the future of his people upon religion, nationality, and love of country And on this basis alone, will the welfare of mankind bloom and flourish! on no other! none! All other means of deliverance will be eternally fruitless! But the representation, the government of a nation, must set up a higher aim than the miserable one of making money in the service of the golden calf! Intellectual and moral development through science and art, and self-sacrifice from love of country, are higher aims than to make money for money's sake The government of a nation, that disowns the higher aims of humanity, is unworthy of the freedom in the element of which it supports an existence The highest power, is the human mind! You may see me imprisoned, in chains, and in a capote, (as I have already worn them——) but you will never see doubt in humanity gain the ascendancy over me, for I believe in God! and know myself as a man

"Mr Fitz told me," continued he, after a pause, there was a small schooner brig lying here, suitable for me, but under what flag, I forgot to ask him I believe she is called the Vanda or Vesta Have you heard of her?"

"And you will really go to sea again? probably towards Rio Grande?"

"We will say towards Africa again In general, Mr Vernon, I beg you, from henceforth, to speak of me as a negro trader, for the people on the exchange will comprehend that sooner I am looking for a vessel here, well, tell them that I purchase it, as every other vessel here is purchased, for the slave trade."

"That will be the best way In case any one belonging to government makes allusion to your position, in consequence of the opened letters, I will give such explanations that even these shall serve me to disguise your speculation, as that of a negro trader, as captain of a slave ship

"Admirable! so be it! At least, many will more readily believe that I am speculating as a negro trader, than that, as a man, I sacrifice myself for a ' phantom ' "

"I will inquire about the Vesta, or whatever the vessel is called," said Mr Vernon, and can, from this time, under the mask of serving you in your negro speculation, be at your call unmolested, in case you wish to purchase this or another vessel "

The friends conversed for awhile, on indifferent subjects, and then separated, Mr Vernon to pass the holiday somewhere in the country, while Hinango hastened to read his newly received letters and documents

------·❊·------

CHAPTER XI.

SENHORA GRACIA

THE young lady, whom we observed on that eventful moonlight night, reading the "Pyschology of Love," in her pavilion, sat, on the morning in which the above conversation took place at the Hotel du Nord, on her divan, with open windows and doors, at the Gloria

The fresh, cooling seabreeze played around and kissed her charming neck, while it blew single locks of her equally charming, rich, dark hair, off into the room, like streamers of a line of battle ship, and then letting them fall, it took up the neighboring locks, to play with them in the same manner

The innocent, but enviable seabreeze!

The lady was dressed in a full white robe, with Grecian sleeves, which only in part covered the shoulders, and was girt at the back, while the front remained loosely enveloping the ideal form of youthful beauty

She was sitting, occupied with a very prosaic employment. by a basket of freshly washed little stockings, part her own, part for the little girl whom we left in undisturbed slumber the other night, and who was now walking about the garden under the care of the negress Maria

Senhora Gracia,* for so the youthful mother called herself, was busied mending stockings This pastime of domestic wives on the European continent has, as it appears, a peculiar charm, since it affords the thoughts a wide latitude, and symbolically represents the social destiny of woman, "to fill up a gap here and there "

Although a negress, according to our views, could have accomplished the business just as handily, it appears, notwithstanding, to belong

* The Spanish Gracia, instead of the Portuguese Graça.

to the virtues of a domestic wife, to attend herself to the rents which must evidently exist in consequence of a wearing contact with the earth, so far as the feet touch the earth in stockings The employment, however, was by no means Brazilian, since a Brazilian lady hardly puts on a pair of shoes a second time, to say nothing of having her stockings mended, or mending them herself, if they should need it The lives of women in Brazil, resemble the lives of the Turkish ladies in their harems, only with the difference, that the various wives of a man in Brazil do not know each other, and are shut up separately, but, on the other hand, they pass the time of loneliness in the favorite ' costume du métier,' that is, in a light negligée, and mostly, even without stockings

The so called destiny of woman, as the property of her husband, for which neither intellect nor heart are called into requisition, makes this mode of life extremely "practical "

The existence of women sinks to an animal vegetation, in which many find their "domestic happiness," and distinguish themselves, as "exemplary wives, by mending their husbands stockings

Horses' hoofs clattered upon the rocky path up the hill, and stopped at the gate of the chacara "That must be the Sr Inglés!" said Sra Gracia, half aloud, to the negress Anna, who was dusting the furniture in the room, and a heaviness came over the heart of the young lady which she did not know how to account for

The negress Maria, who was in the garden with the child, had already opened the gate, which afforded an insight, through the open door of the pavilion, to the window under which Sra Gracia sat on the divan The pavilion, shaded by mangoes, jacarandas, and gigantic bananas, with tropical flowers of strange form blooming around, enclosed, like a magic frame, the living picture——in the back ground, the bay, with its colossal rocks

"Is the Señora at home ?" inquired the young gentlemen, for it was Mr Robert Walker, who had just dismounted from the saddle and given his horse to the care of a negro who attended him

A significant movement of the negress towards the female in the middle ground, already informed him of the answer by anticipation, and Mr Robert involuntarily drew near the pavilion The lady had left her seat, and appeared at the door. Both seemed to observe each other with a single comprehensive glance, and in consequence of some inward emotion, inexplicable to themselves, appeared to have lost, for the moment, the usual conventional unconstraint

The young lady beheld a youth of some twenty years, whose form was as symmetrically noble as his deportment was imposing A fine profile, with an expression of seriousness and dignity about the well formed lips, harmonized with the deep blue, richly radiant eye, more striking in contrast with the black hair and eyelashes The glances of both encountered each other!

Why did the youth lose, at the moment, that ease and self-possession which at all other times made a part of his nature, and was so peculiar to him ? Was it a movement of the sentiment in the inward depths of that female heart, (which like the magnetic fluid operating like a ray) involuntarily flowing out of her soul, and mysteriously penetrating into the depths of his nature? Who can answer this question? It is even doubtful whether she herself ever arrived at a clear understanding of it

To love at first sight, as when a woman sees a man, or a man a woman, and immediately "falls in love," is one of those absurdities in the usual modes of speech, which contradict all pschyological probabilities and the nature of the human heart A person may, at first sight, make an inexplicable and indescribable impression upon another, may awaken a sentiment or an emotion that is not to be expressed in words, which may afterwards ripen into love, but to call this momentary emotion love, would be ridiculous

There are moments in the excited inward life, in which it seems to us as if we find ourselves, for the second time, in the place that surrounds us, as if we had, at some previous time, seen the landscape which is about us, while we recognise the impossibility that such could have been the case It seems to us, as if we had already seen this or that person with whom we come in contact, somewhere before, that we had heard the voice at some former time, whose tones we now hear, and, nevertheless, no such meeting has ever before taken place on earth It seems to us, upon encountering the glance of an eye, as if it penetrated into the innermost depths of our hearts, as if it read the hieroglyphics of our souls Both Robert and the lady found themselves there in such a moment, without being clearly conscious of the sentiments which we have just mentioned

At length Robert felt that it would only be proper to speak to the lady He uttered in a broken manner, a compliment from Sr Moreto and from his uncle, with the surmise that the former had probably intimated to her the design of his visit

"Sr Moreto sent me word, last evening, that you—that a—that a relative of Sr Thomson—a young Englishman——please to come in," said the young lady interrupting herself, "please to be seated Anna, bring a chair for the gentleman—perhaps the draught of wind is disagreeable to you" While she uttered these fragments of conversation with an exceedingly gentle voice, and a charming embarrassment, the slender British youth had entered the apartment, and now replied, with somewhat more presence of mind

"On the contrary, Señora, I thank you I like the draught of air here in this room" He then appeared suddenly to recollect, that he might have expressed himself better, and remained politely standing, until the Señora had placed herself upon her divan

"Pray, sit down—wait a moment," said she, without knowing why or wherefore she wished that the young Briton would wait, and still less how she came upon the idea of uttering the request

Robert took a seat, and his eye fell upon the piano

"You are musical, I presume?" said he, for the sake of asking a question

"I am a great lover of music, and occasionally practice on the piano, whether I am musical—that is, whether I possess musical talent, I doubt——"

"This very reply leads me to suspect that you possess peculiar talent, for whoever in any department of art has no talent, generally considers himself very talented"

"I have not, for some years, had much time and leisure to occupy myself with music When one is married, and obliged to attend to one's children, there remains little time to indulge the inclination for music"

"I see there the dearest little girl," interrupted Robert, "probably your sister?"

"It is my daughter!" replied the lady, with a self-complacent smile

"Impossible!" exclaimed the youth, while he observed the little one, "It cannot be your daughter"

"How so, sir? Why not?" said the mother smiling

"Because—because—because you are yet a child yourself," replied he very hastily, after he got past the "because"

The young lady blushed, and could not again restrain a smile "Pardon me, sir," said she, with an expression of naïve unconstraint on her beautiful Brazilian lips, "pardon me, I have been married four years, and had three children, two alas! are no more"

Robert was serious, almost vexed, for it appeared to offend him, that the lady should take him for a simpleton To explain to ourselves the cause of this vexation, in the presence of such an amiable young mother, we must mention, beforehand, that Senhora Gracia was married in her thirteenth year, and had become the mother of three children in the first three years Robert Walker did not believe this truth, after the lady had repeatedly assured him of it, and we should hardly have believed it ourselves, since the peculiarly maidenly timid nature of the lady who sat there on the divan, and maintained this "absurd" assertion, plainly contradicted it

The expression, "have had three children," not only peculiarly offended the youth, but it evidently embarrassed him, he had outgrown the shoes in which he stepped—when he was told that the "stork brought children," or that they were "taken out of the well"

The "young girl of seventeen years," at the utmost, who took the liberty to assure him repeatedly that she was married, and had already had three children, appeared evidently to desire to jest with him, he resolved, therefore, to break off from the ticklish subject, and made the inquiry whether the pavilion, which had been spoken of by Senhor Moreto and Mr Thomson, was to let

"The pavilion?" said the young lady, in greater embarrassment than ever, "the pavilion ——to let?——O yes!——I believe not——I ——have certainly expressed a wish——pardon me, I will——" With this obscure fragmentary reply, she had arisen, and laid her little hands upon a pier table, on which stood two vases of artificial flowers, under glass shades, but nothing else that she could grasp at "I will show you the pavilion," added she at length, with extraordinary quickness, and without any farther remark, she ran past the young Briton into the garden

"What a wonderful prospect!" sighed Robert, casting a glance around him, and looking upon the bay, which was alive with vessels and small boats, and was spread out before him, enclosed by the azure mountains

23

"Does it please you here?" inquired the little matron, in a tone that i voluntarily expressed the earnest wish, that the young man might be pleased there, and she just as involuntarily felt, that her tone had betrayed something which guileless and pure is it might be, she would rather not have betrayed, as she herself did not even know what it was. But she became suddenly extremely well pleased, when the youth, surprised by the situation and prospect of the garden, made that exclamation

Was it the generous feeling of joy in her so heavily oppressed heart, which followed the discovery that a being, endowed with sensibility, enjoyed with her this prospect, the charm of this delightful scenery? She had neither time, nor desire, to examine long the cause of this childish joy. It pleased her that the prospect suited the youth so well—that was enough.

Anna now brought the key to the pavilion in question, that stood on a similar terrace, about twenty steps distant from the other. She opened the door, and then the window the prospect was the same that the youth had just found so charming, only more unrestricted, because the pavilion in which they now were, did not occupy a portion of the landscape.

"Wonderful! incomparable!" sighed Robert, who stretched his eyes over the garden, and groups of trees on the slopes of the hills, to where a great part of the suburb of da Gloria lay at his feet, and far and still farther was extended the indescribable landscape composition of nature. The young lady stood near him at a window, and being larger than she, he looked sideways, down upon the nearest object in the foreground. It was her waving hair, floating around her neck.

"Ah! it is so beautiful here!" he again sighed, in all the purity of his youthful heart.

The young lady was silent, but her silence was expressive.

"It depends then on your consent, Senhora," began Robert, after a long, long pause, during which he admired the wonderful prospect—"it depends on your consent, whether I am to enjoy the honor and happiness of inhabiting this pavilion"

"On my consent?" whispered the lady, almost inaudibly, though she could not explain, even to herself, why she had not spoken aloud

"I must say, frankly and decidedly, what—— what stipulation I am compelled to make, Senhor," said she, louder, and very hastily.

"I am ready, Senhora, to accept your stipulations, and will strive to fulfil them punctually"

She stepped back into the apartment, and pointed to a divan, while she took a seat herself

"Sit down, Senhor!" said she, with a tone of decision that appeared distant in comparison to the former tone of her voice, although not less musical. "I live here alone, Senhor, alone! with my child, and two negresses as attendants. My husband is absent, I expect him in two months, if not sooner. I may, perhaps, be able to disclose to you, hereafter, the circumstances that have induced me to shut myself up here Enough! I am here in danger—but in what respect, I cannot explain to you to-day. I wished for a 'man' in my neighborhood, as the occupant of this pavilion, a man to whom I could confide myself—to whom I could entrust my life. You

are as strange to me as any man on earth; but my uncle knows your uncle—both are honorable men. You are the nephew of Senhor Thomson, whom I know myself. Notwithstanding you are strange to me, I feel unbounded confidence in you." Her lip trembled, and her eye appeared dim. "Will you be my protector? I am in danger!" she repeated, in a tone of melancholy and subdued sorrow.

The expression of the lovely countenance, that with nearly every word of this declaration conveyed the impression of a different sentiment, seized as powerfully upon the youth, as the confidence, with which the lady honored him, aroused his manly pride.

Without allowing him time to answer, (which would, besides, have been extremely difficult for him,) she continued. "If you come here, let it remain an impenetrable mystery who I am—what my name is—let it be a secret, as well to you as to the world, until I myself discover it to you. No person, except one friend, whom you probably possess, must visit you. No one, and if he should accidentally know me, he must neither tell you who I am, nor any one else. Should he disturb my incognito, I will immediately leave my pavilion. You are musical, I presume?"

"Why do you presume that, Senhora?" inquired Robert, with all the naïveté that was, at times, at his command

"I have guessed it"

"I confess that I am passionately fond of playing on the piano, and should order an instrument here at once"

"That is what I wished to speak about," interrupted the lady. "Ask Senhor Moreto to send your instrument here, and it must come in while I am invisible—while I shut myself up in my house. And now, yet one more stipulation. I will point out to you a single melody, which you must not play—only one. Besides that, I shall be gratified to hear you play what you like. But one melody you must not play, which you, perhaps, might casually hit upon, and thereby increase my danger. It is a well known elegical composition, called The Last Accords of Weber."

"I will most punctually comply with these conditions. You have honored me with your confidence—I shall know how to prize it, and hope to show myself worthy of it." He uttered the last words with a self-consciousness of his pure heart, that by no means escaped the young lady

"My confidence assures you that I am convinced of this beforehand," replied she, with an expression of oppressed womanhood, which beautifies every noble woman, and imparts the glow of loveliness to even less beautiful forms. A thought appeared suddenly to strike her, she looked before her, without, in reality, seeing any thing—then laid the forefinger of her right hand on her rosy under lip, and said "You are the nephew of Mr. Thomson, of Bota Fogo, my physician, Dr. Thorun, a European, is your uncle's physician. How will it be possible to maintain my incognito, if he learns where you live?"

"Dr. Thorun!" replied Robert, "I have seen him already! one of his friends came from Buenos Ayres with me—a certain Mr. Hinango!"

"Hinango!" cried the young lady, and her countenance lost its color, "Hinango the privateer, the Russian naval officer?"

"The same !" replied Robert, evidently surprised by the inward emotion which this name excited in her. "Perhaps you know this man ? forgive the inquiry."

"I—I know—I know this man by sight—as a countryman of my husband's—I have, however, never spoken a syllable to him—never !"

It was now the youth's turn to become pale. He shuddered inwardly, he pressed his riding-whip with both hands, as if he wished to break it, a sudden connexion of ideas reminded him of a warning of Hinango in respect to 'Madame Closting.' His pulse seemed to stop, for there was something inexplicable in the alarm of the young lady, and in the connexion of ideas.

"I have never spoken to him—never !" continued the latter, with her eyes fixed on the ground, " I have merely seen him."

"Do you suppose that he knows your present abode, and that by this means——"

"No !" returned she hastily, "he certainly does not know where I am now, it would not even interest him."

"Hinango would be the very friend, whom I would have wished to invite—I will not do it."

"Why not ?" inquired the lady, with evident embarrassment. "I will speak to Dr. Thorfin, I am firmly convinced that neither of them would ever say who I am, if I asked them not to, for both are honorable men. I beg you, also, not to inform either Dr. Thorfin, or the privateer, where you live, until I have spoke to the doctor. You understand me."

"Perfectly ! I thank you for your confidence,' said Robert, with an oppressed heart, and held out his right hand in honest English style to the Brazilian lady, who seized it and convulsively pressed it. Suddenly blushing, for fear of betraying her embarrassment to the youth, she sought for words, and said

"Farewell ! inhabit this house, if it suits you, consider my request, which I make a condition, and gratify me by your visits—as often as you are willing—to afford a sufferer the consolation of your presence. Adieu !"

She hastily withdrew, and hurried into her pavilion.

Robert stood for a moment, as if paralysed, and then walked through the garden to the gate, that was bolted on the inside. Old Anna opened it, and he mounted his horse, and rode thoughtfully back to the city.

Madame Closting had hardly reached the divan in her pavilion, when, without being able to declare the cause even before God, she was seized with an inward convulsion, burst into bitter, scalding tears, and sobbed aloud, as old Anna related and affirmed years afterwards.

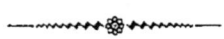

CHAPTER XII

THE SPIRIT OF " YOUNG EUROPE "

Dr. Thorfin entered Hinango's apartment, to invite him and his companions to take a walk. He found his friend with the unfolded letters near him, and with tears in his eyes

" Konarski has been arrested, and is under

Russian torture," sighed Hinango, and handed a letter to the doctor. " That you may better understand its contents, I will first explain to you the position of this friend.

' Simon Konarski was twenty-two years old when the revolution broke out in Poland. He was, at that time, a subordinate officer, and a young man of distinguished education. He was soon advanced to the rank of captain, and received the cross of honor for his personal bravery. He shared the fate of his corps, and reached France as a fugitive, but his spirit remained in Poland, and his glowing patriotism allowed him no rest in exile. In the spring of 1833 he arrived, incognito, with many other Poles, by the way of Germany, in Poland, where a partisan, or guerilla war, was begun, with the design of gradually bringing the whole of Poland again under arms. The bold enterprise failed, priests and executions followed, and entire villages were ordered out to apprehend the ' rebels, who were hunted, like stags, by peasants and hounds. Many were hung and shot, many were escorted to Siberia. Konarski's flight bordered on the miraculous, and one day he only owed his deliverance to the sympathy of a Russian officer who searched the country house where he was concealed. The officer took the owner of the house aside, and whispered in his ear, ' I am one of the followers of Mouravieff,* you understand me ! save your friend.' Konarski arrived at Antwerp, by way of Dantzig when the expedition of Savoy was in preparation, and came to me at Nyon, on the Lake of Geneva, where I was occupied, at that time, incognito, as an emissary of the expedition. I passed some days there with him, which I shall never forget. The expedition failed, and the society of ' Young Europe' arose, like a phenix, from the ashes of the bivouck fires in Savoy. Konarski, long since familiarized with the idea of a ' holy alliance of nations, resolved soon again to return to Poland as an ' apostle of humanity.' With unexampled diligence and perseverance, he learned the trade of a watchmaker in Switzerland and France, that he might more securely undertake his journey under the mask of this profession. Prepared, in all respects, for his mission, he went to London, in the year 1835, where the central committee of ' Young Poland,' as a division of ' Young Europe,' confided to him the mission that he desired. He first went to Cracow, in the strictest incognito, towards the end of the same year. Prepared, at every step, for dungeons, tortures, and the scaffold, he traversed Volhynia, Podolia, and Lithuania—in short, all the provinces of Poland, which, since half a century, had been governed by the Russian knout. Everywhere he found the spirit which he looked for, the field of the heart in which to scatter the seed, that, moistened with blood, will one day spring up in a pure future.' An apostle, the like of whom our association has hardly found, he wrought, with immense effect, upon the hearts that thirsted for consolation. Nature had imprinted on his brow the stamp of his exalted vocation—a noble, open countenance, with the flashing glance of a deep blue eye, coolness and presence of mind in danger, sincerity

---

* One of the heads of the Russian conspiracy, in the year 1826.

and animation in intercourse with his friends, and heart-stirring eloquence in the secret assemblages of the association, united to form a person who awakened unbounded confidence in kindred souls Endowed with divine power, he fulfilled his vocation of strengthening his countrymen in faith in the resurrection of the human race He turned, also, to the female sex, in the consciousness of the exalted worth and the immense influence of woman upon the rising generation, to impress upon the heart of the mother that she should infuse into the suckling at her breast, love of fatherland, faith in God and humanity, and hatred towards all tyranny His personal appearance, which I have described, facilitated his entrance among all classes of the people Not only susceptible youth and females, where he approached them, but, also, priests and functionaries of the government, and officers of the army, joined our association Many officers and functionaries of high rank, manifested the spirit that found harmony and fellowship in them He wrought thus for about two years and a half, sought for in every quarter by the Russian secret police, and only protected by the spirit of the association, which efficiently opposed the element of treachery, and eluded the strictest inquiry At length, however, his fate has overtaken him—that awful fate, to which he always looked forward Read this letter from London "

Thorfin was profoundly impressed by this communication, which, as it appeared shook the heart of his friend in its most secret depths, as it had also newly awakened the sense of his own position in South America

"He was apprehended in the month of May, this year, 1838, in the neighborhood of Wilna," Dr Thorpin read, "after he had so long succeeded, with unexampled adroitness, in eluding the embittered Russian secret police

"All those who had been in personal contact with him, were, very naturally, liable to the same persecutions, but, according to the organization of our association, the discovery of our confederates is, thank God! difficult

"He, as well as his fellow-prisoners, are subjected to the torture, with all its horrors, to extort confessions, in order to renew the arrests

"Konarski undergoes tortures of a barbarity which characterises the Russian government Not only the knout is employed to extort confessions from him, (which can be obtained from him alone,) but the tortures of the middle ages, with all their inconceivable sufferings, were exhausted upon him His fingers have been torn out of joint with pincers, and iron nails driven into the flesh under his finger nails He endures such martyrdom, and holds his peace! Burning sealing-wax has been dropped in the open wounds made by the knout He endures morally, even when he faints from prostration of physical strength Until the present time, not a single confession has passed his lips "

"My God!" sighed Thorfin, "what a man!" He read further .

"The sympathy and reverence which his fate and his almost superhuman steadfastness have produced among the Russians, resembles the effect of his boldest activity among the Poles A Russian captain, on service to guard him, resolved to escape with him—to save Konarski A fellow prisoner, who was let into the plan, found it more advisable to commend himself to the mercy of the emperor, and demeaned himself to be a traitor The captain's name is Koraviefi, he was at once condemned to death,[*] and Konarski, yet more deeply immersed in subterranean dungeons, awaits still more inhuman tortures '

"The Russian government does not yield to Rosas in Buenos Ayres!" sighed Thorfin, but meaner, if possible, than such barbarity in itself, is the cowardice of the creatures of these governments, who deny the reality of such persecution Every Russian ambassador, or his lowest lackey or secretary, would deny it to our faces, and maintain that this intelligence is false, that there is no such torture in Russia, while the same creatures would gladly avail themselves of an opportunity to assist in delivering us up, to obtain thereby an order, or a better post While Rosas reiterated two dozen times in every number of his official Gaceta de Comercio, his curse, "Mueran los salvagos Unitarios,' his ambassador here denies that there is any political persecution in the Argentine republic Fugitives by hundreds land upon the coast of Brazil to elude the executioner's axe of Rosas, and, notwithstanding, the friends of the Gaucho here deny that a man has ever been executed in Buenos Ayres for political crimes!"

"Absolutism and slavery,' remarked Huango, ' continue always as consistent in their operation in politics, as in marriage without love Here is the same case that we touched upon last evening A slave of Rosas, or of the emperor of Russia, with star and orders, will as steadily and firmly deny the barbarity of his master, as a wife in a new hat or shawl denies the blows which she herself has received from her husband Who can explain these absurdities of the demoralization of all legalized slavery? Have you read this part " he asked, pointing to some lines in the letter Dr Thorfin read "Awaking from a swoon, after such torture, Konarski turned towards his executioner, and cried ' Wretch! I have already declared to you, I know nothing! I am acquainted with nobody! Am I guilty? Well! I have at least no accomplices!" He often said to the governor, who wished to persuade him to confess ' Seek for new torments! find out a yet more horrible torture, and we shall see whether you can extort a single syllable from me' The governor, a hardened servant of tyranny, proverbially known for his obduracy, related this expression of Konarski, and added ' The man must be of iron!" and Konarski's fate and his unexampled steadfastness, became known in this manner among the Russians "[†]

* According to later intelligence conducted to Siberia,
† Simon Konarski was executed at Wilna, on the 27th of February, 1839 His death was such as his character, his life, and the spirit of the association that inspired him, would lead us to expect With similar tranquillity of soul, as, some years later, the two Bandieras, at Cosenza,(a) in Italy, and like the three brothers Pizarro, who, as apostles of humanity, were executed in Buenos Ayres, he saw his open grave with a smile, and looked death firmly in the face

A pamphlet, "Quatrieme Anniversaire de la Mort de Simon Konarski, celebree a Londres le 27 Fevrier, 1843, Paris, imprimerie de F H Briard, Rue des Six Jetons, 34", contains many interesting particulars, as a contribution to the history of our time

a See "Ricolti dei Fratelli Bandiera et dei loro Compagni di Martirio in Cosenza, il 25 Juglio, 1844, etc, etc Parigi Wiart, Editore Via d'Enghien, 10, 12. 1845]

Horatio and Alvarez came in, to inquire when they should take their walk. Himango hurried to complete his toilet, and gave to his two companions one of the letters, written in French, to impart to them the fate of Konarski.

The leaf trembled in Horatio's hand, whilst Alvarez read the lines with him. Both interrupted their reading with sighs and exclamations, until at length they looked at each other, and Horatio said: "Does it not seem as if we were reading a leaf out of the history of the first martyrs of Christianity in the first century, before the church overcame this spirit, and sought to bury it in forms?"

"What a spirit must lie at the foundation of this association of "Young Europe," and prevail in its apostles, when it counts such men as this among its martyrs!" sighed Alvarez. "And what fate should I have shared, and our Dolores, if the slaves of Rosas had discovered us, and conducted us to the prisons in Buenos Ayres!"

Himango re-entered, prepared for the walk. Alvarez hurried up to him, and pressed him to his heart. The friends left the hotel, and walked, under Dr. Thorfin's guidance, to the "Passeio Publico," the public garden of the city of Rio, with a terrace on the shore of the bay, presenting shady alleys, and a prospect of the wonderful Organ Mountains. They met there, at the appointed hour, the "air pump controller," Mr. Fitz, in his invariable good humor, who gave them this rendezvous, for inspecting together the schooner brig Vesta, which he had recommended to the ex-Russian naval officer, as a privateer for Rio Grande, or as a slave trader for Angola and Loango, according to either use that Himango might make of it, which was quite indifferent to the astronomer.

CHAPTER XIII

THE PARTNER AND THE YOUNG SWISS

ABD EL KADER, the Congo servant of the house of Rossbruck & Co., in the Rua da Alfandega, informed all the business people, on the holiday morning, that the breakfast was ready, and Mr. Doubly sent him into the cabinet of the young man, who gave himself out for a certain William Rossbruck, to invite him to breakfast likewise. The "gentleman" seemed of the opinion that he should compromise himself less, if he spoke a word to a "nigger" than to a clerk, and asked the servant when Mr. Rossbruck or Mr. Dumpling (a partner in the concern) would come home.

"Don't know," answered the negro, "they at chacara—both senhors—far away—in San Christova. Be sure to come Monday—be here early Monday."

The gentleman seemed to consider what he should do, and Abd el Kader repeated his invitation to breakfast.

"I shall not come, I will not breakfast with——," he grumbled, suppressing the words that wavered upon his tongue, and turning his respectable back upon the negro, who did not honor him long with the contemplation of the faceless latitude of his body, but withdrew, to carre to his young masters, who were already assembled around the covered table, the result of his mission.

"Then he may let it alone!" said Mr. Doubly, and all looked intently at each other. After the conclusion of the breakfast the young men made their toilet, and left the house, to enjoy the aromatic air of the environs. Some of them desired that the dinner should not be kept waiting for them, as they were going to visit Praya Grande.*

Mr. Doubly was left at home alone, and sat reading a volume of poetical poems, written by a young European, when the "gentleman" came out of his room door, which admitted of a view into the interior of Mr. Doubly's apartment. "I am satisfied," thought he, interrupting his reading, "that this young European will write no political poetry!"

The "gentleman" stared at the clerk, who looked up from his book and into his eyes, but bade him no good morning; he only pressed his patent gloves a little deeper between the fingers, and left the room and the house without saying a word.

"Go to the devil! and greet your gentlemen in their private hell!" muttered the young man, as the gentleman slammed the door of the gallery behind him, and stumbled down the steps.

Where the stranger went to, who called himself Mr. William Rossbruck, whether he sought a breakfast in some hotel, or café, was indifferent in the highest degree to the young man who guarded the house of Rossbruck & Co. An hour afterwards, there was a tap at the door which divided the corridor from the steps. Abd el Kader opened it, the gentleman walked in again, did not even look around him, (while the negro observed him from head to foot,) and retired to his cabinet.

The forenoon passed off, and it was two o'clock, the table was covered for dinner, and a friend of young Doubly appeared, whom he had invited to keep him company. The negro informed the gentleman that dinner was ready, "I shall not come!" muttered he, in the same surly tone with which he had declined the breakfast, and Abd el Kader again brought the refusal to young Doubly.

"Only wait!" said he, half aside to himself, "I see now who I have to deal with! If you feel too good to sit at table with us, I will show you that I am at home here. Wait now!"

The guest of the clerk, a young Italian, director of a musical chapel in Rio, learned superficially who was in the cabinet, and took as little notice of the unknown as Mr. Doubly did, apart from the indirect offence.

"Do you know that the Scandinavian is here again?" inquired the Italian, as they seated themselves at the table.

"I have already sent my card to him at the Hotel du Nord, as I could not go out to-day to call on him," replied Mr. Doubly. "He is an early friend of my former principal, in whose society I became acquainted with him. I would gladly have invited him to-day, but my present principal is afraid of being compromised in case

---

* Opposite to the shore of the city, a favorite place of recreation.

he enters this house   Even his name frightens him, if he reads it in the European newspapers "

" I must keep away from him, on account of my situation," said the Signore Maestro, as he ate his soup   " They would suspect that I belonged to the association of ' La Giovine Italia,' and displace me—take my situation from me and that would surely be dreadful "

" As concerns myself,   returned the young Swiss, " I had just as lief it would be known here that I belong to ' Young Switzerland, and be seen walking with an associate of ' Young Europe,' as not, and it my principal should take my situation away from me on that account, I should soon find another , and if ' Old Europe' should ever break loose, I am convinced that we, Swiss in Brazil, could equip a small man-of-war, and a part of us would embark, provided the crisis had come on in Europe, that must follow, sooner or later "

" Certainly, when it comes to that, I will do my part, but ' prudence can do no harm ,' and I promised my father to keep away from ' Young Italy ' My father has a post at the Court of Modena "

" There is the difference   I have promised my father and myself to continue a Republican, wherever I might be   You know that we Swiss, here in Rio de Janeiro, maintain our love of fatherland, by social confederation, in a Riflers' Union   To be sure, there are many among them, likewise, that would tremble to eat a plate of soup with a confederate of ' Young Europe ' There are cowards amongst all nations   The Swiss, however, have preserved, until this time, the spirit of freedom, and if our republics are insignificant, our people are not the most insignificant in Europe   Switzerland yet contains some republicans "

The two young people, (though, to be sure, with apparently different views of life,) chatted away the hour at table, and a portion of the afternoon, without quarrelling about their political differences

Towards five o'clock, the stiff figure of the gentleman in black patent gloves, again appeared in the parlor, again stared at the young Swiss, and walked out of the door

" The clown has certainly been bitten by a mad Englishman," said Mr Doubly, laughing, as both looked after him

" He feels his nullity, and would gladly be something," remarked the Italian , " and as it is easier to play the deaf and dumb gentleman, than the intelligent Frenchman, it is easily explained how he came to wear this mask   As to the rest, the foreign nature peeps awkwardly forth from the mask   No Englishman would ever take him for a countryman "

" This is just the crazy side of the German Anglo-mania," said Mr Doubly, " and evinces the narrow-mindedness of those who are ashamed of being Germans, and ape the English   Will a Briton ever deny his nationality, and assume the least of a foreign form, let him be in what country he may ?   The Germans, however, have no nationality , how can they maintain it ?   As a nation of full thirty millions of men, the Germans might, truly, just as well be self-existent and independent, as the French, the Spanish, or the English."

" The British is, undoubtedly, the first nation on earth—no one can deny that," remarked the Italian

" Certainly, in material respects," replied Doubly , " but there are two sorts of greatness— material and intellectual   The giant of eight feet, who excites the astonishment of the rude populace in some suburban theatre, is certainly great

" The English characterize their own greatness by their acknowledgment and admiration of any, or all, other material greatness   An Englishman respects no intellectual greatness, because he is a stranger to it, he honors no talent, no science no art, no intellect, but only the *result* of talent or of intellect—the result in money

" On the contrary, he admires and honors material greatness, let it be as spiritless as it may Great wealth, a great ox, a great cheese, a great vessel, a great hog, a great plum cake, a great pumpkin, a great *boxer*   all greatness of this sort interests the Englishman, if the ox or the cheese is English   As a positive consequence he not only has no notion of any intellectual greatness, but it appears ridiculous to him— without money '

" If ' the Son of Man were to come again, and were to make his appearance in England, without an equipage with four horses, and without being recommended to Rothschild, he would hardly find an English Christendom," observed the Signore Maestro

" I will read to you, as an Italian, a fragment from a poem, that is certainly written in a dead language, and had to be first translated into English, to be read "

The young Swiss brought a book from his room, and read, in an impressive voice

" Sidon and Tyre have once been great in traffic,
And Carthage, too, has had her Hannibal
The storms of time that mighty foe to form,
Have swallowed all, even to the smallest trace
Of their magnificence, first weak, then weaker,
Their splendor died even to its last faint beam,
Mysteriously extinguished by a power
That sweeps off, in an instant, towns and states
   A single hour—one battle's dire event,
Has oft cut down a kingdom's palmy bloom,
And crushed its firm foundations in themselves,
And all its power and splendor made extinct
Preserved from all decay, Idea stands—
Idea, God's own light in human souls '
Babel, once great and powerful, has fallen ,
Rome, Sparta, Athens, mock at such a fate.
   From Tyre, from Sidon, and from Babylon,
All that remain are, ruins of the past ,
All, save the saying—' Here a throne once stood,
Here kings with wanton Phrynes revelled once—
Here stood the exchange, and there rot far removed,
The slave mart—here the jeweller's bazaar ,'
No more is said of them in history ,
Than—' Here great traffic once was carried on ''
   From Rome, from Athens, and from Ithaca,
More than the name is handed down to us ,
The human intellect, in brilliant splendor,
In arts and science, gleams upon us thence,
Displaying culture's bright meridian path,
In opposition to the tragic silence
Of other cities' ruins—other states,
Once great in gold and stones, in hirelings and in brokers'
   Athens and Rome, and Sparta still survive ,
Vain are all efforts to extirpate Mind
The Greeks still bid defiance to the yoke
Of servitude—the Spartans, (the Mainotes,)
Are roused again in freedom's sacred cause ,
The Italians may be mocked by parasites
The Vatican and Peter's haughty dome,
Eternally enclose the mighty spirit of Rome '
   Behold we not virtue in Italy —
While freedom's martyrs pine in dungeons there ,
Youths who, in words and deeds, have boldly dared
To sacrifice themselves for fatherland ?

Dungeons and exile have no power to blight
The bloom of mind—despots may ever strive
To slay a people and to shame a land,
But Rome's Nemesis will not lie entombed
No nation's dead, that worthy martyrs count,
For God and freedom—honor—fatherland!
No nation's dead that suffers in its chains,
Scourged and dismembered by the hangman's hand,
If nationality still serves the spirit's strength
Een should the nation's fame and splendor vanish,
Should treachery destroy it all as sons
Through nationality shall rise again

The spirit, in the strife with mine, fills
The bloody book of the world's history,
'Tis from the feelings that all action springs,
Tyranny can do nought, against strength of mind
Mysteriously enclosed in mourning crape,
Sits justice in the judgement of the world,
Surrounded by all nations' martyr shades,
Deciding on the rise and fall of states
And what a nation does, and what intends,
All, as a nation, that it strives to effect,
Shall be made known—Long as the earth revolves,
So long shall filthy selfishness be scorned,
Mind will be recognised, and gather fame
But despotism still remains accursed,
For it the sentence from that judgement seat
Shall be—To pass from memory to Oblivion!
Oblivion clouds the splendor of those states,
Which love to man, in spirit, have denied,
Which, nation after nation have betrayed,
Appropriating land on land by fraud

No fruit can ever arise from any seed,
Unless the germ receives the Spirit's ray
All that is mortal fleets away with time;
The spiritual, alone, gains immortality!

There was another rattling and knocking at the door of the corridor and Abd el Kader again opened it The gentleman strode slowly and gravely, with wooden stiffness, through the salon, and disappeared in the passage that led to his room, the two young men again looked after him, and Mr Doubly now declared

"I will invite the clown once more to tea, this evening If he refuses, upon my soul! I will lock him in his cabinet, and take upon myself, voluntarily, the care of the house to-morrow, and he shall sit there until early the day after, till Mr Rossbruck comes home He may knock and call as much as he will, any one might walk in here, and give himself out for William Rossbruck, and, after all, be some clever thief, who may there hide things about his person, and carry them out of the house I know what I have to do for the security of the property of our house If the fellow behaves himself this evening, as is to be expected from a relative of the house, and if he gives me sufficient evidence that he is the person that he pretends to be, well if not, then I shall take the measures towards him that I have resolved on '

The young Italian found this resolution as original as just, since no thief could certainly have chosen a better mask, to cover his entrance into a house, and enable him to carry on his business with all convenience The Sr Maestro withdrew towards evening, and some of the inmates of the house appearing at tea time, Mr Doubly informed them that he should assume the watch for the following day, and sent to invite the gentleman once more to tea The same churlish answer was again returned—"I will not come!" and the young Swiss kept his word

Mr Robert Walker went, towards sundown, to his house in the Rua Direita where a young Englishman kept watch in the same manner as did Mr Doubly in the house of Rossbruck & Co
The sun had hardly gone down, and its last rays ceased to linger on the bare rocky masses of the Corcovado when a clapping of hands was heard in the corridor of the house of Walker & Co At this intimation that some one required admission, a negro opened the door, and Sr Forro announced himself, and enquired if Mr William Walker, from Buenos Ayres, was there

The negro conducted him to a room which Mr Thomson kept as an office when he had any thing to do in town

"No one has announced himself," began Mr Forro, after the usual salutations," and we are now ready to lay before you the plan of this business, to carry out which important steps have already been taken "

" The business relates to mines of metal ?" inquired Robert, as the two seated themselves opposite to each other

" I herewith hand you the necessary documents, which will afford you a clear insight into the whole project The mines are the principal object, as the working of them will be the basis of the industry, which is to support the colony Iron and lead are found there in great abundance The ground, covering the mines is rich in furniture wood of excellent quality, and both sources are nearly inexhaustible The climate is similar to that of the south of Europe, and the luxuriance of the vegetation admits of the cultivation of nearly all the most profitable European fruits In case you enter upon this business, two vessels must immediately be freighted in Europe, to bring out the laborers and emigrants who are already engaged there, as well as the necessary machines and manufactured products of all sorts for the colony Regular vessels from Europe can then ply back and forth as the domain of the colony lies almost in immediate contingency to the ocean "

" Very well!" replied Robert, when the agent of the naturalist had ceased speaking, and appeared to expect an answer "When do you desire a definite answer on our part, after we shall have looked over the documents and materially weighed the whole affair ?'

' This is Saturday,' answered Mr Forro, " Monday morning, at nine o'clock, I shall wish to hear your decision "

"Very well," concluded Robert, " I shall expect you here on Monday morning, at nine o'clock, and will, in the meantime, consult with my uncle, Mr Thomson, about the plan, that we may then give you our fixed determination "

The two men of business parted from each other with businesslike brevity, and Robert mounted his horse to hurry towards Bota Fogo, to lay before his uncle the affair, of which he had already given him previous notice He galloped past the hill of da Gloria, and looked hastily upward at the two pavilions, one of which he was to inhabit on the coming night For this purpose, he had despatched thither his carpet bag, as the examination of his trunks and boxes at the Alfandega was postponed, on account of the holiday

The wish, or, rather, the command, of the amiable young lady, in relation to the maintenance of her incognito, hardly permitted him even to ask himself the questions, who she was, and what was the danger to which she was exposed It was sufficient for him that he was honored by her confidence, and summoned to her protection Notwithstanding this, however, an indescribable uneasiness came over him, when he recurred to the warning of his friend Hinango, and the singular impression which this name had made upon the fair unknown

The thought that the natural connexion of ideas was founded upon the reality that this young lady was Madame Clostiug, gained more and more probability, and caused him to shudder with that indefinable feeling for which he could find no name The secret of the young Brazilian lady, however, whatever circumstances might make it necessary, was sacred to him She was in danger, and the suspicion that she might be the lady whom Hinango had mentioned, could not deter him from occupying the pavilion, as he, in his youthful purity, was unconscious of the danger which might threaten himself

The image of the distressed unfortunate came before his soul with ineffaceable liveliness, and the melodious tones of the voice in which she had requested for herself the consolation of his presence, resounded in the depths of his throbbing heart He thought that he had trotted too rapidly, and restrained his horse to a slower pace, partly to draw his breath more freely, partly to have a longer sight of the pavilion on the Gloria, which, at length, disappeared behind trees and houses

CHAPTER XIV

SECRET BUSINESS

In one of the quiet by-streets extending to the four winds from the Campo da Santa Anna (perhaps the largest square in any city upon earth,) an antiquated garden wall arose, with bananas rustling above it, and protected by a covering of broken bottles, to prevent unbidden guests from climbing over it A narrow opening in this wall formed a gate, or door, on which, in contrast with the undeniable antiquity of the massive wood work, as well as of the wall, a brass bell-handle glittered, which had been placed there but a short time before

It was late in the evening The rockets and blue-lights, in honor of the saint whose name-day had just ended, whizzed and snapped about, and filled the clean tropical atmosphere with powder smoke Empty casks, and even whole piles of wood, blazed, and crackled, and burned, in the middle of the streets, corrupting with soot and smoke the air, that for many men there was, indeed, much too pure There was hissing, and crackling, and clatter without end, like—— a holiday evening in Rio de Janeiro

A little thin short fellow, in a black dress coat, just then glided along by the antiquated wall, and pulled the brass knob, whereupon a bell sounded in a far distance After a time, proportioned to the space that evidently extended between the gate and the bell, something living stirred inside of the old door, and a voice, that appeared to proceed from a broken pot, cried out, tolerably loud

"Que ah?" (who's there?)

"Amigalhâo!"* snarled the little fellow

---

* Intimate friend.

through his nose, and a key grated in the lock of the old door

"Ah! Senhor de Monte Video! welcome, walk in! Dabedi! dahbedikademlafuganita!" cried an old negress, whose voice bore this broken sound

The little man stepped over the threshold, and very carefully ascended two extremely old steps, almost worn out from long use, into a "botanical garden, whose 'scientific wealth' had grown up so confusedly together, that it became difficult for the little man, notwithstanding his contracted latitude, to work his way through it, without being wounded by the thorns of a gigantic aloe

The "Senhor de Monte Video," an "intimate friend of the house" that was so concealed by trees and bushes of all sorts, was told, without asking, that he was welcome, (at least to the old negress,) and that the baron was there

"But he is with the senhora!" whispered the old porteress in his ear, "with the senhora! in the back room! Dahbedibadatupichabanifi—dabitunamnalabamda—hihihi!" said she, with imitable rapidity, in a sort of Ethiopian mother tongue, in which, early and late, she discoursed with herself

"What do you say?" said the little stranger, turning towards her

"I speak my Killomandambisch, hihihi!" laughed the old woman, and drew her visage, otherwise not peculiarly charming, into a hideous grimace

"Yes! but what did you say in your language? you said something to me"

"Not at all! I speak my Killomandambisch, that I may not forget my language! the language of my nation! hihi!"

"What was the meaning of what you said just now?"

"That I do not know, but I always speak my mother tongue, that I may not forget it, as I have forgotten the sense of the words Hihihi! Baindadipumanuadduntucicadembutis"

"Have you then no countrymen or women of your tribe, with whom you could speak your language?"

"Women? ladies? none! I am the only one! for they are much too dear! because we are very handsome! very handsome! too dear! Baditubabenkikadotaludamiduli! hihihi! Senhor Baron Blanco is up there with Senhora Fortuna Dadicabem! pst! still! Senhor de Monte Video! hihihi!"

The little man had reached the steps of a dwelling in the back ground of the natural unartificial botanic garden, and now entered an apartment that was, at the same time, corridor and entrance hall, after the mode of building Brazilian houses

The lighting of the apartment was in accordance with the naturalness of the arrangement of the garden, and very cheap The myriad of stars, glittering more and more in the firmament, generously sent their shining rays through an open window, increasing thereby the saving of gas lights to the occupant, notwithstanding which, it was evidently lighter in that apartment, than it is at times in many shops in London, at twelve o'clock in a November day, with a blaze of gas, almost extinguished by the mass of fog

Senhora Bebida* was a splendid specimen of Ethiopian originality, a shrunken, dwarfish figure, of about four feet high. Her entire apparel consisted of an old coarse coffee sack, with a hole for the neck, and two others for the two arms. The cloth did not quite cover the entire pedestal of this antique figure, but was confined over the hips by a half withered vine, whose leaves and ends hung, Bacchus-like, over her narrow drapery. Her head, overgrown with gray wool, was two-thirds mouth, always grinning, the rest was nose, and some little forehead. Her cheeks and temples were tattooed with Ethiopian hieroglyphics, and decorated with remarkably sparkling little eyes.

Bebida desired the stranger (who appeared to be extremely well known as an 'intimate friend' of the house) to take a seat, and ascended a narrow stairway to a door which was locked.

"Go in the front room and clear away the table," cried a female voice on the inside.

"Front room! clear away table! Danbedipapima," repeated Bebida, "Sr. de Monte Video is below! Dutipaluchugalida."

"What do you say?" inquired the same voice.

"Sr. de Monte Vi-de-o is below! wants to speak to S. Baron! Dapulchatihatchuti!"

"Tell him to wait! I will come down," cried a male voice, which had sounded opposite to old Mr. Thomson in the Hotel Furoax, and belonged to the so called Baron de Spandau, as his 'lawful property,' to say nothing as to whether he possessed much 'lawful property' besides.

"Wait! I'll come! Dapilacolmaliquhetebu!" murmured Bebida, and went into the designated front room, where the relics of a tête-à-tête supper stood upon a round table before a sofa.

Without long hesitation, Bebida seized a champagne bottle, which caught her eye, held it up in the starlight, weighed it in her hand, muttered some phrases of her mother tongue, and pushed the neck of the bottle into her tolerably capacious mouth. "Bonito! bonito!"† murmured she, when not a drop more flowed out, and then removed the oyster shells, and aromas, orange and other rinds, into her apron, which was nothing else than the front part of her single sack garment. She continued muttering to herself, as she went prudently down the steps.

The friend of the house had, in the meanwhile, seated himself at a similar round table, in the middle of the hall, which likewise served as a reception room.

"Bebida! light the lamp! Dapalaradamba," she muttered as she now again made her appearance. "Baron come! senhor must wait!" She tried a chemical match, and laughed unmoderate-

ly, when it snapped and took fire. "Bonito'! bonito'!' fire! fire! bonito'!' Dabelikatapakurbadem!'"

After a moment there was a wax light burning under a glass shade, which, in contrast with the starlight, seemed rather to make it darker than lighter, but near which the friend of the house was able to read the compressed writing of some papers, he had already laid down before him on the table.

The apartment was a Brazilian reception and sitting room, with an alcove in the back ground, near which a passage led into the back part of the house below a staircase that divided it from the front.

A stuffed sofa, some chairs, and an ornamental table, with artificial flowers covered with glass shades, composed the furniture. Some coarse colored lithograph prints, in glass and frames, ornamented the walls, as Bonaparté on the bridge of Arcola, la Belle Suisse, the Prodigal Son, Paul and Virginia, and some interesting images, which properly belonged in the alcove, or in the back room of the upper story. An old, very interesting copper plate engraving above the sofa, was of peculiar value, it represented Rahab calling out the spies from under the flax on her roof, to assist their flight.*

All remained tolerably quiet over the head of the 'intimate friend of the house,' until nearly half an hour had elapsed; footsteps were then heard, without finances, or boots, or shoes, and after some minutes the baron appeared, the point of his nose directed heavenward, and his cheeks highly colored, in a Brazilian dressing gown 'à la Guizot," and a truly national German nightcap of white North American cotton. The intimate friend of the house arose, and drew an armchair near the table, for the baron.

"It is very agreeably cool this evening," began the visiter, as the first word on either side, while the baron was still busied with the capuchin girdle of his dressing gown.

"Very pleasantly cool this evening, Senhor Prole. Have we letters from Buenos Ayres?"

"One for you, baron, and one for me. Mine is from Falsodo. Important intelligence, but nothing decisive, as yet."

"I will write to Buenos Ayres in regard to what you refer to. Do you remember what I dictated to you, three weeks ago, which you copied as a letter? Do you remember that, Senhor Prole?"

"As well as if I had written it yesterday, baron. You informed the Director General of the Secret Cabinet-Police, that you were able to give information concerning the authorship of the 'Elegias dela Plata,' and offered, under certain stipulations, to place the person who wrote the 'Elegias' at the disposal of justice in Buenos Ayres."

"Well, then, you need not be surprised, if the awkward Senhor Falsodo has, until now, written nothing decided. Nevertheless, its all the same. What does he write?"

"This, among the rest," replied Senhor Prole, and read. 'I avail myself of the letter bag of a Swedish brig, to inform you, in all haste, that Senhor Alphonso de P—— is condemned to death, and will be shot to-morrow, at sunrise.

---

* A disgusting drink," as she was named by some wag Bebida—and nearly all the other characters of this novel, from the most important to the most insignificant, are portraits drawn from nature, and inwoven in this composition.

This novel, in itself, may meet the reproach of considering many social and anti social relations, from the most unfavorable side, and throwing a sharp light upon them—wherefore the author gives the assurance, once for all, that all its characters, relations, and events, are founded upon real facts. On the other hand, however, the author's endeavor has been, to arrange and to mark the original materials as the strictest discretion required, without thereby injuring in the least, the psychological and social truth on which this work is founded as a "character painting of our epoch."

† Beautiful, agreeable.

* Joshua, chap. ii.

21

The Franciscan monk, Padre Fernando, has not been able to get any thing out of him, and the said Alphonso has requested a Benedictine monk, named Celeste—in his former worldly relations Senhor Lorenzo de V——.' "

" Now all is arranged," interrupted the Baron, " ' I have further notice of his worldly relations——' "

—" ' worldly relations,' " continued Sr Prole, reading, " ' named Senhor Lorenzo de V——, might be admitted to him, and his request has been granted I have spoken with Senhor Borrachezo respecting the fatality that occurred to you in Monte Video ' "

' Respecting the drubbing that you received in the printing office there? That is a personal matter "

" Certainly, a personal matter, Baron, insomuch as I received it in my own person '

" Is that all he has written to you? All? "

" ' I commend to your particular observation,' " Senhor Prole continued to read, " ' Senhor Horatio de P——, nephew of the traitor Alphonso, who has received permission to be banished from the Argentine Republic—— "

" Unique style, that !" observed the Baron

" ' To be exiled, and has shipped to-day on board of this same Swedish brig, Nordstjernan ' Further ' Likewise suspicious, but without direct accusation, a Russian captain, formerly a naval officer, wished to purchase here a Danish vessel from St Thomas, named Ormur Olafur Hinango——' Is that the name of the brig, or the fellow ?" said Prole, interrupting himself

" I know best about that, the two are already here Does he write you nothing about the other passengers of the Nordstjernan "

" No ! nothing at all !"

" The jackass ! Well, so much the better ! so much the better ! There was then no other suspicious person on board ! none at all ! If my letter, however, does not contain something of more interest than yours, I shall begrudge the postage To be sure, I cannot yet have an answer to my stipulations, I must wait for the next English packet "

He broke open and read the letter, which had likewise been enclosed under cover to Sr Prole, and appeared not to be at all edified by its contents

" Well then, they are busy in Patagonia, as well as in Lapland ! the cursed fellows !" said he, interrupting himself during the reading of the letter, " and what is worse, amongst the sons of the ocean in the Mediterranean sea, as upon the Southern Atlantic !" He read half aloud: " ' The privateer Mazzini, Captain Barigaldi, is on the coast, destined for Rio Grande ' Yes, we know the fellow, I will hand him over to you yet. On Monday I will go to the Minister of Marine, and have a corvette sent towards Rio Grande We must have him, alive or dead——! Is the note despatched to the German beetleman? the invitation to breakfast to-morrow in my room at the Hotel Faroux ?"

" It has been sent ! he will come—Dr. Mer—Mer—what is his name ?"

" Merbold ! Very well, have you looked up a pair of beetles, at Sr Forro's, from the collection of Mr Closting? a very rare specimen ?"

" All has been done, and is ready for you at the Hotel Faroux, since six o'clock this evening A

pair of ' Spinoza hoods,' as they are called, the rarest that Sr Forro found on Mr Closting's register, they cost twelve millreis "

" Twelve millreis " cried the baron, in peevish surprise " Forro is a Jew ! whether baptized or not ! Six pesos for a pair of worthless beetles ! Oh, well ! they will pay for themselves, and if they were not something peculiar, I could not offer them to Dr Merbold, at least I should fail in my object Bebida ! Bebida !" cried he, and rang a small handbell that stood near the light

" Senhor ! senhor !" resounded on the threshold, " Dabikidabinlegomahifu !"

" Shut your wide mouth, and bring us a bottle of the long light green, in the right hand corner of the cellar !"

" Wide mouth—long bottle—light green—right hand corner—cellar—Dabedi ! Dabedikaduhbula !" she muttered, and hurried out

" Have you nothing else ?"

" Yes, indeed !" the famous Organization Act, which has made all our investigations so difficult '

" That must be the same that was printed long ago I know the fellow who planned it "

" He has outwitted us with his ' Temples !' " interrupted Sr Prole " There is the paper, and here is also the famous National Manifest of the ' Humanita ' "

" Read them to me, but first wet your lips—there is Bebida with the Rhenish "

" Senhor ! Rhenish ! and two glasses ! is it so? Badilikademsahifu ! !" She made a profound courtesy, laughed heartily without any special occasion, and brought two bottles, three wine glasses, and a small liquor glass. Both looked silently at her, as if they were waiting to see what Bebida would do, she placed two wine glasses near the two men, took the third in her right hand, and the small one in her left, and remained standing, like a bronzed idol image When the baron had filled his glass, she held out the two glasses, and began her murmur " One for Sra Fortuna—up stairs—the big one ! and for Senhoraça* Bebida the little one ! Fifidabedikadembepumfidabila ! thank ye ! thank ye ! too much !"

" You have none yet !" said the baron, laughing

" Sra Fortuna up stairs, tired ! very tired ! worked hard, Dababedikademsabifili ! must have a glass !"

" There ! she may help herself, and you too, and bring the bottle back directly !" cried the baron, as he handed it to her, " but if Bebida drinks on the stairs, there hangs the chigote, out there !"

The old woman laughed immoderately, made a profound courtesy, took the bottle with the two glasses and hurried away with her " Dabedikademba," etc

" Now, Sr Prole, read the Organization Pity the fellow will not enter into our service, handsome offers are made to him ! he would have invented a new organization of the secret police ! I confess, that this organization of their Union is famously conceived, for even under the torture they can denounce no more than the few persons whom they know. Read it, Sr Prole "

* Senhoraça, a Portuguese word for a person who plays the great lady

The police spy, Sr Prole, from Buenos Ayres, driven from Monte Vidio, with a thrashing, and become a "political refugee" in Rio, and besides, appointed as the secretary and perambulating factotum of the Baron de Spandau, through a secret recommendation from Buenos Ayres, drank his glass of wine, and read as follows

ORGANIZATION,

Of the Union. The "Humanita"

1 Eleven men and youths, who acknowledge themselves bound to the* * * * * * an nationality, unite and choose a leader for a definite period of time

2 Apart from all symbols, we require names to designate things, and will call the union of these eleven persons a Rock

3 Eleven such Rocks, (each of which is to be known by a definite number,) form a Foundation, (121 persons,) the eleven leaders of which form a committee, (fundamental committee,) and elect from among them a leader, a secretary, and cashier

4 Eleven Foundations form a Pillar, (1,331 persons,) the eleven leaders of which likewise meet and choose a leader, a secretary, and cashier

5 Eleven Pillars constitute a Hall, (14,641 persons,) whose eleven leaders likewise meet, and choose the three above mentioned officers from their number

6 Eleven Halls constitute a Temple, (161,051 persons,) whose eleven leaders likewise meet in committee, and choose the three said officers

7 The national union, can choose their general committee in the same manner, as fast as the number of members increases.

8 For inasmuch as despotism declares patriotism "high treason," the national union organized as above, can shield itself from publicity, as the members of the union are unknown, for if, in spite of all precaution, a spy should steal into the union, he can never discover more than ten persons, should he be chosen leader, he can never know the names of more than twenty, among 121 persons, of thirty among 1331 persons, and among 14,641, of only forty persons

9 In case the union, in the above form, should ever become a perfect Temple, the resolutions of the general committee (directory) can very soon bring 161,000 persons into action.

10 Should our nation, by a decisive contest, clear the way to liberty, a speedy organization of the different races will be necessary to found the representation, this can be done in a few days without difficulty, by means of the above arrangement Every province may, in such case, organize itself in Temples The Rocks will be formed with reference to the residence of the members Besides the eleven Hall leaders, (committee §6,) they will also choose twenty-two known patriots from their number, who, together with the Hall leaders, form a Directory, or Council, thirty-three persons who choose their own officers

11 As soon as several Temples of the different races constitute a nation, the Council of the People, (Provisorial Congress) organizes itself The number of the members of this Congress will be determined according to circumstances

12. All elections shall be made for a definite

* South American—Central American, Scandinavian, etc., etc.

term Intrigue and bribery in an election, under this organization, are very difficult. It is very improbable that an unworthy member should get into a committee, and still more improbable that, by four successive elections, he should become Hall leader or representative to a National Congress

13 The election of a national representation (Congress) can, by means of the above organization, be made in a few days, without disorder, as never more than eleven persons meet at once. Public meetings can, however, take place, the preparation for, and regulation of which, may easily be managed under the above organization.

"There we have it! Take yourself off! set down the bottle, and go away!" cried he to the old Behida, who just then came in and lightly muttered, " Dabedicademlamalilipiji! Senhora Fortuna says thank ye! Bonito!" made a more profound courtesy than before, and withdrew, with " Dabedikadembuh!"

" There we have it!" repeated the baron "If it be true that the men of former centuries, rise again, then the spirit of Jacques Molay exists in the fellow who invented this organization If we could only have him imprisoned and burned, like Molay of old!"

" That is a singular thought which you expressed, that the men of former centuries live again in spirit!"

" A thought that comes very close, when we consider the prominent personages here and there For example, Casimir Perrier is evidently Martin Luther, who has discovered the 'juste milieu,' that the other only imitated

" The sensual poet king Solomon, with all his wives, is the poet king Louis of Bavaria 'All is vanity,' is his motto, and he builds splendid temples, like the other

" Nebuchadnezzar, who at length ate nothing but salad, is the old Charles the Tenth, who could endure nothing but vegetables at the last

' Jeremiah is the German poet Boerne, who laments the destruction of his people

" Judas, the last of the Maccabees, is Abd el Kader, if the latter be not even braver still

" Nero is our Rosas, who persecutes the Unitarians, as the other did the first Christians

" Moses, who, with sword in hand, taught nationality and the faith in the only God, is Mazzini.

" John the Baptist, is De-Lamenais

" Balaam's ass that spoke, is Dr Merbold, who takes the crown prince of Prussia for an arch liberal!"

The secretary's laugh accompanied that of his chief

" And do you know who is the ox of Luke the Evangelist ?" inquired the baron, with emphasis

" No!" replied Senhor Prole, after earnest deliberation

" It is you"—and both laughed heartily, and again emptied their glasses

Sr Prole, having emptied his glass once more in private business, continued to read the following:

NATIONAL MANIFEST,

Of the Union The "Humanita"

1. We the undersigned, * * * * * * ans, unite ourselves into a union of equality and brother-

hood, in the spirit of our nationality and call this union * * * *

2 We believe in the primitive spirit of mankind, which reveals itself as the principle of progress, development, and melioration, in the history of all nations and of all times

3 We believe in mankind as a whole, consisting of nations—the nations consisting of different races, united by the bond of patriotism

4. We recognise, as a historical truth, the existence of particular traits of character in every nation, which is shown by all history, from the most ancient to the present time

5 The bond of nationality is the oldest and most sacred bond that unites man to mankind, whilst the idea "mankind" disappears, in a formless chaos, with the denying of the nationality of peoples, whereof it consists

6 We believe that our position, our duties, and our dignity, as men, in the great union of mankind, are the conditions of our nationality

7 We believe that the bonds of nationality are the basis of humanity "Whoever does not love his own nation, cannot love mankind," which consists of nations

8 We believe in the union harmony, and unity of races related in their nationality, and in the fraternity of nations in the great union of mankind

9 The principle of equality is the basis of freedom, freedom, the means of all development and melioration

10 We recognise our fatherland * * * *, in a geographical point of view, as it was formed of itself, by population of kindred races, from * * * * to * * * *

11 We thus recognise, as * * * * ans, the races of * * * * * *

12 We believe in the principle of the equality of all races, without prerogative or distinction, as we also recognise the principle of equality in all the nations of the earth, united in the spirit of humanity

13 We recognise man upon earth, as an independent and morally free being, the dignity of man as founded in the consciousness of his nationality, and the essence of all duties towards mankind, in the fulfilment of the fundamental conditions of humanity

14 We believe in the primitive spirit of mankind, which reveals itself in cultivation and melioration, from century to century We believe it to be the sacred duty of all nations, in consequence of this spirit, to strive and work for the noble end of the emancipation and ennoblement of the human race

15 We recognise the primitive spirit of mankind as the spirit of love, light, and power, as a Unity, and consequently no resisting second power, no "evil spirit"

16 We believe in the principle of freedom in man and in nations. We believe in the moral freedom of man to choose what is good, and in the political freedom of every nation, that man may be able to act in conformity to his moral freedom. We recognise the light of the primitive spirit within us as "reason," and the sentiment of patriotism as the basis of every noble action.

17. In consequence of the principles of freedom, man can be morally free, when he wills, and a nation can be politically free, when it reveals its will for unity, through the union of its powers in the spirit of nationality

18 We recognise a spiritual and formal union of the moral powers of a nation, and a union of nations founded upon the principle of humanity, as absolutely necessary to operate against despotism, which robs the people of their sacred rights, and declares patriotism " high treason "

19 We recognise the sacred " right " of a nation to develop itself in the element of freedom, but, at the same time, we also recognise the duty" of every man to work for the deliverance of the oppressed people, and the duty of every nation to assist and to support the struggle for the deliverance of another nation

20 We recognise the historical truth, that a nation has never yet obtained its liberty and independence, without an obstinate struggle for its sacred rights

21 We understand it as the interest of despotism, to nourish and strengthen national hatred and disunion in the different races of each nation—to keep them separate from each other, in order more easily to keep them in subjection

22 We recognise the principle of love, as the basis of humanity—the band of family, as the basis of morality

23 In consequence of the principle of equality, we acknowledge no prerogative of birth and blood

24 We recognise no lord, but the Lord of the Universe, and no earthly power, but the Power of the People

25 No government is " legitimate," which is founded on the prerogative of birth and blood

26 We recognise it as the right of a nation to rule over its own concerns, by means of reasonable organization, and representation by free election

27 We believe that the development of a nation, in the element of freedom, can only progress on the basis of popular education and national legislation

28 In consequence of the principles of honor and virtue, we do not measure the " worth ' of a man, by his money or property.

29 Apathy and indifference in the character of man, and prejudice and moral slavery in society, are the greatest evils of our age, inasmuch as they tend to bar every advance towards freedom and melioration

30 We believe in the self-consciousness of man, and the power of conviction as the foundation of every advance in humanity We recognise the opposite conviction of enemies, and we honor an enemy, when he defends his conviction, in life and death, as we do ours.

31 In contending for the sacred rights of mankind, we demand a fair, unconditional decision, a denying of all selfism by patriotism. We honor in our enemies the same self-denial, if they, like us, sacrifice their lives and property in contending against us We despise indecision, apathy, and indifference, and declare ourselves uncompromising enemies of all treason in the cause of the nations

32 We adopt, for our universal union, the motto· "Dios y Humanidad," (God and mankind,) and as for our National branch, the motto;* * * * *

_____

* The Italians "Ora e sempre"—The Scandinavians: "Aut pro aut contra," etc , etc.

33 We recognise the plan of an organization of the Union, of the 12th of August 1834, as the basis of our Union, and recommend it to the consideration of all members

34 We recognise a committee as * * * * an national, which consists of eleven * * * * ans, and which is formed according to the aforesaid organization, to be connected with the Central Committee of " * * * * ," on * * * * an soil

35 We recognise a Central Committee of eleven * * * * ans, on * * * * an soil, according to the above organization, as nationally binding

36 We acknowledge the necessity of a national symbol, and consequently, we recognise the colors * * * * * * * * , as national colors , also, a national ensign a * * * * * * *

37 We acknowledge it necessary, that every member of our union, on * * * * * an soil, should provide himself with arms

38 We believe in the special duty of every * * * * * an, on foreign soil, in his position as citizen, or inhabitant of a foreign country, in so far as he acknowledges himself spiritually bound to the * * * * * an national union We recommend to him the strict observance of the law of that state which affords him personal security and protection

39 We are impressed with the necessity of keeping our union a secret on * * * * * an soil, until the day when the people s voice calls us to arms We leave the policy of making public the transactions of a * * * * an committee on the free soil of foreign countries, to the consideration and prudence of its members

40 We adopt as an insignia for the seal of the * * * * * an Union, a * * * * * with the circumscription, * * * * * (See §32)

41 We found this Union, when despotism has anew gained the victory over the cause of the nations But instead of despairing for the fate of mankind, we, on the contrary, declare our faith in God, who governs the destiny of nation's, who leads men and nations from night to light, from slavery to freedom

42 We recognise the Act of Fraternity, of April 15th, 1834, and are prepared to join the offensive and defensive alliance of nations

43 We believe that God reveals himself in mankind, the history of all nations and of all ages to be the impress of the primitive spirit of humanity, in the working and striving of the nations for melioration and perfection

44 As sons of our fatherland, * * * * * , we acknowledge it as our duty to sacrifice ourselves on the altar of patriotism We declare ourselves resolved and ready to seal the covenant of our nationality with our blood, when our hour has come to die for God and Mankind in the spirit of humanity Amen. August, 1838

" They seem to be thorough-going fellows, baron ' those Humanitarios '" began Sr Prole, after a pause , " and according to this devilish organization we can devise little against them '"

" And we can learn even less by the control of their letters in relation to the associates ; no devil can comprehend their mode of writing who has not the key , it is impossible "

" Dabidekademlakonifatumkabanfitopudam'— Bonito ' Vinho bonito ' Dabedikadem '" whispered Bebida, and laughed a Hihihi afterwards,

as she appeared, uncalled, and brought the third bottle She went close to the baron, tried to force her comical black mask to the most profound seriousness of which she was capable, and whispered in his ear, " Sra Fortuna sent to request that you would come up—to her—soon—right away—waiting—wants—will—Debedikadem '"

" I will come right away ' just tell her so ' and do you go to bed ' I will fasten the door myself "

"Dabedikademlafakatibaha, hihihi '" answered Bebida She made a profound courtesy, and took with her the two first bottles, in which there still remained a few drops of " vinho bonito " for her

" Can the Russian Hinango be an emissary of the Humanitarios '' inquired Prole, when they were once more alone, and had again emptied their glasses

" Jackass—there are many in the city of Geneva, in Switzerland '" cried the baron, softening with great presence of mind the word, which might have somewhat offended the assistant spy. " We know his position '"—-" but it will not do to arrest him yet '" said he, interrupting himself " The Russian ambassador here had him under his own surveillance two years ago, his secretary sought admittance in the neighborhood of the pavilion where he lived, but the fellow is too cunning It was all in vain ' He takes care of himself, and the government here even protect him, so long as he undertakes nothing directly against them Well ' then you have appointed the beetleman to meet me at the Hotel Faroux, and the two beetles are ready for him '"

" According to your orders, baron '"

" Take notice yourself of all the passengers who arrived in the Nordstjernan, and observe them sharply, excepting the German ape, who plays the Englishman , he is as harmless to us as any real Englishman upon the European continent I cannot understand the narrow-mindedness of governments that see a demagogue in a Briton ' Every ' gentleman' is naturally a royalist and will not be apt to compromise himself, as an apostle of the idea of the future The real young gentleman, however, from the Nordstjernan, forms an exception, as he was brought up at Buenos Ayres, in association with Unitarians You may keep an eye upon him. And now, good night Take another glass It is midnight, we will conclude our labors "

Sr. Prole emptied another glass, and then the chief agent of European and Argentine espionage, accompanied him through the garden to the gate, locked it behind him, then the house door, and then mounted the narrow stairs, and disappeared in the alcove of the back room

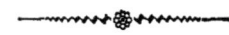

CHAPTER XV.

THE WEIGHT FROM THE HEART

On the Sunday immediately following the Saturday before referred to, all was in movement in the country house of old Mr Thomson, at Bota

Fogo. It is true that no one was particularly invited, except Monsieur le Baron de Spandau, and Dr Thorfin, but, nevertheless, all went "festively on," because Miss Fanny, and Mr. Robert had arrived from Buenos Ayres, and because Mr. George Thompson had been three years a widower for the fourth and a half time It was by no means the day on which his last incomparable, comfortable wife had departed this life—by no means ' Similar days, of which he had five to keep, (for he counted in the day of the death of his West Indian betrothed, one,) had been, for three years, spent very seriously and lonesomely The scales, on the left of the door that led from the "green parlor" into the garden, were on such days hung with myrtle and crape.

Mr Thomson had, on the day before, (after long consultation with an English hair dresser,) caused his thin hair to be cut à la Romeo, and had already appeared at breakfast in "half gala" dress, because he had casually dressed himself earlier than usual, and because Miss Fanny, from Buenos Ayres, was seated next to him

It was towards one o'clock Dr Thorfin and Mr Robert had already arrived on horseback, the blue carriage retured from the city, and brought Miss Susan and Miss Fanny from the English church, where the Catholic lady from Buenos Ayres had perhaps worshipped with as much devotion as the British, who belonged to a sect that ate no meat, and tolerated no musical instruments Love makes people tolerant, and since Miss Susan believed that the Baron de Spandau loved her to distraction, she considered all "no Christians," (that is to say, all who did not belong to her sect,) with far greater indulgence than before

The baron had, from the first, announced himself as a Catholic in Rio de Janeiro, as that was the religion of the court, and he lived in the hope of obtaining a permanent situation under the government, such as had been obtained there by adventurers who were far more stupid than he Of course he regularly visited the court chapel, near the imperial residence, and the Carmelite church, near the court chapel, as both churches were close to each other, and the elegant female world of each rivalled the other Whether the baron was baptized as a Catholic or a Protestant, very naturally concerned nobody, it only the money for the baptism had been duly paid forty years before The sponsors, who, according to the regulations of the church, had, after this or that ritual, solemnly pledged themselves to take care of the spiritual and corporeal welfare of the new member of Christendom, had probably long since forgotten this promise at the altar, and would have considered it indiscreet and silly, in the highest degree, for any one to have reminded them of it

The said Baron de Spandau (as he called himself in Brazil) did not let them wait long for him, and trotted up to the garden gate on his Marscharduro,* just as the blue coach with the two ladies, attended by a colored maid, (who had likewise "renounced all the lusts of the flesh,") had stopped there.

Old Achilles, who had been in a gloomy me-

* Literally, hard runner A race of Brazilian horses, small, but of excellent quality—amblers The race of Minas horses is larger and more hardy.

lancholy mood since his arrival in Bota Fogo and was dressed in his Sunday's state livery, jumped down from the box, he had, as duplicate coachman at the side of Mr. Thomson's "horsebreaker," at least been in the neighborhood of his mistress, whom he would, in no case, have suffered to go alone, even to an English church

Before Achilles, however, had laid his hand upon the coach door, Corinna, who, for the first time in years, had been separated from her mistress, had already opened it

Corinna had been weeping Why? what cause had she to be sad? Had she, perhaps, not had her regular supper, breakfast, and dinner, at Bota Fogo?

On the contrary, Mr Thomson's house was known as very sumptuous, since Miss Susan no longer kept the keys, which Mr Thomson had given over to a black housekeeper Corinna had grown up with Dolores on the banks of the La Plata, so to say, in the garden of a quinta Well, then! and she was now in Bota Fogo, which likewise lay on the water's side Instead of the La Plata, here was a bay, and the quinta was here a chacara, and the garden was a park Where was the great difference? Her mistress was exiled, and, must not return to the garden on the bank of the La Plata—was that a reason for weeping on a fine Sunday morning? Thousands of both sexes leave home, and garden, and fatherland, and seek, in foreign countries, money— money! and if they make money—a little more money—they obtain with it the privilege of stupidity and dullness

It would, indeed, be in vain to institute further inquiry upon the question, why Corinna wept, besides, she was only a negress

The baron had hardly time to spring from his saddle, and hurry to the carriage, before Corinna so suddenly stood by its steps He succeeded, however, in appearing at the proper moment to take his lady's hand, and offer her his arm, whereupon Dr Thorfin, who stood by with Robert, took the liberty to offer the same civility to his sister, after he had been introduced by her brother as a friend of Hinango

And Miss Fanny, also, had been weeping! Strange! She was dressed in black silk, with her hair à l'enfant Miss Susan was in green satin, with an extremely tasteful coiffure à la jeune Anglaise, in which an unpretending white rose was conspicuous She entered the garden gate, on the arm of her friend, and remained standing, with all due politeness, to offer the precedence to her niece from the La Plata, whom Dr Thorfin waited upon

Dolores had remarked this stranger in Hinango's company on board the Nordstjernan, and now learned who he was The presence of this man wrought in her a certain composure, for which she could only account as an indirect communication with the Scandinavian, who had, as it were, appeared to her at the scaffold of Alphonso, and was so nearly akin to her in the element of humanity

Dr Thorfin conveyed to her the most heartfelt greeting from Horatio, and cordial compliments from Hinango and Alvarez, whereupon she inquired after them all, with unaffected interest, and desired to know, especially, whether Horatio had found a residence in the country, in the neighborhood of the city.

"Horatio and Alvarez will to-morrow occupy apartments in the country house in which I reside," replied Dr Thorfin, "and we shall certainly lead a very agreeable life Unfortunately, however, Hinango will not long remain with us, since he intends, as you probably are aware, to go to sea again. Perhaps you are acquainted with his destination," said he in a low tone, with a stolen glance at the baron, who strode before him, as if he were studying the role of Mephistopheles walking in the garden with Martha

"I know his intention,' returned Dolores in as low a tone, "and feel that it proceeds from the depths of his heart, that points out to him his future How I envy him in his position as a man, even although I am not quite certain, in myself, whether I would exchange my female soul for a manly spirit"

Dr. Thorfin was just about to reply, as Mr Thomson approached them, having for a long while observed the confidential conversation, and heard the name of Hinango. He had intentionally deferred selecting his niece, that he might, if possible, arrive at some idea of her connexion with the "notorious privateer," of whom he had occasionally heard first one thing, and then another

He now thought, however, that the two had talked together "enough," and almost regretted having invited his family physician to dinner But who could have suspected that he was to become the electro-magnetic conductor of a spiritual "rapport" between Dolores and the privateer?

The old widower now greeted the two, as if he just perceived them, welcomed his guest, and took the opportunity to give his niece an earnest pressure of the hand, which, from pure heartiness, was almost too strong

"I must introduce the Baron de Spandau to you," cried he, as a thought suddenly struck him, permit me to present him to you Hardly had he said these words, when he had already seized the baron's arm, to the especial vexation of Miss Susan, who was enjoying his agreeable presence, so perfectly after her heart's desire

Instead, however, of leading his future brother-in-law directly to his niece and Dr Thorfin, Mr Thomson took a circuit with him through an alley of the park, as he had something to say to him

"My niece has arrived, as you know, Baron," he began, after coughing, and panting for some time, as if something stood in the way of the words that he wished to utter

"Ah! Your amiable niece from Buenos Ayres! who arrived yesterday in the Nordstjernan, as I heard!" replied the baron

"And will remain here with us for sometime, with my nephew, Mr Robert Walker"

"She seems a very interesting person, your amiable niece, Miss Walker?"

"Miss Fanny Walker, at your service, Miss Fanny is her name Will you permit me to make you acquainted with her?"

"You will flatter me infinitely, for I do not recollect to have seen her in Buenos Ayres, I was not, indeed, introduced at your brother-in-law's ——"

At these words, the baron turned his steps, to meet the proposal for an introduction, when Mr Thomson seized him by the button, coughed again, and at length said, in a peculiarly low voice. "You remember a brochure of poetry baron, which I handed to you as a novelty some weeks since?"

"Brochure of poetry?" repeated the spy, staring at the sky, as if his memory contained no brochure at all, nor a single thing of the sort.

"To be sure, baron, you must remember, you must recollect the Elegies? the "Elegias dela Plata?" as the little book was called

"Elegias dela Plata? no, surely not, I must have entirely forgotten it"

"That is strange!" whispered the old widower, "Did I not give it to you one evening in the Hotel Faroux, when we were supping there with the guarda mor? when I first received it?"

"No! you are mistaken this time!" replied the baron hastily, and with peculiar decision

"Then I will never rely on my memory again," said Mr Thomson, sunk in profound endeavors to read the singular riddle

"It seems to me as if you once told me of a brochure, as if you had the goodness to say to me, that you would give it me to read But it is obscure to me——"

"I said nothing to you, then, of the authoress of the Elegies? nothing at all of the sort"

"Not a word! not a syllable?"

"Hem! singular that! Then I must have spoken of it to you in a dream"

"It is very easily possible! even very probable, but you have not, when awake, and especially in the Hotel Faroux, as you suppose, said a word to me about the authoress, and I never saw the brochure"

"So much the better, then! Now, baron, I will just beg you, of all things in the world, not to let it be perceived in the presence of my niece, that you have ever heard any thing of—of the Elegies——for—for it is a secret, the relations in Buenos Ayres, as you know, between the Confederados and the Unitarios, are—are very critical, and the Argentine ambassador here in Rio, or some spy, might learn something——"

"A spy? some spy or other?" interrupted the agent of the secret police "Do you really believe that there are foreign spies here in Rio? Can that really be the case?"

"They say so! people suspect it, and even maintain it"

"Mr Thomson! whoever says that, fabricates chimeras I ask you, what is a foreign spy to observe here in Rio? Perhaps he is to count the bags of coffee, that are appraised at the alfandega? or listen to the babble of Peter and Paul, in the Café de Commerce in the Rua Direita? or smell at what we eat in the Hotel Faroux? I should like to know what a foreign spy could find to do here in Rio?"

"It certainly appears very ridiculous to me, also," replied Mr Thomson, "the more I reflect upon what a spy could properly spy out here, so much the more improbable does it seem to me, that there should be foreign spies here— although, on the other hand, I have learned that they have found out where the brochures for Rio Grande were printed—who printed them I mean—for example, the epistle of Mazzini, and the like."

"Have the like pamphlets or tracts been printed here in Rio," inquired the future brother-in-law of the old widower. "That is entirely new to me !"

"You do not appear to concern yourself much with political reading, as I observe !"

"I ! with political reading !" laughed the other. "What an idea ! I have something else to do here ! You have long been aware that your brother-in-law, has formed the plan of founding a British viceroyalty in Parà , to connect the River Amazon with the Paranà by a canal, and in this manner to bring the whole of South America, by degrees, under British protection——"

"Ah, indeed !" interrupted the old man astonished in the highest degree, "and you are perhaps here to——?"

"To play into the hands of your brother-in-law ; as I am trying to carry out the plan of transferring the Signal Mountain over there, to British ownership I mean to promote the contract of sale ; to have the government sell the Signal Mountain to England "

Mr. Thomson stopped and stared at the baron, with his mouth wide open, perfectly astonished that he had, at length, quite accidentally, learned the object of his coming to Rio

"Is that possible ? you are, then, so to say, a secret agent in the English service ?"

"Mr Thomson !" whispered the spy, "one confidence is worthy of another You offer me, so to speak, unlimited confidence in family relations, and the like , I, also, owe you mine. What I have just revealed to you, must remain the strictest secret between us , do you understand ? I had an audience yesterday, with the Minister of Finance—a private audience—and can give you the assurance that the affair is going forward. Let that suffice you ! And I do not concern myself with political reading—not I ! But introduce me to your amiable niece "

A great weight had fallen from the heart of good old Mr Thomson, as he had now not only convinced himself that the baron did not concern himself about political brochures, but that, also, he did not know the least about the Elegies of La Plata, and of course could not entertain the least suspicion in relation to the incognito of the young lady from Buenos Ayres

They then hastily approached the family group, and the formal introduction took place The baron did not seem to give any more attention to the niece than politeness on his part required, and paid all the more to Miss Susan, who, on this day, appeared ten, if not fifteen years younger She availed herself of many opportunities to laugh at the baron's jokes, in order to display her beautiful teeth, which the latter, with incontestible justice, had once admired.

"How much do you weigh, doctor ?" cried the old widower in a peculiarly happy mood, the weight having been removed from his heart "Come doctor ! we will see how heavy you are, and you, also, Miss Fanny ? we will all be weighed ; we have still time before dinner !" After this invitation, he started away from the family group, ran to a private door, which led into a front hall, and into the green parlor, arranged the platform scales, and waited for his niece, whom he would not exactly name first, but to whom, of course, the doctor gave the precedence.

Dolores, not coming within a thousand miles

distance of the idea which lay at the foundation of such social amusement, stepped upon the eventful scales with perfect unconcern, and was just as far from remarking the expression of anxiety and expectation on the good humored countenance of her protector, who solemnized this moment as " an event in his life."

"One hundred and thirty-six !" he exclaimed, with inexpressible satisfaction "A hundred and thirty-six pounds ! and I'll bet that she'll weigh a hundred and ninety-six in a year ! for you have a tendency, Miss Fanny ! a tendency to corpulency, I assure you——!"

The baron laughed out loud, and looked at Dr Thorfin, as if he wished to remind him of their "table talk" in the Hotel Faroux

"A youthful glow flushed the cheeks of the old widower, as he felt that he had nearly betrayed himself to his two table companions.

"I would not have believed that you were so heavy !" said Robert, laughing, as he reached his hand to his "sister,' when she jumped down from the scales

"I feel at times that I possess strength," replied Dolores, smiling likewise, "but whether I am of material weight ? that question never occurred to me "

Old Achilles, who was invested with the office of valet, just then announced that dinner was ready The baron offered his arm, with all due ceremony, to his fair future, the old uncle led in his niece, and Dr Thorfin and Robert walked together into the family apartment, in which hung the four portraits of the old widower's sainted wives, who, altogether, in their bloom, weighed eight hundred and forty-three and three-fourth pounds avoirdupois

————✳————

CHAPTER XVI

THE ALFANDEGA AND THE CHEESE

THE three travelling companions, from the La Plata river, sat again in their common parlor, over their aromatic coffee It was Monday morning They were expecting Dr Thorfin, who was to accompany them to the alfandega, where they had agreed to meet Robert Walker, to take joint possession of their travelling effects

The bustle of the lively business street, Rua Direita, become more and more varied The singular monotonous cry of the coffee laden negroes, ascended with a peculiar sound, into the open windows, and brought the strangers to the balcony

They saw a train of some thirty Ethiopians, in national costume—that is to say, naked, all but short quasi pantaloons, which enveloped the hips, without covering the thighs Each carried on his head a heavy bag of coffee, and trotted along, with his body bent forward, one arm raised to the bag, the other elbow drawn up with the fist stretched forward, all the while staring straight before him, with downcast eyes, and at each rapid step, ejaculating sounds nearly like " Doi-doy—Doi-doy ! " forming, in thirty-fold gradations, from the deepest bass to the highest alto, a singularly original, but sadly striking chorus.

In front of this noisy concert, sprang a negro, in the same garb, who represented the orchestra, his instrument was a funnel with leather drawn over it, in which rattled a handful of coffee grains, as a suitable accompaniment to the chorus, or rather to mark the time, instead of the drumstick of the tambour major. With this monotonous cry of Doi-dov, the poor devils trotted on, pursuing their course with as much diligence as if the fate of Brazil depended upon their not losing a moment

"Mournful lot of colored humanity!" sighed Hinango, to whom this spectacle, although no novelty, was always painful "And have these men heads, only for the purpose of carrying a coffee bag, of some one hundred and fifty pounds weight, on a trot, from the warehouses to the alfandega, and from the alfandega to the lighter that conveys the freight on board? while the majority of the citizens here are negroes and mulattoes, who are distinguished for their honesty, diligence, and morality!"

"I cannot even conceive the economy of such transportation,' remarked Horatio, looking after the train "Could not these thirty sacks of coffee be as easily carried on a single dray with some horses, as in such a manner by thirty men?"

The entrance of Dr Thorsin interrupted the conversation He waited until the friends had prepared to go out All four left the hotel, although Alvirez had no baggage to take possession of They walked to the neighboring building of the alfandega, where the captain had sent all the travelling effects of the passengers

They had hardly found the expected objects, before Robert Walker, according to agreement, entered likewise, to open his own trunks, as well as the trunks and boxes of his "sister," which were now overhauled and examined

The crowd of functionaries, tradespeople, and carrier negroes, in the spacious halls and courts, and passages of the buildings, which served as warehouses of the alfandega, moved around the strangers A thousand objects, from foreign countries, here and there attract the attention of one and another

"There is the elegant negro, with his white servants," whispered Horatio, in the ear of his friend Hinango, "the same that lately went past our hotel with the young lady——"

"An interesting countenance," returned Hinango, "draw him in crayon, without reference to color, and every cultivated European would acknowledge him as his equal, and admire his intellectual expression"

"What is in this box?" enquired a custom house officer of young Walker, touching a considerably large, flat box, which was just opened

"An old family picture," replied Robert, "the portrait of one of my aunts"

"It must pay duty, the frame also, the picture twenty-five per cent, the frame one hundred per cent on the value"

"Art seems to be treated here like a hated foreigner," whispered Horatio."

"Even if such a system should foster art in Brazil," replied Hinango, "it is at least difficult to procure for young artists, good originals of the old masters for study"

The box was opened, and the living image of Dolores, in an old fashioned dress, appeared It was the picture of her deceased mother, painted in Madrid, shortly before her marriage, when she accompanied her father, who went to Europe as ambassador from the Spanish colony

The worth of the picture and the frame was specified, and it escaped many, that the distinguished negro joined the group, and observed the picture with evidently heightening interest

Horatio and Hinango were the first to remark the attention of the Ethiopian, who, absorbed in the contemplation of the picture, did not observe them He was a tall, thin man, of a regular Ethiopian figure, with the above specified humane countenance He was dressed, according to Brazilian custom, in white linen with a fine white beaver hat His shirt buttons, watch chain, rings, etc, were ornamented with valuable jewels At a distance behind him stood a white servant, apparently Portuguese in blue livery, with gold buttons

A custom house officer threw the cover over the picture, and the negro gentleman roused himself, as if from a dream, looked hastily around upon the bystanders, as if he would ask forgiveness for having taken the liberty of looking at the picture, and stepped backward some paces without a word

"Do you know this man?" inquired Hinango, in a low tone, of the custom house officer who was inspecting his effects

"To be sure!" replied he, "it is a millionaire from Goa, in the East Indies, who, on his arrival here, paid duty on a thousand contos in gold coin * as travelling money, besides the cargo of the vessel, which belonged to him He has two daughters with white governesses, and lives in the Rua do Valongo, where he has a palace I am not surprised that he looked at the portrait, he appears to be a connoisseur and admirer of paintings If I am not mistaken, he brought out many valuable pictures with him He very often walks around here in the alfandega, and occasionally has something to send off"

The information was certainly sufficient, as it indicated the standing of the negro gentleman, but how the portrait of the mother of Dolores could so highly interest him, as was evidently the case, as to make him forgetful of the whole alfandega around him, remained a riddle, that involuntarily occupied the travellers from La Plata

The interesting millionaire from Goa remained standing at a distance, as if he was observing other objects — not belonging to the passengers of the Nordstjernan Horatio's boxes were opened, and the various apparatus of an artist, or dilletanti in oil painting, were unpacked The negro from Goa now appeared to have made sufficient observations once more looked at the South American to whom the painting apparatus appeared to belong, and slowly withdrew — first looking at one thing, and then at another, that caught his eye

The resemblance of the picture to the daughter of the lady whose portrait it was, evidently endangered the incognito of the poetess, in case the Indian negro (which still remained inexplicable) had inspected the picture as a portrait, and not merely as an interesting oil painting, and, (what was equally inexplicable,) perhaps, connected with it peculiar recollections

* Gold and silver coin pay two per cent duty in Brazil, (import and export,) as these metals are considered productions of the country, and articles of commerce.

25

Alvarez conversed with Horatio about the singularity of this meeting, and reminded him of an involuntary exclamation of Dolores, on board the Nordstjernan, when he mentioned to her the name of his mother. "She has taken the secret with her to the grave!" she said, at that time, half aloud, to herself

"Granting," returned Horatio, "that the interest of this Indian negro in the portrait of her mother is, in some way or other, connected with this secret, no one can give us any information respecting it but just this Senhor from Goa, and it will not answer for us to approach him on this subject, inasmuch as Dolores passes here for Miss Fanny Walker"

"A true portrait has, many times already, given occasion to the most singular discoveries," observed Hinango, "and it appears to me that this gentleman from Goa will not be wanting in discretion, if he should be disposed to approach us on his part We must wait for that"

"Inconceivable!" exclaimed Alvarez, suddenly awaking from a train of ideas "Señora Dolores said those words when I mentioned the name of my uncle, Garringòs, whose traces I sought for years in Madrid, and in all Spain. This picture, you say, was painted in Madrid, prior to the year 1812, when my uncle disappeared thence Can this expression of Señora Dolores, in relation to her mother, have any connexion with the name of my uncle, and, of course, with his fate?"

"'She has carried the secret with her to the grave,'" replied Horatio, "is all that we have learned, and probably Señora Dolores, also, knows no more in relation to the secret"

The friends had completed their business at the alfandega, and the requisite 'négres de gagne' were loaded, to carry away their effects Robert was very serious, and appeared self-absorbed The lively unconcern with which he had greeted his fellow voyagers, only a few evenings before, had vanished The friends who surrounded him, expected that something disagreeable had occurred at his uncle's house, in consequence of the arrival of Dolores.

"I will send my trunks for the present with yours, to the Hotel du Nord," said he to Ormur "I occupy a pavilion in the neighborhood of the city, but, henceforth, I also wish to live incognito. I have given up my room at my uncle's country house to my 'sister,' that is the reason why I occupy a separate dwelling I will tell you the rest by and by."

"I thank you again for your friendship," returned Hinango, "and hardly know how I have acquired it"

"I cannot even explain to myself," asserted the youth, "wherefore I feel so drawn towards you! It seems to me, however, as if the association with you, during our voyage, had given a new 'sounding-board' to my inward being! as if all the tones of life, which come in contact with me, reverberate with deeper harmony You see I am obliged, involuntarily, to express myself poetically.

"If my individuality," replied Ormur, "operates upon you with a certain attraction, my dear young friend, it is a proof to me that your mind, or your inner life, as I may call it, is unfolded in youthful purity, and feels itself drawn towards me, through affinity with me. For you

must know that there are men, who, notwithstanding their advance in age, preserve in themselves all purity and depth of mind, in spite of all their bitter experience, in spite of all the storms of life! The world declares such a state of mind, to be 'infirmity, over excitement, nervous weakness,' and——"

A man of business approached the group from the Nordstjernan, interrupting the conversation It was Mr Forro, who greeted young Walker, and inquired after his health He had just come from Mr Thomson's office, where he had provisionally arranged the new business

Hinango and his friends left the alfandega, to despatch their effects to the chacara in which Dr Thorfin had prepared rooms for them Robert Walker exchanged some words with the agent of the naturalist, and then mounted his horse From necessary caution in relation to the incognito of the lady, he deferred the transportation of his effects to da Gloria until late in the evening, but hurried out there himself, to speak to her, if only to ascertain whether the villa was ready for him

"How in the world could you be such a jackass, as to shut yourself up, and by that means ruin the whole business that occasioned your coming to Rio?" These words were addressed by a man to his younger companion, as they passed Robert Walker at one of the gates of the Alfandega, just as he had given his horse the spur This was Mr Franz Rossbruck, and the "jackass" was his nephew, our "gentleman"

"I did not shut myself up!" replied the latter, "The young man, the Swiss, locked me in, he admits that himself"

"Mr Doubly has related the whole affair to me, circumstantially, and I can only praise his conduct I should, in his place, have done the same A young fellow comes in, speaks English, and gives himself out for a connexion of the house, considers himself too good to sit at table with his equals, and what was still more odd, to exchange a word with them, goes out and in, and all the time, without saying a word, and shuts himself up again in the interior of the apartment, allotted to him as a connexion of the house! Mr Doubly then simply said to me, 'When this 'would be gentleman' had four times declined our invitation to your table, I doubted that he was your nephew. I thought him an impostor, or a deranged person, and, in either case, it was incumbent on me to take measures to prevent his injuring us As an impostor he might rob us, and as a crazy man, he might do, God knows what! I therefore had bread and water placed in his room, and locked the door with my own hand, to await your return"

"And I sat there from Saturday evening, until this morning, two nights and a day, with bread and water," growled the "gentleman," with a visage a yard long

"You deserve to be locked up for a year, on bread and water, with some of the real English dandies whom you try to ape—without possessing a spark of English business skill You may go back again to Europe! We can make no use here of such a gentleman as you!"

"Good morning Sr. Rossbruck! how are you? it's a coolly pleasant morning!" sounded near the dandy's uncle, who beheld, to the heightening of his just displeasure, Senhor Forro's well known confiscable business physiognomy

"Good morning, Senhor Forro! how are you?" grumbled he, half over his shoulder

"Your nephew, I presume?" continued the other, with a sort of mischievously friendly smile, looking at the young man, who pressed down his patent gloves between the fingers

"I have just left your office, Senhor Forro, and hear, to my great dissatisfaction, that you deny us the signature to the contract"

I regret, extremely, that you did not sign the contract at the right time We waited until the last moment appointed by the last agreement The partner of your house, whose arrival was announced by the 'Jornal do Commercio,' might have done us the honor only to send a negro to us with the information that he was here, and the business would still have remained at your disposal

The uncle of the gentleman bit his lips, in the overflow of his gall, but found not a word of reasonable objection

"You know, however, that Mr Closting has received a considerable advance from us, as earnest in this business—about two contos di reis!" he, at length said, with a peevish air

"Senhor Closting! advance!—I know nothing about that Senhor Francisco! that is a private affair You have no claim on our firm, it does not concern me in the least It's a fine coolly pleasant morning Good morning, Senhor Francisco! may I offer you a pinch?" inquired he, with the utmost politeness, as he was about to depart, and took out his box

"I thank you!" grumbled the uncle of the Angleised nephew, and Mr Forro took a pinch himself, and, mingling with the crowd of the alfandega, vanished behind the loaded negroes

The "gentleman" made a face as if he was endeavoring to invent a powder which "should put millions in circulation" He trembled for the moment when his uncle might find out that he had given a hint to a young Englishman on board the Nordstjernan, in regard to the undertaking, an imprudence, on his part, which he perceived himself, although he had done it with the best intention in the world—to make known the "respectability" of his house He walked on with his uncle, like a school boy who has taken the premium for stupidity, and at length looked for his English baggage, with the caligraphic inscription "William Rossbruck, Esq"

While these scenes took place in the halls of the alfandega, Dr Merbold sat with the Baron de Spandau, in the private parlor of the latter, in the Hotel Faroux, at a breakfast, at which fresh Minas cheese, the favorite dish of the naturalist, was conspicuous

"So you have remarked, Herr Baron, that I am fond of new cheese!" laughed the German savant, as he cut himself a thick slice

"I confess that I am a great friend of cheese myself, and this Minas cheese has really a great resemblance to our German cream cheese"

"More than the Germans to the Mineiros!" returned the entomologist "We Germans are peace-loving, faithful subjects of the most glorious confederate princes, and do not trouble ourselves with politics like the turbulent Mineiros up there, in the mountains They are truly a rebellious set! One cannot catch a beetle there without meeting some hotheaded fellow They are like the French, and the Spaniards, and the Italians, and all the Catholic nations of Europe! who are always rebelling! Our Protestants in Germany deserve praise for that! they do not allow themselves to be so easily excited!"

"That is true!" interrupted the baron, "Protestantism is a good fulminating powder against revolutionary schemes! Since Dr Luther called upon the German princes to shoot down the rebellious peasants in Thuringia and Suabia, peace and order have pretty generally prevailed in all Protestant countries! We have our universities to thank for that! especially our professors of theology! and also the 'pastors!' Fathers of families will not willingly allow themselves to be disturbed in their official diligence in the nuptial bed!"

"You are right, upon my soul!" cried Dr Merbold, astonished by this observation, "that is true, too!"

"The Protestant ecclesiastics are generally demagogues as students If, however, an arch demagogue takes a wife, all is over with his patriotism! Among a thousand, there will not be three exceptions to this rule The Protestant dogmatic of marriage,' my dear doctor, has a very peculiar, mysterious power"

"That is just what physiologists assert!" affirmed Dr Merbold, "and I once disputed, for an hour, with a professor in Gottingen, who wished to maintain that wedlock was more interesting than entomology—which he endeavored to prove, on the ground of experience, as he was both married and a good entomologist! As relates to myself, I merely took the position, that entomology had always so confined me, that I never had time to make the necessary acquaintance and experience which ought to precede marriage My acquaintance and experience are confined, as you know, entirely to the beetle world"

"Then I presume you know this married pair?" inquired the baron, handing him, with a significant look, a neat paper box, ornamented with Fanny Elssler's portrait in lithograph

"Hey! the devil! a pair of Spinoza hoods!" cried Dr Merbold, springing up from his chair, and letting a great piece of Minas cheese fall on the floor "Hey! the devil! that would be something for the entomological museum at Berlin!"

"Will you accept them, as a present from me, doctor? you can send them, in your own name, to whatever government you like!"

"No, baron! you are too good! too generous! I will guarantee you, through this pair of beetles, the title of a 'Real corresponding member' of some royal academy of science or other, and will you relinquish such an advantage to me? Really, are you in earnest, baron? really in earnest?"

"Why not? as I tell you, the pair of beetles is designed for you, and no one else!"

"Then I thank you a million times!" cried the entomologist, and pressed the hand of the spy, while his little gray eyes sparkled through tears

"They shall go to Europe with my 'Simplex

Merboldensis,' with all the treasures that I brought with me from Buenos Ayres ' where the abominable revolutionary war with the Patagonians, or cannibals, or Orientals, as they call the rebels, unfortunately hindered my researches What canaille the people are here in South America, Herr Baron ' Such a revolutionary rabble, that one cannot even quietly collect beetles, without being taken for a rebel ' and that, even on board of a Swedish vessel "

" On board of a Swedish vessel '" exclaimed the baron, as if he was extremely surprised " You did not encounter a visitation on board on account of rebels ·"

" Visitation ' Herr Baron, I can tell you something about that ' I believe I came here with a whole cargo of rebels ' at least, I would not give a patack for the loyal sentiments of all the cabin passengers, with the exception of one, who, to the honor of our nation, was a German ; a Mr. Pferdebruck, or Rossbruck as he is called "

" What is that you say? You came in the Nordstjernan, did you not? with a young Englishman and his sister, as I see by the newspaper."

" With a young Englishman, certainly, and there was a young lady there, also, but whether she was the sister of the young Englishman— the police knows best The clerk of the English house, who lodged with me in a " private cabin," did not have much to say, when I began about the young lady It seemed to me a sort of political abduction. A Russian naval officer, who appeared to have escaped from hunting the sable in Siberia—Hinango is his name—he seemed to me to be very intimate with the young lady ; and they two *politicised* and philosophised in Spanish, by moonshine and daylight, and a fugitive came on board, like Roller in Schiller's ' Robbers,' direct from the gallows '— he had even yet ' the rope around his neck,' that his guitar hung to "

The spy allowed the entomologist to talk on, undisturbed, and seizing a number of the " Jornal do Commercio" which lay on his writing table, he ran over the list of passengers on board the Nordstjernan, and inquired, incidentally " Do you not know the name of the fugitive ? It was not Horatio de P——, who is here among the passengers '"

" Oh, no ' that is the young man whose uncle was shot the morning when we sailed, he is a silent, good-natured young man ; it is a pity he has fallen into such bad company Oh, no ' he did not come on board as a fugitive It was a fellow called Alvarez von der Barca, or something like it The captain had drawn him out of the water, just as we were going to sea, and I nearly had a quarrel with the Russian when the vessel came after us and would have taken him off, and I believe they had also some designs upon the young lady —for that she is the sister of the young Englishman, no one shall make me believe No ' Dr Merbold is not so stupid ' And they were all good friends with the privateer, or pirate, when he came on board ' all went on merrily ' and we saluted each other when we went to sea in company "

" You do not eat any cheese, doctor You entirely forget your cheese and your coffee ' and your beefsteak is getting cold '"

" It's no matter for that, Herr Baron, thank you ! I tell you that was a rebellious passage ' The corsair was called Barrigallows, or something of the sort ' He seemed to me, also, to be ' ripe for the gallows '" And then there was murder on the fishing boat, or some such thing that would have taken us ' The crew rebelled They threw one of the officers overboard, and gagged the other Mr Daily saw the whole of it, and then told me all about it, and explained to me what had been going on around us, for I, myself, Herr Baron, had enough to do with my beetles, and could not give much heed to the rebels ' but Mr Daily remarked, if he were captain of the Nordstjernan, he would make money by this opportunity He said there were two heads on board, either of which was worth a thousand pounds sterling I, however, would certainly not have given these two Spinoza hoods for them I believe he meant the young lady and myself, for he attached great value to my entomology, which certainly is in my head, and has its worth, to be sure '"

Dr Merbold ate cheese, and drank coffee, contemplated his Spinosa hoods from time to time, and answered all the queries of the spy, in regard to the passengers of the Nordstjernan, and their interesting voyage from the river La Plata to Rio de Janeiro

DOLORES.

BOOK V.

CHAPTER I

YANA KIARM

WE now find ourselves amongst the Toldos, of a Patagonian tribe of the Inaken, between the Lago Grande and Lago de Tchuel, at the outlet of the Cusu Leova, in the Rio Negro, in about 38° south latitude, and 67° longitude west from Greenwich—nearly 100 hundred miles W S W from Buenos Ayres, where the European can only determine his route by means of the compass

To make the scenes intelligible, which unfold themselves before us, it will be necessary that we should, with all brevity, institute a geographical and statistical review of the strange locality in which this race of people move about

The Patagonians—one of the most fabulous nations on earth, insomuch as for centuries the most singular descriptions have been disseminated of their gigantic size—inhabit the northern plains, extending from the Straits of Magellan to the Rio Negro, and from the eastern declivities of the Cordillera de los Andes to the shores of the South Atlantic Ocean

They call themselves, in their sonorous language, Tchuelches, (the northern,) and Inaken, (the southern,) and border, towards the mountains of the Andes, upon the Aucas, or Aroncanas, who call themselves Huilichi, likewise a southern race, and towards the coast they adjoin the Puelchus, little distinguished from them in manners and character.

The total number of these tribes of the Patagonians, which has gradually diminished through their struggles and wars among themselves, about the right of hunting, and water, and meadows, and through the war of extermination on the part of humane and Christian Europeans, hardly amounts to 10,000 fighting men, who, however, have as yet maintained their independence against the Europeans

The fabulous physical size of these Patagonians has decreased, as if in proportion to their former numbers, according to the reports of travelling Europeans who have observed them with reasonable eyes, to a certainly considerable grenadier height, to which is joined a well proportioned muscular frame, and a certain natural dignity The complexion of these tribes is dark olive brown, with a slight reddish tint, their faces rather round than oval, with a flat profile, an arched forehead, and small, horizontally cut, dark sparkling eyes without the least expression of falsehood, the short flat nose partly discloses the nostrils, and the thick lips cover the national decoration of beautiful pearly teeth

More striking than many other properties which they share with the neighboring tribes, is the luxuriant richness of their raven black, soft hair, that retains its color and thickness to advanced age, and generally quite covers the back, and, given to the winds, floats about in the element of freedom

The designation of Patagon (big foot,) seems as little accordant with reality, as the long since refuted rumor of their superhuman size On the contrary. the Patagonians are distinguished for their small hands and feet, as well as manifesting, in their whole being, something that pleases and inspires confidence, instead of either physical or moral coarseness, thereby distinguishing themselves from the ox—the proper "cosmopolite"—who grazes, and ruminates, and bellows in all countries, and everywhere remains——Ox.

The customs, like the character of these tribes, evidently resemble those of the patriarchal world of bygone centuries, and show us man in his natural condition, with the innate principle of humanity, which authenticates itself in some form or other of human society

Apart from the fatal hostilities which necessity engenders, these tribes hold together, among themselves, with undeniable nationality All stand up for one, or one for all, at every assault on their independence, which they resist with decided energy, on the contrary, however, they entertain unconcealed distrust against all Europeans, excepting Spaniards and Italians, and perhaps on very just grounds Although, under the former monarchial government of the neighboring Spanish colonies, they were not unfrequently chased with hounds like wild beasts, and forced back to their pampas, their natural human understanding led them by degrees to the knowledge whereby they distinguish despotic ill usage on the part of bloodthirst, conquerors, from peaceful intercourse with free men, who renounce such a system of government. They consider their guests from the south of Europe as men like themselves, who at times innocently and peaceably erect their toldos in the New World, as they do, and barter with them their oxen, against all sorts of useful, and often " really curious " implements

A so called horde of the Inaken, consisting of about a hundred fighting men, with numerous families, some thousands of oxen, and some hundreds of horses, guanacoes,* sheep, and goats, had more and more slowly descended from the southern plains, not far from the Andes, to the right bank of the Rio Negro, to carry on their barter there

The toldos (tents of buffalo hides) formed, in picturesque disorder, a considerable village on the declivity of a hill, which hardly deserved the name, since it was one of those elevations, of miles in width, which, interrupted by depressions of equal extent, form an undulating tract of country, unvarying for hundreds of miles, partly overgrown with luxuriant grass, " a waving grass-sea," partly interrupted by extensive patches of sand, and ornamented here and there with scanty woods and low thickets From the hills, the eye perceived a uniform desert landscape, whose undulating, green foreground, interrupted in the above named manner by patches of sand, lost itself by degrees in the less green middle ground, and at length in the light blue of the distant horizon

Rhabukih, called by his European and pampas friends El Rojo, (the red,) the venerable cacique of his free tribe, sat in an oriental posture upon a thick buffalo hide in front of his toldo, with his left elbow supported by a sort of saddle, that also served him for a pillow at night.

His countenance was purely national, such as we have already generally described A red and white handkerchief, bound about his head, covered the upper part of the high forehead, and formed behind each ear a long end of artistically arranged points, that fluttered behind over his long dark hair. Three stripes of dark red paint decorated each cheek, from the corners of the mouth to the ear and the temple Excepting the upper lip, the countenance was beardless, as his beloved, according to the custom of the country, had taken the pains to pluck out the beard in his early youth He was a respectable figure, of advanced age, of conspicuous Patagonian size, and of course half a head taller than the Emperor Nicholas of Russia, who, like king Saul of old, " is higher than all the people." His dress was as original as the entire scene around him He wore, as his choicest garment, the national poncho, whose form the Brazilians have borrowed from these tribes, as we have already described it at Villa Tasso, at the time of Serafini's arrest. But this poncho of the Cacique El Rojo was not of European stuff, but a home made article, the costly product of the domestic industry of his daughters

Whoever conceives of this patriarchal world of South America, as an anti-social desert, remote from all civilization, errs, like so many Europeans, who often prize far too highly the hot house civilization of our whitewashed age, in comparison with " half savage nations "

The condition of women in Patagonia has, certainly, so far, a similarity with the slavery of many nations on the European continent, insomuch as woman is considered the first and most indispensable of " domestic animals," who performs all the labor, for the convenience and comfort of man, fatigues herself through the day, and hardly finds rest at night

As woman evidently rules in many countries, and (in opposition to this degrading slavery) is considered as a doll, to be fed and dressed, and then undressed and put to bed again—so we consider woman in Patagonia, not as the ruling, but the administrative, power

Woman, in Patagonia, shears the guanacoes and spins the wool, seeks the coloring matter and dyes the yarn, weaves or knits the cloth, embroiders the trimming of the imported linen or white calico, takes care of the cooking, cleans the toldos, &c , &c , and fulfils, besides, all the female household and conjugal duties, as soon as she has arrived at the appointed age, which event is distinguished by great festivity The marriageable girl is proclaimed capable to love, by the cacique and a sort of priestess, and is tattooed on different parts of her well formed body, like leaving the " finishing school," and being " brought out into the world " as marriageable

The poncho of the cacique was a long, four-cornered piece, some six feet wide, and eight or nine feet long, artfully woven from sheep and guanaco wool, striped lengthwise with various colors, and decorated with ornaments The prevailing tints of the several stripes were brown, red, dark green, light green, yellow, and white The decorations in the stripes themselves, of various gradations displayed (to the surprise of Europeans, accustomed to the artistic forms of antiquity) evident antique arabesques in their complicated squares, which, borrowed from the Grecian decorations, have passed over to our modern borders The garment which (to borrow the tone of virtuous transatlantic civilization) wound its folds " nearest the body " of the cacique, was a piece of British, or French, or Helvetian calico, three yards long, doubled together, like Senhora Bebida's coffee bag, and the poncho, provided with a hole for the neck The piece of clothing that British discretion finds " inexpressible," (as if it would thereby directly turn the attention to the precise portion of the person which it covers,) was, on our cacique, indeed inexpressible, and could the less be called (without hypocrisy) pantaloons, since the notion of pantaloons signifies something quite different It was a valuable shawl of guanaco wool, whose quality ranged between the finest merino and cashmere—likewise manufactured at home, by the " princesses of the house " The undyed wool presented a natural color, in so called broken tint, between light gray and a light brownish yellow—the stuff itself was delicate and soft as cashmere How this shawl was wound round the hips and partly covered the legs, like pantaloons was " inexpressible," we could, at the utmost, form a model with our own hands out of a large lady's shawl, but the description would be too long * From below these " inexpressibles,"

---

* Guanaco, a sort of sheep camel, or lama, whose wool is of excellent quality.

* These guanaco shawls, like the ponchos of the Patagonians, were occasionally sent to Europe as rarities An ordinary poncho, even though it had been worn, cost always, among Europeans, over forty Spanish

a pair of white pantaloons descended, trimmed with a border of embroidery—a sort of lace, not sewed on, but wrought, à jour, by means of threads skilfully drawn out of the calico. A pair of half boots, or rather "leather stockings," cut from the two hind shanks of a horse, in such a manner that the joint covered the heel, (of course, without sewing,) completed the picturesque costume of the Cacique El Rojo. A small leather bag, with fire implements, consisting of flint, steel, and fungus, (which latter was carefully deposited in the hornlike hinder part of a small armadillo, two or three inches long, ornamented with silver,) bow and arrows, some knives, likewise with silver on the handles, and a sling, the favorite national weapon, hung, and were stuck about and near him. This is a tolerably exact portrait, *en tableau de genre*, of our Cacique Rhabukih el Rojo.

It was about sundown, and the numerous family of the stout, venerable old man, in various toldos near him, were employed in their domestic occupations, while he lay there upon the buffalo hide, smoking a cigarette, and from time to time looking at a very common silver watch, for which he had bartered twenty oxen with a European. Some tame ash grey ostriches, serving his grandsons as riding horses, wandered about near him, ruminating philosophically. Here and there, before the entrance of a toldo, boiled the "ever full fleshpot," the single but nourishing dish of the Patagonians, which is every hour at the service of every guest. To reckon according to the national fleshpot, it would, of course, always be "mid-day" in Patagonia, in so far as the hand of the noonday hour amongst the working classes of almost all nations points to the fleshpot, which is occasionally empty.

Some "princes and princesses" of the reigning house of Rhabukih approached their papa, or grandpapa, and at the same time the fleshpot before his tent, seated themselves, after the oriental fashion, for an intimate interview with the old man and the fleshpot, while they took knife and spoon in hand, and though without a plate, to be sure, began to eat their soup tolerably decently.

A sort of governess, or waiting woman, prepared the tea, which is called Chà de Mattè,* from a South American plant that grows principally in the province of Paraguay, always, however, an article of luxury in Patagonia.

The tea leaves were shaken into a bullet formed cup, (Guja,) and boiling water poured on them. This cup is for the most part a cocoanut shell, the stem of which serves like the handle of a pan. These gujas are often ornamented with all sorts of figures and hieroglyphics. A silver tube, ten inches long, with a perforated hollow globe, is immersed in it, and the drink, as hot as the gums can bear it, is sucked through it, while the leaves remain in the cup.

The old cacique sucked his guja, and comfortably enjoyed this "modern drink," recommended it to his family as very strengthening to the breast, and then smoked his cigarette again.

The females were dressed in the above described

piastres. There are guanaco shawls worth more than a hundred piastres. They have endeavored to imitate this material in Europe, but could not succeed, as they have no guanaco wool, and the fabric is quite peculiar.
* Or. Mattè.—Chà is the Chinese word for tea.

national garb, only with the difference, that the ladies merely wore white richly adorned calico "inexpressibles" and carried in their tinder bags, the implements for knitting and embroidery. The young members of the family were hardly to be distinguished from each other by their sex, as the maidens were not yet tattooed, and a certain national family likeness prevailed in all their faces. Men, women, and children of the nation moved about with democratic unconcern, around the tent of the cacique, all stamped with the above national resemblance as members and descendants of a single family.

Peaceful guanacoes were straying around at pasture, while in the far distance the numerous masses of horned "four-footed cosmopolites," likewise *en famille*, bellowed at the setting sun in manifold gradations of tone, to the interruption of their ruminating lives. Domesticated horses, saddled for hourly service, appeared through the fetters of habit to desire the halter, and wandered with slow steps around the tents, in expectation of the riders, who mounted them every few minutes, and then left them again to themselves. Hunting dogs, of distinguished breeds, stood in groups near the young family of the cacique, in close companionship, while the howl of savage bloodhounds (introduced by the Spaniards, and degenerated to beasts of prey) joined in, from a distance, with the lowing of oxen and the neighing of the horses. The dense smoke of fresh kindled turf (which, for want of wood, serves as the national fuel) rose, here and there, around a colossal fleshpot, and gave a dark shading to the monotonous but highly pleasing picture, in contrast with the cloudless azure blue heavens, through which countless flocks of birds were flying.

In opposition to the "nobility" of the tribe of Inaken, (who, as to that, had no hereditary privileges,) appeared the "people," in the natural condition of nakedness, clothed with a single garment, the poncho, which the men wore in the manner of the cacique, with the hole for the neck.

The poncho of the women, suitably to its object, was considerably longer than the men's, and was wound round the hips and shoulders like a sort of carbonaro mantle, or antique drapery, (similar to the before described garment of the negresses,) whereby the form of the body was more or less displayed in its natural contour, and a portion of the shoulder remained at times uncovered.

"Yana Kirym has prophesied," said the cacique to himself, "that he would come again before the sun had disappeared for the third time behind the distant plains, and the longest of these little pieces of metal upon this circle of figures has only to creep round it twice more, and then the sun shall go down, having shone upon our Oregham hither at home."

"There comes Yana Kirym, herself!" exclaimed a princess of the house, "and Oregham will come too, if she has foretold it."

Yana Kirym was the sibyl of the tribe of Inaken, a sort of personified "principle of the mysterious," which, as religion, (or as faith in a higher divine power,) appears more or less, in the so called state of nature, in all nations.

The Patagonians acknowledge a single supreme being, whom they call Ach-éKenat Kanet, to whom they ascribe all good and all (apparently) evil effects, which latter, according to their convictions, only "seem" evil, and lead to some unknown good object

Their religion is simple in the highest degree They acknowledge no evil principle, but believe in continuance after death, and in eternal blessedness In accordance with this belief, death appears to them like a passage into a better life, and they lay in the grave of the departed his weapons and implements, which he may perhaps require on his passage to another world The sacrifice of death of all the oxen, horses, guanacos, and sheep, which the deceased possessed in life, is peculiarly singular, they are all killed upon his grave, for he wants nothing more on earth, and Ach-éKenat Kanet takes care of his family, who do not yet know the "worth of man" by property.

Yana Kirym maintained the rank, or, as it were, the office of high priestess The gifts of clairvoyance, of prophecy, and of the interpretation of dreams, were alike bestowed upon her She prophesied from the blood of a young cow in the decline of the moon, ordered the funerals, took care of the sick, prepared medicinal herbs, and led the migrations of the tribe by the stars, as the cacique carried no compass

The seeress approached She was a thin figure, of Patagonian height, whose profile, like all the others, formed nearly a perpendicular line, she had a high, deeply furrowed forehead, and a sharp, penetrating glance in her brown eyes A black handkerchief, fastened in the manner before mentioned, covered the upper part of her head, the long hair of which, parted in two masses, hung down upon her breast, fastened in a knot She was a relative of the cacique, and of course wore a clean calico garment next to her olive brown skin, a pair of richly embroidered pantaloons and half boots, of the form above described, (from which the great toe peeped out,) stuck into a stirrup strap without metal—for Yana Kirym was on horseback, like every male and female Patagonian who wished to move over a space of five steps or farther She carried a single long arrow, without a bow, and the national bag, with fire implements and cigarettes, one of which she was just then smoking

"If the bloodthirsty chief on the river La Plata has slain my Oregham, we will break up and cross the pampas to his toldo, and he shall find out whose son he has killed" cried the old man to the sibyl

"They come!" said she, seriously, and in a hollow, guttural tone. "They come! thy son, my Oregham, and the 'friend of man' from the seashore, and yet another comes with them, whom they have saved from death."

The cacique and his children listened silently to the words of the Inaken sybil, and looked at each other Every countenance spoke silent reverence, and the features of the old man brightened with the anticipation of meeting again his eldest son, who had travelled to Buenos Ayres, with Signore Testa, to become acquainted with the stone toldos of the gaucho cacique, and the many other wonders of the world, on the river La Plata.

"Dost thou see them come?" inquired the old man, as he raised his arm from the saddle,

and sat erect, as if he intended to leave his buffalo hide

"I have already seen them long; not by daylight, but at night, when my kingdom opens itself," replied Yana Kirym, slowly and earnestly "I saw them fourteen days ago, when they rested themselves, after riding thirty leagues. They changed horses with our people All slept, and our friend from the seashore, took an instrument and cut off the hair entirely from the head of the friend he had saved, for a round spot of the crown was made bare before, as a mark in case he wished to escape, and the Matoperros* of the cacique from La Plata would have known him by that The fugitive wore Oregham's second dress, which he took with him, to appear in the stone toldos of the gaucho chief. The stranger anointed his head with ostrich fat, and bound the cloth on it, after our manner, that the hair might grow again, until he comes amongst the white men who fight against the matoperros of the prince that lives far away to the north

When the stranger from the seashore had shorn the head of his friend, they both lay down to sleep for some hours, and the youngest daughter of the cacique drew near the toldo of the man with the shorn head, and heard him pray aloud, and she knelt down before the toldo, and prayed to Ach-éKenat Kanet that he would protect him from the matoperros of the bloodthirsty cacique of the gauchos, who hunts our people with hounds, and murders the white people that will not acknowledge him as their Ach-éKenat Kanet here below The stranger slept peaceably, and before the sun arose again, they all laid their saddles upon fresh horses, and came galloping in a straight line to the southwest, towards us, with arrow speed, without resting, nearly forty leagues every day, and changed their horses when they arrived at toldos, and left the tired ones behind, and many horses sank exhausted under them, before they could unbuckle the saddle

"So saw I them in my dream-world, and nothing evil has happened to them since then, or I should have known it They rode and galloped on in their flight, and changed horses, and then rode and galloped on again, coming nearer and nearer to us here, swift as arrows, without rest and repose, and the hair of the man who seeks our protection grows again as fast as they ride, and the trace of the mark on his crown, has already vanished, and they will soon be here"

"Dost thou know the man that seeks shelter with us? dost thou know the man among his people?"

"I know who he was, and what he is I saw his heart in a dream, and read the inscription of his soul. He is a spirit acquainted with Ach-éKenat Kanet as I am, but he sees not things to come like me, only in his manner judging the future by the past Ach-éKenat Kanet gave to our Oregham the thought to travel to the far, far distance, because this man, with the 'mark of slavery,' required our aid, and without him he would have been lost there, for

---

* Literally "dog killers"—a nickname of the military, who formerly took the field against the wild hounds above mentioned.

the blood-thirsty cacique of the gauchos had sworn his death"

"Didst thou know all this at that time," said a daughter of the cacique, "when Oregham insisted that he would travel far, far away with the white friend, didst thou know then with what object it was done?"

"No!" answered Yana Kirym with all candor, "I knew it not, but I suspected that his journey must have some particular object unknown to himself, because he could give no other reason, wherefore he wished to accompany the white friend, than to see the stone toldos on the Plata river, and the great boats wherein a hundred men or more can journey over the great waters that never end"

Yana Kirym answered some more questions of the cacique and his children, who listened with reverential attention to her words, and then suddenly gave her horse a thrust with the shaft of the arrow, and galloped in flying haste towards the shores of the Rio Negro

CHAPTER II

ASYLUM IN PATAGONIA

NEARLY an hour had elapsed since Yana Kirym had silently departed, and El Rojo still lay, with his watch in hand, on the buffalo hide before his toldo A little maiden near him was trying to embroider a new pattern of her own design, à jour, upon a piece of calico, as she drew out the threads here and there with admirable dexterity, and brought out leaves and flowers, without in the least detracting from the tenacity and firmness of the material A little grandson of the old chief, some seven years old, had mounted an ostrich, to take his after supper ride for his better digestion, and turned in the direction in which Yana Kirym had disappeared

"Why dost thou work so late to-day?" inquired the cacique of the diligent little maiden near him "Thou hast embroidered enough for to-day, long sitting is not good, thou wilt become corpulent, and that is not pretty"

"No, my father! that is not pretty—to become corpulent, but tall and slender, and broad across the breast, and well fleshed here and there, that is pretty! And I do not wish to be less handsome than Vala Limi She is pretty, my father, is she not? But I am working this border for the guest who is coming here this evening When Yana Kirym told me, the day before yesterday, that Oregham would come to-day, I determined to work these pantaloons for him, but now the stranger-guest shall have them, and thou, my father, wilt give him a beautiful poncho, of the best we have But it was very bad for friend Testa to cut off his hair! Think, my father, of an Inake without long hair! with a bald head! that must look like a meadow without grass! The poor, bareheaded guest! I would give him the half of my hair, if it could be, that the poor man might not look so ugly"

"Thou mayest marry him, if he stays here," said the old chief. "His hair will soon grow again"

"I must see him first!" replied his granddaughter "If he is young and good—if I suit him—if he will be good to me, so right good, my father, so good, and so pleased, with me that he can hardly go to hunt without me—as good as our Oregham is to Vala Limi—then I would be good to him, and——"

"And journey with him far away?" interrupted the patriarch.

"No! my father. Journey with him? leave you all? how can you think so? that would not please me I would nowhere be so happy as with you, and no one would love me so well!"

Thus the little one prattled on, and the old man smilingly listened to her, smoking his cigarette

The little boy on his ostrich had galloped past the more distant toldos, accompanied by Oregham's favorite dog, which had, for the first time since her lover's departure, left the tent of Vala Limi. He was a beautiful, glossy black hunting dog, with erect ears, (broad and hollow,) shaped like a spoon, (and therefore sooner perceiving the slightest, most distant sound,) with white feet, and other white spots Dogs of this breed serve their masters without arms in the chase, as they catch, with indescribable dexterity, the wild fowl, which nestle, in countless numbers, in the undulating "grass waves" of Patagonia A single one of these dogs, led to the chase by a boy, is able to supply the fleshpot of a whole family with the most exquisite birds, and is, of course, a most valuable gift of nature.

The boy trotted about on his ostrich in child-like unconcern, looked from time to time at "Rosas," (so was Oregham's favorite named,) and suddenly saw him no more Let him call as loudly and as often as he might, with his tender voice, Rosas was off The poor boy steered his ostrich in circles and crosswise, hither and thither—Rosas was nowhere to be found. The thought that Oregham was coming home, and would not find his Rosas, came upon the poor child with deadly anxiety, he wept bitterly, and embracing the neck of his ostrich, allowed it to carry him wherever it would Rosas appeared to be lost in the boundless desert waste of the waving "sea of grass," perhaps suddenly strangled by a crafty, lurking bloodhound, or at least exposed to the danger of being strangled and devoured The disconsolate boy rode about, with tearful eyes, and dared not go home without Rosas The sun had already sunk behind the horizon and similar dangers to those which beset the favorite, threatened him. Suddenly, swifter than the flight of thought, Rosas reappeared, and sprang upon the ostrich, as it were giving a sign that it must follow him, and then flew, with lightning speed, in leaps some fathoms long, over the grass-sea in the direction of the village. The boy tried his two legged courser, and followed him As soon as Rosas had reached the first toldo, the population was also set in motion; "Rosas! Rosas!" cried old and young, "Oregham is coming!" Rosas hastened to Vala Limi; and the names "Rosas!" "Oregham!" and "Vala Limi!" resounded with hundred-fold intonations in the evening stillness of the Inaken village on the shores of the Rio Negro

Rosas hurried past the toldo of the cacique, to Vala Limi's tent, where she still sat at her portable loom, working upon a splendid poncho, to be a wedding dress for her beloved Although possessed of considerable Patagonian strength, and " here and there cushioned over" with noble muscular roundness, (according to the naive expression of the old cacique's granddaughter,) Vala Lami was, nevertheless, almost thrown prostrate on her buffalo hide, when Rosas brought her the intelligence that Oregham was in the neighborhood

The "friend" of her beloved thereupon took the " canine liberty" of covering her handsome face with kisses, or at least of licking it wherever his light red tongue would reach, whining and howling round her, and then springing on her again After a moment he left the tent and disappeared, flying back by the way he had come

Vala Lami sought, with all haste, to arrange her splendid locks in the best manner possible, plaited them in two masses, slung them under her arms, and fastened them in a knot on her heart Rosas had literally torn the poncho from her body With technical adroitness she held one end on the left hip, passed the right end through from beneath, and threw the rest over the right shoulder. After such a provisionary toilet, by which the proud form of her Juno-like figure stood out for the most part in natural fullness, she stepped forth from her tent, that was set in an open place where the toldos of the cacique formed a semicircle

" The nobility and the people" had already assembled in a numerous crowd, all on horseback—as a matter of course The little boy, with his eyes still wet, considered himself a chief personage in the assembly, and laughed through his big tears, beside himself with joy that Rosas was not lost, and besides, certainly very much pleased with Oregham's return , but " Rosas" was naturally the principal thing with him

Many turned about back and forth in evident impatience, and would gladly have left the square, to ride towards the travellers, but the cacique remained before his tent, and respect required them to remain in his neighborhood, until the son of the house arrived

Oregham at length appeared, sitting proudly on his horse, and near him Signore Testa, and Celeste-Lorenzo Before them rode Yana Kirym, and behind them five Patagonians, as travelling companions, and a crowd of people of all ages, and of both sexes, who closed around them as they sprang through the toldo village

A shout of joy and rejoicing, in well articulated Inaken tones, greeted the " prince of the house," who had returned from his first great journey to the far, far distance, and soon Oregham, Vala Lami, and old Rhabukih formed, as it were, a single mass of embraces

Celeste dismounted from his horse, and stood, with Testa, opposite to the sibyl of the Inaken tribe   " Welcome man of death !" cried Yana Kirym, with a subdued voice, in the Spanish language, observing Celeste with a keen glance She then pressed his hand, and laid her left upon his right shoulder ; " Welcome ! man of death ! escaped from death to seek thy grave ! I know thee and thy path ! the cacique will relate to thee that I saw thee, and where and when I saw thee   Ach-éKenat Kanet hath protected thee until now ; and he will protect thee further—— to thy grave !

" Welcome to our protection—rest and tarry here , I would say , remain with us, and take thee a wife, and live with us in rest and peace, and repose in the lap of a family , but that is not thy calling , that is pleasant and not hard , that is charming and alluring, for our maidens are beautiful, and our men are happy , but that is not thy path   Three days shalt thou abide here, in all quiet and recover thyself after thy long, long journey , and when I have, during three nights, traversed my realm to obtain information concerning thy future lot, then will I tell thee when thou shalt depart and whither thou shalt ride   Let thy pack be unbuckled from the led horse there, and take thence the sacred cup that thou carriest with thee, and I will prepare chà de matté for thee, that thou mayest drink from thy cup this evening , for it is a sacred hour, the hour of thine arrival among the tents of Rhabukih, the cacique of the Inaken !"

She departed hastily, and went to her fireplace

Celeste looked with evident amazement at his friend Testa, when Yana Kirym mentioned the cup, of the existence of which it was impossible she should have been informed by any ordinary method   Testa, who had held intercourse for years with this race of people, appeared as little surprised by the whole deportment and tone of the seeress, as by the hint in respect to the cup.

We left Celeste on that eventful night in the prison edifice at Buenos Ayres, and indirectly learned through Señor Domingo and Padre Fernando, that he was still in the chapel, when the latter so urgently inquired about him

The last hours of Alphonso wrought with a decided revulsion upon the mind of the man who had "renounced the world to live to the Lord," which might, very naturally, be a suddenly approaching crisis in his inward life

Celeste had seen a martyr to the idea of freedom take leave of the world with his eyes unbound, as his associates have been executed in our epoch, in almost all countries where humanity strives and struggles to release itself from the chains and bonds of absolutism—of the church, as well as the throne

Lorenzo had once renounced the world at the grave of his betrothed, the sister of Dolores, after his heart had been incurably wounded by the breaking, at her death, of the earthly bond of love which enchained him

It may certainly appear ridiculous, or at least overstrained, in our civilized age, when all the more profound sentiments are despised, that a youth, or a man, can be so deeply penetrated by a sentiment of pure love, that, overpowered by the prostration of grief, he forms a resolution, at the grave of his betrothed, to bury himself alive in the cells of a monastery

We have advanced so far in " civilization," that faith and love, in whatever form we find them on earth, are generally taken for weakness, for nervous disease, enthusiasm, and the like, and nothing is so peculiarly ridiculous as sentiment.

Celibacy, as the renunciation of all domestic relations, and especially of the conditions of nature, could only have become, through a singular misconception, an ordinance of the church, after the spirit had disappeared which inspired the apostles for their mission, and led to such renunciation from conviction Men, whose lives are pervaded by an idea that is more exalted than their time, and who expose themselves to persecution unto death by the advocacy of this idea, can have no claims to domestic relations— to domestic happiness

When Paul declares, "He that marries does well, but he that marries not, does better," he speaks in his office as apostle loosed from the fetters of human society, which despised the idea for which he had sacrificed his claims on life The apostle of Christendom recognised the unconditional necessity to keep himself at a distance from the fettering bonds of domestic relations, that he might work more powerfully, and not burden himself with the reproach of uniting a noble being to his fate, or exposing a woman to the persecutions that beset him Notwithstanding this, however, there are, in the early statutes of Christendom, no traces of a celibacy such as the church, in later times, has held up

It would carry us back too far, to insert here our observations on the foundation of monastic life, which originated in the inward desire of individual men for external repose and seclusion from the world, that they might resign themselves, undisturbed to spiritual contemplation, and intellectual research Such an individual direction however, with the renunciation of love in its earthly form, pre-supposes an unshakeable strength of mind, that borders on the superhuman, as it despises the requirements of nature and the fundamental stipulations of human society Only the inspiration of an exalted idea the dissolving of human individuality in this idea itself, whether it takes the form of faith, of love, or of freedom, is able to arouse such a moral force in man, which, when it is awakened, is declared by the profane world to be enthusiasm and over-excitement, whether in or out of the cloister There is a love in earthly form, that is able to enchain the heart of a noble man to that degree, that the unlimited renunciation of terrestrial happiness, on separation from the beloved object, or at her grave, becomes, to the honour of the human heart, very natural

There is a love in earthly form, so pure and so exalted, that the heart which experiences it parts, by a separation from the beloved being, equally from every hope of terrestrial felicity

Lorenzo renounced the world, and became a monk, because he had received the Christian religion, is "religion," according to the fundamental principle from which it sprung He occupied himself in the solitude of the cloister with the study of church history, and sought for the spirit of religion in the forms of the church, and looked for Christians in the monks around him He found in neither the one, nor the other, what he had sought He saw the colossal edifice of the third century extended in earthly splendor and magnificence—a temple of luxury, in which stupidity and sensuality had erected their altars He saw the idea and the spirit of the Christian religion here and there glimmering forth in former centuries, through this night of obduracy and darkness, when it was yet able to manifest itself as idea and spirit, before absolutism had thoroughly taken possession of the church, and fused itself with her—making of

every priest an executioner, to murder the soul of man before it wakes in faith and love

The everyday event of our time, that a servant of the Lord in any state should be called upon to attend, in his official capacity, a sinner to the scaffold, who doubting the legitimacy of monarchy, "for justice's sake" had been condemned to death as a traitor, had ended the long struggle through which Celeste had striven for years in his cell

With the salvo of musketry, that terminated the life of his friend, terminated also his union with the forms of a church that tolerated, approved, and in a manner accomplished, such a murder He left the corpse of his friend, when it had been thrust into the pit, and returned to the chapel, to collect himself for the fulfilment of the purpose that he had matured within him

After he had approached the Lord in prayer, to whose glory one martyr after another has shed his blood, he departed with hasty steps, and went, by a private way, through lanes and gardens to Mr Walker's, whom he found still in bed

With all the calmness and presence of mind that belonged to his character, and the calling he sustained, he revealed his "secret" to the old Briton, who was, very naturally, prepared immediately to consider it as his own, and assist him in his flight

An embarkation on board the Nordstjernan was, however, impossible, or at least too critical and dangerous, and Mr Walker had instantly another plan in readiness A box was sent to the cell of Celeste, that contained a few books, but principally clothing, and Signore Testa was induced to leave Buenos Ayres, some days earlier than he had intended

Mr Walker had already sent a person to Sr Testa's hotel, to request him to come to him, when the two encountered each other at the shallop of Captain Finngreen Some words in the letter, which Testa had given to young Walker for Finnango, intimated that he had himself simultaneously conceived the idea of taking with him to Patagonia, Lorenzo, whose life was in undoubted danger

All the preparations for flight, were made with the rapidity of lightning Sr Testa, upon Mr Walker's hint, hurried to the chapel of the monastery, where Celeste awaited him, and then to his hotel, where he confided all that was necessary to young Oregham, whose co-operation he required throughout Without Oregham's attendance, the journey through the pampas would have been impossible, while his presence facilitated it, as they only required to reach the first Indian settlement, to receive fresh horses, and, in case of need, the conduct of a guard They got happily past the outposts of the "matoperros," and reached the first settlement of the Patagonians, about thirty leagues from Buenos Ayres, where the seeress of the Inaken saw them in her dream

Yana Kuym stirred her fire, and placed a small copper teakettle on a Delphic tripod, to prepare for the guest the cha de matté, of which she carried a supply with her

The old and young world of the Inaken village, pressed as near as possible to "Prince Oregham" and his two white friends, always, however, maintaining a due distance, which was a natural effect of the innate discretion of this amiable tribe

All three excited, in the highest degree, the interest of the nation Oregham, because he had been far—far away on the La Plata river, and seen the stone toldos of the bloodthirsty cacique of the gauchos Young and old observed him, from his turban to his big toe, that peeped forth from the boot, to discover if any thing about him were altered, but nothing was found that was worth the trouble of looking at him so long At the utmost, he had become six or seven weeks older, which was hardly to be observed on his youthful countenance Perhaps Vala Lin found some sprouts of hair germinating on his well formed chin—very possibly, but the repose and leisure for a confidential hour of Patagonian love, in which the sproutings of the youth's beard would disappear, was not to be thought of for some time These caressings may, perhaps, not be so painful as they appear, since they say, that every little hair from the beard is paid for with a kiss Whether the bride kisses the youth, or the youth the bride, we have not, hitherto, been able to learn

The information diffused through the revelations of the sybil, that Celeste was a fugitive, whom the bloodthirsty chief of the gauchos had condemned to death, particularly excited the universal sympathy of the good people for him. No name filled with such horrors the traditions of the Indians, as the murderous deeds of Rosas, who, under the pretence of a "war against the savages," had shown his so called bravery, and risen from gaucho, or clerk, to "general" The history of these Indian tribes affords, like so many others, facts as interesting as horrible, in relation to a war of extermination, by which "pure and civilized Christians" have oppressed the nationality and the primitive religion of so called savage nations Only the hypocrisy of a characterless age, like our own, could throw a veil over the disgrace of such a Christianity, which, however, notwithstanding this, is everywhere apparent in its shameless selfishness.

Celeste's personal appearance had something imposing, and commanding reverence, that involuntarily fixed upon him the eyes of the toldo population The dignity and elevated stature of his noble form, the pallid countenance, stamped with suffering, and embrowned by the wind of the pampas, which had blown around him in his flight of weeks on horseback, harmonized with his dark, monastic beard, which a broad cravat had concealed until he arrived at the Indian settlements, and which was there, as here, a recommendation to him

The old, dignified cacique hastened to meet him, with a formal greeting, offering him his tribe as his nation, and all Patagonia as a free fatherland, in case he, as an adopted son, should wish to make use of them So called uncivilized nations, more or less in a state of nature, not unfrequently surprise us by their keen and just judgement of the men with whom they come in contact The undeniable principle of attraction and repulsion, often indicates itself in the minds of men in a state of nature, by agreeable tokens Only the unfortunate misunderstandings which have induced foreigners to resort to arms

where they had been met with hospitality, destroy the bond of humanity, which is held more sacred in the heart of many uncivilized nations, than in our civilized world

The Inaken cacique, Rhabukih, distinguished two species of men men with mustaches, and men without The history of the Indian races had given him an idea of European civilization, that encourages shaving He had, once for all, denied himself all communication with any European whatever of the " razor civilization," and evinced, like the negroes in Brazil, an admirable tact in distinguishing the nationality of the Europeans

This tact of the so called half savages, may be partly grounded on the fact, that they always find opportunity to judge of the various national physiognomies of their own and other tribes, and pursue the same course towards Europeans No Briton would easily have deceived the old cacique, in case he should have given himself out, with a natural beard, to be a Spaniard, a Frenchman, or an Italian "Any one can let his mustaches grow " said Rhabukih, in very distorted Spanish, as he conversed with Celeste about the bearded and the beardless, " but every face does not agree with them I can paint my face white, but I should not therefore be a European, I can fasten a horse's mane upon an ox, but he would not then be a horse "

Yana Kihym had prepared the refreshment for Celeste, who, at her intimation, looked for this cup, which he had brought with him as a sacred memorial of the farewell from his friend, and from Dolores He placed himself under the medical care of the mysterious old woman, without having attained a clear knowledge of herself and her prophetic gift It had certainly been long known to him that similar prophetesses were found among the tribes of Patagonians ; but he was as far from all superstition in respect to them, as he was on the other hand inclined to satisfy himself of a peculiarity, which, as a so called " sixth sense,' or " second sight," is evinced in many races of people by undeniable facts

The old cacique led the strangers to the nearest steaming fleshpot, and by degrees began to inquire of his son concerning the wonder-world of stone toldos on La Plata river, and the murderous acts of the Cacique Rosas, and his friendship with the razor nation

CHAPTER III

PHILOSOPHY AND RELIGION

OREGHAM had relinquished his tent to the two guests, and furnished it with all the conveniences that the customs and mode of life of his tribe permitted The habitation itself was set in the ground about the depth of two feet, and the earth thus thrown out formed a low wall, with the stems of trees set in it, after the manner of a Gothic roof, supporting the buffalo hides, which presented an opening above, likewise covered at night with hides The topmost layer of the hide roof resembled the cover upon a saddle, and afforded the necessary passage to the rain

On both sides, in the interior of the toldo, elevations of earth were left, which, covered with buffalo hides, formed a sort of divan

The saddle of the Patagonians, a piece of wood with a heap of thongs which meet together in two rings, serves (as before mentioned) for a pillow, and the poncho for a covering In relation to the breakfast of the guests, it may be remarked is a peculiarity, that the Patagonians, surrounded by thousands and thousands of cows, use no milk,* they of course prepare neither cheese nor butter Their drink is fresh water and chã de matté, which they, like the Brazilians, receive from the before mentioned provinces in leather bags, and obtain by barter

Flesh or fowl, cooked with a celery plant, a sort of bulb, and its broth, which forms a well relished " bouillon," is their principal food The mode of life of these hordes is peaceful and simple Strife and dissension are very rare in the society of a tribe, of course lawyers find no opportunity of " making money " among them If, nevertheless, a disagreement occurs, the cacique decides it, according to his views and experience, and generally with undeniable sagacity

Although each possesses his own property, stealing and cheating are not only unknown, but a stranger's handkerchief cannot be lost, without arriving again into possession of the owner On the other hand, dishonesty and intentional pilfering is all the more the order of the day, on the inhabited coasts of the country, and in the European settlements It will there serve as a rule for every stranger, not to allow the least thing of any value whatever to be seen, since it would undoubtedly disappear, even in as mysterious a manner as at times precious stones are turned to pebbles ———

It would certainly lead to mournful reflections, if we should throw light on the position of the European settlers, who there, as in almost every transatlantic colony, seek in every way to " make money," under pretence that they have left their fatherland on account of the restriction of their "industrious activity," or have sought the New World " from love to freedom ".——

Where the notion of liberty includes the permission to steal in a cunning manner, and to pilfer their property from natives and strangers, the civilization is not particularly advanced, with which the Europeans would bless the so called " savage nations "

No circumstance shows us this civilization of the Europeans in a stronger light than their position in the New World, in regard to the natives, with whom we must not find fault, if they, like the Patagonians, look upon every white man, by anticipation, as a selfish cheat, who comes among them to transact business after his own manner

The toldo village of the Cacique El Rojo lay about eighty English miles from the outlet of the Rio Negro into St Matthias Bay, where the harbour of St Antonio admitted of commerce with the northern provinces of South America, by an exportation of the productions of the country, amongst which salt, obtained by the evaporation of sea water, predominated.

The navigation, however, is dangerous, from

sandbanks and pamperos, and only enterprising seamen are induced to take freight from Buenos Ayres, St Catharina, Rio de Janeiro, Rio Grande, &c., there and back The Danish flag, one of the most numerous in Rio de Janeiro,* is also the best known on the coast of Patagonia

Signore Testa had, for years, freighted many vessels for St Matthias Bay, under the above mentioned circumstances, and had once more undertaken this journey towards Buenos Ayres, for such an object

He had there again engaged a Danish vessel, to sail for St Matthias Bay, which was to return to Buenos Ayres, and the contract was already concluded, when he was made acquainted with the circumstances of the persecuted individuals whom we designate by the general name of " Humanitarios "

According to all regulations for the freighting of vessels, and under the circumstances of this unpretending contract, it remained a critical affair to make the proposal to the Danish captain, to steer towards Rio de Janeiro, instead of St Antonio, or, even by a circuitous passage, and with loss of time, to set a passenger on shore at Monte Video, while, at the same time, a visit from the Argentine vessels of war, at the mouth of the La Plata, was to be feared

Lorenzo's resolution to go, if possible, to Rio Grande, there, sword in hand, to preach the gospel of the future, (and, in case Providence had so determined, to seal his testimony with his blood,) was already matured at the grave of Alphonso

During the three days which Yana Kuym had set apart as a period of mysterious inquiry, she kept herself in the strictest seclusion from all the toldo world

Lorenzo felt, for the first time, the consequences of such unusual exertion, and all the discomforts of a ride à la Mazeppa, when he came to repose himself For the first day, he remained on his buffalo hide divan, under the careful attendance of Vala Lima, and the little ostrich rider, who hardly moved from his side

Testa availed himself of the absence of the priestess, to occupy himself with very prosaic matters, sorting ostrich feathers and ox horns, which he had received in exchange for Swiss calico and head-handkerchiefs, for transportation to the bay of St Matthias

Of course all went on in the usual manner, and the doings amongst the toldos were carried on upon the customary footing, as at the similar arrival of any Spaniard or Italian amongst an Indian tribe on the borders of the Rio Negro

Two nights had passed, and Signore Testa lay, on the third evening, on his divan of buffalo hides, opposite to his friend, and smoked his cigarette, and drank, with him, the aromatic chã de matté Their conversation turned upon the spiritual contest of our age, which is here and there already carried on with weapons, and which, according to Lorenzo's view, will pass into a universal religious war, or contest of faith

The Italian had, until now, from consideration

---

* Wildness of the herds is given as the cause of this singular privation, but single cows could be tamed easily enough.

* According to the Annual Harbour Reports, the majority of vessels there are under Scandinavian flags. In the year 1813, there were at one time, owing to the very low freight, 23 Danish and 32 Swedish and Norwegian vessels in the bay of Rio

for Celeste's state of mind, intentionally avoided leading him to detailed communication of his politico-religious convictions, but appeared not the less inclined to receive his confession of faith in this respect so soon as the other found himself fit for the exertion

"Since my childhood," began Lorenzo, "the spiritual life has stirred within me, which unfolds itself in us more and more, as an eternally moving, searching power, striving upward more and still more to the light of truth, the more we are penetrated by the mysterious ray of a higher existence Thought, which seems to harmonize this earthly existence with a higher world, endeavoring to conceive of it established as an element of being, and eternally leading back upon the unrevealed mystery of the idea of Divinity, was manifested in me as a powerful force, and carried me forward in inquiry and contemplation, with burning soul-thirst after knowledge

"My education was entrusted to a European, a Spaniard, who had been persecuted by the church in Europe, because he followed the spiritual direction pointed out by the philosophy of the former century I was more or less acquainted with the various philosophical systems, which, in rigid contradiction to each other, indicate the unfettered strivings of the spirit, that seeks to enclose in " forms," what no human intellect has, up to the present time, been able to apprehend under any fixed form

"At length I recognised all philosophy as the highest vital element of reason in the urgency of self-contemplation But I recognised, at the same time, all philosophical systems, as the designs and plans of various architects to carry up an edifice, in which was a point of view, where man expected the voice of *truth*, but heard only his own voice, as the organ of the spirit that spoke out of himself

"I placed myself upon this point of the basis of the various systems, leaned my ear to the indicated places in the *acoustic rotunda* of the earthly and spheral universe, and the echo of all knowledge, led me back to myself, to the consciousness within me, that a higher spirit, in myself, spoke to me I recognised " reason " as the highest evidence upon earth, and reason itself forced into the acoustic edifice of this or that philosophical system Thought appeared to me like a prisoner crippled in a dungeon

"And upon no basis, upon no point of view of philosophical perception, did I find more clearness than I was able to develop in myself

"I distinguished three sequent acoustic edifices of philosophic doctrine

"I entered one, whose arch was closed at the top by the architectural key-stone that held the edifice together, but admitted of no prospect into the interminable spheral world of higher regions, the gloomy darkness of the grave surrounded me It was the edifice of Atheism, based on the "system of denial," without foundation, inasmuch as the contradictions of atheism have no support in themselves, for it denies Spirit as the source of all being, and of course denies also the foundation of its own edifice.

"I entered another philosophical acoustic edifice, likewise closed in its arch, but with high windows on all sides, looking out upon the animated earthly erection, the edifice of cold Pantheism, whose basis, brought together from all the realms of nature, showed to me, as a man the position in which I saw myself, as a man on earth, separated from the higher idea of being, existing as an isolated creature, as an I—as a *Myself*, in the dreary desert of Individualism

"In the edifice of atheism I was conducted by the leading-strings of contradiction to the abyss of insanity, for I was to deny a primitive power, whose effects in my own spiritual existence I was not able to deny

"In the edifice of pantheism I was chilled by the arrogance of egotism, the notion of a son that denied the father, and the notion of spirit contracted within itself, denied the source from whence it streamed through me

"I wandered around in the desire for light, I sought and struggled on in the thirst after truth, and I entered the third edifice of philosophy It was a higher, more exalted, more splendid temple, with similar bow windows around, with delightful prospects of animated nature, but in the cupola, a far, wide view up into the zenith of the universe, and my spirit felt itself drawn upward to the mysterious source of the light, whose glimmering rays shone about me, and awakened my soul to the joyful consciousness of a relation with the inscrutable zenith-idea Deity It was the edifice of Spiritualism, founded upon the granite of the existence of a higher power, proceeding from the idea God, the source of all being, uniting the Son, (humanity) with himself, through the Spirit of life

"Thus I involuntarily recognised the triad of the existence of our incarnation, in spirit, soul, and body, represented by the three different combined systems of the philosophy of all ages, Spiritualism, Pantheism, and Atheism

"I recognised the body as a form, as the material instrument of the soul, spirit, as the consciousness of the divine power in man, which unites the soul and body with each other I had become as clear in myself, as the human spirit in a shell of clay can attain to clearness, and my perception led me to Faith

"I believed, and I loved ' You know, superficially," continued he, after a pause, " the history of my past life I found a being whose love strengthened me, in the long struggle with doubt, which I passed through, until I attained the perception that I have endeavored to explain to you But even although penetrated by the ray of spiritualism, I nevertheless felt myself entangled in the flowery garlands of pantheism, which pointed out to me, (as an egotist under the demands of individualism,) life as an incontestible possession, and the enjoyment of life as the highest aim I experienced the reciprocal love of a being who understood me, and in this blending of our two beings through attraction, upon an equal scale of spiritual life, I recognised Love

"Theresa died—and it was with me, as if a part of my existence had been torn away from me in her person If you have ever loved—if you have ever been loved—in the highest, holiest sense of the word, you will understand me, and can explain to yourself the crisis which decided my future upon her bier I chose the tonsure and the monastic cell from conviction,

Penetrated by Faith, I sought in religion, as the centre of spiritualism, consolation and support for my inward life, and an asylum in the lap of the church, under the foolish illusion, that the church was founded on religion, which she should represent

"I received consecration, with a holy inspiration for my future calling—I busied myself in the uninterrupted study of church history, and recognised the unity of all religion, as I had recognised the unity of the conception God I traced the Christian religion, and arrived, through Mosaism—at—the—mystery—of—the—Egyptian—idea of Unity, (which was concealed from the people through the high priest of Isis)—and was led backward to Buddhism, in which I again recognised the Christian myth of Trinity

"I now sought religion in the church, and, very naturally, first in Catholicism, and I beheld the idea of Christianity in the blood of the martyrs of those first ages, when Christianity arose out of the ruins of Mosaism, like a phenix from the ashes of a destroyed temple I beheld the Christian religion, throughout centuries, as the element of movement, of progress, of the ennoblement of mankind, until the church (as the instrument of absolutism) issued the false coin of dogmatic statutes, which prescribed forms to men, to choke the Spirit, that threatened danger to all absolutism

"I saw the spirit of the Nazarene enchained and bound down by the canons of the church, and the church, by degrees, became a prison for the spirit, with subterranean dungeons, with racks and torture, for the extirpation of the idea for which the Son of Man had laid down his life

"I recognised in Jesus the *man*, who, when suffering under the pangs of death, breathed forth the sigh 'My God! my God! why hast thou forsaken me?' a sigh that soars upward from the whole of supplicating humanity Honouring in Jesus the man who offered his life for the deliverance of mankind, since he sealed with his blood the doctrines of equality, of love to man, and of justice, I looked for Christianity in our age, on earth—and for disciples of Jesus, in the lap of the church And I found no trace of Christianity

"The church has become an Augean stable, filled with the rubbish of intolerance and unbelief, heaped up in the dark night of stupidity, kept humid with the blood of freedom's martyrs in all nations, and with the wine spilled at priestly orgies and bacchanals to the 'remission of sin,' through the well paid 'absolution' of a shamefully betrayed Christendom

"I beheld, however, apostles of the doctrine of Jesus coming forward, from century to century, in the consciousness of their sacred mission, to point to the Augean stable of the church, that mankind might cleanse it And I beheld these apostles outlawed and burnt—Jacques Molay, and John Huss, and I recognised De Lamenais, as their follower I beheld in De Lamenais, the union of spiritualism as philosophy, with Catholicism as religion, in rigid opposition to the *juste milieu* of Protestantism and the absolutism of popery The notions of Catholicism and popery appeared to me as rigidly separated from each other as the notions of "religion" and of "church"

"I beheld in the struggle of the Templars and the Hussites, the idea 'religion' contending against the absolutism which the popedom (as church and state) combines in itself, and I recognised in De Lamenais, a phenomenon which will perhaps bring on a yet longer, and even as bloody a struggle, in all nations upon earth, as the struggles of the Templars and the Hussites

"I beheld the central evil indicated by De Lamenais, which burdens mankind with Monarchy and Priesthood, but at the same time, also, the misery of subjugated humanity in consequence of both evils, which can only be resisted and conquered by a subversion of the existing social prejudices, by Social Reform, which presupposes political and religious reform

"I recognise, and would die for the truth, that all the endeavors and struggles of noble men, who seek to alleviate the miseries of mankind by social reform, will remain fruitless, without political and religious reform, without an overthrow of all social evil existing until now I merely avail myself of the word Reform instead of Revolution

"I recognise the basis of Society of our age as false, as vile, and, moreover, as defiled, and the prevailing maxims and prejudices, as evidently in contradiction to nature and reason I recognise every crime as privileged under the firm of virtue, in so far as church and state give men free leave to sin, so that they do not disturb the defiled basis of their hypocritical existence.

"I behold the virtue of all virtue 'the love of man to mankind,' pointed out as vices and crimes, materialism and egotism, as the ruling principles, the chigote and the yard measure swinging for the subjugation of the people and the spirit, in republics as well as in monarchies!

"I see the abyss to which mankind is hastening with forced steam power, by water and by land, while they acknowledge no higher element of life than that of sensuality, loveless beastiality, under the pretence of propagating such an unintellectual human race The worth of man is estimated by money, and in all history of mankind, until our epoch, man never availed himself of this dishonorable measure towards men—never!

"But Mankind will not decline, for it is only the animated form of a higher idea of deity, revealed to us in its effects

"Humanity will awaken, and the Augean stable of the church will be swept out, and the hundred moleheaps of money-making sects, who desecrate the word 'religion' as the firm of their extended Business, will be trodden down like moleheaps, when the angel with the drawn sword shall come!

"The salvation of human nature shall come again, not as a person, but as an event in the world! It will drive out the usurers and shopkeepers, the traders of men and buyers of souls, from the temple of humanity——!

"When can we travel to Rio Grande?" said Celeste, interrupting himself, as he sprang from his divan of buffalo hides

Testa was just about to answer, as Yana Kirym called his name on the outside of the tent; he went to meet her, and begged her to come into the tent, and take a seat by him

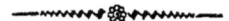

CHAPTER IV.

SECOND SIGHT

INSTEAD of accepting the invitation to seat herself on the earthen step within the toldo, Yana Kirym beckoned to her old acquaintance to come out to her, and with a second wave of her hand, she signified that Lozenzo also might appear

Both now stood near the old woman, who directed their attention to a crowd of people, that surrounded a group of riders. It was a white man, in Patagonian costume, heavily armed, and accompanied by some Inaken and Puelches, whose horses steamed and snorted under them

Loud murmuring and talking were heard in the crowd, who moved nearer so soon as the traveller perceived the Italian Testa in front of the Toldo.

The tired horse galloped the last fifty paces to where the Italian stood, and then feeling himself disburthened of his rider, dropped his head from exhaustion

Oregham, who had received the rider, and was likewise on horseback, beckoned to some of his people to unsaddle the poor animal, and throw a buffalo skin over him, for the evening was cool, and the horse steamed, and had been overridden

"Thank God that I meet you, Signore Testa!" began the traveller; " and this gentleman is probably the one expected," added he, with a glance to Lorenzo

The person who spoke thus, was a slender, lean man, of middle age, and with a serious countenance, Mr. Farren, a North American, who had formerly carried on the whaling business at the Falkland Islands, and had lived for some years in Port St. Antonio, on the Bay of St Matthias, in intimacy with the Italian, as his neighbour

Signore Testa could hardly reply for astonishment, to the address of his friend, who put his hand into his Patagonian sack, and gave him a letter. Then turning to Prince Oregham, he begged for a drink of water, for he was very thirsty, and the folds of his head-handkerchief, as well as his eyebrows and whiskers, were powdered with sand

"From a friend who is not personally known to you—Captain Barigaldi, of the schooner Mazzini, lying in our harbour since the day before yesterday," added he, while Testa broke the seal, whose device, " Ora e sempre," expressed beforehand the character of the sender

Some boys had, at Oregham's bidding, brought a jar of fresh water, and a silver cup with cha de matté. Mr. Farren drank, and Signore Testa read as follows ,

"PORT ST ANTONIO, Oct., —, 1838
     On board the schooner ' Mazzini '
"God with us !

"I met a Swedish brig, the Nordstjernan, fourteen days ago, on the English bank, at the mouth of La Plata river, with fugitives on board, from Buenos Ayres for Rio de Janeiro, under the escort of one of our friends, Hinango, a Scandinavian.

"I learned from him, that you had the noble-minded intention to take with you, on your departure from Buenos Ayres, if possible, an associate who was in danger there, over the pampas, to this coast I accompanied the Nordstjernan to the latitude of Rio Grande, and Hinango gave me your address for Port St Antonio

"I considered it my duty to direct my course hither, for the possible case that you may have accomplished the deliverance of our comrade

"Our flag brought the bearer of this on board to me, when I had cast anchor here, and I satisfied myself that he is your friend, and is ready, as a man, to serve the cause which we represent I learned from him, that you would probably not return direct to St Antonio, but by way of the toldos of an Inaken tribe on the other side of the Lago de Tehuel He offered himself to carry you the intelligence that I was here, or to leave with the cacique of the tribe the information and this letter, in case you have not yet arrived there

"In case you are still on the way, and should receive this letter within three days after the arrival of the bearer at the settlement of El Rojo, then know that I shall await you here until then, and reckon thirty hours more for your journey from Lago de Tehuel to Port St Antonio Unhappily, the position of affairs in Rio Grande, and my individual duty, will not permit me to remain here longer God grant that I may not be here in vain, and that you have succeeded in delivering our brother, whose standing and worth are known to me

"The bearer will communicate to you many particulars of the voyage of the Nordstjernan, and of a rencontre with an Argentine cutter, as far as I have been able, in all haste, to impart them to him

"In the hope of soon embracing our associate, Senhor Lorenzo de V——, perhaps in your company,   Your Brother,
                                    BARIGALDI."

Hardly had Signore Testa read the first line of this letter, than he shared it with the brother whose deliverance it concerned, and both read it together, while the evening twilight by degrees veiled the handwriting Lorenzo looked silently towards heaven, without being able to find words to speak his thanks for such care and sympathy on the part of the " young European' for him, and for the cause of South America to which he had devoted himself

"I am ready to depart with you instantly," said he, pressing a hand of each Every form of thanks appeared feeble and insufficient to express his feelings

"Ye shall stay here to-night," said Yana Kirym, who had, until now, earnestly observed every motion and every look of the three white men

"Thou must repose here this night," said she, turning particularly to Mr Farren, " for thou art weary and worn out with thy ride, and I have yet a word to say, in all quiet, with this friend of Ach-éKenat Kanet," pointing to Lorenzo

"The son of the ocean who has sent thee, will not expect thee so soon as ye shall reach him Sit down then by the flesh pot and eat, and smoke a cigarette with thy friend from the seashore, while I reveal to the friend of Ach-éKenat Kanet what He hath revealed to me, for him, and for you all "

With these words she beckoned the Spaniard to follow her, and walked with him through the toldos, to a hill clothed with a group of trees, where she seated herself, and Lorenzo did the same. Behind them lay the Inaken village, with its glimmering fireplaces and dark clouds of turf smoke rising in the still night, by degrees embracing its sister twilight in the peaceful bonds of repose. Before them spread the waving, illimitable plains, of similar mile-wide hills, with groups of trees and thickets, scarce perceptibly interrupted by sandy bottoms. The direct line of the far, far distance was separated, like the horizon on the open sea, from the transparently clear evening sky, which here and there reflected its gradually fading splendor in the wide stream.

Countless swarms of fowl of various species whirred through the mild summer air, and sank to their repose in the waving sea of grass. The lowing of the herds subsided by degrees, and the neighing of the horses became less frequent. Louder and louder sounded the howlings of the wild dogs, and the watchers of the Inaken horde rode slowly about, with loaded slings, prepared to encounter this "barbarized European race" with their maiming contents.

Long did Yana Kirym sit beside the friend of Ach-éKenat Kanet without a word. She seemed to allow him the time, to receive within himself the impression of a grand and strangely foreign nature, and then lifted up her voice and spoke in broken Spanish.

"I have asked of Ach-éKenat Kanet who thou art? and he has told it to me in dreams. I know thee, and thy mission to thy people, thou comest from a grave, and goest where graves will be filled. Thy future is clear to me, but it must remain dark to thee according to the will of Ach-éKenat Kanet. But that I know thy future I will show thee, because I will tell thee some things about the lot of others who are dear to thee, but not all that I know.

"I saw about thee and the friend from whose grave thou comest, a woman and a youth. Both go from danger into danger, especially the woman, for she is a woman, and the world of the white people in which she lives is corrupt in its morals and regulations, and does not acknowledge the dignity of woman; and those who desire to protect thy friend are preparing for her downfall.

"When the moon that now rises there, has turned its full face four times upon us, and when she has then vanished entirely for the fourth time, then will evil days come for many—for all that Ach-éKenat Kanet hath bound by his spirit to thee and to each other—those whom thou dost not yet know."

She paused, and then continued in a gentle, sad tone. "The little that Ach-éKenat Kanet has revealed to me in a dream concerning thy future, and the fate of those who are united with thee, I may not reveal to thee, I can only warn thee, but in this case warning is of little avail.

"All might have ended otherwise, if your manners and laws had been different," she continued, with a deep sigh. "But your wretchedness lies in the slave trade of women, in the willingness and haste of the slaves to sell themselves, and in the difficulty which the slaves, who feel themselves free, find in protecting themselves before sale. There lies the misery, and there lie the bodies of the slain; and ye call that civilization in your tongue, and would introduce such civilization

amongst us, through your missionaries with beards and without beards.

"The bearded call themselves Christians, and show us a piece of wood or metal, and say, it is your God, the image of a man nailed to a cross, and tell us of the virgin that bore him, and call this virgin the mother of God, whose lover was a Holy Spirit, and that that spirit was even God himself, and that the virgin then bore him—God himself.

"The white people may comprehend all that, but we Inaken understand that Ach-éKenat Kanet is almighty, and that we shall live after death, and will have to give an account in another world to Ach-éKenat Kanet. The story of the holy virgin we do not comprehend.

'Then come the missionaries without beards, who also call themselves Christians, and carry a thick book that they call the Word of God, and affirm that the mother of God is not then Deity, and that the doctrine of the missionaries with beards is false, and they will not have any thing to do with the mother of God, but preach only of the Son, and say his blood redeemed the world two thousand years ago. And these same whites, who call themselves Christians, with beards and without beards, come here over the sea, and trade in men, and show us the image of their God and the thick book, and fall upon us in our toldos, and help the cacique from La Plata river to kill us, and have brought bloodhounds here and firearms and seek to exterminate us and steal our cattle, and kneel down before their wooden God, or their metal God, and swear by the thick book, and kiss the leather on the thick book, and entice our virgins into their toldos, and call that Christianity!

"If I had not my duty to fulfil here in my nation, I would journey into the country of the whites, over the sea, and teach and preach of Ach-éKenat Kanet, the only God, of whom no image can be seen, because no one has ever seen him, but who reveals himself to us in the flowers of every grassy mound, and in the stars that glitter there above!

"Our virgins have no intercourse with holy or unholy spirits, but with youths and men, and choose their lovers, and the youth or man chooses his wife, and often both choices meet, and the children of our people are healthy and strong, and thou seest no men amongst us that are born cripples, no wretched beings who owe their existence to intoxication, for we are not acquainted with the stimulants of civilization.

"None of our virgins would prefer one man to another because he has more oxen, but because he loves her more than another. And then come the whites, and call themselves Christians, and want to give us burning water poison for our oxen, and to poison our men and our women with poison water, and feed our virgins with pepper and vanilla, and call that civilization.

"Tell the white women slaves, where thou findest them. 'I greet you from Yana Kirym, the friend of Ach-éKenat Kanet, of the tribe of the Inaken, and say to you. If you cannot live without burning water, and pepper, and cantharides, and vanilla, remain single and be ashamed in your white skins. And if you give yourself to a man, because he has many oxen and horses, then will your children not be men! And if you give yourselves to a man who cheats his brother and breaks his word, and ye know it, then will your children be cheats and word-breakers, by your example ! and your people will point at them with the finger, for As the bull so is the calf !

" ' And if ye hasten to attach yourselves to a man, for fear that ye shall remain single, then know that Ach-éKenat Kanet has ways and means to convey the seed-dust of the flower from chalice to chalice, although the flower may remain fastened to its stem, and the stem to its root !

" ' As Ach-éKenat Kanet, fills the cup of a flower with pollen by a gentle breeze, and, in the case of need, through butterflies and bees that carry it from the male to the female flower, so will he also find ways and means to convey your feelings from your hearts to those of the men, and awaken love for you, if your hearts are aroused to love !

" ' Therefore, be not over hasty, and do not sell yourselves for daily bread, or earthly goods, for what you as virgins give to your husbands is your highest and holiest, and you can only give it *once* ! no power on earth can replace it, when once ye have yielded it !'

" Tell all this to your white women slaves, and lay it to their hearts, that they may believe in Ach-éKenat Kanet, and in the evening breeze, and in the butterflies and bees that fly from flower to flower and bring their love together !

" And tell your youths and men to take example from our people, in the consciousness of their dignity—to know and feel to what tribe they belong, and that all kindred tribes form one people, united by manners and language ! Tell them to love each other, as the sons of one people, and exercise hospitality towards every son of another people, when he approaches them in peace in Ach-éKenat Kanet Let all recognise each other as brethren, and unite themselves as a nation, to fight against the bloodthirsty caciques, who conquer countries and slay nations, and treat the subjugated tribes like animals !

" Tell the youths and men to stand up as the sons of their nation, all for one, and one for all, like my people in Patagonia, in the struggle against the cacique of the gauchos from the Plata river, and against the whites with beards and without beards, who call themselves Christians, and traffic in men, in mockery of Ach-éKenat Kanet, who directs the stars above, and calls us at death to himself in a better world "

She sighed deeply, and continued " As concerns the fate of thy friend, and those who are involved in it, Ach-éKenat Kanet has placed guards here and there, and what is to be saved will be saved—if it be not in life, then in death For where men will neither hear nor see, and establish and maintain laws in contradiction to nature, and to the spirit of Ach-éKenat Kanet—there the fruit develops itself from the flower, and where thorns are sowed as the germ, Ach-éKenat Kanet will not bring forth roses !"

" If I may save a life that is in danger, then give me a hint when and where I must step forth," said Lorenzo, when the priestess ceased to speak.

" Thou shalt stand forth in thy nation, as a wayfarer on the bloodstained field of the present. Thou must testify of Ach-èKenat Kanet, the only God, and convey to thy people the legacy of the friend from whose grave thou comest ! As to the danger of those whom I have pointed out, thou knowest thyself that their lives, like them, belong to your nation, and what Ach-éKenat Kanet has determined for the deliverance of thy friends, will be done through a being from whom you do not expect it The forms of my dream float around me— I may not disclose it to thee—but I see a ship as it were, sailing over the ocean, and I see the danger upon the ship—and two small vessels are near the large one for safety and protection Whatever may take place—and whatever shalt happen to thee—know and feel, in thy last hour, that thou shalt live after death where the spirit of Ach-éKenat Kanet will shine around thee ! Rely on him, and live here on earth for thy nation !"

Lorenzo heard this effusion of the singular being with more tranquillity and patience than perhaps many friendly or unfriendly readers will receive it with, who, as Catholic or Protestant, will declare many assertions to be " evident blasphemy," which we, however, can overlook in a half savage Patagonian, from whom, indeed, little else was to be expected

As concerns the dark intimations from the realms of second sight, we shall see their import in the progress of the story, and can only, in this place, give the assurance, that we have met with facts of this kind in our personal experience, which are far more decided than these, and whose accomplishment could be confirmed by many witnesses

The last glimmering of the evening red had long since vanished below the horizon, and the cloudless sky was by degrees sown with stars

Like a glowing ball, whose circle was a little indistinct on one side, the moon ascended above the dusky line of the horizon, rising higher and higher, and looked sadly down in the same night upon Yana Kuym and Lorenzo—— upon the ruins of the guimpeiro village in the interior of Brazil—— upon the villa of the young lady on da Gloria, who fired the pistol—— and upon the Swedish brig Nordstjernan, as Habakkuk Daily left her in the character of an English officer

Single fires of the domestic " vestals" of Patagonia, (which they maintained through the night for the prosaic purpose of having them ready to prepare the breakfast in the morning without the trouble of rekindling,) smoked and blazed here and there, for there was no thunder cloud in the sky, and no pampero was to be feared, that would drive the destructive element amongst the dry hides of the toldos Lorenzo sat, self-absorbed, beside the strange being, who had not spoken a word after the above close of her singular discourse

The friend of Alphonso at length arose, and pressed the hand of the old woman She pointed in the direction of the toldos where his companions had remained, and then directing her gaze upward at the stars, continued seated under the trees, while Lorenzo followed her intimation, and slowly withdrew

He found his companions, with the cacique and his son Oregham, reclining, in a semicircle, upon buffalo skins before his toldo, smoking cigarettes, and near them the aromatic cha de matté, to which they gave him a friendly invitation, without alluding to the cause of his absence

Not far from the group sat an old Inake, diligently employed in finishing a pair of national boots, or leather stockings, for the white guest whom the friend from the seashore had brought to them, they were the shank skins of a horse, stripped off in the aforesaid manner, macerated with salt and wood ashes, scraped bare on a board, and then dried, and the old man was just then busied in rubbing them supple with dry ashes and sand

The little maiden, whom we saw beside the cacique, at work embroidering the border of the "inexpressibles" which she designed for the stranger, had completed her masterpiece, and had likewise secretly placed it in his toldo

The projected journey of the three guests was comfortably talked over and the old Il Rojo and his son, prince Oreghain, begged Lorenzo to consider the national costume which had served him on his flight, as an insignificant present on their part, without denying him the satisfaction which he requested, of leaving behind some object or other, as a memorial of his arrival under their hospitable protection

After Signore Testa had related much to his old friend, concerning the chief of the gauchos, and his war of extermination against Monte Video, and of the excitement in all South America for the establishment of a national central government, they all wished each other good night, and betook themselves to their toldos

Early on the next morning the whole Inaken tribe was in motion, to give a farewell greeting to the three white men Old and young, and great and small, endeavored to make them understand their hearty wishes for a prosperous journey

Vala Lini appeared, to repeat in person her thanks to the stranger from the seashore, that he had taken such good care of her beloved Oreghain when far away, and brought him back safely to their toldos again

The three white men mounted their horses, accompanied by Oreghain and some hundred Inaken of both sexes, forming a picturesque cavalcade, as an escort half way to the next settlement, of a tribe of Puelches

There the travellers changed their horses, leaving their own behind, without debating long over the difference in value, which would not have amounted to a dollar in money at the utmost—a convenient mode of travelling in Patagonia, which will hardly subsist long after European "civilization" shall have been introduced there

Towards the evening of the second day, Lorenzo found himself on board the Mazzini, in Baragaldi's brotherly society, who immediatly made preparations to get under sail, and directed his course towards the coast of Rio Grande

CHAPTER V.

FORTUNATE BUSINESS.

UNTIL now, we have moved in a unity of time, from the first appearance of Lorenzo, as a Benedictine monk, in the prison edifice at Buenos Ayres, until his embarkation in Patagonian costume on board the Mazzini, in the Bay of St Matthias All that has occurred within the limits of our relation is included in the same time

The sybil of the Inaken intimated a crisis in the FATE of many of the principal persons whose position in human society we have from the first sought to investigate We hasten to concentrate in a short retrospect, what occurred in the widely extended circle of our characters, and, more or less, brought on the crisis, which (without any prophecy of Yani Kyimi) must proceed sooner or later, from the various elements of the social world in which they move

According to the Bible, in which we are told that "the last shall be first," and with a recognition of the insuperable distance which separates men from each other in their social position, we would gladly begin our retrospect with Pat Gentlebov, Achules, or Corinna, if their relations were not in just as natural a social sequence, dependant on the fate of others, whom we must necessarily first touch upon

Notwithstanding this, we shall still begin "below," and first observe our Mr Daily, who now called himself Mr James John Stone Dressed like a gentleman, he announced himself on the day of his arrival in Rio at the counting-room of his "house," which had, of course, an entrance in Rio, another in Buenos Ayres, and here and there, in the world, concealed private entrances, which were not all known even to himself He conversed freely with Mr Thomson on business matters, and alluded to the permission of Mr Walker, of Buenos Ayres, that he should be allowed to make a journey into the interior of the country, "on private business," as soon as the cargo of the Nordtsjerman was discharged, which required his presence as supercargo

Mr Thomson found "no objection" to the agreement of the clerk with his brother-in-law, and now learned, that Mr Daily's father and grandfather lived somewhere in Brazil, at least Mr Habakkuk had received no intelligence of their death The contemplated journey had, of course, for its object, to inform himself personally of the welfare of his relatives, and besides, to try if he could not obtain an advance on his supposed inheritance, to establish himself somewhere The object of such a journey was recognised on both sides as " very reasonable, and very practical," and Mr Daily took a most cordial leave of the partner of a house to which he had for some years rendered much important service, though it had been oftentimes " quite in private "

We find Mr Stone, after some days, in a small private house, in an unpretending street, occupied in packing, systematically, a valuable collection of superior Chili stones A quantity of neat little boxes, filled with cotton, lay around him, and he put in order, and fastened up, the rubies, emeralds, sapphires, topazes, etc., which lay in deplorable confusion under the concealed false bottoms of his two colossal trunks, as he had, until now, had no time to arrange them there systematically There was a knock at the door, Mr Daily left the small apartment in which he was busied, slipped into the alcove, locked the door behind him, and appeared in the corridor of the narrow house, where two persons were seeking admittance

"Is that you, Mr ———' what's your name?" inquired he of one of the men,

"Dick Vail, as you will recollect, and here is the man whose acquaintance you wished to make, the commission merchant, who does a greater business here in Rio, than Dick Vail will ever do in his life!"

The spokesman was, then, Dick—Dick Vail, the old acquaintance of Pat Gentleboy in the English navy, whom we remarked on board the Nordstjernan, on the night Mr Daily stepped into the sumacca to go on shore

Mr Daily was endowed with that mysterious instinct which so often puts practical men of business on the right track, when they are "looking for somebody or other" to employ in this or that business

The unfortunate intelligence that Mr Closting was absent, had, as is known, put him in a little perplexity Mr. Dick Vail had become, from the moment of his entering the sumacca to the arrival in Rio, his travelling companion and conductor He had learned to know him as a former boatswain in the British navy, who had "followed his business" on the coast of Brazil, and he did not require the intercourse of two nights and a day, to discover in him the man whom he just then required

Mr Dick Vail, "first mate" of a smuggling sumacca had sufficient acquaintance in the "mercantile world" of Rio, and especially in its subordinate classes, to be able to render a service to his countryman, from whose seaman's uniform the smuggler peeped forth as soon as he felt himself comfortable, among his equals, on board the sumacca The necessity of the stranger, as a "foreign merchant" from Chili, to find in Rio a creditable commission merchant, was in itself so simple and natural, that Mr Dick Vail found "no objection" to bring such a person to his countryman

"Come in!" returned Mr Stone to the above greeting, and led the two friends into a back room of his house, that, like thousands of others in Brazil, appeared built after the selfsame model of the garden-house of Senhora Fortuna, whose acquaintance we have yet to make

"This man here, who has known me for years," began the third person, as they seated themselves in the armchairs in the back room, "this man has told me about your business, and I am ready to serve you as a commission merchant You can inquire about me all over the city. I am well known as a business man of honor, and honesty, and credit."

"The credit is the principal thing!" interrupted Mr Stone, with a smile on his lips "What is your name? Where do you live?"

"My name is Isaac Schweinfurter, and I live in the Rua do San Pedro, No 237, just below the Campo de Santa Anna, if you know where that is! Here is my address." Mr Stone received the card of the man of business, and appointed him to come to him again on the following morning, and the two men now took their leave

Mr. Stone then went out, and arriving at the Hotel Faroux, he gave to one of the butlers a card with the name of the commission merchant in a disguised hand, and requested him to obtain information, if possible, "where this man lived" He soon learned what he knew already, and besides, that Mr. Schweinfurter was a well known broker in stones and jewels, who had pretty good credit Mr Stone required to know no more Mr Schweinfurter appeared at the hour agreed upon, and the "merchant of Chili" handed over to him a considerable business in costly stones.

Mr Schweinfurter found the quality of the wares superior, and the quantity considerable He required five per cent commission on the stipulated price, which he considered reasonable as did Mr Stone also, for they were both experienced men of business

Mr Schweinfurter took with him some samples of the various species, and on the third day received all the boxes of precious stones in return for 1643 pounds sterling ready money, and the business was completed

One day, when Mr Stone was in the packing room of the Messrs Walker & Co, as usual, Mr Thomson came and whispered in his ear "Come, by and by, to my room at the counting-house, and take a glass of sherry with me, I have something to show you You are a connoisseur in stones I made a bargain yesterday, I can tell you! A collection of Chili stones such as you hardly ever saw. I paid 1613 pounds sterling, and I'll wager that we make fifty per cent on it. Mr Robert assures me that we have just as fine a collection in Buenos Ayres, on on the way to St Petersburg, that are nearly, if not quite, as brilliant as these! but I doubt whether we ever made a bargain of this sort"

"I doubt it, beforehand," said Mr Daily, smiling "I will make free to try a glass of sherry, thank you kindly, Mr Thompson I will give my opinion of the value of the stones I am rejoiced that you've made such a good bargain! Thank you kindly, Mr Thomson, for your reliance upon my opinion."

Mr Daily took a glass of sherry in Mr Thomson's office, admired the superior precious stones, and the peculiarly fortunate bargain of the house of Walker & Co, prepared himself for a journey in the interior of the country, and joined a tropa, destined for the province which his father had inhabited for years

To what category a ship captain belongs when on shore, is a peculiar question, since, at the utmost, the merchant invites him to dinner, if he has made a successful voyage for him, and wishes him at sea again as soon as possible, when he has his freight aboard.

We take it upon our conscience to consider the gallant Captain Finngreen next to the clerk or supercargo, as we must take our leave of him

With the elevated consciousness which every noble action leaves behind it in the human heart, Captain Finngreen looked down from the latitude of his fortunate arrival in Rio, upon the various degrees of danger which he had escaped with his cabin passengers

Indifferent as many passengers remain to the captain, whom they annoy with the wearisome inquiry, "When will the vessel arrive in port?" and with their criticisms of the provision chest, etc, Captain Finngreen had become very much attached to his passengers from the river La Plata, of whom some of them evidently had to thank him for their deliverance.

The Nordstjernan had for years plied between

Northern Europe and Buenos Ayres, or Rio de Janeiro, and was now freighted for the return voyage up the English Channel

Captain Finngreen did not omit to invite his friends to a farewell dinner on board, and with Hinango, Alvarez, Horatio, and Robert Walker, appeared Dr Thorfin and the ever good humored air pump controller of the imperial princesses

All sorts of " healths' were drunk, and first " Miss Fanny's" whose incognito remained carefully preserved, and next, to the toast " To the freedom of South America," resounded as loud a viva " To the unity of Scandinavia as a republic, for the employment of a naval power which she possesses from nature "

" May our divided races," cried Captain Finngreen, with glass in hand," recognise their dignity and their vocation to do their part as a united nation, with a powerful fleet, towards the deliverance of Europe and speak with the cannon's mouth when it shall once break out there—when Russia and England, united, desire to sustain the cause of despotism

" Scandinavia ! Scandinavia ! ' Star of the North, break brightly forth !'" added he, with animation, and all the Scandinavians joined in, and emptied their glasses with their companions

" England and Russia united !" said Robert, interrupting the ensuing silence, and looking around him with an expression of amazement " That would be a singular alliance ! the freest nation united with despotism personified !"

" And nevertheless, the most natural alliance in the world !" asserted Hinango " as you will yourself perceive, friend Robert, when you weigh the position of England and Russia Both states are only strong and great at the expense of freedom, through the slavery and subjugation of other nations and their own people "

" What ?" interrupted the young Briton, " do you then assert that the freest nation in Europe, we English, are subjugated ?"

" Your pardon, my good friend Robert, I do most distinctly assert it Your people are not only under the escutcheons and yard sticks of your aristocrats and tradesmen or manufacturers, but lie in deeper wretchedness than the Russians The Russian serf is at least clothed and fed In England, the poor are, from childhood, systematically crippled in manufactories, or starve in the streets or almshouses, notwithstanding all the ' philanthrophy' and all the ' piety' of your higher classes "

Robert appeared at a loss to refute this, and observed that a great proportion of his countrymen were aware of these facts, and were striving for a change.

" I am far from denying that," replied the Scandinavian, " I never confound the misfortunes of a nation with the principles of the government that represents the people, but these governing principles of Great Britain are closely united with the absolutism of Russia, and when the people of Europe shall one day arise to struggle for their freedom and independence, these two powers will stand opposed, for life or death, against the cause of mankind !"

" As cabinets—it may be ! I will grant that," rejoined Robert, with a certain decision of manner peculiar to him, " but not the British nation ! There is in our people too much straightforward perception of right and wrong, for them

to be blinded at such a crisis ; they have been hitherto led by the nose, perhaps I must admit that we have, until now, falsely understood and falsely recognised the principle of freedom, but I will not relinquish the belief in my nation ' '

" Bravo !" cried Dr Thorfin, " in you speaks the noble Briton of a rising generation ! Here's to the future of the British nation ' ' added he, and raised his glass " The young Britannia of the future, in the spirit of humanity !'"

All shared the faith of the young Briton, and the hope of the Scandinavian, and emptied their glasses, while Hinango heartily pressed the hand of the gallant youth

Robert began, with a voice of youthful strength, the wonderfully impressive melody of his native hymn

" Rule Britannia ! Britannia rule the waves !'"

and those who knew the words joined in festively with him

The Scandinavians then sang their national hymn, whose first lines Captain Finngreen had recited, and the powerful baritone of Alvarez accompanied the soft tenor of Horatio in their South American hymn of curse

" The waves of La Plata are beating
On the shore—and with horrors they're gone— etc.

The thermometer of the astronomer's gaiety rose with every every glass, until it reached the temperature of extravagance, and as a comical interlude to the serious vocal entertainment, he sang, with true devotion, his well known favorite song

" No general has such powerful might—" etc., etc

At last a " prosperous voyage" was drank to Captain Finngreen, who was preparing to go to sea again in a few days after this hearty leave-taking from his friends

CHAPTER VI

THE POWER OF ATTORNEY FROM GOA.

SENOR ALVAREZ ought properly to have stood below Mr Daily, and according to the above-designated system of classification from below upward, ought to be named next to Achilles, for he was only a type setter and besides a music teacher, a twofold very subordinate quality in the scale of the social world of British civilization Properly Alvarez, as type setter and music teacher, did not belong at all to " the social world," according to British notions

Every talent, let it show itself in whatever province of art it may, belongs very naturally in the subordinate class of all other " serviceable agencies," and compromises the man who has the misfortune to be endowed with it, if he has not, at the same time, a considerable property at his command, through which he obtains admittance into the social world and masks his talent

Señor Alvarez had announced the resolution, to seek immediately for a place as type setter, whereupon Dr Thorfin met him with the proposition, to procure him some pupils for the guitar, which would not be difficult in Rio de Janeiro

Apart from the national or provincial talent for music, as for example in the province of St Paolo, the predilection for musical entertainment (especially on stringed instruments) is unmistakable in the great cities of Brazil

Instruction in music is there a part of the system of education, which, like the whole of social life generally in South America, wavers (like Hercules at the cross-roads) between British fashion and French intellect, more, however, inclining to the latter, where peculiar cases of absolute paucity of intellect do not recognise for themselves the cultivation of a finishing school of British dullness as more suitable and comfortable

Alvarez gave lessons on the guitar in different families of different nations, and was, among Brazilians and strangers from the European continent, considered with peculiar respect and sympathy, as a " political refugee,' who endeavored to lighten his existence in exile by his distinguished talent On the other hand, amongst the Britons, with whom he became acquainted through Mr Thomson's " patronage," he was treated as a " teacher," who gave instructions for a stipulated price, as the footman cleaned the boots for stipulated monthly wages

In the transatlantic world of British civilization, the teacher, in any department whatever of science or learning, appears to belong, not even to the category of footmen, but to that of negro slaves, as Señor Alvarez learned, in the most characteristic manner, at an English academy in Rio He presented himself there, one day, in the garb of a gentleman, and handed to the principal of the establishment (formerly a ship carpenter) a letter of recommendation from Mr Thomson Hardly had he read the contents of the letter, than he declared, with businesslike despatch ·

" I am very thankful to Mr Thomson for this recommendation, but I cannot use it I am just about selling my academy, with the entire inventory, tables, and chairs, and benches, instruments and-books, and teachers of all sorts—my guitar teacher amongst the rest I am sorry—very sorry, pardon me—I am just now very busy——"

Notwithstanding this summary dismissal, as the saleable slave of a ship carpenter, who had established a finishing school for young ladies, the good Alvarez by no means wanted for congenial employment, while he occupied his room in the chacara of Dr Thorfin, and passed his leisure hours there with the latter and Horatio

Horatio, likewise in the estimation of the British civilized world " only an artist," and of course below zero in the scale of British respectability, visited the Academy of Arts,[*] where the collection was certainly not of particular

value But in itself the academy represented an intellectual authority, which, according to the notions of British civilization, is not exactly directly " useful "——

The nephew of Alphonso lived in the secluded intellectual world which all true talent forms around itself, and out of which, also, it contemplates life from a higher point of view

Serious and melancholy by nature, the events which he had of late encountered were by no means calculated to increase his spirits The peculiar circumstance, however, that he was entirely cut off from all intercourse with the friend of his uncle, whom he had accompanied in exile, added little alleviation to the sufferings which he experienced at the remembrance of his home

As related to these sufferings, a well meant, friendly counsel was imparted to him on his first arrival in Rio, " to drive them out of his head," and this counsel came from the jovial mouth of Mr George Thomson, his banker

" You have saved a pretty property," observed Mr Thomson, as Horatio sat with him in his office, receiving the amount of a bill of exchange, " be reasonable, and drive from your head the fantasies of freedom, and fatherland, and the like , and, if I may advise you, throw your painting stuff aside ' A young man, like you, with such a capital, should give up the pencil I cannot conceive what sort of civilization exists in Buenos Ayres, when your relations could allow you to employ yourself in such a manner You must perceive, Señor P——, that I mean well to you You are commended to my care by Mr Walker, and I am, so to say, responsible for you here—for your career and your prosperity I beg you to consider what sort of career lies before you—for prosperity is out of the question ! If, instead of painting, you would take up statuary, a business might always be established, with marble, and sandstone, and the like ' Apply yourself to sculpture Set up a statuary establishment for gravestones, doorsills, and the like saleable articles ! Buy a dozen negroes, and I will send out to England for a machine to saw marble, and apply yourself to the practical part of sculpture Deliver solid wares, even if required from Carrara marble Let all the sawing be done by negroes, and keep up your respectability Do not put your hand to any thing except in your office Keep an able foreman, who understands the practical business, that is requisite for such an establishment, until you acquire the necessary knowledge to distinguish Carrara marble from Brazilian granite I can tell you, that with your capital, you would be a made man here ' I advise you as a friend What the devil will you do with the pencil ? In the first place, you must do all the painting yourself, for you cannot have portraits and the like made by negroes, at least, not so easily as squares of marble for floors , and you know that such handwork as painting injures your respectability, and will entirely undermine it You are, and will always remain, ' only an artist,' and if your pictures should even be admitted into a salon, people will not admit you there, as you must know !"

The youth would have replied to the Briton, that in Buenos Ayres, as in Rio, another standard prevailed in relation to talent and human worth

[*] This institution was founded in Rio by a resolution of the Brazilian Chamber of Deputies The requisite professors in the various departments were written for to Paris, and established as State functionaries The edifice of the academy, in the neighbourhood of the Largo do Francesco de Paolo, was erected for this especial object It contains the necessary collection of plaster casts from the best known antique statues and busts, and a picture gallery of ancient and modern masters, which will be increased according to ability. The worthy director of the academy at that time was Mr Taunay, brother of the French Consul General in Rio

than perhaps in England, but he had hardly uttered a word, when Mr Thomson interrupted him

"What is your fashionable world in South America, my good Senhor Horatio? How can you compare that with our English respectability? Pardon me, but I mean well by you! Even if—even if, in this semi-barbarism, among Spaniards, and Portuguese, and Frenchmen, and the like—even it a painter, or musician, or a teacher of languages, or even a mechanic, finds admittance into some house or other, let me ask, what sort of a house is it? Perhaps the gentleman, as he calls himself, was formerly nothing else but a teacher, or artist, or even a mechanic, and besides, and in all cases, he is a foreigner! for even an Englishman, in his case, who, as a parvenu establishes a so called respectable house, would admit no artist or teacher to his salon, that he might not expose himself to the embarrassment of having him seen there by some gentleman whose portrait he had painted, or whose daughter he had instructed on the piano. My good Senhor P——, think where you are working with your pencil!—— You are working yourself down into the basement, into the society of the footman, who places the money in your hand for your portraits or your lesson in drawing. You must at length receive money for your handwork, and the gentleman who sends the pay to you, will be little apt to inquire whether you are descended from an old Spanish family or not! You are, and will remain, 'an artist,' and there's an end of it, and it gives me pain, with your capital—it might be turned to something better."

One day, as Horatio sat in one of the cool apartments of the Academy of Arts, and worked at a drawing after the head of Niobe, Alvarez stood near him, having come to take him to dinner. Horatio was just giving an account of his interesting interview with Mr Thomson, about the position of an artist, and the respectability of a stone cutter or a marble merchant, at least in the English mercantile world, when a white servant, in blue livery, with gold buttons, accompanied by a porter of the academy, entered the room

"That is Senhor P——," said the porter, in a respectful low tone to the white footman, who drew a billet from his pocket, and handed it to the nephew of Alphonso, with the words "From Senhor Vera, Rua do Valongo"

Both recognised, at the first glance, the servant of the interesting negro from Goa, and looked inquiringly at each other, while Horatio opened the billet

"My compliments to Senhor Vera," said he, turning to the negro, "I will take the liberty to make my visit to-morrow about eleven o'clock."

The footman withdrew, attended by the porter who had conducted him in

Horatio imparted to his friend the contents of the billet. It was a polite invitation from Senhor Bernardo Vera, from Goa, that he would do him the honor of calling upon him, since he desired to consult with him as a friend of art, about a picture. Both suspected that the consultation about a picture might be only a pretence, to enter into communication with Horatio, in consequence of the impression that the portrait of the mother of Dolores had wrought upon the Ethiopian

"Go with me to-morrow!" said Horatio to his friend, to whom the solution of the riddle might not be less important than to the other, inasmuch as the family name of his mother, on board the Nordstjernan, had wrought just as singular an impression upon Dolores

"I will introduce you as my friend, who likewise possesses judgement in the arts," said Horatio, "and perhaps your acquaintance is of more importance to him than mine, a suspicion which the name of your uncle, who disappeared, inspires me with"

"Certainly!" remarked Alvarez, "it seems to me, myself, as if light might dawn upon me, according to all that has hitherto appeared possible to me"

The two sons of Apollo went on the following day, at eleven o'clock, to the before mentioned palace, and were led by the same servant into a salon, furnished in the old fashioned style of European luxury of the last century, like similar buildings of the sort in Rio

After some moments, Senhor Vera appeared, the same negro whom they had seen before the picture in the picking room of the alfandega. He received the two friends with the suitable demeanor of a man of the world, greeted them in Spanish with a Portuguese accent, and especially fastened his penetrating glance on Alvarez, whose countenance, as it seemed, he had not observed in the alfandega, from pure absorption in the contemplation of the picture

Senhor Vera evidently spoke with a perturbed heart, and seemed not to find the words that he sought, for the opening of his subject

"Your countenance, sir," said he, after a short introduction, "assures me beforehand that I have not deceived myself in my hopes. Will you have the goodness to go with me now to my room, and look at a picture"

The two friends walked on before the negro, and soon stood with him in his study, at least the room rather resembled the library of a savant than the counting-room of a merchant

Senhor Vera drew aside the green curtain that covered a picture, and Horatio and Alvarez started backward as they beheld the same portrait of the mother of Dolores, or at least a duplicate painted by the same master, as it had appeared in the box at the alfandega

"You are then a nephew of Señor Gabriel Garingòs?" said Senhor Vera to the astonished Alvarez, "for your features resemble his, as they do the portrait of your mother, which I know. And you, if I may inquire?" added he, turning to Horatio. "You can both of you, gentlemen, perhaps give me information concerning the life or death of the lady whose portrait you see here, the duplicate of which I beheld, not long since, at the alfandega?"

"Señora Paula de C—— is dead," replied Horatio, deeply moved by the mystery which still enveloped this encounter

"Did she leave children?" inquired Senhor Vera, hastily

"A daughter, named Dolores"

"Where does she live?" inquired the negro with evident anxiety

Both South Americans now fell into the most singular perplexity, they looked at each other with the same expression, which implied the duty of preserving, in the strictest manner, the incognito of Dolores

"My God!" exclaimed the negro, "she lives? and your glance reveals to me that you must conceal her abode from me! Then she is probably in danger, perhaps proscribed, like so many others, as a participatress in the cause of the Unitarians, Republicans, or Humanitarios!"

The two friends were silent Señor Vera hurried to a writing-desk, took some papers from a concealed drawer, and asked Alvarez, in a decided tone

"Pardon me, sir, are you a son of Dona Maria Juana de Garringòs, whatever name she might have borne after her marriage?"

"My name is Alvarez de la Barca, my mother's name was Maria Juana de Garringòs," replied he

"Have you sisters?"

"One sister, Maria Juana Angelica"

"Where is your sister?"

"Unhappily I do not know! she left Corrientes when I went to Europe five years ago, she went to Bahia, as governess with an Italian family I have only a short time since returned from Europe. My letters were intercepted in Spain, as I took part in the struggle of the nation against Don Carlos I have written to Bahia, and expect an answer daily"

"According to the station of your sister, I may then presume that you do not possess an ample property?"

"We are poor," returned Alvarez with dignity, "but Providence gave us talent, and we are independent"

"The question which I allowed myself," continued the negro, after a pause, "would be indiscreet, if I had not the right to ask it, through this power of attorney, on the part of Señor Gabriel Garringòs, your uncle in Goa."

"My uncle Gabriel!" cried Alvarez, in a voice trembling with emotion, "in Goa! Then he is alive? living in Goa?"

"He is living as one of the most distinguished physicians in Goa, is a millionaire, and has commissioned me, by this document, to inquire about his family, and to bring you this intelligence, in the case that Señora Paula de C—— was not living In the other case, if the lady whose picture you see here were still in life, it would not have been permitted to me to give you information of the existence of your uncle The causes which lie at the foundation of these instructions to me, which may, perhaps, appear strange to you, rest in the grave of this worthy lady As little as we will for the present touch upon a secret which 'rests in the grave,'" continued he, "so little will I permit myself a question concerning the fate of this lady's daughter I desire you, however, to mark well where I live, in case Señora Dolores, as you called her, should need the succor of a friend, for life or death for Señor Gabriel is my bosom friend, I am indebted to him for my intellectual improvement through intercourse with him, and through my improvement, I am indebted to him for the suitable application of the wealth which my father bequeathed to me I am commissioned to open an unlimited credit with the children of this lady, and of the sister of my friend, in whatever circumstances I might find them; that is to say,

advances in ready money, as an earnest of the inheritance that will one day accrue to them Take notice, then, of my abode, come and see me soon and often Communicate this intelligence, if possible, to the daughter of the lady whose portrait has led me to this fortunate discovery, which I have sought through a correspondence with Buenos Ayres Give her, then, this intelligence, if possible, and," added he to Alvarez, "consider me as the banker of your uncle—and write to him through me And above all things, procure me intelligence of your sister I am ready to go to Bahia, to accompany you there, in case you believe that it would be suitable"

Alvarez was too much surprised with all he had heard, and with the reality of the portrait that he saw, to be able to talk over, tranquilly, the necessary measures

The negro handed him a duplicate of his uncle's power of attorney, dated from Goa, and added. "Only through this picture, or through its duplicate, was information to be obtained concerning the life or death of this lady, without betraying Señor Gabriel's incognito, which he wished to maintain strictly, so long as Señora Paula lived"

The two friends comprehended this, and understood all the sooner the necessity for the transportation of the picture, which, more than any written document, confirmed the commission of the Spaniard, who, even in Goa, lived under another name

The negro repeated his urgent wish to find an oppportunity, as soon as possible, of fulfilling, at least in part, the especial commission of his friend in relation to his property, and Horatio and Alvarez withdrew for the present

CHAPTER VII

THE TWO PAVILIONS

Robert Walker had taken possession of the pavilion in the garden of Madame Closting, and passed the greater part of his time there, as he was only occupied in his counting-house from ten in the morning until two in the afternoon

The exchange and alfandega were closed at this hour, and the mercantile people then either betook themselves to their chacaras, or to their several dwellings in the bosom of their families; and those who had not the good fortune to be married, either went to dine at a hotel, or, as bachelors, passed their time in some way or other, with or without a friend

Most of the commercial houses kept, besides their chacaras, particular family tables for the clerks and partners, as we have seen in the case of Messrs Rossbruck & Co, and a repast seldom went off without guests, since X sometimes ate with Z, while Z, without the fear of compromising himself, seated himself at table with the clerks of the friendly house of X, and partook of the roast meat.

Excepting the regular visits to his uncle in Bota Fogo, and to Dr Thorfin and his fellow voyagers of the Nordstjernan, which he repeated several times in the week, Mr Robert Walker was seldom seen anywhere in society, or as above named, as a self-invited guest From a dislike to the confusion at the Hotel Faroux, he had made the arrangement to enjoy his dinner quietly and comfortably in the company of his hostess, and the little creature "whom she wished to pass for her daughter" According to English custom, he drank his tea late in the evening, and in the morning his Brazilian coffee, alone, in his pavilion

He had, a long time before, studied the German language, and now, since his acquaintance with Hinango and Dr Thorfin, pursued, with a like zeal, the study of the Swedish and Danish languages, the rich literature of which excited a particular interest in him

He lived in this manner in tranquil retirement, in social intercourse with the young lady, who had found in him a friend and protector, and felt himself more than ever attached to the forte piano, since he practised four-handed compositions with her, an innocent entertainment, that no police mandate prohibited

Robert had not only developed to practical readiness a decided talent for music, but enclosed within the depths of his soul that "sounding board of sentiment," (as he had on one occasion expressed himself,) on which all the tones of art and nature reverberated in their mysterious purity, as harmony of the soul in its spiritual element

This inward feeling in him resembled a diamond, whose solution had been attempted in all methods, by the chemical matter of education, and, to Aunt Susan's great indignation, without success In whatever fold of the heart this diamond, the sense of the beautiful, had concealed itself, it had remained uninjured, and more than ever asserted its moral worth, since the undeniable crisis in the life of the noble youth, at his arrival in Rio, as friend and protector of the exiled poetess from La Plata river

Robert's inclination for music would perhaps not have developed itself in so great a degree, if (as we have already intimated) it had not been stimulated by Aunt Susan

Miss Thomson, who had had the boy under her superintendence for years, in consequence of her sectarian spirit declared all music to be a sinful propensity to worldly dissipation, and strictly prohibited him from musical exercises

It happened with the boy, as with so many men, who often first experience the worth of freedom through despotic restrictions, and feel the moral force within them the more powerfully, the more strictly it is repressed

The less the boy was able, according to his youthful perceptions, to recognise the practising of music as sinful and depraved, and cursed before God, the oftener did he slip away to his music master, and linger at the piano forte for hours

After Aunt Susan's departure from Buenos Ayres, he became his own master in the above respect, since his father, with whose religious views we are acquainted, gave himself little trouble about it, whether Robert played the piano or cards, if his teachers were satisfied with him, who were to form him into a capable business man

Robert had never found his undeniable ex-

pertness on the piano so entertaining, as in accompanying the favourite compositions of his pretty, and truly amiable hostess, who, on her part, quite unaccountably to herself, had never before moved her little fingers over the keys with such readiness, as when she accompanied the young Englishman It only happened occasionally, that she suddenly, and certainly in the least difficult passages, made a mistake, or missed the time, and then, involuntarily, partly in apologetic civility, her glance was turned sideways upon her friend, either to excuse the mistake, or to ask his indulgence

The empire of tone on the planet Saturn, may be, as Hinango affirms, of an extension and elevation of which we poor mortals on the earth are not able to form a conception; but music has ever appeared to us incontestably powerful, even on earth, as a medium for the expression of sentiment and thought, and the fragmentary intimation of the Scandinavian "enthusiast" may, perhaps, have for itself some ground of probability

In this instance, it was remarkable that the musical pair, in the comparison and selection of the ancient and modern compositions of their united musical store, discovered a singular accordance in the character and spirit of the compositions—a coincidence of taste and judgement in art, which proved an undeniable affinity of mind, as well as an intimate communion of soul. The musical portfolios of both, contained in preference, masterpieces of serious and profoundly sentimental composition, in opposition to the superficial and often characterless mixture of stolen fragments, "put together," and combined into an *allegro*, which are liked in so many families, under the pretext, that "life is serious enough, and, of all things in the world, people must not hear any thing serious or mournful upon an instrument'"

Whether Mr Robert's piano was of better quality, or more conveniently situated for two stools, or the daylight coming through less foliage was brighter at his window, or the glass cylinders to his wax lights were cleaner than all these things appeared in the apartment of Senhora Gracia, she had, all at once, experienced a particular preference for Mr Robert's piano, and as it was difficult to move, and there was no better place for it in her villa, the instrument remained where it was, and Senhora Gracia often remained by Senhor Roberto, upon his comfortable chair, long after they had ceased playing their four-handed compositions

This confiding unreserve, which (according to the observations of so many travellers) forms a part of the character of the Brazilian women, and manifests itself in their natural naiveté in social intercourse, operated with magic power upon the stranger youth Being endowed by nature with similar unreserve, in a few weeks he felt himself as if at home with the young lady, whose circumstances he never allowed himself to touch upon, as he respected her secret

When Robert came home, he regularly found the traces of a careful disposing hand, which arranged the smallest trifles for his accommodation the vases on the pier table filled with fresh flowers, the blinds closed on the sunny side, and the shaded windows opened, in short, all the preparations for his return, and, occasionally, a peculiarly delicate flower left upon the keys of the piano, as if in forgetfulness

The windows of the sitting-rooms in the two pavilions, whose insignificant distance from each other we have before intimated, casually afforded a prospect (or rather insight) into each other, besides which, they commanded a view of the Bay and the gigantic Organ Mountains The Brazilian sun regularly took its course, from east to west, through the northern hemisphere, and shone upon the two pavilions, towards evening, in such a direction that Senhora Gracia's window, where, as it seemed, was her favorite seat, happened to be enveloped in shade, and of course could remain open unhindered On the other hand, the window at which stood the writing-desk of her neighbor was partly covered by some bananas, whose fanlike crowns first commenced at a height not reached by Senhor Roberto's forehead when he sat at his usual place at home

Senhora Gracia occupied herself with the art of making flowers from the feathers of parrots and "colibris," and many other birds, an art which (as we shall soon know) she had acquired when a child amongst the nuns, and had since then often turned to the lightening of her solitary existence

She worked from sunrise until Robert came to dinner, and often employed the remaining hours until sundown, to complete an unfinished flower, or to begin the composition of another, according as she felt inclined "Senhor Roberto" generally seated himself at his writing-desk, as he had the habit, when he was not writing, of reading there, perhaps because the slanting direction of the desk was particularly convenient for him, as a support to his book?

A young Brazilian woman is as little able always to make flowers, as a young Englishman is to read or write for ever, without once looking up and around from the flowers, or from the paper, whether it be written or printed paper, that is a matter decidedly settled, which requires no citations from Aristotle, or Jesus the son of Sirach, or Lord Chesterfield

Heaven knows how it chanced that Senhor Roberto, almost without exception, encountered the glance of the lively, inquisitive eyes[*] of the young Brazilian lady, whenever, quite casually, he looked up from his writing or reading, and out of the window. Without further pursuing the question how it chanced, we will, for the present, take for granted that it was accident—altogether accident, as there are so many thousand singular accidents in life, which are certainly not so interesting as this meeting the glance of the young lady appeared, at least we infer, that, in case the accident had not appeared interesting to her, she would probably have avoided the encounter of glances

By Robert's door stood a young banana, close to the wall Senhora Gracia's attention had been drawn to it by Dr Thorfin's remark, that the leaves of this colossal plant will often grow from ten to fourteen inches in a night,[†] while

they do not grow at all during the day To convince himself of this, Robert daily bent the so called tube-leaf, which developed itself from the chalice of the crown, against the wall, by means of a cane of sufficient length, and scratched a mark with the same cane It was the Brazilian spring, it was quasi May. in Guenabara, and Senhora Gracia appeared to delight, with peculiar love, in the wonderful richness of nature A mysteriously powerful force of nature seemed to spread itself through her being, with similarly speedy development, a sentiment of the joy and happiness of existence unfolded itself in her, as the chalice leaf of the young banana struggled upward from night to night—heavenwards—starwards—up to the ethereally clear zenith, which was touched by an arm of the milky-way, whose myriad stars our human eyes only know by hearsay

Shall we explain it to ourselves by the childish love of a pure female heart for the wonderfully rich mysterious nature, that Senhora Gracia at times suddenly rose from her work and ran to the young tree, merely to see whether it did not indeed grow in the day time? And shall we count it amongst the thousands and thousands of insignificant accidents, that she must pass directly by Robert's door, to arrive at the sun-avoiding and starlight-loving banana, not to mention that the doors of chacaras or pavilions in Brazil stand open the whole day? Senhor Roberto concerned himself as inquisitively and scientifically about the growing and not growing of the tropical botanic world as Senhora Gracia If we only put all these insignificant circumstances and accidents together, it will surprise nobody, that they both met, from time to time, under the young banana, before Robert's door, and the justice of the peace for the parish of Nossa Senhora da Gloria would not have easily decided whether the young Brazilian lady found the young Senhor Inglez, or the young Senhor Inglez found the young Brazilian lady there Both stood there, and contemplated the young banana, and conversed about the tropical strength of nature, about the influence of the starry and spheral world upon our earth, and about the disturbing, paralysing effect of the sun, which extinguished the coals under old Anna's coffee kettle, if she did not interpose herself, or some other object that cast a shadow, between.

Robert's thermometer hung outside of the window at which he had his seat Senhora Gracia had no thermometer, and appeared like a travelling Briton in Russia, (who would look at the thermometer to see when it froze him,) just as willing to examine at times it it was hot, or how hot it was, in their neighborhood To look at the thermometer, she must step to Robert's window, and her little chin just rested, exactly convenient, on the sill

That was only blind chance, just as incontestably as all besides that we have incidentally alluded to, and it would be silly and pedantic to take the least notice, in any history whatever, of such little accidental circumstances But good manners, politeness, the complaisance of neighborhood, required, imperatively, that Robert should spring up from his seat, and lean out of the window, or on the window, which Senhora Gracia almost touched with the delicate chin of her delicate little face, whereupon he would say a word to her, or she to him, and often one word produced another, and a quarter of an hour was chatted away

The thermometer might rise or fall, but with such casual encounters, the "thermometer of mutual confidence" at least rose in nearly equal proportion with the tropically rapid development of the banana and of sentiment

An exhausless material of mutual entertainment was afforded by the little lizards, which every evening pursued their youthful sports, pairwise, among themselves, here and there, on the white painted walls seeking to surprise each other, slipping away again, and not tiring, for hours, of showing each other all conceivable marks of attention

This species of little mosquito lizards, belong amongst the prettiest, most delicate, and most amusing little "domestic animals" we could name The mysterious manner in which they paralyze a mosquito by a glance, and then dart upon and swallow him, fettered the young Englishman, as it does many Europeans in Brazil, for hours, in observation and contemplation Without this mysterious power of the glance, a lizard, which cannot fly, would hardly be able to catch a mosquito, that would betake itself to the air at its slightest approach

Robert contemplated, with unwearied attention, the adroit movements of the fairylike, delicate little animals, running about like flies on the ceiling, as they glided round a mosquito, until they could direct a glance at his head from a distance, such a "glance in glance" as instantly bound the insect, fastened it to the spot, and allowed it to be caught

Who will find it remarkable or surprising, that Senhora Gracia partook with Robert, in a neighborly manner, of this amusement in the contemplation of nature, especially when the advancing cool of the evening permitted them to remain in the open air?

Whom does it surprise, that by degrees, through so many chances and little accidents and opportunities, an agreeable relation of neighborly intimacy grew up between the two, which became more intimate every day, before Robert had yet received any information about the outward relations and inward life of his indisputably amiable neighbor?

The connexion of ideas awakened in Robert, as he mentioned the name of Hinango at his introductory visit, and infused into his mind the suspicion that this young lady might be Senhora Closting in person, had by degrees been established within him to a probability On the contrary, the impression that this female made upon him, loudly and forcibly contradicted the tangible reality, that she was the mother of the little creature, or mother and wife at all

Senhora Gracia appeared to him a maiden, early developed in a tropical climate, breathed upon by some mysterious soul-suffering, that rather spiritually heightened than physically spoiled her charming bloom In consequence of all this confusion of ideas, he fell into a maze of the most singular contradiction with himself and the reality, that he would not recognise as such He was as little able to comprehend the thought that the young lady was the mother of the little girl, as on the other hand to give an account of the degree in which this question generally interested him, and wherefore it seemed impossible for him to recognise the reality, as such If the connexion of ideas led him within the limits of the probability in which the young lady appeared to him as Madame Closting, he was shocked, and notwithstanding this, was obliged to admit to himself that this young lady would perhaps have remained more distant to him, if he had not surmised in her a being so boundlessly unfortunate as to belong to such a man as Mr Closting was described to him He could not even deny that he had all the more carried out his momentary design of entering indirectly into business connexion with Mr Closting, to give to his friend Hinango, whose sympathy had always been valuable to him, an after proof that he could transact business with the other, without incurring the danger which his fellow voyager had quite incidentally indicated, by way of conversation, and more in jest than earnest

The expression of inward suffering which Hinango had designated, in respect to Madame Closting, spoke incontestibly from the whole being of the young lady, who, as a woman in danger, had made demands on his protection

We will not examine whether this expression which presupposed a heart that was capable of suffering, might not originally have more powerfully attracted the sensitive youth than even conspicuous beauty, without soul in expression, (and armed with icy coldness against all the impressions of life,) would ever have been able to do

The position of Robert as protector of the young lady, who had so confidingly claimed his sympathy, was founded on a coincidence of singular circumstances, which were partly foreign to him, and partly proceeded from his personal relations, without his being able to prevent them

Senhora Gracia had one day revealed to her physician, Dr Thorfin, that a young Englishman, whose uncle had introduced him to her uncle, inhabited the pavilion, and he soon afterwards learned, to his no small astonishment, that this neighbor was no other than Mr Robert Walker, the fellow voyager and friend of Hinango Had his patient imparted to him this intelligence the day before Robert took possession of this abode, he would probably have taken it on his conscience to break off the contract for the lease under some pretence or other, without casting the least doubt upon the blameless deportment, or the pure and noble character of the young lady The physician knew his patient and her sufferings, the cause of them, and their effect upon such a heart as hers

To explain Dr Thorfin's perception of things, we remark, that he would not have entertained a scruple, for example, about quartering the young gentleman, William Rossbrück, in the pavilion, since, according to his psychological judgement, he would have taken upon himself the responsibility, in respect to this young man, that no element of spiritual attraction threatened the young lady with danger, as in the other case he was fully satisfied that there could be no question of any other attraction for his patient, out of the province of inward life

Dr Thorfin had, from personal experience, but too clearly seen the rigid difference of woman's position, contrasted with that of man, which the judgement of the world seldom or never consider—we mean, the difference of a mutual approach and intercourse of the two sexes, which rests on sympathy of soul, contrasted with another approach and intercourse, which is as foreign to the former, as the higher soul's life is to the lowest materialism, in a word, we thus distinguish "Love and Animalism," (in case we may be permitted to form a positive word for an abstract notion.)

How little Dr. Thorlin had erred or deceived himself in such perceptions, may, perhaps, be proved by the bullet which, on that eventful evening, whizzed through the garden gate, under circumstances that we shall find, in due time revealed, in the progress of our story.

The so called weak woman, in the consciousness of her dignity, is endued by nature with a strength which, as repulsion, bids defiance to all mortal power, and repels every frivolous approach with the "sentence of death, expressed by a single *glance* ——

CHAPTER VIII

SOCIAL QUESTIONS

It may be considered a philosophic truth, that man, in every age, and in every zone, remains "man," and we understand, by this term, the inhabitant of the earth, in preference to all other creatures of our planet, endowed with susceptibility for a higher idea than that of animal life, with free power of will, with capacity for thought, and judgement, and sentiment, capable of the moral and physical ennoblement which the consciousness of his divine nature points out to him. In accordance with this truth, however we behold man in the various zones of the earth incontestably thrown under the influence of climate, of customs, and, especially of human regulations. The latter often appear more a satire on reason and the divine nature, in rigid contradiction with themselves, and oppressive of the moral freedom of man, than they authenticate reason, and promote nature.

Should it appear possible, in consequence of the philosophical result of the considerations and researches of all ages, to arrive at a definition of the term, *man*—to answer, with tolerable logical tenability, the question "What is man?" all logical tenability would be suddenly at a loss by the half of the question "What is woman?"

With all respect and veneration towards the intellectual judgement of all the classical and modern philosophical cultivation of European academies and universities, (among which we give the "Institute de France" the first place,) we doubt, nevertheless, whether if this were proposed as the prize question for the year 1846, a satisfactory answer would be given, by all the white or coloured* literati on earth.

The more Socialism is recognised in our epoch,

as a subject of the most profound research, and the future transformation of existing social regulations is acknowledged to be an undoubted necessity in all nations, so much the more clearly does the question arise, as to the destiny and the dignity of woman. By "socialism," we understand the consideration and profound investigation of the dignity and high destiny of mankind, the discussion and designation of the duties of both sexes towards human society and towards themselves, and the announcement of all possible means and ways of arriving, through moral ennoblement, at the aim of their social destination.

It is a consequence of our material age, as interesting as it is natural, that socialism (in whatever form, and with whatever aim it presents itself here and there) prefers to concern itself with the material interests of individual classes, rather than to hold up the moral ennoblement of the whole nation as the chief thing.

As a result of nationality, would proceed the reformation of the statutes, which circumscribe the material interests of the so called subordinate classes, and degrade them as slaves to the selfishness and prejudice of the so called privileged classes, who keep them in wretchedness.

It seems to us strange, remarkable, and inconceivable, that philosophers of high standing can consider a social edifice of the future to be practicable, and answerable to the requisitions of society, whose foundation rests upon individualism instead of humanity.

It seems to us impossible to produce a social transformation without overthrowing the political regulations of prerogative, without establishing the freedom of a nation. And it seems to us just as impossible, in countries where the element of political freedom on the basis of nationality is attained, to bring about a social reformation through material improvements, without a recognition of moral and intellectual ennoblement, the exalted and true destination of man, as his aim on earth.

Association upon association may form themselves, on funds or voluntary contributions, with or without community of goods, to supply temporary nourishment and employment to some thousands of breadless mechanics—speculators upon speculators, (proceeding to the practical application of this or that philosophical system) may establish and promote one or the other philanthropic social enterprise—the social world, or the basis of individualism, will forever remain the same, so long as the nation does not, in the element of freedom, set up ordinances of humanity, in consequence of which the legislation of the state, and the education of the rising generation, shall be recognised as the first and only means of all social improvement, and all ennoblement of the human race.

By the side of the material degeneracy of the men of our age, which confounds the means with the end, and recognises no higher aim than "to make money," even despising talent and intellect, as subordinate to this object—stands woman, "the riddle of creation," which, judging by the records of Scripture, even God (as it appeared) was not able to solve. The singular prophecy which he united with it, is as obscure as the riddle itself: "Therefore shall a man leave

---

* A coloured man, Mr Linstant, LL.D., of Hayti, obtained, in consequence of an anonymous dissertation, in the year 1839, the prize of the Academy of Paris, upon the question "What is the cause of the antipathy of the whites against coloured people?"

father and mother, and shall cleave to his wife, and they twain shall be one flesh."

Had Dr. Thorfin, in his discussion about the psychological enigma of the moral degradation of woman in marriage without love, recollected this passage of the Bible, it would, at least, have advanced him some steps nearer to the solution of this social question. It has been many times juridically proved that a morally vile man, when it comes to the point at which the unfortunate wife might separate from her husband, literally "cleaves" to his wife, and if she desires the separation, in a hundred cases to one he refuses, because she has become "one flesh" with him, and is, as Mr. Thomson expressed himself, perhaps, particularly "comfortable" to him as a wife.

We see, likewise, millions of cases in which the wife, as Mr. Fitz said, "cannot be separated from her husband by a steam engine of sixty horse power," although he is sunken in demoralization, a fact, the reason of which is perhaps to be sought in the above passage of Scripture—because both have become "one flesh."

If the original Hebrew text, in the above place, has been correctly translated, (which we submit to the researches of classic philologists,) then "the riddle of creation," woman, stands out only the more inexplicable, since God, according to another Scripture passage, "created man in his own image," and it repeats "In the image of God created he him." And this man, created in the image of God, "shall leave father and mother, and cleave to his wife." That is, in fact, as great a contradiction as woman is in herself.

It stands, also, in Scripture: "It is not good for man to be alone." To be sure not. This truth has been recognised for many thousand years. "It is not good." The Apostle Paul, as an apostle who, here and there, in his flight, must "slide out of a window in a basket,"[*] could only maintain, as an exception, "he that does not marry does better," since there might not always be room enough in such a flight-basket for two persons, and his apostolic office required resignation.

That the Apostle Paul, however, recognised clearly the powerful influence of woman upon man or youth in general,[†] is confirmed, amongst many similar passages, by his fatherly or brotherly warning to the youthful apostle Timothy "to beware of the young widows,"[‡] etc., since he beheld the young Timothy (like so many other apostles) in danger of hanging his apostolic office "on the nail" so soon as he should "cleave" to a young widow! We may conclude, from Paul and all the epistles of the apostles, that the woman of eighteen hundred years ago, was the same woman who, some thousands of years before, gave her Adam to eat of the forbidden fruit, and then, with female inconsistency, cast the guilt upon the serpent.

Poor, unfortunate woman! thou hadst, at least, of course, so much love of truth, and sense of honor and openheartedness, as to admit, "I first allowed myself to be seduced, and then I seduced."

Perhaps she was seduced by a Mephistophel—by one of those fallen angels, who lived with them in Paradise, as the "children of God."

[*] 1 Corinthians, chap. 7, v. 8, 9, 32, 37, 38, 40
[†] 2 Corinthians, 11, v. 33   [‡] Timothy, chap. 5, v. 11

"Noble, but much to be pitied woman! If I, like Adam, had had the luck to be seduced by such a woman,' (observed Hinango, in conversation with Dr. Thorfin on the above social questions,) "I would have sustained the loss of earthly paradise, and in the love of such a noble woman, would have found my spiritual paradise, even in the desert——'

'That I believe—it is probable," added Dr. Thorfin, and both found themselves at the garden gate of Madame Closting, when Hinango withdrew, and rode out towards Bota Fogo.

———

CHAPTER IX

THE BRAZILIAN WOMAN.

It was towards evening. Dr. Thorfin found the young Englishman from the Nordstjernan in the sitting-room of his hostess, who was occupied with her flower work while the "little creature" who must "by all means be her daughter, was playing at her feet, and trying to make flowers likewise, with the clippings of some feathers.

The physician, who had already, for some weeks, often met young Mr. Walker in the same domestic circle, took a seat by him, and expressed, in the first place, his professional gratification at the indisputable revival of strength in his patient.

"For the present, you require no more medicine,' said he, after a short conversation upon the state of her health, ' if you should relapse, however, Æsculapius would be in perplexity, and leave me in the lurch."

"Relapse! be so ill as I was lately!" cried the young lady, with a heartfelt expression of anxiety and dread, "God forbid!" and laid her feather flowers out of her hand.

' What book have you there, Mr. Walker?" said Dr. Thorfin, hastily seeking an object on which to turn the attention of the sufferer.

"Luckock's Notes on Rio de Janeiro and Southern Brazil—1820," replied Robert, "and I was just going to read, for Senhora Gracia, a portrait, as I find here, although in a very bad style, a delineation of the characteristics of the Brazilian women."

"I fear, however, that the Senhor Inglez observes us through English spectacles, which, perhaps, magnify or diminish, or are green or blue. Honestly speaking, I feel that we are no more perfect than the female sex in other countries, and fear I should fall into a little embarrassment, if this sketch is correct."

"You will permit me to read it to you, Senhora?" inquired Robert, smiling.

"I beg you to do so, and promise not to interrupt you. If, however, I find accusations against my countrywomen, I shall allow myself to make our apology after you have ended."

The little one went up to Dr. Thorfin, and showed him her flowers. Robert began, and read as follows:

"Of their dress and appearance, we strangers were more competent judges than of their minds The former is of the lightest sort Among their familiar friends, they are seen with a shift only, and the bosom of it often falling off from one shoulder. They wear no stockings, and seldom either slippers, or the wooden clogs, with brown upper leather, called tamancas Their hair is long, bound with a riband close behind the head, the end turned up to the crown, and there twisted about a sort of bodkin Sometimes a wreath of artificial flowers is added, ingeniously made by themselves of silk, beads, coloured paper, tinsel, and the wings of some of the brilliant insects of the country They are arranged and worn with taste They have few opportunities of conversing with the other sex, and what good fortune offers they use with eagerness

"The ornaments of these females have a pleasing effect, and set off the charms of a face, the features of which are round and regular, a black, lively, inquisitive eye, a smooth and open forehead, a mouth expressive of simplicity and good temper, furnished with a white and even set of teeth, united with a moderately handsome figure, a sprightly, laughing air, and a demeanour gay, frank, and unsuspicious Such is the appearance of a young lady of about thirteen or fourteen years of age, a period when she usually takes upon her the cares of a household At eighteen, in a Brazilian woman, nature has attained to full maturity, a few years later, she becomes corpulent, acquires a great stoop in her shoulders, looses the good humour of her countenance, and the eye and mouth both indicate that they have been accustomed to express the violent and vindictive passions

"Early corpulence appeared to me to arise from their secluded and indolent habits They are seldom seen out of doors, except when going to mass, so early as four o'clock in the morning, and even then the whole form and face are so wrapped in mantles, as to preclude the enjoyment of fresh air, and to conceal every feature, except perhaps a wickedly talkative eye The exercise which these ladies take, is almost wholly confined to the house "

Senhora Gracia had listened to the reading the most quietly possible, even though at times a slight flush passed over her Brazilian complexion, and Dr Thorfin had, by anticipation, so to say, counted her replies "upon his fingers"

"I will tell the Senhor Inglez my opinion, point for point," began the lady, smiling, when Robert had concluded She requested the book, to read over the several places, that she might correct them Robert appeared to hand it to her reluctantly, as he feared, with justice, that she would read further than he had proposed He could, however, find no consistent pretext for withholding the book from her, so he handed it to her, and she read over the places she had marked for herself.

"As concerns our negligée, I should like to know in what sort of ladies' society your Inglez was an 'intimate friend' That we cannot, in so warm a climate, tie ourselves up in many tight garments, while we, as your Inglez himself admits, pass most of our time at home, I find as suitable as natural, but I demand of you both, to decide whether you have ever seen me in a lighter negligée than this in which I am sitting here, and whether it has ever 'partly fallen from my shoulder,' in your presence '"

The two friends, according to the truth, gave the required affirmation, and Senhora Gracia continued

"As regards our tamancas, they are not always of brown leather, as your Inglez asserts, but as you see, and have long known, of all conceivable colors, and often very tastefully ornamented " She thrust out the point of a tamanca below the trimming of her negligée

"And for the most part very small and delicate," returned Dr Thorfin, "at least yours are so "

"What is it to your Inglez whether we wear stockings in the house or not ?" she continued

"Perhaps he is a knight of the Order of the Garter," interrupted Mr Robert

"He may have the honor He will hardly have seen at our balls here an empress or lady of the court without stockings, in case he had been permitted to attend them I thank him that he at least allows us commendable hair I do not wear mine, however, twisted up 'in buckskin,' but as you see, for the most part, confined on the forehead with a velvet band, and fastened in a knot behind '

"And that it is certainly very becoming to you," affirmed the doctor,' only I find the velvet band too wide, it conceals too much of your open forehead "

"I thank you doctor ' That we can make flowers you see, but we seldom use paper for them, and the English paper there that asserts our 'eagerness to converse with gentlemen,' if it were even colored, I would not convert into a thistle leaf As regards our portrait, we owe the Inglez national thanks indeed ' he is very gracious ' very flattering ' only I find our faces more oval than round Perhaps the Inglez saw them all round, because he was accustomed to his own reflection in the glass A moderately handsome figure '" continued she, with naïve emphasis "Then it is moderately handsome ' Thanks ' thanks ' in the name of my countrywomen ' mo-de-rate-ly handsome ' I find this judgement admirably just "

The two friends could not restrain their laughter at the expression on the oval countenance of the young lady, who suddenly rose, placed herself before the mirror, and contemplated her figure, with the exclamation "Yes, sir, mo-de-rate-ly handsome '"

"'Gay, frank, and unsuspicious '" Frank and unsuspicious we are, that they must allow us Gay ' Ah ' yes, I was gay once At thirteen or fourteen, we are burdened with the cares of a household, that is true Whether we are mature matrons at eighteen, and some years later become corpulent, and lose our good humour, that may, also, be partially true, although I have not become corpulent; I have, unhappily, already, before eighteen years, lost my good humor " She read further "'Accustomed to express violent and vindictive passions '" "Is that true ?" inquired she, with incomparable naïveté "Have you seen me so violent, doctor ? say frankly ?"

"If Mr Robert lives near you for some months, I will beg him to answer the question "

"Senhor Roberto," now began the young lady, with an expression of voice and countenance as original as goodhearted, "Senhor Roberto, you know that I, also, am a Brazilian woman, now listen to my request, in the presence of you and my friend I hope that I shall long enjoy the pleasure of your neighborhood, and if you should ever see me in an outbreak of passion—an outbreak of passion against you, then pardon me! Will you, Senhor Roberto—will you forgive me, in such a case? I beg you now to do so, in case I should ever vex you, to ask forgiveness when I have vexed you, would be hard for me, for I am a woman—a Brazilian woman, and, so far as I have heard, your European women seldom or never admit that they have done wrong, when they offend a friend through their ebullitions."

The inimitable naturalness, and the sad tone with which Senhora Gracia uttered this request, affected both her auditors.

"You will not vex me, nor can you offend me in any manner, that I should expect a request for pardon from you," replied Robert, "there may occur cases when you will mistake me, and when the pain of being mistaken by you, will make me unhappy, that is all forgiven in anticipation, I give you my hand thereupon."

"You are a noble man," sighed the lady, and pressed the hand of the Briton, "I envy the woman that ——" She interrupted herself, and read silently.

"——the unnatural, and shamefully early age at which they are allowed to marry. Their early good humor, or the show of it, soon wears away, they often become the very reverse of what they were, and exhibit the alternative too plainly. They seem to be regarded by the men as dolls, or as spoiled children, whose whims must be gratified, and even anticipated, and she who has the greatest number, obtains the most attention. The generality of ladies, treated in this way, become, almost of course, fretful and peevish, and vent their spleen upon their slaves."

While she scanned over these lines, all the contradictory emotions which their impression wrought in her, were depicted upon her delicate countenance.

"The unnatural and shamefully early age," whispered she, and suddenly threw the book from her. A deadly paleness overspread her face, a fever chill appeared to pass over her.

Dr Thorfin and Robert looked at each other with an expression of heartfelt sympathy, and remained silent.

"God forgive me! it was not my fault," she at length exclaimed, and leaned herself hastily out of the window, to hide a flood of tears.

The two friends found it convenient to withdraw for an instant, and went into Robert's pavilion, where the little one, with her feather flowers, accompanied them.

"Is that really her daughter?" inquired Robert of the physician, after a long pause. "I permit myself this question, without desiring to intrude upon the incognito of this lady, which was the condition under which I came here."

"To be sure," replied Dr. Thorfin, laughing, "I thought you knew that, long ago."

"Call it spleen, or what you will, I cannot believe it, and will not believe it!"

"Why not?"

"Because I cannot think that she is married."

Thorfin again looked at the youth with a smile, and observed "You may be willing to believe it or not—be able to think it or not, it nevertheless is and will remain so Your neighbor has been married four years To whom, I may not tell you, as you well know Besides this little one, she has had two others, sickly, suffering creatures, who did not live long"

"You may make another believe that?" grumbled Robert. "You will at length try to persuade me that I myself am already a grandfather!"

Senhora Gracia had dried her tears, and now called to the little one at the entrance of the pavilion under the young banana, both gentlemen went out to her before the door, and led the child towards her.

"I thank you for the book, doctor," she began, as she handed him a small duodecimo volume, it was the "Psychology of Love," which she had thrown her tamanca after on that eventful night.

"Whoever the author may be, and in whatever part of the world he may live, he means well by us, by the women, and I hope that a worthy individual of our sex may long since have rewarded him with her love"

"I doubt that extremely," said Dr Thorfin laughing, "for, so far as I know his circumstances his property is confiscated, and 'Without money, no mouths of honey'"

"Doctor! how can you quote such a proverb? Are you in earnest?"

"Perfectly in earnest, through manifold experience, confirmed also around us here"

"And have you made no experience from observation, which tells you of the contrary? I know also that men get through the world better in relation to their outward existence, when they are married than if they remain single"

"Certainly! I grant you the last," assented the doctor, "the man makes demands upon social sympathy for his wife; demands which he dares not make as a so called single person Where love cements the union, I find such demands just But to bind a noble being to us, as a 'sign of family paternity,' without love, I pronounce to be unmanly, and as a man of honor I, myself, would be ashamed of such a privilege"

"And as is indicated in this book, also," added the lady, with a sigh

"If I had a free fatherland, I would propose a marriage court in every parish, consisting of women and men,"* continued Dr Thorfin. "Each couple should announce themselves as betrothed, and should not marry until a year after the announcement, if both kept to their resolution If they became convinced, during the year, that mutual love did not prevail, then many unhappy marriages would be avoided Before the same court, all complaints and accusations for divorce should be received, investigated, and decided on.

"Very naturally, however, the necessary establishment of a universal Popular Education should precede this. As government in general should regard education as the foundation of its spiritual and material prosperity, care should also be taken, by various public institutions, for the welfare of the children of divorced parents.

* See Social World, Book VI, chap iii, Dolores.

: "If man considers liberty as the privilege to do or to leave undone whatever pleases, without the higher aim of human ennoblement, the youthful generation will grow up like nettles upon the open fields, and if the children inherit nothing else, they will, at least, inherit the selfishness of their parents" —

"Don Pedro the Second will hardly introduce popular education in Brazil on such humane principles," observed the young lady.

"No monarchy, whether despotic or constitutional, will sustain a principle of humanity that contravenes its establishment, and in countries which boast of their freedom, man is so extremely occupied with 'business and money making,' that, until now, he has found no time to reflect upon the idea of freedom, and to ponder his duty, as a man, towards mankind"

"I used to believe that England was free, and was proud of our freedom," remarked Robert, "but I feel, more and more, that we are governed by a power which more rigidly resists the foundation of a rational system of popular education than absolutism; it is Prejudice, which recognises the aristocracy and the priesthood as the highest authority, and so long as these prevail, no social transformation is to be thought of"

"Your old England, my dear Mr Walker, is, in relation to moral freedom, at least two centuries behind France, and will yet pass through a crisis like the year '93, before prejudice is overthrown"

"Our Chartists appear to know what is required——"

"And your socialists stand opposed to them, since in England, as everywhere, they hold a social reform possible without political and moral freedom, that is the mistake!"

"Papa will come soon!" said the little one, interrupting the philosophical physician, "and bring a gold chain for mamma, and then we shall go to the theatre"

The young lady colored at the inapropos interruption, took the little creature gently by the hand, and led her to her attendant, the negress Maria"

Dr Thorfin took leave of the young Englishman and his convalescent patient, and rode down the hill, past his dwelling, towards Bota Fogo, where he was to meet his friend Hinango according to agreement

CHAPTER X

NATURE AND CHURCH

It was difficult for Robert to find a word of excuse for having, by his lecture of the characteristics of the women of Brazil, touched a string in the mind of his friend, which so clearly awakened within her the tone of discord.

"Pardon me, Senhora," began he, as he was walking with her in the garden, "I considered the whole sketch, so far as I read it, beforehand, from the comic side, and did not suspect——"

"O, I know that, Senhor Roberto! It was not your intention to wound me—I feel that—

you gave me the book unwillingly. I thank you, however, that you have given me an opportunity——" She paused, and then continued "You know too little of my fate, to be able to imagine what anguish stirs when I——when I look back upon a step—that I—took once—and —have regretted often enough"

"You have really been married then? if I may be allowed the question I have, until now, not been able to believe it, and just because I did not believe, I had the less fear of reading"

"Let us sit down," said she, after a pause, and pointed to a stone bench near the young banana. "To-day I am at length forced to give you information about my position, about my inward life Listen to me quietly, and condemn me, if you find me culpable"

An expression of pleasure passed over Robert's countenance, at the prospect of receiving the long desired communication, which, from strict discretion, he would never urge.

The young lady commenced, interrupting herself, from time to time, as she was led aside into the mazes of retrospection, and related as follows:

"My father was a superior officer at the mines of Minas Geraes He was surrounded by gold, but he was an honorable man, and acquired no property His income was hardly sufficient for our support My mother was the daughter of an officer of high rank, who likewise left nothing behind but the name of a brave soldier We were three sisters My brother entered the military service, and fell, as an ensign, in the campaign in the south, in the war against the rebels I lived, when a child, with my sisters in the Minas Mountains, until my mother died, ten years ago We were helpless, for the pension of my mother ceased at her death, and we had no protectors at court Some relatives, among the rest Senhor Moreto, in Rua dos Ouvives, took us, and provided for our education in a convent school, where young girls of the first families were instructed in all that was found suitable My sister was afraid to go into the world without property, and shrunk from the thought of being unhappy in marriage She knew as little as I what was to become of her when she left the institution, and remained in the cloister She took the veil, "to have a living." Ah! it would perhaps have been better if I had done the same, but it was quite difficult to place one of us there, for we were poor, and my sister could give no donation to the convent. Besides, I felt no inclination for cloister life, I could not dissemble, and I could not believe what the church required as faith Ah! I often felt so unhappy! As a child I had so loved the whole world The whole of grand, exalted nature, with all its mountains, and streams, and flowers, and butterflies, had become so familiar to me. I played all day, and until late at night, with my flowers, whose buds I watched before they unfolded, and gave every favorite a particular name, and laid myself down by them, and often prattled to them for hours I admired mysterious nature in the life of the flowers, observed many of the chalices, as they slowly closed at sundown, and hurried in the morning to the same flower, before it awakened, and laid down by it, and said to it: 'Oh, thou dear, good little flower, wilt thou soon awake? how hast thou slept ? hast thou dreamt much—much and pleasantly ?" Pardon me these childish reminiscences, I lived entirely in my flowers, it seemed to me as if I was related to them   I was then obliged to part from all that I loved there, and lived five whole years in the convent   The religious sentiments which I had derived from sublime nature, were declared to be sinful, heathenish notions, abominable, and blasphemous   I must now consider as culpable, what had so purely developed itself in me as a child, in reverence and worship of the God who made my flowers

"Ah! I cannot and will not tell you of the pain I felt when they called me a heathen, who would be 'eternally damned' unless converted   As a child of seven or eight years old, I must comprehend religious dogmas, which the nuns themselves, who taught them, did not comprehend them   I was merely to believe them, believe in relics and miracles, and pray in words whose meaning I did not understand, and secretly observe my playfellows, and report to the nuns what this or that one said or did   Hell was depicted to me as a means of binding me to the so called duties of faith and espionage   I recognised our whole so called religion as a system of terror, that holds up fear instead of love, and the Devil instead of God   But why should I relate to you any more of my sufferings as a child ?   I prayed to the God whom I had acknowledged in my childish innocence, that he would open my heart to faith—faith in the miracles of the church, and in all that I should believe in   But God heard me not, and I could not respect the nuns, who wished to compel me to listen secretly to my playmates, and to be the cause of their punishment, when I saw no sin in all that was described as culpable   At length I was confirmed, and left the convent

"An aunt took charge of me, but I came 'out of the rain under the eaves'   I had, until now, only seen the world through the window grates of our convent, the whole great city was a strange world to me, and no Botocudan maiden, that may casually come to Rio, can be more astonished with all that surrounds her here, than I was   I was curious to see all, to become well acquainted with every thing, and my aunt declared me a worldling, and wept over my 'thwarted education,' and when I told her that I was passionately fond of playing on the organ, and wished for a piano that I might practice diligently, then my misfortunes were complete '

"A singular accordance with my position towards my aunt in Buenos Ayres," remarked Robert, as she paused   "I beg you tell me more "

"I longed to hear an opera—to visit the theatre   One of my relatives took me, occasionally, here and there, and I soon learned our national dances from my young friends, in whose society I lived   I attended family balls, and I found life so new, and so charming by its novelty, and now desired nothing so much as to be 'independent,' that I might enjoy life   I called it being independent to remove from my aunt, who was hourly tiring me with telling the rosary, and depicted all the enjoyments of the world as sinful and culpable.   I durst read nothing but my convent books, which I had read a hundred times, and I thought so much the more.   I had an aptitude for flower-making, and not to be a burden

to my aunt for the expenses of clothing, and the like, I gave my attention to the trade, and sold my work to the business people, who dealt in them   A stranger came to live at my aunt's, who had hired the second story   I made his acquaintance   He was a naturalist, and had formerly been a soldier in the German legion   He always had all sorts of singular things to show me—minerals, and animals, and insects, that were strange to me, and attracted my curiosity   Sometimes he had a tiger cat, whose frightful wildness terrified me, and yet I lingered willingly before the cage, to accustom myself to the horrible   He kept great boa constrictors, rattlesnakes, and the like monsters   I gradually became accustomed to the naturalist, and his disagreeable company   He was more polite and complaisant to me than any other man had ever shown himself, and—and—God knows I only desired a friend in the world, a friend who should accompany me through life   I did not know what I wanted, I did not know any thing of life—I had no idea of my destiny as a woman—I was, with all my education, so stupid, so excessively stupid, in all that the future was to lead me to, so unconscious with regard to all social relations, that I—that I did not even know what step I took when I married the man in whom I sought a friend "

'Then you married Mr Closting ?'" inquired Robert, involuntarily, but started when he had uttered the name

"Mr Closting! my God! you know, then, that I——"

"That you are Madame Closting," interrupted the youth, "that is, I might have known it long ago, but—until to-day I did not even yet believe that you were married, and, consequently, not that you were Madame Closting   I cannot, and will not, and never shall believe it!" added he, with a degree of violence

Notwithstanding the seriousness which the lady's state of mind, and which the communication occasioned, she could not avoid a smile, since the contradiction of his assertions bordered on the comic

"Dear Senhor Roberto," began she, after a pause, "in the convent I was required to believe what no man can know, and you refuse to believe what you knew beforehand "

"Well," said the youth, after he had for a long time gazed before him, "explain it as you will, I cannot conceive the thought that you are the mother of that little one, that you have ever pressed the hand of a man—to say nothing of giving your hand away——   I had forgotten to say to you this morning," continued he, "that I am going away in a few days "

"Going away! you will go away?   Senhor Roberto, do not put such a bitter jest upon me   You cannot be in earnest !"

"However, I ——"

"I understand you," she would have said, but she restrained the words on her tongue, that would have expressed too much.

"No," continued she, after long reflection, "No, it cannot be! you will not go away, you have hardly been here six weeks   Six weeks! it seems to me as if it were six days   You must stay here, Senhor Roberto, at least, until my husband comes.   You ought not to leave me   I have not yet told you all.   I will reveal to you the situation in which I am placed here, and I am certain, beforehand, that you will not leave me to the danger that threatens me if I remain here alone."

"It is true," interrupted he, "I have promised you my protection—it is true I will remain here until—until the business of our house calls me away It will happen some of these days Tell me, I beg you ——"

"There is a man here who sought the acquaintance of my husband," continued Madame Closting, "a baron from Europe, who is travelling for his pleasure, as he says, he lives at the Hotel Faroux, a man in whose presence I was always more uncomfortable than before the cage of the rattlesnakes and the tigercats, and it has become evident, latterly, that my antipathy towards this man was not unfounded This man leads here a very wild, dissolute life, and keeps several mistresses This man visited us often before my husband went into the interior of the country, and transacted business with him We lived in the city, and I remained alone with my two negresses The baron, as he called himself, continued his visits under the mask of being a friend of my husband, after he had gone away, I received him according to my antipathy, without, at the same time, violating hospitality Perhaps he remarked that his presence was not exactly desired by me, and he remained away for a long time My husband has an agent here, who takes care of his business, his name is Senhor Forro; his mother-in-law is a very low woman, who unfortunately visited me occasionally, because I could not show her the door My husband left me a sum for my support, he is very particular in all that relates to money matters, you will become acquainted with him, and find a friend in him, he is the best man in the world, and universally respected, he has enemies, like all other men—and especially enviers—amongst his countrymen particularly, because he is fortunate in business and a very experienced business man——"

"And the agent's mother-in-law?" said Mr Robert, interrupting the "exemplary wife" of the respected man of business, "the woman of whom you were going to tell me——."

"I came upon the subject of my husband because he is very punctual in money matters, and very naturally would not have gone away without having left word with Senhor Forro to give me the necessary sum monthly that I required for my housekeeping."

"Pardon me for interrupting you," remarked Robert, "I find it very strange that your husband should leave you under the guardianship of an agent whose mother-in-law is a bad character; incorrect associations were to be feared."

"Certainly—but—the men stand in business connexion between themselves, and their family regulations they consider as—as secondary—the one never concerns himself with the family of the other."

"Just so I think; therefore Senhor Forro, also, should have had no occasion to concern himself with you Go on, I beg."

"The baron then remained away a long while My husband has now been gone eight months, and should already have returned four months ago He wrote, however, that his business required a still longer journey, and he desired or ordered Mr Forro to continue to pay me the monthly sum There must have been a misunderstanding," continued she, with evident embarrassment, "evidently a mistake, for my husband is known here as a man of property and credit, and universally respected as such, you must make his acquaintance——"

"And Senhor Forro refused you the money, and gave out that he had no funds of Mr Closting?" said Robert, again interrupting the "exemplary wife"

The embarrassment of the lady increased at these words of the young merchant, who had sufficient knowledge of affairs and of the world, to see through the circumstances

"Some misunderstanding must have taken place, Senhor Roberto, for I assure you that my husband——"

"And the mother-in-law came then instead of Mr Forro, and declared that no credit was opened for you? I will anticipate you, and relate to you what further occurred The baron appeared again — repeated his visits — offered his services to you, as the friend of your husband, to make an advance to you—and thereupon appeared this low woman, as a friend of the baron——"

"My God!" interrupted she, "you know the whole story, then? Through whom? if I may ask, through whom did you learn it? not from Dr Thorin?"

"From you! Senhora, from yourself, since you have just told me enough to enable me ' to read the rest on the leaves of a banana' The bad woman made her appearance as mediatrix, and by degrees came forward with certain propositions—with base, shameful importunities? Have I guessed it?"

The unfortunate woman sat suffused with purple at the recollection of a baseness which the youth had exactly and truly pointed out Her wounded feelings at length found expression in bitter tears "You have truly delineated my terrible situation, Senhor Roberto, but you do not yet know the end," continued she, when she had at length recovered composure "Think of the unheard of audacity of the baron, as he calls himself Instead of considering himself as dismissed by the answers which I repeatedly gave to the negotiatrix, he appeared himself, took me by surprise, so to say, in my own house—and wished—to force money upon me" She was again interrupted by tears, and at length continued again "Senhor Moreto, whom your uncle knows, is my relation, I hurried to him, and sought protection, without naming the baron There existed a relation between him and my husband that was not agreeable to me all sorts of calumnies, even before my marriage, intrigues of those who envied my husband, especially of some young Brazilians who—who were very polite to me——"

"I can understand it all," concluded Robert, "gallant young men who desired to possess your hand, told the truth to your uncle in relation to Mr. Closting——!"

"The truth!" cried the "exemplary wife," "Senhor Roberto! what do you mean by that?" and her high forehead drew itself into wrinkles between the eyebrows "You cannot surely believe that my husband——"

"Pardon me, Senhora," interrupted he, "I

believe that you love your husband, as only a wife can love her husband "

" I—I—I love my husband ?" returned she in a confusion which spread a paleness over her countenance, " I—love him ? I can neither love him nor esteem him—horrible ! Oh, God !" sighed she " Oh, if I could but love him as he loves me ! if you only knew how he clings to me—how he——"

Robert arose, the lady seized him convulsively by the hand " Senhor Roberto !" sighed she, as she arose also, and as it were literally held fast to him " Forgive me ! forgive me ! for Heaven's sake do not misapprehend me, I beseech you do not ! no ! I do not—love him He has—disappointed me He should have chosen a different woman—quite different—not a woman of sentiment—not a woman that—had a heart—like this "

She said these words, and gazed fixedly before her Pressing his arm with her right hand, she leaned her left, and her forehead, on his shoulder Her limbs seemed to fail

Robert trembled " Sit down, Senhora Will you go into your room ? Shall I give you my arm ?"

No ! no ! not in my room—I will finish—my relation—you must know all My uncle then, is I call Senhor Moreto, reproached me about my marriage, there was a violent scene, but he took my part as a man, and proposed to me to occupy this pavilion, which belonged to him I had hardly moved in here, when the baron discovered my asylum, perhaps through my negresses, who are obliged to go into the city occasionally, and whom he has followed at a distance ; perhaps even by my committing the imprudence of playing the melody which I designated to you Enough he endeavored to force himself in here, and one evening, very late, nothing else remained for me, but to fire a pistol through the garden gate above his head "

" Why did you not aim lower ?" inquired the young Briton, " he is not very broad, to be sure, but you might then perhaps have hit him somewhere "

" You are acquainted with him then—you know of whom I speak ?"

" Of the Baron de Spandau," answered Robert, " and I thank you, with all my heart, that you have given me this information The miserable fellow has sneaked into our house I know his views "

" I concealed even from my uncle the name of the scoundrel who persecuted me, because I—because I did not want to accuse him, as he was an acquaintance of my husband and my uncle."

" I can account for that ! and admire your delicate consideration for a fellow who does not deserve it "

" You now understand, noble Senhor Roberto, the ground of my petition that you will remain here, until my husband comes. If I—if I even do not love him, he is yet a good man, and——"

" You just said, however, that he had deceived you ! and whoever deceives a woman, acts, in my opinion, neither honorably nor well "

" Pardon me ! he loves me indeed ! as well as he can love He provides for me, however, and for our children."

Robert made a movement to withdraw

" Stay ! stay ! Senhor Roberto, stay by me !"

cried the unfortunate " I mean do not go away ! do not forsake me !" She uttered the last words with such deep feeling, that Robert could not find it in his heart for the moment to deny such a request

" Senhora Gracia !" answered he, after a pause, in a decided tone, " I will then remain here until—until Mr Closting returns, upon one condition "

" Whatever it may be, I will comply with it "

" Upon the condition, then, that you never mention your husband in my presence—never allude to your relation to him—never ! Either not speak another word to me from this hour, except what the usual salutation of a neighbor requires, or never mention that man's name to me again Do not require others to respect him, whom you yourself cannot respect You must either avoid him or me. Do not condemn me to the most horrible fate with which a man was ever burdened Decide for yourself and for me "

" I promise you that I will decide," sighed the unfortunate woman, pressing his hand convulsively, and gazed with a moistened glance into his eyes Her forehead was near his lips, she felt his breath, both trembled It was night. Robert lowered his head, she lingered near him as if his pulse was hers As if awakening from a dream, Robert rose and attended her to the door of her pavilion, she tottered into her apartment, her protector entered his, where he threw himself on his divan, sunk in that chaos of feelings which now prevailed in him, to work out his eventful future

---

CHAPTER XI

ALL SORTS OF COMMUNICATIONS

HORATIO and Alvarez went from the palace of the negro from Goa, to their abode at Dr Thorfin's, the mediator of their connexion with Dolores, to whom, in such a case, they would certainly have gladly spoken in person After they had made their northern friend acquainted with this singular invitation, and what had occasioned it, the question arose whether it would be proper to discover to the plenipotentiary the present abode of the exile Hinango, who almost every evening, at least for a moment, sought his friends, in case they did not visit him upon St Theresa, came in just as the matter was under discussion He was " on business," as Dolores was translating some fragments of a literary work of " Young Europe," which passed from hand to hand through Thorfin, and was set up by Alvarez in a French printing office, to be despatched to Rio Grande Dr Thorfin delivered the manuscript which he received from Dolores, and Alvarez carried a proof sheet with him But Hinango was soon diverted from his business by the communication to him of what had taken place in the Rua do Valongo

" At any rate I will endeavor to procure a private interview with Dolores to-morrow," continued Dr Thorfin, in their general consultation, " though it is every day becoming more difficult Since we, as it seems, have no treachery to fear on the part of Senhor Vera, Dolores may perhaps desire to confide in him, to receive the information about the relation of Senhor Garringós to her deceased mother I am myself not the less curious to procure an explanation of this affair, as lately a circumstance surprised me in conversation with Dolores We were talking about magnetism in Miss Susan's presence, who considers the belief in magnetic power 'sinful' Dolores smiled, and observed 'The priests in Spain were likewise of that opinion,' but suddenly recovered herself, however, and returned to her rôle of 'Miss Fanny' before me, and merely asked me, if I knew a brochure, the oldest and first that Mesmer had published about his discovery' I replied to her by repeating the title 'Mémoires sur la Découverte du Magnétisme animal,' under Mesmer's name—in the titlepage, 'Genéve et Paris, 1779' She seemed as if she wished to say more, but her incognito did not admit of it Miss Susan had already remarked that her niece was acquainted with a great many worldly books, and, in short, believed in animal magnetism—what no 'church' allowed

" 'Because all the miraculous cures that Jesus performed would then admit of explanation,' added I, and Aunt Susan would gladly have ordered me instantly thrown out of the window

"Whether the intimated persecution in Spain stands in connexion with the incognito of the physician in Goa, I hope soon to learn I know so much as this, that a Jesuit in Vienna, Pater Hell, and an Englishman by the name of Ingenhouse, endeavored, by all sorts of intrigue, to appropriate to their objects the discovery of Mesmer, and to announce it as their own, another interesting example, by the way, that a Jesuit and a Briton often pursue the same path, and endeavor to arrive before each other at the goal "

"We have also to do with them both, here in South America," said Hinango, smiling, "and I do not know which is the bitterest foe to the future of this country As concerns Dolores, she is at present in greater and more especial danger from a good Briton, who has taken into his head the idea of marrying her "

"Are you at length convinced of that '" inquired Dr Thorfin, laughing

"From all that I hear by you, and must conclude from the conduct of the old widower, I have not a doubt remaining, and I cannot see, what is to be done, to save Dolores "

"Unless particular circumstances intervene, nothing, nothing is to be feared for the present," observed Thorfin, "for Mr George goes slowly to work, that he may the more surely attain his object What is odd in this whole affair is, that the old man as confidently believes in the carrying out of his 'fixed idea,' as if Dolores really stood with him at the altar "

The friends were interrupted in their conversation, by an old acquaintance from the mouth of the La Plata, Patrick Gentleboy, who had sought Hinango, without finding him, on St Theresa He already nearly knew the haunts of his future captain, and found him where he had expected

Patrick, with the aid of Captain Finngreen, converted the cutter which Barigaldi had presented to him, secretly into money, without exciting observation, and accepted Hinango's proposal to enter into his service, as he was negotiating for the purchase of the schooner brig Vesta, and could then employ him on board as port guard. Until then, he kept secret his acquaintance with the stout red-haired Irishman, not to increase the suspicions of the Baron de Spandau, who had, unfortunately, learned more about the mouth of La Plata, from Dr Merbold, than was even necessary

"I ax pardon, your honor '" began the capstan pipel, "I have come to your honor about something, quite intirely by ordinary "

"Now '" said Hinango, what's the matter' what news '"

"Faith, your honor, that has happened to me that an ould sailor does not often meet with I am promoted from the foremast to a horse, or rather to the stable By your honor's lave, I'll just tell ye what I mane This morning I was sitting with Jemmy O'Halloran, my landlord, and a countryman, too, from ould Ireland, your honor, when in comes a spalpeen that spoke some sort of English, your honor, and he stares at me like a sailor at the land he is steering for, and then he turns about, and makes his course for Jemmy O'Halloran, that was behind the bar, your honor, and cries, 'Ship ahoy '' and takes a glass of cachaz,* and then goes on to speak him without trumpet, and axes if he doesn't know a man, may be a sailor, that could take a sirvice on shore He said he knew somebody that could employ such a man. 'There sits a man that looks like a sailor,' said my countryman, Jemmy O'Halloran, and winks at me, because he knowed well enough that the fellow meant me, he saw that, as well as I, your honor' But I won't tire your honor with a long yarn, but go into port at the rate of 'nine knots an hour' The Dutchman, Baron de Span-dau, wants to make a groom of me' Did your honor ever hear the like of that' captain' And so I went to look for you, becase the air didn't look jist clear to me, there's a bank ahind, a bank of clouds, and there's a storm brewing, I'll lay any wager, begging your honor's pardon'

"Did the baron inquire what ship you came in '" interrupted Hinango

"To be sure, your honor, he axed more questions than aver a Dutchman on the open sea, when he meets a vessel after a hundred days' voyage, but I answered him as a smuggler does a custom house cutter I said I had been at sea two years with Captain West, in the Rose of Peru, and last with Captain Drewes of the barque Julia, of Hamburgh and was only waiting here for news of my brother Tom, from the coast of Patagonia, and when he wanted to see my papers, I told him that the cursed Brazilian rats, that here in port run over your feet, had eaten up my tin box with all the papers, and my sail maker's thimble into the bargain He told me—the baron I mane, your honor—that he wanted to get a boat, or a shallop, to fish here in the bay, and axed me would I be his boatswain, and for the present I could find employment here in the stable with the care of his horses I told him that I was not willing to have any thing to do with a four-legged craft that carried the bowsprit behind and steered by the head The thing didn't plase me at all, at all, and so I toult him, but I would

---

* Brazilian white rum.

think about it, and so I came straight to look for your honor   Do you know what I suspect, captain? what the spalpeen wants? He wants to use me for a spy! and I'm all ready, at his sarvice!"

The friends smiled, and looked at each other Patrick continued.

"If the spalpeen of a baron takes me to be stupid, and bad enough to sarve him as a spy, I will do it, but I'll sarve him in such a way that he shall have something to tell of! I'll act as stupid as he thinks me, I tried it on him to-day already   I axed him if he could tell me where the English governor here lived   'You mane the ambassador,' sez he. 'No, your honor, the governor,' sez I 'for sure there must be an English governor upon an English island!'' and then he tells me that the country here was not an island, and that the name of it was Brazil, and that a prince lived here! I gave him many thanks for telling me, and promised to give him an answer after I found out how much I was owing to my landlord, and came away from the Hotel Farouge, where he lives, the Dutch spalpeen!

"Now, your honor, what d'ye say till it? will I take the place? for he axed me if I had not lately been on La Plata river? accidentally as a passenger may be? I axed him if the La Plata river ran round Cape Horn, or in amongst the West Indies, and then sure the leak in my skull was plain enough for a blind man to see"

"Do you not think that he knows well enough how you came here, if he wishes to take you into his service?" inquired Dr Thorfin

"I don't doubt it at all, at all, your honor," replied Patrick, turning his flat straw hat like a tiller rope before him, "ought I to tell him, then? I ax pardon, your honor, but ought I to tell the Dutch spalpeen I am Patrick McCaffray, from the Ar-gentile man of war? the same that shot down the officer on board the cutter, when the *Mazzini* came up with us, and when we were ordered to blow up the schooner? ought I to say that your honor? and have myself shut up in prison here at the command of the Ar-gentile consul, or ambassador, or whatever he may be?"

"Certainly," observed Hinango, "you could not well do otherwise than briefly deny that you ever had been in communication with us"

"And begging your honor's pardon, I have always heard that whoever wants to make his way on shore, must appear stupid, stupid as possible, and then he will do the best"

"You may be in the right," interrupted Hinango, "but the baron has undoubtedly remarked that you are not so stupid as you wish to appear"

"And begging your honors' pardon, it is exactly such people, that ar'n't just as stupid as they are thick or long, and know how to turn their stupidity to account, that can sail in all water, and don't run so easily upon sand and reefs"

The friends looked at each other again, and smiled their approbation of the Irishman's wit

"As the Dutchman found out where I was, I'm sartin he knows who I am, and what use he wants to make of me I know very well, for mayhap he commands a *signal ship* here on shore, that reports at Buenos Ayres or elsewhere, and he wants people to look out, and

see what sails pass. But I must keep close when I once enter the sarvice. I cannot come here any more, nor see you, captain, but must keep a report cutter, and I have one already under sail   There is a seamstress sits with the daughter of my landlord, an Irish girl too, she is, and her mother washes for us sailors, her name is Lucy, and she's a nate honest girl. She must, by your lave, take care of your honor's linen, and go in and out of your house, you understand   and when I have anything to tell your honor, I will tell it by Lucy"

"Have you already made such acquaintance with her that you can count upon Lucy, Patrick?" inquired Hinango, "that she will not deceive you?"

"Oh! as to that, captain, I'll risk my head on Lucy, for isn't she an Irish girl, and all she wants to know is, that there is a young lady from La Plata river in danger, as I saw pretty plainly when I was behind you in the Ar-gentile brig Lucy need only know the part that Pat Gentleboy played in the cutter, and she will show that she's an Irish girl, I'll answer for it!"

The friends again exchanged glances, and indicated more by looks than words, their approbation of all that the gallant Irishman proposed

"Here, captain, here is the tin case with my papers," continued Patrick, "the baron must not find those upon me, keep them till your next muster roll, and let my name stand in your memo-raundum as boatswain for your schooner brig   She's an inviting little thing, the Vanda! I looked at her yesterday at a distance   She desarves to have a boatswain like Patrick McCaffray"

Dr Thorfin summoned a negro, to hand a glass of wine to the honest fellow, who took it with thanks, and "poured it over the ballast in his hull," as he expressed himself.

"Then captain, it's a bargain that I'm to sarve *you* as an informer, and the baron is to *pay* me for it, and the money for my cutter Mr Walker has got, and the *obliquidation* papers you will find in the tin box"

Hinango hastily examined the papers that were committed to his keeping, and found all in the best order   He thanked Patrick for his confidence, and especially for his diligence in serving the good cause after such an original fashion. "But are you not afraid that the baron will send you to Buenos Ayres?"

"Me! Pat Gentleboy, is it, that he'll be after sending me to Buenos Ayres?" said he, laughing, "and faith, before he'll do that he must have me to send, and before he, or three of his fellows, or even a dozen, take me alive, the blood will run from some of them, I promise your honor! No, captain, they don't hang a man at the *yard* until they *have* him, and in the mane whilst, I'll take care they don't catch you, or the young lady from La Plata river! that shall be my business, and Lucy will come to you, to take care of your linen   Farewell, captain! Farewell to your honors!" said he to the three others, and hastily withdrew.

Dolores had lived, until this time, in Mr. Thomson's country house, at Bota Fogo, in tranquil retirement, as his niece, and found her situation, if not exactly agreeable, yet endurable. She occupied herself, uninterruptedly, with literary labors, arranged a collection of her poems for an edition, and filled up the time which she had to spare from her own productions, by translating Childe Harold, as she intended to translate the whole of Lord Byron's works into her mother tongue

Severely as Miss Susan might cry out against such unheard of proceedings, and exclaim about the Catholic who had evidently been conceived and born in heathendom, Dolores had, nevertheless, known how to secure her moral independence from the beginning At the first opportunity that a loud remark of Aunt Susan in presence of Mr Thomson afforded, she declared, with the decision peculiar to her, according to her rule, however, of the betrothed of Robert towards his aunt

"I yield, under existing circumstances, to the parting from my friend Robert, because my position requires it The sacrifice I make must be conceivable to you—do not require yet greater I was, so to say, brought up with your niece, Miss Fanny, and have learned and studied the English language and literature as my own"

"Good heavens!" interrupted Miss Susan, "you have studied English literature?"

"And entertain the highest reverence for your authors and poets, especially those who are misconceived in England, and only in part understood, like Byron"

Miss Susan shrank back at this name, and exclaimed, with a glance at her brother, "Lord have mercy upon us, you have then even Byron's works among your books!"

"And am translating his Childe Harold into Spanish, and shall dedicate the edition to my Robert"

The old widower twitched his face, as if an enormous beetle had suddenly alighted upon his cheek, not on account of the literary occupation, which he allowed to take care of itself until after his marriage—he was merely shocked and thunderstruck by the words, "my Robert" Although absolute necessity required, in relation to the aunt, that Dolores should, with all consistency, carry out the part of the betrothed of his nephew, there could hardly have been found a more painful situation for Mr Thomson, than the one which compelled him to have this mask of betrothal daily before his eyes He hoped, or rather firmly believed, that nothing would stand in the way of his realizing, in his own time, his anticipated courtship of Dolores, when some months had passed, which would certainly be necessary, that such a step might not be considered as "youthful precipitancy" on his part

So far as he had hitherto been able to observe, he had certainly not discovered the slightest ground of suspicion that a love relation subsisted between Dolores and Robert, a consolation that at times made the sight of the mask endurable. Robert, to be sure, made his appearance regularly several times a week, and deported himself, in presence of his aunt, towards Dolores, as her betrothed; a demeanor which, delicate and discreet, as it ever was, occasionally made the old widower's hair stand on end, especially when he kissed her on the forehead at parting To the reiterated consolation of Mr Thomson, Robert not only in general very soon departed, but appeared at the tea table, as in the

garden, always quite strangely occupied with himself—absent minded—somewhere else ——

Mr Thomson observed more and more sharply, and by degrees beheld, in the far, far distance a beacon towards which Mr Robert had directed his course, although the port was blockaded by a hostile legitimate navy

People like Mr George, who, notwithstanding their "youthful age," have sailed for full forty years laden with matrimonial thoughts, have, for the most part, a particularly sharp eye for recognising vessels, far and near, bound on a similar course; if, on the other hand, many steer for the altar, without carrying *love* as ballast, many sail laden with love, who must renounce it in anticipation if they would ever enter the port of matrimony

Mr George took occasion to inquire of Dolores, in a confidential tone, as uncle and friend, whether Robert had left a so called "acquaintance" behind in Buenos Ayres, and learned that his nephew, so far as Dolores knew, had held, except with her and her sister, little or no intercourse with young ladies, and had passed most of his leisure hours in their society The sensation which this information excited in the old widower was divided,—in so much as no former observation had satisfied him that no love understanding existed between Robert and Dolores, if, on the other hand, the affair still appeared suspicious to him

Accident at length showed him the beacon in the far distance,—as the talkative baron once turned the conversation upon Mr Robert's neighbor——and the latter, from youthful diffidence, or awkwardness, could not prevent a sudden flush, which, besides his uncle, nobody present observed

A light then suddenly dawned upon the old man, as we have said—the beacon, probably, towards which his nephew was steering his course The result of a business transaction that should suddenly have brought him half a million, would not have surprised him so joyfully, so consolingly, and so tranquillizingly, as this discovery He had learned, incidentally, from Sr Moreto, that this young neighbor was a young lady of the highest *respectability*, and he required to know no more If she were unmarried, or a widow, so much the better, if she were a wife seeking a divorce, (for Sr Moreto had already intimated that she was there on legal business,) it was very well This case, even, was no misfortune ! whatever might be the circumstances of the young lady, it was enough for the old man that Robert, as it appeared, had directed his eye upon her instead of Dolores All the rest was, and remained, to the old experienced matrimonial practitioner, a secondary matter—entirely a secondary matter—which would finally admit of being accomplished by the means which were at Robert's command, in case of need, and which had already set aside far greater difficulties than proceedings for divorce and the like

Dr. Thorfin sought an interview with Dolores on the day after Alvarez had revealed to him the communication of the negro from Goa, and availed himself of some moments in the garden, while Miss Susan had withdrawn to her room

Dolores appeared in the highest degree surprised and affected by the news from Goa.

"What relation existed between my mother and Gabriel Garringòs in Madrid, was always a riddle to me," said she, after long reflection. "I will in part to you what I know. I once found, after my mother's death, a little book—the title of which you lately mentioned to me *correctly*—among some of my mother's papers that she had kept carefully put away. In this book was written the name of 'Gabriel Garringòs, Dr. Med., Madrid, 1810,' and I learned, in answer to my a little too naïve questions, that the physician was a friend of my mother, who treated her in a nervous sickness, and had saved her life by magnetism. I admit that this science was at that time strange to me, and I first obtained an intimation of this mysterious sphere through that little book.

"I heard, from a friend of my mother, that she had been in a state of clairvoyance, and had given her physician the most singular information, which remained entirely strange to her out of the magnetic sleep. She had admitted that she experienced a wonderful personal inclination for her physician, and knew of his approach even while he was yet at a great distance, or had traced him as he came near the house. She appeared to avoid looking back upon this situation and these relations, or at least to speak of them unwillingly. I only learned that the circumstances which controlled her at that time, made the separation from her friend obligatory, which suddenly and inexplicably took place. The phenomenon of animal magnetism in the person of the young physician, however secret it was kept, had drawn upon him the observation of the ecclesiastics, and his life was in danger. The fate of her friend remained obscure, and up to this hour no one in Spain or in South America knows in what manner the magnetizer was saved, or put out of the way, who, on the night of the 24th of May, 1812, did not arrive at home, after having left the residence of my grandfather about ten o'clock.

"That is all that I ever knew about Dr. Garringòs. The illness of my mother had vanished. She soon after accompanied her father back to Buenos Ayres, and was married. If I judge correctly, from many passages of her fragmentary correspondence, so far as I became acquainted with it afterward, this mysterious inclination for Garringòs, which she endeavored to struggle against as a consequence of her sickness itself, disappeared after her marriage, but awakened afterward, as a friend has since assured me. Some years after my birth, my mother lost her health, and died when I was about ten years old."

Dr. Thorfin heard this communication with fixed attention, and then inquired.

"What is your determination in regard to the confidant of Dr. Garringòs? May I inform him of your abode?"

"According to all that Alvarez has informed you of, concerning the duplicate of the picture, and the inferences from this letter of attorney, we may confide in him certainly. He ought to know my fate, and you, doctor, will have the goodness to visit him, with Alvarez, but urge him to strict discretion in regard to my incognito."

"That is a matter of course," answered he, hastily, for Aunt Susan approached with a criticising air at the long interview of her niece with the foreign doctor, which certainly did not appear absolutely necessary.

"Present my hearty greetings to Mr. Robert when you see him," continued Dolores, aloud, and with unconcern, as Aunt Susan approached her, "and my fellow voyagers likewise, all of them. How is Horatio?"

"Very well, so far as I know," replied Dr. Thorfin.

"Have you seen the baron lately?" inquired Aunt Susan. "He is not ill, I hope?"

"So far as I know, the baron is also very well, I shall probably meet him to-day at the Hotel Faroux."

"Give my compliments to him, then, we hope to have the pleasure of seeing you both on Sunday."

"I thank you Miss Thomson, on my own part, I will have the honor, and will then take the liberty to bring you the book of which we were just speaking," added he to Dolores.

"What sort of a book?" inquired the quasi gouvernante, of the poetess, with pardonable female curiosity.

"'Spiridion,' the last work of Madame Sand," answered Dr. Thorfin, to the vexation of the lean aunt.

"Of Madame Sand! Do you read the books of Madame Sand, Miss Fanny?"

"I consider Madame Sand as the first authoress of our epoch, and there are few men who can stand beside her."

"Shocking!" sighed the well educated Englishwoman, "translates Byron, and reads Madame Sand," added she, half aloud. "Did I ever hear any thing like it?"

Dr. Thorfin now took leave, and left the poetess to the ill humor of her gouvernante, which mounted higher than ever, since Dr. Thorfin had named an authoress, whose philosophical work, 'Spiridion,' would be alone sufficient to immortalize her name in the literature of her nation.

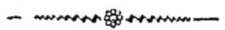

CHAPTER XII.

THE MOONLIGHT NIGHT

It was such a tropical moonlight night as surrounded the two pavilions when we first beheld the desecrated wife on her divan. Two months had passed by since then.

The dense foliage of the groups of trees on the declivity of the hill, formed broad masses of shadow, above which the magically lighted landscape appeared in wonderful magnificence. The distant mountains raised their dark and downy summits to the star sprinkled sky, and the bay, like a mirror of polished crystal, displayed the reflection of the moon, whose light formed the glistening pearls and diamonds of the silver veil, that was hardly ruffled by a zephyr. Here and there a boat floated slowly towards the shore at the foot of the hill, and with every stroke of the oar, that sounded clearly and distinctly in the deathlike silence, a phosphorescent gleam, like flaming oil, dripped back into the watery element, and again expired on the almost motionless surface.

Hundreds of magically shining insects flitted through the deep dark foliage of the perfuming coffee shrubs and blossoming orange trees, whose aroma, mingled with that of innumerable other blossoms, filled the atmosphere, and afforded a balsamic odor, which, as it were, strengthened the breast and the heart, while the magic forms of the landscape fettered the eye, and elevated the soul in blissful contemplation

Star upon star sparkled immediately in the neighborhood of the moon, and the myriads of orbs filled the blue of ether to a glittering, colourless expansion of the idea space, in unfathomable boundlessness

The harmony of a composition of Beethoven audible for miles in the slumbering distance, resounded through the silent night from the pianoforte of Robert, who, at the side of his friend, animated the strings

Both played   The spirits of both appeared to float upward, on the wings of tone, to Saturn, to the natal sphere of spiritual melody   The hands of both moved as if guided by inward harmony, which diffused itself through their being, even to the nervous fluid of the finger ends that glided over the keys   Both, as with a spiritual glance, looked over the passages and runs of the composition, whose mysterious expression, no written music is able to give—which no master can teach, and no scholar can learn, if the soul do not comprehend the melody, and return it from itself, as there occurred in the four-handed execution from the musical dream-world, in the pavilion of the serious youth and the unfortunate Brazilian lady

Slow, and still slower, sounded and lingered the final accord, in trembling pianissimo, and the last note floated off, and expired in the far, far distance, in the motionless, deathlike silence

Both looked at each other, from an involuntary impulse, to confirm, by a glance, what the spiritual harmony had so undeniably expressed in tones

"Ah !   if you could always accompany me thus , always !" sighed Gracia, reaching her hand involuntarily to her friend

Robert's eyes received the ray of hers •   it seemed a magnetic band, embodied as a ray, even though invisible, and soul appeared to stream forth into soul

"If I could accompany you for ever, remain near you for ever !" sighed the unfortunate, again repeating the earnest pressure of the hand she held

"We are separated upon earth," at length the youth found words to say , "separated until death !" and he arose, as if he would remove into the air ——

The lady also rose from her seat, stared before her with motionless eyelids, then started back, and shuddered

"God pardon me the thought ! God pardon it to me ; how it rushed through me I cannot myself conceive," said she, slowly, and in a low tone.

"What thought ?" inquired Robert, with an agitated voice, for the glance of the sufferer shocked him.   Her countenance, lighted by the bright beams of the moon, grew as pale as the face of a corpse, only an inexpressible brilliancy lingered about the eye, her lips quivered , with folded hands she stood there like a statue—a supplicating angel

"I entreat you, tell me what suddenly struck you ; confide it to me ?" said Robert, after he had contemplated her for a long time, as if with holy reverence

"A thought that is frightful, but which yet awakened within me, as the most inward desire of my soul   I wished to be changed into a lizard, still preserving my spiritual existence, that I might accompany you everywhere—to glide around you everywhere, even although unnoticed by you , to hide myself at evening over against you, like these, and peep forth from my hiding-place, and merge my glance in yours, as these are looking out upon us from behind your books "

"Great God !" sighed Robert, lost in the depth of the abyss, from which had ascended this thought of disconsolate despair, of unconquerable longing   "What have I done ? what crime have I committed, that I have awakened a sentiment in you which I dare not return ?"

"And you do not return, because you 'will' not return it," added the woman, with a sharp intonation

"Senhora !" cried the youth, in an excited voice, "Senhora, do not taunt me !   If I have hitherto given no utterance to the sentiments which rage within me, which are even destroying me, it is because I recognise the position in which we stand in the world, and before the world !"

"Before the world !" interrupted she, with a tone of scornful contempt, "before the world ! Ah! if you could suspect how far the world—what we designate with this wretched word—how far the world, with its judgement and condemnation, lies below me now !   how indifferent men have become to me, with all their scorn and uncharitableness !   Oh, you suspect not what has passed within me until now, since I—since I knew you, since I have only lived in you, and must be ever and eternally, as if fettered, as if bound, in your neighborhood !   Is the world capable of condemning me ? of judging me ? a world that does not comprehend me ?" added she, with an expression of elevated dignity "   Robert was silent

"I do not know what has happened to me, since you have been about me, by what influence you have operated upon me "

"Will you not allow me to utter the same inquiry ?" said the youth

"No ! no ! Robert ! that I will not allow, for you would do an injustice   Oh ! I well know that I possess nothing that could awaken your sentiments   If they are awakened, it is only compassion, and not that feeling which binds me to you, ah ! that I must not even once express it, name it, much less nourish it " She said these words with thrilling anguish, and pressed her folded hands together with inward despair

"By all that is sacred, you do me injustice !" exclaimed Robert, advancing towards her , "what demon of diffidence has again taken possession of you, that you despair, as you once despaired five years ago, of being worthy the love of a man—who—who might be worthy of you, and gave yourself away without love, renouncing love ? What is that in you as woman ?" continued he, in a tone that bordered upon reproach, "what is that inconceivable feeling that expresses itself in you as unbelief, as despair of love? If you do not believe in your heart, if your feelings do not tell you that you are beloved, then you also do not love. The heart feels that it is loved, and requires no oath."

"So may God judge me!" returned Gracia, after a pause, and stretched her folded hands towards heaven, "so judge me God, if this be not love, that exalts my soul!"

She faltered at these words, and raised her hand to her forehead, her glance fell, her limbs tottered.

"Gracia!" cried the youth, putting his arm round her, as she was evidently near fainting. Her limbs refused their office, she sank on Robert's breast, willess, motionless, her arms hung down as if broken. Her glance, brilliant as before, soared upward to his eyes, her lips, pale, as if under the kiss of death, quivered and exhaled the respiration of a stagnating life into the breath of the youth, who, carried away by overpowering feeling, hardly retaining his consciousness, sank his head lower and lower, and intercepted the convulsively quivering soul in his breath ——

The eye of the guiltless woman broke, as if in a last struggle, and closed as if to a dream.

Minutes elapsed. "Just Heaven!" she suddenly exclaimed, looking wildly around her. "Where am I? What is that? Is it you Robert?" As if floating downward from another world, she suddenly gazed at the youth—and then gradually regained her consciousness—a glance, expressing the thousand fold contradictions in her mind the fear of being mistaken, and the delight at the perception of being understood in her unhappy feelings. Despair and joy, belief and doubt, touched Robert's inmost being.

"For ever!" sighed she, pressing his hand, and sinking on his breast. "I never yet gave my heart. I give it to you for eternity!" ——

"For eternity!" repeated she, with a confirming glance and with the swiftness of an arrow she left the pavilion.

There stood the youth, like a statue, gazing before him, as if he read his unfortunate future; as if he read his sentence of death in the fibres of the straw matting under his feet.——

DOLORES.

BOOK VI.

CHAPTER I

FIVE SHIPS AT ANCHOR

SOME days after the interrupted interview of Dr Thorfin with Dolores, Alvarez conducted him to the palace in the Rua do Valongo

The physician stood long absorbed in contemplation of the picture, whose twofold existence had occasioned the mental discovery, and now explained, according to the commission of the exile, what he judged proper concerning her fate

"Then she lives here in the neighborhood?" inquired Senhor Vera, in joyful surprise

"In the family of an Englishman at Bota Fogo," replied Thorfin "Her incognito, however, and peculiar circumstances which it is necessary for us rigidly to observe, will not admit of her receiving a visit from the friend of her uncle

"I can understand them," began the negro, "and for the present renounce this pleasure, earnestly as I desire it Should circumstances occur which may occasion Senora Dolores to change her asylum, I bid you to make known to her, that my house stands open for her reception My daughters live here with me in the society of their governess, and although they bear the Ethiopian tint, their hearts will vie with those of any English woman in sympathy and respect for the 'niece' of our friend. I have to inform you about the circumstances which have generally been the cause of my commission

"Some twenty and odd years ago, Señor Gabriel de Garringòs arrived in Pondjern* under an assumed name. He was recommended to our house. My parents received him with hospitality, according to the custom of the country A mutual friendship soon arose, in which I was included—then but a youth

After some years, he first gradually disclosed to us his former position in Europe, and afterwards his inward being We then learned that the application of animal magnetism was at that time prohibited in some countries of Europe, by church and state, and drew down persecutions upon many who treated this discovery

as a science You may be aware that this mysterious power has, for a long time, not been unknown in India, and plainly lies at the foundation of many compositions of Indian poetry, as, for instance, "Kamrup," and others Magnetic *rapports* as a dream life, is not a strange or surprising appearance in India, without being treated as a science, like in Europe Garringòs found many opportunities of pursuing his studies in this department, and after we had observed him, and been astonished at several cures which he undertook in our neighborhood, he revealed to my father and to me what had driven him from Europe

"I am in possession of several documents, which he confided to me in the certainty that a daughter of his friend was living, whose portrait we see here These documents may now be delivered into the hands of Señora Dolores, and will, perhaps, not be uninteresting to you likewise, as you are a physician One document contains, if I may so call it, a peculiar, and perhaps in Europe unknown, System of Magnetism, which may be made public—on condition, however, of keeping secret the name of my friend

"From another document, which encloses the history of his inner life, you will perceive that Garringòs foresaw (or rather foreknew) the death of his female friend, and then first resolved to inquire concerning the fate of her daughter, whom he, by a singular spiritual relationship, ranked among the descendants of his own family"

Dr Thorfin received the designated papers, whose perusal would interest him the more, as he regarded magnetism as a favorite study He therefore endeavored to seek an early opportunity to convey the communications to the young lady, for whom they were first intended, that he might thereafter digest them at his leisure

Senhor Vera touched upon the circumstances of Alvarez, and then again urgently sought for information in regard to the residence of his sister, concerning whose fate he had unfortunately learned nothing

He declared that he was firmly resolved to go to Bahia, to discover the traces of the young lady by some means, unless he should soon receive a satisfactory answer He expressed the supposition that the correspondence was probably very

---

* The East Indian name of Goa.

unsafe, on account of the political relations of Brazil, as many would fear to compromise themselves by any communications not relating to commercial matters After a long conversation concerning the circumstances of the family of Garringòs, Dr Thorfin and Alvarez left the palace The former hastened to Bota Fogo, in the hope of being able to deliver to Dolores the papers from Goa, and the latter directed his steps to Hinango's, where he was to meet him and Horatio, for a political consultation

Hinango's "mission" in South America, which he had taken upon himself, in his peculiar relations to the central committee of Young Europe required some papers to be despatched to Rio Grande, which he could indeed take with him on board of his well armed vessel, were it not that peculiar circumstances, in regard to the safety of Dolores, detained him personally in Rio

Horatio and Alvarez, both full of glorious zeal for the cause of their fatherland, vied in offering to undertake the mission to the headquarters of the insurgents, the materials of which had for some time employed them The translation and copying, and also the preparation for the press, gave them plenty to do

Hinango was in negotiation for the purchase of the schooner brig, which had hitherto borne the name of Vesta, to take her as a privateer to the coast of Rio Grande and the Banda Oriental

The strange position in which Dolores was placed, imposed upon him, on the other hand the moral obligation not to go to sea until her personal safety was made more certain than was the case under the existing circumstances Her embarkation from Buenos Ayres to Rio, had been more the result of concurring circumstances, than her own will and plan She would have preferred going to Mount Video, where she, at least in a social respect, could await her intellectual element The necessity of her speedy departure, and the difficulty of finding a safe passage for her under a neutral flag, had hastened the sailing of the Nordstjernan, which was favored by Mr Walker's " passion for secrets," and his just as undeniable desire to be obliging and serviceable He had no direct commercial connexion with Monte Video, and would consequently have been obliged to give up the whole secret. A certain pride to " despatch" the friend of his daughter, in such danger, from his own house on board of a vessel, to his own house in Rio, might have been at the bottom of the willingness which he manifested so zealously in this matter

Although Mr Walker had hinted at the secret of the authorship in the most cautious manner, and with all due importance, to his brother-in-law in Rio, he did not in the least doubt of the personal security of the persecuted poetess, under the protection of Mr Thomson He had, like so many business people of his sort, too little insight into the political relations which surrounded him, to perceive the danger of his protegé in Rio Men of his class, who do not take a decisive part in any political contest, and belong to neither the one nor the other party, (but to secure their personal safety, in a *juste milieu*, by which they are never compromised,) seldom comprehend the extreme of a political or religious persecution Similar men, in whom no principle has arrived to the clear-ness of inward moral conviction, for whose support they would stake their external existence, not to mention their fortune or life, cannot conceive of the " power of conviction," which is so dangerous to the principle opposed to it

As every man judges others by himself, he can seldom represent to himself a higher degree of moral strength than that which he possesses A man without patriotism or religion, cannot, with the best will, have any idea of a sacrifice for the sake of patriotism or religion ; it is psychologically impossible No material egotist can have an idea of an action or a connexion from love, for what he calls love, is selfishness and animal instinct, as far as the feeling is extinct in him which lies at the foundation of love

In this psychological and logical impossibility of correct judgement on the part of material men, is founded that loveless "judgement of the world," which, in a thousand instances, falls upon the man who, penetrated by a principle, acts from conviction, or from love in harmony with himself As a moral consequence, the "world breaks most mercilessly the staff over him who is not understood —— Far beside the judgement or critics of the social world, (founded upon prejudices and adopted regulations,) stands " public opinion,' the judgement of sound common sense and natural feelings The world gives its judgements generally very loud, public opinion judges sometimes in silence

Decided enemies, often more considerate, judge each other with less narrow mindedness, when opposed in a political or religious contest Both recognise the force of the principle which contends against them, as well as the effect and consequences of sacrifice from conviction

Let the "practical *juste milieu*" believe in a reconciliation of despotism with the idea of liberty, a reconciliation of materialism with spiritualism, a union of fire with water, without injury to either of the hostile elements ——the *juste milieu* only manifests, by such a belief, its own want of character, if not its narrow-mindedness

The word of every author, the poem of every poet, in the spirit of liberty, remains a thorn in the eye of despotism, until the author or poet becomes converted to the opposite principle, or is bought over to silence ; and, until then, his person is morally and civilly condemned to death The *juste milieu* can as little comprehend such a man's contempt of such a sentence of death, as it can conceive of the maintenance of a moral conviction, in spite of such a sentence The *juste milieu* does not recognise the power of such a conviction, because it has none itself

Mr Thomson had hastily read the Elegies of La Plata, upon a time, and had thought them very interesting, very beautiful, very pretty, and that they displayed quite a poetical tendency, as he afterward thought the authoress very interesting, very beautiful, very pretty, and far from being so thin as her little pamphlet, but with a decided tendency to corpulency But he had had neither time nor occasion to reflect upon the spirit of conviction that breathed throughout the work, because that spirit had nothing at all to do with his business

Mr Thomson, like thousands of his kind, very seldom, if ever, thought. He calculated and calculated, as his business required, and his whole life was a Business, which his father had quite accidentally happened to found. He had not an hour to spare to reflect upon any thing, not directly belonging to his business, that did not affect him personally.

In the first weeks after the arrival of Dolores, he had almost forgotten that she was the authoress of those Elegies, as the baron had, luckily for himself, got the idea out of his head that he had ever shown him the pamphlet. This forgetfulness and absent-mindedness in all that does not concern his department, in which the Briton lives, is to be found, without exception, among all business men who move in the narrow sphere of their calculations, whose atmosphere is like a chemical substance that dissolves in itself every thing foreign, and annihilates all that does not belong to their business.

Such men as Mr. Thomson are like the wheels of a machine, which fit to a hair between the cogs of another wheel, in which they fall mechanically, and, when set a going by the "perpetual motion" of calculation, turn positively about their axes, as long as some fatal effect from without does not disturb them, or cause another wheel to stop, a misfortune that makes them as useless as the separated wheel of a broken machine.

Mr. Thomson recognised physical existence as the principal condition of every business. He did not conduct business in order to live from its profits, but he lived only to "do business." He considered the principal objects of physical existence to be breakfast, lunch, dinner, supper, soda water, pepper, mustard, castor oil, Morrison's pil's, sherry, port, ale, and a large English family bedstead.

No reasonable man will ever maintain that such claims on life could have been in the least extravagant. On the contrary, we find few men who do not make nearly the same demands for their earthly existence, although many do not see them satisfied.

Mr. Thomson had now proposed to himself to marry Señora Dolores, and Mr. Thomson was a man who generally endeavored to carry out what he had once proposed to do, let it be what it would; it was all one—M. Thomson was a man of energy. He had five times in his life obtained the hands of ladies whose tendencies to corpulency were just as attractive as was here the case, and he thought that the devil would be to pay, if she should this time be obliged to abandon his purpose.

Hinango had seen through this individuality of the old widower, and as clearly understood the position of his female friend, who (as he expressed himself in his seaman's way) lay under convoy of an old corvette, between cliffs on every side, to be escorted into the port of matrimony, and could not separate from it without exposing herself to the danger of being sunk by a broadside of desperation from the old corvette, called the "Energy." Dolores must get out of this dangerous spot, lift anchor under the flag of moral freedom, and go out upon the ocean of life, to seek some other port.

There seemed to be no social navy at hand to save "Dolores," by giving battle to the old corvette. The condition of "Dolores" was critical and became every day more and more so, since the suspicious guard ship "De Spandau" had approached the old corvette under a false flag,

likewise to tow into the port of matrimony an old English brig, called "Miss Susan," laden with dullness and intolerance, and a deck load of hope, deceived a hundred times. The old "Miss Susan" was indeed newly rigged and painted, but did not make a move as if she meant to run away from the longed for convoy, but the guard ship kept both under close watch. These four sails lay in a safe anchorage, but a few short English miles distant from the port, whose lighthouse was the top of a stately steeple to which the convoy bore down.

There seemed to be no obstacle in the way of the two captains, to prevent them from running in with the first favorable wind, as both, from long seaman's experience, knew their sailing ground. The captain of the "Spandau" did not always observe the port laws, nor punctually report himself to the worldly or spiritual authorities, but sometimes escorted a brig into the Port of Betrothed, without paying the duties for anchorage, buoys, lighthouse, and the like, although he was, notwithstanding, by no means wanting in practice.

Both were sufficiently practical captains, acquainted with the coast, among whose rocks they lay. They had duly examined the cables and chains of their convoys, and from their long experience, considered them strong enough to withstand the breakers, which they declared to be quite insignificant, at least "Miss Susan" lay as comfortable at anchor before the port of matrimony as ever an old vessel of the kind did, that had been over forty years at sea, and had never found a pilot or a convoy for its destination.

"Dolores," according to the inspection of the captain of the "Energy," very lightly laden with poetical enthusiasm, religious and political exaggeration, fantastic ideas concerning the social world and the destiny of woman, had hitherto appeared very little inclined to submit to the convoy. But the "Energy" considered the escort as secured, as soon as the flag of the "Dolores" could be properly hoisted up again, which, alas! under the prevailing mourning, had, until now, floated at half-mast.

Such weeks or months of mourning were so natural, and happened so often in the merry navigation of life, that this circumstance scarcely came into consideration, when the captain of the "Energy" sat before his special chart, and very comfortably compared with the reality the deep upon which he was anchored, the reefs that surrounded him, and the light from the church steeple of matrimony. According to his view, an old seaman, under Hymen's flag, would not easily have so fortunately cast anchor, as he, favored by tide, wind, and weather, had succeeded in doing. He regarded his "Energy" and the stately "Dolores" at his side with a satisfaction, of which a land hero, who never cast anchor under that flag, on the coast of matrimony, can form no idea.

Hinango could not and would not desert Dolores in such a situation, and, nevertheless, the difficulties of a formal abduction were evidently increased at every visit of the captain of the "Spandau," at the side (if not on board) of the old brig "Miss Susan." Both captains seemed to have a secret understanding, to improve a good opportunity when the period of mourning of the "Dolores," should have expired, of running in together into the safe port   There had been, until now, a calm, a motionless calm, and the sea was only moved in beating against the reefs and cliffs, by the mighty current of time

The supposition of Hinango and his friends, in relation to the above plan, was so far well founded as the captain of the "Energy" made use of the strange guard ship, to keep "Dolores" in their midst, while "Miss Susan," somewhat nearer to the entrance of the harbor, lay quite comfortably, held by solid chain cables, and did not need scarcely any watching

Hinango saw the case before his eyes, that the "Energy" would some day take the liberty to attempt to command the "Dolores" by signal, and that the latter would then (with undeniable dislike to the company of the "Energy") consequently lie between two fires, within shot of the Spandau

The most necessary step on his part, as privateer, for such a case, to come to the assistance of the hard-pressed "Dolores," was the preparation of the Vesta, the schooner brig, which he had purchased through Vernon's agency This vessel, of about two hundred tons, had, before that, belonged to a corpulent Portuguese, who used it in his slave business, and had not spared it. It was constructed after the French model, elegantly shaped, and built for a fast sailer, and had proved its original strength and solidity through many a storm, although it sometimes, perhaps, had leaked

It lay upon the water in a manner pleasing to every seaman, and obeyed, with admirable ease, the slightest pressure of the helm ; it sailed close to the wind, like an American pilot boat, required strong canvass when upon its course, and seemed jealous of every sail that endeavored to outrun it   The corpulent son of Lusus,* her owner, knew the good qualities of his Vesta, as well as every other seaman or captain did his comfortable vessel, but she was too small for the slave trade, and he finally resolved to dispose of her.   The conscientious journal of the Vesta, under the command of the Lusiado, showed her excellent sailing, of which he, like every other seaman, was not a little proud, as he ascribed a part of her good qualities to his own nautical skill, which every sailor thought just and right

Hinango made several pleasure trips with his favorite, without actually going to sea, which, under the existing circumstances,† would certainly have been difficult, but he had sufficient judgement to calculate what would be her sailing upon the broad ocean, under full sail, with a favorable wind, from his trial excursions   He seemed, for the present, not to desire a better ship, as it, on the other hand, having been new rigged, and a fresh coat of paint put on it, since coming into his possession, really appeared as one of the finest slave ships in the bay of Rio The Vesta, fitted out for a Haytien man of war, and Mr. Vernon's hints, that it, like so many others, was secretly intended for its former purpose, the slave trade, was sufficient to satisfy

the curiosity of the inquirers who chanced to notice the vessel

Hinango, without ceremony, took possession of the cabin of the corpulent Portuguese, as captain of the Vesta, the name of which he changed to Astrala, when he got his ship papers made out in order under the Haytien flag

The insurrection in Rio Grande, a Brazilian province, would clearly prevent his return to any port of the empire, as soon as he should be seen there, openly taking part in the cause of the people   He would, consequently, have to delay his departure from the Bay of Rio, until the crisis in Dolores' fate should have shown itself

He had sufficient to do until that time, to procure the translation into Spanish of those pamphlets which he had arranged from his papers as an author of "Young Europe," if it should only be to answer, before friend or foe, the question "What a life like his was really intended for ?"   In this manner originated a short extract from a literary work "on nation and government"

Alvarez had resolved, as soon as the work should be completed, to undertake a journey by land to Rio Grande, in order, as a member of the association, the Humanidad, to bring the gift of a young European to the insurgents   This offer was the more to be prized, as the departure of the Astrala (as the Vesta was now called) was deferred to an indefinite time, and the little work, perhaps, contained much that might be welcome to the insurgents, and of practical utility to them   But the uncertainty respecting the fate of the sister of Alvarez, was a circumstance which Hinango took into consideration, and regarded as a strong reason against his departure   It nevertheless appeared necessary to open a communication by land with Rio Grande, for the safe arrival of the Astrala on the coast of Rio Grande, watched as it was by the Brazilian men of war, or cruisers, seemed somewhat doubtful, as soon as it should have fired the first shot for the cause of the people

Hinango had, as an answer to the question of conscience, what he, and men of his position, really intended to do in the world ? explained the spirit and object of his mission in a sort of epistle to the insurgents in Rio Grande   This document, as well as the pamphlet to which it was to serve as an introduction, may the sooner find a place in this novel, as we owe the reader an account of the real object of life, and the travelling about of a man, who, "without any regular business," had, as it would seem, even roamed about through half-a-dozen planets ——

We therefore improve the calm on the coast of our events, before which the five ships are lying at anchor, at some distance from each other, to give the reader the necessary information in regard to the above "questions of conscience," by here inserting the epistle in the style of a privateer, and the little book without a title

The two following chapters are to be considered as the ballast of the Astrala, as their contents are heavy enough, and would, perhaps, be sufficient to keep a ship of state, at whose helm a man of head and heart should be placed, in course, under the flag of humanity, towards the point of its destination.

* The Portuguese style themselves the sons of Lusus, as the Germans call themselves the sons of Hermann, the Swiss the sons of Tell.
† According to the port laws of Rio, no ship can pass the fortress Santa Cruz, without having been cleared at the custom house, or, in a particular case, with a written permit from the guarda mor (port captain)

CHAPTER II.

THE EPISTLE OF ORMUR,

TO THE INSURGENTS OF RIO GRANDE

" God and mankind "

Ormut, a European, of the tribe of the Scandinavians, called to be an apostle of humanity offereth unto you the greeting of the spirit which inspireth him, and sendeth unto you, in the performance of his duty, a little book, without title, concerning nation and government

Let humanity prevail in the spirit of God, and manifest its existence in striving after perfection Amen

We have beheld you for years contending openly and heroically for your freedom and independence—for the extension of republican boundaries in South America

We know that the Brazilian monarchy hath, by means of a legitimate band of pirates, of the alfandega, burdened, oppressed, and almost destroyed all commerce on your coast with an oppressive duty, hath forced millions from you without securing its own existence thereby, because the most of the plundered money fell into the left pocket of the alfandega

We know that ye are tired of such monarchical disorder, that ye, in the proud consciousness of your strength, made short work with the aforesaid piracy of the alfandega, that ye drove away your plundering guests, and lit the matches of your cannons with the monarchical tariff

The history of the world of the last centuries showeth " similar instances " of so called colonies, of this or that monarchy, throwing overboard the monarchical custom house officers, douaniers, gens d'armes, officers of the alfandega, or whatever they were called, as well as all other kinds of officers, and proclaiming a republic, or even a constitutional monarchy

Such occurrences are considered great events in the history of the world, but mankind are little benefited by the result, so long as no Principle proceeds from such a declaration of independence, that is higher than the personal liberty of " making money "

Every republic that has arisen out of the ashes of a monarchy, after a long and obstinate struggle, is continually exposed to the danger of sooner or later being precipitated into the mines of selfishness—if it counts no Republicans

I therefore feel myself called, in sending unto you the accompanying little book, concerning nation and government, to impress upon your hearts what is needful, and what will be needful, in every nation which, having acquired its independence, declares itself a " republic "

A Republic is not a country in its geographical position, between this or that latitude and longitude, a republican is not every man born in such a country, without a throne, that is called a republic Think not so There are as less republicans by birth as there are aristocrats by birth, and whoever imagines that he is a republican, because he was born in a country without a throne, is like the arrogant aristocrats, who pride themselves upon the chance of their birth

Know ye, a republican is not born such, but must develop himself from the germ of humanity that was born within him A republican may be born in an absolute monarchy, as we behold royalists, and so called aristocrats, in every republic, who were born there

The first conditions of a republic, and of any republican, are, respect for himself, and justice to others !

Know ye, that it will signify little, if ye cry out " We are free, no king and no emperor can command us ! we can act and do as we please ! we live in a free country ! hurrah for the republic !"

Know ye what the word republic meaneth ? whence it cometh ? If there should be those among you that know it not, I will explain it to you

The word republic is derived from the Latin words " res," the cause, and " publica," public, therefore " republic " is the public or general cause, the general welfare, the welfare of the people, the commonwealth

Republican is, consequently, according to the original signification of the word, a man that sacrificeth his own personal interest, to the public, common cause, to the welfare of the people

Consider ye this, and call ye not yourselves republican, before ye recognise the spirit of the word, and fulfil the duties which the term implieth

Think not that your contest is ended, when ye have succeeded in driving the hirelings of the enemy beyond your borders, who did not become the " food for powder" of the power of your people When ye shall have apparently obtained your political freedom, then first beginneth your contest for "moral freedom," without which the other will be worthless

When ye shall have disarmed the hirelings by which monarchy endeavored to subjugate you, ye will not have likewise disarmed the Prejudices remaining among you, after they had taken root under the corrupting influence of monarchy, and its prop—the priesthood

Know ye, that it is easier to obtain a brilliant victory over the bayonets of despotism, than to eradicate the lurking poison of prejudice and hypocrisy, after it hath flown through the veins and nerves of a people for centuries

It is easier for a nation to free itself from monarchical slavery than from the chains of moral slavery under the mask of freedom

Freedom consisteth not in the personal liberty to do, and to omit, what ye will, to live for your personal and frequently very sordid interest, and to call to your brother " Help thyself do as I do make use of the confidence and the stupidity of others in thy business make money as I do thou art free "

Freedom is not the permission to wear your hats on your heads before every body, and not to be obliged to salute any person whom ye may chance to meet in the dwelling of another, and who is "nothing to you," because ye do no business with him

Freedom consisteth not in the rude independence sustained by credit, nor incivility to creditors and foreigners, nor in the privilege of taking your ox hides and horns to market without excise, and to export them without duty to king or emperor

Freedom consisteth not in your Declaration of

Independence, whereby ye absolve yourselves from the statutes of the crown

Freedom is something else

Know ye, that political freedom is founded upon your fatherland, and moral freedom in your hearts It is the condition in which ye are hindered by no external subjugation from developing and improving your moral and spiritual powers, from fulfilling your duties towards yourselves, towards your nation, and towards mankind.

Let moral freedom abide in your hearts, it is the consciousness of your dignity as men, and of your power of will, the acknowledgement of your higher destination, with the renunciation of all prejudices, which circumscribe it, and prevent you from attaining it

Freedom is consequently no most gracious present, that an emperor, or a king or queen can grant or guarantee by a sheet of paper, called a Constitution,

Freedom is your Birthright, that no despot can grant unto you, no tyrant needeth guarantee It is not a gift, for which men should beg in servile suppliant petitions, it is then most sacred and inviolable Possession, which they may maintain against every attack in battle, for life and death

Moral freedom and personal liberty, are founded on equality The violation of the moral equality of a fellow man is a violation of his liberty It is not the end of a nation, but the means for the fulfilment of all the duties of humanity

Therefore, when ye shall have laid the foundation stone of your political freedom, be also morally free, and make use of the element of freedom for the general welfare, in honor of the term Republic

Moral freedom can prevail in the heart of a slave fettered in chains, and many so called republicans do not know even what is moral freedom !

Think not that ye are free, while ye value your worth by oxen and ox hides, and by the money that ye get for them ! for ye are slaves unto mammon.

Think not that ye are free, while your priests lead you about by the noses, and prohibit you to read books dictated by sound reason ! for ye are the slaves of the priesthood.

Think not that ye are free, while you seek after offices and dignities in the service of one or the other party of your state, to beg for yourselves (under the protection of the Faroupilhas, or of the Moderados, or of the Caramuros) comfort at the expense of your nation Verily I say unto you, ye are slaves unto your selfishness

Think not that the freedom of a future generation will arise from the stinking slough of your party spirit, from revilings and defamatory speeches against persons of this or that party in your state. Freedom recogniseth no person, it is a principle, it recogniseth no popular party, but the People only !

Think not that your children will grow up to be republicans, as a palm tree groweth up to be a palm tree, and a thistle a thistle Bring up your children to be Men, and your fatherland will bloom as a republic

Ye despise the "mob" of your nation in its rudeness and coarseness, and the ruder and coarser is your mob, the greater is your own shame for a republic knoweth not the term, "mob" The republic, like a mother, shall care for all her children, with equal love, and the neglect of a single one is a crime against humanity —— mark ye that !

We hear much said about the rights of man and the rights of nations, but no one speaketh of the duties of man towards his nation, and of the duties of nations towards mankind

Know ye, a nation that proclaimeth its freedom, and doth not at the same time recognise and fulfil its duties to mankind, is a selfish nation, and stands very low.

The duties of your nation to mankind, next, consist in this that ye make laws in accordance with the progress of the age, for the improvement and ennoblement of your generation, and as an example for other nations, that ye reveal the destination of man, which is a loftier one than the animal gratification of material wants, that ye manifest the spirit of freedom, and teach it in your schools, that ye assemble the wise men of your nation in universities, and offer prizes for the honor of mankind, as ye have, hitherto, prizes for the improvement of cattle For verily I say unto you, mankind hath claims on every people, and every people hath claims upon the last of its sons ! consider ye that !

Where the worth of man is only reckoned by money, there man himself is a saleable creature purchasable by every despot, and such a generation serveth, at the utmost, as manure for a future one For by deceit and cheating can ye "make money," and a stupid blockhead can be rich

If ye as a people recognise no loftier aim than the misuse of liberty "to make money," it were better ye should remain the serfs and slaves of an emperor or of a queen ! and not disgrace the term "republic" for ye are unworthy of liberty, and deserve to have your per centage of traffic and gain counted out to you with the knout ——

Beware of the mania of money-making, lest the negroes spit after you, and cry after you, "money ! money ! sovereigns ! gentlemen ! respectable ! fashionable ! money ! money !" as they do alter the English in the Rua Direita at Rio de Janeiro, where I have seen it, and can therefore personally testify thereto

Therefore, beware of those gentlemen who bleat, "God save the king !" or, "God save the queen !" (God save the queen, and let us shave the people,) and come to you, and say unto you "We will teach you civilization "—— Ye must know that the nation of these gentlemen has become the most powerful of all others, by theft, robbery, and fraud, by murder and incendiarism, committed in all parts of the world, by the so called cabinet of this Christian nation, and the rich there call poverty a crime, and a great part of the people are maimed and starved in manufactories, and have scarcely strength enough to cry, "God save the queen ?" and fifty thousand miserable sinners wander about in the capital of this gentleman nation in privileged misery, and cannot tell where or how they live

When such gentlemen offer you their "civilization," thank them kindly, and place them under police supervision, and watch their steps for their business is to shave nations, and they have done a great business with razors, and races of men and horses

Take heed that ye be not like the aristocrats, in splendor, and luxury, and effeminacy, for that showeth the enervation of your republics, and your venality to every despotism

Take heed that ye do not show your "republican principles" out of ragged elbows and dirty linen, for ye only manifest thereby the raggedness of your consequence and the dirtiness of your inward being

Take heed that ye do not hate and despise foreigners, who, after being disarmed in the contest for their fatherland, seek a refuge among you, and sojourn under your roofs, for (except the Cibocles and Mamalocos) your fathers were foreigners themselves in your land, and if ye will be republicans, pride yourselves not of the privilege of birth

Beware of the "Cosmopolites," who come unto you, and say "We know nothing of fatherland, and need no fatherland, only land' we come among you to do our business under the protection of your laws

Beware of the "yardstick people," who come unto you, and say "We will not become citizens of your state, for we 'do not meddle with politics,' but we want only to make money, and therefore do we dwell without your cities, and thereby save the taxes we would have to pay as citizens"

Let your lazos be thrown about the necks of such cosmopolite rabble, to hang them on the branches of a jacaranda, where they are highest

Beware of the "Philanthropists," who come unto you, and say "We advise you, not to introduce any social improvements, but to maintain the principles of prerogative, that your poorer classes may remain poor, and we may have opportunities to build poor-houses, and to appoint our protegés as poor-house guardians, and as officers of all kinds For it is a pity to let your beef bones rot Let the poor continue poor, that they may eat our bone soups Let us give alms publicly, and inscribe our names beside the emperors whom you have dethroned, for he was a philanthropist, and ye have greatly misunderstood him" Cast your lazos about the necks of this philanthropical rabble, to hang them

Beware of the Priests, who come unto you, and say "We are sent hither by our most gracious emperor, or by our most gracious good king, or from our most gracious queen, to preach Christianity unto your people after the text 'Render to Cæsar the things that are Cæsar's, that nothing remain that is the people's,' allow yourselves to be trodden under foot, and flogged alive on earth, and let the 'wool be pulled over your eyes' by the mighty ones of the earth, in Christian humility, and slavish subjection; for then ye will die happy and go to heaven, and every day secure your mock-turtle, and ale, and plumb pudding, in a private paradise, separated from your rich, (as you have been separated from them in your royal churches,) whose "protection" will despise you even there

Fling your lazos about the necks of such a priestly rabble, and hang them

And now I deliver unto you the little book, without title, on nation and government, that ye may read it, and multiply it, and distribute it, among your people, and erect schools in the spirit of this book, in honor of the Republic, and for the welfare of mankind Amen

Written on board the schooner brig Astrala, under the flag of Humanity
January the 9th, 1839
ORMUR OLAFUR

CHAPTER III

THE BOOK OF ORMUR,

ON PEOPLE AND GOVERNMENT

INTRODUCTION

A nation cut up in powerless parts, governed to its own ruin, and to the destruction of its nationality, by insolent princes, hostile to the interests of the people, will surely one day awake, and assert its independence as a nation It will recognise its own dignity, and feel the disgrace of slavery, it will no longer endure tyranny, but shake off the ignominious yoke, free itself, and represent itself

If we should belong to a nation, that had attained its freedom after a decisive contest, we would take the liberty of submitting the following plan for a national representation, with the motto "Prove all things, hold fast that which is good"

I

FORM OF A NATIONAL REPRESENTATION AND GOVERNMENT

1 A large country must of necessity be divided into separate parts, (provinces or districts,) to facilitate the administration of government Such divisions already exist in almost every country, as distinct races of people generally maintain their original character in all its peculiarities, and distinguish themselves from each other accordingly, without prejudice to the whole

These Districts generally bear the name of their original inhabitants Each District will consist of several Shires, the boundaries of which may be determined by mountains, rivers, or other accidental circumstances

2 The inhabitants of each shire shall elect by a majority of votes (without distinction of property) a Shire-man, and in every district a District Governor If the shire-man, or chief-man in the shire, should be advanced to the office of district governor, his place shall be filled by a new election

3 The shire-men shall be, at the same time, district deputies, and assemble for about three months in every year, as a District Chamber, in the capital of the district, for deliberation, and the transaction of the affairs of the district

The before mentioned organization of the people in Temples* (or whatever name may be thought appropriate) shall be the basis of every election

* See the document, "Organization of the Union," &c, Dolores, page 187.

242 DOLORES.

4 A District Secretary shall be elected by the people for the term of five years, who shall take precedence, in the deliberations, and at the same time keep the archives of the district

The governor shall preside in the district chamber, and have two votes

5 After their general deliberations shall be concluded, the deputies will return to their homes But this body must be consulted so that one-fourth of their number are retained as a committee for deliberations in unforseen emergencies The discharge or leave of absence of members shall be determined by lot

6 The President of the Nation shall be elected for five years He must first have been governor of a district

7 Every district shall send its deputies to the capital These deputies will form a Congress, over which the president shall preside The election shall be conducted by the people of the districts, the number to be determined according to the population, their term of office to last three years

8 The congress shall transact all affairs of the state, both internal and external, and be empowered to decide upon all matters, being, however, responsible to the people for its acts

9 One-third of the congress shall be yearly replaced by other deputies

10 After the expiration of five years, the president cannot be re-elected for the next five years, unless by a majority of four-fifths

11 At the end of each year, a commission shall be nominated by congress to hear all complaints against the president, and to lay them before congress for investigation

12 The president shall reside in the capital

13 The governors shall reside in the capitals of their respective districts.

II

MILITIA, MILITARY, AND NAVY

1 The defence of the country shall devolve upon the national guard, and the navy, which are to be divided into so called active and inactive corps

2 Every native of the country, from the age of 18 to the age of 40, shall belong to the active guard Those residing on the coast shall belong to the navy

3. Every citizen, on passing his fortieth year, will enter the inactive guard, or navy, which, in time of war, is to remain for the defence of the place, and is not to take the field, or proceed to sea, as does the active At the age of 50, the citizen may retire from service

4 The art of war, navigation, military tactics, fortification, etc, are to be taught in the high schools, (universities)

5 The science of war will form a department in the high schools The choice of study shall be free, like every other

6. Gymnastic exercises are to be taught and practised as a necessary part of education, to prepare for military service At the same time, a swimming school may be instituted

7. A fencing school shall be attached to the gymnastic department, at which there are to be weekly public exhibitions

8 Horsemanship shall likewise be made a part of education in the national schools. It shall be taught by experienced teachers, in connexion with instruction concerning the structure of the horse, (anatomy, etc)

9 The necessary military required to be in service for the maintenance of order, shall consist of the national guard, drawn by lot for three years, (from the 20th to the 23rd year)

10 The officers of the guard shall be elected by the latter, but they must, nevertheless, pass the necessary examination before the military examiners

11 All the officers of the active guard (except engineers) shall draw, without distinction, the same pay from the treasury, and shall be named, according to their position, without priority of rank.

12 The officers of the corps of engineers, and of the navy, shall draw a salary proportionate to the extent of their studies and attainments, and when not in service, a third part thereof

13 The number of engineers and officers of the navy shall be regulated by the condition of the active guard and navy

14 Rank and title in the guard and navy will confer no distinction, but, nevertheless, every subordinate officer will owe unconditional obedience to his superior during service

15 In particular cases, the chief of a division of a brigade, or of a regiment, as well as the commander of a frigate, corvette, etc, can be ordered to take an inferior service without injury to his honor

16 The general national military exercises of the national guard shall take place every year, at the close of the harvest, but, nevertheless, in such a manner, that only one-half of the militia shall be assembled at once, so that every citizen will be exercised about three weeks every other year, in a camp

17 No superior officer will be authorized to chastise a subordinate for any offence that he may commit It shall be his duty to report it to his superior

There shall be in every division, as on board of every man of war, a court of honor, chosen by election, which shall hold public sessions The punishment shall be determined by the law applying to the case

18 Should the offence of an officer be of such a nature as to require a dismission from service, the court of honor shall decide whether the criminal shall longer remain in the national guard or navy, without rank

19 No citizen can, even after having passed an examination, become an officer, until he shall have served three years in the national guard or navy (II § 9)

20 The war and naval departments, together with the topographical bureau connected with them, shall be stationary

The members thereof shall be paid by the state, like other officers

21. The active cavalry also shall draw, when out of service, a small salary, as a compensation for the keeping of the horses, in case the number of cavalry men should not be sufficient

III

ORGANIZATION FOR ARMING THE PEOPLE

1 The leader of each rock shall deliver to the foundation the list of names of those youths

and men who, in case of war, would belong to the active corps (See Organization Act, page 187)

2 The secretary of the foundation shall retain the eleven lists, and report the number of warriors to the secretary of the hall

The organization of the army shall take place in a manner similar to the organization of the whole nation

Ten men and a leader will form a band

Eleven bands (121 men) shall form a company, or squadron of cavalry

A company shall keep ten bands (110 men) in the line, the remaining eleven to be employed as pioneers, officers, drummers, mechanics, and the like

3 Eleven companies (1,331 men) will form a column, but as each company will have only 110 men in the line, the line of the column shall consist of only 1,210 men, the remaining 121 to constitute the corps of officers, musicians, officers of the bureau, staff, (état major,) etc

Two columns will form a battalion, 2,420 men, in the line

4 The organization of the people is not to be affected by the calling out of the army Every individual will keep his number in the "rock of the temple" until death, unless he shall have been expelled for crime or misconduct, etc

To avoid confusion, every pillar, etc, can choose some suitable name, as, for example, rock 1, pillar Hope, hall 7, temple Rio Negro

5 The operation of this organization in temples is three-fold.

(a) As a means of representing the state in the election of officers

(b) As a means of arming the inhabitants of the districts, towns, etc

(c) As a means of promoting the interests of humanity, as liberty is thus founded on the basis of equality

The two first affect the country the last, mankind

IV

INTERNAL ADMINISTRATION — OFFICERS OF GOVERNMENT

1. The president and governors shall draw a fixed salary, the senators and district deputies an allowance per diem, for the time they remain together

2 Officers of government must have completed a course of legal studies

3 Every nomination of officers shall proceed from the choice and proposal of the people residing in the district over which the office is exercised

4. All the officers of the general government of the interior, shall draw their pay from the general treasury, and not from the district

5 The election of administrative officers shall take place *viva voce* The district candidates shall send their certificates to the administrative departments, or personally report themselves The five best shall be designated from the proposed number, of whom the citizens of the district shall elect one

6 The president shall have no right to transfer officers from one district to the other, unless by consent of the heads of the district

7 Every officer may appoint his deputies

and subordinates, public protestation being reserved to the people

8 The necessary number of lawyers, notaries, professors, physicians, surgeons, etc, employed in the public institutions, are to be officers of government, paid by the state

9 The appointment of physicians and surgeons, not in the public institutions, may take place according to the requirements of the number of inhabitants of a place or district

10 The candidate for either of the learned professions must undergo a public examination

11 Official salaries to be regulated by moderation, but yet so that a subordinate officer shall receive an adequate support Whoever does not wish to serve the state for a moderate salary, is not compelled to seek an office

12 The appointment of the officers of government, in regard to salary, will fall into three classes, but without in the least affecting the rank or standing of the officers All officers and citizens of the government will stand upon an equal footing

13 The clerks, etc, in the public offices, are to be selected from the candidates of the institutions of learning, (V § 26,) and paid by the state

V

SOCIAL WORLD — LEGISLATION, INSTITUTIONS OF LEARNING, PROMOTION OF THE SCIENCES, ARTS, AND INDUSTRY

1 There will be, besides the legislative and administrative, a Controlling, or Social Power The legislative power will be represented by the congress, to whom the legislative body will be subjected It will not be able to make laws without the assent of the congress

2 The legislative body will consist of a certain number of worthy men, elected by the people (as officers of government) for ten years, and shall assemble in the capital All propositions in regard to laws, are to be laid before this body for deliberation, and the chairman thereof shall submit them to the senate (congress)

3 The administrative or executive power will be composed of all the officers of government except the congress, the legislative body, and the district deputies

4 No district deputy nor general deputy can be appointed to an administrative office

5 The third, controlling, or social power, will consist of a national council of a proportionate number, elected from the people, according to the before mentioned organization

6 The duties of the national council will be to lighten the labors of the legislative body, to promote the intellectual and social improvement of the people, and to meliorate their social condition

7. No member of the national council can at the same time be a member of congress, or an officer of the government, but may be a shireman or district deputy A building shall be erected for the council in the capital, to be used as a bureau for archives, a library, etc

8 The council shall elect from their body a president, a cashier, and a general secretary, who are to be paid by the people, from contributions to the temple fund, without resort to the state treasury

9 These three officers shall reside in the

capital   The national council shall assemble three months in every year, in the different capitals of the district, alternately, and elect a chairman from their body The chairman shall direct the propositions and labors, with the help of the secretary   The council will deliberate and decide

10 The destination of all classes of the people shall be regulated by the council   It will not only represent, what is properly the department of education, (as far as its propositions shall be submitted to the congress,) but control all public institutions, provide for the intellectual development of the laboring classes, and promote mental activity, in science, literature, and the arts

11 While men may, of their own accord, and from inward impulse, be busied day and night in intellectual employment, mental activity in literature and the arts, let it be provided that no one of the so called laboring classes shall be employed longer than eight hours a day, that he may devote the remainder of his time to recreation and intellectual improvement

12 Every laborer shall enjoy a proportionate part of the profits of his industry

13 The national council shall control the profits of laborers, as far as the latter can bring their complaints before them, whereupon an inspector (one of the council) shall be directed to institute an investigation

14 Associations with community of property can exist   They shall be proposed to the national council, who shall consider the proposition, and, in case of approval, shall lay the same before the congress for confirmation

15 The property or possessions of every association shall be considered private property, and as such shall be honored with the property tax, by which the state is supported, which protects the association

16 The property tax shall be progressive All who do not possess a certain fixed amount of property (to be determined by the council) shall not be obliged to pay any property tax

17 Personal and moral freedom is the fundamental condition of all development every man has a right and claim to a proportionate result of his labor, and shall also be required to contribute his proportion towards the support of the state

18 Every person shall be at liberty to convey his property to an association, but no association shall have the right to violate private property

19 The first and most sacred property bestowed upon man, is his body   Personal freedom is founded on the law of nature, as the condition of all development

20. Community of property can naturally only be limited to an association, however extended it may be, and the possessions of such an association will consequently always remain the property of the association

21 No association can exempt itself from its duties towards its nation and fatherland There can be no " state within a state "

22. Education, as the most sacred duty of government, shall promote the development of the physical, as well as intellectual powers and moral ennoblement

23. The system of education shall be planned by a national committee of education, to be sub-

mitted to the people, and confirmed by the national council

24 Considering the value of time, instruction in the living languages will be preferred to the study of the dead, as only those persons require the latter, who intend to devote themselves to one of the learned professions (law, medicine, and divinity *)

25 Besides the country, town, and high schools, (universities,) there shall be, in every shire, a general house of education for the male, and another for the female youth

26 In the general house of education, the male youth will obtain a fundamental instruction in all the departments of science, and receive an education in accordance with his natural disposition and his talents, for the occupation which he may choose

27 Besides teachers of science, artists and mechanics of all kinds shall be appointed in the necessary instruction, and be paid by the state

28 In the houses of education for females, instruction will be imparted (besides in the necessary sciences) in all branches required in a female education

29 All children, without exception, will find in this institution a dwelling and support, without distinction of condition and the circumstances of their parents   The pupils of the female sex are to remain in it until the end of their sixteenth year, and those of the male sex until the end of their eighteenth year

30 Public instruction in these institutions, as in all others, shall be without charge

31 A Bazaar shall be connected with the house of education, for the exhibition of all work delivered by the pupils in the arts and trades, and female work

Every article prepared by a pupil, shall be conscientiously appraised, and the amount, after a deduction of the material, divided into three parts, two of which shall be deposited in the public savings bank, as the property of the pupil, and the other shall go to the institution   The pupil's earnings shall bear the usual national per centage, and be reserved for him, as a fortune, until he shall arrive at his twenty-fifth year   The female pupils may receive the amount of their earnings, at their marriage, or at the end of their twentieth year

32 An Academy of Fine Arts, (sculpture, painting, architecture,) and an Academy of Music, shall be established at the capital.

33 The products of art, of the academy, are to be bought by the national Art-union, and disposed of to its members

34 A university shall be established in every district for the study of law, medicine, theology, philosophy, etc

35 As an inducement to effort, medals shall be bestowed for the most excellent works. A travelling stipend for three years will be given with the highest medal

36 The erection and adornment of public and private edifices, representations from the history of the people, in statues and fresco, will offer to talent opportunity for activity and development

37 It shall be the duty of the congress to use

---

* No sectarian shall be allowed to preach, until he shall have shown his acquaintance with ecclesiastical history, etc , in a public examination before the university

their best endeavors to promote the bloom of all sciences and arts, and of industry, and not to neglect any branch of education

.5. There shall be in every capital of a district, as well as in the capital of the country, a building for a national theatre. The company belonging to the former, shall change their locality every three months. The theatre is to be a school of improvement for the people, and at the same time, a support to rising poetic talent. The aim of all the arts will be the strengthening of the national spirit and moral ennoblement. The dramatic artists shall be considered officers of government.

VI.

MARRIAGES, AND COURTS OF MARRIAGE.

1. Bad marriages are an essential cause of the corruption of mankind, for the greater part are contracted for pecuniary purposes, like a business transaction, or originate from base motives.

2. So called "reasonable" and heartless marriages have a pernicious influence upon the next generation, and in them lies founded the greatest evil of the present and the future.

3. In every shire there shall be established courts of marriage, chosen by the inhabitants of both sexes, consisting of four married men and six married women.

4. A citizen shall preside, who is to be chosen by lot, and shall have two votes.

5. The court shall hold weekly sessions, generally Sundays.

6. Females shall have a free choice of marriage, as well as males.

7. Every couple wishing to be married shall report themselves to the court, and be approved for their correct moral and civil conduct, and to declare their free consent. Their marriage can first take place a year afterwards, should they not separate before that time.

8. No couple can contract marriage, the difference in whose age is more than thirty years.

9. No young man or woman shall be forced into marriage of speculation by their relations. The injured party can complain before the court.

10. Marriage shall be concluded before this court by contract, and then confirmed by the authority of the district, and the clergyman chosen by the couple.

11. Divorces can at any time be granted by this court, for legal grounds.

12. The guilty party, whose offence shall have given a cause for the divorce, shall be liable to damages at the suit of the injured party.

13. The children of divorced persons, shall be brought up in the general institution of education, for the security of their morals, without distinction of age and condition.

14. Adultery shall be followed by divorce.

15. Difference of religion shall not be an impediment to marriage. A couple resolved upon marrying, against whom there is no other objection, can have recourse to this court, in case the parents give this as a ground of objection.

VII.

FREEDOM OF CONSCIENCE.

1. There shall be no predominant, so called Religion of State ——

2. Every form of worship shall be permitted, unless it should contradict morality.

3. All natives of the country, or those who shall have acquired the right of citizenship, shall be under equal obligations to the state, under the protection of the laws.

4. All intrigue of proselytism, of whatever nature, shall be prohibited, and be punished by law.

5. Religious instruction shall first commence at the twelfth year, when youth is sufficiently matured to comprehend the sublimity of revelation. Every sect can pay their particular teacher, who will be allowed the use of a room in the school building, an hour each day, under the control of the national council.

6. Interments in churches are prohibited. No corpse can be buried within the city.

VIII.

UNIVERSAL PRINCIPLES.

1. One code of laws shall prevail throughout the whole country, designed and carried out according to the requirements of the age, and founded upon nature and reason.

2. There shall be no civil oaths. The love of country in the heart of the citizen shall be his obligation. The lost idea " honor " shall be restored to life.

3. Every office holder shall be obliged to the people faithfully to support the laws, without the formula of an oath. Offences against the people by neglect of duty, shall be grounds of legal complaint.

4. Every foreigner shall be under the protection of the laws as soon as he touches land.

5. Government shall be supported by progressive taxes upon property.

6. There shall be no taxes upon necessaries, (indirect taxes.)

7. There shall be no duties, nor excise, etc.

8. Import duties upon articles of luxury will be rendered superfluous by the progressive property tax.

9. Highways and railroads shall be under the care of the state.

10. The perfection of all products of the country, as well of nature as of industry and art, shall be encouraged by premiums.

11. The state shall propose yearly prize questions in all the sciences.

12. Universal liberty of occupation. Abolition of all compulsion of trade. No association, with a community of goods, shall enjoy exclusive privileges.

13. Every department of culture and industry shall be represented and promoted by especial district councils for that purpose.

14. Lotteries and stamps on paper are abolished.

15. Luxury is a worm at the foundation of the state.

16. The simplest national costume shall prevail among all classes. No gold or silver shall be worn on military uniforms.

17. All foreign fashions are infidelity to nationality.

18. Whoever shall accept a rank, title or order from any foreign monarchy, shall forfeit the honor of serving in the national guard, and likewise claims to office in fatherland.

19 Offences against morality and persons by the free press, shall, like all others, be a cause of legal complaint

20. Capital punishment shall only be inflicted in cases of treason; all other crimes shall be punished by confinement in the house of correction

21 The house of correction for criminals will be an institution of industry, in which they are to be treated as sufferers A third of the proceeds of the articles produced by the sufferer in the house of correction, shall be laid aside for him in the "national savings bank," to be given to him at the expiration of his term of punishment

22 Legislation and education are the first duties of government In education lies the germ of the succeeding generation legislation maintains the dignity of the state

23 All male and female teachers shall be regarded as officers of the government of the noblest calling. Their existence, until their decease, shall be secured by an especial savings-bank, under the protection of the state

24 Woman will be revered as the noblest work of creation To woman is confided the improvement of the people to an elevated degree, by the influence of females upon the education and moral perfection of mankind

25 The maiden should be conscious of her dignity, and entrust her heart to no one who shall not have shown himself a man in the nation

26 The mother should regard her children as her choicest possession, which she consecrates to fatherland. The feeling of love to fatherland (patriotism) should be nourished and strengthened in the tender heart of the child, as the purest and holiest after faith in God.

27 The highest aim of a maiden should be to render the man happy, who belongs to the nation, as if to thank and reward him for his efforts

28 The purest endeavors of a youth should be directed towards the development and perfection of his being, as a man in his nation, which includes all virtues in itself

29 A man's highest and noblest aim should be to live and die for fatherland

IX

SENTENCES

1 Intellectual activity is the highest Hand-labor stands higher than capital Money has no value in itself, but only as the means to a noble end.

2 Property and possessions, unaccompanied by mind and heart, are the brand on the forehead of a criminal

3 As difficult as it is for a rich man " to enter the kingdom of Heaven,' so difficult is it for a merchant to be a republican A merchant recognises only his personal interest; the republican principle requires personal sacrifice

4 " There is no friendship in business," and no principle on 'change

5. A republic that recognises commerce as the highest aim, and money as its element, is not a republic, but a monarchy of the venal slaves of mammon

6 When money is an article of speculation, man also is venal

7 As long as it is no disgrace to be nothing else than rich, there is no hope for mankind

8 The greatness of a nation does not consist in the motion of its machines, nor in the extension of its commerce, nor in the enlargement of its boundaries, but in the spirit with which it represents the cause of humanity

9 Private institutions, establishments, and foundations, what noble purpose they ever may intend, will always remain " private," without influence of the development and progress of the nation as a moral and spiritual power

10 The greatness of a state depends not on the number of its inhabitants, but upon the spirit that animates the people in their efforts after ennoblement

11 Millions of slaves moulder in the grave of oblivion A single man may raise the name of his nation in the annals of mankind

X

THE NATION AND HUMANITY

1 Every man in the nation shall pay a fixed, or a voluntary tax, for the promotion of humanity, which the treasurer of the pillar shall send by the treasurer of the hall to the treasury of the temple * The directors of the temple shall annually deliver a public account

2 Every temple shall establish the necessary printing presses, which are to be conducted by chosen officers

3 A separate printing press shall be established on behalf of the national council, in their building (See V § 7)

4 A popular newspaper shall appear every five days, as the organ of the national council, at the same time faithfully translated in several languages

5 As soon as a national council shall be organized, it shall appoint as many " messengers of communication " for other nations, as shall have organized themselves in a similar manner, and shall have joined the Humanita

6 As each nation recognises but one national council, it requires but one messenger for every neighbouring or distant nation

7 National hospitality will provide for the dwelling and subsistence of the " messengers of communication "

8 The messengers of communication shall draw a salary, proportioned to their necessities, from the treasuries of the temples, by which they were appointed

9 The messengers of communication (popular ambassadors) shall endeavor more and more to strengthen the union of the nations, and promote great enterprises for the welfare of mankind

10 The organ of the national council (see § 4 above) shall especially endeavor to avoid confusion in their necessary labors, and particularly to lighten the work of legislation

11 There shall be a provisional committee, on laws created in the usual manner Members of the council, of the government, and of the chamber, can also be elected to the committee on laws

12. The committee on laws, shall prepare an

* See the Organization Act, page 187, Dolores In case the " Book of Ormur " should be printed separately, the Organization Act must precede it, as an introduction.

edition of a condensed extract from all writings, of all nations, in all ages, which relate to legislation, or refer to useful laws. The form of these extracts shall be limited to paragraphs. The spirit of the law, and not the mass of what is written, is to be taken into consideration. Every individual, who considers himself competent, can take part in this compilation. Each extract shall bear the name of the original author, and shall be entitled "book," as, for instance. The book of Moses, Samuel, Solon, Socrates, Plato, etc., the book of Jesus, Muhammed, Marcus Aurelius, Cicero, Beccaria, Montesquieu, Volney, Rousseau, David Hume, Locke, etc., Herder, Seume, etc., the books of the Chinese, Persians, etc., etc. The whole compilation to form the " Books of Humanity."

13 After the completion of these labors, (about a year,) the melioration of the laws can be proposed. Until that time, the statutes of the organization, and the various provisional laws, shall continue in force.

14 It would be ingratitude on the part of mankind, not to improve the treasures, which have been bequeathed to them, by the men of all times, who have lived and died for them.

15 The presses of the temple (of the nation) can be employed, in the mean time, on the above Books of Humanity. The nations of the nineteenth century may be ashamed that they do not make use of what is before them for rational legislation.

16 As a temple consists of 11,611 men, the distribution of the editions of similar works, can be arranged accordingly, apart from private orders. It is of course understood, that besides the national printing presses, there may be as many private presses, as may be requisite.

17 The regular meetings of the rocks and pillars among themselves, or in committee, shall be determined by the statutes. The committee (council) of a pillar or hall can appoint popular meetings, and announce the time and place, through the national newspaper.

18 These popular meetings shall be designed to animate the spirit of the nation, and promote the cause of humanity, by festive military exercises and public addresses. Similar national festivals shall take place for the yearly distribution of prizes, for the promotion of industry, the arts and sciences, agriculture, improvement in the breed of cattle, etc.

We believe that it would not be so difficult to promote the welfare of a nation, and to effect the deliverance of all mankind, if man would manifest the will to be free. We deliver these words to the nations of the earth, and hope to be understood, in whole and in part. We hope that our pure intentions, which dictated these words, may meet with the spirit of sympathy to be expected in the nobler nature of man.

We acknowledge, at the same time, that we have to contend against egotism, and that our work, which would be so simple and easy of accomplishment, will meet with all the difficulties which selfishness on earth opposes to virtue. But we, nevertheless, do not despair of mankind.

We believe in nature and reason, and therefore we act. May the nations comprehend the spirit of these " words of a man," and may this spirit spread among every people, that the word may become deed. Amen.

CHAPTER IV

THE ESCORT.

IT was two o'clock, one afternoon, when the alfandega was closed, and the saloon of the exchange was gradually being vacated.

A numerous train of coffee negroes trotted along the Rua Direita, towards the Largo do Pazo, to receive, be sure some door there, the payment for so many coffee sacks sent, whereby each negro would, perhaps, obtain for himself a glass of cachaz, while he truly and honestly delivered to his master every vintém that he received.

The train was a brilliant one that time. A little old negro danced before, with a parti-colored plaster image upon his gray wool, it was the statue of Napoleon, whose head was (very naturally) colored black, as a sort of Ethiopian divinity, with the "little corporal's" hat, and arms crossed over each other, in high bottes fortes—Napoleon himself, as emperor and as negro.

Near the "office bearer" ran the "tambour minor," with his funnel instrument filled with dry coffee beans, and bound over with a piece of leather, whose rattle sounded afar, in the tropically clear atmosphere, more noisily than a child's ivory rattle in a small family room.

Next followed the "chief standard bearer," a "fine fellow," big as a small Goliath, with an old crownless Hanoverian infantry shako on his head, ornamented with a quantity of worthless ostrich feathers, which had arrived in a chest from Rio Negro, and had been swept out of the alfandega with the sand.

In the right hand of the proud quasi giant, fluttered a ragged old handkerchief upon a rocket stick, and a half hundred of sweating Ethiopians, naked as the wretchedness of their fate, with make-believe "culottes" on their hips, trotted behind the three principal personages, and sang their monotonously melodious "Doy-doyh! Doy-doyh!" half out of breath, for it was the beginning of January, and the thermometer pointed to above a hundred degrees of Fahrenheit.

A cavalcade of some thirty men, in uniforms, rode past the negro train, it was the lifeguard of the prince, Don Pedro Pecino, (the little,) as the negroes usually called the boy. Behind the "infantry on horseback," of which one lost a chacot, another a stirrup, and another even a sword, (for they went upon the full gallop,) rolled the carriage of the future emperor, Don Pedro the Second. The state carriage was followed by two others, less brilliant, filled with gold bedecked court functionaries, while a train of galloping "infantry on horseback" endeavored to follow, as quickly as possible; each did his best, to go as well as ever he could, without slipping from his saddle.

The three passengers from the Nordstjernan, Hinango, Alvarez, and Horatio, had agreed to meet Dr Thorfin at the Hotel du Nord, to make arrangements for the voyage of Alvarez to Rio Grande. They contemplated, from a balcony, the tumult of the Rua Direita, the train of slavery, and the train of the empire.

"A guard of cavalry who cannot ride! here in Brazil, where there are provinces that possess the most famous riders in all the world!" exclaimed Alvarez, observing the flying stirrups,

and the downfall of chacot and sword "I cannot comprehend that '"

"We may easily comprehend it, my dear Mr
Daily," answered Dr Thorfin, employing the
name of Alvarez' Titulo de Residencia, (police
documents ,) "we may very well understand it,
when we reflect that the cavalry of Rio Grande
and St Paolo are famous republicans, to whom,
at this time, the little person of the future emperor would hardly be entrusted"

"There comes some more cavalry '" interrupted Horatio, and the eyes of all were directed to a third train, that entered the Rua Direita
from the Largo do Pazo

"What is that '' cried some of the four

"Come down ' we must see that nearer,
down below," observed Hinango, and all hastened down to the troop in front of the hotel

It was a train of captive "rebels," faroupilhas,
from the interior of the country, arrived from
Porto Seguro, in a vessel of war, landed on the
place in front of the Hotel Faroux, and there
taken in custody by permanentos and gens
d'armes, to be registered before the commandant, and escorted to a prison

The "peaceful citizens" of the principal
streets of Rio ventured in part to step out of
their doors, or upon their balconies, to contemplate the train, which was certainly as interesting as imposing

Slowly and gravely rode an officer, with a corporal and twelve men in advance, casting threatening glances around, as if he would say,
"Look ' what these gentlemen have come to,
may happen to you also, if you are not servile "
The officer, as well as his people, were white
It appeared that they would not honor any mulatto, or negro, with the bailiff's office, for fear
that their uniform might cover a free human
heart, and endanger the state The vanguard
was followed by the captives, with heavy chains
on their hands, that were fastened to one foot
on a ring

According to the grade of criminality, men
walked in advance, whose countenances bore
the impress of the higher classes in the social
world, in coarse capotes, partly barefooted, and
partly in tamances Some yet wore their valuable ponchos. Broad brimmed Minas hats, of
beaver or straw, covered their heads, which most
of them, in the consciousness of worth, held
proudly upright, while others, depressed by
grief and trouble, looked fixedly before them
As if in irony, a half naked negro was thrust into
rank with his former master, who walked as a
criminal next him, because he had given freedom to him, and hundreds of other slaves, to lay
the foundation of the freedom of his fatherland

A strong detachment of "infantry on horseback" closed the train, which numbered some sixty captives, among whom were several women
and children

The stillness of death reigned in the whole
street. The cabriolets, and carriages, and riders, who casually came into the neighborhood, halted; the foot passengers remained
standing . all contemplated the escort, no one
said a word. Many avoided betraying by their
looks, what they thought and felt

Among the first captives, walked a tall, nobly
formed young man, with a pale, dignified countenance, whose expression evinced moral force

and tranquillity of soul He wore a slave' capote
without a poncho, and a fine Minas hat Next
him walked a young delicate woman, in a rich
dress, without ornaments A Minas beaver hat
covered her head, whose hair, well arranged,
waved in the breath of the gentle wind She
raised with her right hand the heavy chain which
descended from the left arm of her husband to
the ring on his foot, to lighten his bonds for him
Her lovely countenance, formerly of Brazilian
whiteness, at the mercy of wind and storm for
months, had lost its blooming complexion, and
the legible traces of suffering and despair were
displayed on her features of exalted womanhood.

All eyes lingered, as if riveted upon this pair,
and here and there, on a high balcony, a feeling
Brazilian woman pressed her handkerchief to her
lips, in the pain of sympathy, and turned away
from this picture of sacred love and constancy

Hardly had Alvarez directed his glance upon
this lady, than a ray penetrated him like lightning when it sets fire to a palm tree His countenance became of a deadly paleness, he leaned
on Hinango's arm, shrank within himself, and
then, carried quite beside himself, exclaimed,
'It is she '" half aloud, and crossed to the middle of the street where the train walked along

His sister, the wife of Serafini, had hitherto
gazed, from time to time, upon the countenance
of her husband, whose glance met hers All
that surrounded her remained strange, and appeared indifferent to her , she looked not around
her

Suddenly a young man stepped into the path,
and, at the same instant, some gens d'armes also,
from the rear guard, came up to them both

"Angelica '" cried Alvarez, in a tone that she
had only ever heard as a "voice of home " The
lady looked at the stranger, her countenance became rigid with an inward convulsion, all at
once, however, she seemed to recognise her
brother

"Alvarez' is it you? My God! Alvarez '"
cried she, and sank senseless into his arms

"Forward '' commanded a corporal, touching with his sword the shoulder of Serafini,
who remained standing near his wife, and did
not obey the order

The commanding officer of the vanguard had
remarked the so called tumult, and galloped
back

"Who are you?" inquired he of the refugee
from La Plata, with a brutal mien and harsh
voice

"I am the brother of this lady," said he,
trembling, as his sister hung upon him, bereft
of consciousness "Help ' help," exclaimed
he, without troubling himself with the bailiff

Hinango and Dr Thorfin had not failed to
follow the steps of Alvarez, and now hastened
to carry the lady into a neighboring apothecary's shop

The officer ordered her brother, with a commanding voice · "Remain here '"

"I remain here? leave my sister in such a
situation?" returned Alvarez, with violence

"You will remain here ' Who are you?
Where is your police certificate?" inquired the
other, briefly and dryly

We must recollect that Alvarez, like all strangers, was obliged to have a titulo de residencia
from the police, that he might not be exposed

to the danger of being taken up as a vagabond, and placed amongst the permanentos In consequence of this necessity, Robert Walker had given him the pass of his clerk, Habakkuk Daily, upon whose name he had received his certificate.

"What is your name? what are you called? who are you?" inquired the officer, as Alvarez, in the singular perplexity in which he found himself, did not wish to show his police certificate, or announce its existence

"My name is Alvarez de la Barca, from Corrientes, on the Parana I am the brother of this lady," returned he, with self-possession

"And you have no titulo de residencia?" interrupted the officer

'De la Barca!" cried Serafini, who stood at some distance in his rank, separated from Alvarez by gens d'armes

The expression of this exclamation, which comprised all the stormy sensations of the moment, penetrated the brother's heart, who had, as yet, received no answer from Bahia, to his manifold inquiries about the fate of his sister

His letter from Rio had arrived there simultaneously with the intelligence that Signore Serafini had been arrested at his plantation, as a faroupilha, and escorted to Porto Seguro No one dared to acknowledge, in a letter, that he had even heard the name of Madame Serafini, or been in correspondence with her or her husband He was a prisoner, a state criminal, and most correspondents in Bahia loved their personal safety

Notwithstanding that the same prudence and fear also prevailed in many of the "peaceful" citizens in Rio, a crowd had collected about the group, and the officer appeared to feel that "a storm was brewing," in relation to the security of his prisoners

With sufficient presence of mind, therefore, he commanded a corporal to bring the escort in order, and hold the carbines "ready to fire" He then turned again to the "suspicious fellow," who announced himself as the brother-in-law of the most culpable criminal, and informed him that he was a prisoner

At the same instant, a young Englishman pressed through the crowd, and hastily stepped up to the officer It was Robert Walker, with a disturbed countenance, already vividly interested in the passage of the train, which he had been gazing at from under the porch of the exchange He was now afflicted in the highest degree by the group, in which he saw his friend from the Nordstjernan involved

"What's the matter here?" inquired he of the bailiff on horseback, while he seized the hand of Alvarez

"Don't you touch the prisoner, or ——" cried the other to him, with a look that expressed the conclusion of his threat "Who are you?" said he, interrupting himself

"My name is Robert Walker—Englishman."

"Go home!" growled the gens d'arme

"You have no right to order me," replied the young Briton "Why have you seized this gentleman?"

"That's no concern of yours"

"That certainly is my concern, because I am his friend, and I will guaranty for him, if bail will be received for him, on his account"

32

"Then attend the prisoner to our bureau," growled the officer

"No," cried Alvarez, "I beseech you, Señor Roberto, hasten to my sister, she is there at the apothecary's"

"Your sister!" cried the youth, with an expression of amazement that bordered on terror

"It is my wife!" resounded from the train of captives "It is Signora Serafini, my wife, I beseech you take care of her."

This petition of the unfortunate was evidently occasioned by the explanation of the young Englishman, as that revealed in him the upright character of a noble young man, who, in such a strait, was ready to act for his friend, and was favored by his national and social position

The petition was not, however, requisite to heighten Robert's sympathy, who now, with equal presence of mind, gave his card to the officer, and said "Here is my name, our counting house is well known, I will be at your bureau in a moment" With the same despatch with which he had spoken these words, he once more pressed the hand of Alvarez, and whispered in his ear "I will hasten to your sister, and then come immediately to you" He then pressed through the crowd that had assembled in front of the apothecary's

An officer of the national guard, on duty in the neighboring guard house, had approached the officer of gens d'armes, and inquired what was passing He learned that this man carried no titulo de residencia, and, as the relative of a state criminal, stood in connexion with "rebels," and was arrested in consequence

The citizen of Rio in uniform now inquired of the Argentine refugee whether he had acquaintance in the city

"No!" answered Alvarez, who possessed too much discretion to name, in his present situation, any one whom his acquaintance would compromise.

"You do not know this young man, then, the young Englishman, Mr Walker?" inquired the gens d'arme officer, looking at the card which the latter had handed to him

"No!" replied Alvarez, briefly and dryly, as before

The citizen heard the name of a well known English house, and without appearing to be satisfied, noted the name of the prisoner

The officer of gens d armes pushed the "vagabond," Alvarez, into the train of faroupilhas, and ordered some soldiers of his cavalcade to ride near him

The train now put itself in motion The corporal breathed more freely, and threw out his chest again, since his officer was again in the ascendant The crowd had retreated to the sidewalk, without bringing the security of the faroupilhas in question.

Angelica had accompanied her husband from the moment when they left Villa Tasso. The journey led through inhospitable campos and densely wooded valleys, through ravines and gullies, over trackless mountains, whose summits occasionally overhung abysses, the view from which, alone, was sufficient to make a man's head swim, while the horse or mule, left to itself, found the way in an inconceivable manner, and often planted its four hoofs on a ledge of rock, whose surface hardly comprised two square feet Exposed by day to the burning heat of the sun, and often to pouring thunder-showers, the lady passed the night where the prisoners were guarded, sometimes in an out-building of a venda, chacara, or fazenda, in a negro hut, or in the lonely, desolate dwelling of a "criminoso," who had committed murder in some place, and, not being politically suspicious, had evaded justice, betaken himself to the wilder-ness, and there established a fazenda, recognised as a " criminoso," but not further molested

Brazilian hospitality, which, as a national cus-tom, stands as greatly to the honor of the people as to the convenience of travellers, certainly af-forded every attention to the delicate lady, where the escort met with men, and she encountered many touching traits of heartfelt sympathy, where she could have hardly expected it But seldom, almost never, did she quit the neighbor-hood of the place where her husband was guard-ed, and positively refused to occupy a conven-ient apartment, when he was obliged to repose his grief burdened head under the open sky, a rest that seldom strengthened him

In the town which the escort reached after some days journey, more captive faroupilhas were added to the planter from Villa Tasso, and their number increased, until they arrived at Porto Seguro, and particularly in that depot of rebels, to such compass as we have remarked in the Rua Direita

A man-of-war transported the whole band of " scoundrels " (as the royalists contemptuously designated them,) towards Rio de Janeiro, where they at length arrived, after full two months of such wearisome and troublesome travel The vessel was anchored near the fortress of Vil-ganhon, where the prisoners were to obtain " free quarters," so soon as they had passed the inspection of the authorities in the capital, who were constantly occupied with criminal investi-gations against the rebels of all the provinces

Angelica found herself, at her debarkation, in a nervous state that requires no further descrip-tion, when we look back upon the physical exer-tion and endurance of such a journey, and upon the state of mind which must undoubtedly have overpowered her

The choice was afforded her, to remain for the present, on board with her attendants, and go on shore alone with them, or to separate her-self from her people, in case she was resolved to accompany her husband into the city, as there would be no place for her four servants in the " prison building," where she might alone, per-chance, find a cell ——

Her choice was soon decided, she gave her effects to the charge of a black chambermaid, who had, with touching constancy and steadfast-ness, borne all the hardships of the journey at her lady's side, and she appeared with her hus-band in the escort, where we have seen her

Alvarez had five years before departed for Bar-celona, while she remained in Corrientes, and after their mother's death, sought a situation as governess Her talents and character were a sufficient recommendation to procure her such employment anywhere It happened that a relative of Signore Serafini, from Bahia, on a visit in Buenos Ayres, wanted a young lady in her capacity as a companion; she travelled with this family, where Signore Serafini became ac-quainted with her, and after a year of social intercourse, offered her his hand She lived in the midst of domestic happiness at Villa Tasso, where we first observed her, and had since made every endeavor to impart the intelligence to her brother in Europe, and invite him to her house

Alvarez travelled about in Spain for a long time, prosecuting the slightest trace of his uncle wherever it glimmered upon him—but soon be-came an object of attention to the same priestly party, who, as it appeared, still well remembered his uncle

He labored here and there as a type setter, and occasionally accepted an engagement as chorus singer at the opera, under some dramatic name or other

The uninterrupted struggle between the Chris-tinos and Carlists, separated every year more and more, upon the Castilian peninsula, the principle of absolutism from its opposite one of freedom, and it is well known that a republican party developed itself, in whose battalions many members of " Young Europe" carried arms, who, after the failure of the " Expedition of Savoy," were scattered with the organization of the Union into all parts of the world

Alvarez harmonized with the spirit of the Union, while he recognised its principles as his own

We may recall to ourselves the reminiscence of Hinango about their former acquaintance, and so the more easily explain to ourselves the circumstances which subjected the correspon-dence of the South American in Spain to the control of the police It was not surprising that no letter from him reached his sister, and that he received no answer from Bahia He returned to his own country, and with respect to the secret police, came " out of the frying pan into the fire "

There exists* a European secret police, in all parts of the world, which controls, with the greatest consistency, the movements, travels, and correspondence of proscribed persons, whose character and consequence is sufficiently known to despotism to deserve its attention

No political combination, since the society of Illuminati, founded in Germany by Weisshaupt, (and, by the way, betrayed by the German author of " Solitude," Dr Zimmerman, physician to the court of Hanover,) has been persecuted with such strictness and watchfulness, on the part of European courts, as " Young Europe," and, perhaps, for very natural reasons —

Despotism, recognising its position as royalty, may very well heap curse and ban upon a union (and sentence to death those members who sus-tain the spirit of the union in their individuality) whose principles are plainly and clearly spoken in literary works, threatening danger to " Old Europe" and to the principle of nation-devouring legitimacy, especially by struggling, with intel-lectual power, against ordinances which contra-dict nature and reason

Although Hinango had given to his associate, Barigaldi, on board the Nordstjernan, a confi-dential report concerning the extension of the Union, which, strictly speaking, should belong

* In a novel of our epoch—the author is obliged to speak in *present time*

to the materials of this work, we can, nevertheless, only contemplate these documents from a distance, since it would be difficult to force our way into the cabin of the well armed Mazzini, and read them there We may, however, intimate that a transatlantic republic, peopled by Spaniards, offered to the committee of " Young Europe" a loan of four millions of French francs, in case the Union would again rear its standard in Europe, and enter into alliance with the republics of South America, as the Union of Humanity

Through what medium this historically memorable offer was made, and what hindrances lay at that time in the way of the fulfilment of such a plan, must remain unknown, until perhaps future events shall bring about a similar alliance of humanity, and reveal facts which will tend to the honor of the spirit of the Union, before friend and foe ——

Hundreds of the proscribed individuals of " Young Europe," escorted toward England from the continent, through the above mentioned consistent persecution on the part of despotism, dispersed into all parts of the world, and many separated from the spirit of the Union, as their fate separated them from their associates Of course these could no more be dangerous to the enemy

Here and there, however, one remained true to the cause for which he had declared himself, and whereever fate led him—he stood under the inspection of European espionage

We may now, all the more readily, explain to ourselves how it occurred that neither Angelica nor her brother had been able to procure that intelligence of each other which each so earnestly desired.

Signora Serafini had valid grounds for believing her brother dead, or for the surmise that he was in chains, in a similar manner with her husband

Dwelling with him in spirit more than ever before, during the journey from Villa Tasso until her arrival in the Rua Dieita, in Rio, she had often recalled all the remembrances of her childhood passed at his side Suddenly a man appeared to her there, in whose features she certainly recognised an evident family resemblance—whose appearance, however, as a living creature, in the principal street of the Brazilian imperial city, was as a phantom to her Hardly had her name sounded, in that voice which comprised in one single tone of sorrow all the remembrances of childhood, than her physical strength, suffering and shattered by the circumstances that surrounded her, sank under the nameless effect of this impression. She fell senseless, and only regained her consciousness in the loja of the apothecary, where she now remained in an armchair, under Dr. Thorfin's attendance

" Where is Carlo? where is my husband?" inquired she, when she at length unclosed her eyes, and saw entirely strange faces, as she gazed wildly round her

Hinango and Horatio, with Dr Thorfin, who stood nearest to her of the sympathizing group, looked at each other, as if consulting how they should answer the question.

" —Where am I?" how came I here?" inquired the sufferer, after a pause, becoming more and more conscious of the objects that surrounded her. " Have we arrived in Rio de Janeiro?" continued she " Does this building belong to the prison where my husband lies in chains?"

Dr Thorfin now mildly explained to her, that she had been seized with a fainting fit, and was separated for the moment from her husband, whom she would see again, so soon as her strength would permit.

She remained silent, and appeared absorbed in the contemplation of an image which she saw with her spiritual eye All partook of the silence

" I recollect now, how I became ill here," continued she, after a long pause " We have been upon the journey for two months—my strength has been overcome by manifold hardships—and—and I have been obliged to leave my two children behind, at home—it was impossible for me to bring them. All these sufferings have destroyed my nerves—a fever seized me—a paroxysm of delirium, there—out there—when I was—walking along beside my husband I thought of Alvarez, my brother—felt what a consolation it would be for me, if I knew him to be there at home with my children, while I was here with Carlo, in the neighborhood of his prison—then I was seized with a feverish fancy, and it seemed to me as if I saw a man before me—so like my deceased mother—and as if I heard the voice of Alvarez——

" But it was, unhappily, only a feverish fancy !" sighed she, sinking back in her armchair

Robert now entered, and Dr. Thorfin beckoned to him to be silent

" Will you have the goodness to accompany me to my husband?" continued she, after another pause

" Your husband has sent me to you," said Robert, now speaking " My name is Walker. I am an Englishman, lately from Buenos Ayres, here on a visit to my uncle Honor me with some commission May I conduct you, for the present, to my hotel, just here in the neighborhood? Shall I take your effects from on board the vessel, and bring them to you?"

" From Buenos Ayres —— ?" returned Angelica, half to herself " From La Plata river?" from my home?—I thank you—you have then spoken to my husband? Where is he?"

" He has just been taken into the bureau, and will soon receive permission to see you "

" I thank you, I will avail myself of your sympathy I must beg you to send some one on board of the vessel in which we arrived to-day from Porto Seguro I must order my servants—they are blacks—to come on shore with my effects—my waiting-maid is named Helena May I trouble you with these requests? Helena might—bring some linen for my husband—if the effects are not all delivered. I hope they will allow him to change his linen—this evening—and his bed, his mattress—Helena must bring that on shore likewise. May I trouble you with these requests?"

Robert protested his readiness to fulfil her commissions, and repeated his wish to be allowed first to conduct her to a hotel, to which the lady assented

A Portuguese cadeira (an old fashioned postchaise, with curtains, drawn by two negroes) was procured, in which the lady took her seat, and soon arrived in front of the neighboring Hotel du Nord

Dr Thorfin procured female attendance in the apartment of the lady, and prescribed, as physician, the necessary means for refreshing and strengthening her

_ Before Robert hurried on board, the doctor gave him a hint to keep the existence of Alvarez in Rio secret from the lady, for the present, as she considered the encounter a feverish fancy, and the intelligence of her brother's arrest would only, at this moment, heighten her sorrow.

The friends from the Nordstjernan lingered in a saloon of the hotel, in consultation concerning the event which had led to the dangerous arrest of Alvarez.

The Baron de Spandau, "everywhere and nowhere," where there was "any news," rushed into the saloon where they were sitting, and inquired, with great animation, after the health of the lady of whose fainting he had just heard

The friends answered him as coldly as the warm climate of Brazil permitted, which did not seem at all to surprise the obtrusive spy

"And your friend, I hear, has also been accidentally arrested," said he to the doctor "The young man that lives with you—Mr Daily, or whatever his name is—the musician, or type setter, or whatever he is"

"Arrested! I do not believe that!" replied the other, with the utmost indifference "I was in the apothecary's shop when the escort went off, I believe he only followed the crowd We know nothing about his arrest"

"Indeed! you did not know that he had been arrested? but you know that he recognised the young lady, the wife of a faroupilha, as his sister, and she declared him to be her brother?"

"I do not know his family relations," replied the other, with the same indifference as before

"If I can be of service to him, through my acquaintance here, perhaps in obtaining his release, it shall be done with pleasure You know, doctor, I take a warm interest in the unfortunate, especially when I find that they have respectable connexions, as, for example, this young Mr Daily, your guest"

"He will certainly be much obliged to you for your sympathy, Senhor Baron Perhaps you may sooner learn his relations through your acquaintance than through us, for, although he lives with me, my discretion has prohibited me from prying into his secrets It is well known, that almost every man has his own peculiar secrets, or family affairs—affairs of the heart, and political affairs, and there are people in our time who make a business of such secrets"

"Certainly, doctor," replied the baron, a little embarrassed, for he had remarked, long since, that the doctor entertained suspicion against him, "Certainly, doctor! every diplomatist even makes a business of secrets"

He took his leave in all haste, to inform himself, in some of the bureaux, "from pure sympathy," of the particulars of the arrest, in the hope of soon seeing Dr Thorfin again, and left the hotel.

CHAPTER V.

THE LOVING HEART

SINCE the moment in which a suffering wife of a practical man, who had once led or seduced her to the altar, had lost in Robert's arms the consciousness of the world of sense, and awaked to the consciousness of love, the latter found himself in the circumstances of a man who has received his sentence of death, and looks forward to the hour of his execution

The next morning after that memorable night, he left his pavilion very early, to ride, as if seeking at a distance that tranquillity of soul which was now for ever destroyed within him

Robert had never been beloved The sentiment of love, which, in our material century, is ridiculed as "sentimentality," (while without this sentiment, every social connexion of both sexes is a crime against nature,) had long ago seized him, since, in daily confidential intercourse with this unfortunate woman, he had become acquainted with her mind, and attracted towards her by mutual sympathy of soul His love was pure.

It could never be to his reproach, to be penetrated by a feeling, the reciprocation of which might lead to a so called social crime, (in so far as the pure love of Senhora Gracia passed for such) Feeling depends not on our will, and if the will is able to extinguish "feeling" it has never been feeling

It remained in this, as in a thousand similar cases, difficult to decide which of the two had the most to reproach themselves with, or whether both did not stand irreproachable before their own consciences, as before God,

Gracia recognised in Robert's society, in the retrospect upon her married life, that she had not been beloved, that she had never loved The case occurred in her, which Dr Thorfin, in his theory of "conjugal apathy," placed in the third class, among thousands and thousands of similar cases, in the social world of all civilised countries

Both loved each other Gracia's love, also, was pure; so pure as a heart was able to love, under destroying influences of social bonds—which "condemned her love to death," together with her inward life—her soul But an eternal labyrinth of contradictions and inquiries of original womanhood was now revealed to the unfortunate woman—while the question arose whether Robert's love was not rather a consequence of her inclination to him, a result of his noble-minded sympathy in her misfortunes, than original affinity of soul?

This question, perhaps the most original of female originality, (we know no other term for this inexplicable weakness,) now created in her that just as womanly original self-torture, by which she embittered, for herself and her lover, a life that had already become wretched enough through her love.

Gracia had never known love—her heart had no idea of love, as that sympathy of soul which "believeth all things, endureth all things, hopeth all things"—whilst it, as love, at the same time, comprises within itself religious surrender—belief in love.

And that is just the effect of sympathy of soul,

to elevate men into the element of the higher spiritual existence

Materialism denies love, because it denies the Deity, it names "love" sexual instinct, which is proper to every animal, and follows the instinct in the formation of social connexions

But wo to those who make a mistake in their choice, uniting with themselves for ever a being whose inward life stands as rigidly opposed to them as love is to instinct, as spirit to matter.

It is, however, a remarkable and almost inexplicable phenomenon, that men, by their abstract materialism incapable of love, in thousands of cases, choose to form a social connexion with exactly those beings whose individuality stands as rigidly opposed to them as fire to water, and that such beings, in thousands and thousands of cases, allow themselves to be deceived, confounding love with instinct

According to the ordinances of the social world, woman is robbed of her personal and moral freedom, As a maiden with property, she is exposed to the speculations of a man who makes advances to her in order to marry her property As a maiden without fortune, she is the care of her parents, whose so called social duty consists especially in providing for their daughter—in getting her well married An orphan without property, like Gracia, is the most unfortunate creature that can exist upon any one of the planets for a higher destination, since the despotism of social regulations robs her of the right of maintaining her personal and moral independence by a free choice in her love, and often exposes her, besides, to the ill usage of heartless relatives

To an orphan in such a situation, only two ways remain open either as soon as possible to sell her body for life to sustain her outward existence, or, in case no one desires in all haste to purchase her, to seek, in some way or other, according to the measure of her cultivation and her talents, a more worthy situation, provisionally renouncing her "social destination" as woman, to maintain her moral freedom through the avails of her industry

In the latter position, a female would be less likely to fall into the possession of a proprietor, as an article of merchandise, if social regulations did not burden her with the absurd contractions of personal freedom, which (apart from all companionable intercourse) even refuses her the correspondence with any youth or man, or regards it as a social offence in case she has not already proclaimed herself to be the property of the correspondent

The more deeply we penetrate into the absurdity of similar regulations of our age, so much the more striking appears the inexplicable phenomenòn that an intellectual female, in thousands of cases, voluntarily allows herself to be deceived, availing herself of the first approaches of a man, to guaranty her "social destiny as woman," since she at least binds herself by a promise, if the social union at the altar does not take place until years after.

Opposed to the female nature, often distinguished by a touchingly unpretending modesty, we see, in a thousand cases, the impudent arrogance of selfishness apparent in the choice of the man; since, let him be as unintellectual and soulless as he may, he takes to himself a female who in intellectual respects surprisingly exceeds him, although he be not "a man of quality," who might presume to make pretentions to such a woman! In the natural, unpretending modesty of the woman, and in this impudent arrogance of the man, is not only to be found in part the solution of this inexplicable phenomenon, but unhappily, also, in great part, the evil of social incongruities, the source from which manifold social crimes are derived ——

Robert had ended his ride on that morning, and betook himself as usual to his counting house, more than ever oppressed with inward disquietude, and struggling against the impulse which attracted him towards home, to inquire after the health of his friend He was about to leave the city earlier than usual, as he stood, after two o'clock, under the porch of the exchange, and perceived the train of arrested faroupilhas, and soon after the crowd around the group, in which he recognised Alvarez as the principal person

We know to what offers he was impelled by his noble heart, that throbbed more warmly and actively than ever with the exalted sentiments which the glance of his beloved had consecrated within him

Connected with all the other circumstances, there were two negroes and negresses (whose transportation from one province of Brazil into another is charged with duty and excise) to be landed as merchandise from on board the vessel of war Habituated as Robert was to all sorts of business, the landing and visitation of the effects nevertheless demanded time A special permit must be obtained from the guarda mor, as the offices of the alfandega were already closed He had to run and to explain, and hour after hour passed over, until at length, towards sundown, he arrived with the attendants and effects of Senhora Serafini at the hotel

With more eagerness of impatience than ever before, and with such inward longing as perhaps a woman has rarely experienced while waiting for her friend, Gracia looked forward to the return of Robert, as the hands of her watch had reached the hour at which he generally appeared to dinner

A whole hour had elapsed beyond the usual time—and yet another—and another—and still Robert did not appear

In what a labyrinth of care, of fear, and of anxiety, was the poor unfortunate woman sunk, during those hours? Robert had disappeared in the morning without greeting her after breakfast, or saying adieu to her, as he had always done before

What had passed within him since the last eventful meeting? (which she remembered with about the same indistinctness, as did Senhora Serafini her meeting with her brother,) which presented itself to her mind like a dream of delirium Had he formed the resolution to forsake her, to part from her for ever? Perhaps because she now appeared unworthy of his love? Perhaps because she had lost his respect after she, the wife of another, seized with faintness, had lost her conciousness on his breast?

Did he perhaps love her, notwithstanding? Was love the cause, the reason of his resolution to separate from her? And whither had he fled? Where was he? Where did he linger? Who now shared his society, which always wrought so animatingly upon her? Who now, in conversation with him, gazed into his eye, whose glance had obtained such a mysterious power over her? Perhaps a woman—perhaps a female friend? These, and similar heartrending anxieties, considerations, and questions, tormented the unfortunate woman She saw the table covered for three hours, and soon it was three and a half The negresses came with a —stupid question · whether the Senhora would not dine alone, as Senhor Roberto probably would not come?

"Not come!" resounded in her sorrowful breast, and perhaps she would not have seated herself alone at this table for weeks, we will not say never, for Senhora Gracia was a woman, and a woman is more strongly supplied with philosophical self-control than man——

There lies an error in the designation · the "weaker sex" There are more women who declare Werther to be a fool, and cannot conceive why he shot himself, than there are men who, capable of such love, would be able to endure the horrible lot of knowing the woman to whom they were attached by love, to be in the arms of another.——

The sun went down in tropical splendor and magnificence A purple veil was thrown over the whole chain of mountains, behind which it disappeared. Suddenly the glowing red of the mountain summits faded into violet, then into a dusky, azure blue, which became even more dusky, and the mountain ridges now glittered, like a sharp "silhoutte," upon the green and yellowish blue horizon

Horse hoofs clattered up the rock upon the terrace on which the pavilions stood The heart of the sufferer found hardly room enough in her breast for its violent movement "It is he!" cried she, and hurried into Robert's pavilion, while Maria opened the gate, through which a passing confidant of the baron might have been able to see her, if she had remained in the garden

Robert relinquished the bridle of his horse to the negro who usually attended him, and hurrying through the garden to the pavilion of his friend, did not find her, but beheld her through the open window at his writing-desk. He flew over the space that divided them, and found himself immediately in the presence of Madame Closting.

Pale as a marble statue, Senhora Gracia rose from her seat With downcast eyes, she tottered to her friend, moved her hand tremblingly to meet the pressure of his, endeavored to speak, and could utter nothing but the low, hardly audible words. "Robert, can you still respect me?"

"My God, Gracia! respect you?" exclaimed Robert, while he struggled against the violent motion which this question of feminine innocence excited within him. "How came you by this question? by the thought which lies at the foundation of this apprehension? poor, dear, noble woman!" he sighed, pressing her hand, and (the utmost that he durst permit himself in his discreet shyness) imprinting a kiss upon her forehead, as her head sank upon his breast.

"What anxiety have I endured on your ac-count!" began now the tender creature "Where were you so long? I feared that you had——"

"Gone away?" said Robert, smiling, "no, my friend—when I am going away I will take a farewell kiss from you with me, and leave behind with you, instead, what will do you no good—and what I can never obtain again upon earth!—never!"

"Horrible!" sighed Gracia—and Robert found it salutary to interrupt, by a relation of the causes which had prevented him from appearing at the usual time, the situation in which both found themselves So soon as he had uttered the words "the arrival of a lady," the poor woman shrank back convulsively

"A lady has arrived?" cried she, "a lady of your acquaintance—a female friend? How long is it since you have seen her?" inquired she, hastily, gazing at him with a confused glance

"Come to dinner, and I will tell you all about it quietly How could you be so terrified at the first word of my report?"

Both walked into the dining-room of the "Villa Gracia," as Robert named her pavilion He bound the napkin around the little neck of the "little one," seated her upon her little chair next himself, and the "little one" ate her soup, while the friend of her mother continued · "A young lady from the interior of the country——"

"Young? a young lady, do you say?—you ought not to look at a young lady!" interrupted the amiable Brazilian, with all the vivacity of her tropical temperament.

Robert could not restrain his hearty laughter, and proposed an agreement that she should listen to him quietly, until he had arrived at a pause in his relation

"But you must not tell a long story about the young lady; that I will not allow I can and will hear nothing about a young lady for whom you ran about three hours, and—left me here alone"

"Well, then, I will tell you quickly You know what a persecution prevails in the interior of the country, as well as here, against the faroupilhas——"

"Against the rebels! Yes, I know that; they deserve no better"

"Then you are a royalist, as I just now hear!" inquired Robert, with amazement "Is it possible! I did not know that"

"My husband is——" she was just finishing the sentence she had begun, when she suddenly stopped, and with a crimson blush concealed her face, and for a long time did not dare to look up again,

The involuntary allusion to her social position shocked Robert not less than it startled her The thought that a man existed, to whom the earthly covering of the soul that loved him belonged as lawful property, agitated him all the more in contrast with the emotion in the mind of the woman, which the slightest suspicion occasioned, that he, on his part, had only spoken to a female

"Forgive me!" repeated Gracia, offering him her little hand, "I was over hasty——"

"Yes, indeed, you were over hasty," interrupted Robert, taking the word in an entirely different signification, with reference to an event that occurred five years before, "you certainly were over hasty, and might as well have waited until—— nevertheless," pursued he, "I will continue my relation. The arrests in the interior nre going forward, and to-day an escort arrived here with faroupilhas The greater part were from the higher classes of society, among others, a Signore Serafini——"

"An Italian, then?" interrupted his friend "I cannot bear the Italians—that you know"

"I know that many, besides you, cannot bear them," remarked Robert, "and that pains me, for I feel that it is as hard for a nation to be un-understood as it is for a man On the river La Plata there are many Italians, and I love them as I do their nation, apart from the glory of the nation in science and arts Serafini is, be-sides, a Brazilian, born in Brazil, like thousands of Portuguese—will you suppress, for a moment, your natural antipathy, you little Portu-guese·"

"I Portuguese?" exclaimed the young lady, half serious, half laughing "That I deny! I am a Brazilian! and you may see, by my com-plexion, that Indian blood flowed in my ances-tors—genuine Brazilian—and I am proud of it"

"That is true," said Robert, laughing "I have long since made the observation that you were proud—and that particularly pleased me, as I, also, am a 'proud Englishman,' as they call us"

"And you appear to be a republican!" which they are not generally—the English—so far as I have heard

"I have had a tendency to republicanism, since I must admire the struggles of the Orientals against Rosas," replied the "young Englishman," "and I became more and more clear upon the voyage and since I have been here—especially by manifold contact with the fugitives from La Plata river—on board the Nordstjernan——and through the example——of my sister"

"Sister!" interrupted Gracia, with her cus-tomary vivacity, "then you have a sister—indeed? who came with you from Buenos Ayres? I read her name in the Jornal do Commercio, in an old number, lately, in your pavilion, as I arranged the flowers Is your sister handsome?"

"You little simpleton!" answered Robert laughing heartily, "what thought led you to that question? You cannot surely become jeal-ous even of my sister?"

"Become? become?" said Gracia smiling, "as if I should first 'become' jealous! I am jealous! jealous as a loving Brazilian woman—jealous of every being that meets your glance—even of that cat, if you should take her upon your lap—of that aloe, out there, if you look at it too long!—and I should not be jealous of your sister!—— You often, no doubt, give her your hand—— and kiss her on the forehead!—— I will not suffer that! you shall no more press the hand of your sister!"

Robert contemplated, with evident involuntary satisfaction, the glowing of a female nature that loved him, calmly listened to her remarks and commands, and at length said, slowly and with significance· "You will undoubtedly give your hand to some man beside me, and kiss him—— not as I kiss my sister—— and must not I also be jealous?"

A long pause ensued

"Pardon me!" at length began the poor wo-man, laying down her fork and sinking back in her chair.

"Do you know that the thought has occurred to me· never to see him again! never! since I feel that you love me and that I love you But I would also live apart from you I would not burden your name with the disgrace of having dissolved a bond——that has never bound my heart——never!—— I would live retired, in solitude——and read your letters——and write to you—and work as I do now—to be indepen-dent by my industry——to be with you in spirit ——to accompany you in spirit——wherever you may abide'"

"Mother! please to give me another piece of pigeon," sounded the voice of the dear little one shrilly in her ears She shrank back, as if a stroke of lightning had darted into the pavilion She again covered her face with her handker-chief, and wept

Robert had heard the significant revelation of his friend with surprise and sorrow, as it inti-mated to him the sphere of sympathy in which her mind dwelt He had prepared himself for a reply as significant and decided as the result of the impression which this communication wrought upon him, when the word "mother," although uttered in a soft childish voice, also filled his soul with the same discord

The impression of this revelation from the heart of his beloved, in relation to a separation from her husband, was twofold

The purpose of separation, in itself, appeared to the youth on the one hand as the most natural consequence and requisition of that declaration in which the unfortunate woman had affirmed with a sacred oath her love to him, and dedicated to him her heart "for eternity"

The mere thought that Gracia had ever lived in private connexion with a man, (which the existence of the little one unfortunately but too plainly confirmed,) always wrought such bitter and disgusting sensations in the heart of the deeply loving youth, that he, for this very reason, (as we long ago remarked,) even endeavored to deny the reality But so much the more horrible and even unheard of, must the thought be for him, that the woman who, in a state of exalted spiritual life, had avowed her love for him—given him her heart for ever—should demean herself, sooner or later, to the so called fulfilment of conjugal duty in the arms of another—a thought that he could not entertain—that was far from him—since he honored in his beloved the dignity of woman—and woman in the noblest sense of the word

The secondary effect of the impression of the revelation was the suddenly awakened care for Gracia's future, in case she, in the consciousness of her pure love, should feel herself strong enough to despise the judgement of the world, as she had intimated in that hour with such de-termined decision

It appeared evident to him that a third person, whether of the male or female sex, is never able to dissolve a union, if an inward separation, or dissolution of the bond to which the sacrament of marriage was perverted, has not already taken taken place.

If the element of separation has not long since carried through its chemical fermenting and separating process in the interior of the social relation, (that until then had passed for mar-riage,) no third person whatever can effect the disturbance of a union, much less a separation.·

The cause of every divorce lies in the interior of marriage itself, and frequently becomes, as it were, the germ of future disturbance and dissolution in one or in both natures It is carried to the altar with them, as far as it lies in the rugged contrast of both natures, which a sacrament of the church can as little bind to each other as water and fire can unite The germ of such inward separation unfolds itself the more rapidly into blossom and fruit, the more deeply the feelings glow in the one heart that discovers in the other, instead of a return of love, the waste desert of indifference

The external separation of such a compact of propagation, which never existed as a union of souls, is, of course, only a natural realization of the inward dissolution of the marriage, which just as naturally requires no dissolution, since it never was a union of souls

If it were even possible to keep a register over the interior relations of the marriages of our civilized era, which a Parisian Terneau or cashmere shawl (instead of the mantle of Christian love) generally covers in the most discreet manner possible, it might occur that the number of internally dissolved unions would exceed, at least a hundred fold, the number of public separations from bed and board, or formal divorces .

This result of such a (certainly difficult) registration may appear the more natural, the more we observe the shameless levity or dishonorable speculation which marriage involves on the one hand, as a guarantee of existence, or a satisfaction of sensual demands , on the other hand, as a money concern, without regard to sympathy or harmony of character—without love.

As certainly as " no steam engine of sixty horse power " is able to carry off a woman when she herself does not determine and accomplish the carrying off of her lover, just as certainly would a third person never occasion a separation, if the foundation of it had not, as above intimated, long ago been laid in the grounds of the union itself.

Love is nourished by a reciprocal love No man of honor will ever allow a woman who is fettered by social bonds, to perceive a sentiment that, from some unfortunate cause, he may experience towards her, if he has not become convinced, by the most delicate shades of intercourse, of her love to him ; and, even then, the thought of an influence on his part upon the dissolution of the social bond will be far from him.

The same sense of honor, however, which in such a case prescribes the man's duty of action—condemning him to silence, to self denial, and not unfrequently, to death—demands just as unconditionally from the unfortunate woman, in such circumstances, a physical separation from her husband, apart from the consideration whether a public or formal divorce can, under existing circumstances, immediately take place

This alternative presents itself to the woman in the moment of her declaration, and in no manly heart can the sentiment of pure love ever be more sacredly, profoundly, powerfully, and inalienably aroused and nourished, than just through such a declaration of mutual love The love of a man of honor is heightened in such a case, by the accountability with which

destiny has burdened him, in the consciousness of the love of an unfortunate female, who recognised highly valued and involuntary love in him, the man of honor, and to the man of honor revealed her love, and gave herself for ever

Natural as the physical separation of Gracia from her present possessor, or proprietor, appeared to the noble young man, he yet was, for the moment, severely shocked by the thought of becoming, according to the views of the world, the proscribed cause or occasion of a divorce Only Gracia's proud contempt, expressed on that night, for the world and its judgement, could have so suddenly enabled him to soar upwards to a similar elevation, in the consciousness of his love and his duty, in relation to the future of the female who had, with such confidence, placed herself for ever in his heart

We know that in the singular contradiction of his sentiments, Robert sought constantly, and with determination, to banish the thought that the amiable little one was the daughter of Gracia , since his present cognisance of the past night he was less than ever able to allow its natural rights to the often contradicted reality

" No !" cried he, as he saw Gracia's tears flowing, and sprang from his seat , " no ! it is impossible !—it cannot be ! One lie prevails here, conceal it as you may Confirm the sentence of death that seems to have fallen upon me, and in my last hour, I cannot and will not believe that ever a man has embraced you—that this, or any other being upon earth can call you—mother ! You are yourself but a child ! a child whose heart is a bud, which has but just unfolded itself as a flower under the spirit-breath of love !"

" That you should ever have lost your consciousness in the arms of a man without love—! Gracia, you have led me to the brink of lunacy— no !—not you—God forgive me ! not you—you are innocent , and not myself, for my heart is pure, and conscious of no guilt , but if ever an hour should come, in which you should be forced to feign love for a man, to grant him that which only love makes sacred, then—may God forgive you what you have done to me——through your oath !"

The unfortunate woman held out her hand to him, and convulsively pressed his, incapable of returning a word

Some one knocked at the gate, and a negress opened it. It was a confidant of old Moreto, in the Rua dos Ourives, with a note to Senhora Gracia The messenger departed as hastily as he came

She broke open the note with a trembling hand, cast a glance on the first lines which it contained, and her hand fell into her lap, as if paralyzed The note lay on the floor

Robert took it up, and laid it near his friend upon the table

" Read it—I beseech you, read it !" said she, with a broken voice Robert obeyed her request It contained the intelligence, on the part of Senhors Forro and Moreto, that Senhor Closting had arrived in Porta d'Estrela, and would probably be in Rio on the ensuing day

Robert laid the note again beside Madame Closting, and would have left the room " Go to Maria and tell her to make coffee," whispered she in the ear of the little one.

Hardly had the child left the room when Gracia sprung up, threw herself on the breast of her friend, gazed into his eyes, and then sank back again into her chair Robert, who could not avoid partaking of the coffee which the little one had ordered, seated himself again in his place, seized the hand of his friend, and lingered, as before, in her society—banishing, with all the power of his will, the thought that the paper of the note just received was paper, and that the little one was the daughter of the "child" with whose hand he played as if it never—had been thown away

———⁓⁓⁓⁓✿⁓⁓⁓⁓———

CHAPTER VI

BLUESTOCKING

Miss Susan Thomson had hitherto developed as little talent for observation and perception as any English young lady from one of the finishing schools, where she is impressed with the idea that she must not notice nor observe any thing, in order not to compromise her respectability by taking notice of an object not belonging to the fashionable world She had, nevertheless, in the first week that she was in the company of Miss Fanny from Buenos Ayres, (or Senhora Isabella, as she was generally called there,) made the observation that that young lady was a bluestocking—an extravagant bluestocking

The basis of the English social relations rests upon the massive materialism that looks upon every intellectual or spiritual tendency as superfluous, every talent, no matter what, as a subordinate object, which can be paid for with money, and consequently is, in itself, a branch of industry, like any other manufacturing or productive labor

A man or youth in England, who is distinguished for any talent, or a desire for intellectual development, is on that account a "misfortune to his family," which, in proportion to the degree of its "respectability," becomes the more sensitive, the more such a talent asserts its intellectual originality

In consequence of these laws of English prejudice, the English author, on appearing before the public, wraps himself in the strict incognito of anonymousness, and often hides from his nearest relatives, the mental activity that inspires him

Only in particular cases, when extraordinary success crowns his efforts, or his personal independence with rank and title enable him to overcome the judgement of his family, does he appear in his true name His position then becomes an object of curiosity, for the world only tolerates him at most, and treats him in his presence as one suffering under a nervous disease, but by anonymous attacks, and when his back is turned, mercilessly treads him into the dust where he belongs.

If an author in England, without fortune, is placed on the same footing with a servant, and stands proscribed, it is no wonder that a woman in England, whether poor or rich, fashionable or not, finds a hell upon earth when she manifests any intellectual or spiritual tendency, or occupies herself with literature

In accordance with the above prerogatives of condition, rank, and title, a Lady Morgan, Lady Blessington, etc , is merely tolerated, because she may defy, in her social position, the world that fawns about her , but such a spirit, nevertheless, remains subjected by the "rigid supervision" of the absolute despotism of British regulations, to the condition of not rising by any literary step or mental flight above the barriers which prejudice and fashion have placed there as British

These barriers of British prejudice and fashion are a Chinese wall, by which every Englishman is constantly surrounded, wherever he transports his home.

An Englishman, impelled by "unfortunate inclination" to scientific, intellectual, or literary labors, (however they may be named,) is regarded by his relatives as a patient, and they consider it to be their duty to make every endeavor to cure his disease, in which, alas ! they do not always succeed The undeniable "British consequence" with which the Englishman carries about with him, to all parts of the world, the element of his British existence, (as if it were a portable atmosphere,) stamps the Englishman as "English," and as such he lives and moves everywhere, whether as a travelling gentleman, or as a man of business, in the fast bound Chinese barriers of British prejudices

Dolores, besides her many prominent qualities, (which we have occasionally before spoken of,) possessed a certain unity of being, such as few men have, which consists in clearness of self-knowledge, in the consciousness of moral and spiritual strength, and in the strong necessity of making our actions and course of life correspond with our convictions and our knowledge

This unity of being is a rarity, and is generally misunderstood, as refractoriness and exaggeration, for social despotism desires a general levelling, above which no moral independence shall elevate itself in contradiction to the universal prescriptions of fashion and prejudice

This spiritual unity of being is the strict reverse of "British originality" The first rests upon moral freedom, the last is founded on moral and social slavery The former acknowledges the intellectual as the basis of existence ; the latter form fashion

As "original" as the personal originality of an Englishman may appear, it is, nevertheless, characterized by the unconditional slavish observance of form—British fashion.

The spiritual unity of being is manifested in the moral strength of conviction, in the consciousness of moral freedom, which directs all its actions in accordance with nature and reason British originality acknowledges no moral freedom, much less its power , and all the laws of nature and reason, all freedom of will and action, are subjected to the laws of British fashion, the violation of which is the crime of all crimes

Should a being possessing such spiritual unity come in contact with the British social world, they would judge it according to the first law of human judgement, (which we have mentioned before,) after him or herself, and, consequently, entirely falsely, because the Briton, influenced in his judgement by his British element, remains always · a Briton.

Therefore moral freedom and mental independence appear to the Briton, wherever he finds them, as prejudice ; for, in his British preoccupation he is incapable of a logical conclusion. He draws his conclusions in regard to others after himself, and in case he meets with an individuality which he (with the best will in the world) does not understand, he regards it as a " queer originality "—a result of spleen.

Dolores was considered by the Thomsons as a young lady who, taken up with prejudices, suffered from "spleen," which Miss Susan Thomson wished, by some means, " to drive out of her head "

But, alas ! Miss Susan soon perceived that all her efforts were lost on Miss Isabella, and that she was the most extravagant bluestocking that ever took a worldly book or pen and ink in hand Such a " misfortune in Miss Susan's family," appeared to her greater every day, especially as the bluestocking was to marry her nephew. She even remarked, when she quite unintentionally went into Miss Isabella's room, that she sometimes wrote verses without having Byron's Childe Harold before her, and consequently must, indeed, be an intellectual productive poetess. It was almost incredible, but alas ! it was true ; Miss Susan had seen it with her own light gray eyes

Señora Isabella had become an abomination to the mistress of the heart of the Baron de Spandau , she wished her out of the house, in short and good If this " strange person " was to marry her nephew, it should only take place upon the condition that the baron should marry her—herself—Miss Susan Thomson. That was her resolution , that was the rule of all her actions towards the " strange person," as well as towards the amiable baron , and she hoped, after prudent and clever reflection, to break a way for her own marriage by promoting that of Isabella

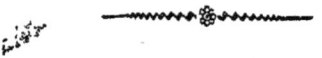

CHAPTER VII.

THE DECLARATION

One day the baron visited the lady of his heart. She sat in her myrtle bower on the garden terrace, and hastened, as usual, as joyfully to meet the object of her longing as the laws of fashion permitted. It was towards evening, and, in fact, not so oppressively warm as it had been some hours before in that same day ; but the baron found it " very warm" in the arbor, and proposed to accompany the lady into the house. He seemed to " have something upon his mind," from which he would certainly prefer to unburden himself between four walls, rather than in a transparent myrtle bower The baron was a man of feeling—of soul—and there are conferences which excite the feelings, agitate the soul, and can bring tears into a man's eyes, which the black gardener and other negroes

did not need to see The baron said but little until they entered the green parlor, he walked silently along by the side of Miss Thomson his silence only spoke the more He evidently had something on his mind that must now come out —must come out at last—at last—for he had now been her brother's " intimate family friend " long enough, and if he really "had a design upon his sister," it was at last time to declare himself The laws of the social world required a declaration

Miss Susan's countenance expressed a heaviness of heart, as she stepped by the side of Monsieur le Baron, and into the green parlour , she then sank upon the sofa At the same time he found the warm draught of air a little too cool, and shut to the side doors which offered a view of the famous platform scales

All was then right , the adorer of Miss Thomson was now about to come to the point, and to make his declaration

If this is a case that takes place a million times a year, in different parts of the world, and, of course, may seem quite an ordinary occurrence, this case was, nevertheless, no ordinary occurrence to the young lady—who was driving from the quarantine of her maidenly condition into the open roads of hopelessness. On the contrary, it was to her the most novel and strange event that could ever happen to her , it never had occurred to her—no, never, in the whole course of her life—and she had lived long enough to have had time for such a case to arrive

These thoughts or considerations were substantially those which were unconsciously expressed in Miss Thomson's thin, but, for all that, (according to her own conviction,) very handsome face

The baron had closed the doors, and at her very hospitable invitation, had seated himself by her side, in a very wide armchair, close by the end of the sofa, upon which her left arm rested She had, quite accidentally, so placed herself that her right hand remained free, in case that in any particular result of the confidential conference politeness should require her to give her hand to the baron

" Miss Thomson," the baron at last began, and turned, quite accidentally, a ring which he wore, among others, on the little finger of his left hand, and which she had never observed there before , " Miss Thomson, I have had the honor, for more than a year, of being considered as the friend of your brother, and as a friend of your family, and I can partly ascribe it to the respectability of my family relations in Europe, that I am allowed to visit at your house, a position which I can appreciate as it deserves "

The baron had brought forth this masterly, rhetorical introduction with so much ability, that he could not help admiring himself, and for that purpose, paused a moment Miss Susan's *fraise*, or chemisette, over that flat portion of her body which generally (somewhat more rounding) covers the female heart, moved It was evidently some inward emotion, which had penetrated into Miss Thomson's being, some agitation of feeling, (what she was never before conscious of possessing,) or a physical emotion of the heart, in consequence of a strange oppressiveness and anxiety; or, be it what it may, the emotion was there. The snow white muslin, about a span below the hollow of the neck, moved and moved, in such a manner that it was plainly to be seen that she was laboring under some anxiety She was anxious that the baron would not turn about when he got half way, but safely arrive at his destination, and " propose "

" You are sufficiently well acquainted with me, Miss Thomson, with my character as a gentleman, with my behavior as a man of honor, and with my respectability, which alone gave me courage to approach you with a revelation, or rather a declaration, which my character as man requires of me, and which, Miss Thomson, can neither surprise nor offend you, if you consider the impression that you have never failed to make upon me "

At the second period of this rhetorical proposal, the muslin moved more violently than before The face of the young lady was suffused by a deep red, which is only to be seen in Brazil in the reflection of sunset upon the horizon, (without any allusion to the approaching evening of life of the young lady on the sofa near the baron)

" Miss Thomson," he at last continued, " I like, as a man, to pursue a straightforward course, and therefore take the liberty of disclosing to you, in all brevity, that my adoration for you, of which you have long been aware, was connected with a feeling that no language can express, but which has brought me to the resolution of placing my future life in your hands, to choose you to judge me and this step, while I declare to you, that I would consider it as my greatest happiness to offer to you, Miss Thomson, my future existence, my life, my fortune, my Self, to lead at your side a quiet, peaceable, retired life, to prepare such a life for you, to enjoy it with you, under the protection of Providence, which knows the purity of my heart, and in its mysterious ways has conducted me into your presence " The baron had happily completed this third and concluding period of his rhetorical composition, fetched a long breath, seemed much affected, and wiped his eyes—as if that was necessary

Miss Susan likewise drew a long, long breath, and the eyes of both met

Far be it from us to say that an expression of reply, or of inward emotion, was apparent in Miss Susan's look, as it met that of the baron Miss Susan's muslin was moved, she suffered anguish—the anguish of death, but merely from uncertainty in her highly wrought expectation Her anguish was passed ; the sum of sums, the addition of all the rhetorical forms with which Monsieur le Baron decorated his proposal, satisfied her calculation Miss Thomson now knew where she stood ; but it would have been contrary to all tact and *ton,* to let the baron know where *he* stood She therefore took a long, long breath, looked upon the baron with the most maidenly timidity and embarrassment that was at her command, since she had systematically learned in the last lessons of her finishing school (to be sure a very long time before) what behavior was proper for such an occasion, which, sooner or later, must present itself at least once in the life of every young lady, unless the devil should have entered the family papers instead of the swine.

She replied with a kindness and mildness, but with a seriousness and dignity that no one but a lady of such respectability would be capable of expressing

" I thank you, baron—for the confidence with which—you have just honored—me, and will endeavor to—consult with my God and—with my self about this step of—my life, so important for you as for me, and I shall—take the liberty to inform—my brother of this affair, and will give you—my answer through—through Mr Thomson—to-morrow—if possible "

The baron, from his business knowledge in such matters, had not anticipated any other answer, and had prudently informed his friend, Mr Thomson, of his resolution, some hours before, at their common dinner in the Hotel Farou Mr Thomson, as a man of experience in this department of social business, received the preliminary communication of his future brother-in-law as one which he had long expected, and wished the baron " success in the result of his visit at Bota Fogo "

However, he did fail to ask him, incidentally, to be allowed to inspect his family documents, from which it might be seen that his mother had been a countess so and so, his aunt a marchioness so and so, his father the Baronet de Spandau, Knight of the Order of the Black Eagle, of the Order of Wladimir of the first class, and of the Order of the Danish Elephant and the Austrian Rhinoceros, and as to his fortune, Mr Thomson could inquire at the Russian Consul's, who " knew his circumstances," and would at any time give the necessary information respecting him, in person, to such a man as Mr Thomson.

The importance and originality of the baron's visit, in itself, did not allow him, for this time, to remain longer in Miss Susan's bewitching society He took his leave with all the ceremony that had become a second nature to him as a former ensign of the royal Prussian infantry, and which is universally acknowledged as the mark of a " refined education."

It was well known that Miss Thomson was an English woman, and had passed through the first years of youthful levity. Long consideration, reflection, deliberation, viewing the matter on this side and that, consultation with herself, her brother, and her God, was not so requisite as the formal betrothal at the expiration of the stated time, and the " to-morrow " which she had appointed—(for, alas ! she could not consistently set a shorter term)

As it is much more difficult in England for a female to get a husband than in any other country in the world, an English woman can appreciate the act of betrothal ; and only in England, and among people of English descent, are " suits for breach of promise of marriage" ever thought of, which would offend the feelings of delicacy of the women of other nations

---

CHAPTER VIII

" ALL RIGHT "

MR. GEORGE THOMPSON returned home to tea, and found Miss Fanny and Miss Susan walking in the garden, arm in arm, a thing that had never happened before Miss Susan appeared unusually cheerful

"How are you, Miss Thomson?" the old widower called out to her, smiling mischievously, "I congratulate you"

The most maidenly blush that ever suffused Miss Susan's cheeks, "since the memory of man," rose close up under her light gray eyes It was the first blush of maidenly self-satisfaction that she had ever experienced, the blush of a virgin whose virginity was embellished by that social solidity which time alone can give, and which we find in Old England indicated in large letters and figures on a dairy (milk shop) or other " institute," where we read

" ESTABLISHED 1787 "

As little expression as Miss Susan manifested in her look when the baron had completed his proposal, so much expression now appeared about the corners of her mouth, as she, with an ineffably naïve smile, gave her brother to understand, that he should not be indiscreet, and betray, before Señora Isabella, that she was, so to say, "a bride"

"Can I invite the baron to dinner to-morrow, with a few friends? say Dr Thorfin, and His Excellency the Ambassador of His Highness of Kniphausen?" Mr George asked, after he had heartily shaken the hands of both ladies, and played a moment with Miss Fanny's hand

That was a delicate question, Miss Susan now had to give a decisive yes or no She considered, as long as her inward impatience was able to keep itself down, (to avoid the least appearance of youthful levity,) and at last lisped "Yes"

Mr Thomson now introduced his sister to Miss Fanny, "as the betrothed of the Baron de Spandau," just as Robert entered the garden, the old widower then informed him, in his liveliest manner, and with the greatest formality, of the betrothal, which was to be celebrated the next day

Robert's face suddenly lost its color, and then became overspread with the manly red of the ebullition of suppressed bitterness He looked back upon Senhora Gracia's communication, as well as the many remarks of Dr Thorfin, concerning the future member of the family—the spy, in whose hands lay the fate of Dolores, and this last circumstance enforced upon him—silence

We have long since observed that Mr George Thomson was a "man of business," who usually carried out what he undertook or had resolved upon He had, as is well known, resolved to marry Señora Dolores, and now resolved that three weddings should be celebrated on one day, somewhere in common, on board of some vessel—namely, his, the baron's, and Robert's wedding Robert had this evening happened there very opportunely, as he wished to speak with him about this business, as far as Mr Robert Walker was personally interested in it

The young Englishman had drank his coffee after dinner in Senhora Gracia's company, as usual, and had smoked a Manilla segar, the scent of which was very agreeable to her when a part of it came from Robert's mouth He had left his friend, in order to pay a hasty visit to his relatives.

"Bob!" cried his old uncle to him, as the ladies went into the green parlor, where the tea was ready "Bob, I have a word to say to you in haste——' We will come to tea in a moment," he interrupted himself, calling to the ladies through the open window

Robert remarked that what his uncle had to say to him must be something important, because he wished to despatch it in a hurry, and because he had placed both hands behind his back—an evidence of deep reflection on his part

"Why do you not bestow your confidence upon me" he commenced, after Robert had stepped upon the terrace, where nobody heard them

"How so, Uncle George?"

"I mean why do you not confide to me what you carry in your heart? for you need the advice of a friend"

"I carry something in my heart? What makes you think so?"

"Well, now, there is no need of shooting around the corner, we might as well fire at the mark at once You are in love, and must get married"

Robert stared at his good old uncle with unfeigned astonishment

"Well, indeed! you need not wonder at my second sight, I have long known that you are in love, and, if I am not mistaken, are loved in return All right, there is nothing in the way I have inquired about her, unknown to you She is an excellent woman, of good family, of sufficient respectability she has been circumvented and seduced into marriage by a man whose baseness she found out after it was too late, she has separated from him, can procure a divorce, and then, after a few months, you can marry her If you need money until that time, if she should need money to arrange matters with her previous husband, who knows how to value money—don't hesitate to take what you may require, a couple of thousand pounds or so, to buy her off Don't hesitate in the least I will advance to you from my private funds, it will have nothing to do with our house, nor your father But endeavor to bring it about soon Hark ye, Bob! lose no time Be quick about it And now come to tea"

The decided, dry exchange manner with which Mr Thomson treated this "business," proved to him but too plainly that the whole affair was sober earnest

Robert had become more and more surprised at every word he heard, and was about to utter the most solemn protestation, that he was not in love with any woman who was the lawful property of another, when his uncle added the invitation, "come to tea," and hastily left him The thought that his relation to Madame Closting had been discovered by some to him inconceivable means, and as it seemed had already been spoken of somewhere, startled the noble youth, whose delicacy equalled his love. But as soon as he came to himself again after—such a surprise, his uncle's conduct did not appear at all strange to him He knew the old man, and his way of doing business; he might be assured that he had conducted himself in this affair with the greatest prudence, for he regarded it as a matter of business, and nobody could keep a business secret better than Mr. George Thomson

Robert was aware of this characteristic of his uncle, and remained self-absorbed, standing upon the terrace, until he was again called to tea.

Uncle George had awakened a thought in him that was not entirely new to him, since Senhora Gracia had informed him of her intentions in that regard—the thought of realizing his spiritual connexion with Gracia by a social tie. He enclosed the whole train of ideas in the sanctuary of his heart, and walked towards the green parlor to tea.

"I hear that one of your travelling companions of the Nordstjernan, has been arrested to-day," remarked Mr Thomson, continuing his relation of the news of the day, as Robert entered the room.

Dolores, to whom these words were directed, grew pale. "One of my travelling companions of the Nordstjernan? not Hinango?" she asked, with involuntary animation.

Robert felt that it was too late to give his unsuspecting uncle a criticising look, who, besides, had not the least idea of a spiritual connexion between the passengers of the Nordstjernan.

"Oh! no!" replied the old man in answer to Dolores' question, "by no means, Captain Hinango is well, and at liberty; I spoke to him to-day in Mr Vernon's company. The music-teacher has been arrested—Alvarez. He has found his sister here, the wife of a very rich fazendeiro, who was brought here as a prisoner of state from Porto Seguro. He is a very respectable man—very rich—but he has unfortunately "meddled with politics." He is a republican, and is in chains. And his wife must be a noble woman—an excellent woman—a pattern of a woman, she accompanied him two whole months upon the journey, in the greatest misery. I have made inquiries; there are houses here from Bahia that know what he is worth—Senhor Serafitini, or whatever is his name."

Women, no matter of how contracted a mind, have a peculiar "instinct" to control the affairs of the heart of others, and of getting hold of this or that secret, a quality in which they might put to shame many an agent of the secret police, in respect to men's secrets.

Dolores had no sooner uttered the word Hinango, in the above question, than Miss Susan would have bet her head that she was in secret connexion with no one else than Hinango. How and by what means she arrived at this certainty, can more easily be illustrated by the example of the most narrow-minded woman in a similar instance, than we can explain.

If love makes tolerant, (as we have before remarked in relation to Miss Fanny and the religious differences of those around her,) the eve of a betrothal makes a liberal philanthropist of a selfish old maid, and an obliging, magnanimous friend of a suspicious aunt. Dolores became lost in reflection at this detached relation of her old friend, and imagined herself in the position of Alvarez' sister.

The first and most natural consequence of her thoughts, was to wish nothing more ardently than to visit that lady, to seek her friendship, and console her. Before she found words to reply to the old man's communication, Miss Susan took up another thread of the discourse, and turned to her brother with peculiar good nature:

"Then you saw Captain Hinango to-day in company with Mr Vernon? will you not invite him with Dr Thorfin? it seems that they are very intimate friends?"

"Who?" replied the old widower, who had received this last remark in an entirely different sense from that in which it was intended, "who are intimate friends?"

"I mean Dr Thorfin and Captain Hinango."

"That may be," replied Mr George, very coolly, with a glance at Dolores, who, likewise a woman, had as readily remarked "what quarter the wind came from," that now so suddenly filled the sails of hospitality of the "young lady" who poured out the tea.

"I have long designed to request you, uncle, to invite Mr Hinango here," interposed Robert, "for he was very polite to Miss Fanny and me—as attentive as a gentleman could be."

"So!" remarked the old man, with a peculiar intonation, turning to Miss Fanny, "so he was very polite to you—very attentive, indeed!"

"He does his nation honor as a gentleman on his travels," replied Miss Fanny, with indifference. "I hear that he is a Russian, and the Russian gentlemen are universally known by a certain *savoir vivre.*"

"That must be admitted, they are almost as well bred and polished as our Englishmen," affirmed Mr Thomson.

"In other respects," continued Miss Fanny, "Hinango is a visionary, one who is always soaring in the upper regions, and often becomes rather tiresome to us here on earth."

"So I hear, so I hear, just as you say," interrupted the old man, while Robert endeavored to keep from smiling, and Miss Susan did not allow herself to be in the least deceived by Miss Fanny's tactics.

"That is the very reason why I will not invite him here to-morrow," continued Mr Thomson, "otherwise it would not be inadvisable, for there cannot be too many witnesses at such a ceremony, and because Captain Hinango has done business with us to-day. He bought some cannons of us, six twelve-pounders, some Scotch sail-cloth, and a chest of small arms, and the like, for his Vesta. He is going to the coast of Africa for negroes, and will load for St. João de Macahé, we will then, probably, have other business to do with him."

"Don't let them stand in the way of your inviting the Russian Captain," observed the niece from La Plata, "on the contrary, I cannot only endure his society, but I find him at times quite sufferable, and he even amuses me."

"Well, then, he shall amuse you to-morrow," said Mr Thomson, smiling, who for the last two months had not had the least cause to be jealous of Hinango.

"So, then, to-morrow?" added Robert, and arose to go home. "I can call at Dr Thorfin's, in my neighborhood, this very evening, and invite him and Hinango to dine with us to-morrow."

"And I will invite the baron myself," rejoined Mr Thomson, with a significant glance at his sister; "and I will likewise personally invite the ambassador from Kniphausen."

"Let him stay away, uncle," observed Robert, "he is so strange to us."

"But he is a diplomatic person, and the whole is to be a diplomatic dinner," said Mr Thomson, smiling; "and besides, we shall do his excellency of Kniphausen a service, for he lives at the hotel, and selects his dishes from a bill of fare. He saves every dinner that he is invited to eat. If his position would allow it, he would invite himself to dine at a different place every day, but the clerks here eat at the same table with their principals, and that incommodes him, and when he has to go in the country, the carriage or boat hire costs more than his dinner at the Faroux, and that he will be glad to save to-morrow by our invitation."

"Well, then, to-morrow at four o'clock?" Robert again asked, as he took his hat—but he suddenly remained a moment, sunk in deep thought. It occurred to him, that Mr Closting would probably return, while he would be assisting at the baron's betrothal. He pressed his sister Fanny's hand with unusual agitation, and she remarked that his trembled violently, and was of a feverish heat.

"What is the matter with you, Robert?" she asked, with a tone in which was mingled sisterly affection and love. "What ails you?"

"Nothing—nothing," he exclaimed, and hurried away.

"Strange!" said Miss Susan, looking after her nephew for some time; "I never saw him so before—never!"

"He'll soon get over that, I know what ails him!" exclaimed Mr Thomsom, "it is your betrothal to-morrow, and no letter yet from Buenos Ayres. Why should that not make a little impression on him?"

"If news and consent do not come soon," remarked Dolores, in her character of runaway betrothed, "we will make short work, and follow your example, Miss Thomson."

"Yes, that we will, indeed!" cried the old widower, "that we will! pity that it cannot take place to-morrow!"

"Do not forget to invite his Reverence for to-morrow, whispered Miss Thomson," "you ride directly by his door."

"That's very true!" replied he, "an ecclesiastic must be present at the betrothal! that is an old Anglo-Saxon custom." And the tea session was raised.

CHAPTER IX.

THE CAST-AWAY.

It was about ten o'clock, on the evening of the same day, when the Baron de Spandau was seated at supper with his friend Fortuna, in the old garden house, not far from the Campo da Santa Anna. This friend was likewise an English woman——Miss Sarah * * * *, who at that time bore in Brazil the name of Fortuna. She had sailed from England in a vessel with full three hundred passengers, bound for Sydney, they had arrived at about 20° south latitude, when a fire broke out on board, and nothing but the young captain's presence of mind saved the ship and the passengers, of whom two young girls had already thrown themselves overboard in the first moment of terror. The ship was still four

hundred miles from the coast of Brazil. The captain resolved, if possible, to go into the harbor of Rio, and happily succeeded. The case was examined, and it was discovered that some of the outer planks were burnt in many places to the depth of half an inch.

Sarah had not thrown herself overboard. She found in Rio a friend of old acquaintance from Europe, who solemnly promised her marriage, which induced her to remain there when the ship set forth on its voyage. Hers was the everlasting old story of a poor betrayed girl. Sarah, who could find no employment where negro slaves were preferred to white people, threw herself into the arms of another friend, who had compassion on her, and remained her "friend" until he left her. She then became the friend of a man who called himself Mr Albert ——, and gave her for a residence the garden house, in which he transacted his private business with all sorts of agents.

Sarah was very pretty, she passed for beautiful, and was noticed for her gracefulness in Rio. She was a blonde, tall and slender, with a dazzlingly fair complexion, and strong and rapid in her manner and movement. Her real English national countenance was adorned by a peculiarly mild, good hearted expression.

Senhora Fortuna sat next her friend, on a well stuffed sofa, in lightest négligé, though with well arranged hair, she ate oysters, and ananas, and turtle soup, and confectionery, and drank one glass of champagne after another, and was very talkative.

Besides some lithographs from Walter Scott's "Heart of Mid-Lothian" and "Pirate,' a well toned guitar hung on the wall. As a Suabian once answered, who was asked "Can you play on the Violin?" "I don't know, really—I have never tried"—so had Sally been musical before she learnt any instrument, and after a few hours of instruction, accompanied her natural voice very harmoniously with the guitar.

"You need only say," continued the Baron in conversation, "that you accidentally learned her address—when she comes to you in the morning, but if you ever let it be perceived that you know me, or are in communication with me, then we are two! mark that!"

"Oh, yes, I mark that!" replied the poor creature, "and her name is Pusy, and she's an Irish woman?"

"Lucy is her name, not Pusy! and she is a daughter of the "ever green Erin"—and her friend is called Patrick Gentleboy——a boatman on the bay. And because I want to know what is in the fellow—you understand me?—I find it necessary that you should spy him out a little."

"Spy him out!" said Miss Sally, laughing loudly, "what may not a passably handsome English woman become, when the vessel gets on fire under her in the midst of the ocean?— now I am to become a spy at length! that is a neat office!—Drink! spy!—drink!—you are a spy! are you not? there, take your glass! long life to espionage! I don't want to know who you spy for."

"How came you by the idea that I might be a spy?" inquired the Baron with evident surprise.

"How did I come by the idea? I smelt it. You have often admired my fine nose, and said it was Grecian !— whether it is Grecian or Turkish—it is all the same ! but fine it is ! Drink then ! Albert !—my Prince Albert !— oh how you please me to day !— long life to you Prince Albert, drink ! don't be a fool ! how can you think that I take you for a spy ? you don't appear clever enough to me for that !— and if you were one, and wanted to engage me to spy with you and for you, you would have come to the right person !— but I do nothing gratis ! that you know !—— Drink ! and don't be a fool ! Do you want me to believe that you are a spy or that you are not a spy ? I will believe whatever suits you, so long as I suit you ! and so long as you have money and provide me with champagne ! Drink, spy or no spy !"—

"Bebida !" cried she with a high intonation, and ringing at the same time her table bell The waiting woman appeared in her coffee sack, with a similingly grinning countenance, murmuring her "Senhora——Dabedikademlcfedanalafi —hi-hi-hi ! Vinho ? Senhora, vinho ?" inquired she, as Sarah pointed out to her the empty bottle "Senhor de Montevideo is waiting below—— Senhor—— Dabedikademlienla——"

"Let him wait ! and bring wine ! of the same sort !" Shame-pain !

"Yes, Senhora, Shame-pain !" grinned Bebida, and turning towards the door, stuck the neck of the empty bottle into her little mouth, and let the last drops fall upon her tongue

"There, drink the glass out ! and bring another up with you !" cried Fortuna to her, handing her the glass she had just filled

"I wish I had always been a woman like Bebida !" said she, half aside, "just like Bebida—as ugly as night, and dry and dwarfish like Bebida."

"How so ? for what ?"

"Then I should not be here in your arms and should need no champagne that I might fulfil my service—and forget——"

"The devil take me-lan-cho-ly,"

interrupted she herself, singing with a melodiously clear voice

"The devil take me me-lan-cho-ly ;
Only one life on earth is allowed us
And when for the grave they enshroud us,
Too early it ever will be, will be ?
Too early it ever will be !"

repeated she, throwing herself back on the sofa

"Then you are not willing to be in my arms ? I did not know that," said the baron

"Have I not said 'that you were not famous for wit in your own country !" If I am only in your arms, wheher willing or unwilling, it is all the same to you, as it is to every man who only wants to have a woman in his arms ! Swig ! swig ! I tell you, and hide your stupidity ! You know that I am yours because you give me what I require, and many thousands of women partake of my lot ! but they are more clever than I was and not so open hearted as I.—— Have I ever teased you to marry me or to give me a living, to secure my future ? Since one man deceived and circumvented me, I love you all, as cannibals ! My Scot, who took possession of me here on board the vessel as an old friend, that was a gentleman ! who deceived me, like a gentleman—and I shall never allow myself to be deceived again "

Bebida came in with a bottle, and handed the Senhora at the same time the guitar also While the Baron started the cork, Sarah sang, with peculiar expression .

"A health then, to true sym-pa-thy !
You may purchase or sell what is human,
Making—Heaven knows what, of a woman—
But a traffic in hearts cannot be ? "|

Bebida laughed loudly, as if the song was given for her particular entertainment "Senhora—sing—bonito—sing !— vinho, more vinho —more sing bonito ! dabedikadem—— lapitafikadembedi—hi-hi-hi !" murmured and laughed she and withdrew

The spy had opened the bottle with masterly ability Fortuna held forth the glass, and the medicine which is recommended to married women by so many physicians pearled and foamed

"Had you ever a mother ?" inquired Sarah of the Baron, without looking at him, as she carried the glass to her burning lips

"How so, you little fool ?"

"Oh, because ! I only think she must have been a sigular woman !"

"How so ?"

"Because she had a son who cannot love "

"How do you know that I cannot love ?"

"Because you would then offer a woman something else besides money and champagne

' The devil take me-lan-cho-ly !'"

continued she, suddenly singing out, and striking powerfully on the strings

"The devil take me-lan-cho-ly—'
What's the use of the 'holy alliance ?'
I'll rather set forms at defiance,
Than be sold out of hy-po cri-sy ' ||:

The devil take hy-po cri sy—'
Whoever herself is deceiving,
Or flatters a man for a living,
Soon or late very wretched will be "

"Drink spy ! and go down to your deputy spy, and send Lucy to me to-morrow, and I will spy for you so that you shall never forget me But you must send me the shawl that I saw to-day in the Rua do Ouvidor ! for I am a woman, and will do any thing for a shawl It is only two hundred millreis You know I'm modest You know the shop, the shop under my patronage ! The shawl hung right at the entrance—with a sky blue ground—and a million colors—in the border and centre ! I will use it for the present as a bed covering, because it is too hot here to wear a shawl, but I will not live forever in this land of lizards ! Your health spy ! and now go down stairs and come again soon "

The baron withdrew, seeming not exactly to understand his confidante He was almost sorry that he had recommended Lucy to her through a third person as seamstress But he had remarked that Patrick resorted in the evening to the house where she worked, and had seen her one evening in the neighborhood of the chacara where Dr. Thorfin lived.

"If it does no good, it can do no harm," thought he, as he went to Señor Prole in his audience chamber.

Although it is well known that the secret policy of the state, as well as of the church, in all countries where they organize their web, seek the particular co-operation of a certain class of the female sex, and menials of all classes, yet experience shows that many mistakes are nevertheless made in this manner.

If we consider the element of female nature as the basis of all social relations, (as we have formerly explained the influence of woman upon every age,) the duty of humanity would lead us to lighten a degradation of the female sex, whose guilt is not borne by the woman alone as an individual, but will fall upon the conscience of the whole social world, if it have a conscience in our age

We behold woman robbed of all social independence, as the slave of the regulations which restrict her moral freedom, robbed of the right of a free choice with respect to the most sacred connexion, and all these regulations and restrictions springing from the hypocritical pretence of the " promotion of morality "

A girl in Sarah's circumstances leaves her country with a hundred other families, that they may not starve there on the threshold of an episcopal palace, which is sustained by a yearly income of from fifty to sixty thousand pounds sterling She seeks some honest existence afar off, instead of falling a prey to poverty in London, where the Statistics number from eighty to a hundred thousand publicly degraded females, in a population of about a million and a half, independently of the hundred thousand degraded in private ——

This prompts the searching question for humanity Did a single one of these unfortunate creatures choose degradation voluntarily ? did a single one cast herself voluntarily upon such moral wretchedness, without gliding down, step by step, (through shameful seduction and breach of faith in man, or moral destruction by education and example,) into the abyss of ruin, in which the heartless condemnatory sentence of the world loads her with contempt and scorn ?

Where Di Thoufin maintains as a psychologist, " married women seduce, maidens are seduced," every keen observer will not only agree with him, but will recognise the logical conclusion that the demoralization of our epoch lies founded in the immorality of the man, since no female would become degraded if she were not seduced, and then, being forsaken by the man, left a prey to open disgrace and wretchedness

On the other hand, we venture to affirm that no wife would intentionally seduce a youth or man, if she had always been allowed the right of moral independence and free choice for the most sacred of all bonds But always, and above all, however, the guilt falls upon the man who seduces a female without love, whether it be with or without the permission of the church

It would be a painful subject of psychological research, to decide whether the moral wretchedness of a woman, the suffering of her heart, be more keen, more terrible in the openly degraded woman, in whom feeling more or less is blunted, or in the unfortunate wife, who, retaining the profoundly delicate sentiment of noble womanhood, is, without love, placed by social regulations at the disposition of a man whom she can neither love nor respect ——

Is not every physical surrender of woman without love, Prostitution, whether the rights of the man are secured by ordinances or not ?

These are questions which we lay before all mankind, whose sanctuary they concern ——

We inquire further, whether, among thousands of these unfortunate, seduced beings, who are now a prey to public disgrace, there would not be many who would immediately leave their horrible position, if the social world would permit them to re-enter the element of morality ?

Although exceptions may be found here, as to all other rules, yet at least many credible reports of the British administration of the criminal Colony of Botany Bay, bear witness that not only hundreds of such cast-away creatures become, under wise measures, not only morally improved, but exemplary wives and mothers

It may be true that a second generation of such a population may not only be particularly distinguished for morality, but the social world of England itself, affords not a few examples that such unfortunate beings become, through the sympathy, confidence, respect, and love of a man, virtuous wives and happy mothers

The position of woman obtained a humane recognition, first through the legislation of Moses, and the principle of love first developed itself, manifested for the protection of women, in Jesus In all earlier and later religious codes, woman appears robbed of all dignity, more or less considered as a being without a soul, (as in the code of Muhammed) in a degree of abject degradation which delicacy forbids us closely to describe

If we read with attention the mémoires of the Evangelists, which have come down to us in the four Gospels, and the   ries, and epistles of the Apostles of Jesus,   shall perceive, running through them, a d   icate thread of the love and sympathy which woman displayed for the Nazarene in so many eventful moments of his ministry—in accordance with the sympathy with which he himself received woman—when the Scribes and Pharisees brought the fallen one to him that he should judge her   Not less touching and significant, as the answer of Jesus in this case, are the important and elevating historical facts which appear in so many places in the letters of the Apostles, with relation to the sympathy and co-operation of the female sex for the dissimination of the persecuted and despised doctrines of primitive Christianity

But as the spirit of the doctrine of Jesus has become more and more dissolved, and has disappeared, by degrees, in the forms and formalities of the church, and as the church, (as an instrument of absolutism) has gradually renounced the spirit of Christianity, so has the principle of humanity also disappeared from the social regulations which church and state have established

Woman not only loses the original sacred protection of the religion of Jesus, under the " police institution of the church," but is subjected to the moral intolerance of the social world of such a Christendom

The church, as an absolute, despotic power, degrades the sacrament of marriage into a cheap article of traffic, to bind human beings indissolubly, for ever, by an outward form, whose inward life is often more or less in rigid opposition, and whose so called choice, in thousands of cases, recognised as an " unfortunate error," often leads to crime, which the church does not by any means judge as Jesus considered it, in the spirit of humanity

Here as there we find the woman, as a purchased slave, the property of a man whose presence often works, in time, with repulsion upon her, or, as the despised cast-away, judged and condemned the most strictly and uncharitably by her own sex, and cast out from the social world.

We behold woman in our age in a state of oppression, of despair, from which only a rational legislation, and a general system of popular education, in the spirit of humanity, will ever be able to produce help and deliverance

------〰〰〰❀〰〰〰------

CHAPTER X

THE ALCOVE

MONSIEUR LE BARON DE SPANDAU was private agent to several governments of the European continent, in a similar position with the Baron von Schweizer, from Frankfort, for Russia, Mr Malten, in Aarau, and a Mr Adam Kuszkowski, (called Anton Kuberski,) for Prussia, Mr Francis Napoleon Szostakowski, for Russia, a General Ramorino, for France, Austria and Sardinia, a Monsieur le Comte de George de Bertola, for Austria and France; a Monsieur Conseil, for France, a Signore PARTESOTTI, for Austria, a Mr Lessing for Prussia, and hundreds of others whose position is not revealed and unmasked like these, partly through their own awkwardness, partly through the energy of those whom they observe, pursue, and occasionally would deliver to the torture

Many of the papers of these spies have fallen into the hands of the persecuted, and have been here and there published Similar engagements offered a rich and splendid remuneration to industry, (especially since the political crisis in Europe, in consequence of the July revolution,) to many ex-diplomatists, literary gentlemen, chevaliers d'industrie, and penitentiary culprits *

A new faculty of study has been in a measure revealed in the progress of our civilization, for whose examinations the greatest proportion of "legitimate proofs" of the lowest crimes serve as a recommendation, and whose sphere of operation enjoys of itself the privilege of sustaining by demoralization the monarchial principle, which has established itself upon demoralization.

Monsieur le Baron de Spandau had found the opportunity to avail himself in the "high places" of Buenos Ayres as well as of Rio de Janeiro, of his talent as a bloodhound, and had, it appears, been recognised as serviceable While he was commissioned in the pay of some European governments to observe the interior state of the political movements of South America, the ambassadors of the courts, whose ministerial authorities had despatched him, were placed under his espionage, as well as the Argentine chargé

---

* The above designated "Anton Kuberski," who was sent to France as a Prussian spy, in January, 1832, had been, for example, condemned to twelve years confinement in a penitentiary for forgery, but was set at liberty as a useful subject of the Prussian government, and was sent to Strasbourg with comprehensive instructions, where he played his part with ability, until he was seen through!

d'affaires in Rio de Janeiro, to whom his position as spy in the service of the cabinet of Rosas remained unknown

The important *agent des deux mondes* had despatched his report to his secret authorities in Buenos Ayres soon after the arrival of the Nordstjernan in Rio, and, as it appeared, received copious instructions for private proceedings, according to which he had acted hitherto

He found his factotum in the designated audience chamber, almost impatient from his long attendance, with dry mouth The condescending chief remarked his ill humour, and immediately called out to Bebida, over the threshold, to bring wine and two glasses

"Si Senhor! vinho! vinho!" croaked she, somewhere in the background, where she was smoking her little pipe

The Baron took his seat at the round table, and cast a glance upon the letters which Senhor Prole had brought

"A vessel arrived from Buenos Ayres?" inquired he, as he began to open the envelope

"Not direct from Buenos Ayres An Argentine man of war lies before Santos—these letters were forwarded from there"

"What, the devil! not the Caza?"

"I believe the brig is called La Caza, if I am not mistaken"

The Baron read with increasing attention one of the beforementioned letters, sunk, from time to time, in consideration and reflection, then read again, and said, half to himself "that may all be arranged, and we shall see an end of the whole affair

"——— Difficult—very difficult, that I admit, but so much the more interesting, and the consequences, also, so much the more brilliant " He read again, half aloud "As concerns that, I beseech you not to be over hasty, you may go more surely to work, to allow her time, but in that case, not only to possess yourself of her papers, but especially her person, since from to-day, M le Baron, I hold you responsible in this respect "

"An unheard of responsibility, which forces the sweat from my brow ' said he, in the above mentioned tone, with a breath that almost resembled a sigh

"Dabedicademlafodunicalafi—hi-hi-hi' Vinho! do Rhino '—not shame-pain '" muttered Bebida, who came in with two bottles of Rhenish wine, and four glasses

"Out, out, old hag '" grumbled the baron to her, too much occupied with Dolores to be able at this time to pay her the smallest attention

Bebida, however, remained standing there, with a glass in each hand, like a Babylonian Belus, or dragon cast in bronze, with a short candle in the right claw Senhor Prole, as an "intimate friend of the house," gently uncorked a bottle, poured out some wine, without disturbing the meditations of his master, (burdened from this hour with so heavy a responsibility,) and the bronze Belle also received the balsam of life

She whispered then, very low, and hardly audibly, her "Dabedicademlofimago, hi-hi-hi," and disappeared trippingly from the scene

The baron looked again into the letter, and read "Should it be impossible for you to escort the condemned in safe custody to Argentine ground, and should the danger occur of loosing her out of your power, it remains with you, in such a case, to take your measures." He shrank back, severely shocked, and his countenance lost its color. Prole seized a glass and bottle, helped himself again, and acted as if he had not observed his employer.

According to the formerly described construction of Brazilian dwellings, like the one in which we now find ourselves in spirit, a little door led from the alcove under the stairs, through into the alcove of the back room.

In an entirely peculiar state of mind in which we have already contemplated her, Sarah had left her timancas standing where they were when she lay, with naked feet, according to Brazilian custom, on the wide sofa, and had slipped down stairs slowly and softly, while Beuida brought the wine. For the case that she might be observed, she had taken her guitar with her, that she might, as before, sing her favorite song there, as if she had wished to surprise the baron. She arrived at the door of the alcove, whose antiquated keyhole afforded a convenient view of the baron, who sat opposite to the alcove, at the designated round table, on which stood the wax candles, by whose light he read the letter. Although he murmured very low, and the letter was written in French, in which language he likewise also conversed with Prole, Sarah attained her design—of spying for the present the spy himself.

A girl in Sarah's situation would be likely to trouble herself little about what her friend or owner does when he is away from her, still, a certain female curiosity might, in the beginning, have turned her attention to the secret meetings of the baron with the amigalhão, who, according to appearances, might be less his friend than his servant. Abstractly from the contracted education of a common English country girl, she had, nevertheless, developed a certain natural understanding, which is at times rightly designated by the name of "mother wit," insomuch as it embraces hereditary or native talent.

As little capable as a young girl, transplanted from an English village into the capital of a foreign country, might be to form an idea of the political and religious struggles, or of the positions and sacrifices of parties, she had, notwithstanding, as an English woman, so much notion of the people's party, and of their oppression by the "powerful of the earth," of radicals, and whigs, and tories, as every English country girl has, who, from her childhood, hears politics talked about, and regularly, even if only from curiosity, runs through a weekly or daily paper.

The word "traitor" embraces in England, to the honor of the English national character, an idea so decidedly contemptible, that it is difficult, especially among the middle classes, to find a man who does not partake of the above feeling of contempt.

This undeniable sentiment of rectitude, which abhors all treachery, and rouses the heart against the traitor, is a characteristic of the British people, that the monarchial government which there, as everywhere, stands rigidly opposed to the people) does not always partake of.

Sally would probably have been as little likely on that evening, as hitherto, to take into her head to trouble herself with the business of her "friend," if his suggestion, that she should take a personal share in his espionage, had not brought her to the resolution to observe him, to ascertain his position.

In the hiding place above mentioned, she could not only contemplate at her ease every expression upon the countenance, but understand, for the most part the meaning of those passages in the letter which he read in fragments.

A superficial knowledge of the French, (for which her second acquaintance had afforded an opportunity,) as well as the analogy of the two languages in many important words, enabled her to presume, if not thoroughly to perceive, beyond all expectation, circumstances and relations whose effect and impression were from time to time vividly expressed on the fully lighted countenance of the baron.

Sally had perceived that the affair concerned a she—that it was about a female. The poor creature might be whatever men and her fate had made of her, still she was, and ever remained, a woman. As woman, she took as lively an interest in one of her sex, as yet entirely unknown to her, as many protected by the favor of fortune, and by a misimprudence in their intercourse with men, would perhaps have shown for her.

Sally was unfortunate—despairingly unfortunate, and in such a situation a lively interest in the danger and sufferings of others is often less foreign to the female heart than in the giddiness of pleasure and the lap of comfort. She heard the word Buenos Ayres, and had been sufficiently long in Brazil to be aware of the war and struggle for life and death, which went on upon the river La Plata.

The baron who appeared to have recovered from the first shock, and to have found himself again in the consciousness of his executioner's office, cast another glance upon the letter and read:

"As relates to Himango, it will be of little avail to arrest him so long as he does not take an active part in the events in Brazil, or here with us, since as yet we possess no testimony against him. If you are able to obtain such, and will take the consequences of the arrest upon yourself, then do what you think proper—it is your affair."

"I thank you exceedingly," said he, tolerably loud, "it is my affair, certainly. My life is also my affair, and I am not the least inclined at present to hazard it against a 'Young European.' I will here have nothing to do personally with a 'Young European,' who may belong to the central committee and have his associates here. The suspicion of an accusation would fall upon me—it would then come to light, and my game would then be ruined here forever! No, your excellency, I am no fool, I will keep watch of him, and take care that he shall be put out of the way before he, with his Astrala, shall fire upon the Brazilian or Argentine flag—but so long as he is in the neighborhood and commands a vessel, even as a privateer, I cannot accomplish my work here—that is very evident."

Sally was shocked—a man was then to be put out of the way—a "Young European"—who appeared to maintain a peculiar position—whom the baron feared—he was to be murdered if she had rightly understood

"The Astrala will take cannon on board, and small arms," remarked Prole, who heard the name

'I know that already, thank you, nevertheless, for your heedfulness," rejoined the other, filling his glass

"The young man, Senhor Horatio de P——, visits the negro from Goa in the Rua do Valongo, Dr Thorfin too Both still live on the Gloria," continued Prole

"Do many Brazilians go in and out at Dr Thorfin's?"

"But few, according to appearances patients, under his treatment"

Sally was all ear—not a word escaped her, and the simple sentences were very intelligable to her Then Dr Thorfin, a physician—lives on the Gloria She noted this address without knowing yet whether some other would not follow that might serve in case of need

"Young Mr Walker goes very often to Dr Thorfin's——"

"I know that, 'tis well, however, that you know it also He is very dangerous to us," continued he, half to himself, "especially if the embarkation should take place, he would then accompany the condemned, and that would be bad—that must not be, and to put him out of the way, that would not answer, he is an Englishman and I will not meddle with the English, for the future less than ever"

Sally heard the mention of a young Englishman—who stood in the way of the plot—which still, to be sure, remained obscure to her—but she heard, also, for the second time, the words "for the future,' what might they signify?

"Young Mr Rossbruck has sailed for Europe again"

"That's no concern of ours—you knew that long ago, he may go, and attend to his business better in Europe than he did here'"

"Your Patrick appears to watch the Vesta or Astrala, as she is called, very attentively I see him very often upon the island of Cobras"

"I don't trust the fellow, I have made arrangements to have him watched—he is not so stupid as he appears, and I am more clever than he probably believes me But nothing can be done to that fellow either, he is only a sailor to be sure, but an English subject, and has his ambassador and consul here—and if I were to have him arrested to send him to Buenos Ayres, he would be set at liberty right away again I had hoped that the fellow was dissipated,and thought I had found in him the right person, but it was a great mistake He drinks, to be sure, his glass of grog like any other Irishman, but he is not a drunkard, do does not revel nor steal, and will deceive nobody but me I must see and get him aboard of some vessel for a long voyage —that he may be out of our way I do not trust the fellow"

Sally had again heard much, and understood a great deal—Patrick was then the subject—whom she was to spy through Lucy! She had heard that Patrick was an honest fellow, well, perhaps she could employ him directly to take some step, as soon as she should have formed any resolution.

"Those are all our passengers from the Nordstjernan," continued Prole, "for you know already that Alvarez is arrested"

"I know that, his sister is Madame Serafini I knew that long ago, through Mr Closting, but I was obliged to wait for the arrival It was to be foreseen that he would compromise himself then The name of Daily has hitherto availed him merely upon his ticket of residence I had respect for him—on account of Walker and Thomson—and must for the future have still more"

Sally heard again the words "for the future," what did he mean by that? Had they reference to the contents of a letter which he had just named? How should she find out?

"About the lady who came in the Nordstjernan. I need, also, make no report to you?' asked Prole, with a significant glance, "as you ordered me"

"Thank you, I will observe her myself"

"But to convince you that I am more serviceable than you usually believe I will tell you who she is"

"Indeed," cried the chief, with a smiling mien, "then you, also, have found that out?"

"It is Senora Dolores—the author of the famous Elegies, condemned to death in Buenos Ayres—whom you, Monsieur le Baron, are to produce alive upon Argentine ground," said the deputy spy, slowly, and very significantly

Sally trembled and shuddered The matter concerned, also, the delivery of a lady who was condemned to death—a poetess who had arrived with the Nordstjernan

"What more did the poor girl require to know, to confirm in her the resolution to do her best for the deliverance of the condemned"

"Bravo!" exclaimed the baron, when Prole had revealed his mystery, "that does you honor, I will render a brilliant report about you, to Buenos Ayres—about you, Senhor Prole, I say; you shall receive an appointment there as soon as you return But you must go, at present, to Santos, on board the man-of-war that lies there —you must hold personal communication with the captain It is the brig La Caza—the same for which Patrick was impressed—the same that was sent after the Swedish brig The captain's name is Tumble This letter here is from him, he has claims upon the reward that is set on the head of Dolores He has had a fellow on board who knew nearly as much as I, and who was thrown overboard from the cutter Captain Tumble had found out a great deal in Buenos Ayres, had conceived similar suspicions of Dolores, when it came out that she had gone away with Mr Walker as his sister He only lays claim to half the reward, and has received orders to be helpful to me—that is the commission! But Dolores is guarded and protected on all sides, surrounded by attendants, and armed. How to bring her from Bota Fogo—on board the Caza—that, Senhor Prole—that is a problem that you truly cannot solve"

Sally trembled more violently than before. The whole affair became clearer and clearer—at the same time, however, she found re-assurance and consolation in the difficulties which the betrayer himself recognized

"You must then go to-morrow to Santos—no, the day after to-morrow—to-morrow I have no time to send you To-morrow I celebrate my betrothal."

" With Miss Thomson, if I may inquire ? "

" With Miss Thomson," replied the baron , " and therefore I cannot go myself to Santos at present "

Sally was near fainting, not that she by any means had ever conceived the idea that the baron would marry her She had never thought of that, and would now have hardly accepted such a proposal But this man was about to celebrate his betrothal on the morrow—to unite himself with a female, who (let her be who she might) would marry a rascal in him —— She had now learned enough, and her resolution was more than ever confirmed. But she must put her hand to the work She must, if possible, obtain possession of this letter from Buenos Ayres, for some hours, to employ it at the risk of her own life How and in what manner? that also she had already planned out She left her post quickly but softly, slipped back up the stairs, made a noise there as if she came from above, and sang, with a loud voice .

> " The Devil take me-lan-cho-ly—'
> I'll not live on so lonely for ever—
> Myself to a man I'll deliver,
> And not love him unless he loves me." ‖

Without having altered her toilet (which was properly less than a toilet) she flew into the room, seized the Baron around the neck, and cried " Bebida ! bring some champagne, the Dutch wine does not suit Sally ! Where are you staying this evening, Prince Albert? my Albert ! I've dreamed charmingly, God knows how long, up there, upon the elastic divan I dreamed I was *Queen Victory*, and you were the real Prince Albert, and that all England belonged to us two, and Scotland and Ireland ! and Robert Peel was our chamberlain and O'Connell our coachman, and Lord Melbourne was our pensioned groom out of service, and Lord Palmerston was a Chasseur on the box in a Russian green livery, and Great Britain was a well stuffed armchair like that in which you are sitting Come, let me sit by you, or upon you '—so—now I sit well ! Now, Bebida ! where does it stay? that forlorn oyster without a shell ?—— How are you Senhor Prole? what is your wife doing in Monte Video ? and your children ? I mean your wife's children, that's true ! you don't understand much English Albert, be my interpreter, I will pay you for it as honestly as an interpreter would be paid by Queen Victoria when the Turkish ambassador tells her about his three hundred wives in Constantinople —— Albert its a pity you are not Sultan—you have a talent for Sultanhood !— There's Bebida ! Now, Prince Albert, knock off the head of a bottle—be an executioner for once '"

" Dabedicadem—vinho—*shame-pain* ' hi-hi-hi—vinho bonito !" grinned Bebida, placing two bottles on the table

" Now one more, right away !" cried the slave of the traitor, who now thought of her freedom ! " One more, right away, Bebida ! I have a thirst for shame-pain, a thirst to-night ! My heart is like a burnt coal, but it glimmers and glows yet ! I will quench it out entirely '—— The devil take me-lan-cho-ly !" she exclaimed, and threw the Dutch night cap off the baron on the engraving of Rahab and the two persecuted men of Isreal, which we formerly designated.

Bebida brought the " fancy perruque" back again, Sarah pulled it down over the nose of the spy, then emptied a glass of champagne, and seized her guitar After some wild chords, she accompanied her voice in tempo furioso in the following strophes

> " A health now , to phi lo so phy —'
> If you lie, none will ever believe you,
> If you cheat, they are sure to deceive you,
> But deception of souls cannot be '—
> ——Deception of souls cannot be '

> 'Long life, then, to phi lo so phy —'
> The church still her payment is taking
> For the weddings each night she is making,
> While champagne drowns anti pathy '—
> ——While champagne drowns anti pa thy '"

She rasped in ascending furioso a final chord, and emptied her glass again with equal fury

" Isn't that a beautiful song, Prince Albert ? that was written by a Saxon princess, and Don Pedro the First set it to music when he had completed his celebrated " Brasilienne "* It is an imperially royal song ' and has great resemblance to the high song of Solomon " His left hand lies under my heart, and his right embraces me " And where in it is once said " My friend is white and ruddy, the chief among many thousands '"— that's you, Prince Albert ' and where-in it is further said " I am a wall, and my breasts are towers !"— that's me, Prince Albert —that's your Sally, from Norfolkshire, in Old England Long live Sally of Norfolkshire ! Your health Senhor Proletary or Secret-ary But now I want to be serious, and talk to you about business," she began, after a pause, while " Prince Albert" contemplated her profile with peculiar satisfaction, as it balanced before his turned up nose

" You told me about a Pussy or Lucy that I must spy on account of your boatman, Patrick Gentleman, or whatever he is called I have though over the thing What's the use of my having a long talk with Lucy first I propose another way , but drink, Prince Albert ' don't you see your Queen Victory drink also? then you want to know what Patrick is about, or something of that sort. Tell me what you want to get out of him, and I ll take upon myself to bring out what's in him—only there'll hardly be much money got out of him "

" You see, child," replied the Baron, " I'm a spy—I spy the negro traders here, that go back and forth between here and Africa—you know already that the slave trade is prohibited."

" To be sure—to be sure ; you can't carry off any more *blacks*, but as many *white* female slaves as you will Well, go on "

" You see then, child, I have appointed Patrick as deputy spy, he is to observe a slave trader for me, who is fitting out here to go to Angola—Patrick is to watch him when he goes to sea—then we shall go after him, out to the Sugar Loaf, and take him !"—

" We ? we also? we two and Bebida, out to the Sugar Loaf, on the negro hunt? the thing pleases me—I'm agreed to it ' The devil take me-lan-cho-ly !' " said she, and took her glass and drank.

The baron found the extravagance of Sally so natural, and her proposal to deal directly with Patrick so entirely corresponding with her

---

* The " Brasilienne," as is well known, was composed by Don Pedro.

mother wit, that he entered into the plan without the slightest suspicion

"I will tell you why I want to speak directly with Patrick You wish it to remain secret that I know you or that you know me, or that we both know each other —— The devil take hypocrisy," said she, interrupting herself again, and seizing her guitar, she sang.

"The devil take hy-poc ri sy —!
I'm bound to show love and affection
And to hide every crime from detection—
Champagne here' that blots out all an ti pathy

"And you will perceive,' continued she, as if she had not interrupted herself, "that it is easier to maintain my incognito without Pussy or Lucy, than with her"

"How so ' explain that to me"

"I will explain that to you, Prince Albert," continued she, with a very serious tone, seating herself the most comfortably possible in his lap "Here is one person, and yet another, to be admitted behind the curtain—Lucy and Patrick Now a man is ten times better to leave behind the curtain than a woman—and if the woman be also only a poor Lucy that sews for money—or does no one knows what for money, the matter is very plain' therefore, my prince, I would rather admit your Patrick directly behind the curtain, than to risk that Lucy should lead you and me behind the curtain, around the left hand corner—do you understand me ' Oh how handsome you are to-night' and how I love you, so long as you give me plenty of champagne ' how interesting you are, when you have on your Dutch nightcap '

Long life, then, 'o phi lo-so phy —'
The church still her payment is taking—

and besides, my pet, I would like to see what sort of a youth Patrick is' if he is a fellow that looks like something in his sailors' jacket, then I will take him to the court tailor of the Prince de Joinville,* in the Rua do Ouvidor, and have a gentleman made out of him—a dandy—as elegant as any one to be found in the botanical garden, and he shall then be my ' cavaliere servente,' or, properly, your ' cavaliere servente,' as the Catholics in Rome call it when the Pope's lady has her

friend ' do you understand ' That is my plan with Patrick, and now drink—and let your tiresome Senhor Prole-tary go home and to bed, and do you lie down and go to sleep, and let me alone, for I have politics in my head—a whole two legged Irishman, named Patrick, is running about in my head"

"Very well, Sally, I thank you for your attention, and will entirely follow your plan How will you manage to speak to him ' shall he come here '"

"Do you think I ought to go to him ' perhaps in his room, if he occupies one '" inquired she with all the humor which was peculiar to her "You mean me to visit a gentleman ' What's come over you ' But jesting aside, ask our Amigalhão to say to Patrick that an English lady has inquired about him—an English lady ' mind that '—who lives in such a place, and is called so and so But I must have a name ready for him ' Well, then, my name is Lady Hamlet What name have you given me to Lucy '"

"Why, the first name that occurred to me, 'I wrote the name of Mrs Adams on a card, with the name of this street, and sent it by a negro to the little tavern"

"Well then, Prince, if Patrick comes I am Lady Hamlet, if Lucy comes, I am Mrs Adams, and I will receive Lucy in the front, and Patrick in the back room Lady Hamlet and Mrs Adams are sisters, and look very much alike—all that will do nicely Now only give the Amigalhão the address of Lady Hamlet quickly, and go to bed, and don't disturb me in my politics—for this night '"

Sally twanged again her favorite melody, "the devil take," &c, and disappeared

The Amigalhão had yet much to report about Rio Grande, and the arrival of a monk, in Patagonian costume, in the camp of the rebels, not far from the town of Laguna, where he commanded a body of cavalry "It is the Benedictine Celeste, the friend of the traitor Alphonso, who gave him the sacrament in prison," added he

"Very well '" assented the chief, writing the name and address of Lady Hamlet in a feigned hand upon a card, with which the Amigalhão took his leave

Bebida had long ago fallen asleep on her straw pallet in the back room The master of the house locked and bolted the garden gate and the house door with his own hand, and betook himself likewise to rest—at least to bed.

---

* This is not by any means an anachronism. A Parisian tailor bore this title upon his large sign in Rio, years before the marriage of the prince with the Brazilian princess

DOLORES.

BOOK VII.

CHAPTER I

SPIRITUAL "RAPPORT"

GRACIA awaited the return of her friend from Bota Fogo with greater impatience than ever. It was late in the evening. Her soul resembled an ocean of sentiment, excited to its fathomless depths by the hurricane which, as the heaven-storming and hope-destroying "power of circumstances," beat around the weakly manned bark of her love, to swallow it up, or to dash it in pieces against some one of the rocks on the neighboring coast.

Her heart throbbed and fluttered, and her pulses seemed overpowered by the predominating force of the nerve fluid, which streamed through her frame from the thought-embracing fibres of the brain, down to the executing organs of the trembling finger ends.

The intelligence that her husband was only a day's journey from the capital, and would be there the next evening, had renewed a destroying struggle within her heart, that seemed long ago subdued—long ago interrupted by a truce, but eternally renewed—and after long bluster and fury, left the hostile forces in the same position in which they stood when the "declaration of war" took place, through Robert's entrance into her asylum.

The question of the existence or non-existence of her inward life again arose, as a so called "vital question." She had felt long since that she only belonged to one, that only one sacrificial flame could rise from the altar of her heart. She had long since received the mysterious commandment of love "Thou shalt have no other gods but me." She had recognised in Robert the unity of love, in its operations from his mind upon herself, and in the reaction of her soul upon him. Led by this mysterious, irresistible power of love, she had admitted to him that she loved him, when in a state of mind that was a riddle to herself, and remained a riddle to her while on earth.

But opposed to the unity of love, the despotic, many headed monster of "social duty" now reared itself—a duty which she herself had originally assumed, and since then fulfiled in every respect, with the willing subordination of a slave.

She must now choose, and had long since chosen, she must now put her choice in execution, and was, nevertheless, unable to do so.

She had believed it possible to detach and separate the spiritual life from her clay—to rend her soul from her body—to give her love to the one, and herself to the other—and the indissolubility, the unity of her being, contradicted such a possibility. The "either or" arose again, as the absolute demand of necessity, with this demand, in opposition to the many headed monster of social duty, arose just as sacred a duty of love. Her love had penetrated the life of a man in its deepest depths, and found in those depths its spiritual existence—while social duty bound her to a man whom, according to her own admission, she did not love, and whose heart was "a rock, from which no magic rod of love had been able to lead forth a fountain of reciprocal affection, nor a drop of sentiment."——

She pondered over her future, cursed her past—but no contemplation of the one, and no curse upon the other, could extricate her a hair-breadth from her present position.

The raging hurricane of the heaven-storming and hope destroying "power of circumstances" roared on, and the weakly manned skiff of her love now mounted to the black clouds, which had long since concealed the last star of the future, and was now again flung down into the sepulchral night of her marriage without sympathy.

When Robert was not at home, she lingered in his pavilion. The light for her flower-making seemed better to her there. Robert's armchair at his writing-desk appeared more comfortable. His window afforded her a prospect of the picturesque entrance between the colossal granite rocks of "Santa Cruz" and the "Sugar Loaf," less concealed by near standing bananas and jacarandas, than at the east window in her own pavilion. She found Robert's piano better sounding than her own, (as we knew long since,) and had a peculiar satisfaction in arranging his apartment with her own hand, placing fresh flowers in his vases, and putting away his books, and papers, and music, to make the room homelike for him before he returned.

In the above intimated state of mind which is indescribable in words, she found herself in

Robert's pavilion, on the evening when he left her and rode towards Bota Fogo

She endeavored at length to reassure, to compose, to amuse herself, and turned over Robert's music, and here and there a written copy of a song. A leaf came to her hand, a poem in Spanish which lay in a half open envelope, in the form of a letter. It was not Robert's handwriting, it was a hand stamped by a character of manly firmness, and yet it had about it something womanly—a certain peculiar delicacy. But she soon forgot the handwriting in the impression of the poem, which she first read hastily, and then once more, and then another time. It bore the superscription "El Desterrado," (The Exile,) and was as follows

> "Kindred and fatherland
> Ne'er shall I see
> By fate's relentless hand
> Severed from me
> Only to me remains
> Life, with its cares and pains,
> And until I am dead,
> Nought but the bitter bread,
> Of the sad exile.
>
> Glory, hope earthly good,
> Love's golden chains,
> Vainly for aught I sued,
> Nothing remains,
> But in this foreign land,
> Sore wounded, hardly scanned,
> Lonely to lay my head,
> And eat the bitter bread
> Of weary exile.
>
> I wander on the shore
> Where the waves dash,
> And surging evermore,
> Mournfully plash,
> Ever reminding me
> Of my sad destiny,
> While o'er the sands I tread,
> Loathing the bitter bread
> Of gloomy exile.
>
> No friendly form appears
> To soothe my woes,
> None but me dry my tears
> And find repose
> I must forgotten be,
> None care remember me,
> They think of me as dead,
> While mine's the bitter bread,
> Of the lorn exile.
>
> Where'er I wind my way,
> Sadly and slow,
> To sorrow still a prey,
> Lonely I go;
> While the cold world to me
> Giveth no welcome free,
> But, with averted head,
> Grudges the bitter bread
> Of the poor exile.
>
> When my last hour shall come,
> Cold and serene
> When for the silent tomb
> I quit the scene,
> Then in a foreign land,
> On the deserted strand
> Washed by the ocean wave
> Shall be the lonely grave
> Of the worn exile.
>
> No cross my tomb will bear,
> No loved one weep,
> And offer pious prayer,
> Where I shall sleep.
> Thus banished and alone,
> Comfortless and unknown,
> His days of bitter grief,
> To which death brings relief,
> Ends the poor exile."

"By whom was this poem? Why had Robert never imparted it to her? To whom was it addressed? where was it written? In Rio de Janeiro, upon the same paper that Robert always used, which his negro brought from his counting-house to the garden gate, it was of the same form, the same bluish tint, it bore the same English mark. By whom was the poem? How could Robert bring this wonderful Elegy home without immediately communicating it to her, allowing her the enjoyment of reading it with him? Did he believe her incapable of feeling, with him, the unspeakably touching elevation of this intellectual sigh.

Gracia had never felt what exile was, she had never reflected upon the idea of fatherland What should occasion her to reflect upon it? She had never concerned herself about politics, and like a child with its mother's milk, she had imbibed, as a woman in conjugal life, the modes of thinking and views of her husband, in all that related to politics. Her husband, denying patriotism, declared the struggles of the patriots in Brazil to be rebellion against the ruling powers, and transitory occurrences

Her husband appeared to have had no feeling for fatherland, and she herself had, until this moment, never reflected that the paradise of her wonderful home lay in Brazil, that her fatherland was where her nation lived, where her cradle had stood, where as a child she had played and prattled with her flowers A singular, strange, untrodden region of perception was revealed to her through this Elegy, the perception of a position of man, united to mankind by the sacred bond of patriotism, which even asserted its influence at a far, far distance, as love

She perceived the idea of fatherland—consecrated by the first impression we receive of life—made sacred by the first sentiment that ever awakes within us, by the first pleasures we enjoyed, by the first tears we shed, in joy or sorrow, and by the first anguish that pierced our loving souls

She read the poem yet once more, and it was to her, as if suddenly the ray of a never suspected strength of mind streamed through her Her "interior clairvoyance" suddenly awoke, as a somnambulist awakes, with covered eyes, in that cloud-formed element of light, whose splendor surrounds her, and in whose distance move the forms and transparent images of the mysterious, higher existence—the abode of the soul-life!——

She found herself suddenly in the real world of her spiritual existence, cut off and rigidly separated from the petrified, dreamy form of material vegetation

Robert returning, cast a glance from the threshold of the gate through the open door of his pavilion, and immediately remarked his friend seated in his armchair, by his round table, with the candles lighted She hastened towards him with the sheet in her hand, greeted him with the heartiness peculiar to her, and said: "I have again been indiscreet! I have been looking through your papers again, to find love letters, and found this admirable Elegy! Who wrote it? To whom is the Elegy addressed?"

---

* This Elegy, as well as the "Hymn of Curse," "Dolores," pages 59, 60, are not mine, but Spanish originals of a poetess from the river La Plata, whose name I am not authorized to give.   HARRO

"To an exile," replied Robert, smiling

"I thank you for the information!" replied Gracia, "but I shall not allow myself to be put off so, I must know who the Elegy is from, and to whom it is addressed"

"In case I could even answer the first question—in case I knew from what collection the poem was copied—how could I then know, exactly, to whom it is addressed Has Lord Byron given the name of the ladies to whom many of his Elegies are addressed?"

"Then the poem has been transcribed from some book here in Rio?" continued Gracia, as she re-entered the pavilion with him "Well! then bring me the book, I beseech you! will you! will you bring me the book?"

The naïve earnestness which spoke in this request, disarmed Robert's resolution to conceal from her the origin of the poem He could not tell her an untruth—he could not lie, especially when Gracia addressed a question to him It cost him a sufficient effort long ago, when he had occasion to speak of his "sister" to her

"It would have its difficulties to bring you the book," replied he, "yet you may, nevertheless, become acquainted with it some time or other. it is a copious book, but a living one"

"Then the poetess is here, if that is her handwriting!"

"How so? she may even be somewhere else!"

"Then she has been here, however"

"Why do you suppose so?"

"Because the poem is written upon your counting-house paper"

Robert started "You women are truly born for spies," said he, smiling ' Then you have already made that discovery? Well, the poem is by my sister"

"By your sister!" cried Gracia, with an expression of amazement and wonder "Then your sister writes poems in the Spanish language?" added she, with a certain coldness, as a doubt of the truth of this assertion took possession of her mind, just as involuntarily as the impression from the reading of the Elegy had seized her. Easily as it might be possible for an English woman, living in Buenos Ayres from her childhood, to become as familiar with the Spanish as with her mother tongue, still there was something about it that contradicted probability, and this something was just as inexplicable to her, as the impression of the poem itself upon her mind

"I do not know, Robert," began she, after long silence, "I do not know how I shall express myself about this Elegy, I have read so many poems in different languages, but none ever wrought upon me like this one I doubt whether it is the poem alone that has so thrilled me, is it not in some way the spirit of the authoress, in all its purity and elevation, that speaks in this poem, and calls into requisition a certain sympathy of my soul—draws my whole being upward to itself—involuntarily and irresistibly fetters and attracts me towards it? It is soul, and whoever is not attracted by this poem, has no soul. May I know who it is by?" inquired she, with that indescribably mild voice which characterized the childishness of her nature, in undeniable contradiction to the existence of the "little creature," who just then

34

bade good night to her mother and the neighbor, as she was carried to bed

Robert found himself in singular embarrassment His relations to Gracia had long ago annihilated every secret between them He breathed as a part of her being, and lived only in her heart, neither suspicion nor mistrust against her, lay within the scope of his existence The pleasing sadness that prevailed in her, in consequence of the reading, was as unfeigned as every expression of her inward life Notwithstanding this, however, he had laid himself under a sort of moral obligation to preserve a secret which had become more urgent than ever before

Gracia remarked, by means of the spiritual organ of her womanhood, (for which a determinate word fails us,) that she had come in contact with a secret, and suddenly, though involuntarily, altered her tone, which was not by any means less gentle, but had in it all the more sadness

"Well, Robert," said she, after a renewed pause, "the poem then is by your "sister,' and it is addressed to Hinango"

"But how in the world did you come to suspect that? Have you become clairvoyant this evening?" inquired he, retreating a step, and contemplating her with wonder

"My state of mind may be something of the sort," replied Gracia, "I have also found it out In that case, this poem will prove the effect which the mind of your sister would probably have upon me Greet your sister," continued she, with a tremulous voice, "and greet Hinango, to whom, after to-morrow, it will no longer be of any use to keep my residence a secret"

Suddenly shocked by the connexion of ideas in relation to the return of her husband, she sank into an armchair, covered her face, and wept

Robert trembled A long pause followed, voiceless as the deathlike silence of the moonlight night that surrounded them

"Hinango and my husband are foes," continued she, at length, "without ever being angry or quarrelling There is an enmity of natures that requires no quarrelling They speak to each other when they meet Neither speaks ill of the other, and Hinango," added she, in a wifelike tone, "Hinango could find no cause to speak ill of Senhor Closting"

"You were about to speak of the effect of the Elegy," interrupted Robert, who had taken a seat by her and seized her hand, which he now dropped, while his youthful forehead was suffused by a gloomy shadow Another long pause ensued The minds of both were long ago so deeply entwined together, that each suspected, felt, and shared the other's lightest emotion without words—almost without a glance

Gracia understood Robert's movement The harmony with which she would have offered her greeting to the spirit, (which in a manner lived in the unknown poetess and in Hinango,) was disturbed by the involuntary mention of a man who, estranged from this spiritual region, belonged nowhere less than there, while the same man had, nevertheless, become "a part of her own being" This tragical reality appeared once more to reveal itself to her; she seemed to feel that she was banished from those regions, in being fastened upon earth to a corpse.

The chain which, as it were, fettered her like a female Prometheus to the rock of matter, pressed upon her more injuriously than ever before. Her glance sought the eyes of Robert, and her bitter anguish found utterance without words

"I wished" she said, after a long silence, "to request you, dear Robert, to convey my soulfelt greetings to the poetess of this Elegy, and to her and your friend Hinango, and——I am suddenly aroused to the tragical consciousness of the necessity that removes me spiritually, as well as socially, from you all." She sank into reflection, her eye was again troubled.

"If Hinango has hitherto suspected our friendship, he has at least never by a syllable intimated it," observed Robert

Gracia sighed, and her glance again lingered in his

"Offer my greeting, nevertheless, to the spirit," continued she, "that speaks in this Elegy, and in which both live—your sister and Hinango, say to them, that I perceive this spirit, though I cannot yet comprehend it, say to them, that your friendship to me, my unrestrained intercourse with you, has unlocked the susceptibilities of my mind, to perceive this spirit of sacrifice for the love of fatherland—which I shall comprehend more and more—through your love. But do not tell them the last. I recognise those two beings, your sister and Hinango, as spiritual appearances from a higher sphere, and therefore I talk to them through you, as unrestrainedly, as confidentially, as freely, as though they did not live on earth. And that is just the effect that similar works, in verse or prose, have upon us——they lead us off from our world of clay, from the bonds and fetters which bind us to this earth—bear us upward for the moment into the region of the soul's life, where spirit greets spirit."

She seemed again lost in reflection, and with the peculiar rapidity with which the ebullitions of her nerve-life, so to speak, vibrated from one pole to the other, she changed also her tone, the expression of her glance, and her whole nature, without in the least degree losing her amiability.

"But I will not have your sister to be a living person, I want her to be a book, as handsomely bound as the case may be—something like the edition there of Thomas Moore's Irish Melodies, in velvet, with gold spangles, and with admirably spiritual contents, but not living! There must be no woman that writes upon the selfsame paper that you use; I will not suffer such paper fellowship! I will not have her write any more on your paper, or you in short, upon hers! my nerves could not endure it! I should know it here on the Gloria, if she scribbled on your paper in Bota Fogo. When she touched the paper there, it thrilled through all my nerves, this effect heightened the impression of the poem. Yes, laugh at me—it is simple truth! All your stories about your 'sister' do you no good—and if the poem were not adressed to Hinango, as I knew immediately—you might look out for yourself! I would throw the elegantly bound book into the bay! drown it! Yes! don't look at me! you don't know me yet! When I touch this paper, I tremble in every limb! Don't laugh at me! I will not know how handsomely the book is bound!"

"Have I ever yet asked you how that book is bound, in which you have read during four years, and whose contents appear, nevertheless, to be unknown to you?" inquired Robert, with a significant glance "And you appear to be unable to endure the 'thought,' the realization of which I must now suffer with respect to you?

After a long silence, he arose, and began in a decided tone. "I stand in business with Senhor Forio and Mr Closting; I am obliged to see Mr Closting immediately when he arrives—so soon as he arrives. Our business is of importance, it concerns a colony on Santa Catharina. And I am going there——soon——very soon——"

"Oh no, Robert! stay here!—stay here!" interrupted she, "stay for my sake!—— who knows what the future——what may happen?"—

"Good heavens! Gracia! what contradiction in you and in me!" exclaimed Robert, "it does not require your fearful request to keep me here!—I am fettered here—— I cannot go away—and, nevertheless, it would be better that I should, even this very night—this night—depart ——it were better——"

"It is the reverse, Robert," sighed Gracia, I am fettered by you, that I feel."

"Be it action or reaction," returned Robert, "our misfortune is ever the same. The soul *rapport* exists—only the difference prevails, that in you it will soon be interrupted—while in me it will still exist. My life will be, from henceforth, a martyrdom, that knows no expression.—But I shall be able to die without the fear of hell! for I am already undergoing a hell upon earth."

"Horrible!" sighed Gracia! "horrible! I understand you!"

"You will yet understand me better, by reading some biographical and psychological fragments from the domain of Magnetism. I have in my possession, some documents from Goa, which disclose a singular, but consistent system, concerning the relations of the inward life, of the soul's life, to physical nature. Dr Thorfin has handed it to me, to translate from Spanish into English. I have it here. Read it to morrow at leisure. I shall, besides, not be at home to dinner to-morrow."

He arose, went to his desk, and handed an envelope to his friend

"You will not be here to-morrow?"

"No, Gracia, I am invited to a betrothal My aunt declares her betrothal to the Baron de Spandau."

Gracia sank back in her armchair, not knowing whether she should laugh aloud, or continue in the terror that seized her. "No! you jest!" cried she at length. "You are in good spirits, and that delights me, Robert."

"It is no jest! it is simple, infamous truth. The man has known how to avail himself of his social position here in Rio, to make my not very young aunt CRAZY. She declares her betrothal, but, before he marries her, I will, it is to be hoped, have a word to say to Uncle George."

"Good heavens! and can you not now exert yourself to prevent the betrothal?"

"No! I am fettered—bound by circumstances. The baron is a spy, a hireling of Prussia, and in the pay of Rosas, and has here the lives of some persons in his hand—for whom I could sacrifice my life "

" Great God !" sighed Gracia, rising and seizing Robert's hand, " and he was so intimate with—with Mr Closting ' "——

" That is easily explained," returned Robert, briefly and abruptly " Now one more question, for it is late, and we must part for to-day "Lay your hand upon your heart, and answer me before God, Gracia whom do you love ? Mr Closting or me ? Answer me as for life and death !"

" Do you still ask ?" replied Gracia, in tones that conveyed the answer " Can you still doubt ?"

" I require a decided answer "

" Have I not then assured you often enough, I never have loved him !—never ! He never possessed my heart—never I love you, as perhaps no woman ever loved a man So may the Lord judge and condemn me, if you still doubt my love !'" cried she, with a tremulous voice

" I must and will doubt it, so long as you are his wife "

Gracia sank back in her armchair Robert walked back and forth in the room

" Forgive me, as I forgive you," began he, after a long pause, as he went up to her and took her hand " You have been ill, and are ill, and ought to have known yourself as a woman You are not the first, and will not be the last woman who has destroyed, or will destroy, the life of a man—guiltlessly—innocently—without being aware of it, or desiring it

" You did not know what you were doing four or five years ago O that your sex would once learn to know itself, and to value itself, that no woman would fasten such a bond, in which, as you have just expressed it, " she gives herself, and retains her heart " There lies your crime, and yet you have committed none ! you are pure before yourself, and before God, and, as to myself, I must enter a new hell upon earth, after having enjoyed heaven in the dream of our love—in the belief of your love

" My strength yet to live upon earth, I must receive from above You will now destroy rather than confirm it. Now go to rest, for it is late !" He imprinted a kiss on her forehead, and pressed her hand

Gracia arose and lingered for a moment, sighing " You are a noble man, Robert Good night ! but never repeat the question of your doubt God knows my heart Good night !'"

Robert accompanied her to her door, and returned with slow steps to his pavilion, sought slumber, and only found torturing dreams, of murder near, and murder in the distance, and he longed for death.

CHAPTER II

MAGNETISM

THE fragmentary leaves which Dolores received from Goa, through Senhor Vera, and communicated to her friends, were the following, " *Manuscripts from Goa* "

I ELEMENT OF MAGNETISM *

1 Man is a spiritual being soul Our body is the instrument, the covering of our being, to connect it with matter, the world of senses

2 The magnetic fluid in our nerves is the organ of the soul, the instrument of the will for the movement of the body, (matter) Every movement of any part of our body takes place by means of the nerves, every nervous fibre is an organ of the will

3 The term *animal* magnetism arises from misunderstanding In order to express myself clearly in this communication of my researches in the department of magnetism, I will employ the word *animatic* magnetism, (from anima, soul †) in opposition to the term " animal "

4 There is but one power, the animatic Physical power is an erroneous expression Matter has no power when not in motion, unexerted power is not power, motion is animatic

5 All life is animatic, and appears to us in its different gradations, in all the departments of nature, as animatic power the principle of life, of motion

6 The Nerve system in our body is opposed to the Blood system The nerve fluid embraces life Blood is the material opposite to the necessity of motion.

7 For what purpose is iron in our blood ? Physiology has heretofore given vague and unsatisfactory answers to this question ‡

Why do we hang iron to a magnet ? That the magnetic power may continue in motion Iron is the anti-magnetic principle, it draws the magnetic power to itself, and in itself, as a sponge does water, and sends it off again, in a radiating motion

8 Iron in the blood is the unconditionally necessary antithesis to the motion of animatic power the condition of life Without iron in the blood the animatic power would depart from us, be lost, escape, as the magnet dies away without iron, (its antithesis)

9 The motion of all animatic power is radiating The motion of all matter circular, (rotary) The magnetic fluid, the magnetic light, (invisible to the eye beyond the magnetic sphere,) is radiating in its operation Electricity is radiating in its operations, also the light of the spheres

The thought, (the rays of spirit,) like the timeless motion of the electro-magnetic element, radiates to the most distant space, nearly without time The stars move in a circle, (like all masses of matter) and the blood circulates within us, as the antithesis to the radiating motion of animatic life

10 The twofold motion · the ray and the circle, is the inscrutable secret (but also the condition) of life The whole universe reveals this twofold motion

11 Man is a spiritual and not a material being

12 The entire creation is a formation of the spirit—not a self-moving material world

---

* The author of Dolores herewith delivers to the forum of science a theory, a system, founded upon a hypothesis, the tenability or intenability of which, can only be determined in the department of science.

† This expression has been applied already in Dolores, pages 144 and 164

‡ Scholastic learning thus answers this question iron gives to blood its red color But this is no answer at all, for the blood might as well be blue

13 Which first commences our body or our life? (the form of existence or our existence as soul?)

Life first commences in its everlasting, mysterious moment of creative power The consciousness of the earthly existence of two beings disappears in that moment in a more elevated life, from whose source our life proceeds, as it it were brought down, as a soul

14. After life has originated, the animatic creative power first develops and forms the body —originally an organization of nerves, comparable to a tube, to a flower stalk, whose blossom is the brain, and whose root, the later organ of generation, connects life with the world of the senses Physiologists understand me

15. After the commencement of life, in such a formation the heart first developes itself, and takes its shape, as the centre of the circulation of the blood, for the preservation of life

16 The animatic power of the nerve fluid represents the soul, the spiritual, original being of man The blood represents matter, (the form of being,) the means of connexion with the corporeal world

17 According to the principles of phrenology, man's nervous organs are developed in proportion as they are brought into action and exercise, as the natural condition of power in its movement the spiritual life is also thus developed in the nerve organization, in proportion as it is exerted and brought into action, according as the soul (as a power) exercises its abilities in thinking, perception, feeling, etc

18 As phrenology goes hand in hand with physiognomy, both rest upon the basis of the superior Psychology, and this science is in its infancy It embraces many other branches, and its object is *Man* as a spiritual being, as soul, in his position and relations to the corporeal world, to himself and to mankind

19 All human diseases can be divided into two categories in animatic and animal diseases

20 Animatic diseases are those in which the nerve organization is affected in disproportion to the world of senses, those are the moral sufferings. They are founded in the inner (soul) life, and can only be treated or cured by remedies derived from the higher psychology

21 Animal diseases are those which have their origin in the injury, disturbance, or in the disproportion of individual organs of the body, (as the form or covering of the soul,) and indirectly bring about disorders of the nerve organization, (as far as they are executive instruments of the spiritual power, instruments of the soul,) without being based upon moral sufferings

22 The science of medicine is not conceivable without psychology, as it is of the first and most unconditional necessity to know the disease, to see through its nature or existence, before applying any remedy to cure it

23 Psychology in its higher branches, is the philosophy of medicine It is an all-embracing department—an inexhaustible study in itself, inasmuch as it embraces its object, the being of Man, in all his relations to the corporeal world, unfathomable in *its* basis, immeasureable in *its* extent.

24. Animatic magnetism is the element of the inward life, separated from the corporeal world;

the movement of animatic power in its proper sphere, elevated above time and space

25 Animatic magnetism (as a science) is the acknowledged thesis of the higher psychology at the gate of the spiritual temple of humanity It authenticates the existence of animatic element and of the spiritual radiating motion in its proper sphere It is not an object of faith, but a fact of reality, of experience—an object of knowledge

26 The animatic life in man, (as a development to spiritual power,) is subjected to infinite variety in every individual, in a particular gradation, like the shapes of life in general, in their endless variety of form, in all the departments of nature

27 As seldom as two leaves can be found on the same tree, which are perfectly alike in their fibrous formation, so seldom can two men be found in whom animatic life is developed in an exactly equal degree But as there are classes (categories) in the province of every science, so also in the higher psychology—in magnetism

The magnetic or animatic nature of man, falls into four categories, which may be designated from the four elements, as the fire, air, water, and earth, magnetic natures, which find their relationship in the four temperaments

28 In the fire and air magnetic natures, the element of animatic life is predominant, insomuch as it overcomes the antithesis of the iron particles of the blood, which, notwithstanding, can be relatively strong, (like the quantity of iron which this or that magnet bears for the preservation of its own power)

29 In the water and earth magnetic natures, the iron element in the blood governs the animatic (nerve) life, the animal nature is predominant, the inward life in its thousand gradations, more or less kept under These two degrees are related to the sanguinary and phlegmatic temperaments

30 The fire and air magnetic natures, predominate in choleric and melancholy temperaments, yet under the condition of individuality A fire and air magnetic nature may be choleric and melancholy, but it by no means follows that the element of animatic life is always predominant in choleric or melancholy men

31 Between the two categories of the animatic and animal natures, lies the equator of magnetic susceptibility, of the faculty of somnambulism, magnetic clairvoyance Only the animatic (fire and earth magnetic) natures are capable of clairvoyance, and, on the other hand, of magnetic influence on others Water and earth magnetic natures cannot produce any magnetic effect upon others, nor can they enter the spheres of clairvoyance in case they should be put into a magnetic sleep (by a proportionately strong magnetic influence from without)

32 All convulsive appearances, as the effect of the approach of certain individuals to somnambulists, (or clairvoyants in their magnetic sleep,) are to be explained by the above mentioned contrasts of the magnetic classes The earth and water magnetic natures produce convulsions in somnambulists by their approach—as does iron when brought near them.

33. On the contrary, a lock of hair from a fire and air magnetic individual, when laid below the pit of the heart (upon the centre of the plexus

cœliacus) of a somnambulist, produces a direct magnetic *rapport*, and a beneficial influence *

34 The property of Rhabdomancy—the effect of concealed iron upon certain men, is just as naturally to be explained by the above principle, as the repulsion of the anti-magnetic element upon the animation

35 As this repulsion and attraction appears undeniable and decidedly in the state of magnetic sleep, the same repulsion and attraction of animatic and animal (magnetic and anti-magnetic) natures† also exist in the external " every day life," without men being conscious of it and sometimes present themselves in remarkable cases of sickness

36 It would be a singular prejudice or misunderstanding which would assert that magnetic natures are in themselves cases of disease, and that a fire, or air magnetic (nervous) man is " disordered in his nerves "

It could just as well be asserted that a noble man is diseased, because in him the organ of humanity, of benevolence—and that a musician is diseased, because in him the organ of music, has been especially developed

37 A man carefully educated, physically and morally, according to the demands of nature and reason, without effeminacy on the one side, and without brutalization on the other, will sooner become nervous than animals—without respect to the degree of his intellectual cultivation

38 Experience shows, in a thousand cases, that men whose nervous system is cushioned over with more than the necessary quantity of matter, (which cannot pass for nervous,) are subjected to a multitude of diseases, which arise from excessive fullness, and the corruption of the animal juices On the contrary so called nervous men (in whom animatic life is predominant) who lead a rational manner of life, with a natural repulsion for every injurious substance,‡ are often patterns of health

39 Physical and moral influences upon the development of man, induce and form either his animatic or animal nature—apart from his intellectual dejection Experience offers cases of prominent degrees of fire magnetic natures in a very subordinate state of intellectual cultivation, as well in somnambulists, as in men who (without a scientific education) can operate as magnetizers.

40 Animatic (inward) life, is an element without the material world Experience shows that men who from childhood have been subject to severe diseases, have often cultivated§ their inward life, their minds, to a high degree

41 The term " soul sufferings " is frequently understood erroneously, as disorders of the nerve organization are frequently confounded with soul-sufferings

All our soul-sufferings are trials of our moral power, for its development, for our ennoblement, and the more deeply we feel soul-sufferings, the more susceptible are we also to receive in us the ray of the higher idea of being, to nourish in us the glow of sincere love

We have here again the contrast of phlegmatic lifelessness and of sanguine levity The first knows nothing of soul-sufferings, the latter passes lightly by them, enjoys earthly existence, and ' cares for nothing "

42 While the earth and water magnetic natures find parallels in phlegmatic and sanguine temperaments, (with a suppression of the feelings, and an inclination to sensuality,) the fire and air magnetic natures afford parallels with men in whom the soul (the higher or deeper inward life) is predominantly developed

43 The choleric temperament is manifest in the violent ebullition of feeling at the least injury of inward self-consciousness, it can easily be mistaken for sanguine passionateness, which, as an opposite principle, is foreign to the animatic element

44 The deeper soul-life is manifested in the melancholy temperament, (in the gloomy contemplation of the night of earth, whose occurrences, impressions, and contacts, often in rigid material contradiction to the conditions and demands of itself,) surrounded by forms of external life as if with a black mourning veil, this temperament, also, can very easily be mistaken for inanimation of the inward life—for absolute phlegm Many a phlegmatic man appears melancholy, while his deadened, slumbering soul feels nothing, and his sleeping or lifeless spirit has arrived to neither a gloomy nor a cheerful view of life

45 Fire and air magnetic natures, more or less related to these temperaments, feel, in proportion to their animatic life, mutual attraction towards each other, and repulsion towards opposite natures

46 Animatic (nerve) life, and spiritual (inward) life are certainly two distinct conceptions, but the last stands so much the higher, in proportion as the first is developed Spiritual (inward) life in the absolute phlegm of an earth-magnetic individual, would be a contradiction itself—an impossibility

47 Animatic (nerve) life in a man, as well as the spiritual life, can be heightened, decreased, and gradually entirely lost by internal and external impressions We are acquainted with men, who, animatic in their youth, were not without soul, and who, having gradually become phlegmatic and soulless, the reverse of what they were, went down as earth magnetic natures, in materialism Opposed to these, we also find

---

* The author of these fragments has experienced the most singular effects from the *rapport* of a fire magnetic nature with a somnambulist in the highest crisis of clairvoyance, and in this communication generally, he only moves in the province of science and personal experience
† See § 28, 29
‡ This natural repulsion of healthy (nervous) men, is shown to a remarkable degree in the dislike to all strong drinks and spices, which collectively operate injurious ly upon the nerves, and many of them prejudicially upon the blood The English feed and poison their children from the cradle with outrageous doses of opium, pepper, &c , and thus bring about an overfullness of the blood, and a diseased state of the nervous organization, which are manifested in the deadening of the inward life, and in the blunting of the intellect, and promote that dullness which characterizes phlegmatic individuality
§ A strong proof of this is afforded by the author of this

novel, in himself Sickly and miserable from his cradle, with a constant affection of the breast and of hemorrage, and in danger of consumption, the right side of his body became totally paralyzed in his eighth year This lasted two years He was cured by magnetism Nevertheless, mind and soul were developed in the boy He wrote his first poem with his left hand, the right being paralyzed (See " Harro Harring, a biographical sketch by Alexander H. Everett ") men in whom animatic life was first developed when an exalted sentiment or a divine idea in some form took possession of them, and in a measure raised their souls above the mass of matter

II. SUPERIOR PSYCHOLOGY

48 Man as a spiritual being (soul) is a unity The body is but our covering, our instrument, and without soul would have neither strength nor life, and consequently no existence

49 Dualism rests upon error There is but one power—and what appears to us as opposing, power is only matter itself, the development and cultivation of which is the task of animatic power—the principle of life—life itself

50 Creation is an imbodiment, an incorporation of the original idea of Deity, who, as the primitive spirit, created life, which, as a working (animatic) power, forms and shapes matter

51 All life, all being, (existence,) proceeds from the primitive source of spirit, the source of strength, of light, of love, as an eternal mystery—impenetrable to human research

52 As our body is related to the soul, the mass of matter of the universe is related to the soul of the universe—to animatic power—which as life, flowed from the source of spirit

53 As our soul is related to spirit, (reason in its higher power,) so is the soul of the world (the animatic power in creation) related to the primitive spirit—to Deity

54 In men animatic power reveals itself as the organ of the soul—which proceeds from the source of spirit, provided with the self-consciousness of spirit (reason) and the presentiment of the divine original idea of being, as soul, in the principle of faith, of love

55 Spirit, Soul, and Body, are consequently three distinct conceptions in the unity of life

56 The soul is the unity of our being, from which the spirit is developed as the higher power of reason, and strives upwards to its source by attraction

57 Feeling, Will, Understanding, and Spirit are the four elements of our human existence, which, if they were all equally cultivated, could show man as God created him, " in his own image."

58. There is no evil principle The evil does not lie in man, much less any where else in nature, but in the regulations of men, in human society, which nourishes and strengthens egotism and ignorance, from which the evil proceeds

59. The unity of our being lies in the consciousness of our power of will, and manifests itself as moral freedom No power in heaven nor in earth can bend or destroy the mental power of will, for it is the consciousness of our divine nature itself

60 Millions of men live along in a state of animalism, as neither their feeling, nor their will, nor their understanding, nor their spirit, have been cultivated, and yet they pass for " reasonable men." They are not men, much less reasonable ones.

61 Mankind can as little make demands upon those creatures as men, as the social world in which they move makes a demand on their feeling, on their will, on their understanding, or on their spirit The social world only urges its claims on man's egotism.

62 Materialism denies the soul According to its rules, man is " a digesting and propagating machine, endowed with instinct, by which he moves, on the urgency of necessity, to preserve his life and to enjoy sensuality " Such is the man of materialism—the materialist himself—" in his own image "

63 Although man, as a soul, is born with all the faculties of feeling, of will, of understanding, and of spirit, and is left to his development as a man by education, there is, nevertheless, an endless variety in his individuality, in his very origin

64 LOVE (without which no man should receive his life, unless he supports his existence in consequence of a crime against nature) is a Magnetic *Rapport* without the sphere of magnetic clairvoyance

65 Love, as attraction of soul, cannot take place without development of inward life, and consequently not without a predominance of animatic (nerve) life An animal nature feels the instinct of propagation, (sensuality,) but not love

66 As violent as is the repulsion of an animatic being in the magnetic sleep, on the approach of an animal individuality,* just as decided is the repulsion† of an animatic (fire or air magnetic) female against an animal (earth and water magnetic) man, so soon as she is conscious of her existence as a soul, or *vice versa*.

67 This awaking to a consciousness of the animatic nature can take place from internal and external influences, as the effect of a pure love, and as a natural result of excessive sensuality and destructive contact with an opposite animal nature—often in consequence of both causes at the same time In both cases, a diseased state of the nerve organization ensues, for which the healing art has hitherto applied iron as a palliative remedy

68 In the case of physical disease, disturbance of the nerve life from " unfortunate love," a union with the beloved being would be the first and only condition of cure If this union does not take place, and the longing of love (founded in the inward life itself) is powerfully suppressed from external influences, a momentary physical recovery can only be effected at the expense of the inward life and of morality, with paralyzation and deadening of the animatic power, under the predominance of the animal nature—of sensuality

69 Should the unfortunate love, braving all external circumstances, connect itself with the inward life as unity of feeling, animatic power would remain predominant,—and no remedy could restore the equilibrium of the nerve fluid and of the iron particles in the blood.

Patients of this class manifest a decided disinclination for sensual enjoyment, a mastery over the animal nature, repulsion of physical contact

70 The application of iron as a known palliative remedy for the before mentioned nervous diseases, when they proceed from excessive sensuality, is a confirmation of my theory, as regards the object of iron in the blood

* This repulsion, which is manifested by convulsions, very simply lies in the superabundance of iron in the blood, in the heterogenous nature See § 28, 29
† The repulsion seems to have been acknowledged by the legislation of the ancients, in the *odium invincibile,* as a legal ground for divorce.

71 The science of medicine has recognised iron as a "strengthening" remedy, without accounting to itself how it operated, and from what cause It considered as a remedy that which is only a dangerous stimulant, and should never be applied, or at least only with great caution, always with psychological insight into the nature of the disease, and the individuality of the sufferers In the application of iron, the science of medicine seemed to follow (without perhaps knowing it) the homœopathic principle, for it uses the same element as a remedy which, as an anti-magnetic element, (as a superabundance of iron in the strange individuality of an earth or water magnetic nature,) brought about the derangement of the nerve organization by physical contact, by influence from without upon the fire or air magnetic being

72 Iron applied as a so called remedy in hysterical diseases, can only operate as a palliative when the disease proceeds from physical causes, from derangements of certain organs by the excessive enjoyment of sensuality and of propagation—weakness and prostration of the animal nature—but never when it proceeds from the inward life, as a retroaction upon the animatic life In the last case it produces, in proportion to the dose, more or less convulsions—as iron operates upon a somnambulist, in whose presence it is brought

73 As an external remedy, applied in baths, it produces a momentary irritation, an ebullition of sensuality—sensual desire—and can thus far promote conception, but never restore the equilibrium of animatic life. There follows after the application of iron, as after every stimulant, an after prostration of the animal life, a derangement and deadening of the animatic, and indirectly of the inward life * A hysteric patient, suffering from longing for love, (or in consequence of unfortunate love,) momentarily excited to sensuality by iron, loses his animatic (spiritual) strength in the same proportion as his animal nature is elevated in sensuality

74 We every day hear it asserted, that "the most opposite characters produce the best and happiest marriages" This is nonsense, and probably originated from a typographical error, as it might read, instead of characters "temperaments," and even then the assertion would not be tenable

The character of man, is the shaping of his inward being under the thousand-fold influences of education, of circumstances, of experience—in short, of all the impressions of life which form the man, or destroy him, it is his moral or immoral existence

The temperament of man, is founded in the physical relation of the nerve organization and of the blood, and has a bearing upon his character, so far as the different elements, which embrace the temperament, receive in themselves the different colors in different reflections

An animatic union of noble characters can take place, upon an equal degree of development, in opposite temperaments—and opposed to this, the greatest difference of temperament can manifest one and the same ebullition of noble passion, when the basis of the inner being of the characters bears a spiritual relationship

75 Put, on the contrary, an isolation of any one of the four temperaments is only imaginably in the phlegmatic—which characterizes the abstract imagination of the inward life—so unsusceptible to all impressions from without, as to an admixture with any one of the other temperaments within All the other temperaments appear very seldom, "scarcely ever," isolated in an individual, but more or less form that happy equilibrium of the human character, the less this or that temperament predominates

76 Even admitting the typographical error spoken of, the above rule would not be tenable An obsolete phlegm connected with its own element would only enjoy a so called "happy marriage," which would indeed be subjected to few disturbances from without, as both beings would vegetate along in material insensibility. As striking as this picture may appear, every observing psychologist will concede that it is to be met with in the reality, in a thousand resemblances, in all parts of the world it is man in the condition of animalism, propagating his race like an animal, it is the union of the earth magnetic natures of two beings in their own element.

77 It often remains difficult in the psychological analysis of the temperament, to distinguish correctly the inward being in the envelope of the temperament, for it often happens that the greatest calm of soul and presence of mind, of a so called sanguine or choleric man, is mistaken for phlegm, as, on the other hand, this or that action of a man is ascribed to his choleric or sanguine temperament, when it proceeds from abstract phlegm, from want of feeling, from denial of soul.

78 Every noble act or deed arises from feeling, the heart, (mind) A bad act or deed generally proceeds from insensibility or heartlessness, from a so called "hardened mind"

79 A pure, noble man can commit a great crime when his moral freedom of will is overcome by the ebullition of his feeling On the contrary, acts are done from moral freedom of will, which, according to social regulations, appear as crimes *

80 But no one will be disposed to place similar crimes on a parallel with a coolly calculated bad act, or with a murder which proceeds from the denial of feeling, from a hardened heart, as a tragical appearance of demoralization

81 As a murder may be committed from ebullition of feeling, in a passion, (whilst it would be difficult to deny the morality of the "criminal,") social crimes may take place which are ascribed to sensuality, whilst just the opposite element—animatic (inward) life, in its excited preponderance—is the cause of such crimes

82 Fire and air magnetic natures are less sensual than earth and water magnetic natures, for the iron in the blood (which represents the animal sensual natures) is kept in equilibrium, or controlled by the magnetic fluid

83 It is another great error, when even phy-

---

* We know cases in which physicians ordered chalybeate baths to women suffering under distraction of the nerve organization from animatic causes—unknown to the physicians. The effect of the baths was a momentary disposition to sensuality, and then total nervous and moral destruction.

* That this paragraph may be better understood, we add, for examples, Charlotte Corday, Lewis Sand, Allbeaux, Tschech, &c.

sicians consider many female nervous diseases to be the effect of unsatisfied sensuality, whilst they are often just the reverse—the effects of the unsatisfied demands of the soul—the effects of unreciprocated love

84 A sensual (earth and water magnetic) individuality, with a low degree of animatic (inward) life, does not become affected by that nervous derangement from longing for love, which is foreign to it.

85 Animal sensuality, and "enjoyment of the senses," are distinct notions. The more animatic life is developed, the purer is the enjoyment of the senses in every respect, which embraces whatever is beautiful and exalted in nature and art, but has nothing in common with animal sensuality, with bestiality

By the term "animal sensual nature" we understand predominant sensuality, with a greater or less inanimation of the animatic life, of unsusceptibility for the more noble and spiritually elevated. Every healthy man is capable of sensual enjoyment, but, "to the pure all things are pure, and the noble ennobles every thing in itself. Men who know no higher enjoyment than the sensual, are of animal natures, and their individuality corresponds with the phlegmatic and sanguine temperament—the earth and water magnetic categories

It is well known that the Turks are peculiarly sensual. The phlegmatic sanguine temperament predominates in them, their bodily fulness, their prevailing, predominating animal life, suppress the animatic power, the development of spiritual life. In accordance with this, the Turks manifest the attraction and repulsion of the magnetic categories. The Turk likes female corpulency, the terms *fat* and *beautiful* are to him synonymous, whilst a delicate form of body, of nobler animatic nature, presents little attraction for him. Opium destroys the animatic power, and indirectly increases the particles of iron in the blood

All heating, stimulating spices operate in a similar manner. Fish, (especially when salted,) and shell fish, as oysters for instance, produce a sensual effect. Hence the numerous propagation of the population on coasts abounding in fish, and likewise their phlegm is remarkable. Half raw beef, and strong beer, likewise effect a predominancy of animal nature, to the suppression of animatic power. The blood of some Turks, very superficially chemically analyzed, showed three, four, and five times the quantity of the iron particles to be found in an ordinary animatic individual. Science may pay attention to these facts, and investigate them further

86 The animatic spiritual life is the "sixth sense" of man, (the origin of which is the nerve fluid,) and the union of souls by love can only take place in this element of animatic life.

87 The love and reciprocated love of an animatic to an animal being is as abstract impossibility. What is called love, is in a thousand cases sensuality, and repulsion arises when that is satisfied · on the contrary, however, a deceptive attraction of an animal (anti-magnetic) nature (from the predominance of iron in the blood) can be imagined, which may stun and attract an animatic nature, as a mass of magnetless iron, draws the weaker magnet to itself. By this hypothesis alone, the innumerable matrimonial connexions of entirely different natures could be explained, which were a riddle to sound reason, inasmuch as it was inconceivable how a spiritual being could be fettered to a more or less soulless mass of matter

88 The above certainly strange hypothesis finds in reality such thousand-fold supports of experience, that it at least, like my hypothesis concerning the object of iron in the blood, deserves the attention of psychologists

89 In a thousand cases of such unnatural connexions, the fettered animatic life becomes gradually lost in animal existence, or it awakes in nervous convulsions when unnaturally overpowering, and degradation to the service of sensuality, of vulgar animal nature, deranges the organization

90 The hypothesis of the attraction of the predominant iron in animal natures, finds its support in the want of consciousness of the animatic nature, (of the inward life,) which (having become a sacrifice to deception) first awakes when the effect of marriage without love has destroyed the nerve organization—manifesting the existence of the inward life as an unsatisfied demand of love

91 The development of the inward life and of moral freedom through education, elevates man more and more from an animal existence to the consciousness of animatic life, which prevents, by repulsion, the crime of an unnatural union of two hostile natures

92 Enlightenment concerning the spiritual nature and the higher destiny of man, and the rational education of the rising generation, can alleviate the misery of the social world—prevent crimes, which the regulations of the world and the animal degradation of man in the element of materialism have hitherto systematically promoted, "under the protection of the laws"

93 The consciousness of animatic life is often suppressed by the sexual instinct, love is confounded with sensuality. But man was endowed with moral strength, freedom of will, as a spiritual being, to control the animal element within him. No pretext of "convenience," of "reasonable motives" or of circumstances, excuses the intentional union of opposite elements, from whose connexion proceed physical and moral disturbance, social and criminal offences. The cause and reason of such appearances are consequently not "the influence of Satan upon the evil nature" of man, they are founded in the unnatural regulations made by the social world, which immediately promote those disturbances

94 The unnatural union of opposite natures, in the sanctuary of generation, by animal demands and resignation without love, is in a measure "the sin against the holy spirit", of love for it affects the "crime of crimes"—the life of a future generation—the lot of all mankind.

APPENDIX TO CHAPTER II, BOOK VII.

STATEMENT OF DR ADLER, MEMBER OF THE GERMAN SOCIETY OF PHYSICIANS AND NATURALISTS, AND PRACTISING PHYSICIAN IN NEW YORK.

Mr. HARRO-HARRING laid before me his views "concerning the effect of iron in our blood," (manifesting his restless mental exertions,) for my examination and opinion, in a general medicinal respect

Believing that I have made myself sufficiently acquainted with the course of ideas, and the style of the author, I venture to express the conviction that the hypothesis established by him, concerning the department of physiology, chemistry, pathology, therapeutics, is peculiar and original, not borrowed from any medicinal school of Europe, nor taken from any to me known doctrine belonging thereto, and that, on account of its undeniable importance, it is worthy the consideration of scientific investigation

But as several premises upon which rest the connexion of the whole, are liable to important objections of science and experience, and as the author's manner of treating the subject offers a loose, not a strictly scientific connexion, (which according to his intention could not be otherwise,) I therefore feel called upon to give a statement of the reasons and limitations, under and with which I have adopted the author's views, and given this opinion to publicity.

Although I do not always partake in his opinion in regard to principles and deductions, my objections may give occasion to scientific discussion, and thus only heighten the interest for the author's hypothesis My so far complete observations, concern the views § 8, 67, 70, 71, 72, 73, 82, 83, 87, and 88, belonging to the main question, § 7 As it did not appear to be in accordance with the purpose of a novel, nor the plan of the author, to give my remarks here, I will deliver them to the public in a separate pamphlet.

F G ADLER, M D.
New York, Dec 6, 1845.

CHAPTER III

GABRIEL GARRINGOS

Biographical Fragment—Manuscript from Goa

—" I PURSUED the study of magnetism in the years 1810–12, in Madrid, where this science, at that time placed in the same category with sorcery and witchcraft, laden with curse and ban by church and state, was severely persecuted on the part of the inquisition

I had to thank a casual acquaintance with a French physician, for the perusal of some books and pamphlets which appeared to have little value for himself, since he, as he declared, only carried them with him as curiosities

Hardly had I entered the element of magnetism as a branch of science, than I obtained enlightening information concerning my own individuality, and recognised the existence of animatic force within me

I magnetized without a magnet, by means of the glance and the fluid of the hand, and produced the most interesting and instructive effects upon nervously diseased, and upon healthy persons, who, notwithstanding the threatened danger of falling under the power of the inquisition, confided themselves to me

There was living at that time in Madrid, a family of distinction from Buenos Ayres, who, on being informed of my studies, sought my acquaintance in a confidential manner The only daughter of this family, Señora Paola de C——, suffered from a liver complaint, which many physicians, pronouncing her symptoms consumptive, had treated falsely

After I had at the first glance satisfied myself of the animatic (fire and air magnetic) temperament of the patient, I undertook the cure by Mesmerism The patient arrived by speedy transition at the highest crisis then known to me, that of " clairvoyance with free motion "

After four operations by means of the hand fluid, repeated at the same hour, (in the evening,) it became easy for me to produce magnetic sleep by means of the glance fluid She gave me a clear perception of her disease, while she, like a soul, as it were, floating outside of the body, beheld it transparent, and pointed out to me the remedies which would cure the disturbances occasioned by former false treatment, and the disease itself, and which did, in fact, thoroughly cure them

During the crisis of her somnambulism, her spirit moved in a sphere of perception which had until then been strange to myself, and whose visions surprised to the utmost degree her parents, who were present every evening

These revelations attached me to this being by indissoluble bonds of reverence

This spiritual reverence, united with the attraction of kindred natures, and with animatic reaction on her part upon me, awakened the feeling of sympathy in me, which gave my life the direction I have pursued since that time.

This accordance of animatic nature, formed a bond of soul-union in the sphere of magnetism, which soon evinced itself in a similar degree in the life out of the state of somnambulism, although this state was entirely unknown to the sufferer (as to all other somnambulists) so soon as she returned from it to the outward world

I had learned, at the moment of my introduction to the family, that Señora Paola was betrothed for a " marriage of convention "—and guided my deportment towards her according to this discovery, so eventful to me.

Her powerful sympathy for me soon found utterance in the crisis of her clairvoyance, to the great terror of her parents, to whom I explained the circumstance that a somnambule, when without the magnetic sphere, is conscious of no phenomena within that element, and remembers not a single syllable, which she may have spoken in magnetic sleep

The parents soon satisfied themselves of the truth of my information, and saw it confirmed by the fact, that Señora Paola denied, in the strongest manner, her sympathy for me, in consequence of the will of her parents in relation to her " destiny "——

Paola's father had been sent in state affairs of the South American colony to Madrid His position subjected him to the usual intrigues and cabals of a cabinet, whose ministry endeavored to render his whole mission abortive

The somnambule once, in her state of spiritual perception occupied herself with some surprising particulars of the circumstances which threatened the future prosperity and fate of her father—and gave information that placed it in his power to disarm the intrigues of his opponents. This served to protect the interests of the colony against the encroachments of despotism, and Don A. de C—— at least attained this object of his personal satisfaction.

The riddle how he had been able to penetrate into the deepest mysteries of his enemies, and to convict them of their contradictions, was inexplicable to them.

The suspicion fell on me, and my life was more than ever in danger. The rack and tortures of the inquisition awaited me.

But the same genius who had in the sphere of spiritual perception given us this information, saw just as clearly my nearest, as well as my most remote future. Paola recognised in her visions the unavoidable necessity for our separation on earth, and beheld just as clearly the steps and measures of the enemy, whose persecution surrounded me with snares.

The mother had, on pretence of a journey into the country, taken a secret dwelling, in which I observed the last crisis. My friend desired me one evening, (it was the 24th of May, 1810,) not to go home as usual, but to pass the night with a friend, who had sought after me, and expected me. She saw my dwelling surrounded by military ——

I took leave of Paola, in her crisis of clairvoyance. She returned to real life—and what she had seen and said as a somnambule—remained as strange and unknown to her as ever.

The friend to whom I was recommended by the counsel of the somnambule, occupied a position in which he would not easily be suspected of sympathy with me. I remained carefully concealed in Madrid, until they no longer sought for me there. My flight was arranged and carried out. I arrived at Cadiz, and thence on board a vessel to Goa.

The magnetic *rapport* with my friend still continued.

For the first month she regularly fell, at the same time, into a magnetic sleep, and awoke just as regularly about midnight. During those hours I found myself in a state of waking dreaminess, which I cannot here describe.

I could imagine what impression this still existing spiritual *rapport*, between Señora Paola and myself, must produce upon her parents, and struggled with myself, for life and death, to dissolve it—or looked for the accomplishment of the determination which she nourished in her somnambulism—of following me to Goa.

Whether or not this longing was as powerful in her waking state, as it manifested itself in the crisis of her somnambulism, I learned notwithstanding, at a later period, that she always, with wonderful self-control, denied her sentiments I had, at my sudden departure, strictly enjoined it upon the parents not to call in an anti-magnetic physician in case she (as I surmised) fell of herself into magnetic slumber, and should perhaps experience convulsions and cramps This request and warning rested upon my purpose, if possible to employ outward means of dissolving a magnetic *rapport*, which had led to a union of souls forbidden by convenience.

I sought to break up this regularly recurring sleep, by external methods, I took chalybeate baths—surrounded myself with iron. The consequence was a violent disturbance of my nerve organization, and severe convulsions in my somnambule, as I afterward learnt, since (without her knowledge in the waking state) I corresponded with her mother.

As I was with her in spirit, and perceived the reaction of her convulsions by the employment of such remedies, so did she as a spirit float around me in my waking state, and from the hour of our separation until this day—through a quarter of a century—her essence has never left me. It floats around me wherever I go or stay. It has become a part of my being. It lives in me, as I lived in her entity.

She appeared to me at that time in a waking dream, and besought me not to torment her, not to remove myself spiritually from her by the employment of disturbing remedies,* which was a thing impossible in itself, and contrary to the primitive laws of the higher soul's life.

" You may employ external means to destroy the organism of our soul's life, but you are as little able to destroy the *bond* that unites us, as you are able to destroy our souls '" said she, in a dream, shortly before my embarkation from Cadiz.

" *The soul is indestructible*. It knows no time—no age. No suffering is able to change its entity. It may remain undeveloped, suppressed, like a germ, in men; the soul may be extinguished to the last spark through materialism, but the germ cannot be annihilated—the spark cannot be extinguished. It slumbers on in the mass of matter, and at its awakening, after the physical death of the shell that enveloped it, it discovers that it was incumbent for it to have fought the fight of its development on earth. It must begin from below in another world, in the scale of imperfection to which it has sunk back through failure in the development of its force of will—through failure in self-consciousness upon earth —— Through the consciousness of our reason, and through the perception of our soul, does the spirit within us develop itself, and strive upwards to the source of light, from which it is derived.

" Whoever lives on earth without the recognition of reason, and without perception of the soul, lives on in the element of materialism; he does not live, he vegetates, and at the moment of awakening after death, an account will be required from each one, of how he has developed or neglected the sacred pledge of the inward life.

" The consciousness of inward life or death, or the soul's suicide on earth, is the heaven and hell beyond the grave——in the awaking."

With similar consolations did the spirit of my friend strengthen me in my dream-life, and I discontinued the employment of disturbing and destructive remedies, for the dissolving of our animatic unity, as no external methods would have been able to destroy our unity of soul.

Paola followed the will of her parents on her return to Buenos Ayres, and gave her hand to

---

* In accordance with the facts upon which these communications are founded, we know also a fact in the contrary case, in which a man in animatic union with a lady, separated from her, fell into a state of nervous disturbance in consequence of iron in several forms, applied on her as medical remedies. The " effects in distance," of many hundred miles, could be proved by letters and diaries

her betrothed a year after our separation Her soul remained also united to mine, notwithstanding she was twice a sufferer from disturbing physical causes—— and her state of magnetic *rapport* was interrupted

I experienced what no mortal on earth suspects, who does not know the sphere in which my being for ever moved I saw her then afterwards in a dream, as the mother of two daughters The oldest was strange to me—the second my spiritual image The first died—and it has seemed to me for some years, as if Paola no more lived on earth, since she speaks to me in my dreams in a more elevated spiritual language, and my soul has found peace upon earth

My relatives left Spain likewise, and went to South America I have one sister, whom I love infinitely, as she loves me But in the possibility that a human error may occur in my dream-life, and Paola still live, I remain faithful to my resolve, not to allow a syllable to be heard from me, until I obtain the assurance of her death, or that which I have longed for—to bear my silence to the grave It was my design, not even through the news of my existence to disturb in the least degree a social relation, which, from all that I could learn, was not so painful for Paola as the effect it produced upon me at a distance

At her departure from Spain, Paola's mother sent me the duplicate of a portrait of my somnambule which a talented artist had copied from her own original

Since Paola's marriage I have no more intelligence from her mother, as I broke off the correspondence on my part

GABRIEL GARRINGÒS TO SENHOR H VERA

Goa, January 13th, 1838

My friend—

I transmit you the two accompanying manuscripts, the Element of Magnetism, etc, and *Autobiographical Fragments*, and permit me here to repeat my verbal request and commission to you, at your departure for Rio de Janeiro

After having been made acquainted, since your youth, with all that concerns my inward and outward life, I desire you carefully, but in secret, to make inquiries in regard to the fate of my friend and my sister—under the guidance likewise of the accompanying family papers and the aforesaid portrait

Should my forebodings be well founded that a being lives on earth, who, as a wonderful phenomenon in the province of the spiritual spheres, is so nearly akin to me spiritually, as to be a copy of my inward being, the confirmation of this would be a singular compensation for all the sufferings I have endured on earth, in consequence of an indissoluble spiritual bond

Should you succeed in discovering traces of my friend, then conceal entirely this commission, in case she still lives, and gladly as I would fulfil my duty as a brother towards my sister, I must, in such a case, still further maintain my incognito, even towards her I doubt whether Señora Paola knows my sister, but even if she have remained a stranger to her until now, a chance might reveal that I still live, and where I live This discovery might even yet endanger my friend's peace of mind—which remains sacred to me

Should my forebodings, however, not have deceived me, should Paola have passed over into that sphere of light whose existence as a spiritual reality became certainty to us, I then desire you to make use of the accompanying power of attorney, and to control and dispose of the half of my possessions, or to be equally divided among the children of my sister and Señora Paola, remarking, by the way, that the other half will accrue to these my heirs at my death, for which purpose I have named you, my dear Vera, as the executor of my testament

Your friend, etc, etc

— · —⟞⟞⟞⟞⟞⟞ ❦ ⟝⟝⟝⟝⟝⟝— · —

CHAPTER IV

PATRICK AND SALLY

HARDLY had Senhor Vera heard, through Dr Thorfin and Horatio, of the arrival of Signora Serafini and the arrest Alvarez, than he went to the Minister of the Interior, and sought a private audience, which was granted to him without particular difficulty He legitimated himself as the attorney of an uncle of the lady and the prisoner, commissioned to take an interest in them in every respect, in any case that might occur

The Minister of the Interior was always—Minister of the Interior, and this position, in a monarchy or at a court, embraces a legitimate or quasi legitimate importance, which troubles itself little with the family relations of any arrested type setter or guitar teacher, especially when he is the companion in guilt of a *sans culotte*, or even his brother-in-law. The Minister promised to "inform himself about the matter" of the two prisoners, and allowed the millionaire from Goa to undertake another excursion to the portal of his ministerial palace Senhor Vera made use of this permission, and found his excellency colder and more laconic than before

"The release of the prisoner, De la Barca, is not to be thought of," replied he to the negro from Goa "With regard to the faroupilha, Serafini, he will probably be condemned to death, and I will endeavor to soften the sentence to perpetual exile from Brazil But his process must take its course, I cannot set him at liberty not even with guarantee of a million As regards the young man, De la Barca, accusations from Europe are pending against him, through an ambassador I will, upon your intercession, and from considerations for his sister, take care that he is not given up Your wish to visit the prisoners cannot be complied with. Neither you, nor the lady, nor any one else, can hold any intercourse with them so long as their sentence is not pronounced Tell the lady, however, that I will undertake the twofold affair, and, if possible, will soften the sentence of death against her husband as a traitor, as I told you already "

The minister turned to a secretary, who had remained during the interview, and Senhor Vera took his leave

He went to the Hotel du Nord, where Dr. Thorfin and Horatio awaited him, to accompany him on a visit to Signora Serafini She had gradually received from Dr Thorfin a communication concerning the existence and the fate of her brother, which could not be withheld from her, as Senhor Vera urged it, that he might when it was possible, fulfil the commission of her uncle as his attorney Angelica learnt, to her highest surprise, the intelligence from Goa, and at the same time also received the revelation concerning the singular bond which placed at her side a female, as a sister, who lived in her neighborhood in the strictest incognito

We consign the unfortunate wife and sister to the consolation and care of those friends who arranged for her a country house in Prava Grande, where she was to await the time that should decide the fate of those so dear to her

Patrick Gentleboy received a card of a certain Lady Hamlet through the medium of a negro, who could not tell him much about the occasion of the invitation But Patrick had heard all sorts of long stories told by one sailor and another during tedious night watches before the mast, on board of one or another slow sailing ship on a long, long voyage stories of wonderful lucky accidents, by which this or that poor devil by some chance or other was suddenly taken out from the mire of his miserable life, and became a "gentleman" without knowing how

Patrick made his toilet as carefully as a Dutch sailor when he is ordered "to the helm" on board an Admiral's vessel, dressed himself clean from head to foot, and even drew the two long ends of his neck handkerchief through a gold ring which he had bought for himself as a memorial of his charge as "commanding officer of a cutter" at the mouth of the La Plata Connoisseurs assert, to be sure, that Patrick was cheated, that the ring was false, but having paid for it as gold, he wore it as gold He thrust a new Chili hat that cost ten milliers on his head, and swaggered along in a broad sailor's step through the suspicious Rua do Sabão to the Campo da Santa Anna, and arriving at length in the open space, sought the street near it, where Lady Hamlet must live It was about one o'clock in the day The great fountain in the apparently interminable square swarmed with negroes and negresses, who drew the water and rinsed their linen, and told each other all sorts of things about whites, and blacks and mulattoes, and caboclos! and often laughed in chorus

To his great amazement, he met a female, poorly but cleanly dressed, with a black straw gipsy, and a real strongly marked Irish countenance, that was rather handsome than otherwise It was Lucy, attended by a droll little old negress, dressed in a coffee sack with a water ewer upon her head, and a little pipe in her little mouth "What, the devil! Lucy! where did you come from?" cried he to her, "and what sort of a faymale two legged mole is that creeping along by you there?"

"I've been to see a Mrs Adams that was after wanting a white woman to do some sewing for her, but to my notion she seems more like a Miss than a Mistress She is a kind lady for a Saxon, and I've got some work from her"

"And I am bid to go to a Lady Hamlet Only see what sort of an admiralty order that is, that brings me into this latitude! and sure there's enough of that same here, and longitude besides, plenty of room to beat against without touching land "Do you know where this street is? then read once No 9 Rua do—do——where is it?"

"And sure that's the same house that I m after coming from?" cried Lucy "Is there ever a Lady Hamlet lives in your garden?" inquired she of old Behida, who had been very attentively observing the long red-haired branco

"Si Senhora?" replied the old woman with a deep breast voice "Yes, Senhora Amlet lives with Senhora Adams Si Senhora? Dabedicademlasimaqulipatu?"

"Will you show this gentleman the way there? There, there are four vintéms for you," continued Lucy, taking out her purse to bestow the gentle gift from pure compassion for the poor creature

"Thanks! thanks, Senhora! thanks!" croaked Behida in the alto voice which she had at command when she was pleased, "Dabedicadempatigumati! I ll show the Senhor Branco! bonito Senhor Branco grande big! hi-hi-hi! red hair! red beard! bonito! Dabedicadem—hi-hi-hi!" said she, laughing loudly, and turning towards the corner of the little countrylike street, in which Senhora Sally Fortuna Adams Hamlet resided

Patrick had not much time to chat with Lucy, he promised her to come to O Halloran's in the evening, and tell her what his fate had prepared for him, and then hurried after the female mole, who had not drawn any water, as she wished first to earn the four vintéms she had received beforehand

Behida had been prepared at the gate for such inquiries by Miss Sally, and now led the "fine red branco" to Lady Hamlet, who sat in the audience chamber in the wide armchair "Great Britain," dressed in decent negligé, and absorbed in Dickens's "Oliver Twist"

Patrick looked at the Lady, and looked at her again, and showed his card, and asked if "this was the place!"

"Sit down," began Sally, in a low voice, and with a seriousness of expression that offered a singular contrast with the lascivious extravagance of the Bachante of the preceding night

"You are an Irishman, and your name is Patrick——"

"Patrick McCaffray at your service, but they call me mostly Pat Gentleboy, plase your Ladyship!"

Sally sighed, for it was difficult for her to make the preface which must precede her revelation

"You are in the service of a man here who calls himself the Baron de Spandau, who is a spy?" began she at length

Patrick had seated himself, and was pulling his Chili hat in all manner of ways, and looking at the lady as sharply as if she were a buoy or tun which he wished to steer past

"The man is called the Baron de Spandau what's taken me in tow, sure enough, your ladyship,' replied he at length, "and sure I found out he was a spy before iver I took sarvice wid him, and didn't I tell that same to Captain Hinango and Dr Thorfin——?"

"Captain Hinango and Dr Thorfin!" interrupted Sally with considerable vivacity, "that's right—those were the names——"

"But if I might be so bould as to ax your ladyship who are you? for I'm a stranger here and—" He looked all around, as if to satisfy himself that all which surrounded him was in fact strange to him

"I am a poor girl from Norfolkshire in England," replied Sally, with a reiterated sigh "My name is—" she suddenly hesitated and blushed. A womanly sentiment of shame seized her at the thought of the position in which she was placed in regard to the seaman

"My name is Caroline," continued she. "Can an English woman rely upon you, Patrick, in a matter which concerns the saving of several lives?"

"Is it whether you can rely upon me when there are lives to be saved?" repeated Patrick, rising hastily, "well, then, be Jasus! my name is Patrick McCaffray, and may sorrow be my portion if ye cannot rely upon me when there are lives to be saved, whether male or female, begging your ladyship's pardon for speaking so loud, but its the truth! I came here with the Nordstjernan, a Swedish brig, of 100 tons, strong, heavy, and a fine sailer, Capt Fingreen, and before I went on board I—fired with this finger a carbine, and burnt down an Argentile officer in the stun of our cutter, who wanted to make an incendiary out of me, to bring honest people, gentile people, to the gallows a young lady from La Plata river, beautiful as the moon when it rises in the first night watch! and before I came on board the Argentile brig I was pressed, with a South American gentleman—a gentleman, if ever a cabin passenger was one. And now your ladyship knows who I am and where I came from, and I'll take your orders if you plase"

Sally beckoned to old Bebida, who showed herself at the door with wine and water, and a large glass. She came in, placed the refreshments on the table, murmured very softly her "Dabedicadem," and glided out again

"Help yourself to a drink," continued Sally, "it is warm, and you must go a long distance, to the Gloria, or does Captain Hinango live somewhere near?"

Patrick had used the large glass for what it was good for, wiped his lips with the ends of his black silk neck handkerchief, and replied, "I ax your ladyship's pardon, Captain Hinango has been living at Santa Theresa, but is now on board the Astrala, which lies out there by the Cobras island, between the Cobras and the Patriot's Fortress, Devil-call-you,* as I believe it is the name"

"Well, which do you believe you can find the most certainly at this hour, Captain Hinango or Dr Thorfin?"

"Shure and it would be Captain Hinango, on board the Astrala, but if I go to him, and the baron knows it, there'l be a storm brewed"

"The baron knows that I have sent for you, I was to spy you concerning Captain Hinango's voyage. You can, then, go undisturbed on board to him, and in case the baron should ask you about it afterwards, you could say that you went there to inquire of him if he had not known a Mr McDonald in London, the brother of Lady Hamlet, that this lady was here, and thought that she had heard his name mentioned by her brother, then you can come back again undisturbed, as I must spy you still further"

"Now I begin to see how the land lies, and

* Do-Vilcalhon.

I'll steer my course accordingly. And what will I carry for Captain Hinango?"

"This letter, on which hangs his life and the life of the young lady from Buenos Ayres—and my life," added she in a low voice, trembling, as she handed the envelope to the Irishman, which contained the order from Buenos Ayres, under a false name of the baron, addressed to Señor Prole

"I got possession of these letters at the risk of my life last night, and must lay it back again before this evening, where I took it from. If it were missed, I should be poisoned without ceremony, for the scoundrels would know then that I saw through their plan, and knew their position"

"Och! and that's thrue for you then, it's that same they'd be doing," returned Patrick, shoving the letter into the breast pocket of his blue spencer, and buttoning it up. "Miss Caroline," said he, after a pause, "I must hoist anchor, and get under sail to come alongside of the Astrala. I'll come back here in an hour, but if I don't find Captain Hinango, what then? will I go to Dr Thorfin?"

"Yes," assented Sally, "go to one of the two, but of all things in the world, bring the letter back to me before this evening"

"In two hours you shall have the letter again, I promise your ladyship, and may God reward you for what you are doing to save Captain Hinango and his friend!—Your health, Miss Caroline" added he, while he again availed himself of the large glass, and then cordially took his leave

He hurried out across the Campo da Santa Anna, into the Rua do Sabio, and still out, and further out, to the Praya dos Poscadores where he stepped into a negro boat, and steered over to the Astrala. He found Captain Hinango in his cabin, employed with the expedition to Rio Grande, whither Horatio was to go in a few days. After a short and very incomprehensible preface about a Lady Hamlet, and Miss Caroline, and Campo da Santa Anna, and a long, long street called the Rua do "Sabottes," and about the young lady from La Plata river, and the risk of life, and the like, Patrick drew out the letter, and handed it to the captain of the Astrala. The worthy Patrick was by no means tipsy, the two drops of wine at Miss Sally's had not given him the least appearance of intoxication, but what he said had very little meaning

Hinango opened the envelope and began to read, in the hope of learning more from the letter than from Patrick's "speech from the throne" in the name of "Queen Victory." Hardly had he glanced over the first periods, when he looked at the sheet on both sides, turned it over again, then looked at Patrick, and inquired:

"Where did you get this letter?"

"Ax pardon, your honor," replied Patrick, "it's the most natural thing in life. A young girl that calls herself Caroline, from Norfolkshire in England, gave the letter to me, and runs the risk of her life if I wouldn't bring it back again in an hour. As for what's in the letter, that I don't know, for I can't spake French, but I only know that Miss Caroline has a good intintion to save the lives of some people that she doesn't know intirely, and that's the whole thruth, axing your honor's pardon—

that's all I had to say before. And now, your honor, 'll be afther understanding the letter, and all about it"

Hinango now read further, and the sheet trembled in his hand, not by any means that personal fear took possession of him—he knew no fear. His courage rose with every danger, when it only concerned himself, but he transferred himself, with all the vivacity of his northern imagination, into the position of the poor girl who had sent him a document which contained his own death sentence, and that of Dolores, and without personal interest, had, in such a manner, exposed herself to danger to save them both

"Where is the girl who gave you this letter?" inquired he, hastily and urgently, seizing a pen and copying some passages of the letter, while he spoke to Patrick

"In the little quiet street round the left hand corner, from the great wide long place, where the nigger women 'wash," replied he, and Hinango wrote further

"Do you know whether I can speak to her? whether she would receive a visit?"

"I doubt it, captain,' said Patrick, "for doesn't your honor see, if you went there, the baron might find it out'

Hinango started, and looked at him intently "The baron?" cried he, "the girl knows the baron then? This letter is directed to the baron, that I can comprehend, but I do not comprehend the girl, therefore I would like to speak to her You are a fellow who has seen many craft, tell me then, Patrick, what do you think of this girl? the Caroline—to what class does she belong?"

"Och then, captain," replied Patrick, "I'll make bould to say that she holds a good course, when she's trying to save your honor and the young lady, and that's a great deal, for the rest, she seems to me a right solid, well built, and good sailing brig, who has not been many years in service, but hardly used, as it seems to me, your honor, and run ashore by some captain or other, and left there till another one goes to sea with her, and runs her ashore again So that's what I think about the fine English Caroline of Norfolk But it's time, your honor, for me to be getting into the boat agin, to take back the letter."

Hinango had, meanwhile, noted what was necessary, again placed the letter in the envelope without address, and rising, said to Patrick with all the earnestness of his nature, "Patrick, now take this letter to the worthy girl, and greet her from me Tell her that I thank her in the name of the young lady, and that I desire to thank her myself for her noble minded behavior towards me Tell her that whoever she may be, she holds a high and sacred place in my esteem, and if I can do the smallest thing for the promotion of her happiness, she must not refuse to talk with me about it, whenever and wherever it may be Nevertheless, I leave all that with her, and now see that you lose no time."

"I'll see to all that, your honor,"said Patrick, confidently, and hurried into his negro boat, which awaited him at the side of the Astrala

"Strange," thought Hinango, when he was again alone, "this is the third case in my experience in which a poor creature of this class has taken an interest in the persecuted, risking her own life to save the lives of men, without expecting, under the existing circumstances, any acknowledgement whatever! Is the female heart so noble by nature, that no social wretchedness can lay it waste? or does misfortune heighten the nobleness of the heart?"

Amid similar contemplations he locked his writing desk, took with him the copy which he had just written, and entered his boat

We already know that he had been invited, with Dr Thorfin, to the betrothal at Mr Thomson's

The fate of Dolores lay nearer to his heart than the danger which evidently threatened him personally He turned to Dr Thorfin, and informed him of what he had just learned Horatio was present

"What is to be done to save Dolores?" was the question, and a long pause of mutual consideration followed

"I must take Dolores on board, and conduct her to Monte Video," began Hinango, at length

"That would be the only method," observed Thorfin, "but the embarkation cannot take place here in Rio For the future, the Baron is, so to say, a member of the Thomson family, and Dolores has long since been considered as such How in the world shall we bring her away from Bota Fogo, without pursuit on the part of the old widower, who wishes to marry her, and on the part of the baron, who wishes to deliver her up?"

"Old Mr Thomson must go with her," observed Horatio, "Dolores must act as if she entered into his plan"

"That she will not do," interrupted Hinango, "it is worth her life, but, as a woman, she will undertake no such part"

"I feel that," assented the youth, "but do you know any other way?"

"She must take a voyage with the Thomson family, may be to Santa Catharina, where Mr Thomson has business now besides You, Horatio, must go as quickly as possible to Rio Grande. Celeste is there Bangalih must cruise before Santa Catharina with the Mazzini, I will meet him there with the Astrala, and we must take Dolores either peaceably or by force"

"The plan is not bad," observed Thorfin, "but Robert must accompany Dolores, and conduct the whole expedition We can confide Dolores to him, and if the Baron should even go with them, Robert would bring off Dolores, either by cunning, or by his decided deportment in defiance of him"

"Could not this take place here in Rio?" inquired Horatio, after a renewed pause

"It would be very difficult, almost impossible," observed Thorfin Admitting that Robert should find it possible to undertake a trip on the bay with her, and conduct her on board the Astrala, would not Spandau immediately suspect where she had been carried to? Under the pretence that you had "chains and cramps" on board for the slave trade, he would immediately institute a search Although many ships are equipped here, and intended for this purpose, the pretence would serve the secret police to seize the condemned from La Plata river The circumstance that she is here under a false name would make her arrest lawful, and then she would be in the baron's hands, and Mr Thomson would not even then believe that De Spandau was a spy De Spandau would do every thing as Thomson's brother in law, to be helpful to him, to compel Dolores to marry him, and the old man would be gratefully obliged to the Baron for his rascality So soon as Dolores takes a single step to leave Thomson's, she incurs the risk of falling into the hands of the police "

" I perceive all that," assented Hinango , " but now for one question will Robert tear himself away from the fetters which paralyze him here ? Will he be able to save himself in order to save Dolores ?"

Horatio looked inquiringly at his friend, for he, in his inexperience, had not seen through the relation of Robert to his neighbor, having less quicksightedness than the others

" I hope," replied Thorfin, " that exactly and simply this, and only this occasion, will tear him away from the tragical circumstances which surround him We know him hitherto in the depth of his noble nature I am satisfied that the safety of Dolores lies near his heart, for he loves her like his sister, and reverences her like a saint But I admit also that a powerful motive must be aroused within him, to separate him from his neighbor, if it be only for a time, and if he does not soon separate himself from her—I fear—more than I will express to-day."

" In that case, my dear Horatio, you must now immediately set off for Rio Grande, may be by water to Santa Catharina, and so along the coast, under the good pretence of your art, may be as a landscape painter "

" I am ready" replied Horatio, " and will go all the more gladly, now that I know that Celeste is already there We shall then soon find an opportunity of receiving Dolores in Santa Catharina "

" De Spandau has at least no authority there, as he has here," observed Hinango " Even if there be a police there, it is at least no secret police, at his service Under Robert's orders, old Achilles will always be his man in case of need, and gladly as I would take Patrick with me as boatswain of the Astrala, he appears on the other hand as indispensable for such an expedition in Robert's service and for the safety of Dolores "

" The fellow is indispensable," added Thorfin " It remains for us now to obtain the consent of Dolores to this plan, and if possible to arrange the voyage to Santa Catharina before you go away, Señor Horatio, that we may then be able to decide when the Mazzini must cruise before Santa Catharina "

" If possible, I will be on board of the Mazzini myself," replied the youth , " I hope to arrange it so "

The three friends still conversed about the many particulars for the preparation and carrying out of the plan, until the time arrived which summoned Hinango and Thorfin to the betrothal Horatio felt more painfully than ever the bitterness of his social separation from Dolores, who, in the " castle" of an English house, must renounce all acquaintance, and least of all durst receive a " foreigner" like Horatio, who was " only an artist," as a guest at the house

Nothing else remained for the youth but to send his hearty greeting to his friend, who, through the fate of his uncle, stood as near to him as any being on earth

CHAPTER V

THE DIPLOMATIC DINNER

THERE are words in every language which cannot be translated in the same sense in any other language by any single word, because the idea is strange which the word expresses, and many a language has no words for ideas, which are current in every other language. Thus the two English words, " humbug" and " dullness," cannot be translated in any other language without lengthy description, because the ideas which these words represent, are national English, and at the same time inseparable

The English language, originally brought together on the basis of the Anglo-Saxon tongue, by a certain system of piracy, (as the possessions of the British have been acquired in all quarters of the globe,) wants a multitude of words, the ideas of which are foreign to the nation, because it does not exactly require them in its business. Thus, for instance, the word " fatherland " was first introduced by Lord Byron, until which an Englishman was unacquainted with the term. He was acquainted with the word " native country," the land where he, as an individual, was born—the word " home," where he finds his comfort, which he can transport to all parts of the world , but the Englishman as little knew the word " fatherland," as he did the term " love of fatherland," which is something quite different from his patriotism The Greek word, Æsthetic, (the science of the intellectually beautiful,) long since current in the German language, and in a measure " incorporated " in it by Lessing's " Laocoon," is foreign to the English language, because the sense for the intellectually beautiful is wanting in the nation, while this science has its professorship in every university of the European continent

It would be an endless task, and the object of a particular literary work, to analyse the disfiguration of foreign ideas in the reception of foreign words in the English language, but such a work would be instructive

We have been invited to Miss Thomson's betrothal dinner, and have here only to do with the words and ideas, humbug and dulness

The bridegroom represents humbug, the bride dulness

What is humbug ?

The word seems to have originated in latter times, from the development of " civilization "

Aristotle-Johnson was not acquainted with it Is the word composed from hum and bug ? The hum of a carrion beetle over a foul morass ? or is it perchance the name of the inventor of humbug, by whom the word was applied to the invention, or to the thing as, for instance, the words Daguerreotype, Mesmerism, Fourierism, Paletot, Garrick, Guillotine, and so many others ? Perhaps it is really the name of an immortal man—immortal by the mischief which his invention has caused in all parts of the world to which English civilization has extended But in such a case, if it were his name, like Fulton, Guttenberg, Hahnemann, Berthold Schwartz, &c , &c It is inconceivable that humbug itself has not long since hit upon the speculation of

---

* Translated into English about ten years ago.

placing a monument to its inventor—to humbug with his birthplace, the house in which he was born, the little sh: he wore when a child, the nightcap in which he slept, in short, " to humbug" with all the relics of its immortal inventor What " a new world" of humbug would be opened to humbug by this apotheosis of its inventor It is indeed a thought which cannot be sufficiently discussed, as the episode of a novel We must therefore look, for its investigation, to another literary work, to be as comprehensive as possible

As every creature requires its elements of existence, as the bird lives in the air, the fish in the water, amphibious animals in both elements, the swine in the mire, the muckworm in the 'stench of manure, Humbug exists in its element —Dullness Without the element of dullness, humbug cannot exist

What is dullness ?

Aristotle-Johnson says " Dullness is stupidity, indocility, dimness " Well, very well But neither stupidity, nor indocility, nor dimness, is dullness. The word dullness embraces rather all the conceptions which lie at the foundation of all these three significant words But also the thorough and satisfactory discussion of the term dullness cannot be treated as the episode of any novel, but only as the element of humbug, as the so called " life question of humbug," in a philosophic novel—" Humbug "*

Monsieur le Baron de Spandau, a former apprentice to an apothecary, then a Prussian ensign, and then sentenced to imprisonment for the practical development of his talent in the visitation of the portfolios of others, was, in the last capacity, recognised as a useful subject in the service of the royal Prussian secret police, in the department of foreign affairs

He was an intimate friend of Signore Partesotti,† from Mantua, the celebrated Austrian spy at Paris, who had acquired a certain " honorable position" in the history of the secret associations (of the police as well as of republican conspiracies) of our epoch, and of right deserves his place in a biographical dictionary of the " bearers of court and gallows dignities "

Monsieur le Baron de Spandau had then been betrothed to Miss Susan in the same very natural manner, as the book publisher's clerk, Monsieur le Comte de B—— from Milan, married a Miss *——, and the Billiard Maker, Monsieur le Comte de —— from Smyrna, married a Lady *—— in London, in the years 1832–1835.

"With humbug nothing is impossible," could very well pass into a proverb, by the side of the old proverb, "With God nothing is impossible "

It was much more brilliant in Mr Thomson's country house at Bota Fogo, on this day of betrothal, to which we now return, than it was once on that festive Sunday, when Mr Thomson's hopes, and expectations, and claims on life were " weighed," and Señora Isabella de Campana was weighed.

As soon as the morning had fairly commenced, " all hands were called on deck," to clean and sweep all the rooms, chambers, and closets of the " Villa Thomson," to turn about every thing that was in them, to dust all the furniture, to fix and fold all the curtains and other drapery, as if right should be done for the reception of such respectable guests, at the head of whom was his Excellency the Minister of his Transparent Highness the Prince of and at Kniphausen

The old portraits of Vasco de Gama, and the no less immortal poet Camoês, in valuable copperplate engravings in glass and frame, (remains of the decayed property of a former possessor of the villa, of Portuguese nationality,) were as carefully wiped off and cleansed from musquito spots, as the magnificent picture of Queen Victoria, which had only arrived a few months before, as a selected impression " avant la lettre," from London, direct to Bota Fogo, and was displayed in a broad rosewood frame, with gold borders, under crystal glass, in a small vice cabinet, next to the often mentioned " green parlor "

His excellency the ambassador of Kniphausen, made his appearance as early as half-past one, although he well knew that the main business, to which he had been called, would first begin at four or half-past four

He made use of the excuse of offering to the extraordinarily hospitable Miss Thomson his especial congratulation at her betrothal, in the form of a morning visit, whereby he would partake of a sort of lunch, which, if eaten at the Hotel Faroux, would cost, by the bill of fare, three milliers, without wine As we here introduce this European and Brazilian important personage, it is right and proper to specify the qualities of his excellency at the introduction

We therefore remark, beforehand, that there are, in the diplomatic world, ambassadors who are not diplomatists, and diplomatists who never become ambassadors

Far be it from us here to engage in a detailed, systematic and categorical account of the various qualities of diplomatic characters, as there are. Ambassadors and ministers, ministers plenipotentiary, resident ministers, and ministers without a residence, envoyés extraordinaires, and envoyés bien ordinaires, chargés d'affaires, and chargés sans affaires, conseilliers de legation, and legation without either counsel or counsellor ; first secretaries of the embassy, secretaries of legation, public and private attachés, and secret attachés, agents d'administration of the embassy, and secret agents of the ambassador, valets de chambre of the embassy, and femmes de chambre of the ambassador, &c , &c , and however they may all be entitled

Such a systematical, categorical classification would be altogether too diplomatically tedious for an episode to the betrothal of Miss Susan, who had had enough of maidenly tediousness for the last twenty years

His excellency, the minister of " his transparent highness," the Prince of Kniphausen, (and of some other princes of the Germanic Confederation inclusive,) was actually ambassador, or resident minister of his princes at the imperial Brazilian court, and drew a yearly salary (apparently by " voluntary contributions" on the part of the courts which he represented) of about ten thousand dollars, with extra table-money (for the maintenance of legitimate hospitality) of about two thousand dollars, a salary with which he could have very respectably represented the splendor and magnificence of his Prince of Kniphausen, and the aforesaid other princes But his excellency's favorite study had always been Political Economy, and, as a branch of this system, he had passionately studied Private Economy, one of the most interesting and lucrative studies that any ambassador can pursue, who draws a yearly salary of twelve thousand dollars His excellency did not at all comprehend for what purpose he should, so to say, "run through" this yearly income in Rio de Janeiro, He inhabited a chamber with a closet, in the third story of the Hotel Faroux, and had the privilege of receiving a friend in one of the parlors of the first story when he chose, without thereby enjoying the right of sending anybody out of the room, who, likewise, might be receiving a friend there just at that time He kept a carriage with four horses, a coachman, and two servants in livery, for particular audiences and gala days, at a celebrated livery stable on the Largo do San Francisco de Paolo, and paid so and so much——for every harnessing and gala ride

As to the expenditure of the extra table money, he had, once for all, adopted the principle, to invite no one to dine with him, but as often as possible to invite himself here and there, to put himself in the way of being invited, and (in case this could not be done every day) to eat in the large dining room at the Hotel Faroux, with all private economy of a bill of fare This "carte de restaurant" was extremely well adapted to his diplomatic station, in which he, like every other diplomatist, was a declared partisan of every "restauration"

The ambassador was a tall, slender man, with a somewhat reddish, real diplomatic, that is to say, unspeaking face, as far as Silence is the first quality of diplomatic dignity He always appeared dressed in black, with black gloves, like many other gentleman, and never wore white or yellow gloves, from principle, from private economy He was a man of principle

He lived as a bachelor, (which proceeds from the above,) and as to his intercourse with the female sex, his connexions of that sort remained a diplomatic secret, as a matter of course He was actively occupied in colonization, in exploring mines, and the like—as projects, without ever taking a share in any of them He had at least so much sentiment of honor, as a diplomatist, that he never engaged in commerce He had studied, was classically educated, and consequently knew that the Greeks, in the bloom of their states, despised commerce, and committed it to their slaves, while they occupied themselves in science and arts, to the honor of their republic

His excellency had partaken of his lunch, with all the presence of mind, and calm of soul which an ambassador (although not a diplomatist) can manifest on similar public and private affairs He was just then promenading in the park, with the principal person, or "heroine of the day," Miss Susan Thomson, the future "Baroness de Spandau," and was playing upon the Portuguese national instrument, the Palito, just as the mar-

chardura of Monsieur le Baron de Spandau, stamped at the garden gate

The aforesaid Portuguese national instrument, the palito, is a small, thin, flexible, but stiff piece of wood, about three inches long, of the thickness of a knife, smooth, and pointed at both ends It is played with the thumb and the two longest fingers of the right or left hand, on being passed between two teeth of the upper or lower jaw and gives out no sounds — Such is the Portuguese national instrument the palito, in profane English, "tooth pick," the practical use of which (as of every musical instrument, with or without sound) requires a particular degree of artistical skill, which is a national peculiarity of the Portuguese

This well known musical entertainment, "of good tone" without sound, is genuine diplomatic in its nature, for being connected with noiseless silence, it is of assistance in a thousand cases, where a man of bon ton does not know what to do with the other hand, a case which happens but too frequently in the unbusied "great world"

The predominant passion of the Portuguese, "translated into Brazilian,' made an article of commerce of this instrument, which is "imported" from Europe in an incredible number of boxes, with other Nuremberg toys, as a "very important article"

The ambassador was just then playing the palito, beside the future Baroness de Spandau, when the stamping of a horse's hoofs was heard, that had carried the baron from the city to Bota Fogo It is self-evident that Miss Susan could not possibly receive the baron in the presence of a third (and even diplomatic) person, under the present (and to her never before happened) circumstances, notwithstanding the State of Silence which this person represented Miss Susan therefore left the ambassador, with a short "beg pardon," and hurried by the sweet scented shrubbery, through the park, into a side wing, and through all sorts of doors and passages, to her chamber in the main building of the Villa Thomson

Mr Thomson had delivered Miss Susan's reply to the baron personally, early in the morning, who, at her slightly intimated wish, sent a written word by his negro on horseback, to his bride, at eleven o'clock in the forenoon of the same day

So Miss Thomson had something written, something legal, and legally binding on the part of her betrothed, which, if necessary, could be made valid 'before court"

Far be it that Miss Susan in the least feared such a case of the future By no means But experience showed so many unfortunate cases, that a young girl, declared by this or that man to be his bride, and then deserted by the bridegroom, had become a subject of conversation at the expense of her good name, a tragic contrast, to being a subject of conversation, to the acknowledgement of her fair fame as a betrothed For it is entirely undeniable, that the good name of a young girl is never established more brilliantly than by her betrothal

The baron ran through the principal alley without noticing the ambassador, whom he perhaps saw. The latter was possible, for his excellency was "visible" as he hurried by him at a short distance But the baron did not notice any Ambassadorship, when he hastened into the villa, and a negro in livery conducted him to Miss Susan's private apartment The "written" assurance of the betrothal on his part had taken place, and the betrothal " by mouth" was now to be celebrated How a betrothal after the English custom is celebrated by mouth, is to us a diplomatic secret The materials of our novel observe a strict diplomatic silence upon this point

The ambassador walked from the park back into the green parlor, where, according to Brazilian custom, various kinds of wine, and also water, stood upon a small table, for the general use of the visiters who might go in and out This Brazilian " going in and out" of the visiters was not exactly an English custom, and contradicted the closed garden gate, fastened with thick English bolts But on this particular day, the Brazilian table of refreshments was loaded in proper order The ambassador did not, indeed, like the Brazilians, (for they were a rebellious nation, and he was the ambassador of several monarchies,) but he liked many Brazilian customs, and likewise the Madeira, and port, and sherry, in the clear shining crystal decanters upon the small table

He went to the small table, did his best, " pour passer le temps," and had scarcely entered the park again, when the Baron de Spandau presented his betrothed bride to him

What an event in Miss Susan's life of forty years !— She was not only the future Baroness de Spandau, but was presented, as such, to His Excellency, the Resident Minister of " his Transparent Highness ' the Prince of Kniphausen It was clearly one of the most interesting subjects for an article of " high life ' of any English court newspaper, at least the most interesting article for Miss Susan Thomson

Towards four o clock the blue coach rolled up to the garden gate Mr Thomson had ridden to the Gloria, according to agreement, where he had taken in Dr Thorfin, Captain Hinango, and Robert Immediately after them appeared the invited clergyman, the Reverend, in a dusty hired cab

The introduction act of the bride and bridegroom—of his Ambassadorship, of the condemned Russian ex-naval officer, and of the clergyman, was performed with all ceremony

His diplomatic excellency, the ambassador who had been invited to this dinner, was introduced to the other guests, as his Excellency, etc He was, as such, to take a seat of honor at the table, (as a personified diploma, to increase the respectability of the house,) had of course performed his first duty, and now waited with a certain legitimate right for the second service, the dinner itself, that should do him its service The affair was quite in order, and no " Intervention " was to be feared

The clergyman was a minister of the Church of England, et voilà tout He represented the " Church ",—which (as is said in Faust) " has a large belly, and has already devoured whole countries " The meagre English clergyman, (like so many others, treated by the mother church, with all her fat bishops, in a very stepmotherly manner,) had likewise a legitimate right to await the betrothal dinner, for he had been invited to it.

Mr Thomson went off for a moment to arrange his toilet, and then appeared again in the park, and on his arm also appeared his neice, Miss Fanny Walker, from Buenos Ayres, whom he introduced to the ambassador and to the clergyman, and who also made a most gracious and stiff courtesy to her former travelling companion, Captain Hinango Her right hand trembled to be reached to her intimate friend and protector, and to press his—but it must remain by her side without accomplishing it—for Miss Fanny was an English woman, and a solemn scene of introduction of entire " strangers " was taking place about her All eyes were directed upon her—she must remain " Miss Fanny," and, as such, look before her

Robert alone had the right to step up to her, to shake her hand, and to ask, with all heartiness, " how do you do, Fanny ?" for he was her brother, whom Mr Thomson, to-day more than ever, wished " to the devil," notwithstanding he was his own nephew

A large genuine English bell sounded, and the company went into the green parlor, the future baroness on the arm of her baron, Miss Fanny on the arm of old Mr Thomson, (who was not certainly so very old,) " Church and State " walked beside each other, and Dr Thorfin arm in arm with Hinango The seats were occupied Corinna stood behind the chair of her mistress, Achilles behind that of Hinango, and behind every guest was stationed a negro in livery, for the green parlor was very spacious A turtle soup a la Faroux opened the dinner

The ambassador suffered from a weak stomach, and had a tumbler of Madeira poured out for him, before taking the soup That was quite in order, and did not increase the bill At first the conversation was dull, as usual at every first " course " of a diplomatic dinner After a while a word was taken up, and became a thread of social discourse about the various events of the day, which did not particularly interest any one, least of all the two betrothed, whom henceforth (as a future married couple) nothing interested—nothing in the wide world but themselves

" How are you getting along with your colonization in St Catharina ? does it go on well ? if I may ask ?" inquired the ambassador, of the master of the house, after he had, during a full quarter of an hour, done his part at the table with diplomatic silence, and let his jaws rest a little, in order to commence again all the better

" Pretty well," replied Mr Thomson " Two ships are now loading at Antwerp, they will bring out laborers, and there is one ship in Liverpool, which will take on board necessaries for the colony, and we now expect our main geologist, or engineer, Mr Closting, whom you perhaps know by name I even believe that he will come to-day "

Robert had just then a pair of turkeys (a male and female) before him, in violet sauce, à la Duchesse de Kent, to carve, and tore apart with real fury the artificially enfolded wings, which the cook had unnecessarily locked in each other. His youthful brow was drawn up in wrinkles on account of the difficulties of separating the vexatious wings

" I have heard of him," answered the diplomatist, in a tone of indifference

" He is said to be a skilful man of business, a

smart fellow, " observed Dr Thorfin, with a sharp glance at Robert, who worked away at separating the wings of the turkeys

" A remarkable man," asserted the baron, " a man of much talent, of solid learning, and of respectable connexions here at court, as I hear "

" That is easily understood," exclaimed Mr Thomson, " It would besides be a great pity, if such a man was not prized for his business talent As to the rest," he added, with a peculiar tone, " as to the rest, I do not know him, except in my business transactions with him indirectly, through his partner Otherwise I am not acquainted with him at all "

By this explanation Mr Thomson protected himself from every appearance of being connected with a man, concerning whom this and that report was afloat, whereby he maintained his British principle, " a business acquaintance is no connexion

" You will probably soon undertake a journey to Santa Catharina, yourself," the ambassador again asked " It is called one of the finest provinces of Brazil, as I hear "

" It is a wonderful country, a paradise, a real paradise,' asserted Mr Thomson, ' I shall make a journey there—in about five or six weeks—or in two months—when it is a little cooler I shall take Miss Fanny then , she has seen but little of Brazil yet You will accompany me, Miss Fanny, will you not ' to Santa Catharina '"

" It will certainly be very agreeable to me to accompany you," replied the niece with British prudishness

" It will certainly be very agreeable to me to accompany you " repeated Mr Thomson silently to himself, for he placed much in these words—much—very much ' if one should rightly consider the " To accompany you " What was there not in these words ' And then even, " It will be very agreeable to me !" In fact, Mr Thomson could not expect a more satisfactory answer

" Then we will travel together, my future brother-in-law !" exclaimed the bridegroom, " will we not my dear '" (said he, turning to his bride,) " and celebrate our wedding in Santa Catharina !"

If a virgin face was ever suffused with a legitimate purple red, or ever smiled with joyful self-satisfaction, that face was Miss Susan's, for she had a legitimate right to blush, and she had waited long enough for that right—that God knew

" An excellent idea," said Mr Thomson, laughing, with an inquiring look at Miss Fanny-inquiring so far as she was to give her consent to accompany them to Santa Catharina " If it suits you, in about two months, Miss Fanny '" he now asked with a certain exacting decision

" I shall always gladly accompany you, dear uncle !" was her answer, and Mr Thomson seemed more than content, apart from the fatal " dear uncle," an appendix that the circumstances of her present incognito indeed very naturally made requisite

" It shall be a real journey of pleasure !" he exclaimed,-and filled himself a glass The ambassador, (as a matter of course, well acquainted with English customs,) had immediately after the first course " requested the honor " to empty a glass to the health of the lady of the house. Just

as little did his ambassadorship neglect to drink to Miss Fanny's health, and as there was no other lady present, his ambassadorship afterwards drank Mr Thomson s health, and Robert's health, and Dr Thorfin's health, and so on, with and without " health," as many times as he was representative of courts that salaried him

" To our prosperous journey to Santa Catharina ! Miss Fanny," exclaimed Mr Thomson, and cast a glance at his niece, that expressed as much " uncleish" satisfaction as an old widower ever cast at a young lady

Miss Fanny nodded a tender English approval.

" And you must go along Robert," exclaimed Mr Thomson, as he emptied his glass to the last drop, " you must go too, and must look you up a bride by that time, and we will make a wedding—we will " celebrate" a wedding, I would say—Aunt Susan s wedding and yours at the same time !"

Robert blushed again and again Dr Thorfin looked him sharply in the eye Hinango, who sat by him, remarked that the youth trembled " I will naturally go with you," he replied, and endeavored to conceal his embarrassment, " if my sister goes, I never separate from her, you know that uncle , and if you were going to Constantinople altogether, I would accompany my sister "

Dr Thorfin cast a glance at Hinango—— expressing all they had said before dinner in relation to Robert's accompanying on such a journey

Mr Thomson had long since felt all personal security in regard to his purpose, as he had more than sufficiently convinced himself that Robert was any thing but his rival, what he had once feared , notwithstanding, he could not bear to see him press Dolores' hand

" You will leave us soon too, captain ?" Thorfin asked his friend Hinango, to give him an opportunity to intimate that he would leave the field clear for the baron

" I shall probably return to Hayti in about a fortnight, he replied in a conversational tone My ship is getting fitted out gradually, and will increase our unpretending fleet of the negro republic

" You have been long in the service of the Haytian republic, if I may ask ?" said the baron to him, with the mildest tone imaginable as bridegroom

" Ever since I left the Russian service, baron," was the unsatisfactory answer

" It will be best to determine immediately the day of our departure to Santa Catharina !" exclaimed Mr Thomson, as the champagne was poured out, " we are now in the middle of January—then comes February, March—we will appoint the 15th of March as the day of our departure from the Bay of Rio We will take some convenient vessel I have, besides, a cargo to load for my colony there, and after to-morrow I will make my arrangements accordingly Have any of you any thing against it, gentlemen and ladies ? the 15th of March, under sail for Santa Catharina ? He addressed the four relations with this parliamentary proposition, (inasmuch as the baron might be included amongst them) and no particular contradiction appeared upon the countenances of any one On the contrary, the baron joyfully gave his assent, and Miss Fanny's countenance could very naturally express no denial

She was · her uncle's niece, the child of the house, for whose pleasure this proposition was originally made

"So it is agreed upon," he repeated. "We will sail on the 15th of March, and His Reverence can by that time have provided us with a worthy clergyman for our colony at Santa Catharina, as I requested you to do this very morning—" he continued, turning to the clergyman, who had until then eaten and drank more than he had talked

"If I am not mistaken, there has been an English clergyman for some time at Santa Catharina, or at least at the island of that name—a missionary," he repeated slowly and in a dry pulpit manner. "But I shall, nevertheless, not omit to do my best, at your command, for the extension of the gospel and our High Church," he added as slowly, and worked on at the pudding that had been served up in its turn. The conversation became more lively, the "journey of pleasure" afforded abundant material

Robert sat as if upon coals—he would have wished that the long sitting at table had been shorter, and yet—a thought penetrated him—perhaps now—perhaps at that very moment Mr Closting had returned home—and the woman who had once breathed in his ear "for eternity!" lay perhaps in the arms of a man whom he wished in England, that he might "transact business" with whom he liked ——

Hour after hour passed at table. At last the ladies retired, according to English custom, and the drinking was to commence. But it was a betrothal dinner, and the baron soon followed his bride into the garden. Robert found occasion thereby to rise, and likewise to accompany his friend Hinango to the open air. Dr Thorfin "stuck" to the table, that the whole company should not go out in the air, where Hinango and Dolores might at least say a few words to each other.

The bride and bridegroom walked about the "labyrinths" of the park, and Dolores enjoyed the society of a confidant, with whom she had until then lived almost uninterruptedly in spirit, for she prepared with him the literary expedition to Rio Grande, which was carried to and fro between both by Dr Thorfin. Her first inquiry concerned Horatio, the favorite of her soul, the boy who had become a man at the scaffold of his relatives, and whom she would so gladly have seen from time to time

Hinango answered the question dictated by the warmest friendship, as explicitly as he could, and then proceeded with compressed brevity, on account of the danger of being disturbed by the old widower, to the disclosure of a plan concerning the future of Dolores, that he had consulted about with Horatio and Dr. Thorfin before the blue coach took them in. "Dr Thorfin," said he, "will communicate much to you, when you next see him, in relation to your position here in Rio. You must depart, and no better opportunity could present itself than Mr Thomson's projected journey to Santa Catharina. Horatio will soon go to Celeste in Rio Grande. Get your letter ready for him. The province of Rio Grande is for the present secure from subjugation on the part of monarchy. You will find an asylum there with some respected family of the country, unless you should prefer Monte Video. I shall go to sea in a fort-

night, and shall steer for Bahia, in order to ward off the espionage that watches us. Celeste stands in Rio Grande at the head of a patriotic committee, and at his request Barigaldi will cruise before Santa Catharina with the Mazzini, where I will join him, and take you on board, to assist you to Rio Grande or Monte Video. This is our plan for your deliverance. You are in danger here, but compose yourself—fear nothing. Robert will accompany you. Achilles will remain with you; and the stout Irishman, who took the cutter on the river La Plata, will likewise be near you in Robert's service, if necessary to collar the baron. You know his position? I mean the baron's!"

"Can it be possible? is he a spy?" asked Dolores, in as low a voice as Hinango had spoken to her

"As certainly as I am Hinango," he affirmed

"And I will do my duty that the scoundrel shall never become my uncle," whispered Robert. "I will accompany you, Señora Dolores, to Rio Grande, or to Monte Video, there is my hand upon it"

"You consent to our plan, then," Hinango again asked

"Entirely! to all that you have resolved upon and shall command, for my deliverance," replied Dolores, and pressed the hands of both

Mr Thomson just then came around the corner of some shrubbery with the ambassador, and considered it very superfluous that Miss Fanny should give Captain Hinango her hand in conversation

Coffee was presented, according to Brazilian custom, and the company amused themselves with all unconstraint at the celebration of the betrothal

CHAPTER VI

HORROR.

THE company at Bota Fogo remained together until late, for a cheerful, social tone prevailed, notwithstanding the different elements of which it was composed, or, perhaps, for the very reason that it was composed of such different elements, and each one sacrificed himself for the company. The ambassador even became talkative towards Hinango, and spoke of his former social relations, which were no secret in Rio

Towards midnight the blue coach and a cabriolet, with Mr. Thomson's livery, took the guests to the Gloria, and into the city

Robert made use of his gate key with a throbbing heart. He found all in the garden dead and silent, no light in Gracia's pavilion, who had, on no former evening, retired to rest without bidding him "good night"

The negress Anna appeared with a lamp to light Robert's candle with.

"Senhora Gracia has gone to the city, Senhor has come," remarked Anna, and looked upon the ground, for she did not venture to read the effect of her words in Robert's countenance.

The poor old negress had a heart. The youth trembled—a shudder passed over him.

"Well, Anna, go to bed, I have matches, I will light my candle myself," he replied, and Anna wished him good night

"Good night," he repeated, partly in reply to the well meant wish, partly speaking to himself, and entered his pavilion "I would not wish my worst enemy a good night like this—and those which are to follow!" he sighed

A visiting card lay upon his desk, with the inscription, "Mr Forro & Co," and under this was written, with a lead pencil, "Mr P C L Closting"

So the husband of his female friend had taken his wife away, and had already learned from Mr Forro that Robert was her neighbor, that he was the same Mr Walker with whom his partner, and he likewise, (of course,) were doing business.

So far all was in order

He went to his closet, and found a white rose upon his dressing table It seemed to be a natural one Robert raised it up to enjoy the scent, and found it singularly heavy It was one artificially arranged from Cacadu feathers, but how could the Cacadu feathers be so heavy? He examined it, and discovered that the cup of the inner leaves could be taken out, he took it out, and a ring fell upon the floor, with the inscription, "Gloria"——

It was a name he had given his female friend, as he jestingly called her "Nossa Senhora da Gloria" The gift and the symbol agitated him, he followed the connexion of ideas, and the image of his beloved, which was never absent from him a second, appeared to him in spirit, in the arms of a man ——

It was late—past midnight His fancy wandered to the reality which surrounded his friend He put the ring on his hand, the blood seemed to leave his veins, he stared fixedly about him—his eye caught the pistol which, loaded as usual, hung by his bed He thought of his duty in regard to the deliverance of Dolores —— and trembled

At last he threw himself in an arm chair beside his bed, in which he was still sitting when the morning dawned upon him

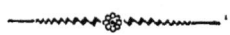

CHAPTER VII

THE HAPPY MARRIED COUPLE

PATRICK had brought back the letter to Sally, and talked a great deal to her She now learnt from him, for the first time, as circumstantially as he could relate to her, who the young lady was whose life was in danger, to whom the baron was betrothed, and nearly what sort of a man Hinango was—whose life was the next subject of consideration

"If a nagur was to be hired for two patacks to stab him," said Patrick, "be Jasus and I'd as lave take the strike meself, to kape it aff from Captain Hinango I tell you what, Miss Caroline, that same's a jintleman quite intirely, in troth, a rale sailor, I tell you, as iver walked the quarter deck in navy uniform, and cast a 'keep-course' to the man at the helm into the compass.

"And now couldn't you give us a hint about what goes on here fornenst, and I'll give you a chance to make reports to the baron, so as he shall niver be the wiser but you're spying me all the time"

"Patrick," interrupted the poor girl, "I have yet a commission to give you If I should resolve to see Captain Hinango or Dr Thorfin, it would be because I seek their protection, to return with some family to Europe, but it must be with a family, and not alone And that I can do only through the recommendations of such men as the two friends, as they will grant me the necessary confidence, to which I may perhaps lay claim, after all that the friends have until now learnt from me and by me"

"And faith, its that same they'd be glad to do, ither of 'em, the captain or Dr Thorfin, if so be they can, and sure I'll send 'em word all about it be Lucy, for I ll not be going there meself, or the baron'd be after finding out that it's under a false flag I m sailing"

"Can you rely upon Lucy, Patrick?"

"Is it Lucy? be Jasus, Miss Caroline, and I'm sure of her as I am of Captain Hinango! She's niver been a navy officer, to be sure, like him; but I know her heart like me own pocket —and troth that's often empty, and I know Lucy right well, and that's the truth, Miss Caroline, and I'd thrust her wid the whole red-haired Pat Gentleboy, and its good care she'd be taking of him, be day and be night!"

Sally could hardly restrain a smile, although she was by no means in a situation which was calculated to excite one

"Well, Patrick," replied she, "then communicate, by Lucy, to Captain Hinango and Dr Thorfin, what I have told you Lucy may come to fetch work from time to time, and in this way she can give you intelligence"

"And that's thrue for you, ma'm and so I know now what course I'll be steering, and shure I'll not lave the helm till Captain Hinango goes to sea wid the Astrala Farewell, Miss Caroline—but stop a bit—and shure you'll not be going away from this so long as Captain Hinango's here We must both of us save the baron, and he must save us 'till the young lady and all the lave of them have clawed out of the harbor We must hold on so long, be night and be day!"

"I see that," sighed Sally, and Patrick took leave and withdrew

We pass over the events of the night which took place after the betrothal and the return of Mr Closting, and find Robert on the following morning in his office in the Rua Direita, as pale as death, perhaps the result of a cold that he might have taken in his uncle's park, at Bota Fogo ——

He was just then busied in correspondence in relation to the colony at Santa Catharina, as two gentlemen approached the grate of his "cage" One was Mr Forro, who introduced the other to him as Mr Closting

Mr Robert Walker looked up from his writing paper, and saw beside Mr Forro a man whose exterior manifested no prominent quality. He was a short, robust, square built man, whose piercing look roved about unsteadily

"I am happy to make your acquaintance,"

replied Robert, as he laid down his mother-of-pearl penholder, and involuntarily turned the ring, which since a certain hour had remained on his finger, and perhaps a little embarrassed him

"I hear from my wife that she has, for several months, had the honor of living in your neighborhood and under your protection, and I thank you heartily for every attention which you have shown her," said Mr Closting, in the polite manner of a man of the world of some refinement.

A slight blush overspread Robert's countenance—as is often the case where one hears a compliment, and should answer it by another He arranged his reply as aptly as his present situation, and the indisposition under which he now labored allowed, which latter made his utterance difficult.

"I yesterday took the liberty of leaving you my card, when I brought away my wife, who sends her respects, and requests that you will dine with us to day. You must have become acquainted with my house in the city, through Senhor Forro"

Robert had a hard struggle to undergo The resolution which circumstances forced upon him, to avoid henceforth the friend from whom he in spirit could never more be separated, wavered at this hospitable invitation, at the thought of seeing that friend again, although in the presence of a man whose company was disagreeable to him, and affected him as iron does a somnambulist

"I thank you," he replied, after a pause; "I thank you and your lady for your kind invitation, and will take the liberty of calling. Please give her my respects"

Mr. Forro now introduced the subject of business, as far as it was necessary for them to consult together, about many particulars of the commenced enterprise

Robert improved the opportunity to conduct the two men of business into Mr Thomson's office, to whom Mr Closting was now likewise introduced

The young man handed over the affair to his uncle, and returned to his cage, to his correspondence

Mr Fitz, the air pump controller of their Imperial Highnesses the Brazilian Princesses, sat this forenoon as usual in his large atelier, and chanced to be again singing his favorite song

"No general has so powerful might," etc,

just as Dr Thorfin and Hinango entered, who visited him from time to time The captain of the Astrala had confided some instruments to him which he wished to have finished in a short time The everlasting good humor of the astronomer lengthened out the conversation concerning this and that, and at last the company was increased by Mr. Closting, who saluted his countrymen with much politeness, and related, in answer to Mr Fitz's inquiry in regard to the interior of Brazil, what might interest him and those present

Mr Fitz, among other things, questioned him about the young man whom the naturalist had brought over as secretary from Europe, and heard that he had dismissed the "impertinent fellow" full two months before from his service, and did not know what had since become of him

"He seemed, in other respects, to be an intelligent young man," remarked Dr Thorfin, "of much talent, and very eager after knowledge"

"He was, indeed, very inquisitive," said Mr Closting, smiling "he concerned himself altogether too much about things that did not belong to him Otherwise I do not deny his good qualities—not at all"

To turn the conversation upon another subject, he informed them of a rarity that he had brought with him—a diamond of the second class that he had bought for gold dust "Honor me, gentlemen, all three of you," he added, "with your company at dinner to-day, and I will make it a pleasure to show you the diamond; it is something very distinguished!"

Mr Fitz and Dr Thorfin accepted the invitation. Captain Hinango politely excused himself, on the ground that he was unfortunately obliged to go to Praya Grande, and should not return until late in the evening—which the naturalist "much regretted."

Both had always stood upon the singular footing of social contact of two men who mutually felt the most decided repulsion of their nature, and found no cause "to break" with each other, because they had in fact never been connected Mr Closting was but too well aware that Hinango knew of his "youthful pranks," by which he had acquire the name of a "second Cartouche," but he likewise knew Hinango's former position, and gladly improved the opportunity to take him by the arm, in the Rua Direita and in the Rua do Ouvidor, to appear intimate with him, to use him as a folio to his somewhat wormeaten reputation

Robert incidentally told his uncle that he had been invited to dine with Mr Closting, and that he had accepted the invitation. "I don't like that at all," replied the old Englishman, "and would have been better pleased if you had declined it. Never forget the difference of contact with men in business and in intercourse We can do business with men, and we do business with men, whose intercourse we must avoid, because it would compromise us You understand me, Robert; there lies the distinction"

"Is Mr Closting's reputation then so bad?" asked Robert, "that I must be embarrassed in knowing him?"

"My boy, I have informed myself sufficiently about him, and know the history of his whole life pretty accurately If he were not such a thorough scoundrel as to know how to make himself respectable, I would not have entered into business with him. Besides, we are properly only in business with Mr Forro, his name is not mentioned The tricks that he has played in Europe are whispered about here, but people know to a certainty that he has three times become bankrupt, in a skilful manner, in different provinces in the interior of the country, and has cheated and stolen "by note"—and that's sufficient But we would not do much business in large places, if we only dealt with people who enjoy an unsullied reputation, we should soon keep limited books, my dear Robert The commercial world in our days is composed of very rotten elements, and the paper of a bill of exchange is often effected by the bad odor of the man who endorsed it. As to your intercourse with Madame Closting, as a neighbor, I have nothing against that," he continued, after a pause, " that is another thing, and you can keep up your friendship with her, as before—and—as I lately told you, you can marry her as soon as she is divorced from Mr Closting—I have nothing against it "

Robert sat down beside the old man as if his knees would break under him He had never given the slightest information to a living soul in regard to his unfortunate relation It was a secret that he kept most sacredly, but his Uncle George appeared to have seen through it—and, without violating it on his part, he could listen to what his uncle had to say to him in confidence.

" Yes, yes, dear Robert! that is my view—and my advice, and I repeat to you endeavor to bring about this affair, go to work the right way—declare yourself to the handsome wife, if you have not done it long since—for I have long ago remarked which way the hands pointed Propose to her to accompany you to Santa Catharina I will build you a beautiful villa there One of our house must live there, as general superintendent of the colony You are well fitted for it It is a paradise—the finest part of Brazil What the devil should hinder you from living happily there, with a pretty young wife, who has been a widow ?"

The magic picture of such a future (in contradiction to his own previous views) entered into Robert's soul and occupied his thoughts

He saw the possibility of such an existence, for he presumed that Senhora Gracia's reciprocation of his feelings originally rested upon the ground of her moral dislike to Mr Closting, and this ground seemed in part as logical as probable, for no wife would be able to swear love to another man, unless she abhorred her husband excessively Whether this logical conclusion is true with the female sex, which generally embraces more contradiction within itself than logic, may be left for the present undecided The inconceivable obstinacy with which Gracia always endeavored to magnify the virtues of her husband, when the least mention was made of him, confused Robert in regard to all that concerned this female and his own future But on the other hand he bore on his finger a symbol which showed the bond of soul, louder than words, and more plainly than any glance He resolved to do his best to clear up the matter, as soon as possible

" I will enter Mr Closting's house in the city to-day, and no more hereafter," he remarked to those propositions, " and afterwards determine if I will ever see Madame Closting again at Da Gloria "

" I will answer for it that such will be the case, dear Robert," replied the old widower, " and if you should move to Praya Grande to-to day, Madame Closting would find the air healthier there, and hire a villa near you day after to-morrow My dear Bob ! I have more experience in such matters than you imagine, only act as if you would separate from your friend, and you will see if she will be so easily separated from you, if she will, then she will prove that she only led you around by the nose, and ' trifled with you '"

" Trifled ?" repeated Robert, " trifled with the life of a man ?"——and he returned to his cage

The dinner in celebration of Mr Closting's arrival took place

Robert appeared there, and found the married couple sitting upon an elegant sofa, engaged in cordial conversation The lady was in a gala dress, richly adorned after the Brazilian fashion with gold chains and diamonds, but was peculiarly pale and changed, perhaps from the contrast of the ornaments, which he had not seen her wear before ——

She received Robert with all cheerfulness and naïveté, and when Mr Fitz and Dr Thorfin made their appearance, she bestowed upon her husband all the pleasing attentions and civilities which an exemplary wife in the social world owes, in Brazil as in other civilized countries Robert seized the first and last means of maintaining his self-possession, by imagining to himself, as always, that his friend was a young girl, that had never in her whole life kissed any man but him He could have thrown any man out of the door, who would have asserted that that man " who searched into the mysteries of nature " was the husband of the young girl, and not her eldest brother

But such a powerful and forced perversion of the power of conception, seized upon and deranged the nerves of the young man's brain, more violently than he himself anticipated ——

The naturalist showed his diamond to the guests, and, at the same time, all the presents which he had brought to his wife, and she scarcely found words to express her joy at the extraordinary attention and providence of her husband, and leaned upon his arm as if there was not a more happy married couple in the world

After supper, Mr Closting led the guests into a side room, to admire a great variety of natural curiosities, which he had likewise brought with him

Robert found time and opportunity to whisper in his friend's ear, that, for particular reasons, he would not again visit her at that place, but that he would expect her in her former neighbourhood of Da Gloria, in case the symbol which she had confided to him had its meaning, as he presumed, from the seriousness of her nature

Gracia appeared surprised, and a little embarrassed, and was about to give him a low answer, just as Mr Closting and Dr Thorfin accidentally came up

' Do you not think, doctor," asked Madame Closting, " do you not think that it would be better for my health to keep my dwelling on Da Gloria, at least to pass most of my time there ? The air here in the city is more oppressive to me than it ever was before "

" That is very natural," replied the physician, " the atmosphere on Da Gloria, and especially where you reside, is certainly more beneficial to your nerves than in any of these damp streets in the city Mr Closting will surely comprehend that, and not desire you to leave the pavilion

" That is a matter of course," replied the husband, " you will live where you are now, and I will move there likewise, it was my plan, and I hope that Mr Walker will remain our neighbor for the present," he added, looking at the youth, who scarcely heard what was said

" I shall hope so also," exclaimed the lady.

"Senhor Walker will likewise remain constant to our piano, that I will presume—will you not, Senhor Walker? You will stay with us on Da Gloria, and we will continue our piano playing?"

The young man now understood the drift of the conversation, and answered, that he should not remain long in Rio, and therefore should probably retain the dwelling until his departure because he had a dislike to "moving."

The lady sought an indifferent subject as the material to interrupt the conversation and was as polite and friendly to Mr Walker as her position allowed

The company separated after a few hours

When Robert was taking leave, the lady remarked that she expected that very evening to have the pleasure of executing with him a four-hand composition, an indirect invitation, which he accepted

Mr Closting found young Mr Walker's acquaintance, and the business connexion with his house, important in many respects, and made use of both to conclude a new business, for he sold the celebrated diamond to Mr Thomson shortly after his return, and received about twenty-two contos for it

Mr Thomson laid the jewel aside as his private property, and intended to dispose of it advantageously in Europe, as he contemplated, soon after his marriage with Señora Dolores, to undertake a journey to London in her company

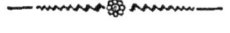

CHAPTER VIII.

MASS MELTING AT RIO GRANDE

The province of Rio Grande, one of the most interesting countries on the face of the earth, on account of its natural productions and picturesque beauty, extends from the Atlantic Ocean about four hundred miles into the interior, and five hundred miles along the coast, from San Paulo and Santa Catharina, southerly to the Banda Oriental, on the borders of which is the principal port, Rio Grande do San Pedro, at the entrance into the Lagoa dos Patos

This province, originally settled by Vincentists,* towards the close of the sixteenth century, after the Indians had been forced to retire more and more into the interior, became, from its position between the Spanish and Portuguese possessions, gradually peopled by emigrants from both nations. It was a frequent cause of quarrel between the two crowns, of which one was as little able to enforce its claims as the other, until Great Britain finally had pity on this paradise of the earth, and Sir Samuel Auchmuty planted the British flag in the productive soil, in the year 1804. "The lessons in Spanish," which the English received in Buenos Ayres, the "exercises" of which were very legibly written with their own blood, soon made this possession uncomfortable for them, and they saw themselves constrained to give it back to the

---

* Brazilians from St. Vincent.

"miserable Spaniards," from whose hands it was finally transferred to Portugal, without any actual consent on the part of the people

There are provinces in all parts of the world, the population of which acquire a love of freedom and independence, as it would seem, from the air, or the evaporation from the soil, or, God knows how, which they manifest more than the inhabitants of other countries, who are exchanged by this or that prince, in treaties of peace, like wethers and ewes, for other wethers and ewes, and vegetate as exemplary "faithful subjects," and think of any thing except "liberty" or "rebellion"

As the province of St Paulo has, up to this time, had the glory to unite that spirit of liberty with an undeniable striving after intellectual perfection, and exhibits a population that reminds us partly of the Spartans and Athenians, and partly of the Swiss, the province of Rio Grande is also elevated to a like degree of moral freedom, although the state of education among the people does not indeed equal that of the Paolists

The philosophical education of a Celeste, as the librarian of a monastery in Buenos Ayres, will not greatly surprise us, when we find seminaries and universities in St. Paulo, in which the professors pursue various philosophical systems, as, for instance, Antonio Ildefonso Ferreira, already at the beginning of our century, transplanted Kant's system of philosophy, in the Portuguese language, to Brazil. The intellectual life which undeniably characterises those provinces, and manifests itself in so many forms, opens to our view a world as original as strange, which may be more or less foreign to the northern nations of transatlantic soil, because the spirit of philosophy is not an article of commerce ——

All the so called revolutionary movements of South America since 1817, to which we have before alluded, evidently proceed less from material questions, than from the spirit which is there developed from itself, even though in oppressed forms

The inhabitants of the province St Paulo, and in a measure their neighbors in Rio Grande, are famed for their noble physical appearance, as well as for their noble character, which shows itself in every contact, and cannot be denied by their bitterest enemies. As the inhabitants of the province of Minas Geraes are distinguished for a certain fondness for French luxury, and the imitation of refined European manners, we find in St Paulo and Rio Grande the simplicity of patriarchal life, which contents itself with solid furniture, made there from the wood of the country. In accordance with the external social forms which recommend themselves by neatness and cleanliness, we are met by an upright, open, frank, and hearty manner of the serious inhabitants

The population of St Paulo and Rio Grande, descendants of Spaniards and Portuguese, is distinguished from those races in Europe by a fresher blooming complexion and a taller shape while that Spanish "grandeza" is retained, which appears as "the respect of a man towards himself," and degenerates into ridiculous stiffness where it is wanting and is spiritlessly imitated.

The contest about boundary and territory, which has excited the Spanish and Portuguese provinces for centuries, and was intended to keep alive the national hatred, (by which monarchy seeks to isolate one people from another,) disappeared of itself the more the spirit of liberty was developed in the people

While the Spaniards and Portuguese, wherever they come in contact, meet each other with a certain mutual distrust, both elements, in the luxuriant and favored province of Rio Grande, melted down into a harmonious efficient whole, that had stood four years as a " people," when the schooner Mazzini had landed the passenger Celeste in the neighborhood of the city Laguna

The Brazilians of the province of Rio Grande assert their sacred rights against the encroachments of monarchy, with a similar decided resistance as the Greeks once defied the Turks—as the Circassians oppose the Russians—and the Bedouins reject the " civilization" of the French We call this people the " Grandes," that we may have a name for them when we shall hereafter speak of them among the Paulists, Orientals, Mineiros, Cabocles, etc

The standing article in the day's history of Brazil at that period, was the famous "campanha do sul," the campaign in the south, that consumed more " food for powder" than the Brazilian monarchy could keep in the field

One Brazilian man-of-war after another landed in the principal ports, so called, " regular troops, or standing army," which could not be brought into rank and file from pure " irregularity," and (as a biting irony on the word) could not " stand" upon their legs as an army

We have already beheld a sample of Brazilian permanentos in the interior of the country, at the arrest of Signore Serafini, and can the more easily give an idea of an entire army, consisting of similar " barefoots" driven together, who hung their shoes on their bayonets after their feet had become so sore from marching that they could not get them on again

The province, as a country in a military point of view, offered every advantage to the insurgents The mountainous chains which extend along the coast of Brazil, (in places at some distance from it,) from Para upwards beyond the equator, penetrate several hundred miles into the district of Rio Grande, to Lake Patos, which is about two hundred miles long, and, separated from the ocean by a long tongue of land, offers a single entrance

The chief town, Rio Grande do St Pedro, at this entrance, remained for years in the possession of the monarchical troops, but all endeavors on their part to put down the insurrection were as difficult as fruitless

Extensive plains and hilly country, surrounded by high mountains, favored the movements of the cavalry of the insurgents who, so to say, " grown up on hors back," could await the enemy in the open field, and not only attack him with the same weapons, but also with lazos, as they would do to catch horses and oxen

If the royalists attempted an invasion of the coast, the landing was rendered difficult by small vessels of war, like the schooner we mentioned, for the troops had to disembark in longboats, and frequently sustained a total defeat before they reached land The insurgents, on the other hand, kept possession of all the small harbors, which afforded them communication with other provinces, and their rear was, as we may say, covered by the mountains in which the " not standing" army could not easily penetrate

In connexion with these advantages, the product of the country, celebrated for agricultural and grazing purposes, and favored by the finest climate in the world, (which may be compared to that of Southern Europe,) afforded subsistence and bestowed the blessing of peace during the contest

It often happened, under similar circumstances, that a division of troops sent off from Rio Janeiro, only brought an addition of force to the insurgents, instead of strengthening the cause of monarchy by victory

The Brazilian government had long sought a support in the German " food for gunpowder," as we have mentioned in the course of this novel. A traffic in human flesh was carried on, on the coast of Germany, similar to that on the coast of Africa, and the only difference between the slaves was—in their color

As tragically as the Germans appear in many chapters of the history of the world of the last century, as sold hirelings, and have left behind them in Europe and the New World blood-spots which do not tend to the honor of the mass who sold themselves to the service of tyranny, the German troops in Brazil, on the other hand, stand in a better light

A large number of individuals of disbanded regiments had settled in Rio Grande, and built up German towns and villages there, the population of which were increased by prisoners of war who went over to the cause of the people, as well as by deserters who went over, " with bag and baggage "

The imperial government had at that time sent two other corvettes to Rio Grande do St Pedro, and several thousand men again took the field " to put down the rebellion "

The insurgents remained quiet in their towns and villages, awaiting an attack, while a strong detachment of cavalry was posted behind hills and woods, to fall upon the enemy's rear, if he should again take a notion to show a naked spot.

We now enter upon the free soil of the blooming province of Rio Grande, in a region on the shores of the Mambituba, which in its character clearly calls to mind the northern provinces of Italy, where the Alps form a similar background to fruitful plains and hilly country, as do the Serros of the interior of Brazil, and towards the east the Serro do Mar

The insurgents had repulsed an attack of the permanentos, and had returned victorious home to their towns and villages

Before a Venda in the neighborhood of the flourishing village San Rafael, shaded by lofty trees, rich in its fields and meadows, with murmuring brooks running serpentine through it into the rushing river, there was a scene, attended by all the liveliness of a revolutionary epoch

A concourse of men, from nearly every nation of Europe, and from all the provinces of Brazil, which were united in a contest for life and death, pressed upon each other

Tall lean Mineiros, with oval expressive faces,

in broad brimmed hats, spencers, and ponchos, high buckskin boots heavily loaded with silver spurs, and with silver handles to their swords and diggers, contrasted with the less lean Paulists, whose blooming complexions, browned by the sun in the long campanha, were visible in a similar costume, no less heavily encumbered with silver weapons

Grandes, with long raven black hair, serious, sharply defined features, appeared in the proud carriage of their well shaped bodies, at the side of innumerable shades of colored persons and Indians, in strong contrast with the Brazilian-bleached Germans and other Europeans, whose hair was as variously marked in color as the skin of the negroes, from the blackest Mosambique to the white bred colored offspring of whites and cabocles

It was a Sunday morning, before the commencement of a great mass meeting

Among the so called "heroes of the day" was an "unknown" person, who some months before had arrived in the schooner Mazzini, at the seaport town Laguna, from Patgaonia, and since then had taken a part in the battles of the people All sorts of questions passed around from mouth to mouth, concerning the former relations of a man whose outward appearance was characterized by a solemn seriousness, joined with that intellectual dignity which imposes without intending it

The unknown, our Celeste, had been wounded by a ball in the left shoulder several weeks before, and had received careful attention at the hands of a family on their plantation in the neighborhood of the village St Rafael

A similar accident had befallen a German, who had gone over from the imperial army, and had fought the enemy at the side of the unknown But the wound of the German was less important, and had confined him to his bed but a short time He was a mechanic, a blacksmith by trade, a cavalry man by nature, and a republican from the spirit of the times, which he had acquired in different countries of Europe since the revolution of July He was one of those stereotype patriots of southern Germany of the years 1831-32, "every inch a rebel," and capable of every momentary sacrifice from pure love of liberty He was Mr Wartling, a cousin of the famous "tailor Preuss," proscribed in the states of the Germanic Confederation for "demagoguish principles"

He escaped to France, and sailed from Havre de Grace to Rio de Janeiro When there, Mr Wartling had one evening, in patriotic poetic enthusiasm, drank a glass of wine too much, (although he was generally extremely temperate and abstinent,) and fell into the hands of the patrol, who "packed him off," without long examination, as food for powder, to Rio Grande, as had happened in Buenos Ayres to the two friends Falsodo and Perezoso

Mr Wartling had been four years in the Brazilian service, and was resigned to his fate He also worked at his trade, learned Portugues with the aid of a grammar, in which he had lon acquired such a proficiency as even to propagate republican ideas in Brazil

He was a man of strong mind, a clear intellect, and a warm heart He had long believed that a smith like him had just as good a right to be a "man" as the minister of state, "Vast Councillor," as he styled him, to whom the emperor had presented a fazenda with two hundred negroes, and who corresponded as an intimate friend with Prince Metternich—which Mr Wartling thought superfluous

Our blacksmith was as good a republican as any that ever wore imperial uniform, whether Russian or Brazilian, and he was far more dangerous and injurious in his circle, to despotism, is a demagogue, than many authors whose language has been taken from them by censorship, and who live in quiet upon a pension from court

The owner or landlord of the fazenda, which supported a brilliant reputation as a vende, was likewise a German, formerly a sergeant in a German battalion in Rio de Janeiro

Mr Bolz, as the fat landlord was called, just then stood upon the veranda of his hotel, in conversation with Mr Breit, the schoolmaster of the village St Rafael, to whom he was telling the "cursed affair of the Campo da Santa Anna," at Rio de Janeiro

"Yes, yes, Mr. Breit, I assure you, that my hair stands on end when I think of it I tell you the damned negroes bore the fire of our closed square, let those drop by their sides who could no longer stand, and then rushed upon us without giving us time to load again! and disarmed us, as God is my judge! disarmed us! and the half of our corps were left upon the spot, killed with the butts of their own muskets, stabbed with their own bayonets! the damned negroes, they were in a perfect fury against the escravos brancos, as they called us Yes, when I think of it, I drink a glass cachaz to brace my nerves!"

"Uncle" Bolz did as he said, poured himself out a glass of cachaz and emptied it in memory of "that cursed affair of the Campo da Santa Anna," just as Mr Wartling joined them

"Well, have you studied out your speech?" his friend, Mr Bolz, called to him, "i am desirous to hear you, and what you will bring to market"

"I will read something out of a popular German book that I have translated into Portuguese, you will hear what it is"

"Is it anything historical?" asked the schoolmaster, a former German or Prussian student at Berlin, who had likewise taken up teaching, after having been in the German legion in Brazil

"You are one of those who keep to the letter which deadens, who do not know the spirit which gives life," said Mr Wartling, smiling "I know you learned historians! It is indeed something historical which I shall offer, but not out of Zschockkes history of the Wittelsbacher, or Raumer's history of the Hohenstauffen, nor from the Prussian history of Frederick the Great, the author of which also happens to be called 'Preuss,' as if he had been baptized so for that purpose, it is nothing of that sort, but something historical about another king"

"Say nothing against Prussia and the Prussian royal house, I am a Prussian, and shall continue so!"

"Then please to clear out of Rio Grande this very day, you double rascal you! a royalist and a Prussian besides!"

The landlord laughed to split his sides.

"I was only joking, my dear Mr Wartling," replied the schoolmaster, much alarmed at having, in his historical zeal, forgotten that he was for the time in Rio Grande, where many a royalist had been hoisted up to a pine tree for having opened his mouth too wide, and discussed royalist principles.

"Joke at Jacobi's, in Berlin, when you are drinking your small beer, but here in Rio Grande you had better keep your royalist principles to yourself"

"But you will acknowledge the "historical law," which most learned men in Germany consider the first," cried the schoolmaster, who had no idea of being silenced by a common smith Y u know there are several kinds of law for instance, the Roman law, and a law of succession the civil law, and the law of nature, a municipal law, and a historical law, and in consequence of the historical law, we stand here upon Prussian soil and ground '

"What!" exclaimed the smith, "are you sea sick ashore? or are you out of your head? what kind of royal Prussian nonsense is that you are talking ?"

"I am neither the one nor the other, but I speak the real historical truth," replied Mr Breit "You must know that a Prussian prince was once to marry a Portuguese princess !"

"No, I don't know any thing about it,' replied the smith

"That I can excuse you for, for your historical studies do not seem to have been very extensive But what is historical, remains historical The marriage did not take place, because the princess would not turn Protestant, or Prussian—I say Prussian, for there is a royal Prussian religion, and that is likewise historical and it has its church in Rio de Janeiro Well, Portugal endeavored to conciliate the Prussian prince, and Prussian monarchy, after the marriage had failed, and presented this province Rio Grande to Prussia, as a compensation for the unconcluded matrimonial alliance That is historical, and in print, and by historical, we understand every thing that is related historically, under proper censorship "

"The devil you do !" said Mr Wartling, smiling, and listened to what he had further to say

"You see, Mr Wartling, I am, to be sure, here as a republican, as you may say, in the service of government, as teacher, or professor, as you wish, but for all that, my historical knowledge is not to be called in question This province is Prussian, according to historical law The historical documents are in Berlin, and a Prussian prince will, one of these days, come out here and make good his claims, you may depend upon it, and it will finally be all one to the people whether they are Brazilian, Spanish or Prussian, as long as the historical law remains in force "

"Are you possessed, Mr Schoolmaster ?" exclaimed Mr Wartling, "have you been drinking too much cichaz ?"

The landlord again laughed until his sides shook, and the smith continued

"Schoolmaster, take care ! What you have just said to me remains among ourselves, but if I should translate into Portuguese to those Mineiros or Paulists, what you have just been saying, they would, as God is my judge, bring you before a court martial and hang you up—hang you, until you would swing like a needle to the thread, when a tailor holds it up "

The schoolmaster saw that it was a serious matter, and felt considerably uneasy in his royal Prussian loyalty

"Well, then," he said, "let it remain among ourselves, and I will keep within my place until Prussia makes valid the historical law "

"You had better go to-day to one of the outposts of the permanentos, and have an imperial capote thrown over you, it will become you better than a poncho of the Grandes "

"There comes the hero from Patagonia," exclaimed the landlord, looking in the distance, and the people put themselves in motion towards a hill, that was appointed as the place from which the addresses were to be delivered.

Mr Wartling and the landlord mounted their horses, and likewise went to the place, where the committee of arrangements were just then receiving the unknown

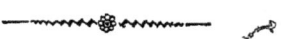

CHAPTER IX

MONARCHY.

LORENZO appeared on horseback in the dress in which we have already seen him in Patagonia, attended by officers of different detachments in the picturesque costume of those provinces which would offer to the artist an inexhaustible study for *tableaux de genre*

Ladies on horseback, in the dark national overcoat; with pointed black broad brimmed fur hats and long black locks, at the side of others in black mantillas, their small feet in stirrups made out of the horns of oxen, their bridles and saddles covered with silver, thick sheepskins, with long wool dyed in indigo, for saddle coverings, or sitting upon tiger skins, whose lively colors contrasted with their dark dresses, and the bright white of their horses—country people in the costume of the last century, a kind of Polish chamara, worked with lace, and buttons made from Spanish half and quarter piastres, in shoes with broad silver buckles—Mineiros and Paulists, in the before described ponchos, part of them made from products of the country, (like those of the Patagonians,) part of them of a light blue color, with bright red under-lining thrown over the arm, in high buckskin boots, buckled under the knee, and projecting far above the knee, forming a pocket, out of which shone the silver handle of a dagger, silver spurs and stirrups of more than a pound in weight, high broad straw hats at the side of the broad brimmed fur hats of the Paulists—half savage mountaineers, of different complexions, in the costumes of their different tribes, armed with bows and arrows · formed a while, in picturesque grouping, on the side of a hill, that afforded a most charming prospect, over blooming flax fields and meadows, to the back ground of the gigantic mountains, which traversed Rio Grande in all directions.

The clear atmosphere of a sultry summer day

in February, favored a festival that proceeded from the events of the times, whose spirit more or less animated the multitude, who now, in solemn silence, arranged themselves on horse-back and on foot, to hear the expected addresses

The governor of the comarca appeared on horseback among the gigantic jacarandas on the top of the hill, accompanied by Celeste and the smith, Wartling, and attended by an escort that formed a sort of staff or festival committee

The smith made the remark, that a speech to a large public in the open air would be better heard and understood if the speaker should stand lower than the people, for sound went upwards, and in the other case it would be lost in the air above the public

The governor thought this remark correct, and its application very practicable. The whole committee then descended the hill in great order, and occupied a place in the midst of the people, who now, being in a sort of amphithe-atre, head above head, could see the speakers, and hear their voices much better. The presi-dent of the festival committee, an opulent fazen-deiro, in his rich poncho, with a pointed fur hat, his arms and his horse-trappings richly ornamented with silver, now spoke in a low voice with the governor, and then rode forward to open the festival and address the people

All eyes were now turned towards him, and he seated himself in his saddle, and spoke

"South Americans!

"Citizens of the State of Rio Grande! God be with us, and victory to the republic!

"We celebrate to-day the restoration to health of two men who have joined us from remote countries of the earth, from pole and pole, and bearing arms with us in the contest for freedom and independence. I speak of the citizens Lo-renzo Celeste and August Wartling"

A joyful viva interrupted the speaker. He waited until the hurrahing ceased, and then pro-ceeded

"The citizen August Wartling, who has been several years in South America, and out of en-thusiasm for the cause of the people came over to us from the ranks of the mercenaries, among whom his hard fate had placed him against his own will, has fought for years in our ranks for the freedom and independence of our state as a future free state of South America! August Wartling is a man from the so called "working classes" of the people, by which we understand those who work with their hands, opposed to those classes who do not work—or work with money—and opposed to that most unfortunate class who cultivate the field of the mind, who live in the realms of thought, in a restless men-tal activity, working for a future generation, without recompense or profit for themselves

"Wartling appears here amongst us as the representative of all those collected masses of hand-workers, of all nations and countries, and brings to you the spiritual greetings of all his brethren in distant Europe! A representative of the intellectual power will follow him."

Another loud viva resounded in the air, and the president retired among the district commit-tee. Smith Wartling gave his horse a pressure with spur and bridle, and took the place which the other had just left, seated himself comforta-bly in his saddle, and spoke, saying:

"Republicans!

"Free citizens of South America! I first thank you for the sympathy and the regard that I have found among you, especially since I was wounded at the side of a man who will address you after me"

A loud bravo interrupted the speaker, after which he proceeded

"We here contend against the monarchical principle opposed to us. Yonder, behind those advanced posts, there stand the hirelings of the empire, and their leaders assert the right 'by the grace of God'. That you may know what mon-archy is, and how monarchy was established, which assumes its right 'by the grace of God,' from the Bible, I will here read to you some fragments from a little popular book of 'Young Europe,' 'The old history of king Saul'' Give heed and listen! and take the word to heart"

He then drew out a manuscript, and read in the Portuguese language as follows.

"'The people of God,' whose history contains the documents of truth, were, from their com-mencement, a people under popular govern-ment, and we find no trace of monarchy in the whole plan of creation. The people were gov-erned by judges and the 'elders' among the people, and no individual dared to step forward with the impudent assumption of being called 'by the grace of God' to be absolute ruler over any nation

Samuel, a venerable representative of the peo-ple, whose historic writings have come down to us, was a man of great wisdom, the son of a mod-est, God-fearing mother. He was, as a child, in favor both with the Lord and with men. His spi-rit lived in the exalted knowledge of the Divine Being, in immediate consultation with him who had called him to be a support unto his people, and endowed him with the everlasting light of reason, and every thing that his reason sug-gested to him, was considered by the people as the voice of God, and the people recognised in the man the prophet the sage whose word sounded as prophecy, as the oracle of the con-ception of pure reason

'And all Israel, from Dan even to Beer-sheba, knew that Samuel was established to be a pro-phet of the Lord, and the word of Samuel came to all Israel

'And it came to pass when Samuel was old,' as we read in the first book of Samuel, (ch viii,) 'that he made his sons judges over israel

'And his sons walked not in his ways, but turned aside after lucre, and took bribes, and perverted judgement

'Then the elders of Israel gathered themselves together, and came to Samuel unto Ramah,

'And said unto him, Behold, thou art old, and thy sons walk not in thy ways: now make us a king, to judge us like all the nations

'But the thing displeased Samuel, when they said, Give us a king to judge us. And Samuel prayed unto the Lord

'And the Lord said unto Samuel, Hearken unto the voice of the people in all that they say unto thee: for they have not rejected thee, but they have rejected me, that I should not reign over them

'According to all the works which they have done, since the day that I brought them up out of Egypt even unto this day, wherewith they have forsaken me, and served other gods, so do they also unto thee

'Now, therefore, hearken unto their voice howbeit yet protest solemnly unto them, and show them the manner of the king that shall reign over them

'And Samuel told all the words of the Lord unto the people that asked of him a king.

'And he said, This will be the manner of the king that shall reign over you He will take your sons, and appoint them for himself, for his chariots, and to be his horsemen, and some shall run before his chariots

'And he will appoint him captains over thousands, and captains over fifties, and will set them to ear his ground, and to reap his harvests, and to make his instruments of war, and instruments of his chariots.

'And he will take your daughters to be confectionaries, and to be cooks, and to be bakers

'And he will take your fields, and your vineyards, and your olive yards, even the best of them, and give them to his servants

'And he will take the tenth of your seed, and of your vineyards, and give to his officers, and to his servants

'And he will take your men-servants, and your maid-servants, and your goodliest young men and your asses—and put them to his work

'He will take the tenth of your sheep, and ye shall be his servants

'And ye shall cry out in that day, because of your king which ye shall have chosen you, and the Lord will not hear you in that day.

'Nevertheless, the people refused to hear the voice of Samuel and they said, Nay; but we will have a king over us,

'That we may also be like all the nations, and that our king may judge us, and go out before us, and fight our battles

The developement of mankind, then as in our own time, did not advance equally among all nations, many heathen races were governed by rude despotism, as entire nations are in our days The people of God appeared to be led astray by the splendor of royal magnificence — They desired a martial leader in their warlike excitement, one who would 'go out before them,' a king 'And Samuel heard all the words of the people and he rehearsed them in the ears of the Lord,' (chap viii, v 21,) that is, he consulted God, through the reason which enlightened him

'And the Lord said to Samuel, Hearken unto their voice, and make them a king, and Samuel said unto the men of Isreal, Go every man unto his city'

It would scarcely require an especial discussion to enable you to behold in the words of the Lord his decided dislike to the monarchical principle, after we attentively regard the above objection as a formal threat

The bitter declaration of Providence against the voice of the people, who in their foolish blindness desired a king, the decided answer of the Lord to Samuel, 'They have not rejected thee, but they have rejected me that I should not reign over them,' manifests the strongest resentment

A time will come, said Samuel, and the nations of the earth who acknowledge the word of the Lord, shall sigh under the oppression of the arbitrary rule of an enemy of the people,

and they will lament and despond, and will cry to the Lord in their need against their king whose unlimited power they have approved of, but the Lord will not then hear them, but refer them to his declared word, which they rejected and would not respect, as they have rejected him, that he should not reign over the nations of the earth

'Nevertheless, the people refused to obey the voice of Samuel; and they said, Nay, but we will have a king over us,' etc

'And Samuel heard all the words of the people, and he rehearsed them in the ears of the Lord

'And the Lord said to Samuel, Hearken unto their voice, and make them a king'

And who was chosen in God's bitter irony, to be king over the infatuated people? The wisest among the people, that he might rule for the people in divine illumination of heart? Nay.

The Lord in his anger had given his consent to the stubbornly demanding people, and his insulting justice gave the people such a king as the proud obdurate people deserved, that they might learn what it was to oppose the will of Providence ——

'Now there was a man of Benjamin,' (chap ix, v 1, 2, &c,) 'whose name was Kish, the son of Abiel, the son of Zeror, the son of Bechorath, the son of Aphiah, a Benjamite, a mighty man of power

'And he had a son, whose name was Saul, a choice' (elegant) 'young man and a goodly, and there was not among the children of Isreal a goodlier person than he from his shoulders and upward he was higher than any of the people'

So this interesting young man, distinguished by his—length of body, was chosen to be king over an infatuated people, and his appointment took place after the following manner, (chap ix., v 3, &c)

'And the asses of Kish, Saul's father were lost, and Kish said to Saul his son, take one of the servants with thee, and arise, go seek the asses

'And he passed through mount Ephraim, and passed through the land of Shalisha, but they found them not and they passed through the land of Shalim, and there they were not and he passed through the land of the Benjamites, but they found them not

'And when they were come to the land of Zuph, Saul said to his servant that was with him, Come and let us return, lest my father leave caring for the asses and take thought for us

'And he said unto him, Behold now, there is in this city a man of God, and he is an honorable man, all that he saith cometh surely to pass, now let us go thither, peradventure he can show us our way that we should go'

In this manner came, Saul the tallest and choicest youth among the people, before the prophet Samuel—he sought for some runaway asses, and found —— crown and sceptre —

And when Samuel saw the elegant Saul, the voice of the Lord spoke in his mind, 'Behold the man whom I spake to thee of, this is same shall reign over my people' (v 17)

And Samuel conversed with Saul, and invited him to eat with him, and quieted him about his asses and said, (v 20,)

'And as for thine asses, that were lost three

davs ago, set not thy mind on them for they are found ”——

Thou hast instead of them found a kingdom, with a great many asses

And Samuel prepared the young man to be be monarch over the children of Israel, and took a vial of oil, and poured it upon his head and annointed him king

And after all preparations had been made, ‘ Samuel called the people together unto the Lord,’ (to divine service,) ‘ to Mizpeh ,

‘ And said unto the children of Isreal,’ (chap x , v. 18–26,) ‘ Thus saith the Lord God of Israel, I brought up Israel out of Egypt, and delivered you out of the hand of the Egyptians, and out of the hand of all the kingdoms, and of them that oppressed you :

‘ And ye have this day rejected your God, who himself saved you out of all your adversities and your tribulations and ye have said unto him, Nay, but set a king over us Now, therefore, present yourselves before the Lord, by your tribes and by your thousands

‘ And when Samuel had caused all the tribes of Israel to come near, the tribe of Benjamin was taken

‘ When he had caused the tribe of Benjamin to come near by their families, the family of Matri was taken, and Saul the son of Kish was taken and when they sought him, he could not be found

‘ Therefore they inquired of the Lord further, if the man should yet come thither And the Lord answered, Behold he hath hid himself among the stuff

‘ And they ran and fetched him thence and when he stood among the people, he was higher than any of the people, from his shoulders and upward

‘ And Samuel said unto all the people, See ye him whom the Lord hath chosen, that there is none like him among all the people ? And all the people shouted, and said, God save the king‘

‘ Then Samuel told the people the manner of the kingdom, and wrote it in a book, and laid it up before the Lord And Samuel sent all the people away, every man to his house

‘ And Saul also went home to Gibeah ; and there went with him a band of men whose hearts God had touched

‘ But the children of Belial said, How shall this man save us ? And they despised him, and brought him no presents. but he held his peace ’ (v 27)

The public appointment of Saul to be king, bears so strongly the impression of the tragic-comic, that we are not surprised that some so called ‘ sons of Belial,’ whose perceptions were, perhaps, clearer than those of the people, made themselves somewhat merry at the new king

The tribes of the people were assembled as to a ‘ church parade,’ as a foretaste of the military method of government , and the venerable Samuel arose and addressed the people, and repeated the threatening of the Lord

‘ Thus saith the Lord God of Israel I brought up Israel out of Egypt, and delivered you out of the hand of the Egyptians, and out of the hand of all the kingdoms that oppresse you, and subjugated you And you have this day rejected your God, who himself saved you out of all your adversities. and your tribulations,

and ye have said unto him, Nay, but set a king over us

‘ Now, therefore, present yourselves before the Lord, by your tribes and by your thousands ’

This terrible voice of the Lord from the mouth of Samuel, had so scared the anointed of the Lord, that he could easily see what he had before him, to reign as king against the will and under the express displeasure of the Eternal

And as the families came near, the family of Matri was taken, of the tribe of Benjamin, and they sought the tall Saul, the son of Kish, but he could not be found Then they consulted together, and said, ‘ Will he yet come hither ?’ And the Lord answered, through Samuel, ‘ Behold he hath hid himself among the stuff ’

Then they ran and fetched him out of his hiding place among the stuff, where he had concealed himself in a natural feeling of ‘ royal fear,’ and when he stood among the people, he was higher than any of the people from his shoulders upward

And Samuel said unto all the people, not without some contempt and irony ‘ See ye him whom the Lord hath chosen , that there is none like him among all the people !”

And all the people shouted and said, Viva! Hurrah ! God save the king ! But Samuel repeated once more to the people all the rights of monarchy, and delivered the book of laws, and then sent all the people away, every man to his house

And Saul also went home, and there went with him a band of men, whose hearts God had touched by the terrible voice of threatening, wherefore they, from fear of the Lord, would not immediately leave the king, whom they had demanded in their obstinacy towards God

But some ‘ sons of Belial,’ who had quite well understood the Lord, and comforted themselves that the new monarchy had not been their wish, made themselves a little merry at the courageous king who had hid himself among the stuff, when he should have shown himself in his royal majesty ‘ How shall this man save us ?” said they They laughed and despised him in the bottom of their hearts, because they could not see any thing in him, except the length of his goodly, stately figure, that should require them to revere his royal majesty The republicans, the so called ‘ sons of Belial,’ also formed an opposition, and— brought the king no ‘ presents,’ as did the rest of the people But Saul behaved with monarchical prudence—‘ he held his peace ,’ for he was now king and relied upon his royal strength and power, without regarding the voice of discontent among the people, just as now-a-days kings and princes are accustomed to do, after the example of the first king—of the tall and stately King Saul

Had it been the will and plan of Providence to give the people a king, to establish monarchy for the welfare of the people, All-ruling Wisdom would have looked for other qualities in the anointed than length of body, by which the king should, as it were, ‘ stand above’ all the people

The irony of God is confirmed, from century to century, down to the present day, for little is asked about the character and wisdom of a king: t there is only a king there, all the people shout and say: ‘ God save the king !’

Had Providence selected the wisest from among the people, to rule with discretion and judgement, then indeed would the defenders of the monarchical principle have a reason for asserting their opinions

But the fate of the first king confirms the unmistakeably spoken dislike of God to monarchy

If Providence had given the people who in their stubborn obstinacy desired a king, a worthy, so called " good king," it would have shown monarchy to the people in an advantageous light, and such would have been a contradiction by God of himself, who had refused the desire of the infatuated people, with powerful threats

' Wait now infatuated ungrateful people—ye have not rejected my prophet but me, that I should no longer be your king—just wait, I will show you what the monarchy is that ye desire, I will send upon you the hard oppression, of monarchy, *and ye shall cry out in that day because of your king which ye shall have chosen over you, and the Lord will not hear you in that day*'

After such a threat, the Lord could not contradict himself, and—made the people a king in his wrath—such as we see the kings in the history of all nations, from Saul down to the present day "

The voice of the smith now fell without any particular rhetorical conclusion and he continued

" There are so called ' free states'—republics—which arrogate to themselves democratic principles, as they call their mask, and carry on a slave trade, a man-trade, with black and with white slaves If this state here, for whose freedom we shed our blood, should ever become such a free state, a German smith would be ashamed that he had sacrificed his life for such so called freedom

May Rio Grande sustain the principle of freedom in the reasonable and natural form of a republic, in despite of all the glittering bayonets of a rotten and wormeaten monarchy, may Rio Grande, as a flourishing republic, become attached to the future Grand Union of the United States of South America—attached by the sacred bond of Humanity, whose spirit manifests itself in our hearts, in our conviction and in our faith, now and forever . *Ora e sempre* "

Wartling had been interrupted in many parts of his address, by the loud applause of the people, and the like happened when he had reached the above end He drew back, and Celeste rode forward on horseback, as he had appeared there, and took his place

The eyes of all rested upon him Since his arrival so many things had been said among the people about him, that a particular curiosity was excited in many to see him The ladies especially had taken a lively interest in him, and had endeavored to manifest their sympathy in every way, while he lay sick of his wound

Celeste now appeared before the people, and the impression of his presence caused the silence of death to prevail, instead of the loud tumultous applause which greets the people's favorite when he mounts the speaker's stand His countenance was pale, in consequence of moral and physical sufferings—exposed to wind and weather in the open field since his flight from Buenos Ayres.

The Patagonian head-handkerchief enveloped his head, from under which appeared a few of the growing hairs on the temples But so much the longer was his dark beard which fell upon his breast, and covered the upper lip in proportionate length He looked around about him upon the assembled multitude, then laid the bridle of his horse over the tiger skin which covered the saddle

The deathlike silence continued A holy spirit of devotion seemed to accompany him, and to render the hearts of all susceptible for the expected word

------

CHAPTER X

THE SPEECH FROM THE SADDLE.

AND Lorenzo seated himself conveniently in his saddle, and spoke, saying .

" Strange and peculiar days have come for
   earth,
In course of things , most wonderfully moves
A spirit in the hearts of human kind,
With shape and form it seeks to clothe itself,
T' assume a substance somewhere , and to mould
What human beings call Society
The spirit that we have no word to name,
Which we can but anticipate—not prove,
Endeavors, in its working here on earth,
The statutes of the future to set forth ,
To lay the groundwork of a better culture,
To bring to pass a kingdom long foreseen,
I mean *the kingdom of our God on earth.*

Cast we a desultory glance behind,
O'er the world's history—we recognise
Mankind originally raised above
The situation of minority
Through the idea which we call Religion.
  We see religions multiplying still ,
Each *after*, or from *out* of others formed,
From one eternal primitive religion,
In whatsoever form it shows itself
At the same time we mark transitions strange
In the world's epochs —periods waste and void,
Without all faith, *without idea ;*—epochs
When, as it were, hardly the breath of life
Rules at the moment ,—periods, I say,
In which mankind is moved by nought beside
Outward appearance , while a sore disease
Spoils, as it were, and wastes the very life
Of mental vigor, that should rouse them up
Anew, and which, as *spirit* of the *future,*
Must first destroy and put away old forms,
As happened twice, thousands of years ago.

Profoundly sunk in slavery and in serfhood,
Mankind once lay, in rude idolatry
Of mammon and of sensuality
Men paid their homage to the golden calf
  And Moses came, sent forth by God himself,
A nation to construct *without* a king,
Who were to recognise one king alone,
Him, only *Him—Jehovah Zebaoth* '
And through long ages did the spirit still
Unfold itself in the Mosaic law.

The worship of one God, which stood opposed
To heathenish idolatry, and spread
Itself abroad, as the renewing spirit
Of *life* and *energy ;*—but *love* was wanting
Reason and revelation shadowed forth,
The dawn of a new epoch for the world,
The prophets bodings now became more loud
Than faith in forms and cold formalities,
Which only by the priesthood were maintained,
And, 'midst the prophets' lamentation, rose
The comforting announcement of the future.

Waste, ruin, now extended everywhere,
The heart of man still throbbed, but did not
　　live
Like some fair marble statue then stood man
Upon this rich and beauteous earth of ours—
So lifeless, and inspired by no soul
All in those days was marble—man, as well
As the proud fanes of his magnificence—
And cold and unsusceptible as stone
Man, and the world, and life, and nature, all,
All was one heap of stones—*Creation petrified*

Now, sent by God, the Son of Man appeared,
The Word, by prophets' visions long announced,
Was now made flesh, and *Love* came down to
　　earth,
And justice and equality were taught
By the scorned Nazarene, who now proclaimed
The reign of peace—*the kingdom of our Lord*
　The Son of Man sealed and confirmed his word
By dying on the cross a martyr's death

Jesus' disciples, wonderfully moved
By love's blest spirit, taught continually
After his death, still seeking to extend
The doctrines of Equality and Love,
The claims of earthly *Justice*　And they lived
In harmony and fellowship together,
Pattern alike to heathen and to Jew
　When Jesus had been dead some sixty years,
The name of *Christian* first originated ;
And those who bore this name, the company
And fellowship of the disciples, grew
And gathered strength, while despot's vainly
　　sought
To weaken and uproot them : strong they grew
Through all the persecuting hate of tyrants,
While all the mighty of the earth pursued,
With bitterness and rage, the principle
Of that *Equality* which Jesus taught.

　The Christians bled　Victim on victim fell,
Blood flowed in torrents, and one martyr died
After another—crucified and burnt
And with the crisped and burning bones of one
The pile was kindled to consume the next
　But out of all the martyrs' blood and death,
The spirit of true holiness arose
And waxed strong and powerful through itself
　The thrones of princes then began to shake,
And trembling moved about the crowned heads
Now were the opposing principles displayed,
The power of *selfishness*, and that of *love*.
The *might of spirit* soaringly arose
From earthly clay up to its own bright sphere

　At length the Emperor Constantine assumed
Dominion o'er the persecuted Christians,
And with him came the *fathers* of the *church*,
To mould the *forms* of such a novel doctrine.

Bathed in the blood of martyr's, faith had now
Become *religion*, and was called the *church*.

　But tyranny remained unable still
To uproot Faith, and tear down the Idea
From that exalted spirit height whence she
Dispensed her light to all the human race

　Impossible it was quite to suppress
Jesus' pure doctrine, therefore Despotism
Possessed itself of the "Idea"—prudently
Impressing with it "a false coinage," which
It gave the people—and that was the *Church*,
Which, as "religion," passes now on earth

　From day to day the elements fermented,
Of Selfishness and Love, while here and there
Truth's Spirit, dignified and great, appeared
In forms, as events of the centuries
The brilliant epoch of mankind shows forth
In Christian combat for the Holy Grave.

　The Primitive Idea remained in force,
The human Heart was full of inspiration,
And penetrated by the light of Faith,
Man then despised the paltry gauds of earth,
Life's splendor and magnificence, from love
To God, whom in the Son of Man he knew

　And the two elements fermented still,
And in the Templars was evinced the spirit
Of life and energy—and Jacob Molay,
With three companions, fell beneath the power
Of despotism, which had long ago
United with the church,—Molay was burnt ;
And on the band of Templars now abide
The curses of all crowns, and Molay's dust
Strewed to the winds, is execrated still

　The church was now a worldly sov'reignty,
A government that ruled o'er all the nations
Which owned themselves as so called *Chris-
tendom* ,
And blood-stained popery's chief officer
Was to its shame—the *executioner*
　Johannes Huss appeared, to rend Bohemia
From such disgraceful servitude, and he
Was burnt like Molay, but his spirit lived,
It struggled on and onward, forty years,
And to this day it is not quite extinct

　Three centuries ago, truth's spirit rose
And stirred itself in human hearts —Some priests
And monks seceded from the Papal chain ;
Nevertheless, they still continued priests
They preached reform—but wanted alteration
Only in forms—the substance still remained :
The *church* as it had been ; and as we see
Significantly in the English church——
The brilliant fruits of priestly reformation.

　The old building was new timbered and re-
paired
With wooden balconies, and, like old *women*,
They wrangled and contended about *words*,
Those men of reformation, separated
For phrases—ne'er having recognised
The *spirit* that inspired the *Son of Man*
They pieced new cloth upon old garments, and
Like the five virgins, they went out to meet
The bridegroom—destitute of living oil
To trim their lamps, and so they went astray.

The rich and splendid edifice anew
With earthly trappings was adorned, but still
Remained a temple of despotic power,
Of every tyrant's arbitrary will,
And by degrees the church has settled down
Into an *instrument of state*—become
A *police court*—religion and the glow
Of faith are now extinct within her pale.

The priests preach loudly of the nullity
Of earthly goods, of patience, and denial,
While they live impudently on in splendor,
Enjoying luxury and sensual revels
They preach uprightness and equality,
And serve with venal and disgraceful duty
The throne, and monarchy, and tyranny,
Which they support,—thus murder upon mur-
    der,
Accomplishing on men, who struggle for
Humanity, and, most unheard of baseness,
Murders on murders they commit upon
Whole nations who are striving after freedom.
    They preach humility—submissiveness
And slavery—and subjection to the axe
Of the anointed executioner,
Who, smeared with blood, maintains his so
    called right,
By 'grace of God,' and loads with curse and ban
Honor, and virtue, and the love of man

    —This is the state of Christian doctrine now,
But clear as light, and still unfalsified,
Th' idea of his divine original
Displays itself in man, and even now
Does the blest spirit of the Nazarene,
Like a pure ray of light, the source of being,
Gleam forth, and draw men upward to itself,
Above the mass of gross *materialism*

    —— Nations there are, and have been, who
    have called
Themselves 'God's chosen people,' and who
    claim
Pre-eminence in goodness above others
In former times the Jews appeared so, now
They are the English—and in history
They play the selfsame part
                    But those who think
They're better than all others, prove themselves
Worse than all others by the thought itself.
    This thread conducts us to the following curse,
Which God pronounced by Samuel on the Jews
'In my just anger will I cast you off!'
Thus said the Lord ' 'for ye've rejected me
From ruling over Israel as your king !'
    And when the carpenter's poor son appeared,
Preaching contempt for every earthly good,
To send away from human kind the chains
Of mammon, and of sensual delight,
The venal Jews sold their deliverer ——
——The Jews then disappeared as a nation.

    And Christianity—Christ's doctrine—now
Is falsified to priestcraft, and ere yet
Two thousand years have passed, we find on earth
But a dark trace of Christianity:
Love's spirit is opposed by *calculation;*
Materialism overrules the *Spirit;*
And on the edifice of *selfishness,*
Colossal as the tower of Babel, stands
Britannia, greater than all states on earth
Through usury and shameful peculation.
    39

The English make a traffic of mankind
And of Christianity, religion is
Only an article of trade with them !
And in contempt of Jesus' doctrines, there
The people starve while priests luxuriate !
    ——And thus two dominations rear them-
    selves.
The Popedom and the *Church of England,* still
The two are only *one;* 'tis but the priesthood
In twofold form—the garments only differ
Of the well nourished priests, and if the Popedom
Is hated by the English high fanatics,
The hatred 's only caused by jealousy

    Britannia has already set her foot
In South America—our struggle here
Has lasted twenty years, for death and life,
And here and there disarmed, we've armed anew,
Since first in Pernambuco we proclaimed
That a Republic was the end we sought
    Disgracefully betrayed and sold, we see
The people's strength in South America
Through Britannia—through *Britannia* !

    Curses on
The *throne* that to its state hypocrisy
Perverts Christianity—in maintenance
Of a vile system of deceit and lies !
Curse on *Britannia's* cabinet, upheld
By priests, and scorning its own suffering people,
It seeks, in countries far remote, to span
The nations in the yoke of slavery.
    ——Far as the waves of ocean foaming roll,
Great Britain girdles towns, and lands, and
    countries
Nation on nation, trades in realm on realm,
Unnerves the orient, and threatens now
T'appropriate the fruits of twenty years
Of struggle here, as *British Property*

    ——And now, my brethren ! know for what
    we fight,
And know against *what enemy* we struggle.
    The time will come, when over all the earth
Nation on Nation rouse themselves to fight,
The freedom of all countries to establish
On pure religion's primitive idea;
And then all enmity, and scorn, and rage,
Shall concentrate themselves within Great
    Britain
The English will stand forth as enemies
Of freedom and of mankind, and the struggle
Will grow more fearful than it e'er has been,
And with more bitterness be carried on
    Then shall the spirit of humanity
Be armed for life and death against Great Britain.
The name of Briton then, shall be a curse,
The world will turn away from all who bear it;
And wheresoe'er a Briton wends his way,
T'escape the scaffold, or evade a shot,
Britons themselves will close their doors against
    them—
Who never pity their own countrymen,
When splendid, rich, as is Great Britain now.
    Accursed in selfishness and infamy,
The Briton in despair shall curse himself—
And as Britannia in her blindness now
Commits a suicide on her own poor people·
A Castlereagh on Castlereagh shall then,
With his own blood, inscribe Britannia's end,
In the great book of the world's history—
And then Great Britain shall no more be found.

Dispersed o'er all the world, as now the Jews,
The British people then shall chaffer with
The jewels of the crown, and with the mantle
Of the last king of England—and the sceptre,
Britannia's, for old silver shall be sold,
By Britons in a foreign land   And thus
You see Britannia's present situation,
And this will also be Britannia's end '

But Erin's sons and Caledonia's sons
Shall stand as people in their sacred right,
Delivered from ' Britannia's golden chains'
Upon the ruins of ' Britannia's throne,'
In brotherhood receiving in their arms
' The rest of English' to reconciliation,
All hatred and all vengeance disappears,
Before the spirit of humanity,
When mankind will awake in resurrection
Thus is my prophecy of future days
The Revelation of Humanity

                                         Amen "

Hardly had Celeste uttered the last words, with the glow of inspiration which characterized his whole discourse, and had from time to time seized upon the hearts of the people with threatening effect, when a youth came forward from a group of citizens, and approached the circle which now surrounded the speaker

A musical choir began, by the arrangement of the standing committee, the world-famed Marseillaise and many hundred voices accompanied the powerful " Allons-enfans" !—

A stati officer in Celeste's neighborhood informed him that a youth had arrived from Rio de Janeiro, who desired to speak to him. Celeste had dismounted from his horse to lie down on the grass, exhausted by the physical exertion of his speech, and still weak in consequence of his wounds   He turned around, as if he did not comprehend what they announced to him

" Did you say that a youth had arrived from Rio de Janeiro," inquired he, after a pause, " it surely is not——."

" It is Horatio," said a gentle voice in the crowd near him, and the nephew of Alphonso flew into his arms

CHAPTER XI.

THE WOMAN'S CURSE.

GRACIA lived on in those eternal convulsions and struggles of all the powers of her wounded soul. Little as she was able to explain to herself how it was possible that a sentiment which contradicted her social duties, could overpower her to such a degree as it had drawn her towards the kindred soul, still less had she been able hitherto to suppress it. She recognised in this sentiment the support of her inward life, which was first aroused when her social relations had destroyed her peace of mind   The more, however, she now endeavored to maintain this *point d'appui* of her spiritual existence, the more deeply did she stray into the labyrinth of the rigid contradiction between her heart and the forms of social life.

The more she became clear in the conscious-

ness of loving Robert, the more deeply did she feel the degradation of herself in a union which rested upon deceit, and whose consequences and conditions she had first seen through when it was too late   In these struggles and convulsions, which she had hitherto, as far as possible, endeavored to conceal from her beloved, arose, (according to her views,) the monster of necessity, sustaining itself upon animal relations without love

In the most evident contradiction with herself, she continued a connexion which lay founded upon the regulations recognised as the basis of the social world, while, on the other side, she at the mere touching of the paper on which a female had written, trembled and shrank before the thought that Robert might have only given his hand to another woman in conversation   Even her excessive jealousy was a contradiction in herself

The natural sentiment of jealousy, which is founded upon human weakness, disappears in two extremes of circumstances

Love, (in the sense of the word which we have so often designated, and in the idea of which we maintain,) nourished and confirmed in the being whom a bond of mutual love has fastened forever, knows no jealousy   Indifference—which misuses a social form to content the animal demands of nature, and in rigid opposition to the sentiment of love, requires neither soul nor intellect, but only a body—knows just as little of this sentiment

Jealousy proceeds not so much from suspicion, as from the diffidence of a heart which is mattered by the anxious uncertainty, the painful doubt whether it is capable and in a condition to answer all the demands of its kindred heart in every respect whether the beloved recognises and returns its love in the degree in which itself feels it · whether no being on earth has ever been able to produce a similar effect on the beloved heart, as the loving heart experiences within itself

Jealousy, of course, vanishes where such a blessed conviction prevails, of the love that " believes in love" and never doubts , and in the other case, where love was never the question, where animal instinct in the place of love formed a bond that rested upon egotism   The egotist overrating all his powers and capabilities, knows no jealousy, because he cannot imagine that there exists a man in the world who would be able more punctually to satisfy all the demands of the so called love of a being than himself   In the self-conciousness of infallible egotism, (which as arrogance, knows how to make itself pass,) lies in part the ground of the inconceivable deception by which a man is able to fascinate a being who is as strange to him in heart and intellect, is the egotist himself is foreign to the inward life

Egotism knows as little jealousy as love, because the former considers itself perfect in the above respect, and the latter, in the conciousness of mortal imperfection, lives in the conviction of the mutual love, which " believeth in love, endureth all things, hopeth all things ," which dissolves itself in the unity of the kindred soul, and interweaves the existence of love, with the idea of Eternity.

We will not institute the question, whether a

being like Gracia, united in happy social relations with such a man as Robert, would ever have experienced jealousy We doubt it, since we recognise in both that original affinity of soul upon which their love rested

We will, however, institute the question how the interior of a being like Gracia must be disturbed, when she trembled before the thought of finding occasion for the slightest jealousy, while she maintained before the eyes of her beloved, a relation that inflamed in the youth, of whose love she was conscious, not exactly jealousy, but a sentiment of injured honor for which psychology has, as yet, found no significant word ——

The thought of the possibility of a realization of his love in social forms had never occurred to the youth till she herself awakened this idea within him, which was afterwards confirmed by his uncle.

This gentleman considered every thing in life, and life itself, only from the practical side,— even marriage was to him a business, and what appeared here and there as love, was only to him the introduction to business Mr Thomson in his relations to the female sex, upon the point of matrimony, was as great an egotist as ever possessed himself of the hand of a female He felt, in proud self-contentment, that he was in a condition to satisfy all the external demands of a woman, and as he himself knew of no demands of the heart, he could, very naturally, not conceive that the heart had in general its demands.

Robert loved Gracia in the purest sense of the word The thought which his uncle had awakened within him required the dissolution of the connubial bond, which had, so to say, infused the individuality of his beloved into a stranger, since she, to speak in Scripture language, had become "one flesh" with this foreign element

Gracia's relations to Robert, however, required not so much a public divorce, as a physical separation from the man whom she had never loved, and by whose connubial contact she was degraded

Sufficient moral grounds of divorce had existed, long before Robert came into Gracia's neighborhood, and every woman in her situation, possessed of moral self-consciousness, would be in duty bound to part from a man whose influence could only more and more demoralize her Senhora Gracia appeared to have perceived this, before she made advances to Robert, and gave him her explanation But the longer the demoralizing influence of a mean nature upon a noble one, in the physical bond of matrimony, endures, so much the more does the woman (or in an opposite case the man) lose in moral self-consciousness and honorable sentiment The woman imbibes, without knowing or desiring it, the worldly perceptions and views of life of the demoralized, characterless husband—through the "unity of the flesh," whilst she gradually suppresses her moral delicacy of sentiment in all that regards the characterlessness and the crimes of her husband. There are few wives who do not soon, with natural penetration, (a certain female instinct,) see through the individuality of their husbands, because the inward life

(as we formerly intimated) is universally more easily and highly developed in woman than in man, but there are few women who, with the cultivation of the inward life, at the same time develope their moral force—and come forth as morally independent—against the characterlessness and meanness of the husband—who clothes and feeds them, and is to provide for their children The demoralization of marriage without love lies founded (as we have likewise formerly intimated) in the ordinances of the church and state, which have instituted marriage as a covenant of propagation, without taking into consideration the natural consequence of such a covenant upon the rising generation

Although Robert had never given utterance to the thought of separation, still the distracting feeling pressed upon him for which we know no word, and which urged the dissolution of an animal relation that (according to Gracia's declaration) had never been founded in love, and so long as it subsisted, remained a twofold crime against nature and love

Robert found himself in his pavilion on that evening after the family dinner, when his friend was announced, and greeted him with her customary heartiness and unconstraint It was difficult for him to find a proper mode of reply, since a tenfold impression raged within him from the reception of the ring and the return of the husband

As a reply to the first impression, he had a like symbol ready since that morning, as the present required The return of the personified inimical principle of his sentiments—was a subject he had determined to touch upon, when the ring gave him exactly the occasion he desired The unhappy youth followed the natural promptings of his character, and thanked his friend in the first place with undissembled openness for the symbol he had received, adding that he possessed a like one, in case she had recognised in sacred earnest its signification. He dared not, however, give utterance to the natural stipulation, abstractly from a public separation, the possibility of which affected him as a foreign suggestion

Gracia accepted the symbol of "Eternity" with expressions of sincere joy, and anticipated him by requiring an explanation of wherefore he would not visit at her husband's house in the city The young Englishman fell into the most painful embarrassment He must give a wife only the lightest intimation of the position of her husband as a citizen He looked back upon his entrance into the dwelling, and upon the manifold information and assertion of his friend that she had never loved her husband, and would love him, and him only, to eternity. He hinted in the most delicate expressions at the valid grounds that must subsist, through which she herself experienced so decided a repulsion against Mr Closting as she had at least asserted, and brought it home to her perceptions whether many others might not be deterred from seeking personal intercourse with him upon the same grounds which caused her repulsion

Madame Closting sank into an armchair and gazed inquiringly at her friend "What do you mean to say by that?" said she, with an expression of amazement.

"What you sufficiently understand yourself, since you have manifested that valid grounds of the repulsion on your part exist "

"What have the grounds of my repulsion to do with the standing of my husband as a citizen?" inquired she, with evidently wounded self-love "You will not undertake to impugn the character of my husband, as you hint at reasons that should occasion people to avoid his society? If you say a single word to the prejudice of my husband, I must doubt your character, since you traduce him from envy, while he is worthy as a man, of all respect and friendship on your part "

Robert turned pale, and sank likewise upon a chair opposite his friend

The declaration of the wife was simple, brief, and concise It was the declaration of a woman—in her social position as a wife and mother, and so far right, if it had only not concerned a man who had long since lost his credit as a citizen—and been directed to a man who was placed in such delicate relations towards her, to whom she had given her heart for ever, or at least had sworn to do so.

"You will not surely regard the reports and tattle which the mean envy of some countrymen of my husband has put in circulation, who are wanting in practical ability for business, and endeavor, on that account, to cast suspicion upon his character, because they are less successful than he, who is making his fortune here?"

"Do you mean by this Hinango, madam?" inquired Robert, suddenly, in a tone of injured honor.

Gracia trembled at the sound of this ice-cold word—she sprang up and seized Robert's hand

"Robert, you do not love me, and wish to part from me?" cried she, with tears starting from her eyes

"Gracia! are you deranged?" inquired the youth, pressing her hand between both of his

"You love another—you love Dolores "

"Dolores!" cried Robert, springing as if struck by lightning, "how did you know that name, which has not passed my lips?"

"See! now I only see how violent you are! is not my suspicion well founded? if the poetess were indifferent to you, how could you then be so shocked at my words?"

"I conjure you to tell me how you learned the name Dolores? from whose mouth did you hear it?"

"From the mouth of my husband," replied the wife, smiling, "he knows your so called 'sister,' and——"

"And stands in connexion with the Baron de Spandau, to deliver her to Rosas in Buenos Ayres."

It was now Gracia's turn to tremble. She sank into her armchair again, and gazed earnestly at Robert

"In connexion with the Baron de Spandau, to deliver her to Rosas," repeated she slowly, with an inquiring tone of the most profound horror

"Gracia! Gracia!" now cried the young Englishman "a shameful game has been played with you until now, and even now they are playing the same towards you! Do you know who Dolores is? Dolores is the being—who from the scaffold of her beloved on the river La

Plata, saved her own life by flight, to escape a similar fate, and as her protector, together with Hinango, Providence led in to Brazil, to this precipice on which I now stand—in relation to you ——

"Through my reverence for Alphonso and his beloved, and through Hinango's friendship for me, I believed myself to be worthy of your love, and of being understood and appreciated by you,—and now doubt me still' repeat that exclamation of unheard of doubt—whether I love you!"

"Forgive me, Robert," said the woman, after a long pause, with a feeble, tremulous voice A web of hell encloses me and—you, but be assured that my husband is as little connected in this respect, with the infamous Baron de Spandau, as I am, I pledge myself for that —I know him too well to believe him capable of a base transaction—to say nothing of such treachery in regard to the life of a female "

Robert's brain was in danger of bursting. The domain of absolute lunacy revealed itself to him so far as this woman must be an inhabitant of this domain, thus to bring forward declaration upon declaration, which must either be against her convictions, or the result of an inward disturbance, in which the soul's mirror received the appearances of the outward world distorted, and returned their reflection again in the colors of a foreign element.

"Let your husband have learnt the circumstances of Dolores where and through whom he may, I conjure you, for the sake of our love, (if it be still sacred to you,) to tell me in what respect he spoke to you of her—what he has said to you about her?"

"Nothing—but that you ran away with her from Buenos Ayres, and that she has hitherto passed for your sister in Bota Fogo He said it was a secret—but he knew the reality "

"And you then immediately believed this communication, and probably believe in it now?"

"No—no, Robert! by all that is holy, I do not believe that you love this being—who, besides—— stands too high—for me——ever ——to be only worthy of raising my eyes to her——if you had ever considered her as other than your sister "

She spoke the last words with a certain muscular convulsion of her countenance, which expressed itself around the lips, and large tear drops fell suddenly down upon her pale cheeks

Robert was again agitated and impressed by the tone of profoundest sadness which accompanied these words, as well as by the declaration itself, which revealed to him the unhappy pangs of jealousy in the depths of her heart.

"Gracia! Gracia! I cannot comprehend you, and who will ever dare to boast that he does comprehend a woman? Shall I now set before you your parallel in relation to the characters of Mr Closting and myself, as you have expressed it? shall I explain the grounds of my repulsion——?"

"Do not speak of him! do not mention his name!" cried the poor woman hastily, and with violence, "I conjure you be silent about him!—be silent about him!"

"Well, I will be silent about him, but the

sentiment that you have confirmed and consecrated in me, will not be silent, it will speak aloud in my soul for ever ! Do you remember your words—' for ETERNITY '""

"I have said it once,' replied Gracia, with decision, "and I do not recall it—if I even feel," added she, with the same sadness as before, and with tears, "if I even feel that you never——would have made advances to me——if this unfortunate heart had not first revealed its sentiments to you "

"Good heavens '" cried Robert, clasping his hands, "what is this in you that is for ever and eternally torturing you with doubts of my love for you ? You make me regularly mad by every revelation of your heart If the belief in love is wanting in you, then you do not love, for faith and love are one If you are unable to think or to conceive that my being resolves itself into the consciousness of your reciprocal love, then the sentiment of love is foreign to you—that is bringing me—to the grave '"

"Yes, I can conceive it, Robert ' I understand you ' your sufferings are unheard of—and I have caused them "

"Not you—and not myself I can as little reproach you as myself, but I require justice from you, and in that you are wanting ' You are unjust towards me, while you tremble before a thought—which nourishes your jealousy, and require from me the endurance of a reality,—that I should suffer what I suffer, that I should endure what I endure '"

"*Can* I do otherwise ?" inquired she, with profound anguish, seeming to have forgotten what she had remarked, while reading the "Psychology of Love," since she, in case she had not forgotten it, now proclaimed herself "to be a goose, or her husband a monster "

"Yes, you can do otherwise if you will I repeat this assertion ' You are morally free as a woman; even if a slave of social regulations, a slave of him who bought you at a nominal price ' A negro slave maintains, in such a case, her moral freedom , and do you not possess the same force ?"

"Frightful ' frightful '" sobbed the unfortunate woman , "to compare me with a negro slave—to call me a slave—to treat me so ' No ' you do not love me ' you never loved me ' an unaccountable delusion has fooled me '—thank God '—it is past—it is torn away ' It is well that it has happened so—that it has come to this ' Think God ' it is well—to treat me so ' No ' that is too hard ' *He* would not have treated me so ' *he* never has used me so ' *he* has too much feeling ever to treat me in such a manner ! Frightful '—unheard of '"

Robert stood there like a statue whose foundation is undermined But instead of being agitated, he heard with all tranquillity the language of a feverish delirium which had possession of his friend He approached her, to take her hand consolingly

"Back ' back ' monster !" cried she, with a savage glance, the ray of which was physically perceptible to him , "back ' touch me no more ' never again—never more, with your devil's claws, which look like human hands ' Get away from me, Satan ' I curse you as the most treacherous being on earth ' take yourself off, or I will call the negresses to put you out !"

Robert made his study in the domain of the higher psychology, as a young physician observes the paroxysms of fever in a patient of whose cure he entertains the most well founded hopes

The whole manliness of his character displayed itself at this moment in all its grandeur, as he (contrary to former ebullitions) did not in the least lose his self-possession, but tranquilly heard all these objurgations, and would have withdrawn, if he had not happened to be in his own apartment, which the patient appeared to have forgotten

Madame Closting gazed around her with a broken glance, through her tears, looking without seeing, then recovered herself, and rising from the armchair, hastened to the door She cast a wandering glance back upon her friend, while she cried out to him, "Monstre que vous êtes," and slammed the door after her

Robert endured the explosion of this "mysterical" mine with all the tranquillity of a young artillerist, who would be ashamed of himself if, from the fear of being blown up into the air, he were to resign or desert a position which he had, in the proud consciousness of his manly character, once assumed or entered upon His heart appeared endued with sublime force It bore such moments, but his nerves would not endure them ; they became physically diseased, through the impression of the scene—the occasion of which was dated four years before, and in which he felt himself blameless He sank into reflection

An hour afterwards, as he left the pavilion to enjoy the coolness of the evening air, he beheld Madame Closting on the arm of her husband, walking up and down in the garden, in conversation upon domestic affairs, for the improvement of their comfortable arrangements, as if the young lady had never exchanged a word with her neighbor

Mr Closting greeted the young Englishman, and inquired after his health, while the lady contemplated him with a glance of coldness and contempt—that might be pardoned in her as a woman Robert felt and endured He was one of those men who willingly excuse every evil, in so far as they look back upon its origin, and do not in the least forget what they have once met with of beautiful, and good, and noble

Robert recollected in this hour the childlike earnest request of the young Brazilian lady, in the presence of Dr Thorfin, "that he would pardon her if she should ever wound him by her passionate violence," as he had, by anticipation, long ago fulfilled this request. The peculiar inward nature of his friend did not appear to him in the least disfigured through these convulsions, which he regarded as the tragical consequences of an incurable nervous disturbance, whose cause he recognised, and whose effect he endeavoured to bear, as far as his human strength would admit—because he loved.

CHAPTER XII.

SECRET MEASURES

Mr. Habakkuk Daily had directed his journey into the interior of the country, towards that town whose charming environs had once so peculiarly fascinated the naturalist's secretary, and arrived at the place of his destination the more safely, as the caravan was ordered thither to which he had joined himself at Porto d'Estréla

After he had, as Mr Stone, concluded his successful business with Mr Schweinfurter, he bore the name of Dujour, under which he could, in case of need, legitimate himself by some family papers. On his arrival at this flourishing town, he casually made the acquaintance of a young man who was politely helpful to him in obtaining information respecting his father. This young man was Mr. Bankoff, (or Banko, as the Brazilians pronounced his name,) who had a situation in a *magasin des beaux arts*, there. He obtained leave of absence for a week, from his principal, to accompany the grandson of the unfortunate old grimpeiro in to the mountains, and Mr. Habakkuk at length entered the dwelling of his murdered father, and found his grandfather occupied with his gold washing, as we have before seen

The four wives of the murdered man thanked young Mr Banko with all the lamenting expressions of feeling of good humoured negresses. that he had conducted to them their four-fold stepson, and rejoiced above measure at finding him so well grown and manly, stronger, and already almost larger than his deceased father

Mr. Habakkuk had learned, through the authorities of the flourishing town, that his father had been murdered in such a place, and buried in such a place; that the investigation, and burial, and other expenses, had amounted to so and so much, which sum a certain Senhor Closting had punctually paid, as the former friend of the murdered man

Mr Banko kept a close mouth and a fixed countenance in every conversation with Mr Habakkuk in relation to the murder—about which he alone could give information, but lent a serviceable hand to the son in all that concerned the neglected administration of the miserable fazenda, which included the living and lifeless property of the murdered man, that had now fallen into possession of Mr Habakkuk as heir.

Strictly as Mr Banko endeavored to govern glance and speech, and deportment, when the murder became the subject of the daily conversation, it, nevertheless, by no means escaped the clever Mr. Habakkuk, that he knew more than he had told as yet. He learned from his four stepmothers, that a valuable diamond belonging to their man must be hidden somewhere—which was valued at about twenty contos. This sum was no trifle, and agreed with all that Mr Habakkuk had by degrees heard of the "worth" of his father, (as it is called in English)

Mr Closting, as the intimate friend of the murdered man, had during some days before and after his interment, put the books and papers of the grimpeiro in order, and handed them over to the four women, none of whom could either read or write.

Mr Dujour had passed his life as a man of business, and as such had had no friend, for absolute egotism, which recognises nothing but personal interest, dissolves and disperses all friendship according to the old proverb "no friendship in trade" He had recognised no higher aim than to amass property, and no higher enjoyment of life than the satisfaction of his animal necessities in fourfold conjugal life No one in the neighborhood has sought intimate association with him, as he held himself aloof from the world—contracted within his business, which had been his world. No one had been intimate with him in life who might be able to give information about his "worth" after his death

Mr Habakkuk repeatedly conversed at large with Mr Banko about the inquiry after the diamond—which had now become the principal thing with him As the result of all these consultations, the latter revealed to him the possibility of falling upon the trace of the diamond in case Mr Daily would permit him to carry through the affair as he might think best In consequence of the heir's remarking, as above mentioned, that the young man who had been acquainted with his father in the last days of his life, knew something which he kept secret, he agreed all the sooner to. this proposal—and it was resolved that they should return to Rio de Janeiro in company

Mr Banko had desired that the negro Francisco might attend them, since he had not only often held in his hand the diamond in question, but had been employed from his childhood in diamond mines, and possessed in the business a certain technical knowledge, by which he might serve as an "*expert*" in case of need

We find the two travellers, attended by Francisco, in the small German tavern in the Rua do Cano—at Rio, where Mr Habakkuk first appeared when he arrived from Buenos Ayres

Mr. Banko had made the stipulation that he was to act entirely independently in this affair, and desired his companion to call himself thenceforward, Mr Stone, or to assume some other name, and to hold himself aloof from all communication with strangers

Mr Habakkuk promised to follow his directions, excepting as far as he was obliged to announce his arrival to the house of Walker & Co

Mr Banko had no objection to this, and after this visit of announcement had been made, Mr Daily in a peculiarly excited mood, entered the billiard room in which we once found the Botocudan Prince and Di Merbold

Merbold lived from time to time in Rio, and was just playing a game of billiards with Mr. Banko as Mr Habakkuk called the latter aside.

The lawful inheritor of the diamond was obliged to restrain his impatience until the game was played out, as the discreet young German wished to avoid all appearance of having anything important to say to the Englishman or Frenchman from Buenos Ayres

"Hey ! the devil !" cried Dr Merbold, looking up from his balls, "there is my fellow voyager of the Nordstjernan ! How are you——Mr ——? what's your name——"

"Mr Vaily," interrupted Habakkuk, inquiring likewise after the health of the entomologist.

"Mr. Vaily, sure enough ! Have you met Mr. Closting, and done any business with him? He's here now He has been home about a fortnight Mr Fitz will tell you where he lives '''

The son of the murdered man was much embarrassed, at the retrospect upon his business with Mr Schweinfurter in the absence of the naturalist—but soon collected himself, however, and with his peculiar assurance answered exactly as he thought suitable

Mr Banko had finished his game, and now slowly betook himself to an adjoining apartment, where Mr Habakkuk seated himself beside him

"Only think——!" began he, "Mr Thomson has just been talking with me about my journey into those diamond mountains, and told me incidently that he had, within a fortnight, purchased a diamond for twenty-two conto di reis, from a naturalist, and when I asked him, quite by accident, what the name of this man was, he mentioned Mr Clostng''

Banko started, but collected himself, however, and whispered in his ear "I counsel you once more, observe my doctrines Be silent! Do not let it be observed that you have ever heard the name of Closting It's bad enough that this old granny, that the entomologist knows you Remember, as soon as we take a single false step here, we are lost! our lives are at hazard You knew long ago that a man's life only costs two patacks to end it"

Habakkuk acknowledged the danger, and promised to keep himself passive

"Stay at home for some days," whispered the young German, "and I will say that you are sick, exhausted with your journey—they will bring you your meals into your room"

Mr Banko returned to a conversation on indifferent subjects with Dr Merbold in the billiard room, and the-heir of the gimpeiro retired to the solitude of his sleeping apartment

The Baron de Spandau walked with hasty steps back and forth in his private garden before the house of Fortuna It was midnight, and the clear starlight came glimmering down He seemed to expect some one, and did not remove but a few steps from the gate—that he might be at hand himself when the bell rang The blinds of the upper story were closed Bebida tottled round in the lower part of the house, otherwise all was dark and still

There was a gentle ringing, and the baron hurried to the gate Senhor de Monte Video came down the steps—with him was a young negro

"That is the Senhor who wants to speak to you, take notice of him that you may know him again," whispered Senhor Prole

"Si Senhor," said the negro "What is your name?" inquired the baron

"Moloch"

"I wish to order you to come to the island of Cobras, and will designate the place to you Will you know me again?"

"Si Senhor,' replied the negro, staring sharply at the "Senhor Branco"

"There's a milreis for your walk this evening, now you can go"

"Si Senhor," said the negro again, and Senhor de Monte Video give him a rendezvous for the next day, and let him out of the gate

A long pause ensued A lean snake glided obliquely across the path upon which both stood The leaves of the bananas rustled slowly in the zephyr of the tropical midnight Nothing else stirred

"He is going to sea about this time," began the principal spy, "or at least designs to go to sea If he takes this Astrala outside of the Sugar Loaf, then an expedition to Santa Catharina is of no avail, or at least its consequences are very uncertain "——

"He must then be despatched beforehand, I see that," replied Senhor Prole, "and this negro is safe He is horribly ill used, and would stab ten whites instead of one for a trifle—if they are only white The fellow breathes nothing but revenge "

"Very well I rely upon your choice—and besides, 'dead men tell no tales,' especially as the fellow whom he is to despatch, is more mischievous than ten faroupilhas "

"That will very naturally be our protection," assented the blood broker

"Come in and take a glass of wine !" said the baron, after a long pause

Senhor Prole accepted the invitation, and both seated themselves at the round table in the front room of the villa

"Dabedicendem," muttered Bebida, as she brought glasses and bottles, and awaited a glass for herself, and a second for Senhora Fortuna

Her wish was complied with, but she found the door fastened which led into Sally's room—and supposed that it was bolted on the inside and that Senhora Fortuna was asleep She placed the glass upon the table in the front room of the upper story, and went into the garden and laid down upon a bench—to rest after the day's work

Sally was at her post at the key hole of the alcove, and observed the countenance of the baron and the movement of his lips when he spoke, as soon as he had taken his place at the table He was singularly pale, as if he were ill

"He cannot very well be despatched until the evening of the day after to-morrow," began the spy, after he had emptied a couple of glasses

"He will not be ready before then either," replied Prole, drinking likewise "Mr Fitz is still arranging an instrument for him—an astronomical circle, or whatever the thing is called—and he often works a little slowly "

"Moloch must then wait in the evening until he steps into his boat from the stairs at the quay Dos Pescadores, and hand him the—— and give him the rest," continued the Baron, looking uneasily around him, as if he wished to satisfy himself that he spoke unheard

"He must then step into a boat in the neighborhood," said Prole, "row up to the captain's boat, give him the stroke, and pull him immediately into the water—before his people can prevent it "

"Very well, very well," replied the chief, rising. It seemed as if something wrought upon him, as if he must look around after the doors which led into the alcoves—but nothing was there ——

Sally had remarked that her looking through the old hollowed out keyhole without a metal guard, had produced this effect upon the man which he experienced, as our glance is able, perhaps, in the box of a theatre, to cause a person to look around at us—if it possess sufficient magnetic fluid.

She feared, by a continuance of this eye-strike, to expose herself to danger, and leaving the alcove, she found herself upon the stairs in an instant, and soon in the front room, where Bebida had placed the wine. Then she felt herself in security, since she could easily regain her own room. She had heard enough—more than enough. Her heart throbbed almost to bursting. She looked around her as if seeking for help. She felt herself alone and forsaken, and consoled herself with the thought that Lucy would be there on the next day for more work.

"A young German has arrived with Mr. Daily, who was formerly in Mr. Closting's service, and will go out in the Astrala—as a cadet, or something of the military sort."

"That's like him. The fellow is also infected with the ideas of "Young Europe"—reads prohibited books, and sings rebel songs at his wine!"

"Our Patrick does not appear to stand in connexion with the opposite party——"

"Why do you think so?"

"Because he stays with you, and does not go out in the Astrala."

"Hem," returned the baron thoughtfully, "I don't take that for any proof of his doctrine. He may conceal something else behind it; at least I shall not take him with me on board the Santa Catharina. Apropos," continued he, "have you taken care of the letter for Captain Tumble?"

"I sent it to the post by Patrick."

"Why did you not take it yourself?"

"Because I then saw the negro, Moloch, passing, just as I had sealed it—and was obliged to hurry after him and call him aside——. It was impossible for me to go to his furious masters after him, and it was exactly the time to put the letter in the mail bag for Santos."

"Well, we will hope that it may be taken care of. I see very well that you could not be in the two places at once. Patrick has not yet given any ground for suspicion. He is very punctual in all that we entrust to him—nevertheless—prudence on our part is always necessary——. How did you find the Captain of the Caza? what sort of fellow is he?"

"A brutal Englishman—coarse towards everybody that is subordinate to him; but he was tolerably cordial with me. It seemed to be of importance to him to capture Dolores—and Hinango, if he could catch him! I believe he would even let Dolores go for that, for he knows all that happened to the cutter. A sailor has returned to Buenos Ayres, and reported that Hinango commanded the Nordstjernan at that time, and cut away the masts of the cutter."

"The cursed fellow, nevertheless, belongs to me. Captain Tumble may have claims upon Dolores—I know what price is set upon Hinango's head, and of that no one shall receive a per centage but you, Senhor Prole."

"I thank you, Monsieur le Baron. You are very right. I deserve also, in fact, an indemnification for the caning in Monte Video."

"That you shall have, if Moloch aims his stroke well."

"Captain Tumble will not, however, wait an hour after the arrival of the mail from Rio. He is a decided fellow. I explained to him, however, that you are just as punctual, Monsieur le Baron, and just as decided."

"Even allowing that the letter should miss him in Santos, it would be sent directly to Buenos Ayres, the address of the Caza is sufficient, and there are yet six weeks—seven weeks—— He can still easily come back from La Plata river to Santa Catharina."

"Certainly," assented Senhor Prole, emptying his glass, and after drinking another, took leave, for it was very late.

CHAPTER XIII.

THE INVISIBLE HAND

HINANGO had received, through Patrick, the baron's letter, which should have been despatched by mail to Captain Tumble, of the brig La Caza, in the road of Santos. He hastened to communicate it to his friend Dr. Thorfin. It ran as follows:

"At your desire, which has been made known to me by Senhor P——, and as you expect a written assurance on my part, before you seek, under some pretence or other, the permission of your admiralty to anchor at the appointed time in the road of Santa Catharina, I take the liberty to offer you the following explanation.

"The expedition for the appointed object cannot take place from here before the 15th of March. I pledge myself, however, (in case sickness or death should not overtake me before that time,) to manage the embarkation here on the said 15th of March, and to set sail for Santa Catharina on the same day.

"I desire you, therefore, to calculate the time which a sailing vessel (dependant on wind and weather) will require to arrive there, and to await me there in company with the appointed object.

"That you may know the vessel on board of which I am, I will cause a white flag with a green wreath to be hoisted on the foremast so soon as I see a vessel of war which is likely to be yours.

"I will take care that the schooner brig which is equipping here as a man-of-war, under the X***** flag, shall not take me under convoy, nor arrive there before me. Should, however, this (or any other man-of-war under an enemy's flag) obstruct the delivery of the aforesaid object on board of your brig, then I desire you to do all in your power to destroy the hostile sail, and in case of urgent necessity I will land first at Santa Catharina.

"According to your desire, I also declare that I am ready to share the sum with you, which is held forth for the expedition of the object, and empower you to make this document available as a guarantee in this affair, according to your pleasure.

"Should it be impossible, for me (notwithstanding all my cares and endeavors) to deliver the person aforesaid to you, on board of your vessel, I have, nevertheless, claims upon the sum which is offered for the discovery of the same, and offer in the above case to share the same with you likewise, as I shall, on the other hand, take care in the same case to fulfil the commission—with which those in high places have honored me," etc , etc ——

" Our Patrick deserves to be set in gold!" observed Dr Thorfin, when he had read the above letter, "and we know now where we are ' '

" The affair is now in our hands ' ' remarked Hinango, " since Captain Tumble evidently will not come to Santa Catharina, as this document is wanting for his guarantee, which he, as we perceive has made a stipulation   Horatio must be in Rio Grande now, and we may reckon with certainty that the Mazzini will be found at Santa Catharina before the 15th of March—let him be where he may, even if he were now in Monte Video, our communication through Horatio will find him "

" Fewer difficulties appear now to stand in the way of our plan than I had feared at the beginning," observed Thorfin   " In any case, however, Robert must be on board, for without him Dolores would be constantly exposed to the so called care of the old widower, and to the villany of the baron "

" I see that well," assented Hinango   " If Robert's attendance she can, perhaps, in case of the most urgent need, fly to Barugaldi or to me, and save herself   Robert could, in such a case, show all the firmness of his character, which we have hitherto become acquainted with, apart from his unfortunate relations to his neighbor "

The doctor was silent, and seemed not willing to express the anxiety which Hinango himself participated in, without giving way to it for the moment

" I am, above all things, now anxious about you, however," said Dr Thorfin, interrupting the ensuing silence   " Take care of yourself Ormur you may expect a dagger—a stab at two patakos any evening '"

" I am convinced of that   It must be a sudden attack backwards, over the shoulder, if I do not ward off the blow   You know I never go unarmed, and especially in the evening "

Mr Fitz interrupted the conversation , he made his appearance with Mr Banko, who had begged him to conduct him to Dr Thorfin's

Banko requested the doctor to allow him a few words in private, which request was immediately granted, and the doctor went aside with him

The young German explained, after a brief preface, that he came about a particular affair, in which he required the confidence of a man like Dr Thorfin, in order to be able to fulfil his duty

" You know Mr George Thomson," continued he   " I have learnt that this gentleman has not long since purchased a diamond worth about twenty contos   Without expressing the least suspicion, accusation, or assertion, against any person whatever, I beg you to procure me the opportunity of seeing the diamond, in company with a negro who serves me, and in your presence—I require nothing further   The result of this inspection will then perhaps lead to something more "

Dr Thorfin observed the young man with peculiar attention as he listened to him. The open unembarrassed mien which we have already designated in Mr Banko, had something prepossessing   The subject of the request was, moreover, not so significant in itself as the result

might prove to be, according to a sudden suspicion which was aroused in the doctor

" When do you wish me to introduce you to Mr Thomson ?" inquired he, after a brief reflection upon the awakened suspicion

" So soon as possible, perhaps to-day or tomorrow if it is agreeable to you   I will be here as soon as you like it "

" Very well," replied Dr Thorfin, " then I will desire Mr Thomson to take the diamond to town with him, to save us the distance to Botafogo," and both again returned to the room to Captain Hinango and Mr Fitz

Mr Fitz had conducted the young German to Captain Hinango the day before, that he might engage him as " a fifth wheel to the waggon," on board the Astrala, (as the air pump controller expressed himself,) which Senhor Prole, like a zealous deputy spy, had already learnt, since having been introduced to the astronomer by Mr Clostmg, and often went there. Hinango did not appear disinclined to place the young man under some charge or other, either as clerk or purser, or as cadet of the marines, and concluded the engagement, in case Mr Banko could be ready for departure in three days

The latter was in the highest degree rejoiced at this, since his plan stood in connexion with the undertaking for the designation of the murderer—that he might, in case of need, immediately find safety somewhere, in the event that a dagger might also be directed against him

We leave the chacara in the neighborhood of Nossa Senhora da Gloria, and hasten into the lonely silent street near the Campo da Santa Anna, where Sally awaited Lucy, her seamstress, with increasing impatience, upon whose appearance Hinango's life now depended—insomuch as she alone could be made the medium of warning

The forenoon passed away, and still Lucy did not come   A little negro girl made her appearance in her place, with the insignificant garment which was carried back and forth as a pretext for intercourse

" Senhora Lucy sick—hab fever—can't come," reported the negro girl

Sally had already, since that moment in the alcove, experienced likewise a sort of fever, and truly a very violent one, and now was almost in despair, as good counsel was more precious than ever

How in the world should she, directly or indirectly, convey to Captain Hinango the warning which might protect him from the stroke of Moloch's dagger ?

The baron had already almost conceived suspicions, as the result of Sally's espionage had not fallen out entirely to his satisfaction   Should she write a few words and send them to the post ? through whom ? through the negro girl, who hardly knew whether a post office was " eaten with a fork or a spoon ?"

Should she send her chamber maid, Bebida, to Da Gloria ?   Little as Dabedicadem might be worth, (according to English human valuation,) Sally might, nevertheless, be certain that Dabedicadem would be stolen, as she had never been in the street yet, excepting when she had been taken to auction to be sold, or when she went out to get water from the next fountain, or when she was sold again .

40

Sally had hitherto strictly declined entering into personal intercourse with Captain Hinango or Di Thorfin, on manifold grounds, amongst which prudence predominated, which she was obliged to observe for the rescue of Dolores

She dismissed the negro girl, with the request that she would, in any case, come again on the following day, dressed in her best, as she desired her attendance* for a walk, without having as yet formed any resolution what she should do, and whom she should seek

At the hour which he had designated to Moloch, through Prole, the Baron de Spandau went to the island of Cobras, to the southeast corner of the wall of the "house of correction," the most suitable rendezvous which he could possibly have appointed—for it was silent, and deserted, and solitary there

Three wandering negro musicians, slaves of a speculator, who made use of their talent for his own gain, had formed a group in the shade of a high wall, for a general rehearsal of their interesting concert

One, a gloomy Mandengo, played the melancholy sounding Marhimba, the half of a gourd, with nine steel springs of different strength inside, which, touched like the keys of a pianoforte, produced a hollow, expressive harmony A tall Congo played his favorite national instrument, the Oro-Congo, the gourd fiddle, whilst a robust Kabenda beat the Sacca-socca, a half dozen or quasi kettle-drums, likewise the halves of gourds, of various sizes, covered with leather, and variously tuned All these seemed wholly absorbed in their art, with true enthusiasm, and without regarding the unhappy Kirraboo, who, for the time, alone formed the sole audience to the concert It was Moloch, he stood there, with his empty basket beside him, as nègre de gagne,† who was going about in pursuit of business

The Senhor Branco whom he had seen the evening before by moonlight, now appeared to him in the clear light of the sun as bad as he was

The Kirraboo approached him in a quiet, isolated, and solitary corner of the colossal walls

Moloch was a distinguished young negro from the race of the Kirraboos, in the interior of Africa, near the equator—an Ethiopian aristocrat—a young man "of good family," descended from parents who were richer in gold dust than the baron in baseness—and that is saying a great deal He was about seventeen years old, with a perfectly well made body, of middling stature, and well knit His countenance was adorned with artificial wails, from the middle of the forehead, down to the point of the nose

In the endless wars of the Ethiopian tribes amongst themselves, he was transported to the coast as prisoner, there sold or exchanged for a couple of pieces of calico, and not long before, had been disembarked, with three or four hundred of his black country people, from various tribes, not far from the bay of Santa Anna

Moloch had never seen a white man until he fell into the hands of the slave trader, who put him in chains, and brought him chained across the ocean He had been ill used by white men, and treated, while on board, as one of a drove of cattle that is taken to market—abused by whites before he had been sold to a white man in Rio de Janeiro, who required of him to understand what he was ordered to do in Portuguese, and ordered him daily some hundred lashes "because he was a stupid headstrong brute, that would not hear and would not obey " Senhor Prole, the accidental witness of such usage, had recognised in him "his man," and given him to understand what was necessary

Moloch, with every hour, foamed with more savage fury against the whites, and the opportunity of despatching a single white man was to him a real joy, as a diminution of the debt which he and his colored brethren claimed from the whites

"Your name is Moloch, and you know me " said the baron to him

"Si Senhor," replied the distinguished negro from the equator

"Do you see the schooner brig there, with the blue and white flag ?—blue, like the sky, and white, like my linen , do you understand "

' Si Senhor—little—black—mast, so —— " he indicated the oblique direction of the masts of the Astrala

"Do you know where the stairs Dos Pescadores are—the landing place up there ?"

"Si Senhor ' landing place Dos Pescadores boat—canoe—much—capitaons—much '"

"Well, take notice of the boat of the captain from the schooner brig , pass over to-day, and to-morrow, and the day after to-morrow "

"Si Senhor ' boat—schoon—brig—capitaon —to-day—to-morrow—si Senhor, and to-morrow again ' Si Senhor "

The spy took his hat, and made use of it as the model of a boat "See here, the boat is black outside, with a white stripe on the edge "

"Si Senhor—black—white stripe on edge "

"Inside yellow, like this straw hat "

"Si Senhor—inside yellow, like this straw hat.

"And behind them is a star, painted on the left here '"

"A star, si Senhor—left—here '"

"The captain is something taller than I— slender—dark hair—straight nose—with moustaches "

"With moustaches ?" exclaimed the negro inquiringly, and did not appear rejoiced by this intimation, which may be explained by the peculiar preference which the negroes universally entertain for those whites who wear moustaches —since they distinguish them from the English and other trades-people who consider and treat the negro as merchandise

The baron appeared not to remark this scruple of the Ethiopian, and continued ,

"He is dressed like me—in black merino frock coat—entirely black—and wears a straw hat, like this."

"Dressed like me—black—all black—si Senior," reiterated the Ethiopian

"Like me ' stupid fellow—you are almost naked, and your pantaloons are a grayish white !" interrupted the baron, and now designated to

---

* No woman, of whatever class she may be, excepting slave, walks out in Rio without the attendance of a man or maid servant

† These formerly designated negres de gagne carry, without exception, on their heads, a flat wide basket, of about four feet square

him the hour when the captain on the following or third evening would probably get into his boat at the stairs Dos Pescadores. All the rest he had already arranged through Senhor Prole.

Moloch now received for the present, five millreis to buy himself a digger, in case he could not hire one. Five millreis, was a monstrous capital for a négre de gagne—and the two separated.

Moloch hastened to the shore and entered a negro boat hollowed out of the trunk of a single tree, with whose conductor he made an agreement that he should take him on an excursion, and then rowed around one vessel after another, till they came to the Astrala, where he observed very attentively the captain's boat which lay alongside, so that he might know it again at the stairs Dos Pescadores. It was now so much the easier for him to find "his man," who would step into this boat as captain.

Sally did her best at the baron's nightly visit to manifest her jovial humor, and to mount to the highest possible extravagance. She played the guitar with true passion, and sang her favorite song, "The devil take melancholy," etc., and jestingly informed her friend of the expiration of her service, as she observed she had claims upon an eternal "leave of absence," as she had served him sufficiently, and announced her intention of going to sea as sailor, to hunt for snipes in Australia.

The baron made earnest out of the jest, without suspecting that she in fact entertained the design of parting from him, since he informed her that he was going to Bahia after a few weeks, and unhappily could not very well take her with him.

She managed as well as she could to express her sorrow on that account, in the most touching manner possible, and had now the desired occasion for sinking into reflection, for which she had rich materials in her troubled mind.

The time arrived at which Dr. Thorfin, with Mr. Banko and the negro Francisco, from the diamond mountains, made their appearance in Mr. Thomson's cabinet, where the latter showed them the diamond.

"That's he!" cried the expert negro, as he contemplated the stone, "that's he!" and durst say no more, since the young German had strictly forbidden him to betray, even by a look, on what grounds this inspection took place.

"Can this diamond have been sold to a third or fourth person, and originally stolen?" inquired Mr. Thomson of the doctor, who was contemplating, with a searching glance, the countenances of the negro and the young German.

"Very possible, replied Thorfin, how often has such a diamond already been transferred by unrighteous means!"

"As regards my purchase," continued Mr. Thomson, "I have it from very honest hands—from a man whom you know, and against whom I cannot naturally entertain any suspicion."

"That is certainly not the question," remarked Thorfin, in an indifferent tone.

"To be sure not," affirmed Mr. Banko, "although the honesty of many Europeans who transact business here with large sums is frequently not so genuine as the diamond."

"Very acutely and justly observed," replied the Englishman—and Mr. Banko returned thanks for the favor, apologized for having interrupted Mr. Thomson in his business, and withdrew with his negro.

"Can there have been unfair dealing with this diamond?" began Mr. Thomson, in a low voice to Dr. Thorfin, when they were alone. "One hears so much and so many things about this Mr. Closting, and—nevertheless he stands in high repute here with some of the ministers, and has been a sort of chargé d'affaires accredited from here to different legations, concerning colonization and the like, as I have learned through our friend, His Excellency Von Kniphausen."

"All that may very well agree with rascality," observed the other, "it is well known that the most thoroughgoing intriguants pursue in our time the most fortunate career, especially at monarchical courts, which could not longer subsist without such creatures."

"That becomes more and more clear to me," returned Mr. Thomson. "But in our commercial world also, we have most confoundedly clever fellows. Just think what has happened to us. We had two boxes of Chili stones—a very superior assortment, there were sapphires among them worth fifty pounds sterling a piece; they were smuggled from on board a vessel before Buenos Ayres, and back again into the city, because the captain would not take them with him—were well-seated—carefully kept. The boxes went to Hamburg, and were destined for St. Petersburg, exported as minerals, and what do you think! when the boxes were opened in Hamburg, there was just nothing in them but worthless minerals! as they were called on the smuggling bill of lading. Is not that a cursedly clever theft? But where did it take place? and who has carried it through? God knows. We have perfectly safe people in our service, upon whom no suspicion can fall! the captains were just as honest, and now explain the joke, if you can!— Old Mr. Walker, in Buenos Ayres, laughed himself almost ill about the clever fellow who has so imposed upon us— Let him! be who he may, he is a clever fellow, that all must admit!"

Dr. Thorfin could not avoid laughing with Mr. Thomson at himself, and at the letter of old Mr. Walker, which he communicated to him. He accompanied his friend to the exchange, where they parted—with the expectation of soon seeing each other again in Bota Fogo.

Sally could hardly await for the arrival of the little negro girl on the same forenoon. The little one appeared neatly washed and dressed, to walk behind Senhora Fortuna, or Mrs. Adams, as deputy chambermaid. But, whither should Sally turn her steps? to captain Hinango, on board the Astrala? That would be as improper as unsuitable. To the young painter at the academy, under the pretext of observing the paintings and statues? He had gone away to Rio Grande, long ago. To Alvarez de la Barca? He was in the fortress Do-Vilcalhon as a state prisoner. To Dr. Thorfin, whose dwelling she certainly could probably find, as Lucy had described it to her? He appeared the only person to whom she could confide Hinango's fate. But to arrive at the Gloria she would be obliged to go through the principal street, which led past there towards Bota Fogo, and she knew long ago that her successor, the future Baroness de Spandau, lived there, and that her friend rode back and forth through the street daily, at various times.

If he should meet her, what pretext should she assume, in case he encountered her not far from the abode of the physician? To meet her out there would be sufficient to create suspicion against her, for in case she required a physician, her friend would see to it that one should come to her.

All these considerations remained in her way, and she did not know what was to be done. Suddenly it occurred to her that Lucy had told her of Signora Serafini, to whom she had been recommended as seamstress by Dr Thorfin.

"Did you ever wait upon Miss Lucy to the lady from Bahia, whose husband is a prisoner here in the fortress upon the bay?" inquired she of the little negro girl.

"Si Senhora! at Pray' Granda. Si Senhora!"

"You know her house then? you know where she lives?"

"Si Senhora! know where she lives—little house—yellow—door green—know where she lives."

"In Heaven's name then!" sighed Sally, and hastily made her toilet as simply and properly as her destination and the aim of her visit required.

CHAPTER XIV.

FEMALE CHARACTER

SALLY walked over the Campo da Santa Anna accompanied by her little female servant, through the brilliant Rua do Ouvidor, the long, narrow, coquettish and self-selling Brazilian Paris. Rich in *bijouterie*, luxury, and milliners' shops, and not less rich in materials for a dozen novels, if the female inhabitants would reveal their Mysteries, which they have transported to Brazil from Havre, or Marseilles, or Bordeaux.

She walked slowly further and further around the right hand corner, into the Rua Direita—across the Largo do Pazo, where the German "Philosopher* of the Largo do Pazo" was walking back and forth, as usual, with his harlequin cap, who, while he lived quite comfortably on the benevolence of the citizens, made himself very merry behind their backs about the "fools without caps, who worked for him that he might go promenading."

Sally arrived at the Imperial Palace, and at length on board the steamer that went to Praya Grande.

After a delightful excursion, she stepped out on the opposite shore of the bay, and followed the little negro girl to the garden-house which Signora Serafini inhabited.

Difficult as it might have been in any other case to obtain admission (under existing circum-

* A well known beggar in Rio.

stances) to the lady of a state prisoner, who, watched by the secret police, dreaded all intercourse with strangers, the name and the little attendant of Lucy, nevertheless, served to obviate all difficulty.

But there, for the first time, as she was obliged to encounter the searching and inquiring gaze of the servants, did the danger to which she had exposed herself fall heavily upon her heart ——

The prudence of the lady, in not permitting the entrance of any person who might serve the police as a spy, intimated to the poor girl the watchfulness with which the police probably observed her, and if the baron should ever learn that she had been there——she would be lost.

Signora Serafini inhabited a chacara upon an elevation at Praya Grande, not far from San Domingo, whose site afforded a view of the fortress Do-Vilcalhon, where her husband was confined in chains.

The window of an unpretending furnished apartment overlooked that wonderful "composition of nature," which the variously animated bay in the foreground, and the colossal chain of mountains offer, above which the jagged points of the "Corcovado" and the "Tijouca" rose so majestically.

The wife of the imprisoned faroupilha chose this window as her favorite spot, and seemed to be similarly fettered there with invisible chains, as he in his dungeon to an iron ring in the floor.

Angelica's body sat there at the embroidering frame, at her writing desk, or before a book, while her soul lingered near that "half of her being," whose unity neither the space nor any violent separation could dissolve.

The before mentioned chain of mountains did certainly rise majestically above the here and there cultivated and luxuriously verdant hills and slopes, at the foot of which lay the capital of the empire, with its shining cupolas and steeples. The moveable "staffage" of the magnificent painting was changed every moment in manifold variations, by the innumerable sails of every size, from the "floating world" of a ship of the line, to the miserable negro canoe, in which the Ethiopian fisherman fastens a piece of linen to the broken shaft of a young tree. The restless, stirring life fluctuated up and down, in all imaginable forms, before Angelica's sight, from the first suddenly streaming rays of the morning sun, until the evening twilight, or the transition in the day-bright moonlight.

A thousand objects, from that world of sails upwards into the clouds, which rested from time to time upon the tops of the mountains, would have attracted the attention of any observer at that window. Angelica's look flew over the earthly paradise from San Christova to the "Sugar Loaf," without lingering upon any point of the inexhaustibly rich picture—except one. It was the mass of stone, which, rising upon rocks, formed the fortress Do-Vilcalhon, washed and surrounded by the mirror clear element, that splashed at the foot of the hill upon which she dwelt, and had, in a measure, become a means of connexion between the prisoner and his wife.

Angelica's gaze rested for hours upon the perpendicular, gigantic walls, distant from her several English miles, from whose port holes the colossal mouths yawned towards her, whose rattling thunder would be the only language that would bear any greeting from her husband in the fortress to her at Praya Grande

Those magic charms of nature around about her seemed to have lost their attractive effect upon Angelica's mind As far as they heightened by the contrast of the splendor and magnificence, of the beauty and luxuriousness, of the grandeur and variety, so much the more the pain of separation, the consciousness of the loneliness that penetrated the unfortunate lady

There is a threefold unity of being upon earth, we will describe it here The platonic, (or spiritual,) the animatic, (or unity of the soul,) and the animal, (unity of the flesh,) but the last is only a momentary union

The Platonic Unity is the spiritual connexion, without a particular merging into one, of the animatic life, by the nerve fluid

The Animatic Unity is formed by the merging and mutual dissolution of two souls in the mysterious moments of the outstreaming and receiving of that vital fluid, of the ray of the glance, that seems to flow from the whole body. It is the unity by a mutual giving and receiving of the " fluid of life," the dissolution of the existence of both in one being

The animatic unity presumes the platonic (spiritual) unity, it is founded upon it, and cannot take place without it, as it requires a like depth of feeling, a like degree of development, of the inward life

The platonic unity of two beings of different sexes involuntarily strives after animatic unity, it is the natural condition of the attraction of the inward life itself

The third (so called) unity, is the " Unity of the flesh" as the scriptures designate it and the church privileges it It is a ' formal unity" without regard to mind and soul, about which the church concerns itself the least, when it receives the " flesh tax '

The platonic unity represents the Spirit, (mind,) the animatic the Soul, the Mosaic, (unity of the flesh,) the Body, (sensuality)

In pursuance of this definition, the sacrament of marriage (as the privilege of the Mosaic unity of the flesh) is also confined, in accordance with the New Testament, only to physical existence, without reference to the inward life either here or hereafter

The Mosaic unity (of the flesh) shows us man in the state of animal desire, (lust,) as far as he leaves father and mother and cleaves to a woman from sensuality The church privileged sensuality, when it fixed the sacrament of marriage without regard to soul and mind, to character, heart, or morality ——

Animatic unity is the bond of Divine love, illustrated in human nature This unity is the triumph of life In accordance with the regulations of the world, it does not generally evade the marriage ceremony, it is of too noble a nature to cheat the church of its " tax " The formal social ceremony of marriage, appears to the lovers in animatic unity subordinate in the highest degree, for there is certainly no need of any compulsory measures of " ecclesiastical police" to " force" the wife in animatic unity to

any " performance of duty," nor to bind the husband to his post The term " love" dissolves in itself the term " duty " The mother watches her sick child, not from duty, but from love. Moral freedom recognises no duty of slavery Slavish service and bond of love, are different things

The term " love" presumes mutual consciousness, the recognition of inward dignity, upon which " respect" is founded. Where there is no respect there can be no love, and where the first is procured by deception, disappears at undeception, and love, having no foundation, vanishes, the " duty" also ceases—to which the " church of sensuality" made the woman the man's " subject "

As man is distinguished from the animal by the consciousness of the inward life, the animatic unity is distinguished from the unity of the flesh, of animal instinct The " love" of many a mother to her children is often only animal instinct, in which many animals are known to excel even woman But where spiritual love tied the bond, and the inward life of the man was developed in the child, the love of the mother is elevated to a higher degree, to self-consciousness, that is wanting in " instinct " The mother, without the consciousness of the sympathy to her husband, loves " herself ' in her child, and her love is egotism The mother, on the contrary, bound by the spiritual tie of sympathy, loves in her child " her husband " from whose embrace sprung the " pledge" of love The mother without sympathy will, in decisive cases, sooner abandon her husband than her children A wife in the animatic bond leaves her children to share the dangers of the fate of her husband, when circumstances oblige her to choose one or the other *

Signora Serafini received this " strange girl, who came on an errand from Miss Lucy " Sally begged for a private audience, and after a brief introduction, revealed the occasion of her coming

The wife of the state prisoner, whom Dr Thorfin and Hinango occasionally visited looked earnestly at the " strange girl," and first inquired whether she knew Captain Hinango?

" Only by name I have never seen him "

" What moves you then to expose yourself to such danger as evidently threatens you in case it should be discovered that you have been with me, and the object of your visit should be suspected ? '

---

* The history of Russia affords a remarkable confirmation of this assertion In consequence of the conspiracy at the death of Alexander, (in the year 1825,) there were, among others, about thirty confederates of Mora viteff, from the higher classes, condemned to hunt sables and to work in the mines of Siberia The most of these young princes and counts were married Many of their ladies were unacquainted with the others, and several were separated from each other many hundred miles Without any reciprocal understanding, each wife resolved to follow her husband in chains They committed their children to the care of their relatives or friends, But one of these high-hearted ladies did not accompany her husband, she was the wife of a well known prince, (T―k―y,) who had offered to betray the conspiracy to the Emperor Nicholas, to obtain favor and pardon He was, notwithstanding his offer, sentenced to Siberia He bore the chains of his companions, but instead of the company of true love, he had carried with him the contempt of a woman of whose love he had never been worthy

" I know that Captain Hinango's life is worth more than mine, and if I lose mine, and save him thereby, perhaps Eternal Justice will weigh my pure intentions—against many errors into which my lot has drawn me "

The lady appeared surprised, and contemplating the unhappy girl with sadness, she said " Dr Thorfin told me of a warning for the rescue of our female friend—whose name perhaps you know Did this warning come also from you ?"

" You mean the poetess, Dolores? I have also endeavored to do for her what I held to be my duty "

Angelica was silent, and again sank into reflection, her eyes became moist—her lips quivered.

" Poor unfortunate—noble girl," said she at length, it is you also then of whom Dr Thorfin has spoken to me, who wished to return to England in company with a family "

" I have expressed my wish to Dr Thorfin and Hinango, through an Irish sailor, who is respected by those gentlemen "

" Will you not go to my fazenda in the mountains, on the borders of Goyaz? I have left my children behind there, under safe care, to be sure, but perhaps it would be of service to you to forget, somewhere withdrawn from the world, that you have been betrayed and injured as a woman.

" I have come here, Senhora to beg you, to implore you, if possible, to send the warning to your friend, Captain Hinango, not to go alone and unarmed to night or to-morrow evening, and in general, so long as he may be here, to the stairs Dos Pescadores

" His murder is determined upon, the negro is engaged who is to stab him As regards my future, I thank you for your sympathy, and may speak to you about it hereafter A man in whose hand my life also fluctuates, will go away in the middle of March—perhaps you will permit me then—when I am free—to trouble you again with my visits "

The wife of the prisoner found few words to reply, excepting the sacred assurance that she would immediately do her utmost with respect to Hinango, she then pressed the hand of the poor girl, and accompanied her through her garden to a gate, to draw off, as much as possible from her the eyes of observers

Sally betook herself to the Cirque Gymnastique of Signore Chiarini, whose tumultuous music was just then drumming into the air the stormy overture of the " Escape from the Seraglio "

No one appeared to have remarked what she had particularly wanted in Praya Grande, and even the baron was very well satisfied with the pretext—that she had visited the circus of the celebrated Signore Chiarini—when he found her at the right time of the evening, in a négligé, on her sofa

DOLORES.

BOOK VIII.

CHAPTER I.

NEMESIS.

THE force of the nerve fluid in the glance of man, (as the organ of the soul,) manifests itself in animatic magnetism, insomuch as its operation is capable of producing magnetic sleep The communion of kindred souls between themselves by means of this organ is a mutual receiving and giving, a transfer of interior being, whose alternate operation, as it were, increases the substance of the nerve fluid of two persons with each other, forming an animatic unity, in which (so to say) one soul, attracted into the other, lives in that other.

A single glance may give us information of the most secret emotion in the sanctuary of the soul, and the impression of such a glance, which (in a manner) infuses soul into soul, is able to accompany us indissolubly throughout our whole lives—inwoven with our being, as part of our souls

Spirit and spirit can unite without the encounter of the glance, as, for example, we feel ourselves akin to the spirit of an author, or enter into relationship with him, by reading his works The medium of connexion for the union of souls is the organ of the soul · the magnetic fluid of the glance

The youth Robert, whose individuality would belong in that category which we have designated as fire or air magnetic, had lived until this time (so to say) in Gracia's soul, from which he, as it were, had received a portion into himself, in exchange for a like portion of his animatic existence.

A similar exchange of the inward life can of course only take place between animatic (fire and air magnetic) beings, and is, on the contrary, impossible between animal (earth and water magnetic) natures, or on the part of one such in intercourse with a being of the first category, for no glance fluid can operate where the animatic force is not developed The glance of an animal nature is certainly capable of the expression of the element in which it moves, whether this element be sensuality, instinct, frivolity, etc ; but the animal nature, like its operations, is rigidly opposed to the element of the inward life, in which it is deficient

It follows from the above, that an animatic being of either sex experiences no mutual operation of animatic fluid in connexion or intercourse with animal nature, to whom this element is foreign, since it cannot operate where it does not exist

On the other hand, many phenomena of the social world around us are explained through the above principle, in which beings united in the most intimate manner with each other through this mysterious bond of animatic life—exist spiritually in each other, and, so to say, " fast bound, are fettered to each other "— Similar phenomena, which in the middle ages were counted in the category of Witchcraft, according to the above, have their foundation in natural causes

The countless number of suicides, (which heartless materialism ascribes to everyday Love stories, and scoffs at as laughable occurrences in the ridiculous province of sentimentality,) in a thousand cases find their explanation in a diseased state of the nerves of those unfortunate beings, who, in the manner above designated, feel their animatic existence injured, suddenly disturbed and interrupted, or relaxed, through the opposing hostile principle of the animatic element

The reality of the " distant effect ' in the animatic sphere is a matter of experience, which belongs neither to the province of witcher ft nor to that of " ridiculous sentimentality or foolish love stories "

The Distant Effect in magnetic *rapport* is similar to the timeless movements of an electro-magnetic telegraph ! thought and sentiment operate timeless in far distance

Robert endured (in his physical existence) the operation of a similar animatic *rapport* through the month-long exchange of the glance fluid, in so much as the animatic life prevailed in him, and had, as it were, overpowered his entire being

The neighborhood of Gracia had in a manner become a necessity of his existence. He felt himself fettered by that mysterious bond, (founded upon the higher entity in man,) in so far as we (according to the system of Garringos) recognise the soul's life as primitive existence, whose form or instrument is the subordinate shell of the body.

Robert became physically ill by the disturbance of his nerves, through the distant operation of the voluntary or intentional injury of his nature, by the woman in whose existence he lived animatically

Similar to the above mentioned effect of the electro-magnetic telegraph, the unfortunate felt every contact of the inimical animal principle with the separated part of his being, which systematically ruined and disturbed it The destruction of his mind became reciprocally a destruction of his nerves, and his existence upon earth, undermined by such sufferings, was nearly a physical impossibility

Every psychologist, in traversing the province of animatic magnetism, would have found his illness as natural as the wound fever after an amputation, without being able, as a physician, to prescribe a recipe for replacing the separated portion of his being The misfortune of such sufferings lie specially in the mystery which they occasion, and many a sufferer would be rescued in such cases, if the cause in itself did not require at the same time, also, the stipulation of endurance without soothing participation

Robert passed some days in self-abstraction, in the mechanical performance of his daily business, which did not make very serious claims upon his intellect He endeavored to conceal his illness from himself He passed through the garden which surrounded the two pavilions at his departure and return, and occasionally met his friend, in company with her husband or the little one, and instead of the former greetings, encountered a contemptuous glance, with which she turned her back upon him

The youth observed the tone of social civility towards the lady, as towards her family, now as before He considered his friend as an invalid, a sufferer who was overtaken by a fever which had robbed her of her interior self-consciousness, as a high fever deprives a person of exterior consciousness He had become acquainted with her being as a soul, and was so much the more convinced of her noble nature, since he felt the operation of her spiritual life in himself, which, according to logical consistency, could not have taken place if it had not existed in her

By what means, and with what powerful disturbance the woman endeavored to tear herself asunder from the " monster," who had not dared originally even to allow his sentiments of sympathy towards her to be perceived, may be conjectured ——

Perhaps, however, the unfortunate being experienced a not less violent reaction of the sufferings of her friend, notwithstanding she, seized by a delirium, endeavored suddenly to break a bond which might certainly be violated by female caprices, to an agitating degree, but could not be rent in her.

The intentional dissolution of the animatic unity of the two beings, through the deadening and destruction of the inward life in the woman, by the subjection and solution of her nobler nature in the element of animal vegetation, was murder, undeniable murder, of the kindred spiritual life of the youth Only such an animatic suicide of the woman, (more horrible, than any physical one,) was able to dissolve the *rapport* in the kindred being, as occurs in hundreds

of cases, and at the same time, also, causes physical suicide at a more remote period

Eight days had passed since their separation, when Gracia entered Robert's apartment one evening, under the pretext of asking for some pieces of music which she had forgotten there Her quivering lips were hardly able to utter the request

She remained standing in the middle of the room, gazing before her with a convulsively disturbed countenance, and appeared then to perceive that Robert approached her to hand her the leaves of music She seized them, and allowed them to drop on the floor beside her

Her glance raised itself to the glance of her friend, and a second of such communion embraced what an hour of similar effusion in words would have been incapable of expressing

" Robert——!" was at length the single sound which the unhappy woman exhaled from her oppressed heart, as she sank on the breast of her friend in a similar swoon as in that hour when the acknowledgement of her sentiments forced itself from her

It was a state of inward convulsion, which extended itself to all the physical organs, and of course dried the tears and suppressed the words within her

It was the unfortunate woman, impressed with the guilt of an unheard of wounding of the friend on whom she had once bestowed her most sacred confidence, and who had always shown himself worthy of it It was the wordless petition for forgiveness, in the singular consciousness that the petition was already fulfilled It was the swoon of shame in retrospect upon herself

" You have not wounded me—you have not injured me," began Robert as the unhappy one regained her physical consciousness " I have once known you, and have never deceived myself I feel that, in the operation of your nature upon me I separate character from temperament—nature from a state of suffering I love you, and in this word lies all—all that I can say at this moment for your consolation I live in you, and your sufferings are mine Your boundless misfortune is my—— " He witheld the gloomy word, and gazed in the eyes of his friend, who, still absorbed, heard his words, and hardly dared encounter his glance.

Mr Closting had returned to Rio at the intimation of his partner that his presence was necessary for the business in Santa Catharina.

Without wandering into the prosaic province of the money business of a man who began in Brazil with nothing, and had got so far through his " praiseworthy industy," that his " worth " amounted to a considerable sum, (as he at least himself intimated, that he might sustain his credit,) we merely remark that some indiscreet people, as, for example, Mr Francis Rossbruck and others, announced themselves to him so soon as his return became known.

The indiscretion of certain people proceeded so far, as to consider him their debtor for tolerably large sums, which he had received here and there for one undertaking or another, partly as an advance, and partly as exchange which people had confided to his credit, and the punctual payment of which, upon reception, or at the appointed time, he had "forgotten from sheer business perplexity."

A clerk of the triple headed business house of "Cerberus & Co," in the "lower world," might commit to paper the scenes which occurred in the private office of Mr Closting in those days immediately after his arrival, but we gladly omit them here, since they would bring with them a nomenclature and registry of manifold coarseness and brutal dismissals, for which the poorest paper under our pen would always be too good.

One day Mr Closting sat in his natural history business office, absorbed in correspondence with various imperial and royal academies and institutes, whose correspondent and honorary member he was, (or at least called himself,) when a man entered whom we have already seen before—Mr Nols, his travelling factotum. After he had satisfied himself that his former master was alone, (for he had peaceably left his employ,) he beckoned through the open door into the front room, and two more persons entered—Mr Banko, and Mr Habakkuk Daily. When both had crossed the threshold, Mr Nols closed the door, and placed himself before it.

Mr Closting observed this manœuvre of entrance with a sort of surprise, through which an internal feeling of uneasiness was perceptible, and looked with an inquiring glance, first at one, and then at another of them.

Banko took up the word, and said, in a quiet tone. "I take the liberty of introducing to you Mr Habakkuk Daily, son of the buried Mr Xavier Dujour-Daily, employed in the business of the house of Walker and Co, who has a demand upon you, Mr Closting."

"A demand upon me?" inquired the other, with unfeigned amazement.

"A demand on you, Mr Closting, to the amount of two-and-twenty conto di reis!"

Mr Closting's countenance lost color. "A demand for exchange, then, perhaps from Europe?" inquired he with hesitation, "will you show me the document?"

"Primo and secundo bill of exchange, in due order," replied the young German, laying the two sympathy birds upon the writing table, before Mr Closting, while all three gazed at the murderer with an unaverted glance, and ob-observed every shade of his expression.

There is a "tactic of surprise," which in the art of war is considered to be the best and safest, and by which many generals, with contracted forces, have beaten an enemy who exceeded them tenfold in military strength.

Hardly had the naturalist perceived this duplicate specimen of sympathy birds, prepared with unusual care, and well preserved, than the whole garrison of the intrenched leaguer of his evil conscience (as if siezed with an apoplexy,) grounded arms, and no brutal command of defiance was able to bring the array of impudence again "à la bayonette."

The murderer, as if paralyzed by a stroke of electricity, became still more pale, and instantly sank back into his armchair—and the attacking hostile party had conquered ——

"You will be so good, Mr Closting," continued Mr Banko, when he had for a sufficient time contemplated the surrender of the enemy,

"you will be so good as to pay the before named sum to-morrow morning before ten o'clock, in the cabinet of Mr Thomson, to Mr Daily, on the receipt of his aquittance. Until then we take our leave, farewell."

He then replaced the two birds in his hat, and all three left the cabinet as speedily as they had come.

The naturalist had discovered a province in nature into which his investigations had not until this time extended, the province over which dominates the revengeful Nemesis, who, enveloped in the gloomy veil of night, comes forth here and there as a fearfully terrible sovereign, and occasionally avails herself of the most insignificant circumstances to assist her power.

Mr Forro came into the cabinet of his partner, to consult him upon some matter of business, without noticing the visit which had just taken place, since so many persons passed in and out who "had business with Mr Closting alone."

"My God! are you not well?" exclaimed he, when he saw his partner in his armchair, still pale—pale as death, and half unconscious, gazing on vacancy.

"I must have taken something poisonous," replied the naturalist, "perhaps last evening at supper—some damn'd leaf or herb, or something of the sort, that got among the vegetables, and happened to come upon my fork."

"Shall I send to Dr Thorfin?" inquired Senhor Forro, with friendly sympathy, "or will you prescribe something yourself? You look very suspicious."

"I will go over to the apothecary," observed the other, "and take an antidote, or something, and move about a little in the fresh air. I hope it is nothing to speak of—that it will be nothing of consequence."

At these words he seized his hat, drew it low over his eyes, and left the office and the house.

The first requisite for the moment was to gain composure, to smother, if possible, the disturbance of the physical organism, and calmly to deliberate upon what was to be done. It was necessary in this case to rescue his honor as a citizen, which unhappily was at hazard, abstractly from the fatal consequences of this visit, which might draw after it an accusation of murder, in case he did not take speedy measures against it.

The miserable damned little sympathy birds—the sight of which had suddenly replaced him in the scene where he had expressed to Mr Dujour Daily his views concerning the sympathy of Signora Serafini for her husband—these wretched preparations were now also a testimony to him that somebody had observed him in that moment when he made the shot that legitimated him as the inheritor of the diamond.

Who of those three travelling companions had followed him there? whether the "impertinent fellow" Banko? or the laconic Nols? or the miserable negro Francisco? it was in fact all the same—the infamous bill of exchange upon the twenty-two conto's had been laid before him; and unhappily he could not "protest it," high as he stood in credit with the authorities from one cause and another.

Mr Closting hurried through streets and lanes, to the livery stable where his horses stood, saddled his Minas galloway with his own hand,

41

and took a ride, out towards Bota Fogo, to get some fresh air.

We will allow him to ride until he himself finds it convenient to turn back, and betake ourselves, in the meanwhile, to Dr Thorfin, who had just then received by a negro the invitation from Signora Serafini, to favor her with a visit as soon as possible

The doctor hastened to Praya Grande, and now learnt the object which caused Sally's appearance there The intelligence was not in itself surprising to the friend of Hinango, since the latter, under existing circumstances, had nothing else to expect.

It was already two o'clock in the afternoon when Thorfin returned to the city In the neighborhood of his abode, on the Gloria, he met the naturalist who begged him in all haste to inform his wife that he should probably come very late to the chacara in the evening, as he was overpowered with urgent business, but was otherwise very well

The doctor promised, with peculiar readiness, to make the visit to his neighbor, and the naturalist gave his Minas galloway the spur, and galloped back to town.

Within two hours after the visit he had "composed his mind," as the English say, (which had evidently been discomposed,) if we can call that a mind which vegetated within him After ripe deliberation, he seemed less to have lost his presence of mind than the hope of coming to terms with this indiscreet and bold creditor, who had come under his eye in the square person of Mr Daily.

Mr Closting had considered and weighed what was to be done, and had now resolved to do what he had considered upon and weighed The whole affair hung upon the avoidance of the ordered encounter in the cabinet of Mr Thomson as partner of the house of Walker & Co ; a rendezvous whereby Mr Banko gave him to understand, plainly enough, that the affair would be made public in case he did not comply with the demands of the heir.

Mr Closting would certainly have found the pretext of requiring first the proof that the diamond was the same which had belonged to the grimpeiro, Mr Xavier Dujour, but the two cursed sympathy birds were in the way, which had been used as proof against him in quite another respect.

It now behoved him, if possible, to see and speak this very day with the impertinent creditor and his counsellor Banko—to enter into treaty with them to give up the rendezvous at Mr Tompson's

Mr. Closting betook himself to his cabinet, and wrote two cordial notes to the two amiable young people, wherein he invited them at any rate to speak to him that evening in his office, as he was ready to bring the exchange business with Mr. Habakkuk Daily to an immediate conclusion He added, that he would remain at home, and not leave his office before ten o'clock

A negro was sent to leave the notes to their address in the German tavern in the Rua do Cano, and if possible to deliver them personally to the young gentleman The negro brought the information that he found neither of the two senhorites at home, but the landlord "expected them every moment to dinner, and would then deliver the notes."

Dr Thorfin made a hasty visit to Madame Closting, and found her relapsed into her illness, more suffering than she had been for some months He inquired after the health of their mutual friend, Senhor Roberto, and learned that he was in the city, and, alas! not very well The doctor then returned home, provided himself with two double pistols and a dagger, hurried down to town, entered a boat at the landing place Dos Pescadores, and went out on the bay on board the Astrala

Captain Hinango was occupied at his writing table, composing a farewell letter to Dolores, whose neighborhood he was now about to leave, and which was to be then only leave-taking, as customs and conventionalism denied them intercourse Thorfin appeared The privateer learned from his friend what had brought him there, and again sank into contemplation upon the disinterested devotedness of this despised female, who had hitherto decidedly rejected every approach on his part to a personal assurance of his gratitude

"I must go on shore, however," remarked he, in pursuance of the conversation which had ensued "I have still urgent business to transect, and must by all means go to sea to-morrow—to-morrow noon"

"Well," replied his friend, "then arm yourself well—thoroughly, and we will endeavor to seize the negro who is to despatch you, if possible, to bring him to confession, and unmask the baron in the background"

"That will hardly take place," observed Hinango; "it depends upon circumstances, if we succeed in catching the negro when he throws himself upon me, then, to be sure—then we should have grounds to take a decided stand But remember, besides, that the police, the courts, the government, would take the attempt at murder under their protection, because it took place towards an exile whom the monarchical principle has honored with a sentence of death"

The cabin boy of the Astrala announced Mr Banko's arrival Hinango desired him to come in.

"I have come with my effects, captain," began the young German, "and have here with me an acquaintance, and a negro, both would gladly remain on board to-night if you will permit There are peculiar circumstances, which I can only relate to you when we shall be safely at sea. I beg pardon for troubling you with this request"

Dr Thorfin accompanied the two on deck, and saw the same stranger and the same negro in a boat, whom he had remarked the day before in Mr. Thomson's cabinet Without hinting by a syllable at certain relations, he thought his part, nevertheless, and found much material for singular suspicions

The captain of the Astrala consented to the presence of the two attendants of his future clerk or midshipman on board, so long as they wished, and then went on shore well armed

The overseer of the altandega, who generally examined every one that came on shore, in order to confiscate concealed weapons or contraband goods, knew the captain in his position as captain, and spared himself the trouble of incommoding him and his friend.

Mr Closting remained as if upon coals in his office, and neglected his dinner, as he, very strangely, had no appetite at all, but occasionally a burning thirst

It was about three o'clock when he betook himself to this post Four o'clock came, and six o'clock, and still no Mr Daily He looked out of the window upon the opposite sidewalk, right and left, up and down, but no one stepped obligely across the street, who resembled either of these two The house in which he was, cast a broad shadow upon the opposite walls of the tiresome old houses, the shadow rose even higher and higher The old gray walls of the buildings opposite to him became even grayer and gloomier, and suddenly entirely dark, as the sun had disappeared——and still no one came He again sent one of his negroes to the little tavern in the Rua do Cano, to inquire whether Mr Banko and the stranger had not returned

The negro came again, and announced that both had been there to dinner at three o'clock Mr Banko had taken his baggage on board the vessel, he had said, moreover, that he would soon be on shore again

Strange ' then the notes had been received, and no notice taken of them ; the cursed clown seemed determined not to arrange the affair elsewhere than in Mr Thomson's presence—an impertinence without equal

Mr Closting had once for all declared that he would not leave his office before ten o'clock He must, of course, wait—wait quietly, until ten o'clock, and then—well, then he would have had time enough to consider what was to be done ,

Nothing else remained to him, nothing at all, but to go on board the Astrala, where Mr Banko was then to be found That he was there to be found, Mr Closting concluded from some words of Mr Prole, and from the obstinate delay The thoroughgoing lubber had looked out for his personal safety Mr. Closting comprehended such measures

It struck eight, and nine, and at length ten o'clock——and no one appeared

The naturalist then locked his desk, and drank another glass of water—and remained thirsty, notwithstanding He locked his door, and ordering the negro to wait for him, hastily left the house.

CHAPTER II.

THE MISTAKE

MISS SUSAN THOMSON lived after the happy betrothal dinner in a never-ending tumult of maidenly expectation of the things or the hours " that should come," when at last the middle of the month of March drew nigh. Although she, like a good Christian, had until now, concerned herself very little with heathen mythology, the god Hymen had, nevertheless, not remained unknown to her She even looked in the fishing library of her brother for some old book of mythological contents, to obtain, if possible, still more information about the signification of this or the other heathen divinity At length she found an old French book, " Leçons de Mithologie," etc , and learnt that Amor was a son of Venus and Mars, without conceiving in her narrowmindedness the ingenious symbol of this derivation , still less did she comprehend the mysterious marriage of Amor with Psyche, nor the significantly difficult prediction of the oracle, that the tender, ardent Psyche should be married upon earth to a monster whom she sought to elude by her flight to the island of Cyprus, where the loving Amor visited her incognito every night

' Miss Susan understood all this as little as the Apocalypse, which she had, nevertheless, frequently read She learnt, however, that Hymen was a brother of Amor, who was represented with a torch, with which he kindled the fire upon the altar of matrimony—in case it would not immediately burn of itself, which may occasionally be the case

Her days passed away admirably, and in joy, since she could now receive the visits of her baron without restraint, and make her appearance publicly on his arm, which was an unceasing " satisfaction " to her, as she could thereby evince to the world that she was a betrothed bride, and future Baroness de Spandau '

This allegory of mythology, in relation to the poor Psyche, would rather have found its exemplification in the Gloria than in herself

In accordance with this ingenious myth of antiquity, may Psyches, (or souls,) with and without the oracle, appear to be cast upon a monster in marriage, and it is not every Psyche who rescues herself at the right time, upon an island of Cyprus, or Santa Catharina, but is subdued by the monster upon a peninsula like the Gloria

Far from us be the design of instituting a parallel between the excellent and generous old Mr Thomson, and a monster of the Greek mythology ' Why should not Mr Thomson be able to lay as good a claim to the tenderest Psyche of reality, enveloped in a beautiful form, resembling her mother Venus, (as we are told in the myth,) especially when the mortal shell, in correspondence with his taste, is endowed with a tendency to corpulency ? On the contrary, we leave it to the decision of all young ladies, from fifteen to full forty years, who are desirous of matrimony, whether Mr. Thomson, in such a respectable standing, with a large property, with real estate and houses, and carriages, and livery servants, and apes, was not capable of satisfying all the demands and requisitions which any maiden or young lady whatever could reasonably institute ?

This question, long since decided by anticipation by the sound reason of the female sex, tranquilized Mr Thomson in the joyful prospect of his voyage to Santa Catharina

The baron rode and walked, and ran and went in and out at Mr Thomson's, in Bota Fogo, and regularly informed himself, though incidentally, of the health of Miss Fanny, and heard, from time to time, that she " thanked him for his kind inquiries, and found herself tolerably well "

The Baron was at Mr Thomson's when Mr. Closting rode past the villa upon his excursion. He inquired, more earnestly than ever, after the health of " his friend," Miss Fanny, and seemed to show a singular, almost urgent inclination to present his compliments to her in person   Miss Susan then seized her bridegroom's arm in a very bridelike manner, and ran beside him up the broad stairs, to Miss Fanny's door, on the first story

Corinna appeared at the knock, and the bridegroom was announced   The baron convinced himself that Miss Fanny was still alive, and seated at her writing-table at Bota Fogo—and further he did not wish to know

The Astrala was to go to sea the next day It was still possible that Dr. Thorfin and Hinango might, notwithstanding all the vigilance on the part of the spy, have attempted the bold stroke of carrying off Dolores on board the Astrala, in which she might even then escape alone, if Hinango should personally remain on shore The Astrala was already manned, first and second mate were on board, as Mr Closting had reported to the baron ; the elopement would not have been so impossible , but he had likewise taken his measures for such a case, that the Astrala should not pass the fortress of Santa Cruz without a visitation from topmast to keel ——

The baron had made his visit, and found himself again in the park with Miss Susan

" Do not go out anywhere this evening," whispered he in the ear of his young bride, (who, as a bride, was certainly not three weeks old,) " and keep Miss Fanny at home !   I enjoin it upon you , for I have prepared a surprise for her   We will have a concert in the garden this evening——" whispered he, still lower, playing in the most intimately affectionate manner with a riband paraded in a bow on the flat chemisette " I love such surprises, and have a forte at making them   Stay at home both of you ! you are accountable to me for the pleasure "

Miss Susan more than willingly assumed such responsibility, and was also able to carry it out, inasmuch as only one gate led into the garden, and the surrounding wall was very high—a circumstance which certainly did not come into consideration with relation to Miss Fanny, as she feared no abduction on the part of Robert Walker

All the measures for securing the person of Dolores were of course taken, her possible flight on board the Astrala was hindered, and besides, the baron had the necessary connexion with the officers of the port, which placed the means in his hands of directing the visitation before Santa Cruz *

Hinango had given his friend Thorfin a rendezvous at the Hotel du Nord for a friendly farewell supper, to which Mr Fitz also invited himself when he heard of it

All three sat according to appearance comfortably together, talking about one thing and another   The conversation fell upon Mr Closting's return, and his great success in business, and Mr Fitz observed " that he would succeed yet further in Brazil, as he was an uncommonly clever fellow, and had great protection, and was well known to have been long in the secret service of one functionary or another "——

* Every vessel that quits the bay of Rio has a so called password given to it, which is required from the captain by means of the speaking trumpet, when he passes the fortress of Santa Cruz   In case he should slip out without a password, he receives some shots from the fortress.

We leave the three Northmen in the Hotel du Nord, and betake ourselves to the street where Mr Closting left his house

A thunder storm was pouring down in streams The whole Rua da Alfandega, and all the Rua Direita, " swam with water "   Here and there yet stood a group of negroes at a street corner, to carry the passers-by upon their backs across the rushing rivulets which separated one pavement from another, and much discordant laughter resounded, and many Senhor Brancos slipped sideways down from the backs of the " two legged beasts of burden," with one foot in the rivulets, or with both, according to the greatness of the misfortune

A crowd of captains' boats, with dripping sailors, waited at the broad stairs Dos Pescadores for their old man, amongst the negro canoes and felouques, whose conductors, ready for service, beset the stairs and sprang to meet every one who approached somewhat near, with offers of their services

Patrick, without having been informed through the invalid Lucy of the design of murder against Captain Hinango, had instinctively mingled among the negroes and sailors, who, notwithstanding the pouring rain, exchanged their wit among each other—the negroes laughing loudly at the European sailors for having wet garments, which could certainly not occur to the Ethiopians, as the girdle around the hips was hardly a garment

Patrick availed himself of the pretext of observing the captain of the Astrala, in case the baron should learn that he had been there—since he had hitherto apprized him with the utmost exactness what had been taken on board there.

Mr Closting had some days before made a visit on board the Astrala, in company with Mr. Fitz, and had met some sailors among the crew whom he had formerly recognised as his countrypeople on board of other Scandinavian vessels

At length he reached the place of the Rua dos Pescadores, and hurried to the stairs

" The boat of the Astrala ! is it here ?" cried he, in a Scandinavian language

The two sailors in the Astrala's boat, heartily glad to get on board at length, out of the rain, replied to him, " Here captain ! here !" since they believed that Hinango had appeared at length   Mr Closting sprang down the slippery wet stairs into the boat, and cried to the sailors .

" Will you row me quickly on board ? I have something to say to your mate !"

The two sailors were Scandinavians, of course countrymen of the naturalist, and patriotically rejoiced to hear their own language

" Right willingly !" replied one of them

" Is it you, Mr Closting ?" returned the other, as the former seated himself in the stern, to guide the helm

" It rains fast this evening," remarked one of the sailors

" Very fast," assented Mr Closting

Moloch, who had already from a distance taken notice of the man with moustaches—who so quickly flew upon the stairs, and called for the boat of the Astrala—now stood upon his post.

Patrick, without remarking Moloch, who looked black like any other negro, and especially at night, soon discovered that this voice was not the organ of his captain, and allowed the naturalist to step into the boat Moloch, without exciting observation, stepped hastily down the stairs, sprang across boat after boat, into his canoe which he had long had in readiness, and sculled himself, with Ethiopian dexterity, to the boat of the Astrala, just as it pushed off, and the sailors had raised the oars for the first stroke

In a second the negro's dagger was planted in Mr Closting's breast, and the place in the stern was empty, as the Kirraboo drew the body backwards overboard into the water

"My God! murder! murder!" shrieked the two sailors, and instantly threw themselves into the water to draw the wounded man out, who convulsively held fast with both hands to the rope at the rudder, although he had lost his consciousness

Moloch had, in the same instant in which he accomplished the stroke, slung his dagger out into the bay, thrown himself after it, and disappeared under the water, swimming out into the gloomy, dark, deserted, rainy night, to take the opportunity of gliding on shore somewhere unremarked

Upon the cry of murder from the two sailors, every living thing that was in the neighborhood sprang down the steps, and many were crowded and overthrown

The overseers of the alfandega and the police, who were at their posts notwithstanding the pouring rain, hastened to assert their authority, and to bring the wounded man, or the corpse of the murdered one, to land

"Is that your captain?" inquired an officer of the alfandega of the two dripping seamen of the Astrala "What vessel are you from?"

"This gentleman is not our captain," was the answer, "he is acquainted with our captain, and wished to go on board in a hurry, his name is Closting"

"Senhor Closting? Closting?" repeated a functionary of police, turning to his colleague of the alfandega," the son-in-law of our colonel from Minas Geraes—who has the handsome wife? Murdered from jealousy, or something of the sort!" added he, in a low voice

A lantern was brought from the nearest loja or venda Another functionary now held the light over the corpse of the wounded person, and affirmed

"I thought, to be sure, I knew him! it is Mr Closting, the naturalist He lives yet, thank God!"

"He stirs! perhaps the wound is not mortal," whispered several

Patrick had crowded himself into the group and likewise contemplated the body, and satisfied himself more and more that he had not erred—that Mr Closting was not his Captain Hinango

The functionaries and inspectors made hasty arrangements to carry the wounded man to a house, and sent after a surgeon, apothecary, or physician, whichever was first to be found

"What's the matter there? what's going on there?" inquired Mr Fitz, who, at the same moment, with Hinango and Thorfin, passed the corner of the Rua do San Pedro

"It's only some one shot or wounded," replied a Portuguese, enveloped in his mantle, drenched with rain "A branco with moustaches; no merchant, and no negro," added he, and allowed the Northmen to pass before him

This conclusion of the Portuguese requires an explanation as a negro is always in Brazil worth from six to eight hundred millreis, or even a full conto, and a man with moustaches is generally not publicly for sale Such a one may of course be stabbed without an owner losing his negro capital, and without disturbing the business of any mercantile house—without moustaches

Thorfin, in his quality of physician, pressed through the crowd, and soon found himself beside the before mentioned " body,'

Hinango and Fitz followed immediately after him, and all three at once recognised their countryman Patrick showed himself to his captain, but immediately drew back, as Mr Fitz was present, whom he did not trust

"They're country people of the Senhor——friends—countrymen," whispered the functionaries in each others ears "One's a physician I know him—a very celebrated physician! it's well that he is here"

In this manner, well known, the first place by the wounded man was yielded to Dr Thorfin, and his orders were obeyed A surgeon and an apothecary soon appeared, and it was announced that the wound was certainly very dangerous, and would probably be mortal, but, nevertheless, a cure might be hoped for

"Who will prepare Madame Closting, that she may not learn it too suddenly, before Dr Thorfin goes home, who lives in her neighborhood?" inquired Mr Fitz, who had stepped aside with Hinango

"You hurry out there! you are acquainted there already," observed Hinango

"It would be better for you to go, and bespeak the necessary prudence with Robert Walker," was the view of the astronomer

"I have never visited them yet!" said Hinango, "and besides, I wish to go on board now. However, if you think it would be better that Mr Walker should know it first, then I will go out?"

"Are you the captain of the Astrala, in whose boat the Senhor there has been murdered, or wounded?" inquired of him the police officer, who remembered the family of Madame Closting "I am a police officer," added he politely

"Your servant," returned Hinango, "I am the captain of the Astrala, but now, for the first, learn through you, Senhor, that this murder took place in my boat Under what circumstances did that happen?"

"In your boat?" inquired Mr Fitz, "how in all the world came Mr Closting in your boat?"

"Do you know the wounded man?" further inquired the police officer

"I have known him from my youth, without being particularly intimate with him We have occasionally seen each other here accidentally," replied Hinango

"You must take the trouble to appear at eight o'clock to-morrow morning at the police office, with the two sailors, who are down there in the boat It is on account of the *procès verbal*, your evidence will be taken, and you can then go to sea. I know the family of the lady of this Mr. Closting—a very respectable family. As I hear, there is a young Englishman living in the neighborhood, the son of a very well known house —— May I offer you a pinch of snuff——? '

The officer, who, as a Brazilian functionary, could not suitably exist without a snuff-box, offered the two countrymen of the wounded man his box, and both took a pinch, without, as he expected, "biting" at the conversation, which he had endeavored to turn upon Mr. Walker.

Hinango stepped up again to Dr. Thorfin, and explained to him that he had concluded to prepare the lady of the wounded man indirectly for the shocking intelligence, inquiring at the same time what the other intended in relation to the place whither Mr. Closting should be carried.

The doctor observed that the wounded man must be immediately taken where he could remain for his treatment, since the transportation would always be more dangerous at a later period. "Hasten to his lady, therefore," added he, "and endeavor, as prudently as possible, to convey the intelligence that Mr. Closting has been thrown by a horse. He must have a couch ready for him in a light room, on account of the examination of the wound afterwards. If you can avoid it, say nothing about the attack and stabbing.

Hinango assented to these measures, and hastening to the next stable, where horses and carriages stood ready to hire, mounted a horse himself, and sent a carriage to Dr. Thorfin, for the wounded man.

The open loja into which Mr. Closting had been temporarily conveyed, was closed, and the crowd, whom curiosity and idleness had assembled outside, were obliged to satisfy themselves with their own remarks and whisperings.

The dagger had been driven in directly under the heart, but had, nevertheless, injured no blood vessel. The wounded man gained by degrees his entire consciousness, and now expressed a desire to speak with Dr. Thorfin entirely alone, which was gratified.

"This dagger stroke was intended not for me, but for another," began Mr. Closting, in a feeble voice. "As concerns myself, doctor, you cannot expect any desirable result of your professional treatment, so long as my mind is not tranquil. I have some business to transact with a stranger, whom young Mr. Banko was to bring to me this evening. He did not come, and I heard that he was on board of the Astrala. Send some one there immediately, and let them tell him that he must come here with the stranger. I will arrange the matter this evening. Before I have spoken to these two, I will not be carried home."

The decision of this declaration, which the wounded man uttered significantly, although with a weak voice, was a command to the doctor. He hastened to commission Mr. Fitz to go on board the Astrala in her boat, and, if possible, to bring Mr. Banko and the stranger immediately there, in case the latter was in the neighborhood.

The astronomer fulfilled the commission, and soon stepped upon the deck of the Astrala.

How surprising the intelligence of the attempted murder sounded to the two opponents of the wounded man, may be imagined, at least, however, the matter was to them in itself easily explained. They recognised the necessity of accepting the invitation, and soon found themselves beside the temporary couch of the wounded man, they were then left alone with him.

Mr. Closting now began, in a low voice, and with emotion.

"The state in which I lie here, makes demands upon your consideration. Promise me never to utter a syllable about——about——the matter——on which you came to me to-day. You, Mr Dujour-Daily—will receive the sum which you demand,——but I require consideration from you——as the ' father of a family '——

" In a portfolio there in my coat pocket, you will find the document which secures to you the sum as a possession——under the stipulation that you enter into business temporarily with my partner, Senhor Forro, and the twenty-two contos will remain there as your property until some time hence, or be used wherever you desire to place them, in order that a sudden intimation and payment to your order, should not reveal an affair which should not be spoken of, which ought to be forgotten, from consideration for me as the ' father of a family.' Will you do this? Then look for the documents here directly, and, after a year, you can take your money out of our business, or remain in it with the money, at your pleasure."

Mr Habakkuk Daily heard this " proposal for his good" with increasing attention. The considerable property of twenty-two contos, (eleven thousand dollars,) was the principal thing to him. The murder of his father was a " tragical event," which, however, already belonged to the past.

It was a question whether his father would have placed this sum immediately at his disposal in any business whatever, in case he had met him here living. The business of Forro & Co. was not insignificant, and, especially through the respectable connexions with the house of Walker & Co., its credit had latterly been peculiarly favored. Habakkuk had, consequently, the brilliant prospect of placing himself the next morning, dressed like a gentleman, as a partner of the house of " Forro & Co.," or even as the representative of the wounded Senhor Closting, under the porch of the exchange, with both hands stuffed into the pockets of his spencer, and looking down upon the world in Rua Direita, as a " made man !" This prospect was no trifle.

He examined the designated papers with the greatest apparent indifference, restraining the expressions of his satisfaction. He found the obligations in all order and security, and declared his perfect satisfaction with such an arrangement. The excitement of his feelings, which lay founded in surprise, led him even into an act of liberality, (in remarkable contradiction to his mercantile principles,) as he declared that he would only take twenty contos of the amount, and leave the other two contos in Mr. Closting's possession, as " commission per centage for the arranged business."

Mr. Closting was satisfied with this, and desired to have the sum in ready money ; that is, he wished Mr Daily to bring it to his bedside on the following morning, since he, as the "father of a family," in such a situation, required money, and besides, the affair would be completed with that, and no more agitated

Both parties now gave each other a hand, and promised inviolable silence about what had occurred   It was arranged that it should be said that Mr Xavier Dujour, the grimpeiro had named Mr Closting his "executor,' and his son Habakkuk had returned to Rio to enter into business with Messrs Poiro & Closting, as a partner of their house

M. Binko would, under any other circumstances, have still whispered a word in the ear of the naturalist for his personal satisfaction, but he saw the unfortunate man on his deathbed, and reached him his hand for his consolation, and remained silent   He required from Mr Daily the freedom of the negro slave Francisco, and that his "manumission papers' should be executed on the following day, to which the other willingly agreed

Both returned on board the Astrala, because it was more comfortable for them there than in the noisy little tavern in the Rua do Cano, and they had also much to say to each other ——

Hinango arrived on horseback at the garden gate of Madame Closting It was already nearly half-past twelve o'clock, the storm was past—the sky was full of stars Some one knocked, and to the inquiry of a negress, "who was there?" he mentioned his name, and added, that he wished to speak to Senhor Roberto

"Capitâon Y-nang-hoh!" reported old Anna, as Senhora Gracia and Robert approached the gate at the noise, who hitherto, as in former times, had been walking back and forth in the garden, enjoying the wonderful mildness of the starry night   Both looked inquiringly at each other   Something peculiar must have occurred What could have brought the captain of the Astrala there so late?   He had never been there before   "He has come to take leave,' observed Robert, after a momentary reflection   "He is going out, or——something must have happened in relation to Dolores"

"Ever Dolores!" sighed the jealous woman, "his first thought is ever Dolores'—terrible!" sighed she again

Robert's reply was repressed by Hinango's entrance, as the gate was opened   He dismounted from his horse, and greeted the lady and his young friend, who conducted him into his pavilion   The window was open, and the old confidential sacred place under the thermometer outside of the wall was still there!   Gracia's jealousy demanded that Robert should have no secret towards her, and whatever Hinango might have to announce to him, she must know it, and would gladly have gone directly into the room with the two friends, it this familiarity could have found any apology before the melancholy misanthropic corsair   She took it then upon her conscience to slip into her old accustomed place under the thermometer, and there entirely undisturbed, to listen a little to what the countryman of her husband might have particularly upon his heart

The night was as noiseless and deadly silent as a night after a thunder shower on the Gloria at Rio. The rose leaves hardly moved, not to mention the heavy banana curtains   Gracia could then hear every breath of the two friends, and understand their lowest word

Robert had already been informed of all that concerned Dolores and Hinango, the Astrala, and the mission to Rio Grande   He knew that Hinango intended to go to sea the next afternoon, and had resolved, notwithstanding his indisposition, to pay him a visit in the morning

Hinango's appearance might be a farewell' visit, Robert was inclined to consider it as such; but this surmise soon vanished

"The dagger that was intended for me has found another," whispered the Scandinavian

"My God! how so? what has happened?" interrupted the youth

"I come to beg you, friend Robert, to undertake a difficult commission   You must prepare Madame Closting for the arrival of her husband, in Dr Thorfin's company, wounded!"

"Wounded   by the stroke of a dagger that was designed for you ——I beg you explain yourself clearly"

"Wounded in my boat, at the stairs Dos Pescadores—mistaken for me, as he was hurrying on board to me, but what he wanted there, is inexplicable to me   Enough—a hired negro, whom our baron had engaged, was waiting for me, as we learnt through an indirect warning The negro took Closting for me, and wounded him instead of me"

"Mortally?" inquired Robert, trembling in every limb, and a shriek was heard in the neighborhood of the pavilion

Hinango delayed with the answer   Robert hurried to the window, and beheld Gracia lying insensible under a rose bush   He rushed out of the door   Hinango followed him   They carried the unfortunate wife, lifeless, into her pavilion.

The negresses hastened to them   All the remedies which were at hand were employed to recall her to life   She awakened in delirium, without any consciousness of the reality   After a half hour, the carriage came slowly up to the gate   The wounded man was laid in an apartment which the friends had arranged for him Dr Thorfin hastened to Senhora Gracia, and found her still without consciousness, in wild delirium.

CHAPTER III'

FEMINALITY

THE fatal boat of the Astrala, in the stern of which the murderer of the grimpeiro received the dagger-stroke of the mysteriously disposing Nemesis, waited a long while at the stairs Dos Pescadores for its real captain, who at length appeared, about two o'clock in the morning, and went on board, accompanied by Dr Thorfin The latter deemed this precaution of attendance necessary, since an attack was even yet to be feared, in case the baron, informed of the mistake, should have resolved, in all haste, upon some other plan for the accomplishment of his commission

The doctor, on his way back, procured the necessary additional medicines at an apothecary's, and returned thereupon to the pavilion on the Gloria, where, with Robert he watched till day

On the next morning, Captain Hinango appeared with his two men at the police, and was conducted into an office of the department to which this event appertuned A functionary took down every answer to his questions, they referred to the relations of the captain to the wounded man, and to all the communications which had ever taken place between them

At length the sailors were examined, who were just as fully questioned, and just as punctually answered each question through an interpreter, of which latter, sufficient provision is made in Rio in almost every bureau of the administration

The occasion on which Mr Closting was hurrying so late at night, in a pouring thunder-storm, on board of the Astrala, remained a riddle, which only Mr Banko and Mr Daily were able to solve. The result of the examination appeared to bring forward no ground of suspicion against Captain Hinango, he was, therefore, dismissed, and his already prepared passes for Hayti were recognised as sufficient He hurried once more to the Gloria, to take leave of Dr Thorfin, and again to conjure the noble Robert to conduct the whole expedition to Santa Catharina in the best manner possible, to accompany their friend Dolores, and not to leave her, for life and death

Robert promised this, adding, " I will endeavor to fulfil my duty, with God's help, and hope that he will grant me strength——until I see Dolores in safety "

Hinango did not wish to inquire after the obscure signification of these words, but took leave of his two friends, went on board of his vessel and weighed anchor

At midday Robert saw from his window the Astrala, under sail, pass the Gloria, steering out of the bay, and his heart beat with singular perturbation at the thought of again beholding this vessel, at the appointed time, before Santa Catharina ——

The baron had on the same night received the intelligence of the miscarried enterprise, on his return from Mr Thomson's to the garden-house which Sally inhabited He related to the latter, as city news, that a Mr Closting had been mortally wounded, just as he had taken his seat in the boat of a Captain Hinango, to go on board to him

Sally was obliged to use all her endeavors to reply to this information with as much indifference as she could without heartlessness—as a woman could manifest at murder in general She saw Hinango rescued, and now sighed forth a prayer that Dolores might also be saved

Gracia had returned to consciousness, and was able to leave her apartment Her glance appeared as if broken, and had not its former expression of animatic life. Her whole countenance was changed, and showed no trace of that youthful bloom, which once contradicted the idea of her being a wife and mother No one would have have recognised two faithful portraits, the one taken at this time, the other at that time, as representations of the same original Her soul was compressed within itself. Her body tottered about

She greeted and met Robert as if it were not he—as one of the most intimate friends of her beloved—from whom she had taken leave, and he appeared valuable to her because he was the kinsman and friend of her Robert

As Robert's heart, or rather his soul, had always participated in every motive, every secret feeling, every sentiment of Gracia, he perceived, even now, what was passing within her He read in her soul, as in an open book, his own sentence of death

Those struggles and convulsions which ever tortured her, and ever renewed themselves, appeared now once more overcome The inward sadness of sympathy with which she had only lately thrown herself on his breast, had been overpowered by another sentiment, for which neither she nor we could find a significant word

It was a sentiment that fettered her to the sick or dying couch of a man whom she had never loved, and who had never loved her, who had never recognised her value, as she felt that he had deceived and circumvented her, when she herself did not yet know what was the female vocation, nor what was love The approach of this man excited her repulsion as she had formerly assured her friend, and, nevertheless, she had thrown herself intentionally into his arms, in spite of the love of a heart that was fettered to her for ever by a mysterious attraction

She appeared to have again conquered, in the convulsion and struggle of love and of so called duty One heart, one life, must here be sacrificed; and, very naturally, that heart encountered the fate which had not yet enjoyed the happiness of being fettered by social bonds, which are more important upon earth than all the bonds of love or sympathy of soul ——

Gracia fulfilled her duty as wife and as mother, and stirred not from the sick bed of her husband, whose wound was soon pronounced not mortal

On the other hand, Robert sank upon a sick bed, with a deadly wound of his heart A violent nervous fever seized him, which soon passed into wild delirium, while his inward life freed itself from the fettering clay, and by anticipation flowed upward to the abode of the soul

Dr Thorfin remained the physician of both, although Aunt Susan was determined to send her English physician to Robert's couch, who was acknowledged to be very experienced and practical in such " diseases of climate, stomach complaints," fevers, and the like

Old Mr Thomson, whose way led him daily past the Gloria, lingered twice a day beside Robert's bed, and soon Dolores also appeared, as " Miss Fanny," in company with Miss Susan

Madame Closting saw the "stranger," whose spirit she had once so cordially greeted, and the fury of jealousy again awakened within her, in the inexplicable contradiction of the female heart, which had thought the bond severed that fettered herself to Robert ——

The external appearance of Dolores, the seriousness and indisputable dignity which her deportment evinced, wrought like poison upon the unhappy woman, who endeavored to elude the consciousness of reciprocal love—and manifested this consciousness only so much the more violently in her jealousy

With every approach of Dolores, in the carriage, on horseback, or on foot, the unhappy one trembled—and her countenance contracted itself to a convulsive expression of bitterness, when she saw her walk through the garden to Robert's pavilion, while, on the other hand, she must feel that he was struggling with death from love to her, and that he would not have been exposed to such a state, if he had been capable of loving any other woman except herself. But we are wandering into the analysis of a province that admits of none—the province of the contradictions in the female heart.

What had become of that feeling in which the unfortunate woman once beheld the world, with its sentence, lying like a mass of shadow at her feet? when she wished to be a speechless heard, to accompany her friend, to live until her death, unseen, upon the glances of his eyes, wherever he might be? What had become of that feeling in which she had expressed the longing to live in quiet retirement—separated from the man whom she could neither love nor respect—with him, in spirit, in whose soul her soul was glowing? ——

Was this feeling extinguished? It could not be, so long as her heart still throbbed at the approach of a female to Robert's sick bed. If it had been extinguished, this person, as well as Robert himself, would have been indifferent to her ——

Week after week passed, and the wings of time flitted slowly over Robert's sick bed. Mr. Closting's state gave every hope of speedy recovery under Dr. Thorfin's treatment, who, as a physician and a man, unceasingly fulfilled his duty.

After four weeks, his cure appeared beyond a doubt, and with this prospect, awakened in Gracia the eternal contradiction of the female heart, the sentiment of sympathy for Robert, and her jealousy towards Dolores, knew no bounds. So soon as she believed her husband saved, she gave herself up, with all the unrestrainedness of her former behavior, to the care of Robert, and hardly stirred from his side, excepting when she turned her back upon him in savage anger, so soon as the demon of jealousy seized upon her, which happened (in the waning moon) at least twice in the week, if not oftener.

Robert remained in his pavilion, weak and feeble, though convalescent. The only means for his immediate cure lay in Gracia's power. Her animate removal had disturbed his nervous life; her sympathy, and her moral and personal freedom, would have been able to save him.

Instead of this, however, her struggles and convulsions contended and balanced on in the same proportion as her love again acquired force and her jealousy asserted its supposed right. The smallest trifle which led by means of a remote connexion of ideas to Dolores, or to any other female, put her out of humor, and she was then no longer mistress of herself.

Among twenty cases of the sort, we will here describe one. One day she desired Robert's judgement in the choice of a veil, of which several had been sent to her. Her friend was wanting in the technical expression by which to designate his taste, and with the purest intentions, wishing to point out to her a still more beautiful pattern than any before them, he remarked, in

the simplicity of his nature, "I cannot express myself very clearly in this matter of ladies' dress, when my sister comes the next time, you can look at her veil—the pattern will please you, and she will tell you where she bought it."

That was enough! it required no more to increase the flame to a burning glow, which, as a smothered spark, slumbered in the depths of her troubled heart.

"There we have it again!" cried she, her eyes filling with tears. "No! that is too bad! it is terrible! always the strange person nearest to him—always Dolores! There are no handsomer veil than the veil of this stranger, who, under the title of his 'sister,' has pressed his hand upon his sick bed! nothing pleases him in me, not even this veil, because I might wear it! How could I have been so foolish as to suppose that any thing, any thing whatever, in me, could please him—still less myself, and that this man could ever make me believe that he loved me!"

"Gracia! Gracia! where are you wandering to again?" cried Robert, smiling, though hardly able to raise his hand jestingly, to threaten her with his finger. "Gracia, be good now!"

"And he despises me in my insignificance! he laughs at me, above all things!—gives me to understand that I must compare myself with the stranger, who always lays near his heart. I must feel right bitterly how insignificant I am compared with her—compared with his stranger! No, Robert! no woman ever can or will love you—it is impossible! This intentional wounding—this endeavor to wound me—this trait in your character is unendurable! That woman would be unhappy for ever who was fettered to you—thank God that it is not I! My husband would never have done so—that he never would. He has more consideration, more delicacy of feeling than such an elevated spirit as you, who have to do with ideas, who live in the stars, with such strange people, and can find nothing upon earth handsomer than her miserable veil! No, thank God! I have nothing to do with such idealists! No—he would never treat me so! No—he has too much delicacy of feeling for that! Unheard of! that I could ever be so foolish as to believe that you loved me!—unheard of! No! no woman will ever love you! never! never! never!"

After this soliloquy, Madame Closting left the pavilion, and could not control herself sufficiently to give her friend his medicine at the appointed time. She sent a negress. The patient sent to beg her to take the trouble to come to him—he had a request to make. The lady sent back word, "that he might say to the negress what he wished—she had no time then."

Robert beckoned to the slave to leave him. His "cursed head" fell back upon the couch as if it were of lead, his eye gazed at the sky, as if his soul would there make good its claims upon love. A large tear pearled upon his eyelashes, his bleeding heart felt the response of sympathy, which it, notwithstanding, was not able to dissolve.

42

CHAPTER IV.

MANHOOD.

On the next day, Gracia made her appearance on a visit to Robert, in the best humor—happy, unrestrained, and jesting, diligently occupied with increasing all the conceivable comforts of the patient

Robert felt himself obliged to express once for all, the demands of his injured and deeply wounded sense of honor as a man, with respect to the woman He desired his friend to take a seat, and began, in a low voice

"Gracia, listen to me! I will unfold to you my inmost heart as a man, as you once opened your heart to me, and allowed me a glimpse into your soul

"This illness in which I am lying, threatens my life—I feel that I will not look back upon its origin, but I require from you to look back upon those moments in which your soul had, as it were, put off its mortal integument, upon that moment in which you felt the bonds of the social world rent asunder—when the world and its misery was far from you—lay deep below you—as you looked down upon it from the height of your spiritual existence, those moments formed the crisis of my life—they decided my future.

"As you appeared to me at that time—as a spiritual being, as a soul, your entity was interwoven with mine—in love The bond of soul-sympathy was confirmed, and only in this declaration lies the explanation of the power which fetters me, that I cannot separate myself from you, that, in spite of all injuries, in spite of all ill usage on your part, I cannot leave you—I cannot hate you Your existence, like human life generally on earth, is twofold—the soul's life, and the vegetation of the clay tenement. I recognised your essence in that higher sphere, and have even endured, hitherto, the view of the "caricature of your existence, in seeing you sacrificed to your social relations, in the unfortunate connexion of marriage without love, whose influence appears to destroy your nobler nature So soon as you descend from the sphere of the soul's life, and feel the fetters which bind you to a man whom you, as you say, 'can neither love nor respect,' you torture me with your convulsions, and the appearance of your image becomes a curse to me

"You assert your prerogative as a woman, I assert no prerogative as a man, but my right and my dignity Your eternal doubt in my love is deceit, I know that you are convinced of my love, but this contradiction in you, perhaps, characterises exactly in you the woman Look into yourself, ask yourself what fluctuates, and rages within you? What for ever stimulates you to torture me, and to torment yourself? It is your unhappy consciousness of having received within yourself a foreign, vulgar, common element, which distorts your noble being—which taints your pure nature; it is the influence of a man whom you do love, notwithstanding—as the father of your children!"

"Robert!" interrupted she, with a tone of bitter sadness, and wrung her hands

"Until now you have never known love,' continued the sufferer, "no love of a man! You have confounded the care of an egotist for his property with the sentiment of love, and this fellowship on your part with the foreign element of materialism, which degrades you to the lowest service effects the moral disturbance in you—the fearful consequence of such a loveless union If I could tear myself away from you, if I could hate and despise you, I should suffer less But that I am unable to do, since the moment when I recognised you as a spiritual being, as a soul worthy of my love Your pure claim upon the love of an honorable man, has thrilled me all the more, as it found its way out of the boundless wretchedness of the relations which involved you The thought of separating from you, would be a contradiction in myself—a crime against the spirit of love! The appearance of your pure being, as it seized me in those moments, has become a part of myself, your image is always before me—in me—as if magically bound—as it appeared to me at that moment, and to my unheard of wretchedness, to my despair, no power in heaven or upon earth is able to tear it away—to destroy it in me, not even the woman's curses, the woman who stands in eternal contradiction with this image—with that spiritual being which I love in you"

"Robert!" sighed the unfortunate, while her lips quivered, and a stream of tears impeded the word

"I have often asked myself," continued he, "how I should be able to bear the ill usage of a woman, as a man, with proud self-consciousness, and now the twofold existence, as a soul in paralyzing bonds, and as a woman who denies her soul in marriage without love, has given me a foundation upon this question I repeat for ever, what I have often asserted to you I separate that spiritual image—yourself, your nobler nature—from the degradation of the woman who showers upon me reproach upon reproach. These curses do not touch me, the soul that I love does not send them forth the heart that loves me shares not in them That essence in you that fetters me in a mysterious manner, is a phenomenon in the domain of clairvoyance, foreign and distant from this earthly misery That being—yourself—does not know that the humiliated woman reproaches me, curses me, that woman who curses me knows nothing of our soul's sympathy, nothing of the spiritual existence in which our love lies That is the solution of the riddle of my love to you And perhaps there are hundreds of unfortunates in my situation, who feel themselves fettered in the same manner, and are unable to free themselves, without, like me, being able to give an account of their nameless, fearful state. I behold it! Torture me no more henceforth. I endure sufficient torments in my existence itself However, I do not reproach you, but I pray God that he will end my life But as long as I am condemned to live on earth, I shall maintain my sentiment of honor, as a man before you as a woman Shall I esteem you as a soul—respect yourself as a woman"

Gracia seized his hand, and moistened it with her tears Both were silent Robert felt a moment an alleviation of his sufferings, after having given them utterance, and powerfully endeavored to extricate himself from the chaos of contradiction which produced them. He begged his friend to read something to him She appeared to understand the intention of the request Although she was by no means in a condition to turn her attention immediately to any foreign subject, she constrained herself all the sooner to comply with the request She knew that she afforded him pleasure when she read to him, not so much by the reading itself, as by the spiritual intercourse which it produced, since the minds of both, then in some foreign idea, as it were, recognised each other again She was familiar with his favorite books, and taking one in her hand, she seated herself near him, and read The works which enchained Robert were such as were founded upon a profound thought, an exalted idea, which his mind pursued, or on which he could soar aloft into a domain that lay far from the miseries of this earth

The oftener he enjoyed similar lectures with his friend, so much the more did he feel the intellectual relationship of their natures, and so much stronger appeared the contrast of those convulsions in which a "nail on the wall," or the pattern of a veil, could deprive the poor woman of her self-possession, and which would be as inexplicable to the psychologist, as it was to the lover himself, who separated the spiritual being from the suffering woman This spiritual bond, in contrast to the fetters of social relations, proved, on the other hand, all the more strongly, the extremes in the woman, who was convinced within herself of the sentiments belonging to that sphere in which her spirit soared, while life fettered her to a mass of matter, from which she vainly sought to tear herself The solidity and profundity with which, in their common readings, she comprehended and penetrated their subjects, always surprised the youth less than they enchanted him These convulsions of the sufferer were of course the sooner explained by the contrast in the individuality of the vulgar man, who had, through social regulations, become one flesh with her, and whose contact must, very naturally, systematically disturb the interior of a being, which the former had no occasion for, and set aside with the greatest indifference

The bitter feeling of being separated from Robert by social bonds, was the ground of all similar convulsions with those which we have observed, and which, of course, would never have taken place, if the unnatural connexion with a foreign element had never existed

"Can you read this little poem, without a fit or convulsion of jealousy ?" asked Robert, interrupting the reading, opening the portfolio, and giving to his friend a manuscript

"Oh, I know it already !" exclaimed Gracia, smiling "Believe not that there is a single piece of paper in any secret pocket of your portfolios which I have not examined I know this strange dear little poem," continued she, and read, with a peculiar melancholy expression, the following verses, without title, bearing only the date

——, July 4th, ——
What Heaven on earth could'st thou impart
Unto a loving female heart !

How melted at thy glance's light
The icy chains that held my heart,
How flew the demons of the night,
Which, by sad doubts and fearful blight,
Had wrought my wo with fiendish art

Those tears, that fell from thy dear eyes
Like dew upon a dying flower,
Woke my chill heart to sweet surprise,
Bidding new, fair, grand life arise
In the sick soul, held by love's power.

And at the pressure of thy hand
Whose touch so magically bound us,
I felt my soul again expand,
Saved, far from grief, on lofty land,
Where reconciling angels hover round us *

"And what do you think of this poetry ?" asked Robert

"It is a spirit's kiss—a real poem, but not of a poet, it is of a poetess, of a young lady becoming poetess from love, it is also addressed to the famous privateer, to Hinango, but certainly not by your so called 'sister' ?"

"How do you know that ?"

"This time there is no mystery in my knowledge—no second-sight Did Hinango not send it to you with another poem ? the most horrible Elegy I ever did read, I mean the poem 'Astrala's Sentence,' which you have translated into English "

"Well—but you have not yet answered my question what do you think of this lady, as far as you know now the destroying effect of her so called love upon Hinango's mind "

"My judgement ? Know for the first, my good Robert, you may judge every thing in the world but a woman "

"Why not ?"

"Because a woman cannot judge herself; how then can another judge her ? Even a woman cannot judge another woman "

"Nevertheless," observed Robert, "there seems to be a certain judgement in your opinion of this lady You may be right, and I am strengthened in my belief that a woman can never commit a crime, a woman is always innocent, because she knows not what she is doing —she cannot judge herself "

"Beautifully explained, my dear Robert, for this opinion alone you merit to be loved by a woman as I love you "——

"And to be wounded in the sanctuary of my soul by a woman, like my friend Hinango, and to be persecuted from minute to minute, from second to second, restless and hopeless, by the image, the phantom of a being that once as a soul became a part of my own-being,-of-my-existence—and that, as a wife, resigns herself to the disposition of another man in sensuality

"Yes, I feel it, there must exist a heaven upon earth in love, in true love, in the dissolution of two kindred beings into one soul, into one existence, but I also feel there is no hell upon earth—no curse on the lip of a demon— no torture in hell, like the curse of such a love, of which the remarkable poem, "Astrala's Sentence," gives an idea—but only a faint idea !"

"Terrible ! horrible !" sighed Gracia, pressing her hands as if in prayer, staring upwards, " but——' she interrupted herself, after a long silence, "nevertheless, I should like to have known, or to know, that witch of a female creature that ever exercised such power upon a man like Hinango "

"That is the mystery which Hinango, as a

* This poem is translated in several languages to mask the original, the beauty of which the above translation give a clear idea

man of honor, bears to his grave In every case, she must have been a peculiarly strange being, if a conclusion is allowed from the effect to the cause And this beautiful little poem, though a very insufficient translation, may serve as a proof that the unknown amiable being at least has once had a soul, before her soul, as it seems, became dissolved in a soulless mass of matter, as the essence of a feeble magnet cleaves to a mass of iron "

" But I cannot believe that any woman would ever have compromised her sex, in acting treasonably against a man like Hinango "

" I am glad to hear your expression of such a confidence in the character of my friend, it seems that you know him particularly well "

" I know your friend Hinango, the countryman of my husband, rather more by his enemies than by his friends ; but I have a clear idea of his position—of his political, social, and moral standing in the world and I conclude my opinion of his character, of his heart and mind, in consequence of his position '

" Very well—extremely well," interrupted Robert, smiling, " and now to what conclusion have you arrived in regard to this lady, the poetess of this ' dear little poem,' as you call it ?"

" If I myself, as a woman, should allow myself an opinion of another woman, without giving my judgement—you understand '—then, with my hand upon my heart, I would declare, in regard to this strange and unknown being it must have been a woman of no ' juste milieu,' as the French call it in their politics. The authoress of this little poem, having been honored with the love of your friend Hinango, must have been one of the most noble beings of our sex, or one of the most degenerated. The love of a man like Hinango, judged by his enemies, is a pearl, which is not given to every woman There must have been spiritual attraction—sympathy, because only such a bond would be able to bind Hinango, a man who would not stand alone in the world, if material or physical qualities would ever have exercised the least attraction upon him Not knowing the conduct of the so called ' Astrala,' in connexion with Hinango, I can certainly not judge her, but I believe that the authoress of this dear little poem, addressed to Hinango, would act, and has always been acting, as a woman, in any situation or position, whatever her fate might have been I hope she has always done honor to our sex "

" I thank you, for the sake of Hinango and all manhood," replied Robert, " I shall take notice of your womanlike opinion of your ' sister-in-love,' Astrala, and I shall allow myself to add your noble expressions of confidence, to the manuscript of this dear little poem—to the honor of your sex "

" May I ask you, dear Robert," she interrupted, " for what purpose did you translate that horrible poem, ' Astrala's Sentence ' into English ? May I ask you for what purpose ?" repeated she, with her usual naiveté

" To be deposited in the foundation or corner stone of an ' Asylum for hysterical women,' " answered Robert, with a certain positive intonation——and Gracia blushed

" Yes, my dear," continued the sufferer; pressing her little hands, " I feel it is at last very necessary that asylums, with strong iron bars, should be established for hysterical women, who once have cast themselves away, without love, for a miserable living, and then demand the love of a man of honor, who, perhaps, after their own views, would be able ' to prepare a heaven upon earth for a loving heart ' It seems to me to be time at last that human society, which establishes quarantine institutions against the cholera and other plagues, should pay attention to the ravages and destruction of nervous disease, the origin of which lies in the regulations of the social world, and the extension of which is increasing with the conditions of so called civilization

" May every woman," he continued, with a rising, threatening voice, " may every woman—who knows best the wretchedness of her own heart—may she beware of crime and murder, may she content herself with conjugal sensuality, when she once has delivered herself, without heart and without soul—as a machine—to a man who wanted nothing but a machine "——

" Robert !" cried Gracia, in a painful voice, folding her hands in despair

" Gracia ! do not interrupt me now ! to-day I claim my right as a man May every woman," he continued, " who has cast herself away with resignation of love, separate herself from the man whom she despises, before she claims love, or declares her love to another The law of nature demands it, to say nothing of the nameless fate of the man in whose soul the image of a being lies ' for eternity,' whilst the same being upon earth degrades herself in the arms of another man in sensuality

" As in a well governed state the physician is bound to indicate to the authorities the cases where cholera and plague threaten destruction, the physician, also, should be bound in such cases of dangerous nervous derangement to declare, after his exact information ' In this case, Separation is the single condition to prevent increasing physical destruction and social crimes, and to execute immediately the orders of the worthy physician, ' Asylums for hysterical women should exist in every well governed state

" May legislation at last enter into the province of destruction and despair, into the abyss of which descends sacrifice upon sacrifice, happy when death at last delivers them from an existence for the sufferings of which the man finds no word—bound by his sentiment of honor to silence—to 'silence for eternity !'"

" Notwithstanding, and nevertheless I love you, my dear and good Robert," interrupted the interesting Brazilian woman, escaping (in the full originality of her character) from the depths of sorrow and melancholy, into which Robert's sufferings conducted her, to the extreme of a childlike happiness and self-contentment " I love, you my dear Robert and I am convinced that you love me as ever a man did love a woman—and that you will never love a woman upon earth except me ! Yes, my dear Robert—I feel it, and I could become mad as soon as I enter into reflection upon my fate to be attached to a man——who is as strange to me as any person under the sun, and at whose approach I tremble and I shudder in all my nerves ! Sometimes his approaches cause me physical cramps, and I beg him with tears to leave me, but in vain. He declares he will not leave me, and——" suddenly she changed the intonation of her words like the variation of a musical instrument, by touching the "pedal," and continued, in the most hearty voice of kindness and love. "And if you are going away—far away—I shall discover your residence, I shall go travelling also—by water and by land I shall find you out wherever you would hide yourself, and one day you will see me where you never expected it."——

The old negress Anna appeared on the threshhold in the open door, announcing the visit of the friends of Bota Fogo, arrived at the gate in the well known blue coach.

CHAPTER V

VIEWS OF EXPERIENCE

THE visit of the family from Bota Fogo interrupted this intercourse. The time for the voyage to Santa Catharina approached.

The Baron de Spandau made his appearance with his bride and Miss Fanny, together with Mr. Thomson and Dr. Thorfin, to convince himself that Robert was hastening "with giant strides' towards recovery, and would be able to go on board in a fortnight.

Dr. Thorfin was of opinion that the sea voyage, and the well known mild climate of the island, would operate beneficially upon the invalid, and give the family permission to make this arrangement for the voyage, in so far as he, in his capacity of physician, must previously countersign Robert's travelling passport.

"And you will accompany us too, I hope, Senhora!" continued Mr. Thomson, in conversation with Madame Closting. "Is it not so? you will go with us to Santa Catharina?"

"If Mr. Closting can sit up by that time, and goes with you, I shall very naturally be glad to make the excursion. I have heard so much of the beautiful scenery of that place—it must be even more lovely than the environs of Rio."

"The island of Santa Catharina" replied the old man, "bears the motto, 'it is good to be here, let us build tabernacles here!' one for my nephew, one for the baron, and one for me! and out of the tabernacles we will make English cottages, and arrange them right comfortably!"

The young lady smiled, and considered the whole conversation as a jest of the old widower. The baron contemplated this interview with sharp side glances, as he had long since known, through indirect communication from the talkative old man, the plan, which the latter had attributed to his nephew. "It was "water to his mill," and formed at the same time a wheel which entered into the machinery of his secret intentions, as if it had been cast or turned for the purpose.

Dolores spoke to Robert's friend, and repeated her thanks as his sister, for all the sympathy and care which she had bestowed upon her brother during his severe illness. The hearty sincerity of the words, as well as of the looks and whole deportment of the poetess, touched and agitated the poor woman. She felt, more than ever, how little cause she had to entertain any sentiment of hatred, or envy, or bitterness, toward a being who, under other circumstances, would perhaps have become her most intimate friend on earth.

Whether Dolores, before Robert's illness, had known of the bond of friendship which fettered the playmate of her childhood to this young lady, cannot be decided, but by means of that female property of suspecting and recognising a similar bond at the first glance so soon as an opportunity offers itself of observing the two enamoured beings, she had long known how both were united with each other. An inexpressible sentiment of foreboding and of anguish seized the bereaved friend of the martyr Alphonso, when she saw the invalid in such a horrible though morally pure relation, and she trembled when the thought of his future urged itself upon her. No one knew the noble nature of the youth so well as Dolores, through whose society and intellectual influence it had been developed. No one, however, knew the self-destroying omnipotence of his feelings, which, mocked by the British system of education, had reached the extent which occasionally manifests itself among British characters, misunderstood by their own nation, and admired by men who prize and honor the man in whatever nation they find him.

It has been often asserted, "a Briton as a friend is capable of every sacrifice, and if nothing else remains for him to offer in confirmation of his friendship or love, he sacrifices himself." We believe it, for nowhere do we find so sharp a contrast as in the prejudices and regulations of the British social world, and the grandeur of British intellect, and the depth of feeling which evinces itself in their national literature, and in the characters of their immortal authors and poets. Only the aim of a confused incompleteness, which has exercised itself since the reformation in England in social chains, (and recognises in the element of materialism the external greatness and magnificence,) could form this rigid contradiction. This contradiction is, in exact proportion, as colossal as British dullness on the one hand, and the grandeur of British literature on the other, which latter is founded upon the (in itself) insulted national intellect ——

The appearance of the baron as a member of the young Englishman's family, was one of the most singular encounters which Madame Closting could ever have experienced, in retrospect upon the "memorial' in the garden gate.

The baron did not omit to make a visit likewise to the sick bed of the celebrated naturalist, and the lady of the house saw herself placed under the necessity of politely accompanying him thither. She went, difficult as it even was on one hand to control herself—on the other hand, to leave out of sight the "sister" of her friend, who, with Aunt Susan, remained at Robert's couch—where, of course, the beam of his eye could fall upon her.

Although she had long known that such an encounter of glances could take place unhindered, at every visit of her friend in Bota Fogo, still the feeling that a single soul-utterance of the sort could occur now in her neighborhood, and as it were in the "topographical domain of her sympathetic sovereignty," had something in it indescribably painful for her, the explanation of which, could only be found in the mystery of her femininity.

Madame Closting had very naturally, at the return of her husband, explained the circumstance which induced her to remove to the pavilion of a relative, of which we have become sufficiently informed from her former communication to Robert

Mr Closting found himself a little embarrassed about the refusal of credit by his associate, in respect to her subsistence in his absence, but excused himself by all sorts of apologies in relation to his business, which, after the principle of the modern mercantile world, was carried on by "wholesale," which sets aside numerous payments of insignificant sums as indifferent in the highest degree, so long as credit is maintained; and the creditor is obliged to content himself with the "respectability" of the debtor He declared that "a mistake" had taken place in the correspondence, that Mr. Fono had not understood him, and, as concerned the importunity of the Baron, "he had already spoken to him about it—it had all been good will and jesting on the part of the baron; good will in making her the advance, and a jest to rally and bring her the money in person"

The wife was very naturally satisfied with the explanation, because her husband gave it to her, and she had not the right to doubt the validity, substantiality, and truth of any declaration of her husband ——

The visit of the baron took place in the measured, polite manner of the civilized world, which is not wanting in phrases to express sympathy and commiseration, and wishes and hopes for the health and happiness of the persons to whom a visit is made—in good society

The family from Bota Fogo departed, and Gracia alone remained behind with the invalids, where she, as ever, stayed with one, when the other sank to sleep

Occupied in mind with Dolores, she continued the reading in which she had been interrupted

The two ladies went back to Bota Fogo in Dr. Thorfin's attendance; Mr Thomson and the baron rode into town

"You think, then, that our Robert will really take the little Brazilian with him to Santa Catharina?" inquired the spy of the old widower

"Why not? But all this must remain between ourselves, baron. I hope that our present family connexion gives me a right to talk plainly with you about such affairs"

"Does that require to be mentioned now?" inquired the other, in a tone of the greatest intimacy, "have I ever given you occasion to doubt my sincerity?"

"Never, baron! if that had been the case, we should not have arrived at the position, with respect to each other, in which we find ourselves at present I have, then, (between ourselves be it said,) long ago given my counsel to Robert, for the gaining of his object; for that both understand each other, that both are foolishly fond of each other, that they love each other as well as ever a young man or a pretty woman have loved, that requires no explanation."

"That she has him in her net," remarked the baron," is as true as that I sit here on my saddle, that I have long ago observed in our Robert,

without having seen them together But whether she is so firmly attached to him that she would for his sake give her suspicious husband his congé, or quietly take her leave of him 'sans adieu,' as the French say, that is the question Many have already believed themselves in the possession of a woman, and at length possessed nothing else of her but a lock of hair, or, at the utmost, a garter!"

"I assert, however, according to my experience," observed Mr Thomson, "that both have long ago understood each other"

"I by no means doubt that," exclaimed the baron, "in relation to a certain point, one must be as blind as a mole, if one does not remark that, or as contracted as many husbands, who consider themselves perfect, as husbands, and of course fear no concurrence"

"Do you really believe that Mr Closting does not see through this connexion? or do you think that he sees through it, and pretends ignorance of it, because it is the most innocent that can ever occur"

"Mr Closting, so far as I know him," replied the baron, "is an egotist, and took a wife for economy, because he required a woman. But even granting that he observes a mutual sympathy between the lady and the young man, why should he trouble himself about the heart of a woman, so long as she only serves him in that for which he took her? An egotist knows no jealousy, because he knows no love"

"The French, to be sure, laugh about such an 'Amour d'un jeune Anglaise,'" replied Mr Thomson, "and find it inconceivable that we, in such cases, respect social relations, so long as they are not dissolved on both sides, and of course are no longer social bonds Notwithstanding this, however, every Frenchman would respect a young man like Robert in such a position"——

"And commiserate him, so long as he does not attain his object!" said the bridegroom, laughing.

"That affair at the return of Mr Daily—the inspection of the diamond on the part of the astronomer, the claim of the house of Rossbruck on Mr Closting, and a hundred other circumstances, gives me the suspicion that the unfortunate woman would rather separate herself to-day than to-morrow from the man, who——"

"Who is, nevertheless, a clever fellow, and, as a man of business, knows how to provide for his family And more is neither required by the world nor by the wife"

"That's true, to be sure, and if every woman desired to part from a husband who sustains a bad name, the advocates and notaries would make a rich business out of the divorces, that's clear."

"You have not yet had an opportunity to inquire of Robert alone how far he has progressed in his plan?"

"Not yet, but I shall ride past this evening, and arrange the matter then He seems to be afraid of a falling out with his father, who imparted to him certain "Private Instructions," wherein he particularly insists that Robert shall only take an English woman for his wife; not a foreigner, in any case Now Mr Walker is a singular person; he has his spleen like all of us, and wishes me to the devil with my preference for foreign women!"

"You are in high favor with Señora Isabella,

are you not, Mr Thomson ?" inquired the spy, in a very confidential tone

"With 'Miss Fanny,' as we call her ? to be sure, so far as I know—certainly I postpone my declaration until we are in Santa Catharina, and have never yet despaired of a happy result I have never yet received the 'basket,' Monsieur le Baron, and in this case I do not fear it in the least '

"So far as I hear from Miss Susan, you have little cause to fear a repulsive answer "

"Is that true ?" cried the old widower, very much delighted "is that true ? has Miss Susan sounded, at a distance, how the heart of my Señora Isabella is inclined ' whether it is hard or soft ?"

"Soft, very soft," replied the other, with significance "But what I say to you, now, Mr Thomson, must likewise remain between ourselves—do you understand ? 'Confidence begets confidence,' says the King of Saxony, and I have the same right to your discretion as you have to mine, and more than the King of Saxony has to the confidence of his people "

"I understand—I understand '' replied the old widower, very hastily and impatiently , "then Miss Susan has sounded——?"

"Has sounded, and has found out what was to be expected Señora Isabella is attached, very much attached, and only awaits your declaration, but if you ever allow it to be perceived, Mr Thomson, that I have, even only by a look, revealed this secret to you, then, naturally, your whole undertaking will fail '"

"Fail—the—whole—under—ta—king ? grumbled Mr Thomson to himself, while he, in a trot à l'Anglaise, jumped up with every syllable "You think that it may yet fail ?" inquired he, as the horse again went at a more quiet pace

"That is natural · you have yourself too much experience as a man, not to perceive this critical state Even Miss Susan must not know that I have exchanged a word with you on this affair, by no means ' never ' for she will not allow that she knows who Dolores is, she will not allow it to be seen that she suspects what is hidden behind 'Isabella'—do you understand ?"

"I understand you, baron, and I promise you that I will hold my tongue, I give you my hand upon it "

He held out his hand to his future brother-in-law, and the two already found themselves in the Rua d'Ajuda, and broke off from the important conversation, as the noise of the city disturbed them

Captain Hinango had escaped the baron The object now was to deliver Dolores, or to put her out of the way, according to the order from Buenos Ayres, in spite of all resistance on the part of the Humanitarios, whom he had to fear in the "Mazzini" and the "Astrala "

Robert alone stood in the way, his recovery almost warranted the certainty that he would accompany Dolores, and if this should be the case, the personal delivery of the condemned would be a difficult problem

Robert must then be detained in Rio de Janeiro at any rate. To put him out of the way, as had been attempted against Hinango, would be ill advised, especially as the family relations of the baron to his uncle impeded him; in so far as

sooner or later a suspicion might fall upon him The baron had another plan, which appeared less dangerous to him, and which proceeded almost entirely of itself from the events around him

He betook himself to the police functionary, with whom he was in communication in his peculiar position as secret agent of the Brazilian government, and again conversed with them upon the hitherto fruitless researches for the discovery of the abortive attempt at murder against Mr Closting

"We have hitherto not developed the slightest trace " declared the functionary, in the course of conversation ' Circumstances so singularly favored the flight of the negro, that it seems an impossibility even to take up a single thread of the investigation It was pitch dark, the rain poured in torrents, the negro threw himself into the bay, and such a fellow will swim for a couple of hundred feet under the water like a dolphin—and then pop up and swim on, and creep up, God knows where, on the shore, and go quietly home The digger also lies in the bay, and if we had it, it would do us little good "

"To be sure, the circumstances were very favorable, but, notwithstanding this, what would you say, if I had made the discovery of who engaged the negro ? "

"It would be another evidence of your distinguished talent in the service of the state, and the discovery would do you honor "

"Promise me, then, that the criminal shall not be arrested until I designate the day and hour to you, and I will engage that the guilty person shall not escape us before that "

"I promise you, Monsieur le Baron, I give you my word thereupon "

"Well, and I will keep my word as you do yours "

"A police agent," continued the functionary, "who was on service that evening on the stairs, expressed, to be sure, immediately the next morning, a vague surmise, since he believed that the act had its origin in an *affair d'amour*," that a young Englishman ——"

"I understand you, and must not and cannot at present say another word about it You know my future family connexions here—my whole situation You know my zeal in my correspondence with the interior You know how many taroupilhas are here lodged in Do-Vilganhon, who have found their quarters there through me , and you know also my private relations to Mr Closting, who took my place in the interior of the country, because it is impossible for me to be in two or six places at the same time. You know the most remote thread of the police association whose web is conducted by me, and that is enough for you

"Where church and state come in account, and are even placed in danger, all personal considerations cease, and all family bonds loosen of themselves, where church and state require it for their maintenance "

"I am perfectly of your opinion, Monsieur le Baron, and thank you again for your zeal in the affairs of our government, which will be grateful to you for it "

"I hope so, Senhor, and now farewell , the matter is settled I undertake the arrest of the originator of this scandalous plan for murder · and so, it's settled "

" You may command me, when you require a detachment of permanentos to accomplish the arrest "

" All right ! adieu !'" whispered the baron, and departed hastily, while the police functionary, *Chef de Bureau* of a private branch, sank into reflection, in acknowledgement and admiration of a talent such as the Baron de Spandau evinced

CHAPTER VI

RELIGIOUS CEREMONY

Mr Thomson freighted an English brig, the " Bride of Abydos," for Santa Catharina, and further for Buenos Ayres, since the vessel, as it often occurs, was to exchange her cargo in the former port, before it sailed for its proper place of destination

Dolores lived, as hitherto, in her country retirement, engaged in literary occupations, in the preparation of all her productions, in verse and prose, for an edition, which she would willingly have issued in Rio de Janeiro, if her incognito had permitted her to do so in person

It was a natural consequence, that any undertaking of the sort (even under the protection of the freedom of the press) would draw the observation of the authorities upon the poetess, and disturb her asylum—who, on the other side, stood just as strictly under the protection of the laws, which offered an asylum and personal safety to all political fugitives

The " liberal institutions " of a constitutional monarchy stand, however, for the most part, in opposition to monarchical governments, which make a show of them, in order more effectually to suppress the germ of liberal principles Constitutional monarchy, as a transition epoch in the history of many states from an absolute monarchy to a republic, serves, as it were, only as an evidence that this monarchical principle (founded on the prerogative of birth) contradicts nature and reason, since every man, through his birth, equally partakes of the right of cultivating his moral freedom in the element of political freedom, and a violation of equality is an indirect violation of freedom Constitutional monarchy (as the attempt at an alliance between the principle of selfishness and civic virtue) bears in itself the worm of self-destruction, for by demoralization alone can it nourish the egotism which, publicly or in secret, sells itself for any service A system which cannot maintain its existence without the dissolution of all morality, in the position of its servants, to which venality of conscience leads them, bears within itself the death against which it seeks to protect itself through treachery and murder

Dolores entertained no suspicion against Mr Thomson, and even although she had long ago learnt, through Dr. Thorfin, the fixed idea of the old widower, the realization of which was to lead her to the altar, still the matrimonial plan appeared more to her as a comic episode in her exile, more as entertaining material for laughter, than a matter that would ever occur to her to contemplate in a serious point of view.

Mr Thomson went in to see Robert that evening, and came out with his inquiry in relation to his steps towards a union with Senhora Gracia. The youth, already pale in consequence of his long illness, became suddenly colorless as the white cravat of his old uncle, and raised himself in his armchair to give a decided answer

" My dear uncle, you mistake my relations to a lady whom I love Your demand compels me to give you this explanation But exactly because I love Senhora Gracia as I love her, my sentiments require the devotion on my side which make my self-denial necessary Whether this lady loves me, in the sense that you suppose, I ought not, as a man, to give you any intimation, even if I myself were aware of it But whether she would ever resolve to rend a social bond, which, founded on the past of her life, would extend itself by a living memorial as a gloomy shadow over her future, whether Senhora Gracia would ever separate from her husband, I doubt, and this doubt is a sacred ground on my side, never, never to offer such a proposal to her Such a step, in such circumstances, is for the woman, and not for the man, in my position "

Mr Thomson appeared in the highest degree struck by this confession of his nephew, which showed him in a light that, as it were, displayed his heart and his character in a magical grandeur

" I understand you Bob," replied he, after a long pause, with a hearty pressure of his hand, " and I must also admire you I had hoped in this plan, which I once intimated to you, to have laid the corner stone of your future happiness, and of the health and welfare of your unfortunate friend, but I perceive that I was in error Forgive me, if my worldly views have not accorded with your feelings, or with your conscience I always meant well by you, and even now I am still your warmest friend As to what concerns your relations to this young lady, however, you are my nephew, and as an uncle I must give you my views Let the relation be what it may, it is no concern of mine She is, however, still a woman, and only two cases are conceivable Either she loves you— has confessed her love to you, and from the hour of her declaration, already physically parted from her husband, as your love demands, or she has confessed her love to you in " mysterical convulsions," and still continues to live with her husband, with or without " mysterical convulsions " All other cases, let them be masked as they may, and call them what they will, are humbug ! humbug, my dear Bob ! female humbug ! and Mr George Thomson thinks too much of his nephew to see him allow himself to be led by the nose, or ill treated by a woman who has once been satisfied with a mean fellow No, Bob ! you can transact business in the Rua Direita with whom you will, but to enter into partnership with a good for nothing fellow, in the possession of a female heart—for that you are too good, for you are my nephew, and I am your friend—your warmest friend, your uncle, George Thomson."

" I am convinced of your sympathy," sighed Robert, evidently struck with this language of experience, " and hope to justify myself towards you in every situation in life—even in death."

"You know, Bob," continued the man of experience, "you know I have hitherto not had the least objection to your relations, in so far as I took it for granted, that the young lady had separated as a wife from her husband, from the moment when she confessed her love to you, or gave you her word, or whatever else may have taken place between you. That you appeared to doubt whether she still lives with her husband, surprises me, for you are my nephew, and I do not desire that a woman should consider you as—heaven knows what! I know womankind, I have had four of them, and hope soon to have a fifth!'"

Robert could hardly restrain a smile. The old man continued gaily: "I have experience in this business, Bob! experience in matrimony, and could write a book about it of four thick volumes. I have lived to see a similar instance, Bob! One of my wives suddenly became nervous, grew thin, lost her corpulence, and even confessed to me that she had never loved me, and doubted if I had ever loved her. There was an end of our union. She passed as my wife—before the world, but we lived separate, as follows of course, for the 'No' of a woman must be as sacred to every man of honor as once her 'Yes.' But all these are convulsive phenomena—nervous disease—chills of the heart—fixed ideas of the brain—female spleen! and no physician has found remedies as yet against such a love catarrh. Believe me, I speak from unhappy experience."

"But I am morally satisfied that she does not love her husband, and that she may act from compulsion," replied Robert.

"Poor, poor Robert! you have not had my experience of the strength of woman's will, you make me sad," sighed the good old man, sinking into silent contemplation. "I can now explain to myself how you stand—now for the first time, and may God forgive me that I ever brought you to this pavilion! I have experience—experience—but such a case I could never have imagined.

"I know men who live separate from their wives, while they pass before the world for married people, but each of these men respects the woman and himself, and I need say no more. Such instances of female nervous disturbance, of repulsion, as the physicians call it, are not rare, and I should like to be acquainted with this Mr Closting, he must be the meanest fellow on God's earth, and capable of every crime, or the young lady must be the most——"

"Pronounce no sentence against my friend!" interrupted the unhappy young man quickly, and deeply moved, "for the hour in which I must become convinced that——that she does not love me, will be my last."

"Bah! bah! don't talk in that way, remember always that you have to do with a woman. You will go with us, then, to Santa Catharina?—the voyage will do you good," said the old man hastily, to lead the invalid from the subject.

"To do with a woman," repeated Robert, half aside, "may the just God forbid that I should ever lose the sacred reverence for woman which I entertain, which attaches me to my friend. She has injured me—wounded me for ever, she may destroy me, but I will, even in death, love the soul, which here struggles within her as a woman, in eternal contradiction——with the wife!"

"I will accompany Dolores, as I have once promised her in my heart,' he then said aloud, "I will not leave Dolores, so long as she has not found a safe asylum."

"That is noble of you—noble and excellent, Bob. We will settle ourselves upon Santa Catharina, either on the island or the main land, wherever we find the most beautiful situation, and the baron will build himself a house near ours."

Robert involuntarily made a movement in his armchair, as if a physical pain seized him, which occasioned him to alter his position, he sighed deeply, and at length resumed the conversation.

"You have then consented to Aunt Susan's marriage with the so called baron?"

"So called baron?" inquired Mr Thomson, smiling: "how so? do you doubt if he is really a baron?"

"I not only doubt his barony, but I know positively that he is a spy of several European powers, and likewise serves some of the governments of South America as a spy. I know him in every respect, in his entire reprobateness, and will not, now nor ever, permit him to enter our family."

"Good bye, my dear Bob! Dr Thorfin has forbidden you to talk much, or to be excited; it may delay your recovery, and cause a relapse. Good bye, then, my dear Bob! As concerns the baron, we will talk of that in Santa Catharina. You have now a high fever, my poor boy! take good care of yourself, that you may be able to go with us, for I cannot leave you here ill. You must accompany us, by all means."

"I feel that I must go with you," sighed Robert, in another signification than his uncle intended, who again heartily pressed his hand, and departed in haste.

The baron had dismissed Sally, as he was preparing himself for the voyage to Santa Catharina, and passed his nights during the short intervening time here and there, in other occupations, while he still retained the house as a temporary locality for his consultations with Senhor Prole, and other agents in his employ.

Sally ventured a second visit to Senhora Serafini, to present her thanks for the nobleminded offer with respect to a situation upon her estate. She explained that her presence in Brazil was constantly attended with danger, as accident might reveal her cooperation for the rescue of Dolores and Hinango, and she would then undoubtedly be exposed to the baron's revenge. The lady acknowledged the consistency of these grounds, and assented therefore to the unfortunate girl's design of returning to England. She renewedly offered to consult with Dr. Thorfin in what manner a passage was to be procured for her, as the attendant of a respectable family, and asked of Sally her address, that the doctor might know where to find her. The noble conduct of this unfortunate girl, which stood out in such natural purity from the background of the demoralization of our epoch, was recognised in its full value by the person for whose rescue it had availed.

Earnestly as Hinango had always desired to

express personally his inextinguishible gratitude, yet the existing circumstances in them
selves, prevented the occurence of a meeting
which was in other respects denied by the delicate feelings of the noble girl   The position as
an outcast from the social world would not permit her to make the slightest allusion to her per
son or her fate in an interview with Hinango
Notwithstanding this, she appeared satisfied, by
anticipation, that Hinango, as well as Dolores
was able to distinguish the disinterested devotion
on her part, from the world's prejudice and unlov-
ing sentence of condemnation, which broke the
staff over errors produced as natural effects from
the contradiction of its own social regulations

It so happened that Dr Thorfin was in communication with a family from Northern Europe,
who were preparing to return thither   He
availed himself of the mutual confidence which
prevailed between himself and the lady of this
house, to describe, so far as his prudence per
mitted, the noble conduct of the unfortunate girl
in its purity and devotion, in order to commend
her to her sympathy   The lady agreed, therefore, to take her as a companion, and to leave it
to her whole conduct during the voyage, whether
she should further enjoy her sympathy, which in
such a case would be perpetually secured to her

Sally yielded, with all submission, to these
stipulations, and felt only too deeply that such a
doubt in her morality was certainly founded on
her position, in compensation for which, her
self-conciousness confirmed her in the idea, that
neither she nor many other females would voluntarily, and of their own impulse, have stepped
outside the boundaries of the social world, if
they had not been seduced out of them by men

The baron had been for the last week in full
occupation, and had, of course, scarcely had an
hour to talk with and caress his bride
Miss Susan Thomson appeared not to be unacquainted with the proverb, according to which
" certainty should be preferred to uncertainty,'
and once, in a confidential hour, made the proposal to her lover to celebrate the ecclesiastical
ceremony of marriage before their embarkation
She produced, one after another, her important
and very reasonable grounds   One of these
grounds was, that the good which a man ought
to do could never be done too soon, and as marriage was not only something good, but, accord-
-ing to her view, the best that both of them were
able to do for the present, this was one reasonable ground for completing the ceremony
Another ground was, that they were going to
Santa Cathaiina in a merchant vessel, and not
in a proper packet ship or steamer.   There was
generally, on board of such a vessel, a deficiency
of room in the cabin, and particular divisions
for single young ladies and single gentlemen
were always attended with difficulties.   The
thoughts of separating herself, even only for a
moment, from her lover, she observed, would be
terrible to her, and all sorts of consequent disagreeable occurrences through seasickness, and
storm, and the like, might make his presence in
her private cabin absolutely necessary   That in
such a case it must, on both sides, be of great
importance to be united with each other by lawful bonds, which dissolve all constraint, and all
the restrictions that separate a young man from

a seasick or not seasick young lady   It was to
be hoped that the baron would see this for himself, Miss Thomson observed   The third good
ground was that the " Bride of Abydos (which
God forbid ') might suffer shipwreck before she
arrived at Santa Catharina, (which might God
forbid to fold ') that in such a case, one or the
other of them might become the victim of a
tragical fate, and then it must certainly be as
hard for him as for her, that they had lived for
months in a happy courtship and had delayed
so long the performance of the various ceremo-
nies which must then be too late, if only one of
the pair, or if both, should have found their
grave in the waves—or if singular occurrences
should have separated them   Miss Susan had
properly ten grounds more, all of which she revealed to her bridegroom, who did not reject a
single one, but determined upon the marriage,
as he and she desired

On a fine Sunday, in the month of March the
ceremony of coupling was performed by an English clergyman, and then a second by a Catholic
clergyman, since the baron, as is known, was a
Catholic, and attached a great importance to religion ——

With what feelings the young baroness of
Spandau seated herself in the carriage, as she
left the English church after the conclusion of
the marriage ceremony, we leave to the perception of all young ladies of her age, (or some
years younger,) who have been betrothed to a
baron, and have ever gone from a church home,
or to another church, to be doubly married

The Convent of the " Sisters of Mercy," which
happened to be opposite to the English church,
presented at that moment to the young baroness
a singular aspect, since she could not avoid the
silent reflection, what a tragical fate it must be
to live on as a " Sister of Mercy" in a convent,
or, as a sister among " unmerciful men," to live
any where in the world, especially to pass a virgin life, without having used a single myrtle
wreath, in a country like Brazil, where myrtle
grows by the wayside like thistles and nettles

The ceremony of the Catholic ritual took place
immediately after the Anglican marriage, in the
court chapel in the Rua Direita, and was very
briefly concluded   His Excellency the Ambassador of Kniphausen was invited as witness on
the part of the baron, but, to the regret of all, he
had been ill for some days, and was obliged to
renounce the honor   There were, however,
more than enough of highly respectable witnesses, among the highly respectable friends and
acquaintances of the baron, and there were not
wanting, likewise, two English ladies, who
piqued themselves upon their high rank, to accompany a Miss Thomson into the church, for
the purpose of conducting her, as a lawful Baroness de Spandau, out of the church

On their drive back to Bota Fogo, the young
married pair visited the convalescent Mr Robert
Walker, to receive his congratulations   The
shock that seized him when he learned the occasion of this visit, was very naturally to be ascribed to the excited state of his nerves, and to
no other cause ——

They found him improving in health, and left
him in all haste, with the wish, that he might
not relapse before the departure of the " Bride
of Abydos."

CHAPTER VII.

THE TWO CORPSES

THE days hastened on, and the fifteenth of March drew nearer and nearer. The ' Bride of Abydos ' had taken in her cargo, and was prepared to weigh anchor, so soon as Mr Thomson and his family had taken possession of the cabin.

Mr Closting's state had manifested very bad symptoms, and instead of his expected speedy recovery, his life was more than ever in danger. Dr Thorfin required a consultation of several physicians, since the case was important in itself, and the entire treatment might be subjected to a judicial investigation, so soon as the researches of justice succeeded in coming upon the traces of the murderer.

Senhora Gracia was thrown, by the increased danger of her husband, and the approaching departure of Robert, into a state of mind which we can so much the less describe, as she confined within herself every emotion, and less than ever before opened to her friend the heart that was broken for ever ——

Robert begged his friend to give him some lines in his album, as he was now preparing himself for a separation. He found, one day, the following, written with a tremulous hand upon the last leaf of the splendidly bound book, which he had given her for such a purpose.

" Le cœur de l'homme est un abime de souffrance, dont la profondeur n'a jamais été sondée et ne le sera jamais *   —c.

Those five months which Senhora Gracia had spent in confidential intimacy with her friend, now lay before her as past, like a lovely dream, over whose texture, however, many future images of terror were woven, whose impressions now fixed themselves upon her heart like forebodings, with heavy anxiety. She often observed Robert, while he was occupied with the insignificant arrangements for his departure, without approaching him, as if his appearance were not a reality, as if she must touch him with her hand to satisfy herself that he was a living man—the real Robert. She saw him occupied, and going in and out, to arrange one thing and another for his departure, and by degrees single objects were taken out from the pavilion, which appeared to her as " frames around the pictures of the past," or as background or attribute of his image, inwoven with his entity. The parting from such insignificant trifles gave her a presentiment of the moment in which he himself should, for the last time, pass through the garden, and the gate should rattle behind him.

The increasing danger in which her husband lay from his wound, increased the perplexity and convulsive contradictions which oppressed her heart. Sunk in abstraction, she sat for hours beside the sick or dying bed of her husband, gazing with a fixed glance into the abyss of her future, and came to her recollection with a repressed cry of anguish, when the name " mother" casually sounded in her ears from the mouth of the dear little one.

Who will venture to penetrate into Gracia's feelings, when the consciousness of a social connexion through a third being thrilled her with

horror, and she was then obliged to admit to herself that this union had been formed without sympathy, and that the realization of the idea of unity with a man who was always strange to her, bloomed forth as an imbodied contradiction—in their child !

If we contemplate the state of mind and the sufferings of the unfortunate woman from the point of view of the higher psychology, we behold the thousand-fold reiterated so called social aberrations, over which the world breaks the staff, without examining the ground of the evil. Gracia's crime lay in that thoughtless and characterless over-haste with which she had once entered into, a social bond whose sacred significance seems to have been unknown to her, or whose eventful importance she controverted by syllogisms—that she might be " independent." She appears never to have considered that she only obtained the apparent independence at the cost of her purity.

In this crime against nature, and in this contradiction in themselves, are founded the social crimes and all the inward contradictions which thousands of unfortunate wives in our civilized world commit, and against which they vainly endeavor to struggle.

Gracia's awakening to love, her relation to Robert, was evidently the natural phenomenon in the province of the soul-attraction of the animatic sphere, which Dr Garringos has sufficiently described. It was the awakening of love in its longing after love, as a natural consequence of her existence. Her wretchedness lay in a failure of decision for the realization of this demand, with reference to the social regulations to which she had thoughtlessly or " reasonably" become subjected in earlier youth. Her pardonable indicision effected the inward disturbance of a noble man, who, fettered to her in animatic *rapport*, was with her made a prey to despair. Gracia's confession of her love—her oath, by which she bound Robert to herself " for eternity"—resembled the effusion or communication of a somnambulist in the province of the magnetic dream-world, in rigid opposition to the profane reality. Returning from this magnetic dream-world to everyday life, she felt herself fettered like a slave—as it were chained to a soulless corpse, whose meanness and whose moral annihilation, she was in duty bound to partake of, according to the laws of the state and the church. But neither church nor state had ever inquired whether this union was originally grounded upon reciprocal morality.

Just as rigidly as the domain of the inward life in the sphere of magnetism stands opposed to the outward profane life of the corporeal world, appeared to the unfortunate woman now, also, her love to Robert. Her heart, so soon as she became conscious of her position in love to Robert, (the sustaining of her inward life,) demanded separation—the fulfilment of her oath, holy faith to the heart which she had recognised and wounded by her love—— So called social duty, on the other hand, required degradation of herself for the fulfilment of an unnatural service—endurance and excuse of all the aberrations and crimes of the man whose property she was—a merging of her own individuality in the meanness of a foreign nature—mortification of her inward life—moral death.

---

* George Sand.

During the last days, Robert remained in the city as before his illness, and returned, as in foregoing times, when the sun was near going down. Gracia felt herself drawn by an irresistible impulse to hurry to his pavilion, and then, with the little one in her hand, to inquire whether one thing or another for his departure was to be provided for, which she or her servants might perform. There were moments in which, notwithstanding such inquiries, she could not believe that this friend was now about to leave her, that she was to remain alone by the death-bed of her husband.

Robert observed, according to the demands of his heart, all the outward forms of the most intimate friendship towards the sufferer, whose awakening in love had aroused his inward life, and whose internal convulsions and cramps had destroyed the peace of his soul.

From the above point of view we behold Robert's mind laid waste, since the diseasing of his animatic (nerve) life, as a reaction of the convictions of his beloved, remained incurable so long as she was not able, in the consciousness of her moral freedom as a woman, to rescue herself from the bonds of physical degradation.

As we behold in Gracia the woman, with her claims upon a certain prerogative of her femininality, in the abyss of despair, drawing dagger upon dagger of jealousy and contradiction against Robert—so in Robert appears to us the man, violated in the sanctuary of his higher self-consciousness—his honor. In this feeling of the love which "endures and suffers all things," Robert bore, as we knew long ago, all the outbreaks and convulsive ebullitions of these absolute contradictions—and was silent. No reproach, no bitter reply to such taunts passed his lips. He had (as we mentioned at the time) recognised the entity of his beloved in its original purity—and separated (as we likewise know) external influences from inward worth—temperament from character.

But Gracia's parallel between him and the man into whose arms she had even thrown herself, when the struggle and convulsion of her soul had shown her all the appearances of the outward world in the distorted mirror of her passion, violated Robert's honor as a man, and shook his faith in the female heart.

Logically impossible as it must always remain to find " sense in nonsense," just as impossible must it be, to explain the behavior of a woman in such cases — Gracia's convulsions more and more disturbed by their reaction his animatic life, and lighted all the appearances of the social world around him, as it were with a clear animatic light. This glow of light from the inward life, turned upon the reality, resembled the gas light of a solar microscope, which reveals the animalculæ of a drop of water as hideous monsters—that pursue and devour each other, like a symbol of the eternal struggle in the mysterious essence of nature.

If love, as a religious principle, is to be sustained in the sacrament of the church as a social bond, then at least the social bond must be founded upon love. If the latter be not the case, then the sacrament becomes abused, unhallowed, desecrated. Where no bond of the soul exists, none can be violated or broken; the

gradation of human nature; it is a desecration of the sanctuary of generation, " a sin against the holy spirit of love."

Love can only exist as sympathy in similar developments of the inward life. Gracia had never loved her husband. Instead of consanguinity of being, there existed opposition of the two natures—antipathy.

Robert had once received this oath, " for eternity," in the higher (natal) sphere of the soul's life, and as such, its sacred signification had penetrated him. Doubt in the validity of the oath, would have led him to doubt in the soul's life itself—to doubt in God. Robert believed, because he loved.

In opposition to him, we behold the unfortunate woman awakened to love, without belief in love, led to that contradiction in herself which excuses by all unworthy conduct of the heads of families, and judges the beam in the eyes of men who have never cheated or betrayed a woman, and never for a mean object degraded themselves by alluring a lovely woman into matrimony.

If Gracia had believed in love, she would never, never for a moment, have doubted in Robert's love, nor in himself. We behold in Gracia one of the noblest beings who ever proceeded from the workshop of creation, inwardly destroyed and wasted by an unnatural connexion. Having become diseased in such a situation, as a natural effect of circumstances, she met with Robert.

We now look back to Dr. Thorfin's apparently singular intimation, that a woman in Madame Closting's position would do well to part from her husband, before she had, led by spiritual attraction, endangered the inward life of a guiltless man, and perhaps committed an indirect murder, even if it were not a physical one.

Even though our system concerning sympathy and antipathy, and our hypothesis concerning repulsion and attraction, should be honored by similar opposition like Mesmerism, (upon which both rest,) still the position and the fate of a woman like Senhora Gracia, is repeated a thousand-fold in all countries of the civilized world. Gracia's lot may call in question the sense of honor in both sexes, where it exists. And where no sense of honor exists, the principle of humanity will also be wanting, which this relation calls for.

No formal bond of the church can consecrate a connexion which (let it exist on whatever grounds it may) has been formed without love. The crimes against nature, which in thousand-fold reiteration proceeds from such unions, are those secret sins whose natural effects descend " to the third and fourth generation."

It was on the evening before the embarkation, when Gracia entered the desolate apartment, from which even the writing-desk had disappeared from the window at which she had so often silently contemplated Robert, and even occasionally tickled him on the cheek from a distance with a long spear of grass, to frighten him.

The thermometer was likewise already packed up, and the pictures of Byron and Walter Scott which decorated the apartment, had vanished

Robert went over for a moment into Mr Closting's pavilion, to take a temporary leave of him
in case he might be asleep at a later hour
Gracia remained alone with the little one upon
Robert's divan He found the patient, as ever, in
wild delirium, in which the murder of the
grimpeiro tormented him, which the wife naturally considered as the image of a feverish fancy,
severely as the eternal repetition of the same
fancy always shocked the poor woman beside
his couch

The wounded man lay on a "camp bed" in
the middle of his apartment, a negro sat by him
as watcher Robert greeted him, and inquired
after his health, but he was far away in his delirium, and stared around with the expression
of a lunatic Like so many Europeans, who in
foreign countries lay aside their own language,
and, even to their children, speak the language
of the nation in which they transact their business, Mr Closting also had, for years, assumed
the Portuguese as the language of his thoughts

"Take away the two birds, there—the two
sympathy birds," he muttered to himself "I
shot one of them, and strangled the other—that
is all right, but it must remain secret, my wife
must not know it, for then she would never
come near me again What? not come near
me any more? that would be something new!
Is she not my wife? my lawful wife? is it not
her duty? ought she to part from me? ought
she to go away from me? I have committed
murder, as you call it! Take the two birds away
I tell you! I have shot the miserable grimpeiro—Mr Dujour! Well, that was all right!
what did I do it for? What for? because I am
the father of a family—because I must make a
fortune for my family! Take the two birds
away, I say! Am I not the father of a family?
have I not duties as the father of a family? My
wife is young——I have only three children, but
one every year, and may have ten in ten years
Take the two birds away, or I shall die And
must I not leave property behind? and whether
I do or not, take the two birds away, for I must
provide for my family, and who does not know
what that means?—to provide for a family that—
that——take the two birds away!——Come Gracia, come to me! I have been away long enough!
come and kiss me! You resist? stupid goose!
the two birds will do nothing to you! and that
—blood!——infamous mulack! why do you
not bring me water to wash——my hands——
Gracia! come I say, do you not hear? Gracia,
come, you are as handsome as a sympathy
bird!——that is true, beautiful! you are beautiful!
and—and——"

The youth compelled himself to listen thus
far to this information of the wretched man,
and then withdrew He went back to his pavilion It was to be perceived that his eyes had
been wet He pressed the hand of his friend,
kissed the little one, and dried his eyes anew

A singular noise was audible in the neighborhood, it sounded like the clang of weapons,
and the stamp of hoofs, and the footsteps of
armed men

"Almighty God! what is that?" cried Gracia, when the gate was opened. Several police
officers, with four officers of the permanentos,
entered the garden, and beset the outlet with
guards.

"Compose yourself! be calm! Dolores is betrayed!" whispered Robert in urgent haste;
"they arrest me on her account, but to-morrow
I shall be free again, I am an Englishman, and
our ambassador will know his duty"

During this time, the officers had approached
and entered the apartment Gracia clasped her
child, as if she sought upon the wide earth one
point of support for her oppressed, fluttering
heart, which now hardly throbbed Inexplicable
deathlike anxiety, and the most fearful forebodings, agitated her

Robert asked the officer whom they were seeking, and what brought them there

"Senhor Robert Walker from Buenos Ayres,"
began an officer, producing a document

"I am Senhor Robert Walker, from England,"
replied he, with a firm tone

"Arrested in the name of justice, on account
of an attempt at murder upon the person of
Senhor Louis Closting"

"Great God!" shrieked Gracia, involuntarily
thrusting the child from her, as if only one
grief disturbed her soul Terrified by the anguished cry of her mother, the little one wept
and held fast to her

"Senhora!" cried Robert, "Senhora, compose
yourself!" and a gleam of holy innocence passed
over his countenance

"Almighty God!" cried the disconsolate one
again, gazing around her, as if in a dream, looking towards Robert, and then to heaven, and
wringing her hands in despair

"I will follow you, gentlemen," began Robert, turning to the officer with all composure,
"only allow me a few moments to arrange my
effects"

"Take your own time," replied an officer

"Senhora Gracia," said he then, seizing the
hand of his friend, and looking into her eye,
which hardly recognised what it saw, "Senhora! I ask you here in the presence of these
witnesses, I ask you before God the omniscient,
do you hold me capable of the deed with which
they charge me, of which I am accused?"

"No! no! never! never!" shrieked the unhappy woman, and sank on Robert's breast, without fear of being falsely understood by those
present.

The officers, touched by this scene, looked at
each other with a humane expression on their
petrified countenances

"I repeat the question before the omniscient
God, at my farewell from you Senhora Gracia,
do you consider me capable and guilty of the
deed? I recognise your judgement as the judgement of God?"

"No! oh no! Robert—Robert," sobbed she,
concealing her face upon his breast.

"Then farewell! farewell! I thank you before God, and in the presence of these gentlemen, for the sympathy and friendship, for the
goodness and gentleness, with which you have
kindly treated me as a stranger God be with
you and with me"

He kissed the lady on her forehead as she lay
lifeless in his arms, and relinquished her to the
care of the officers, who appeared more and
more puzzled by all that they saw and heard.
They sent for the female attendants to employ
outward remedies as speedily as possible, to
restore the lady to consciousness.

"Then I can go before my judge," said Robert, and added, in a low voice, turning to the officer, " I will go into the cabinet to dress myself, and write a few lines, to be delivered by you to the Minister of Justice, the door may remain open"

The officers, almost deprived of their presence of mind by the thrilling scene, occupied themselves, together with the negresses who had hurried in, in arousing the unfortunate woman from her swoon; but her nerve life appeared destroyed, and the connexion with the corporeal world rent asunder

obert went into his cabinet, an officer stepped to the threshold after him, and convinced himself that there was no outlet there through which the prisoner might possibly escape He remarked that the latter took up paper and lead pencil, and some garments, and then returned again to his comrades The officer then again cast a glance into the cabinet, saw Robert was writing, and again left the door

A sound like a sigh was audible in the cabinet, and ceased Some officers hurried to the threshold—they found Robert's corpse ! He had pressed a small poisoned dagger into his heart. Near him lay a sheet of paper One of the officers hastily seized it, and read the following lines, written with lead pencil·

"A man who calls himself the Baron de Spandau, a spy of monarchy, engaged a negro to stab my friend Hinango, who has been condemned to death in Russia as a republican The negro mistook Senhor Closting for Hinango I am of course innocent, but I should have been esteemed guilty, as appearances are against me, and my accusers are powerful The regulations of the social world require a victim—I bring it by my death My heart is pure, God knows my sentiments and my sufferings !
　　　　　　"ROBERT WALKER."

"He is dead !" said the officer half aloud to himself, as he touched the body, and put the important paper in his pocket

"He is dead ! he has stabbed himself !" exclaimed one officer to another, who stood in the garden The sound of these words pierced the ear of the hitherto insensible woman, and suddenly effected her recovery

"Dead! who is dead? is my husband dead?" inquired she, gazing before her with an unsteady glance, and groping around with her hand, as if seeking some object on which to lay hold

No one answered

"Where am I ?" inquired she, with an expression of deadly alarm, " I am in Robert's room ! Where is Robert? where is Robert?"

"Roberto is dead !" sobbed the little one, clasping fast hold on her mother, and weeping aloud.

"Just God !" exclaimed she, wringing her hands in inconsolable despair ; "dead?—no ! no !——

She raised herself, as if she was looking for his body: "Where is Robert? where is my friend, the young Englishman—whom you accused of the murder?" inquired she of the surrounding officers

"Dead !" sighed several, and were unable to add another word.

"Dead——," whispered the dying woman, staring before her like a corpse standing upright, and sinking at the same instant back into her chair, she said, in a broken voice· "It was a dream—the dream has become reality '

She felt around her with tremulous hand, seized her little daughter, and exerted her last strength to press her to her heart !

"Mother ! mother !" screamed the little one ' "mother !"

But the mother heard her no more—Gracia was dead.

CHAPTER VIII.

CONSIDERATE WARNING

WHILE this fearful scene was taking place on the Gloria, a police officer, in a civil dress, made his appearance at Mr Thompson's country house in Bota Fogo, where all was in a movement to send the last trunks and boxes aboard the "Bride of Abydos"

The officer inquired for Mr George Thompson, who made his appearance in a white spencer, having been occupied in putting up, with his own hands, and with great care, some little boxes of his " niece's " jewellery

"I regret that I am commissioned to disturb you," began the functionary, " and must beg you to step aside with me a moment "

"What can I do to serve you?" inquired Mr. Thomson, wiping his forehead, for he had severely exerted himself

"I come in the name of the director of the police, with his particular compliments to yourself, Mr Thomson."

"I thank the police director, what are his commands?"

"It has been long known to the police director, that a young lady, Senora Dolores de * * * *, has lived in your family under an assumed name as your niece, Miss Fanny Walker, or as Isabella de Campana, and it must likewise be known to you, that this young lady has been condemned to death in Buenos Ayres, on account of political crimes against the government of the Argentine republic "

Mr Thomson was evidently frightened

The officer continued " The police director has hitherto permitted this young lady to reside in Bota Fogo the more readily, as while she lived in your house, in your family, and under your responsibility, no political crime against our government was to be feared on her part "

Mr Thomson seemed to wish to express his particular thanks for such confidence, but could not, however, find words in his anxiety, and remained silent

The police functionary continued: " Particular circumstances, especially inquiries on the part of the Argentine government, in regard to the residence of the young lady, place the police director under the-necessity of being obliged to impart this intelligence to you the most speedily possible, that he may not be under the necessity of instituting a search in your house, and arresting the lady on account of a falsification of her name. The police director requests you, therefore, to assist the young lady on board a vessel, for her protection, and from personal consideration for you, Mr Thomson, that he may be able immediately to assure the commissioned agent from Buenos Ayres, that the young lady does not live in Rio de Janeiro, nor anywhere in the environs"

Mr Thomson heard this extremely anticipative and polite warning of the police functionary with loyal anxiety, on account of the transgression of any law, a thought which was a horror to him as an Englishman, and at length listened to the advice for embarkation with the highest satisfaction

He overflowed with assurances of his thankfulness and gratitude towards the police director, and the functionary who stood before him "You know, perhaps, that I am just on the point of going on board a vessel to sail for Santa Catharina, and if you had come one hour later, you would not have found either the young lady or myself on shore I beg you to communicate this intelligence to the police director In the course of an hour, the young lady will be on board of the brig, the "Bride of Abydos," and she will only remain in Santa Catharina until I have freighted a vessel there, which shall take us to England, of course the young lady will not seek an asylum on Brazilian ground"

"Well, very well,' replied the functionary, "I am commissioned to repeat, that you will become subject here to an accusation on account of a falsification of passports, if you do not immediately avail yourself of this well meant warning on our part"

' Accusation on account of falsification of passports!' cried old Mr Thomson, embracing in this expression the entire significancy of such an injury to his reputation and his English respectability

"I should be glad, Senhor, if you ——," replied he, in evident embarrassment, "if you would have the goodness personally to communicate this information to the young lady, as she herself is condemned to death, and I, for my part, am only her protector, and should be unwilling that there should be any mistake—— mistake in the person to be executed"

"I had the commission to speak to the lady herself, but one does not willingly trouble——," replied the polite functionary

' Will you have the goodness to follow me -" said Mr Thomson, hastening before the officer, into the apartment of Dolores

The officer saluted the young lady with Brazilian politeness, and repeated to her, word for word, what he had just said to Mr Thomson

Dolores appeared collected and prepared for such a warning, and commissioned the functionary to convey her thanks to the director of police for the consideration that he had hitherto observed towards her, in permitting her to enjoy the hospitality of the Thomson family The officer then withdrew

Mr Thomson had arranged for the embarkation, by means of a shallop immediately in the neighborhood of his country house The effects were carried out, and Dolores entered the shallop, attended by Corinna and old Achilles

The Baroness de Spandau found herself under the necessity of crossing the bay to the "Bride of Abydos," without the attendance of her husband as the latter was still occupied in the city, and was to follow them directly from the Hotel Paroux

Mr Thomson did not stir from the side of Dolores

"Will you not have the goodness to send some one to Robert?' inquired she of her old friend "Robert will presently come to Bota Fogo, and be disappointed at not finding the shallop there It will be better for us to send him word that we have already gone aboard, and then he will take a boat at the Gloria'

Mr Thomson considered this message proper, and in the highest degree necessary, and commissioned one of his negroes to deliver it The shallop put out from the shore, and steered across to the fortress of Vilganhon, in the neighborhood of the "Bride of Abydos'

Hardly were they all on board, when the baron also made his appearance, bringing a message from Robert to Mr Thomson, whom he called aside on the quarterdeck; to communicate to him something of importance Mr Thomson was very inquisitive, and gave his attention

"I have just been with Robert, to bring him off, he commissioned me to impart to you what follows In the moment of farewell from Senhora Closting, the bond of sympathy which has hitherto enchained them both, rendered the parting of the lady from our Robert 'impossible.' in brief, your plan, Mr George, that the lady should accompany our Robert, will be carried out, but not to-day, not to-morrow Mr Closting lies at his last gasp, given up by the physicians, Robert remains with the lady until her fate shall be decided, or if not, in case Mr Closting should be cured, she will go with him wherever he may take her"

"Did I not say so?" exclaimed the old widower, "did I not say so? I know the women, and I knew very well that she would not let him go, that she would not part with him, I knew that! Now then, in God's name'—— He was still weak, besides, and does well to remain on the Gloria But do you know what has happened to us, also? Do you know the order about Dolores?"

"I know all! all! dear George!" replied the scoundrel, "and more than you do! And do you know also," whispered he very low, "that you have nobody to thank but me for this warning? You know my position with the Minister of the Interior, in regard to the purchase of the Signal mountain there as British property! I long ago employed my acquaintance with the Minister to obtain his protection for Dolores But a requisition has now probably been made for her delivery—to Buenos Ayres, and unhappily the government could do nothing more than to give you and her the well meant hint to take yourselves out of the way"

"That was very noble indeed of the government—and very noble on your part Mr Brother-in-law, very noble!" whispered Mr Thomson

"Can we get to sea, captain?" inquired the baron, abruptly breaking off

"If you expect nothing more from the city, I have been ready since noon, we have wind enough to go out," cried the captain, with animation -

"Then do not delay on our account," observed the baron, "is it not so, Mr Thomson? you expect nothing more from the city, do you?"

Mr. Thomson returned a negative answer, and informed the captain that his nephew remained on shore on account of indisposition

The captain now ordered the anchor to be weighed, and the noise brought Dolores on deck

The baron explained to her Robert's pretended commission—which he had just related to the uncle

" Then Robert is not coming ?" inquired she with astonishment

" As I have just made free to explain to you, he remains for the present with his lady, until her fate is decided You already know, long ago, the circumstances "——

Dolores sank into profound and gloomy meditation, but hitherto no thought of suspicion had been aroused with respect to her embarkation She thought of Robert She had observed him in his illness, she had seen through all his sufferings, and now trembled for his life After the first painful forebodings awakened by this intelligence, she thought of herself, of her own lot, of her present situation , again on board of a strange vessel, alone, without Robert—without Hinango—without Horatio or Alvarez, alone, confided to the protection of an old man, who, although he certainly might be a very practical business man, in moments of danger, such as impended over the exile, might very easily loose his presence of mind She had long ago been informed by Dr. Thorfin of the standing of the baron, as Robert, however, was to attend her, the friends had not thought it proper to intimate to her the particulars of the danger that threatened her Robert's presence of mind was to protect her, and Robert—was no more ——

She inquired if no one had seen Dr Thorfin, for even he had not made his appearance for a farewell visit

Mr Thomson now said that he had met him in the city, and that it had been his intention to have accompanied them on board He had, however, been summoned to Signora Serafini at Praya Grande, and could not decline the invitation

This information was consistent with the truth, but Thorfin supposed that the brig would not go to sea until the next morning, and intended to accompany his friend on board, and take leave of Dolores there.

Dr Thorfin returned from Praya Grande late in the evening—hurried to the two pavilions, and found the faithful Patrick beside the two corpses, and the wounded Mr Closting in the delirium of death

Patrick had appeared at the appointed hour, to take the last effects of Robert on board, and, in spite of the baron, to go on board himself in the dress of a livery servant of the young Englishman.

Patrick foamed and raved for some minutes with fury He explained in good English to the police officers *Who* had employed the negro who had wounded the confidant of the spy, the noble naturalist But the functionaries understood no English, and thought the red-haired Irishman intoxicated

Dr. Thorfin hurried down into the city to Senhor Moreto the relative of the unfortunate Gracia, who had already learned the fearful intelligence. The doctor begged the family to confide the little daughter of the departed to Signora Serafini, who, separated from her children, would receive the poor little one with maternal tenderness, which was carried into effect the following day, and the dear little creature found a second mother

Dr Thorfin now relied upon a fortunate meeting of the Mazzini and the Astrala before Santa Cathaiina, for the reception of Dolores, and upon her own presence of mind, as Robert, through the satanic intrigues of the baron, had not accompanied her

——————— ❦ ———————

CHAPTER IX.

THE EXECUTIONER'S OFFICE

EIGHT days after the " Bride of Abydos" passed the fortress of Santa Cruz and the Sugar Loaf, she reached the two little islands of Gal and Alvaredo, at the entrance of the safe harbor of the island of Santa Catharina

It was an admirable Brazilian morning In its picturesque splendor and magnificence, lay the coast of the main land, with its pointed mountains, partly adorned with milk-white cloudy crowns, which the ascending sun gradually chased away The wind was faint The Baron de Spandau had been on the quarterdeck with his perspective glass since four o'clock in the morning, while it was still dark He looked out at all points into the distance, in search of the Argentine man-of-war La Caza Several barks and schooners, and a crew of fishing shallops showed themselves, but nowhere, nowhere did he see a brig that resembled a brig of war

Instead of this, however, to his deadly alarm, two small vessels displayed themselves to his piercing gaze, anchored close to each other, not far from the island of Alvaredo They were the schooner Mazzini and the schooner brig Astrala

Fortunately the spy found himself still alone upon the quarterdeck No one observed him with particular attention The man at the helm took as little notice of him as the mate who had the watch, and the sailors of the foremast watch troubled themselves still less about " the fellow with the impertinent nose." No one remarked that he was indisposed, that he was really pale

At length, however, he was noticed by some one. The cabin boy had risen, and came tottering, half asleep, on deck " Are you seasick, Senhor Baron ?" inquired he, yawning from pure sympathy, and rubbing his eyes The baron made no reply. He could not answer for anger, and rage, and fury—least of all, a miserable cabin boy

He looked again through the perspective glass, as if he hoped that both vessels had been only phantoms, perhaps only little " flying Dutchmen," and might now have disappeared But there they still lay. The schooner brig Astrala, which he had daily seen in the Bay of Rio, and the schooner Mazzini, which Dr Merbold had described to him as fully as he was able to describe a vessel which was not a beetle

The single consolation of the seller of souls,

was the light wind, which sustained the hope that the Caza might still appear before the Bride of Abydos had made the short distance into the harbor This hope was, however, combined with the fear that the two "cursed corsairs" would "cut off" the Bride of Abydos from the Caza, and make the communication between them impossible, in case Captain Tumble should even appear in the distance with a fresh breeze

It was a situation which might put an honest man in despair, to say nothing of a scoundrel The matter here did not merely concern the full price which was set upon the head of Dolores He was to receive half the reward if he were obliged himself to accomplish the order of the ministerial executioner at Buenos Ayres, and of this half he had, as is known, again promised the half to Captain Tumble The object in this case was particularly the delivery itself, the honor attached to such a work for sustaining the monarchical principle!

It struck eight bells, as the captain stepped upon the quarterdeck He was a small, friendly Scot, from Aberdeen—Captain White, a seaman who had experienced many changes of wind, and many storms, and seen many foreign shores

"Halloo!" cried he, "two vessels at anchor," and had some water brought to make his toilet, as the Baroness de Spandau occupied his cabin with the baron, and he slept in a berth where the mate otherwise had his quarters

' These are a couple of vessels of war—privateers from Monte Video I suspect," remarked he, as the mate approached him " Hoist the flag!" added he, " let us see at once what fire we are coming under England is not at war here with the Republicans, as far as I know I hope we have nothing to fear '

The flag was hoisted Dolores appeared, notwithstanding the early hour, leaning on the arm of Corinna, and seated herself on a barrel near the helm Hardly had she beheld the two vessels, than a gleam of joy overspread her countenance, and without concerning herself about the baron's proximity, she exclaimed, "thank God! that is Captain Hinango and Captain Barigaldi!"

" You know these two sail then, if I may ask," said the captain, who had often conversed with Dolores during the voyage

"Yes, indeed," sighed she, "very well I know both vessels, captain, the small schooner is the Mazzini from Monte Video, the schooner brig is the Astrala of Hayti, both captains have shown me great civility Captain Hinango came as passenger with me from Buenos Ayres to Rio "——

"Then I will steer close by them," returned Captain White, "perhaps we may hail them "

"The schooner brig is making sail already!" cried the man at the helm

" The schooner also," cried the mate

" The crews manœuvre well! excellently!" added the captain! "that goes like the devil! halloo! there! they've done it already—weighed anchor already! If we only had a wind now "

"The flag of MonteVideo—light blue, striped with white," said the mate to himself, while he looked through the telescope, " and the flag of Hayti—blue also—dark blue and white," added he, " two cursedly neat vessels! in good trim! fine rigging! both carry flags on the foremast

44

the schooner—green, red, and white, the other, the brig—blue, white, and yellow, and a star in the blue "

" That is the flag of the Scandinavian Union," remarked Captain White, " the Haytian captain is probably a Scandinavian; the Scandinavians are fine seamen "

" That he is!" assented Dolores, " the captain of the Astrala is a Finn, formerly a Russian marine officer "

" A Finn? Captain Hinango? formerly a Russian marine officer?" inquired the captain, meditating, " is not his name Ormui Olafui Hinango?"

" To be sure," cried Dolores, " do you know him?"

" I know a Russian marine officer of that name, who has been condemned to Siberia, to the lead mines, on account of political crimes, as a republican "

" That's the same!" cried Dolores

" He went as passenger with a friend of mine, Captain Allan, of the brig Ivanhoe, from London to Bahia, some years since I lived in his society there for some weeks He is an agreeable man—a strong republican!"

" That he is!" assented Dolores, more and more happy and joyful, from the neighborhood of her friends, and from Captain White's casual acquaintance with her protector

After long reflection upon her situation, and the danger that threatened her, Dolores had already, in the first days of the voyage, formed the resolution to confide her position, in case of need, to the captain of the Bride of Abydos, as she recognised in him a man who was a true seaman She had as yet, however, found no occasion to make demands upon his protection

The police or government had not refused her a residence on Brazilian ground in order to deliver her up, (that contradicted the constitution,) but that they might be able to answer the allied quasi constitutional government of the Argentine republic, " that the lady was not there " Only the so called " cabinet system," according to which a government concludes one affair or another " entirely underhand," (as a diplomatic secret,) could in such a case endanger the personal safety of any one whatever, who ought to have claims upon the protection of the laws. But exactly in this characterless inefficiency with which constitutional monarchy endeavors to evade the laws in all which sustains the principle of despotism, and voluntarily employs them in all that can suppress the principle of freedom, lies the contemptibleness of such a system—the wretchedness of a government that has neither the courage nor the force to maintain a principle, as it ever shows itself in such cases in its full extent Constitutional inefficiency offers the hand to every despot from cowardice, and endeavors to mask its want of character before the nation, as if it acted liberally. This inconsistency of constitutional monarchy, fills the history of our characterless epoch with its contradictions and miseries, as it fills the dungeons in free countries with exiles, and chases the victim of such inefficiency into the hands of the executioner by " expulsion "

It is in such cases not by any means the person, who is persecuted as an exile—it is the principle of freedom and of humanity, which, condemned to death by absolutism must be eradicated, and, nevertheless, will not be eradicated so long as the idea of the divinity lies in man We behold in such persecutions the blindness and obduracy of the creatures in the pay of monarchy, who can forget nothing, because they have learnt nothing, in relation to the history of nations—as the history of mankind, it is British dullness translated into diplomacy, which, from the throne downwards, fills the art of the cabinet with a contagious infection, and endues the ablest jurists or diplomatists with dullness, so soon as they obtain a portfolio under the arm, and roll towards the court in their carriages

If "Ministerial Excellencies" would reflect that a century intervened between John Huss and the Reformation, they would perceive that neither expulsion nor execution is able to exterminate the spirit, that once led the Israelites out of Egypt, and drove the Britons from the United States

The baron stood at the bulwark of the quarterdeck, at some distance from Dolores, while she was talking so confidentially to the friendly little Captain White He seemed still very much indisposed He had for the last month managed all things so admirably that could lead to his object.

He had obtained from Mr Thomson's own mouth the confession that Robert stood in peculiar relations to Madame Closting, and thought to carry her off, at least he might assert as much He had, upon this confession of the uncle, made the revelation to the authorities, that no other than Mr Robert Walker was the originator of the murder which had been attempted on Mr Closting, and was now slowly arriving at its accomplishment He had given the Minister of Police a hint, that the exile from Buenos Ayres occupied herself with the edition of her republican poems, and obtained, through Miss Susan, some sheets of her manuscript, which he used for his purpose, and then replaced, so that their removal could scarcely be remarked

He had written to Captain Tumble to Santos, when the Caza lay there, to take under convoy an English vessel that was to carry arms to Buenos Ayres He had thereby informed Captain Tumble where the two "cursed miserable sail of the Humanitarios" now lay, and all was now to be wrecked

He had just reached the port of treachery, and then not to enter it—to be forced to sea again with a contrary wind? No! he stood at his post, and knew what still remained for him to do

The two privateers approached the "Bride of Abydos" He might expect that Hinango would come on board immediately, and carry off Dolores—to take her to Monte Video The baron must hasten to action—he was on service—it was his duty

"John, will you be so good as to bring me an orange?" cried Dolores to the cabin boy, as he came up from the cabin, and made preparations for breakfast

"Directly Señora," replied John, and would have turned back again

"Do you wish to discharge me from service Señora?" cried the baron, who had hitherto prepared two oranges every morning, one for the baroness, and one for Dolores, as they, according to Brazilian usage, took care to enjoy an orange every morning regularly before breakfast.

"Don't trouble yourself, Senhor Baron," cried she after him, as he hurried down into his private cabin, where the baroness still lay in sweet gentle slumber—for she had gone to rest very late

The baron selected two beautiful oranges—stuck each, according to Brazilian method, upon a fork, and cutting a small circular piece from each, divided the rind lengthwise in such a manner that it formed a flower, of which the orange was the chalice, and then, opening with a trembling hand his private medicine chest, he took out two little flasks, and dropped some drops, and a substance like a grain of salt, into an incision in the middle of one of the oranges This done, he went with both oranges on deck, and stepped before Dolores, with peculiar politeness, and with a jesting, happy deportment, as if he were in particularly good humor

"Which do you please to have?" inquired he, as he turned his back towards the bulwark, and held both hands behind him, "will you have the orange in the right or the left hand?"

"You are very kind, baron," said Dolores, guilelessly and unconstrainedly, "give me the one which is nearest your heart, the left, if the baroness does not protest against it"

The baron exchanged the oranges, as he happened to have the prepared one in his right hand, and presented it to the condemned with peculiar ceremony, but with a trembling hand

Captain White, and the mate, and the man at the helm, observed the free choice of Dolores, and thought the jest sportive

Dolores sucked the rich juice of the orange with peculiar enjoyment from the unfolded flower, and shivered, for the fruit was very cool and fresh

The baron found himself again indisposed, he leaned against the bulwark, holding the second orange in his hand, which was intended for his lady "Shall I give you another, Señora?" inquired he, stammeringly

"Thank you, baron—one orange before coffee is enough I never take but one in the morning I am much obliged to you"

She turned again to Captain White, and talked to him about Captain Hinango, and told him of Captain Finngreen, who had taken her from Buenos Ayres to Rio

The cabin boy asked the baron if he would awaken his lady for breakfast—the table was set, and the coffee ready, or whether he should knock himself

The baron nodded his head, and John made a noise at the private cabin, to awaken the Baroness de Spandau from her sweet dreams of the honeymoon

"How beautifully the two vessels glide along there, near each other," said Dolores, "it is an image of fraternal concord—exposed to all the storms of life I am so pleased, captain, at the sight of these two vessels I almost regret that I am not a man to conduct a third with these two, it should be called "El Desterrado," and should be a terror to monarch's"

Dolores talked on thus gaily, until uncle George appeared, and led her down to breakfast.

CHAPTER X.

THE VICTIM.

It was about ten o'clock in the forenoon The wind was still light—very light The two vessels of the " Humanita " had slowly, very slowly, pursued their course to meet the " Bride of Abydos, and now were almost side by side Mr Thomson was smoking his segar, and rejoicing once more right heartily over the singular concurrence of circumstances under which Señora Dolores could the less refuse him her hand, as she evidently required a safe asylum, and nothing else remained for her, but to go to England with him The clergyman whose attendance had been bespoken at the betrothal dinner had not been brought along, as the wedding of the baroness had already taken place, and Mr Thomson had inquired and satisfied himself that an English ecclesiastic lived at Santa Catharina, who knew how to manage his business right practically Mr Thomson found himself in a state of boundless gratification The view of the wonderful landscape, which now lay before him, it is true, interested him very little, for during his whole life he had scarcely had an hour to himself, in which to turn his eyes upon mountains, and valleys, and rocks, and trees, and the like, unless to a piece of ground for a purchase He was all the more interested, however, with the prospect of his fifth marriage, which was now to take place there, there—on the charming island of Santa Catharina, and he longed to be on shore, " to arrange the business with the clergyman," and to hire a private residence, until the " Bride of Abydos," or another vessel, should convey him and his lawful, charming, blooming wife, to England He was determined, in case Dolores wished it, to retire from business, and hire a palace in Florence, or somewhere else, and live right comfortably in nuptial felicity The appearance of the two privateers in the latitude of Santa Catharina, which, anchored there, were evidently waiting for something, occasionally passed through his head They were the Astrala and the Mazzini—Barigaldi and Hinango, two " fellows with hair on their teeth," with hair on the upper lip, with moustaches, and, so far as was generally known, they carried their hearts in the right place. The thought that perhaps Hinango " had an eye to Dolores," (as people express themselves in matrimonial affairs,) had hitherto been far from the old widower He had remarked no love passages between Dolores and him so long as she resided at Bota Fogo Nevertheless, however, the approach of the two privateer vessels, appeared to him suspicious and doubtful He racked his brains about the occasion of their blockade of the entrance to Santa Catharina, and talked over the matter with Captain White

The captain remarked that the mainland of the province of Rio Grande commenced directly below the province of Santa Catharina, hardly sixty miles distant from their present latitude, and the two privateers were probably destined for Laguna, and were taking ammunition, or something of that kind, on board here, without having any designs upon the Bride of Abydos. The two vessels of the " Humanita " now

floated towards each other, and all eyes were directed upon them

Hinango stood on his quarterdeck, and beside him Horatio, who had travelled from Rio Grande to Monte Video by land, and conveyed the request to Captain Barigaldi to go, if possible, towards Santa Catharina, arrived there, he had gone on board the Astrala, where the cabin was now arranged in the best manner possible for Dolores and Corinna

The baroness was leaning on the arm of the baron, she looked very pale, but very interesting, in the highest degree interesting, as every young woman generally looks in the first days or weeks after marriage She was dressed in a very tasteful negligé, with a little hat " à la Duchesse de Berry," over which was thrown a green veil

The Astrala steered nearest, and Captain Hinango called through the speaking trumpet the seamanlike " Brig ahoy '"

Captain White, upon his post in expectation of this summons, answered, and the captain of the Astrala, in all due form inquired, although he knew the answer beforehand

" Where are you from ?"

" From Rio de Janeiro "

" Where bound ?"

" For Santa Catharina and Buenos Ayres "

" Have you passengers on board ?"

" My whole cabin full, and a lady whom you know, Captain Hinango, and you know me also, I am Captain White—' Bride of Abydos,' the friend of Captain Allan of the Ivanhoe "

" I am glad to hear it—very glad ; I'll come on board of you '" returned the captain of the Astrala

There was silence again on the quarterdeck of the ' Bride of Abydos '

" A fine man '" said Captain White, smiling, " this Captain Hinango ' a naval officer of the first class ' Where's our Señora ?" inquired he, looking around him, " she hasn't become seasick ' Strange that she is not on deck '"

" She is asleep," replied the Baroness de Spandau, " she desired me to awake her if the two vessels came near us " The baroness was going down into the cabin to awaken Dolores. The baron stepped before her, and observed that it was time enough yet, she might still repose until her friend was on board of the vessel

Captain Hinango now called to the captain of the Mazzini to hold himself in readiness ; he would lower his boat, and take him off to go on board the ' Bride of Abydos ' All three vessels now laid themselves " by the wind," which, moreover, did not disturb them very much

" You also know Captain Hinango," continued Captain White, in conversation with Mr Thomson

" To be sure I know him ' a respectable man, a gentleman, is Captain Hinango ! I know him very well ' The cannon of the Astrala were furnished by us, he equipped the Astrala in Rio ; and took a great deal of us, from our stores ; the new schooner's sail was bought of us ! it's cloth from your native place—from Aberdeen "

" One may see that '" observed Captain White, " and very well fitted, and she comes to beautifully !"

The baroness was walking up and down on the arm of the baron, as the Bride of Abydos lay, nearly motionless on the surface of the water, as well as the two privateers. The baron, however, reeled notwithstanding this, and could hardly keep his feet. He required the support of his lady, instead of her leaning upon him, he was feverish, and his lady deeply lamented that he was not well.

The boat of the Astrala, in whose stern Mr. Closting had received the stroke of the dagger, now lay alongside. The two officers of the "Humanita," in dark blue uniform, with white anchor buttons, and snow white nether garments, stepped upon the deck. Both wore flat naval hats, and each carried his national cockade, small swords in silver scabbards appeared on their hips. Horatio accompanied them.

"Captain White!" began Hinango, "you know our flags. My schooner brig is the Astrala, of Hayti, cruising against the slave trade, and the schooner is the Mazzini, of Monte Video—Captain Barigaldi," added he, introducing his friend to the captain of the Bride of Abydos.

"Mr. George Thompson! how do you find yourself? how are you?" said he now to the freighter of the vessel; "I congratulate you on your fortunate arrival before Santa Catharina, I did not think that I should have the pleasure of meeting you here."

"You have been to Bahia, as we saw by the papers?" returned Mr. Thompson.

"To Bahia, and there found orders from my government, which pointed out to me another course. But where is Robert? our Robert? my friend Robert? and where's Miss Fanny?" inquired he, looking around him with peculiar anxiety. "I recollect your plan of making this voyage *en famille?*"

"Miss Fanny is in Buenos Ayres, and the young lady whom you have known under this name is called Isabella de Campana, and is here on board; she is asleep just now."

"We will take the liberty to have her awakened, it will give her great pleasure to see you," said Captain White. "John bring two bottles of port, and glasses, and biscuit!—and biscuit out of the tin box!"

The baroness again offered to awaken her friend, and went down into the cabin. The baron accompanied the lady to the stairs, and then leaned there at the entrance, he was again very much indisposed, it was plainly to be seen. Hinango directed his gaze upon him—he could not endure it, and looked on the ground.

Mr. Thomson now informed Captain Hinango, that Robert had remained behind in Rio from indisposition, that he had had a nervous fever since the departure of the Astrala, but was already convalescent, and would probably soon follow them.

A shriek sounded upwards from the open skylight, and then another, and then it became as still as death.

"My God, what's that?" cried several with one voice, and Captain White hurried past the baron into the cabin. The two privateer captains and Horatio followed, with Mr. Thomson, all silently, and with palpitating hearts.

"Dead! dead! dead!" passed from mouth to mouth. "A stroke of apoplexy!" cried the baron. "My God! my God! and my wife! dead also!—dead also!"

"No!" cried the baroness, awakening from her swoon, "no! but horrible! horrible! to die here on board, of apoplexy!—dead!"

All gazed upon each other. Hinango and Barigaldi recollected themselves first, and bore the body on deck, in the hope that rescue might yet be possible. But Dolores was lifeless—her exalted soul had forsaken its shell of clay; the orange had done its work. Her lips were bluish, as well as her cheeks.

"Poisoned! poisoned!" passed from mouth to mouth, and Horatio sank senseless beside the body. Achilles and Corinna wrung their hands and wept disconsolately. Burning tears sparkled in the flashing glances of the two "corsairs," and their lips quivered.

The whole crew had crowded around the mainmast, and silently and speechlessly all gazed on the body of the noble young lady, who had been honored like a saint on board, from the captain down to the lowest sailor.

The baroness had remained in the cabin, and the baron with her, wailing and lamenting "over the terrible misfortune—over the death of the amiable young lady in blooming youth, on board the Bride of Abydos—of apoplexy!"

"Murder! murder through treachery!" cried Hinango at length, after a deathlike silence, "and the murderer is here on board. Captain White, you sail under the British flag, and we are both lawful republican privateers. We respect your position, your flag, and will not by any means forget our standing as officers under neutral or allied flags,—we respect England, Monte Video, and Hayti. But we 'would have' a right to demand that a murderer be sent from on board, —the murderer of this young lady, Dolores, condemned to death as a republican poetess by Rosas, and betrayed and poisoned by a creature who calls himself the Baron de Spandau. Here, Captain White, is a letter that this scoundrel despatched from Rio to Captain Tumble, commander of the Argentine brig La Caza, who should have met him here at this time to take the condemned on board, and carry her to Buenos Ayres to the scaffold."

Captain White stared at Mr. Thomson, who had long ago been deprived of speech. Both read the letter, which Hinango had received through Patrick, which was sufficient to unveil the murder.

Mr. Thomson beckoned to the captain of the Bride of Abydos, and both descended into the cabin. They found the baron upon the sofa of the large outer cabin, deadly pale, and gazing on vacancy, with the baroness beside him, her face concealed in his half opened vest, clasping him firmly with both hands, as if she feared to lose her young husband, as if he might be stolen from her—a terrible thought for the young baroness in the honeymoon!

"Mr. Spandau! or whatever your name is!" began Mr. Thomson, placing himself directly in front of the trembling nuptial pair! "Mr. Spandau, here's your letter to Captain Tumble. Take yourself from on board!"

With these words he held the well known letter under the nose of the murderer, who, like Mr. Closting at the sight of the sympathy birds, lost his presence of mind, and was unable to utter a word, or even a syllable.

Instead of him, however, the baroness raised her pale face from the open vest of her husband,

CHAPTER X.

THE VICTIM

It was about ten o'clock in the forenoon. The wind was still light—very light. The two vessels of the "Humanita" had slowly, very slowly, pursued their course to meet the "Bride of Abydos," and now were almost side by side. Mr Thomson was smoking his segar, and rejoicing once more right heartily over the singular concurrence of circumstances under which Senora Dolores could the less refuse him her hand, as she evidently required a safe asylum, and nothing else remained for her, but to go to England with him. The clergyman whose attendance had been bespoken at the betrothal dinner had not been brought along, as the wedding of the baroness had already taken place, and Mr Thomson had inquired and satisfied himself that an English ecclesiastic lived at Santa Catharina, who knew how to manage his business right practically. Mr Thomson found himself in a state of boundless gratification. The view of the wonderful landscape, which now lay before him, it is true, interested him very little, for during his whole life he had scarcely had an hour to himself, in which to turn his eyes upon mountains, and valleys, and rocks, and trees, and the like, unless to a piece of ground for a purchase. He was all the more interested, however, with the prospect of his fifth marriage, which was now to take place there, there—on the charming island of Santa Catharina, and he longed to be on shore, "to arrange the business with the clergyman," and to hire a private residence, until the "Bride of Abydos," or another vessel, should convey him and his lawful, charming, blooming wife, to England. He was determined, in case Dolores wished it, to retire from business, and hire a palace in Florence, or somewhere else, and live right comfortably in nuptial felicity. The appearance of the two privateers in the latitude of Santa Catharina, which, anchored there, were evidently waiting for something, occasionally passed through his head. They were the Astrala and the Mazzini—Barigaldi and Hinango; two "fellows with hair on their teeth," with hair on the upper lip, with moustaches, and, so far as was generally known, they carried their hearts in the right place. The thought that perhaps Hinango "had an eye to Dolores," (as people express themselves in matrimonial affairs,) had hitherto been far from the old widower. He had remarked no love passages between Dolores and him so long as she resided at Bota Fogo. Nevertheless, however, the approach of the two privateer vessels, appeared to him suspicious and doubtful. He racked his brains about the occasion of their blockade of the entrance to Santa Catharina, and talked over the matter with Captain White.

The captain remarked that the mainland of the province of Rio Grande commenced directly below the province of Santa Catharina, hardly sixty miles distant from their present latitude, and the two privateers were probably destined for Laguna, and were taking ammunition, or something of that kind, on board here, without having any designs upon the Bride of Abydos.

The two vessels of the "Humanita" now floated towards each other, and all eyes were directed upon them.

Hinango stood on his quarterdeck; and beside him Horatio, who had travelled from Rio Grande to Monte Video by land, and conveyed the request to Captain Barigaldi to go, if possible, towards Santa Catharina, arrived there, he had gone on board the Astrala, where the cabin was now arranged in the best manner possible for Dolores and Corinna.

The baroness was leaning on the arm of the baron; she looked very pale, but very interesting, in the highest degree interesting, as every young woman generally looks in the first days or weeks after marriage. She was dressed in a very tasteful negligé, with a little hat "à la Duchesse de Berry," over which was thrown a green veil.

The Astrala steered nearest, and Captain Hinango called through the speaking trumpet the seamanlike "Brig ahoy!"

Captain White, upon his post in expectation of this summons, answered, and the captain of the Astrala, in all due form inquired, although he knew the answer beforehand·

"Where are you from?"

"From Rio de Janeiro."

"Where bound?"

"For Santa Catharina and Buenos Ayres."

"Have you passengers on board?"

"My whole cabin full, and a lady whom you know, Captain Hinango: and you know me also, I am Captain White—' Bride of Abydos,' the friend of Captain Allan of the Ivanhoe."

"I am glad to hear it—very glad; I'll come on board of you!" returned the captain of the Astrala.

There was silence again on the quarterdeck of the 'Bride of Abydos.'

"A fine man!" said Captain White, smiling, "this Captain Hinango! a naval officer of the first class! Where's our Señora?" inquired he, looking around him, "she hasn't become sea-sick? Strange that she is not on deck!"

"She is asleep," replied the Baroness de Spandau, "she desired me to awake her if the two vessels came near us." The baroness was going down into the cabin to awaken Dolores. The baron stepped before her, and observed that it was time enough yet, she might still repose until her friend was on board of the vessel.

Captain Hinango now called to the captain of the Mazzini to hold himself in readiness, he would lower his boat, and take him off to go on board the 'Bride of Abydos.' All three vessels now laid themselves "by the wind," which, moreover, did not disturb them very much.

"You also know Captain Hinango," continued Captain White, in conversation with Mr Thomson.

"To be sure I know him! a respectable man, a gentleman, is Captain Hinango! I know him very well! The cannon of the Astrala were furnished by us, he equipped the Astrala in Rio; and took a great deal of us, from our stores; the new schooner's sail was bought of us! it's cloth from your native place—from Aberdeen."

"One may see that!" observed Captain White, "and very well fitted; and she comes to beautifully!"

The baroness was walking up and down on the arm of the baron, as the Bride of Abydos lay nearly motionless on the surface of the water, as well as the two privateers. The baron, however, reeled notwithstanding this, and could hardly keep his feet. He required the support of his lady, instead of her leaning upon him, he was feverish, and his lady deeply lamented that he was not well

The boat of the Astrala, in whose stern Mr Closting had received the stroke of the dagger, now lay alongside. The two officers of the "Humanita," in dark blue uniform, with white anchor buttons, and snow white nether garments, stepped upon the deck. Both wore flat naval hats, and each carried his national cockade, small swords in silver scabbards appeared on their hips. Horatio accompanied them

"Captain White!" began Hinango, "you know our flags. My schooner brig is the Astrala, of Hayti, cruising against the slave trade, and the schooner is the Mazzini, of Monte Video—Captain Barigaldi," added he, introducing his friend to the captain of the Bride of Abydos

"Mr George Thompson! how do you find yourself? how are you?" said he now to the freighter of the vessel, "I congratulate you on your fortunate arrival before Santa Catharina, I did not think that I should have the pleasure of meeting you here"

"You have been to Bahia, as we saw by the papers?" returned Mr Thompson

"To Bahia, and there found orders from my government, which pointed out to me another course. But where is Robert? our Robert? my friend Robert? and where's Miss Fanny?" inquired he, looking around him with peculiar anxiety. "I recollect your plan of making this voyage *en famille!*"

"Miss Fanny is in Buenos Ayres, and the the young lady whom you have known under this name is called Isabella de Campana, and is here on board, she is asleep just now"

"We will take the liberty to have her awakened, it will give her great pleasure to see you," said Captain White. "John bring two bottles of port, and glasses, and biscuit!—and biscuit out of the tin box!"

The baroness again offered to awaken her friend, and went down into the cabin. The baron accompanied the lady to the stairs, and then leaned there at the entrance, he was again very much indisposed, it was plainly to be seen. Hinango directed his gaze upon him—he could not endure it, and looked on the ground.

Mr Thomson now informed Captain Hinango, that Robert had remained behind in Rio from indisposition, that he had had a nervous fever since the departure of the Astrala, but was already convalescent, and would probably soon follow them.

A shriek sounded upwards from the open skylight, and then another, and then it became as still as death

"My God, what's that?" cried several with one voice, and Captain White hurried past the baron into the cabin. The two privateer captains and Horatio followed, with Mr Thomson, all silently, and with palpitating hearts.

"Dead! dead! dead!" passed from mouth to mouth. "A stroke of apoplexy!" cried the baron. "My God! my God! and my wife! dead also!—dead also!"

"No!" cried the baroness, awakening from her swoon, "no! but horrible! horrible! to die here on board, of apoplexy!—dead!"

All gazed upon each other. Hinango and Barigaldi recollected themselves first, and bore the body on deck, in the hope that rescue might yet be possible. But Dolores was lifeless—her exalted soul had forsaken its shell of clay; the orange had done its work. Her lips were bluish, as well as her cheeks

"Poisoned! poisoned!" passed from mouth to mouth, and Horatio sank senseless beside the body. Achilles and Corinna wrung their hands and wept disconsolately. Burning tears sparkled in the flashing glances of the two "corsairs," and their lips quivered

The whole crew had crowded around the mainmast, and silently and speechlessly all gazed on the body of the noble young lady, who had been honored like a saint on board, from the captain down to the lowest sailor

The baroness had remained in the cabin, and the baron with her, wailing and lamenting "over the terrible misfortune—over the death of the amiable young lady in blooming youth, on board the Bride of Abydos—of apoplexy!"

"Murder! murder through treachery!" cried Hinango at length, after a deathlike silence, "and the murderer is here on board. Captain White, you sail under the British flag, and we are both lawful republican privateers. We respect your position, your flag, and will not by any means forget our standing as officers under neutral or allied flags;—we respect England, Monte Video, and Hayti. But we would have a right to demand that a murderer be sent from on board, —the murderer of this young lady, Dolores, condemned to death as a republican poetess by Rosas, and betrayed and poisoned by a creature who calls himself the Baron de Spandau. Here, Captain White, is a letter that this scoundrel despatched from Rio to Captain Tumble, commander of the Argentine brig La Caza, who should have met him here at this time to take the condemned on board, and carry her to Buenos Ayres to the scaffold"

Captain White stared at Mr Thomson, who had long ago been deprived of speech. Both read the letter, which Hinango had received through Patrick, which was sufficient to unveil the murder

Mr Thomson beckoned to the captain of the Bride of Abydos, and both descended into the cabin. They found the baron upon the sofa of the large outer cabin, deadly pale, and gazing on vacancy, with the baroness beside him, her face concealed in his half opened vest, clasping him firmly with both hands, as if she feared to lose her young husband, as if he might be stolen from her—a terrible thought for the young baroness in the honeymoon!

"Mr Spandau! or whatever your name is!" began Mr Thomson, placing himself directly in front of the trembling nuptial pair! "Mr Spandau, here's your letter to Captain Tumble. Take yourself from on board!"

With these words he held the well known letter under the nose of the murderer, who, like Mr Closting at the sight of the sympathy birds, lost his presence of mind, and was unable to utter a word, or even a syllable.

Instead of him, however, the baroness raised her pale face from the open vest of her husband,

and soon after that, she raised her voice, while she stared at her brother, and exclaimed "What is it? what is the matter?"

"The matter is," replied Mr Thomson, "that an infamous scoundrel has circumvented, deceived and betrayed you, and me, and all of us, and has murdered our Dolores—my Dolores—poisoned her—as clearly and truly as that her body lies up there, and the murderer in your arms"

"What a shameful, infamous calumny!" now shrieked the exemplary wife of the of the baron, "what an infamous thing! to call my husband a scoundrel! and even to accuse him of murder!"

"A twofold murder!" interrupted Hinango, who had followed the two, and stood beside Mr Thomson "I know Mr ————, whatever your name is," said he now to the baron, "I know very well that you hired a negro named Moloch to stab me on the evening before my departure, and that his dagger pierced your friend Mr Closting You serve in an exemplary manner the secret police of the monarchial principle, but there rules a Nemesis, a mysterious power of Providence! I have nothing further to say to you"

"Who is this man? the foreigner? that he dares to come down into our cabin with his moustaches, and insult my husband?" screamed the baroness with the voice of a fury "Who is this foreigner? what does the fellow want here? is he a passenger here or captain? Come baron! let's pack up and go on shore! Call a fisherman's boat, Captain White! you have men here on board, with whom one cannot come in contact without the risk of injuring their respectability!—it is shameful!—fie! infamous! infamous! to calumniate my husband so! And who is the foreign person, after all, that has died of apoplexy? Who is she? a foreigner—who travelled around the world under all sorts of false names, and had acquaintance with God knows who, and corresponded in verse and prose with suspicious persons—and belonged to no church, neither the English nor the Catholic, and read Lord Byron, and Madame Sand, and——"

"Hold your hellish tongue! you miserable woman, who are unfortunately my sister!" interrupted Mr Thomson, "hold your tongue, I tell you, or I'll throw you overboard!—you first, like a cat, and then this fellow here, like a dog! Now pack up your duds, and then get ready to on shore Come Captain White, come captain," said he, suddenly recollecting himself, to the two witnesses, and all three mounted to the quarterdeck,

Captain White penetrated, with the sharp look of a seaman, the peculiar conflict of circumstances under which the treasonable murder was committed, arrived on the quarterdeck with the two naval officers and old Mr Thomson He expressed his decided intention to keep the murderer as a prisoner on board, and to deliver him for trial to the British consul, or to another British authority in the next place to his present station He added to his explanation to the two captains: "Your decision in regard to this miserable scoundrel is, to be sure, an action of generosity on your part as captains, to the honor of your flag. Your action is fair, noble—really generous—but the murderer is a 'murderer,' and his crime has been committed 'on board of my vessel,' under the British flag, and therefore——"

Mr Thomson interrupted the worthy seaman with the single remark, to take in consideration that the so called "Baron de Spandau" was unfortunately his brother-in-law, and the captain resigned his personal obligation as a British captain, leaving the whole cause, and the murderer and his lady, to the disposition of the two generous "corsairs" of the "Humanita"

Captain White ordered all the baggage of the baron to be brought up, that they might be ready for debarkation, and now turned his attention to the neighboring fishing boats, one of which might set the two passengers on shore

No one spoke, the countenances of all were pale, and all eyes were moist

Hinango ordered the body for the present to be taken into the cabin, to withdraw it from the sun Achilles and Corinna, who went about in a dreamlike state of terror and despair, fulfilled the order, and the silence of death prevailed as hitherto upon the deck

The flag of the Bride of Abydos was lowered to half-mast, as a signal of mourning, and immediately after, the flags of Hayti and of Monte Video on the two privateers were also lowered

"There comes a fishing shallop, or sumacca!" said Captain White interrupting the prevailing silence "We will hail them I know very well that I ought not to set any one on shore until I have undergone the visit from the alfandega—but in this case the devil take the whole alfandega, and the baron first!"

"We shall not receive the visit of the alfandega here," said old Mr Thomson, in a voice of emotion, "we shall not cast anchor before Santa Catharina—not now So soon as we are freed from the two passengers, you will lay your course for the coast of the province of Rio Grande, Captain White, there we will make land, and commit the mortal shell, the body, to the earth. Our papers, to be sure, are made out for Buenos Ayres, but this officer of the Oriental marine, Captain Barigaldi, will have the goodness to procure us anchorage there under such circumstances The two provinces are at friendship with each other, no danger impending"

Captain White agreed with the freighter of the vessel A sailor crept out on the bowsprit with a flag, which he had found on deck, and beckoned the fishing shallop, to come alongside. It was the designated flag with the myrtle wreath, which the baron had brought to the forward deck in the night, and laid under the long boat, to have it at hand, when the Caza should show herself The fishing shallop was at the side. Captain White asked the man who conducted her whether he would set a lady and gentleman on shore on the neighboring island of Alvaredo, or wherever it might suit them. The man was very ready, and Captain White went down into the cabin

The amiable baroness soon appeared, thickly veiled, leaning on the arm of her husband, and tottered with very unsteady steps over the gangway, and was handed down into the shallop The baron followed her Neither he nor she cast a glance around them. The whole baggage of trunks and boxes was let down after them, which had been placed in readiness on the gangway. John, the cabin boy, just then brought the writing-desk and the little mahogany medicine chest of the baron past the quarterdeck,

"Stop!" cried Himango to him, drawing a piece of paper from his pocketbook, and taking his silver pencil, he wrote upon it a receipt for these two pieces, and ordered the mate to hand the paper to the baron, with the remark that he would send both boxes to the Prussian or Russian consul in Rio de Janeiro, when he had examined their contents

The baron received the paper with a trembling hand, and said not a word

All the effects were now from on board, and the shallop pushed off, and steered towards the island of Alvaredo

The seabreeze had strengthened a little, and admitted of their laying their course. The two captains agreed upon signals with Captain White, that they might arrive at Laguna in company, and returned again to their quarterdecks

Slowly, and then by degrees more rapidly, the three vessels floated along near each other, and soon lost sight of the coast, with the islands of Gal, Alvaredo, and Santa Catharina, as they went further out to sea in search of a little wind for the course to Laguna

The body of Dolores was covered with moist cool sails, which they did not remove until the ship's carpenters had completed a plain coffin, in which Corinna laid the victim to eternal repose

Among the papers of the murdered one, was found a letter to Horatio, which declared him, in case of her death, the heir of all her literary manuscripts, the spirit of which appeared in the "Hymn of Curse," and the Elegy "El Desterrado," which are preserved in these pages

CHAPTER XI.

REST IN THE GRAVE.

Towards midnight of the same day the mourning squadron arrived at the bay near the harbor of Laguna, and came to anchor. Captain Barigaldi went on shore, and sought an officer of the armed coasters, to explain to him the unfortunate occasion of their approach

It so happened that a strong body of the insurgents were quartered in the neighborhood to guard the coast against a landing on the part of the imperial troops, and among the commanders of the cavalry appeared Celeste. The latter soon learned from the mouth of Barigaldi all the particulars of the history of Dolores, from the time of her departure from Buenos Ayres to her death, and entered the boat of the Mazzini, attended by a functionary of the republic of Rio Grande, that he might, with him, make arrangements for the landing of the corpses, in order to exempt the captain of the Bride of Abydos from all responsibility

On the silent shore of the country whose people have struggled for years for life and death, to render themselves independent of the disgrace of monarchy—a lonely grave was dug for the South American poetess of the "Humanita"

Solemnly, and in the deathlike silence of the starlight night, was the interment completed. A mute prayer from the breast of all, to the Primitive Spirit of Creation, who governs the world and the fates of men, and guides the nations, superseded the expressions of mourning, which were suffocated by overpowering grief in the hearts of the sorrowers

After the fulfilment of the last tragical duties to the earthly shell of an exalted spirit, the navigators and Mr. Thomson returned on board their vessels, and Celeste, accompanied by Horatio went back to the camp of the insurgents

Before the sun, on the following morning lighted the foaming waves on the border of the silent coast, the three vessels had disappeared—each upon its particular course

Doctor Thorfin had superintended the interment of the corpses on Da Gloria, and two graves, beside each other, covered the bodies of the two mortals whose souls had become a unity upon earth, while the body of the broken female heart, so long as it beat, was the lawful *property* of a man who looked for *no soul* in a woman

The bones of the two unhappy ones now rested beside each other, whose spiritual being, had become united upon earth by an all powerful bond of mysterious attraction, without enjoying the terrestrial felicity of such a unity of soul. The curse with which their love was burdened here below, was now dissolved by the transition to a realm of light beyond the grave, where, according to the declaration of Jesus, no bond of terrestial marriage avails, where the soul recognises itself as soul, and strives onward towards eternal perfectibility, from step to step, in the element of love

Mr. Closting expired in delirium, some weeks after these interments, and found his place of repose at a distance from his deceased so called wife, proportioned to that by which, as a man, he had been separated from her on earth.

Mr. Daily did not neglect to procure an extremely solemn funeral for the skilful man of business, who had aided him to acquire money and credit, and to cause a tombstone of solid worth to be placed on his grave, upon which the virtues of the deceased, as a GOOD CHRISTIAN, A GOOD NATIONAL GUARD, AN EXCELLENT HUSBAND AND FATHER OF A FAMILY, ETC., ETC., appeared in very legible, deeply cut letters

Alvarez obtained his freedom through the decided steps of Senhor Vera, so soon as the Baron de Spandau had left Rio de Janeiro, and lived with his sister in Praya Grande, until Serafini's sentence of death was softened to "eternal exile from Brazil." He then accompanied his relatives to Portugal, whither they were shipped, in the same manner as the Brazilian exiles of high rank in the year 1842—since the young monarchy, as it appears, considered her motherland as a sort of Botany Bay for honorable men

Mr. George Thomson returned to Rio Janeiro, and learned at his arrival in the bay, through Senhor Pedro, the obliging officer of the alfendega, what had occurred on Da Gloria, shortly before his embarkation for Santa Catharina. Six months afterwards, he received intelligence of the Baroness de Spandau from Europe, and transmitted her property, according to her order, to a house in London, where she lives very comfortably with her husband, as a happy wife, and as a "baroness." The baron established a gambling house. His hospitable saloon offered a social circle for foreigners of various nations,

to the protection of celebrated court singers, and imperial royal "virtuosi," who were introduced there by force. All the guests found the baroness very amiable, the baron very polite, and many withdrew in the most civil manner possible, annoyed by all sorts of suspicious reports.

Mr. Habakkuk Daily did a flourishing business as partner of the house of Torio & Co., and soon married a young widow from the family of Madame Forro.

Bebida was again sold at auction for a nominal price, and became the property of a French woman in Santa Theresa, where she muttered her Dabedikadem from early in the morning till late at night.

Patrick went as a sailor to Rio Grande, by the way of Santa Catharina, and sought for and found his Captain Hinango, who granted him his place of boatswain, which he had long ago held upon the muster roll.

We have received less decided intelligence of the Astrala than of the Mazzini, which, under the flag of the insurgents of Rio Grande, was nearly sunk in a severe battle with a Brazilian corvette.

Captain Barigaldi and his crew saved themselves by swimming, while a fire of musketry was directed upon them. Barigaldi received three bullets in the right shoulder, and entrenched himself on shore in a house, where he resisted, during fourteen hours, the attack of the royalists, until Celeste came to his assistance with a troop of cavalry and destroyed the enemy.

Horatio complied with the request of Celeste, to withdraw himself from the armed struggle of Rio Grande, and cultivate his talent for art as much as possible by study and travel. He designed to go to Europe and establish his "atelier" in Rome.

Dr. Thorfin and Mr. Fitz lived in Rio de Janeiro as before. The latter went from time to time to San Christova, examined and controlled the air pumps, and other philosophical* instruments of the two princesses, of whom it is known that the youngest, some years afterwards, was married to a European prince for the further development of her "physique expérimentale." Mr. Fitz sang afterwards, as before, with a barbarous voice, several times each day, his favorite song, "No general has so powerful might, &c.," in which he often became melancholy, and then went and took a walk.

Doctor Merbold still lived and travelled as before, in Brazil, as an entomologist, and occasionally delighted himself with a slice of Minas cheese and a bottle of Bavarian beer, that arrived at Rio de Janeiro by the way of Bremen, to his great national joy!

Achilles and Corinna planted trees around Dolores' grave, and remained in the region of Laguna until the uncle of Dolores in Buenos Ayres decided upon their future position, and sent them the means to arrange a home for themselves somewhere, and cultivate a little piece of land for the satisfaction of their unpretending wants.

It was a natural consequence, that having been involved in the fate of Dolores, they could not

return to the domain of the "Cacique of the Gauchos" so long as his axe governed there as a sceptre.

Mr. George Thomson, after some months, made the acquaintance of a young Portuguese lady of respectable family, of respectable connexions, and with a decided tendency to corpulency, who became enamored of his equipage, and gave him her delicate hand upon his lightest approximation.

——————⁕——————

CHAPTER XII

WOMAN'S MAGIC

ROBERT'S journals and private papers, in the absence of his relatives, came into the custody of Doctor Thorfin, who, as a contribution to the study of Psychology, prepared extracts from them, which have been used as materials in this novel. Interesting and instructive as many pages among Robert's papers might be, manifold circumstances, nevertheless, will not admit of the publication of extracts. The fragment of a single letter, which, shortly before his death, he wrote to his father, may, however, find its place here, as the youth's confession of faith upon marriage and love.

—— "You ask me if I have delivered your letter of introduction to Mr. F——, and how I was received. Freely and open-heartedly, as I have always dealt towards you, my dear father, I answer you, that I have laid aside this well meant letter, and shall avoid the acquaintance of the respectable family of F——. I know your unexpressed thought, of one day hearing the intelligence that I would lead Miss F—— to the altar, as the property of this young lady, as you have with paternal good intentions intimated to me, "sustains about an equal weight with my future possessions," and as you add, 'because Miss F—— is a true Englishwoman.'

With all respect towards our amiable countrywomen, I allow myself, once for all, the declaration, that I deem marriage as the most sacred covenant of humanity, which should only be concluded from love, and from no other consideration whatever.

Sincerely as I honor the 'Private Instructions' which you imparted to me, as the individual view of an Englishman, I will never, in the above matter, set aside the claims of my heart as a man. I am of opinion, that, in this most important step of the two sexes, nationality does not come so strictly under consideration, as morality and love, and declare every matrimonial union to be immoral, which is concluded upon any material ground whatever. The social world around me here, gives me occasion enough to reflect upon the demoralization which directly and indirectly proceeds from a marriage 'à la mode,' or 'marriage de raison,' and so far as I am hitherto acquainted with the world, I hold such a marriage to be a crime. I recognise such a union, as a privilege of all demoralization, even the vilest fellow sustains himself upon this privilege, according to which no one dares to

---

* This English expression, which would sound like *nonsense* in every other language, signifies apparatus for the study of *physique.* *Physique* is the science for the investigation of the powers of nature.

make his wife acquainted with his masked position, and of course the scoundrel always finds a support for his villainy in his Wife, as a so called ' head of a family '

If I do not find a woman, who, recognising in me a man of honor, loves me, and respects my honesty, I shall probably never marry As to the rest, I am tolerably well, etc "

Himango learned, through correspondence with Dr Thorfin, whatever could be of importance to him with respect to Robert's relations to Gracia, and the cause of his death, whereby involuntary succession of mutual philosophical remarks ensued The extracts from some letters of Himango, as a designation of his social position, and as a retrospect upon the sufferings of Robert, may likewise here find a suitable place

——" As you know my ' absurd' views concerning death and life, it will not surprise you when I give you the assurance that it is difficult for me to think that Dolores is dead Does not her spirit live in her poems and songs, and is not every human heart that shares her sentiments and participates in her inspiration a sanctuary of life, in which her spirit continues to operate for the cultivation and for the ennoblement of the human heart ; for the development of the exalted idea—God ' and Humanity '

——I am strengthened by the inspiring thought that the spiritual bond which unites kindred souls cannot be rent asunder by space nor time, by separation nor death ; that we shall once more, upon some brighter planet, meet again those with whom we lived here in spiritual union ; that we shall approach each other there, beyond the grave, by the spiritual bond of attraction—of love—and, less enchained and palsied by material shell, more susceptible of divine love, more clear in knowledge and in the perception of God, striving forth from degree to degree, from planet to planet '

——Young Banko has told me a great deal about a Madame Fesh, with whom he became acquainted in Closting's company somewhere in the interior of Brazil, a woman in all her excellence as a ' propagating machine ' Thus we have, in a retrospect upon the fate of Dolores, become acquainted with woman in her sixfold social position, in Dolores, Angelica, Gracia, Susan, Sally, and Madame Fesh, a singular chance. In these six categories may be classed all the women upon earth

I hear the staff broken over Dolores, upon her grave, as during her lifetime, condemned by anticipation as an ' extravagant enthusiast '' That is very natural A woman who shows head, and heart, and character, will everywhere encounter scorn from the crowd, who possess neither head, heart, nor character.

The deliverance of the female sex from the bonds and chains of unnatural regulations and prejudices, is a problem that our age will not solve, so long as it pursues the direction of a false civilization, which denies the aim of the cultivation of mankind, and departs from it more and more.

As a nation can only be free through the self-consciousness of its dignity, and the exertion of its own strength, and as no tyrant will ever voluntarily descend from the throne and lay down his sceptre and knout, or chigote, before the people, in the touching outbreak of a return to humanity—so does the deliverance of the female sex from the regulations and bonds of a degrading slavery, under the sovereignty of sensuality without love, remain within the power of woman herself

Hitherto many a woman, renouncing moral freedom has sold herself, under the protection of church and state, and under the pretext of fulfilment of conjugal duty, for a living in sensuality

The demoralization of woman does not lie as well outside of matrimony, as particularly, in matrimony itself, as this, contracted as a mean Speculation for a Living, at the expense of morality, privileges any extravagance of sensuality. In a seduced woman, (often less sensual than a lawful wife,) the crime is judged which the Man committed first upon the unfortunate female

So long as the notion of ' housewife' is almost synonomous with a suckling brute or domestic animal, so long as it is taken very ill of a woman if she reads and writes, there is little hope for the development and cultivation of a 'future generation

So called ' virtuous housewives,' who have long ago smothered, ' from reasonable motives,' the remnant of delicacy of feeling which after an education à la mode might casually remain in them, will raise the stone of reproach to cast it with ' fitting contempt' upon Gracia's grave. We cannot learn to know a man better than in his judgement upon others , and so also a woman

The judgement of a man upon the offences of others, is the reflected image of his own nature, whether it be elevated or common, whether it be morally pure, or perturbed by passion and disfigured by crimes, whether it be spiritually great and noble, or soulless, mean, and hypocritically contemptible The deeper a woman is sunk in demoralization and hypocrisy, so much the more intolerant does she appear in her uncharitable sentence upon the aberrations and unmerited sufferings of her sex The hypocrisy of Pharisaism has become the monopoly of the so called Christian church, and has been distributed by anticipation, with the sacrament which privileged marriage à la mode

A woman who has become spiritually short-sighted and insensible, through the influence of her husband, does not see the beam in his eye, but judges in the bitterest manner the mote in the tear-moistened eye of one of her own sex, or in the heaven-soaring glance of a man who has never seduced a woman, and whose heart, perhaps, a woman has broken ——

——Robert was a pure man, a youth such as, God be thanked ' we find in all nations, and in all parts of the world, as single appearances, who, like so many, by their entrance into the world, deny their nobler nature according to the demands of civilization, and either morally or (like Robert) physically succumb.

What many may declare to be weakness in Robert, appears to me, on the contrary, as strength, as the strength of his inalienable love; and so much the more disgustingly does the ill usage of the woman stand forth as the return of such love. It requires certainly the penetration of a psychologist, to recognise in this mixture of temper, contradiction, and inconsistency, the to the protection of celebrated court singers, and imperial royal "virtuosi," who were introduced there by force All the guests found the baroness very amiable, the baron very polite, and many withdrew in the most civil manner possible, annoyed by all sorts of suspicious reports

Mr Habakkuk Daily did a flourishing business as partner of the house of Forro & Co, and soon married a young widow from the family of Madame Forro

Bebida was again sold at auction for a nominal price, and became the property of a French woman in Santa Theresa, where she muttered her Dabedikadem from early in the morning till late at night.

Patrick went as a sailor to Rio Grande, by the way of Santa Catharina, and sought for and found his Captain Hinango, who granted him his place of boatswain, which he had long ago held upon the muster roll

We have received less decided intelligence of the Astiala than of the Mazzini, which, under the flag of the insurgents of Rio Grande, was nearly sunk in a severe battle with a Brazilian corvette

Captain Barigaldi and his crew saved themselves by swimming, while a fire of musketry was directed upon them Barigaldi received three bullets in the right shoulder, and entrenched himself on shore in a house, where he resisted, during fourteen hours, the attack of the royalists, until Celeste came to his assistance with a troop of cavalry, and destroyed the enemy

Horatio complied with the request of Celeste, to withdraw himself from the armed struggle of Rio Grande, and cultivate his talent for art as much as possible by study and travel He designed to go to Europe and establish his "atelier" in Rome

Dr Thorfin and Mr Fitz lived in Rio de Janeiro as before The latter went from time to time to San Christova, examined and controlled the air pumps, and other philosophical* instruments of the two princesses, of whom it is known that the youngest, some years afterwards, was married to a European prince for the further development of her "physique experimentale" Mr Fitz sang afterwards, as before, with a barbarous voice, several times each day, his favorite song, "No general has so powerful might, &c ," in which he often became melancholy, and then went and took a walk

Doctor Merbold still lived and travelled as before, in Brazil, as an entomologist, and occasionally delighted himself with a slice of Minas cheese and a bottle of Bavarian beer, that arrived at Rio de Janeiro by the way of Bremen, to his great national joy !

Achilles and Corinna planted trees around Dolores' grave, and remained in the region of Laguna until the uncle of Dolores in Buenos Ayres decided upon their future position, and sent them the means to arrange a home for themselves somewhere, and cultivate a little piece of land for the satisfaction of their unpretending wants

It was a natural consequence, that having been involved in the fate of Dolores, they could not

---

* This English expression, which would sound like *nonsense* in every other language, signifies apparatus for the study of *physique* Physique is the science for the investigation of the *powers of nature.*

---

return to the domain of the "Cacique of the Gauchos' so long as his axe governed there as a sceptre

Mr George Thomson, after some months, made the acquaintance of a young Portuguese lady of respectable family, of respectable connexions, and with a decided tendency to corpulency, who became enamored of his equipage, and gave him her delicate hand upon his lightest approximation

CHAPTER XII

WOMAN'S MAGIC

ROBERT's journals and private papers, in the absence of his relatives, came into the custody of Doctor Thorfin, who, as a contribution to the study of Psychology, prepared extracts from them, which have been used as materials in this novel Interesting and instructive as many pages among Robert's papers might be, manifold circumstances, nevertheless, will not admit of the publication of extracts The fragment of a single letter, which, shortly before his death, he wrote to his father, may, however, find its place here, as the youth's confession of faith upon marriage and love

———" You ask me if I have delivered your letter of introduction to Mr F——, and how I was received Freely and open-heartedly, as I have always dealt towards you, my dear father, I answer you, that I have laid aside this well meant letter, and shall avoid the acquaintance of the respectable family of F——. I know your unexpressed thought, of one day hearing the intelligence that I would lead Miss F—— to the altar, as the property of this young lady, as you have with paternal good intentions intimated to me, " sustains about an equal weight with my future possessions," and as you add, ' because Miss F—— is a true Englishwoman '

With all respect towards our amiable countrywomen, I allow myself, once for all, the declaration, that I deem marriage as the most sacred covenant of humanity, which should only be concluded from love, and from no other consideration whatever

Sincerely as I honor the ' Private Instructions' which you imparted to me, as the individual view of an Englishman, I will never, in the above matter, set aside the claims of my heart as a man I am of opinion that, in this most important step of the two sexes, nationality does not come so strictly under consideration, as morality and love, and declare every matrimonial union to be immoral, which is concluded upon any material ground whatever The social world around me here, gives me occasion enough to reflect upon the demoralization which directly and indirectly proceeds from a marriage ' à la mode, ' or ' marriage de raison,' and so far as I am hitherto acquainted with the world, I hold such a marriage to be a crime I recognise such a union, as a privilege of all demoralization, as even the vilest fellow sustains himself upon this privilege, according to which no one dares to make his wife acquainted with his masked position, and of course the scoundrel always finds a support for his villany in his Wife, as a so called ' head of a family '

If I do not find a woman who, recognising in me a man of honor, loves me, and respects my honesty, I shall probably never marry. As to the rest, I am tolerably well, etc '

Hinango learned, through correspondence with Dr. Thorlin, whatever could be of importance to him with respect to Robert's relations to Gracia, and the cause of his death, whereby involuntary succession of mutual philosophical remarks ensued. The extracts from some letters of Hinango, as a designation of his social position, and as a retrospect upon the sufferings of Robert, may likewise here find a suitable place

——" As you know my ' absurd' views concerning death and life, it will not surprise you when I give you the assurance that it is difficult for me to think that Dolores is dead. Does not her spirit live in her poems and songs, and is not every human heart that shares her sentiments and participates in her inspiration a sanctuary of life, in which her spirit continues to operate for the cultivation and for the ennoblement of the human heart, for the development of the exalted idea—God! and Humanity '

——I am strengthened by the inspiring thought that the spiritual bond which unites kindred souls cannot be rent asunder by space nor time, by separation nor death. that we shall once more, upon some brighter planet, meet again those with whom we lived here in spiritual union, that we shall approach each other there, beyond the grave, by the spiritual bond of attraction—of love—and, less enchained and palsied by material shell, more susceptible of divine love, more clear in knowledge and in the perception of God, striving forth from degree to degree, from planet to planet '

——Young Banko has told me a great deal about a Madame Fesh, with whom he became acquainted in Closting's company somewhere in the interior of Brazil, a woman in all her excellence as a ' propagating machine ' Thus we have, in a retrospect upon the fate of Dolores, become acquainted with woman in her sixfold social position, in Dolores, Angelica, Gracia, Susan, Sally, and Madame Fesh, a singular chance. In these six categories may be classed all the women upon earth ——

I hear the staff broken over Dolores, upon her grave, as during her lifetime, condemned by anticipation as an ' extravagant enthusiast !' That is very natural. A woman who shows head, and heart, and character, will everywhere encounter scorn from the crowd, who possess neither head, heart, nor character

The deliverance of the female sex from the bonds and chains of unnatural regulations and prejudices, is a problem that our age will not solve, so long as it pursues the direction of a false civilization, which denies the aim of the cultivation of mankind, and departs from it more and more

As a nation can only be free through the self-consciousness of its dignity, and the exertion of its own strength, and as no tyrant will ever voluntarily descend from the throne and lay down his sceptre and knout, or chicote, before the people, in the touching outbreak of a return to humanity—so does the deliverence of the female sex from the regulations and bonds of a degrading slavery, under the sovereignt, of sensuality without love, remain within the power of woman herself

Hitherto many a woman, renouncing moral freedom, has sold herself, under the protection of church and state, and under the pretext of fulfilment of conjugal duty, for a living in sensuality

The demoralization of woman does not lie as well outside of matrimony, as particularly, in matrimony itself, as this, contracted as a mean speculation for a Living, at the expense of morality, privileges any extravagance of sensuality. In a seduced woman, (often less sensual than a lawful wife,) the crime is judged which the Man committed first upon the unfortunate female

So long as the notion of ' housewife' is almost synonomous with a suckling brute or domestic animal, so long as it is taken very ill of a mother if she reads and writes, there is little hope for the development and cultivation of a future generation

So called ' virtuous housewives,' who have long ago smothered, ' from reasonable motives,' the remnant of delicacy of feeling which after an education à la mode might casually remain in them, will raise the stone of reproach to cast it with ' fitting contempt' upon Gracia's grave. We cannot learn to know a man better than in his judgement upon others, and so also a woman

The judgement of a man upon the offences of others, is the reflected image of his own nature, whether it be elevated or common, whether it be morally pure, or perturbed by passion and disfigured by crimes, whether it be spiritually great and noble, or soulless, mean, and hypocritically contemptible. The deeper a woman is sunk in demoralization and hypocrisy, so much the more intolerant does she appear in her uncharitable sentence upon the aberrations and unmerited sufferings of her sex. The hypocrisy of Pharisaism has become the monopoly of the so called Christian church, and has been distributed by anticipation, with the sacrament which privileged marriage à la mode

A woman who has become spiritually short-sighted and insensible, through the influence of her husband, does not see the beam in his eye, but judges in the bitterest manner the mote in the tear-moistened eye of one of her own sex, or in the heaven-soaring glance of a man who has never seduced a woman, and whose heart, perhaps, is broken ——

—— Robert was a pure man, a youth such as, God be thanked ' we find in all nations, and in all parts of the world, as single appearances, who, like so many, by their entrance into the world, deny their nobler nature according to the demands of civilization, and either morally or (like Robert) physically succumb

What many may declare to be weakness in Robert, appears to me, on the contrary, as strength, as the strength of his inalienable love; and so much the more disgustingly does the ill usage of the woman stand forth as the return of such love. It requires certainly the penetration of a psychologist, to recognise in this mixture of temper, contradiction, and inconsistency, the

noble being whom Robert originally acknowledged as worthy of his love, and who fettered
him to herself for ever These peculiarities of
Gracia were undoubtedly the consequences of
her social position, and every ill usage of Robert
was only an effect of foreign meanness, which
she had received within herself Her state of
mind revealed in strong features the disturbing
influence, which again in other respects operated destructively on Robert Gracia not only
misunderstood and injured Robert, but the whole
male sex, since in Robert she contemned the
character and love of a man of honor But who
will raise the veil that covers the sufferings of
Gracia ? whose philosophical self-control could
only have been exercised at the expense of her
heart This noble female, who revealed herself
to her lover in a state of 'magnetic dream-wa-
king,' might well shrink from herself in the
realities of social life, in the arms of a man
whom she despised, and if she did not despise
him, then how does she appear to us on Robert's
breast ?

Who will solve for us the riddle of creation,
in the woman who here, in the impulse after
love, sported with a human life ? May the unfortunate be forgiven, for she knew not what
she did ——

Robert's death did not so much surprise me,
as it would have astonished me if he yet lived
I envy him It is well for him his sorrows are
ended

As faithfully as I believe in God and eternity,
I believe also in an Eternal Divine Justice, and
therefore I fear by no means Robert's awakening, Robert's future existence beyond the grave
I fear not that he should be degraded to an inferior existence of a subordinate star, in a state of
penitence. Oh no ! I believe in Eternal Justice,
who knew him, and his sufferings here upon
earth, and who called him away in an hour of
despair, to a higher sphere, in his innocence,—
as a man, as a sacrifice for the honor of a kindred soul, suffering like himself, in the form of
a woman, here upon earth

The more, however, I perceive the decided
influence of woman upon the entire development of the human race, from generation to
generation, the more deeply do I feel, from early
experience, as well as through observation and
similar suffering, the mighty, I might say, the
all-embracing influence of woman upon our inward nature I recognise the principle of love
not only as the basis of all noble social relations,
as far as the development and ennoblement of
the human race proceeds from it, but as the
basis of all religion I recognise the social
bond of matrimony as the most sacred which
can be formed on earth, when it is founded on
love In the opposite case, however, it is an
effectual system for the demoralization of the
human heart.

You inform me that Mr Closting has left
behind him the reputation of being an admirable father of a family, and that his gravestone
bears testimony to this quality It does not
surprise me at all, as his wife herself, so far as
I know, gave him the name of an 'exemplary
husband '

Beside the prize question, 'What is woman ?' I would place the request for information, about the idea of 'husband,' which

until now I cannot comprehend The real
shows us all over the world, that neither int
lect nor heart, neither character nor tale
neither understanding nor sentiment, neith
honor nor honesty, are required to make a m
pass for 'a good, or even an excellent hu
band '

Fragment of another Letter

——" As regards myself I endure the gloo
feeling of my earthly existence, as a ' fettered
habitant of a Planet,' in the consciousness
that divine strength which is required by
lot, that burdens me, from pure resignation
the cause of humanity, with a life without lo
rich in injuries and insults, whose expiation
genius in terrestrial form will ever effect

I am convinced that the ennoblement of
human race, under the influence of woman,
only begin when woman, recognising her o
dignity and the elevation of her destiny,
more voluntarily sells herself as a slave, to
dishonoring of her noble nature

To man upon earth is given the anticipati
of a higher degree beyond the grave, with
consciousness of his spiritual power to devel
this in the element of moral freedom is
duty, abstractly from the contracted med
crity of our earthly state, in comparison w
the more perfect inhabitants of other plane
less contracted and fettered by clogging matt

Man upon earth bears in himself, ' undeniab
too many peculiarities of the subordinate bei
of Mercury and Venus, for the struggle not
be extremely difficult, for him to raise him
upwards to the consciousness of his more e
vated divine nature, which makes him capa
of the transition into the blessed spheres
eternity But the harder the struggle, the m
exalted is the victory Those men in wh
the spiritual life unfolds itself, more or l
through the attraction of the Primitive Idea
existence, encounter the mean gibes of m
rialists—as the lame, in the country of
limping, (according to the fable,) mocked
ridiculed the stranger with sound limbs, v
was casually brought into their society

My individual longing for death, my ' hor
sickness after the Astral world,' whose influe
upon my existence may appear to many m
rialists as a ' sublime lunacy,' has been pecu
to my entity from childhood. I cannot recol
an hour of my life in which I have not lon
to be away from this earth, upon one or
other of those stars whose rays mysteriously
tracted me to themselves.

Let this confession be as sacred to you, a
might appear ridiculous to many, whose jud
ment would, for that matter, be in the hig
degree indifferent to me

I believe in God and Humanity, in an ete
progression from degree to degree, and in
expiation of a loveless life like mine—bligh
in the anticipation of love I believe in re
ciliation through the principle of Divine L
from whose source our existence originated

In a more recent letter of Thorfin to Hina
we find several passages, with the enclosur
a poem, which appear important in a psych
gical point of view :

"As I was arranging Robert's papers," writes *horfin*, "I found the translation of the poem, Astrala's Sentence,' which you transmitted to im when it was already too late to protect him om a fate designated only too truly and fearilly in this elegy. The portentous poem, with those origin you yourself are more deeply and ntimately acquainted than I am, led me again serious reflection on the facts from which is founded, and from which it undoubtedly roceeded

It reminds me, as a poem, of Astarte's incation in Byron's 'Manfred' Instead of an itation, however, it bears, unhappily, the amp of an unfortunate originality, as the nguage of an incurably wounded mind, hich seeks for such an effusion, as it were, to scue itself momentarily from despair, to prore alleviation by utterance, without the intenn of composing a poem Originating in such manner, it is a document for the archives of e higher psychology, and as such, I would sire that it might be preserved It is a rewed intimation of a mysterious reality,—the ychal combination of an image in spiritual lity with a kindred being, which Walter Scott, nong others, treats of in his work on 'Demongy and Witchcraft,' and which well deserves rther research, as a phenomenon in the doin of psychology This blending of a beloved age with the inward entity of a man, ' crysized, as it were, in the glow of sentiment,' is ely to be explained as the animatic operation a powerful strength of mind, as the effect of nighty Animatic Power upon an other, in the te of magnetic *rapport*, with more or less nsciousness of outward life

It is explicable, that the image of a beloved ng, as well in its external form as in its inor psychal entity, in such moments of spiritunion, is able to impress itself for ever upon kindred soul

It is likewise explicable, that such an imssion, having become a psychal unity with kindred soul, will remain behind for ever as image, in those depths of the inward life, n when the being, so united, has long since urned from such a state of magnetic crisis to erior life, and perhaps even lost the clear conusness of the spiritual union'

Who will be astonished that this transfortion or infusion of a being in the entity of ther, as a horrible reality, should have been isidered, in the unenlightened times of the ddle ages, as mysterious, Sorcery and been idemned by blind fanaticism, whose sentence ught people of both sexes to the scaffold, o were, perhaps, unable to account to them-ves for the strength of soul which they so lly manifested

It is in the nature of things, that the infused age exists more vividly in the mind of the ortunate, the more profoundly his inward is developed, and that, on the other hand, h a transformation cannot take place in mate-natures, more or less stupified or unsuscep-e of psychal impressions

The more profound, however, the mind that fures such influence, so much the more fearful state, which no medicinal remedy, no power

This frightful state becomes evidently increased by a forced withdrawal, turning away, and estrangement of the being who, in a crisis of animatic magnetic deliverance from the bonds of the earth, has effected this ' sorcery '

The latter was evidently the case with Robert, and hastened his end Gracia, just as undeniably supported by the physical influence of the animal element, showed in proportion as strong a female inconsistency in suppressing her sympathy for him, as she had once manifested animatic power to fetter him, and this infusion of being, by means of her whole strength of will, (like the operation of a magnetizer,) turned upon him

You envy Robert his death I understand you, and can only agree with you, as I doubt whether his nervous organization would have granted him similar strength as was manifested by Gabriel Garringòs, to bear a lot which was more horrible than death, and not seldom terminates in lunacy Robert's physical disease began with the symptom unhappily but too well known to you, of the oppressive chilling pain at the central point of the nervous texture, (plexus cœliacus,) the organ of clairvoyance in somnambulism In hundreds of cases this symptom is mistaken by material physicians for a disease of the stomach, or of the liver, and falsely treated It is not to be denied that the liver may be indirectly attacked by a reciprocal operation of the interior organs through disease of the ganglionic texture, but it always depends upon the psychological knowledge of the physician to distinguish the cause from the reciprocal effect

I could have treated Robert by magnetism, and perhaps might have rescued him, if the cause of his illness (by well known distant influence) had not rendered all magnetic treatment fruitless beforehand, for Gracia's physical connexion with the inimical earth magnetic element, wrought just as destructively on Robert, as she thereby powerfully suppressed her own animatic life Gracia committed suicide upon her own moral force, and murder upon Robert Her sudden death was a natural consequence of the interior and physical disturbance, which terminated her unfortunate life in a convulsion.

But if her physical nature had endured the convulsion, and she had lived on under the conjugal influence of her husband, (had he likewise been cured,) she would probably have gradually considered her love for Robert as ' an unfortunate nervous disease, that she had happily passed through,' and Robert's death as ' a consequence of a remarkable coincidence of singular circumstances, in which she herself was the least to be blamed ' Physical unity of her female nature with the foreign element of vulgarity, would in such a case have at last just as naturally entirely overcome her inward life, and destroyed her soul She would have entered into the number of ' excellent wives,' whom a husband would not have to ' compel' to any performance of duty.

I send you here Robert's English translation of the designated elegy, as a memorial of the epoch of his sufferings " tant letter to Hinango. As we here communicate the translation of the poem, we will at the same time, satisfy the poetic justice of the novel with respect to Barigaldi's intimation of Hinango's state of mind. He was himself author of the elegy, mentioned already in the intercourse between Gracia and Robert. The elegy was the following.

ASTRALA'S SENTENCE *

Translated from a Scandinavian Language

" Though thy slumber may be deep,
Yet thy spirit shall not sleep
There are shades which will not vanish—
There are thoughts thou can'st not banish,
By a power to thee unknown,
Thou shalt never be alone '" BYRON

Man ! though from the stars descended,
Spirit ! with my spirit blended,
Soul ! whose inmost vital ray,
Penetrates my shell of clay,
Hearken to my loving verse,
Be it blessing, be it curse

Where you wander, where you stray,
If you hasten or delay,
What you do, or what indite,
If you either read or write,
If in armed host you be,
Or for freedom fight on sea,
Still alike, by day or night
I retain you in my might

Where you labor, where you rest,
Whate'er thoughts may fill your breast,
What you long for, or esteem,
Whatsoever you hope or deem,
As a portion of your being,
I am near you, seen, unseeing,
In the soul-world's magic round,
Self unconsciously I'm bound

Though thou† wouldst mine image flee,
Ever near thee I shall be,
Though thou wouldst my glance elude,
Still on thee it will intrude,
As a *ray* from yonder sphere,
Still to thee it will appear

Like a spirit unannealed,
Circled by a shell of clay,
I am even to thee sealed,
And thy longings feed, each day,
Me once more in life to see,
And unite thyself with me

As a soul akin to thee,
Here to female form confined,
Since thy glance has wounded me,
I my fate accursed find ;
By a man to be betrayed,
Who can only me degrade,
Who no mind nor soul requires,
To supply his sensual fires,
And with him " one flesh" to be,
Makes me terrible to thee

When you wake, and when you **sleep**,
If you laugh, or if you weep,
You must ever see me still,
Creature of a husband's will,
While to him myself I give,
Must this image in you live

If you climb the mountain height,
In the vale the image lies,
To your terror and affright,
You descend, to see it rise
If you seek, by change of scene,
From my hapless form to flee,
You shall only find, I ween,
That your bonds unsevered be
If you turn from me away,
I pursue you with the *ray*,
Whose effect controls your powers,
In the soul's eternal hours

If you on the ocean flee,
Then the image, to your dread,
Lifted on each wave you see,
In each star-beam o'er your head,
And when you, a martyr made,
Seek from life to haste away,
In the flood you see my shade,
Turn on you its living ray,
And th' attempt you dread to dare,
Since you still must find *me* there

If for distant climes you sail,
To a tropic paradise,
Ever thine, I shall not fail,
Still to float before your eyes
In your soul I must abide,
Though I from myself would hide,
That I e'er an oath have made,
Left you—wounded and betrayed

If you seek the desert dreary,
Should a savage meet you there,
And, when you are faint and weary,
Offer you his homely fare ;
If his eye shall kindly greet you,
Even then your heart shall feel,
That my glances there must meet you,
That your wound can never heal
Than such desecrated union,
Sure no suff'ring can be worse,
Living without soul's communion,
Is my horror—and your curse !

If you move in worldly throng,
There you find me too, ere long,
When to solitude you flee,
Still you cannot part from me
I pursue you to your grave,
True, to whom my heart I gave ;
But, that I have e er done so,
Scarce in outward life I know

Should you think in quiet sleep,
Calm your weary lids to close,
In your dreams my place I keep,
And deprive you of repose.
When you strive to offer prayer,
Tauntingly my form is there,
Draws you back by chains of sense,
Makes your worship a pretence,
Since your soul, with me allied,
E'en in prayer, has nought beside.

---

* The author of this elegy preserved also his incognito.
† The change of *thou* and *you* has been a *poetic license* of the translator, to maintain the spirit and the metre of this poem.

If despairing you cast
From this world to speed away,
Still shall your expiring gaze,
See me through death's in my hair.

Thou hadst never, till *that* hour,
Known a woman's fateful power:
Love had ne'er been strange to thee—
Thou didst learn its woes from me:
When athwart thy path, I come
And compelled a mournful doom,
Now thy tears may fall for aye,
Thou may'st, trembling turn away,
'Tis I feel that thou art mine,
And, to curse thee—I am thine.

Should'st thou seek thy natal sphere,
In yon starry worlds on high,
Even there 'tis waste and drear
Till to join thee I can fly—
Till released from earthly night,
I from such a curse am freed
By whose dread mysterious might
Both our souls are made to bleed
Till as soul, released once more,
To thy starry home I soar.

What as soul and mind I be
Well I ween, is known to thee
And what I shall be above,
When I meet thy soul in love
But while here, a shell of clay
Still detains me far away
Here, a soul in mortal pain,
I'm a *woman*—to thy bane.

inango replied to his friend, after the receipt
the above translation, among other things, as
ows:

—"It was one of about a hundred poems,
ch I called 'the Book of Astrala.' The
ter part were committed to the flames, and
as even the original of this elegy, the only
of that collection which any person has ever
Even the unfortunate being, whose eyes
y forced these complaints from my poisoned
t, remains unacquainted with them, as she
ains unacquainted with my sorrows and my
rings, with the state of torture, which this
y not sufficiently designates
was the only woman upon earth that ever
ared herself to me in love—the only woman
exercised an influence upon me for which I
no name—no expression

The crime of this unfortunate was Marriage
without Love. The curse which she thereby drew
upon herself was transmitted to me by her longing after love—when it was too late.

In hours of despair pursued by this image, the
genius of Earth has cut on me the chalice of my
tears which I once shed, and which the soul, in
me, ile form——but art understand.

You desire to publish the translation of the
elegy. I leave it to you to do so. If it is able to
save only a single tender from such a lot, and to
protect a single tender from such a curse, under
which I long for death, then shall I not have
suffered in vain.

Such was the language of Hinango's heart, who
is a spirit soared higher than his epoch, and as a
man was perhaps worthy of the love of a noble
being. We have observed him in his position as
a man contending for the cause of humanity,
and acknowledge to the honor of the male sex,
that neither the image of a soul, nor the curse of
a woman nor the sentence of death of a tyrant,
were ever able to bend or break the force of his
spirit, the power of his mind——

——Celeste fought for several years in Rio
Grande where we have seen him, and ended his
manly life in one of the last battles in the year
184?, by which the Brazilian empire temporarily
suppressed the spirit of the age in that province,
to the great joy of all men of business, who spec-
ulate in ox hides and tallow, and to whom revolution, and rebellion, and the like, are a horror,
as may be easily understood.

Celeste fell sword in hand, at the head of a
body of cavalry which he commanded, and his
last words were the joyous exclamation

"Por Dios y Humanidad."

The wreck of the schooner Mazzini was, after
the formerly described battle, carried in "triumph of the empire" to Rio de Janeiro, where
many sons of the ocean from distant ports saw it,
and many of the sons of Italy greeted it with
three cheers, and the jubilant exclamation
'Viva Mazzini!' Viva la Giovine Italia!
Viva l'Umanita!'"

Mr. George Thomson purchased as a curiosity
the plank from the stern of the captain's boat of
the Mazzini with the inscription

"ORA E SEMPRE."

END

Printed in the USA
CPSIA information can be obtained
at www.ICGtesting.com
LVHW080521271123
764997LV00006B/741